Make the Grade.
Your Atomic Dog Online Editio

The Atomic Dog Online Edition includes proven study tools that expand and enhance key concepts in your text. Reinforce and review the information you absolutely 'need to know' with features like:

- **Review Quizzes**
- Key term Assessments
- Interactive Animations and Simulations
- Notes and Information from Your Instructor
- Pop-up Glossary Terms
- A Full Text Search Engine

Ensure that you 'make the grade'. Follow your lectures, complete assignments, and take advantage of all your available study resources like the Atomic Dog Online Edition.

How to Access Your Online Edition

- **If you purchased this text directly from Atomic Dog ....**
  Visit atomicdog.com and enter your email address and password in the login box at the top-right corner of the page.

- **If you purchased this text NEW from another source....**
  Visit our Students' Page on atomicdog.com and enter the **activation key located below** to register and access your Online Edition.

- **If you purchased this text USED from another source....**
  Using the Book Activation key below you can access the Online Edition at a discounted rate. Visit our Students' Page on atomicdog.com and enter the **Book Activation Key in** the field provided to register and gain access to the Online Edition.

э sure to download our *How to Use Your Online Edition* guide located on atomicdog.com to learn эout additional features!

This key activates your online edition. Visit atomicdog.com to enter your Book Activation Key and start accessing your online resources. For more information, give us a call at (800) 310-5661 or send us an email at support@atomicdog.com

216QTWP93

PKG

*Some online Editions do not contain all features.

MARKETING, 11E

MARKETING, 11E

marketing in the 21st century

Joel R. Evans
Hofstra University

Barry Berman
Hofstra University

CENGAGE
Learning™

Australia • Brazil • Japan • Korea • Mexico • Singapore • Spain • United Kingdom • United States

CENGAGE
Learning™

Marketing, 11e: Marketing in the 21st Century
Joel R. Evans and Barry Berman

V.P. Product Development:
Dreis Van Landuyt

Developmental Editor: Greg Albert

Custom Production Editor: Kim Fry

Technology Project Manager:
Angela Makowski

Permissions Specialist: Todd Osborne

Marketing Specialist: Lindsay Shapiro

Manufacturing Manager:
Donna M. Brown

Sr. Production Coordinator: Robin Richie

For product information and technology assistance, contact us at
Cengage Learning Academic Resource Center, 1-800-423-0563

For permission to use material from this text or product,
submit all requests online at **www.cengage.com/permissions**
Further permissions questions can be emailed to
permissionrequest@cengage.com

Library of Congress Control Number: 2009921769

BOOK ISBN-13: 978-1-426-64764-2
BOOK ISBN-10: 1-426-64764-6

PACKAGE ISBN-13: 978-1-424-05518-0
PACKAGE ISBN-10: 1-424-05518-0

Cengage Learning
5191 Natorp Blvd.
Mason, OH 45040
USA

Cengage Learning products are represented in Canada by Nelson Education, Ltd.

For your course and learning solutions, visit **www.academic.cengage.com**

Purchase any of our products at your local college store or at our preferred online store **www.ichapters.com**

Printed in the United States of America
2 3 4 5 6 7 8 9   15 14 13 12 11

To

Linda, Stacey, and Jennifer

Linda; Glenna, Paul, Danielle, Sophie, and Joshua; and Lisa, Ben, Emily, and Philip

Brief Contents

Contents

Part VI
Promotion Planning 523

Preface

With this fourth Atomic Dog edition, *Marketing* continues its transformation into a state-of-the-art multimedia package. Our subtitle, *Marketing in the 21st Century*, is not just a catchphrase. It signifies our focus on the marketing concepts that are essential for the future success of any organization or person, presented in a technologically advanced pedagogical format. We are proud to lead the principles of marketing textbook market into full reader interactivity—at a value price point.

Marketers in the 21st century, more than ever before, need to understand and properly apply new communication technologies, especially the World Wide Web. Although the media have widely reported on the difficulties associated with *E-commerce* (referring to online sales transactions), the potential uses of *E-marketing* (encompassing any marketing activities conducted through the Internet, from customer analysis to marketing-mix components) are truly enormous.

With this in mind, *Marketing in the 21st Century* not only covers emerging topics in detail, it does so in an interactive, dynamic manner. Here's how: The book can be purchased in two ways: (1) in a four-color print format with access to a full-featured Web site or (2) as a subscription to the full-featured Web site. The print version has all the elements that you expect from *Marketing*: comprehensive topical coverage, colorful design; cases; career material; and so forth. The Web site has the complete text, chapter by chapter, in a reader-enticing format. It has 2,000 hotlinks to actual Web sites, distributed throughout the book; more than 100 animated in-chapter figures that visually display flowcharts, bar charts, and so on; a clickable glossary so the reader can instantly see definitions of key terms; a list of "Web Sites You Can Use" in each chapter (which also appears in the print text); hotlinks to a strategic marketing plan outline, by part of the book; an online Web exercise in each chapter; and more!

These are challenging times for all of us. We have seen the true arrival of the PC age and the World Wide Web, the steady movement in the United States and many other nations around the globe toward service- rather than production-driven economies, a growing understanding and interest in customer service and customer satisfaction, more attention to consumer diversity, the emergence of free-market economies in Eastern Europe and elsewhere, business and government grappling with such ethical issues as the consumer's right to privacy, the impact of deregulation on society, and a host of other actions.

The years ahead promise to be even more intriguing, as the European Union adds more member countries; nations in the Americas make their markets more accessible to one another, other foreign opportunities grow, technological advances continue, and we try to cope with slow-growth economies, scarce—and expensive—resources, and political uncertainties in various parts of the globe. As we prepare for the future, an appreciation of marketing (and its roles and activities) becomes critical.

We believe a 21st-century principles of marketing textbook must incorporate both traditional and contemporary aspects of marketing, carefully consider environmental factors, address the roles of marketing and marketing managers, and show the relevance of marketing for those who interact with or are affected by marketing activities (such as consumers). We also believe such a textbook should describe marketing concepts to readers in a lively, comprehensive, and balanced way. As we indicate at the start of Chapter 1, marketing is "fast-paced, contemporary, and seldom boring."

Although the basic components of marketing (such as consumer behavior, marketing research and information systems, and product, distribution, promotion, and price planning) form the basis of any introductory marketing textbook, contemporary techniques and topics also need to be covered in depth. Among the contemporary topics with full-chapter coverage in *Marketing in the 21st Century* are devising and enacting strategic marketing plans; societal, ethical, and consumer issues; global marketing; marketing and the Web; final consumer demographics, lifestyles, and decision making; organizational—b-to-b—consumers (manufacturers, wholesalers, retailers, government, and nonprofit institutions); goods versus services marketing (including nonprofit marketing); integrated marketing communications; and coordinating and analyzing the marketing plan. Environmental effects are noted throughout the book.

Marketing in the 21st Century explains all major principles, defines key terms, integrates topics, and demonstrates how marketers make everyday and long-run decisions. Examples based on such diverse organizations as Apple, BMW, Coca-Cola, Federal Express, Google, Hilton Hotels, Nestlé, Sephora, United Parcel Service (UPS), Visa, and Wal-Mart appear in each chapter. The examples build on text material, reveal the dynamic nature of marketing, and involve students in real-life applications of marketing.

The New Tradition of *Marketing in the 21st Century*

We are as dedicated today as in the first edition of *Marketing* to having ***the*** most contemporary principles of marketing text on the market. We have listened carefully to the feedback from our colleagues, our students, and our Atomic Dog Publishing team. And we have acted on this feedback. The world is evolving and so are we.

Interactive Learning Brings *Marketing* to Life

During the time that we have worked on *Marketing in the 21st Century*, we have been amazed by the technological skills of Atomic Dog Publishing. We hope you will be, too. As was already noted, *Marketing* has a full-featured, highly interactive Web site that we believe will motivate students to learn about marketing principles in a way that encourages their participation in the learning process. **Our goal is to move the reader from passive learning to active learning.**

These are just some of the ways in which our Web site brings *Marketing* to life:

- The complete text is online. Material may be accessed via concise, simple instructions. A drop-down screen in every chapter lets the reader easily move between topics in the chapter.
- Animated figures in each chapter illustrate key concepts. For example, in Chapter 1, the reader can see how selling and marketing philosophies differ; in Chapter 10, the contrasting approaches to target marketing are highlighted through a series of moving images; in Chapter 12, the various types of services are easier to understand through a visual depiction; and in Chapter 22, the stages of integrated marketing planning are enlivened.
- The figures are not only animated; they are also highly interactive. Through the use of "mouseovers" and "clickovers," the reader can access more information (such as definitions and examples) about the topics in the figures. This means that the online design of the figures is less cluttered, and that instant self-testing is possible.
- All in-chapter key terms are linked to the glossary. With just a click, definitions appear onscreen.
- Through a drop-down screen, the reader can do a key word search for any topic in the book from any chapter in the book.
- Each chapter integrates Quick Checks—true-false questions to test comprehension—throughout.
- The end of each chapter features a full study guide for the chapter, with multiple choice, true-false, and fill-in questions.
- A simple click connects the reader to one of 2,000 hotlinks noted throughout the book. These links deal with a wide range of organizations and information. At the end of every chapter, online and in print, there is a "Web Sites You Can Use" section, as well as a Web-based exercise.
- At the beginning of each part of the online book, there is a hotlink to the relevant section of a strategic marketing plan.
- Eighteen computer exercises (keyed to important topics) are available through an online download.
- There is a comprehensive computerized strategic planning exercise (keyed to Chapter 3).
- Our Web site contains a series of Excel spreadsheets that can be used as individual or integrated market planning analyses. They add a financial dimension when used along with *StratMktPlan*.

Content Changes for the 21st Century

Here is a synopsis of the content changes we have made for *Marketing in the 21st Century*. We hope you are pleased with them.

1. All of the opening vignettes are revised. The vignettes deal with major events in the history of some of the world's leading companies, including American Express, Coca-Cola, Dell, Walt Disney, General Electric, Google, Procter & Gamble, and Toyota.
2. All chapter boxes are revised or new. The boxes have three themes: "Ethical Issues in Marketing," "Global Marketing in Action," and "Marketing and the Web." The boxes' thought-provoking nature has been retained.

   a. Ethics Boxes:
      1. The Ethics of Monitoring Customer Service Calls
      2. Walt Disney Company: A Corporate Philanthropist
      3. Profiting from Corporate Social Responsibility
      4. The Survey Respondents' Bill of Rights
      5. U.S. Entrepreneurs Seek to Help Solve Social Problems
      6. Building a Modern Mall in Nigeria
      7. Graduate Management Admission Council 1, ScoreTop.com 0
      8. Marketing to Children in a Digital Age
      9. Nike's Green Sneakers: Air Jordan XX3
      10. Tips for Marketing to the Hispanic Market
      11. Addressing the Flood of Counterfeit Products
      12. Improving the Integrity of Banking Practices
      13. Do Consumers Really Care About "Ethical" Products?
      14. Chargebacks and Markdown Money: Suppliers Fight Back Members
      15. Protecting Legitimate Film Wholesaling
      16. Barnes & Noble "Discovers" New and Underappreciated Authors
      17. Are Pharmaceutical Firms Overspending on Promotion?
      18. What's the Proper Approach to Negative Publicity?

19. Are Frequent-Flier Programs Still a Good Deal for Consumers?
20. Whom Do Below-Cost Laws Protect?
21. Challenging Visa and MasterCard over Credit Card Fees
22. The Rights of Whistle-Blowers Under the Sarbanes-Oxley Act

b. Global Boxes:

1. NBA Europe Live: Marketing U.S. Sports on the Global Stage
2. Ford Motor Company's Plans for India
3. Chevron: Introducing a New Gasoline Additive Worldwide
4. Neuromarketing Experiments: A New Tool for Marketing Research
5. Modern Marketing Practices Come to India
6. Avon Calling: Shining a Global Star
7. Live 8 and Live Earth: The Global Power of the Internet
8. Marketing "Affordable Luxury" for the Masses
9. Specialty Malls for Wholesale Buyers
10. Coach Drives into China
11. The Globalization of Chinese Brands
12. The Kenya Tourist Board Ramps Up Its Marketing Efforts
13. Successful Branding Practices in China
14. Making Lenovo's Supply Chain a Key Asset
15. Product Safety: Purchasing Products Made in China
16. Retailing in Russia: Opportunities, But Be Cautious
17. The Long-Term Effects of Buy-One Get-One Free Offers
18. MTV: Worldwide Powerhouse
19. Selling Camrys in China
20. Are You Attracted by easyGroup's Anti-Luxury Approach?
21. The $100 Computer Finally Comes to the Marketplace
22. Repositioning Long-Time Companies and Their Brands

c. Web Boxes:

1. Craigslist: Building a User-Driven Online Community
2. Welcome to the Weekend Web
3. "Traditional" Media Refashion Their Strategies
4. Pros and Cons in Doing Marketing Research Online
5. Trying Again to Make the Can-Spam Act Work Better
6. Europe's Expanding Use of the Web
7. Why Yahoo! and MySpace Are Opening Their Data Bases to Others
8. Businesses Embrace Blogging
9. Grainger's Top-Notch B-to-B Web Site
10. Consumer Satisfaction with Online Sales
11. How to Enhance a Brand Image on the Internet
12. Online Reservations: An Effective Tool for Hotels
13. Photo-Sharing Web Sites Revolutionize the Picture Business
14. eBay and Its Sellers: Big Firms Happy, Small Firms Not So Much
15. Source 1: Selling Aftermarket Products to Distributors
16. The Lifestyle Center: An Offline Response to the Internet
17. Spyware and Adware Undermine Online Communications
18. Web-Based Advertising Comes of Age
19. The Boom in Online Coupon Usage
20. Comparison Shopping Web Sites: On Target for Careful Shoppers
21. What Pricing Approach Is Best for Online Music Downloads?
22. Assessing E-Commerce Web Sites

3. "Web Sites Use You Can Use" is a very reader-friendly, in-text feature. The end of every chapter lists valuable Web sites related to marketing. These new chapter-related sites range from search engines to shopping venues to benchmarking practices.

4. All of the short cases are revised or new:

Part 1 1: Why Isn't Customer Service Better?
        2: Every Customer Is NOT a Good Customer
        3: Southwest Airlines: Staying Ahead of Competitors
        4: Continental Airlines: A New Emphasis on Business Intelligence

Part 2 1: Deception Through Ambush Marketing
        2: How Can Consumers Be More Attracted to Green Marketing?
        3: Will the Smart Car Succeed in the United States?
        4: Online Ticket Sales Keep on Climbing

Part 3 1: J.C. Penney: Appealing to the Middle Market
        2: What Does It Take to Be a B-to-B Value Merchant?
        3: Conducting Lifestyle Segmentation with PRIZM NE
        4: Jumping on the Micro Segmentation Bandwagon

Part 4 1: What Practices Are OK in the Product Positioning of Diamonds, Gemstones, and Pearls?
        2: Private Brands Move Upscale
        3: Reckitt Benckiser's Keys to Speeding Innovations in Household and Personal-Care Products
        4: Under Armour: Trying to Keep the Hits Coming

Part 5 1: Making a Multichannel Strategy Work Better
2: Verizon's FiOS Technology Moves to Enterprise Clients
3: Costco: Carving Out a Strong Retail Niche
4: Walgreens: Competing in a Tougher Retail Drugstore Environment

Part 6 1: The Growth of Web Advertising
2: In-Store Marketing: An Integral Part of the Promotion Mix
3: Attracting Generation Y Consumers to Music Festivals?
4: Are Rebates Running Out of Steam?

Part 7 1: What's Ahead for iTunes' Video Pricing Strategy?
2: How Should Parking Be Priced in Downtown Areas?
3: Trading Up Shoppers Through the Aggressive Use of Price Points
4: Is Cutting Down on the Use of Markdowns a Losing Battle?

Part 8 1: Apple: The King of Innovation Marches On
2: Marketing Effectiveness and the Small Accounting Firm

5. The eight comprehensive part cases are all new:

Part 1 Case: Customers at the Core
Part 2 Case: E-volution to Revolution
Part 3 Case: Two Target Markets for the Price of One
Part 4 Case: How to Survive in Today's Marketplace
Part 5 Case: Is Channel Collaboration Feasible?
Part 6 Case: Campaign Trail
Part 7 Case: Launching the Proper Pricing Strategy
Part 8 Case: Formulating Your Company's Next Big Innovation and Growth Strategy

6. All data and examples are as current as possible.
7. The careers appendix (Appendix A) has been updated and has a number of hotlinks.
8. The 18 computer exercises are summarized in Appendix C. They may be downloaded from our Web site. These exercises are extremely easy to use, are self-contained, and operate in the Windows XP environment. All directions are contained on computer screens and are self-prompting.

Building on the Strong Foundation of *Marketing*

Marketing retains these **general features** from prior editions:

- A lively, easy-to-read writing style.
- A balanced treatment of topics by size of firm, goods- and service-based firms, profit-oriented and nonprofit firms, final and organizational consumers, and so forth.
- Comprehensive coverage of all important marketing concepts, including 11 chapters on the marketing mix (product, distribution, promotion, and price planning).

- A full-color design throughout the book, including lots of photos and figures. These illustrations are all keyed to the text, as well as visually attractive.
- Part openers that provide integrated overviews of the chapters in every part.
- Many definitions from the American Marketing Association's online *Dictionary of Marketing Terms*.
- Early coverage of societal, ethical, and consumer issues, and global marketing (Chapters 5 and 6).
- Service marketing coverage in the section on product planning (Chapter 12).
- A mix of short and long cases, 38 in all (30 short cases and 8 comprehensive cases).
- An appendix on careers in marketing.
- An appendix on marketing mathematics.
- An appendix on computerized exercises that accompany the text. A computer symbol in the relevant chapters keys the exercises to the concepts involved.
- A detailed glossary.
- Separate company, name, and subject indexes.

These features have also been retained and are contained **in each chapter**:

- Chapter objectives that outline the major areas to be investigated.
- An opening vignette that introduces the material through a real-world situation.
- An introductory overview that sets the tone for the chapter.
- Thought-provoking boxed extracts on key marketing topics.
- Descriptive margin notes (in the print version) that highlight major concepts.
- Boldface key terms that identify important definitions.
- Many flowcharts and current figures and tables that explain how marketing concepts operate and provide up-to-date information.
- Numerous footnotes to enable the reader to do further research.
- Chapter summaries keyed to chapter objectives. These summaries are followed by a listing of key terms, with text page references.
- End-of-chapter questions divided into separate "review" and "discussion" categories.

The *Marketing in the 21st Century* Package

A complete package accompanies *Marketing in the 21st Century*. For students, there are online computerized exercises, a study guide, numerous hotlinks to career information, current events, and more. To aid the classroom learning experience, hundreds of PowerPoint transparencies accompany the text. For professors, lecture and resource materials, as well as testing materials, are available.

How *Marketing in the 21st Century* is Organized

Marketing in the 21st Century is divided into eight parts. Part 1 presents marketing in today's society, describes its environment, presents strategic planning from a marketing perspective, and discusses marketing information systems and the marketing research process. Part 2 covers the broad scope of marketing: societal, ethical, and consumer issues; global marketing; and marketing and the Internet. Part 3 deals with marketing's central thrust: understanding final and organizational (b-to-b) consumers in a diverse marketplace. It examines demographics, lifestyle factors, consumer decision making, target market strategies, and sales forecasting. Both final consumers and organizational consumers are included.

Part 4 covers product planning, branding and packaging, goods versus services marketing, the product life cycle, new products, and mature products. Part 5 deals with distribution planning, value chain management, logistics, wholesaling, and retailing. Part 6 examines integrated promotion planning, the communication channel, advertising, public relations, personal selling, and sales promotion. Part 7 looks at price planning, price strategies, and applications of pricing. Part 8 integrates the elements of marketing planning—including benchmarking and customer satisfaction measurement—and looks ahead.

We are pleased that previous editions of *Marketing* were adopted at hundreds of colleges and universities nationwide and around the world. We hope the fourth Atomic Dog edition, *Marketing in the 21st Century*, is satisfying to continuing adopters and meets the needs of new ones. Thanks for your support and encouragement.

Please feel free to communicate with us. We welcome comments regarding any aspect of *Marketing in the 21st Century* or its package: Joel R. Evans or Barry Berman, Department of Marketing and International Business, Hofstra University, Hempstead, N.Y., 11549. You can E-mail us at **mktjre@hofstra.edu** or **mktbxb@hofstra.edu**. We promise to reply to any correspondence we receive.

Joel R. Evans
Barry Berman
Hofstra University

A Brief Walk Through

Marketing, 11e: Marketing in the 21st Century

You will find an overview of several distinctive features of *Marketing in the 21st Century* in this walking tour. Through these features, we present the most complete coverage possible of the field of marketing—and do so in an interesting, interactive, and contemporary way.

It's all covered—from absolute product failure to yield management pricing.

Marketing in the 21st Century introduces and integrates key marketing concepts, many of which have grown in importance, such as strategic planning, data-base marketing, marketing and the Internet, integrated marketing communications, and value chain management.

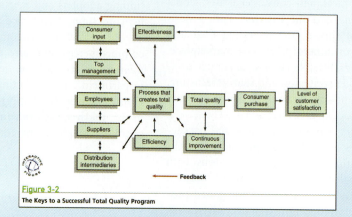

Figure 3-2
The Keys to a Successful Total Quality Program

We look at total quality from a marketing perspective.

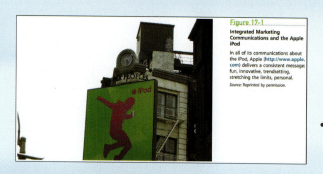

The value of integrated marketing communications is an underlying theme in *Marketing*.

7-3 THE MULTIFACETED POTENTIAL MARKETING ROLES FOR THE INTERNET

After reviewing the company benefits of the Internet in marketing, it should be clear that the Web has the potential to serve several marketing roles, as shown in Figure 7-5 and discussed next. Each firm must determine which roles to pursue and how to prioritize their importance.

Projecting an image—A firm can project an image at its Web site through the site's design (colors, graphics, etc.) and the content presented. Have you ever heard of Accenture (http://www.accenture.com)—formerly Andersen Consulting? No? Well,

The Internet can serve many marketing roles for farsighted firms.

Table 14-1	Selected Distribution Goals by Party	
Party	**Distribution Goals**
Suppliers/ Manufacturers	To gain access to the distribution channel
	To ensure that all distribution functions are performed by one party or another
	To hold down distribution and inventory costs
	To foster relationship marketing with distribution intermediaries and customers
	To obtain feedback from distribution intermediaries and customers
	To have some control over the distribution strategy
	To optimize production runs and achieve economies of scale

The importance of the value chain and the value delivery chain are highlighted.

We believe marketing's vital role should be shown in varied situations. So, we have worked especially hard to present a balance of examples on domestic and international marketing, large and small firms, goods and services, and final consumers and organizational consumers.

This exemplifies our extensive coverage of global marketing.

Figure 6-9

Forward Invention by Colgate-Palmolive

The firm has introduced a number of products especially made for its foreign markets and not sold in its home base of the United States.

Source: Reprinted by permission.

Small firms, as well as large ones, are involved with marketing and strategic planning.

Although a small company, Moonstruck Chocolate has a detailed strategic marketing plan.

3-6b   Moonstruck Chocolate Company: A Strategic Marketing Plan by a Small Specialty Firm

In 1993, Bill and Deb Simmons opened Moonstruck Chocolate Company[24] (then known as Moonstruck Chocolatier) in Portland, Oregon. When it began, Moonstruck was exclusively a maker of truffles for the wholesale market. It sold to retailers such as Neiman Marcus, Marshall Field, and Starbucks. The firm introduced it first retail store in 1996 and sales rose rapidly. Today, Moonstruck is a successful firm that specializes in chocolate-based products, with annual sales of several million dollars and high-powered goals for the future. Why? The firm has created, implemented, and monitored a solid strategic marketing plan. Let's look at the highlights of Moonstruck's plan.

Chapter 12 ("Goods Versus Services Planning") integrates services marketing into product planning.

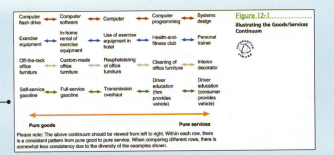

Figure 12-1

Illustrating the Goods/Services Continuum

Computer flash drive	Computer software	Computer	Computer programming	Systems design
Exercise equipment	In-home rental of exercise equipment	Use of exercise equipment in hotel	Health-and-fitness club	Personal trainer
Off-the-rack office furniture	Custom-made office furniture	Reupholstering of office furniture	Cleaning of office furniture	Interior decorator
Self-service gasoline	Full-service gasoline	Transmission overhaul	Driver education (firm provides vehicle)	Driver education (consumer provides vehicle)

Pure goods   **Pure services**

Please note: The above continuum should be viewed from left to right. Within each row, there is a consistent pattern from pure good to pure service. When comparing different rows, there is somewhat less consistency due to the diversity of the examples shown.

Both final and organizational consumers are important to marketers.

In Chapters 8 to 10, we cover the concepts needed to understand consumers in the United States and other nations, to select target markets, and to relate marketing strategy to consumer behavior. Chapter 8 examines final consumer demographics, lifestyles, and decision making. *Final consumers* buy goods and services for personal, family, or household use. Chapter 9 looks at *organizational consumers*, those buying goods and services for further production, usage in operating the organization, or resale to other consumers. Chapter 10 explains how to devise a target market strategy and use sales forecasts.

Final consumers buy for personal, family, or household use; organizational consumers buy for production, operations, or resale.

For *Marketing in the 21st Century*, we have three thought-provoking boxes in every chapter:

- "Ethical Issues in Marketing."
- "Global Marketing in Action."
- "Marketing and the Web."

Each box presents a real-life situation and asks the reader to be a decision maker and state a position or make suggestions.

Ethical Issues in Marketing

Chapter	Title
1	The Ethics of Monitoring Customer Service Calls
2	Walt Disney Company: A Corporate Philanthropist
3	Profiting from Corporate Social Responsibility
4	The Survey Respondents' Bill of Rights
5	U.S. Entrepreneurs Seek to Help Solve Social Problems
6	Building a Modern Mall in Nigeria
7	Graduate Management Admission Council 1, ScoreTop.com 0
8	Marketing to Children in a Digital Age
9	Nike's Green Sneakers: Air Jordan XX3
10	Tips for Marketing to the Hispanic Market
11	Addressing the Flood of Counterfeit Products
12	Improving the Integrity of Banking Practices
13	Do Consumers Really Care About "Ethical" Products?
14	Chargebacks and Markdown Money: Suppliers Fight Back Members
15	Protecting Legitimate Film Wholesaling
16	Barnes & Noble "Discovers" New and Underappreciated Authors
17	Are Pharmaceutical Firms Overspending on Promotion?
18	What's the Proper Approach to Negative Publicity?
19	Are Frequent-Flier Programs Still a Good Deal for Consumers?
20	Whom Do Below-Cost Laws Protect?
21	Challenging Visa and MasterCard over Credit Card Fees
22	The Rights of Whistle-Blowers Under the Sarbanes-Oxley Act

Global Marketing in Action

Marketing and the Web

Marketing in the 21st Century has 30 short cases and eight comprehensive part cases. These cases cover a wide range of companies and scenarios. All are extremely current.

Case 3: Southwest Airlines: Staying Ahead of Competitors[c1-3]

Since 1971, Southwest Airlines' (http://www.southwest.com) operating strategy has been simple. In return for its mechanics, pilots, and flight attendants outhustling its competitors, Southwest provides job security and rewards employees with company stock. In 2007, Southwest posted its 35th consecutive year of net income growth. This was an "amazing feat" due to the highly cyclical nature of the airline business. Southwest also garnered the number 12 spot on *Fortune's* 2008 "American's Most Admired Companies" listing. *Note:* Due to steep increases in 2008 fuel prices, Southwest's profit fell. However, it was the only U.S. carrier to earn a profit during that year.

Southwest's overall strategy focuses on several components: operational simplicity due to the use of one type of aircraft—the Boeing 737 series (this keeps mechanics' training costs and spare parts inventories low), a companywide devotion to having low costs and fares, and an emphasis on efficiency (due to the fast turnaround of its aircraft between arrival and departure). Though most major airlines use a hub-and-spoke system that collects passengers from multiple locations (spokes), flies them to a central hub, and then redistributes the passenger to spokes, Southwest relies on nonstop direct flights. This strategy reduces delays at hubs and enables Southwest Airline flights to be in the air (versus the ground) for more time than any similarly sized aircraft operated by a network carrier. Southwest is also able to unload a flight, clean it, refuel it, and board new passengers in as few as 20 minutes. In contrast, many of its competitors require as much as 90 minutes.

Southwest's strategy was very distinctive in the past. However, it has been copied by airlines such as JetBlue (http://www.jetblue.com) and AirTran (http://www.airtran.com). Southwest faces competition from these upstarts, as well as the entrenched legacy carriers. Carriers such as JetBlue initially borrowed Southwest's one-airplane model and added such goodies as leather seats, individual TV screens, and fancy snacks. JetBlue's costs for available seat mile (8.3 cents as of third quarter 2007) were lower than Southwest's (9.1 cents). And the legacy carriers Delta (http://www.delta.com), with costs of 14.0 cents per mile, and United (http://www.united.com), with costs of 13.3 cents per mile, have cut their cost of flying a passenger mile. The bankruptcy filings by Delta, Northwest (http://www.northwest.com), United, and US

Airways (http://www.usairways.com) enabled these airlines to cut unprofitable routes, reduce interest payments for aircraft, reduce pension obligations, and lower employee wages.

One way that Southwest is seeking to better compete is by expanding its routes. This enables Southwest to lower personnel costs by hiring new, lower-paid employees and spreading its administrative overhead costs over more seats. Southwest recently increased its presence in Chicago by adding flights at Midway airport. Its purchase of a share in ATA (http://www.ata.com), a bankrupt carrier, gave Southwest's customers greater access to such cities as Boston, Denver, Minneapolis, and Honolulu. Southwest also started flying to Philadelphia and Pittsburgh.

Southwest seeks to improve its efficiency through employee attrition, a hiring freeze, and generous severance packages to long-time employees. Another source of savings is through technology that automates certain functions or provides self-service opportunities to customers. Among Southwest's high-tech applications are its Southwest Web site (responsible for over $3 billion in annual bookings), its self-service kiosks, and software that keeps gate agents up to date on a passenger's status and special needs.

Recently, Southwest further streamlined its boarding procedures, added a deluxe program aimed at highly profitable business travelers, introduced onboard wireless Internet access, and installed devices to reduce jet fuel use. Through the successful use of hedging, Southwest paid $1.98 for jet fuel in the first quarter of 2008, versus $2.73 paid by American Airlines (http://www.aa.com) and $2.83 by United. Southwest's hedging profit in that first quarter was $291 million.

Questions

1. Discuss the strategic benefits of Southwest Airlines' low-cost strategy.
2. Describe how the strategies of others airlines are reducing Southwest's low-cost advantage.
3. Should Southwest sustain its low-cost strategy?
4. What else should Southwest do to maintain its leadership position in the U.S. airline industry?

End-of-part cases integrate the material discussed in the group of chapters in particular parts of the text.

Part

7 Comprehensive Case

Launching the Proper Pricing Strategy[pc-7]

INTRODUCTION

Innovation is the fuel that drives growth. Any good sales executive can tell you that the quickest path to revenue growth is through new-product innovation rather than fighting for share in existing markets. Innovation offers immediate differentiation and the chance to command a premium price. Yet the risks of failure are high. A new-product launch enjoys many proud parents: the development team that followed a rigorous staged development process, the manufacturing organization that trained quality experts, the marketing team that developed creative promotions and toured with industry trade shows, the public relations team that built a compelling publicity campaign, and the sales team that enthusiastically extolled the product's virtues to customers. So why are there high failure rates?

THE ROLE OF PRICING IN PRODUCT FAILURES

Many companies' innovation efforts are inwardly focused. The results are billions of dollars wasted developing offerings that have little to no appeal to customers. In business-to-business markets there are three principal reasons for that.

Failure to Connect Customer Needs to Value

The now-defunct PictureTel was an early innovator in the videoconferencing industry 20 years ago, developing a breakthrough technology enabling live videoconferences. Its product launch focused on its impressive technical capabilities. Yet, after PictureTel's great investment and product differentiation, the market did not beat a path to its door. The early value propositions failed to translate the cost of the system into clear value for customers: revenue benefits of reaching more customers or cost savings from travel. In 2000, PictureTel lost $100 million; in 2001, a smaller and more profitable rival purchased it.

Use of Product-Based Value Propositions Centering on Technical Ability Over Market Needs

Iridium (http://www.iridium.com) was a triumph of rocket science. In 1987, the wife of a senior Motorola technology leader fumed because she couldn't call home from a boat in the Bahamas. Eleven years and more than $2 billion later, Motorola (http://www.motorola.com) had successfully launched a necklace of 66 satellites linking

$3,000 phone sets for $7-a-minute calls. However, cell phone customers wanted increasingly small units, not 1-pound "shoe phones," and the market for people who needed a dedicated satellite system for $7 a minute calls was tiny. In 2000, the network was sold for around $25 million—about a penny on the dollar for Motorola's investment.

Overemphasis on the Role of Pricing in Driving Customer Adoption

Petrocosm launched as an oil industry transaction platform with a $100 million investment from Chevron (http://www.chevron.com) and top leadership from the oil equipment industry. It offered a cheap source of high-technology drilling equipment. But in an industry requiring billion-dollar offshore platforms poised over explosive hydrocarbon reservoirs, replacing the trust and experience that trained sales and service representatives offer with a low-cost transaction failed to gain a customer base. The customer base didn't want cheap; it wanted cost-effective. Petrocosm faded away.

The Good News

The pricing process is straightforward and will improve the returns on investment in innovations. Most successful innovators follow a few simple rules:

- Define the financial benefits that customers receive from adopting the new solution.
- Align price levels with financial and psychological drivers of customer value.
- Align pricing strategy with the specific nature of the innovation and the product category life cycle.
- Create outstanding launches—taking emphasis off price by reducing customers' perceived risk.

Companies that adhere to those principles enjoy significant benefits over competitors, including (1) a more effective screening process that enables them to focus resources only on innovations that provide superior value to customers, (2) compelling launches that communicate the business value of innovations, and (3) a coherent pricing strategy that prevents panic discounting to drive sales. Together, the benefits translate to greater success rates for new offerings and better pricing for those that make it to market.

THE VALUE-ON-INNOVATION PARADOX

In b-to-b markets, technological possibility often drives innovation, not defined customer needs. Living on the uncertain edge of technology, it should be less risky to focus on what's possible rather than

[pc-7] Adapted by the authors from Mark Burton and Steve Haggett, "Rocket Plan," *Marketing Management* (September–October 2007), pp. 32–38. Reprinted by permission of the American Marketing Association.

Table of Cases

All of the short cases are revised or new; the eight comprehensive part cases are all new:

At the time that Anne M. Mulcahy, a Xerox (http://www.xerox.com) executive with 30 years of experience at the firm, was chosen chief executive officer, the company was struggling. Xerox was losing $300 million a year, had $14 billion in debt, and faced tough competition from Hewlett-Packard (http://www.hp.com), Canon (http://www.canon.com), and other copier companies.

Mulcahy repositioned Xerox from being a firm that just sold copiers to all kinds of consumers to a provider of applications that can digitally scan and store documents. Today, Xerox likes to be known as "The Document Company," instead of "The Xerox Machine Company." It generates two-thirds of its technology revenues from products that are three years old or younger (more than 100 such products). One interesting new technology involves self-erasing reusable paper. Prints made on this paper have temporary images that enable paper to be reused many times over. Another new technology makes it easier to access documents on cell phones and other small-screen devices.

One way Xerox was able to return to profitability was by carefully studying the needs of its key customers. After analyzing a large insurance company that was a major customer, Xerox learned that the information-related costs in acquiring new business were very high. Xerox showed the client how it could tag the information earlier so it could be reused on an automated basis. This process cut the cost of getting new business for the insurer by 40 to 50 percent.

Mulcahy is also investing in color printing. New digital technology has reduced the costs of color printing so much that production volumes can be more efficiently printed. High-tech diagnostics for color printers enable Xerox engineers to notify customers when their machines need servicing. Xerox makes 15 times as much profit from a color page as from one that is black and white.

As a tribute to her performance, in 2008, Anne Mulcahy received the "CEO of the Year" award from *Chief Executive* magazine. She was the first woman CEO to achieve this distinction.[1]

In this chapter, we will study the complex environment in which marketing decisions are made. We will see that an organization's level of success (or failure) is related not only to its marketing efforts, but also to the external environment in which it operates and its ability to adapt to environmental changes.

Chapter Objectives

1. To examine the environment within which marketing decisions are made and marketing activities are undertaken
2. To differentiate between those elements controlled by a firm's top management and those controlled by marketing, and to enumerate the controllable elements of a marketing plan
3. To enumerate the uncontrollable environmental elements that can affect a marketing plan and study their potential ramifications
4. To explain why feedback about company performance and the uncontrollable aspects of its environment and the subsequent adaptation of the marketing plan are essential for a firm to attain its objectives

[1] Various company and other sources.

A key goal is to reinforce the principles in *Marketing in the 21st Century* in a real-world, lively way. So, we've got all the in-text pedagogy you could want: part openers, chapter outlines, chapter objectives, chapter vignettes, highlighted key terms and marginal notes, photos and line art, bottom-of-page footnotes, useful Web links, summaries linked to chapter objectives, review and discussion questions, appendixes, and more!

Chapter-opening vignettes engage students in marketing in a very reader-friendly manner. These vignettes cover diverse organizations and situations.

Web Sites You Can Use

The U.S. government has the most comprehensive collection of Web sites in the world. It makes available all sorts of information on a free or nominal fee basis. What a wealth of data! One general-access site (http://www.usa.gov) provides access to several hundred million government Web pages. Here are the addresses of several specialized U.S. government sites.

- Bureau of Economic Analysis (http://www.bea.gov)
- Bureau of Labor Statistics (http://www.stats.bls.gov)
- Census Bureau (http://www.census.gov)
- Consumer Product Safety Commission (http://www.cpsc.gov)
- Department of Commerce (http://www.commerce.gov)
- Department of Labor (http://www.dol.gov)
- Economic and Statistics Administration (https://www.esa.doc.gov)
- Environmental Protection Agency (http://www.epa.gov)
- Federal Communications Commission (http://www.fcc.gov)
- Federal Reserve Board (http://www.federalreserve.gov)
- Federal Trade Commission (http://www.ftc.gov)
- Fedstats (http://www.fedstats.gov)
- Fed World (http://www.fedworld.gov)
- Food and Drug Administration (http://www.fda.gov)
- International Trade Administration (http://www.trade.gov)
- Library of Congress (http://www.loc.gov)
- Securities and Exchange Commission (http://www.sec.gov)
- Small Business Administration (http://www.sba.gov)
- Women's Bureau—Department of Labor (http://www.dol.gov/wb)

In each chapter, there is a feature entitled "Web Sites You Can Use," which lists valuable Web resources specifically related to marketing.

About the Computer Supplements Accompanying

Marketing, 11e: Marketing in the 21st Century

Online and in Print

Marketing, 11e: Marketing in the 21st Century is available online as well as in print. The online version demonstrates how the interactive media components of the text enhance presentation and understand. For example,

- Animated illustrations help clarify concepts and bring them to life.
- QuickCheck interactive questions and chapter quizzes test students' knowledge of various topics and provide immediate feedback.
- Clickable glossary terms provide immediate definitions of key concepts.
- References and footnotes "pop up" with a click.
- Highlighting capabilities allow students to emphasize main ideas. They can also add personal notes in the margin.
- The search function allows students to quickly locate discussions of specific topics throughout the text.
- An interactive study guide at the end of each chapter provides tools for learning, such as interactive key-term matching and the ability to review customized content in one place.

Students may choose to use just the online version of the text or both the online and print versions together. This gives them the flexibility to choose which combination of resources works best for them. To assist those who use the online and print versions together, the primary heads and subheads in each chapter are numbered the same. For example, the first primary head in Chapter 1 is labeled 1-1, the second primary head in this chapter is labeled 1-2, and so on. The subheads build from the designation of their corresponding primary head: 1-1a, 1-1b, etc. This numbering system is designed to make moving between the online and print versions as seamless as possible.

Finally, next to a number of figures and exhibits in the print version of the text, you will see an icon similar to those below. This icon indicates that this figure or exhibit in the online edition is interactive in a way that applies, illustrates, or reinforces the concept.

Computer-Based Marketing Exercises

As noted in the preface, *Marketing* has a series of computer exercises that may be downloaded from our Web site. These exercises are extremely easy to use, are self-contained, and operate in the Windows environment, including Windows XP. All directions are contained on computer screens and are self-prompting.

The *Computer-Based Marketing Exercises* are designed to apply and reinforce specific individual concepts in *Marketing*. The exercises are explained in Appendix C; and throughout *Marketing*, a computer symbol signifies which concepts are related to the exercises:

1. Marketing Orientation
2. Boston Consulting Group Matrix
3. Questionnaire Analysis
4. Ethics in Action
5. Standardization in International Marketing Strategy
6. Vendor Analysis
7. Segmentation Analysis
8. Product Positioning
9. Services Strategy
10. Product Screening Checklist
11. Economic Order Quantity
12. Wholesaler Cost Analysis
13. Advertising Budget
14. Salesperson Deployment
15. Price Elasticity
16. Key Cost Concepts
17. Performance Ratios
18. Optimal Marketing Mix

There is also a detailed computer exercise, *StratMktPlan*, that encompasses all major elements of a strategic marketing plan. It is explained in the Chapter 3 appendix and is linked to the part openers throughout *Marketing*. This exercise may be downloaded separately from our Web site.

For professors who like to demonstrate how Excel may be applied in marketing situations, there is a special download at the Web site with a variety of simple Excel-based exercises.

Acknowledgments

Throughout our professional lives and during the period of time that the various editions of this book have been researched and written, a number of people have provided us with support, encouragement, and constructive criticism. We would like to publicly acknowledge and thank many of them.

In our years as graduate students, we benefited greatly from the knowledge transmitted from professors Conrad Berenson, Henry Eilbirt, and David Rachman, and colleagues Elaine Bernay, William Dillon, Stanley Garfunkel, Leslie Kanuk, Michael Laric, Kevin McCrohan, Leon Schiffman, and Elmer Waters. We learned a great deal at the American Marketing Association's annual consortium for doctoral students, the capstone of any marketing student's education.

At Hofstra University, colleagues Benny Barak, Andrew Forman, William James, Songpol Kulviwat, Keun Lee, Anil Mathur, Charles McMellon, Rusty Mae Moore, James Neelankavil, Elaine Sherman, Salvatore Sodano, Shawn Thelen, Rick Wilson, Boonghee Yoo, and Yong Zhang have provided the collegial environment needed for a book of this type.

We would especially like to thank the following colleagues who have reviewed *Marketing* and *Principles of Marketing*. These reviewers have made many helpful comments that have contributed greatly to this book:

Wayne Alexander (Moorhead State University)
Rolph Anderson (Drexel University)
Julian Andorka (DePaul University)
Kenneth Anglin (Mankato State University)
Thomas Antonielli, Sr. (Strayer College)
Harold Babson (Columbus State Community College)
Ken Baker (University of New Mexico)
John Bates (Georgia Southern University)
Stephen Batory (Bloomsburg University)
Richard Behr (Broome Community College)
Kurt Beran (Oregon State University)
Wanda Blockhus (San Jose State University)
John Boos (Ohio Wesleyan University)
Jeff Bradford (Drake University)
Donald Bradley, III (University of Central Arkansas)
James Brock (Susquehanna University)
Harvey Bronstein (Oakland Community College)
Sharon Browning (Northwest Missouri State University)
John Bunnell (Broome Community College)
Jim Burrow (North Carolina State University)
Gul Butaney (Bentley College)
Stephen Calcich (Hampton University)

Robert Chapman (Orlando College)
Yusef Choudhry (University of Baltimore)
Gloria Cockerell (Collin County College)
Barbara Coe (University of North Texas)
Linda Jane Coleman (Salem State College)
Kenneth Crocker (Bowling Green State University)
James Cronin, Jr. (Cape Cod Community College)
John Cronin (Western Connecticut State University)
Richard Cummings (College of Lake County)
Benjamin Cutler (Bronx Community College)
Homer Dalbey (San Francisco State University)
Betty Diener (University of Massachusetts, Boston)
Peter Doukas (Westchester Community College)
Rebecca Elmore-Yalch (University of Washington)
Mort Ettinger (Salem State University)
Roland Eyears (Central Ohio Technical College)
Frank Falcetta (Middlesex Community College)
Lawrence Feick (University of Pittsburgh)
Benjamin Findley, Jr. (University of West Florida)
Frank Franzak (Virginia Commonwealth University)
Stanley Garfunkel (Queensborough Community College)
Betsy Gelb (University of Houston)
Donald Gordon (Illinois Central College)
Jill Grace (University of Southern California)
Harrison Grathwohl (California State University at Chico)
Blaine Greenfield (Bucks County Community College)
Thomas Greer (University of Maryland)
Charles Gulas (Wright State University)
Gregory Gundlach (University of Notre Dame)
Robert Gwinner (Arizona State University)
Rita Hall (Sullivan Junior College)
Robert Hammond (Lexington Community College)
G. E. Hannem (Mankato State University)
Nancy Hansen (University of New Hampshire)
William Harris, III (Quinnipiac University)
Douglas Hawes (University of Wyoming)
Jon Hawes (University of Akron)
Dean Headley (Wichita State University)
Allen Heffner (Lebanon Valley College)
Thomas Hickey (State University of New York at Oswego)
Nathan Himmelstein (Essex County College)
Patricia Hopkins (California State Polytechnic University at Pomona)
Jerry Ingram (Auburn University at Montgomery)
Laurence Jacobs (University of Hawaii)
Rajshekhar Javalgi (Cleveland State University)
Norma Johansen (Scottsdale Community College)

Edna Johnson (North Carolina Agricultural and Technical State University)
Paul Joice, Sr. (Walla Walla College)
Mary Joyce (Emerson College)
Albert Kagan (University of Northern Iowa)
Ruel Kahler (University of Cincinnati)
Bernard Katz (Oakton Community College)
J. Steven Kelly (DePaul University)
John Kerr (Florida State University)
Bettie King (Central Piedmont Community College)
Gail Kirby (Santa Clara University)
Charles Knapp (Waubonsee Community College)
John Krane (Community College of Denver)
R. Krishnan (University of Miami)
Darwin Krumrey (Kirkwood Community College)
J. Ford Laumer (Auburn University)
William Layden (Golden West College)
Marilyn Liebrenz-Himes (George Washington University)
Robert Listman (Valparaiso University)
James Littlefield (Virginia Polytechnic Institute and State University)
Yusen Liu (University of St. Thomas)
John Lloyd (Monroe Community College)
William Locander (University of South Florida)
Kenneth Lord (Niagara University)
Robert Lorentz (Florida Institute of Technology)
William Lovell (Cayuga Community College)
Keith Lucas (Ferris State College)
Scott Marzluf (National College)
Jacob Manakkalathil (University of North Dakota)
Michael Mayo (Kent State University)
Ken McCleary (Virginia Polytechnic Institute and State University)
Elaine McGivern (Bucknell University)
James McMillan (University of Tennessee)
H. Lee Meadow (Eastern Illinois University)
John Mentzer (University of Tennessee)
Jim Merrill (Indiana University)
James Meszaros (County College of Morris)
Ronald Michael (University of Kansas)
Ronald Michman (Shippensburg State University)
John Milewicz (Jacksonville State University)
Howard Mills (Ulster City Community College)
Edward Moore (State University of New York College at Plattsburgh)
Linda Morable (Richland College)
John Morgan (West Chester University)
Linda Morris (University of Idaho)
Ed Mosher (Laramie County Community College)
Carol Stewart Mueller (Nassau Community College)
Paul Murphy (John Carroll University)
Margaret Myers (Northern Kentucky University)
Donald Nagourney (New York Institute of Technology)
Peter Nye (Northeastern University)
Kenneth Papenfuss (Ricks College)

Dennis Pappas (Columbus State Community College)
Terry Paul (Ohio State University)
William Perttula (San Francisco State University)
Michael Peters (Boston College)
Ann Pipinski (Northeast Institute of Education)
Robert Pollero (Anne Arundel Community College)
Edward Popper (Bellarmine University)
William Qualls (University of Illinois)
S. R. Rao (Cleveland State University)
Lloyd Rinehart (Michigan State University)
Edward Riordan (Wayne State University)
David Roberts (Virginia Polytechnic Institute and State University)
Mary Lou Roberts (University of Massachusetts at Boston)
Scott Roberts (Old Dominion University)
Donald Robin (University of Southern Mississippi)
John Rogers (California Polytechnic State University at San Luis Obispo)
Randall Rose (University of South Carolina)
Barbara Rosenthal (Miami Dade Community College)
Thomas Rossi (Broome Community College)
Nancy Ryan-McClure (Texas Tech University)
Barbara Samuel (University of Scranton)
Peter Sanchez (Villanova University)
Alan Sawyer (University of Florida)
Robert Schaffer (California State Polytechnic University at Pomona)
Martin Schlissel (St. John's University)
Stanley Scott (University of Alaska at Anchorage)
Donald Self (Auburn University at Montgomery)
Mohamad Sepehri (Sheperd College)
Rajagopalan Sethuraman (Southern Methodist University)
Reshma Shah (University of Pittsburgh)
Richard Sielaff (University of Minnesota at Duluth)
M. Joseph Sirgy (Virginia Polytechnic Institute and State University)
Richard Skinner (Ashland University)
Michael Smith (Temple University)
Norman Smothers (California State University at Hayward)
Gregory Snere (Ellsworth Community College)
Michael Solomon (Auburn University)
Patricia Sorce (Rochester Institute of Technology)
A. Edward Spitz (Eastern Michigan University)
Thomas Stafford (Texas Women's University)
Gary Stanton (Erie Community College)
Margery Steinberg (University of Hartford)
Jeffrey Stoltman (Wayne State University)
Robert Swerdlow (Lamar University)
Richard Szecsy (St. Mary's University)
Donna Tillman (California State Polytechnic University at Pomona)
Ed Timmerman (Abilene Christian University)
Frank Titlow (St. Petersburg Junior College)
Charles Treas (University of Mississippi)

David Urban (Virginia Commonwealth University)
Anthony Urbaniak (Northern State University)
Richard Utecht (University of Texas at San Antonio)
William Vincent (Santa Barbara City College)
Gerald Waddle (Clemson University)
Donald Walli (Greenville Technical College)
John Walton (Miami University)
J. Donald Weinrauch (Tennessee Technological University)
Colleen Wheeler (St. Cloud University)
Mildred Whitted (St. Louis Community College at Forest Park)
Jack Wichert (Orange Coast College)
David Wills (Sussex County Community College)
George Winn (James Madison University)
Martin Wise (Harrisburg Area Community College)
Joyce Wood (Northern Virginia Community College)
Gene Wunder (Washburn University)
Richard Yalch (University of Washington)
Anthony Zahorik (Vanderbilt University)
William Ziegler (Seton Hall University)

To the many students at Hofstra who have reacted to the material in *Marketing in the 21st Century*, we owe special thanks, because they represent the true constituency of any textbook authors.

We are pleased to recognize the contributions of Diane Schoenberg, our editorial associate; Matthew Wettan, our graduate research assistant; and Linda Berman, for comprehensive indexes. Our appreciation and thanks are extended to Chip Galloway for his continued outstanding work on the computer exercises and Mid Semple for her initial work on many of the PowerPoint slides that accompany this book. We also thank the American Marketing Association, Retail Forward, and Susan Berry for their cooperation and the right to reproduce case materials and photos.

To our families, this book is dedicated—out of respect, love, and appreciation.

Joel R. Evans
Barry Berman

About the Authors

Joel R. Evans, Ph.D., is the RMI Distinguished Professor of Business and Professor of Marketing and International Business in the Zarb School of Business at Hofstra University. Before joining Hofstra, he worked for a *Fortune 500* firm, owned a business, and taught at Baruch College and New York University. Dr. Evans is author or editor of numerous books and articles and is active in various professional associations. At Hofstra, he has received four Dean's Awards and the School of Business Faculty Distinguished Service Award. Dr. Evans has also been honored as Teacher of the Year by the Hofstra M.B.A. Association.

Barry Berman, Ph.D., is the Walter H. "Bud" Miller Distinguished Professor of Business and Professor of Marketing and International Business in the Zarb School of Business at Hofstra University. He also serves as the Director of Hofstra University's Executive Master of Business Administration program. Dr. Berman is author or editor of numerous books and articles and is active in various professional associations. At Hofstra, he has received two Dean's Awards. Dr. Berman has also been honored as Teacher of the Year by the Hofstra M.B.A. Association.

Joel R. Evans and Barry Berman are co-authors of several best-selling texts, including *Marketing in the 21st Century* and *Retail Management: A Strategic Approach* (Prentice Hall). They have co-chaired numerous prestigious conferences, including an American Marketing Association Faculty Consortium on "Ethics and Social Responsibility in Marketing" and the Academy of Marketing Science/American Collegiate Retailing Association Triennial Retailing Conference. Each has a chapter in Dartnell's *Marketing Manager's Handbook*. Drs. Evans and Berman have been consultants for such firms as Fortunoff, NCR, Olympus USA, Simon Properties, and Tesco Ireland. Both regularly teach undergraduate and graduate marketing courses to a wide range of students.

About Atomic Dog

Atomic Dog is faithfully dedicated to meeting the needs of today's faculty and students, offering a unique and clear alternative to the traditional textbook. Breaking down textbooks and study tools into their basic "atomic parts," we then recombine them and utilize rich digital media to create a "new breed" of textbook.

This blend of online content, interactive multimedia, and print creates unprecedented adaptability to meet different educational settings and individual learning styles. As part of *Cengage Learning*, we offer even greater flexibility and resources in creating a learning solution tailor-fit to your course.

Atomic Dog is loyally dedicated to our customers and our environment, adhering to three key tenets:

- **Focus on essential and quality content:** We are proud to work with our authors to deliver a high-quality textbook at a lower cost. We focus on the essential information and resources students need and present them in an efficient but student-friendly format.
- **Value and choice for students**: Our products are a great value and provide students with more choices in 'what and how' they buy—often at savings of 30 to 40 percent less than traditional textbooks. Students who choose the Online Edition may see even greater savings compared to a print textbook. Faculty play an important and willing role—working with us to keep costs low for their students by evaluating texts and supplementary materials online.
- **Reducing our environmental "paw-print":** Atomic Dog is working to reduce its impact on our environment in several ways. Our textbooks and marketing materials are all printed on recycled paper. We encourage faculty to review text materials online instead of requesting a print review copy. Students who buy the Online Edition do their part by going "paperless" and eliminating the need for additional packaging or shipping. Atomic Dog will continue to explore new ways that we can reduce our "paw-print" in the environment and hope you will join us in these efforts.

Atomic Dog is dedicated to faithfully serving the needs of faculty and students—providing a learning tool that helps make the connection. We hope that after you try our texts, Atomic Dog—like other great dogs—will become your faithful companion.

An Introduction to Marketing in the 21st Century

In Part 1, we begin our study of marketing and discuss concepts that form the basis for the rest of the text.

1 Marketing Today

To begin our journey, we look at marketing's dynamic nature, broadly define "marketing," and trace the evolution of marketing. Special attention is paid to the marketing concept, a marketing philosophy, customer service, and customer satisfaction and relationship marketing. We also examine the importance of marketing, as well as marketing functions and performers.

2 The Environment in Which Marketing Operates

This chapter covers the complex environment within which marketing functions, with an emphasis on both the factors that can be controlled and those that cannot be controlled by an organization and its marketers. We show that without adequate environmental analysis, a firm may function haphazardly or be shortsighted.

3 Developing and Enacting Strategic Marketing Plans

Here, we first differentiate between strategic business plans and strategic marketing plans, and present the total quality approach to planning. Next, we examine different kinds of strategic plans and the relationships between marketing and other functional areas. We then present the steps in the strategic planning process. A sample outline for a strategic marketing plan is presented and the actual strategic marketing plan of a small firm is highlighted.

4 Information for Marketing Decisions

In this chapter, we discuss why marketing decisions should be based on sound information. We describe the role and importance of the marketing information system—which coordinates marketing research, continuous monitoring, and data storage and provides the basis for decision making. We also cover the steps in the marketing research process, and show that marketing research may involve surveys, observation, experiments, and/or simulation.

After reading Part 1, you should understand elements 1–5 of the strategic marketing plan outlined in Table 3-2 (page 73).

Chapter 1

Marketing Today

The Walt Disney Company (http://www.disney.com) is a huge media conglomerate that owns the ABC television network (which has affiliation agreements with more than 230 local stations that reach 99 percent of all U.S. television households), as well as ESPN. It also produces and distributes live action and animated television programming under such brands as Walt Disney Television, Buena Vista Productions, and ABC Family Productions. And Disney's Walt Disney World and Disneyland are among the most popular family resort destinations in North America.

One of Disney's hidden jewels is the Disney Institute (http://www.disney institute.com), a training facility that teaches Disney's obsession for customer service to other firms. Over the years, the Disney Institute has trained millions of leaders from more than 35 nations. As a Disney spokesperson says, generating a passion for customer service requires "creating the ultimate guest experience" that reaches consumers on an emotional level. A typical Disney Institute program costs $3,895 per person for a three-and-a-half day program (not including hotel-related expenses or theme park admission fees).

Among the strategies taught at Disney Institute are the following:

- Customer satisfaction is based on well-trained and dedicated "cast members," as the firm refers to its employees. "You can build, create, and design the most wonderful place in the world, but it takes people to make it work," according to a Disney Institute programming director.
- Disney is a great believer in the cross-utilization of employees and managers. In peak periods, a high-level executive may sell popcorn or even stock shelves. This facilitates a corporate-wide message among all Disney employees as to the importance of their jobs.
- Disney invests heavily in training. Sweepers are trained in body language so they can offer help before being asked. They also receive training in recognizing signs of child abuse.
- All of Disney's staff members, not just those playing Snow White or Mickey Mouse, are taught to view themselves as characters playing to an audience: If staff members smile, so will customers.[1]

In this chapter, we will learn more about the importance of service in generating customer loyalty. We will also look at the roles of marketing, see how marketing has evolved, and look at its scope.

Chapter Objectives

1. To illustrate the exciting, dynamic, and influential nature of marketing
2. To define marketing and trace its evolution—with emphasis on the marketing concept, a marketing philosophy, customer service, and customer satisfaction and relationship marketing
3. To show the importance of marketing as a field of study
4. To describe the basic functions of marketing and those who perform these functions

1-1   OVERVIEW

The field of marketing is fast-paced, contemporary, and seldom boring. We engage in marketing activities or are affected by them on a daily basis, both in our business-related roles and as consumers. Okay, but what exactly does "marketing" mean? Well, it is not

---

[1] Various company and other sources.

just advertising or selling goods and services, although these are aspects of marketing. And it is not just what we do as supermarket shoppers every week, although this, too, is part of marketing.

"Marketing"—as formally defined in Section 1-2—is involved with anticipating, managing, and satisfying demand via the exchange process. As such, marketing encompasses all facets of buyer/seller relationships. Specific marketing activities (all discussed later in this chapter) include environmental analysis and marketing research, broadening an organization's scope, consumer analysis, product planning, distribution planning, promotion planning, price planning, and marketing management.

In a less abstract manner, here are two examples of real-world marketing—one from a business perspective and one from a consumer perspective:

Business perspective: Bill Norman, a 2003 BA with a graphic arts major, is a creative director for a large advertising agency. The agency serves both small businesses and corporate accounts on a national basis. Norman oversees the creative end of all print advertising at his agency. This involves graphics, headlines, and copy. He is now ready to open his own firm but must make a number of decisions: Who should his clients be? What kinds of advertising services should he offer? Where should he open his office? How will he attract clients? What fee schedule should he set? Is it ethical to try to attract clients he worked with at his old firm? *Each of these questions entails a business-related marketing decision.*

Let's look at some of Bill Norman's marketing options:

- *Clients*—He could target small or medium businesses (consistent with his work experience).
- *Kinds of advertising services*—He could open a full-service agency and offer a wide array of services, including preparation of advertising graphics and copy for all kinds of media, advice on media selection, media buying, and so on; or he could focus on print ads, as he has done before.
- *Office location*—He could have an office in a downtown office building, a suburban professional building, or his home. He could also do client visits, making the choice of location less important.
- *Attracting clients*—He must determine the best way to reach his potential clients, such as sending out direct mail pieces to prospective clients, making appearances at professional events (such as a local meeting of dentists), running ads in local newspapers, and so on.
- *Fee schedule*—He must rely on his own experience with his previous firm and look at what competitors are doing. Then, he could price similar to others or lower/higher than them (depending on his desired image and a realistic reading of the marketplace).
- *Ethics*—He must weigh the personal dilemma of "stealing" clients from his old firm against the difficulty of starting a business from scratch without any client base.

Consumer perspective: At the same time that Bill Norman is making decisions about his new ad agency, Nancy Willis is reappraising her status as an advertising client. She owns a three-unit restaurant chain and has been a client of a mid-sized ad agency for 10 years. That firm has prepared and placed all of Willis' newspaper advertising (the only medium she uses). Willis spends $250,000 per year on ads; the agency fee is 15 percent of this. Yet, she is now unhappy. She feels the agency takes her for granted. But before switching firms, these questions must be answered: What kind of agency should she select? What services should she seek? Where should the new agency be located? How will she learn more about possible firms? What fees should she be willing to pay? Is it ethical to show prospective firms the bills paid to her present agency? *Each of these questions addresses a consumer-related marketing decision.*

Let's look at some of Nancy Willis' marketing options:

- *Kind of firm*—She could select a small, medium, or large ad agency. Given her current dissatisfaction, she might want to avoid medium and large firms.

> Marketing is a dynamic field, encompassing many activities.

Marketing and the Web

Craigslist: Building a User-Driven Online Community

Craig Newmark, a computer security architect at a brokerage firm, began using the Internet to tell readers about interesting events in San Francisco in 1995. Responding to viewer suggestions, Newmark started including other services such as job openings. Soon, the listings were changed from an E-mail to a Web-site format that could automatically add E-mail postings to the craigslist (http://www.craigslist.org) site. Newmark began to devote himself full-time to craigslist as of early 1999.

Each month, craigslist is used by more than 40 million people (including 30 million in the United States), and lists more than 30 million new classified ads. And monthly, it receives more than 10 billion page views, making craigslist the 8th leading Web site overall in terms of English-language page views. There are now in excess of 500 craigslist sites in all 50 states and in more than 50 countries.

Classified Intelligence (http://www.classifiedintelligence.com), a research firm, found that craigslist brought in $81 million in revenues in 2008 (up from $55 million in 2007). These revenues were from real-estate brokerage firms that advertise apartments and houses for sale, as well as rent and help-wanted listings in ten cities. Ad prices are very low. For example, job-related ads are only $25 in nine cites and $75 in San Francisco. Despite its free or low-cost ads, craigslist is extremely profitable. It has a staff of 25 employees and profit margins that have been described as "astronomical." Just under 25 percent of the firm is owned by eBay (http://www.ebay.com).

Sources: Based on material in Jon Fine, "Can Craigslist Stay Offball?" *Business Week Online* (May 8, 2008); and "About Craigslist Fact Sheet," http://www.craigslist.org (July 7, 2008).

- *Advertising services*—She could continue to have a single ad agency prepare and place all advertising; or she could use one agency to prepare the advertising and another to buy advertising space in newspapers.
- *Office location*—She could look for an ad agency that makes on-site visits (as her present firm does) or seek an agency that has an office near to one of her restaurants.
- *Learning about firms*—She could ask prospective firms for references, check out credentials, interview candidates, and/or require firms to perform a sample task.
- *Fee schedule*—She could continue to pay a standard 15 percent fee; or she could negotiate for a lower amount. She recognizes that you get what you pay for; and she wants great service.
- *Ethics*—Willis believes she, as the client, has the right to show any information about her past advertising practices and fees to prospective agencies.

> We are all involved with or affected by marketing.

A marketing match? For "marketing" to operate properly, buyers and sellers need to find and satisfy each other (conduct exchanges). Do you think that Bill Norman and Nancy Willis would make a good marketing match? We do—but only if their strategy (Norman) and expectations (Willis) are in sync.

The bottom line: Goods and service providers ("sellers") make marketing-related decisions such as choosing who their customers are, what goods and services to offer, where to sell these goods and services, the features to stress in ads, and the prices to charge. They also determine how to be ethical and socially responsible, and whether to sell products globally in addition to domestically. Marketing-related activities are not limited to large corporations or people called "marketers." They are taken on by all types of companies and people.

As consumers ("buyers"), the marketing practices of goods and service providers affect many of our choices, as well as those made by our parents, spouses, other family members, and friends and associates. For virtually every good and service we purchase, the marketing process affects whom we patronize, the assortment of models and styles offered in the marketplace, where we shop, the availability of knowledgeable sales personnel, the prices we pay, and other factors. Marketing practices are in play when we are born (which doctor our parents select, the style of furniture they buy), while we grow (our parents' purchase of a domestic or foreign car or sports utility vehicle, our choice of a college), while we conduct our everyday lives (the use of a particular brand of toothpaste, the purchase of status-related items), and when we retire (our consideration of travel options, a change in living accommodations).

An in-depth study of marketing requires an understanding of its definition, evolution (including the marketing concept, a marketing philosophy, and customer service), importance and scope, and functions. These principles are discussed throughout Chapter 1.

1-2 MARKETING DEFINED

In late 2007, the American Marketing Association introduced a revised definition of marketing, calling it "the activity, set of institutions, and processes for creating, communicating, delivering, and exchanging offerings that have value for customers, clients, partners, and society at large."[2]

For purposes of clarity, this shorter, more direct definition of marketing forms the basis of our text:

> *Marketing* is the anticipation, management, and satisfaction of demand through the exchange process.

It involves goods, services, organizations, people, places, and ideas.

Anticipation of demand requires a firm to do consumer research on a regular basis so it can develop and introduce offerings desired by consumers. *Management of demand* includes stimulation, facilitation, and regulation tasks. Stimulation motivates consumers to want a firm's offerings due to attractive product designs, distinctive promotion, fair prices, and other strategies. Facilitation is the process whereby the firm makes it easy to buy its offering by having convenient locations, accepting credit cards, using informed salespeople, and enacting other strategies. Regulation is needed when there are peak demand periods rather than balanced demand throughout the year or when demand exceeds supply. Then, the goal is to spread demand throughout the year or to demarket a good or service (reduce overall demand). *Satisfaction of demand* involves product availability, actual performance upon purchase, safety perceptions, after-sale service, and other factors. For consumers to be satisfied, goods, services, organizations, people, places, and ideas must fulfill their expectations. See Figure 1-1.

Marketing can be aimed at consumers or at publics. **Consumer demand** refers to the attributes and needs of final consumers, industrial consumers, wholesalers and retailers, government institutions, international markets, and nonprofit institutions. A firm may appeal to one or a combination of these. **Publics' demand** refers to the attributes and needs of employees, unions, stockholders, the general public, government agencies, consumer groups, and other internal and external forces that affect company operations.

The marketing process is not concluded until consumers and publics *exchange* their money, their promise to pay, or their support for the offering of a firm, institution, person, place, or idea. Exchanges must be done in a socially responsible way, with both the buyer and the seller being ethical and honest—and considering the impact on society and the environment.

A proper marketing definition should not be confined to economic goods and services. It should cover organizations (Big Brothers and Big Sisters), people (politicians), places (Hawaii), and ideas (the value of seat belts). See Figure 1-2 and Figure 1-3. A consumer orientation must be central to any definition. And from a societal perspective, a firm should ask if a good or service should be sold, besides whether it can be sold.

Marketing includes anticipating demand, managing demand, and satisfying demand.

Demand is affected by both **consumers** and **publics**.

Exchange completes the process.

[2] Lisa M. Keefe, "Marketing Defined," *Marketing News* (January 15, 2008), pp. 28–29.

Figure 1-1

Customer Satisfaction Is Job One

Dunkin' Donuts (**http://www.dunkindonuts.com**) is quite customer-driven. Customer satisfaction is earned every day. That is why it steadily updates its product mix, offers an extensive value menu, and prides itself on prompt service.

Source: Reprinted by permission.

1-3   THE EVOLUTION OF MARKETING

Marketing's evolution in an industry, country, or region of the world often entails a sequence of stages: barter era→production era→sales era→marketing department era→marketing company era. In some industries, nations, and regions, marketing practices have evolved through each stage and involve a good consumer orientation and high efficiency; in others, marketing practices are still in infancy.

Marketing's origins can be traced to people's earliest use of the exchange process: the ***barter era***. With barter, people trade one resource for another—like food for animal pelts. To accommodate exchanges, trading posts, traveling salespeople, general stores, and cities evolved along with a standardized monetary system. In the least developed nations of the world, barter is still widely practiced.

> Marketing can be traced to the **barter era**.

The modern system of marketing begins with the industrialization of an industry, country, or region. For the world's most developed nations, this occurred with the Industrial Revolution of the late 1800s. For developing nations, efforts to industrialize are now under way. Why is industrialization so important? Without it, exchanges are limited because people do not have surplus items to trade. With the onset of mass production, better transportation, and more efficient technology, products can be made in greater volume and sold at lower prices. Improved mobility, densely populated cities, and specialization also let more people share in the exchange process: They can turn from self-sufficiency (such as making their own clothes) to purchases (such as buying

clothes). In the initial stages of industrialization, output is limited and marketing is devoted to physical distribution. Because demand is high and competition is low, firms typically do not have to conduct consumer research, modify products, or otherwise adapt to consumer needs. The goal is to lift production to meet demand. This is the *production era* of marketing.

At the next stage, companies expand production capabilities to keep up with consumer demand. Many firms hire a sales force and some use advertising to sell their inventory. Yet, because competition is still rather low, when firms develop new products, consumer tastes or needs receive little consideration. The role of the sales force and advertising is to make consumer desires fit the features of the products offered. Thus, a shoe manufacturer might make brown wingtip shoes and use ads and personal selling to persuade consumers to buy them. That firm would rarely determine consumer tastes before making shoes or adjust output to those tastes. This is the *sales era* of marketing. It still exists where competition is limited, such as in nations recently converting to free-market economies.

Supply begins to exceed demand as competition grows. Firms cannot prosper without marketing input. They create marketing departments to conduct consumer research and advise management on how to better design, distribute, promote, and price products. Unless firms react to consumer needs, competitors might better satisfy demand and leave the firms with surplus inventory and falling sales. Although marketing departments share in decisions, they may be in a subordinate position to production, engineering, and sales departments. This is the *marketing department era*. It still exists where marketing has been embraced, but not as the driving force in an industry or company.

In the **production era**, output increases to meet demand.

In the **sales era**, firms sell products without first determining consumer desires.

The **marketing department era** occurs when research is used to determine consumer needs.

Figure 1-3

Marketing Savannah, Georgia, as an Attractive Place for Business

Source: Reprinted by permission.

The **marketing company era** integrates consumer research and analysis into all efforts.

Over the last several decades, firms in a growing number of industries, nations, and regions have recognized marketing's central role; marketing departments at those firms are now the equal of others. The firms make virtually all key decisions after thorough consumer analysis: Because competition is intense and sophisticated, consumers must be aggressively drawn and kept loyal to a firm's brands. Company efforts are well integrated and regularly reviewed. This is the *marketing company era*. Figure 1-4 indicates the key aspects of each era in marketing's evolution.

The marketing concept, a marketing philosophy, customer service, and customer satisfaction and relationship marketing are the linchpins of the marketing company era. They are examined next.

Figure 1-4

How Marketing Evolves

1-3a   The Marketing Concept

As Figure 1-5 shows, the ***marketing concept*** is a consumer-oriented, market-driven, value-based, integrated, goal-oriented philosophy for a firm, institution, or person.[3] Here is an example of it in action:

> Three billion times a day, Procter & Gamble (P&G) brands touch the lives of people around the world. Our goal is to delight consumers at two "moments of truth": first, when they buy a product, and second, when they use it. To achieve that, we live with our consumers and try to see the world and opportunities for new products through their eyes. At P&G (http://www.pg.com), the CEO is not the boss—the consumer is. Great innovations come from understanding the consumer's unmet needs and desires. Regardless of the market, innovation must be consumer-led. That is not the same thing as consumer-decided. As Henry Ford once put it, if he had listened to the marketplace, he would have built a faster, cheaper horse. He understood that what people really wanted was a better way to travel. Consumer insights lead to innovation opportunities. You must develop an appreciation for who your consumers are and how they live, to know their needs and also their aspirations. Only then can you figure out how to deliver a product that can improve their lives.[4]

> The **marketing concept** is consumer-oriented, market-driven, value-driven, integrated, and goal-oriented.

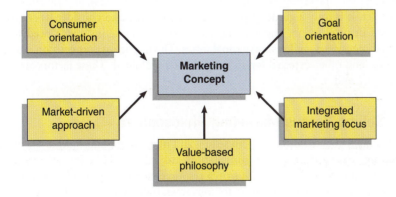

Figure 1-5

The Marketing Concept

---

[3] For an analysis of the marketing concept and its applications, see Frederick E. Webster, Jr., "Defining the New Marketing Concept," *Marketing Management*, Vol. 2 (Number 2, 1994), pp. 23–31; Dave Webb, Cynthia Webster, and Areti Krepapa, "An Exploration of the Meanings and Outcomes of a Customer-Defined Market Orientation," *Journal of Business Research*, Vol. 48 (May 2000), pp. 101–112; Geraldine Fennell and Greg M. Allenby, "Specifying Your Market's Boundaries," *Marketing Research* (Summer 2003), pp. 32–37; Malte Brettel, Andreas Engelen, Florian Heinemann, and Pakpachong Vadhanasindhu, "Antecedents of Market Orientation: A Cross-Cultural Comparison," *Journal of International Marketing*, Vol. 16 (June 2008), pp. 84–119; Steven Ward and Aleksandra Lewandowska, "Is the Marketing Concept Always Necessary?" *European Journal of Marketing*, Vol. 42 (January 2008), pp. 222–237; and Adam Rapp, Niels Schillewaert, and Andrew Wei Hao, "The Influence of Market Orientation on E-Business Innovation and Performance: The Role of the Top Management Team," *Journal of Marketing Theory & Practice*, Vol. 16 (Winter 2008), pp. 7–25.

[4] A. G. Lafley and Ram Charan, "The Consumer Is Boss," *Fortune* (March 17, 2008), pp. 122, 124.

The marketing concept's five elements are crucial to the long-term success of a good, service, organization, person, place, or idea: A *consumer orientation* means examining consumer needs, not production capability, and devising a plan to satisfy them. A *market-driven approach* means being aware of the structure of the marketplace, especially the attributes and strategies of competing firms. A *value-based philosophy* means offering goods and services that consumers perceive to have superior value relative to their costs and the offerings of competitors. With an *integrated marketing focus*, all the activities relating to goods and services are coordinated, including finance, production, engineering, inventory control, research and development, and marketing. A *goal-oriented firm* employs marketing to achieve both short- and long-term goals—which may be profit, funding to find a cure for a disease, increased tourism, election of a political candidate, a better company image, and so on. Marketing helps attain goals by orienting a firm toward pleasing consumers and offering desired goods, services, or ideas.

These are some of the things that managers can do to adhere to the spirit of the marketing concept:

- Create a customer focus throughout the firm.
- Listen to customers.
- Define and cultivate distinctive competences.
- Define marketing as market intelligence.
- Target customers precisely.
- Manage for profitability, not sales volume.
- Make customer value the guiding star.
- Let the customer define quality.
- Measure and manage customer expectations.
- Build customer relationships and loyalty.
- Define the business as a service business.
- Commit to continuous improvement and innovation.
- Manage the company culture along with strategy and structure.
- Grow with partners and alliances.
- Destroy marketing bureaucracy.[5]

Through the marketing concept, a firm analyzes, maximizes, and satisfies consumer demand. Yet, it is only a guide to planning. A firm must also consider its strengths and weaknesses in production, engineering, and finance. Marketing plans need to balance goals, customer needs, and resource capabilities. The impact of competition, government regulations, and other external forces must also be evaluated. These factors are discussed in Chapters 2 and 3.

1-3b Selling Versus Marketing Philosophies

Figure 1-6 highlights the differences in selling and marketing philosophies. The benefits of a marketing, rather than a sales, orientation are many. Marketing stresses consumer analysis and satisfaction, directs the firm's resources to making goods and services consumers want, and adapts to changes in consumer traits and needs. Under a marketing philosophy, selling is used to communicate with and understand consumers; consumer dissatisfaction leads to changes in policy, not a stronger or different sales pitch. Marketing looks for real differences in consumer tastes and devises offerings to satisfy them. Marketing is geared to the long run, and marketing goals reflect overall company goals. Finally, marketing views customer needs broadly (such as heating), not narrowly (such as fuel oil).

Consider Wahl Clipper Corporation (**http://www.wahlclipper.com**), which makes electric shavers, hair trimmers, and other personal-care products. The company was founded nearly 100 years ago and now operates around the world. How has it been able

> With a marketing orientation, selling helps to communicate with and understand consumers.

---

[5] Frederick E. Webster, Jr., "Executing the New Marketing Concept," *Marketing Management*, Vol. 3 (Number 1, 1994), pp. 9–16.

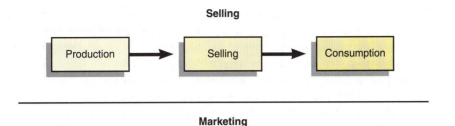

Selling

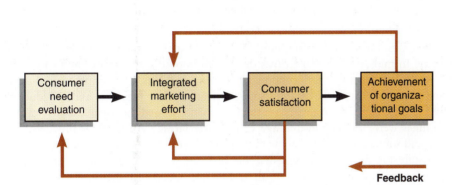

Marketing

Feedback

Figure 1-6

The Focus of Selling and Marketing Philosophies

to prosper for so long? According to former president Jack Wahl, "I realized the difference between sales and marketing. That's a big thing for a small company. Sales means simply presenting the product and collecting money. Marketing means stepping back and looking for the needs of the customer, and for the best way to get through to that user." The firm is now led by Jack's son Gregory, who knows that "To maintain our leadership position in the personal-care categories we serve, we must have vision. Vision to continually improve our existing products. Vision to bring new products to market which meet the wants and needs of consumers. Vision to stay innovative and ahead of our competitors, and vision to support our customers, the retailers, with sales and marketing programs that make it easy, fun, and profitable for them to sell more Wahl products. Leading with Vision means constantly being alert to new opportunities. By sharing the vision, we can make tomorrow absolutely extraordinary."[6]

1-3c Customer Service

Customer service involves the identifiable, but rather intangible, activities undertaken by a seller in conjunction with the basic goods and/or services it offers.[7] In today's highly competitive marketplace, the level of customer service a firm provides can greatly affect its ability to attract and retain customers. Nonetheless, firms often have to make customer service trade-offs. For instance, supermarkets must weigh the potential loss of business if waiting lines are too long versus the cost of hiring more cashiers.

Unless a consumer is happy with *both* the basic good (such as a new PC) or service (such as the installation of computer software) offered by a seller *and* the quality of customer service (such as polite, expert sales personnel and on-time appointments), he or she is unlikely to patronize the seller—certainly not in the long run. And today, unhappy consumers have more ways to vent their anger than ever before:

> Meet today's consumer vigilantes. They are arming themselves with video cameras, computer keyboards, and mobile devices to launch their own personal forms of insurrection. Frustrated by the usual fix-it options—obediently waiting on hold, gamely chatting online

Customer service tends to be intangible, but quite meaningful, to many consumers.

---

[6] Jerry Flint, "Father Says, 'Jump,'" *Forbes* (August 14, 1995), p. 144; and "About Wahl," **http://www.consumer.wahl.com/about.cfm** (April 3, 2009).

[7] "Dictionary," **http://www.marketingpower.com/_layouts/Dictionary.aspx?dLetter=C** (March 22, 2009).

with a scripted robot—more consumers are rebelling against company-prescribed service channels. After getting nowhere with the call center, they're sending "E-mail carpet bombs" to companies with their complaints. When all else fails, a plucky few are going straight to the top after uncovering direct numbers to executive customer-service teams not easily found by mere mortals. And of course, they're filling up the Web with blogs and videos, leaving behind venom-spewed tales of woe. Behind the guerrilla tactics is a growing disconnect between the experience companies promise and customers' perceptions of what they actually get. Consumers already pushed to the brink by evaporating home equity, job insecurity, and rising prices are more apt to snap when hit with long hold times and impenetrable phone trees.[8]

According to consumer surveys, perceptions about the overall level of customer service at U.S. businesses are declining. Why? Let's look at the case of the U.S. airline industry. In mid-2008, several airlines decided to impose a $15 fee on the first checked bag (which had been free) for economy fliers on many flights. The airlines viewed the fee as one reasonable way to cover the soaring increase in their fuel costs and to reduce the weight of their flights. Consumers, on the other hand, viewed the fee as another way that the airlines were "nickel-and-diming" them—after already charging for previously free snacks and sometimes doing away with pillows and some other amenities.[9]

Despite the preceding comments, lots of firms do positively address the issue of customer service. They also know it can be difficult: "Good customer service would seem to be a simple matter. Make policies flexible. Don't force customers to play call-center phone tag. Hire friendly people, train them well, and reward them with healthy pay and benefits. But delivering the right level of customer service turns out to be hard. Some companies struggle to find smiling teenagers who are willing to work for the minimum wage flipping burgers. Others have the difficult task of ensuring their customers get the same message whether they're online, on the phone, or in the store."[10]

> To offer better customer service, some firms are **empowering employees**.

Some of the best practitioners of customer service, such as Ritz-Carlton and Federal Express, are ***empowering employees***, whereby workers are given broad leeway to satisfy customer requests. With empowerment, employees are encouraged and rewarded for showing initiative and imagination. They can "break the rules" if, in their judgment, customer requests should be honored: All Ritz-Carlton hotel (**http://www.ritz-carlton.com**) employees (including housekeepers) are trained to listen for customer complaints and to be familiar with possible solutions. Similarly, Federal Express (**http://www.fedex.com**) drivers can help customers pack breakable items. PARKnSHOP (**http://www.parknshop.com**), Hong Kong's leading supermarket chain, has a strong customer service approach—including a delivery policy that says: "With PARKnSHOP, you carry what's fresh. We deliver the rest. Free."

Ace Hardware (**http://www.acehardware.com**) has been adding a new "customer quarterback" into a number of its stores. This customer coordinator strives to help shoppers when the stores are especially busy: "If there's an influx of shoppers, the coordinator alerts sales associates to drop everything and focus on customers. Using an earpiece, he or she radios ahead so the right expert is waiting when the customer gets to the aisle." If a shopper is just looking, the staff is given an audio heads up to "give him or her 5 or 10 minutes before asking if the person needs help."[11]

1-3d Customer Satisfaction and Relationship Marketing

Customer satisfaction is a crucial element in successful marketing. It is the degree to which there is a match between a customer's expectations of a good or service and the actual performance of that good or service, including customer service.[12] As two experts

> Firms cannot usually prosper without a high level of **customer satisfaction**.

[8] Jena McGregor, "Consumer Vigilantes," *Business Week* (March 3, 2008), pp. 38–39.

[9] Suzanne Kapner, "Flying the Unfriendly Skies," *Fortune* (July 7, 2008), p. 30.

[10] Jena McGregor, "Customer Service Champs," *Business Week* (March 3, 2008), pp. 37.

[11] Aili McConnon, "Calling the Right Play for Each Customer," *Business Week* (March 3, 2008), p. 50.

[12] "Dictionary," **http://www.marketingpower.com/_layouts/Dictionary.aspx?dLetter=C** (March 22, 2009).

Figure 1-7

Factors That Affect Customer Satisfaction

Source: Steven Hokanson, "The Deeper You Analyze, the More You Satisfy Customers," *Marketing News* (January 2, 1995), p. 16. Reprinted by permission of the American Marketing Association.

note: "Successful firms know that the customer is the ultimate judge of the quality of a shopping experience. Consumers enjoy more choice than before—in stores, brands, and channels—and have access to an ever-increasing amount of information upon which to base their buying decisions. Capturing the purchasing power of these sophisticated consumers is a difficult and constant challenge."[13] Figure 1-7 shows 11 representative factors that affect overall customer satisfaction.

This is how daunting it can be to keep customers fully satisfied:

> For the past few decades, customer satisfaction has been the mantra by which firms have tried to manage the relationship between their products and customers. Much to their disappointment, managers are discovering that high levels of customer satisfaction do not necessarily translate into high levels of customer loyalty. For example, they might be surprised to find that more than 60 percent of customers who switch to another brand classify themselves as "satisfied". This points to an important question: Why does customer satisfaction with products translate into such low levels of customer loyalty? Moreover, how can this be improved? A possibility is that customers want more than mere satisfaction; perhaps they want to be "delighted" in exchange for greater loyalty.[14]

If a customer becomes upset, several actions can be taken: (1) "If you have answered the phone on behalf of the company, you have accepted 100 percent responsibility. So get off the 'It's not my fault' syndrome." (2) "Saying you're sorry won't fix the problem, but it definitely does help to defuse it immediately." (3) "When someone is angry or frustrated with your company, the one thing he or she needs is someone to agree with him or her—or at least show understanding." (4) "Don't make a customer wait for good service. Get him or her whatever is needed immediately." (5) "Ask the customer what would make him or her happy." (6) "Service recovery is not just fixing the problem. It's making sure it won't happen again." (7) "After you feel the problem has been fixed, follow-up on it."[15]

Companies with satisfied customers have a good opportunity to convert them into loyal customers who purchase from those firms over an extended period. From a consumer-oriented perspective, when marketing activities are performed with the conscious intention of developing and managing long-term, trusting customer relations, ***relationship marketing*** is involved.[16] Why is this so important? "Several years ago, in

> Through **relationship marketing**, companies try to increase long-term customer loyalty.

---

[13] Theresa Williams and Mark J. Larson, "Preface," *Creating the Ideal Shopping Experience* (Bloomington, IN: Indiana University, 2000), p. 1.

[14] Ravindra Chitturi, Rajagopal Raghunathan, and Vijay Mahajan, "Delight by Design: The Role of Hedonic Versus Utilitarian Benefits," *Journal of Marketing*, Vol. 72 (May 2008), p. 48.

[15] Nancy Friedman, "Check Out These Seven Steps to a Service Recovery," *Tire Business* (June 6, 2005), p. 9.

[16] "Dictionary," **http://www.marketingpower.com/_layouts/Dictionary.aspx?dLetter=R** (March 22, 2009).

Ethical Issues in Marketing

The Ethics of Monitoring Customer Service Calls

Call-monitoring firms have the ability to tap into their clients' phone lines and capture what is on each operator's screen during his or her conversation with a customer. Most such calls are monitored without the need to enter a client's office. New technologies, such as Voice over Internet Protocol (VoIP), also enable firms to search for keywords used by customer service personnel and interpret speech patterns.

Those who favor using "professional eavesdroppers" say it's one of the most effective means of improving customer service levels. If done properly, call monitoring can improve consumer experiences, reduce callbacks, better focus training efforts for call-center personnel, and facilitate employee development. Many clients use data from call-monitoring firms – such as how often a service representative repeats a customer's name and whether a service representative takes the time to verify that he or she is talking to the customer (as opposed to a spouse) – to reward excellent staff members. Call-monitoring firms can also provide tailored training sessions based on their specific call-monitoring experiences with a particular client.

Those concerned about call monitoring feel that consumers need to know that their conversations are being taped and that their identities may be shared with others. Some marketers even feel that having too much information about their customers may be harmful to good long-term relationships. They argue that customers should be able to opt out of having their conversations monitored and feel that a customer may inhibit his/her comments when he/she knows that the conversation is being monitored.

Source: Based on material in "Call Quality Practices 2008," *Business Wire* (April 7, 2008).

The Loyalty Effect, Bain & Company documented the outstanding financial results you can achieve by cultivating customer loyalty: A 5 percent increase in customer retention increases profits by 25 to 95 percent. It costs so much to acquire customers that many of them are unprofitable in the early years. Only later, when the cost of serving loyal customers falls and the volume of their purchases rises, do relationships generate big returns."[17] See Figure 1-8.

Office Depot (**http://www.officedepot.com**), the giant chain of office supplies and equipment stores, is one of many firms that has mastered relationship marketing, especially with its Web sites. For example,

> Tech Depot (**http://www.techdepot.com**) is a direct marketer of computer and technology products. We have over 100,000 business, government, and education customers. Our account management team, combined with our robust online catalog, saves customers time and money. We offer qualified customers many advantages such as flexible credit terms, dedicated account managers, and Extranets. *Multibillion Dollar Buying Power*: As a subsidiary of Office Depot, we have direct relationships with leading manufacturers and distributors to ensure that our customers obtain the most competitive prices each and every day. *Broad Selection*: 100,000+ products, including PC hardware, software, networking, and supplies. *Total Purchasing Convenience*: Security and privacy are assured; bill-when-ship policy; powerful search engine. *Incomparable Service*: Personalized, one-on-one account management; dedicated customer care teams; free-sales technical support; no restocking fees.[18]

Scion, one of Toyota's auto divisions, is another leader in relationship marketing due to its hassle-free sales process, its customer-friendly Web site (**http://www.scion. com**), and other factors:

> Scion is unique because both the products and buying process are designed to create a whole new culture that will change the car buying experience. We respect your time by creating a

---

[17] Darrell K. Rigby, Frederick Reichheld, and Chris Dawson, "Winning Customer Loyalty Is the Key to a Winning CRM Strategy," *Ivey Business Journal*, Vol. 67 (July-August 2003), pp. 1–5.

[18] "About Us," **http://www.techdepot.com/pro/static/aboutus.asp?iid=211** (May 17, 2009).

The best drinks ice
could hope for.

Available inside now.

Figure 1-8

Starbucks: Bringing a Relationship Marketing Philosophy to the Coffee Shop Marketplace

Starbucks (**http://www.starbucks. com**) does everything it can to encourage long-term customer relationships: "We always figured that putting people before products just made good common sense. So far, it's been working out for us. Our relationships with farmers yield the highest quality coffees. The connections we make in communities create a loyal following. And the support we provide our baristas pays off every day."

Source: Reprinted by permission.

simple, straightforward, easy-to-understand approach called "Pure Price." This means no haggle, no hassle. Our customers told us they want a shorter, simpler process with less pressure—and we listened. With the Scion Pure Price Solution, you don't have to negotiate price—or sit around the dealership waiting for someone to "crunch the numbers." In many cases, you'll deal with only one person for the entire transaction—start to finish. That makes it easier on you—and easier on us. We can devote more time and attention to getting you the car you want—and getting you on your way.[19]

Sephora (**http://www.sephora.com**) is a retail concept intent on generating loyal customers. Founded in France, Sephora is one of the world's leading chains of perfume and cosmetics stores. In addition to France, it has stores in Canada, China, the Czech Republic, Greece, Italy, Luxembourg, the Middle East, Monaco, Poland, Portugal, Romania, Russia, and Spain; and it is growing rapidly. Sephora came to the United States in mid-1998 with its New York and Miami stores. There are now about 120 U.S. stores nationwide. The key to Sephora's success is its unique selling approach:

The unique, open-sell environment features over 250 classic and emerging brands across a broad range of product categories including skincare, color, fragrance, makeup, bath and body, and haircare, besides Sephora's own private label. To build the most knowledgeable and professional team of product consultants in the beauty industry, Sephora developed "Science of Sephora." This program ensures that our team is skilled to identify skin types, have a

[19] "Pure Price—No Haggle—No Hassle Scion," **http://www.scionofconcord.com/Pure-Price.aspx** (May 17, 2009).

knowledge of skin physiology, the history of makeup, application techniques, the science of creating fragrances, and most importantly, how to interact with Sephora's diverse clientele. Sephora's highly trained beauty experts are available to assist clients wherever they shop—in stores, online, or via 1-877-SEPHORA.[20]

Many Web sites can help client firms improve their level of customer satisfaction and relationship marketing. Examples include Business Research Lab (**http://www. busreslab.com/consult/custsat.htm**), CustomerSat.com (**http://www.customersat.com**), Customer Value, Inc. (**http://www.cval.com**), and Relationship Marketing, Inc. (**http:// www.rmarketing.com**).

1-4 THE IMPORTANCE OF MARKETING

This section discusses several reasons why the field of marketing should be studied: A basic task for marketing is to generate consumer enthusiasm for goods and services because a key marketing task is to stimulate demand. Worldwide, $70 trillion of goods and services are produced annually (expressed in purchasing-power-parity), with the United States accounting for more than one-fifth of that sum.[21]

> Marketing stimulates consumers, constitutes a large part of selling costs, employs many people, supports industries, affects all consumers, and plays a major role in our lives.

A large portion of each sales dollar goes to cover the costs related to such marketing activities as product development, packaging, distribution, advertising and personal selling, price marking, and administering consumer credit programs. Some estimates place the costs of marketing as high as 50 percent or more of sales in certain industries. Yet, it should not be assumed that the performance of some marketing tasks by consumers would automatically lead to lower prices. Could a small business really save money by having the owner fly to Detroit to buy a new truck directly from the maker rather than from a local dealer? Would a family be willing to buy clothing in bulk to reduce a retailer's transportation and storage costs?

Tens of millions of people work in marketing-related jobs in the United States alone. They include those employed in the retailing, wholesaling, transportation, warehousing, and communications industries (including the Internet), and those involved with marketing jobs for manufacturing, service, agricultural, mining, and other industries. Projections indicate future employment in marketing will remain strong.

Marketing activities also involve entire industries, such as advertising and marketing research. Total annual worldwide advertising expenditures approximate $500 billion. Many agencies, such as Omnicom Group (**http://www.omnicomgroup.com**) and Interpublic Group (**http://www.interpublic.com**) of the United States, WPP Group (**http:// www.wpp.com**) of Great Britain, Japan's Dentsu (**http://www.dentsu.com**), and France's Publicis Groupe (**http://www.publicis.com/corporate/en**) have worldwide billings of several billion dollars each. More than $25 billion worldwide is spent yearly on various types of commercial marketing research. Firms such as the Nielsen Company (**http:// www.nielsen.com**) and IMS Health (**http://www.imshealth.com**); TNS Global (**http:// www.tnsglobal.com**) of Great Britain; GfK Group (**http://www.gfk.com**) of Germany; and Ipsos (**http://www.ipsos.com**) of France each generate yearly worldwide revenues of more than one billion dollars.

All people and organizations serve as consumers for various goods and services. By understanding the role of marketing, consumers can become better informed, more selective, and more efficient. Effective channels of communication with sellers can also be established and complaints resolved more easily and favorably. Consumer groups have a major impact on sellers.

---

[20] "About Sephora," **http://www.sephora.com/help/about_sephora.jhtml?location=sephora** (May 17, 2008).

[21] "World Economic Outlook Data Bases," **http://www.imf.org/external/pubs/ft/weo/2008/01/weodata/index.aspx** (April 2008).

Global Marketing in Action

NBA Europe Live: Marketing U.S. Sports on the Global Stage

To stimulate interest in the sport, several NBA (http://www.nba.com) teams have participated in NBA Europe Live. For example, in 2008, the Miami Heat, New Jersey Nets, New Orleans Hornets, and Washington Wizards played preseason games in Barcelona, Berlin, London, and Paris. Besides the games, the NBA conducted a series of community events and programs in each of these cities. Annually, NBA Europe Live games attract more than 10 TV million viewers and 75,000 spectators, and are supported by many marketing partners, such as Adidas (http://www.adidas.com) and EA Sports (http://www.easports.com).

According to the CEO of Euroleague Basketball (http://www.euroleague.net), "Euroleague Basketball is always seeking to participate and help in making the sport of basketball grow across the globe. We are happy to be participating and making the bridges between Europe and USA stronger."

The NBA has 30 teams in the United States and Canada and is one of the largest suppliers of sports television and Internet programming in the world. During a typical season, the NBA distributes its games and programming material to about 215 countries and territories in more than 40 languages.

Euroleague Basketball includes 24 clubs from about a dozen countries. Euroleague recently launched **Euroleague.TV**, an online broadcast platform/service offering both live and on-demand coverage. Although this service blocks some live broadcasts to protect rights holders, subscribers to Euroleague.TV are otherwise able to watch Euroleague Basketball on an on-demand basis. Subscribers can choose from different subscription packages that offer live games, highlights, weekly magazines, daily news, and exclusive interviews.

Source: Based on material in "NBA Teams to Tour Europe for Third Consecutive Year as Part of 2008 NBA Europe Live Presented by EA Sports," http://www.nba.com/global/europelive_release_080327.html (March 28, 2008).

Because resources are scarce, marketing programs and systems must function at their peak. Thus, by optimizing customer service, inventory movement, advertising expenditures, product assortments, and other areas of marketing, firms will better use resources. Some industries may even require demarketing (lowering the demand for goods and services). The latter often include energy consumption.

Marketing impacts strongly on people's beliefs and lifestyles. In fact, it has been criticized as fostering materialistic attitudes, fads, product obsolescence, a reliance on gadgets, status consciousness, and superficial product differences—and for wasting resources. Marketers reply that they merely address the desires of people and make the best goods and services they can at the prices people will pay.

Marketing has a role to play in our quality of life. For example, marketing personnel often encourage firms to make safer products, such as child-proof bottle caps. They create public service messages on energy conservation, AIDS prevention, driver safety, alcohol abuse, and other topics. They help new goods, ideas, and services (such as Apple iPhones [http://www.apple.com/iphone], improved nutrition, and YouTube [http://www.youtube.com]) to be recognized and accepted by people and organizations.

Knowledge of marketing is extremely valuable for those not directly involved in a marketing job. Marketing decisions must be made by:

> Marketing awareness is invaluable for those in nonmarketing jobs.

- *Doctors*—What hours are most desirable to patients?
- *Lawyers*—How can new clients be attracted?
- *Management consultants*—Should fees be higher, lower, or the same as competitors' fees?
- *Financial analysts*—What investments should be recommended to clients?
- *Research and development personnel*—Is there demand for a potential "breakthrough" product?
- *Economists*—What impact will the economy have on how various industries market their offerings?
- *Statisticians*—How should firms react to predicted demographic shifts?
- *Teachers*—How can students become better consumers?

- *City planners*—How can businesses be persuaded to relocate to the city?
- *Nonprofit institutions*—How can donor contributions be increased?

Each profession and organization must address patient, client, consumer, student, taxpayer, or contributor needs. And more of them than ever before are performing marketing tasks such as research, advertising, and so on.

1-5   MARKETING FUNCTIONS AND PERFORMERS

> Basic **marketing functions** range from environmental analysis to marketing management.

There are eight basic *marketing functions*: environmental analysis and marketing research, broadening the scope of marketing, consumer analysis, product planning, distribution planning, promotion planning, price planning, and marketing management. They are shown in Figure 1-9, which also notes where they are discussed in the text.

Here are brief descriptions of the functions:

- *Environmental analysis and marketing research*—Monitoring and adapting to external factors that affect success or failure, such as the economy and competition; and collecting data to resolve specific marketing issues.
- *Broadening the scope of marketing*—Deciding on the emphasis on and approach to societal/ethical issues and global marketing, as well as the role of the Web in a marketing strategy.
- *Consumer analysis*—Examining and evaluating consumer characteristics, needs, and purchase processes; and selecting the group(s) of consumers at which to aim marketing efforts.
- *Product planning (including goods, services, organizations, people, places, and ideas)*—Developing and sustaining products, product assortments, product images, brands, packaging, and optional features; and deleting faltering products.
- *Distribution planning*—Forming logistical relations with distribution intermediaries, physical distribution, inventory management, warehousing, transportation, the allocation of goods and services, wholesaling, and retailing.
- *Promotion planning*—Communicating with customers, the general public, and others through some form of advertising, public relations, personal selling, and/or sales promotion.

Figure 1-9
The Basic Functions of Marketing

- *Price planning*—Determining price levels and ranges, pricing techniques, terms of purchase, price adjustments, and the use of price as an active or passive factor.
- *Marketing management*—Planning, implementing, and controlling the marketing program (strategy) and individual marketing functions; appraising the risks and benefits in decision making; and focusing on total quality.

Typically, a firm should first study its environment and gather relevant marketing information. The firm should determine how to act in a socially responsible and ethical manner, consider whether to be domestic and/or global, and decide on the proper use of the Web. At the same time, the firm should analyze potential customers to learn their needs and select the group(s) on which to focus. It should next plan product offerings, make distribution decisions, choose how to communicate with customers and others, and set proper prices. These four functions (in combination, known as the *marketing mix*) should be done in a coordinated manner, based on environmental, societal, and consumer analysis. Through marketing management, the firm's overall marketing program would be planned and carried out in an integrated manner, with fine-tuning as needed.

Although many marketing transactions require the performance of similar tasks, such as being ethical; analyzing consumers; and product, distribution, promotion, and price planning, they can be enacted in many ways (such as a manufacturer distributing via full-service retailers versus self-service ones, or a financial-services firm relying on telephone contacts by its sales force versus in-office visits to potential small-business clients by salespeople).

Marketing performers are the organizations or individuals that undertake one or more marketing functions. Included are manufacturers and service providers, wholesalers, retailers, marketing specialists, and organizational and final consumers. As Figure 1-10 shows, each performer has a distinct role. Although responsibility for marketing tasks can be shifted in various ways, basic marketing functions usually must be done by one performer or another. They often cannot be omitted.

Sometimes, one marketing performer decides to carry out all, or virtually all, marketing functions (such as Boeing analyzing the marketplace, acting ethically, operating domestically and globally, having a detailed Web site (**http://www.boeing.com**), seeking various types of customers, developing aerospace and related products,

> Usually at least one **marketing performer** must undertake each basic marketing function.

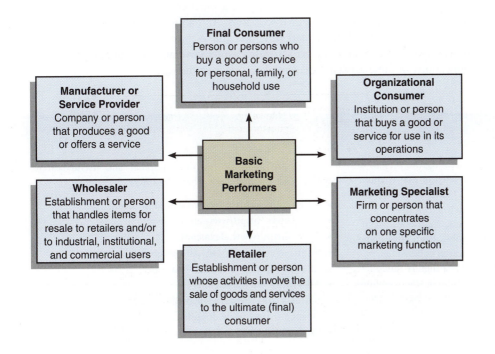

Figure 1-10

Who Performs Marketing Functions

distributing products directly to customers, using its own sales force and placing ads in select media, and setting prices). Yet, for the following reasons, one performer often does not undertake all marketing functions:

- Many firms do not have the financial resources to sell products directly to consumers. They need intermediaries to share in the distribution process.
- Marketing directly to customers may require goods and services producers to offer complementary products or sell the complementary products of other firms so distribution is carried out efficiently.
- A performer may be unable or unwilling to complete certain functions and may seek a marketing specialist to fulfill them.
- Many performers are too small to do certain functions efficiently.
- For numerous goods and services, established distribution methods are in force and it is difficult to set up other methods (such as bypassing independent soda distributors to sell directly to retail stores).
- Some consumers may want to buy in quantity, visit self-service outlets, and pay cash to save money.

1-6 FORMAT OF THE TEXT

Marketing in the 21st Century has eight parts. The balance of Part 1 focuses on the marketing environment, preparing marketing plans, and the information needed for marketing decisions. Part 2 covers topics related to the broadened scope of marketing: societal, ethical, and consumer issues; global marketing; and the Web. Parts 1 and 2 set the stage for the specific aspects of marketing.

Part 3 deals with marketing's central orientation: understanding consumers. It looks at the demographics, social and psychological traits, and decision process of final consumers; organizational consumer attributes and decision making; and developing a target market and sales forecasting. Parts 4 to 7 discuss the marketing mix (product, distribution, promotion, and price planning) and the actions needed to enact a marketing program in depth. Part 8 considers the marketing management implications of the topics raised throughout *Marketing* and discusses how to integrate and analyze an overall marketing plan.

Numerous illustrations of actual marketing practices by a variety of organizations and individuals are woven into our discussions. And although such topics as marketing and society, global marketing, marketing and the Web, organizational consumers, and goods versus service marketing get separate chapter coverage to highlight certain points, applications in these areas are presented throughout the text.

Web Sites You Can Use

In every chapter of *Marketing in the 21st Century*, we present a variety of links to worthwhile Web sites related to that chapter.

An important tool for any Web "surfer" looking for information about a topic related to marketing is a search engine. This tool enables the user to generate a clickable list of Web links on virtually any subject imaginable, from advertising to zero-based budgeting. Dozens of free search engines are available on the Web. Because each one has a slightly different method of searching, you should rely on multiple search engines if you want to do comprehensive research on a subject. After experimenting with various search engines, many users settle on a few that they really like.

Here are many of the most popular and useful search engines. Visit them and see what they offer.

- 1st Headlines (**http://www.1stheadlines.com**)
- About.com (**http://www.about.com**)
- Alexa (**http://www.alexa.com**)
- All the Web (**http://www.alltheweb.com**)
- AltaVista (**http://www.altavista.com**)
- Ask (**http://www.ask.com**)
- Business.com (**http://www.business.com**)
- Dogpile (**http://www.dogpile.com**)
- Excite (**http://www.excite.com**)

- ExpressFind (http://www.expressfind.com)
- Fagan Finder (http://www.faganfinder.com)
- Fazzle (http://www.fazzle.com)
- Findspot (http://www.findspot.com)
- Go.com (http://www.go.com)
- Google (http://www.google.com)
- HighBeam Research (http://www.highbeam.com/library/index.asp)
- HotBot (http://www.hotbot.com)
- Inbox Robot (http://www.inboxrobot.com)
- Internet Archive (http://www.archive.org)
- iTools (http://www.itools.com)
- Iwon (http://www.iwon.com)
- Ixquick (http://www.ixquick.com)
- Live Search (http://www.msn.com)
- Looksmart (http://search.looksmart.com)
- Lycos (http://www.lycos.com)
- Mamma (http://www.mamma.com)
- Metacrawler (http://www.metacrawler.com)
- My Way (http://www.myway.com)
- Scrub the Web (http://www.scrubtheweb.com)
- Search Bug (http://www.searchbug.com)
- Search.com (http://www.search.com)
- Vivisimo (http://www.vivisimo.com)
- Webcrawler (http://www.webcrawler.com)
- Wikia Search (http://www.re.search.wikia.com)
- Yahoo! (http://www.yahoo.com)
- Yellow Book (http://www.yellowbook.com)
- Zenith Optimedia Marketer's Portal (http://www.marketersportal.com)

Summary

In every chapter, the summary is linked to the objectives stated at the beginning of that chapter.

1. *To illustrate the exciting, dynamic, and influential nature of marketing* Marketing may be viewed from both business and consumer perspectives; and it influences us daily. As goods and service providers, we make such marketing-related decisions as choosing who customers are, what goods and services to offer, where to sell them, what to stress in promotion, what prices to charge, how to be ethical and responsible, and whether to operate globally. As consumers, the marketing process affects whom we patronize, choices in the marketplace, where we shop, the availability of sales personnel, the prices we pay, and other factors.

2. *To define marketing and trace its evolution—with emphasis on the marketing concept, a marketing philosophy, customer service, and customer satisfaction and relationship marketing* Marketing involves anticipating, managing, and satisfying demand via the exchange process. It includes goods, services, organizations, people, places, and ideas.

   Marketing's evolution can be traced to the earliest use of barter in the exchange process (the barter era); but, it has truly developed since the Industrial Revolution, as mass production and improved transportation have enabled more transactions to occur. For many firms, modern marketing has evolved via these eras: production, sales, marketing department, and marketing company. Yet, in developing nations, marketing is still in its early stages.

   The marketing concept requires an organization or individual to be consumer-oriented, market-driven, and value-based; have an integrated effort; and be goal-oriented. A marketing philosophy means assessing and responding to consumer wants, real differences in consumer tastes, and long-run opportunities and threats—and to engaging in coordinated decision making.

   For a company to do well, emphasis must be placed on customer service: the identifiable, rather intangible, acts performed by a seller in conjunction with the basic goods and/or services it offers. A number of firms now empower employees so as to improve the level of customer service. Customer satisfaction occurs when consumer expectations are met or exceeded. After customer satisfaction is established, firms then have opportunities to attract loyal customers by paying attention to relationship marketing.

3. *To show the importance of marketing as a field of study* Marketing is a crucial field because it stimulates demand; marketing costs can be high; a large number of people work in marketing positions; it involves entire industries, such as advertising and marketing research; all organizations and people are consumers in some situations; it is necessary to use scarce resources efficiently; marketing impacts on people's beliefs and lifestyles; and marketing influences the quality of our lives. Some marketing knowledge is valuable to all of us, regardless of occupation.

4. *To describe the basic functions of marketing and those who perform these functions* The key marketing functions are environmental analysis and marketing research; broadening the scope of marketing; consumer analysis; product, distribution, promotion, and price planning; and marketing management. Responsibility for doing tasks can be shifted and shared among manufacturers and service providers, wholesalers, retailers, marketing specialists, and consumers. Due to costs, assortment requirements, specialized abilities, company size, established distribution methods, and consumer interests, one party usually does not perform all functions.

Key Terms

marketing (p. 7)

consumer demand (p. 7)

publics' demand (p. 7)

exchange (p. 7)

barter era (p. 8)

production era (p. 9)

sales era (p. 9)

marketing department era (p. 9)

marketing company era (p. 10)

marketing concept (p. 11)

customer service (p. 13)

empowering employees (p. 14)

customer satisfaction (p. 14)

relationship marketing (p. 15)

marketing functions (p. 20)

marketing performers (p. 21)

Review Questions

1. Explain the
   a. anticipation of demand.
   b. management of demand.
   c. satisfaction of demand.
   d. exchange process.
2. Give an example of a good, service, organization, person, place, and idea that may be marketed.
3. Describe the five eras of marketing.

4. What are the five components of the marketing concept? Give an example of each component.
5. What is employment empowerment?
6. What is customer satisfaction? Why is it so important to any firm?
7. What is relationship marketing? Why is it so important to any firm?
8. What are the basic functions performed by marketing?

Discussion Questions

1. a. As Bill Norman, a new advertising agency owner, what business-related marketing decisions would you make? Why?
   b. As Nancy Willis, an advertising agency client, what consumer-related marketing decisions would you make? Why?
   c. Develop a plan for Bill Norman to attract Nancy Willis as a client.

2. As the manager of a local pharmacy, how would your customer services differ from those offered by a national pharmacy chain? Why?
3. Develop a seven-item questionnaire to assess the quality of a firm's relationship marketing efforts.
4. What would a nonmarketing major learn by studying marketing? Give examples for three distinct majors (including at least two nonbusiness majors).

Web Exercise

The American Marketing Association is the leading U.S. professional association for marketers. Visit its Web site (**http://www.marketingpower.com**) and "surf" two sections:

(a) Resource Library and (b) Career Management. Discuss what you learn from your visit.

Practice Quiz

1. Which activity is a central aspect of the definition of marketing?
   a. Manufacturing
   b. Outsourcing
   c. The exchange process
   d. Advertising

2. During the production era of marketing,
   a. research becomes necessary to determine consumer desires and needs.

   b. consumer research and analysis are integrated into all efforts.
   c. business manufactures and sells products without first determining consumer desires.
   d. businesses increase supply to keep up with demand.

3. The current era is known as the
   a. marketing company era.
   b. post-industrial era.
   c. sales era.
   d. Internet era.

4. A value-based philosophy is a key component of
   a. a selling philosophy.
   b. mass marketing.
   c. the marketing concept.
   d. barter.

5. A consumer orientation does *not* usually focus on
   a. production capability.
   b. market needs.
   c. planning.
   d. goals.

6. Although the marketing concept enables an organization to analyze, maximize, and satisfy consumer demand, it should be realized that the concept
   a. does not apply to nonprofit organizations.
   b. is only a guide to planning.
   c. is unnecessary in a competitive marketplace.
   d. is only a theory.

7. The last step for a firm that practices a marketing philosophy is
   a. consumption.
   b. feedback.
   c. consumer satisfaction.
   d. relationship marketing.

8. Customer service activities are
   a. unidentifiable, but relatively tangible.
   b. unimportant to consumers.
   c. identifiable, but relatively intangible.
   d. unrelated to the success of goods and services.

9. Workers can "break the rules" to honor customer requests with
   a. employee empowerment.
   b. a selling philosophy.
   c. power selling.
   d. demarketing.

10. Which statement is *incorrect*?
    a. Consumers today are more satisfied with customer service than ever before.
    b. Consumers today have many mechanisms by which to complain.
    c. Customer service has a large effect on customer satisfaction.
    d. Employee empowerment often leads to greater customer satisfaction.

11. The degree to which there is a match between customer expectations and the actual performance of a good or service is known as
    a. marketing functionality.
    b. customer service.
    c. consumer marketing.
    d. customer satisfaction.

12. Which statement about relationship marketing is correct?
    a. It is short-run oriented.
    b. It cannot be conducted with final consumers.
    c. It places an emphasis on customer loyalty.
    d. It is not a good policy for nonprofit organizations.

13. According to some estimates, marketing costs can be as high as what percentage of a firm's sales?
    a. 15 percent
    b. 25 percent
    c. 35 percent
    d. 50 percent

14. Basic marketing functions
    a. are usually performed by one party.
    b. can be eliminated in most situations.
    c. can be organized in only a limited number of ways.
    d. cannot be shifted and shared.

15. Marketing directly to customers would often require a company to
    a. seek a marketing specialist.
    b. make or sell complementary products.
    c. eliminate many marketing functions.
    d. share distribution of high-volume sales items.

For the answers to these questions, please visit the online site for this book at **http://www.atomicdog.com.**

1 Appendix

Hints for Solving Cases

At the end of each part of *Marketing*, there are a number of short cases and one longer, more provocative case. All of the cases are intended to build on text discussions, improve your reasoning skills, and stimulate class discussions.

Our cases describe actual marketing scenarios faced by a variety of organizations and people. The facts, situations, and people are all real. The questions following each case are designed to help you pinpoint major issues, foster your analysis, have you cite alternative courses of future action, and have you develop appropriate marketing strategies. The information necessary to answer the questions may be drawn from the case and the text chapter(s) to which the case relates.

Keep these hints in mind when solving a case:

- Read (observe) all material carefully. Underline or take notes on important data and statements.
- List the key issues and company actions detailed in the case.
- Do not make unrealistic or unsupported assumptions.
- Read each question following the case. Be sure you understand the thrust of every question. Do not give similar answers for two distinct questions.

- Write up tentative answers in outline form. Cover as many aspects of each question as possible.
- Review relevant material in the appropriate chapter(s) of the text. In particular, look for information pertaining to the case questions.
- Expand your tentative answers, substantiating them with data from the case and the chapter(s).
- Reread the case and your notes to be sure you have not omitted any major concepts in your answers.
- Make sure your answers are clear and well written, and that you have considered their ramifications for the organization.
- Reread your solutions at least one day after developing your answers. This ensures a more objective review of your work.
- Make any necessary revisions.
- Be sure your answers are not just a summary ("rehash") of the case, but that you have presented a real analysis and recommendations.

Chapter 2

The Environment in Which Marketing Operates

At the time that Anne M. Mulcahy, a Xerox (**http://www.xerox.com**) executive with 30 years of experience at the firm, was chosen chief executive officer, the company was struggling. Xerox was losing $300 million a year, had $14 billion in debt, and faced tough competition from Hewlett-Packard (**http://www.hp.com**), Canon (**http://www.canon.com**), and other copier companies.

Mulcahy repositioned Xerox from being a firm that just sold copiers to all kinds of consumers to a provider of applications that can digitally scan and store documents. Today, Xerox likes to be known as "The Document Company," instead of "The Xerox Machine Company." It generates two-thirds of its technology revenues from products that are three years old or younger (more than 100 such products). One interesting new technology involves self-erasing reusable paper. Prints made on this paper have temporary images that enable paper to be reused many times over. Another new technology makes it easier to access documents on cell phones and other small-screen devices.

One way Xerox was able to return to profitability was by carefully studying the needs of its key customers. After analyzing a large insurance company that was a major customer, Xerox learned that the information-related costs in acquiring new business were very high. Xerox showed the client how it could tag the information earlier so it could be reused on an automated basis. This process cut the cost of getting new business for the insurer by 40 to 50 percent.

Mulcahy is also investing in color printing. New digital technology has reduced the costs of color printing so much that production volumes can be more efficiently printed. High-tech diagnostics for color printers enable Xerox engineers to notify customers when their machines need servicing. Xerox makes 15 times as much profit from a color page as from one that is black and white.

As a tribute to her performance, in 2008, Anne Mulcahy received the "CEO of the Year" award from *Chief Executive* magazine. She was the first woman CEO to achieve this distinction.[1]

In this chapter, we will study the complex environment in which marketing decisions are made. We will see that an organization's level of success (or failure) is related not only to its marketing efforts, but also to the external environment in which it operates and its ability to adapt to environmental changes.

Chapter Objectives

1. To examine the environment within which marketing decisions are made and marketing activities are undertaken
2. To differentiate between those elements controlled by a firm's top management and those controlled by marketing, and to enumerate the controllable elements of a marketing plan
3. To enumerate the uncontrollable environmental elements that can affect a marketing plan and study their potential ramifications
4. To explain why feedback about company performance and the uncontrollable aspects of its environment and the subsequent adaptation of the marketing plan are essential for a firm to attain its objectives

---

[1] Various company and other sources.

OVERVIEW

The environment within which marketing decisions are made and enacted is depicted in Figure 2-1. The ***marketing environment*** consists of five elements: controllable factors, uncontrollable factors, the organization's level of success or failure in reaching objectives, feedback, and adaptation.

Controllable factors are those directed by an organization and its marketers. First, top management makes several broad decisions. Then, marketing managers make specific decisions based on those guidelines. In combination, these factors lead to an overall offering (*A* in Figure 2-1). The *uncontrollable factors* are beyond an organization's control, but they affect how well it does (*B* in Figure 2-1).

An organization's level of success or failure in reaching its goals is determined by the interaction of controllable factors and uncontrollable factors. Feedback occurs when a firm makes an effort to monitor uncontrollable factors and assess its strengths and weaknesses. Adaptation refers to the changes in a marketing plan that an organization makes to comply with the uncontrollable environment. If a firm is unwilling to consider the entire environment in a systematic manner, it increases the likelihood that it will have a lack of direction and not attain proper results.

The environment should be considered from two perspectives: The ***macroenvironment*** includes the broad demographic, societal, economic, political, technological, and other forces that an organization faces. The ***microenvironment*** includes the forces close to an organization that directly impact its ability to serve customers, including distribution intermediaries, competitors, consumer markets, and the capabilities of the

> The **marketing environment** consists of controllable factors, uncontrollable factors, organizational performance, feedback, and adaptation.

> Both the **macroenvironment** and the **microenvironment** must be understood.

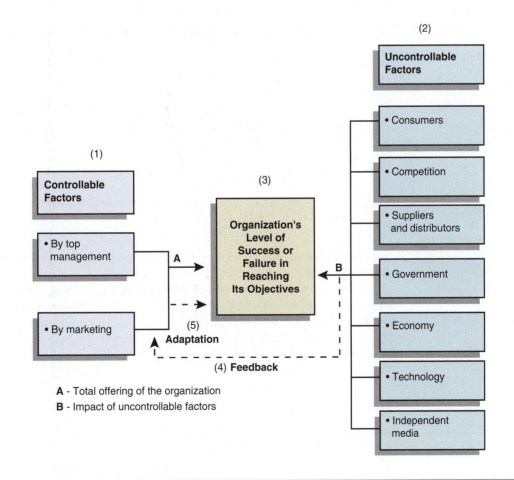

A - Total offering of the organization
B - Impact of uncontrollable factors

Figure 2-1

The Environment Within Which Marketing Operates

Marketing and the Web

Welcome to the Weekend Web

Research conducted by M:Metrics (http://www.mmetrics.com) on 1,861 U.S. "smart phone" owners found that people access different Web sites on weekends than mid-week. They are also more prone to access sites via wireless devices on weekends. The number of unique visitors to mobile Web sites peaks on Saturdays (an 8 percent increase over Fridays and 4 percent greater than on Mondays, the next busiest day). According to M:Metrics, mobile Internet browsing has more than doubled since 2006, with mobile page views increasing by triple.

During the week, many people use Yahoo (http://www.yahoo.com) and Google (http://www.google.com) searches for work- and school-related activities—with comScore (http://www.comscore.com) reports that the Web's fast-growing sites relate to pharmacies, food, cosmetics, and job search. In contrast, on weekends, people are more apt to look at sites related to weather, entertainment, games, and music. On weekends, many U.S. cell-phone users spend more time on craigslist (http://www.craigslist.com) than on any other site. The number two site visited in a mobile manner is eBay (http://www.ebay.com); and the Weather Channel (http://www.weather.com) also rates high on the number of unique visits. In contrast, Yahoo! (http://www.yahoo.com) is the number one site visited from a fixed-location PC, while eBay is the eight-most visited site, Craigslist is in ninth place, and the Weather Channel ranks 26th.

To better appeal to mobile consumers, Verizon Wireless (http://www.verizon.com) has introduced a new Verve Wireless online channel (http://www.vervewireless.com). Through Verve Wireless, Verizon's mobile customers can easily access news, entertainment, restaurant guides, and community event listings from daily newspapers, local weekly magazines, and city-based magazines.

Source: Based on material in Olga Kharif, "Welcome to the Weekend Web," http://www.businessweek.com/technology (May 29, 2008).

organization itself.[2] The Marketing Plan Success Web site gives a good overview of the macroenvironment (http://www.marketing-plan-success.com/Articles/Macroenvironment). The Learn Marketing site highlights the microenvironment (http://www.learnmarketing.net/microenvironment.htm).

Throughout this chapter, the various parts of Figure 2-1 are described and tied together so that the complex environment of marketing can be understood. In Chapter 3, the concept of strategic planning is presented. Such planning establishes a formal process for developing, implementing, and evaluating marketing programs in conjunction with the goals of top management.

2-2 CONTROLLABLE FACTORS

> The organization and its marketers can manage **controllable factors**.

Controllable factors are internally directed by an organization and its marketers. Some of these factors are directed by top management; these are not controllable by marketers, who must develop plans to satisfy overall organizational (top management) goals. In situations involving small or medium-sized institutions, both broad policy and marketing decisions are often made by one person, usually the owner. Even then, broad policies are often set first and marketing plans adjust to them. A person could decide to open an office-supply store selling products to small businesses (broad policy) and stress convenient hours, a good selection of items, quantity discounts, and superior customer service (marketing plan).

2-2a Factors Directed by Top Management

Top management is responsible for numerous decisions, five of which are quite important to marketers: line of business, overall objectives, role of marketing, role of other

---

[2] "Dictionary," http://www.marketingpower.com/_layouts/Dictionary.aspx?dLetter=M (March 22, 2009).

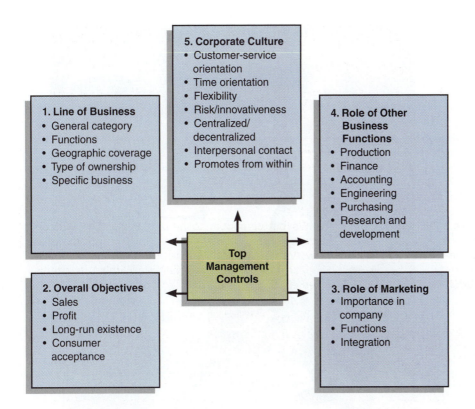

Figure 2-2

Factors Controlled by Top Management

business functions, and corporate culture. They impact on all aspects of marketing. Figure 2-2 shows the types of decisions in these areas.

The *line of business* refers to the general goods/service category, functions, geographic coverage, type of ownership, and specific business of a firm. The general goods/service category is a broad definition of the industry in which a firm seeks to be involved. It may be energy, transportation, computing, or a host of others. The business functions outline a firm's position in the marketing system—from supplier to manufacturer to wholesaler to retailer—and the tasks it seeks to undertake. A firm may want to be in more than one position. Geographic coverage can be neighborhood, city, state, regional, national, or international. Ownership ranges from a sole proprietorship, partnership, or franchise to a multiunit corporation. The specific business is a narrow definition of the firm, its functions, and its operations, such as Ben & Jerry's (**http://www.benandjerrys.com**)—the maker and retailer of premium ice cream, frozen yogurt, and sorbets.

Overall objectives are broad, measurable goals set by top management. A firm's success or failure may be determined by comparing objectives with actual performance. Usually, a combination of sales, profit, and other goals is stated by management for short-run (one year to two years or less) and long-run (several years) periods. Most firms cite customer acceptance as a key goal with a strong effect on sales, profit, and long-run existence. The Business Owner's Toolkit gives a good synopsis of the considerations in goal setting (**http://www.toolkit.com/small_business_guide/sbg.aspx?nid=P01_0350**). See Figure 2-3.

Top management determines the role of marketing by noting its importance, outlining its activities, and integrating it into company operations. Marketing's importance is evident when marketing personnel have decision-making authority, the rank of the chief marketing officer is equal to that of other areas (usually vice-president), and proper resources are given. It is not considered important by a firm that gives marketing personnel advisory status, places marketing personnel in a subordinate position (such as reporting to the operations vice-president), equates marketing with sales, and withholds the funds needed for research, promotion, and other marketing tasks. The larger marketing's role, the greater the likelihood that a firm has an integrated marketing

A firm's **line of business** refers to its business category.

Figure 2-3

New Goals for the New Marketplace

Heinz (**http://www.heinz.com**) recognizes that consumers are becoming more and more conscious of the benefits of healthier food. Thus, an important goal for Heinz has been to eliminate trans fats from its Ore-Ida product line and to add such products as the new Steam n' Mash potatoes.

Source: Reprinted by permission.

organization. The smaller its role, the greater the possibility that a firm undertakes marketing tasks on a project, crisis, or fragmented basis.

The roles of other business functions and their interrelationships with marketing need to be defined clearly to avoid overlaps, jealousy, and conflict. Consider one business expert's observation: "The marketing section of a business needs to work closely with operations, research and development, finance, and human resources to check that their plans are possible. Operations will need to use sales forecasts produced by the marketing department to plan production schedules. Sales forecasts will also be an important part of the budgets produced by the finance department, as well as the deployment of labor for the human resources department. A research and development department will need to work very closely with the marketing department to understand customer needs."[3] Production, finance, accounting, engineering, purchasing, and research and development departments each have different perspectives, orientations, and goals. This is discussed further in Chapter 3.

Top management strongly influences a firm's ***corporate culture***: the shared values, norms, and practices communicated to and followed by those working for the firm. It may be described in terms of:

> **Corporate culture** involves shared values, norms, and practices.

- *A customer-service orientation*—Is the commitment to customer service clear to employees?
- *A time orientation*—Is a firm short- or long-run oriented?

---

[3] "Role of Marketing in Business," **http://tutor2u.net/business/gcse/marketing_role_in_business.htm** (n.d.).

- *The flexibility of the job environment*—Can employees deviate from rules? How formal are relations with subordinates? Is there a dress code?
- *The level of risk/innovation pursued*—Is risk taking fostered?
- *The use of a centralized/decentralized management structure*—How much input into decisions do middle managers have?
- *The level of interpersonal contact*—Do employees freely communicate with one another?
- *The use of promotions from within*—Are internal personnel given preference as positions open?

Nordstrom (**http://www.nordstrom.com**) expects employees to treat customers very well. Dudley Consulting (**http://www.dudleyconsulting-inc.com/CultureLanding-Page.html**) is one of many firms to offer consulting services that help clients enhance their corporate culture, and *Fortune* annually publishes a list of the best U.S. employers (**http://money.cnn.com/magazines/fortune/bestcompanies**).

Google (**http://www.google.com**) "is a public and profitable company focused on search services at many international Web sites. Its breakthrough technology and continued innovation serve the company's mission of 'organizing the world's information and making it universally accessible and useful.'" Google has been widely honored for its progressive corporate culture and the driving forces behind it:

> There's little in the way of corporate hierarchy and everyone wears several hats. The international Webmaster who creates Google's holiday logos spent a week translating the site into Korean. The chief operations engineer is also a licensed neurosurgeon. Because everyone realizes they are an equally important part of Google's success, no one hesitates to skate over to a corporate officer during roller hockey. Hiring is non-discriminatory and favors ability over experience. Google has offices around the globe and recruits local talent from Zurich to Bangalore. Dozens of languages are spoken by Google staffers. As Google expands its development team, it continues to look for those who share an obsessive commitment to creating search perfection and having a great time doing it.

After top management sets company guidelines, the marketing area begins to develop the factors under its control.

2-2b Factors Directed by Marketing

The major factors controlled by marketing personnel are the selection of a target market, marketing objectives, the marketing organization, the marketing mix, and assessment of the marketing plan. See Figure 2-4.

One of the most crucial marketing-related decisions involves the choice of a ***target market***, which is the particular group(s) of customers a firm proposes to serve, or whose needs it proposes to satisfy, with a particular marketing program. When selecting a target market, a company usually engages in some form of ***market segmentation***, which involves subdividing a market into clear subsets of customers that act in the same way or that have comparable needs.[4] A company can choose a large target market or concentrate on a small one, or try to appeal to both with separate marketing programs for each. As a rule, these questions must be addressed before devising a target market approach: Who are our customers? What kinds of goods and services do they want? How can we attract them to our company? For some interesting insights on target markets, visit the Web site of the Edward Lowe Foundation (**http://www.edwardlowe.org/index.elf?page=sserc&storyid=6378&function=story**).

At marketing-oriented firms, the choice of a target market affects all other marketing decisions. A book publisher appealing to the high school science market would have a

A target market is the customer group to which an organization appeals.

Market segmentation is often used in choosing a target market.

---

[4] "Dictionary," **http://www.marketingpower.com/_layouts/Dictionary.aspx?dLetter=T** and **http://www.marketingpower.com/_layouts/Dictionary.aspx?dLetter=M** (March 22, 2009).

Figure 2-4

Factors Controlled by Marketing

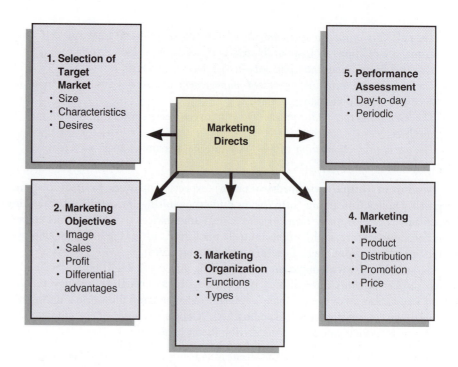

different marketing approach than one appealing to the adult fiction market. The first firm would seek an image as a well-established publisher, specialize its product offerings, make presentations to high school book-selection committees, sell in large quantities, and offer books with many photos and line drawings that could be used for several years. The second firm would capitalize on well-known authors or publish books on hot topics to establish an image, have books on a variety of subjects, use newspaper ads and seek favorable reviews, distribute via bookstores, sell in small quantities (except if large chains are involved), and de-emphasize durability, photos, and artwork to produce books as efficiently as possible.

Marketing objectives are more customer-oriented than those set by top management. Marketers are quite interested in the image consumers hold of a firm and its products. Sales goals reflect a concern for brand loyalty (repeat purchases), growth via new-product introductions, and appeal to unsatisfied market segments. Profit goals are related to long-term customer loyalty. Most important, marketers seek to create ***differential advantages***, the unique features in a firm's marketing program that cause consumers to patronize that firm and not its competitors. Without differential advantages, a firm would have a "me-too" philosophy and offer the consumer no reasons to select its offerings over competitors' products.

Differential advantages can be based on a distinctive image, new products or features, product quality, customer service, low prices, availability, and other factors. Snapple (**http://www.snapple.com**) is known for offbeat flavors such as White Tea Raspberry, Levi's Dockers (**http://www.us.dockers.com**) for a comfortable fit, Sony (**http://www.sony.com**) for high-tech electronics, Tiffany (**http://www.tiffany.com**) for top-line jewelry, Wal-Mart (**http://www.walmart.com**) for selection and prices, and Chase (**http://www.chase.com**) for mobile ATM locations for the convenience of customers. See Figure 2-5. Build-a-Bear Workshop lets customers build their own stuffed animals, which they can even do online (**http://www.buildabear.com**): "Shop online for your beary best pal. When you find the pawfect pal, add a Build-A-Sound personal voice greeting by selecting 'Build-A-Sound' under the 'Add Sound' menu options. As you complete your order, you will be instructed to call a toll-free number and record your beary own personalized 10-second message! Your message will play from inside your bear or other furry pal every time it's hugged!"

A ***marketing organization*** is the structural arrangement that directs marketing functions. It outlines authority, responsibility, and the tasks to be done so that functions

Differential advantages consist of the firm's unique features that attract customers.

A **marketing organization** may be functional, product-oriented, or market-oriented.

Figure 2-5

Chase: Creating Differential Advantages in Banking

Can't get to the bank or supermarket? Maybe your bank will come to you.

Source: Reprinted by permission of Susan Berry, Retail Image Consulting, Inc.

are assigned and coordinated. As illustrated in Figure 2-6, an organization may be functional, with jobs assigned in terms of buying, selling, promotion, distribution, and other tasks; product-oriented, with product managers for each product category and brand managers for each brand, in addition to functional categories; or market-oriented, with jobs assigned by geographic market and customer type, in addition to functional categories. A single firm may use a mixture of forms.

A *marketing mix* is the specific combination of marketing elements used to achieve objectives and satisfy the target market. It comprises decisions regarding four major variables: *Product* decisions involve determining what goods, services, organizations, people, places, and/or ideas to market; the number of items to sell and their quality; the innovativeness pursued; packaging; product features; warranties; when to drop existing products; and more. *Distribution* decisions include choosing whether to sell via intermediaries or directly to consumers, how many outlets to sell through, how to interact with channel members, the terms to negotiate, the tasks assigned to others, supplier choice, and more. *Promotion* decisions include selecting a combination of tools (ads, public relations, personal selling, and sales promotion), whether to share promotions with others, the image sought, the level of personal service, media choice, message content, promotion timing, and more. *Price* decisions include choosing overall price levels, the price emphasis, the relation between price and quality, the emphasis to place on price, how to react to competitors, when to offer discounts, how prices are computed, what billing terms to use, and more. A marketing mix is used by all firms, even farmers selling at roadside stands.

> The **marketing mix** consists of four elements: product, distribution, promotion, and price.

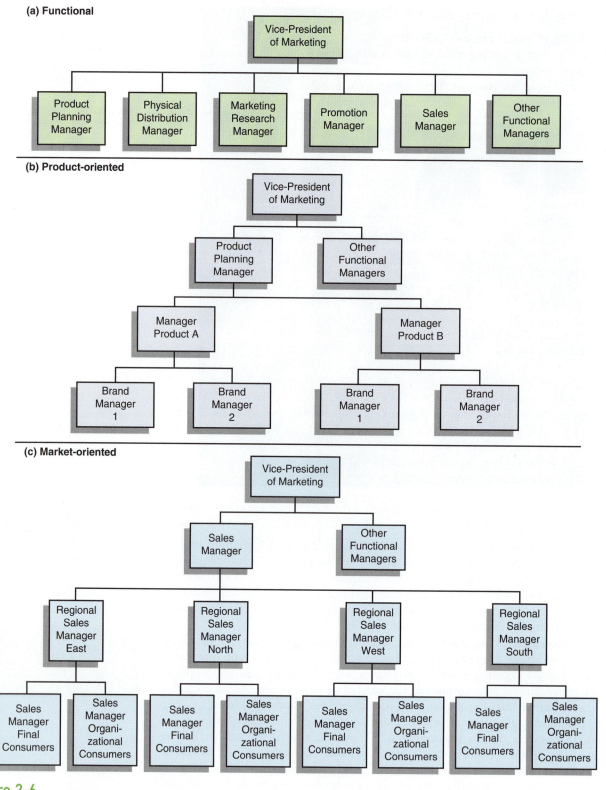

(a) Functional

(b) Product-oriented

(c) Market-oriented

Figure 2-6

Illustrations of Marketing Organizations

When devising a marketing mix, these questions should all be considered:

- Is the target market precisely defined?
- Does the total marketing effort, as well as each element of the mix, meet the target market's needs?
- Are marketing mix elements consistent with one another?
- Do the elements add up to form a harmonious, integrated whole?
- Is each marketing mix element being given its best use?
- Does the marketing mix build on the firm's cultural and tangible strengths? Does the marketing mix imply a way to correct any weaknesses?
- Is a distinctive personality in the competitive marketplace created?
- Is the company protected from the most obvious competitive threats?[5]

Canon (**http://www.canon.com**) is an example of a firm applying the marketing mix concept well. It has distinct marketing mixes for different target markets. For beginners, it offers "Easy and Fun" PowerShot A-model point-and-shoot cameras with automatic focus and a built-in flash. The cameras are sold in all types of stores, including discount stores. Ads appear on TV and in general magazines: "You'll quickly discover that the easiest way to capture a great image is to simply 'point' and 'shoot.'" The cameras typically sell for $100 to $150. For serious amateur photographers, Canon has advanced cameras with superior features and attachments. They are sold in camera stores and finer department stores. Ads are in specialty magazines: "High-end PowerShot digital cameras incorporate the creative performance of a professional digital SLR camera and the compact convenience of a point-and-shoot." These cameras sell for several hundred dollars. For professional photographers, Canon has even more complex cameras with top-of-the-line features and attachments. They are sold at select camera stores. Ads are in trade magazines: "With exceptional speed, rugged durability, and advanced features, Canon 35mm EOS cameras make picture-taking feel professional." The cameras are costly (the EOS-1Ds is about $8,000). In sum, Canon markets the right products in the right stores, promotes them in the right media, and has the right prices.

The last, but extremely important, factor directed by marketers involves performance assessment: monitoring and evaluating overall and specific marketing effectiveness. Evaluations need to be done regularly, with both the external environment and internal company data being reviewed. In-depth analysis of performance should be completed at least once or twice each year. Strategy revisions need to be enacted when the exter1nal environment changes or the company encounters difficulties.

> **Performance assessment** involves monitoring and evaluating marketing activities.

2-3   UNCONTROLLABLE FACTORS

Uncontrollable factors are the external elements affecting an organization's performance that cannot be fully directed by that organization and its marketers. A marketing plan, no matter how well designed, may fail if uncontrollable factors have too adverse an impact. Thus, the external environment must be regularly observed and its effects considered in any marketing plan. Contingency plans relating to uncontrollable variables should also be a key part of a marketing plan. Uncontrollable factors that especially bear studying are consumers, competition, suppliers and distributors, government, the economy, technology, and independent media. See Figure 2-7.

> **Uncontrollable factors** influence an organization and its marketers but are not fully directed by them.

---

[5] Benson P. Shapiro, "Rejuvenating the Marketing Mix," *Harvard Business Review*, Vol. 63 (September-October 1985), p. 34. See also Boonghee Yoo, Naveen Donthu, and Sungho Lee, "An Examination of Selected Marketing Mix Elements and Brand Equity," *Journal of the Academy of Marketing Science*, Vol. 28 (Spring 2000), pp. 195–211; Håkan Håkansson and Alexandra Waluszewski, "Developing a New Understanding of Markets: Reinterpreting the 4 Ps," *Journal of Business & Industrial Marketing*, Vol. 20 (No. 3, 2005), pp. 110–117; Shiou-Yu Chen and Tzong-Ru Lee, "The Corresponding Strategic Marketing Mix to the Relationships Between National Culture and Consumer Value," *International Journal of Management & Enterprise Development*, Vol. 5 (No. 3, 2008), p. 3; and John Graham, "The New Marketing Mix: Where Will You Meet Your Customers?" *American Salesman*, Vol. 53 (March 2008), pp. 16–20.

Ethical Issues in Marketing

Walt Disney Company: A Corporate Philanthropist

For more than 50 years, the Walt Disney Company (http://www.disney.com) has been involved with community philanthropic programs to help local nonprofit organizations. Since then, annual donations by its Disneyland Resort (http://www.disneyland.disney.go.com) and Disneyland's 20,000 employees in Anaheim, California—just one of the firm's locations—have reached $12 million.

In one recent year, Disneyland and its employees contributed more than $8 million in merchandise and equipment donations and more than 94,000 hours of volunteer service to community projects and events. Disneyland employees also donated 5,000 care packages and letters of encouragement to active duty military personnel as part of the Disneyland Resort Military Care Program.

Disneyland is sensitive to assisting community residents in times of crises. It recently became a partner of Operation Orange County, a group of nonprofit

organizations which includes the American Red Cross (http://www.redcross.org) to help those displaced from their homes by California wildfires. As part of this program, employees contributed nearly 5,000 pounds of nonperishable foods and bottled water. They also visited with families in local shelters to cheer them up in their time of need.

The Attractions Maintenance employee team, which works on the night shift to maintain attractions, collects gifts and plans a special holiday visit for residents of a nearby nursing home. According to the home's executive director, "The reception from the staff and residents was overwhelming. I hear things like, 'I love you Mickey' and 'Thank you Mickey for being here.' It just brought tears to my eyes."

Source: Based on material in "Public Affairs: Disneyland," http://publicaffairs.disneyland.com (April 30, 2009).

2-3a   Consumers

Although a firm has control over its target market selection, it cannot control the changing characteristics of its final or organizational consumers. A firm can react to, but not control, consumer trends related to age, income, marital status, occupation, race, education, place and type of residence, and the size and power of organizational customers. For example, health insurers must deal with the fact that many of their largest business customers are downsizing; thus, fewer employees need insurance.

Interpersonal influences on consumer behavior need to be understood. People's purchases are affected by the corporate culture at their jobs as purchasing agents; their

> Organizations need to understand consumer trends, interpersonal influences, the decision process, and consumer groups.

Figure 2-7

Uncontrollable Factors

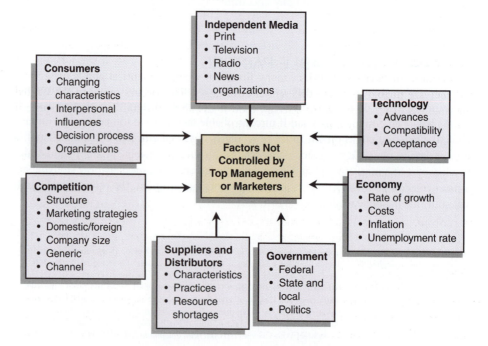

family, friends, and other social contacts; and the customs and taboos shaping culture and society. For instance, in some states, liquor sales are more regulated (as to outlets, prices, other goods that can be sold, and days open) than they are in others through state liquor boards (**http://www.atf.treas.gov/alcohol/info/faq/subpages/lcb.htm**).

Because people act differently in buying various goods and services, the consumer decision process—the steps people go through when buying products—affects the way that products are marketed. In the case of company cars, a purchasing agent carefully looks for data on a number of models, ranks several alternatives, selects a favorite, negotiates terms, and completes the purchase. On the other hand, with an inexpensive meal, a person looks at a watch, sees it is lunch time, and goes to a nearby fast-food outlet.

Consumer rights groups speak on behalf of consumers at public hearings, at stockholder meetings, and with the mass media. To avoid some negative consequences from active consumer groups, a firm must communicate with customers on relevant issues (such as a product recall), anticipate problems (such as order delays), respond to complaints (such as poor service), and be sure it has good community relations (such as sponsoring neighborhood projects). Consumers Union (**http://www.consumersunion. org**), which publishes *Consumer Reports*, is one of the largest consumer advocacy groups.

2-3b   Competition

The competitive environment often affects a company's marketing efforts and its success in reaching a target market. Thus, a firm should assess its industry structure and examine competitors in terms of marketing strategies, domestic/foreign firms, size, generic competition, and channel competition. Each year, *Business Week* (**http://www.businessweek. com**) publishes an overview of the trends occurring in a number of industries. It also makes its forecasts available online.

A company could face one of four possible competitive structures: With a *monopoly*, just one firm sells a given good or service and has a lot of control over its marketing plan. This occurs in the United States when a firm has a patent (exclusive rights to a sell a product it invented for a fixed number of years) or is a public utility, such as a local power company. In an *oligopoly*, a few firms—usually large ones— account for most industry sales and would like to engage in nonprice competition. The U.S. carbonated beverage industry is a good example of this. According to Beverage Digest (**http://www.beverage-digest.com**), Coca-Cola Company, PepsiCo, and Dr Pepper Snapple Group account for almost 90 percent of U.S. soft drink sales. In *monopolistic competition*, there are several firms in an industry, each trying to offer a unique marketing mix—based on price or nonprice factors. It is the most common U.S. industry structure, followed by oligopoly. Service stations, beauty salons, stationery stores, garment makers, and computer-clone makers are some industry sectors with monopolistic competition. In *pure competition*, many firms sell virtually identical goods or services and they are unable to create differential advantages. This occurs rarely in the United States and is most common for selected food items and commodities (and happens if numerous small firms compete with each other).

> Monopoly, oligopoly, monopolistic competition, and **pure competition** are the main types of competitive structure.

After analyzing its industry's competitive structure, a firm should study the strategies of competitors. It should look at their target markets and marketing mixes, images, differential advantages, which markets are saturated and which are unfulfilled, and the extent to which consumers are content with the service and quality provided by competitors. See Figure 2-8. Hoover's Online (**http://www.hoovers.com**) is an excellent source of information on thousands of firms around the world. Brief company profiles are free.

Both domestic and foreign competition should be examined. For instance, in the United States, Bank of America (**http://www.bankofamerica.com**) competes with Citigroup (**http://www.citigroup.com**), American Express (**http://www.americanexpress. com**), and others for financial services business. Many U.S. and West European industries are mature; the amount of domestic competition there is rather stable. In some industries, competition is rising due to the popularity of innovations such as notebook PCs. In others, domestic competition is intensifying as a result of government

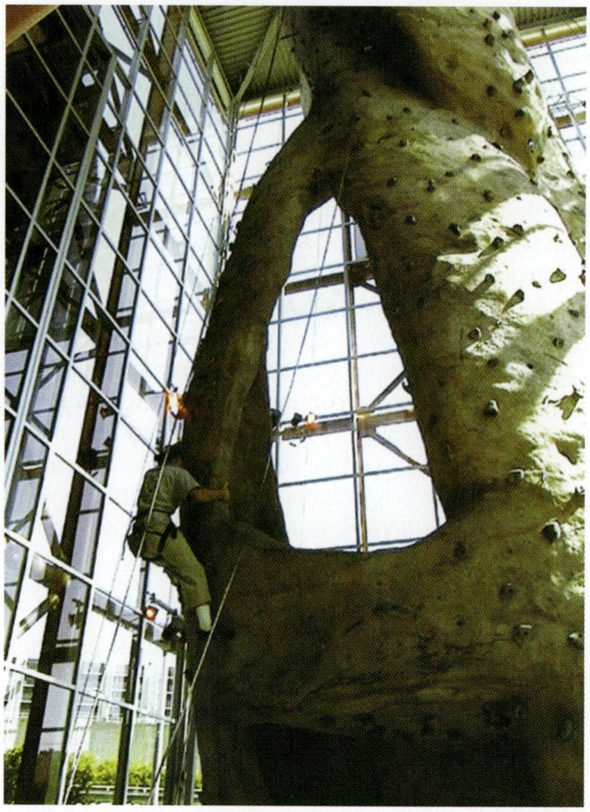

Figure 2-8

REI: Succeeding in a Highly Competitive Marketplace

REI (http://www.rei.com) is a retailer of high-end gear, clothing, and footwear for camping, bicycling, climbing, paddling, and other outdoor activities. Although it competes with scores of other firms, from Sports Authority to North Face to L.L. Bean to Lone Arrow, REI stands out. Its stores are exciting (as this photo shows), it has strong guarantees, and its members can save money on the products carried.

Source: Reprinted by permission of TNS Retail Forward.

> Foreign competition is intensifying.

deregulation. For instance, hundreds of companies offer long-distance telephone service in the United States alone.

Foreign competitors now play a major role in many industries. In the United States, foreign-based firms have large market shares for steel, pharmaceuticals, office machines, telecommunications equipment, apparel, consumer electronics, and motor vehicles. At the same time, competition in foreign markets is more intense for U.S.-based firms than before as rivals stress innovations, cost cutting, good distribution and promotion, and other factors. Nonetheless, U.S.-based firms remain strong in such areas as aerospace, chemicals, information technology, transport equipment, scientific instruments, and cereal.[6]

For many industries, there has been a trend toward larger firms due to mergers and acquisitions, as well as company sales growth. Mergers and acquisitions have involved telecommunications firms such as Cingular (http://www.cingular.com) being acquired by AT&T (http://www.att.com); media firms such as the New York Times Company (http://www.nytco.com) acquiring About.com (http://www.about.com); food manufacturers such as Nestlé (http://www.nestle.com) acquiring Gerber (http://www.gerber.com); retailers such as IHOP (http://www.ihop.com) acquiring Applebee's (http://www.applebees.com); and many others. Internal sales growth has been great for such firms as Wal-Mart (http://www.walmart.com), Apple (http://www.apple.com), Toyota (http://www.toyota.com), and Dell (http://www.dell.com)—each with annual sales of several billion dollars.

From a small firm's vantage point, personal service, a focus on underserved market segments, an entrepreneurial drive, and flexibility are differential advantages; cooperative ventures and franchising let such firms buy in bulk and operate more efficiently. To large firms, widespread distribution, economies of scale, well-known brands, mass-media ads, and low-to-moderate prices are competitive tactics.

---

[6] "Industry Trade Data and Analysis," http://ita.doc.gov/td/industry/otea/OTII/OTII-index.html (May 8, 2009).

Every organization should define competition in generic terms (as broadly as possible). *Direct competitors* are similar to the firm with regard to the line of business and marketing approach. *Indirect competitors* are different, but still compete with it for customers. Both types should be accounted for in a marketing plan. A movie theater not only competes with other theaters—direct competitors—but with indirect competitors such as online firms (such as **http://www.netflix.com**), video stores, TV and radio shows, video games, sporting events, live theater, amusement parks, bookstores, restaurants, and schools. A theater owner should ask, "What must I do to compete with a variety of entertainment and recreation forms, in terms of movie selection, prices, hours, customer service, refreshments, and parking?"

A company should also study the competition from its channel members (resellers). Each party in the distribution process has different goals and would like to maximize its control over the marketing mix. Some wholesalers and retailers carry their own brands in addition to those of manufacturers.

> Competition should be defined generically—as widely as possible.

2-3c   Suppliers and Distributors

Many firms rely on their suppliers and distributors (wholesalers and retailers) to properly run their own businesses. Without their ongoing support, it would be hard, if not impossible, for a company to succeed.

Suppliers provide the goods and services that firms need to operate, as well as those that the firms resell to their customers. In general, a firm is most vulnerable when there are relatively few suppliers, specific goods and services are needed to run a business or satisfy customer demand, competitors would gain if the firm has a falling-out with a supplier, suppliers are better attuned to the desires of the marketplace, suppliers informally take care of maintenance and repair services, the turnaround time to switch suppliers is lengthy, and suppliers have exclusive access to scarce resources.

For firms unable to market products directly to consumers, distributors (wholesalers or retailers) are needed. As a rule, a firm is most vulnerable when there are relatively few distributors in an area, the distributors carry many brands, shelf space is tight, the firm is unknown in the marketplace, particular distributors account for a large part of the firm's revenues, distributors help finance the firm, distributors are better attuned to the marketplace, and competitors are waiting in the wings to stock the distributors.

These are among the supplier/distributor practices that a firm should regularly study: delivery time or requests, product availability, prices, flexibility in handling special requests, marketing support, consistency of treatment, returns policies, and other services. Unsatisfactory performance in one or more of these areas could have a lasting impact on a firm and its competence to enact marketing plans.

A firm's ability to carry out its plans can be affected by the availability of scarce resources—regardless of suppliers' good intentions. Over the past three decades, periodic shortages and volatile price changes have occurred for many basic commodities, such as gasoline, home heating oil, other petroleum-based products, plastics, synthetic fibers, aluminum, gold, chrome, silver, tungsten, nickel, steel, glass, grain, fertilizer, cotton, and wool. And despite efforts at conservation, some raw materials, processed materials, and component parts may remain or become scarce over the next decade.

If resource shortages and/or rapid cost increases occur, one of three actions is possible: (1) Substitute materials might be used to construct products, requiring more research and product testing. (2) Prices might be raised for products that cannot incorporate substitute materials. (3) Firms might abandon products if resources are unavailable and demarket others where demand is greater than can be satisfied.

> Suppliers and distributors can have a dramatic impact on an organization.

2-3d   Government

Worldwide, governmental bodies have a great impact on marketing practices by placing (or removing) restrictions on specified activities. Rulings can be regional, national, state, and/or local. For example, the European Union sets rules for its member nations.

In the United States, for 120 years, federal legislation has been enacted that affects marketing practices, as highlighted in Table 2-1. This legislation can be divided into three groupings: antitrust, discriminatory pricing, and unfair trade practices; consumer protection; and deregulation.

The first group of laws protects smaller firms from anticompetitive acts by larger ones. They seek a "level playing field" by barring firms from marketing practices that unfairly harm competitors. The second group of laws helps consumers deal with deceptive and unsafe business practices. They protect consumer rights and restrict certain marketing activities. The third group of laws has deregulated various industries to create more competition. They allow firms greater flexibility in their marketing. The Federal Trade Commission (FTC) is the major U.S. regulatory agency monitoring restraint of trade and enforcing rules against unfair competition and deceptive practices (http://www.ftc.gov).

> U.S. federal legislation involves interstate commerce; each state and local government has its own regulations, as well.

Besides federal regulation and agencies, each state and local government in the United States has its own legal environment. State and local laws may regulate where a firm can locate, the hours it can be open, the types of items sold, if prices must be marked on each item, how goods must be labeled or dated, the amount of sales tax (http://www.salestaxinstitute.com/sales_tax_rates.php), and so forth. State and local governments may also provide incentives, such as small business assistance, for firms to operate there.

The political environment often affects legislation. Marketing issues such as these are often discussed via the political process prior to laws being enacted (or not enacted): Should certain goods and services be stopped from advertising on TV? Should state governments become more active in handling consumer complaints? Both firms and consumer groups can have input into the process. The goal is to market their positions to government officials. A strength of the U.S. political system is its continuity, which lets organizations and individuals develop strategies for long periods of time.

> Privatization is changing the number of businesses in foreign countries.

Internationally, one of the biggest legal and political challenges facing nations that now have free-market economies—after decades of government-controlled markets—is how to privatize organizations that were formerly government-run: "In the short-term, privatization can potentially cause tremendous social upheaval, as privatization is often accompanied by large layoffs. If a single large firm or many small firms are privatized at once and upheaval results, particularly if the state mishandles the privatization process, a whole nation's economy may plunge into despair."[7]

Global Marketing in Action

Ford Motor Company's Plans for India

Ford Motor Company (http://www.ford.com) plans to invest $500 million in India. Ford wants to increase its annual Indian production capacity from 50,000 engines and 100,000 cars to 250,000 engines and 200,000 cars. The expanded capacity will be used to make small, inexpensive cars that can be sold in India as well as other developing markets. In 2007, Ford India (http://www.india.ford.com) sold about 40,000 vehicles, up from 22,000 in 2005. Overall passenger car sales in India have doubled in the past several years.

In India, the least expensive cars have been best-sellers. Until recently, the lower end of the Indian car market was dominated by Maruti Suzuki India Ltd. (http://www.marutisuzuki.com), which is affiliated with Japan's Suzuki Motor Corporation (http://www.globalsuzuki.com/globallinks/index.html). As Arvind Mathew, the president and managing director of Ford India, says: "There is a huge population of two-wheeler owners who are aspiring [to drive] cars," and they usually start with small ones.

Although both Ford and General Motors (http://www.gm.com) have had car manufacturing operations in India for more than a decade, the two firms have not been as successful as they hoped since they lacked a low-cost car. Ford's new car for the Indian market will be priced between $7,600 and $10,200, which is less than the price of any of Ford's current models. Toyota (http://www.toyota.com) and Nissan (http://www.nissan.com) also have plans to launch a $7,000 car for the Indian market. In contrast, a new car model made by India's Tata Motors Ltd (http://www.tatamotors.com) sells for $2,500.

Source: Eric Bellman, "Ford to Invest $500 Million in India," *Wall Street Journal* (January 9, 2008), p. A13.

[7] "Privatization," http://www.bambooweb.com/articles/P/r/Privatization.html (July 16, 2008).

Table 2-1 Key U.S. Legislation Affecting Marketers

Year	Legislation	Major Purpose
A. Antitrust, Discriminatory Pricing, and Unfair Trade Practices		
1890	Sherman Act	To eliminate monopolies
1914	Clayton Act	To ban anticompetitive acts
1914	FTC Act	To establish the Federal Trade Commission to enforce rules against restraints of trade
1936	Robinson-Patman Act	To prohibit price discrimination toward small distributors or retailers
1938	Wheeler-Lea Amendment	To amend the FTC Act to include more unfair or deceptive practices
1946	Lanham Trademark Act	To protect and regulate trademarks and brands
1976	Hart-Scott-Rodino Act	To require large firms to notify the government of their merger plans
1989	Trademark Revision Act	To revise the Lanham Trademark Act to include products not yet introduced on the market
1990	Antitrust Amendments Act	To raise the maximum penalties for price fixing
1995	Interstate Commerce Communication Termination Act	To require the Federal Trade Commission and the Justice Department to file periodic reports to assess and make recommendations concerning anticompetitive features of rate agreements among common carriers
1994	International Antitrust Enforcement Assistance Act	To authorize the Federal Trade Commission and the Justice Department to enter into mutual assistance programs with foreign antitrust authorities
2002	Sarbanes-Oxley Corporate Responsibility Act	To prevent accounting fraud by requiring greater accountability by companies and their senior executives
2004	Antitrust Criminal Penalty Enhancement and Reform Act	To amend the Sherman Act to increase maximum prison sentences (from 3 to 10 years) and raise the maximum fine for individuals (from $350,0000 to $1 million) for restraint of trade among the States, monopolizing trade, and other restraints of trade
B. Consumer Protection		
1906 1906	Food and Drug Act Meat Inspection Act	To ban adulterated and misbranded food and drugs, and to form the Food and Drug Administration (FDA)
1914 1938	FTC Act Wheeler-Lea Amendment	To establish a commission and provisions for protecting consumer rights
1939 1951 1953 1958	Wool Products Labeling Act Fur Products Labeling Act Flammable Fabrics Act Textile Fiber Identification Act	To require wool, fur, and textile products to show contents and to prohibit dangerous flammables
1958 1960 1962	Food Additives Amendment Federal Hazardous Substances Labeling Act Kefauver-Harris Amendment	To prohibit food additives causing cancer, require labels for hazardous household products, and require drug makers to demonstrate effectiveness and safety
1966	Fair Packaging and Labeling Act	To require honest package labeling and reduce package-size proliferation
1966	National Traffic and Motor Vehicle Safety Act	To set safety standards for autos and tires
1966 1969 1970 1972	Child Protection Act Child Toy Safety Act Poison Prevention Labeling Act Drug Listing Act	To ban hazardous products used by children, create standards for child-resistant packages, and provide drug information
1966 1970	Cigarette Labeling Act Public Health Smoking Act	To require warnings on cigarette packages and ban radio and TV cigarette ads
1967 1968	Wholesome Meat Act Wholesome Poultry Act	To mandate federal inspection standards

(continued)

1968	Consumer Credit Protection Act	To have full disclosure of credit terms and regulate the use of credit information
1970	Fair Credit Reporting Act	
1970	Clean Air Act	To protect the environment
1972	Consumer Product Safety Act	To create the Consumer Product Safety Commission (CPSC) and set safety standards
1975	Magnuson-Moss Consumer Product Warranty Act	To regulate warranties and set disclosure requirements
1975	Consumer Goods Pricing Act	To disallow retail price maintenance
1980	Fair Debt Collection Practices Act	To eliminate the harassment of debtors and ban false statements to collect debts
1980	FTC Improvement Act	To reduce the power of the FTC to implement industrywide trade regulations
1990	Clean Air Act	To expand the 1970 Clean Air Act
1990	Children's Television Act	To reduce the amount of commercials during children's programs
1990	Nutrition Labeling and Education Act	To have the FDA develop a new system of food labeling
1991	Telephone Consumer Protection Act	To safeguard consumers against undesirable telemarketing practices
1992	Cable Television Consumer Protection and Competition Act	To better protect consumer rights with regard to cable television services
1996	Credit Repair Organizations Act	To prohibit misleading representations associated with credit repair services
1998	Children's Online Protection Act	To protect children's privacy by giving parents the tools to control what information is collected from their children online
1998	Telemarketing Fraud Protection Act	To strengthen penalties for telemarketing fraud
1999	Gramm-Leach-Bliley Act	To protect the privacy of consumers' personal financial information
2002	Best Pharmaceuticals for Children Act	To amend the Federal Food, Drug, and Cosmetic Act to improve the safety and efficacy of pharmaceuticals for children
2003	Do Not Call Registry Act	To authorize the FTC to set up a federal registry of consumers who do not want to be called by telemarketers
2003	Can Spam Act	To make it illegal to send junk E-mail (spam) that fails to meet several conditions [new rules introduced by the FTC in 2008]
2003	Medicare Prescription Drug, Improvement, and Modernization Act	To provide for a voluntary program for prescription drug coverage under Medicare and to allow a deduction for amounts contributed to health savings accounts
2004	Sports Agent Responsibility and Trust Act	To make it unlawful for an agent to recruit a student athlete by giving any information, making a false promise, or providing anything of value
2005	Junk Fax Prevention Act	To require that unsolicited faxes include "a clear and conspicuous notice on the first page" explaining how the customer can be removed from that distribution list
2006	Dietary Supplement and Nonprescription Drug Consumer Protection Plan	To protect users of dietary supplements and other nonprescription drugs by requiring manufacturers and distributors to report serious adverse effects to the government within 15 days of their discovery
2007	The Food and Drug Administration Amendments Act	To ensure that the FDA has sufficient resources to properly review new drugs and devices

C. Industry Deregulation

Over the last 40 years, various laws and regulations have been enacted to make the natural gas, airline, trucking, railroad, banking, electricity, telecommunications, and other industries more competitive.

2-3e   The Economy

The rate of growth in a nation's or region's economy can have a huge effect on a firm's marketing efforts. A high growth rate means the economy is strong and the marketing potential large. Quite important to marketers are consumer perceptions—both in the business and final consumer sectors—regarding the economy. For instance, if people believe the economy will be favorable, they may increase spending; if they believe the economy will be poor, they may cut back.

In 2008, consumer perceptions about the U.S. economy reached the lowest level in 28 years—mostly due to high gas prices and a severe downturn in the housing market.[8] To measure consumer perceptions, the Conference Board (**http://www.conference-board.org/economics/consumerPubCCS.cfm**) and the University of Michigan (**http://www.sca.isr.umich.edu**), among others, conduct consumer confidence surveys to see if Americans are optimistic, pessimistic, or neutral about the economy. In uncertain times, many organizational consumers are interested in preserving their flexibility.

A country's economic growth is reflected by changes in its **gross domestic product (GDP)**, which is the total annual value of goods and services produced in a country less net foreign investment. These are the estimated 2009 GDPs (in U.S. dollars and at purchasing parity) for 10 selected nations: United States, $14.3 trillion; China, $8.5 trillion; Japan, $4.5 trillion; India, $3.5 trillion; Germany, $3.0 trillion; France, $2.2 trillion; Brazil, $2.0 trillion; Italy, $1.9 trillion; Mexico, $1.4 trillion; and Canada, $1.3 trillion.[9] In recent years, the yearly growth in most of these nations has been 2 to 5 percent; and when industries such as autos and housing speed up or slow down, the effects are felt in insurance, home furnishings, and other areas. The United States is expected to have real GDP growth averaging 2 to 4 percent annually during the next few years.[10]

> Economic growth is measured by the **gross domestic product**.

Some business costs—such as raw materials, unionized labor wages, taxes, interest rates, and office (factory) rental—are generally beyond any firm's control. If costs rise by a large amount, marketing flexibility may be limited because a firm often cannot pass along all of the increase; it might have to cut back on marketing activities or accept lower profits. If costs are stable, marketers are better able to differentiate products and expand sales because their firms are more apt to invest in marketing activities.

From a marketing perspective, the real income of consumers is critical. Whereas actual income is the amount earned by a consumer (or his/her family or household) in a given year, **real income** is the amount earned in a year adjusted by the rate of inflation. For example, if a person's actual income goes up by 4 percent in a year (from $50,000 to $52,000) and the rate of inflation (which measures price changes for the same goods and services over time) is 4 percent for the year, real income remains constant [($52,00) − ($52,000/1.04) = $50,000]. If actual income increases exceed the inflation rate, real income rises and people can buy more goods and services. If actual income goes up by less than the inflation rate, real income falls and people must buy fewer goods and services.[11]

> **Real income** describes earnings adjusted for inflation. Both inflation and unemployment affect purchases.

A high rate of unemployment can adversely affect many firms because people who are unemployed are likely to cut back on nonessentials wherever possible. Low unemployment often means substantial sales of large-ticket items, as consumers are better off, more optimistic, and more apt to spend earnings.

2-3f Technology

Technology refers to developing and using machinery, products, and processes. Individual firms, especially smaller ones with limited capital, often must adapt to technological advances (rather than control them).

> **Technology** includes machinery, products, and processes.

---

[8] Sudeep Reddy, "Consumers Are Downbeat on Economy," *Wall Street Journal* (May 17, 2008), p. A2.

[9] Authors' estimates, based on *World Factbook*, **https://www.cia.gov/library/publications/the-world-factbook** (July 17, 2009).

[10] To obtain ongoing information about the U.S. economy, visit the Web site for the *Survey of Current Business*: **http://www.bea.doc.gov/bea/pubs.htm**.

[11] For more information on the impact of inflation, visit "Overview of BLS Statistics on Inflation and Consumer Spending," **http://www.bls.gov/bls/inflation.htm**.

Many firms depend on others to develop and perfect new technology, such as computer microchips; only then can they use the new technology in products, such as automated gasoline pumps at service stations, high-definition television sets and DVDs, or electronic sensors in smoke detectors for office buildings. With new technology, the inventor often secures patent protection, which excludes competitors from using that technology (unless the inventor licenses rights for a fee).

In several areas, companies have been unable to achieve practical technological breakthroughs. For example, no firm has been able to develop and market a cure for the common cold, a good-tasting nontobacco cigarette, a commercially acceptable electric car, or a truly effective and safe diet pill.

When new technology first emerges, it may be expensive and in short supply, both for firms using the technology in their products and for final consumers. The challenge is to mass produce and mass market the technology efficiently. In addition, some technological advances require employee training and consumer education before they can succeed. Thus, an emphasis on user-friendliness can speed up the acceptance of new technology.

Certain advances may not be compatible with goods and services already on the market or may require retooling by firms wanting to use them in products or operations. Every time an auto maker introduces a significantly new car model, it must invest hundreds of millions of dollars to retool facilities. Each time a firm buys new computer software to supplement existing software, it must see if the new software is compatible. For example, can the firm's PCs run all the computer programs the firm uses?

To thrive, technological advances must be accepted by each firm in the distribution process (manufacturer/service provider, wholesaler, retailer). Should any of the firms not use a new technology, its benefits may be lost. If small retailers do not use electronic scanning equipment, cashiers must ring up prices by hand even though packages are computer-coded by manufacturers. *Time* magazine has published a list of the 20 most important technological developments of the 20th century, ranging from the automobile to the Internet (**http://www.time.com/time100/builder/tech_supp/tech_supp. html**).

2-3g   Independent Media

Independent media affect perceptions of products and company image.

Independent media are communication vehicles not controlled by a firm; yet, they influence government, consumer, and publics' perceptions of that firm's products and overall image. Media can provide positive or negative coverage when a firm produces a new product, pollutes the air, mislabels products, contributes to charity, or otherwise performs a newsworthy activity. Coverage may be by print media, TV, radio, the Internet, and news organizations. To receive good coverage, a firm should willingly offer information to independent media and always try to get its position written or spoken about.

Although the media's coverage of information about a firm or information released by a firm is uncontrollable, paid advertising is controllable by the firm. Ads may be rejected by the media; but, if they are accepted, they must be presented in the time interval and form stipulated by the firm.

2-4   ATTAINMENT OF OBJECTIVES, FEEDBACK, AND ADAPTATION

An organization's success or failure in reaching objectives depends on both how well it directs its controllable factors and the impact of uncontrollable factors. As shown in Figure 2-1, it is the interaction of an organization's total offering and the uncontrollable environment that determines how it does.

To optimize marketing efforts and secure its long-run existence, a firm must get *feedback*—information about the uncontrollable environment, the organization's performance, and how well the marketing plan is received. Feedback is gained by measuring consumer satisfaction, looking at competitive trends, evaluating relationships with government agencies, studying the economy and potential resource shortages, monitoring the independent media, analyzing sales and profit trends, talking with suppliers and distributors, and utilizing other methods of acquiring and assessing information.

> **Feedback** provides information that lets a firm **adapt** to its environment.

After evaluating feedback, a company—when necessary—needs to engage in *adaptation*, thereby fine-tuning its marketing plan to be responsive to the environment, while continuing to capitalize on its differential advantages. The firm should look continually for new opportunities that fit its overall marketing plan and are attainable by it, and respond to potential threats by revising marketing policies.

For instance, many small optical shops are struggling due to the growth of such large chains as LensCrafters (**http://www.lenscrafters.com**), Sterling Optical (**http://www. sterlingoptical.com**), Pearle Vision (**http://www.pearlevision.com**), and others. The latter advertise extensively, buy in quantity to get special deals, and offer fast service and good prices. To operate in this environment, small optical shops use adaptation strategies like this one by Eyetique (**http://www.eyetique.com**), a five-outlet chain in Pennsylvania:

> Eyetique Edge is a corporate benefits program offered to a variety of Pittsburgh area employers, schools, and other organizations of 25 members or more. The plans provide special employee rates on vision and hearing examinations, eyewear, hearing aids, and more, with no cost or paperwork for the employer. Because of this, Eyetique Edge is extremely popular. Features include a 21-point comprehensive eye exam by independent doctors of optometry, 20 percent employee discounts on all products and services (excluding disposable contact lenses), minimal paper work, ease in adding new employees, acceptance of many insurance plans, no exclusions for pre-existing conditions, no employee claim forms, no lapses or limitations in coverage, no limit to the number of times a member or their immediate family may use this benefit, no waiting period, and no deductions.[12]

In gearing up for the future, a firm needs to avoid *marketing myopia*—a short-sighted, narrow-minded view of marketing and its environment. Consider this:

> **Marketing myopia** is an ineffective marketing approach.

> In today's global economy, knowledge is king. The booming business of flat-panel displays is a prime example. American and European display makers who weren't watching developments in Japan with an eagle eye, and who did not integrate technologies and skills from both America and Asia, have been left behind, too late to master the technologies and customer understanding required to catch the "slim-line," flat panel wave. Only alliances between Asian and Western companies succeeded; every one of the competitors who used only the know-how available in their home country fell by the wayside. To learn from the world, a company needs to come up with new ways to work in the international environment. It must become a global prospector, looking for hotbeds of emerging technology or bellwether customers that foreshadow future trends. But tapping into new pockets of knowledge around the world usually requires more than just short-term visits, 'study missions,' searching the Internet, or a visit to the Patent Office.[13]

---

[12] "Eyetique Edge," **http://www.eyetique.com/edge.html** (May 17, 2009).

[13] Yves Doz, Jose Santos, and Peter .J Williamson, "Marketing Myopia Re-Visited: Why Every Company Needs to Learn from the World," *Ivey Business Journal*, Vol. 68 (January-February 2004), pp. 1–6. See also Len Tiu Wright, Chanaka Jayawardhena, and Charles Dennis, "Editorial: Marketing Myopia," *Journal of Marketing Management*, Vol. 24 (February 2008), pp. 131–134; Kevin Morrell and Chanaka Jayawardhena, "Myopia and Choice: Framing, Screening, and Shopping," *Journal of Marketing Management*, Vol. 24 (February 2008), pp. 135–152; and John D. Nicholson and Philip J. Kitchen, "The Development of Regional Marketing—Have Marketers Been Myopic?" *International Journal of Business Studies*, Vol. 15 (No. 1, 2007), pp. 107–125

Web Sites You Can Use

The U.S. government has the most comprehensive collection of Web sites in the world. It makes available all sorts of information on a free or nominal fee basis. What a wealth of data! One general-access site (http://www.usa.gov) provides access to several hundred million government Web pages. Here are the addresses of several specialized U.S. government sites:

- Bureau of Economic Analysis (http://www.bea.gov)
- Bureau of Labor Statistics (http://www.stats.bls.gov)
- Census Bureau (http://www.census.gov)
- Consumer Product Safety Commission (http://www.cpsc.gov)
- Department of Commerce (http://www.commerce.gov)
- Department of Labor (http://www.dol.gov)
- Economic and Statistics Administration (https://www.esa.doc.gov)
- Environmental Protection Agency (http://www.epa.gov)

- Federal Communications Commission (http://www.fcc.gov)
- Federal Reserve Board (http://www.federalreserve.gov)
- Federal Trade Commission (http://www.ftc.gov)
- Fedstats (http://www.fedstats.gov)
- Fed World (http://www.fedworld.gov)
- Food and Drug Administration (http://www.fda.gov)
- International Trade Administration (http://www.trade.gov)
- Library of Congress (http://www.loc.gov)
- Securities and Exchange Commission (http://www.sec.gov)
- Small Business Administration (http://www.sba.gov)
- Women's Bureau—Department of Labor (http://www.dol.gov/wb)

Summary

1. *To examine the environment within which marketing decisions are made and marketing activities are undertaken* The marketing environment comprises controllable factors, uncontrollable factors, the organization's level of success or failure in reaching its objectives, feedback, and adaptation. The macroenvironment includes the broad societal and economic forces facing a firm; the microenvironment includes the more direct forces that affect a firm's ability to serve its customers.

2. *To differentiate between those elements controlled by a firm's top management and those controlled by marketing, and to enumerate the controllable elements of a marketing plan* Controllable factors are the internal strategy elements directed by a firm and its marketers. Top management decides on the line of business, overall objectives, the role of marketing and other business functions, and the corporate culture. These decisions affect all aspects of marketing.

   The major factors directed by marketing personnel are the selection of a target market—the group(s) of customers a firm proposes to serve; marketing objectives—more customer-oriented than those set by top management; the marketing organization; the marketing mix—a specific combination of product, distribution, promotion, and price decisions; and performance assessment—monitoring and evaluating marketing outcomes. It is important for marketing personnel to strive to create differential advantages—the unique features that cause consumers to patronize one firm and not its competitors.

3. *To enumerate the uncontrollable environmental elements that can affect a marketing plan and study their potential ramifications* Uncontrollable factors are the external elements affecting a company's performance that cannot

be fully directed by the top management and marketers of a firm. Any marketing plan, no matter how well conceived, may fail if uncontrollable factors negatively affect it too much.

Among the key uncontrollable variables are changing consumer traits, interpersonal influences on consumer behavior, the consumer decision process, and consumer groups; the competitive structure of the industry in which a firm operates (monopoly, oligopoly, monopolistic competition, or pure competition) and such competitor attributes as marketing strategies, country of origin, size, generic competition, and channel competition; suppliers and distributors, their traits and practices, and resource shortages; government legislation and the political environment; the rate of economic growth (as measured by the GDP and real income), the costs of doing business, and other economic factors; technology, which refers to the development and use of machinery, products, and processes; and independent media, the communication vehicles not controlled by the firm.

4. *To explain why feedback about company performance and the uncontrollable aspects of its environment and the subsequent adaptation of the marketing plan are essential for a firm to attain its objectives* A firm's level of success or failure in reaching its goals depends on both how well it directs and enacts the factors under its control and the impact of uncontrollable factors on the marketing plan. In enacting a marketing strategy, a firm should get feedback (information about its overall and marketing performance and the uncontrollable environment) and adapt the strategy to be responsive to the surrounding environment while continuing to exploit its differential advantages. Marketing myopia, a shortsighted view of marketing and its environment, must be avoided.

Key Terms

marketing environment (p. 29)

macroenvironment (p. 29)

microenvironment (p. 29)

controllable factors (p. 30)

line of business (p. 31)

corporate culture (p. 32)

target market (p. 33)

market segmentation (p. 33)

differential advantages (p. 34)

marketing organization (p. 34)

marketing mix (p. 35)

uncontrollable factors (p. 37)

monopoly (p. 39)

oligopoly (p. 39)

monopolistic competition (p. 39)

pure competition (p. 39)

gross domestic product (GDP) (p. 45)

real income (p. 45)

technology (p. 46)

independent media (p. 46)

feedback (p. 47)

adaptation (p. 47)

marketing myopia (p. 47)

Review Questions

1. Explain the five elements of the environment within which marketing operates.
2. In the environment of marketing, what are the two major types of controllable factors for a company? How do they differ?
3. What criteria would you use to assess the role of marketing in a company?
4. Why should a firm select a target market before developing a specific marketing mix?
5. What is the most important marketing objective for an organization? Why?
6. Describe the four components of the marketing mix.
7. What is the intent of each of these categories of federal legislation?
   a. Antitrust, discriminatory pricing, and unfair trade practices
   b. Deregulation
   c. Consumer protection
8. Why is technology an important uncontrollable factor for many companies?

Discussion Questions

1. How does a firm's corporate culture influence the performance of its personnel? Relate your answer to a national pharmacy chain.
2. What are the differential advantages for each of these? Explain your answers.
   a. National Football League (**http://www.nfl.com**)
   b. Wii game system (**http://www.wii.com**)
   c. Visa Student Card (**http://www.usa.visa.com/ personal/student/index.jsp**)
3. Distinguish between the marketing mixes used by Ford (**http://www.fordvehicles.com**) and Lincoln (**http://www. lincoln.com**), two car lines of Ford Motor Company.
4. Deregulation presents both opportunities and potential problems for companies. Offer examples of both for the airline industry.

Web Exercise

The Food and Drug Administration (FDA) is the U.S. agency responsibility for overseeing food and drug safety. Visit these two sections of its Web site: (a) Information for Consumers (**http:// www.fda.gov/cder/info/consumer.htm**) and (b) Information for Healthcare Professionals (**http://www.fda.gov/cder/info/ healthcare.htm**). Discuss what you learn from your visit.

Practice Quiz

1. Which of the following is *not* a factor primarily controlled by top management?
   a. Line of business
   b. Role of marketing
   c. Advertising strategy
   d. Overall objectives
2. When it is considered important by a firm, marketing is
   a. heavily involved in consumer research.
   b. equated with sales.
   c. given staff status.
   d. controlled by a production vice-president.

3. In selecting a target market, marketers usually
   a. ignore competitors.
   b. engage in market segmentation.
   c. control the marketing plan.
   d. determine the marketing mix.

4. Which of the following is *not* a form of marketing organization?
   a. Functional
   b. Product-oriented
   c. Market-oriented
   d. Coordinated

5. Product, price, promotion, and distribution decisions are components of the
   a. marketing protocol.
   b. marketing mix.
   c. marketing organization.
   d. marketing philosophy.

6. Whether to sell via intermediaries or directly to consumers, how many outlets to sell through, and whether to control or cooperate with other channel members are examples of decisions marketers must make about
   a. selling.
   b. production.
   c. distribution.
   d. price.

7. The most effective approach to the uncontrollable factors in the marketing environment is
   a. product innovation.
   b. insulating the marketing plan from them.
   c. continuous monitoring of their effects.
   d. constantly reorganizing the marketing organization.

8. In a monopoly, one firm
   a. seeks to engage in price wars.
   b. has no control over price because merchandise is standardized.
   c. finds that consumer demand is quite elastic.
   d. has a lot of control over the marketing plan.

9. Where a few large firms comprise most of an industry's sales, the competitive structure is best described as
   a. oligopoly.
   b. competitive monopoly.
   c. monopolistic competition.
   d. monopoly.

10. A firm has the least control over its pricing strategy in
    a. pure competition.
    b. monopolistic competition.
    c. oligopoly.
    d. monopoly.

11. Which of these statements is *not* correct?
    a. Pure competition occurs much less often than does monopolistic competition.
    b. Foreign competitors now play a declining role in many industries.
    c. It is necessary to study the competitive strategies of other firms.
    d. There is now a trend toward larger firms.

12. When a firm defines its competition in generic terms, it
    a. looks at competition as broadly as possible.
    b. examines its existing channel partners.
    c. focuses on patent expiration dates.
    d. analyzes the competitive structure within a specific industry.

13. Which type of competition most closely resembles generic competition?
    a. Direct competition
    b. Indirect competition
    c. Intermodal competition
    d. Bimodal competition

14. Which statement about technology is true?
    a. Patents provide exclusive rights to sell new products for virtually limited time periods.
    b. Small firms can control the technological advances that affect them.
    c. Technology cannot reduce the impact of resource shortages.
    d. Loss of patent protection decreases competition.

15. To attain its objectives, a firm is well advised to
    a. acquire feedback from the environment.
    b. maintain its existing strategies at all costs.
    c. ignore uncontrollable factors.
    d. bypass the independent media entirely.

For the answers to these questions, please visit the online site for this book at **http://www.atomicdog.com.**

Chapter 3

Developing and Enacting Strategic Marketing Plans

General Electric (GE) (**http://www.ge.com**) is one of the largest and most diversified technology, media, and financial services corporations in the world. Its products include aircraft engines, power generators, water processing, and business and consumer financing. GE comprises six operating segments: Infrastructure, Commercial Finance, GE Money, Healthcare, NBC Universal, and Industrial.

GE regularly ranks high on *Fortune's* "America's Most Admired Companies" list, *Fortune's* "Global Most Admired Companies," and *Forbes'* "World's Most Respected Companies Survey." Over the years, GE has been a major force in many strategic planning theories that have been adopted by business planners worldwide, including the concept of strategic business units as the building blocks of a corporate plan, the need for a strong mix of businesses, and the value of assessing business strength and market opportunities in evaluating an overall strategy.

In September 2001, when Jeffrey R. Immelt succeeded John F. Welch as GE's chief executive, annual earnings were $28 billion on $130 billion in sales. By 2007, GE's revenues exceeded $170 billion, and GE's earnings per share from continuing operations grew by 18 percent over the prior year. Unlike Welch—who stressed cost-cutting, efficiency, and buying and selling businesses—Immelt focused on risk taking, sophisticated marketing strategies, and innovation.

Recently, GE devised a "Growth as a Process" plan focusing on strong initiatives in technology, commercial excellence, customer focus, globalization, innovation, and developing growth leaders. As a result, GE has increased its research and development investment, more aggressively applied well-known quality management principles, and built strong management teams to tap into global growth markets. Through its "Imagination Breakthroughs" program, GE is developing 20 new "1 billion dollar businesses" involving such major technological breakthroughs as the "very light jet engine," low-cost desalination plants, and energy-efficient applicances.[1]

In this chapter, we will consider strategic planning from a marketing perspective and review, in depth, each of the steps in the strategic planning process. We will also examine the use of strategic planning by both small and large firms.

Chapter Objectives

1. To define strategic planning and consider its importance for marketing
2. To describe the total quality approach to strategic planning and show its relevance to marketing
3. To look at the different kinds of strategic plans and the relationships between marketing and the other functional areas in an organization
4. To describe thoroughly each of the steps in the strategic planning process: defining organizational mission, establishing strategic business units, setting marketing objectives, performing situation analysis, developing marketing strategy, implementing tactics, and monitoring results
5. To show how a strategic marketing plan may be devised and applied

[1] Various company and other sources.

3-1 OVERVIEW

As described in Chapter 2, the marketing environment includes a number of factors directed by top management and others directed by marketing. To coordinate these factors and provide guidance for decision making, it is helpful to engage in a formal strategic planning process. For marketers, such a process consists of two key components: a strategic business plan and a strategic marketing plan.

A *strategic business plan* provides "the overall direction an organization will pursue within its chosen environment and guides the allocation of resources and effort. It also provides the logic that integrates the perspectives of functional departments and operating units, and points them all in the same direction." It has (1) an external orientation, (2) a process for formulating strategies, (3) methods for analyzing strategic situations and alternatives, and (4) a commitment to action.[2]

A *strategic marketing plan* outlines the marketing actions to undertake, why they are needed, who is responsible for carrying them out, when and where they will be completed, and how they will be coordinated. A marketing plan is carried out within the context of a firm's broader strategic plan.

Our discussion of strategic planning in marketing is presented early in this book for several reasons. The strategic planning process

- gives a firm direction and enables it to better understand the dimensions of marketing research, consumer analysis, and the marketing mix. It is a hierarchal process, moving from company guidelines to specific marketing decisions.
- makes sure each division's goals are integrated with firmwide goals.
- encourages different functional areas to coordinate efforts.
- requires a firm to assess its strengths and weaknesses and to consider environmental opportunities and threats.
- outlines the alternative actions or combinations of actions a firm can take.
- presents a basis for allocating resources.
- highlights the value of assessing performance.

Figure 3-1 highlights how a firm can have a clear and directive strategic vision. Marketing's contribution to strategic planning is a crucial one:

> Marketing plays a vital role in the strategic management process of a firm. The experience of companies well versed in strategic planning indicates that failure in marketing can block the way to goals established by the strategic plan. When the external environment is stable, a company can successfully ride on its technological lead, manufacturing efficiency, and financial acumen. As the environment shifts, however, a lack of marketing perspective makes the best-planned strategies treacherous. Indeed, marketing strategy is the most significant challenge that firms of all types and sizes face. As one study noted, 'American corporations are beginning to answer a "new call to strategic marketing," as many of them shift their business planning priorities more toward strategic marketing and the market planning function.'[3]

For example, mass merchandisers such as Wal-Mart (**http://www.walmart.com**) recognize that each element of their strategy must reflect a customer orientation. Thus, Wal-Mart discount department stores place most sales personnel in product categories where customers want assistance, not evenly throughout stores.

In Chapter 3, we discuss a total quality approach to strategic planning, various kinds of strategic plans, relationships between marketing and other functional areas, and the strategic planning process—and show how strategic marketing plans may be outlined

Strategic planning includes both a **strategic business plan** and a **strategic marketing plan**.

Marketing should have a key role in strategic planning.

---

[2] "Dictionary," **http://www.marketingpower.com/_layouts/Dictionary.aspx?dLetter=S** (March 22, 2009). For good background information on strategic planning, see David J. Collins and Michael G. Rukstad, "Can You Say What Your Strategy Is?" *Harvard Business Review*, Vol. 86 (April 2008), pp. 82–90.

[3] Arnold Scott, "Aspects of Strategic Marketing," **http://www.web-articles.info/e/a/title/Aspects-of-strategic-marketing** (June 6, 2007).

About Atomic Dog Publishing

Atomic Dog Publishing was founded to provide instructors and learners with a completely unique teaching and learning tool. We began by breaking down books into their basic parts–their atomic parts–as it was clear that these components could be recombined to create a new and better kind of publication by using the rich capabilities of digital media.

Atomic Dog blends online content delivery, interactive multimedia components, and print to form a completely unique learning and teaching tool. Our online textbooks (HyBred Media™) contain interactive elements that allow instructors and students to customize their text to meet course objectives and fit individual learning styles. Identical core content found in the online edition is also available in the print edition with iconic references to interactive material found online.

We give authors and instructors a clear content alternative, while providing students superior choice and value. As part of Cengage Learning, we can provide you with premium content and superior learning solutions tailor-fit to the way you teach. We are loyal and dedicated to our customers—we hope that our publications, like great dogs, become your best friends.

Figure 3-1

The Clear Strategic Vision of Atomic Dog

Source: Reprinted by permission.

and applied. Chapter 22, which concludes the text, deals with how marketing plans are integrated and analyzed in a total quality framework.

A general planning Web site (**http://www.businessplans.org/topic10.html**) from Business Resource Software provides good planning materials from a small business perspective.

3-2 A TOTAL QUALITY APPROACH TO STRATEGIC PLANNING

> All firms should adopt a **total quality** approach, thereby becoming more process- and output-related in satisfying consumers.

Any firm—small or large, domestic or global, manufacturing- or services-driven—should adopt a total quality viewpoint when devising a strategic plan. **Total quality** is a process- and output-related philosophy, whereby a firm strives to fully satisfy customers in an effective and efficient manner. To flourish, a total quality program needs a customer focus, top management commitment, an emphasis on continuous improvement, and support from employees, suppliers, and distribution intermediaries:

- *Process-related philosophy*—Total quality is based on all the activities that create, develop, market, and deliver a good or service for the customer. A company gains a competitive advantage if it offers better-quality goods and services than competitors or if it offers the same quality at a lower price.
- *Output-related philosophy*—Although process-related activities give a good or service its value, the consumer usually can only judge the total quality of the finished product that he or she purchases. Many consumers care about what they buy, rather than how it was made.
- *Customer satisfaction*—To the consumer, total quality refers to how well a good or service performs. Customer service is a key element in a person's ultimate satisfaction, which is affected by the gap between that person's expectations of product performance and actual performance.
- *Effectiveness*—To a marketer, this involves how well various marketing activities (such as adding new product features) are received by consumers.
- *Efficiency*—To a marketer, this involves the costs of various marketing activities. A firm is efficient when it holds down costs, while offering consumers the appropriate level of quality.
- *Customer focus*—With a total quality viewpoint, a firm perceives the consumer as a partner and seeks input from that partner as it creates, develops, markets, and delivers a good or service.

- *Top management commitment*—Senior executives must be dedicated to making a total quality program work and to ensuring that corners are not cut in an attempt to be more efficient. In the best firms, "total quality" becomes ingrained as part of the corporate culture.
- *Continuous improvement*—A firm must continuously improve its quality because, in most cases, today's total quality will become tomorrow's suboptimal quality. A complacent company will be hurt by the dynamics of the marketplace and fast-paced technological and global marketplace trends.
- *Employee support and involvement*—Employees must "buy into" a total quality program for it to work. Empowering employees not only gets them involved in the total quality process, but it also assures that customer problems are promptly addressed and resolved in the customer's favor.
- *Supplier and distributor support and involvement*—Suppliers and resellers can greatly affect total quality due to their involvement in creating it. They too must "buy into" a firm's total quality efforts.

Figure 3-2 shows how a total quality program should work. At the left are the participants who create total quality. There is an interchange among the parties and between the parties and the process. In this way, a good's or service's effectiveness and efficiency are influenced. Total quality is the output. The process and total quality itself are regularly improved. If a consumer feels a product has superior total quality, a purchase is made. When experience with a purchase is pleasing, customer satisfaction occurs. Because one measure of effectiveness is customer satisfaction, there is an impact arrow.

Satisfaction is feedback that places consumer input into the process. The consumer's central focus is evident because this party appears three times: consumer input, consumer purchase, and customer satisfaction. At the Ritz-Carlton hotel chain (**http://www.ritzcarlton.com**), the only hotel company to twice win the Malcolm Baldrige National Quality award, total quality is imperative: "The Ritz-Carlton is a place where the genuine care and comfort of our guests is our highest mission. We pledge to provide the finest personal service and facilities for our guests who will always enjoy a warm, relaxed, yet refined ambience. The Ritz-Carlton experience enlivens the senses, instills well-being, and fulfills even the unexpressed wishes and needs of our guests. At Ritz-Carlton, 'We are

> For a totally quality program to work, every party in the process must participate.

Marketing and the Web

"Traditional" Media Refashion Their Strategies

The multi-billion dollar U.S. online advertising market has been dominated by Google (**http://www.google.com**), Yahoo! (**http://www.yahoo.com**), and Microsoft (**http://www.microsoft.com**). Some analysts estimated that as much as 85 percent of all online advertising dollars went to the "Big Three" in 2007. And less than one-third of this amount was passed onto partner sites within their networks. Google has also consistently increased its market share. It currently accounts for nearly one-half of all U.S. online advertising dollars.

The online world of advertising is rapidly changing. Older tactics, whereby advertisers aggressively sought banner ads with the hope of getting clicks from interested viewers, are no longer very popular. Print publishers and TV media executives are also increasingly aware that their audiences are spending more time online. Many traditional media now own Internet sites: Rupert Murdoch's News Corporation owns Myspace.com (**http://www.myspace.com**), Fox Broadcasting Company formed Fox Interactive Media (**http://www.fox.com**), and *The Washington Post* (**http://www.washingtonpost.com**) plans to increase Internet advertising through its Web sites.

To enhance their competitive positions, four of the nation's largest newspaper owners have developed quadrantOne (**http://www.quadrantone.com**), a combined advertising network representing about 175 small newspapers and other publications. This network facilitates the process of buying space on dozens of small Web sites. According to quadrantOne's CEO, "Local publishers just don't have the scale to compete with the big portals." In contrast to the major portals, quadrantOne shows its advertisers exactly where in their network their ads appear.

Source: Based on material in Catherine Holahan, "Old Media Takes Aim at Web Goliaths," **http://www.businessweek.com/technology/content/feb2008/tc20080224_102524.htm** (February 25, 2008).

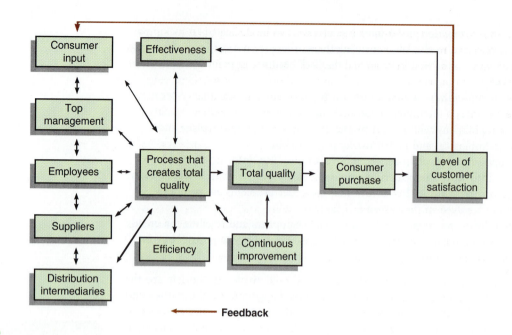

Figure 3-2

The Keys to a Successful Total Quality Program

Ladies and Gentlemen serving Ladies and Gentlemen.' Our Ladies and Gentlemen are the most important resource in our service commitment to our guests. By applying the principles of trust, honesty, respect, integrity, and commitment, we nurture and maximize talent to the benefit of each individual and the company."[4]

Sometimes, the total quality process breaks down in a way that may be difficult to fix. For example, many firms have had glitches with their Web sites, including heavy traffic causing system overloads, poor inventory and shipping coordination, too long a time for replies to E-mail, and so forth. These problems require expensive and time-consuming solutions. To learn more about the strategic aspects of total quality management (TQM), visit the U.S. Chamber of Commerce Web site (**http://www.uschamber. com/sb/business/P03/P03_9000.asp**). It highlights the role of marketing in TQM.

3-3 KINDS OF STRATEGIC PLANS

Strategic plans can be categorized by their duration, scope, and method of development. They range from short run, specific, and department generated to long run, broad, and management generated.

Plans may be short run (typically 1 year), moderate in length (2 to 5 years), or long run (5 to 10 or even 15 years). Many firms rely on a combination: Short-run and moderate-length plans are more detailed and operational in nature than long-run plans.

Japan's Canon (**http://www.canon.com**), the maker of cameras, machines, and optical products, has taken this planning approach:

> We aim to become a truly excellent global company, joining the ranks of the world's top 100 firms. (1) As we celebrate Canon's 70th anniversary, we aim to achieve the overwhelming No. 1 position in existing businesses that have supported our growth to date. To enhance our market competitiveness, we will secure a new technological edge with the development of key components and key devices and the reinforcement of platform technologies. (2) To maintain and increase global competitiveness, Canon believes it is

> Short-run plans are precise; long-run plans outline needs.

---

[4] "Gold Standards," **http://corporate.ritzcarlton.com/en/About/GoldStandards.htm** (March 22, 2009).

necessary to shift toward equipment-intensive processes by introducing highly productive automated systems and robots. We aim to introduce a new production system centered on automated assembly lines that operate around the clock. (3) Looking to further diversify, we are seeking out promising new areas—such as displays, office imaging solutions, and commercial printers—while pursuing business activities outside our established fields. Regional headquarters in the United States and Europe are investing capital and human resources to establish new businesses that capitalize on the technical expertise and characteristics unique to each region. (4) To continue to grow beyond 2010, Canon is stepping up research to discover new technologies and develop new business domains. We are expanding collaborations with leading research institutes and universities, so as to develop cutting-edge technologies. (5) To become a world-class firm, our employees must strive for excellence. Thus, we will further enhance our training programs to cultivate capable employees who are trusted by society and encourage them to put into practice Canon's guiding principles. At the same time, we will step up efforts to develop insightful global leaders and business managers who also contribute to the business world and society as a whole.[5]

The scope of strategic plans also varies. There may be separate marketing plans for each of a firm's major products; a single, integrated marketing plan encompassing all products; or a broad business plan with a section devoted to marketing. Separate marketing plans by product line are often used by consumer-goods manufacturers; a single, integrated marketing plan is often employed by service firms; and a broad business plan is often utilized by industrial-goods manufacturers. A firm's diversity and the number of distinct market segments it seeks both have a strong influence.

> Consumer-products firms often have plans for each line.

Last, plans may be devised by a bottom-up, top-down, or combination approach. In bottom-up planning, input from salespeople, product managers, advertising people, and other marketing areas is used to set goals, budgets, forecasts, timetables, and marketing mixes. Bottom-up plans are realistic and good for morale. Yet, it may be hard to coordinate bottom-up plans and to include different assumptions about the same concept when integrating a company-wide plan. Shortcomings of bottom-up plans are resolved in the top-down approach, whereby senior managers centrally direct planning. A top-down plan can use complex assumptions about competition or other external factors and provide a uniform direction for marketing. Input from lower-level managers is not actively sought and morale may diminish. A combination of the two approaches could be used if senior executives set overall goals and policy, and marketing personnel form plans for carrying out marketing activities.

> Bottom-up plans foster employee input; top-down plans are set by top management.

3-4 STRENGTHENING RELATIONSHIPS BETWEEN MARKETING AND OTHER FUNCTIONAL AREAS IN AN ORGANIZATION

An organization's strategic planning efforts must accommodate the distinct needs of marketing and other functional areas. This is not always simple, due to the different orientations of each area, as shown in Table 3-1. Marketers may seek tailor-made products, flexible budgets, nonroutine transactions, many product versions, frequent purchases, customer-driven new products, employee compensation incentives, and aggressive actions against competitors. This may conflict with goals of other functional areas to seek mass production (production), stable budgets (finance), routine transactions (accounting), limited models (engineering), infrequent orders (purchasing), technology-driven new products (research and development), fixed employee compensation (personnel), and passive actions against competitors (legal).

> The perspectives of marketing and other functional areas need to be reconciled.

Top management's job is to ensure that every functional area sees the need for a balanced view in company decision making and has input on decisions. Although a degree

[5] "Excellent Global Corporation Plan Phase III," http://www.canon.com/about/strategies (November 3, 2008).

Table 3-1	The Orientations of Different Functional Areas
Functional Area	**Major Strategic Orientation**
Marketing	To attract and retain a loyal group of consumers through a unique combination of product, distribution, promotion, and price factors
Production	To utilize full plant capacity, hold down per-unit production costs, and maximize quality control
Finance	To operate within established budgets, focus on profitable items, control customer credit, and minimize loan costs for the company
Accounting	To standardize reports, detail costs fully, and routinize transactions
Engineering	To develop and adhere to exact product specifications, limit models and options, and concentrate on quality improvements
Purchasing	To acquire items via large, uniform orders at low prices and maintain low inventories
Research and Development	To seek technological breakthroughs, improvements in product quality, and recognition for innovations
Personnel	To hire, motivate, supervise, and compensate employees in an efficient manner
Legal	To ensure that a strategy is defensible against challenges from the government, competitors, channel members, and consumers

of tension among departments is inevitable, conflict can be reduced by encouraging interfunctional contact; seeking personnel with both technical and marketing expertise; forming multifunctional task forces, committees, and management-development programs; and setting goals for each department that take other departments into account.

3-5 THE STRATEGIC PLANNING PROCESS

> The **strategic planning process** includes steps from defining a mission to monitoring results.

The *strategic planning process* has seven interrelated steps: defining organizational mission, establishing strategic business units, setting marketing objectives, performing situation analysis, developing marketing strategy, implementing tactics, and monitoring results. Because the process encompasses both strategic business planning and strategic marketing planning, it should be conducted by a combination of senior company executives and marketers. The strategic planning process is depicted in Figure 3-3.

This process applies to small and large firms, consumer and industrial firms, goods-and services-based firms, domestic and global firms, and profit-oriented and nonprofit-oriented institutions. Planning at each step in the process may differ by type of firm, but using a thorough strategic plan is worthwhile for any company. Sample plans for three businesses—manufacturer, service provider, and retailer—are available at the Business Owner's Toolkit site (**http://www.toolkit.com/tools/bt.aspx?tid=buspln_m**).

The steps in strategic planning are discussed in the following sections.

3-5a Defining Organizational Mission

> A firm sets its direction in an **organizational mission**.

Organizational mission refers to a long-term commitment to a type of business and a place in the market. It "describes the scope of the firm and its dominant emphasis and values," based on that firm's history, current management preferences, resources, and distinctive competences, and on environmental factors.[6]

---

[6] "Dictionary," **http://www.marketingpower.com/_layouts/Dictionary.aspx?dLetter=C** (March 22, 2009).

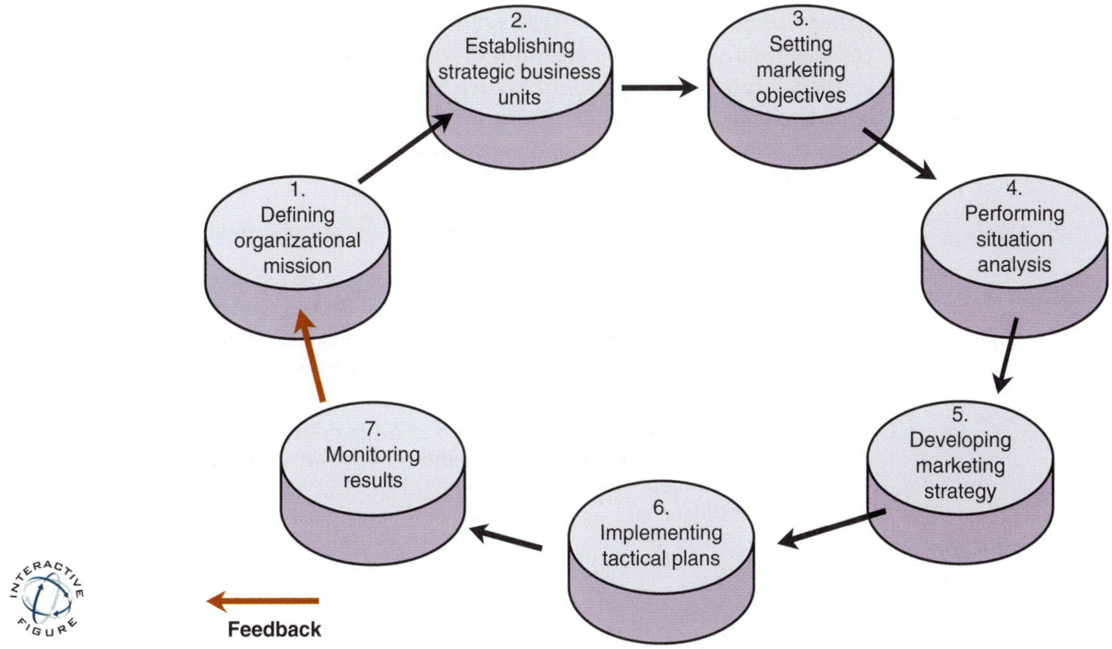

Figure 3-3

The Strategic Planning Process

An organizational mission can be expressed in terms of the customer group(s) served, the goods and services offered, the functions performed, and/or the technologies utilized. It is more comprehensive than the line-of-business concept noted in Chapter 2. Organizations that diversify too much may not have a clear sense of direction. The mission is considered implicitly whenever a firm

- seeks a new customer group or abandons an existing one,
- introduces a new product (good or service) category or deletes an old one,

Ethical Issues in Marketing

Profiting from Corporate Social Responsibility

For the most part, firms can no longer afford to ignore social responsibility or to keep quiet about their efforts in raising funds for charities. A recent study by IBM, involving more than 250 business leaders, found that 68 percent of the businesses surveyed have already focused on corporate social responsibility activities that generate additional sales and profits. Let's look at three examples of firms that "do well by doing good."

Cemex (http://www.cemex.com), a Mexican firm that specializes in construction materials, now has a savings club that enables its low-income customers to pay for items on a weekly basis at discounted prices. Although Cemex sells these goods at two-thirds the regular price, this strategy has expanded the market for Cemex. As a result, this market segment is growing at 250 percent per year.

Catalyst Paper (http://www.catalystpaper.com), a Canadian company, uses byproducts of paper and pulp production to power its operations. This process also reduces carbon emissions through recycling waste water generated by heat. Thus, Catalyst Paper has saved millions of dollars (U.S.) in fuel consumption—and lowered greenhouse gas emissions.

Great Britain's Marks and Spencer (M&S) (http://www.marksandspencer.com) recently launched "Behind the Label," an advertising campaign that shows the firm's commitment to ecological and social issues. Among the topics addressed are safety issues relating to mad cow disease and sustainability issues with wood products used in furniture. The end result was a rejuvenated M&S brand with sales increases of 10 percent and profit increases of 22 percent in one recent year.

Source: Based on material in George Pohle and Jeff Hittner, "The Right Corporate Karma," http://www.forbes.com/leadership (May 16, 2008).

- acquires another company or sells a business,
- engages in more marketing functions (a wholesaler opening retail stores) or in fewer marketing functions (a small innovative toy maker licensing its inventions to an outside company that produces, distributes, and promotes them), or
- shifts its technological focus (a phone manufacturer placing more emphasis on cellular phones).

Here are two diverse illustrations of a clear organizational mission:

1. Atomic Dog Publishing (**http://www.atomicdog.com**) [the publisher of this book] blends online content delivery, interactive multimedia components, and print to form a completely unique learning and teaching tool. Our online textbooks contain interactive elements that allow instructors and students to customize their texts to meet course objectives and fit individual learning styles. Identical core content found in the online edition is also available in the print edition with iconic references to interactive material found online. We give authors and instructors a clear content alternative, while providing students with a superior choice and value. As part of Cengage Learning (**http://www.cengage.com/highered**), we can provide you with premium content and superior learning solutions tailor-fit to the way you teach. We are loyal and dedicated to our customers—we hope that our publications, like great dogs, become your best friends.[7]

2. The mission of Southwest Airlines (**http://www.southwest.com**) is dedication to the highest quality of customer service delivered with a sense of warmth, friendliness, individual pride, and company spirit. This mission has always governed the way we conduct our business. It highlights our desire to serve customers and gives us direction when we have to make service-related decisions. It is another way of saying, "we always try to do the right thing!" We have achieved the airline industry's best cumulative consumer satisfaction record, according to U.S. Department of Transportation data. It is *never* our wish to inconvenience our customers. We tell employees we are in the customer service business—we just happen to provide airline transportation. Southwest is proud to incorporate its voluntary customer service commitment in its official contract of carriage reinforcing our pledge to provide safe, affordable, reliable, timely, courteous, and efficient air transportation and baggage handling service on every flight, as well as produce a fair return on our shareholders' investments.[8]

3-5b   Establishing Strategic Business Units

Strategic business units (SBUs) are separate operating units in an organization.

After defining its mission, a firm may form strategic business units. Each *strategic business unit (SBU)* is a self-contained division, product line, or product department in an organization with a specific market focus and a manager with complete responsibility for integrating all functions into a strategy. An SBU may include all products with the same physical features or products bought for the same use by customers, depending on the mission of the organization. Each SBU has these general attributes:

- A specific target market
- Its own senior marketing executive
- Control over its resources
- Its own marketing strategy
- Clear-cut competitors
- Distinct differential advantages

The SBU concept lets firms identify the business units with the most earnings potential and allocate to them the resources needed for growth. For instance, at General Electric, every SBU must have a unique purpose, identifiable competitors, and all its major business functions (manufacturing, finance, and marketing) within the control of

[7] "About Atomic Dog Publishing," **http://www.atomicdogpublishing.com/AboutUs.asp** (March 11, 2009).

[8] "Southwest Airlines: Customer Service Commitment," **http://www.southwest.com/about_swa/customer_service_commitment/customer_service_commitment.pdf** (July 15, 2008).

that SBU's manager. Units not performing up to expectations are constantly reviewed and, if necessary, consolidated with other units, sold, or closed down.

The number of SBUs depends on a firm's organizational mission and resources, and the willingness of top management to delegate authority. A small or specialized firm can have as few as one SBU; a diversified firm can have up to 100 or more. The rather specialized WD-40 Company (http://www.wd40.com) has three main SBUs: multipurpose lubricants (WD-40 and 3-in-One), heavy-duty hand cleaners (Lava and Solvol), and household products (such as Carpet Fresh, Spot Shot, and 2000 Flushes). And the highly diversified Johnson & Johnson (http://www.jnj.com), with 250+ SBUs, is "the world's premier consumer health company, the world's largest and most diverse medical devices and diagnostics company, the world's 3rd-largest biologics company, and the world's 6th-largest pharmaceuticals company."[9]

Firms sometimes eliminate SBUs that do not fit for them. After careful consideration, PepsiCo (http://www.pepsico.com) spun off its restaurant SBUs—KFC, Pizza Hut, and Taco Bell—to concentrate on three businesses: carbonated beverages, snack foods, and noncarbonated beverages. PepsiCo then acquired Quaker Oats, with its Gatorade drinks and other food products.

3-5c Setting Marketing Objectives

A firm needs overall marketing objectives, as well as goals for each SBU. Objectives are often described in both quantitative terms (dollar sales, percentage profit growth, market share, etc.) and qualitative terms (image, level of innovativeness, industry leadership role, etc.).

> Marketing objectives may include quantitative and qualitative measures.

For example, Hewlett-Packard (http://www.hp.com) is a 70-year-old "technology company that operates in more than 170 countries around the world. No other company offers as complete a technology product portfolio as HP. We provide infrastructure and business offerings that span from handheld devices to some of the world's most powerful supercomputer installations. We offer consumers a wide range of goods and services from digital photography to digital entertainment and from computing to home printing." It has a solid base of marketing goals that complement its overall corporate objectives:

Passion for customers—We put our customers first in everything we do.

Customer loyalty—We earn customer respect and loyalty by consistently providing the highest quality and value.

Profit—We achieve sufficient profit to finance growth, create value for our shareholders, and achieve our corporate objectives.

Growth—We recognize and seize opportunities for growth that builds upon our strengths and competencies.

Market leadership—We lead by developing and delivering useful and innovative products, services, and solutions.

Speed and agility—We are resourceful and adaptable, and we achieve results faster than our competitors.

Meaningful innovation—We are the technology company that invents the useful and the significant.

Commitment to employees—We demonstrate our commitment to employees by promoting and rewarding based on performance and by creating a work environment that reflects our values.

Leadership capability—We develop leaders at all levels who achieve business results, exemplify our values, and lead us to grow and win.

---

[9] "Our Company," http://www.jnj.com/connect/about-jnj/?flash=true (April 27, 2009).

Global citizenship—We fulfill our responsibility to society by being an economic, intellectual, and social asset to each country and community where we do business.[10]

Small firms' goals may be less ambitious than those set by their larger counterparts, but they are no less important. Goals are necessary to focus the firm and allow it to monitor the level of success or failure. Without goals, how can a firm really measure its performance?

3-5d Performing Situation Analysis

> **Situation analysis** investigates a firm's strengths, weaknesses, opportunities, and threats.

In *situation analysis*, also known as SWOT analysis, an organization identifies its internal strengths *(S)* and weaknesses *(W)*, as well as external opportunities *(O)* and threats *(T)*. Situation analysis seeks to answer: Where is a firm now? Where is it headed? Answers are derived by recognizing both company strengths and weaknesses relative to competitors, studying the environment for opportunities and threats, assessing the firm's ability to capitalize on opportunities and to minimize or avoid threats, and anticipating competitors' responses to company strategies. The Business Owner's Toolkit site (**http://www.toolkit.com/small_business_guide/sbg.aspx?nid=P03_8020**) provides an in-depth discussion of many of the factors to be reviewed during a situation analysis.

Situation analysis can, and should, be conducted at any point in a firm's life. Consider this example, as reported by Datamonitor:

> P&G (**http://www.pg.com**) has leading market positions across most of its businesses. P&G is also one of the world's most successful brand-building companies with one of the largest portfolios of trusted brands. More than 80 percent of P&G's total sales and profits come from 41 of its largest brands, the brands that generate more than $500 million each, in annual sales. P&G has one of the most diversified product portfolios in the world. It participates in more than 40 product categories with 300 brands in over 60 markets. P&G has witnessed failures in its quality controls occasionally. In September 2006, P&G suspended sales of the cosmetics in China after they were found by the authorities to contain the banned substances. A significant portion of the revenues from the sale of products is derived from a few customers and high-frequency stores. Sales to Wal-Mart Stores (**http://www.walmart.com**) and its affiliates represent about 15 percent of its total revenue. Just seven retail customers account for about 30 percent of total unit volume. Hence, the loss of any of these customers will lead to a sharp decline in P&G's revenues and also a loss of its market share.
>
> The consumer products business is driven significantly by population growth, household formation, and income growth. These factors are now yielding strong growth in many of P&G's developing markets, including India and China. The health-care industry is likely to grow due to changing U.S. demographics. P&G faces intense competition from major firms such as Colgate-Palmolive (**http://www.colgate.com**), Johnson & Johnson (**http://www.jnj.com**), and Unilever (**http://www.unilever.com**). P&G also faces competition from local, low-cost manufacturers in developing countries as well as from increasing private-label brands introduced by large-format retailers and discounters worldwide.[11]

Here's what a small new consulting firm's SWOT analysis might look like: *Strengths*: "We are able to respond quickly as we have no red tape and no need for higher management approval. We can give really good customer care, as our current small amount of work means we have a lot of time to devote to customers. Our lead consultant has a strong reputation. We have low overhead." *Weaknesses*: "Our firm has no market presence. We have a small staff with limited skills in some areas. We are vulnerable to vital staff becoming sick or leaving. Our cash flow will be erratic in the early stages." *Opportunities*: "Our business sector is expanding, with many future possibilities for success. Our local chamber of commerce recommends local businesses for work where

---

[10] "HP Corporate Objectives and Shared Values," **http://www.hp.com/hpinfo/abouthp/corpobj.html** (April 27, 2009).
[11] "Company Spotlight: Procter & Gamble," *Datamonitor* (July 2008), pp. 129–134.

possible. Competitors may be slow to adopt new technologies." *Threats:* "Will developments in technology affect this market beyond our ability to adapt? A small change in focus of a large competitor might wipe out any market position we achieve."[12]

Situation analysis may sometimes reveal weaknesses or threats that cannot be overcome, and a firm drops or sells a product line or division. In the mid-1990s, General Mills (**http://www.generalmills.com**) sold its popular restaurant division—comprised of the Red Lobster, Olive Garden, and China Coast chains. Why? Fifty-five percent of General Mills' food profits were used to fund the restaurant business; and the firm decided to focus instead on its leading food brands. This is the focus today: "General Mills gets its Kix as the number two U.S. cereal maker (behind uber-rival Kellogg, **http://www.kellogg.com**). Among its cereal brands are Cheerios, Chex, Total, Kix, and Wheaties. General Mills is a brand leader in flour (Gold Medal), baking mixes (Betty Crocker, Bisquick), dinner mixes (Hamburger Helper), fruit snacks (Fruit Roll-Ups), grain snacks (Chex Mix, Pop Secret), and canned and frozen vegetables (Green Giant). It is also a leading maker of branded yogurt (Colombo, Go-Gurt, and Yoplait). Its 2001 acquisition of Pillsbury from Diageo (**http://www.diageo.com**) doubled the company's size, making General Mills one of the world's largest food companies. Its foods are available in more than 100 countries."[13]

Figure 3-4 highlights BMW's strong move into "pre-owned" cars, after a SWOT analysis.

3-5e Developing Marketing Strategy

A *marketing strategy* outlines the way in which the marketing mix is used to attract and satisfy the target market(s) and achieve an organization's goals. Marketing-mix decisions center on product, distribution, promotion, and price plans. A separate strategy is necessary for each SBU in an organization; these strategies must be coordinated.

A marketing strategy should be clear to provide proper guidance. It should take into account a firm's mission, resources, abilities, and standing in the marketplace; the status of the firm's industry and the product groups in it (such as laptop PCs versus all-in-one printers); domestic and global competition; such environmental factors as the economy and population trends; and the best growth options—and the threats that could dampen it. For instance, McDonald's (**http://www.mcdonalds.com**) does a lot of image advertising as part of its overall marketing strategy to enhance its stature in the business community.

Four strategic planning approaches are presented next: product/market opportunity matrix, Boston Consulting Group matrix, General Electric business screen, and Porter generic strategy model.

The Product/Market Opportunity Matrix
The *product/market opportunity matrix* identifies four alternative marketing strategies to maintain and/or increase sales of business units and products: market penetration, market development, product development, and diversification.[14] See Figure 3-5. The choice of an alternative depends on the market saturation of an SBU or product and the firm's ability to introduce new products. Two or more alternatives may be combined.

Market penetration is effective when the market is growing or not yet saturated. A firm seeks to expand the sales of its present products in its present markets through more intensive distribution, aggressive promotion, and competitive pricing. Sales are increased by attracting nonusers and competitors' customers and raising the usage rate among current customers.

> A good **marketing strategy** provides a framework for marketing activities.

> The **product/market opportunity matrix** involves market penetration, market development, product development, and diversification options.

---

[12] Adapted by the authors from Advanced Integrated Technologies, "SWOT Analysis," **http://www.scribd.com/doc/2673524/SWOT-Analysis?query2=enron%20swot%20analysis** (2006).

[13] "General Mills, Inc.," **http://www.hoovers.com/general-mills/–ID__10639–/free-co-factsheet.xhtml** (February 28, 2006).

[14] H. Igor Ansoff, "Strategies for Diversification," *Harvard Business Review*, Vol. 35 (September-October 1957), pp. 113–124. See also "The Ansoff Matrix," **http://www.mindtools.com/pages/article/newTMC_90.htm** (March 9, 2009).

Figure 3-4

Profiting from SWOT Analysis

After studying the marketplace, BMW decided to place greater emphasis on the sales of used cars ("certified pre-owned").

Source: Reprinted by permission.

Market development is effective when a local or regional business looks to widen its market, new market segments are emerging due to changes in consumer lifestyles and demographics, and innovative uses are discovered for a mature product. A firm seeks greater sales of present products from new markets or new product uses. It can enter new territories, appeal to segments it is not yet satisfying, and reposition existing items. New distribution methods may be tried; promotion efforts are more descriptive.

Product development is effective when an SBU has a core of strong brands and a sizable consumer following. A firm develops new or modified products to appeal to present markets. It stresses new models, better quality, and other minor innovations closely related to entrenched products—and markets them to loyal customers. Traditional distribution methods are used; promotion stresses that the new product is made by a well-established firm.

Diversification is used so a firm does not become too dependent on one SBU or product line. The firm becomes involved with new products aimed at new markets. These products may be new to the industry or new only to the company. Both distribution and promotion orientations are different from those usually followed by the firm.

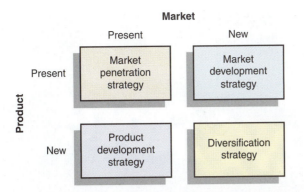

Market

Figure 3-5

The Product/Market Opportunity Matrix

Source: Adapted from H. Igor Ansoff, "Strategies for Diversification," *Harvard Business Review*, Vol. 35 (September–October 1957), pp. 113–124.

Here is how the product/market opportunity matrix can be applied to United Parcel Service—UPS (http://www.ups.com):

- Market penetration—UPS is the world's largest package-delivery firm. It advertises extensively on TV and in magazines. The U.S. slogan is "What Can Brown Do for You?" The slogan elsewhere is "Deliver More." Annually, UPS handles more than 4 billion packages for 8 million customers.
- Market development—It is stepping up efforts around the world, where client use of delivery services tends to be much less than in the United States. In 1990, UPS International operated in 40 nations; now, it operates in more than 200 countries and territories. The firm's Web site is accessible in 23 languages and dialects, and has dedicated content for more than 100 countries.
- Product development—UPS now offers more shipping choices than ever before, including Express Critical, Next Day Air Early A.M., Next Day Air, Next Day Air Saver, 2nd Day Air A.M., 2nd Day Air, 3 Day Select, Ground, Hundredweight Service, and various Worldwide Express services.
- Diversification—Though the major focus of UPS is package delivery, it has such subsidiaries as UPS Supply Chain Solutions (http://www.ups-scs.com)—offering supply chain support, from transportation to customs; UPS Capital (http://www.upscapital.com)—a provider of financial and insurance solutions; UPS Customer Solutions (http://www.ups-psi.com)—a global management consulting group that delivers business solutions; and the UPS Store (http://www.upsstore.com) and Mail Boxes Etc. (http://www.mbe.com), which together operate 6,000 stores.[15] See Figure 3-6.

The Boston Consulting Group Matrix The *Boston Consulting Group matrix* lets a firm classify each SBU in terms of market share relative to key competitors and annual industry growth. A firm can see which SBUs are dominant compared to competitors and whether the industries in which it operates are growing, stable, or declining. The matrix comprises stars, cash cows, question marks, and dogs, as well as the strategies for them.[16] See Figure 3-7.

The presumption is that the higher an SBU's market share, the better its long-run marketplace status because of lower per-unit costs and higher profitability (http://www.bcg.com). This is due to economies of scale (large firms can automate or standardize production, service tasks, distribution, promotion, and so on), experience (as operations are repeated, a firm becomes more effective), and better bargaining power. At the same time, the industry growth rate indicates a firm's need to invest. A high growth rate means a substantial investment will be needed to maintain or expand the firm's position in a growing market.

The **Boston Consulting Group matrix** uses market share and industry growth to describe stars, cash cows, question marks, and dogs.

[15] Various sections, http://www.ups.com (March 9, 2009).
[16] "Portfolio Management Based on Market Share and Market Growth," http://www.12manage.com/methods_bcgmatrix.html (August 17, 2008).

Figure 3-6

The UPS Store

The UPS Store (**http://www. upsstore.com**) is just one of the mechanisms utilized by UPS to facilitate its wide-ranging delivery services.

Source: Reprinted by permission.

A *star* is a leading SBU (high market share) in an expanding industry (high growth). The main goal is to sustain differential advantages despite rising competition. It can generate substantial profits but needs financing to grow. Market share can be kept or increased by intensive advertising, product introductions, greater distribution, and/or price reductions. As industry growth slows, a star becomes a cash cow.

A *cash cow* is a leading SBU (high market share) in a mature or declining industry (low growth). It often has loyal customers, making it tough for competitors. Because sales are steady, without high costs for product development and the like, a cash cow

Figure 3-7

The Boston Consulting Group Matrix

Source: Adapted from Bruce D. Henderson, "The Experience Curve Reviewed: IV. The Growth Share Matrix of the Product Portfolio" (Boston: Boston Consulting Group, 1973). *Perspectives*, No. 135.

Relative Market Share

	High	Low
High Industry Growth Rate	**SBU** **Designation:** Star **Marketing Strategy:** Large marketing efforts to maintain or increase market share	**SBU** **Designation:** Question mark **Marketing Strategy:** Intensify marketing efforts or leave the market
Low	**SBU** **Designation:** Cash cow **Marketing Strategy:** Use profits to aid growing SBUs, maintain position	**SBU** **Designation:** Dog **Marketing Strategy:** Reduce efforts or divest

Relative market share is an SBU's market share in comparison to the leading competitors in the industry. Industry growth rate is the annual growth of all similar businesses in the market (such as sugarless gum).

yields more cash (profit) than needed to hold its market share. Profits support the growth of other company SBUs. Marketing is oriented to reminder ads, periodic discounts, keeping up distribution channels, and offering new styles or options to encourage repurchases.

A *question mark* is an SBU that has had little impact (low market share) in an expanding industry (high growth). There is low consumer support, differential advantages are weak, and competitors are leaders. To improve, a big marketing investment is needed in the face of strong competition. A firm must decide whether to beef up promotion, add distributors, improve product attributes, and cut prices—or to abandon the market. The choice depends on whether a firm believes the SBU can compete successfully with more support and what that support will cost.

A *dog* is an SBU with limited sales (low market share) in a mature or declining industry (low growth). Despite time in the marketplace, it has little customer interest— and lags behind competitors in sales, image, and so on. A dog usually has cost disadvantages and few growth opportunities. A firm with such an SBU can appeal to a specialized market, harvest profits by cutting support, or exit the market.

IBM (**http://www.ibm.com**) operates in four main segments: global services— technology support and consulting; systems and technology—mainframe computers, servers, and more; software—mostly for businesses and institutions; and global financing—client funding for systems, software, and services. The firm applies the principles suggested by the Boston Consulting Group matrix. It examines SBUs in terms of expected industry growth and market position, and then sets marketing strategies. In recent years, there has been a shift away from hardware—which contributed less than one-quarter of IBM's overall revenues in 2008 (down from 43 percent in 1998)—and toward global services, which accounted for 55 percent of sales in 2008 (up from 36 percent in 1998). The shift is due to a combination of declining hardware sales in a stagnant industry and the strong opportunities for information technology services.[17]

The General Electric Business Screen

The *General Electric business screen* categorizes SBUs and products in terms of industry attractiveness and company business strengths. It uses more variables than either the product/market opportunity matrix or the Boston Consulting Group matrix. Industry attractiveness is based on market size and growth, competition, technological advances, and the social/legal environment. Company business strengths encompass differential advantages, market share, patent protection, marketing effectiveness, control over prices, and economies of scale. An SBU may have high, medium, or low industry attractiveness, as well as high, medium, or low business strengths; it would be positioned accordingly on the business screen in Figure 3-8.[18]

SBUs in green are investment/growth areas. They are in strong industries and performing well. They are similar to stars in the Boston Consulting Group matrix. Full marketing resources are proper, and high profits are expected. Innovations, product-line extensions, product and image ads, distribution intensity, and solid price margins are pursued.

SBUs in yellow are selectivity/earnings areas. They are not positioned as well as investment/growth SBUs. An SBU may be strong in a weak industry (as a cash cow), okay in a somewhat attractive industry, or weak in an attractive industry (as a question mark). A firm wants to hold the earnings and strength of cash cows, and use marketing to maintain customer loyalty and distribution support. For question marks, a firm must decide whether to raise its marketing investment, focus on a specialized market niche, acquire another business in the industry, or trim product lines. The medium/medium SBU is an opportunity to appeal to underserved segments and invest selectively in marketing.

SBUs in red represent harvest/divest areas. They are similar to dogs in the Boston Consulting Group matrix. A firm can minimize its marketing effort, concentrate on a few

The **General Electric business screen** measures industry attractiveness and company business strengths.

---

[17] Various *IBM Annual Reports*.

[18] "Marketing Strategy Matrix," **http://www.brs-inc.com/models/model17.asp** (August 17, 2008); and David A. Aaker, *Strategic Marketing Management*, Eighth Edition (New York: Wiley, 2008).

Figure 3-8

The General Electric Business Screen

Source: Maintaining Strategies for the Future Through Current Crises (Fairfield, CT: General Electric, 1975).

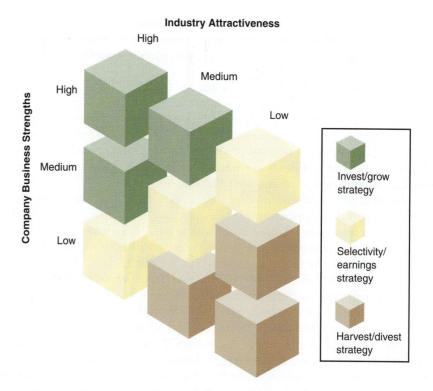

products rather than a product line, divest, or close down the SBU. Profits are harvested because investments are minimal.

Bausch & Lomb (**http://www.bausch.com**) applies the fundamentals of the business screen. It is building its current eye care businesses, as well as pursuing new opportunities within the global eye care market: "Bausch & Lomb is the eye health company dedicated to perfecting vision and enhancing life. We offer the world's most comprehensive portfolio of eye-health products, and we have one of the oldest, best known, and most respected healthcare brands in the world." Bausch & Lomb "began in 1853 as a small optical shop that grew to become a multi-billion dollar corporation with 13,000 employees worldwide and products sold in more than 100 countries." Its "history of innovation continues today as we invent new materials, engineer new technologies, and create pioneering ways to help people see better." The firm has five broad product categories: contact lenses, lens care, pharmaceuticals for eye conditions, cataract and vitreoretinal surgery instruments and devices, and products for use in laser surgery.[19] To concentrate on its main businesses, Bausch & Lomb sold its sunglass SBU (featuring Ray-Ban), its Miracle Ear hearing aid SBU, and its animal research SBU.

Visit the "GE Innovation Timeline" (**http://www.ge.com/innovation/timeline/index.html**) to learn about the varied major contributions made by the firm that has given us the GE business screen.

The Porter Generic Strategy Model The *Porter generic strategy model* identifies two key marketing planning concepts and the options available for each: competitive scope (broad or narrow target) and competitive advantage (lower cost or differentiation). The model pinpoints these basic strategies: cost leadership, differentiation, and focus.[20] See Figure 3-9.

> The **Porter generic strategy model** distinguishes among cost leadership, differentiation, and focus strategies.

---

[19] "About Bausch & Lomb," **http://bausch.com/en_US/corporate/corpcomm/general/about_bauschandlomb.aspx** (April 3, 2009).

[20] Michael E. Porter, *Competitive Advantage: Creating and Sustaining Superior Performance* (New York: Free Press, 1985), pp. 11–26; Michael E. Porter, *Competitive Strategy: Techniques for Analyzing Industries and Competitors* (New York: Free Press, 1980), pp. 34–46; and "Porter's Generic Strategies," **http://www.mindtools.com/pages/article/newSTR_82.htm** (March 9, 2009).

Competitive Advantage

Firm pursues
a **COST LEADERSHIP
STRATEGY** by targeting
the mass market and
featuring low prices.

Firm pursues a
**DIFFERENTIATION
STRATEGY** by targeting
the mass market and
featuring distinctive
attributes in goods
and/or services.

Firm pursues a COST
FOCUS STRATEGY by
targeting a niche
market and
featuring low prices.

Firm pursues a
**DIFFERENTIATION
FOCUS STRATEGY**
by targeting a niche
market and featuring
distinctive attributes in
goods and/or services.

Competitive Scope

Figure 3-9

The Porter Generic Strategy Model

Source: Tables developed by the authors based on concepts in Michael E. Porter, *Competitive Advantage: Creating and Sustaining Superior Performance* (New York: Free Press, 1985), pp. 11–16.

With a *cost-leadership strategy*, an SBU aims at a broad target market and offers goods or services in large quantities. Due to economies of scale, a firm can reduce per-unit costs and have low prices. This gives it higher profit margins than competitors, allows better responses to cost increases, and/or lures price-conscious consumers. Among those using cost leadership are UPS (**http://www.ups.com**), DuPont (**http://www.dupont.com**), and Wal-Mart (**http://www.walmart.com**).

In a *differentiation strategy*, an SBU aims at a large market by offering goods or services viewed as quite distinctive. The goods or services have a broad appeal, yet are perceived by consumers as unique by virtue of features, availability, reliability, and so on; price is less important. Among those using differentiation are Federal Express (**http://www.fedex.com**), Seiko (**http://www.seiko.com**), and Caterpillar Tractor (**http://www.cat.com**).

With a *focus strategy*, an SBU (which could be a small firm) seeks a narrow market segment via low prices or a unique offering. It can control costs by concentrating on a few key products aimed at specific consumers (cost focus) or by having a specialist reputation and serving a market unsatisfied by competitors (differentiation focus). Printek Direct! (**http://www.printekdirect.com**) markets refurbished printers to cost-conscious customers, while the Baby Jogger Company (**http://www.babyjogger.com**) makes a line of strollers for those who like jogging with their babies and toddlers. A neighborhood hardware store usually has a good combination of service, convenient location, and long hours; a local radio station may cater to an over-50 audience by playing mostly rock music from the 1960s, 1970s, and 1980s.

The Porter model shows that a small firm can profit by concentrating on one competitive niche, even though its total market share may be low. A firm does not have to be large to do well.

Evaluation of Strategic Planning Approaches

The strategic planning approaches just discussed are widely used—at least informally. Many firms assess alternative market opportunities; know which products are stars, cash cows, question marks, and dogs; recognize what factors affect performance; understand their industries; and realize they can target broad or narrow customer bases. Formally, strategic planning models are most apt to be used by larger firms; and the models are adapted to the needs of the specific firms employing them.

The approaches' major strengths are that they let a firm analyze all SBUs and products, study the effects of various strategies, reveal the opportunities to pursue and the threats to avoid, compute marketing and other resource needs, focus on key differential advantages, compare performance with designated goals, and discover principles for improving. Competitors can also be studied.

> Strategic models have pros and cons, and should be only part of planning.

The approaches' major weaknesses are that they may be hard to use (particularly by a small firm), may be too simplistic and omit key factors, are somewhat arbitrary in defining SBUs and evaluative criteria (such as relative market share), may not be applicable to all firms and situations (a dog SBU may be profitable and generate cash), do not adequately account for environmental conditions (such as the economy), may overvalue market share, and are often used by staff planners rather than line managers.

These techniques are only planning aids. They do not replace the need for managers to engage in hands-on decisions by studying each situation and basing marketing strategies on the unique aspects of their industry, firm, and SBUs.

3-5f Implementing Tactical Plans

> A marketing strategy is enacted via **tactical plans**.

A *tactical plan* specifies the short-run actions (tactics) that a firm undertakes in implementing a given marketing strategy. At this stage, a strategy is operationalized. A tactical plan has three basic elements: specific tasks, a time frame, and resource allocation.

The marketing mix (specific tasks) may range from a combination of high quality, high service, low distribution intensity, personal selling emphasis, and above-average prices to a combination of low quality, low service, high distribution intensity, advertising emphasis, and low prices. Each SBU should have a distinct marketing mix, based on its target market and strategic emphasis. The individual mix elements must be coordinated for each SBU, and conflicts among SBUs must be minimized.

Proper timing (time horizon) may mean being the first to introduce a product, bringing out a product when the market is most receptive, or quickly reacting to a competitor's strategy to catch it off guard. A firm must balance its desire to be an industry leader with clear-cut competitive advantages against its concern for the risk of being innovative. Marketing opportunities exist for limited times, and the firm needs to act accordingly.

Marketing investments (resources) may be order processing or order generating. Order-processing costs involve recording and handling orders, such as order entry, computer-data handling, and merchandise handling. The goal is to minimize those costs, subject to a given level of service. Order-generating costs, such as advertising and personal selling, produce revenues. Reducing them may be harmful to sales and profits. A firm should estimate sales at various levels of costs and for various combinations of marketing functions. Maximum profit rarely occurs at the lowest level of expenditure on order-generating costs.

Tactical decisions differ from strategic decisions in these ways. They

- are less complex and more structured.
- have a much shorter time horizon.
- require a considerably lower resource commitment.
- are enacted and adjusted more often.

PepsiCo's Frito-Lay (**http://www.fritolay.com**) "is the undisputed chip champ of North America. The company makes some of the best-known and top-selling snack-foods around, including Cheetos, Doritos, Fritos, Lay's, Rold Gold, Ruffles, SunChips, and Tostitos. Frito-Lay also makes Grandma's cookies, Funyuns onion-flavored rings, Cracker Jack candy-coated popcorn, and Smartfood popcorn. The company offers a light line of chips (formerly WOW!) made with fat substitute, olestra."[21] At Frito-Lay, tactical planning means regularly introducing new versions of its products, informing delivery people and retailers about these products, aggressively promoting products, and maintaining profit margins—while not giving competitors a chance to win market share by maintaining lower prices, advertising heavily, and servicing retail accounts very well. On the other hand, small manufacturers may need outside food brokers to gain access to food retailers. Even then, they may have difficulty getting chains as customers.

---

[21] "Frito-Lay, Inc.," **http://www.hoovers.com/frito-lay/–ID__48009–/free-co-profile.xhtml** (March 2, 2009).

3-5g Monitoring Results

Monitoring results involves comparing the actual performance of a firm, business unit, or product against planned performance for a specified period. Actual performance data are then fed back into the strategic planning process. Budgets, timetables, sales and profit statistics, cost analyses, and image studies are just some measures that can be used to assess results.

> Performance is evaluated by **monitoring results**.

When actual performance lags, corrective action is needed. For instance, "When it comes time to implement a strategy, many companies find themselves stymied at the point of execution. Having identified the opportunities within their reach, they watch as the results fall short of their aspirations. Too few companies recognize the reason. Mismatched capabilities, poor asset configurations, and inadequate execution can all play their part in undermining a company's strategic objectives."[22]

Some plans must be revised due to the impact of uncontrollable factors on sales and costs. For this reason, many farsighted firms develop contingency plans to outline their potential responses in advance, should unfavorable conditions arise.

We discuss the techniques for evaluating marketing effectiveness in Chapter 22. These techniques are covered at the end of our book so that the fundamental elements of marketing are thoroughly explored first.

3-6 DEVISING A STRATEGIC MARKETING PLAN

A firm can best create, implement, and monitor a strategic marketing plan when it has a written plan. This encourages executives to carefully think out and coordinate each step in the planning process, better pinpoint problem areas, be consistent, tie the plan to goals and resources, measure performance, and send a clear message to employees and others. A sample outline for a written strategic plan and an application of strategic planning by a small firm are covered next.

3-6a A Sample Outline for a Written Strategic Marketing Plan

What are the ingredients of a good strategic marketing plan? It should

- be integrated into an organization's overall business plan.
- affect the consideration of strategic choices.
- press a long-range view.
- make the resource allocation system visible.
- provide methods to help strategic analysis and decision making.
- be a basis for managing a firm or SBU strategically.
- offer a communication and coordination system both horizontally (between SBUs and departments) and vertically (from senior executives to front-line employees).
- help a firm and its SBUs cope with change.[23]

> Written documents aid strategic marketing planning and are useful for all sorts of firms.

Table 3-2 presents a sample outline for a written strategic marketing plan. This outline may be used by firms of any size or type. (*Please note: There is a comprehensive strategic marketing plan exercise accompanying this book. It is described in the appendix at the end of the chapter. If you are online, you may access the exercise by clicking on the special computer icon. In addition, at the beginning of each part of the text, there is a planning icon. If you are online, click on the icon to review the implications of what you learn in that part from a strategic marketing plan perspective.*)

---

[22] Tsun-yan Hsieh and Sara Yik, "Leadership as the Starting Point of Strategy," *McKinsey Quarterly* (Number 1, 2005), p. 67.

[23] Adapted by the authors from Aaker, *Strategic Marketing Management*.

Global Marketing in Action

Chevron: Introducing a New Gasoline Additive Worldwide

After Chevron's merger with Texaco, Chevron (http://www.chevron.com) began marketing gasoline under the Texaco (http://www.texaco.com) brand name. Texaco stations supplied with gasoline by Chevron now sell gasoline with the ingredient Techron at its U.S. gasoline stations and in close to 90 percent of all branded gasoline sold by Chevron worldwide. Chevron will be the first oil company to include a branded additive in all of its global markets. This strategy enables Chevron to use standardized promotions in all countries. It also raises its level of gasoline performance worldwide.

Techron helps prevent engine deposit build-up on intake valves and fuel injectors that can impact a vehicle's performance and emissions. Techron also cleans an engine's intake system while it minimizes combustion chamber deposits that can cause knocking, the loss of power during acceleration, and higher levels of emissions. Techron is included in all grades of Texaco gasolines.

As a result of the merger of Chevron and Texaco that occurred in 2001, both Chevron and Shell had the rights to use the Texaco brand in the United States market until July 1, 2006. As of that date, Chevron acquired exclusive rights to the Texaco brand in the United States. Chevron acquired exclusive rights to the Texaco brand outside the United Sates as of 2005. The process of adding Techron to all gasolines worldwide began in 2005. In 2008, Chevron launched Chevron Diesel with Techron D, an additive specially formulated for diesel engines in 48 Chevron stations in Sacramento.

Sources: Based on material in "Texaco Launches Techron Globally," *Business Wire* (May 2, 2005); and "Chevron Launches Premium Diesel Pilot Program in Sacramento," *Business Wire* (March 19, 2008).

3-6b Moonstruck Chocolate Company: A Strategic Marketing Plan by a Small Specialty Firm

In 1993, Bill and Deb Simmons opened Moonstruck Chocolate Company[24] (then known as Moonstruck Chocolatier) in Portland, Oregon. When it began, Moonstruck was exclusively a maker of truffles for the wholesale market. It sold to retailers such as Neiman Marcus, Marshall Field, and Starbucks. The firm introduced it first retail store in 1996 and sales rose rapidly. Today, Moonstruck is a successful firm that specializes in chocolate-based products, with annual sales of several million dollars and high-powered goals for the future. Why? The firm has created, implemented, and monitored a solid strategic marketing plan. Let's look at the highlights of Moonstruck's plan.

> Although a small company, Moonstruck Chocolate has a detailed strategic marketing plan.

Organizational Mission Moonstruck has a clear mission: to bring the higher European standard for chocolate to the American marketplace and to create chocolate cafés that serve as a meeting place in a busy, impersonal world. To do so, Moonstruck is "romancing" the cocoa bean and educating customers, as Starbucks did with coffee.

In 2001, Dave and Sally Bany acquired the firm. They were searching for a small business to take national: "One taste of Moonstruck's products and they were hooked. To make fitting use of a well-worn phrase, they liked it so much they bought the company." The Banys want to grow the cafés, the wholesale business, direct sales (through 1-800-557-MOON), and sales from the Web site.

Organizational Structure The Banys play a role in helping develop new products, planning marketing strategies, and ensuring overall quality. However, the firm is now

---

[24] The material in this section is based on http://www.moonstruckchocolate.com (March 1, 2009); Elizabeth Fuhrman, "A New Moon," *Candy Industry* (June 2004), pp. 28–33; Edward O. Welles, "The Next Starbucks," *Inc.* (January 2001), pp. 48–53; "Moonstruck Chocolate Co. Selects New CEO," http://www.bizjournals.com/portland/stories/2008/03/24/daily11.html (March 25, 2008); "Moonstruck Chocolate Co. Welcomes Highly Acclaimed Chef as New Master Chocolatier," http://www.reuters.com/article/pressRelease/idUS50684+08-Jan-2008+PRN20080108 (January 8, 2008); and "First Moonstruck Chocolate Café in New Jersey Celebrates Grand Opening," http://www.reuters.com/article/pressRelease/idUS117281+20-Jun-2008+PRN20080620 (June 20, 2008).

Table 3-2	A Sample Outline for a Written Strategic Marketing Plan

Using as much detail as possible, please address each of these points for your organization:

1. Organizational Mission
   a. In 50 words or less, describe the current mission of your organization.
   b. In 50 words or less, describe how you would like your organizational mission to evolve over the next 5 years. Over the next 10 years.
   c. How is the organizational mission communicated to employees?

2. Organizational Structure
   a. State and assess the current organizational structure of your organization.
   b. Does your organization have strategic business units? If yes, describe them. If no, why not?
   c. Does each major product or business unit in your organization have a marketing manager, proper resources, and clear competitors? Explain your answer.

3. Marketing Objectives
   a. Cite your organization's overall marketing goals for the next 1, 3, 5, and 10 years.
   b. Cite your organization's specific marketing goals by target market and product category for the next 1, 5, and 10 years in terms of sales, market share, profit, image, and customer loyalty.
   c. What criteria will be used to determine whether goals have been fully, partially, or unsatisfactorily reached?

4. Situation Analysis
   a. Describe the present overall strengths, weaknesses, opportunities, and threats (SWOT) facing your organization.
   b. For each of the key products or businesses of your organization, describe the present strengths, weaknesses, opportunities, and threats.
   c. How do you expect the factors noted in your answers to (a) and (b) to change over the next 5 to 10 years?
   d. How will your organization respond to the factors mentioned in the answer for (c)?
   e. Describe the methods your organization uses to acquire, distribute, and store the information necessary to make good marketing decisions.

5. Developing Marketing Strategy
   a. Compare your organization's overall strategy with those of leading competitors.
   b. Describe your organization's use of these strategic approaches: market penetration, market development, product development, and diversification.
   c. Categorize each of your organization's products or businesses as a star, cash cow, question mark, or dog. Explain your reasoning.
   d. For each product or business, which of these approaches is most appropriate: invest/grow, selectivity/earnings, or harvest/divest? Explain your reasoning.
   e. For each of your organization's products or businesses, which of these approaches is most appropriate: cost leadership, differentiation, cost focus, or differentiation focus? Explain your reasoning.

6. Societal, Ethical, and Consumer Issues
   a. What is your organization's view of its responsibilities regarding societal, ethical, and consumer issues?
   b. How are organizational policies developed with regard to societal, ethical, and consumer issues?
   c. Discuss your organization's social responsibility approach in terms of the general public, employees, channel members, stockholders, and competitors.
   d. State your organization's code of ethics and how acceptable ethical practices are communicated to employees.
   e. Describe your organization's strategy for dealing with consumers' basic rights (information and education, safety, choice, and to be heard).

7. Global Marketing
   a. What is the role of global marketing in your organization's overall strategy?
   b. Describe the cultural, economic, political and legal, and technological environment in each major and potential foreign market that your organization faces.
   c. Describe your organization's strategy in terms of which and how many foreign markets your organization should enter.
   d. Develop an appropriate organizational format for each current and potential foreign market.
   e. State the extent to which your organization utilizes a standardized, nonstandardized, or glocal [both global and local] marketing approach in its foreign markets.
   f. Explain how your organization's marketing mix varies by foreign market.

8. Marketing and the Internet
   a. Does your organization use the Internet (Web) in its marketing strategy? If no, why not?
   b. If your organization uses the Web, does it engage in E-marketing rather than just in E-commerce? If no, why not?
   c. If your organization uses the Web, what are the marketing-related goals?
   d. If your organization uses the Web, is a systematic Internet marketing strategy applied? If no, why not?

(continued)

Using as much detail as possible, please address each of these points for your organization:

9. Consumer Analysis and Target Market Strategy
    a. What are the demographic characteristics of the target market segments served or potentially served by your organization?
    b. What are the lifestyle and decision-making characteristics of the target market segments served or potentially served by your organization?
    c. Do you market to final consumers, organizations, or both? How does this approach affect your overall marketing strategy?
    d. Describe the important consumer trends that could have a major effect on your organization.
    e. Explain the demand patterns that exist for your organization's products (homogeneous, clustered, or diffused).
    f. Describe your organization's choice of target market strategy (undifferentiated, differentiated, or concentrated marketing) and target market(s).
    g. Does your organization understand and utilize such concepts as derived demand, the heavy-usage segment, and benefit segmentation? Why or why not?
    h. State how your marketing mix(es) is (are) appropriate for the target market(s) chosen.
    i. What sales forecasting procedures are used by your organization? How are they related to your target market strategy?

10. Product Planning
    a. Describe your organization's products from the perspective of tangible, augmented, and generic product concepts.
    b. Are your organization's products viewed as convenience, shopping, or specialty products by consumers? How does this placement affect the marketing strategy?
    c. Discuss the rationale behind the width, depth, and consistency of your organization's product mix.
    d. Describe your organization's product management organization.
    e. Discuss your organization's competitive and company product positioning for each product/brand.
    f. Describe your organization's use of corporate symbols and its branding strategy.
    g. Outline your organization's overall packaging strategy.
    h. What kinds of goods (durable and/or nondurable) and services (rented-goods, owned-goods, and/or nongoods) are sold by your organization? What are the ramifications of this for the marketing strategy?
    i. How are your organization's products positioned along the goods/service continuum? What are the ramifications of this for the marketing strategy?
    j. Describe your organization's new-product planning process.
    k. In what product life-cycle stage is each of your organization's major product groupings?
    l. How can your organization extend the life-cycle stage for those products now in the introduction, growth, and maturity life-cycle stages?

11. Distribution Planning
    a. How are channel functions allocated among distribution intermediaries and your organization?
    b. Explain how relationship marketing is used in your organization's channel of distribution.
    c. State your organization's distribution approach with regard to channel length (direct or indirect) and channel width (exclusive, selective, or intensive distribution), and whether a dual distribution strategy is appropriate.
    d. Present an approach for your organization's achieving and maintaining channel cooperation.
    e. Describe your organization's overall logistics strategy (including transportation modes, inventory management, and foreign distribution).
    f. Explain your organization's choice of wholesaler type and your choice of specific wholesalers.
    g. Explain your organization's choice of retailer type and your choice of specific retailers.
    h. How are wholesalers and retailers evaluated by your organization?

12. Promotion Planning
    a. State your organization's broad promotion goals and the importance of each one.
    b. Discuss your organization's overall promotion plan from the perspective of integrated marketing communications, and describe the roles of advertising, public relations, personal selling, and sales promotion at your organization.
    c. Describe how your organization determines its overall promotional budget.
    d. For each element of the promotional mix (advertising, public relations, personal selling, and sales promotion):

        ☐ Set specific goals.
        ☐ Assign responsibility.
        ☐ Establish a budget.
        ☐ Develop a strategy (such as themes/messages/selling techniques/promotions, media choice, timing, cooperative efforts).
        ☐ Set criteria for assessing success or failure.

    e. Describe how your organization's promotion efforts vary by target market and product.
    f. At your organization, what is the role for new communications formats and technologies (such as the World Wide Web, electronic in-store point-of-purchase displays, and hand-held computers for salespeople)?

(continued)

Using as much detail as possible, please address each of these points for your organization:

13. Price Planning
    a. Explain your organization's overall pricing approach (price-based versus nonprice-based) and how you determine the "value" your organization provides to consumers.
    b. Categorize your organization's target market(s) in terms of price sensitivity, and state how this affects the pricing strategy.
    c. What is your organization's pricing philosophy for dealing with cost increases or decreases?
    d. What practices does your organization follow to ensure compliance with all government rules about pricing?
    e. Describe the role each channel member (including your organization) plays in setting prices.
    f. Explain the competitive pricing environment your organization faces.
    g. State your firm's specific pricing objectives.
    h. Describe your organization's price strategy with regard to its use of cost-based, demand-based, and/or competition-based pricing.
    i. When your organization implements a price strategy, which of these elements does it use: customary versus variable pricing, one-price versus flexible pricing, odd pricing, the price-quality association, leader pricing, multiple-unit pricing, price lining, price bundling, geographic pricing, purchase terms, and price adjustments?

14. Integrating and Analyzing the Marketing Plan
    a. Describe your organization's processes for integrating and analyzing its marketing plans.
    b. Detail how the long-term, moderate-term, and short-term plans are compatible.
    c. Explain how the elements of the marketing mix are coordinated.
    d. Are ongoing marketing budgets sufficient? Does your organization differentiate between order-generating and order-processing costs? Explain your answers.
    e. How do you expect competitors to react as you implement your organization's strategy?
    f. Discuss how your organization utilizes benchmarking, customer satisfaction research, marketing cost analysis, sales analysis, and the marketing audit.

15. Revising the Marketing Plan
    a. What contingency plans does your organization have in place for handling unexpected results?
    b. Are marketing plans revised as conditions warrant? Explain your answer.
    c. Is your organization reactive or proactive in its approach to revising marketing plans? Explain your answer.

Note: Points 1-5 relate to Part 1 in the text.
Points 6-8 relate to Part 2 in the text.
Point 9 relates to Part 3 in the text.
Point 10 relates to Part 4 in the text.
Point 11 relates to Part 5 in the text.
Point 12 relates to Part 6 in the text.
Point 13 relates to Part 7 in the text.
Points 14-15 relate to Part 8 in the text.

headed by a professional staff that includes chief executive Dan Hossley, who has 25 years of retail experience, and "Master Chocolatier" and Director of Research and Development Julian Rose, who has more than 25 years of experience as a pastry chef and chocolatier. The firm's team of chocolatiers "quietly work away on a variety of confections, hand-crafted, dipped, and decorated, ranging from toffee to truffles to chocolate bars."

Marketing Objectives Moonstruck has ambitious goals. Sales have been increasing nicely due to the debut of various popular new chocolate lines, the opening of new stores, and expansion of the wholesale portion of its business. As Sally Bany says, "We want to be a national brand and we're well on our way to that as long as we keep making great products."

Situation Analysis Founders Bill and Deb Simmons formulated their strategic plan based on Starbucks, the retail coffee giant. They did a comprehensive analysis of Starbucks' business model before opening Moonstruck. As they commented in *Inc.*, "What really lit a fuse under Starbucks was not just its commitment to better beans but its move into retail—selling coffee by the cup. The stores were decorated with bins of coffee beans, photos of coffee trees, and shelves of gleaming coffee paraphernalia. Employees were trained to educate customers about what they were drinking and why it tasted good. For many, the experience was so engaging that Starbucks became a natural gathering place, and that made the brand familiar. The more we poked at the Starbucks model, the better it looked." Today, Moonstruck has carved out its own distinctive flourishes.

Developing Marketing Strategy The two strategic planning approaches with the most relevance for Moonstruck are the product/market opportunity matrix and the Porter generic strategy model. The firm is engaged in both a product development strategy (producing distinctive new chocolate products for current chocolate customers) and a market development strategy (seeking out those who have not thought of chocolate beverages as "must have" drinks). It is a great believer in a differentiation strategy (superior products at a premium price).

Societal, Ethical, and Consumer Issues Moonstruck uses the highest-quality ingredients. It treats employees and customers courteously, honestly, and respectfully. The firm stands behind all of the products it makes and sells, and is socially responsible.

Global Marketing Moonstruck searches the globe for the best cocoa beans, consistent with its organizational mission: "Our chocolate products are made with only the finest, freshest ingredients. The company's chocolate originates from rare cocoa beans that are among the highest quality produced anywhere in the world. When properly fermented and roasted, the cocoa seeds achieve fine profiles of unique flavors with nuances of fresh flowers, ripe fruits, and rich woods."

Marketing and the Internet Moonstruck has a colorful, interactive, well-planned Web site (**http://www.moonstruckchocolate.com**) that describes the background of the company, customer service policies, and the products it makes. The site also lists the firm's retail locations and permits online ordering.

Consumer Analysis and Target Market Strategy Moonstruck appeals to customers who are interested in quality, uniqueness, assortment, and service—and are willing to pay for it. The firm has three market segments: retail customers who buy at the firm's company-owned-and-operated stores, Web and telephone shoppers (1-800-557-MOON) who buy directly from the firm, and independent retailers that resell Moonstruck products to those stores' customers.

Product Planning Moonstruck has greatly expanded its product line since the early days, adding products that complement each other well. Today, the product line includes chocolate truffles, chocolate bars, chocolate pecan clusters, chocolate pops, chocolate mints, toffee, hot cocoa mixes, chocolate and espresso drinks (at its cafés), and lots more.

Distribution Planning As already noted, Moonstruck offers products in many venues: its own cafés, retail stores, telemarketing, and the Web. Its retail cafés now operate in Oregon, Illinois, Michigan, California, New Jersey, Virginia, and Massachusetts. The cafés feature the firm's moon logo, chocolate-colored swirls woven into the ceiling and carpeting, and seating for about 20 to 25 people. See Figure 3-10. Macy's (**http://www.macys.com**) and Balducci's (**http://www.balduccis.com**) are among the traditional retailers carrying Moonstruck products.

Promotion Planning Moonstruck uses in-store tastings and demonstrations to draw customers into impulse purchases. It also does some print advertising. But its biggest promotion effort revolves around the publicity it receives from newspaper, magazine, TV, and radio coverage. In 2005 and 2006, the firm obtained a lot of publicity by being included in the Annual Academy Award Gift Basket, which was given to celebrities for attending the awards show ("chocolate for the stars"). In 2007, National Public Radio (**http://www.npr.com**) chose its Valentine Day Love Letter Collection as the winner in a taste test. The *Ellen DeGeneres Show* (**http://www.ellen.warnerbros.com**) has featured Moonstruck in the gift bags given to guest celebrities.

Price Planning Moonstruck has above-average prices, reflective of the quality and status accorded its products. Most revenues are from high-margin chocolate truffles and drinks. For example, one 24-piece truffle collection in a special gift box retails for $50 and one 9-piece truffle collection in a standard box retails for $19.

Figure 3-10
The Allure of Moonstruck Chocolate Cafés
Source: Reprinted by permission.

Integrating and Analyzing the Plan The Banys and their management team constantly keep their eye on the ball. They recognize that every decision they make reflects on the image and performance of Moonstruck Chocolate. They regularly monitor performance and look for ideas that fit within their overall vision for the firm.

Revising the Marketing Plan Unlike Bill and Deb Simmons, the Banys are not big believers in franchising as a mechanism for future growth in Moonstruck Chocolate Cafés. As Dave Bany says, "I understand it's pretty difficult to control quality, and that makes me hesitant." Retail expansion will be funded by the firm and, perhaps, some outside investors.

Web Sites You Can Use

A variety of Web sites provide step-by-step advice on strategic planning and many even have free, downloadable, easy-to-use templates. Here, we present a number of such sites, divided into two categories: strategic business plans and strategic marketing plans.

Strategic Business Plans
- BizMove.com: *Developing a Successful Business Plan* (**http://www.bizmove.com/small-business/business-plan.htm**)
- Bplans.com—*How to Write a Business Plan* (**http://www.bplans.com/dp**)
- Business Owner's Toolkit—*Writing Your Business Plan* (**http://www.toolkit.cch.com/text/p02_5001.asp**)
- Center for Business Planning—*Planning Guidelines* (**http://www.businessplans.org/guide.html**)
- Inc.—*Writing a Business Plan* (**http://www.inc.com/guides/write_biz_plan**)

- Edward Lowe Foundation—*How to Create a Long-Run Plan* (**http://www.edwardlowe.org/index.elf?page=sserc&storyid=0054&function=story**)
- PlanWare—*Writing a Business Plan* (**http://www.planware.org/bizplan.htm**)
- Tutor2You—*Strategy: What Is a Strategy?* (**http://www.tutor2u.net/business/strategy/what_is_strategy.htm**)

Strategic Marketing Plans
- BizMove.com—*Small Business Marketing* (**http://www.bizmove.com/small-business/marketing.htm**)
- Bplans.com—*Sample Marketing Plans* (**http://www.bplans.com/sp/marketingplans.cfm**)
- Business Resource Software—*Marketing Plan* (**http://www.businessplans.org/Market.html**)
- Inc.—*Marketing Guides* (**http://www.inc.com/guides/marketing**)

- Edward Lowe Foundation—*How to Gain a Competitive Edge* (**http://www.edwardlowe.org/index.elf? page=sserc&storyid=8869&function=story**)
- Morebusiness.com—*Marketing Department* (**http://www.morebusiness.com/running_your_business/marketing**)
- Morebusiness.com—*Sample Marketing Plan* (**http://www. morebusiness.com/templates_worksheets/bplans/printpre. brc**)
- U.S. Chamber of Commerce—*Building a Successful Marketing Plan* (**http://www.uschamber.com/sb/business/ P03/P03_8000.asp**)

Summary

1. *To define strategic planning and consider its importance for marketing* Strategic planning encompasses both strategic business plans and strategic marketing plans. Strategic business plans describe the overall direction firms will pursue within their chosen environment and guide the allocation of resources and effort. Strategic marketing plans outline what marketing actions to undertake, why those actions are needed, who is responsible for carrying them out, when and where they will be completed, and how they will be coordinated.

   Strategic planning provides guidance via a hierarchical process, clarifies goals, encourages departmental cooperation, focuses on strengths and weaknesses (as well as opportunities and threats), examines alternatives, helps allocate resources, and points out the value of monitoring results.

2. *To describe the total quality approach to strategic planning and show its relevance to marketing* A total quality approach should be used in devising and enacting business and marketing plans. In that way, a firm adopts a process- and output-related philosophy, by which it strives to fully satisfy consumers in an effective and efficient manner. Customer focus; top management commitment; emphasis on continuous improvement; and support and involvement from employees, suppliers, and channel members are all involved.

3. *To look at the different kinds of strategic plans and the relationships between marketing and the other functional areas in an organization* A firm's strategic plans may be short run, moderate in length, or long run. Strategic marketing plans may be for each major product, presented as one company-wide marketing plan, or considered part of an overall business plan. A bottom-up, top-down, or combined management approach may be used.

   The interests of marketing and the other functional areas in a firm need to be accommodated in a strategic plan. Departmental conflict can be reduced by improving communications, employing personnel with broad backgrounds, establishing interdepartmental programs, and blending departmental goals.

4. *To describe thoroughly each of the steps in the strategic planning process* First, a firm defines its organizational mission—the long-term commitment to a type of business and a place in the market. Second, it establishes strategic business units (SBUs), the self-contained divisions, product lines, or product departments with specific market focuses and separate managers. Third, quantitative and qualitative marketing objectives are set. Fourth, through situation analysis, a firm identifies its internal strengths and weaknesses, as well as external opportunities and threats.

   Fifth, a firm develops a marketing strategy—to outline the way in which the marketing mix is used to attract and satisfy the target market(s) and accomplish organizational goals. Every SBU has its own marketing mix. The approaches to strategy planning include the product/market opportunity matrix, the Boston Consulting Group matrix, the General Electric business screen, and the Porter generic strategy model. They should be viewed as planning tools that aid decision making; they do not replace the need for executives to engage in hands-on planning for each situation.

   Sixth, a firm uses tactical plans to specify the short-run actions necessary to implement a given marketing strategy. At this stage, specific tasks, a time horizon, and resource allocation are made operational. Seventh, a firm monitors results by comparing actual performance against planned performance, and this information is fed back into the strategic planning process. Adjustments in strategy are made as needed.

5. *To show how a strategic marketing plan may be devised and applied* Strategic marketing plans work best when they are integrated within the overall strategic business plan and prepared systematically and comprehensively—as illustrated in Table 3-2. This is exemplified by Moonstruck Chocolate, a small confectionary firm.

Key Terms

strategic business plan (p. 53)

strategic marketing plan (p. 53)

total quality (p. 54)

strategic planning process (p. 58)

organizational mission (p. 58)

strategic business unit (SBU) (p. 60)

situation analysis (p. 62)

marketing strategy (p. 63)

product/market opportunity matrix (p. 63)

Boston Consulting Group matrix (p. 65)

General Electric business screen (p. 67)

Porter generic strategy model (p. 68)

tactical plan (p. 70)

monitoring results (p. 71)

Review Questions

1. Distinguish between the terms "strategic business plan" and "strategic marketing plan."
2. Explain Figure 3-2, which deals with the total quality approach.
3. Why are conflicts between marketing and other functional areas inevitable? How can these conflicts be reduced or avoided?
4. Under what circumstances should a company consider reappraising its organizational mission?

5. In situation analysis, what is the distinction between strengths and opportunities and between weaknesses and threats? How should a firm react to each of these factors?
6. Distinguish between the General Electric business screen and the Porter generic strategy model.
7. Explain how tactical decisions differ from strategic decisions.
8. Why is it important to monitor the results of a marketing plan?

Discussion Questions

1. Do you think your college bookstore is following a total quality approach? Why or why not? What total quality recommendations would you make for the bookstore?
2. What issues should a movie studio study during situation analysis? How could it react to those issues?
3. Give a current example of each of these strategic approaches: market development, product development,

market penetration, and diversification. Evaluate the strategies.
4. Develop a rating scale to use in analyzing the industry attractiveness and company business strengths of a local travel agency, a leading printer manufacturer, or a medium-sized DVD manufacturer.

Web Exercise

Bplans.com (**http://www.bplans.com/sp/marketingplans.cfm**) offers several free sample marketing plans at its Web site. Take a look at the sample marketing plan for Boulder Stop

(**http://www.bplans.com/spv/3336/index.cfm?affiliate=pas**), a sports equipment retailer and café. What could a prospective competitor learn from studying this plan?

Practice Quiz

1. An organization's direction within its chosen environment and its allocation of resources is usually determined by
   a. marketing tactics.
   b. marketing myopia.
   c. strategic planning.
   d. strategic business units.

2. Separate marketing plans for each product line are most often used by
   a. service firms.
   b. industrial-goods manufacturers.
   c. local governments.
   d. consumer-goods manufacturers.

3. Which of these is a way to drop tension among functional departments?
   a. Setting objectives for each department that are interdependent with other departments' goals
   b. Minimizing interfunctional contact
   c. Seeking employees who do not blend technical and marketing expertise
   d. Establishing independent task forces and committees

4. Organizational mission refers to
   a. a long-term commitment to a type of business and a place in the market.
   b. specific actions undertaken to implement a given marketing strategy.
   c. an approach in which a firm seeks greater sales of present products or new product uses.
   d. a philosophy by which an organization individually assesses and positions every strategic business unit.

5. According to the strategic planning process, the next step after a firm defines its organizational mission is to
   a. establish strategic business units.
   b. set marketing objectives.
   c. perform situation analysis.
   d. outline a budget.

6. An example of a qualitative term that can be used to describe objectives is
   a. profit as a percentage of sales.
   b. sales growth.
   c. market share in the industry.
   d. level of innovativeness.

7. Which of the following questions does situation analysis seek to answer?
   a. In what direction is a firm headed?
   b. How will resources be allocated?
   c. Who is responsible for carrying out marketing actions?
   d. What sales personnel should be hired?

8. As part of a market development strategy, a firm could
   a. develop new models of existing products to appeal to present markets.
   b. reposition existing products.
   c. become involved with new products aimed at new markets.
   d. seek to attract nonusers of its existing products.

9. A strategic business unit with a high market share in a mature industry is a
   a. question mark.
   b. star.
   c. dog.
   d. cash cow.

10. The General Electric business screen looks at two major dimensions: company business strengths and
    a. industry attractiveness.
    b. target market features.
    c. market share.
    d. profitability.

11. Strategic business units shown in the selectivity/earnings areas of the General Electric business screen are
    a. performing well in unattractive industries.
    b. performing well in strong industries.
    c. performing poorly in unattractive industries.
    d. performing poorly in highly competitive industries.

12. According to the Porter generic strategy model, with a differentiation focus strategy, a strategic business unit
    a. aims at a narrow target segment through low prices or a unique offering.
    b. aims at a narrow market by offering goods or services viewed as distinctive.
    c. aims a new product at a new market.
    d. aims at a broad market and offers products at low prices and in large quantities.

13. A major weakness of the strategic planning approaches discussed in this chapter is that they
    a. prevent a firm from analyzing all its business units and products.
    b. do not focus on creating and keeping key differential advantages.
    c. are sometimes difficult to implement.
    d. do not allow a firm to follow competitors' actions.

14. The level of investment in specific marketing activities and the timing of marketing actions are decisions relating to
    a. implementing tactics.
    b. establishing SBUs.
    c. developing marketing strategy.
    d. monitoring results.

15. Monitoring results involves
    a. creating new strategic business units.
    b. setting corporate and marketing objectives.
    c. comparing actual performance to planned performance for a specified time period.
    d. identifying internal strengths and weaknesses, as well as external opportunities and threats.

For the answers to these questions, please visit the online site for this book at **http://www.atomicdog.com**.

3 Appendix

Strategic Marketing Plan

In Chapter 3, we presented a detailed sample outline for preparing a written strategic marketing plan (Table 3.2). Throughout *Marketing*, the part-opening pages refer to the specific sections of the sample plan that apply to each of the eight parts in the book.

To provide you with more insight into strategic marketing plans, we have prepared the special computer exercise that is described in this appendix. It is called *StratMktPlan*. You may access the exercise by clicking on the icon or by going to our Web site.

StratMktPlan is based on the sample outline in Chapter 3. From that outline, we have selected a cross section of questions for you to address. You will be assigned to a specific firm and gear your answers toward it. Answers are typed directly into easy-to-use drop-down windows. The exercise outline is shown in Table 1.

By answering all *StratMktPlan* questions, you prepare a comprehensive strategic marketing plan. Depending on your professor's goals, different students or student teams can be assigned to competing companies in the same industry, or assigned to companies with totally different strategies and resources. One student or team can be assigned to a national firm selling mass-appeal products, while another group is assigned to a local firm selling a product for a niche market.

You are encouraged to use secondary sources (including the Web) to devise a marketing plan when working on the *StratMktPlan* computer exercise. SWOT analysis (strengths, weaknesses, opportunities, and threats) should include data derived from secondary sources.

There are two ways in which your professor can assign the *StratMktPlan* exercise: (1) You or a team of students can be

---

Table 1	*StratMktPlan* Exercise Outline

Develop an integrated strategic marketing plan for the assigned company by addressing each of the questions below.

Organizational Mission
- In 50 words or less, describe the current mission of your organization.

Marketing Goals
- Cite your organization's overall marketing goals for the next 1, 3, 5, and 10 years.

Situation Analysis
- Describe the present overall strengths, weaknesses, opportunities, and threats (SWOT) facing your organization.

Developing Marketing Strategy
- Compare your organization's overall strategy with those of leading competitors.

Societal, Ethical, and Consumer Issues
- What is your organization's view of its responsibilities regarding societal, ethical, and consumer issues?

Global Marketing
- What is the role of global marketing in your organization's overall strategy?

Marketing and the Internet
- Does your organization use the Internet (Web) in its marketing strategy? If no, why not?

Consumer Analysis and Target Market Strategy
- What are the demographic characteristics of the target market segments served or potentially served by your organization?
- Do you market to final consumers, organizations, or both? How does this approach affect your overall marketing strategy?
- Describe your organization's choice of target market strategy (undifferentiated, differentiated, or concentrated marketing) and target market(s).

(continued)

Product Planning

- Describe your organization's products from the perspective of tangible, augmented, and generic product concepts.
- Discuss the rationale behind the width, depth, and consistency of your organization's product mix.

Distribution Planning

- Explain how relationship marketing is used in your organization's channel of distribution.
- State your organization's distribution approach with regard to channel length (direct or indirect) and channel width (exclusive, selective, or intensive distribution), and whether a dual distribution strategy is appropriate.

Promotion Planning

- State your organization's broad promotion goals and the importance of each one.
- Discuss your organization's overall promotional plan from the perspective of integrated marketing communications, and describe the roles of advertising, public relations, personal selling, and sales promotion at your organization.

Price Planning

- Explain your organization's overall pricing approach (price-based versus nonprice-based) and how you determine the "value" your organization provides to consumers.
- Categorize your organization's target market(s) in terms of price sensitivity, and state how this affects the pricing strategy.

Integrating and Organizing the Marketing Plan

- How do you expect competitors to react as you implement your organization's strategy?

Revising the Marketing Plan

- What contingency plans does your organization have in place for handling unexpected results?

requested to hand in *StratMktPlan* assignments one part at a time, with submissions spaced out over the term. (2) You or a team of students can be requested to work on StratMktPlan as a comprehensive course assignment, with one overall submission at the end of the semester.

We have included in the *StratMktPlan* computer exercise an illustration of a strategic marketing plan for Sporting Goods and More, based on the Table 1 questions in this appendix. Assume that Sporting Goods and More is a large (40,000 square feet),

privately-owned, for-profit store located near a major shopping mall that is 5 to 10 miles from your campus. This retailer competes with all nearby firms that carry sporting goods, sports apparel, sports-related consumer electronics, sports-related publications, sports drinks and snacks, and similar merchandise. Although the specific answers in this illustration may not be directly applicable to another company, the example should stimulate your thinking and give you a better idea of how to handle the questions.

Chapter 4

Information for Marketing Decisions

About 85 years ago, Arthur C. Nielsen, Sr., pioneered many key concepts in marketing and media research. He is credited with developing equipment to determine which TV programs consumers watch, known as the Nielsen Television Ratings. He also developed a scanning device that enables manufacturers and retailers to collect timely data on weekly sales by item. Prior to Nielsen, radio stations would ask listeners to mail in postcards to let the stations know if they enjoyed particular programs. Firms such as Post Cereal and Kellogg would monitor their sales by counting the number of freight cars going in and out of their warehouse.

A major initial obstacle to the development of marketing research at A.C. Nielsen (http://www.acnielsen.com) was getting retailers to give the firm access to data. Some large grocery chains were concerned that competitors would use the data to learn their specific strategies. Nielsen eventually was able to convince these retailers that they needed to know their market share, as well as what was selling in their total market area—while protecting their proprietary data.

One of Nielsen's leading current products is Consumer Panel Solutions (CPS). Through CPS, Nielsen regularly collects data from 260,000 households in 27 countries. The panel data represents all types of consumers who purchase goods at supermarkets, drug stores, warehouse clubs, computer stores, and mass merchandisers. These data enable subscribers to regularly review data on brand loyalty, consumer purchases, and consumer demographic characteristics.

Another significant Nielsen product is a semi-annual global online survey that measures consumer confidence levels, spending habits, and concerns. One recent survey polled 26,312 Internet users in 48 global markets about their purchase behavior for designer brands. Sixteen percent of the respondents stated that they purchase designer brands, and 31 percent stated that they knew a consumer who buys designer labels.

Nielsen became part of VNU, a Netherlands-based information provider, in 2001. In 2007, VNU changed its name to the Nielsen Company in recognition of the value of the Nielsen name.[1]

In this chapter, we will look at the value of marketing information, explain the role of a marketing information system (which gathers, analyzes, disseminates, and stores relevant marketing data), and describe the marketing research process. We will also look at sampling methodologies and online surveys.

Chapter Objectives

1. To show why marketing information is needed
2. To explain the role and importance of marketing information systems
3. To examine a basic marketing information system, commercial data bases, data-base marketing, and examples of marketing information systems in action
4. To define marketing research and its components and to look at its scope
5. To describe the marketing research process

4-1 OVERVIEW

Firms make better decisions when they have good marketing information.

A firm needs to have good information before, while, and after making (and enacting) marketing decisions if its strengths, weaknesses, opportunities, and threats are to be assessed accurately; actions are to be proper for a given marketing environment; and performance is to be maximized. See Figure 4-1.

[1] Various company and other sources.

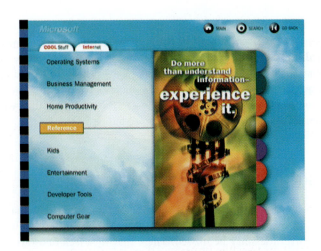

Figure 4-1

Taking a Proactive Approach to Marketing Information

A company's chances for success rise dramatically if it seeks out—and uses—in-depth marketing information.

Source: Reprinted by permission of Retail Planning Associates. Photography by Michael Houghton/STUDIOHIO.

Good information enables marketers to

- gain a competitive edge.
- reduce financial and image risks.
- determine consumer attitudes.
- monitor the environment.
- gather competitive intelligence.
- coordinate strategy.
- measure performance.
- improve advertising credibility.
- gain management support for decisions.
- verify intuition.
- improve effectiveness.

Reliance on "gut feelings," executive judgment, and past experience is not sufficient in making marketing decisions: "A business that wants to remain competitive and be profitable will need to understand the products that their target market is looking for. This kind of information only comes from marketing research. Not only will they need to understand what products should be brought into the market, but also the success of their current products. Information on what they are doing right and what could use some improvement is vital to a firm's success. It is only with the correct data that a business can create a marketing plan or adjust the one they already have."[2]

The *scientific method*—incorporating objectivity, accuracy, and thoroughness—should be followed when collecting and analyzing any marketing information. With *objectivity*, data are gathered in an open-minded way. Judgments are not reached until all data are collected and analyzed. *Accuracy* requires the use of carefully constructed research tools. Each aspect of data gathering, such as the study format, the sample, and tabulations, is well planned and executed. *Thoroughness* deals with the comprehensive nature of information gathering. Mistaken conclusions may be reached if probing is not intense enough.

In this chapter, two vital aspects of marketing information are covered: marketing information systems and marketing research. A marketing information system guides all of a firm's marketing-related information efforts—and stores and disseminates data—on a continuous basis. Marketing research involves gathering and analyzing information on specific marketing issues:

> The **scientific method** requires objectivity, accuracy, and thoroughness.

---

[2] Peter Geisheke, "The Importance of Marketing Tools in Developing a Marketing Strategy," **http://www.articlesbase.com/marketing-articles/the-importance-of-marketing-tools-in-developing-a-marketing-strategy-474107.html** (June 7, 2008).

Simply "taking orders" and gathering data just doesn't cut it. Marketing research can no longer hide behind numbers; it must be out in front of critical business issues. Indeed, the demands and expectations now placed upon marketing researchers require them to possess business acumen, be proactive in identifying needs, and deliver the type of insights that answer the question "now what"? And whether you are a one-person show or a marketing research group of 20, you still need to know how to partner with both internal and external clients to design research projects that address real business needs."[3]

4-2 MARKETING INFORMATION SYSTEMS

The collection of marketing information should not be a rare event that occurs only if data are needed on a specific marketing topic. If research is done this way, a firm faces many risks: Opportunities may be missed. There may be a lack of awareness of environmental changes and competitors' actions. It may be impossible to analyze data over several time periods. Marketing plans and decisions may not be properly reviewed. Data collection may be disjointed. Prior studies may not be stored in an easy-to-use format. Time lags may result if a new study is required. Actions may be reactionary—not anticipatory. Thus, it is vital for a firm, regardless of its size or type, to use some form of marketing information system to aid decision making. See Figure 4-2.

A *marketing information system (MIS)* is "a set of procedures and methods for the regular, planned collection, analysis, distribution, and storage of information for use in making marketing decisions."[4] This means that a firm should:

- actively amass data from internal company documents, existing external documents, and primary studies (when necessary).

> A **marketing information system** regularly gathers, analyzes, disseminates, and stores data.

Figure 4-2

J.C. Penney's Enhanced Marketing Information System

J.C. Penney (**http://www.jcp.com**) uses a sophisticated marketing information to gather customer data and interests, track orders, manage inventory, and assistant company merchandisers. One use of the marketing information system involves the data warehouse needed to effectively operate the TEN different gift registries that the retailer offers its customers— including a wedding registry, baby registry, special occasion registry, anniversary registry, and graduation registry.

Source: Reprinted by permission of TNS Retail Forward.

[3] Gayle Lloyd, "Fedex Your Way to More Effective Marketing Research," presentation to the American Marketing Association Chapter (September 12, 2008).

[4] Adapted by the authors from "Dictionary," **http://www.marketingpower.com/_layouts/Dictionary.aspx? dLetter=M** (March 22, 2009).

Global Marketing in Action

Neuromarketing Experiments: A New Tool for Marketing Research

Neuromarketing experiments integrate neuroscience and clinical psychology to better understand how consumers react to products, brands, and ads. This involves using such state-of-the-art technologies as functional magnetic resonance imaging and electro-encephalograms to learn which areas of the brain are activated when subjects see, hear, smell products, or even test a product. Experiments can also use brain imaging in combination with eye tracking. Though these technologies cannot study consumer motivation, they can determine whether a consumer is attracted, repelled, interested, or indifferent to a product or ad.

Among the firms that use neuromarketing are Nike (http://www.nike.com), Wrigley (http://www.wrigley.com), and Viacom Brand Solutions (http://viacombrandsolutions.co.uk/site.html), which sells advertising on such networks as MTV, VH1, Nickelodeon, and Paramount Comedy in Great Britain and Ireland. Viacom hired Neurosense Limited (http://www.neurosense.com), a British marketing research firm that specializes in using cognitive neuroscientific methods, to better understand consumer behavior.

Neurosense placed into episodes of *South Park*, a cartoon comedy series, and studied the reactions of 18- to 30-year-old consumers. Each subject spent an hour inside a brain scanner while watching four programs. Neurosense found that ads for one product elicited vigorous brain responses from the subjects, while ads for two other products yielded less reaction. It then concluded that ads that were "congruent" with the consumer's environment outperformed those that were "incongruent." Viacom's director of research thinks the insights to be gained from neuromarketing should change the way marketers function.

Sources: Based on material in Amber Haq, "This Is Your Brain on Advertising," http://www.businessweek.com/globalbiz/content/oct2007/gb2007108_286282.htm (October 8, 2007); and "Brain Scans are Helping Advertisers Find Out How to Light Up Customers' Brains," http://www.telegraph.co.uk (February 17, 2007).

- analyze data and prepare suitable reports—in terms of the mission, strategy, and proposed tactics.
- distribute analyzed data to the right marketing decision makers in the firm (who will vary based on the particular topics covered).
- store data for future use and comparisons.
- seek all relevant data that have either current or future marketing ramifications—not just data with specific short-term implications.
- undertake data collection, analysis, distribution, and storage in an ongoing manner.

Figure 4-3 shows how an information system can be used operationally, managerially, and strategically for several aspects of marketing.

Next, we present the components of a basic marketing information system, commercial data bases, data-base marketing, and examples of MIS in action.

4-2a   A Basic Marketing Information System

A basic marketing information system is shown in Figure 4-4. It begins with a statement of company objectives, which provide broad guidelines. These goals are affected by environmental factors, such as competition, government, and the economy. Marketing plans involve the choice of a target market, marketing goals, the marketing organization, the marketing mix (product, distribution, promotion, and price decisions), and performance measurement.

Once a marketing plan is outlined, the total marketing information needs can be specified and satisfied via a *marketing intelligence network*, which consists of continuous monitoring, marketing research, and data warehousing. *Continuous monitoring* is used to regularly study a firm's external and internal environment. It can entail reading trade publications, watching news reports, getting constant feedback from employees and customers, attending industry meetings, observing competitors' actions (competitive intelligence), and filing periodic company reports. Marketing research is used to obtain information on particular marketing issues (problems). Information may be retrieved

A **marketing intelligence network** includes **marketing research, continuous monitoring, and data warehousing**.

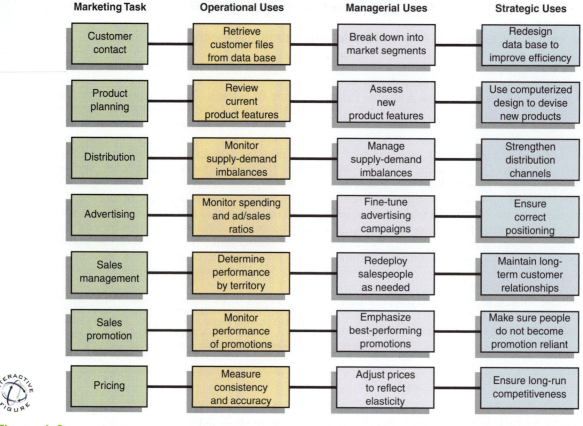

	Marketing Task	Operational Uses	Managerial Uses	Strategic Uses
	Customer contact	Retrieve customer files from data base	Break down into market segments	Redesign data base to improve efficiency
	Product planning	Review current product features	Assess new product features	Use computerized design to devise new products
	Distribution	Monitor supply-demand imbalances	Manage supply-demand imbalances	Strengthen distribution channels
	Advertising	Monitor spending and ad/sales ratios	Fine-tune advertising campaigns	Ensure correct positioning
	Sales management	Determine performance by territory	Redeploy salespeople as needed	Maintain long-term customer relationships
	Sales promotion	Monitor performance of promotions	Emphasize best-performing promotions	Make sure people do not become promotion reliant
	Pricing	Measure consistency and accuracy	Adjust prices to reflect elasticity	Ensure long-run competitiveness

Figure 4-3

How Marketing Information Can Be Utilized

Source: Adapted by the authors from Rajendra S. Sisodia, "Marketing Information and Decision Support Systems for Services," *Journal of Services Marketing*, Vol. 6 (Winter 1992), pp. 51–64.

from storage (existing company data) or acquired by collecting external secondary data and/or primary data. ***Data warehousing*** involves retaining all types of relevant company records (sales, costs, personnel performance, and so on), as well as information collected through continuous monitoring and marketing research. These data aid decision making

Figure 4-4

A Basic Marketing Information System

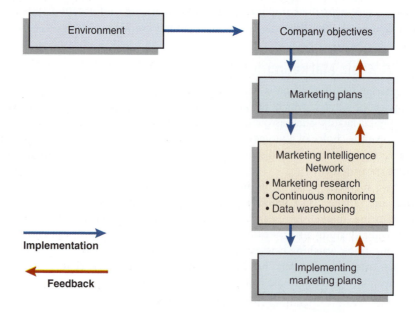

and are kept for future reference. Marketing research is just one part of an ongoing, integrated information system.

Depending on a firm's resources and the complexity of its information needs, a marketing intelligence network may or may not be fully computerized. Small firms can do well if employees and managers read industry publications, attend trade shows, observe competitors, talk with suppliers and customers, track results, and store the findings from these efforts. In any event, information needs must be stated and regularly reviewed, data sources identified, personnel given information tasks, storage and retrieval facilities set up, and data routed to decision makers. The keys to a good MIS are consistency, completeness, and orderliness.

Marketing plans should be enacted based on information from the intelligence network. Through continuous monitoring, a firm might learn that a competitor intends to cut prices by 7 percent during the next month. This would give the firm time to explore its own marketing options (switch to cheaper materials, place larger orders to get discounts, or ignore the cuts) and select one. If monitoring is not done, the firm might be caught by surprise and forced just to cut prices, without any other choice.

A basic MIS has these advantages: organized data collection, a broad perspective, the storage of vital data, crisis avoidance, coordinated marketing plans, speed in gathering the data to make decisions, data retained over several time periods, and the ability to do cost-benefit analysis. Yet, forming an MIS may not be easy. Initial time and costs may be high, and setting up a sophisticated system may be complex.

4-2b   Commercial Data Bases

Because client companies need current, comprehensive, and relatively inexpensive information about the environment in which they operate, many specialized research firms offer ongoing *commercial data bases* with information on population traits, the business environment, economic forecasts, industry and individual companies' performance, and so forth. Such data bases may include newspaper and magazine articles, business and household addresses culled from telephone directories and other sources, industry and company news releases, government reports, conference proceedings, indexes, patent records, and so on. Research firms sell access to their data bases to clients, usually for a rather low fee.

> **Commercial data bases** can provide useful ongoing information.

Data bases may be available in printed form, on CDs and DVDs, and as downloads from the Internet. Several commercial data-base firms exist that concentrate on tracking and clipping newspaper and magazine articles on an orderly basis; unlike with computerized data bases, these firms actually look for information on subjects specified by clients. They offer their services for a fee. There are 1,000 to 2,000 commercial information brokers around the world (many of them in the United States).

Firms such as InfoUSA (**http://www.infousa.com**) provide business and household addresses and other data in CD, DVD, download, and additional formats. InfoUSA gathers data from phone directories, annual reports, and government agencies; it also makes millions of calls each year to keep data bases current. For $2,200, a client can buy an InfoUSA data base of 10,000 small California businesses (having annual sales of $500,000 to $1 million)—with addresses, contact names and titles, phone and fax numbers, Web addresses, number of employees, number of PCs, and more. InfoUSA has more than 4 million customers—from single-person firms to giant corporations. Donnelley Marketing (**http://www.donnelleymarketing.com**), Dun & Bradstreet (**http://www.dnb.com/us**), and Experian (**http://www.experian.com**) are other popular commercial data-base providers.

Many firms, schools, and libraries subscribe to one or more online data bases, whereby users have free access or are charged a small fee. Among the best-known data-base services are ProQuest (**http://www.infolearning.com**), InfoTrac from Cengage (**http://infotrac.galegroup.com**), Factiva (**http://www.factiva.com**) from Dow Jones, and LexisNexis (**http://www.lexisnexis.com**) from Reed Elsevier. With these services, the user can do a search on a particular topic or firm. Full articles or reports may also be accessed and printed, sometimes for an additional fee.

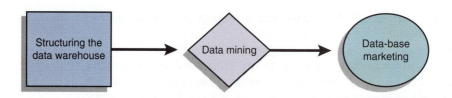

Figure 4-5

Applying Data-Base Marketing

4-2c   Data-Base Marketing

In conjunction with their MIS efforts, many firms are using data-base marketing to better identify target markets and more efficiently reach them. **Data-base marketing** is a computerized technique that compiles, sorts, and stores relevant information about customers and potential customers; uses that information to highlight opportunities and prioritize market segments; and enables the firm to profitably tailor marketing efforts for specific customers or customer groups. This process is shown in Figure 4-5.

Among the three steps in data-base marketing that are described in Figure 4-5, data mining is the most crucial. **Data mining** is an in-depth, computerized search of available information to find profitable marketing opportunities that may otherwise be hidden. The goal is to pinpoint the most attractive customer segments, along with their unique attributes and needs. For example, "Data mining a supermarket data base could reveal that certain items are purchased together, such as beer and chips, or that other items are purchased sequentially, such as basic pet supplies followed by pet food. Data mining can reveal that purchase patterns for some products have a shared seasonality such as angel food cake, whipped cream, and fresh berries. It can reveal that customers with a shared set of demographic characteristics will purchase like items, shop at similar times and frequencies, be equally brand loyal or disloyal, purchase similar groups of items, or respond to a particular type of promotion."[5]

In data mining, a data base

is your own private weapon in the battle for business. It's a source of information compiled about your own customers, past and present, and also about people you believe are genuine prospects. You place into it as many appropriate specifics as you can, including information about past purchasing patterns and whatever else may be relevant to making a sale. Your data base will help identify your most responsive targets and send tailored messages. Data-base marketing provides a level of targeting and personalization that's been a dream. Thanks to today's sophisticated yet inexpensive technology, it can be expedited efficiently, simply, and cost-effectively. It is superb for generating efficient responses, strengthening customer relationships, and setting the foundation for more powerful marketing in the future.[6]

> Through **data-base marketing** and careful **data mining**, companies can enhance customer interactions.

[5] "Data Mining," **http://www.answers.com/topic/data-mining** (April 5, 2009). See also Kurt Thearling, "Data Mining and Analytic Techniques," **http://www.thearling.com**.

[6] "USPS: Data-Base Marketing," **http://www.usps.com/directmail** (April 3, 2004).

Relationship marketing benefits from data-base marketing. A firm can identify those customers with whom it would most like to have long-term relationships, learn as much as possible about them (such as demographics, purchase behavior, and attitudes), customize marketing efforts toward them, and follow up to learn the level of satisfaction. A firm might even compute a "lifetime value" for specific customers, based on their purchase history, and adjust marketing efforts accordingly. See Figure 4-6.

When setting up a data base, each actual or potential customer gets an identifying code. Then, *contact information* such as name, address, phone number, industry code (if a business customer), and demographic data (when appropriate), and *marketing information* such as source and date of contact(s) with firm, purchase history, product interests, and responses to offers are entered and updated for every customer. Data should be distributed to a firm's marketing decision makers and kept in the MIS. Efforts should be coordinated so customers are not bombarded with mailings and a consistent image is maintained.

Many consulting companies are available to help clients with data-base marketing. One is Database Marketing Solutions (**http://www.database-marketing.com/services/index.html**): "Businesses are striving as never before to make the most of each customer relationship. Therefore, marketing data must be managed and interpreted with unprecedented precision and accuracy. With solid information, you can plan, execute, measure, and improve customer-centered initiatives that focus on your most promising targets. That's where our skilled data-base marketing specialists are invaluable. Relying on proven methodology, we unlock the power of your data to drive profitable marketing programs."

Figure 4-6

Using Data-Base Marketing to Foster Customer Relationships

Through its store-based computerized checkouts, Menards (**http://www.menards.com**)—a home improvement retailer—employs a data-base marketing strategy, which enables it to better target opportunities by store location and to get feedback about the behavior of its Menards Big Card credit customers.

Source: Reprinted by permission of Susan Berry, Retail Image Consulting, Inc.

In practice, data-base marketing might actually work like this:

(1) No matter how busy you are, be sure to enter every new customer and prospect name into your data base, along with other pertinent information. Every time you touch base with a customer or prospect, make a notation so you'll have a running log. (2) Organize your prospecting list into a pyramid, with the hottest prospects at the top and the coldest ones at the bottom. This way, you can devote the most time to the prospects that are most likely to buy from you and not waste time on those likely to say no. (3) Once you've started mining your data base, you can get a better handle on which customers are going to buy from you and when. To keep track of pending sales, use an Excel spreadsheet. As potential projects come in the door, type the client's name, type of project, and expected dollar value. (4) An easy, cost-effective way to keep in touch with clients is by sending a weekly E-mail newsletter. It should go not only to your existing customers, but also to prospects, previous customers, and people you meet at trade shows or networking events. (5) No matter what else comes up, be sure to set aside time each day for prospecting and data-base management.[7]

4-2d   MIS in Action

> Information systems are being applied today in various settings.

Millions of organizations worldwide now use some form of MIS in their decision making, and the trend is expected to continue. In fact, as a result of computer networking, progressive firms (and divisions within the same firm) around the globe are transmitting and sharing their marketing information with each other quickly and inexpensively. Most *Fortune 1000* companies engage in data-base marketing.

Among the specific firms using their marketing information systems well are Office Depot and the U.S. Postal Service (USPS). Each devotes considerable time and resources to its system. Here are examples of how they apply MIS.

Office Depot (**http://www.officedepot.com**) sells through stores, direct mail, contract delivery, the Internet, and business-to-business E-commerce in more than 40 countries. To facilitate the flow of information throughout the firm, it recently devised a new marketing information system that combines data from many different sources: "We know what products our customers buy, at what price, and so on. The question is how you use this information. We started out by ranking customers, then identifying and prioritizing the best segments, adding life-cycle analyses and so on. Over time, this approach became increasingly integrated to describe our customer base. Once you can describe your customers, you can move into predicting their future behavior and make investment decisions based on that knowledge." As a result, the company has expanded the role of its MIS "to support our marketing strategy, reduce costs, and individualize offers. In the latter, we started by including targeted messaging on catalogs, then moved into digitally printing catalog covers with a customer's preferred products and special offers. Now, we've extended this approach to telephone account management. This means we can make the customer a really specific offer for a longer term period, if that customer has the potential and we have an opportunity to grow our share of wallet."[8]

Every day, the United States Postal Service (**http://www.usps.com**) handles more than 700 million pieces of mail. This enormous task requires a top-flight marketing information system, one which depends heavily on data scanning: "By combining the passive scanning of various barcodes with improved start-the-clock acceptance information via better bulk acceptance systems, it is possible to measure service performance for all classes of mail. To support service improvements for various commercial products, data from PostalOne!, Delivery Confirmation, CONFIRM, transportation tracking, and product tracking are being integrated and reviewed. In-transit scanning will be enhanced to create better diagnostic data so that bottlenecks can be eliminated throughout the

---

[7] Rosalind Resnick, "Do-It-Yourself Data-Base Marketing," **http://www.entrepreneur.com/article/0,4621,310778,00.html** (September 1, 2003).

[8] "The World's Largest Office Products Supplier Relies on SAS for Customer Intelligence," **http://www.sas.com/success/pdf/officedepot.pdf** (2008).

system. This will assist in reducing cycle times over the entire mail supply chain. Priority Mail service strategies to extend current overnight reach will also be explored. In all cases, the objective is to provide very reliable estimates of service performance while minimizing measurement cost."[9]

4-3 MARKETING RESEARCH DEFINED

Marketing research involves systematically gathering, recording, and analyzing information about specific issues related to the marketing of goods, services, organizations, people, places, and ideas. It may be done by an outside party or by the firm itself. As we noted earlier, marketing research should be used as one component of a firm's overall marketing information efforts. For example, see Figure 4-7.

Several points need to be kept in mind if marketing research is to be effective:

- Research must not be conducted haphazardly.
- The process involves a sequence of tasks: data gathering, recording, and analysis.
- Data may be available from different sources: the firm itself, an impartial agency (such as the government), or a research specialist working for the firm.
- Research efforts may be applied to any aspect of marketing that requires information to aid decision making.
- All results and their implications must be communicated to the right decision maker(s) in a firm.

Just because a firm chooses to use marketing research does not mean it must engage in expensive projects such as test marketing and national consumer attitude surveys. It may get enough data by analyzing internal reports, holding informal meetings with marketing personnel, or purchasing a report from a research company. Marketing research does require an orderly approach and adherence to the scientific method. For every marketing

> **Marketing research** involves collecting, tabulating, and analyzing data about specific marketing issues.

Figure 4-7

Payless ShoeSource: Understanding Its Shoppers

Payless ShoeSource (**http://www. payless.com**) operates about 4,600 stores. After doing marketing research on its customers, Payless found that shoppers in certain areas (such as New York City) are quite diverse. To reflect this, some Payless stores now welcome customers with the multilingual sign shown here.

Source: Reprinted by permission.

---

[9] United States Postal Service, *Strategic Transformation Plan 2006-2010* (September 2005), p. 58.

issue studied, the amount and cost of research depend on the kinds of data needed to make informed decisions, the risk involved in making those decisions, the potential consequences of the decisions, the importance of the issue to the firm, the availability of existing data, the complexity of the data-gathering process for the issue, and other factors.

As an example, consider what a marketing firm targeting to teens could learn from a recent online global study involving more than 58,000 teenagers conducted by Finland's Sulake (**http://www.sulake.com**). The report costs about $750 in U.S. dollars:

> Like an anthropological yearbook, the report painted an intriguing portrait of teens' brand preferences and how they prefer to spend time online. Globally, brands including Coca-Cola (**http://www.coca-cola.com**), McDonald's (**http://www.mcdonalds.com**), and Nike (**http://www.nike.com**) rank as the most popular. Broken down by country, the results could help firms looking to better target customers. Latin American teens, for instance, prefer Avon (**http://www.avon.com**) cosmetics and Americans like CoverGirl (**http://www.covergirl.com**). Despite still being the favored handset maker in 15 of 31 nations, Nokia (**http://www.nokia.com**) lost ground to Sony Ericsson (**http://www.sonyericsson.com**) and Samsung (**http://www.samsung.com**), which are now favored in nations such as Germany, Denmark, and Switzerland. Usage has changed too: In 2006, 38 percent of teens used their phones to listen to music; 71 percent did in 2008.[10]

4-4 THE SCOPE OF MARKETING RESEARCH

> Global marketing research expenditures total several billion dollars each year.

Client companies annually spend more than $25 billion worldwide (40 percent in the United States) for data gathered by marketing research firms. The top 25 research firms (more than one-half of which are U.S.-based) account for three-fifths of the total, with more than 1,000 firms responsible for the rest.[11] These amounts are in addition to research sponsored by government and other institutions and to internal research efforts of firms themselves—which run to billions of dollars each year.

These are the topical areas in which companies are most apt to engage in or sponsor marketing research efforts: industry/market characteristics and trends, customer/product satisfaction, market-share analyses, segmentation studies, brand awareness and preference, purchase intentions, competitive intelligence, and concept development and testing. On average, companies spend 1 to 2 percent of their revenues on marketing research. For example, see Figure 4-7.

Five aspects of marketing research merit special discussion. These involve the rapid rise in customer satisfaction studies, the use of the Internet, the application of single-source data collection, ethical considerations, and the complexities of international marketing research.

Companies now participate in more customer satisfaction research than ever before, in keeping with the customer focus noted in Chapter 1. This form of research has more than doubled in recent years, with some firms doing their own studies and others hiring specialists. Whirlpool (**http://www.whirlpool.com**) sends its own surveys on appliance satisfaction to thousands of households each year. It also pays consumers to "fiddle" with computer-simulated products at its Usability Lab. Whirlpool's research also extends to its European, Latin American, and Asian markets. On the other hand, Maritz Research (**http://www.maritzresearch.com**) has worldwide revenues of several million dollars from doing customer satisfaction studies for clients. As one observer noted, "The answers to the questions 'How are we doing?' and 'What should we do better?' are the building blocks of

---

[10] Matt Vella, "What Do Teens Want?" **http://www.businessweek.com/print/innovate/content/jun2008/id20080620_409689.htm** (June 20, 2008).

[11] Estimated by the authors from "Honomichl 2008: Top 50 Business Report of the U.S. Marketing Research Industry," *Marketing News* (June 15, 2008), special section; and "Honomichl Global Top 25," *Marketing News* (August 15, 2008), special section.

a customer relationship based on measurable value. Answered correctly, they track improvements in the business relationship and identify areas for improvement. Yet, translating answers into meaningful actions is difficult. The issue is not whether or not you are *getting* information about customer satisfaction; it is whether or not you are *using* information about customer satisfaction to act differently."[12]

Over the last several years, spending for online marketing research has grown quite rapidly—from $3.5 million in 1996 to more than $5 billion worldwide in 2009. According to one recent study, more than 90 percent of major companies and about two-thirds of small corporations participate in online research.[13] In fact, one of the largest marketing firms in the United States, NPD Group (**http://www.npd.com**), decided to shift its focus to Web-based research and away from "offline" research: "Our online consumer panel consists of more than 3 million registered adults and teens who have agreed to participate in our surveys, providing NPD and our clients with unmatched insight on trends, purchasing, consumption, ownership, and usage. Our market research information is based on responses from nationally representative samples, and results are demographically balanced."[14] Here are other examples of how online marketing research is being employed:

- Many businesspeople start doing their research by checking out competitors' Web sites, using search engines, and accessing online annual reports and trade publications. Information is current, easy to obtain, and often free.
- Through online subscriptions, Hoover's (**http://www.hoovers.com**) "provides comprehensive, up-to-date business information for sales, marketing, business development, and other professionals who need intelligence on U.S. and global companies, industries, and the people who shape them." It offers proprietary "data-base access to more than 21 million companies and the people who lead them."[15]
- For $599 yearly, a client firm can subscribe to Zoomerang Pro Online Surveys (**http://www.zoomrerang.com**). This enables the client to have Zoomerang software assist in preparing and administering surveys. These features are included: "Unlimited questions and participants. More than 100 survey templates—or the ability make your own. Customize your survey, images, logos, and links. Cross-tabulation, filtering, report downloads, and customizable charts. Premium customer support by phone."[16]

Due to technological advances, *single-source data collection*—whereby research firms track the activities of individual consumer households from the programs they watch on TV to the products they purchase at stores—is now possible. For instance, via its BehaviorScan service, Information Resources Inc. (IRI) (**http://www.infores.com**) monitors the viewing habits and shopping behavior of thousands of households in various markets. Microcomputers are hooked to household TVs and note all programs and ads watched. Consumers shop in supermarkets, drugstores, and other stores with scanning registers and present cashiers with special cards (resembling credit cards). Cashiers enter each consumer's identification code, which is electronically keyed to every item bought. Via computer analysis, viewing and shopping behavior are then matched with such information as age and income.

Because of the unethical practices of some firms, many potential respondents are "turned off" to participating in marketing research projects. In fact, a lot of Americans say they will not answer a survey. To help turn the situation around, many professional

> **Single-source data collection** is a result of high-tech advances.

---

[12] Marian Singer, "What Makes Customer Satisfaction Research Useful?" **http://www.industryweek.com/ReadArticle. aspx?ArticleID=16027** (March 31, 2008).

[13] "About MRA," **http://www.mra-net.org/press/online.cfm** (July 30, 2008).

[14] "NPD Group: Consumer Panel," **http://www.npd.com/about.consumerpanel.html** (April 5, 2009).

[15] "Hoover's Company Information," **http://www.hoovers.com/global/corp/index.xhtml?pageid=10617** (April 5, 2009).

[16] "Zoomerang Pro Online Surveys," **http://www.zoomerang.com/online-surveys/index.htm** (July 30, 2008).

Ethical Issues in Marketing

The Survey Respondents' Bill of Rights

The Council for Marketing and Opinion Research (CMOR) (http://www.cmor.org) has a bill of rights for survey respondents that highlights several important ethical issues that research companies need to address.

Here are some of the areas covered by the CMOR respondents' bill of rights:

- A respondent's privacy should always be maintained. The respondent's name, phone number, E-mail address, and individual responses to a survey are not to be disclosed to anyone outside the research project without the respondent's permission.
- Respondents should be told the name of the research organization and the general nature of the survey.
- Respondents should be contacted in advance if the interview is to be recorded via audio or video. In addition, they should be told how the recording will be used.

- Respondents should not be sold any good or service or asked for money under the guise of research.
- Respondents should be contacted at reasonable times. If a time is not convenient, respondents can ask to be contacted at a more convenient time, if necessary.
- A respondent's decision to not participate in the study, to not answer specific questions, or to discontinue participation should be politely respected.
- Respondents should be assured that the highest standards of professional conduct will be upheld in the collection and reporting of information they provide.

Source: Based on material in "What Your Rights Are If You Are Interviewed," http://www.youropinioncounts.org/index.cfm?p=rights (February 12, 2009).

marketing research associations have toughened their ethics codes. For example, at its Web site, the Interactive Marketing Research Organization (IMRO) (http://www.imro.org/profstds/code.cfm) strongly encourages member firms to adhere to the following practices:

> The IMRO is founded on the principles of upholding the highest standards of both ethical and professional conduct in the use of research technologies. Over and above normal standards of research, our professional activities shall be conducted with particular respect for the individual's right to privacy, both in terms of confidentiality of information collected during the marketing research process and the right to be free from unsolicited and unwanted contact. In all cases, the purpose of research conducted by IMRO members will be clearly and accurately stated along with the limitations of the use of personal information gathered. Individuals will have the right to be removed from potential research respondent lists and given a clear and simple way of communicating such a decision. Members will not willingly and knowingly mislead respondents as to the parameters of the research process including length of survey, incentive, use of data, etc. IMRO members will at all times conform to the 1998 Children's Online Privacy Protection Act (COPPA) and not collect personal data from children under the age of thirteen without the express approval of their parents or guardians. IMRO members pledge to comply with the local, national, and regional laws and regulations regarding the use of all modes of data collection including both interactive and traditional channels of communication in the countries where research is being performed.

With more firms striving to expand their foreign endeavors, international marketing research is now more important. This can be quite challenging. For instance, the language used, respondent selection, and interviewer training are among the areas requiring special consideration.[17] Consider this example.

---

[17] See Robert B. Young and Rajshekhar G. Javalgi, "International Marketing Research: A Global Project Management Perspective," *Business Horizons*, Vol. 50 (March-April 2007), pp. 113–122; and Alex Rialp Criado and Josep Rialp Criado, "International Marketing Research: Opportunities and Challenges in the 21st Century," *Advances in International Marketing*, Vol. 17 (July 2007), pp. 1–13.

Firms deciding how to best market products to the billions of people in Eastern Europe and Central Asia increasingly do marketing research there. Yet, designing and conducting research is hard. Some people have never been surveyed before. Communications systems, especially phone service, may be subpar by Western standards. Secondary data from government agencies and trade associations may be lacking. Thus, firms must be adaptable. When it did research there, a while back, Kodak (**http://www.kodak.com**) could not find relevant consumer data, a photography trade association, or pictures of local cameras for use in a questionnaire. So, to gather data on camera usage and preferences, Kodak took part in a multiclient survey devised by SRG International Ltd. (**http://www. srgicorp.com**). The survey was conducted in nine former Soviet republics; since each had its own language, nine questionnaire versions were prepared.

4-5   THE MARKETING RESEARCH PROCESS

The *marketing research process* consists of a series of activities: defining the issue or problem to be studied; examining secondary data (previously collected); generating primary data (new), if necessary; analyzing information; making recommendations; and implementing findings. Polaris Marketing Research's Web site (**http://www.polarismr. com/edctr_overview.html**) is a useful tool for learning more about the process.

> The **marketing research process** consists of steps from issue definition to implementation of findings.

Figure 4-8 presents the complete process. The steps are to be completed in order. For example, secondary data are not examined until a firm states the issue or problem to be studied, and primary data are not generated until secondary data are thoroughly reviewed. The dashed line around primary data means these data do not always have to be generated. Many times, a firm can obtain enough information internally or from published sources to make a marketing decision without gathering new data. Only if secondary data are insufficient should a firm gather primary data. The research process is described next.

4-5a   Issue (Problem) Definition

Issue (problem) definition is a statement of the topic to be looked into via marketing research. Without a focused definition, irrelevant and expensive data—which could confuse rather than illuminate—may be gathered. A good problem definition directs the research process to collect and analyze appropriate data for the purpose of decision making.

> Research efforts are directed by **issue definition**.

When a firm is uncertain about the precise topic to investigate or wants to broadly study an issue, it uses exploratory research. The aim of *exploratory research* is to gain ideas and insights, and to break broad, vague problem statements into smaller, more precise statements.[18] Exploratory research, also called "qualitative research," may involve in-depth probing, small-group discussions, and understanding underlying trends. Once an issue is clarified, conclusive research, also called "quantitative research," is used. *Conclusive research* is the structured collection and analysis of data pertaining to a specific issue or problem. It is more focused than exploratory research and requires larger samples and more limited questions to provide quantitative data to make decisions. Table 4-1 contrasts the two forms of research.

> **Exploratory research** looks at unclear topics; **conclusive research** is better defined.

4-5b   Secondary Data

Secondary data consist of information not collected for the issue or problem at hand but for some other purpose; this information is available within a firm or externally. Whether secondary data fully resolve an issue or problem or not, their low cost and rather fast accessibility mean that primary data should not be collected until a thorough secondary data search is done.

> **Secondary data** have been previously gathered for purposes other than the current research.

---

[18] "Dictionary," **http://www.marketingpower.com/_layouts/Dictionary.aspx?dLetter=E** (March 22, 2009).

Figure 4-8

The Marketing Research Process

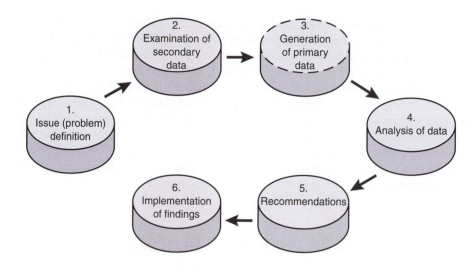

Advantages and Disadvantages Secondary data have these general advantages and disadvantages:

Advantages

- Many types are inexpensive because primary data collection is not involved.
- Data assembly can be swift, especially for published or company materials.
- Several sources and perspectives may be available.
- A source (such as the government) may obtain data a firm could not get itself.
- Data assembled by independent sources is highly credible.
- They are helpful when exploratory research is involved.

Disadvantages

- Available data may not suit the current research purpose due to incompleteness and generalities.
- Information may be dated or obsolete.
- The methodology used in collecting the data (such as the sample size) may be unknown.
- All the findings of a research study may not be made public.
- Conflicting results may exist.
- Because many research projects are not repeated, the reliability of data may not be proven.

Sources Two major sources of secondary data exist: Internal secondary data are available within a firm. External secondary data are available outside a firm. Most companies use each source in some way.

Table 4-1   Examples of Exploratory and Conclusive Research

Vague Research Topic	Exploratory Research	Precise Research Topic	Conclusive Research
1. Why are sales declining?	1. Discussions among key personnel to identify major cause	1. Why is the turnover of sales personnel so high?	1. Survey sales personnel and interview sales managers
2. Is advertising effective?	2. Discussions among key advertising personnel to define effectiveness	2. Do adults recall an advertisement the day after it appears?	2. Survey customers and noncustomers to gauge advertising recall
3. Will a price reduction increase revenues?	3. Discussions among key personnel to determine the level of a price reduction	3. Will a 10 percent price reduction have a significant impact on sales?	3. Run an in-store experiment to determine effects

Internal Secondary Data The information inside a firm should be reviewed before spending time and money searching for external secondary data or collecting primary data. Internal sources include budgets, sales figures, profit-and-loss statements, customer billings, inventory records, prior research reports, and written reports.

At the beginning of the business year, most firms set detailed budgets for the next 12 months. The budgets, based on sales forecasts, outline planned expenditures for every good and service during the year. By examining the sales of each division, product line, item, geographic area, salesperson, time of day, day of week, and so on, and comparing these sales with those of prior periods, performance can be measured. With profit-and-loss statements, actual achievements can be measured against profit goals by department, salesperson, and product. Customer billings provide information on credit transactions, sales by region, peak selling seasons, sales volume, and sales by customer category. Inventory records show the levels of goods bought, manufactured, stored, shipped, and/or sold throughout the year.

Prior research reports, containing the findings of past marketing research efforts, are often stored and retained for future use. When a report is used initially, it is primary data. Later reference to that report is secondary in nature because it is no longer employed for its basic purpose. Written reports (ongoing data stored by a firm) may be compiled by top management, marketing executives, sales personnel, and others. Among the information attainable from such reports are typical customer complaints.

External Secondary Data If a research issue or problem is not resolved through internal secondary data, a firm should use external secondary data sources. Government and nongovernment sources are available.

All levels of government distribute economic and business statistics. Various U.S. government agencies also publish pamphlets on such diverse topics as franchising and deceptive sales practices. These materials are distributed free of charge or sold for a nominal fee. The *Catalog of U.S. Government Publications* (**http://catalog.gpo.gov/F**) lists these items. In using government data, particularly census statistics, the research date must be noted. There may be a lag before government data are released.

Three types of nongovernment secondary data exist: regular publications; books, monographs, and other nonregular publications; and commercial research houses. Regular publications contain articles on diverse aspects of marketing and are available in libraries or via subscriptions. Some are quite broad in scope (*Business Week*); others are more specialized (*Journal of Advertising Research*). Periodicals are published by conventional publishing companies, as well as by professional and trade associations. See below and the next page for a list of the Web sites of more than 50 marketing-related publications.

> A firm's records or past studies comprise internal secondary data.

> Government and nongovernment sources make available external secondary data.

Examples of Marketing-Related Publications

- *Advertising Age* (**http://www.adage.com**)
- *American City Business Journals* (**http://bizjournals.bcentral.com**)
- *Brand Packaging* (**http://www.brandpackaging.com**)
- *Brandweek* (**http://www.brandweek.com**)
- *BtoB* (**http://www.netb2b.com**)
- *Business Week* (**http://www.businessweek.com**)
- *Chain Store Age* (**http://www.chainstoreage.com**)
- *Consumer Reports* (**http://www.consumerreports.com**)
- *CRM* (**http://www.destinationcrm.com**)
- *Demographic Research* (**http://www.demographic-research.org**)
- *Direct* (**http://www.directmag.com**)

- *Display & Design Ideas* (**http://www.ddimagazine.com**)
- *DM News* (**http://www.dmnews.com**)
- *Drug Store News* (**http://www.drugstorenews.com**)
- *DSN Retailing Today* (**http://www.dsnretailingtoday.com**)
- *E-Commerce News* (**http://www.internetnews.com/ec-news**)
- *Entrepreneur Magazine* (**http://www.entrepreneur.com**)
- *Fast Company* (**http://www.fastcompany.com**)
- *Forbes* (**http://www.forbes.com**)
- *Fortune* (**http://www.fortune.com**)
- *Hoover's Online* (**http://www.hoovers.com**)
- *Inc.* (**http://www.inc.com**)
- *Incentive* (**http://www.incentivemag.com**)

(continued)

- *Industry Standard* (**http://www.thestandard.com**)
- *Journal of Advertising Research* (**http://www.jar.warc.com**)
- *Journal of Business Ethics* (**http://www.kluweronline.com/issn/0167-4544**)
- *Journal of Consumer Marketing* (**http://www.emeraldinsight.com/jcm.htm**)
- *Journal of Database Marketing & Customer Strategy Management* (**http://www.palgrave-journals.com/dbm/index.html**)
- *Journal of Marketing* (**http://www.atypon-link.com/AMA/loi/jmkg**)
- *Journal of Marketing Research* (**http://www.marketingpower.com/live/content1054C363.php**)
- *Journal of Services Marketing* (**http://www.emeraldinsight.com/jsm.htm**)
- *London Times* (**http://www.thetimes.co.uk**)
- *Marketing News Blog* (**http://appserver.marketingpower.com/blog/marketingnews**)
- *Marketing Today* (**http://www.marketingtoday.com**)
- *Marketing Week* (**http://www.marketingweek.co.uk**)
- *McKinsey Quarterly* (**http://www.mckinseyquarterly.com**)
- *Monkey Dish (from Restaurant Business)* (**http://www.monkeydish.com**)
- *Multichannel Merchant* (**http://www.multichannelmerchant.com**)
- *Newsweek International Editions* (**http://www.msnbc.com/news/nw-INT_front.asp**)
- *New York Times* (**http://www.nytimes.com**)
- *Nonprofit Times* (**http://www.nptimes.com**)
- *P-O-P Times* (**http://www.poptimes.com**)
- *Progressive Grocer* (**http://www.progressivegrocer.com**)
- *Promo* (**http://www.promomagazine.com**)
- *Sales & Marketing Management* (**http://www.salesandmarketing.com**)
- *Selling Power* (**http://www.sellingpower.com**)
- *Shopping Centers Today* (**http://www.icsc.org/sct**)
- *Stores* (**http://www.stores.org**)
- *Target Marketing* (**http://www.targetonline.com**)
- *USA Today* (**http://www.usatoday.com**)
- *Value Retail News* (**http://www.valueretailnews.com**)
- *Wall Street Journal* (**http://www.wsj.com**)

Books, monographs, and other nonrecurring literature are also published by conventional publishing companies, as well as by professional and trade associations. These materials deal with special topics in depth and are compiled on the basis of interest by the target audience.

Various commercial research houses conduct periodic and ongoing studies and make results available to many clients for a fee. The fee can be low or range into the tens of thousands of dollars (or more), depending on the extent of the data. That kind of research is secondary when the firm purchasing data acts as a subscriber and does not request specific studies pertaining only to itself; in this way, commercial houses provide a number of research services more inexpensively than if data are collected for a firm's sole use. Among the leaders are Nielsen (**http://www.nielsen.com**), IMS Health (**http://www.imshealth.com**), Arbitron (**http://www.arbitron.com**), and Maritz Research (**http://www.maritz.com**).

Two excellent online sources of free marketing information on various subjects are About Marketing (http://marketing.about.com) and KnowThis.com's marketing virtual library (**http://www.knowthis.com**).

4-5c   Primary Data

Primary data consist of information gathered to address a specific issue or problem at hand. Such data are needed if secondary data are insufficient for a proper marketing decision to be made.

> **Primary data** relate to a specific marketing issue.

Advantages and Disadvantages Primary data have these general advantages and disadvantages:

Advantages
- They are collected to fit the precise purpose of the current research topic.
- Information is current.
- The methodology of data collection is controlled and known by the firm.
- All findings are available to the firm, which can maintain their secrecy.
- There are no conflicting data from different sources.

- A study can be replicated (if desired).
- When secondary data do not resolve all questions, collecting and analyzing primary data are the only way to acquire information.

Disadvantages
- Collection may be time consuming.
- Costs may be high.
- Some types of information cannot be collected (e.g., Census data).
- The company's perspective may be limited.
- The firm may be incapable of collecting primary data.

Research Design If a firm decides primary data are needed, it must devise a *research design*, which outlines the procedures for collecting and analyzing data. A research design includes the following decisions.

> The **research design** outlines data collection and analysis procedures.

Who Collects the Data? A company can collect data itself or hire an outside research firm for a specific project. The advantages of an internal research department are the knowledge of company operations, total access to company personnel, ongoing assembly and storage of data, and high commitment. The disadvantages of an internal department are the continuous costs, narrow perspective, possible lack of expertise on the latest research techniques, and potentially excessive support for the views of top management. The strengths and weaknesses of an outside research firm are the opposite of those for an inside department.

> Internal or outside personnel can be used.

What Information Should Be Collected? The kinds and amounts of data to be collected should be keyed to the issue (problem) formulated by the firm. Exploratory research requires different data collection than that for conclusive research.

Who or What Should Be Studied? First, the people or objects to be studied must be stated; they comprise the population. People studies typically involve customers, personnel, and/or distribution intermediaries. Object studies usually center on firm and/or product performance.

Marketing and the Web

Pros and Cons in Doing Marketing Research Online

Online surveys offer some major potential benefits to traditional formats involving telephone, mail, or personal interviews. One major advantage is that the respondents decide when to complete the survey. This enables respondents to devote sufficient time to each question and not feel that they have been interrupted at a bad time. Firms can also ask sensitive questions (such as how often one showers) due to respondent anonymity. Online surveys are also less costly, yield faster results, and lend themselves to savings in tabulation.

Some research firms have used online surveys in conjunction with community sites to replace the traditional use of panels and surveys. One social networking firm, Communispace (**http://www.communispace.com**), has set up more than 300 private Web communities which have been used by such marketing research firms as Virtual Surveys (**http://www.virtualsurveys.com**). Researchers that utilize community

sites believe that members are enthusiasts of either specific goods (such as high definition televisions or digital single-lens reflex cameras) or of specific brands, and that they are especially deliberate in their responses.

One key problem associated with online surveys may be the lack of representativeness of respondents. According to one survey expert, drawing conclusions from online polls can be "like making an automobile out of soft plastic." Other experts are especially critical of online panels where respondents get compensated for every completed questionnaire. They maintain that respondents may be more interested in the rewards than the goods or services.

Sources: Based on material in David Benady, "In Search of an Honest Opinion," *Marketing Week* (March 4, 2008), pp. 32-37; and Burt Helm, "Online Polls: How Good Are They?" *Business Week* (June 16, 2008), pp. 86–87.

Sampling the population saves time and money.

Second, the way in which people or objects are selected must be decided. Large and/or dispersed populations usually are examined by *sampling*, which requires the analysis of selected people or objects in the designated population, rather than all of them. It saves time and money; and when used properly, the sample's accuracy and representativeness can be measured. With *probability (random) sampling*, every member of the designated population has an equal or known probability of being chosen for analysis. For example, a researcher may select every 50th person in a phone directory. With *nonprobability sampling*, members of the population are chosen on the basis of convenience or judgment. For instance, an interviewer may select the first 100 dormitory students entering a college cafeteria. A probability sample is more accurate, but it is more costly and difficult than a nonprobability sample.

Third, the sample size must be set. Generally, a large sample will yield greater accuracy and will cost more than a small sample. There are methods for assessing sample size in terms of accuracy and costs, but a description of them is beyond the scope of this text.

One of the leading firms in client sampling support is Survey Sampling International (**http://www.surveysampling.com**).

What Technique of Data Collection Should Be Used? There are four basic primary-data collection methods: survey, observation, experiment, and simulation.

A **survey** communicates in person, over the phone, or by mail.

A *survey* gathers information from respondents by communicating with them. It can uncover data about attitudes, purchases, intentions, and consumer traits. Yet, it is subject to incorrect or biased answers. A questionnaire is used to record answers. A survey can be done in person, by phone, by mail, or through the Internet. At its Web site, Surveypro.com offers a series of free tutorials on how to design surveys (**http://www.surveypro.com/tutorial**) and dozens of sample questions (**http://www.surveypro.com/sample**).

A *personal survey* is face-to-face and flexible, can elicit lengthy replies, and reduces ambiguity. It may be relatively expensive, however, and bias is possible because the interviewer may affect results by suggesting ideas to respondents or by creating a certain mood during the interview. A *phone survey* is fast and relatively inexpensive, especially with the growth of discount telephone services. Responses are usually brief, and nonresponse may be a problem. It must be verified that the desired respondent is the one contacted. Some people do not have a phone, or they have unlisted numbers. The latter problem is now overcome through computerized, random-digit-dialing devices. A *mail survey* reaches dispersed respondents, has no interviewer bias, and is relatively inexpensive. Nonresponse, slowness of returns, and participation by incorrect respondents are the major problems. The technique chosen depends on the goals and needs of the specific research project. An *Internet survey* researches dispersed respondents, requires respondents to answer all questions in the order intended, and generates quick responses that can be easily analyzed. However, many possible respondents do not have Internet connections, some view online surveys as junk mail, and online surveys that encourage consumers to "drop by" do not present unbiased results.

A nondisguised survey reveals its purpose, whereas a disguised one does not.

With a *nondisguised survey*, the respondent is told a study's real purpose; in a *disguised survey*, the person is not. The latter may be used to indirectly probe attitudes and avoid a person's answering what he or she thinks the interviewer wants to hear or read. The left side of Figure 4-9 is nondisguised and shows the true intent of a study on people's attitudes and behavior about sports cars. The right side shows how the survey can be disguised: By asking about sports car owners in general, a firm may get more honest answers than with questions directed right at the respondent. The intent of the disguised study is to uncover the respondent's actual reasons for buying a sports car.

A **semantic differential** uses bipolar adjectives.

A *semantic differential* is a list of bipolar (opposite) adjective scales. It is a survey technique with rating scales instead of, or in addition to, traditional questions. It may be disguised or nondisguised, depending on whether the respondent is told a study's true purpose. Each adjective in a semantic differential is rated on a bipolar scale, and average scores for all respondents are computed. An overall company or product profile is then

Nondisguised

1. Why are you buying a sports car?
_____
_____
_____

2. What factors are you considering in the purchase of a sports car?
_____
_____
_____

3. Is status important to you in buying a sports car?
_____ Yes
_____ No

4. On the highway, I will drive my sports car
_____ within the speed limit.
_____ slightly over the speed limit.
_____ well over the speed limit.

Disguised

1. Why do you think people buy sports cars?
_____
_____
_____

2. What factors do people consider in the purchase of a sports car?
_____
_____
_____

3. Are people who purchase sports cars status-conscious?
_____ Yes
_____ No

4. On the highway, sports car owners drive
_____ within the speed limit.
_____ slightly over the speed limit.
_____ well over the speed limit.

Figure 4-9

Nondisguised and Disguised Surveys

devised. The profile may be compared with competitors' profiles and consumers' ideal ratings. Figure 4-10 shows a semantic differential.

Observation is a research method whereby present behavior or the results of past behavior are observed and noted. People are not questioned and cooperation is

In **observation**, behavior is viewed.

Figure 4-10

A Semantic Differential for a Color Television

Please mark the blanks that best indicate your feelings about Brand A, your feelings about Brand B, and your ideal rating for a 27" **color console television set**.

	A	B	I	
Expensive				Inexpensive
Innovative				Conservative
Low quality				High quality
Disreputable				Reputable
Unattractive console				Attractive console
High status				Low status
Well-known				Unknown
Excellent picture				Poor picture
Poor value for money				Good value for money
Like other brands				Unique
Reliable				Unreliable
Unavailable				Readily available

Legend: A = brand of the company
B = leading competitor
I = ideal rating for a brand by respondent

unnecessary. Interviewer and question bias are minimized. Observation often is used in actual situations. The major disadvantages are that attitudes cannot be determined and observers may misinterpret behavior.

In disguised observation, a person is unaware he or she is being watched. A two-way mirror, hidden camera, or other device would be used. With nondisguised observation, a person knows he or she is being observed. Human observation is done by people; mechanical observation records behavior by electronic or other means, such as a video camera taping in-store customer behavior or reactions to a sales presentation.

An *experiment* is a type of research in which one or more factors are manipulated under controlled conditions. A factor may be any element of marketing from package design to advertising media. In an experiment, just the factor under study is varied; all other factors remain constant. For example, to evaluate a new package design for a product, a manufacturer could send new packages to five retail outlets and old packages to five similar outlets; all marketing factors other than packaging remain the same. After one month, sales of the new package at the test outlets are compared with sales of the old package at similar outlets. A survey or observation is used to determine the reactions to an experiment.

An experiment's key advantage is that it can show cause and effect—such as a new package increasing sales. It is also methodically structured and enacted. Key disadvantages are the rather high costs, frequent use of contrived settings, and inability to control all factors in or affecting a marketing plan.

Simulation is a computer-based method to test the potential effects of various marketing factors via a software program rather than real-world applications. A model of the controllable and uncontrollable factors facing the firm is first built. Different combinations of factors are then fed into a computer to see their possible impact on a marketing strategy. Simulation requires no consumer cooperation and can handle many interrelated factors. Yet, it may be complex and hard to use; does not measure actual attitudes, behavior, and intentions; and is subject to the accuracy of the assumptions made. For an online, interactive demonstration of a simulation, visit Marketplace Business Simulations' Web site (**http://www.marketplace-simulation.com**) and click "demos."

Table 4-2 shows the best uses for each kind of primary data collection.

How Much Will the Study Cost? The overall and specific costs of a study must be outlined. Costs may include executive time, researcher time, support staff time, pretesting, computer usage, respondent incentives (if any), interviewers, supplies, printing, postage or phone expenses, special equipment, and marketing expenses (such as ads).

A study's expected costs should be compared with the expected benefits to be derived. Suppose a consumer survey costing $10,000 would let a firm improve the package design of a new product. With the changes suggested by research, the firm would lift its first-year profit by $30,000. Thus, the net increase due to research is $20,000 ($30,000 profit less $10,000 in costs).

An experiment varies marketing factors under controlled conditions.

Simulation enables marketing factors to be analyzed via a computer model.

Research costs range from personnel time to marketing expenses.

Table 4-2	The Best Uses of Primary Data-Collection Techniques
Technique	**Most Appropriate Uses**
Survey	When determining consumer or distribution intermediary attitudes and motivations toward marketing-mix factors; measuring purchase intentions; relating consumer traits to attitudes
Observation	When examining actual responses to marketing factors under realistic conditions; interest in behavior and not in attitudes
Experiment	When controlling the research environment is essential, and establishing a cause-and-effect relationship is important
Simulation	When deriving and analyzing many interrelationships among variables

How Will the Data Be Collected? The people needed to collect the required data must be determined and the attributes, skills, and training of the data-collection force specified. Too often, this important phase is improperly planned, and data are collected by unqualified people.

Data collection can be administered by research personnel, or it can be self-administered. With *administered data collection*, interviewers ask questions or observers note behavior; they record answers or behavior and explain questions (if asked) to respondents. With *self-administered data collection*, respondents read questions and write their answers. There is a trade-off between control and interviewer probing (administered) versus privacy and limited interviewer bias (self-administered).

Interviewers administer surveys or respondents fill them out.

How Long Will the Data-Collection Period Be? The time frame for data collection must be stipulated, or else a study can drag on. Too long a time frame may lead to inconsistent responses and secrecy violations. Short time frames are easy to set for personal and phone surveys. Mail surveys, observation, and experiments often require much more time to implement; nonetheless, time limits must be defined.

When and Where Should Information Be Collected? The day and time of data collection must be set. It must also be decided if a study is done on or off a firm's premises. The desire for immediacy and convenience has to be weighed against the need to contact hard-to-reach respondents at the proper time.

Data Collection After the research design is detailed, data are then collected. Those engaged in data collection must be properly supervised and follow directions exactly. Responses or observations must be entered correctly.

4-5d Data Analysis

In *data analysis*, the information on questionnaires or answer forms is first coded and tabulated and then analyzed. Coding is the process by which each completed data form is numbered and response categories are labeled. Tabulation is the calculation of summary data for each response category. Analysis is the evaluation of responses, usually by statistical techniques, as they pertain to the specific issue or problem under investigation. The relationship of coding, tabulation, and analysis is shown in Figure 4-11.

One firm offering data analysis services is 1010data (**http://www.1010data.com/ resources.resources.html**). Visit the site for a "test drive."

Data analysis consists of coding, tabulation, and analysis.

4-5e Recommendations

Recommendations are suggestions for a firm's future actions based on marketing research findings. They are typically presented in written (sometimes oral) form to marketing decision makers. The report must be appropriate for the intended audience. Thus, technical terminology must be defined. Figure 4-11 shows recommendations flowing from completed research.

After recommendations are made to the proper decision makers, the research report should be warehoused in the marketing intelligence network. It may be retrieved in the future, as needed. Sample research reports may be viewed at Envirosell's Web site (**http:// www.envirosell.com**). Click on "Research."

4-5f Implementation of Findings

A research report represents feedback for marketing managers, who are responsible for using findings. If they ignore the findings, research has little value. If they base decisions on the results, then marketing research has great value and the organization benefits in the short and long run.

Figure 4-11

Data Analysis, Recommendations, and Implementation of Findings for a Study on Coffee

1. Do you drink coffee?	☐ Yes	01	300
	☐ No	02	200
2. In general, how frequently do you drink coffee? (Check only one answer.)	☐ Two or more times per day	03	142
	☐ Once per day	04	84
	☐ Several times per week	05	42
	☐ Once or twice per week	06	20
	☐ One to three times per month	07	12
	☐ Never	08	200
3. During what time of day do you drink coffee? (Check all answers that apply.)	☐ Morning	09	270
	☐ Lunch time	10	165
	☐ Afternoon	11	100
	☐ Dinner time	12	150
	☐ Evening	13	205
	☐ None	14	200

Coding: Questionnaires numbered A001 to A500. Each response is labeled 01 to 14 (e.g., Morning is 09; Evening is 13). Question 3 is a multiple-response question.

Tabulation: Total responses are shown above right.

Analysis: 60% drink coffee. About 28% drink coffee two or more times daily (representing 47% of all coffee drinkers); almost 25% of coffee drinkers (74 people) consume coffee less than once per day. 90% of coffee drinkers consume coffee in the morning; only one-third consume it in the afternoon.

Recommendations: The coffee industry and individual firms need to increase the advertising geared toward noncoffee drinkers, as well as infrequent coffee drinkers. Emphasis should also be placed on lifting coffee consumption during afternoon hours.

Implementation of findings: New, more aggressive advertising campaigns will be developed and the annual media budgets devoted to increasing overall coffee consumption will be expanded. One theme will stress coffee's value as an afternoon "pick-me-upper."

Marketing managers are most apt to implement research findings if they have input into the research design, broad control over marketing decisions, and confidence that results are accurate. Figure 4-11 provides an illustration of how a firm could implement research findings.

Web Sites You Can Use

A number of Web sites are valuable for a firm to visit when collecting the information necessary to make the proper marketing decisions. Here is a cross section of general interest sites:

- Annual Reports (**http://www.annualreports.com**)—"Boasting the most complete and up-to-date listings of annual reports on the Internet."

- Competitive Intelligence Resource Index (**http://www.bidigital.com/ci**)—"A search engine and listing of sites-by-category for finding competitive intelligence resources."
- Dismal Scientist (**http://www.economy.com/dismal**)—"Provides daily analysis of the global macroeconomic, industry, financial, and regional trends that affect your business, organization, or investments."

- Google Trends (**http://www.google.com/trends**)—
"Compare the world's interest in your favorite topics. Enter up to five topics and see how often they've been searched on Google over time."
- How Stuff Works (**http://www.howstuffworks.com**)—
"Widely recognized as the leading source for clear, reliable explanations of how everything around us actually works."
- *Information Please Almanac* (**http://www.infoplease.com**)—
"All the knowledge you need."
- Internet Public Library Reference Center (**http://www.ipl.org**)—"The first public library of and for the Internet community."

- LibrarySpot (**http://www.libraryspot.com**)—"To break through the information overload of the Web and bring the best library and reference sites together."
- Marketingprofs.com (**http://www.marketingprofs.com**)—"Marketing know-how from professionals + professors."
- Marketing Today (**http://www.marketingtoday.com/news_feeds/index.htm**)—"The Online Guide to Marketing in the Information Age."

Summary

1. *To show why marketing information is needed* With good information, a firm can accurately assess its strengths, weaknesses, opportunities, and threats; operate properly in the marketing environment; and maximize performance. Reliance on gut feelings, judgment, and experience is not sufficient. The scientific method requires objectivity, accuracy, and thoroughness in research projects.

2. *To explain the role and importance of marketing information systems* Collecting marketing information should not be viewed as an infrequent event. Acting in that manner can have negative ramifications, especially with regard to misreading the competition and other external factors that can affect a firm's performance.

   A marketing information system (MIS) is a set of procedures to generate, analyze, disseminate, and store anticipated marketing decision information on a regular, continuous basis. It can aid a company operationally, managerially, and strategically.

3. *To examine a basic marketing information system, commercial data bases, data-base marketing, and examples of marketing information systems in action* The key to a basic MIS is the marketing intelligence network, which consists of continuous monitoring, marketing research, and data warehousing. The intelligence network is influenced by the environment, company goals, and marketing plans, and it affects the implementation of marketing plans. Marketing research should be considered as just one part of an ongoing, integrated information system. An MIS can be used by both small and large firms.

   Specialized research firms offer valuable information via commercial data bases that contain data on the population, the business environment, the economy, industry and company performance, and other factors. Data bases are available in printed form, on CDs and DVDs, and as downloads from the Internet.

   Many firms look to data-base marketing for improving their customer interactions. Data-base marketing involves setting up an automated system to identify and characterize customers and prospects and then using quantifiable information to better reach them. With data mining, firms seek out hidden opportunities related to specific customers.

   Marketing information systems are being used by firms of every size and type.

4. *To define marketing research and its components and to look at its scope* Marketing research entails systematically gathering, recording, and analyzing data about specific issues related to the marketing of goods, services, organizations, people, places, and ideas. It may be done internally or externally.

   Expenditures on marketing research run into the billions of dollars annually. Five aspects of research are noteworthy: customer satisfaction studies, the growth of Web-based research, single-source data collection, ethical considerations, and intricacies of international research.

5. *To describe the marketing research process* This process consists of defining the issue or problem to be studied, examining secondary data, generating primary data (when needed), analyzing data, making recommendations, and implementing findings. Many considerations and decisions are needed in each stage.

   Exploratory (qualitative) research is used to develop a clear definition of the study topic. Conclusive (quantitative) research looks at a specific issue in a structured manner. Secondary data—not gathered for the study at hand but for some other purpose—are available from internal and external (government, nongovernment, commercial) sources. Primary data—collected specifically for the purpose of the investigation at hand—are available through surveys, observation, experiments, and simulation. Primary data collection requires a research design: the framework for guiding data collection and analysis. Primary data are gathered only if secondary data are inadequate. Costs must be weighed against the benefits of research. The final stages of marketing research are data analysis—coding, tabulating, and analysis; recommendations—suggestions for future actions based on research findings; and implementation of findings by management.

Key Terms

scientific method (p. 85)

marketing information system (MIS) (p. 86)

marketing intelligence network (p. 87)

continuous monitoring (p. 87)

data warehousing (p. 88)

commercial data bases (p. 89)

data-base marketing (p. 90)

data mining (p. 90)

marketing research (p. 93)

single-source data collection (p. 95)

marketing research process (p. 97)

issue (problem) definition (p. 97)

exploratory research (p. 97)

conclusive research (p. 97)

secondary data (p. 97)

primary data (p. 100)

research design (p. 101)

sampling (p. 102)

survey (p. 102)

semantic differential (p. 102)

observation (p. 103)

experiment (p. 104)

simulation (p. 104)

data analysis (p. 105)

Review Questions

1. What may result if managers rely exclusively on intuition?
2. What is the scientific method? Must it be used each time a firm does research? Explain your answer.
3. Describe the elements of a basic marketing information system.
4. Distinguish between commercial data bases and data-base marketing.
5. Differentiate between conclusive and exploratory research. Give an example of each.
6. Why should a secondary data search always precede primary data collection?
7. Outline the steps in a research design.
8. Under what circumstances should a firm use an experiment to collect data? Simulation? Explain your answers.

Discussion Questions

1. A sneaker manufacturer wants to get information on the average amount that U.S. consumers spend annually on sneakers, what types of sneakers they buy, the characteristics of the people who buy sneakers, the time of year when sneaker purchases are heaviest and lightest, the sales of leading competitors, and customer satisfaction. Explain how the firm should set up and enact a marketing intelligence network. Include internal and external data sources in your answer.
2. Kay's is a large jewelry chain. Barbara's Jewelry Boutique is an independent local business. If both wish to gather data about their respective competitors' marketing practices, how would your research design differ for each?
3. Develop a semantic differential to determine attitudes toward the price of gasoline. Explain your choice of adjectives.
4. Comment on the ethics of disguised surveys. When would you recommend that they be used?

Web Exercise

At its Web site, Decision Analysts (**http://www.acop.com/demo/page1.asp**) provides a demonstration of its online survey service. Describe what you learn from this demonstration. Would you recommend Decision Analysts? Why or why not?

Practice Quiz

1. Which of the following is a reason why a firm should continuously collect and analyze information regarding its marketing plan?
   a. To guarantee success
   b. To monitor the environment
   c. To rely more heavily on executive judgment
   d. To maintain secrecy about its operations
2. Which of the following is a component of a marketing intelligence network?
   a. Simulation
   b. Data warehousing
   c. Product design
   d. Marketing entropy

3. Which of these is never a type of commercial data base?
   a. infoUSA CDs
   b. Census data
   c. Primary data
   d. Internal secondary data

4. Marketing research
   a. should be crisis-oriented.
   b. can be applied to only certain aspects of marketing.
   c. must be conducted in a systematic manner to be effective.
   d. includes only data collected from sources outside the firm.

5. The first step in the marketing research process involves
   a. studying competitors.
   b. implementing findings.
   c. establishing the issue to be studied.
   d. surveying consumers.

6. Secondary data should be collected before primary data because
   a. secondary data is generally more easily and inexpensively obtained than primary data.
   b. secondary data will have guaranteed suitability to the current research study, whereas primary data will not.
   c. secondary data will always be current, whereas primary data may be dated or obsolete.
   d. secondary data will not yield conflicting information from different sources, whereas primary data may.

7. Which of the following is not an example of internal secondary data?
   a. Attending trade shows
   b. Sales figures
   c. Customer billings
   d. Inventory records

8. Which of the following is an advantage of primary data?
   a. Information is current.
   b. Primary data are usually less expensive to collect than secondary data.
   c. Most firms are skilled in primary data collection.
   d. Data collection is typically fast.

9. Choosing 125 females ages 18-29 and 125 females ages 30 and older to participate in a research study is an example of a(n)
   a. exploratory research study.
   b. probability sample.

   c. nonprobability sample.
   d. external secondary data search.

10. Which of the following is *not* one of the four basic methods of primary data collection?
    a. Experiment
    b. Observation
    c. Distribution
    d. Simulation

11. Which of the following research methods has the least interviewer bias?
    a. Personal surveys
    b. Observation
    c. Telephone surveys
    d. Internet surveys

12. Among the advantages of conducting a mail survey is the
    a. ability to avoid nonresponse problems.
    b. ability to complete the survey at a convenient time.
    c. speed with which surveys are returned by respondents.
    d. ability to avoid participation by incorrect respondents.

13. If a firm wants to study consumer attitudes through the use of bipolar adjectives, it will most likely use
    a. observation.
    b. a semantic differential.
    c. simulation.
    d. experiment.

14. A major advantage of an experiment is its
    a. ability to show cause and effect.
    b. ability to control all factors in or affecting a marketing plan.
    c. infrequent use of contrived settings.
    d. relatively low costs.

15. The process by which each completed data form is numbered and response categories are labeled is called
    a. tabulation.
    b. analysis.
    c. survey design.
    d. coding.

For the answers to these questions, please visit the online site for this book at **http://www.atomicdog.com.**

Case 1: Why Isn't Customer Service Better?[c1-1]

According to some experts, despite the popularity of such slogans as "Customers Are Number One" and "The Customer Is Always Right," the overall quality of customer service is actually getting worse. For example, the American Customer Satisfaction Index (http://www.theacsi.org) shows that many firms are graded as a "C" for customer service. There is clearly a major disconnect between the quality of customer service that marketers say they are providing and how consumers perceive the level of customer support.

A recent survey of 2,200 U.S. shoppers conducted by the Wharton School of Business found that 82 percent of respondents would definitely continue shopping at a problem-free store. This percentage dropped to 62 percent when shoppers encountered problems. The highest rate of problems were cited by shoppers ages 18 to 29 (68 percent); the lowest rate was by shoppers over 65 (41 percent). Here are the top ten consumer complaints for poor in-store customer service:

1. "That's not my department."
2. "Could not find anyone when needed help."
3. "Customer felt pestered when they wanted to browse on their own."
4. "Customer felt like sales associate was intruding on their time or conversations."
5. "Sales associate was insensitive to long-checkout lines."
6. "Sales associate not interested in helping customer find what they were looking for."
7. "Sales associate was not very polite or courteous."
8. "Product/item was out of stock."
9. "Sales associate didn't listen when customer explained what they wanted."
10. "Customer felt ignored, sales associate did not say hello or make eye contact."

Another study by Wharton had similar findings. One-third of the respondents said that they could not find a salesperson to help them and that this one specific issue could permanently cost a store 6 percent of customers. One-quarter of the respondents also felt ignored by sales associates. They reported not getting a greeting, a smile, or even eye contact: "Customers would walk into a store and the store representative would see them and continue to put items on the shelf or watch the cash register or do administrative work—absolutely ignoring the fact that an actual person was in the store." This problem could result in 3 percent of shoppers permanently defecting. A customer's feeling that he/she was ignored was the customer complaint most likely to be shared with others.

This study concluded that there are four characteristics that are found in ideal sales associates: "engager," "educator," "expeditor," and "authentic" sales help. The engager smiles and stops what he or she is doing to help a customer. The educator makes specific product recommendations based on a buyer's needs. The expeditor helps speed a customer through the checkout process. And though the authentic salesperson lets customers browse on their own, he or she comes across as genuinely interested in being helpful.

There are some solutions to these problems that are not based on sales associate attitudes. One solution is to equip salespersons with handheld devices that can help locate where specific items are to be found in the store. These devices can also be used to reduce long lines at cash registers by scanning items and recording credit- and debit-card sales. Stores can also improve store signage and have centralized information kiosks staffed by helpful and trained personnel.

Questions

1. Comment on the results of the studies described in this case. Why do you think these outcomes occurred?
2. What is the difference between customer satisfaction and customer delight?
3. Explain the statement: "Technology can hinder, as well as help, customer service."
4. Besides the solutions to bad customer service noted in the case, what else would you recommend?

[c1-1] The data in the case are drawn from "Customer Service," http://consumerist.com (October 1, 2008); and "Are Your Customers Dissatisfied? Try Checking Out Your Salespeople," http://knowledge.wharton.upenn.edu/article.cfm?articleid=1735 (May 16, 2007).

Case 2: Every Customer Is NOT a Good Customer[c1-2]

Some firms tend to focus their marketing strategies on the most profitable consumers. Some have tried to reduce purchases—or to even refuse to serve unprofitable customers. Sprint (http://www.sprint.com) recently sent letters to about 1,000 customers to inform them they would no longer be sold wireless phone service. After tracking the number of support calls over a one-year period, Sprint found that these customers would call hundreds of times a month on the same issue that Sprint felt was resolved. Sprint waived the termination fees for these customers and then cut off their wireless phone service.

Delta (http://www.delta.com) is among the airlines that changed their frequent flyer programs to make it more difficult for consumers who continually select the lowest airline fares to earn free trips. Likewise, many retailers have begun to track consumers and refuse to provide refunds to consumers who frequently return merchandise. Some banks have increased usage fees on small and unprofitable accounts.

The electronics chain Best Buy (http://www.bestbuy.com) hired Larry Selden, author of *Angel Customers and Demon Customers,* to help the electronics retailers remove unprofitable customers from its mailing list. One group of unprofitable customers that Best Buy was targeting had a history of abusive returns (such as returning a good in unsalable condition or returning a laptop computer he or she purchased for short-term use instead of renting the unit). In many cases, electronics retailers such as Best Buy now charge restocking fees on selected items to discourage customers from buying cameras or laptops for use on vacations and then returning them after they arrive at home. Best Buy has also instituted a Reward Zone loyalty program designed to recruit its most profitable customers instead of trying to maximize customer participation. Best Buy's Reward Zone members, on average, spend significantly more at the chain than its average customers.

Firms need a systematic strategy to properly manage customer divestment. This process consists of several steps. Potential customer candidates for divestment need to be determined through an analysis that reviews each customer's servicing costs, gross profits, and lifetime purchases. Using this type of analysis, FedEx (http://www.fedex.com) raised the rates of a group of customers after determining that these customers did not meet promised sales revenue levels. In addition, many of these customers had large numbers of residential accounts that required multiple deliveries. Customers who balked at the rate increases were told they could seek competitor quotes.

As an alternative to divestment, some customers merely need to be taught to use the firm's services more effectively. They need to use the Web as a means of checking bank balances, the value of stock market investments, or computer troubleshooting directions.

In some cases, divested customers have been assisted in getting alternative sources by their former suppliers. These new sources can be a lower-cost subsidiary of the parent company or even a competitor that focuses on smaller customers or on niche markets. EchoStar (http://www.echostar.com), a satellite TV service provider, uses prepaid plans to handle customers with poor credit histories. Legal and accounting firms can also shift less profitable accounts to junior associates as opposed to partners.

A final aspect of customer divestment planning relates to how the terminated relationship is to be communicated. One research study found that 80 percent of the divested consumers were angry, frustrated, or embarrassed about being cut off. Seventy percent of these customers did not receive any advance notice. More than one-half of the respondents who received advance notice were informed by mail as opposed to a phone call from a service representative or in person. The majority of terminated customers would have preferred phone or in-person contact.

Questions

1. Comment on the marketing strategies described in this case.
2. What else could be done before terminating a "bad" customer?
3. a. List and describe three examples of unprofitable customers for a retailer of furniture.
   b. List and describe three examples of unprofitable customers for a local florist.
4. Develop a loyalty-card program for a hotel chain that reflects the profitability of different customer segments.

[c1-2] The data in the case are drawn from Vikas Mittal, Matthew Sarkees, and Feisal Murshed, "The Right Way to Manage Unprofitable Customers," *Harvard Business Review* (April 2008), Vol. 86, pp. 94–102.

Case 3: Southwest Airlines: Staying Ahead of Competitors[c1-3]

Since 1971, Southwest Airlines' (http://www.southwest.com) operating strategy has been simple. In return for its mechanics, pilots, and flight attendants outhustling its competitors, Southwest provides job security and rewards employees with company stock. In 2007, Southwest posted its 35th consecutive year of net income growth. This was an "amazing feat" due to the highly cyclical nature of the airline business. Southwest also garnered the number 12 spot on *Fortune's* 2008 "American's Most Admired Companies" listing. *Note:* Due to steep increases in 2008 fuel prices, Southwest's profit fell. However, it was the only U.S. carrier to earn a profit during that year.

Southwest's overall strategy focuses on several components: operational simplicity due to the use of one type of aircraft—the Boeing 737 series (this keeps mechanics' training costs and spare parts inventories low), a companywide devotion to having low costs and fares, and an emphasis on efficiency (due to the fast turnaround of its aircraft between arrival and departure). Though most major airlines use a hub-and-spoke system that collects passengers from multiple locations (spokes), flies them to a central hub, and then redistributes the passenger to spokes, Southwest relies on nonstop direct flights. This strategy reduces delays at hubs and enables Southwest Airlines flights to be in the air (versus the ground) for more time than any similarly sized aircraft operated by a network carrier. Southwest is also able to unload a flight, clean it, refuel it, and board new passengers in as few as 20 minutes. In contrast, many of its competitors require as much as 90 minutes.

Southwest's strategy was very distinctive in the past. However, it has been copied by airlines such as JetBlue (http://www.jetblue.com) and AirTran (http://www.airtran.com). Southwest faces competition from these upstarts, as well as the entrenched legacy carriers. Carriers such as JetBlue initially borrowed Southwest's one-airplane model and added such goodies as leather seats, individual TV screens, and fancy snacks. JetBlue's costs for available seat mile (8.3 cents as of third quarter 2007) were lower than Southwest's (9.1 cents). And the legacy carriers Delta (http://www.delta.com), with costs of 14.0 cents per mile, and United (http://www.united.com), with costs of 13.3 cents per mile, have cut their cost of flying a passenger mile. The bankruptcy filings by Delta, Northwest (http://www.northwest.com), United, and US Airways (http://www.usairways.com) enabled these airlines to cut unprofitable routes, reduce interest payments for aircraft, reduce pension obligations, and lower employee wages.

One way that Southwest is seeking to better compete is by expanding its routes. This enables Southwest to lower its personnel costs by hiring new, lower-paid employees and spreading its administrative overhead costs over more seats. Southwest recently increased its presence in Chicago by adding flights at Midway airport. Its purchase of a share in ATA (http://www.ata.com), a bankrupt carrier, gave Southwest's customers greater access to such cities as Boston, Denver, Minneapolis, and Honolulu. Southwest also started flying to Philadelphia and Pittsburgh.

Southwest seeks to improve its efficiency through employee attrition, a hiring freeze, and generous severance packages to long-time employees. Another source of savings is through technology that automates certain functions or provides self-service opportunities to customers. Among Southwest's high-tech applications are its Southwest Web site (responsible for over $3 billion in annual bookings), its self-service kiosks, and software that keeps gate agents up to date on a passenger's status and special needs.

Recently, Southwest further streamlined its boarding procedures, added a deluxe program aimed at highly profitable business travelers, introduced onboard wireless Internet access, and installed devices to reduce jet fuel use. Through the successful use of hedging, Southwest paid $1.98 per gallon for jet fuel in the first quarter of 2008, versus $2.73 paid by American Airlines (http://www.aa.com) and $2.83 by United. Southwest's hedging profit in that first quarter was $291 million.

Questions

1. Discuss the strategic benefits of Southwest Airlines' low-cost strategy.
2. Describe how the strategies of others airlines are reducing Southwest's low-cost advantage.
3. Should Southwest sustain its low-cost strategy? Explain your answer.
4. What else should Southwest do to maintain its leadership position in the U.S. airline industry?

[c1-3] The data in the case are drawn from "Airlines Hedge Against Rising Fuel Bills; Risky Deals to Lock In Prices Have Paid Off for One U.S. Carrier," *Hamilton Spectator* (July 2, 2008), p. A11; Joe Brancatelli, "Southwest Airlines' Seven Secrets for Success," *Portfolio.com* (July 8, 2008); and Anne Fisher, "America's Most Admired Companies," *Fortune* (March 17, 2008), pp. 65–67.

Case 4: Continental Airlines: A New Emphasis on Business Intelligence[c1-4]

Just as Southwest (http://www.southwest.com) is the airline industry's leader with its low-cost strategy, Continental Airlines (http://www.continental.com) is viewed by many as a leader in business intelligence. It has had a data warehouse since 1998; and the data warehouse achieved global status in 2007. Though one-half of its user community is now based in Houston, Continental's headquarters, the other half is in 75 cities located throughout the world.

The data warehouse is supported by 15 professionals who are responsible for such tasks as data transformation, application interface development, user training and support, and data-base administration. The scope of the data warehouse has grown due to three trends: new business groups are being added to the user base, the user base is increasingly global, and warehouse capabilities are being integrated into Continental's operational business practices.

Continental's data warehouse usage is global in scope. In Japan, this has expanded into price decision making. Predicting airline utilization is especially difficult in Japan because a high percentage of flights are booked by travel agents; the agents are not required to post their bookings into Continental's reservation system until 30 pays prior to the flight's departure. The warehouse is also used by Continental's tax department in Great Britain. All airlines are required to pay a departure tax for passengers who depart from British airports. However, passengers who spend less than 24 hours in Great Britain are exempt from the tax. Prior to the data warehouse being operational, Continental annually overpaid tax authorities due to poor or incomplete records.

Let's look at how using warehouse data can improve ways that Continental handles two important areas: reservation complaint handling and flight performance. Before the warehouse's integration into reservation complaint handling, Continental's 80 person customer-care department had to collect relevant information from customers, print it, and then re-key the data prior to resolving any issues. Not only was this time consuming, but also it enabled some consumers to ask for and receive duplicate payment for the same incident. Now, under Continental's new system, customer service personnel can select a number of inputs from the data warehouse, run them through Continental's rules engine, and generate a recommended customer service action. The new system is faster, eliminates double payment for the same complaint, is more consistent, and only involves 10 people. While many of Continental's competitors continue to only accept complaints via E-mail, Continental's data warehouse allows its customers to use phones. Continental says that many customers want to talk to a live person.

In the past, Continental manually tracked the reasons for specific flight delays (e.g., weather, mechanical problems) by using 100 or so delay codes. When a delay code was not listed, general managers were asked to supply the proper code and reply via telex or E-mail. According to a manager within the operations support group, "It would take forever to track down the information and update the codes into our legacy system." All flights that need delay codes are now automatically listed for each station. A general manager can log onto a flight, click on that flight number, and enter the delay code.

Even though Continental's system is highly functional, the firm must continually respond to a number of potential problems. System users, such as reservation agents, are uncomfortable if the system does not respond in 5 seconds or less. There is a growing amount of data in the warehouse, and large volumes of data can slow the system down. Last, many users also desire real-time data, whereas some data is still uploaded into the warehouse on a batch basis.

Questions

1. What types of commercial data bases should Continental consider for inclusion into its data warehouse?
2. How can Continental utilize data mining?
3. Develop a short survey that focuses on recommended actions for mechanical-related flight delays of varying time periods: 1 to 3 hours, 4 to 6 hours, and 7 hours or more.
4. How can the data warehouse be used in conjunction with a loyalty program that awards airline miles to specific customers based on their total flight miles with Continental?

[c1-4] The data in the case are drawn from Barbara H. Wixom, Hugh J. Watson, Anne Marie Reynolds, and Jeffrey A. Hoffer, "Continental Airlines Continues to Soar with Business Intelligence," *Information Systems Management*, Vol. 25 (Spring 2008) pp. 102–112.

Customers at the Core[pc-1]

INTRODUCTION

Virtually all companies who compete successfully in today's challenging marketplace accept the idea that they should obtain insight from their target customers as they develop their business strategies, segment their markets, and design new products. Companies with a strong external focus on customers tend to be more profitable than companies focused internally on products, technology, or processes. Still, many organizations restrict the focus on consumer insights to their marketing function.

Customer-insight driven companies continually strive to integrate all customer insight into a knowledge base, and widely share this throughout the organization. All decisions are made not only with the goals of the enterprise in mind, but with the needs of the target customer in mind. Investments are made not only in customer-insight infrastructure and tools, but in developing business practices that make customer insights readily available to all functions within the company.

CUSTOMER INPUT INTEGRATION

Companies can be classified along a customer input continuum of five stages ranging from customer oblivious to customer controlled. See Figure 1.

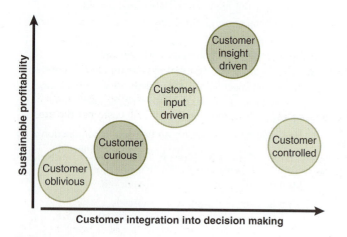

Figure 1

Stages of Customer Insight Integration and Sustainable Profitability

[pc-1] Adapted by the authors from Robert Schieffer and Eric Leininger, "Customers at the Core," *Marketing Management* (January-February 2008), pp. 30–37. Reprinted by permission of the American Marketing Association.

Customer Oblivious

These are often small or internally focused companies. They focus on technology that will support the development of their product line, and feel that customers don't know what they want. Therefore, consumer input is not integrated into the planning process. Their major source of input from customers is customer complaints, and they view them as irritations rather than opportunities to retain valuable customers. Their marketing tactics tend to focus on "selling harder" and "cutting prices to get the business." Since profitability is hard to sustain by these companies, their mortality rate is high.

Customer Curious

Like customer-oblivious firms, they have an unfocused marketing strategy and spend money to serve any customer who wants to buy. However, these companies know that customer input is helpful in some marketing decisions. They hire a marketing staff to learn more about customers, and often differentiate offerings. Their major source of customer input is anecdotal, and their curiosity about customers allows them to avoid gross marketing blunders that doom the customer oblivious. Their unfocused marketing strategy and lack of customer insight only slightly improve their odds for sustainable profitability.

Customer-Input Driven

These companies realize that customer input is critical to most marketing decisions, and make investments in gathering extensive data from customers. They believe that all customer input deserves attention, but often fail to transform the vast amount of input they have into customer insights, planning principles, and marketing strategies. They have developed a segmented view of customers, realizing that different groups respond in different ways to different product and service offerings, but usually target more segments than they can profitably serve. Because these firms lack insights into what their target customers really value, their offerings tend to be of the win/lose variety—great for the company, but less than great for the customer. They invest in marketing research staff to collect customer input, but customer input is often owned by and exclusively utilized by the marketing department.

Customer-Insight Driven

As companies move to stage four, striving to be driven by deep insights into the undermet needs of target customers, who become delighted with the companies' products and services and often pay higher prices to get them, these firms deepen their focus on attractive segments, and develop well-positioned offerings for a manageable group of segments. They create win/win offerings that are profitable for them, and make target customers feel the offering was created especially for them. These companies understand the process of transforming customer input into deep customer insights that drive their entire organizations, not just the marketing departments.

McDonald's Corporation (**http://www.mcdonalds.com**) has revitalized itself over the past several years by returning to its original focus on the customer. A few years ago, new CEO Jim Cantalupo told investors he would return McDonald's to glory by focusing on customer basics: reliable, relevant, and appealing food; clean restaurants; and good customer service. As the *Chicago Sun Times* reported, Cantalupo "immersed himself in reports showing what customers said." His management team (including two men who would later be his successors as CEO) accelerated the customer focus and its application to the core principles of operational excellence, marketing leadership, and financial discipline. Their emphasis? "Face the facts. Listen to your customers because they will tell you what really matters."

Firms driven by deep insights into the needs of target customers have the best opportunity for profitable, sustainable competitive advantages. Companies with a strong external focus on customers tend to be more profitable than organizations focused internally on products, technologies, and processes. A company's satisfied customers are likely to improve both the level and the stability of cash flows and do better than their competition in terms of satisfying customers.

Customer Controlled

Unfortunately, some firms go too far and become customer controlled. They will respond to the dictates of almost any customer and lose focus on target segments in a way that exposes them to indirect competition. They neglect to dig deep for customer insights and abdicate their decision making to their customers. They give the customer what they ask for, often delivering incremental innovations at a lower price. This is hardly the road to sustainable profitability. The sales force usually has a high degree of power in customer-controlled companies, since it is the conduit of customer dictates to the organization. These companies often serve the unprofitable customer segments that other companies try to avoid.

These five stages are summarized in Table 1.

Table 1	Stages of Customer Insight Integration

Assessment tool					
	Stage I Customer oblivious	**Stage II Customer curious**	**Stage III Customer input driven**	**Stage IV Customer insight driven**	**Stage V Customer controlled**
Management view of role of customer insight	Customers don't know what they want Ignore them	Customer insight is helpful in marketing decisions	Customer insight is critical for marketing decisions and helpful for other decisions	Customer insight is to all business decisions All decision makers focused on providing value to target customers at a profit	Forget about customer insight Give the customers what they ask for
Typical market and product strategy	All customers are targeted with undifferentiated offering	All customers are targeted with differentiated offerings	Many customer segments are targeted with Win/Lose offerings	Several customer segments are targeted with Win/Win offerings	Several customer segments are targeted with Lose/Win offerings; product proliferation
Dominant form of customer communication	Customer complaints	Customer anecdotes	Customer anecdotes and some hard customer input	Customer insight	All customer dictates
Practices in business-to-consumer firms	Focus on selling harder Cut prices to get the business	Marketing staff is hired Budget established for marketing research	Marketing research staff is hired Customer input is owned by and resides in marketing	Customer insight is everyone's job Customer insights are captured in a knowledge base and shared throughout the organization	Customer insights are irrelevant and ignored All decisions are abdicated to the target customers
Practices in business-to-business firms	Focus on technology Cut prices to get the business	Marketing staff is hired Focus is on market information and competition	Marketing research staff is hired to study markets Focus is on understanding customer verticals	Customer insight is everyone's job Insights are gathered on needs and beneftis sought among target segments	Customer insights are irrelevant and ignored All decisions are abdicated to salespeople

TEN POTENTIAL PITFALLS

As firms seek to become customer-insight driven, they often invest more resources in their marketing and consumer insight capabilities to accelerate the transition. However, many pitfalls exist that can limit the effectiveness of these investments—or worse, lead to wrong marketing decisions. By avoiding ten pitfalls that happen far more frequently than they should, companies can increase their likelihood of achieving true customer insight, increased brand relevance, and sustainable profitability.

1. **The certainty pitfall.** Upon committing to large investments in marketing research, some executive management expects customer insight to eliminate uncertainty. When marketing mistakes still occur, some executives become cynical about the predictive ability of customer insight efforts and eliminate or gut marketing and marketing research departments. Yet, the best way to think about investments in customer insight is not as eliminating uncertainty, but as improving the odds of marketplace success over the long haul. Investments in understanding consumers will not eliminate uncertainty or guarantee success. So setting the expectations of senior management is important to the success of an ongoing customer-insight program.

2. **The issue of the day pitfall.** Too often, customer insight is treated as a series of unrelated projects, with new learning not integrated into a knowledge base. Consumer and marketplace insight resources are focused on "issues of the day," rather than on foundational issues that will impact the strategic direction of the company. The irony here is that strong foundational studies can usually answer many of the "issues of the day." Further, executive management appreciates the quick turnaround and low cost of answering questions from foundational studies, databases, and simulation tools. Ongoing deep understanding of consumer segments and need states, continuous analysis of advertising impact on attitudes and sales, an up-to-date product quality assessment vs. competition, automated price modeling capabilities, an ongoing competitive monitoring system, and so forth will find many applications in day-to-day work.

3. **Insight hoarding pitfall.** In many companies, customer insights are not shared widely outside of the marketing department. Yet, consumer and marketplace insights should power the entire organization, rather than being hoarded within one area. All functions need to have a connection to meeting the needs of target customers. Finance is assessing relative investments, research and development is balancing technology-driven innovation with customer-driven innovation, sales organizations need to align brand goals with retail customer strategies, and senior management is seeking to keep a finger on the current pulse of the business and understand the future potential of the business. Only by integrating with the entire business can insight leaders fulfill their full responsibility to the organization.

4. **One culture myopia pitfall.** Conclusions about the global appeal of a good or service do not recognize cultural nuance around the world. Too often, companies will assume that successful product launches in a lead country are satisfactory test markets for global rollouts. Building a clear consumer framework that outlines the relative size of market segments, need states, and distribution outlets can help to create hypotheses about which new products will "travel well" across cultures.

5. **Tactics before strategy pitfall.** Many companies neglect the development of a sound marketing strategy prior to developing marketing tactics. Tactical research, such as product optimization, advertising testing, or price testing, is conducted prior to segmenting the market, targeting one or two segments to serve, and clearly positioning the offering to the target segment(s).

   Effective marketing tactics can only be developed by optimizing them to the target market segment, rather than the entire market. Effective tactics can only be developed after the positioning strategy is clearly articulated: Who is the target market, what category is the offering competing in, what is the compelling point of difference, and what is the reason to believe?

6. **Poor problem/opportunity definition pitfall.** Marketing research frequently is conducted without clear objectives and without an understanding of how insights will be used. Management has only a fuzzy understanding of the problem or opportunity they want the marketing research study to address, resulting in poorly framed objectives for the study. Often, key parts of the marketing strategy (segmentation, targeting, and positioning) and the marketing mix are neglected as management focuses on only one or two of these key customer insight areas.

   When Iridium Satellite (**http://www.iridium.com**) launched its global satellite communications system in 1998, it had a clear vision of providing international business travelers with a single telecommunications system that would allow them to place and receive calls "at the ends of the earth." Major effort was placed on developing an advertising campaign (promotion) that would attract the one million customers needed to break even. More than $145 million was spent on the campaign, which generated more than 1.5 million inquiries from potential customers. But Iridium failed to gain and/or act on insight into other keys areas of its marketing strategy and tactics: Were international business travelers the appropriate target market segment, given that the phone couldn't be used inside office buildings, in moving cars, and in urban settings with tall buildings? Would the handset price of $3,000 and the $5–$9 per minute phone service charges be a barrier to adoption and usage by the target market? Would the complexity of learning to use the Iridium phone (and its 220-page user manual) be a negative to international business travelers? Would the size and weight of the phone (described by many as a small brick), and the array of accessories and adapters needed to make the phone work globally, be a negative to the target market?

Iridium appeared to be driven by the incredible technology they were developing, rather than insights from target customers. Iridium filed for bankruptcy just nine months after the system became commercially available. (It has since recovered.)

7. **Rational consumer pitfall.** Some economists believe consumers act in a rational manner when they make purchase decisions, and that they have access to complete information on the product (as well as alternative products) when they make their purchases. However, for most purchase decisions, consumers make decisions involving emotional motivations with limited information. Kraft Foods (**http://www.kraft.com**) has found that Oreos are not just good-tasting cookies, but they are a "magical door which can transport us into a dimension of youth. Within seconds we can reflect back on our own childhood, when a simple pleasure like eating an Oreo cookie was part of every fun-filled day." How large of a role does emotion play in your brand connection to target customers?

8. **Start with a survey pitfall.** By far, the biggest source of disappointment for some marketers is the confusion caused by beginning a customer insight effort with a survey. By skipping the preliminary steps of gaining a shared understanding of a problem/opportunity, assessing the current knowledge base, conducting secondary research, conducting qualitative research, and doing questionnaire pretesting, the data generated by the survey is often incomplete, confusing, and leads to more questions than it answers. Quantitative marketing research surveys should only be conducted after you have developed a clear understanding of what is to be measured. You can't measure that which you don't understand.

9. **Direct questioning pitfall.** Many marketers feel that by asking customers directly about the importance of various product attributes, price sensitivity, and intent to buy new products, they will obtain valid, predictive results. Target customers are asked to rate the importance of a series of attributes. They are asked directly what they would pay for a new product. They are asked how likely they would be to buy a new product, and all of the customers who say they "definitely will buy" and "probably will buy" the new product are expected to buy it in the first year.

In many cases, direct questioning leads to invalid customer insight. It engages the conscious mind of the consumer and leads to shallow, surface, rational responses that make sense to the respondent but often have little to do with their motivations for their purchase decisions.

So how can indirect marketing research techniques tap into the unconscious mind, to yield valid and predictive customer insights? Many indirect techniques have been developed and used successfully. Projective techniques, such as word association and sentence completion, have been used in marketing since the 1960s. One of the most powerful methods to tap into the unconscious mind of consumers is the patented Zaltman Metaphor Elicitation Technique (**http://www.olsonzaltman.com**). It includes several, such as asking the consumer to gather pictures from magazines that capture the feelings and emotions involved in buying and using the product. The respondent is asked to describe the pictures and tell a story about each.

In all consumer insight efforts, consumers generally show "unconscious" excess sensitivity toward whatever they think is being studied. It is important to keep the customer naïve as to the marketing purposes of the study. Circumventing the conscious mind with indirect marketing research techniques can lead to consumer insights that unlock the mind of the market.

10. **Poor stimulus pitfall.** Promising new ideas can be cast aside when the test stimulus materials do not do their job. Susan Lazar of the Lazar Group (**http://www.lazargroup.com**) crystallized this point, based on her deep experience with qualitative research across many industries. Too often, initial concept boards contain unrealistic claims, overcomplicated or unclear benefit statements, and a general lack of application of the discipline of "positioning." We have seen the same idea expressed with poor stimulus material and excellent stimulus material. Great ideas would have been killed if someone had not called out the problems with how the idea was expressed and insisted on re-testing.

Take the time and effort to explain the unique benefits of the offering to the target market—in language that is clear and believable, without overselling the offering. Plan on an iterative approach, where ideas and concepts can be reworked and new insight efforts conducted.

Many cases exist where these pitfalls were ignored, and the misuse of customer input led to decisions that led to marketing failures across a range of industries. Avoiding these ten pitfalls can allow the firm to drive win/win decisions with customer insight that will result in sustainable profitability.

FOCUS ON THE CUSTOMER

Gaining customer insight will not eliminate uncertainty in management decision making. But it can greatly improve the odds of gaining a sustainable, profitable competitive advantage. The odds can be further enhanced by ensuring that all decisions throughout the organization benefit from customer insight and a marketplace perspective, through a relentless focus on the target customer.

When the management team decides to drive the firm's decisions through a deep understanding of the unfulfilled needs of target customers, sustainable competitive advantages, innovation, and revenue growth follow. They differentiate their company on benefits that are highly valued by target customers. They use customer insights as part of their knowledge base to develop planning principles and drive strategic direction, and avoid the many pitfalls on the road to becoming customer-insight driven.

Questions

1. What are the strategic implications of Figure 1?
2. Describe how a firm could evolve through the stages shown in Table 1.
3. How can a firm avoid falling into the undesirable Stage V shown in Table 1?
4. Give an example of a firm that you think is in Stage I in Table 1. What do you recommend for this firm?
5. Give an example of a firm that you think is in Stage IV in Table 1. What do you recommend for this firm?
6. Which 3 of the 10 pitfalls cited in the case do you think are the most important? Explain your answer.
7. How could an effective marketing information system assist a firm in the areas noted in the case?

Part 2

Broadening the Scope of Marketing

In Part 2, we present an expanded perspective of marketing—one that is necessary today.

5 Societal, Ethical, and Consumer Issues

In this chapter, we examine the interaction of marketing and society. We begin by exploring the concept of social responsibility and discussing the impact of company and consumer activities on natural resources, the landscape, environmental pollution, and planned obsolescence. Next, ethics is discussed from several vantage points: business, consumer, global, and teachability. We then turn to consumerism and consider the basic rights of consumers: to information, to safety, to choice in product selection, and to be heard. The current trends related to the role of consumerism are also noted.

6 Global Aspects of Marketing

Here, we place marketing into a global context—important for both domestic and international firms, as well as those large and small. We distinguish among domestic, international, and global marketing. Then, we see why international marketing takes place and how widespread it is. Cultural, economic, political and legal, and technological factors are discussed. We conclude by looking at the stages in the development of an international marketing strategy: organization; entry decisions; degree of standardization; and product, distribution, promotion, and price planning.

7 Marketing and the Internet

At this point, we look at the emergence of the Internet and its impact on marketing practices. We show why the Internet is valuable in marketing and look at the many potential marketing roles for the Internet. Next, we cover how the Internet may be used to enhance a marketing strategy and present several examples. We end the chapter with a discussion of the challenges of the Internet in marketing and a forecast about the future of E-marketing.

After reading Part 2, you should understand elements 6–8 of the strategic marketing plan outlined in Table 3-2 (page 73).

Chapter 5

Societal, Ethical, and Consumer Issues

After Lance Armstrong won the U.S. amateur bicycling championship in 1991, he decided to become a professional athlete. Then, in 1996, Armstrong was diagnosed with testicular cancer and given a 50 percent chance of survival by his doctors. Fortunately, his surgeries and chemotherapy were successful; Armstrong returned to training three months after chemotherapy and to professional cycling in 1998.

In one of the greatest comebacks in the history of sports, Lance Armstrong won his first Tour De France race less than three years after his initial diagnosis with cancer. In total, he won seven consecutive Tour de France bicycle races (1999-2005). The Tour de France is widely acknowledged to be bicycle racing's toughest and most prestigious race.

Among his numerous awards were ESPN's ESPY Award for Best Male Athlete from 2003 through 2006 and the Associated Press Male Athlete of the Year from 2002 through 2005. As one observer noted, "Lance Armstrong is the ultimate athletic brand: an extraordinary winner, a cancer survivor who rebuilt his body into an endurance machine, an effective corporate spokesperson, and an outspoken advocate." Others credit Lance Armstrong with garnering wider U.S. recognition of cycling as a sport.

In 1997, during his cancer treatment, but before his recovery, Lance Armstrong founded the Lance Armstrong Foundation (LAF) (**http://www.livestrong.org**) as a nonprofit organization. This began his commitment as an advocate as well as a world representative for people with cancer. LAF's mission is to enhance the quality of life for those living with, through, and beyond cancer by supporting scientific research, educational community programs, and public awareness efforts. LAF secures contributions from the public by selling bracelets, from direct contributions, and from corporate donors. In 2006, LAF raised $36 million, of which $10.2 million came from special events, $9.5 million from contributions, and $7.3 million from royalties. Some contributions come from the sales of yellow Livestrong wristbands at $1 each. The foundation had net assets exceeding $50 million in 2007. Due to its high efficiency and effectiveness, Charity Navigator (**http://www.charitynavigator. org**) has given LAF a three-star rating.[1]

In this chapter, we will study several issues relating to the interaction of marketing with overall society, as well as with consumers. We will look again at business responses to social responsibility.

Chapter Objectives

1. To consider the impact of marketing on society
2. To examine social responsibility and weigh its benefits and costs
3. To look into the role of ethics in marketing
4. To explore consumerism and describe the consumer bill of rights
5. To discuss the responses of manufacturers, retailers, and trade associations to consumerism and study the current role of consumerism

5-1   OVERVIEW

Individually (at the company level) and collectively (at the industry level), the activities involved with marketing goods, services, organizations, people, places, and ideas strongly

---

[1] Various company and other sources.

influence society. They have the potential for both positive and negative consequences, regarding such factors as these:

- The quality of life (standard of living)
- Natural resources, the landscape, and environmental pollution
- Consumer expectations and satisfaction with goods, services, and so on
- Consumer choice
- Innovation
- Product design and safety
- Product durability
- Product and distribution costs
- Product availability
- Communications with consumers
- Final prices
- Competition
- Employment
- Deceptive actions

> Marketing can have both a positive and a negative impact on society.

In the United States and many other highly industrialized nations, marketing practices have made a variety of goods and services available at rather low prices and at convenient locations. These include food products, motor vehicles, telecommunications services, clothing, entertainment, books, insurance, banking and other financial services, audio and video equipment, furniture, and PCs.

At the same time, the lesser use of modern marketing practices in some parts of the world has often led to fewer product choices, higher prices, and less convenient shopping. For example,

> In Africa, consumption issues cannot be separated from basic development challenges such as poverty alleviation, access to basic services, gender inequality, environmental protection, and the long-term sustainable development goals. African economies are still developing and the struggle to attain such basic goods and services including food, clean water, sanitation and shelter remains largely an un-reached goal for many of its 700 million consumers. Lifestyles, human behavior, and consumption patterns are affected by most of these development challenges. Therefore sustainable consumption programs are needed to equip consumers with tools and opportunities needed.[2]

Yet, even in the United States and other nations where marketing is quite advanced, marketing activities can create unrealistic consumer expectations, result in minor but costly product design changes, and adversely affect the environment. Thus, people's perceptions of marketing are mixed, at best. Over the years, studies have shown that many people feel cheated in their purchases due to deception, the lack of proper information, high-pressure sales pitches, and other tactics. Consumers may also believe they are being "ripped off" when prices are increased. And waiting in store lines and poor customer service are two more key areas of consumer unhappiness.

Consumer displeasure is not always transmitted to companies. People may just decide not to buy a product and privately complain to friends. Usually, only a small percentage of disgruntled consumers take time to complain to sellers. The true level of dissatisfaction is hidden. However, few people who are displeased, but do not complain, buy a product again from the same firm. In contrast, many who complain and have their complaints resolved properly do buy again:

> Statistics show that only 4 percent of unhappy customers actually complain to the firms responsible for the bad service experiences. Rather than complain to companies, unhappy customers, on average, tell 10 relatives, friends, and even strangers about their negative

---

[2] Cathy Rutivi, "Sustainable Lifestyles/Consumption from an African Consumer Perspective," Consumers International: Fifth African Roundtable on Sustainable Consumption and Production (June 2008).

experiences. And 13 percent of them will tell 20 other people! This is justification for the "encourage customer complaints" mantra. If you don't make it easy for customers to complain, you will not hear about most of their unhappy experiences. Remember the old saying, "complaints are gifts, or opportunities?" Without the complaints, you don't have the opportunity to turn a negative into a positive for unhappy customers. Furthermore, and just as important, you don't have the opportunity to identify problems that could be fixed, thus preventing other customers from experiencing the same negative situation.[3]

In this chapter, we divide our discussion into three broad areas: social responsibility—addressing issues concerning the general public and the environment, employees, channel members, stockholders, and competitors; ethics—knowing and doing what is morally correct, with regard to society in general and individual consumers; and consumerism—focusing on the rights of consumers.

5-2   SOCIAL RESPONSIBILITY

> Social responsibility aids society. The **socioecological view of marketing** considers voluntary and involuntary consumers.

Social responsibility is a concern for "the consequences of a person's or firm's acts as they might affect the interests of others."[4] Corporate social responsibility means weighing the impact of company actions and behaving in a way that balances short-term profit needs with long-term societal needs. This calls for firms to be accountable to society and for consumers to act responsibly—by disposing of trash properly, wearing seat belts, not driving after drinking, and not being abusive to salespeople. See Figure 5-1.

From a marketing perspective, social responsibility also encompasses the *socioecological view of marketing*. According to this view, firms, their customers, and others should consider all the stages in a product's life span in developing, selling, purchasing, using, and disposing of that product. And the interests of everyone affected by a good's or service's use, including the involuntary consumers who must share the consequences of someone else's behavior, should be weighed. For example, how much of a scarce resource should a firm use in making a product? What should be the rights and responsibilities of smokers and nonsmokers (as involuntary consumers) to one another?

As two observers astutely noted, social responsibility

> calls upon marketers to balance three considerations in setting their marketing policies: company profits, consumer wants satisfaction, and public interest. Originally, companies based their marketing decisions largely on immediate company profit calculations ignoring public interests. They then began to recognize the long-run importance of satisfying consumer wants, and this introduced the marketing concept. Now they are beginning to factor in society's interest in their decision making.[5]

To respond to the socioecological view of marketing, many firms now use "design for disassembly" (DFD), whereby products are designed to be disassembled in a more environmentally friendly manner once they outlive their usefulness. These firms use fewer parts and less material, and recycle more materials. For example, Hewlett-Packard (**http://www.hp.com**) is quite involved with DFD: The company "now uses a common screw form factor all the way through. In the good old days, subassemblies might have been held together with a Phillips head screw; main assemblies might have been held together with a flathead or a torque screw. So what we found in dissembling is that the person had to keep switching screw drivers." Desktop PC cases for desktop PCs were joined together with five screws. "Today, a lot of business PCs have a latch where you

---

[3] Donna M. Long, "Encourage Consumer Complaints," **http://www.learningjourneyinc.com/nl/august_2006_cs.htm** (August 2006).

[4] Adapted by the authors from "Dictionary," **http://www.marketingpower.com/_layouts/Dictionary.aspx?dLetter=S** (March 22, 2009).

[5] Bernadette D'Silva and Stephen D'Silva, "Use of Societal Concept of Marketing in Corporate Image Building," **http://www.indiainfoline.com** (November 11, 2004).

Figure 5-1

The Positive Effects of Social Responsibility

Source: Reprinted by permission.

pull the latch and the whole side comes off." Battery covers are now built into the battery. HP also uses less plastic and more metal (which is easier to recycle).[6]

At times, social responsibility poses dilemmas for firms and/or their customers because popular goods and services may have potential adverse effects on consumer or societal well-being. Examples of items that pose such dilemmas are tobacco products, no-return beverage containers, food with high taste appeal but low nutritional content, crash diet plans, and liquor.

Until the 1960s, such resources as air, water, and energy were generally seen as limitless. Responsibility to the general public was rarely considered. Many firms now realize they should be responsive to the general public and the environment, employees, channel members, stockholders, and competitors, as well as customers. Table 5-1 shows socially responsible marketing in these areas.

This is how Johnson & Johnson (**http://www.jnj.com**) views its societal role, as highlighted in Figure 5-2. This credo was first enunciated in 1943:

> We believe our first responsibility is to the doctors, nurses, and patients, to mothers and fathers and all others who use our products and services. In meeting their needs, everything we do must be of high quality. We must constantly strive to reduce our costs in order to

[6] Doug Smock, "Efforts Grow to Design for Disassembly," **http://www.designnews.com/index.asp? layout=articlePrint&articleID=CA6496975** (November 19, 2007).

Table 5-1	Illustrations of Socially Responsible Marketing Practices

Regarding the General Public and the Environment
Community involvement
Contributions to nonprofit organizations
Hiring hard-core unemployed
Product recycling
Eliminating offensive signs and billboards
Properly disposing of waste materials
Using goods and services requiring low levels of environmental resources

Regarding Employees
Ample internal communications
Employee empowerment allowed
Employee training about social issues and appropriate responses to them
No reprisals against employees who uncover questionable company policies
Recognizing socially responsible employees

Regarding Channel Members
Honoring both verbal and written commitments
Fairly distributing scarce goods and services
Accepting reasonable requests by channel members
Encouraging channel members to act responsibly
Not coercing channel members
Cooperative programs addressed to the general public and the environment

Regarding Stockholders
Honest reporting and financial disclosure
Publicity about company activities
Stockholder participation in setting socially responsible policy
Explaining social issues affecting the company
Earning a responsible profit

Regarding Competitors
Adhering to high standards of performance
No illegal or unethical acts to hinder competitors
Cooperative programs for the general public and environment
No actions that would lead competitors to waste resources

maintain reasonable prices. Customers' orders must be serviced promptly and accurately. Our suppliers and distributors must have an opportunity to make a fair profit.

We are responsible to our employees, the men and women who work with us throughout the world. Everyone must be considered as an individual. We must respect their dignity and recognize their merit. They must have a sense of security in their jobs. Compensation must be fair and adequate, and working conditions clean, orderly, and safe. We must be mindful of ways to help our employees fulfill their family responsibilities. Employees must feel free to make suggestions and complaints. There must be equal opportunity for employment, development, and advancement for those qualified. We must provide competent management, and their actions must be just and ethical.

We are responsible to the communities in which we live and work and to the world community as well. We must be good citizens—support good works and charities and bear our fair share of taxes. We must encourage civic improvements and better health and education. We must maintain in good order the property we are privileged to use, protecting the environment and natural resources.

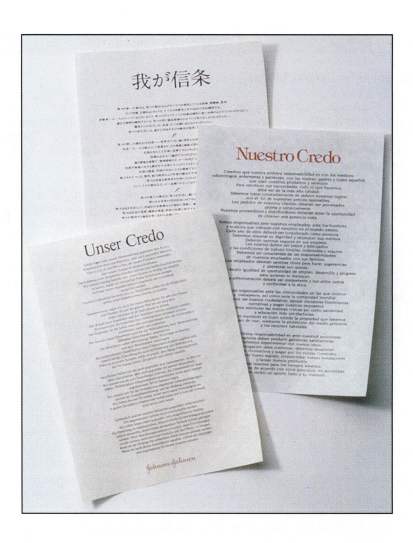

Figure 5-2

Johnson & Johnson's Global Social Responsibility Credo

At Johnson & Johnson, "A shared system of values, known as Our Credo, serves as a guide for all who are part of the Johnson & Johnson Family of Companies. The Credo can be found in 36 languages, each expressing the responsibilities we have to our customers, employees, communities, and stockholders." All of the various language versions of the credo are available at the company Web site (**http://www.jnj.com**).

Source: © Johnson & Johnson. Reprinted by permission.

Our final responsibility is to our stockholders. Business must make a sound profit. We must experiment with new ideas. Research must be carried on, innovative programs developed, and mistakes paid for. New equipment must be purchased, new facilities provided, and new products launched. Reserves must be created to provide for adverse times. When we operate according to these principles, the stockholders should realize a fair return.[7]

Company and consumer activities have a significant impact on natural resources, the landscape, pollution, and planned obsolescence. These areas are discussed next.

5-2a Natural Resources

Today, we are aware that our global supply of natural resources is not unlimited. Both consumer behavior and marketing practices contribute to some resource shortages. Nonetheless, Americans annually discard 1,650 pounds of trash per person—including large amounts of paper, food, aluminum, plastic, tires, furniture, and clothing. Packaging is an especially big component of trash. How do other nations compare? Australians discard 1,525 pounds per person, the Germans 1,325 pounds, the British 1,280 pounds, the French 1,190 pounds, and the Japanese 880 pounds. In the less-industrialized Mexico, the amount is 750 pounds.[8] The U.S. Environmental Protection Agency (EPA) even has an entire Web site devoted to municipal solid waste (**http://www.epa.gov/epaoswer/non-hw/muncpl**).

> Resource depletion can be slowed by reducing consumption, improving efficiency, limiting disposables, and lengthening products' lives.

[7] "Our Credo Values," **http://www.jnj.com/connect/about-jnj/jnj-credo** (n.d.).

[8] *Environment at a Glance: OECD Environmental Indicators*, OECD, Paris, 2006.

Ethical Issues in Marketing

U.S. Entrepreneurs Seek to Help Solve Social Problems

For several years, a growing number of U.S. entrepreneurs have invested in businesses that focus on solving social problems in poor countries. Marketing experts attribute this trend to increased media attention on global social problems, as well as the development of foundations by billionaires. Let's look at how two U.S. entrepreneurial efforts are making a difference.

Dr. Jordan Kassalow, an eye physician with considerable experience in impoverished countries, found through his experiences that most of his patients needed basic reading glasses, not sophisticated eye surgery. Kassalow co-founded the Scojo Foundation, a nonprofit organization, to identify, train, and finance local businesspeople to sell affordable eyeglasses in especially poor areas of the world. Scojo recently changed its name to VisionSpring (http://www.visionspring.org). The organization's target market consists of workers in rural areas who need corrected vision to continue to make a living. Many of these people earn between $1 and $4 a day, and most reside in 13 counties in South Asia, Latin America, and Africa. VisionSpring has sold more than 100,000 pair of affordable glasses, trained more than 1,000 VisionSpring entrepreneurs, and referred more than 90,000 people for advanced eye care.

KickStart (http://www.kick-start.org) is a San Francisco-based nonprofit group that develops and markets new technologies in Africa. These low-cost technologies (such as pumps and oilseed presses) are sold to small businesses. KickStart estimates that the equipment it has sells to more than 64,000 new businesses, which then generate in excess of $80 million in profits annually.

Sources: Based on material in "KickStart: The Tools to End Poverty," http://www.kickstart.org (June 30, 2008); and "Scojo Foundation Changes Name to VisionSpring, Launches $5 Million Prospectus to Build Sustainable Social Enterprise," http://www.visionspring.org (June 9, 2008).

Although Americans spend billions of dollars yearly on garbage collection and disposal—and thousands of curbside recycling programs exist nationwide—only 30 percent of U.S. trash is actually recycled (up from 6 percent in 1960). The world's most ambitious recycling program is in Germany; 72 percent of all beverage containers other than milk must be recycled by law. Germany's Ordinance on the Avoidance of Packaging Waste requires manufacturers and distributors to take back all transport packaging; and retailers are required to have bins for consumers to return all secondary packaging.[9]

Natural resource depletion can be reduced if the consumption of scarce materials is lessened and more efficient alternatives are chosen; fewer disposable items—such as cans, pens, and lighters—are bought; products are given longer life spans; and styles are changed less frequently. Convenient recycling and repair facilities, better trade-in arrangements, such common facilities as apartments (that share laundry rooms, etc.), and simpler packaging can also contribute to better resource use.

Progressive actions require cooperation among business, stockholders, government, employees, the general public, consumers, and others. They also involve changes in lifestyles and corporate ingenuity. As the EPA suggests, businesses and consumers can "produce less waste by practicing the 3Rs: Reduce the amount and toxicity of trash you discard. Reuse containers and products; repair what is broken or give it to someone who can repair it. Recycle as much as possible, which includes buying products with recycled content."[10] See Figure 5-3.

5-2b The Landscape

Garbage dumps and landfills, discarded beverage containers, and abandoned cars are examples of items marring the landscape.

---

[9] "Germany, Garbage, and the Green Dot: Challenging the Throwaway Society," http://www.informinc.org/xsum_greendot.php (June 11, 2009).

[10] "Reduce, Reuse, and Recycle," http://www.epa.gov/epaoswer/non-hw/muncpl/reduce.htm (June 11, 2009).

Figure 5-3

Protecting Scarce Resources

Source: Reprinted by permission of the American Forest and Paper Association.

In the United States, 55 percent of discarded materials are sent to dumps and landfills (the rest is recycled or burned). However, many communities no longer allow new dumps and landfills, existing ones are closing for environmental reasons (there are now 1,750 landfills, down from 8,000 at 1988), and recycling is being stepped up at existing dumps and landfills.[11] Some landfill areas in Europe and Japan are at capacity—hence, those countries have a greater interest there in recycling and incineration.

When no-return bottles and cans were developed, littering at roadsides and other areas became a problem. To reduce litter, many states and localities have laws requiring deposit fees that are refunded when consumers return empty containers. Some manufacturers and retailers feel the laws unfairly hold them responsible for container disposal, as littering is done by consumers—not them. Also, labor and recycling costs associated with container returns have led to slightly higher beverage prices. Container laws are

> Dumps and littering have become major factors in marring the landscape. Various communities have enacted rules to lessen them.

moderately effective; consumers still must be better educated as to the value of proper disposal.

Cars are sometimes abandoned on streets, where they are then stripped of usable parts. One suggestion to cover the disposal of a car is to include an amount in its original price or in a transfer tax. For example, Maryland has a small fee on title transfers to aid in the removal of abandoned cars.

Other ways to reduce the marring of the landscape include limits or bans on billboards and roadside signs, fines for littering, and better trade-ins for autos and appliances. Neighborhood associations, merchant self-regulation, area planning and zoning, and consumer education can also improve appreciation for the landscape. This is a cooperative effort. A merchant cleanup patrol cannot easily overcome pedestrians who throw litter on the street. Here is what Nike (**http://www.nike.com**) is doing to help:

> Every year, across the globe, millions of pairs of athletic shoes end up in landfills or are disposed of in some other way. That's a lot of shoes going to waste. So, we created the Nike Reuse-A-Shoe program in 1990. Since then, we've recycled more than 21 million pairs of athletic shoes and contributed to more than 265 sport surfaces to provide places to play for kids as part of Let Me Play (**http://www.letmeplay.com**), Nike's global community investment program. Reuse-A-Shoe collects worn-out athletic shoes of any brand, including end of life shoes collected through recycling programs, special events, and stores, shoes that are returned from retailers due to a material flaw, and even counterfeit shoes. We also recycle much of our scrap material left over from making Nike footwear. The shoes and shoe materials are ground up and purified to become a material we call Nike Grind. We then partner with leading sports-surfacing companies to incorporate Nike Grind into basketball and tennis courts, running tracks, soccer fields, fitness flooring, and playground safety surfaces.[12]

5-2c Environmental Pollution

Dangerous pollutants must be reduced and substitutes found. Environmental pollution can be generated by spray-can propellants, ocean dumping of industrial waste, lead from gas and paint, pesticides, sulfur oxide and other factory emissions, improper disposal of garbage, and other pollutants. Consider this:

> Through improved treatment and disposal, most industrialized countries have reduced the effects of many pollutants, thus improving water quality. Yet, contaminants from agriculture and development activities in watersheds have kept the cleanup from being complete. In general, national water cleanup programs have not been effective in reducing pollutants such as nutrients, sediments, and toxics that come in runoff from agriculture, storm water, mining, and oil and gas operations. In most developing countries, pollution sources such as sewage and pesticides have degraded water quality, particularly near urban industrial centers and agricultural areas. A lot of wastewater in developing countries is discharged directly to rivers and streams without any waste processing treatment.[13]

Government and industry in the United States, Western Europe, and Japan devote a combined total of several hundred billion dollars annually to environmental protection. And antipollution spending has risen in many less-developed nations in Latin America, Asia, and Africa. The EPA (**http://www.epa.gov**) is the major U.S. government agency involved with pollution; a number of state agencies are also active in this area. Numerous other nations have their own government agencies to deal with the issue.

Both government and business actions are needed to reduce dangerous environmental pollution.

[12] "Reuse-A-Shoe and Nike Grind," **http://www.nikebiz.com/responsibility/community_programs/reuse_a_shoe.html** (May 17, 2009).

[13] Carmen Revenga and Greg Mock, "Dirty Water: Pollution Problems Persist," **http://earthtrends.wri.org/features/view_feature.cfm?theme=2&fid=16** (October 2000).

These are among the voluntary activities of companies and associations:

- New PCs, printers, monitors, and other electronic devices automatically "power down" when not in use to reduce air pollution and conserve energy.
- The American Chemistry Council (**http://www.americanchemistry.com**) has worked with the EPA to keep hazardous compounds out of the environment.
- 3M spends part of its research-and-development budget on environmental protection projects; it has a Web site on sustainability (**http://solutions.3m.com/wps/portal/3M/en_US/global/sustainability**).
- Japan's Ebara Corporation (**http://www.ebara.co.jp/en**) uses its own technology to remove harmful sulphur dioxides and nitrogen oxides from power plants more efficiently.
- Nearly 40 leading firms are members of the Global Environmental Management Initiative (**http://www.gemi.org**), designed to foster an exchange of data about environmental protection programs.
- The Coalition for Environmentally Responsible Economies (**http://www.ceres.org**) is a nonprofit group of investors, public pension funds, foundations, unions, and environmental, religious, and public interest groups working with business to enhance corporate environmental responsibility worldwide.

5-2d   Planned Obsolescence

Planned obsolescence is a marketing practice that capitalizes on short-run material wearout, style changes, and functional product changes.

In *material planned obsolescence*, firms choose materials and components that are subject to comparatively early breakage, wear, rot, or corrosion. For example, the makers of disposable lighters and razors use this form of planned obsolescence in a constructive manner by offering inexpensive, short-life, convenient products. However, resistance is growing to material planned obsolescence because of its effects on natural resources and the landscape.

In *style planned obsolescence*, a firm makes minor changes to differentiate the new year's offering from the prior year's. Because some people are style-conscious, they will discard old items while they are still functional so as to acquire new ones with more status. This is common with fashion items and cars.

With *functional planned obsolescence*, a firm introduces new product features or improvements to generate consumer dissatisfaction with currently owned products. Sometimes, features or improvements may have been withheld from an earlier model to gain faster repurchases. A style change may accompany a functional one to raise consumer awareness of a "new" product. This form of planned obsolescence occurs most often with high-tech items such as computers.

Marketers reply to criticism thusly: Planned obsolescence is responsive to people's desires as to prices, styles, and features and is not coercive; without product turnover, people would be disenchanted by the lack of choices; consumers like disposable items and often discard them before they lose their effectiveness; firms use materials that reduce prices; competition requires firms to offer the best products possible and not hold back improvements; and, for such items as clothing, people desire regular style changes. As Michael Dell once said, "There's no such thing at Dell (**http://www.dell.com**) as finished, done, good enough. We believe we can improve things all the time, so we constantly look for opportunities."[14]

Several firms have enacted innovative strategies with regard to planned obsolescence. Kodak (**http://www.kodak.com**) recycles single-use disposable cameras. Canon (**http://www.canon.com**) has a factory in China to recondition and refill used copier cartridges.

> **Planned obsolescence** can involve materials, styles, and functions.

---

[14] Kevin McKean, "Planned Obsolescence," **http://www.infoworld.com/article/03/09/26/38OPeditor_1.html** (September 26, 2003).

SKF of Sweden (**http://www.skf.com**) is a worldwide bearings maker; to increase the life of its products, it has added more preventative maintenance services.

5-2e   The Benefits and Costs of Social Responsibility

Socially responsible actions have both benefits and costs. Among the benefits are improved worker and public health, as reflected in fewer and less severe accidents, longer life spans, and less disease; cleaner air; better resource use; economic growth; a better business image; an educated public; government cooperation; an attractive, safe environment; an enhanced standard of living; and self-satisfaction for the firm. Many of these benefits cannot be quantified. Nonetheless, expectations are that the U.S. Clean Air Act (**http://www.epa.gov/oar/caa/index.html**) and the laws of other nations will ultimately save thousands and thousands of lives each year, protect food crops, reduce medical costs, and lead to clearer skies.

Although some social-responsibility expenditures are borne by a broad cross section of firms and the general public (via taxes and higher prices), the benefits of many environmental and other programs are enjoyed primarily by those living or working in affected areas. The costs of socially responsible actions can be high; U.S. environmental-protection spending is nearly 2 percent of the annual gross domestic product. Various environmentally questionable products that are efficient have been greatly modified or removed from the marketplace, such as leaded gasoline. Because of various legal restrictions and fears of lawsuits, new-product planning tends to be more conservative; and resources are often allotted to prevention rather than invention. Furthermore, trade-offs have to be made in determining which programs are more deserving of funding. See Figure 5-4.

To be effective, all parties must partake in socially responsible efforts—sharing benefits and costs. This means business, consumers, government, channel members, and others. Sometimes, tragic events bring people together. For example, in September 2005, after the Hurricane Katrina disaster along the U.S. Gulf Coast, the American

> Social responsibility has benefits as well as costs; these need to be balanced.

Figure 5-4

The Benefits and Costs of Social Responsibility

Benefits	Costs
Worker and public health	Unequal distribution of benefits
Cleaner air	Dollar costs
Efficient use of resources	Removal of some goods from the market
Economic growth	Conservative product planning
Improved business image	Resources allocated to prevention rather than invention
Government cooperation	
Public education	
Attractive environment	
Better standard of living	
Self-satisfaction of firm	

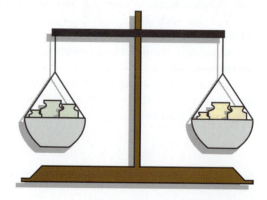

Red Cross (**http://www.redcross.org**) received nearly $1 billion in contributions from hundreds of thousands of private citizens around the world, and numerous businesses contributed large sums of money, goods, and services for relief, relocation, and rebuilding efforts.

5-3 ETHICS

In any marketing situation, ***ethical behavior*** based on honest and proper conduct ("what is right" and "what is wrong") should be followed. This applies both to situations involving company actions that affect the general public, employees, channel members, stockholders, and/or competitors and to situations involving company dealings with consumers.

> **Ethical behavior** involves honest and proper conduct.

Figure 5-5 outlines a framework for ethical/unethical decision making. An individual is affected by his or her background and experiences, social influences, and job. When an ethical dilemma occurs, these factors come into play (consciously or subconsciously). For each ethically questionable issue, the person considers alternative actions, makes a decision, and acts accordingly. He or she then faces the consequences, which affect future decisions. The ethics code of the American Marketing Association (**http://www.marketingpower.com/aboutama/pages/statementofethics.aspx**) is shown in Figure 5-6.

Of great importance in studying ethics are answers to these two questions: How do people determine whether an act is ethical or unethical? Why do they act ethically or unethically?[15] People *determine* (learn) whether or not given actions are ethical through their upbringing, education, job environment, and life-long experiences—and others' responses to their behavior. People may also apply their own cognitive reasoning skills to decide what is morally acceptable. Individuals *act* ethically or unethically based on their expectations of the rewards or punishments—financial, social, and so forth—flowing from their actions. They consider both the magnitude of the rewards or punishments (such as the size of a raise or the maximum fine that could be imposed on a company) and the likelihood of their occurrence (such as the probability of getting a large raise or having a large fine imposed on the firm).

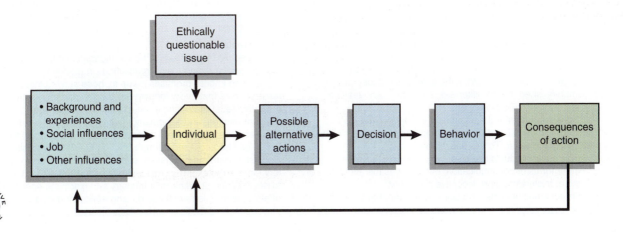

Figure 5-5

A Framework for Ethical/Unethical Decision Making

---

[15] Shelby D. Hunt, "Foundations of the Hunt-Vitell Theory of Ethics," presented at the 1995 AMA Faculty Consortium on Ethics and Social Responsibility in Marketing (Hempstead, NY: Hofstra University).

Preamble

The American Marketing Association commits itself to promoting the highest standard of professional ethical norms and values for its members (practitioners, academics, and students). Norms are established standards of conduct that are expected and maintained by society and/or professional organizations. Values represent the collective conception of what communities find desirable, important, and morally proper. Values also serve as the criteria for evaluating our own personal actions and the actions of others. As marketers, we must recognize that we not only serve our organizations but also act as stewards of society in creating, facilitating, and executing the transactions that are part of the greater economy. In this role, marketers are expected to embrace the highest professional ethical norms and the ethical values implied by our responsibility toward stakeholders (e.g., customers, employees, investors, peers, channel members, regulators, and the host community).

Ethical norms

As marketers, we must:

- Do no harm. This means actively adding value to our organizations and customers through our work, by embodying high ethical standards and adhering to all applicable laws and regulations in the choices we make.
- Foster trust in the marketing system. This means striving for good faith and fair dealing so as to contribute toward the efficacy of the exchange process. Pricing, communication, and delivery of products/services should avoid deception.
- Embrace ethical values. This means building relationships and fostering consumer confidence in the integrity of marketing by affirming these core values: honesty, responsibility, fairness, respect, transparency, and citizenship.

Ethical values

Honesty – to be forthright in dealings with customers and stakeholders. To this end, we will:

- Strive to be truthful in all situations and at all times.
- Offer products of value that do what we claim in our communications.
- Stand behind our products if they fail to deliver their claimed benefits.
- Honor our explicit and implicit commitments and promises.

Responsibility – to accept the consequences of our marketing decisions and strategies. To this end, we will:

- Strive to serve the needs of customers.
- Avoid using coercion with all stakeholders.
- Acknowledge the social obligations to stakeholders that come with increased marketing and economic power.
- Recognize our special commitments to vulnerable market segments such as children, the elderly, the economically impoverished, market illiterates, and others who may be substantially disadvantaged.
- Consider the natural environment in our decision-making.

Fairness – to try to balance justly the needs of the buyer with the interests of the seller. To this end, we will:

- Represent products in a clear way in selling, advertising, and other forms of communication; this includes the avoidance of false, misleading, and deceptive promotion.
- Reject manipulations, and sales tactics that harm customer trust.

- Refuse to engage in price fixing, predatory pricing, price gouging, or "bait-and-switch" tactics.
- Avoid knowing participation in conflicts of interest.
- Seek to protect the private information of customers, employees, and partners.

Respect – to acknowledge the basic human dignity of all stakeholders. To this end, we will:

- Value individual differences and will avoid stereotyping customers or depicting demographic groups (e.g., gender, race, sexual orientation) in a negative or dehumanizing way in promotions.
- Listen to the needs of customers and make all reasonable efforts to monitor and improve their satisfaction on an ongoing basis.
- Make every effort to understand and treat respectfully buyers, suppliers, intermediaries, and distributors from all cultures.
- Acknowledge the contributions of others, such as consultants, employees, and coworkers, to marketing endeavors.
- Treat everyone, including our competitors, as we would wish to be treated.

Transparency – to create a spirit of openness in marketing operations. To this end, we will:

- Strive to communicate clearly with all constituencies.
- Accept constructive criticism from customers and other stakeholders.
- Explain and take appropriate action regarding significant product or service risks, component substitutions, or other foreseeable eventualities that could affect customers or their perception of the purchase decision.
- Disclose list prices and terms of financing as well as available price deals and adjustments.

Citizenship – to fulfill the economic, legal, philanthropic, and societal responsibilities that serve stakeholders. To this end, we will:

- Strive to protect the ecological environment in the execution of marketing campaigns.
- Give back to the community through volunteerism and charitable donations.
- Work to contribute to the overall betterment of marketing and its reputation.
- Call upon supply chain members to ensure that trade is fair for all participants, including producers in developing countries.

Implementation

We expect AMA members to be courageous and proactive in leading and/or aiding their organizations in the fulfillment of the explicit and implicit promises made to those stakeholders. Finally, we recognize that every industry sector and marketing sub-discipline (e.g., marketing research, E-commerce, Internet selling, direct marketing, and advertising) has its own specific ethical issues that require policies and commentary. An array of such codes can be accessed through links on the AMA Web site. Consistent with the principle of subsidiarity (solving issues at the level where the expertise resides), we encourage all such groups to develop and/or refine their industry and discipline-specific codes of ethics to supplement these guiding ethical norms, and values.

Figure 5-6

The American Marketing Association's Code of Ethics

Source: © American Marketing Association. Reprinted with permission from American Marketing Association.

Various ethical theories seek to explain why people and organizations act in particular ways. Here are four of them, applied to marketing:

- *Egoism*—a theory asserting that individuals act exclusively in their own self-interest. Example: A product manager postpones investing in improvements for a mature product because he or she expects to be promoted within the next six months and wants to maximize short-term profits.
- *Utilitarianism*—a theory asserting that individual and organizational actions are proper only if they yield the greatest good for the most people (the highest net benefit). Example: A pharmaceutical company markets an FDA-approved drug with some side effects as long as it helps more people combat a particular disease than the number affected by the (minor) side effect.
- *Duty-based*—a theory asserting that the rightness of an action is not based on its consequences, but rather is based on the premise that certain actions are proper because they stem from basic obligations. Example: A supermarket chain sets below-average prices in a low-income area even though this adversely affects company profits in that community.
- *Virtue ethics*—a theory asserting that actions should be guided by an individual's or organization's seeking goodness and virtue ("living a good life"). Example: A virtuous firm is totally truthful in its ads, packaging, and selling efforts, and does not use manipulative appeals to persuade customers.[16]

Ethical issues in marketing can generally be divided into two categories: process-related and product-related.[17] ***Process-related ethical issues*** involve "the unethical use of marketing strategies or tactics." Examples include dishonest advertising, price fixing, selling products overseas that have been found unsafe in the United States, and bribing purchasing agents of large customers. ***Product-related ethical issues*** involve "the ethical appropriateness of marketing certain products." For example, should tobacco products, sugar-coated cereals, and political candidates be marketed? More specifically, should cigarettes be sold? Should there be restrictions on their sales? Should cigarette ads be allowed? Should cigarette taxes be raised to dampen use? Should smoking be banned in offices, restaurants, and planes?

To maintain the highest possible ethical conduct by employees, senior executives must make a major commitment to ethics, communicate standards of conduct to each employee, reward ethical behavior, and discourage unethical behavior. This example sums up the intricacy of many ethical issues for marketers:

> Information may or may not affect consumption, but one ethical justification given for market systems is that they leave final product selections to informed customers. Ethical concerns arise, however, as to how information is presented. What if information is expressed in a persuasive manner? There is no generally accepted theory of ethics with regard to marketing persuasion, and persuasion is prevalent in marketing. Marketing persuasion spreads through competition. In addition, marketers, as experts in their discipline, often know better what will fulfill customers' needs than do the customers. Do customers want to be persuaded by marketers when something is in the marketers' own best interest? Will customers think this ethical? Most people want to feel that their decisions are their own—with no undue influence from others.[18]

Next, we examine ethics from four vantage points: a business perspective, a consumer perspective, a global perspective, and the teachability of ethics.

---

[16] Gene R. Laczniak and Patrick E. Murphy, *Ethical Marketing Decisions: The Higher Road* (Needham Heights, MA: Allyn & Bacon, 1993), pp. 28–42.

[17] Gene R. Laczniak, Robert F. Lusch, and William A. Strang, "Ethical Marketing: Perceptions of Economic Goods and Social Problems," *Journal of Macromarketing*, Vol. 1 (Spring 1981), p. 49.

[18] Dillard B. Tinsley, "Ethics Can Be Gauged by Three Key Rules," *Marketing News* (September 1, 2003), p. 24.

5-3a A Business Perspective

> Many companies have ethics codes; some have implicit standards.

Most firms in the U.S. *Fortune 500* have formal ethics codes. Some codes are general and resemble organizational mission statements; others are specific and operational. In contrast, French, British, and German firms are less apt to have formal codes; acceptable standards of behavior are more implied. The European Union has been working to clarify the latter situation.

One of the most complex aspects of business ethics is setting the boundaries as to what is ethical. To address this, the following scale was devised and tested with a variety of marketing personnel. The scale suggests that businesspeople make better decisions if they consider whether a marketing action (is):[19]

Fair	_ _ _ _ _	Unfair
Just	_ _ _ _ _	Unjust
Culturally Acceptable	_ _ _ _ _	Culturally Unacceptable
Violates an Unwritten Contract	_ _ _ _ _	Does Not Violate an Unwritten Contract
Traditionally Acceptable	_ _ _ _ _	Traditionally Unacceptable
Morally Right	_ _ _ _ _	Not Morally Right
Violates an Unspoken Promise	_ _ _ _ _	Does Not Violate an Unspoken Promise
Acceptable to My Family	_ _ _ _ _	Unacceptable to My Family

Here are examples showing business responses to ethical issues:

> Cause-related marketing has good and bad points.

- *Cause-related marketing* is a somewhat controversial practice wherein profit-oriented firms contribute specific amounts to given nonprofit organizations for each consumer purchase of certain goods and services during a special promotion (such as sponsorship of a sport for the Olympics). It has been used by such firms as American Express (**http://www.americanexpress.com**) and MasterCard (**http://www.mastercard.com**), and such nonprofits as the International Red Cross (**http://www.icrc.org**). Advocates feel cause-related marketing stimulates direct and indirect contributions and benefits the images of both the profit-oriented firms and the nonprofit institutions involved in it. Critics say there is too much commercialism by nonprofit groups and implicit endorsements for sponsor products.
- U.S.-based Arch Chemicals' (**http://www.archchemicals.com/Fed/Corporate/About/Ethics/letter.htm**) employees must adhere to these standards: "Arch Chemicals is a company of integrity, committed to the highest principles of ethical business behavior. Our customers, suppliers, communities, and shareholders know that they can trust us to do what we say. Our success as a company is built on this trust and on our personal and professional commitment to compete fairly and honestly, in full compliance with the laws and regulations wherever we do business. As we continue to expand our operations globally, we will be faced with an increasingly complex business and legal environment. For this reason, we must always operate under one set of standards—standards that are rooted in our Principles of Integrity and set forth in company policies and the Arch Code of Conduct."
- Mary Kay Inc. (**http://www.marykay.com**) "was one of the first companies to enact a comprehensive corporate recycling program and one of the first companies to ban product testing on laboratory animals" for cosmetics. The firm "has not conducted, or

[19] R. Eric Reidenbach, Donald P. Robin, and Lyndon Dawson, "An Application and Extension of a Multidimensional Ethics Scale to Selected Marketing Practices and Marketing Groups," *Journal of the Academy of Marketing Science*, Vol. 19 (Spring 1991), p. 84. See also Nhung Nguyen, M. Basuray, William Smith, Donald Kopka, and Donald McCulloh, "Moral Issues and Gender Differences in Ethical Judgment Using Reidenbach and Robin's (1990) Multidimensional Ethics Scale: Implications in Teaching of Business Ethics," *Journal of Business Ethics*, Vol. 77 (February 2008), pp. 417–430.

Global Marketing in Action

Modern Marketing Practices Come to India

For several decades after gaining its independence in 1947, the Indian government restricted market growth by such measures as retaining government ownership of companies in many important sectors of the economy, prohibiting foreign investment, developing overly restrictive licensing requirements for business, and restricting imports. Then, from the mid 1980s through the early 1990s, the licensing system was dismantled, government regulations in the information technology and communications sectors were liberalized, and foreign trade and investment barriers were reduced. As a result of these reforms, India's economy has become one of the world's largest as measured by purchasing power parity rates.

The number of Indians living below the poverty level has been reduced, and a large Indian middle class has emerged. The Indian economy has posted an average growth rate of more than 7 percent in the decade since 1997, reducing poverty by about 10 percentage points. India achieved 8.5 percent GDP growth rate in both 2006 and 2007.

Here is a summary of what Indian business leaders still need to do to adopt a more global mindset.

- Reduce labor laws that inhibit job creation in manufacturing and other areas where India should have a major advantage in the world economy
- Cut the bureaucracy that limits firms from more freely entering and exiting markets. Red tape is especially visible in the agricultural, retail, manufacturing, and transportation sectors of the Indian economy.
- Further reduce import tariffs and foreign investment regulations.
- Privatize government-owned firms in such major industries as energy and banking.

Source: Based on material in Ernesto Zedillo, "India Getting On Board," **http://www.forbes.com/forbes/2007/1029/029.html** (October 29, 2007).

---

requested on its behalf, any testing of products or ingredients on animals in more than 15 years and actively supports the research of alternative testing methods." Furthermore, "Mary Kay is an active member of the Personal Care Product Council (**http://www.personalcarecouncil.org**) and supports its Consumer Commitment Code, established to further strengthen industry safeguards for consumers."[20]

5-3b A Consumer Perspective

Just as business has a responsibility to act in an ethical and a societally oriented way, so do consumers. Their actions impact on businesses, other consumers, the general public, the environment, and so on. Ethical standards in marketing transactions can truly be maintained only if both sellers and buyers act in a mutually respectful, honest, fair, and responsible manner.[21]

> Consumers should act as ethically to businesses as they expect to be treated.

Yet, consumers may find it hard to decide what is acceptable—especially with regard to broad societal issues. Daniel Yankelovich (**http://www.dyg.com**), an expert in the area, says a society goes through seven stages to form a consensus on major issues (such as how to deal with health care for older people):

1. The public becomes aware of an issue, but citizens do not yet feel a pressing need to take action.
2. The public moves beyond awareness to a sense of urgency.

---

[20] "Being a Responsible Corporation," **http://www.marykay.com/content/company/beingresponsible.aspx** (March 28, 2009).

[21] For a good overview of the issues involved in consumer ethics, see Aviv Shoham, Ayalla Ruvio, and Moshe Davidow, "(Un)ethical Consumer Behavior: Robin Hoods Or Plain Hoods?" *Journal of Consumer Marketing*, Vol. 24 (Number 4, 2008), pp. 200–210; and Johannes Brinkmann and Ken Peattie, "Consumer Ethics Research: Reframing the Debate About Consumption for Good," *Electronic Journal of Business Ethics and Organization Studies*, http://ejbo. jyu.fi/pdf/ejbo_vol13_no1_pages_22-31.pdf, Vol. 13 (Number 1, 2008).

3. The public begins to look at alternatives for dealing with issues, converting free-floating concern into calls for action.
4. The public is resistant to costs and trade-offs.
5. The public considers the advantages and disadvantages of the available alternatives.
6. The public accepts an idea but is not yet ready to act on it.
7. The public accepts an idea both morally and emotionally.[22]

With regard to consumer perceptions about whether specific activities on their part are proper, consider the actions cited in Figure 5-7. Which of them would you, *as a consumer*, deem to be ethically acceptable? Which would be ethically wrong? What should be the ramifications for consumers engaging in acts that are ethically unacceptable?

5-3c A Global Perspective

Ethical standards can be tough to apply globally due to several factors: (1) Different societies have their own views of acceptable behavior for interpersonal conduct, communications, businesses, and other factors. (2) Misunderstandings may arise due to poor language translations. (3) In less-developed nations, there may be less concern for social and consumer issues than for improving industrialization. (4) Some national governments have questionable rules so as to protect domestic firms. (5) Executives are usually more

> Ethical decisions can be complicated on an international level.

Figure 5-7

Ethical Appropriateness of Selected Consumer Activities

Source: Figure devised by the authors using activities listed in James A. Muncy and Scott J. Vitell, "Consumer Ethics: An Investigation of the Ethical Beliefs of the Final Consumer," *Journal of Business Research,* Vol. 24 (June 1992), p. 303; Sam Fullerton, David Taylor, and B. C. Ghosh, "A Cross-Cultural Examination of Attitudes Towards Aberrant Consumer Behavior in the Marketplace: Some Preliminary Results from the USA, New Zealand, and Singapore," *Marketing Intelligence & Planning* , Vol. 15 (April-May 1997), p. 211; and Russell Belk, Timothy Devinney, and Gina Eckhardt, "Consumer Ethics Across Cultures," *Consumption, Markets, and Culture,* Vol. 8 (September 2005), pp. 275–289.

As a consumer, how would you rate these actions in terms of their ethical appropriateness? Use a scale from 1-10, with 1 being fully ethical and 10 being fully unethical.

Activities	Ratings
Being less than truthful on surveys	—
Changing price tags on merchandise in a retail store	—
Drinking a can of soda in a supermarket without paying for it	—
Exaggerating quality at a garage sale	—
Getting too much change and not saying anything	—
Giving misleading price information to a clerk for an unpriced item	—
Inflating an insurance claim	—
Joining a music club just to get some free CDs without any intention of buying	—
Observing someone shoplifting and ignoring it on a given shopping trip	—
Purchasing a counterfeit product	—
Purchasing a product made by underage workers	—
Purchasing a useful product that is environmentally questionable	—
Repeating store visits to buy more merchandise that is available in limited quantity	—
Reporting a lost item as "stolen" to an insurance company in order to collect money	—
Returning merchandise after wearing it and not liking it	—
Selling a frequent flier ticket	—
Stretching the truth on an income-tax return	—
Using a long-distance telephone access code that does not belong to you	—
Using computer software or games you did not buy	—

---

[22] Daniel Yankelovich, "The Seven Stages of Public Opinion," http://www.publicagenda.org/pages/seven-stages-public-opinion (March 28, 2009).

aware of ethical standards in their own nations than in foreign ones. (6) Global ethical disputes may be tough to mediate. Under whose jurisdiction are disagreements involving firms from separate nations?

Here are some perspectives on global ethical challenges:

- "U.S. officials say they will propose changes in accounting regulations to make U.S. businesses a more attractive investment overseas, but critics say the move could water down ethics regulations passed in the wake of the Enron collapse, according to a report from the *New York Times*. The Securities and Exchange Commission (**http://www.sec.gov**) is preparing a timetable to allow U.S. firms to shift to international accounting rules, a move that may allow for computation of higher rates of earnings, according to the *Times*. Critics warn that some international rules are weaker than U.S. regulations, allowing, for instance, sketchier disclosure about mortgage-backed securities, derivatives, and other complex investment vehicles at the vortex of the current housing crisis."[23]

- "Because ethics are a part of culture, to study ethical choices without considering the cultural context is not realistic. Differing cultural reactions to consumption practices would be expected, not only because moral values are socially and culturally constructed, but also because of cultural differences in social roles, gender roles, institutional structures, welfare expectations, laws, and traditional rights, privileges, and obligations. Culture filters perceptions of what is good or responsible consumption and what is perceived to be the consequences of violating moral norms. Due to varying concepts of what is good for the person and what is good for society, the judgment of what constitutes an ethical breach in the first place would be expected to vary greatly depending on cultural orientation."[24]

- The British version of the Motley Fool investment Web site (**http://www.fool.co.uk**) raised an emerging ethical-investment question: "Is it morally right to speculate on food? Rising food costs, sometimes called 'agflaton,' have been at least partly blamed on speculators—investors who, depending on their strategy, profit when food prices go up or down. Fool columnist Padraig O'Hannelly concludes that while speculators may profit from soaring prices, which are a direct result of food shortages, speculation does not have a cause-and-effect relationship to shortages. But he admits it's a complex area and invites readers to correct him if he's wrong by posting a response on the Fool site."[25]

Firms that market globally need to keep three points in mind: One, *core business values* provide the basis for worldwide ethics codes. These are company principles "that are so fundamental they will not be compromised" in any foreign markets. These include promise keeping, nondeception, the protection of societal and consumer rights, and to not knowingly do harm. Two, *peripheral business values* are less important to the firm and may be adjusted to foreign markets. These relate to local customs in buyer-seller exchanges, selling practices, and so on. Three, if possible, *ethnocentrism*—perceiving other nations' moral standards in terms of one's own country—must be avoided.[26]

Here are some suggestions for firms to engage in globally ethical practices: Include international personnel when setting and enacting ethical practices, and listen to diverse views. View globally ethical practices as a competitive advantage that can be communicated to consumers, the general public, and others. Do not rely only on the law in

[23] "Reports Focus on Ethics in Business and Finance," **http://www.globalethics.org/newsline/2008/07/07/business-and-finance** (July 7, 2008).

[24] Russell Belk, Timothy Devinney, and Gina Eckhardt, "Consumer Ethics Across Cultures," *Consumption, Markets, and Culture*, Vol. 8 (September 2005), pp. 275–289.

[25] "Ethical Investment Dilemmas Probed by World Press," **http://www.globalethics.org/newsline/2008/07/14/investment-dilemmas** (July 14, 2008).

[26] Gene R. Laczniak, "Observations Concerning International Marketing Ethics," presented at the 1995 AMA Faculty Consortium on Ethics and Social Responsibility in Marketing (Hempstead, NY: Hofstra University).

countries where ethical practices are not codified. Use ethical compliance officials wherever business is done. Print ethics codes in various languages. Do not presume that people in other countries are less interested in ethical behavior than those in the home market.[27]

5-3d   The Teachability of Ethics

Given the impact of societal values, peer pressure, self-interests and personal ambitions (and fear of failure), and other factors on people's sense of ethically acceptable behavior, considerable debate has ensued as to whether ethics can be taught.[28] As one expert noted: "A successful ethics curriculum does not guarantee that participants will never behave immorally. Not even churches or prisons boast that kind of effectiveness. So why should we expect it of an ethics class? What we expect is that when students complete an ethics class, they will approach moral problems with more thoughtfulness, as well as be more likely to resolve these problems in the right way. The goal is improvement, not perfection."[29]

Despite the question as to whether ethics can be taught, the following can be transmitted to people so that their ethical perceptions can be positively influenced:

> **Ethical concepts can be communicated.**

- Clear ethics codes
- Role models of ethical people
- Wide-ranging examples of ethical and unethical behavior
- Specified punishments if ethical behavior is not followed
- The vigilance of professors and top management regarding such issues as cheating on tests, misleading customers, and other unethical practices
- The notion that ethical actions will never put an employee in jeopardy (thus, a salesperson should not be penalized for losing a customer if he/she is unwilling to exaggerate the effectiveness of a product)

Consider this view of the role of teaching ethical standards to business students:

Business managers confront unprecedented problems, issues, questions, and predicaments. The techniques of the past are not only difficult to apply to today's demands, but they may be inadequate for, or irrelevant to, tomorrow's requirements; business students need to be prepared to deal creatively with the new and unforeseen, for they will rarely confront the traditional and predictable. Old ethical responses will have to be transformed in unexpected ways and interpreted with imagination. Many managers in leading internationalized businesses explicitly discuss the merits of other-regarding, and even the benefits of altruistic behavior among employees, partners, collaborators, and colleagues. The teaching of business ethics is not likely to be a passing fad, but a long-term responsibility for colleges and businesses. The faculties of the former and the managers of the latter had better develop strategies and tactics to help them convince both students and employees that business ethics is an increasingly key concern in the changing environment of business.[30]

For more ethics insights, visit Institute for Global Ethics (**http://www.globalethics. org**), Applied Ethics Resources (**http://www.ethicsweb.ca/resources**), Center for Ethical Business Cultures (**http://www.cebcglobal.org**), Ethics Resource Center (**http://www. ethics.org**), International Business Ethics Institute (**http://www.business-ethics.org**), and *Business Ethics* magazine (**http://www.business-ethics.com**).

---

[27] International Business Ethics Institute, "10 Mistakes in Global Ethics Programs," *PM Network* (April 2005), p. 51.

[28] For an interesting discussion on this issue, see Shelby D. Hunt and Scott J. Vitell, "The General Theory of Marketing Ethics: A Revision and Three Questions," *Journal of Macromarketing*, Vol. 26 (December 2006), pp. 143–153.

[29] Terry L. Price, "How to Teach Business Ethics," **http://www.insidehighered.com/views/2007/06/04/price** (June 4, 2007).

[30] James W. Kuhn, "Emotion as Well as Reason: Getting Students Beyond 'Interpersonal Accountability,'" *Journal of Business Ethics*, Vol. 17 (February 1998), pp. 297–299.

5-4 CONSUMERISM

In contrast to social responsibility, which involves firms' interfaces with all of their publics, consumerism focuses on the relations of firms and their customers. *Consumerism* encompasses "the wide range of activities of government, business, and independent organizations that are designed to protect people from practices that infringe upon their rights as consumers."[31]

Consumer interests are most apt to be served well in industrialized nations, where their rights are considered important, and governments and firms have the resources to address consumer issues. In less-developed nations and those now turning to free-market economies, consumer rights have not been as suitably honored due to fewer resources and to other commitments; the early stages of consumerism are just now emerging in many of these nations.

U.S. consumerism has evolved through five distinct eras. The first era was in the early 1900s and focused on the need for a banking system, product purity, postal rates, antitrust regulations, and product shortages. Business protection against unfair practices was emphasized. During the second era, from the 1930s to the 1950s, issues were product safety, bank failures, labeling, misrepresentation, stock manipulation, deceptive ads, credit, and consumer refunds. Consumer groups, such as Consumers Union (**http://www.consumersunion.org**), and legislation grew. Issues were initiated but seldom resolved.

The third era began in the early 1960s and lasted to 1980. It dealt with all areas of marketing and had a great impact. Ushering in this era was President Kennedy's *consumer bill of rights*: to information, to safety, to choice in product selection, and to be heard. These rights, cited in Figure 5-8, apply to people in any nation or economic system. Other events also contributed to the era's aggressiveness. Birth defects from the drug thalidomide occurred. Several books—on marketing's ability to influence people, dangers from unsafe autos, and funeral industry tactics—were published. Consumers became more unhappy with product performance, firms' complaint handling, and deceptive and unsafe acts; and they set higher—perhaps unrealistic—expectations.

> **Consumerism** protects consumers from practices that infringe upon their rights.

> President Kennedy declared a **consumer bill of rights**: to information, to safety, to choice, and to be heard.

- To be informed and protected against fraudulent, deceitful, and misleading statements, advertisements, labels, etc.; and to be educated as to how to use financial resources wisely.

- To be protected against dangerous and unsafe products.

- To be able to choose from among several available goods and services.

- To be heard by government and business regarding unsatisfactory or disappointing practices.

Figure 5-8

Consumers' Basic Rights

[31] "Dictionary," **http://www.marketingpower.com/_layouts/Dictionary.aspx?dLetter=C** (March 22, 2009).

Product scarcity occurred for some items. Self-service shopping and more complex products caused uncertainty for some people. The media publicized poor practices more often. Government intervention expanded, and the FTC (**http://www.ftc.gov**) extended its consumer activities.

The fourth era took place during the 1980s as consumerism entered a more mature phase, due to the dramatic gains of the 1960s and 1970s and an emphasis on business deregulation and self-regulation. Nationally, no major consumer laws were enacted and budgets of federal agencies concerned with consumer issues were cut. Yet, state and local governments became more active. In general, the federal government believed that most firms took consumer issues into account when devising and applying their marketing plans, and fewer firms ignored consumer input or publicly confronted consumer groups. Cooperation between business and consumers was better, and confrontations were less likely.

Since 1990, the federal government has been somewhat more involved with consumer issues. Its goal is to balance consumer and business rights. Some national laws have been enacted and U.S. agencies have had mixed efforts in their enforcement practices. At the same time, many state and local governments are keeping a high level of commitment. Unfair business tactics, product safety, and health issues are the areas with the most attention. Today, more firms address consumer issues and resolve complaints than before.

These key aspects of consumerism are examined next: consumer rights, the responses of business to consumer issues, and the current role of consumerism.

5-4a Consumer Rights

As noted, consumer rights fall into four categories: information and education, safety, choice, and the right to be heard. Each is discussed next.

Consumer Information and Education The right to be informed includes protection against fraudulent, deceitful, or grossly misleading information, advertising, labeling, pricing, packaging, and so forth—and being given enough information to make good decisions. In the United States, many federal and state laws have been enacted in this area.

The federal Magnuson-Moss Consumer Product Warranty Act requires warranties to be properly stated and enforced (**http://www.ftc.gov/bcp/conline/pubs/buspubs/ warranty.htm#Magnuson-Moss**). They must be available prior to purchases, so consumers may read them in advance. A *warranty* is an assurance to consumers that a product meets certain standards. An *express warranty* is explicitly stated, such as a printed form showing the minimum mileage for tires. An *implied warranty* does not have to be stated to be in effect; a product is assumed to be fit for use and packaged properly, and is assumed to conform to promises on the label. The FTC monitors product-accompanying information as to the warrantor's identity and location, exceptions in coverage, and how people may complain. A *full warranty* must cover all parts and labor for a given time. A *limited warranty* may have conditions and exceptions, and a provision for labor charges. Implied warranties may not be disclaimed.

Many states have laws regarding consumer information. For instance, cooling-off laws (allowing people to reconsider and, if they desire, cancel purchase commitments made in their homes with salespeople) exist in about 40 states. Unit-pricing laws that let people compare the prices of products coming in many sizes (such as small, medium, large, and economy) are likewise on a state-by-state basis. Government actions involving consumer information are also increasing internationally.

Unfortunately, the existence of good information does not mean consumers will use it in their decision making. At times, information is ignored or misunderstood, especially by those needing it most (such as the poor); thus, consumer education is needed. Most state departments of education in the United States have consumer education staffs. Such states as Illinois, Oregon, Wisconsin, Florida, Kentucky, and Hawaii require public high school students to take a consumer education course. And hundreds of programs are conducted

A **warranty** assures consumers that a product will meet certain standards.

Marketing and the Web

Trying Again to Make the Can-Spam Act Work Better

The 2004 Can-Spam Act regulates the sending of commercial E-mail messages. It states that commercial E-mail must contain the full address of the sender and have an opt-out mechanism (that is implemented within 10 days of receipt). Unsolicited E-mails must also clearly disclose that the message is an ad.

Some critics argued that the original act—which was intended to prohibit spam (junk) E-mail—actually had the effect of demonstrating to companies how to plan and implement spam. They believed that Congress favored the speech rights of E-mailers (the freedom of firms to send unsolicited ads) over consumers' right to privacy (freedom from receiving unsolicited and unwanted ads).

Because the original act proved to be ineffective, in May 2008, the Federal Trade Commission (FTC) (http://www.ftc.gov) approved four new rule provisions to the Can-Spam Act. These are the key provisions:

- To opt-out of future E-mails, a recipient cannot be asked to pay a fee, provide information beyond an E-mail address, or take any other steps beyond sending a reply E-mail or visiting a single Web page.
- The FTC clarified the meaning of "sender" to facilitate which of multiple parties need be contacted.
- Commercial E-mail can use a post office box or private mailbox as a "valid physical postal address."
- The definition of "person" was clarified so that the law is not limited to natural persons.

Sources: Based on material in Chandra Johnson-Greene, "FTC Approves New Rule Provisions for CAN-SPAM," *Circulation Management* (June 2008), p. 9; and Reynolds Holding, "A Spammer's Revenge," *Time*, http://www.time.com/time/magazine/article/0,9171,1574169,00.html (January 5, 2007).

by all levels of government, as well as by private profit and nonprofit groups. The programs typically cover how to purchase goods and services; key features of credit agreements, contracts, and warranties; and consumer protection laws.

Two good online consumer information sources are Consumer.gov (http://www.consumer.gov) and Consumer Affairs.com (http://www.consumeraffairs.com).

Consumer Safety There is concern over consumer safety because every year millions of people worldwide are hurt and thousands killed in incidents involving products other than motor vehicles. People also worry about having a safe shopping environment, one free from crime.

The yearly cost of U.S. product-related consumer injuries is estimated at several hundred billion dollars. Critics believe up to one-quarter of these injuries could be averted if firms made safer, better-designed products.

The Consumer Product Safety Commission, CPSC (http://www.cpsc.gov), is the federal U.S. agency with major responsibility for product safety. It has jurisdiction over 15,000 types of products—including TVs, bicycles, lamps, appliances, toys, sporting goods, ladders, furniture, housewares, and lawn mowers. It also regulates structural items in homes such as stairs, retaining walls, and electrical wiring. The major products outside the CPSC's authority are food, drugs, cosmetics, tobacco, motor vehicles, tires, firearms, boats, pesticides, and aircraft. Each of these is regulated by other agencies. The Environmental Protection Agency (http://www.epa.gov) can recall autos not meeting emission standards; and the Food and Drug Administration (http://www.fda.gov) oversees food, drugs, cosmetics, medical devices, radiation emissions, and similar items.

The CPSC has a broad jurisdiction. It can

- develop voluntary standards with industry cooperation.
- issue and enforce mandatory standards, banning consumer products if no feasible standard would adequately protect the public.
- obtain the recall of products or arrange for their repair.
- conduct research on potential product hazards.
- inform and educate consumers through the media, state and local governments, and private organizations, and by responding to consumer inquiries.

When the CPSC finds a product hazard, it can issue an order for a firm to bring the product into conformity with the applicable safety rule or repair the defect, exchange the product for one meeting safety standards, or refund the purchase price. Firms found breaking safety rules can be fined; and executives can be personally fined and jailed for up to a year. *Product recall*, whereby the CPSC asks—orders, if need be—firms to recall and modify (or discontinue) unsafe products, is the primary enforcement tool. The CPSC has initiated many recalls (**http://www.cpsc.gov/cpscpub/prerel/prerel.html**), and a single recall may entail millions of units of a product. It has also banned such items as flammable contact adhesives, easily overturned refuse bins, asbestos-treated products, and a flame retardant in children's clothing that was linked to cancer.

The U.S. motor vehicle industry, overseen by the National Highway Traffic Safety Administration, NHTSA (**http://www.nhtsa.gov**), has had many vehicles recalled for safety reasons. Over the last 30 years, there have been thousands of U.S. recalls (often voluntary actions under NHTSA prodding) involving millions of cars, trucks, and other vehicles (some of which have been recalled more than once). NHTSA also makes its vehicular testing data available at its Web site (**http://www.nhtsa.dot.gov/cars/testing/comply**).

Consumers also have the right to sue the maker or seller of an injurious product. A legal action on behalf of many affected consumers is known as a *class-action suit*. Each year in the United States, numerous consumer suits are filed in federal courts and in state courts; these include both individual and class-action suits. Consumer suits have been rarer outside the United States. Yet, this too is changing. For example, until the early 1990s, Chinese consumers "had little recourse when they were shocked, burned, or dismembered by shoddy state-produced goods. Now they can sue."[32] Since then, numerous product liability lawsuits have been filed in China.

A firm can reduce the negative effects of product recalls, as well as the possibility of costly class-action suits, by communicating properly when it learns a product is unsafe. This means voluntarily telling affected consumers, citing specific models that are unsafe, making fair adjustment offers (repair, replacement, or refund), and quickly and conveniently honoring those offers.

Consumer Choice   The right to choose means people have several products and brands from which to select. Figure 5-9 illustrates this. As noted earlier, the lack of goods and services (of any brand) is a key consumer concern in less-developed and newly free-market nations where demand often far outstrips the supply for such items as coffee, bread, jeans, shoes, cosmetics, and fresh meat.

The federal governments in many industrialized countries have taken various actions to enhance the already extensive consumer choices there:

- Patent rights have time limits, after which all firms can use the patents.
- Noncompetitive business practices, such as price fixing, are banned.
- Government agencies review proposed company mergers; in some cases, they have stopped mergers if they felt industry competition would be lessened.
- Restrictions requiring franchisees to purchase all products from their franchisors have been reduced.
- The media are monitored to ensure that ad space or time is available to both small and large firms.
- Imports are allowed to compete with domestic-made items.
- Various service industries have been deregulated to foster price competition and encourage new firms to enter the marketplace.

> The Consumer Product Safety Commmission has several enforcement tools, including **product recall**.

> A **class-action suit** can be filed on behalf of many consumers.

> When consumers have several alternatives available to them, they are given the right to choose.

---

[32] Craig S. Smith, "Chinese Discover Product-Liability Suits," *Wall Street Journal* (November 13, 1997), p. B1. See also Michael Palmer and Chao Xi, "Collective and Representative Actions in China," **http://www.law.stanford.edu/display/images/dynamic/events_media/China_National_Report.pdf** (December 17, 2007).

Figure 5-9

The Right to Choose

In the United States, consumers often have a wide range of product choices—including the option to purchase a classic office chair from Design Within Reach (**http://www.dwr.com**). Its "multichannel, integrated sales strategy enables Design Within Reach to maintain a high proportion of products in stock at all times, reinforces brand awareness, and enhances customer knowledge of the products."

Source: Reprinted by permission.

In the United States and many other highly industrialized nations, consumer choice for certain product categories is so extensive that some experts wonder if there are too many options. For instance, "Many marketers believe that competitive differentiation arises from giving customers more choices and options. But through the strategy of 'offering more choice,' marketers may actually end up increasing complexity and costs, and causing customers 'mental fatigue.' With some customers drowning in 'choice,' some companies are finding it easier to meet customer needs by simplifying their offerings."[33]

Consumers' Right to Be Heard The right to be heard means that people should be able to voice their opinions (sometimes as complaints) to business, government, and other parties. This gives consumers input into the decisions affecting them. To date, no overall U.S. consumer agency exists to represent consumer interests, although several federal agencies regulate various business practices relating to consumers. Their addresses and phone numbers, as well as those of trade associations, are available from the Federal Citizen Information Center's Consumer Action Web Site (**http://www.consumeraction.gov**). Most states and major cities have their own consumer affairs offices, as do many corporations. Each encourages consumer input.

Consumer groups also exist that represent the general public or specific consumer segments. They publicize consumer opinions and complaints, speak at government and industry hearings, and otherwise generate consumer input into the decision processes of

> Various federal, state, and local agencies are involved with consumers.

[33] Paul Barsch, "When Less Is More in Consumer Choice," **http://www.mpdailyfix.com/2008/04/when_less_is_more_in_consumer.html** (April 29, 2008).

government and industry. Because a single consumer rarely has a significant impact, consumer groups frequently become the individual's voice.

5-4b   The Responses of Business to Consumer Issues

Over the past five decades, in many nations, the business community has greatly increased its acceptance of the legitimacy and importance of consumer rights; many firms now have real commitments to address consumer issues in a positive manner. Nonetheless, a number of companies have raised reasonable questions about consumerism's impact on them. They particularly wonder why there isn't a *business bill of rights* to parallel the consumer's. Here are some of the questions that businesspeople raise:

- Why do various states, municipalities, and nations have different laws regarding business practices? How can a national or global company be expected to comply with each of these laws?
- Don't some government rules cause unnecessary costs and time delays in new-product introductions that outweigh the benefits of these rules?
- Is it really the job of business to ensure that consumers obey laws (such as not littering) and use products properly (such as wearing seat belts)?
- Isn't business self-regulation preferred over government regulation?
- Are multimillion-dollar jury awards to consumers getting out of hand?

Selected actions by manufacturers, retailers, and trade associations with regard to consumer issues are discussed next.

Manufacturers Many firms have long-time programs to handle consumer issues. Maytag (**http://www.maytag.com**) introduced Red Carpet Service in 1961 to improve its appliance repair service. Zenith (**http://www.zenith.com**) set up a customer relations department in 1968; Motorola (**http://www.motorola.com**) created an Office of Consumer Affairs in 1970; and RCA (**http://www.rca.com**) opened a corporate consumer affairs office in 1972.

Intel (**http://www.intel.com**), the computer technology firm, has customer support centers in five different regions around the around the world: North America; Latin America; Europe, Middle East, and Africa; Japan; and Asia-Pacific. It also offers a sophisticated, but easy-to-use, Web site (**http://www.intel.com/support/index.htm? iid=hdr+support**) for software downloads, product information, parts replacement, warranty assistance, frequently asked questions, and technical support.

In the area of product recalls, many firms are now doing better. For instance, LifeScan (**http://www.lifescan.com**), a Johnson & Johnson company, makes meters that diabetics use to monitor blood sugar levels. When a single meter was found to be defective, LifeScan voluntarily recalled its entire product line and notified 600,000 customers within 24 hours. Because of how it handled the recall, LifeScan's market share has risen since that incident.

Some manufacturers have introduced new products or reformulated existing ones to better satisfy consumer concerns about a clean and safe environment for them and their children. One such firm is Shell (**http://www.shell.com**).

Despite manufacturers' interest in consumer issues, there remain instances when their performance could be better: "The blinking 12:00 has long been a humorous reminder of the difficulty many of us have had programming and configuring consumer electronics. But there's nothing funny about spending thousands of dollars on a high-definition TV only to wind up watching both programming and DVDs in standard definition. There's plenty of blame to go around: confusing, poorly written manuals; overly complex products; consumer laziness; and ignorant salespeople and inept cable and satellite installers."[34]

> Firms have become much more responsive to consumers, yet questions remain about the effects of consumerism on firms.

---

[34] Michael Fremer, "News to Use: HDTV Setup," *Bergen Record Online* (January 22, 2005).

Retailers   Numerous retailers have expressed a positive attitude about consumer issues, some for several decades. J.C. Penney (**http://www.jcpenney.com**) first stated its consumer philosophy in 1913, and Macy's (**http://www.macys.com**) formed a Bureau of Standards to test merchandise in 1927. In the 1970s, the Giant Food (**http://www. giantfood.com**) supermarket chain devised its own consumer bill of rights (paralleling the list of rights articulated by President Kennedy):

- Right to safety—no phosphates, certain pesticides removed, toys age labeled.
- Right to be informed—better labeling, readable dating of perishable items, and nutritional labeling.
- Right to choose—continued sale of cigarettes and food with additives.
- Right to be heard—consumer group meetings, in-house consumer advocate.
- Right to redress—money-back guarantee on all products.
- Right to service—availability of store services and employee attentiveness.

For 25 years, Wal-Mart (**http://www.walmart.com**) has had in-store signs to inform consumers about environmentally safe products. It has also run ads encouraging suppliers to make more environmentally sound products. At 7-Eleven Japan (**http://www. sej.co.jp/english**), top executives regularly sample foods sold at the chain. Target (**http://www.target.com**) donates about $150 million yearly. See Figure 5-10.

Retailers and consumer groups have opposing views involving ***item price removal***, whereby prices are marked only on shelves or aisle signs and not on individual items. Numerous retailers, particularly supermarkets, want item price removal since electronic checkouts let them computer-scan prices through codes on packages. They say this reduces labor costs and that these reductions are passed on to consumers. Consumer groups believe the practice is deceptive and will make it harder for them to guard against misrings. Item price removal is banned in a number of states and local communities. For many years, Giant Food has been a leading advocate of item price removal; it passes cost savings to shoppers.

> With **item price removal**, prices are displayed on shelves or signs.

Figure 5-10

Target: Giving Back to the Community

Source: Reprinted by permission of Susan Berry, Retail Image Consulting, Inc.

Trade Associations Trade associations represent groups of individual firms. Many have been quite responsive to consumer issues through such actions as coordinating and distributing safety-related research findings, setting up consumer education programs, planning product standards, and handling complaints.

The Direct Marketing Association (**http://www.the-dma.org**) sets industry guidelines and has a new program called Commitment to Consumer Choice (CCC) (**http://www.dmaccc.org/About.aspx**), which "supports DMA's strong desire to empower consumers and build trust. Consumers have strongly expressed their desire for choice over the types and volume of mail they receive. Today's consumers want safe and secure shopping experiences and for the many consumers who are environmentally conscious, the CCC gives them the ability to put their beliefs into action." The National Retail Federation (**http://www.nrf.com**) has a Consumer Affairs Committee and offers information to the public. The Alliance Against Fraud in Telemarketing & Electronic Commerce (**http://www.fraud.org/aaft/aaftinfo.htm**) is dedicated to reducing fraudulent practices and consists of consumer groups, trade associations, labor unions, phone companies, federal and state agencies, and telemarketers.

The Better Business Bureau, or BBB (**http://www.bbb.com**), is the largest and broadest business-run U.S. trade association involved with consumer issues. It publishes educational materials, handles complaints, supervises arbitration panels, outlines ethical practices, publicizes unsatisfactory activities and the firms involved, and has nationwide offices. It supports self-regulation. Nationwide, the BBB handles nearly a million consumer-business disputes each year. These disputes are sometimes decided by impartial arbitrators, whose rulings are usually binding on participating firms but not on consumers.

Trade associations may vigorously oppose potential government rules. For example, the Tobacco Institute (funded by tobacco firms) lobbied for many years against further restrictions on tobacco sales, promotion, distribution, and use. Today, due to a civil legal settlement, its Web site (**http://www.tobaccoinstitute.com**) disseminates information. As the site notes, it "is designed to provide the public with access to documents produced by the Tobacco Institute in Attorney General reimbursement lawsuits and certain other specified civil actions, and to documents produced after October 23, 1998 through June 30, 2010 in smoking and health actions, and includes certain enhancements, all as provided for by paragraph IV of the Attorneys General Master Settlement Agreement (MSA)."

5-4c The Current Role of Consumerism

During the 1980s, there was much less U.S. federal government activity on consumer-related issues than during the 1960s and 1970s due to the quality of self-regulation, consumerism's success, increased conservatism by Congress and the American people, and the importance of other issues.

By 1980, many firms had become more responsive to consumer issues. Thus, less pressure existed for government or consumer groups to intervene. A move to industry deregulation also took place as a way to increase competition, encourage innovations, and stimulate lower prices. In addition, consumerism activity was less needed because of the successes of past actions. On all levels, government protection for consumers had improved dramatically since the early 1960s, and class-action suits won big settlements from firms, making it clear that unsafe practices were costly. Consumer groups and independent media publicized poor practices, so firms knew such activities would not go unnoticed. In the 1980s, many members of Congress and sectors of the American public became more conservative about the role of government in regulating business. They felt government had become too big, impeded business practices, and caused unneeded costs; thus, some government agency functions were limited and budgets cut. Consumerism issues were not as important as other factors, including unemployment, the rate of inflation, industrial productivity, and the negative international balance of trade.

After a decade of a "hands-off" approach, many U.S. government leaders, consumer activists, and business leaders felt that the balance between business and consumer rights

Federal U.S. consumerism efforts have picked up after a relative lull in the 1980s.

had tipped a little too much in favor of business. Hence, the federal government assumed a somewhat more aggressive posture toward consumer-related issues than in the 1980s; and states and localities are continuing to be heavily involved.

Here are some indications of the role of the U.S. government:

- In 2008 alone, the U.S. Justice Department (**http://www.usdoj.gov**) reached settlements with health care systems, pharmacies, and physicians involving hundreds of millions of dollars in fines for improper billing practices (mostly involving Medicare); and several international airlines pleaded guilty to fixing prices on air cargo and were fined more than $500 million.

- Each year, the Federal Trade Commission (**http://www.ftc.gov**) tracks consumer fraud complaints from 125 other organizations and provides the complaints to more than 1,600 civil and criminal law enforcement agencies in the United States and abroad through a secure, online database. These are regularly among the most frequent complaint topics: identity theft, shop-at-home/catalog sales, Internet services, foreign money offers, prizes/sweepstakes and lotteries, computer equipment and software, Internet auctions, and health care claims.

- There is now a comprehensive Web site for product recalls (**http://www.recalls. gov**)—"your online resource for recalls"—that enables consumers to learn about recalls involving almost any product in one convenient place.

- The FTC's Bureau of Consumer Protection is promoted at its Web site (**http://www. ftc.gov/bcp/index.shtml**).

- The Securities and Exchange Commission has added an Office of Internet Enforcement, OIE (**http://www.sec.gov/divisions/enforce/internetenforce.htm**): "In general, OIE undertakes formal and informal investigations and initiates SEC prosecutions based on leads culled from the SEC's Complaint Center; performs surveillance for potential Internet securities-related fraud; formulates investigative procedures; provides strategic and legal guidance to enforcement staff nationwide; organizes and maintains the OIE Computer Lab specifically to aid in the surveillance of the Internet for potential securities fraud and to assist in Internet-related securities fraud investigations; acts as a clearinghouse and repository for Internet-related legal and technical policy and developments; acts as a resource, information source, referral source internally within the SEC and externally, to other government agencies and SROs; and organizes and presents seminars, training classes, and speeches within the SEC and to other agencies."

Several states have also increased their activities. For example, more than 35 states have enacted laws to regulate gift cards and gift certificates. These laws involve expiration dates, fees, where the cards or certificates may be used, disclosure of all terms, and so on. Consumers Union has a Web site dedicated to these state regulations (**http://www. consumersunion.org/pub/core_financial_services/003889.html**).

In many nations outside the United States, government, industry, and consumer groups are stepping up efforts relating to consumer rights—as past efforts have often been lacking in foreign markets. Some nations are making real progress, whereas others have a long way to go. No other nation has gone through as many stages or passed as many laws to protect consumer rights as the United States. The worldwide challenge will be for government, business, and consumer groups to work together so the socioecological view of marketing, ethical behavior, consumer rights, and company rights are in balance.

Web Sites You Can Use

The Federal Citizen Information Center makes the most recent copy of the complete *Consumer Action Handbook* available online (**http://www.consumeraction.gov/viewpdf. shtml**) for free. It contains much useful consumer information, including the names, addresses, phone numbers, Web addresses, and E-mail addresses for numerous consumer organizations, local Better Business Bureaus, corporations, trade associations, state and local consumer protection offices, military consumer offices, and federal agencies.

Summary

1. *To consider the impact of marketing on society*   Marketing actions can have both positive and negative consequences regarding such areas as the quality of life and consumer expectations. Various studies have shown that people's perceptions of marketing are mixed. Firms need to recognize that many dissatisfied consumers do not complain; they simply do not rebuy offending products.

2. *To examine social responsibility and weigh its benefits and costs*   Social responsibility involves a concern for the consequences of a person's or firm's acts as they might affect the interests of others. It encompasses the socioecological view of marketing, which looks at all the stages of a product's life and includes both consumers and nonconsumers. Social responsibility can pose dilemmas when popular goods and services have potential adverse effects on consumer or societal well-being.

   Consumers and marketing practices have led to some resource shortages. To stem this, cooperative efforts among business, stockholders, government, employees, the public, consumers, and others are needed. Garbage dumps and landfills, discarded containers, and abandoned autos are marring the landscape. Thus, many areas have laws to rectify the situation. Dangerous pollutants need to be removed and safe alternatives found to replace them; environmental pollution will be an issue for the foreseeable future. Planned obsolescence is a heavily criticized practice that encourages material wearout, style changes, and functional product changes. Marketers say it responds to consumer demand; critics say it increases resource shortages, is wasteful, and adds to pollution.

   Socially responsible actions have such benefits as worker and public health, cleaner air, and a more efficient use of resources. They also have costs, such as the unequal distribution of benefits, dollar expenditures, and conservative new-product planning. Benefits and costs need to be weighed.

3. *To look into the role of ethics in marketing*   Ethical behavior, based on honest and proper conduct, comes into play when people decide whether given actions are ethical or unethical and when they choose how to act. Egoism, utilitarianism, duty-based, and virtue ethics theories help explain behavior. Marketing ethics can be divided into two categories: process-related and product-related.

   Ethics may be viewed from four vantage points: a business perspective, a consumer perspective, an international perspective, and teachability. A major difficulty of ethics in business relates to setting boundaries for deciding what is ethical. For high ethical standards to be kept, both consumers and firms must engage in proper behavior. Ethical standards in a global setting are especially complex. Much debate has ensued as to whether ethics can be taught.

4. *To explore consumerism and describe the consumer bill of rights*   Consumerism deals with the relations of firms and their consumers. It comprises the government, business, and independent organizations' activities that are designed to protect people from practices that infringe upon their rights as consumers.

   U.S. consumerism has seen five eras: early 1900s, 1930s to 1950s, 1960s to 1980, 1980s, and 1990 to now. The third era was the most important and began with President Kennedy's stating a consumer bill of rights—to information, to safety, to choice, and to be heard. The interest now is in balancing consumer and business rights in the United States, as well as in other countries.

   The right to be informed includes consumer protection against fraudulent, deceitful, grossly misleading, or incomplete information, advertising, labeling, pricing, packaging, or other practices. Consumer education involves teaching people to spend their money wisely.

   The concern over the right to safety arises from the large numbers of people who are injured or killed in product-related accidents. The U.S. Consumer Product Safety Commission has the power to order recalls or modifications for a wide range of products; other agencies oversee such products as autos and pharmaceuticals.

   The right to choose means consumers should have several products and brands from which to select. In the United States, some observers wonder if there is too much choice.

   The right to be heard means consumers should be able to voice their opinions to business, government, and other parties. Several government agencies and consumer groups provide this voice.

5. *To discuss the responses of manufacturers, retailers, and trade associations to consumerism and study the current role of consumerism*   Many firms and associations are reacting well to consumer issues. A small number intentionally or unintentionally pursue unfair, misleading, or dangerous acts.

   The current era of consumerism has witnessed somewhat more activism than in the 1980s and less than in the 1960s and 1970s. In the 21st century, government, business, and consumers will continue working together to resolve consumer issues.

Key Terms

social responsibility (p. 124)

socioecological view of marketing (p. 124)

planned obsolescence (p. 131)

ethical behavior (p. 133)

process-related ethical issues (p. 135)

product-related ethical issues (p. 135)

cause-related marketing (p. 136)

consumerism (p. 141)

consumer bill of rights (p. 141)

warranty (p. 142)

product recall (p. 144)

class-action suit (p. 144)

item price removal (p. 147)

Review Questions

1. Define the term *socioecological view of marketing*. What are the implications for marketers?
2. Describe the pros and cons of planned obsolescence as a marketing practice.
3. What is ethical behavior? Distinguish among the egoism, utilitarianism, duty-based, and virtue ethics theories.
4. Why is cause-related marketing a controversial practice?
5. Why are ethical standards of conduct particularly complex for international marketers?
6. How does consumerism differ from social responsibility?
7. Explain the consumer bill of rights.
8. Describe the current role of consumerism.

Discussion Questions

1. From a savings bank's perspective, why is hidden consumer dissatisfaction a particular problem? How would you go about making dissatisfaction less hidden?
2. Present a seven-point ethics guide for operating in Mexico.
3. How would you teach marketing ethics to an introductory marketing class? What topics would you discuss? Why?
4. As an executive for a leading detergent manufacturer, how would you implement a product recall if you discovered that one million boxes of your detergent (already distributed to retailers) inadvertently had a dangerous ingredient in them?

Web Exercise

Mike Moran, a senior engineer at IBM, has posted a short quiz on marketing ethics online: "Do You Pass the Web Marketing Ethics Test?" (**http://www.marketingnewz.com/marketingnewz-22-20080212DoYouPasstheWebMarketingEthicsTest.html**).

Comment on this ethics quiz and the examples cited by Moran. What other ethical questions would you add to this test? Why?

Practice Quiz

1. Which of these statements is incorrect?
   a. Marketing practices rarely encourage unrealistic consumer expectations.
   b. The true level of customer dissatisfaction is usually hidden.
   c. Deceptive actions are not okay if no one is physically injured.
   d. Tobacco products are affected by the socioecological view of marketing.

2. Corporate social responsibility
   a. balances short-term profit needs with society's long-term needs.
   b. does not refer to issues such as product availability and innovation.
   c. considers only the needs of society.
   d. considers only deceptive actions.

3. Which of these countries annually discards the most trash per person?
   a. Russia
   b. United States
   c. India
   d. China

4. A practice that encourages short-run material wearout, style changes, and functional product changes is
   a. product innovation.
   b. price gouging.
   c. product cloning.
   d. planned obsolescence.

5. An example of a process-related ethical issue is
   a. price fixing.
   b. liquor marketing.
   c. food shortages.
   d. cigarette manufacturing.

6. Which of the following statements about cause-related marketing is correct?
   a. Critics say there is too much commercialism by nonprofit groups and implicit endorsements for sponsor products.
   b. Companies participating in cause-related marketing rarely seek any profits.
   c. While its use was once considered somewhat controversial, that is no longer true.
   d. It has not been used by such nonprofits as the Red Cross.

7. Which of the following is *not* one of the basic rights outlined in President John Kennedy's consumer bill of rights?
   a. Mass production
   b. Information
   c. Safety
   d. Choice

8. During the fourth era of consumerism,
   a. cooperation between business and consumers rose.
   b. state and local governments became less active in environmental issues.
   c. there was a reduction in the emphasis on business deregulation.
   d. the budgets of the federal agencies concerned with consumer issues increased significantly.

9. Consumers who need it most
   a. use product information in their decision making.
   b. use product information infrequently.
   c. demand more product information.
   d. use product information to complain to manufacturers.

10. Which of the following products does *not* fall under the jurisdiction of the Consumer Product Safety Commission?
    a. TV sets
    b. Bicycles
    c. Autos
    d. Electrical wiring

11. The primary enforcement tool of the Consumer Product Safety Commission is
    a. adverse publicity.
    b. product recall.
    c. imprisonment.
    d. purchase-price refunds.

12. Which of these statements is correct?
    a. Consumer lawsuits are rare in the United States.
    b. Japan has more consumer lawsuits than any other country.
    c. The CPSC is a legislative branch of the Supreme Court.
    d. Consumers have the right to sue the makers of injurious products.

13. Which of the following is *not* available to consumers in their quest to be heard?
    a. Industry specialists
    b. A directory of federal agencies regulating business
    c. A single overall U.S. consumer agency
    d. Consumer groups

14. The largest and broadest business-operated U.S. trade association involved with consumer issues is the
    a. Chamber of Commerce.
    b. Federal Trade Commission.
    c. Better Business Bureau.
    d. Bank Marketing Association.

15. In contrast to the 1980s, currently,
    a. the Food and Drug Administration is no longer a government agency.
    b. firms are no longer required to report settlements of product-safety lawsuits involving death or disabling injuries to the CSPC.
    c. there is a somewhat more aggressive federal government posture toward consumer-related issues.
    d. state and local governments have reduced their involvement in consumer-related issues.

For the answers to these questions, please visit the online site for this book at **http://www.atomicdog.com**.

Chapter 6

Global Aspects of Marketing

When Kiichiro Toyoda, the founder of Toyota Motor Corporation (http://www.toyota.com), and his younger cousin Eiji, built their first factory in central Japan, they had modest goals. Yet today, Toyota Motor Corporation is the world's largest auto maker. The first plant, located in what is now referred to as "Toyota City," was responsible for introducing such key marketing concepts as just-in-time inventory management, the *kanban* system of parts labeling, and *kaizen*, a continuous improvement process.

Toyota has learned much about international marketing since it first exported the Toyota Crown to the United States in 1957. Although the Crown was too underpowered for the U.S. market, its smaller Corolla model (introduced in the United States in 1968) quickly became popular with American consumers looking for an inexpensive and reliable car. The Corolla became the best-selling car model of all time. And the Camry has been the best-selling car in the United States for most of the last decade.

By 1970, Toyota had become the world's fourth-largest car manufacturer. In 2003, Toyota overtook Ford Motor Company (http://www.ford.com) as the world's second-largest car maker. During 2008, the firm surpassed long-time leader General Motors (http://www.gm.com) as the world's leading auto maker. This is the first time that a non-U.S. company is the global leader.

Toyota is currently focusing on expanding its global manufacturing capabilities. Its strategy is based on producing cars near to or in the same countries where they will be purchased. In recent years, Toyota has opened major vehicle plants in such locations as India (1999), France (2001), China (2002), Mexico (2004), the Czech Republic (2005), and Texas (2008).

Much of Toyota's global focus is on China, which is expected to become the second-largest car market (behind the United States) by 2010. Although Toyota was a latecomer to the Chinese market, in 2007, its Camry became the third best-selling car in China. By expanding the number of Lexus dealerships in China from 13 to 39, Toyota also plans to increasingly sell its Lexus brand there.[1]

In this chapter, we will explore the environment facing international marketers, including data on U.S. imports and exports, and see how to develop an international marketing strategy.

Chapter Objectives

1. To define domestic, international, and global marketing
2. To explain why international marketing takes place and study its scope
3. To explore the cultural, economic, political and legal, and technological environments facing international marketers
4. To analyze the stages in the development of an international marketing strategy

6-1 OVERVIEW

International transactions—including goods and service—generate more than $17 trillion in yearly global sales. And virtually every nation engages in significant international business, whether it be the United States with $4 trillion in yearly exports and imports of

---

[1] Various company and other sources.

goods and services, Namibia (in southern Africa) with $6 billion in exports and imports, or Tonga (in the South Pacific) with $175 million in exports and imports. In many areas, the marketplace has a wide mix of foreign firms competing with domestic ones.[2]

Whether a company is big or small, operates only in its home nation or both domestically and abroad, markets goods or services, and is profit- or nonprofit-driven, it needs to grasp key international marketing concepts and devise a proper strategy. This means having a broadened marketing perspective:

> When Starbucks' (**http://www.starbucks.com**) former Vice-President of Marketing Karin Koonings first joined Starbucks' international team, she found that their local marketers around the world were unimpressed by the firm's global efforts, mostly because they were clueless about them. Koonings' first step was to connect personally with regional and local teams to listen and determine firsthand their challenges and opportunities. She then briefed her teams to better connect with international markets via regular personal visits, telephone calls, and new immersions at corporate and regional offices to offer interaction and strategic planning as often as possible. She took connecting disparate markets even further by promoting a virtual exchange program among employee partners, allowing them to rotate between markets and headquarters. This was crucial given that Starbucks, which opened its first store outside the United States in 1996, now operates in more than 40 countries.[3]

Domestic marketing encompasses a firm's efforts in its home country. *International marketing* involves marketing goods and services outside a firm's home country, whether in one or several markets. *Global marketing* is an advanced form of international marketing in which a firm addresses global customers, markets, and competition. It is used by both multinational and global firms.

A company may act domestically, internationally, or both; efforts vary widely. Here is the range of options that may be pursued:

- A *domestic firm* restricts its efforts to the home market. It believes the base market is both large enough and responsive enough to meet its sales and profit goals.
- An *exporting firm* recognizes that the home market is no longer adequate for it fully to meet revenue and profit goals. A firm typically uses exporting when it seeks to sell its traditional products in foreign markets, often via distribution and sales intermediaries. A relatively low percentage of business is outside the domestic market.
- An *international firm* makes modifications in its existing products for foreign markets or introduces new products there; the firm knows it must aggressively cultivate foreign markets. There remains enough strength in the domestic market for that market to remain the dominant one for the company.
- A *multinational firm* is a worldwide player. Although corporate headquarters are in the home nation, the domestic market often accounts for 50 percent or less of sales and profits—and the firm operates in dozens of nations or more. Geographically, the business scope and opportunity search are broad. Many leading U.S. players, such as Boeing (**http://www.boeing.com**), Citigroup (**http://www.citigroup.com**), Heinz (**http://www.heinz.com**), and McDonald's (**http://www.mcdonalds.com**), are in this category; they market items around the world, but have a distinctly American business culture. See Figure 6-1.
- A *global firm* is also a worldwide player. Yet, because its domestic sales are low, it places even more reliance on foreign transactions. It has the greatest geographic scope. Such firms have been more apt to emerge in smaller nations, where

Margin notes:

Due to its impact, international marketing concepts should be understood by all types of firms.

Domestic marketing involves the home nation, **international marketing** embraces foreign activities, and **global marketing** has a worldwide focus.

A firm may be domestic, exporting, international, multinational, or global.

[2] "World Trade Report 2008," **http://www.wto.org/english/res_e/booksp_e/anrep_e/world_trade_report08_e.pdf**; "The World Factbook," **https://www.cia.gov/library/publications/the-world-factbook** (March 1, 2009); and "U.S. International Trade in Goods and Services," **http://www.census.gov/foreign-trade/www** (March 1, 2009).

[3] Marc De Swaan Arons, "What It Takes to Really Win Globally," *Advertising Age* (May 19, 2008), p. 22.

Figure 6-1

Heinz: An American Multinational Firm

Heinz (**http://www.heinz.com**) markets its products around the world, with non-U.S. revenues now accounting for 55 percent of total company revenues. Emerging markets are showing especially strong growth for Heinz.

Source: Reprinted by permission.

Accelerating Growth in Emerging Markets

Upon receiving his first order for Heinz products in the UK in 1886, Henry Heinz declared, "The World is Our Field." Heinz has been a pioneer among U.S. food companies in exploring global opportunities ever since.

Emerging Markets have become one of the largest growth engines for today's Heinz.

Heinz possesses significant advantages in many of these markets due to our well-established domestic brands, in addition to a growing Heinz® brand in ketchup, sauces, and infant/nutrition. We also enjoy scalable infrastructure, unique distribution capabilities, and strong local management.

THE INFRASTRUCTURE WE HAVE ACQUIRED AND BUILT HAS ALLOWED US TO EXPAND OUR PRESENCE

Heinz was one of the first companies from the western world to operate in China. Our late Chairman Henry "Jack" Heinz II, grandson of the Founder, personally oversaw the opening of our infant cereal factory in Guangzhou in 1986. We remain the trusted leader in the Chinese infant cereal category.

Heinz has initiated a new program in China to expand our fast-growing Long Fong® brand. The Company provides grocers in second- and third-tier cities with freezers in exchange for exclusively merchandising Long Fong's dumplings, dim sum, rice balls, and steam bread. Aided by this program, we have doubled Long Fong sales in less than four years, and expect to continue driving double-digit sales increases for the forseeable future.

In India, meanwhile, a fleet of bicycle salesmen, supported by mobile health clinics and door-to-door promotion, has significantly increased brand penetration for our Glucon-D® energy beverage brand.

In Fiscal 2008, Heinz expanded its freezer distribution program to introduce the Long Fong brand to many new cities.

WE ARE GROWING WITH OUR GLOBAL CUSTOMERS

In Russia, the world's second-largest ketchup market, we recently extended our relationship with McDonald's. Building on the awareness created by this partnership, the Heinz® brand is now the leader in Moscow and St. Petersburg.

---

companies have historically needed foreign markets to survive (in contrast to U.S. firms). A quintessential global firm is Sweden's Ikea furniture store chain (**http://www.ikea.com**), which derives only 7 percent of total sales from its Swedish customers. It has stores in Europe, North America, Asia, Australia, and the Middle East; prints catalogs in about 25 languages; and purchases merchandise from 1,350 suppliers in 50 nations. See Figure 6-2.

It is clear, now that we are in the 21st century, that more domestic firms will need to become exporters and then international in orientation. And multinational firms will need to become more global, thereby acting without boundaries and not dominated by a home-country-based corporate culture.

This chapter looks at why international marketing occurs, its scope, its environment, and the components of an international marketing strategy.

6-2 WHY INTERNATIONAL MARKETING TAKES PLACE

For several reasons, countries and individual firms are engaging in greater international marketing efforts than ever before.[4] These are highlighted in Figure 6-3 and discussed next.

> Countries trade items with which they have a **comparative advantage**.

According to the concept of *comparative advantage*, each country has distinct strengths and weaknesses based on its natural resources, climate, technology, labor costs, and other factors. Nations can benefit by exporting the goods and services with which they have relative advantages and importing the ones with which they have relative disadvantages. Comparative advantages may generally be grouped into two categories: (a) those related to the physical environment of a country (such as natural resources and

---

[4] For more in-depth analysis, see *Journal of International Marketing; International Marketing Review; European Journal of Marketing; Journal of International Marketing & Marketing Research;* and *Advances in International Marketing.*

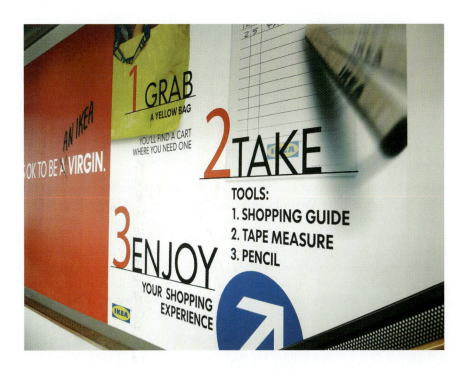

Figure 6-2

Ikea: A Truly Global Firm

Due to the small size of its domestic market (Sweden has a population of just 9 million), Ikea derives well over 90 percent of its sales from outside of Sweden. Therefore, it must think globally and seek expansion in foreign markets.

Source: Reprinted by permission of Susan Berry, Retail Image Consulting, Inc.

climate) and (b) those related to the socioeconomic development of a country (such as technological advances or low labor costs). Among the best U.S. comparative advantages are its agricultural productivity, the level of technological prowess, and service industry expertise.

Economic and demographic trends vary by country. A firm in a nation with weak domestic conditions (such as high inflation) and/or a small or stagnant population base can stabilize or increase sales by marketing products in more favorable foreign markets. Historically, the U.S. market is attractive due to rather low inflation and unemployment, as well as the relative affluence. Developing and less-developed nations are potentially lucrative markets due to their population growth; more than 90 percent of world growth is there. Thus, Heinz (**http://www.heinz.com**) targets developing and less-developed nations due to their growth and nutrition needs. Its brands are established in Africa, Asia, and the Pacific Rim:

> Heinz is extending its first-mover advantage in emerging markets with well-established, profitable, and growing domestic brands, as well as an expanding Heinz-branded ketchup and infant/nutrition business. Our emerging markets represent 13 percent of total Heinz sales and about 25 percent of our sales growth. We expect these markets to grow net sales at

> The domestic economy and demographics affect international efforts.

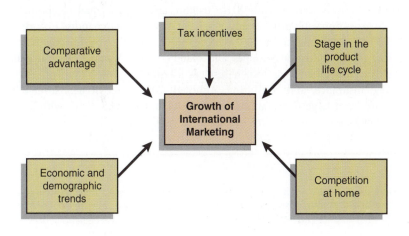

Figure 6-3

Why International Marketing Occurs

high-teen percentage rates for the foreseeable future. We will support this growth with continued investments in R&D, marketing, new capacity, and management talent in these markets. For example, in Indonesia, we are supplementing strong growth in our core ABC®-branded soy sauce and beverage businesses with new cooking pastes. We will also consider entering select new markets, given our proven ability to identify, execute, and grow joint ventures and acquisitions in the developing world. Emerging markets are expected to account for approximately 20 percent of Heinz's overall sales by 2013.[5]

Competition in a firm's domestic market may be intense and lead to its expanding internationally, as these examples show:

- The U.S. optical-products marketplace is highly competitive. So, U.S.-based Bausch & Lomb (**http://www.bausch.com**) has increased its activities in regions with expansion opportunities. Its non-U.S. sales represent about 56 percent of its total sales; and it markets products in more than 100 nations.
- In Europe, Germany's Henkel (**http://www.henkel.com**) is a leading maker of detergents, cleansers, and personal-care items, as well as industrial chemicals. Yet, it faces intense European competition from Dutch-British Unilever (**http://www.unilever.com**) and America's Procter & Gamble (**http://www.pg.com**), among others. So, it has been pumping up efforts in Asia and Africa.

Because products are often in different stages of their life cycles in different nations, exporting may be a way to prolong the cycles. For instance, the U.S. market for tobacco products has been falling, for health and social reasons. To stimulate cigarette sales, Philip Morris International (**http://www.pmintl.com**) and R.J. Reynolds (**http://www.rjrt.com**) have turned more to foreign sales. The two firms have heightened their efforts in Eastern Europe—where cigarette smoking is popular and shortages of domestic tobacco products occur. International marketing can also be used to dispose of discontinued goods, seconds, and manufacturer remakes (repaired products). These items can be sold abroad without spoiling the domestic market for full-price, first-quality items. However, firms must think carefully about selling unsafe products in foreign markets, a practice that can lead to ill will on the part of the governments there.

Some countries entice new business from foreign firms by offering tax incentives in the form of low property, import, and income taxes for an initial period. In addition, multinational firms may adjust revenue reports so their largest profits are recorded in nations with the lowest tax rates.

> **Home competition may lead to international efforts.**

> **International marketing may extend the product life cycle or dispose of discontinued items.**

6-3 THE SCOPE OF INTERNATIONAL MARKETING

> **The United States is both the world's largest goods and services exporter and importer.**

The world's leading export countries are the United States, China, Germany, Japan, France, and Great Britain. Together, they account for $6.5 trillion annually in goods and services exports (nearly 40 percent of total yearly world exports).[6] In 2007, U.S. merchandise exports were roughly $1.15 trillion, an amount equal to about 8 percent of the U.S. gross domestic product and 9 percent of world merchandise exports. Services accounted for $500 billion in 2007 U.S. exports. Among the leading U.S. exports are capital goods, industrial supplies and materials, food grains, medical equipment, and scientific instruments, and such services as tourism, entertainment, engineering, accounting, insurance, and consulting. Although 70 percent of U.S. foreign business revenues are from large firms, almost one-quarter million U.S. firms with less than 20 employees engage in some level of international marketing.

---

[5] *Heinz 2008 Annual Report.*

[6] The data cited in this section are from "The World Economic Outlook Database," **http://www.imf.org/external/pubs/ft/weo/2008/01/weodata/index.aspx** (April 2008); "The World Factbook;" "Most Frequently Accessed Tables;" and "U.S. International Trade in Goods and Services."

The United States is also the world's largest importer, followed by Germany, China, Great Britain, France, and Japan. In 2007, U.S. merchandise imports were about $2.35 trillion—more than one-sixth of total world merchandise imports. In 2007, service imports were an additional $380 billion. Leading U.S. imports include petroleum, motor vehicles, raw materials, and clothing.

Due to the high level of imports in 2007, the United States had a merchandise *trade deficit*—the amount by which the value of imports exceeds the value of exports—of $820 billion. This was by far the greatest merchandise deficit in the world and set a U.S. record. On the other hand, 2007 U.S. services stayed strong, with a service *trade surplus*—the amount by which the value of exports exceeds the value of imports—of $120 billion. By a large amount, this was the greatest service surplus of any nation.

The U.S. merchandise trade deficit is due to a variety of factors:

> The United States has had large merchandise **trade deficits** and large service **trade surpluses.**

- The attractive nature of the U.S. market. Per-capita consumption is high for most goods and services.
- The slow-growth economies in a number of other countries depressing consumer purchases there.
- Increased competition in foreign markets.
- U.S. dependence on foreign natural resources (including petroleum).
- High U.S. labor costs.
- Trade restrictions in foreign markets.
- U.S. firms virtually exiting such markets as televisions and VCRs.
- Making products in the United States with imported parts and materials.
- The complacency of some U.S. firms in adapting their strategies to the needs of foreign markets.
- The mediocre image of U.S. products in the eyes of many Americans.
- The emphasis of many U.S. firms on profits over market share. In contrast, Japanese firms try to keep prices stable to maximize market share—even if they must reduce profit margins to do so.

Because merchandise trade deficits have been so high, U.S. firms are improving their product quality, focusing on market niches, becoming more efficient, building overseas facilities, and engaging in other tactics to improve competitiveness. Some have called for tighter import controls and more access to restricted foreign markets; one outcome of their efforts is the Omnibus Trade & Competitiveness Act that requires the president to press for open markets. The U.S. government has also negotiated with foreign governments to help matters. For example, China has agreed to amend some practices to improve its trade balance with the United States. Yet, the U.S. trade deficit with China exceeds $250 billion a year.

Despite the trade deficit, the United States is the dominant force globally. Between its imports and exports, the country accounts for more than one-quarter of all global trade.

6-4 THE ENVIRONMENT OF INTERNATIONAL MARKETING

Although the principles described throughout this book are applicable to international marketing strategies, there are often major differences between domestic and foreign markets—and marketing practices may have to adapt accordingly. Each market should be studied separately. Only then can a firm decide how much of its domestic marketing strategy can be used in foreign markets and what elements should be modified.

To gain insights about the global marketplace, useful resources such as these may be consulted:

- International Monetary Fund's "IMF Publications" (**http://www.imf.org/external/ pubind.htm**)
- OECD Data Online (**http://oecdwash.org/DATA/online.htm**)

- United Nations' "UN & Business" (**http://www.un.org/partners/business/index.asp**)
- U.S. Census Bureau's International Programs Center (**http://www.census.gov/ipc/www**)
- U.S. International Trade Administration (**http://trade.gov/index.asp**).
- World Trade Organization's "Resources" (**http://www.wto.org/english/res_e/res_e.htm**).

The major cultural, economic, political and legal, and technological environments facing international marketers are discussed next. See Figure 6-4.

6-4a   The Cultural Environment

International marketers need to be attuned to each foreign market's cultural environment. A *culture* consists of a group of people sharing a distinctive heritage. It teaches behavior standards, language, lifestyles, and goals; is passed down from one generation to another; and is not easily changed. Almost every country has a different culture; regional and continental differences also exist. A firm unfamiliar with or insensitive to a foreign culture may try to market goods or services that are unacceptable to that culture. For example, beef and unisex products are rejected by some cultures.

> Inadequate information about foreign **cultures** is a common cause of errors.

Table 6-1 shows the errors a firm engaged in international marketing might commit due to a lack of awareness about foreign cultures. At times, the firm is at fault because it operates out of its home office and gets little local input. Other times, such as when marketing in less-developed nations, information may be limited because a low level of population data exists and mail and phone service are poor. Either way, research—to determine hidden meanings, the ease of pronunciation of brand names and slogans, the rate of product consumption, and reasons for purchases and nonpurchases—may not be fully effective.

Cultural awareness can be improved by employing foreign personnel in key positions, hiring experienced marketing research specialists, locating offices in each country of operations, studying cultural differences, and responding to cultural changes.[7] Table 6-2 shows several cultural opportunities.

Consider this critique regarding the way many Western firms act when dealing with foreign cultures:

> "There's a right and a wrong approach to establishing a business relationship in China," says Sean Wall, a manager director at DHL-Sinotrans, a Chinese express-shipping provider.

Figure 6-4

The Environment Facing International Marketers

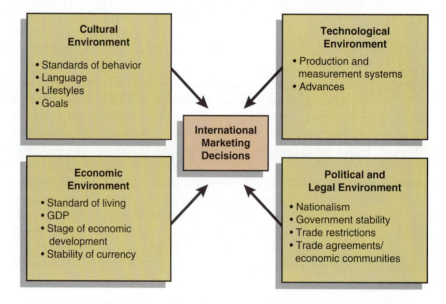

---

[7] See Attila Yaprak, "Culture Study in International Marketing: A Critical Review and Suggestions for Future Research," *International Marketing Review*, Vol. 25 (Number 2, 2008), pp. 215–229.

Table 6-1   Illustrations of Errors in International Marketing Because of a Lack of Cultural Awareness

Cadbury Schweppes, a British confectionary firm, decided to promote its Dr Pepper soft drink in the U.S. through a treasure hunt, in which gold coins were buried throughout the United States. One location was a burial ground in Boston, where such historic figures as Samuel Adams, John Hancock, and Paul Revere were laid to rest.

A U.S. telephone company showed a commercial in Latin America in which a wife told her husband to call a friend and say that they would be late for dinner. The commercial was not successful because Latin Americans would not customarily call a friend about being late.

A golf ball manufacturer packaged golf balls in packs of four for the Japanese market. Since the pronunciation of the word "four" in Japanese sounds like the word "death," four-pack packages are highly unpopular in Japan.

Pepsi broadcast an ad in India showing a young boy serving Pepsi to members of a local cricket team. Unfortunately, many Indians viewed the ad as glorifying the use of child labor.

In the Czech Republic, portable phones did poorly when first introduced because they were perceived as walkie-talkies.

Japanese cars had engine trouble in China, where drivers turned off their motors when stopped at red lights. Because the air-conditioning in these cars kept going with the motors off, the engines malfunctioned.

At the Moscow Pizza Hut, consumers did not purchase the Moscva Seafood pizza, with sardines and salmon. "Russians have this thing. If it's their own, it must be bad."

Pepsodent failed in Southeast Asia when it promised white teeth to a culture where black or yellow teeth are symbols of prestige.

In Quebec, a canned-fish manufacturer promoted a product by showing a woman dressed in shorts, golfing with her husband, and planning to serve canned fish for dinner. These activities violated cultural norms.

Maxwell House advertised itself as the "great American coffee" in Germany, although Germans had little respect for American coffee.

In Mexico, a U.S. airline meant to advertise that passengers could sit in comfortable leather seats; but the phrase used in its Spanish translation ("sentando en cuero") meant "sit naked."

Source: Compiled by the authors from various publications.

"If you're opening a footwear or textile business and at the first meeting tell the Chinese manufacturer how the industry works, and say 'This is how we'll do business'—that's the wrong approach. If you ask direct questions about a business—such as how much money it made in the past—that is the wrong approach. If you expect business decisions to be made quickly at one meeting—that is the wrong approach. Chinese do not discuss or make actual decisions in a business setting." Sean Hurley, Asia Pacific human resources director at Agility Logistics (**http://www.agilitylogistics.com**), says: "In the United States, you never do business with friends. In Asia, you only do business with friends. Before the Chinese will do business with you, they want to spend time getting to know you personally."[8]

One way to learn about a foreign culture is to visit Web-based search engines relating to specific nations or regions. Go to Lycos MultiMania (**http://www.multimania.lycos.fr**)—France, Yahoo! Japan (**http://www.yahoo.co.jp**)—one of three dozen country-based Yahoo! sites, and Terra (**http://www.terra.com**)—Latin America. Most of these sites are in the languages of the nations they represent.

---

[8] Lisa Harrington, "East Meets West," **http://www.inboundlogistics.com/articles/features/0108_feature06.shtml** (January 2008).

Table 6-2	Illustrations of Cultural Opportunities for International Marketers

McDonald's varies its menu worldwide to appeal to tastes, culture, and religious values. For instance, in India, a vegetarian burger, the McAloo Tiki, is served; beer is sold in its German outlets; and in Greece, McDonald's burger is wrapped in pita bread.

General Motors is designing some vehicles capable of being manufactured with either right- or left-hand drive to appeal to driving customs around the world.

Dunkin' Donuts has been successful in Brazil because it understands that Brazilians rarely eat breakfast. It markets donuts in Brazil as a snack, dessert, and party food.

Nokia knows that residents in many developing countries share the use of one phone. It recently launched a phone with call-tracking features for kiosk use as well as multi-phonebook features.

To accommodate the weak electrical infrastructure in India, as well as the low consumer incomes, Hewlett-Packard created an inexpensive and portable solar charger.

Globally, the greatest growth in ready-to-eat cereal sales is in Latin America, where there is new interest in convenient foods.

After one year of employment, in most European countries, people receive 20 to 25 days of vacation (compared to 10 days for Canadians and Americans). This means an emphasis on travel, summer homes, and leisure wear.

Japanese consumers are attracted by high-tech vending machines—such as those that play music, talk, dispense free products at random, and use splashy rotating signs.

In China, the most popular color is red—indicating happiness. Black elicits a positive response because it denotes power and trustworthiness.

French Canadians drink more soda, beer, and wine than their English-speaking counterparts.

Nigerians believe "good beer only comes in green bottles."

PepsiCo expects its international sales to grow at twice the rate of its North American businesses. It's poised to achieve this growth by designing new products in these markets that are tailored to local tastes.

Source: Compiled by the authors from various publications.

6-4b   The Economic Environment

The economic environment of a nation indicates its present and potential capacities for consuming goods and services. Measures of economic performance include the standard of living, the gross domestic product (GDP), the stage of economic development, and the stability of the currency.

> The quality of life in a nation is measured by its **standard of living.**

The **standard of living** refers to the average quantity and quality of goods and services that are owned and consumed in a given nation. United Nations (**http://www.un.org**) and Organization for Economic Cooperation & Development (**http://www.oecd.org**) data show that the United States has the highest standard of living of any major industrialized country. By reviewing a nation's per-capita ownership and consumption across a range of goods and services, a firm can estimate the standard of living there (regarding the average *quantity* of goods and services). Table 6-3 compares data for 11 diverse countries.

> The total value of goods and services produced in a nation is its **gross domestic product.**

As noted in Chapter 2, the **gross domestic product (GDP)** is the total value of goods and services produced in a country each year. Total and per-capita GDP are the most-used measures of a nation's wealth because they are regularly published and easy to calculate and compare with GDP data from other nations. Yet, per-capita GDP may be misleading. The figures are typically means and not income distributions; a few wealthy citizens may boost per-capita GDP, while most people have low income. And due to price and product availability differences, incomes buy different standards of living in

Table 6-3	Ownership and Consumption in Eleven Countries					
	Passenger Cars (per 100 People)	TV Sets (per 100 People)	Telephone Land Lines (per 100 People)	Cell Phones (per 100 People)	Daily Newspaper Circulation (per 100 People)	Electricity Consumption (Kilowatt Hours per Year per Person)
United States	80	80	60	78	21	12,750
Brazil	8	22	20	52	4	1,920
Canada	56	72	65	58	16	16,350
China	5	32	28	35	4	2,200
France	57	60	58	83	22	7,000
Great Britain	48	53	57	115	33	5,725
India	1	10	5	15	6	450
Italy	62	53	46	122	10	5,300
Japan	55	70	56	80	58	7,700
Nigeria	0.1	7	1	23	3	125
Russia	16	41	25	105	11	7,000

Source: Computed by the authors from "InfoNation," http://www.cyberschoolbus.un.org/infonation/index.asp (June 18, 2008); and *World Factbook 2008*, https://www.cia.gov/library/publications/the-world-factbook/index.html (updated as of June 10, 2008).

each nation. According to the World Bank's (http://www.worldbank.org) *World Development Indicators* data base, a U.S. income of $42,000 yields about the same standard of living—purchasing power parity—as $25,500 in Greece, $11,000 in Argentina, $4,100 in China, $2,200 in India, and $800 in Sierra Leone.

Marketing opportunities often can be highlighted by looking at a country's stage of economic growth. One way to classify growth is to divide nations into three main categories: industrialized, developing, and less-developed.[9] See Figure 6-5.

Industrialized countries have high literacy, modern technology, and per-capita income of several thousand dollars. They can be placed into two main subgroups: established free-market economies and newly emerging free-market economies. The former include the United States, Canada, Japan, Australia, and nations in Western Europe; they have a large middle class, annual per-capita GDP of $15,000 and up, and plentiful goods and services to satisfy their needs. The latter include Russia and its former republics, and some Eastern European nations (such as Poland, Romania, and Serbia); though industrialized, they have a smaller middle class, annual per-capita GDP of $6,000 to $14,000, and insufficient goods and services to satisfy all their needs.

In *developing countries*, education and technology are rising, and per-capita GDP is about $4,000 to $9,000. Included are many Latin American and Southeast Asian nations. Although these countries are striving to build their industries, consumers are limited in what they can buy (due to the scarcity and relatively high prices of goods and services). They account for 20 percent of world population and almost one-third of its income.

Less-developed countries include a number of nations in Africa and Asia. Compared to other nations, literacy is lower and technology is more limited. Per-capita GDP is typically below $2,000 (and less than $1,000 for about 50 countries). These nations have

> Countries can be classified as **industrialized, developing, and less developed**.

[9] Adapted by the authors from "Dictionary of Marketing Terms," http://www.marketingpower.com/_layouts/Dictionary.aspx (March 22, 2009), various pages.

Figure 6-5

The Stages of Economic Development

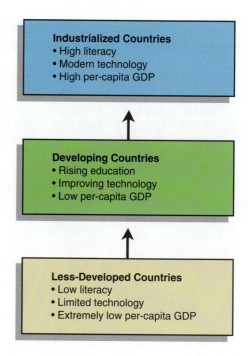

two-thirds of world population but less than 15 percent of world income. According to U.N. data, people in the most affluent one-fifth of the world have 65 times greater per-capita GDP than those in the bottom one-fifth.

The greatest marketing opportunities often occur in industrialized nations due to their higher incomes and standards of living. However, industrialized countries tend to have slow rates of population growth, and sales of some product categories may have peaked. In contrast, developing and less-developed nations tend to have more rapidly expanding populations but now purchase few imports. There is long-run potential for international marketers in these nations. For example, Brazilians have only 80 cars

Marketing and the Web

Europe's Expanding Use of the Web

A recent study conducted by Nielsen (**http://www. nielsen.com**) found that there were more than 315 million Web users in Europe. This represents almost two-fifths of the European population and about one-quarter of worldwide Internet users. As of 2008, eMarketer (**http://www.emarketer.com**) estimated that there will be 136 million Web users in France, Germany, Italy, Spain, and Great Britain, the five largest countries in the European Union. Total online sales in Europe were expected to exceed $100 billion.

The largest online advertising market in the world has been Great Britain, where the Web accounted for as much as 18 percent of all media spending in 2008. According to the Internet Advertising Bureau (**http:// www.iab.net**), British ad spending on the Web now exceeds radio advertising and will soon exceed national print advertising. Some experts attribute the

size of the Web market in Great Britain to strong consumer purchasing activity, low-cost connectivity, and the high incidence of broadband. Internet Trends (**http://www.internettrends.org**) reports that about one-half of all British households now have a high-speed connection; this figure is estimated to reach 77 percent by 2011.

According to other research findings, British use of the Internet involves a multitude of purposes, including product purchases, weather forecasts, business research, legal information, and participation in community sites. One-quarter of British Web users are over 50 years of age. And the Web is more popular there among retired individuals than gardening.

Source: Based on material in Nicola Delasalle, "The Changing Face of the Internet in Europe," **http://www.electronicretailermag.com/info/ere07_face.html** (July 2008).

per 1,000 population and Indians 13 per 1,000. The more than 1.3 billion people of China have 70 million cars—far fewer than in the United States, which has less than one-quarter of the population of China.

Currency stability should also be considered in transactions because sales and profits could be affected if a foreign currency fluctuates widely relative to a firm's home currency. For example, should the value of a foreign currency strengthen relative to the U.S. dollar, then U.S. products become less expensive to consumers in that foreign country (exports) and that country's products become more expensive for U.S. consumers (imports).

The currencies of both industrialized countries and developing and less-developed nations typically fluctuate—sometimes dramatically. As a rule, established free-market industrialized countries' currencies have been more stable than those of other nations.

6-4c The Political and Legal Environment

Every nation and region has a unique political and legal environment. Among the factors to consider are nationalism, government stability, trade restrictions, and trade agreements and economic communities. These factors can be complex, as the growing European Union has discovered.

Nationalism refers to a country's efforts to become self-reliant and raise its stature in the eyes of the world community. At times, a high degree of nationalism may lead to tight restrictions on foreign firms to foster the development of domestic industry at their expense. In the past, some nations even seized the assets of multinational firms, revoked their licenses to operate, prevented funds transfers from one currency to another, increased taxes, and/or unilaterally changed contract terms.

Government stability must be studied in terms of two elements: consistency of business policies and orderliness in installing leaders. Do government policies regarding taxes, company expansion, profits, and so on remain rather unchanged over time? Is there an orderly process for selecting and installing new government leaders? Firms will probably not function well unless both factors are positive. Thus, although many companies have made large investments in developing nations, others have stayed away from some less-developed and developing countries.

A firm can protect itself against the adverse effects of nationalism and political instability. Prior to entering a foreign market, it can measure the potential for domestic instability (riots, government purges), the political climate (stability of political parties, manner of choosing officials), and the economic climate (financial strength, government intervention)—and avoid nations deemed unsuitable. PRS Group (**http://www.prsgroup.com**) provides political risk assessment of nations around the globe and shows a sample report at its Web site. The U.S. Overseas Private Investment Corporation, OPIC (**http://www.opic.gov**), insures American investments in developing and less-developed nations against asset takeovers and earnings inconvertibility; in addition, private underwriters insure foreign investments. Risks can also be reduced by using foreign partners, borrowing money from foreign governments or banks, and/or utilizing licensing, contract manufacturing, or management contracting (which are covered later in the chapter).

Another aspect of the international political and legal environment involves trade restrictions. Most common is the *tariff*, a tax placed on imported products by a foreign government. The second major restriction is a *trade quota*, which sets limits on the amounts of products that can be imported into a country. The strictest form of trade quota is an *embargo*, which disallows entry of specified products into a country. The third major restriction involves *local content laws*, which require foreign-based firms to set up local plants and use locally made components. The goal of tariffs, trade quotas, and local content laws is to protect economies and domestic workers of the nations involved. Embargoes often have political ramifications, such as the United States refusing to trade with Cuba. Here are examples:

> Currency stability affects foreign sales and profit.

> **Nationalism** involves a host country's attempts to promote its interests.

> Tariffs, trade quotas, embargoes, and **local content laws** are forms of trade restrictions.

- The United States imposes tariffs (**http://www.dataweb.usitc.gov**) on imported clothing, ceramic tiles, rubber footwear, brooms, flowers, cement, computer screens, sugar, candy, trucks, and other items. The tariffs raise import prices relative to domestic items. At its Web site, the U.S. International Trade Administration cites tariffs by other nations (**http://www.trade.gov/td/tic/tariff**).
- China has trade quotas on a variety of agricultural products, including corn, cotton, palm oil, rice, soybean oil, sugar, vegetable seed oil, wheat, and fine wool.
- To stimulate domestic production, for nearly a decade, Brazil placed an embargo on most foreign computer products—thus banning their sales there.
- In Italy, such food products as pasta, olive oil, and tomato have strict country-of-origin labeling laws.

Trade agreements and economic communities have reduced many barriers among nations. In 1948, 23 nations, including the United States, signed the General Agreement on Tariffs and Trade (GATT) to foster multilateral trade. By 1994, 115 nations participated in GATT. From its inception, GATT helped lower tariffs on manufactured goods. But members got bogged down since trade in services, agriculture, textiles, and investment and capital flows was not covered; and GATT let members belong to regional trade associations (economic communities) with fewer trade barriers among the nations involved in those associations than with those not involved.

The **World Trade Organization** seeks to eliminate trade barriers.

In 1995, after years of tough negotiations, GATT was replaced by the *World Trade Organization, WTO* (**http://www.wto.org**). About 155 nations have since joined the WTO, whose mission is to open up markets even further and promote a cooperative atmosphere around the globe:

> The WTO is the only international organization dealing with global rules of trade between nations. Its main function is to ensure that trade flows as smoothly, predictably, and freely as possible. The result is assurance. Consumers and producers know they can enjoy secure supplies and greater choice of finished products, components, raw materials, and services. Producers and exporters know foreign markets will remain open to them. The result is also a more prosperous, peaceful, and accountable economic world. WTO decisions are typically taken by consensus among all member countries and they are ratified by members' parliaments. Trade friction is channeled into the WTO's dispute settlement process where the focus is on interpreting agreements and commitments, and how to ensure that countries' trade policies conform with them. This reduces the risk of disputes spilling over into political or military conflict. By lowering trade barriers, the WTO also breaks down other barriers between peoples and nations. At the heart of the system—known as the multilateral trading system—are the WTO's agreements, negotiated and signed by a large majority of the world's trading nations, and ratified in their parliaments. These agreements are legal ground-rules for international commerce. They are contracts, guaranteeing member countries important trade rights. They also bind governments to keep their trade policies within agreed limits to everybody's benefit.[10]

In contrast to the WTO, which promotes free trade around the world, each *economic community* promotes free trade among its member nations—but not necessarily with nonmember nations. As a result, the best interests of the WTO and economic communities may clash.

The two leading **economic communities** are formed by the **European Union** and the **North American Free Trade Agreement**.

The two leading economic communities are the European Union (**http://europa.eu/index_en.htm**) and the North American Free Trade community (**http://www.nafta-sec-alena.org**). The *European Union (EU)*, also called the Common Market, has grown to 27 countries: 15 long-standing members (Austria, Belgium, Denmark, Finland, France, Germany, Great Britain, Greece, Ireland, Italy, Luxembourg, Netherlands, Portugal, Spain, and Sweden), and 12 newer ones (Bulgaria, Cyprus, Czech Republic, Estonia, Hungary, Latvia, Lithuania, Malta, Poland, Romania, Slovakia, and Slovenia).

---

[10] "The World Trade Organization," **http://www.wto.org/english/res_e/doload_e/inbr_e.pdf** (2007).

EU rules call for no trade restrictions among members, uniform tariffs with nonmembers, common product standards, and a free flow of people and capital. The aim is for members to have an open marketplace, such as exists among states in the United States. One of the EU's biggest challenges has been installing a common currency, the Euro, across all of its members. The combined GDP of the enlarged EU is slightly more than that of the United States; the total population is almost 1.7 times that of the United States. And the EU hopes to add even more countries in the future.

The ***North American Free Trade Agreement (NAFTA)*** was enacted in 1994, creating an economic community that links the United States, Canada, and Mexico; it has sought to remove tariffs and other trade restrictions among the three countries. The population of NAFTA countries is about 90 percent that of the expanded EU, while the NAFTA members' GDP is 15 to 20 percent higher. In 2005, the United States also entered into a more limited arrangement to form the U.S.-CAFTA-DR Free Trade Agreement (**http://www.export.gov/fta/cafta**), which includes the United States, Costa Rica, Dominican Republic, El Salvador, Guatemala, Honduras, and Nicaragua.

Other economic communities include the Andean Pact (**http://www.comunidadandina.org/endex.htm**), with 4 Latin American members; Association of Southeast Asian Nations (**http://www.aseansec.org**), with 10 members; Caribbean Community (**http://www.caricom.org**), with more than a dozen members; Central American Common Market (**http://www.sieca.org.gt/site/inicio.aspx**), with 5 members; Gulf Cooperation Council (**http://www.gcc-sg.org/eng/index.php**), with 6 Arabic members; Economic Community of West African States (**http://www.ecowas.int**), with 15 members; and Mercosur (**http://www.mercosurtc.com**), with 4 Latin American members.

The International Monetary Fund gives descriptions of many other economic communities at its Web site (**http://www.imf.org/external/np/sec/decdo/contents.htm**).

6-4d   The Technological Environment

International marketing is affected by technological factors such as these:

- Technology advances vary around the world. For example, in the United States, 72 percent of households have cable TV service and only 15 percent have satellite TV service. In Western Europe, these figures are quite different due to the lack of cable wiring and the growth of TV satellites. Thus, in Great Britain, just 15 percent of households have cable TV service while one-quarter have satellite service.
- Foreign workers must often be trained to run equipment unfamiliar to them.
- Problems occur if equipment maintenance practices vary by nation or if adverse physical conditions exist, such as high humidity, extreme hot or cold weather, or air pollution.
- Electricity and electrical power needs may vary by nation and require product modifications. For example, U.S. appliances work on 110 volts; European appliances work on 220 volts.
- Although the metric system is used in nations with 95 percent of the world's population, the United States still relies on ounces, pounds, inches, and feet. Thus, auto makers, beverage bottlers, and many other U.S. firms make items using metric standards—and then list U.S. and metric measures side-by-side on labels and packages. For the United States to convert to the metric system, the American consumer must be better educated about measurement and learn meters, liters, and other metric standards; the process remains slow (**http://ts.nist.gov/weightsandmeasures/metric/lc1136lv.cfm**).

> International marketing may require adjustments in technology.

On the positive side, various technological advances are easing the growth of international marketing. They involve communications (fiber optics, the Internet), transactions (automatic teller machines), order processing (computerization), and production (multiplant innovations).

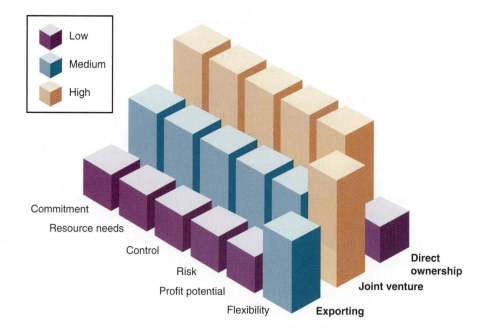

Figure 6-6

Alternate Company Organizations for International Marketing

6-5 DEVELOPING AN INTERNATIONAL MARKETING STRATEGY

The vital parts of an international marketing strategy are explored next: company organization, market entry decisions, the degree of standardization, and product, distribution, promotion, and price planning.

6-5a Company Organization

A firm has three organizational formats from which to choose: exporting, joint venture, and direct ownership. They are compared in Figure 6-6.

With *exporting*, a firm reaches international markets by selling products made in its home country directly through its own sales force or indirectly via foreign merchants or agents. In direct selling, a firm situates its sales force in a home office or in foreign branch offices. This is best if customers are easy to locate, concentrated, or come to the seller. With indirect selling, a firm hires outside specialists to contact customers. The specialists may be based in the home or foreign nation. There are 1,500 to 2,000 specialized U.S. export management firms marketing products in foreign nations (**http://www.ita.doc. gov/td/oetca/emcs.html**). Indirect selling is best if customers are hard to locate or dispersed, if a potential exporter has limited funds, and/or if local customs are unique.

An exporting structure requires minimal investment in foreign facilities. There is no foreign production by the firm. The exporter may modify packages, labels, or catalogs at its domestic facilities in response to foreign market needs. Exporting involves the lowest commitment to international marketing. Most smaller firms that engage in international marketing rely on exporting. For example, Purafil (**http://www.purafil.com**) is a Georgia-based maker of equipment that removes corrosive, odorous, and toxic gases from commercial and industrial environments, as well as museums, libraries, and archives. It relies on local distributors to market its products in more than 60 countries around the globe, and foreign business now accounts for more than 60 percent of the firm's $55 million in annual revenues.[11]

> **Exporting** lets a firm reach international markets without foreign production.

---

[11] Julia Boorstin, "Small & Global: Exporting Cleaner Air," **http://www.fortune.com/fortune/smallbusiness/ marketing/articles/0,15114,643698,00.html** (June 2004); and "Purafil Cleans Air in Buildings Across the Globe," **http://www.gbj.com/content.cfm?Action=story_detail&StoryID=2045** (May 2007).

Global Marketing in Action

Avon Calling: Shining a Global Star

U.S.-based Avon (http://www.avon.com) is a true global company with $10 billion in global sales revenues—three-quarters outside the United States. It sales representative are often British, Russian, or Chinese:

- Avon has sales operations in 66 countries and territories, including the United States, and it distributes its products in 48 additional countries and territories.
- Even though Avon's global research and development facility is located in New York, it has satellite research facilities in Brazil, China, Japan, Mexico, and Poland.
- Avon has manufacturing facilities in Latin America, Asia Pacific, and China.
- Avon views its geographic diversity as a major strategic advantage. It seeks higher growth rates in developing and emerging markets (such as Brazil, China, Columbia, Russia, Turkey, and

Venezuela) than in developed markets such as the United States.

A key competitive advantage for Avon is its direct-selling channel. Avon's 5.4 million active independent sales representatives (about 460,000 of whom work in the United States), along with its promotional brochures, embody the "stores" in which Avon products are sold worldwide. Direct selling enables Avon to quickly set up a sales network by using independent representatives. Avon also sells its products through its Web sites in the United States and other markets. The sites serve consumers who do not have access to or do not wish to buy from an Avon representative. In some countries, such as Brazil, Avon has established cosmetics sales centers to give customers an opportunity to sample products.

Sources: Based on material in "First Avon Door in Brazil," *Latin Beat* (August 2007), pp. 34–35; and *Avon 2007 Annual Report.*

With a *joint venture* (also known as a *strategic alliance*), a firm agrees to combine some aspect of its manufacturing or marketing efforts with those of a foreign company so as to share expertise, costs, and/or connections with key persons. A joint venture may also lead to favorable trade terms from a foreign government if products are made locally and there is some degree of foreign ownership. However, such ventures may not be easy. For example, in China, "Companies pursuing a joint venture need a clear and realistic idea about why they want such an alliance. They should understand the bigger picture—including China's political climate and investment trends. They should also understand the current and potential future motivations of the partner and what the partner can contribute in the short and long run. To do this, foreign companies must conduct thorough due diligence on the potential partner; analysis will require more expertise, time, and effort than is common in more developed markets."[12]

Here are examples of firms engaged in international joint ventures:

> A **joint venture** can be based on licensing, contract manufacturing, management contracting, or joint ownership.

- "Working with the renowned Chinese company Brilliance China Automotive Holdings Limited (CBA), the BMW Group [Germany] has established a production and sales joint venture. Based in Shenyang, China, this extends BMW's international presence" (http://www.bmw-brilliance.cn/bba/en).
- U.S.-based General Electric (http://www.ge.com) has a joint venture with Mubadala Development (http://www.mubadala.ae). This $6 billion agreement involves commercial finance in the Middle East and Africa. The firms also plan to cooperate in other opportunities involving energy, water, and aviation.
- Thailand's Charoen Pokphand (http://www.cpthailand.com) has had a telecommunications venture with Verizon (United States), an insurance venture with Allianz AG (Germany), and a food venture with Indo-Aquatics (India).

---

[12] Jan Borgonjon and David J. Hofmann, "The Re-Emergence of the Joint Venture?" *China Business Review*, Vol. 35 (May-June 2008), p. 34.

Figure 6-7

Gigante: A Good Joint Venture Partner

Mexico's Gigante has joint ventures in that country with various foreign firms, including U.S.-based Radio Shack and Office Depot.

Source: Reprinted by permission of Susan Berry, Retail Image Consulting, Inc.

- Mexico's Gigante (**http://www.gigante.com.mx/content/new-site/home.html**) works with U.S.-based Radio Shack (**http://www.radioshack.com**) and Office Depot (**http://www.officedepot.com**). See Figure 6-7.

Joint ventures operate under several different formats. *Licensing* gives a foreign firm the rights to a manufacturing process, trademark, patent, and/or trade secret in exchange for a commission, fee, or royalty. The Coca-Cola Company (**http://www.cocacola.com**) and PepsiCo (**http://www.pepsico.com**) license products in some nations. In *contract manufacturing*, a firm agrees to have a foreign partner make its products locally. The firm markets the products itself and provides management expertise. This is common in book publishing. With *management contracting*, a firm acts as a consultant to foreign companies. Such hotel chains as Hilton (**http://www.hilton.com**), Hyatt (**http://www.hyatt.com**), and Sheraton (**http://www.starwoodhotels.com/sheraton**) use management contracting. With *joint ownership*, a firm produces and markets products in partnership with a foreign firm so as to reduce costs and spread risk. At times, a foreign government may insist on joint ownership with local businesses as a condition for entry. In Canada, outsiders have been required to use joint ownership with Canadian firms for new ventures.

With ***direct ownership***, a firm owns production, marketing, and other facilities in one or more foreign nations without any partners. The firm has full control over its operations in those nations. Thus, Great Britain's Invensys (**http://www.invensys.com**) owns a factory in Belluno, Italy, that makes electromagnetic timers for washing machines. Sometimes, wholly owned subsidiaries may be established. In the United States, the Stop & Shop and Giant Food supermarket chains are subsidiaries of Royal Ahold (**http://www.ahold.com**) of the Netherlands. Similarly, foreign facilities of U.S.-based firms annually yield revenues of hundreds of billions of dollars.

Under direct ownership, a firm has all the benefits and risks of owning a foreign business. Potential labor savings exist, and marketing plans are more sensitive to local needs. Profit potential may be high, although costs may also be high. Nationalistic acts are a possibility, and government restrictions are apt to be stricter. This is the riskiest organization form.

Formats may be combined. A firm could export to a country with a history of political unrest and use direct ownership in a country with tax advantages for construction. McDonald's worldwide efforts (**http://www.mcdonalds.com/countries.html**)

> **Direct ownership** involves total control of foreign operations and facilities by a firm.

combine company restaurants, franchised restaurants, and affiliate-operated restaurants (whereby McDonald's owns 50 percent or less of assets, with the rest owned by resident nationals). Company outlets are largely in the United States, Canada, France, Great Britain, and Germany; franchised outlets are mostly in the United States, Canada, France, Germany, and Australia; and affiliate restaurants are common in Latin America, Japan, and other Pacific nations.

6-5b   Market Entry Decisions

Various factors must be considered in deciding which and how many foreign markets a firm should enter. Here are several of them:

> A firm needs to determine which and how many foreign markets in which to do business.

Which Market(s) to Enter

- Are there cultural similarities between a foreign nation and a firm's home market? How vital is this?
- Are there language similarities between a foreign nation and a firm's home market? How vital is this?
- Is the standard of living in a foreign market consistent with what a firm would offer there?
- How large is a foreign market for the goods and services a firm would offer there? Is it growing? What is the regional potential (e.g., Eastern Europe)?
- Is the technology in a foreign market sufficient for a firm to do business? Is the country's infrastructure sufficient?
- Are there enough skilled workers in a foreign country?
- Are the media in a foreign country adequate for a firm's marketing efforts?
- What is the level of competition in a foreign market?
- What government restrictions would a firm face in a foreign market? The economic communities?
- How stable are the currency and government in a foreign market?
- Is the overall business climate in a foreign country favorable to a firm?

How Many Markets to Enter

- What are the firm's available resources?
- How many foreign markets could a firm's personnel properly oversee and service?
- How diverse are multiple foreign markets? What is the geographic proximity?
- What are the marketing economies of scale from being regional or global?
- Are exporting arrangements possible? Are joint ventures?
- What are a firm's goals regarding its mix of domestic and foreign revenues?
- How extensive is competition in a firm's home market?

6-5c   Standardizing Plans

A firm engaged in international marketing must determine the degree to which plans should be standardized. Both standardized and nonstandardized plans have benefits and limitations.

With a *standardized (global) marketing approach*, a firm uses a common marketing plan for all nations in which it operates—because it assumes worldwide markets are becoming more homogeneous due to better communications, more open country borders, the move to free-market economies, and other factors. This approach downplays differences among countries. Marketing and production economies exist—product design, packaging, advertising, and other costs are spread over a large product base. A uniform image is presented, training foreign personnel is easier, and centralized control is applied. Yet, standardization is insensitive to individual market needs, and input from foreign personnel is limited:

> Firms sometimes assume that what works in their home country will work in another country. They take the same product, same advertising campaign, even the same brand names and

> Under a **global approach**, a common marketing plan is used for each nation. Under a **nonstandardized approach**, each country is given a separate marketing plan. A **glocal approach** is a combination strategy.

packaging, and try to market it the same way in another country. The result in many cases is failure. Why? Well, the assumption that one approach works everywhere fails to consider differences between countries and cultures. While many firms that sell internationally are successful with a standardized marketing strategy, it is a mistake to assume this approach will work without sufficient research.[13]

With a **nonstandardized marketing approach**, a firm sees each nation or region as distinct and requiring its own marketing plan. This strategy is sensitive to local needs and means grooming foreign managers, as decentralized control is undertaken. It works best if distinctive major foreign markets are involved or a firm has many product lines. Consider T-Mobile's (**http://www.t-mobile.com**) approach: the firm's "heady global strategy is being played out locally with a twist based on each country organization's unique challenges and market. In the face of growing competition in Eastern Europe, the Czech Republic is using a multisite, multimedia environment to manage its customer communications within a single infrastructure; T-Mobile in Germany is increasing sales performance and simplifying business processes by centrally managing all information and communications; and T-Mobile USA is keeping pace with the changing U.S. market-place by arming its contact center agents with the skills and knowledge they need to respond to customers' needs."[14]

In recent years, more firms (such as T-Mobile) have turned to a **glocal marketing approach**—which stands for *think global and act local*. This approach combines stand-ardized and nonstandardized efforts to enable a firm to attain production efficiencies, have a consistent image, have some home-office control, and still be responsive to local needs. This is how Germany's Henkel (**http://www.henkel.com**)—a manufacturer of adhesives and home- and personal-care products that are sold in 125 countries—uses a glocal approach:

> Eighty percent of Henkel's employees are based outside of its home market. Emerging markets account for 35 percent of its sales. In 2004, it bought U.S.-based Dial Corporation, maker of Dial soap and Right Guard deodorant. About 80 percent of the company's brands are global and 20 percent are local. "What makes us different [from some of our competitors] is that we also believe strongly in our local brands. These are often brands that we have acquired in the past, and which may have huge brand equity. When they do, then we keep the original brand name to take advantage of that equity, but use the same packaging that we use for products sold in other markets." One example of a glocal brand is its FA range of deodorants and shower gels. In Sweden, the products are sold under the Barnängen label—a Swedish brand; and in Italy, as Neutromed—another local brand. "We have three different labels for a product that is made in the same factory. "That way, we benefit from the local brand equity as well as taking advantage of the economies of scale that Henkel can provide."[15]

When choosing a marketing approach, a firm should evaluate whether differences among countries are great enough to warrant changes in marketing plans, which elements of marketing can be standardized, whether the size of each foreign market could lead to profitable adaptation, and if modifications can be made on a regional rather than a country basis.

6-5d Product Planning

International product planning (for both goods and services) can be based on straight extension, product adaptation, backward invention, and/or forward invention.

[13] "Global Marketing," **http://www.knowthis.com/internl.htm** (March 2, 2009).

[14] Mila D'Antonio, "T-Mobile's Global Strategy Goes Local," *1to1* (July-August 2005), p. 28.

[15] Emma Barraclough, "Henkel's Global Transformation," **http://www.managingip.com/Article/1933496/Henkels-global-transformation.html** (May 18, 2008).

Ethical Issues in Marketing

Building a Modern Mall in Nigeria

The developers of The Palms (http://www.thepalms shopping.com), a fully-enclosed 215,000-square-foot shopping center in Lagos, Nigeria, have encountered a number of challenges. Because the government bans many imports, including furnishings for the shops and even carpeting for the movie theater, store fixtures must be locally produced. Some shipments have been delayed because the developers refused to bribe local officials. A 9-inch-thick, 8-foot-high concrete block wall was built around the perimeter of the center for riot protection. An electric power generator plant is necessary due to Lagos' frequent electrical outages. And the center needs its own sewage and water purification facilities.

The Palms has about 55 stores, ranging in size from 300 to 6,400 square feet (including Africa's largest grocery store and a major discount store), a six-screen movie theater, and parking for about 700 cars. The center's target market includes middle-class and wealthy Nigerians, as well as foreigners who work in Nigeria, many of whom work in Nigeria's oil industry.

There are now discussions of extending The Palm's size as well as developing three similar malls in Nigeria. According to a property manager, "Nigerians have embraced mall culture." Some attribute the success of The Palms to its affect on people's lives. Where once shopping meant going to an open-air market or a neighborhood small store, consumers can now browse the aisles and chose from vast selections at supermarkets or large discount stores.

Sources: Based on material in Ed McKinley, "Against All Odds," *Shopping Center Today* (April 2005), pp. 55–58; and "Palms Shopping Center," http://en.wikipedia.org/wiki/Palms_Shopping_Mall (July 25, 2008).

In a ***straight extension*** strategy, a firm makes and markets the same products for domestic and foreign sales. The firm is confident it can sell items abroad without modifying the products, the brand name, packaging, or ingredients. This simple approach capitalizes on economies of scale in production. Apple (http://www.apple.com) markets the same PCs in the United States, Mexico, and many other countries. Soda companies use straight extension in many (but not all) countries around the world. Beer makers also use straight extension, and imported beer often has a higher status than domestic beer. Yet, straight extension does not account for differences in customers, laws, customs, technology, and other factors.

With a ***product adaptation*** strategy, domestic products are modified to meet foreign language needs, taste preferences, climates, electrical requirements, laws, and/or other factors. It is assumed that new products are not needed and minor changes are sufficient. This is the most-used strategy in international marketing: Heinz (http://www.heinz.com) adapts its food products to the tastes and languages of the nations in which they are sold–see Figure 6-8. Disneyland Resort Paris (http://www.disneylandparis.com) features Mickey Mouse, Cinderella, and other U.S. Disney characters but also has food concessions and hotels that are adapted to European tastes; KFC (http://www.kfc.co.jp) has grilled rice balls to go with its fried chicken wings in Japan; PepsiCo's Cheetos cheese-flavored puff snack (http://www.cheetos.com) is cheeseless in China (with flavors such as buttered popcorn); gasoline formulations vary according to a nation's weather conditions; and appliances are modified to accommodate different voltage requirements.

With ***backward invention***, a firm appeals to developing and less-developed nations by making products less complex than the ones it sells in its domestic market. This includes manual cash registers and nonelectric sewing machines for consumers in areas without widespread electricity and inexpensive washing machines for consumers in low-income countries. Whirlpool (http://www.whirlpool.com) affiliates build and sell an inexpensive "world washer" in Brazil, Mexico, and India. It is compact, is specially designed (so it does not tangle a sari), handles about one-half the capacity of a regular U.S. washer, and accommodates variations in component availability and local preferences.

In ***forward invention***, a company develops new products for its international markets. This plan is riskier and more time-consuming and requires a higher investment than other strategies. It may also provide the firm with great profit potential and, sometimes, worldwide recognition for innovativeness. With nearly three-quarters of its

> **Straight extension, product adaptation, backward invention,** and **forward invention** are methods of international product planning.

Figure 6-8

Product Modification by Heinz: Adapting to Local Markets

Source: Reprinted by permission.

overall sales coming from foreign markets, U.S.-based Colgate-Palmolive (**http://www. colgate.com**) often engages in forward invention. For example, it developed La Croix bleach for Europe and Protex antibacterial soap for Asia, Africa, and Latin America. See Figure 6-9.

6-5e Distribution Planning

> Channel members and physical distribution methods depend on customs, availability, costs, and other factors.

International distribution planning encompasses the selection and use of resellers and products' physical movement. A firm may sell direct to customers or hire outside distribution specialists—depending on the traditional relationships in a country, the availability of appropriate resellers, differences in distribution practices from those in the home country, government restrictions, costs, and other factors. For example,

- Central cities in Europe often have more shopping ambience than central cities in the United States.
- In Brazil, PepsiCo (**http://www.pepsi.com.br**) markets soft drinks through the domestic AmBev (**http://www.ambev.com.br/eng/index_en.php**) beer and soda company because of its extensive Brazilian distribution network.
- Amway sells its household products in Japan (**http://www.amway.co.jp**) via hundreds of thousands of local distributors (who are also customers); as in the United States, distributors earn commissions on sales.
- In the Philippines, Avon (**http://www.avoncompany.com/world**) uses a special system of branch outlets to service its representatives. See Figure 6-10.

Figure 6-9

Forward Invention by Colgate-Palmolive

The firm has introduced a number of products especially made for its foreign markets and not sold in its home base of the United States.

Source: Reprinted by permission.

Distribution often requires special planning: Processing marine insurance, government documents, and other papers may take time. Transportation may be inefficient if a nation has limited docking facilities, poor highways, or few vehicles. Distribution by ship is slow and may be delayed. Stores may be much smaller than in the United States. Inventory management must take into account warehousing availability and the costs of shipping in small amounts. When Ben & Jerry's entered Russia in the 1990s, it had problems due to the lack of refrigerated trucks and freezers. So, it brought in Western trucks and freezers to store its ice cream. The distribution process turned out to be too costly and inefficient, causing Ben & Jerry's to exit the Russian market. The firm still operates in nearly 25 other countries.[16]

6-5f Promotion Planning

Campaigns can be global, nonstandardized, or glocal. Figure 6-11 shows an example of a glocal ad.

Firms may use global promotion for image purposes. For example, FedEx (**http://www.fedex.com**) introduced a global advertising campaign, "Behind the Scenes," to "reinforce how FedEx helps customers access market opportunities—globally and locally—around the world." The campaign "extended the strong legacy of the FedEx brand globally by reinforcing our commitment to delivering an outstanding customer experience consistently around the world." Ads were placed in "strategic print and online media and appeared in key markets, including Great Britain, France, Germany, Italy, India, Hong Kong, China, Singapore, Taiwan, Korea, Japan, Mexico, Brazil, and Canada."[17]

Companies marketing in various European nations often find that some standardization is desirable due to overlapping readers, listeners, and viewers. For instance,

> International promotion planning depends on the overlap of audiences and languages and the availability of media.

[16] "Our Company," **http://www.benjerry.com/our_company** (March 2, 2009).

[17] "FedEx Launches Global Advertising Campaign," **http://news.van.fedex.com/node/7977** (February 15, 2008).

Figure 6-10

Avon: Meeting Local Distribution Needs

For foreign markets where the distribution structure is underdeveloped, Avon uses a system of branches to help sales representatives receive products for delivery to customers. Avon has "branch supermarkets," like the one shown here in the Philippines.

Source: Reprinted by permission.

German TV shows are received by a large percentage of Dutch households, and *Paris Match* magazine (**http://www.parismatch.com**) has readers in Belgium, Switzerland, Luxembourg, Germany, Italy, and Holland.

There are also good reasons for using nonstandardized promotion. Many countries have distinctions that are not addressed by a single promotion campaign—including customs, language, the meaning of colors and symbols, and literacy. Appropriate media may be unavailable. In a number of nations, few households own TV sets, ads are restricted, and/or mailing lists are not current. National pride sometimes requires that individual promotions be used. Even within regions that have perceived similarities, such as within Western Europe or within Latin America, differences exist. In both regions, several different languages are used, and many consumers want to receive messages in their own language.

Most firms end up utilizing glocal promotion plans:

Standardized strategies seem most apt if a product is utilitarian and the message is informational. Reasons for buying or using the good or service are rational—and less apt to vary by culture. Glue, batteries, and gasoline are such products. A standardized approach would also appear effective if a brand's identity and desirability are integrally linked to a specific national character. Coca-Cola and McDonald's are marketed as "quintessential American products"; Chanel is a "quintessential French product." Yet, it is generally more effective to *glocalize strategies* to local customs and cultures:

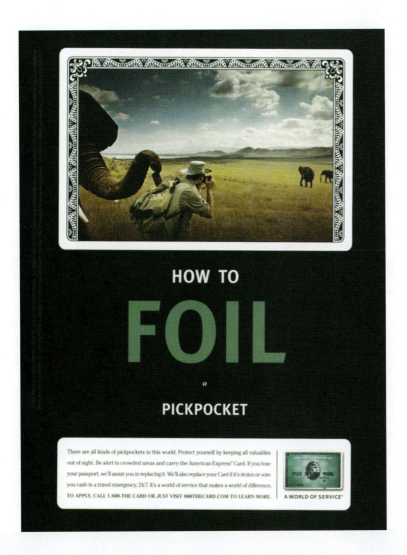

Figure 6-11

A Glocal Ad from American Express

American Express is a worldwide financial services company. It runs English ads, such as the one here, in various English-speaking countries; and it runs ads in the languages of many of the other countries in which it does business. Its advertising themes—such as security—tend to be universal.

Source: Reprinted by permission.

- Product usage often varies according to the culture.
- For many products, benefits are more psychological than tangible, requiring an understanding of the psychologies of different cultures.
- Some societies are demonstrative and open; others are aloof or private.
- Advertisers must consider a multicultural and flexible strategy if a brand is in different stages of development or of varying stature across different markets.
- A commercial for a mature market may not work well in a developing one.
- A commercial in a market where the product/brand is unique has quite a different task than a commercial where competition is intense.[18]

The World Advertising Research Center (http://www.warc.com) offers considerable information on international promotion planning.

6-5g Price Planning

The basic considerations in international price planning are whether prices should be standardized, the level at which prices are set, the currency in which prices are quoted, and terms of sale.

---

[18] McCollum Spielman Worldwide, "Global Advertising: Standardized or Multicultural? *Topline* (Number 37, 1992), pp. 3–4.

Unless a firm operates in an economic community such as the EU (and sometimes, even then), price standardization is hard. Taxes, tariffs, and currency exchange charges are among the costs a firm incurs internationally. For example, a car made in the United States is typically priced at several thousand dollars higher when sold in Japan, due to currency exchange fees, shipping costs, taxes, inspection fees, and so forth. "Homologation" alone (inspections and modifications needed to meet Japan's standards) could add $2,000 to $3,000 to the final selling price.

When setting a price level, a firm would consider such local factors as per-capita GDP. Thus, firms may try to hold down prices in developing and less-developed countries by marketing simpler product versions or employing less-expensive local labor. On the other hand, prices in such industrialized nations as France and Germany can reflect product quality and the added costs of international marketing.

Some firms set lower prices abroad to enhance their global presence and sales or to remove excess supply from their home markets and preserve the prices there. With *dumping*, a firm sells a product in a foreign nation at a price much lower than in its home market, below the cost of production, or both. In the United States and many other nations, duties may be levied on products "dumped" by foreign firms.[19]

If a firm sets prices on the basis of its home currency, the risk of foreign currency devaluation is passed along to the buyer and there is better control. But this strategy has limitations. Consumers may be confused or unable to convert a price into their own currency, or a foreign government may insist that prices be quoted in its currency. Two easy-to-use currency converter Web sites are Universal Currency Converter (**http://www.xe.net/ucc**) and FXConverter (**http://www.oanda.com/converter/classic**). See Figure 6-12.

Terms of sale also need to be set. This involves such judgments as what fees or discounts channel intermediaries get for the tasks they perform, when ownership is transferred, what payment form is required, how much time customers have to pay bills, and what constitutes a proper refund policy.

> Major decisions in international price planning involve standardization, levels, currency, and sales terms. **Dumping** is disliked by host countries.

Figure 6-12

Choosing a Currency

Due to constantly shifting exchange rates, a key decision for a company marketing internationally is the choice of the currency or currencies it uses when selling its goods and services.

Source: Reprinted by permission of Susan Berry, Retail Image Consulting, Inc.

[19] See "Overview of Trade Remedies," **http://ia.ita.doc.gov/pcp/pcp-overview.html.**

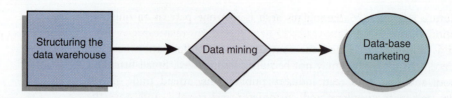

Structuring the data warehouse	Data mining	Data-base marketing
Company compiles, sorts, and stores relevant customer information: • Demographic and lifestyle characteristics • Past purchase behavior • Attitudes • Desired product features • Trends • Etc.	Company: (a) Reviews information in data warehouse to highlight marketing opportunities (b) Derives customer profiles based on most meaningful factors (c) Generates possible market segments with unique needs (d) Prioritizes market segments based on their profit potential	Company pinpoints its marketing efforts to stimulate customer interest, to offer tailored differential advantages, and to maximize customer satisfaction. Relationship marketing is the foundation for all long-run efforts.

An *experiment* is a type of research in which one or more factors are manipulated under controlled conditions. A factor may be any element of marketing from package design to advertising media. In an experiment, just the factor under study is varied; all other factors remain constant. For example, to evaluate a new package design for a product, a manufacturer could send new packages to five retail outlets and old packages to five similar outlets; all marketing factors other than packaging remain the same. After one month, sales of the new package at the test outlets are compared with sales of the old package at similar outlets. A survey or observation is used to determine the reactions to an experiment.

An experiment's key advantage is that it can show cause and effect—such as a new package increasing sales. It is also methodically structured and enacted. Key disadvantages are the rather high costs, frequent use of contrived settings, and inability to control all factors in or affecting a marketing plan.

Simulation is a computer-based method to test the potential effects of various marketing factors via a software program rather than real-world applications. A model of the controllable and uncontrollable factors facing the firm is first built. Different combinations of factors are then fed into a computer to see their possible impact on a marketing strategy. Simulation requires no consumer cooperation and can handle many interrelated factors. Yet, it may be complex and hard to use; does not measure actual attitudes, behavior, and intentions; and is subject to the accuracy of the assumptions made. For an online, interactive demonstration of a simulation, visit Marketplace Business Simulations' Web site (**http://www.marketplace-simulation.com**) and click "demos."

Table 4-2 shows the best uses for each kind of primary data collection.

How Much Will the Study Cost? The overall and specific costs of a study must be outlined. Costs may include executive time, researcher time, support staff time, pre-testing, computer usage, respondent incentives (if any), interviewers, supplies, printing, postage or phone expenses, special equipment, and marketing expenses (such as ads).

A study's expected costs should be compared with the expected benefits to be derived. Suppose a consumer survey costing $10,000 would let a firm improve the package design of a new product. With the changes suggested by research, the firm would lift its first-year profit by $30,000. Thus, the net increase due to research is $20,000 ($30,000 profit less $10,000 in costs).

Customer integration into decision making

**When forest products
are your business,**

**planting 1.7 million trees every day is a
smart investment.**

The Sustainable Forestry Initiative® program is dedicated to the future of the nation's forests, as well as the challenge of preserving rare and endangered forests around the world. Respect for nature and sound business practices are integrated to the benefit of the environment, landowners, shareholders, customers and the people they serve. And that allows us to meet the demand for wood and paper products, while helping to ensure our forests will be around forever.

SUSTAINABLE FORESTRY INITIATIVE®
Growing tomorrow's forests today.®
www.aboutsfi.org

[11] "Municipal Solid Waste: Basic Facts," http://www.epa.gov/epaoswer/non-hw/muncpl/facts.htm (June 11, 2009).

Socially responsible actions have both benefits and costs. Among the benefits are improved worker and public health, as reflected in fewer and less severe accidents, longer life spans, and less disease; cleaner air; better resource use; economic growth; a better business image; an educated public; government cooperation; an attractive, safe environment; an enhanced standard of living; and self-satisfaction for the firm. Many of these benefits cannot be quantified. Nonetheless, expectations are that the U.S. Clean Air Act (**http://www.epa.gov/oar/caa/index.html**) and the laws of other nations will ultimately save thousands and thousands of lives each year, protect food crops, reduce medical costs, and lead to clearer skies.

Although some social-responsibility expenditures are borne by a broad cross section of firms and the general public (via taxes and higher prices), the benefits of many environmental and other programs are enjoyed primarily by those living or working in affected areas. The costs of socially responsible actions can be high; U.S. environmental-protection spending is nearly 2 percent of the annual gross domestic product. Various environmentally questionable products that are efficient have been greatly modified or removed from the marketplace, such as leaded gasoline. Because of various legal restrictions and fears of lawsuits, new-product planning tends to be more conservative; and resources are often allotted to prevention rather than invention. Furthermore, trade-offs have to be made in determining which programs are more deserving of funding. See Figure 5-4.

To be effective, all parties must partake in socially responsible efforts—sharing benefits and costs. This means business, consumers, government, channel members, and others. Sometimes, tragic events bring people together. For example, in September 2005, after the Hurricane Katrina disaster along the U.S. Gulf Coast, the American

Benefits	Costs
Worker and public health	Unequal distribution of
Cleaner air	benefits
Efficient use of resources	Dollar costs
Economic growth	Removal of some goods
Improved business image	from the market
Government cooperation	Conservative product
Public education	planning
Attractive environment	Resources allocated to
Better standard of living	prevention rather than
Self-satisfaction of firm	invention

Ethics theories range from egoism to virtue ethics.

AS ICONIC AS THE TYPEWRITER
[2007]
THE NINE-O SWIVEL ARMCHAIR
DESIGNED BY ETTORE SOTTSASS

THE SOURCE FOR FULLY LICENSED CLASSICS
WWW.DWR.COM | 1.800.944.2233 | DWR STUDIOS

Cultural Environment
- Standards of behavior
- Language
- Lifestyles
- Goals

Technological Environment
- Production and measurement systems
- Advances

Economic Environment
- Standard of living
- GDP
- Stage of economic development
- Stability of currency

Political and Legal Environment
- Nationalism
- Government stability
- Trade restrictions
- Trade agreements/economic communities

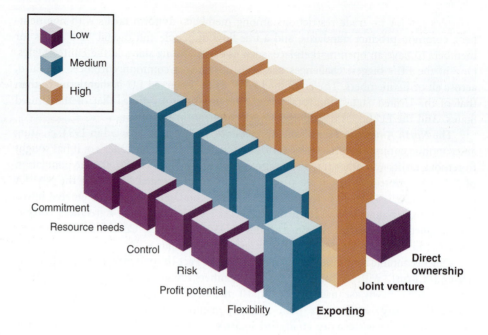

Web Sites You Can Use

Four Web sites pertaining to global marketing are especially noteworthy. The CIA World Factbook (**http://www.cia.gov/ library/publications/the-world-factbook/index.html**) reports current demographic and economic data on virtually every country in the world. The Center for International Business Education and Research (CIBER) at Michigan State University

(**http://www.ciber.msu.edu**), Center for International Business & Travel (**http://www.internationalist.com/business**), and WWW Virtual Library: International Affairs Resources (**http://www2.etown.edu/vl/intlbus.html**) have a number of valuable resources.

Summary

1. *To define domestic, international, and global marketing* Domestic marketing covers a firm's efforts in its home country. International marketing involves goods and services sold outside the home nation. Through global marketing, a firm operates in many nations. A company may be categorized as a domestic firm, exporting firm, international firm, multinational firm, or global firm. For any type of company (whether domestically or internationally oriented) to succeed in today's competitive marketplace, it must grasp key international marketing concepts and act appropriately.

2. *To explain why international marketing takes place and study its scope* International marketing occurs because nations want to exchange goods and services with which they have comparative advantages for those with which they do not. Firms seek to minimize weak economic conditions and attract growing markets, avoid domestic competition, extend the product life cycle, and get tax breaks.

   The United States is the world's largest exporter for both goods and services. Hundreds of thousands of U.S. firms engage in some level of international business. The United States is also the world's leading importer, with a huge merchandise trade deficit. In contrast, the United States has a service trade surplus. Several reasons account for the merchandise trade deficit, ranging from the American market's allure to the emphasis of U.S. firms on profits over market share. Various actions are under way to reduce this deficit; and the United States is the dominant force worldwide.

3. *To explore the cultural, economic, political and legal, and technological environments facing international marketers* The cultural environment includes the behavior standards, language, lifestyles, and goals of a country's citizens. The

economic environment incorporates a nation's standard of living, GDP, stage of development, and currency stability. The political and legal environment includes nationalism, government stability, trade rules, and trade agreements and economic communities like the World Trade Organization, European Union, and North American Free Trade group. The technological environment creates opportunities and problems.

4. *To analyze the stages in the development of an international marketing strategy* In developing a strategy, a firm may stress exporting, joint ventures, or direct ownership of operations. Each approach has a different commitment, resource needs, control, risk, flexibility, and profit range.

   A company should consider several factors in deciding on which and how many foreign markets to enter. These include cultural and language similarities with the home market, the suitability of the standard of living, consumer demand, its own available resources, and so on.

   A firm may use standardized (global), nonstandardized, or glocal marketing. The decision depends on the differences among the nations served, which marketing elements can be standardized, the size of each market, and the possibility of regional adaptation.

   Product planning may extend existing products into foreign markets, modify them, produce simpler items for developing nations, or invent new products for foreign markets. Distribution planning looks at channel relations and sets a network for direct sales or channel intermediaries. Physical distribution features would also be analyzed. Promotion planning would stress global, mixed, or glocal campaigns. Price planning would outline whether prices should be standardized, the price level, the currency for price quotes, and terms of sale.

Key Terms

domestic marketing (p. 155)
international marketing (p. 155)
global marketing (p. 155)

comparative advantage (p. 156)
trade deficit (p. 159)
trade surplus (p. 159)

culture (p. 160)
standard of living (p. 162)
gross domestic product (GDP) (p. 162)

industrialized countries (p. 163)

developing countries (p. 163)

less-developed countries (p. 163)

nationalism (p. 165)

tariff (p. 165)

trade quota (p. 165)

embargo (p. 165)

local content laws (p. 165)

World Trade Organization (WTO) (p. 166)

economic community (p. 166)

European Union (EU) (p. 166)

North American Free Trade Agreement (NAFTA) (p. 167)

exporting (p. 168)

joint venture (strategic alliance) (p. 169)

direct ownership (p. 170)

standardized (global) marketing approach (p. 171)

nonstandardized marketing approach (p. 172)

glocal marketing approach (p. 172)

straight extension (p. 173)

product adaptation (p. 173)

backward invention (p. 173)

forward invention (p. 173)

dumping (p. 178)

Review Questions

1. Distinguish among domestic, international, and global marketing.
2. How can a firm improve its cultural awareness?
3. Differentiate among industrialized, developing, and less-developed countries.
4. If the value of the Kenyan shilling goes from 65 shillings per U.S. dollar to 75 shillings per U.S. dollar, will U.S. products be more or less expensive in Kenya? Why?
5. Define each of the following:
   a. Quota
   b. Tariff
   c. Embargo

6. What are the pros and cons of exporting versus joint ventures?
7. Why would a firm use a standardized international marketing strategy? What are the potential disadvantages of this strategy?
8. Distinguish among these product-planning strategies: straight extension, product adaptation, backward invention, and forward invention. When should each be used?

Discussion Questions

1. Cite three basic differences between marketing in the United States and in Latin America.
2. In India, there are 10 TV sets per 100 people, compared with 80 per 100 people in the United States. What are the ramifications of this from a marketing perspective?

3. What are the advantages and disadvantages of a country's belonging to an economic community such as the European Union?
4. Develop a 10-question checklist by which a toy company could determine which and how many foreign markets to enter.

Web Exercise

It is imperative that firms understand the cross-cultural differences in the nations where they do business. Visit this Web site (**http://www.1000ventures.com/business_guide/** **crosscuttings/ccd_ex_china-us.html**) to see several distinctions between Americans and the Chinese. Discuss what you learn from your visit.

Practice Quiz

1. Companies are more likely to engage in international marketing when
   a. competition in the home country is growing.
   b. the home economy is growing.
   c. the home population base is growing.
   d. the home tax rates are lower.

2. Which of these is a contributing factor to the U.S. trade deficit?
   a. Trade restrictions in foreign markets
   b. The inadequate quality control for U.S.-made products
   c. High U.S. labor costs
   d. Increased competition in foreign markets

3. Cultural awareness most clearly requires marketing research on
   a. literacy.
   b. trade restrictions.
   c. hidden meanings.
   d. size of demand.

4. The gross domestic product
   a. is difficult to calculate.
   b. refers to the average quantity and quality of goods and services consumed in a country.
   c. does not take into account differences in living standards in different countries.
   d. gives the United States an index of 100 against which other nations are rated.

5. Developing countries have
   a. 60 percent of the world's population.
   b. per-capita income of about $4,000 to $9,000.
   c. widespread modern technology.
   d. less than 5 percent of the world's income.

6. Which of the following is *not* a way in which an international firm can protect itself from the adverse effects of nationalism?
   a. Measuring domestic instability
   b. Taking in foreign partners
   c. Insuring itself
   d. Engaging in direct ownership

7. Which of these limits the quantity of specified products allowed into a country?
   a. Embargo
   b. Tariff
   c. Quota
   d. Local content laws

8. Which statement is *not* correct?
   a. NAFTA includes Canada.
   b. The Andean Pact includes countries from Latin America.
   c. The European Union has a larger population than the United States.
   d. Economic communities are now illegal.

9. The highest level of commitment to international marketing is
   a. licensing.
   b. contract manufacturing.

   c. direct ownership.
   d. exporting.

10. Which of the following is a type of joint venture?
    a. Indirect selling
    b. Direct selling
    c. Management contracting
    d. Global marketing

11. The least risky form of organization for international marketing is
    a. joint venture.
    b. direct ownership.
    c. exporting.
    d. management contracting.

12. Standardized international marketing plans
    a. are sensitive to regional needs.
    b. work best when distinctive foreign markets are involved.
    c. involve decentralized control.
    d. present a uniform image.

13. The international product-planning strategy appropriate for laundry detergent formulation is
    a. forward invention.
    b. product adaptation.
    c. backward invention.
    d. straight extension.

14. In which of the following countries does PepsiCo market soft drinks via the domestic AmBev beer and soda company?
    a. Brazil
    b. Great Britain
    c. Japan
    d. Mexico

15. Dumping refers to selling goods abroad
    a. at high prices.
    b. with prices similar to those in the home market.
    c. to remove excess supply from the home market.
    d. so that cheap labor may be used.

For the answers to these questions, please visit the online site for this book at **http://www.atomicdog.com**.

Chapter 7

Marketing and the Internet

Larry Page and Sergey Brin met as computer science doctoral students who were studying methods for searching and organizing large quantities of data. They developed a formula that would order the results of a data search by relevancy. To Page and Brin, early online search engines, which typically sorted Web pages by analyzing words and their positions within a document, were woefully inadequate as the Web expanded. They were convinced that a Web page pointed to by 100 sites would be more valuable than one referred to by 5 linked sites.

In 1998, Page and Brin presented their findings at the World Wide Web Conference. One year later, after raising close to $30 million in funding, they launched Google (**http://www.google.com**). Today, Google is the most widely used site for Web searches, on topics ranging from health-related questions and product reviews to current events. Google's Web Search products enable users to automatically translate text in 12 languages, search by number (such as a shipping tracking number), and search for movie, music, and weather information. It now is the largest Internet-based firm with annual revenues of $20 billion. More than one-half of Google's searches and revenues are from outside the United States.

Google's revenues come from its ability to deliver cost-effective online advertising to clients. Its auction-based AdWords program, for example, enables Google network members to deliver relevant ads targeted to specific search questions. In this program, advertisers bid on the keywords that will trigger their text or display-based ads. Google's keyword tool, which is part of AdWords, suggests helpful keywords that advertisers can use to increase the number of hits. A budget hotel operator may receive related keywords such as "hotel discounts," "motels," or "bed and breakfast." Google also has an AdSense program that positions Web ads in sites that are not owned by Google (such as a link to a site placed within an article).

Google recently joined OpenSocial (**http://www.opensocial.org**), a group of Facebook competitors. Unlike Facebook, which uses proprietary networks and coding language, OpenSocial uses open standards that allow developers to extend their application software.[1]

In this chapter, we will explore the various marketing roles of the Internet. We will also examine how traditional marketers can use the Internet as a vital part of their overall marketing strategy.

Chapter Objectives

1. To demonstrate why the Internet is a valuable marketing tool
2. To explore the multifaceted potential marketing roles for the Internet
3. To show how to develop an Internet marketing strategy
4. To illustrate how the Internet is being utilized to enhance marketing strategies
5. To consider the challenges of using the Internet in marketing and to forecast the future of E-marketing

7-1 OVERVIEW

As an introduction to our discussion of marketing and the Internet, let's define four basic terms.

---

[1] Various company and other sources.

The *Internet*, also known as "the Net," is a global electronic superhighway of computer networks—a network of networks in which users at one computer can get information from another computer (and sometimes talk directly to users at other computers). It is a public, cooperative, self-sustaining system accessible to hundreds of millions of people worldwide. The *World Wide Web (WWW)*, also known as "the Web," comprises all of the resources and users on the Internet using the Hypertext Transfer Protocol (HTTP). It is a way to access the Internet, whereby people work with easy-to-use Web addresses and pages. Through the Web, users see words, colorful charts, pictures, and video, and hear audio.[2] Although the two terms have somewhat different meanings, they both relate to online activities—and are both used interchangeably by the media and by companies. Thus, in this chapter (and book), both terms have the same connotation: online activities.

E-marketing includes any marketing activity that is conducted through the Internet, from customer analysis to marketing-mix components. *E-commerce* refers to revenue-generating Internet transactions. E-marketing is the broader concept, and it does not necessarily have sales as the primary goal.

By virtue of its rather low costs, its wide geographic reach, and the many marketing roles it can serve, the Internet should be a key part of *any* firm's marketing strategy—regardless of the firm's size or characteristics. In the decades ahead, virtually every firm will have some kind of Web presence, much as they now have a phone, a fax machine, an answering machine, and other technological tools.

Since the Internet's inception as a commercially viable business resource, its importance and value have been misperceived by many. At first, a number of experts talked of how Internet firms would soon overwhelm traditional retailers and drive them out of business. They predicted that annual online retail sales in the United States alone would soon reach hundreds of billions of dollars. They were wrong: Online retail sales are only a fraction of what was predicted. Now, some experts underestimate the overall business value of the Internet because E-commerce revenues have not reached the early projections; and they cite the high failure rate of "dot com" firms. Again, they are wrong about the Internet's impact.

These experts have not recognized how long a major new technology takes to permeate the marketplace. The majority of people in the world still do not have a PC, "surf the Web," or shop online. In addition, a lot of people who own a PC, surf, and shop online still prefer shopping at stores due to the purchase immediacy, the hands-on buying experience, the social interaction with others, and so forth.

The true impact of the Internet, and the reason we are devoting a full chapter to this topic, relates to the multiple marketing tasks that can be undertaken, both better and more efficiently—not to the level of sales revenues to be attained. This point underscores why the rush to judge the Internet as a business fad was so wrong. Generating sales revenue is only one of a multitude of benefits that the Internet can achieve for a firm. Most of our focus is on E-marketing, not just on E-commerce.

In this chapter, we will cover several aspects of marketing and the Internet: why the Internet is such a valuable marketing tool, the multifaceted uses of the Internet, developing an Internet marketing strategy, applications of the Internet in marketing strategies, and the challenges and future of E-marketing.

> The **Internet** is a global superhighway of computer networks. Through the **World Wide Web**, people work with easy-to-use Web addresses and pages.

> **E-marketing** involves any marketing activity on the Internet, while **E-commerce** is its revenue-generating component.

7-2 WHY THE INTERNET IS A VALUABLE TOOL IN MARKETING

According to estimates drawn from the Internet World Stats' (**http://www.internet worldstats.com/stats.htm**) data base, by 2010, about 1.75 billion people around the globe

> Web usage is rising rapidly worldwide

---

[2] "Look It Up," **http://whatis.techtarget.com** (March 30, 2009).

are expected to be using the Internet. This signifies great E-marketing opportunities for firms. For just the 9 countries highlighted in Table 7-1, during 2008, there were already 320 million active home users; on average, they typically spent 20 to 40 hours monthly online and went online 30 or more times a month. In the United States, three-quarters of all households go online at least once each month.

People surf the Internet for many reasons besides shopping. They seek out entertainment, health, financial, sports, and news sites. They do product research. They "talk" to one another (many via AOL Instant Messenger, **http://www.aim.com**). They communicate online with firms to register complaints and make suggestions. They send E-mails and greetings cards. The U.S. Postal Service (**http://www.usps.com**) handles more than 700 million pieces of mail daily; in contrast, billions of E-mail messages are sent every day!

Companies (actually, their employees) also surf the Web for a variety of reasons other than shopping. They see what competitors are doing. They read about industry trends and events. They communicate with suppliers. They exchange data among offices anywhere in the world. They monitor inventory levels. They survey customers and measure satisfaction. They do sophisticated analyses of customer data bases.

Bernie & Phyls Furniture (**http://www.bernieandphyls.com**), a family-run, Boston-area chain with six stores and annual sales of $120 million, is a good illustration of how the Internet presents a variety of E-marketing opportunities beyond E-commerce:

> "Our goal was not really to derive sales," said CEO Larry Rubin. "It was to drive people into the stores." That's one of the ways the site has proven its worth. Consumers have the option of purchasing online, but the bigger result is that they're coming into showrooms with photos of items they printed out, saying they want to take a closer look. And when a customer calls with a question or problem, the employee can use a computer to call up an image of the very piece the consumer is talking about. "It's often hard for customers to describe what is wrong with something on the phone, but it's much easier when both are looking at the same thing. The goal is to service the customer at the highest level, and having the entire catalog of merchandise on the company's internal site helps accomplish this," said spokeswoman Amy Blumenthal. If a part has to be replaced, it can be ordered before a service technician goes to the house, possibly saving one diagnostic trip.[3]

Table 7-1	Internet Penetration of the Home Market in 9 Countries			
	Active Home Users (Millions)	**Average Time Spent per Month**	**Average Number of Sessions per Month**	**Active Home Users as a Percentage of Total Population**
United States	154	36 hours, 30 min.	35	51
Germany	37	34 hours, 45 min.	37	45
Great Britain	27	25 hours, 30 min.	28	44
France	25	40 hours, 0 min.	43	39
Brazil	23	36 hours, 0 min.	30	12
Spain	19	42 hours, 40 min.	39	47
Italy	18	22 hours, 30 min.	26	31
Australia	12	35 hours, 30 min.	38	58
Switzerland	4	31 hours, 0 min.	36	55

Sources: Compiled by the authors from *Nielsen//NetRatings*, **http://www.nielsen-netratings.com** (March-June 2008); and U.S. Bureau of the Census, International Data Base.

[3] Clint Engel, "Web Site: Few Sales But Big Payoffs," *Furniture Today* (August 29, 2005), p. 24.

Likewise, Ikea (**http://www.ikea.com**) devotes a lot of attention to its Web site. It has colorful descriptions and photos of its home-furnishings product lines. There is a worldwide store locator. The firm explains its vision. But mostly, Ikea emphasizes in-store shopping as the way for consumers to get the most out of their home-furnishings shopping experience. The Swedish-based retailer places much more emphasis on its E-marketing efforts than on E-commerce.

Let us next examine two specific aspects of marketing and the Internet: the three phases of Internet use by companies and the benefits of using the Internet in marketing.

7-2a   Bricks-and-Mortar, Clicks-Only, and Bricks-and-Clicks

E-marketing is evolving through the three phases shown in Figure 7-1. The phases are (1) bricks-and-mortar firms, (2) clicks-only firms, and (3) bricks-and-clicks firms.

Bricks-and-mortar firms are traditional companies that have not gotten involved with the Internet. Until a few years ago, this was very much the predominant business format, as these companies believed the Internet provided too few benefits relative to the costs and complexity of being online. Now, bricks-and-mortar firms are likely to be small in size and scope.

In the 1990s, a number of innovative *clicks-only firms* entered the marketplace. These companies do business just online. They do not have traditional facilities. Many early clicks-only firms generated good revenues, but had trouble turning a profit. They often expanded too fast and invested heavily in their infrastructures. There was a major shakeup among clicks-only firms, with a number of once-popular companies going out of business. However, thousands and thousands of clicks-only firms are flourishing.

The trend today is toward *bricks-and-clicks firms* that operate in both a traditional setting and on the Internet. Virtually every large retailer (and numerous medium-size and small firms) has a substantial Web presence. This is also true of manufacturers, wholesalers, government entities, nonprofit organizations, and others. The bricks-and-clicks format enables firms to appeal to multiple market segments, maximize customer contact points, leverage the strengths of each form of business, and enter into new alliances.

> **Bricks-and-mortar firms** are not involved with the Internet. **Clicks-only firms** do business just online. **Bricks-and-clicks firms** combine traditional and Internet formats.

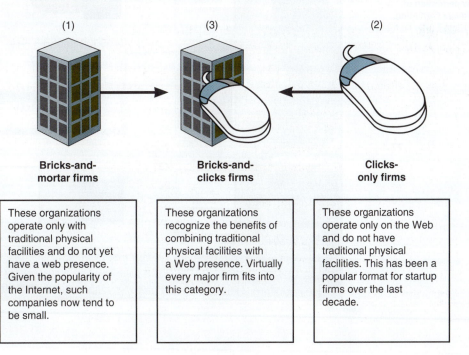

(1)	(3)	(2)
Bricks-and-mortar firms	**Bricks-and-clicks firms**	**Clicks-only firms**
These organizations operate only with traditional physical facilities and do not yet have a web presence. Given the popularity of the Internet, such companies now tend to be small.	These organizations recognize the benefits of combining traditional physical facilities with a Web presence. Virtually every major firm fits into this category.	These organizations operate only on the Web and do not have traditional physical facilities. This has been a popular format for startup firms over the last decade.

Figure 7-1

The Three Phases of Marketing and the Internet

Newsweek, Wal-Mart, and Sephora are organizations that are now active in bricks-and-clicks. *Newsweek* (**http://www.newsweek.com**), founded in 1933, sells 3.1 million print copies each week. Yet, the Internet has become much more important in its strategy: "*Newsweek* offers comprehensive coverage of world events with a global network of correspondents, reporters, and editors covering national and international affairs, business, science and technology, society, and the arts and entertainment. Newsweek.com offers the weekly magazine online, daily news updates, Web-only columns from our top writers, photo galleries, audio and video reports from correspondents, podcasts, mobile content, and archives." At Wal-Mart (**http://www.walmart.com**), the world's largest firm, "Walmart.com is a lot like your neighborhood Wal-Mart store. We feature a great selection of high-quality merchandise, friendly service, and, of course, everyday low prices. We also have another goal: to bring you the best shopping experience on the Internet. But we think of ourselves, first and foremost, as a retailer."[4] French-based Sephora (**http://www.sephora.com**) actively promotes its Web site at beauty stores around the world. See Figure 7-2.

Amazon.com (**http://www.amazon.com**) is one of the increasing numbers of formerly clicks-only firms that now also operate traditional facilities or have alliances with partners having traditional facilities. It has alliances with such leading retailers as Macy's (**http://www.macys.com**), Office Depot (**http://www.officedepot.com**), and Target Stores (**http://www.target.com**), among others. Atomic Dog (**http://www.atomicdog.com**) now markets its texts in college bookstores, as well as online. See Figure 7-3.

Figure 7-2

Sephora Successfully Moves to a Bricks-and-Clicks Strategy

Sephora's Web site (**http://www.sephora.com**) features a huge product selection and most of the popular brands in its beauty care category—just like Sephora's stores.

Source: Reprinted by permission of Susan Berry, Retail Image Consulting, Inc.

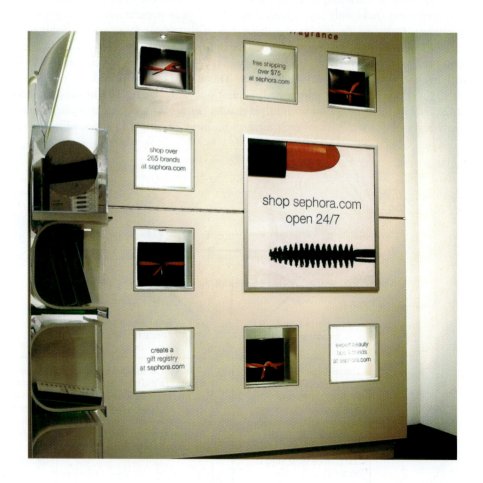

[4] "About Newsweek, Inc.," **http://www.newsweek.com/id/38405** (March 30, 2009); and "An Introduction to Walmart.com," **http://www.walmart.com/catalog/catalog.gsp?cat=542413** (March 30, 2009).

Figure 7-3

Atomic Dog's Clicks-First Strategy

7-2b   The Benefits of a Company's Using the Internet in Marketing

The value of the Internet in marketing is best conveyed by reviewing the benefits that a company may receive by going online. Several of these benefits are shown in Figure 7-4 and described next.

Communicability—The Web makes it easy for an organization to communicate with each of its constituencies: consumers, suppliers, resellers, employees, the media, government bodies, and others. For example, "To communicate more effectively with the community, Big Brothers Big Sisters of Metro Atlanta (**http://www.bbbsatl.org**) decided to launch a more professional looking and informative Web site." This site is its main marketing effort; and it "needed the site to build brand awareness, drive participation, and create emotional connectivity. It was important to leverage existing Web traffic to promote sponsors, as well as effectively inform the audience about recent news and events."[5]

> The potential marketing benefits of the Internet range from communicability to sales revenues.

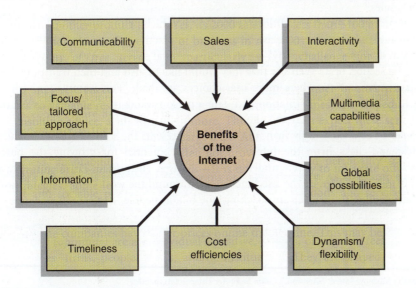

Figure 7-4

Company Benefits of Using the Internet in Marketing

[5] "Improving Marketing and Communication Via the Web," **http://www.npower.org/about/tech-impact-stories/improving-marketing** (July 31, 2008).

Focus/tailored approach—The Web enables a firm to focus on a specific target market and offer a marketing mix especially devised for that target market. The Internet is also especially good for targeted E-mails. One strong practitioner of a personalized approach is MyMMs.com (**http://www.mymms.com**), where site visitors can create their own M&Ms: "This is ideal for weddings and major events."[6]

Information—A firm can amass information about almost any facet of its business from free Web sites, as well as fee-based ones. Both secondary data and primary data can be garnered via the Internet.

Timeliness—With the Internet, a company can operate in "real time," which means the ability to communicate, gather information, and so forth in a contemporaneous manner. The time lags associated with other marketing tools are much shorter on the Web.

Cost efficiencies—Reduced costs are often a result of Internet usage. Postal costs decrease. Inventory costs can be lowered because there is more efficient communication between companies and their suppliers. Sales personnel can follow-up with clients more efficiently. There are no shipping costs for items such as software that are sold via the Web and downloaded by customers.

Dynamism/flexibility—The Internet is a dynamic and flexible medium, which lets a company rapidly adjust its marketing mix. For instance, if a firm sees that a particular product is not selling well, it can instantly change the advertising at its Web site or lower the price until consumer demand reaches a satisfactory level. Likewise, if a firm runs out of a popular item that it is selling, a reorder can be placed immediately through the Web.

Global possibilities—With the Internet, a company can effectively and inexpensively communicate with its constituencies around the world, thereby increasing the reach of the firm's marketing strategy. The expensive part of operating a global E-commerce Web site is often the distribution costs that result from expanding into new geographic markets.

Multimedia capabilities—The Internet offers huge multimedia possibilities for marketers, especially as many users convert to cable, DSL, or other fast connections. More company Web sites will soon be showing 3-D pictures of products that can be rotated 360 degrees, streaming audio and video, photo galleries of product offerings, and so forth: "The proliferation of broadband access has allowed for a new and increasingly engaging way of merchandising products, from high-resolution, close-up product views to full videos and integrated audio feature descriptions with a depth of printable sales collateral. The online product page has become the new point of influence for engaging customers and influencing brand preference. The quality of that experience dramatically impacts sales.[7]

Interactivity—Unlike traditional advertising, which is uni-directional (from company to audience), the Internet can be deployed interactively (from company to audience and from audience to company)—much like personal selling. A firm can ask people to click on a section of its Web site that they would like to visit and then transport them to that particular section, where more user choices are made. For example, an airline site can gather data on the destination and date a person wants to travel to from his or her home area, and then display the alternative flights that fit the person's criteria.

Sales—For a clicks-only firm, the Internet represents the sole source of revenue. For a bricks-and-clicks firm, the Internet offers the potential for growing the business. According to global research undertaken by Nielsen (**http://www.nielsen.com**), as of 2008, 85 percent of those who used the Internet around the world had made at least one purchase online—a number approaching one billion people.[8]

---

[6] Samantha Murphy, "Sweet Sensation," *Chain Store Age* (June 2008), p. 50.

[7] Rick Martin, "The New E-Marketing Must-Haves: Video and Rich Media," **http://www.ecommercetimes.com/story/62961.html** (May 19, 2008).

[8] Nielsen, *Trends in Online Shopping: A Global Nielsen Consumer Report* (February 2008).

Global Marketing in Action

Live 8 and Live Earth: The Global Power of the Internet

The first Live Aid concert, held in 1985, was viewed by 1 billion people and raised $100 million for African famine relief. The most recent Live 8 concert (**http://www.live8live.com**), in 2005, was devoted to debt relief for third-world nations. The concerts took place in Philadelphia, London, Paris, Berlin, Rome, and Barrie, Canada (near Toronto), and viewers/listeners could access the concert via MTV, traditional radio, satellite radio, and the Internet.

The Live Earth (**http://www.liveearth.org**) in 2007 was devoted to changing attitudes about global warming. Concert proceeds were sent to the Alliance for Climate Protection (**http://www.climateprotect.org**), a nonprofit organization. Concert goers were asked to sign a pledge to pressure their countries to sign treaties to reduce global warming, to personally reduce carbon dioxide pollution, and to plant trees.

In July 2007, more than 150 artists—including Madonna, the Police, the Red Hot Chili Peppers, and Alicia Keys—performed concerts at New Jersey, London, Johannesburg, Rio de Janeiro, Shanghai, Tokyo, Sydney, and Hamburg. Between performances, a special Web site (LiveEarth.MSN.com) featured short films, public service announcements, instant messaging, and interactivity. Live Earth parties in 119 countries were held, ranging from home viewings (on NBC, Telemundo, the Sundance Channel, Bravo, MSNBC, and Universal HD) to museum festivals. The concerts were broadcast on XM satellite radio.

Live 8 and Live Earth attracted estimated worldwide audiences of 1 billion people and 2 billion people, respectively, through their various Internet affiliations and events.

Sources: Based on material in Abbey Klassen and Alice Z. Cuneo, "MSN Sets Stage for Live 8 Reprise," **http://www.adage.com/digital/article?article_id=115060** (February 19, 2007); and "Live Earth Aims to Cause Lasting Change," **http://www.washingtonpost.com/wp-dyn/content/article/2007/07/02/AR2007070201007.html** (July 2, 2007).

7-3 THE MULTIFACETED POTENTIAL MARKETING ROLES FOR THE INTERNET

After reviewing the company benefits of the Internet in marketing, it should be clear that the Web has the potential to serve several marketing roles, as shown in Figure 7-5 and discussed next. Each firm must determine which roles to pursue and how to prioritize their importance.

> The Internet can serve many roles besides generating sales.

Projecting an image—A firm can project an image at its Web site through the site's design (colors, graphics, etc.) and the content presented. Have you ever heard of Accenture (**http://www.accenture.com**)—formerly Andersen Consulting? No? Well, you can learn a lot about the firm and the image it projects by visiting its Web site—which explains what Accenture is, what it does, the types of clients it serves, where it does business, and more: "Accenture is a global management consulting, technology services, and outsourcing company. Combining unparalleled experience, comprehensive capabilities across all industries and business functions, and extensive research on the world's most successful companies, Accenture collaborates with clients to help them become high-performance businesses and governments. With more than 180,000 people in 49 countries, we generate annual revenues of more than $20 billion."[9]

Customer service—Many firms use the Internet to supplement their traditional customer service. At its Web site, Staples, the office products chain, has a "Staples Rebates" section (**http://www.stapleseasyrebates.com/promocenter/staples/promo_search.html**)—where a customer can see what rebate offers are available by entering the name of the manufacturer, the product code, a keyword, or a rebate number.

Channel relations—The Internet can help channel members to better understand one another, to coordinate their distribution strategies, to smooth over conflicts, and so forth. To enhance its relationships with small companies that developed games for

---

[9] "Company Overview," **http://www.accenture.com/Global/About_Accenture/Company_Overview/CompanyDescription.htm** (April 29, 2009).

Figure 7-5

How the Internet May Be Utilized in Marketing

its Wii system, Nintendo "launched a new channel for games distribution—WiiWare (**http://www.nintendo.com/wii/wiiware**). Games are downloaded over the Internet by redeeming WiiPoints, which can be purchased at the Wii Shop Channel or at retail outlets. The intention is to give smaller games developers a channel to sell their wares other than the expensive retail distribution methods."[10]

Purchasing and inventory management—The Web can greatly facilitate company purchases and inventory management. Procter & Gamble (**http://www.pg.com**), the consumer products manufacturer, has two distinct password-protected Web sites to assist its retailers in making purchases for resale to final consumers: "The P&G Customer Portal (**https://customer.pg.com**) and Web Order Management (**https://order.pg.com/jsp/login/login_norm.jsp**) systems assist the company's trade partners in purchasing, managing, and promoting P&G products. These Web-based systems are always available. They provide product information, order status, and invoices."[11]

Information gathering and sharing—As previously noted, the Internet has considerable possibilities for providing marketing information. One valuable site is *Quirks Marketing Research Review* (**http://www.quirks.com**): "If you conduct, coordinate, use, or purchase market research or marketing research services, then Quirks.com is the Web site you need. Here you'll find 7,100+ market research companies, 2,000+ market research articles, 600+ market research job openings, 1,300+ definitions of market research terms, 100+ market research industry events, 15+ market research degree programs, and more."[12]

Data-base development—Due to the online interactions between a firm and its suppliers and customers, extensive marketing data bases can be developed. Amazon.com's Web site (**http://www.amazon.com**) has millions of registered customers, many of whom regularly shop at Amazon.com. The firm has purchase data, shopping preferences, and contact information on these customers.

Mass customization—An extremely attractive feature of the Internet involves companies' ability to engage in **mass customization**, a process by which mass-market goods and services are individualized to satisfy a specific customer need, at a reasonable price. According to one systems design firm, "Based on the public's growing desire for product personalization, it serves as the ultimate combination of 'custom-made' and 'mass production.' Simply stated, mass customization is about choice; about giving

Through online **mass customization**, a company can individualize mass-market goods and services to satisfy a specific customer need, at a fair price.

---

[10] James Quintana Pearce, "Nintendo Launches Online Distribution Channel WiiWare," **http://www.paidcontent.org/entry/419-nintendo-launches-online-distribution-channel-wiiware** (May 13, 2008).

[11] "B2B Directory: Retail Customers," **http://www.pg.com/b2b/retail_customers.jhtml** (April 29, 2009).

[12] "Welcome to the Worldwide Market Research Source," **http://www.quirks.com/index.asp** (May 1, 2009).

consumers a unique product when, where, and how they want it. The Internet makes it possible for anyone to compile music CDs containing any combination of songs. Or obtain customized home mortgages. Or design a one-of-a-kind friend of Barbie, complete with unique name, clothing, and personality. Mass customization not only benefits the consumer, it offers the manufacturer significant benefits: a high degree of product/service flexibility, reduced inventory risk, and a competitive edge."[13]

Advertising and sales promotion—A company can promote its goods and services, along with its image, through the Internet. It can use banner ads at portal sites, be listed at search engines, and present multimedia messages and special sales promotions at its own Web site. Consider Google's (**http://www.google.com**) AdWords program, which "aims to provide the most effective advertising available for businesses of any size. We pledge to help you meet your customer acquisition needs by enabling you to reach people looking for your good or service, fully control your ad budget, easily create and edit your ads, and see your ads on Google within minutes of creating them. AdWords gives you 24/7 access to detailed performance reports that help you track the effectiveness of your ad campaigns. We also strive to give you the friendliest, most knowledgeable customer service possible. You can expect a prompt response to your E-mail questions, typically within one business day."[14]

Selling—Generating sales is a key Internet marketing role for many firms. (We've listed it here to re-emphasize that selling is only one role for the Internet.) When engaging in E-commerce, this should be kept in mind: It "is about making it easy to shop, which should make it easy for you to sell. Providing shoppers with an experience that eliminates their anxiety is a step in the right direction. Web commerce is about delivering an experience that replicates offline shopping in a number of ways. It allows shoppers to browse, evaluate, and take action without engaging in a series of steps that requires a commitment early in the process that a shopper may not be ready to make. What we're talking about is an interactive 'single-page' shopping experience that gives a shopper a feeling of control and versatility."[15] See Figure 7-6.

Multichannel marketing—Bricks-and-clicks firms engage in multichannel marketing, whereby they sell their products through more than one distribution format, in this case, the Internet and at least one other format. Barnes & Noble has a Web site (**http://www.barnesandnoble.com**), 800 U.S. stores, an 800 number, and in-store video kiosks. Its Web site offers free shipping on most orders of $25 or more.

7-4 DEVELOPING AN INTERNET MARKETING STRATEGY

To best use the Internet in marketing, a firm should be systematic in preparing and enacting the proper strategy. Figure 7-7 presents the steps to be followed in this process. The six middle boxes relate to the basic components of an Internet marketing strategy. The four outside boxes are key influences in making strategic decisions. Let us explore each of these factors.

> There are six basic steps in developing an Internet marketing strategy.

1. Goal categories are set, drawn from the factors in Figure 7-5. Both quantitative and qualitative objectives should be enumerated. These are the well-articulated Internet objectives of Zeppelin (**http://www.real-estate-tech.com**), a Hong Kong-based real-estate consulting company: (a) "To share real-estate knowledge, information, and experience via research, analyses, commentaries, articles, charts, tables, newsletters, and Web links from our site and those of others." (b) "To introduce our real-estate services such as E-consulting and Web data searches to prospective clients." (c) "To promote our real-estate products such as real-estate reports, E-books, financial

---

[13] Gerber Scientific, "What Is Mass Customization?" **http://www.mass-customization.com** (March 31, 2006).

[14] "AdWords Advantages," **https://www.adwords.google.com/select/advantages.html** (April 29, 2009).

[15] Mercado, *Wired to Shop—Part 2: Liberate, Empower, and Engage the Online Shopper* (May 20, 2008), p. 7.

Figure 7-6

Driving Global E-Commerce

The Internet is transforming the way people work, play, and shop. That is certainly true in Brazil, where Som Livre (assisted by Unisys) is the country's leading online music retailer. It has more than 50,000 Real Audio music files—from 150 recording labels—that customers can sample before buying.

Source: Reprinted by permission. Richard Bowditch, Photographer.

spreadsheets, and technical tutorials to prospective customers" (d) "To enable a real-estate Web communication network for professional, academic, institutional, and individual entities to express their own ideas, share their experiences, announce their latest activities, and/or communicate with one another."[16]

2. The target audience is identified and selected, and its desires are studied. Here are some recent research findings about online users:

- In Western Europe and North America, more than 90 percent of Internet users have made at least one online purchase—compared with 67 percent in Eastern Europe, the Middle East, and Africa.
- Broadband connections vary widely by age. Seventy percent of U.S. adults ages 18 to 29 have a broadband connection—compared with only 20 percent of those ages 65 and older.
- For every $1 spent on Internet purchases, "Web-to-Store" shoppers spend $3.45 offline at local stores. "Web-to-Store" shoppers are those who do research online and then buy at a store. "Online consumers are becoming precision shoppers. They are availing themselves of the wealth of information resources online to discover and evaluate products, compare them, and find where they can be purchased."
- About two-thirds of U.S. cell phone users have engaged in some mobile Internet activities, such as E-mail, text messaging, and purchasing.
- Monthly, social networking Web sites MySpace (**http://www.myspace.com**) and Facebook (**http://www.facebook.com**) attract more than 75 million and 35 million visitors, respectively. About 40 percent of adult Internet users and 70 percent of teenage Internet users visit at least one social networking site each month.

---

[16] "Web Objectives," **http://www.real-estate-tech.com/zeppelin_web_objectives.htm** (April 3, 2006).

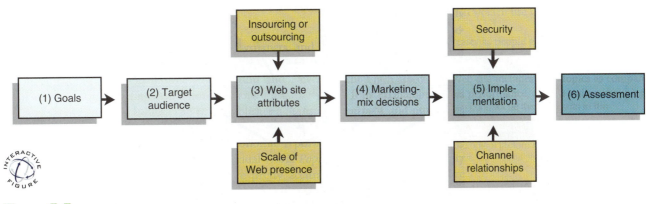

Figure 7-7

The Stages of an Internet Marketing Strategy

- Several types of Internet consumers have been identified, including: active online spenders—comfortable spending online and spend more than most others; thoughtful spenders—careful online and spend less than the most experienced online shoppers; occasional purchasers—focus is on "starter" items such as gifts and flowers; and infrequent and cautious browsers—relative newcomers to the Web who are not very comfortable with online purchases.[17]

As shown in Figure 7-8, people have numerous reasons for shopping online. Different target audiences place a different emphasis on these reasons. That is why consumer desires must be examined carefully before embarking on the specifics of an Internet marketing strategy.

3. Web site attributes are determined. First, the company must decide whether to undertake all Web-related activities itself (insourcing) or to have specialized firms do some or all Web-related activities for it (outsourcing). Most companies outsource technical development and maintenance of their sites; far fewer fully develop sites on their own. Small firms often outsource the entire operation. For a design fee of $1,000 and a hosting fee of $30 to $55 per month, Hoover Web Design (**http://www. hooverwebdesign.com**) will design, host, and maintain "a custom 10-page html Web site designed to represent your business with a user-friendly interface. You can include a photo gallery, a calendar of events, or any other pages which will advertise your business." Second, the company must choose the scale of its Web presence, especially the weight of the site in its overall marketing strategy, the percent of the marketing budget devoted to the site, and how the site is to be implemented. How is the site to be used for customer service, channel relations, selling, and so on? Are all products to be displayed at the site? Is the site to be simple or have a full range of bells and whistles? How widely is the site to be promoted?

> A company must decide between insourcing and outsourcing Web activities, and determine the scope of its Web presence.

After making decisions as to insourcing or outsourcing and the scale of the Web presence, site attributes are chosen. Here are some factors to consider in designing a marketing-oriented Web site:

- *Web address*—The company can have its own Web address or be part of a Web community. It must carefully pick a name to use. This is becoming more complex due to the addition of new domain suffixes (as designated by ICANN, **http:// www.internic.net/faqs/new-tlds.html**): .info and .biz for general use, .pro for

> It is critical for a Web site to be designed well.

---

[17] Nielsen, *Trends in Online Shopping: A Global Nielsen Consumer Report*; Pew Internet & American Lifestyle Project, *Home Broadband Adoption* (July 2008); eMarketer, "Here Comes the 'Precision' Shopper," **http://www.emarketer. com** (February 26, 2008); Pew Internet & American Lifestyle Project, "Data Memo: Mobile Access to Data and Information" (March 2008); comScore, "Top Social Networking Sites in May 2008," **http://www.clickz.com/ showPage.html?page=3629976** (June 20, 2008); eMarketer, "Social Network Marketing," **http://www.eMarketer. com** (June 20, 2008); and CACI Limited, *E-Types Users Guide* (2008).

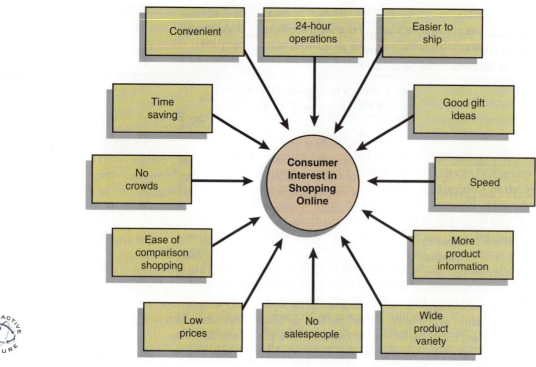

Figure 7-8

Why Consumers Purchase Online

professionals, .name for personal sites, .museum for museums, .aero for the aerospace industry, and .coop for business cooperatives.

- *Home page*—The home page is the gateway to the firm. It projects an image, presents information, and routes viewers to other relevant company pages. It must be easy to navigate and laid out well.
- *Site content*—The content can include some or all of these topics: company background, company vision and philosophy, financial performance, product descriptions, where products are sold, community service involvement, customer service, an online shopping cart, career opportunities, press releases, and more.
- *Use of multimedia*—A site can be rather plain with mostly text and a few graphics, or it can involve the heavy use of photos, animations, audio clips, video clips, and so forth.
- *Links*—Web sites can have two types of links. Almost every company has internal links: a person clicks on an icon on the home page and he or she is then transported to another section within the company's site. There may also be external links: a person clicks on an icon on the home page and he or she is then sent to another site outside of the firm's site, such as a trade association or a search engine. With the latter, the person may or may not return to the company site.
- *Shopping tools*—If a firm engages in E-commerce, there must be a mechanism for directing shoppers through the purchase process, including a secure way of entering personal data. Amazon.com (**http://www.amazon.com**) is widely admired for the "1-Click" shopping option it offers to customers.
- *Electronic data interchange*—A Web site must be able to facilitate the exchange of information among company employees and with channel members. This is especially critical in E-commerce for order shipping and inventory control.
- *Feedback*—Visitors must have a way to communicate with the firm, and there must be a mechanism for the company to respond in a timely manner.

- *Trade-offs*—When designing a site, trade-offs must be weighed. A site with a lot of graphics and photos may take a long time for users to download if they are using a dial-up Internet connection. So, how many bells and whistles should a site have, given the limitations for some users?

4. Internet-based marketing-mix decisions are made while developing the Web site; they must be consistent (synergistic) with offline marketing decisions. These are some examples:

   - *Product decisions*—Which products are listed at the site? Which products are featured at the site? Many firms do not list or describe all items in their product mix. Also, what should be the features of downloadable products (software, music, publications, etc.) that are sold online?

   - *Distribution decisions*—If the company sells at its site, does it ship from one locale or from around the country (world)? How quickly can (should) products be delivered to customers?

   - *Promotion decisions*—Which promotion mix should be used to reach the firm's Internet goals? There are many ways to promote a site and E-marketing efforts, from banner ads to listing Web addresses in traditional ads to E-mail, and more. One highly effective online tool is the ***opt-in (permission-based) E-mail***, whereby Internet users agree to receive targeted E-mail from a firm. It is far more effective than unsolicited E-mail, which turns off a lot of people. As one expert noted: "Given skepticism about E-mail, we know that to earn trust, we must do it intentionally and systematically. In contrast to many marketing campaigns, these customers have already selected themselves as a target audience. Subscribers to permission-based E-mail start out interested in hearing your value proposition."[18]

   > **Opt-in E-mail**, which is sent with the permission of the consumer, is good for both the company and the consumer.

   - *Pricing decisions*—Engaging in E-commerce requires two fundamental pricing decisions: How should online prices relate to those for offline businesses (including those of the firm itself)? How frequently should prices be changed to reflect market conditions? Because so many Internet shoppers are price-driven, online prices have tended to be lower than offline prices for the same products, and online transactions are often not subject to sales tax. Although the technology exists to adjust online pricing by the minute, firms must be careful not to confuse consumers or to get them upset if they visit a site and then return the next day to purchase, only to find that the price has risen.

5. At this point, the Internet marketing strategy is implemented. Again, two factors affect a firm's ability to properly enact its strategy: security and channel relationships. A vast number of Internet users are concerned about Web security, and they are hesitant to provide personal data for fear that "hackers" will obtain the data or that firms will resell the data. The security issue can be dealt with by offering a secure section of a Web site, protected by a well-known firm such as VeriSign (**http://www.verisign.com**) or Cybertrust (**http://www.cybertrust.com**), for entering personal data and credit information. The reselling issue can be handled by having a clear, user-friendly privacy policy—accessible by clicking an icon at the Web site. With regard to channel relationships, a move into E-commerce may place a firm into conflict with its suppliers or resellers, which may view this as a form of competition. The trade-offs must be weighed.

   > A Web site must be secure, protect privacy, and not be a threat to other channel members.

   The firm must be sure that its Web strategy runs smoothly, once it is enacted. It must be alert to several possible breakdowns in the system, such as site crashes, out-of-stock conditions, a slow response to customer inquiries, incorrect prices, hacker invasions, and poor coordination with the offline strategy.

---

[18] Morgan Stewart, "You've Got Permission, Now Be Relevant: How to Use Segmentation, Targeting, and Personalization to Deliver Relevant E-Mail," **http://www.technologyexecutivesclub.com/PDFs/ArticlePDFS/ segmenttargeting.pdf** (2005).

6. The last step in an Internet marketing strategy is to assess performance and make necessary modifications. Assessment should be closely tied to the Web goals (step 1) that have been set in terms of image, customer service, sales, and so forth. These are some measures that can be studied: daily site traffic, average length of the stay at the site, ratings on customer service surveys, sales revenues, costs per transaction, repeat business, the number and type of system breakdowns per time period, and more. The effectiveness of banner ads placed at other sites must be also be judged.

Special attention should be paid to rating the quality of the Web site itself. These are among the factors that should be regularly reviewed from the Internet user's perspective:

- Clarity of site's mission
- Download time
- Time needed to comprehend site characteristics
- Informational value
- Ease of navigability
- Use of graphics/multimedia
- Interactivity
- Currency
- Security
- Simplicity of purchasing
- Printability of site pages
- Creativity

7-5 HOW THE INTERNET IS BEING APPLIED IN MARKETING STRATEGIES

> Internet marketing is being applied in many ways.

We now present several examples of E-marketing in action.

Marketing and the Web

Why Yahoo! and MySpace Are Opening Their Data Bases to Others

According to one report, "openness is the buzzword ringing through Yahoo!'s Sunnyvale, California campus." Yahoo! (http://www.Yahoo!.com) executives want to open Yahoo! programming to outside developers with the expectation that its Web pages will become even more attractive to users. Yahoo! has already released the source codes for its E-mail, hoping that third-party firms will develop small programs, dubbed "widgets," to better coordinate users' address books and other E-mail services. Yahoo! believes this is the first step in a multistage process. For example, a test version of the new My Yahoo! enables users to link to Google's E-mail service, Gmail (http://mail.google.com). Also included are widgets from Netflix (http://www.netflix.com) and the *New York Times* (http://www.nytimes.com) that enable users to view movies and read stories from customized home pages.

MySpace (http://www.myspace.com) has also given developers access to three application programming interfaces (APIs): OpenSocial with MySpace Extensions, Action Script, and REST. OpenSocial with MySpace Extensions lets programmers create applications in JavaScript and HTML. ActionScript enables developers to build Flash widgets. REST assists in server-to-server communications.

Kyle Brinkman, vice president and general manager of MySpace's developer platform, says: "We want to make sure that people get exposed to applications, find them, install them, and benefit from them without being overloaded by them." Under the openness framework, MySpace is hoping that new applications will be embedded into its Web page. These embedded applications are expected to increase loyalty to MySpace.

Sources: Based on material in Catherine Holahan, "Yahoo's Open Invitation," http://www.businessweek.com/technology (September 11, 2007); and Marji McClure, "MySpace Developer Platforms to Serve as Foundation for New Applications," *EContent* (April 2008), pp. 8–9.

7-5a   Consumer Analysis

As Table 7-2 shows, in the United States, slightly more females than males use the Internet and usage is highest for young adults. Two-thirds of Whites and Hispanics use the Internet, compared with 55 percent of Blacks. Higher-income and better-educated people are most apt to use the Internet, though a significant number of those with lower incomes and less education have use of the Internet today. Aside from E-mail, information activities are the most popular Internet tasks. Online purchases are growing rapidly in many categories. The average online order is at least $100 for several categories, led by computer hardware.

According to comScore Networks (http://www.comscore.com), shopping behavior is affected by the length of time a person has used the Internet: "Newbie online shoppers

Table 7-2	Internet Usage: A U.S. Perspective		
Population Attributes	**% Using the Internet**	**Online Activities**	**% of Internet Users Engaging in Activities on a Daily Basis**
Male/female online ratio	49/51	Use Internet	70
18 to 29 years old	83	Send E-mail	56
30 to 49 years old	78	Use a search engine	41
65 years old and over	28	Get news	37
White	68	Surf for fun	28
Hispanic	66	Check weather	22
Black	55	Research products	19
Lower income	48	Engage in instant messaging	10
Middle income	72	Buy products	6
Higher income	93	Download music	4
High school graduate	57	Make travel reservations	3
College graduate	89	Participate in online auctions	3
Selected Products Bought Online	**% of Online Shoppers Buying in a Typical Year**	**Selected Online Sales by Product Category**	**May 2008 Average Order Size ($)**
Books	66	Computer hardware	253
Apparel	57	Computer software	252
Travel arrangements	57	Automotive	179
Gifts	51	Consumer electronics	144
CDs	45	Event and movie tickets	126
Videos/DVDs	42	Office supplies	100
Computer software/games	41	Sporting and outdoor goods	68
Electronics/appliances	40	Home and garden	64
Hobby items	37	Shoes and athletic footwear	53
Computer hardware	36	Apparel	51

Sources: Table developed by the authors based on data from Pew Internet & American Lifestyle Project, various reports, http://www.pewinternet.org/index.asp; USC Annenberg School Center for the Digital Future, *2008 Digital Future Project*, http://www.digitalcenter.org; and Nielsen, "MegaView Retail," http://www.marketingcharts.com (May 2008).

cling to the familiar. They are 81 percent more likely than experienced shoppers to shop only at sites they've shopped at in the past. Willingness to shop at new sites increases with experience. And as experience and comfort grow, spending grows. Research data indicate that 75 percent of online shoppers are willing to try a new Internet merchant."[19]

Marketers can also use the Internet to gain greater insights about their consumers. See Figure 7-9.

7-5b Product Planning

Companies take a variety of product-planning approaches with the Internet, such as these two. Atomic Dog (**http://www.atomicdog.com**), the publisher of this text, is involved with Internet-driven texts and print versions of them. The online texts feature high-tech graphics, animations, interactivity, and other dynamic attributes not found in traditional printed books.

At Pillsbury's Web site (**http://www.pillsbury.com**), it has a section called My Pillsbury Baking. "This is your corner of our site! Everything here is designed to make it more convenient for you in the kitchen." In My Recipe Box, "collect your favorite recipes from around our site or add your own. Access dessert ideas any time!" In the Grocery List, "Keep track of the recipe ingredients you need from the store. Grocery shopping has never been easier!" "When you register with PillsburyBaking.com, you'll have access to your personalized recipe box and grocery lists."[20]

Figure 7-9

MyBestSegments from Claritas

As Claritas notes as its Web site (**http://www.claritas.com/ MyBestSegments/Default.jsp**), "Think of MyBestSegments as a 'photo album' of consumer markets. Each market segment has its own pages that display 'snapshots' of the segment's demographic traits, lifestyle preferences, and consumer behaviors.

Source: Reprinted by permission.

---

[19] James Maguire, "The State of E-Commerce: Online Shopping Trends," **http://www.ecommerce-guide.com/news/ trends/article.php/3524581** (August 2, 2005).

[20] "Welcome to Pillsbury Baking," **http://www.pillsbury.com/AALL/default.aspx** (April 30, 2009).

More firms are also heeding this advice:

On the Web, all goods are not equal. One important dimension on which items differ is in the ability of consumers to ascertain the quality of products in cyberspace. On one end of the spectrum are commodity products, where quality can be clearly and contractually articulated and conveyed. Products such as oil, paper clips, and stock shares all fall under this category. On the other end of the continuum are products for which the perception of quality differs from consumer to consumer and product to product, such as produce, used cars, and works of art. Understanding how hard it is to convey quality, reliability, or consistency for certain classes of products over the Web enables businesspeople to think strategically about the long-term success of different types of E-commerce.[21]

7-5c   Distribution Planning

The use of the Internet in distribution planning varies widely. For example, Terry Precision Cycling (**http://www.terrybicycles.com**) is a small manufacturer of bicycles and related products for women. The firm does relatively little E-commerce business at its Web site, and relies on independent bicycle shops around the country. Office Depot (**http://www.officedepot.com**) is a huge bricks-and-clicks chain. Although its stores generate $11 billion in yearly sales, Office Depot's Web site provides most of its sales growth, with annual online sales hitting $5 billion.

One of the most complex aspects of E-distribution involves business-to-business exchanges that connect sellers and potential buyers. The most successful such exchange is Covisint (**http://www.covisint.com**), initially formed by several auto makers and then acquired by Compuware (**http://www.compuware.com**): "As a global leader of collaboration solutions and services, Covisint turns the extended enterprise into a competitive advantage for more than 45,000 organizations worldwide. It provides an on-demand infrastructure for secure collaboration, interoperability, and access to information. Covisint streamlines and automates business processes, globally connecting business communities, organizations, and systems in the manufacturing, health care, aerospace, public sector, and financial services industries." It "enables companies of any size, location, or technical sophistication to share vital business information and applications across internal and external business partners."[22]

As a result of the distribution problems that a number of online firms have faced, they are now more apt to outsource delivery to such industry powerhouses as UPS (**http://www.ups.com**), which has a significant Internet logistical presence with its UPS OnLine Tools.

7-5d   Promotion Planning

With the demise of such prominent E-commerce firms as Pets.com and eToys.com, many Internet-driven firms have scaled back their TV advertising efforts. These efforts proved too costly and too ineffective. Print and online ads remain popular. In-store kiosks have a role, as illustrated in Figure 7-10. And opt-in E-mail is rising rapidly in popularity.

To learn more about online promotion planning, read these excellent articles: "The Web Marketing Checklist: 32 Ways to Promote Your Web Site" (**http://www.wilsonweb. com/articles/checklist.htm**) and "How to Attract Visitors to Your Web Site" (**http:// www.wilsonweb.com/articles/attract.htm**).

---

[21] John M. de Figueiredo, "Sustainable Profitability in Electronic Commerce," *Sloan Management Review*, Vol. 41 (Summer 2000), p. 41.

[22] "About Covisint," **http://www.covisint.com/about** (March 30, 2009).

Figure 7-10

In-Store Kiosks at Whole Foods

As Whole Foods (**http://www. wholefoodsmarket.com**) notes: "We want to satisfy and delight our customers—every single one. We design our stores, train our Team Members, and select our products with that goal in mind." And that is why it has added kiosks to provide more information for shoppers.

Source: Reprinted by permission of Susan Berry, Retail Image Consulting, Inc.

7-5e   Price Planning

According to Jupiter Research (**http://www.jupiterresearch.com**), 80 percent of Internet shoppers comparison shop before buying, and nearly one-half of Internet shoppers visit 3 to 5 sites before making a purchase. Some firms set their online prices similar to—or slightly below—their offline prices, and count on customer loyalty to their brands and the convenience of Web shopping to stimulate business. Other companies such as eBay (**http://www.ebay.com**) and Priceline.com (**http://www.priceline.com**) focus their appeal on people who like to price shop and get bargains.

Still other companies use the Internet to sell close-out merchandise at deep discounts:

> At SmartBargains.com (**http://www.smartbargains.com**), we believe there's an art to bargain shopping. And it doesn't involve rummaging through bargain bins. Here, you'll discover your favorite brands at smart low prices, ready whenever you want to shop. Since 1999, we've been dedicated to giving you an online, off-price shopping experience that's easy, instantly rewarding, and fun. Every day, our professional buyers search the globe to bring you an edited selection of quality, brand-name goods in home, fashion, jewelry, and more. We've logged the miles, sorted the bargains, and selected only the best for you. Our commitment starts with the quality of our goods and continues to our Web site, our state-of-the-art fulfillment center, and our highly responsive and dedicated customer service team.[23]

---

[23] "What We Do," **http://www.smartbargains.com/Promo/Help/What-We-Do.aspx** (May 2, 2009).

7-6 CURRENT CHALLENGES AND FUTURE PROSPECTS FOR E-MARKETING

In this section, we look at the challenges and future prospects for marketing and the Internet.

7-6a The Challenges of Using the Internet in Marketing

Some challenges faced by Internet marketers are beyond their control (such as slow-speed dial-up connections and the complexity of multichannel marketing); others are self-inflicted (such as poor customer service and overly rapid expansion). Before turning to several specific challenges, both uncontrollable and self-inflicted, let us cite some general reasons why E-marketing can be so daunting:

> Web challenges fall into two categories: uncontrollable and self-inflicted.

- A company's corporate culture may be hard to adapt to the Internet.
- Internet marketing may not capitalize on a company's core competencies.
- The proper roles for E-marketing may not be specified clearly enough—or be realistic in nature.
- Web users can be very demanding.
- The personal touch may be important to many customers.
- Channel partners may be alienated.
- Online and offline systems may be hard to integrate.
- It may be difficult to determine what Internet functions to insource and which to outsource.
- Investment costs and ongoing expenses may be underestimated.

Let us now review a number of specific challenges related to marketing and the Internet.

Consumer resistance to online shopping—Despite the rapid growth of online sales, less than 5 percent of U.S. retail revenues and about 10 to 15 percent of U.S. business-to-business revenues are from Internet transactions. Why? Many final consumers still want personal contact, the immediacy of a store purchase, and the ability to touch products before buying. They also often find the online purchase process to be too cumbersome. From a business-to-business perspective, "Many firms must largely redesign important purchasing processes from the ground up to capitalize on technology. Then they must motivate employees to embrace broad changes while training them in new methods. There is a lack of software integration capabilities between purchasers and suppliers."[24]

> These challenges must be reviewed carefully and in-depth.

Customer service—Web users often feel frustrated by what they perceive as inadequate customer service. According to an Allurent (**http://www.allurent.com**) study on consumers' online experiences, although people may be shopping more online, their expectations are also rising. Why? "I know that technology is constantly changing and improving and I expect that online shopping should also be getting better. I see that most retailers consistently advertise their Web sites so I expect to see them invest in making those sites better than they were last year. I have high-speed bandwidth and expect to see more online stores better presenting products in a way that takes advantage of my faster Internet speed." Allurent also found that "nearly 40 percent of consumers revealed that a frustrating online experience would make them less likely to shop at that retailer's physical store. And 60 percent reported that when they have a frustrating shopping experience online, it negatively impacts their overall opinion of the retailer/brand. An overwhelming 80 percent would not return to the site after having a negative online shopping experience, meaning with most customers, retailers have one chance to make a great impression."[25]

---

[24] "Online Purchasing Continues to Grow," *Supply House Times* (September 2003), p. 40.

[25] "National Survey Finds Online Shoppers' Expectations Are Rising; Retailers Have One Chance to Make a Great Impression," **http://www.allurent.com/newsDetail.php?newsid=38** (January 30, 2008).

System breakdowns—Various system breakdowns have occurred and will continue to occur. Some are caused by companies' lack of attention to their sites, but most are due to the sheer complexity of E-marketing with regard to the number of parties involved in a typical Web site (from Internet service provider to content Web master), the amount of traffic on the Web, the number of links that firms have at their sites (which must be checked regularly to be sure they are not broken), the use of multimedia, and other factors. In addition, firms must constantly be vigilant and protect their sites against intrusions from hackers who may corrupt files, steal customer data, and otherwise be destructive.

Speed of site performance—Slow connections are irritating to both users and companies that have Web sites. Users with dial-up telephone connections—still the mode for some home users—must wait to log on every time they dial-up, face periodic busy signals, and endure long delays when photos or other multimedia tools are featured at the Web site. Some features, such as video clips, may not work at all with a dial-up connection. Firms are disappointed because they must scale down their sites so that downloads are not excessively slow for dial-up users. With the growth of "always on" cable, DSL, and other high-speed connections (already in use by most businesses and the majority of homes in the United States), this challenge will diminish in the years ahead.

Internet connection costs—Although the promise of high-speed connections is great, the prices will have to drop for significantly more users to sign on. As of 2009, Time Warner's Road Runner service (**http://www.rr.com**) charged a monthly cable Internet connection fee of $44.95 ($29.95 for each of the first 6 months); and Verizon's FiOS DSL service (**http://www.Verizon.com/fios**) charged a monthly Internet connection fee of $47.95 (with the first month free). These fees were for those not also subscribing to phone or cable TV service. For dial-up consumers, prices are much less expensive. In 2009, the AOL (**http://www.aol.com**) standard monthly dial-up fee was $9.99 plus taxes.

Legal issues—Because Internet use is relatively new, few legal precedents exist. The legal challenges facing E-marketing fall into two categories: firm versus firm and government activities. In the first category are disputes over copyrights, patents, and business practices. For example, a number of music companies successfully sued Napster (**http://www.napster.com**) to require the firm to stop facilitating the free exchange of copyrighted materials, forcing Napster to change its business strategy. Amazon.com (**http://www.amazon.com**) sued Barnes & Noble.com (**http://www.bn.com**) to prevent the latter from offering one-click shopping, since Amazon.com has a patented process for it. The two firms settled out of court. With regard to government actions, among the most contentious issues are whether to tax items sold over the Internet (in the United States, sales tax is not required unless a firm has a physical presence in a state with a sales tax), whether children should be denied access to undesirable sites, whether there should be rules governing purchase terms and delivery dates, and whether and how to protect individuals' privacy.

Privacy issues—Internet users are willing to provide some personal data. Yet, they are concerned about what information is requested at Web sites and how that information is to be used. The positive: "Visit the Amazon.com (**http://www.amazon.com**) site to buy a book online and your welcome page will include recommendations for other books you might enjoy, including the latest from your favorite authors, all based on your history of purchases. Most customers appreciate these suggestions, much the way they would recommendations by a local librarian." The negative: "Take, for example, the case of Facebook (**http://www.facebook.com**), the popular social networking site. It introduced a system called Beacon that tracked members' purchases on other sites and shared the information with each user's social circle. Within a month, outraged users had forced Facebook to reconsider its unannounced initiative. The company apologized, then introduced new privacy options that require users to 'opt in' to the Beacon program. The result? In a survey by TNS (**http://www.tnsglobal.com**) of U.S. Internet users, "91 percent say that, given the opportunity, they would use online tools to control online tracking of their information."[26] To better address consumer online privacy concerns, a number of organizations have formed the nonprofit Online Privacy Alliance (**http://www.privacyalliance.org**).

Communicating without spam—Opt-in (permission-based) E-mail can be very successful. People respond well when they are asked if it is okay for a firm to communicate with them and what kinds of information they would like to get. What most Web users object to is the extensive use of ***spam***, which is unsolicited and unwanted E-mail. As of 2008, more than 80 percent of all E-mail was spam. Consider this:

> E-mail newsletters are extremely popular and can be a valuable way to keep in touch with your customers or clients or students. However, it's very, very easy to have your E-mail flagged as spam and never reach the recipient. Worse, if your E-mails repeatedly show up in an administrator's spam queue, you're risking having your entire domain banned. So here's some tips to make sure that doesn't happen: (1) Make sure the recipient has agreed to receive mail from you. There is no excuse for sending newsletters to unsuspecting people with whom you have no relationship. (2) Make sure there is an obvious way for the recipient to unsubscribe or otherwise change their settings. Honor all requests to unsubscribe immediately. (3) Include a name along with the E-mail address. This will help the spam filters know that your E-mail is legitimate. (4) Include a subject line that is accurate and relevant to the body content. In the United States, this is required by law. (5) Include an accurate "From" line. (6) Avoid messaging IN ALL CAPS. This is a common spam technique. Also avoid unnecessary punctuation repetition such as !!! or ???[27]

As noted in Chapter 5, a federal anti-spam law was enacted to try to alleviate the spam problem. It has, thus far, been ineffective because "spammers" have been able to circumvent it.

Clutter—There is a lot of clutter on the Web, given the huge number of companies that are now online. It is becoming much tougher for any one company to be noticed and to stand out. For instance, in Chapter 1, we cited nearly 40 search engines; and there are many others. They must work quite hard to differentiate themselves. In general, this means that well-known firms will have an easier time attracting Web visitors and that all firms must keep up their promotion efforts.

Finding a workable business model—Some Internet-based firms have not earned a profit due to excessive investments, overly rapid expansion, system breakdowns, and overestimates about how quickly people would buy online. They need a more realistic and focused business model. For example, a decade ago, Webvan spent $1 billion to develop an online grocery business (which expanded to include electronics, toys, drugstore items, and other product lines). Yet, its 2000 sales were less than $100 million and it suffered enormous losses. It went out of business in mid-2001.

Expectations of free services—A particularly vexing challenge for those that offer online services is how to generate revenues from them. As evidenced by all the free Web sites referenced in this book, there are a huge number of sites that allow free access to valuable resources—including newspapers, magazines, encyclopedias, software, consulting advice, and a whole lot more. Thus, users often expect these services to be free; and they will bypass sites that charge a fee. Attempts to generate revenues at these sites by having paid advertising have often not proven to be very successful.

Integrating bricks-and-clicks operations—It is not always easy to integrate offline and online strategies. Some leading companies have misfired because of insufficient coordination, such as Barnes & Noble, which did not allow in-store returns of online purchases when it began Internet selling. Today, it does. Due to the price-sensitive nature of Web shoppers, some companies have lower prices online than offline. This may be disturbing

> Internet users are really turned off by **spam**, unsolicited and unwanted E-mail.

---

[26] "Privacy on the Web: Is It a Losing Battle?" **http://knowledge.wharton.upenn.edu/articlepdf/1999.pdf** (June 25, 2008).

[27] Jason Friesen, "How to Send an E-Mail Newsletter without Sending Spam," **http://jasonfriesen.ca/news/archives/2008/04/15/how-to-send-an-email-newsletter-without-sending-spam** (April 15, 2008).

Ethical Issues in Marketing

Graduate Management Admission Council 1, ScoreTop.com 0

In 2008, the Graduate Management Admission Council, or GMAC (http://www.gmac.com), was awarded $2.3 million plus legal costs in a case against the now-defunct ScoreTop.com, a firm that sold review materials for the GMAT exam. GMAC's GMAT exam is used by more than 4,000 graduate schools of business to evaluate prospective M.B.A. students. According to GMAC, ScoreTop.com had distributed over its Web site "live" copyright materials that were still in use on the GMAT exam.

GMAC also legally took possession of a hard drive from the server used to run ScoreTop.com's site and shut down the site. GMAC notified business schools of any student prospects who had used the site. Although the hard drive contained about 6,000 names, some people were innocent surfers who did not download the test materials. GMAC vowed to cancel the scores of anyone who used ScoreTop.com, prohibit them from retaking the GMAT, and notify schools that received the test scores of cheaters. The reaction at schools ranged from a "slap on the wrist" to expulsion.

GMAC became aware of the problem when it learned about an individual who bragged that Scoretop.com had given him a competitive advantage. GMAC immediately cancelled the student's score and notified the schools where the student applied. It is unclear how the schools reacted to that student's application. The person at the root of the scandal took the GMAT exam at least three times in 2002 and 2003. He was not represented in court on the copyright infringement case as he returned home to China.

Sources: Based on material in Louis Lavalle, "GMAT Cheating Controversy Grows," http://www.businessweek.com/bschools (June 27, 2008); and Francesca Levy and Matthew Lawyue, "GMAT Scandal Has MBA Students Sweating," http://www.businessweek.com/bschools (July 1, 2008).

to store shoppers who feel they should have the same opportunities for discounts. With store-based transactions, companies need on-premises inventory so products are immediately available. Yet, with Web-based sales, central warehouses can be more efficient.

Global issues—Even though the Internet is a worldwide communications vehicle, cultural, language, currency, legal, and other differences among countries can affect a firm seeking a global Internet strategy. Since global distribution tends to be complicated, there often is a need to outsource tasks.

7-6b The Future of E-Marketing

Here are some projections about the future of E-marketing:

> As a major new technology, the Internet will have a bright future, with some stumbles along the way.

- The impact of the Internet on all parties will continue to be enormous, but somewhat different than originally anticipated. Although Internet-generated revenues will grow, there will be more emphasis on E-marketing (using the Internet to enhance marketing strategies) than on E-commerce (sales from Internet transactions).
- Bricks-and-clicks firms will typically outperform bricks-and-mortar firms and clicks-only firms. Bricks-and-clicks firms with a bricks-and-mortar background will do the best of all, due to their name recognition, customer following, and established physical presence. See Figure 7-11.
- The growth of new high-speed transmission modes such as cable and DSL connection services will allow more multimedia capabilities to be incorporated into company Web sites, creating an exciting environment for browsing, entertainment, and shopping by users.
- Business-to-business E-commerce will continue to far outstrip business-to-consumer E-commerce.
- It is forecast that U.S. online retail sales will rise by one-third between 2009 and 2012.
- Most firms engaged in E-commerce will be profitable, having learned valuable insights over the last several years. See Figure 7-12.

Figure 7-11

Hyatt: A Well-Integrated Bricks-and-Clicks Approach

As one of the world's leading hotel chains, Hyatt (**http://www.hyatt.com**) is always looking for ways to delight its customers. Recently, Hyatt added a new Web site to its bricks-and-clicks strategy: yatt'it (**http://www.yattit.com**) is "where Hyatt Gold Passport members share their insider tips on worldwide travel."

Source: Reprinted by permission.

Figure 7-12

E*Trade: A Master of Online Marketing

E*Trade (**http://www.etrade.com**) averages more than 125,000 transactions per day and receives an average commission of $10 to $11 per trade. The firm is quite profitable.

Source: Reprinted by permission.

- Internet usage and E-commerce will grow more popular around the world. Figure 7-13 shows 2008 data by region. As has been the trend in recent years, the gap among regions will decline.

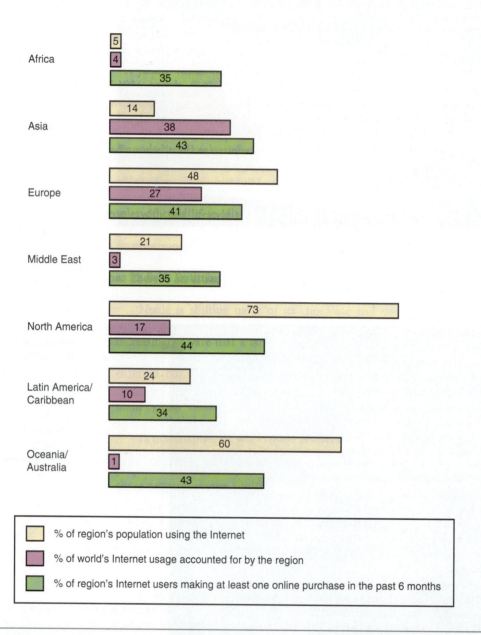

Figure 7-13

Internet Usage in Regions Around the World

Sources: Figure developed by the authors from data reported at **http://www.internetworldstats.com** (November 9, 2008); and Nielsen, *Trends in Online Shopping: A Global Nielsen Consumer Report* (February 2008).

Web Sites You Can Use

Several companies conduct research related to the Internet and provide valuable marketing-related information at their Web sites. These firms include:

- Clickz (**http://www.clickz.com**)—Free articles on all aspects of E-marketing.
- eMarketer (**http://www.emarketer.com/Newsletter.aspx**)—Sign up for the free daily E-newsletter.
- Forrester Research (**http://www.forrester.com**)—Register as a guest to gain access to free sample reports.
- Internet World Stats (**http://www.internetworldstats.com/index.html**)—Worldwide Internet usage data.

- Jupiter Research (**http://www.jup.com**)—Register as a guest to gain access to free sample reports.
- Marketing Charts (**http://www.marketingcharts.com**)—Free charts and data on Internet marketing.
- Nielsen/Net Ratings (**http://www.nielsen-netratings.com/news.jsp**)—Click on "NetView Usage Metrics" to see free current data on Internet usage in 10 countries.
- Plunkett Research (**http://www.plunkettresearch.com/technology/ecommerce_trends.htm**)—Free industry overview.

Summary

1. *To demonstrate why the Internet is a valuable marketing tool* The Internet is a global electronic superhighway of computer networks accessible to people worldwide. The World Wide Web is a way to access the Internet; users see words, colorful charts, pictures, and video, and hear audio. In this chapter (and book), the terms are used interchangeably. E-marketing involves any marketing activity through the Internet. E-commerce refers to sales-generating Internet transactions. E-marketing is the broader concept, and it does not necessarily have sales as the primary goal.

    About 75 billion people around the globe use the Web. They surf the Internet for many reasons other than shopping. For instance, they seek out entertainment, financial, sports, and news sites. They do product research. They "talk" to one another. They communicate with firms to register complaints and make suggestions. They send E-mails and greetings cards. Companies also surf the Web for reasons other than shopping. They check what competitors are doing. They read about industry trends and events. They communicate with suppliers. They exchange data among offices anywhere in the world. They monitor inventory. They survey customers. They analyze customer data bases.

    E-marketing is evolving in three phases: (1) traditional bricks-and-mortar firms, (2) clicks-only Internet firms, and (3) bricks-and-clicks firms that combine the other two formats. The trend is more toward bricks-and-clicks firms because they can appeal to multiple market segments, maximize customer contact points, leverage the strengths of each form of business, and enter into new alliances.

    Firms can achieve benefits by using the Internet in marketing. Benefits include communicability, a focus/tailored approach, information, timeliness, cost efficiencies, dynamism/flexibility, global possibilities, multimedia capabilities, interactivity, and sales.

2. *To explore the multifaceted potential marketing roles for the Internet* The Web can serve multiple marketing roles. Each firm must determine which of these roles to pursue and how to prioritize their importance: projecting an image, customer service, channel relations, purchasing and inventory management, information gathering and sharing, data-base development, mass customization (a process by which mass-market goods and services are individualized to satisfy a specific customer need at a reasonable price), advertising and sales promotion, selling, and multichannel marketing.

3. *To show how to develop an Internet marketing strategy* A firm should use a systematic process in forming a proper strategy. The six steps in the process relate to the basic components of an Internet marketing strategy. There are also four outside influences in making strategic decisions.

    (1) Goal categories are set. Both quantitative and qualitative objectives should be stated. (2) The target audience is identified and selected, and its desires studied. (3) Web site attributes are determined. First, the company must decide whether to do Web-related activities itself (insourcing) or to have specialized firms perform some or all Web-related activities for it (outsourcing). Second, the company must choose the scale of its Web presence, especially the importance of the Web site in its overall marketing strategy, the percent of the marketing budget for the Web site, and how the Web site is to be implemented. Third, Web site attributes (address name, home page, etc.) are ascertained.

    (4) Internet-based marketing-mix decisions are made while developing the Web site, consistent with offline marketing decisions. (5) The strategy is implemented. Two factors affect a firm's ability to properly enact its strategy: security and channel relationships, and they must be dealt with well. Once the strategy is enacted, the firm must ensure that it runs smoothly. (6) Performance is assessed and modifications made as necessary.

4. *To illustrate how the Internet is being utilized to enhance marketing strategies* Many firms actively use the Web in their consumer analysis, product planning, distribution planning, promotion planning, and price planning. Several examples are noted.

5. *To consider the challenges of using the Internet in marketing and to forecast the future of E-marketing* Some challenges are rather uncontrollable (such as dial-up connections) and others are self-inflicted by companies. Attention must be paid to consumer shopping resistance, customer service, system breakdowns, site speed, connection costs, legal issues, privacy issues, spamless communications, clutter, a workable business model, expectations of free services, integrating bricks-and-clicks operations, and global issues.

In the future, Internet usage will continue growing, with E-marketing being even more essential. Bricks-and-clicks firms will succeed best. High-speed connections will lead to more multimedia-rich Web sites. Business-to-business E-commerce will greatly outstrip business-to-consumer E-commerce. There will be a considerable increase in Internet use outside North America.

Key Terms

Internet (p. 185)

World Wide Web (WWW) (p. 185)

E-marketing (p. 185)

E-commerce (p. 185)

bricks-and-mortar firms (p. 187)

clicks-only firms (p. 187)

bricks-and-clicks firms (p. 187)

mass customization (p. 192)

opt-in (permission-based) E-mail (p. 197)

spam (p. 205)

Review Questions

1. Distinguish between E-marketing and E-commerce.
2. Describe the three phases of E-marketing.
3. What cost efficiencies does the Internet offer for companies that use it properly?
4. What is mass customization? Give an example not mentioned in the chapter.
5. Discuss the six basic steps in developing an Internet marketing strategy.
6. Why is it important for a company to monitor the links, both internal and external, at its Web site?
7. Why is opt-in E-mail gaining in popularity by both companies and Internet users?
8. State four major challenges facing E-marketers.

Discussion Questions

1. What can a firm learn by studying Tables 7-1 and 7-2?
2. Visit your school's Web site. Which of the marketing roles cited in this chapter do you think it is performing? Explain your answer.
3. Develop and explain a five-item survey to use in assessing the design of a Web site.
4. What is your favorite social networking Web site? Why?

Web Exercise

eBay (**http://www.ebay.com**) is a very successful online marketer. As an auction firm, eBay has strict rules of behavior—updated regularly—for both buyers (**http://pages.ebay.com/help/policies/buyer-rules-overview.html**) and sellers (**http://pages.ebay.com/help/policies/seller-rules-overview.html**). What are the most important current rules for each party to understand? Why? What other rules should it consider adding?

Practice Quiz

1. The basic difference between the Internet and the World Wide Web is that only
   a. the Internet is a marketing tool.
   b. the Internet is a public system.
   c. through the Web can users see graphics and hear audio.
   d. through the Web can consumers E-mail each other.

2. A consumer request for information on the Web that is helpful in determining the features of a particular refrigerator model is an example of
   a. spamming.
   b. E-commerce.
   c. E-marketing.
   d. logistics.

3. Which of these is the broadest concept?
   a. Opt-in E-mail
   b. Bricks-and-mortar
   c. E-commerce
   d. E-marketing

4. Which Internet marketing format has undergone a major shakeup?
   a. Catalogs
   b. Clicks-only firms
   c. TV shopping
   d. DSL

5. Which one of the following is *not necessarily* a benefit for a firm using the Internet in marketing?
   a. Timeliness
   b. Low system-maintenance costs
   c. 24/7 operations
   d. Global possibilities

6. Which of these Internet attributes relates to the ability of the Internet to have two-way communication?
   a. Interactivity
   b. Hyperactivity
   c. Connectivity
   d. Globalization

7. Which role of the Internet in marketing is best illustrated by a firm maintaining a list of key customers and their purchasing behavior?
   a. Data-based proliferation
   b. Data-base development
   c. Customer service
   d. Channel relations

8. The lot size in mass customization is typically
   a. one unit.
   b. 10 units.
   c. 100 units.
   d. more than 1,000 units.

9. Multichannel marketing is practiced by a(n)
   a. E-commerce firm.
   b. bricks-and-mortar firm.
   c. bricks-and-clicks firm.
   d. clicks-only firm.

10. Which of these statements is correct?
    a. Seventy percent of U.S. adults ages 18 to 29 have a broadband connection.
    b. Far more men than women use the Internet in the United States.
    c. Internet use increases as people get older.
    d. Internet use decreases as household income increases.

11. Which aspect of a Web site includes such topics as company background, financial performance, and an online shopping cart?
    a. (URL) Web address
    b. Site content
    c. Links
    d. Home page

12. An Internet retailer respects a consumer's privacy by
    a. using spam.
    b. using opt-in E-mail.
    c. selling names to mailing list brokers.
    d. trading names and addresses of customers with noncompeting firms.

13. Computing daily Web site traffic, ratings on customer service surveys, and sales revenues are measures to be used in
    a. making distribution decisions.
    b. enacting trade-off decisions.
    c. making promotion decisions.
    d. assessing performance.

14. Which of these factors should *not* be regularly reviewed in evaluating the quality of a Web site?
    a. Download time
    b. Security
    c. Product variety
    d. Currency

15. The large number of search engines, as well as the number of companies that are now online, contribute to
    a. the need to outsource Web decision making.
    b. consumer privacy concerns.
    c. clutter.
    d. system breakdowns.

For the answers to these questions, please visit the online site for this book at **http://www.atomicdog.com.**

Case 1: Deception Through Ambush Marketing[c2-1]

"Ambush marketing" is a practice whereby a competitor piggybacks on another firm's marketing events without its approval and then intends to fool potential customers into thinking that it is the official sponsor of the event. A representative of the ambush firm typically gains access to an event by purchasing tickets, and then erects signs and distributes fliers and merchandise without permission. Ambush marketing is quite popular for some small brands because they can get valuable exposure to a highly targeted audience at a very low cost.

With "guerilla marketing," public spaces and unsponsored events are used to increase awareness or trial of a brand. For example, Red Bull (http://www.redbullusa.com) has used guerilla marketing by giving students a free case of its beverage if they throw a party featuring the energy drink. A common strategy in guerilla marketing is to bypass security guards by befriending the staff or to use disguises to appear to be an authorized entrant (such as a marketer dressing up to resemble a student). A guerilla marketing tactic used by some marketers at the 2008 Olympic Games in Beijing was to convert some popular restaurants near the Olympic center to hospitality centers.

Nike (http://www.nike.com) has used ambush marketing. In one instance, its ambush marketing was so effective that 22 percent of British consumers thought Nike was the official sponsor of the World Cup taking place in Japan and Korea—in contrast to the 19 percent who knew it was actually Adidas (http://www.adidas.com). Nike used ambush marketing at the Atlanta Olympics by handing out Nike caps at transportation hubs that spectators wore into the stadium, purchasing all outdoor poster sites, and setting up Nike Village directly next to the official Olympic Sponsors' Village. In some instances, the ambush marketer achieves higher recognition ratings than actual event sponsors.

Official sponsors of events need to protect themselves from ambush marketing. One way is to have an ambush-marketing clause in every event or sponsorship contract. FIFA (http://www.fifa.com), the world soccer authority, uses contract law that bars tickets from being given out free or allowing attendees to wear clothing with logos from unauthorized sponsors. Spectators who have Pepsi (http://www.pepsi.com) drink containers or caps with Google (http://www.google.com) emblems can be barred from entry to protect an event's real sponsors—Coca-Cola (http://www.coca-cola.com) and Yahoo! (http://www.yahoo.com). Some firms even withhold a percentage of sponsorship monies from the organizer. If the anti-ambush terms of the contract are not properly enforced, these funds may be permanently withheld. Some firms also try to limit the opportunity for ambush marketers by closely examining an event's co-sponsors and refusing to co-sponsor events where a known ambush marketer is a participant.

The concern over ambush advertising is so great that the International Olympic Committee (http://www.olympic.org) has asked those countries bidding to host the Olympics to secure venues close to major events to prevent unauthorized outdoor advertising from being shown on TV. To protect sponsors against ambush marketing, New Zealand passed a Major Events Management Bill in December 2006. One provision of this legislation is to establish "clean zones," roughly 3 miles around event venues and stadiums. No unauthorized advertising (including signs, billboards, banners, hang gliders, parachutes, and aerial displays by aircraft) is allowed during a major event.

Some advertising agencies and marketers prohibit the use of ambush marketing in their code of ethics. An account executive needs to ask: "Is the short-term gain worth your job or your reputation to achieve a quick-hit win against another brand manager? How would your stable of clients feel about this approach? Is there any potential for lost business?"

Questions

1. Discuss the ethical concerns regarding ambush marketing.
2. Discuss the ethical concerns regarding guerilla marketing.
3. Develop a plan for Olympic Sponsors' Village to prevent ambush advertising by Nike or other firms.
4. As a partner in a major advertising agency, discuss the pros and cons of engaging in ambush advertising for a major client at your agency.

[c2-1] The data in the case are drawn from "Combating Ambush Marketing," http://www.marketingmag.co.nx (May 2007); pp. 26–27; and David Wolk, "How Can You Compete with an Olympic Sponsor?" *Media* (March 6, 2008), p. 37.

Case 2: How Can Consumers Be More Attracted to Green Marketing?[c2-2]

When asked the question, "Does green still sell?," one author says that green marketing issues will likely be one of the next big factors in consumer demand. Yet, even though a growing number of consumers report that they care about environmental issues, the key issue is exactly when do these issues become a real driver of demand? Some marketing analysts feel that, today, green marketing is not anywhere near the level of other drivers of demand (such as style, function, or price). For example, many consumers will not pay additional money for food produced in an environmentally friendly farm; and most consumers are not switching to hybrid cars due to the higher price of the vehicle.

One factor that may increase the attractiveness of green marketing is its increased endorsement by celebrities. Leonardo DiCaprio recently released a documentary *The 11th Hour* (**http://www.11thhouraction.com**), which looks at environmental crises caused by humans. Brad Pitt, together with Global Green USA (**http://www.globalgreen.org**), has designed environmentally friendly housing in New Orleans. Green marketing has also been adopted by some of the world's major brands, including Apple and Levi Strauss. Apple (**http://www.apple.com**) announced its "Green Apple" program, which removes toxic chemicals and increases the firm's use of recycling. Levi Strauss (**http://www.levis.com**) launched its "Green Jeans" brand, made from organic cotton that is finished in a chemical-free process. Fruit drink company Innocent (**http://www.innocentdrinks.co.uk**) started a "Buy One, Get One Tree" campaign.

Product categories such as food and cosmetics naturally fit with green campaigns. Brands such as Body Shop (**http://www.bodyshop.com**) and Aveda (**http://www.aveda.com**) are viewed by many consumers as "better for you" and "more luxurious." Fashion and interior design can also create a compelling case through products perceived by consumers as "green and chic," "green and luxury," and "green and good for you."

One "shot in the arm" for certain green marketing efforts is their lower relative cost. Many environmentally friendly products use less fossil-fuel content than nongreen competitors. With high oil costs, the price difference between the green and nongreen alternatives is being reduced. Eco-Products (**http://www.ecoproducts.com**), for example, a firm that produces compostable dinnerware, has seen its sales increase by 400 percent. According to the firm's chief executive,

"Our products are made from corn derivative, and our competition uses petroleum. They are having price increases where our prices are stable." Likewise, TerraCycle Inc. (**http://www.terracycle.net**), a manufacturer of fertilizer, plans to market an artificial fire log made with soy wax. The firm's largest competitor uses petroleum as a key ingredient.

One potential area of ethical conflict relates to the endorsement of green products. Endorsements add credibility to a firm's ecological claims, while they also add revenues to environment groups in need of funding. The Sierra Group (**http://www.thesierragroup.com**), a major environmental group, recently agreed to add its logo and endorsement to five Clorox Green Works products (**http://www.greenworkscleaners.com**), including an all-purpose cleaner and toilet-bowl cleaner. The products were featured on the *Oprah Winfrey Show* and the *Ellen DeGeneres Show*. The products were so successful that Clorox raised its sales forecast five times. However, four Sierra Group local chapters opposed the endorsement. In addition, some in Sierra Group have produced blogs critical of Clorox.

Clorox believed the Sierra Group's endorsement was critical to the success of Green Works. Its initial research showed that 25 percent of respondents worry about the use of harsh chemicals found in cleaning products and that more than 40 percent of the consumers surveyed wished they could find a natural cleaner that is effective. The new products were especially important to Clorox because the nearly $3 billion household-cleaning product market has had stagnant sales levels.

Questions

1. Develop a green marketing policy for an appliance manufacturer marketer based on natural resource utilization.
2. Develop a green marketing policy for a soda marketer based upon landscape considerations.
3. Develop a green marketing policy for a car manufacturer based upon environmental pollution.
4. As a public relations manager for Clorox, how would you handle the criticisms of the Sierra Club endorsement?

[c2-2] The data in the case are drawn from Arden Dale, "Green Products Gain From New Price Equation," *Wall Street Journal* (June 24, 2008), p. B7; Mya Frazier, "Clorox Eco-Friendly Line Finds Green Foes," *Advertising Age* (June 16, 2008), pp. 3, 25; and Jasmine Montgomery, "Can Green Brands Get Sexy?" *Brand Strategy* (March 2008), pp. 42–43.

Case 3: Will the Smart Car Succeed in the United States? ^{c2-3}

The most popular Smart Car (**http://www.smartcarusa.com**) model is a two-seat vehicle built at a Daimler plant in France. Unlike competitive cars in its class, that Smart Car has no back seat. It's also a little less than 9 feet long (3 feet shorter than the Mini). The entry-version of the Smart Car, priced at about $12,000, is powered by a 1.0-liter, 3-cylinder 71-horsepower engine. What's most special about the car to most buyers is its gas mileage, estimated at 40 miles per gallon (mpg). In comparison, the Yaris 5-speed car (**http://www.toyota.com/yaris**) gets 33 mpg and the Mini (**http://www.miniusa.com**) achieves 32 mpg.

When the Smart Car was first introduced in the United States at the beginning of 2008, it already had a waiting list of 30,000 consumers who had placed a $99 deposit to reserve their cars. That number is quite high, considering that the vehicle was launched in the United States with no print or TV ads. Most of Smart Car's initial promotion was based on the car's Web site, press reports on the car, and word of mouth among Americans who had seen the car on a foreign trip. About 770,000 Smart Cars have been sold in 36 countries. An annual target U.S. sales figure of 50,000 Smart Cars may be conservative.

Throughout 2008, demand for the Smart Car was significantly greater than supply. Unlike at other dealerships affected by high fuel prices and a slowing economy, there was a flurry of activity at the Smart Car's first U.S. franchise, in Bloomfield Hills, Michigan, about 20 miles from Detroit. Rich Cortright, the franchise owner, reported that the average Smart Car buyer was different than the young buyers of other budget cars, namely, Toyota's Scion (**http://www.scion.com**) and Volkswagen's new Beetle (**http://www.vw.com/newbeetle/en/us/**): "This is not a young person's car, really. It's something that people who are living with practicalities like. It's something for people who may already have a larger vehicle and want something that's fun and good on gas to get around town in." Though Smart Car has not reported data on the average age of its owners, the typical responses to that question on the Smart Car Community Board ranged between 40 and 73.

A major factor in the Smart Car's successful U.S. introduction was the rapidly rising gasoline prices. Although highly efficient small cars are highly popular in Europe (where gas prices are 2 to 2.3 times higher than in the United States because of high taxes), Americans, until recently, favored large cars and SUVs. The attitudes of Americans began to shift as gas prices accelerated to more than $4.00 per gallon for regular grade. In late 2007, a Kelley Blue Book (**http://www.kbb.com**) research study found that 26 percent of U.S. new car shoppers said they would seriously consider a more fuel-efficient vehicle if gas prices increased significantly. By mid-2008, that percentage increased to 47 percent. As a result, small car sales have been soaring. Toyota's Yaris, which starts at $11,350, reported sales increases of 46 percent in April 2008. Sales of Honda's Fit, (**http://www.honda.com**) whose prices start at $13,950 and gets 31 miles per gallon, rose by 54 percent.

Despite the success of these models and the public's new thirst for gas-stingy cars, the Smart Car's long-term success is far from a sure thing. Unlike the Yaris and Fit, the Smart Car has a tiny advertising budget. There are also detractors who argue that Americans are accustomed to buying a car with two rows of seats—not two seats. Last, several reviews have been less than complementary. For example, the nonprofit National Public Radio (**http://www.npr.org**) has called the car "a cross between a dune buggy and a golf cart."

Questions

1. What factors will determine whether the Smart Car succeeds in the long run?
2. Discuss the Smart Car's features from the perspective of the socioecological view of marketing. From the perspective of product-related ethical behavior.
3. Is the Smart Car an example of straight extension or product adaptation? Explain your answer.
4. In developing a promotional campaign for the Smart Car, would you use a standardized, nonstandardized, or glocal marketing approach? Explain your answer.

---

^{c2-3} The data in the case are drawn from Steve Miller, "Vroom for Two," *Brandweek* (June 2, 2008), pp. 20–23.

Case 4: Online Ticket Sales Keep on Climbing[c2-4]

According to one estimate, the live-event ticket industry in Great Britain accounts for more than $5 billion in annual sales, about $2.2 billion of which is through agents. The same source indicates that about 80 percent of Internet users have bought tickets online. Several firms, such as Aloud (http://www.aloud.com), Live Nation (http://www.livenation.co.uk), See Tickets (http://www.seetickets.com), and Ticketmaster (http://www.ticketmaster.com), have each invested heavily to further develop online ticket sales in Great Britain. Aloud, with 250,000 users attracted over the past two years, is owned and operated by Bauer Consumer Media, part of the Bauer Publishing group (http://www.bauer.co.uk), and the largest privately owned publisher in Europe. Live Nation, another online ticket provider in Great Britain, is the world's second largest online event ticketing service.

In May 2007, TickEx (http://www.tickex.com) launched a search engine that allows consumers to access 95 percent of the ticket content on the Web. Though TickEx specializes in concerts, its search engine will seek out tickets for live music, sports, and theater events from all major ticket Web sites. Users can search for events based on location, date, and price. As TickEx's chief marketing executive notes, "We see us as Google for Tickets." TickEx has initially focused on Great Britain but plans to expand into other English-speaking countries.

In addition to large online ticketing firms, smaller companies such as eFestivals (http://www.efestivals.com) specialize in selling tickets for festivals. As that firm's founder says, "Fans come to the site to see what the lineup is for festivals and there are easy links for them to buy tickets. This way, tickets are just a click away from news about the festival."

There are a number of competitive dynamics in British online ticketing. Eric Baker, a co-founder of StubHub (http://www.stubhub.com), moved to London to start a European-based online ticket agency. After a successful trial, DontStayIn (http://www.dontstayin.com) was rolled out. The site, with 330,000 members, offers tickets to 130 events, mostly clubs. There are also a number of ticket resale and exchange sites active in Great Britain. These include Viagogo (http://www.viagogo.com), Seatwave (http://www.seatwave.com), and MyTicketmaster (http://www.myticketmaster.com). Consumers typically visit these firms after going to Ticketmaster and finding that a concert has been sold out. The sites enable individuals to sell tickets they cannot use or wish to sell at a profit.

Many events allow consumers to use multiple channels to purchase tickets. For example, an event can use its own box office for ticketing and also allow online and telephone sales through its ticketing agency: "If people are at school, college, or work and want to buy a ticket, then having so many different ways of buying them can only be a good thing."

A number of benefits are associated with the use of online ticketing, for both customers and promoters. Customers have 24/7 access to ticketing, can more easily compare seating and pricing alternatives, and can avoid waiting in long lines for tickets (and then finding themselves sold out of a show). The sites also offer important information about people's favorite artists and venues. Promoters benefit from their events being more available to a larger audience, faster transaction times, access to the customer data bases the agencies hold, and outsourcing of back-end functions. Online sales are also an effective medium for selling all of a show's tickets: "Where online ticketing really helps is for shows with 1,000 seats, where 990 of the tickets are guaranteed to be sold. It is those last 10 that are the hardest to sell and where an online presence really makes a difference."

Questions

1. What issues must be addressed when foreign customers visit online ticketing sites to buy tickets for events in their own countries?
2. How can a music or sports event marketer overcome the resistance to online shopping for tickets?
3. Describe the pros and cons of using multichannel retailing by a music and sports event marketer.
4. What should be done to reduce the number of online tickets that are purchased by firms that resell these tickets for prices far above face value rather than by individual consumers?

[c2-4] The data in the case are drawn from "TickEx Aims to Become 'Google for Tickets'," *Music Week* (May 5, 2007), p. 7; "Ticketing Boom Clicks into Place," *Music Week* (July 16, 2005), pp. 9–11; and "Ticketing Traffic Hits New High," *Music Week* (April 19, 2008), p. 2.

E-volution to Revolution[pc-2]

INTRODUCTION

In the decade since the World Wide Web was introduced, the only certainty that marketing managers have faced is uncertainty. A major strategic thrust of business, government, and nonprofits has been implementing technology-based service systems. These service systems have transformed every aspect of our lives—including how we socialize, manage our money, purchase goods and services, and gather information. Yet, any organization that has a stable and functioning E-service model shouldn't become too smug. The pace of change is accelerating—not slowing—as a convergence of cutting-edge technologies, millennial lifestyles, and technology-related demographic shifts is moving the world of E-services from evolution to revolution.

We might soon view the age of the Web in the same way we viewed the "steam age" in the 20th century. The E-services of today will likely appear flat, static, and immobile compared with the technology-based E-services of the future. To a degree, the seeds of the coming revolution are evident in Europe and Asia, where newer generations of information technology have leapfrogged North America. Marketers can benefit by knowing these trends, the opportunities the trends will create, and the obstacles to be overcome. Consumer behavior, in the face of technological change, has implications for them.

Three concurrent trends will heavily shape the future of E-services. They consist of advances in information technology, changing lifestyles (which technology influences in many respects), and demographic shifts. Each trend in the macroenvironment is experiencing significant transformation, which will profoundly affect how consumers adopt and use E-services.

INFORMATION TECHNOLOGY

Technology refers to cutting-edge solutions that have the potential to add value to consumers' lives—in the form of increased efficiency, security, flexibility, or functionality. Boundless technologies are coming to market or in development. Five elements of technology progression will fundamentally transform interactions among consumers, E-service providers, and E-service providers' employees: mobility, portability, convergence, personalization, and collaboration. See Table 1 and Figure 1.

[pc-2] Adapted by the authors from Regina D. Woodall, Charles L. Colby, and A. Parasuraman, "'E-volution' to Revolution," *Marketing Management* (March-April 2007), pp. 29–34. Reprinted by permission of the American Marketing Association.

Mobility

This frees consumers from a fixed venue (e.g., a bricks-and-mortar store) to conduct transactions anywhere they choose. With most of the population owning wireless phones, technology is a way to meet mobile consumers' entertainment and communications needs. According to the 2006 *National Technology Readiness Survey* (*NTRS*), the most desired new feature of wireless devices was global positioning system technology—which allows users to get directions or navigate to a location.

Third-generation (3G) networks' lack of penetration in the United States hampers growth in mobile E-services. This is due to older infrastructure, and government and industry slowness to launch new systems and standards. These 3G networks offer the faster data-transfer speeds needed for advanced functionality and are much further along in Europe and Asia. While the United States catches up with 3G networks, other countries are planning to leapfrog to fourth-generation networks—with richer content.

Another, still in the early stages in the United States, is for Microwave Access (WiMAX) networks. Currently, millions of consumers take advantage of Wi-Fi hot spots, where they log on to the Web with a wireless connection. Unlike the narrow-range and voice-oriented networks of today, WiMAX will supply broadband access from a wider spectrum. This enables faster and richer linkage to digital information.

Portability

This refers to technology's increasing capability to be transported easily, even a small distance—such as from the kitchen to the living room. Wireless networks, which are just starting to take off, make it possible to move freely in the home with a device. Wi-Fi allows consumers to get hold of information and entertainment anywhere—from a local coffee shop to a travel depot. Bluetooth technology (which provides wireless connections) and greater space saving, in the form of flat panels for computers and video, further enhance portability. These technologies afford consumers additional control over their environments, including enhanced privacy to conduct research and access E-services. An example is Sony's LocationFree TV (**http://www.sonystyle.com**), which lets consumers watch their favorite programs anywhere in a residence, be it in the bath or at the dinner table.

Convergence

The convergence of voice, video, and data also presents enormous possibilities. If a service provider offers it, customers can benefit from a greater human experience—a service representative who is available online "24/7," by voice or video, and able to send and receive data to

Table 1 Elements That Influence an E-Service

Element	Enabling technologies	Fulfilled consumer needs	Examples of new E-service solutions
Mobility	WiMAX, 3G, and 4G	Freedom, time, and access	Finance, navigation, and location-free entertainment
Portability	Bluetooth, wireless networks, and flat panels	Freedom, comfort, and privacy	Wellness and location-free entertainment
Convergence	Broadband and videoconferencing	Human touch, organization, and efficiency	E-service representatives and complex transactions involving data sharing
Personalization	Recommendation systems, database integration, and smart cards	Efficiency and opportunity	Personalized mini-brands and high-impact merchandising
Collaboration	Instant messaging, chat, Web conferencing, and gaming/E-learning platforms	Group decision making and involvement of influencers	Web-conferenced interactions and E-learning

enhance the transaction. This will be the best of both worlds for customers: They will receive the high-touch service they usually get in person, and have the convenience of an online interaction. Although the adoption of home videoconferencing has been slow, E-service providers are building the market from the ground up.

Broadband access allows voice, video, and data to flow efficiently in a single pipeline. With penetration at two-thirds of Web users, consumers recognize the benefits it provides in their busy lives and are willing to pay for it. Broadband technology keeps getting faster, with fresh options entering the market—such as fiber-optic

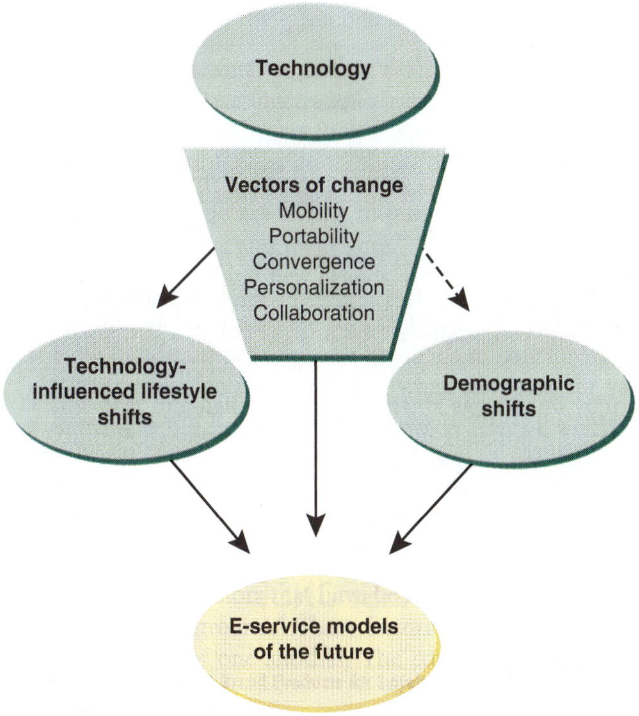

Figure 1

Factors Driving an E-Services Revolution

E-services that can deliver data at accelerated speeds. Cable companies are responding by boosting their system speeds. And in Asia, providers are offering consumers E-services that are available only to commercial users in the United States. With more and more consumers adopting high-speed access, and the speeds continually increasing, E-service providers will be able to add new convergent capabilities to increase convenience and efficiency for consumers.

Personalization

Successful E-service models adapt transactions to the customer's needs, and successful technology-based E-services allow personalization that makes the experience more relevant and responsive. Some of the earliest E-services permitted users to customize a portal to their preferences (e.g., http://my.yahoo.com). Many consumers won't take the time to do this—but technology gives E-services the ability to adapt to their behavior. Personalization hasn't always matched its hype. However, sophisticated data modeling and data-base integration lets E-service providers use customer-specific data to optimize decisions in self-service transactions. For instance, Amazon is well-known for its success in using customer information to merchandise to customers, based on stored and transactional information.

Adding to personalization of automated technologies is the "smart card." More common in Europe than in North America, it contains large amounts of personal data—which self-service devices can access electronically. Examples of applications include verifying users' identities online, storing vital medical information in a wallet, and controlling admission to different parts of a building.

Collaboration

This will affect E-services further into the future, but potentially with greater impact. Most technology-based E-services involve interactions between a consumer and a computer, or a consumer and an employee; soon, it will be increasingly possible to involve several parties in a transaction. E-service models are bringing

217

together groups or communities, in real-time and extended-time transactions. Many interfaces already allow collaboration: Web conferencing (to augment presentations), online education platforms and auctions, and so on. For instance, online consumers share information when shopping. And a college student—living away from home and applying for student loans—can remotely involve his or her parents in the transaction, as advisers and cosigners.

CHANGING LIFESTYLES

As mentioned, technology is altering how consumers do business, access information, and interact with each other—and this has a powerful effect on E-service models. Consumers' lifestyles are changing in many ways: through increased E-commerce activity, information gathering, mobility, and social network creation. These elements will have a strong impact on the growth and future of E-services.

E-Commerce Activity

This has become mainstream among U.S. consumers. Three-quarters of online adults purchased a $10–$100 item on the Web in 2006—up from 64 percent in 2004 and 47 percent in 2000. Consumers also see value in managing their finances via online banking and bill paying. In 2006, 65 percent of consumers checked an account online, compared with 51 percent in 2004 and 26 percent in 2000. Usage of banks' bill-pay E-services jumped from 30 percent in 2004 to 49 percent in 2006.

The primary obstacle to E-commerce has weakened. There appears to be heightened sensitivity to security and privacy breaches, as a result of "phishing" scams, identity theft, and terrorism concerns. Despite this, consumers are less worried now—about the security of their online personal information—than they were two years ago.

Consumers feel that technology gives them the freedom to take care of business on their own schedules, and more efficiently than in person. The real-time nature of online tracking—of purchases and financial account activity—keeps consumers in touch, and offers them peace of mind. They're less likely to give up these E-commerce advantages because of privacy and security fears.

Information Gathering

Technology empowers consumers to obtain the information they need to take care of themselves. During an appointment with the doctor, consumers no longer have to ask the right questions and rely on him or her to tell them everything they need to know; E-services such as WebMD (**http://www.webmd.com**) provide all the details. In 2006, 69 percent of consumers researched health information online.

Mobile Lifestyles

Consumers don't want to limit their entertainment and communications options just because they are on the go, inside and outside of their homes. They're increasingly adopting a mobile lifestyle that takes advantage of technology. In a recent eBrain (**http://www.ebrain.org**) research study, the most important attribute was portability—not price, quality, or brand. Consumers expect technology that they can easily take with them as they move around their homes and travel. There is an increasing number of consumers who are unplugging their landline phones, to solely rely on wireless phones for communication (now exceeding 10 percent of the population).

Social Network Creation

Communities on social and E-learning Web sites are highly popular, particularly among younger consumers who have identities on MySpace (**http://www.myspace.com**) or Facebook (**http://www.facebook.com**). Even though there's concern about diminishing human relationships, online networking has advantages. Students can send instant messages to friends for help with homework. And citizens from different countries can reach out to each other, to gain a mutual understanding. There's also a movement toward narrowly defined communities, which is possible because of a critical mass found on the Web.

DEMOGRAPHIC SHIFTS

The United States is experiencing several demographic shifts that will influence E-services' growth and demand, and technology is driving some of them. The affected groups include Hispanics and immigrants, older Americans, and the remote workforce.

Hispanics were 12.5 percent of the population in 2000, up from 9 percent in 1990. This fast-expanding group, along with recent immigrants, requires new E-services to stay connected and interact with family and friends around the world.

The population is aging, with baby boomers (born from 1946–1964) beginning to retire. The economy will experience a decrease in productivity, and organizations will naturally look to technology to help fill the void. Organizations might also consider technology to serve the increasing number of elderly people with special needs.

Geographically, there's evidence of a "rural rebound," as Americans seek additional space in the face of a growing population. And technology is playing a role, by making it easier to work from remote locations. The degree to which workers are willing or able to work from home has limits, but technology contributes to a more dispersed workforce.

REVOLUTION RESPONSE

Rapid change in macroenvironment trends poses a challenge to service organization managers—to adapt or perish. E-service models in the next decade will need to incorporate the elements of technology progression discussed previously. Strategic responses should be based on full convergence of voice, video, and data;

complete mobility and portability; evolved interfaces; successful personalization; and bringing back the personal touch.

Delivering Full Convergence of Voice, Video, and Data

Ultimately, consumers should have the ability to contact an organization or government agency online, see and listen to an employee if warranted, share information, and conduct tasks such as entering information. Early entrants might delight their more tech-savvy customers. But there's a risk that they will be vulnerable, by offering systems that aren't fully perfected or cutting-edge.

Making Services Mobile and Portable

More service applications will move to being portable devices, which benefit consumers anywhere. Although there's considerable buzz about recent entertainment services (e.g., the video iPod), the greatest potential might be in banking, government, and "E-tailing" services. New mobile applications will emerge, such as sending electronic coupons over portable devices based on the recipient's location.

Developing Evolved Interfaces

Consumers will expect more intuitive and flexible ways of interacting with E-service providers. This mirrors developments in industries similar to video gaming, which cater to tech-savvy customers. Interfaces based on voice recognition, eye tracking, and motion sensing are just a few.

Implementing Successful Personalization

Personalization is a natural element when there's pressure to build loyalty and convert visits into sales. Consider the advantage that a clothing-store salesperson has by being able to see and listen to a customer. Now translate that to a Web-based service, in which providers can make recommendations using knowledge of the customer's age, body shape, and fashion taste. Again, information technology continues to advance. E-service providers can enact practical solutions, such as offering options that reflect natural benefit segments (i.e., groups with similar requirements).

Bringing Back the Personal Touch

Most consumers agree that the human touch is very important when doing business with a company. Technology has an opportunity to come full circle, and reintroduce the human being into the transaction. For example, a first-time home buyer can complete a mortgage application at his or her residence (where there is ready access to records), while conferencing with a professional loan officer who manages expectations and provides assurances. Such a model results in costs higher than those of a fully self-service transaction, but E-service providers should weigh the costs against the increased retention and loyalty. The model also [...] providers to reach lower-cost labor markets.

Customer Enlistment

The greatest partner in adapting to technological change is the customer. To understand how to optimize this relationship, it is important to examine consumer behavior. Buyers in a business-to-consumer or business-to-business context possess varying beliefs about technology. Positive beliefs consist of a tendency to innovate and be optimistic about technology's benefits; negative beliefs consist of a general discomfort in using technology, and an insecurity regarding its safety and privacy. All of us vary in combinations of these beliefs, and it is possible to simultaneously harbor both kinds.

Customers are inclined to fall into segments suggesting unique opportunities. These include partnering, supporting, persuading, and simplifying.

Partnering

Work with your most tech-savvy customers. One out of five U.S. adults is an "explorer." This type of consumer has a strong affinity to cutting-edge technology, and few inhibitions in using it. Explorers enjoy learning and experimenting with recent technology, as well as sharing their knowledge. Marketers should study the behaviors and needs of these early adopters. Research can reveal the new models of behavior they're adopting—either by creating them on their own or by turning to competitors with more state-of-the-art E-services. Explorers will willingly share their insights, in response to traditional market research.

Supporting

Help your most enthusiastic customers manage the latest service technologies. One out of four U.S. adults is a "pioneer." This type of consumer believes in and desires progressive technology, yet has a great deal of insecurity and discomfort in making it work for him or her. Marketers need to single out the enthusiastic-but-challenged pioneers and offer them the latest functionality, educate them on how to use the E-services, and assure them that the technology is benign. Success depends on investing in customer training, documentation, and technical support—areas that frequently get cut back when introducing self-service technologies.

Persuading

Convert "skeptics." One-fifth of the population has little emotional involvement with technology. The good news is that these consumers are uninhibited in accepting it; the challenge is showing them the benefits. Customers can view the same features (e.g., security) as drawbacks or advantages. The trick is crafting messages to turn liabilities into assets. Marketers must show that innovative E-services actually enhance security and control, by offering a real-time and "24/7" connection to information.

Simplifying

Save today's technologies for customers who resist change. One-third of the population sees limited or no benefit to technology, and many obstacles to its use. As an organization aims to upgrade its technology solutions, these "paranoids" and "laggards" are excellent prospects for last-generation technology. An explorer might look for a portable device with the latest features (e.g., broadband access, music downloading, full video capability). But a laggard might desire a less-advanced model, which has voice-only service and is cheap, reliable, and easy to use.

A revolution can be an exciting time. It challenges organizations to continually learn, adapt, and perfect. Understanding the macroenvironment trends, which are transforming E-services marketing and delivery, is critical—as are partnerships. And the first ones that an organization should turn to are with its customers.

Questions

1. Discuss the ethical aspects of three of the issues described in the case.
2. Discuss the global marketing implications of three other issues described in the case.
3. Explain several different ways in which a company could use the Internet as part of its social responsibility efforts.
4. What ethically questionable Internet practices should companies avoid? Why?
5. How should a company participate in Web-based social networking? Give an example.
6. How can technology be used to bring back the "personal touch?"
7. What would you recommend that a company do to drive more customers to its Web site?

In Part 3, we see why consumer analysis is essential and discuss consumer characteristics, needs, profiles, and decision making—and how firms can devise marketing plans responsive to today's diverse global marketplace.

8 Final Consumers

This chapter is devoted to final consumer demographics, lifestyles, and decision making. We examine several specific demographics (objective and quantifiable characteristics that describe the population) for the United States and other countries around the globe. By studying final consumer lifestyles and decision making, we can learn about why and how consumers act as they do. Lifestyles encompass various social and psychological factors, many of which we note here. The decision process involves the steps as consumers move from stimulus to purchase or nonpurchase.

9 Organizational Consumers

Here, we focus on organizations purchasing goods and services for further production, use in operations, or resale to other consumers—business-to-business (b-to-b) marketing. We look at how they differ from final consumers and at their individual characteristics, buying goals, buying structure, constraints on purchases, and decision process.

10 Developing a Target Market Strategy

We now discuss how to plan a target market strategy. Consumer-demand patterns and segmentation bases are examined; and undifferentiated marketing, concentrated marketing, and differentiated marketing are explained and contrasted. The requirements for successful segmentation and the importance of positioning are also considered. We conclude with a discussion of sales forecasting.

Consumer Analysis: Understanding and Responding to Diversity in the Marketplace

After reading Part 3, you should understand element 9 of the strategic marketing plan outlined in Table 3-2 (page 74).

Chapter 8

Final Consumers

Nestlé (**http://www.nestle.com**), the world's largest food and beverage manufacturer, is a long-time global marketer. Popular Nestlé brands include Buitoni, Friskies, Magi, Nestea, Lean Cuisine, Jenny Craig, Ortega, and Poland Spring. Its Nescafé coffee, Perrier bottled water, and Ralston Purina pet foods are the market leaders in their categories. Several Nestlé brands have annual sales of least $1 billion. Its pet food brands, such as Purina and Friskies, account for more than $12 billion in yearly worldwide sales.

Chocolate has always been vital to Nestlé. The firm began selling chocolate in 1904, and in 1920 it purchased Cailler (the first firm to mass produce chocolate bars) and Swiss General (the inventor of milk chocolate). Nestlé developed its Nestlé Crunch bar in 1938, and it purchased the Butterfinger and Baby Ruth candy brands in the 1990s. It recently formed a joint venture with Pierre Marcolini, a Brussels-based maker of premium chocolate. Other premium chocolate products of the firm include Perugina, Baci, and Nestlé Noir. Nestlé chocolate products comprise about 10 percent of its total sales.

To increase its market share in chocolate, Nestlé is carefully monitoring the sales of candies to diabetics and the marketing of chocolate to adults. Nestlé produces the Everyday Eating Web site (**http://www.everydayeating.com**) that features special coupon offers targeted at diabetics. It has also reduced the sugar content of some of its products to better meet the dietary needs of diabetics, such as its Babe Ruth Sugar Free Carb Select candy bar and Nestlé's Coffee-Mate Sugar Free Coffee Creamer.

Nestlé is shifting more of its chocolate and confectionery advertising from children to adults. As with other chocolate and confectionery makers, Nestlé is increasingly aware that a large portion of its target market consists of adults who either consume the products themselves or who buy chocolate candy for their children. For example, when a spokesperson for Nestlé was asked who the target market for Baby Ruth chocolate candy bars was, her response was "Definitely adult men." Other chocolate and confection makers report that women ages 18 to 45 years are their key buyers.[1]

In this chapter, we will explore several key consumer demographic and lifestyle trends, as well as the marketing implications of the trends. This will enable us to pinpoint market needs, reasons for purchases, and changing lifestyles, and purchase patterns among adult consumers and other market segments.

Chapter Objectives

1. To show the importance and scope of consumer analysis
2. To define and enumerate important consumer demographics for the U.S. population and other countries
3. To show why consumer demographic analysis is not sufficient in planning marketing strategies
4. To define and describe consumer lifestyles and their characteristics, examine selected lifestyles, and consider the limitations of consumer lifestyle analysis
5. To define and describe the final consumer's decision process and consider the limitations of final consumer decision-making analysis

---

[1] Various company and other sources.

8-1 OVERVIEW

The consumer is the central focus of marketing, as discussed in Chapters 1 and 2. To devise good marketing plans, it is essential to study consumer attributes and needs, lifestyles, and purchase processes, and then make proper marketing-mix decisions.

The scope of consumer analysis includes the study of *who* buys, *what* they buy, *why* they buy, *how* they make decisions to buy, *when* they buy, *where* they buy, and *how often* they buy.[2] For example, we might study a college student (who) buying textbooks (what) that are required for various classes (why). The student looks up the book list at the school store and decides whether to buy new or used books for each course (how). Just before the first week of classes (when), the student goes to the school store or online to buy the books (where). This is done three times per year—fall, spring, and summer (how often).

In today's diverse global marketplace, an open-minded, consumer-oriented approach is imperative so a firm can identify and serve its target market, minimize dissatisfaction, and stay ahead of competitors. Why is this important? "To gain and maintain competitive advantage in a crowded marketplace, it is important to make customers feel special and unique. We then stand a better chance of retaining their loyalty when they next make a buying decision and of gaining new business through word of mouth and recommendation."[3] See Figure 8-1.

In Chapters 8 to 10, we cover the concepts needed to understand consumers in the United States and other nations, to select target markets, and to relate marketing strategy to consumer behavior. Chapter 8 examines final consumer demographics, lifestyles, and decision making. *Final consumers* buy goods and services for personal, family, or household use. Chapter 9 looks at *organizational consumers*, those buying goods and services for further production, usage in operating the organization, or resale to other consumers. Chapter 10 explains how to devise a target market strategy and use sales forecasts.

> **Final consumers** buy for personal, family, or household use; **organizational consumers** buy for production, operations, or resale.

8-2 DEMOGRAPHICS DEFINED AND ENUMERATED

Consumer demographics[4] are objective and quantifiable population characteristics. They are rather easy to identify, collect, measure, and analyze—and show diversity around the globe. The demographics we discuss here are population size, gender, and age; location, housing, and mobility; income and expenditures; occupations and education; marital status; and ethnicity/race. After studying single factors, a firm can form a consumer demographic profile—a demographic composite of a consumer group. See Figure 8-2. By creating profiles, a firm can pinpoint both opportunities and potential problems.

Several secondary sources offer data on demographics. For U.S. demographics, a key resource is the U.S. Bureau of the Census (**http://www.census.gov**), a federal government agency with considerable national, state, and local data via printed reports, computer tapes, microfiche, CDs, and online data bases. Its American FactFinder Web site (**http://www.factfinder.census.gov**) is quite useful. Many marketing research firms and state data centers arrange census data by ZIP code, make forecasts, and update data. Because complete *Census of Population* data are gathered only once a decade, they must be supplemented by Bureau of the Census estimates (**http://www.census.gov/popest/estimates.php**) and statistics from chambers of commerce, public utilities, and others.

> **Consumer demographics** are easily identifiable and measurable.

[2] Adapted from Leon G. Schiffman and Leslie Lazar Kanuk, *Consumer Behavior*, Ninth Edition (Upper Saddle River, NJ: Prentice-Hall, 2007), Chapter 1.

[3] "Getting Intimate with Customers," **http://www.marketing-magic.biz/archives/archive-marketing/getting-intimate-with-customers.htm** (May 12, 2009).

[4] Unless otherwise indicated, the data presented in this chapter are all from the U.S. Bureau of the Census (various publications); the U.S. Bureau of Labor Statistics; the United Nations (various publications); the Organization for Economic Cooperation and Development (various publications); the *CIA World Factbook*, **https://www.cia.gov/library/publications/the-world-factbook** (August 17, 2008); the Population Research Bureau (various publications); and authors' estimates and extrapolations.

Figure 8-1

Daffy's Message for Shoppers: High Fashion. Low Prices. Cool Customers.

Source: Reprinted by permission.

About.com has a Web site (**http://geography.about.com/cs/uspopulation**) on the "U.S. Population, Census, & Demographics." The annual *Survey of Buying Power* (**http://www.surveyofbuyingpower.com**) has current U.S. data by metropolitan area and state, including retail sales, income, and five-year estimates. Other valuable U.S. sources are

Figure 8-2

Factors Determining a Consumer's Demographic Profile

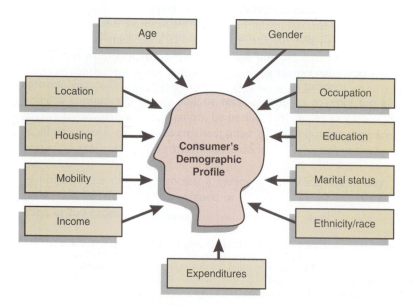

Editor & Publisher Market Guide (**http://www.editorandpublisher.com**), *Rand McNally Commercial Atlas & Marketing Guide* (**http://www.randmcnally.com**), *Standard Rate & Data Service* (**http://www.srds.com**), local newspapers, and regional planning boards.

The United Nations (**http://www.un.org**), Euromonitor (**http://www.euromonitor.com**), Organization for Economic Cooperation and Development (**http://www.oecd.org**), and Population Reference Bureau (**http://www.prb.org**) are four excellent sources for international demographics. The U.N. publishes a *Statistical Yearbook* and numerous other population studies. Euromonitor publishes *International Marketing Data and Statistics*. OECD issues demographic and economic reports on an ongoing basis. The Population Reference Bureau publishes an annual *World Population Data Sheet*. In highly industrialized nations, demographic data are pretty accurate because actual data are regularly collected. In less-developed and developing nations, demographic data are often based on estimates rather than actual data because such data are apt to be collected on an irregular basis.

Information is provided throughout the chapter on both U.S. and worldwide demographics. A broad cross-section of country examples is provided to give a good sense of the diversity around the globe.

8-2a   Population Size, Gender, and Age

The world population is expected to go from 6.87 billion in 2010 to 7.65 billion in 2020, an annual rise of 1.1 percent. Over the same period, the U.S. population will rise from 309 million to 336 million, an annual rise of less than 0.9 percent. The U.S. population will drop from 4.5 percent of world population in 2010 to 4.4 percent in 2020. Figure 8-3 shows world population by region for 2010 and 2020.

Newborns are less than 2 percent of the population (1.4 percent in the United States) in industrialized nations—compared with up to 4 to 5 percent or more in nations such as Afghanistan and the Congo. For the industrialized countries, a large proportion of the births are firstborns.

Males and females comprise roughly equal percentages of the worldwide population. Yet, in many industrialized nations, females are over one-half of the population—mostly due to differences in life expectancy. For newborn females, it is 84 years in Canada, 83 in Italy, 81 in the United States, and 72 in India; it is 79 years for newborn males in Canada, 77 in Italy, 75 in the United States, and 67 in India.

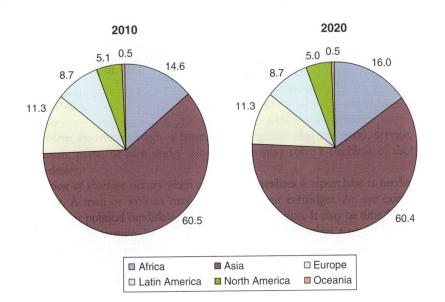

Figure 8-3

The World's Population Distribution, 2010 and 2020

Source: U.S. Bureau of the Census, International Data Base (June 2008).

The populations in industrialized nations are older than in less-developed and developing nations. Today, the portion of the population age 14 and under is 14 percent in Italy, 14 percent in Japan, 17 percent in Great Britain, 20 percent in the United States, 20 percent in China, 25 percent in Brazil, 30 percent in Mexico, and 42 percent in Nigeria.

8-2b Location, Housing, and Mobility

> The world is becoming more urban.

Over the last century, a major move of the world population to large urban areas and surrounding suburbs has taken place. Today, about 25 cities and their suburbs have at least 10 million residents each—led by Tokyo, Seoul, and Mexico City. Worldwide, just over one-half of the population lives in an urban area. But, the level of urbanization varies greatly by country. About 82 percent of the U.S. population resides in cities and their suburbs. It is 45 percent in China, 37 percent in Pakistan, and 14 percent in Nepal.

In many parts of the world, the majority of people own the homes in which they reside. Here are some examples: Bangladesh, Finland, Greece, New Zealand, Paraguay, Sri Lanka, and the United States.

The worldwide mobility of the population is high; annually, millions of people emigrate from one nation to another and hundreds of millions move within their nations. Since 2000, 10 million people have legally immigrated to the United States. Overall, one-eighth of those living in the United States were born elsewhere. Among U.S. residents, about 14 percent of all people move yearly—60 percent within the same county, 80 percent within the same state, and 90 percent within the same region; only 10 percent of moves are to a new region or abroad. Recently, the greatest U.S. population growth has been in the Mountain, Pacific, South Atlantic, and Southwest regions.

8-2c Income and Expenditures

Consumer income and expenditure patterns are valuable demographic factors when properly studied. These points should be kept in mind when examining them:

- Personal income is often stated as GDP per capita—the total value of goods and services produced in a nation divided by population size. This does not report what people really earn, and it inflates per-capita income if a small portion of the population is affluent. A better measure is median income—the income for those at the 50th percentile in a nation; it is a true midpoint. Yet, median incomes are rarely reported outside the United States.
- Personal income can be expressed as family, household, and per capita. Families are larger than households and per-capita income is on an individual basis; thus, data are not directly comparable. Income can also be cited in pre-tax or after-tax terms, which are not directly comparable.
- Because prices differ by country, a comparison of average incomes that does not take purchasing power into effect will be inaccurate.
- Economic growth is cyclical. And at any given time, some economies will perform well while others struggle.
- Although the term "poverty" varies greatly by nation, more than 1 billion people in the world are characterized by malnutrition, illiteracy, and disease.

In 2008, the U.S. median pre-tax household income was between $48,000 and $50,000 (and mean household income was $68,000). Yet, even though one-fifth of all households had incomes of $100,000 or more and one-third of all households had incomes of $75,000 or more, one-quarter of all households had incomes of less than $25,000—and one-eighth of U.S. households were at the poverty level. The United States has one of the greatest spreads between high-income and low-income households of any industrialized nation in the world. Furthermore, in terms of purchasing power, U.S. median household income has risen only slightly over the last 25 years.

The slow growth in real U.S. income (after taking inflation into account) has occurred because the increases in household income have been virtually offset by increases in prices. The price increases have led to a higher *cost of living*, the total amount consumers annually pay for goods and services. Since 1990, the greatest price increases have been for energy, medical care, tuition, and tobacco; the smallest have been for computers, phone services, apparel, and video and audio products.

Many nations monitor their cost of living via a *consumer price index (CPI)*, which measures monthly and yearly price changes (the rate of inflation) for a broad range of consumer goods and services. During the last 25 years, the overall annual rise in the U.S. CPI (**http://www.bls.gov/cpi/home.htm**) has generally been less than 5 percent. The annual CPI has also risen by 5 percent or less in about one-half of the countries around the world in recent years.

Global consumption patterns have been shifting. In industrialized nations, the proportion of income that people spend on food, beverages, and tobacco has been declining. The percentage spent on medical care (including insurance), personal business, and recreation has been rising. In less-developed and developing nations, the percentage of spending devoted to food remains high. Americans spend less than 15 percent of income on food, beverages, and tobacco, while Pakistanis spend more than one-half of their income on food, beverages, and tobacco.

Disposable income is a person's, household's, or family's total after-tax income to be used for spending and/or savings. *Discretionary income* is what a person, household, or family has available to spend on luxuries after necessities are bought. Classifying some product categories as necessities or luxuries depends on a nation's standard of living. In the United States, autos and home telephones are generally considered necessities; in many less-developed countries, they are often considered luxuries.

> Changes in the **cost of living** are measured by a consumer price index.

> Consumption reflects **disposable income** and **discretionary income**.

8-2d   Occupations and Education

The work force in industrialized nations continues moving toward white-collar and service jobs. In less-developed and developing nations, many jobs involve manual labor and are more often agriculture-based.

The total employed civilian U.S. labor force is 145 million people—compared with Japan, 66 million; Germany, 41 million; Great Britain, 31 million; France, 27 million; and Italy, 24 million. For the last 45 years, the percent of U.S. workers in service-related, technical, and clerical white-collar jobs has risen; the percent as managers, administrators, and sales workers has been constant; and the percent as nonskilled workers has dropped. Only about 2.2 million U.S. workers have an agriculture-related job.

Another change in the labor force around the world has been the increase in working women. Forty-five years ago, women comprised one-third of the total U.S. labor force. Today, the figure is 47 percent; and 70 percent of adult U.S. women are in the labor force. In Great Britain, the percentage is comparable, while 27 percent of Turkey's adult women are in the labor force.

During 1970, 40 percent of all married U.S. women were in the labor force. Now, nearly two-thirds are. The percent of married women with children under age six in the U.S. labor force has also jumped dramatically, to 60 percent today. Similar rises have also occurred in other nations.

Unemployment rates, which reflect the percentage of adults in the total labor force not working, vary widely by nation. During 2008, the U.S. unemployment rate was 5 to 6 percent. In contrast, the rate for the European Union nations averaged about 7 percent. Though the U.S. percentage was lower, it still meant millions of people without jobs. Some worldwide unemployment is temporary, due to weak domestic and international economies. Other times, depending on the nation and industry, many job losses are permanent. Unemployment is often accompanied by cutbacks in discretionary purchases.

Great strides are being made globally to upgrade educational attainment, but the level of education tends to be much higher in industrialized nations than in less-developed and

> Women are a large and growing percentage of the worldwide labor force.

developing ones. One measure of educational attainment is the literacy rate, the percentage of people in a country who can read and write. In industrialized nations such as the United States, this rate is 99 percent. Here are the rates for some less-developed and developing nations: Bolivia, 87 percent; Chad, 23 percent; Ethiopia, 43 percent; India, 61 percent; Nicaragua, 68 percent; and Saudi Arabia, 79 percent.

Judged against other large industrialized nations, the United States is the most educated. A higher percentage of U.S. adults have finished high school and college than those in Canada, France, Germany, Great Britain, or Japan. As of 2005, 88 percent of U.S. adults 25 years old and older were high school graduates, and 30 percent were college graduates. Figure 8-4 compares U.S. higher education with other nations (based on 2005 data).

The sharp increase in working women and higher educational attainment have generally contributed to the growing number of people in upper-income brackets; the rather high unemployment rate in some nations and industries, and slow-growth economies, have caused other households to have low incomes.

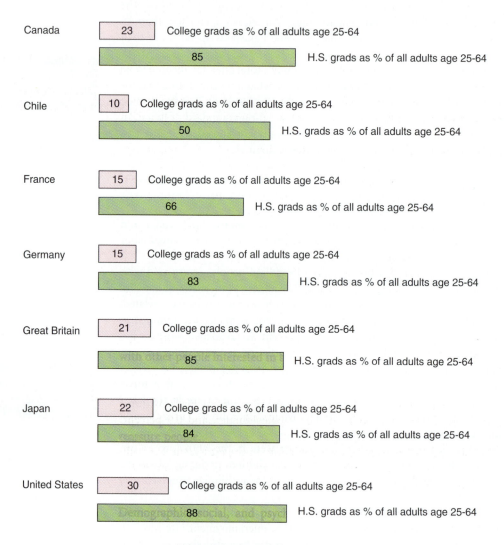

Canada — 23 — College grads as % of all adults age 25-64
85 — H.S. grads as % of all adults age 25-64

Chile — 10 — College grads as % of all adults age 25-64
50 — H.S. grads as % of all adults age 25-64

France — 15 — College grads as % of all adults age 25-64
66 — H.S. grads as % of all adults age 25-64

Germany — 15 — College grads as % of all adults age 25-64
83 — H.S. grads as % of all adults age 25-64

Great Britain — 21 — College grads as % of all adults age 25-64
85 — H.S. grads as % of all adults age 25-64

Japan — 22 — College grads as % of all adults age 25-64
84 — H.S. grads as % of all adults age 25-64

United States — 30 — College grads as % of all adults age 25-64
88 — H.S. grads as % of all adults age 25-64

Note: These statistics are from 2005, the latest common date available. The % of high school graduates includes those who also graduated from college.

Figure 8-4

Percentage of Adults Who Have Graduated from High School and College

Source: Organization of Economic Cooperation and Development data, as reported in *Education at a Glance 2007.*

8-2e Marital Status

Marriage and family are powerful institutions worldwide, but in some nations, they are now less dominant. Although 2.2 million U.S. couples get married each year, just over one-half of U.S. households contain married couples; the percentage of households with married adults in many other nations is much higher. The median U.S. age at first marriage is 28 years for males and 26 years for females, as people wait to marry and have children. The average U.S. family size is now 3.1. Male and female ages at first marriage are much lower in less-developed and developing nations, and their average family is bigger.

A *family* is a group of two or more persons residing together who are related by blood, marriage, or adoption. A *household* is a person or group of persons occupying a housing unit, whether related or unrelated. In many nations, average household size has been dropping. The U.S. average is 2.6—due to later marriages, more widows and widowers, a high divorce rate, many couples deciding to have fewer children, and the growth of single-person households. Nearly 27 percent of U.S. households are one-person units. Family households represent 68 percent of U.S. households (down from 85 percent in 1960).

> A **family** has related persons residing together. A **household** has one or more persons who may not be related.

8-2f Ethnicity/Race

From a demographics perspective, *ethnicity/race* should be studied to determine the existence of diversity among and within nations in terms of language and country of origin or race.

About 290 different languages worldwide are spoken by at least 1 million people each—12 of those are spoken by at least 100 million people (including Mandarin, English, Hindi, and Spanish). Even within nations, there may be diversity as to the languages spoken. Canada (English and French), Chad (French and Arabic), Peru (Spanish and Quechua), and the Philippines (Pilipino and English) all have two official languages. A key issue the European Union faces in its expansion is the multiplicity of languages spoken.

> **Ethnicity/race** is one measure of nations' diversity with regard to language, country of origin, or race.

Most nations consist of people representing different ethnic and racial backgrounds. For instance, among those living in the Philippines are Malays, Chinese, Americans, and Spaniards. Sometimes, the people in various groups continue to speak in the languages of their countries of origin, even though they may have resided in their current nations for one or two generations.

The United States is comprised of people from virtually every ethnic and racial group in the world. The Bureau of the Census uses "Black or African-American," "White," "Asian," "Native Hawaiian and Other Pacific Islander," and "American Indian and Alaska Native" to delineate racial groups; "Hispanic" is an ethnic term, denoting people of any race.

As of 2010, the U.S. population is 78.4 percent White, 13.1 percent Black/African-American, 4.6 percent Asian/Native Hawaiian/Other Pacific Islander, and 0.9 percent American Indian/Alaska Native, with 3.0 percent defined as "Other Race" (including "Multiracial"). Hispanics are 15.5 percent of the population. In the future, the U.S. will continue becoming more diverse, due to both higher birth rates and immigration to the United States by Nonwhites. See Figure 8-5.

8-2g Uses of Demographic Data

As noted at the beginning of the chapter, after studying individual demographics, a firm can form demographic profiles to better focus its marketing efforts. Here are three examples.

The single-person U.S. household is changing: One-quarter of those living alone are divorced. More than one-half are 55 years of age or older. Only 5 percent of 25- to 34-year olds live alone, while 30 percent of those 65 and over live alone (39 percent of the women in this category and 19 percent of the men). The majority of those living alone own a car, live in their own home, and subscribe to cable TV. It is twice as likely for a

Figure 8-5

Marketing to a Diverse Marketplace

More and more companies, such as HSBC (**http://www.hsbc.com**), "the world's local bank," recognize the changing face of the U.S. marketplace and are working hard to appeal to the increasingly diverse consumer population.

Source: Reprinted by permission.

person living alone to own a laptop PC than the average household. Of those living alone, 40 percent use a microwave to do at least one-half of their cooking.[5]

To better market ads in *Southwest Airlines Spirit Magazine* (**http://www.spiritmag. com**), the publisher regularly communicates the demographic profile of readers: Fifty-seven percent are women, 61 percent are married, 72 percent are ages 25 to 54, nearly one-half are college graduates, 45 percent are in managerial or professional jobs, and nearly one-half have an annual household income of $100,000 or more.[6]

Demographic profiles of nations, such as Australia and Turkey, can be contrasted. Australia presents better marketing opportunities for firms targeting older, well-educated consumers, while Turkey presents better opportunities for firms marketing to children:[7]

	Australia	Turkey
Gender ratio (male/female)	0.99/1.00	1.02/1.00
Annual population growth	0.8%	1.0%
Life expectancy	81 years	73 years
Median age	37 years	29 years
Population under 15 years of age	19%	24%
Working women as part of all adult women	70%	27%
Literacy rate	99%	87%

8-2h   Limitations of Demographics

> Demographic data may be dated, unavailable, too general, require profile analysis, and not consider reasons for behavior.

These limitations should be noted in applying demographic data: Information may be old. Even in the United States, a full census is done once per ten years and there are time lags

---

[5] Chris Reynolds, "Me, Myself, and I," *American Demographics* (September 2004), p. D36; and U.S. Bureau of the Census (various publications).

[6] Pace Communications, "Spirit 2008 Demographic Profile."

[7] *CIA World Factbook*, **https://www.cia.gov/library/publications/the-world-factbook**.

Global Marketing in Action

Marketing "Affordable Luxury" for the Masses

For years, luxury has typically meant unique items, beautifully designed and with very high prices. For example, Valextra (http://www.valextra.it), a luxury leather goods store in Milan, sells suitcases starting at about $5,000. The suitcases—which have no wheels, no pull straps, and no retractable handles—come in white leather. When a sales assistant was asked about their durability, he commented that these suitcases were made for those that use private jets.

Recently, such luxury-oriented firms as Cartier (http://www.cartier.com), Chanel (http://www.chanel.com), and Dior (http://www.dior.com) have extended their product lines to cater to the global middle class, which wants the prestige of designer names with lower price tags. Armani (http://www.armani.com) now sells chocolates, Prada (http://www.prada.com) markets a cell phone, and Gucci (http://www.gucci.com) has an $80 box of playing cards. As Gucci's chief executive remarked, "We are

not in the business of selling handbags. We are in the business of selling dreams."

In discussing his firm's current marketing approach, Coach's (http://www.coach.com) chief executive stated that as the firm repositioned itself, it saw its $300 pocketbooks "fly off the shelves." As a result of Coach's revised strategy, "luxury has been democratized." Another key advantage of today's luxury positioning is the 8 to 10 percent annual increase in sales of luxury goods.

One vexing question is whether the sale of less-expensive goods will undermine the image of luxury brands. In answer to this question, one market analyst noted that luxury brands may be viewed as a pyramid with Cartier and Louis Vuitton (http://www.louisvuitton.com) at the top and Coach near the bottom.

Source: Based on material in Peter Gumble, "Luxury Goes Mass Market," http://www.money.cnn.com/2007/08/30/magazines/fortune/mass_vs_class.fortune/index.htm (September 8, 2007).

before data are released. Data may be limited in some nations, especially less-developed and developing ones. Summary data may be too broad and hide opportunities and risks in small markets or specialized product categories. The psychological or social factors influencing people are not considered. The decision process used in purchasing is not explained. Demographics do not delve into the reasons why people make decisions.

Here are some of the questions not addressed by demographic data:

- Why do consumers act as they do?
- Why do consumers with similar demographic characteristics act differently?
- To whom do consumers look for advice prior to purchasing?
- Under what situations do families (households) use joint decision making?
- Why does status play a large role in the purchase of some products and a small role in others?
- How do different motives affect consumer decisions?
- How does risk affect consumer decisions?
- Why do some consumers act as innovators and buy products before others?
- How important are purchase decisions to consumers?
- What process do consumers use when shopping for various products?
- How long will it take for consumers to reach purchase decisions?
- Why do consumers become brand loyal or regularly switch brands?

To answer these questions, more firms now use demographic data in conjunction with consumer lifestyle and decision-making analysis. A final consumer's *lifestyle* represents the way in which a person lives and spends time and money. It is based on the social and psychological factors that have been internalized by that person, as well as his or her demographic background.[8] These factors overlap and complement each other; they are not independent of one another. The consumer's decision process involves the steps a

> Consumer **lifestyles** describe how people live. In making purchases, people use a decision process with several stages.

---

[8] Adapted by the authors from "Dictionary," http://www.marketingpower.com/_layouts/Dictionary.aspx?dLetter=L (March 22, 2009).

person uses in buying goods and services. Demographics, social factors, and psychological factors all affect the process.

8-3 CONSUMER LIFESTYLES

The social and psychological characteristics that help form final consumer lifestyles are described next.

8-3a Social Characteristics of Consumers

The final consumer's social profile is based on a combination of culture, social class, social performance, reference groups, opinion leaders, family life cycle, and time expenditures (activities). See Figure 8-6.

As discussed in Chapter 6, a *culture* comprises a group of people who share a distinctive heritage, such as Americans or Mexicans. People learn about socially proper behavior and beliefs via their culture. The American culture values achievement and success, activity, efficiency and practicality, progress, material comfort, individualism, freedom, external conformity, humanitarianism, youthfulness, and fitness and health.[9]

Cross-cultural differences involving people around the globe must be studied. For instance:

> As Americans, we tend to be much more casual and informal when we meet people. Our natural inclination to be familiar can put some people on edge. Germans and Japanese are unlikely to use first names in business. Asians prefer to use less eye and physical contact. Latins are prone to touching and to smaller personal space, while Asians and Germans enjoy more distance. The Latin hug ("abrazo") is common between men and men and women and women. At home, the Japanese are more comfortable with a bow from the waist. With Asians and Germans, punctuality is a must! Business cards are treated with more respect by

> Each **culture** transmits acceptable behavior and attitudes. **Social class** separates society into divisions. **Social performance** describes how people fulfill roles.

Figure 8-6

Factors Determining a Consumer's Social Profile

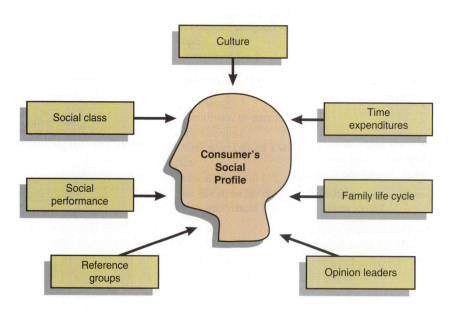

---

[9] Schiffman and Kanuk, *Consumer Behavior*, Chapter 12.

people from other countries, and there is a strong emphasis on titles and positions. It is helpful to have cards printed in their language on the back if you are regularly dealing with a particular country. Germans often include university degrees and the company's founding date on their cards; so you may want to add similar information to yours. Germans, Japanese, and Latins value more formality in manners than Americans. Don't stand with hands on hips or talk with hands in pockets. Be tolerant about smoking, as Japanese and Europeans smoke more than Americans. Avoid speaking in a loud voice. Respect privacy and a sense of order with Germans. Latins enjoy discussing family, whereas Germans and Japanese generally do not.[10]

Social class systems reflect a "status hierarchy by which groups and individuals are classified on the basis of esteem and prestige."[11] They exist all over the globe and divide society into segments, informally or formally grouping those with similar values and lifestyles. Industrialized nations have a larger middle class, greater interchange among classes, and less rigidly defined classes than less-developed and developing nations. Social classes are based on income, occupation, education, and type of dwelling. Each class may represent a distinct target market. Table 8-1 shows the informal U.S. social class system.

Social performance refers to how a person carries out his or her roles as a worker, family member, citizen, and friend. A person may be an executive, have a happy family life, be active in the community, and have many friends. Or he or she may never go higher than assistant manager, be divorced, not partake in community affairs, and have few friends. Many combinations are possible.

A *reference group* is one that influences a person's thoughts or actions. Such groups have a large impact on the purchase of many goods and services. Face-to-face reference groups, such as family and friends, have the most effect. Yet, other—more general—groups also affect behavior and may be cited when marketing products. Ads showing goods and services being used by college students, successful professionals, and pet owners often ask viewers to join the "group" and make similar purchases. By pinpointing reference groups that most sway consumers, firms can better aim their strategies.

> **Reference groups** influence thoughts and behavior. **Opinion leaders** affect others through face-to-face contact.

Firms want to know which persons in reference groups are *opinion leaders*. These are people to whom other consumers turn for advice and information via face-to-face communication. They tend to be expert about a product category, socially accepted, long-standing members of the community, gregarious, active, and trusted; and they tend to seek approval from others. They typically have an impact over a narrow product range and are perceived as more believable than company-sponsored information.

The *family life cycle* describes how a family evolves through various stages from bachelorhood to solitary retirement. At each stage, needs, experience, income, family composition, and the use of *joint decision making*—the process whereby two or more people have input into purchases—change. The number of people in the various stages can be found from demographic data. Table 8-2 shows a traditional cycle and its marketing relevance. The stages apply to families in all nations—industrialized and less-developed/developing, but opportunities are most applicable for industrialized countries.

> The **family life cycle** describes life stages, which often use **joint decision making**. The **household life cycle** includes family and nonfamily units.

When doing life-cycle analysis, the people who do not follow a traditional pattern because they do not marry, do not have children, become divorced, have families with two working spouses (even if there are very small children), and so on, should be noted. They are not adequately reflected in Table 8-2, but may represent good marketing opportunities. As a result, the concept of the *household life cycle*—which incorporates the life stages of both family and nonfamily households—is taking on greater significance. Table 8-3 shows the current status of U.S. family and nonfamily households.

---

[10] Carolyn Luesing, "Appreciating Cultural Differences Makes Good Business Sense," **http://www.media3pub.com/bizonline/articles/culture.html** (February 11, 2006).

[11] "Dictionary," **http://www.marketingpower.com/_layouts/Dictionary.aspx?dLetter=S** (March 22, 2009).

Table 8-1	The Informal Social Class Structure in the United States
Class	**Characteristics**
Upper Americans (nearly one-fifth of population)	
Upper-upper	Social elite; inherited wealth; exclusive neighborhoods; summer homes; children attend best schools; money unimportant in purchases; secure in status; spending with good taste
Lower-upper	Highest incomes; earned wealth; often business leaders and professionals; college educated; seek best for children; active socially; insecure; conspicuous consumption; money unimportant in purchases
Upper-middle	Career-oriented; executives and professionals earning over $85,000 yearly; status tied to occupations and earnings; most educated, but not from prestige schools; demanding of children; quality products purchased; attractive homes; socially involved; gracious living
Middle Americans (nearly two-thirds of population)	
Middle class	Typical Americans; average-earning white-collar workers and the top group of blue-collar workers; many college educated; respectable; conscientious; try to do the right thing; home ownership sought; do-it-yourselfers; family focus
Working class	Remaining white-collar workers and most blue-collar workers; working class lifestyles; some job monotony; job security sought more than advancement; usually high school education; close-knit families; brand loyal and interested in name brands; not status-oriented
Lower Americans (about one-sixth of population)	
Upper-lower	Employed, mostly in unskilled or semiskilled jobs; poorly educated; low incomes; rather difficult to move up the social class ladder; protective against lower-lower class; standard of living at or just above poverty; live in affordable housing
Lower-lower	Unemployed or most menial jobs; poorest income, education, and housing; the bottom layer; present-oriented; impulsive as shoppers; overpay; use credit

Sources: Adapted by the authors from Linda P. Morton, "Upper or Elite Class," *Public Relations Quarterly*, Vol. 49 (Winter 2004), pp. 30–32; Linda P. Morton, "Segmenting Social Classes: The Middle Class," *Public Relations Quarterly*, Vol. 49 (Fall 2004), pp. 46–47; Linda P. Morton, "Segmenting Social Classes: The Working Class," *Public Relations Quarterly*, Vol. 49 (Summer 2004), pp. 45–47; Roger D. Blackwell, Paul W. Miniard, and James F. Engel, *Consumer Behavior*, 10th ed. (Cincinnati: South-Western, 2006); and Leon Schiffman and Leslie Lazar Kanuk, *Consumer Behavior*, 9th ed. (Upper Saddle River, NJ: Prentice Hall, 2007), Chapter 11.

Ethical Issues in Marketing

Marketing to Children in a Digital Age

The Federal Trade Commission's (http://www.ftc.gov) attempts to restrict advertising to children date to 1978, when the agency sought to ban all ads to children under 7 years of age. The FTC was overruled by Congress. A more recent criticism of marketing to children is based on the widespread use of advertising junk food to children and its effect on childhood obesity.

The Joan Ganz Cooney Center (http://www.joanganzcooneycenter.org), a nonprofit research organization, is pushing for new legislation of digital media. There are currently no laws controlling the labeling of online advertising or for any minimum educational content on child-oriented Web sites.

The Cooney Center's research report, *D is for Digital*, calls for "A revitalization of the Children's Television Act of 1990" in order to "modernize the child protections now called for in a digital age." The Children's Television Act was largely designed to increase the quality of programming aimed at children. Since it was enacted in 1990, it predates the Internet, cell phones, iPods, and mobile gaming devices.

In pushing for new legislation, the Cooney Center states that many digital marketing vehicles, unlike traditional TV, are highly interactive, while traditional TV programming is a more passive activity. Firms such as Disney (http://www.disney.go.com) and Viacom's Nickelodeon (http://www.nick.com) have created games and virtual worlds for their products. Webkinz (http://www.webkinz.com), Build-A-Bear Workshop (http://www.buildabear.com), Lego (http://www.lego.com), and Mattel's Barbie (http://www.mattel.com) all have Web sites that are toy-focused. Although Mattel says that it will not run any outside advertising on its Barbie Girls Web site, one critic has argued that the entire site is in fact an ad for the Barbie doll and her accessories.

Source: Based on material in Anastasia Goodstein, "Let's Rewrite the Rules for Kids' Media," http://www.businessweek.com/technology (February 28, 2008).

Table 8-2	The Traditional Family Life Cycle	
Stage in Cycle	**Characteristics**	**Marketing Opportunities**
Bachelor, male or female	Independent; young; early in career, low earnings, low discretionary income	Clothing; auto; stereo; travel; restaurants; entertainment; status appeals
Newly married	Two incomes; relative independence; present- and future-oriented	Apartment furnishings; travel; clothing; durables; appeal to enjoyment and togetherness
Full nest I	Youngest child under 6; one to one-and-a-half incomes; limited independence; future-oriented	Goods and services for the child, home, and family; durability and safety; pharmaceuticals; day care; appeal to economy
Full nest II	Youngest child over 6, but dependent; one-and-a-half to two incomes; at least one spouse set in career; future-oriented	Savings; home; education; family vacations; child-oriented products; some luxuries; appeal to comfort and long-term enjoyment
Full nest III	Youngest child living at home, but independent; highest income level; thoughts of future retirement	Education; expensive durables for children; replacement and improvement of parents' durables; appeal to comfort and luxury
Empty nest I	No children at home; independent; good income; thoughts of self and retirement	Vacation home; travel; clothing; entertainment; luxuries; appeal to self-gratification
Empty nest II	Retirement; less income and expenses; present-oriented	Travel; recreation; new home; health-related items; less interest in luxuries; appeal to comfort at a low price
Sole survivor I	Only one spouse alive; actively employed; present-oriented; good income	Immersion in job and friends; interest in travel, clothing, health, and recreation areas; appeal to productive lifestyle
Sole survivor II	Only one spouse alive; retired; some feeling of futility; less income	Travel; recreation; pharmaceuticals; security; appeal to economy and social activity

Time expenditures refer to the activities in which a person participates and the time allocated to them. They include work, commuting, personal care, home maintenance, food preparation and consumption, child rearing, social interactions, reading, shopping, self-improvement, recreation, entertainment, vacations, and so on. Though the average U.S. workweek for the primary job has stabilized at 35 to 40 hours, some people work at two jobs. Americans enjoy TV, surfing the Web, phone calls, pleasure driving, walking, swimming, sightseeing, bicycling, spectator events, reading, and playing games and sports.

> **Time expenditures** reflect the workweek, family care, and leisure.

8-3b Psychological Characteristics of Consumers

The final consumer's psychological profile involves his or her personality, attitudes (opinions), class consciousness, motivation, perceived risk, innovativeness, and purchase importance. See Figure 8-7.

A *personality* is the sum total of an individual's enduring internal psychological traits that make the person unique. Self-confidence, dominance, autonomy, sociability, defensiveness, adaptability, and emotional stability are selected personality traits. An individual's behavior is strongly affected by his or her personality. As an example, a self-confident and sociable person often will not buy the same goods and services as an inhibited and aloof person. It is necessary to remember that a personality is made up of many traits operating in association with one another.

> A **personality** describes a person's composite internal, enduring psychological traits.

Attitudes (opinions) are an individual's positive, neutral, or negative feelings about goods, services, firms, people, issues, and/or institutions. They are shaped by demographics, social factors, and other psychological traits. One marketing task is to foster favorable attitudes; given the intensive competition in many industries, a firm cannot normally succeed without positive consumer attitudes. When studying attitudes, two concepts should often be measured—the attitude itself, and the purchase intention

> **Attitudes** can be positive, negative, or neutral.

Table 8-3	The Current Status of U.S. Family and Nonfamily Households	
Household Status	**Percentage of All U.S. Households**	
Family Households	67.6	
Married couples, no children under age 18		28.1
Married couples, with children under age 18		22.7
Other types of families, no children under age 18		7.6
Other types of families, with children under age 18[a]		9.2
Single-Person Households[b]	26.7	
Age 24 and under		1.4
Age 25 to 44		6.7
Age 45 to 64		9.2
Age 65 and over		9.4
Other Nonfamily Households[c]	5.7	
Male head of household, with nonrelatives present		3.2
Female head of household, with nonrelatives present		2.5
Total	100.0	100.0

[a] Includes one-parent families in which married couples are separated but not divorced, one-parent families headed by divorcees, one-parent families headed by widows and widowers, and one-parent families headed by never-married mothers and fathers.
[b] Includes people who have never married, as well as those who are widowed, separated, and divorced.
[c] Includes roommates.

Source: Computed by the authors from *America's Families and Living Arrangements: 2007* (Washington, DC: U.S. Census Bureau).

Figure 8-7

Factors Determining Consumer's Psychological Profile

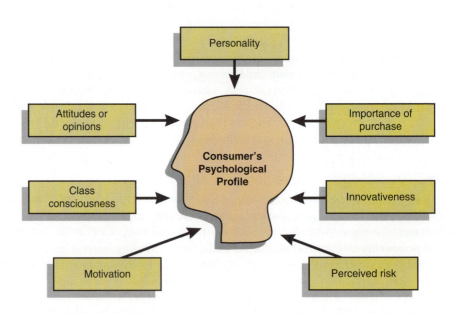

toward a firm's brand. For example: (1) Do you like brand A? Would you buy brand A in the future? (2) How does brand A compare with other brands? Would you buy brand A if it were priced higher than other brands?

> **Class consciousness** is low for inner-directed people and high for outer-directed people.

Class consciousness is the extent to which a person seeks social status. It helps determine the interest in social-class mobility, the use of reference groups, and the importance of prestige purchases. Inner-directed people want to please themselves and are often attracted by products that perform well functionally. They are not concerned with social mobility, rely on their own judgment, and do not value prestige items. Outer-directed people want to please others. Upward social mobility, reference group approval, and ownership of prestige items are sought. These people are often attracted by products with social visibility, well-known brands, and uniqueness. Functional excellence may be less important.

Motivation involves the positive or negative needs, goals, and desires that impel a person to or away from certain actions, objects, or situations.[12] By identifying and appealing to people's *motives*—the reasons for behavior—a firm can produce positive motivation. For example:

> **Motivation** is a drive-impelling action; it is caused by **motives.**

Motives	Marketing Actions That Motivate
Hunger reduction	Television and radio ads for chains restaurants
Safety	Smoke detector demonstrations in stores
Sociability	Perfume ads showing social success due to products
Achievement	Use of consumer endorsements in ads specifying how much knowledge can be gained from a course in real-estate sales
Economy	Newspaper coupons advertising sales
Social responsibility	Package labels that emphasize how easy it is to recycle products

Each person has distinct motives for purchases, and these change by situation and over time. Consumers often combine economic (price, durability) and emotional (social acceptance, self-esteem) motives when making purchases.

Perceived risk is the level of uncertainty a consumer believes exists as to the outcome of a purchase decision; this belief may or may not be correct. Perceived risk can be divided into six major types:

> **Perceived risk** is the uncertainty felt by the consumer about a purchase.

1. Functional—risk that a product will not perform adequately.
2. Physical—risk that a product will be harmful.
3. Financial—risk that a product will not be worth its cost.
4. Social—risk that a product will cause embarrassment before others.
5. Psychological—risk that one's ego will be bruised.
6. Time—risk that the time spent shopping will be wasted if a product does not perform as expected.[13]

Because high perceived risk can dampen customer motivation, firms must deal with it even if people have incorrect beliefs. Firms can lower perceived risk by giving more information, having a reputation for superior quality, offering money-back guarantees, avoiding controversial ingredients, and so on.

A person willing to try a new good or service that others perceive as risky exhibits *innovativeness*. An innovator is apt to be young and well educated, and to have above-average income for his or her social class. The person is also likely to be interested in change, achievement-oriented, open-minded, status-conscious, mobile, and venturesome. Firms need to identify and appeal to innovators when introducing a new good or service.

> **Innovativeness** is trying a new product other see as risky.

The *importance of a purchase* affects the time and effort a person spends shopping for a product—and the money allotted. An important purchase means careful decision making, high perceived risk, and often a large amount of money. An unimportant

> The **importance of a purchase** determines the time, effort, and money spent.

---

[12] "Dictionary," http://www.marketingpower.com/_layouts/Dictionary.aspx?dLetter=M (March 22, 2009).

[13] Schiffman and Kanuk, *Consumer Behavior*, Chapter 6.

purchase means less decision time (an item may be avoided altogether) and low perceived risk, and it is probably inexpensive.

8-3c   Selected Consumer Lifestyles

Many distinct consumer lifestyles will continue, including family values, voluntary simplicity, getting by, "me" generation, blurring of gender roles, poverty of time, and component lifestyles. Their marketing implications are shown in Table 8-4.

A *family values* lifestyle emphasizes marriage, children, and home life. With this lifestyle, people focus on children and their education; family autos, vacations, and entertainment; and home-oriented products. Because the traditional family is becoming less representative of U.S. households, firms must be careful in targeting those who follow this lifestyle. They should also remember that a family values lifestyle remains the leading one in other nations. For instance, in Italy, about one-half of women are in the labor force, and the divorce rate is much lower than that of the United States.

Voluntary simplicity is a lifestyle in which people have an ecological awareness, seek product durability, strive for self-reliance, and buy technologically simple products. People with this lifestyle are cautious, conservative, and thrifty shoppers. They do not buy expensive cars and clothing, hold on to products for long periods, and rarely eat out or go on pre-packaged vacations. They like going to a park or taking a vacation by car, are more concerned with product toughness than appearance, and believe in conservation. There is an attraction to rational appeals and no-frills retailing.

> In some households, family values have a great impact.

> Voluntary simplicity is based on self-reliance.

Table 8-4	Selected Marketing Opportunities of Consumer Lifestyles
Lifestyle Category	**Marketing Opportunities in Appealing to the Lifestyle**
Family values	Family-oriented goods and services Educational devices and toys Traditional family events "Wholesome" entertainment
Voluntary simplicity	Goods and services with quality, durability, and simplicity Environmentally safe products Energy-efficient products Discount-oriented retailing
Getting by	Popular brands and good buys ("value") Video rentals and other inexpensive entertainment Do-it-yourself projects such as "knock-down" furniture Inexpensive child care
"Me" generation	Individuality in purchases Luxury goods and services Nutritional themes Exercise- and education-related goods and services
Blurring of gender roles	Unisex goods, services, and stores Couples-oriented advertising Child-care services Less male and female stereotyping
Poverty of time	Internet and phone sales Service firms with accurate customer appointments Laborsaving devices One-stop shopping
Component lifestyle	Situational purchases Less social class stereotyping Multiple advertising themes Market niches

Getting by is a frugal lifestyle pursued by people due to economic circumstances. They seek product durability, self-reliance, and simple products. Unlike those with voluntary simplicity, they do so because they must. In less-developed and developing nations, most people have this lifestyle; a much smaller proportion has this orientation in industrialized nations. Getting-by consumers like well-known brands (to reduce perceived risk), do not try new products, rarely go out, and take few vacations. They seek bargains and patronize local stores. They rarely feel they have any significant discretionary income.

A *"me" generation* lifestyle stresses being good to oneself, self-fulfillment, and self-expression. There is less pressure to conform and greater diversity; there is also less interest in responsibilities and loyalties. Consumers with this lifestyle stress nutrition, exercise, and grooming. They buy expensive cars and apparel, and visit full-service stores. These people are more concerned with product appearance than durability. Some place below-average value on conservation if it will negatively affect their lifestyle.

Since many women work, more husbands are assuming the once-traditional roles of their wives, and vice versa, thus *blurring gender roles*. According to the *American Time Use Survey*, "On an average day, 83 percent of women and 66 percent of men spend some time doing household activities, such as housework, cooking, lawn care, or financial and other household management. Women spend 2.7 hours on such activities, while men spend 2.2 hours. Twenty percent of men do housework—such as cleaning or doing laundry; and 37 percent of men do food preparation or cleanup."[14] See Figure 8-8.

> When economic circumstances are tough, some people emphasize getting by.

> The "me" generation stresses self-fulfillment.

> Blurring gender roles involves men and women undertaking nontraditional duties.

Figure 8-8

Blurring Gender Roles

More men and women are now engaging in nontraditional activities, such as doing grocery shopping together.

Source: Reprinted by permission of Susan Berry, Retail Image Consulting, Inc.

---

[14] "American Time Use Survey—2007 Results," http://www.bls.gov/news.release/pdf/atus.pdf (June 25, 2008).

A poverty of time exists when a quest for financial security means less free time.

The prevalence of working women, the long distances between home and work, and the large number of people working at second jobs contribute to a *poverty-of-time* lifestyle in many households. For such households, the quest for financial security means less free time. This lifestyle leads people to greater use of time-saving goods and services such as fast-food restaurants, convenience foods, quick-oil-change services, online retailers, one-hour film processing, and professional lawn and household care.

Today, more people employ a *component lifestyle*, whereby their attitudes and behavior depend on particular situations rather than an overall lifestyle philosophy. People may take their children with them on vacation (family values), engage in recycling (voluntary simplicity), look for discounts to save money (getting by), take exercise classes ("me" generation), share shopping chores (blurring gender roles), and eat out on busy nights (poverty of time). As one marketing expert puts it:

With a component lifestyle, consumer attitudes and behavior vary by situation.

> Consumers are more than willing to pay for luxury items in certain categories while at the same time they doggedly shop for deals and wait for items to go on sale in others. What's going on? Consumers are paying close attention to categories that are important to them, making small statements in quality products. An example of this is the higher socioeconomic consumer who appreciates nice furniture, but cannot justify the expense on every piece. He or she will shop at Ikea (**http://www.ikea.com**) for certain items and then at a high-end store such as Luminaire (**http://www.luminaire.com**) for others. Or there's the woman who mixes ready-to-wear apparel from Target (**http://www.target.com**) with her Prada (**http://www.prada.com**) purse and Manolo Blahnik (**http://www.manoloblahnik. com**) shoes.[15]

8-3d Limitations of Lifestyle Analysis

Unlike demographics, many of the social and psychological aspects of final consumer lifestyles are difficult to measure, somewhat subjective, usually based on the self-reports of consumers, and sometimes hidden from view (to avoid embarrassment, protect privacy, convey an image, and other reasons). Ongoing disputes still exist over terminology, misuse of data, and reliability.

8-4 THE FINAL CONSUMER'S DECISION PROCESS

The final consumer's decision process has many stages, and various factors affect it.

The *final consumer's decision process* is the way in which people gather and assess information and choose among alternative goods, services, organizations, people, places, and ideas. It comprises the process itself and the factors affecting it. The process has six stages: stimulus, problem awareness, information search, evaluation of alternatives, purchase, and post-purchase behavior. Demographic, social, and psychological factors affect the process. Figure 8-9 shows the total decision-making process.

Whenever a consumer buys a good or service, decides to vote for a political candidate or donate to a charity, and so on, he or she goes through a decision process. Sometimes, all six stages in the process are used; other times, only a few steps are utilized. The purchase of an expensive stereo requires more decision making than the purchase of a new music video.

At *any* point in the decision process, a person may decide not to buy, vote, or donate—and, thereby, end the process. A good or service may turn out to be unneeded, unsatisfactory, or too expensive.

[15] Paul Marobella, "Contradictions in Consumer Trends," *Direct* (May 15, 2004), p. 32.

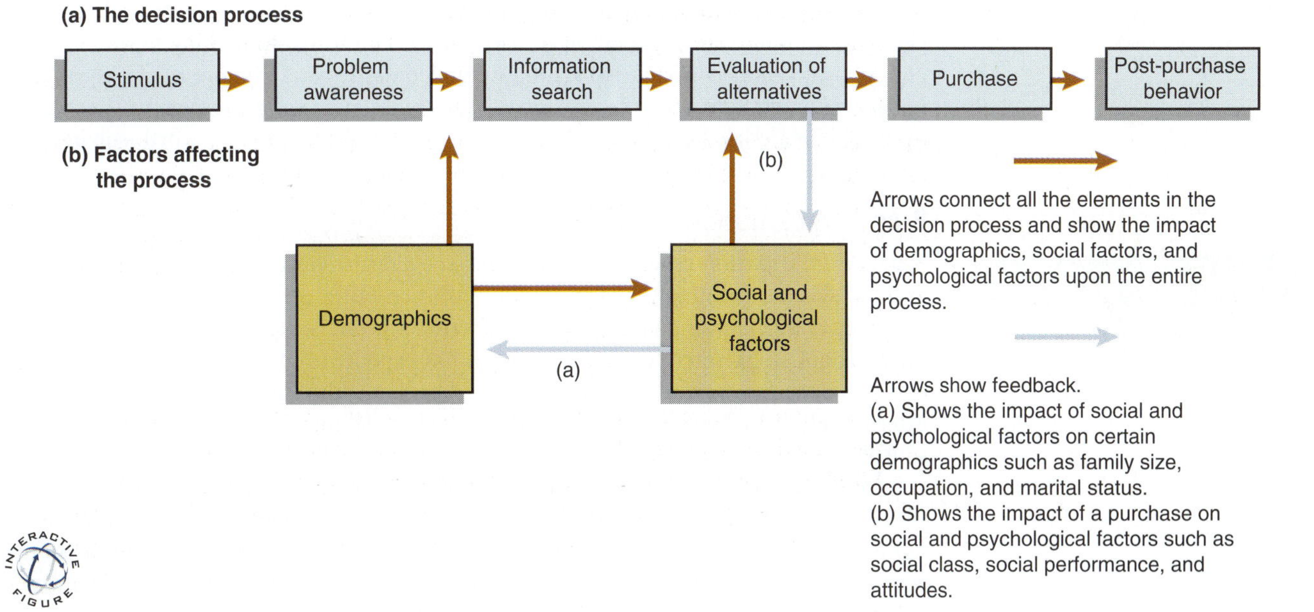

(a) The decision process

(b) Factors affecting the process

Arrows connect all the elements in the decision process and show the impact of demographics, social factors, and psychological factors upon the entire process.

Arrows show feedback.
(a) Shows the impact of social and psychological factors on certain demographics such as family size, occupation, and marital status.
(b) Shows the impact of a purchase on social and psychological factors such as social class, social performance, and attitudes.

Figure 8-9

The Final Consumer's Decision Process

8-4a Stimulus

A *stimulus* is a cue (social, commercial, or noncommercial) or a drive (physical) meant to motivate a person to act.

A *social cue* occurs when someone talks with friends, family members, co-workers, and others. It is from an interpersonal source not affiliated with a seller. A *commercial cue* is a message sponsored by a seller to interest a person in a particular good, service, organization, person, place, or idea. Ads, personal selling, and sales promotions are commercial cues. They are less regarded than social cues because people know they are seller-controlled. A *noncommercial cue* is a message from an impartial source such as *Consumer Reports* (**http://www.consumerreports.org**) or the government. It has high believability because it is not affiliated with the seller. A *physical drive* occurs when a person's physical senses are affected. Thirst, hunger, and fear cause physical drives.

A person may be exposed to any or all of these stimuli. If sufficiently stimulated, he or she will proceed to the next stage in the decision process. If not, the person will ignore the cue and delay or terminate the decision process for the given good, service, organization, person, place, or idea.

> A **stimulus** is a cue or drive intended to motivate a consumer.

8-4b Problem Awareness

At the **problem awareness** stage, a consumer recognizes that the good, service, organization, person, place, or idea under consideration may solve a problem of shortage or unfulfilled desire.

Recognition of shortage occurs when a consumer realizes a repurchase is needed. A suit may wear out. A man or woman may run out of razor cartridges. An eye exam may be needed. A popular political candidate may be up for re-election. It may be time for a charity's annual fundraising campaign. In each case, the consumer recognizes a need to repurchase.

Recognition of unfulfilled desire takes place when a consumer becomes aware of a good, service, organization, person, place, or idea that has not been bought before. Such an item may improve status, appearance, living conditions, or knowledge in a way not tried before (luxury car, cosmetic surgery, proposed zoning law, encyclopedia), or it may

> **Problem awareness** entails recognition of a shortage or an unfulfilled desire.

offer new performance features not previously available (laser surgery, tobacco-free cigarettes). Either way, a person is aroused by a desire to try something new.

Many consumers hesitate to act on unfulfilled desires due to more risk. It is easier to replace a known item. Whether a consumer becomes aware of a problem of shortage or of unfulfilled desire, he or she will act only if the problem is seen as worth solving.

8-4c Information Search

> An **information search** determines alternatives and their characteristics.

Next, an *information search* requires listing the alternatives that will solve the problem at hand and determining the characteristics of each option.

A *list of alternatives* does not have to be written. It can be a group of items a consumer thinks about. With internal search, a person has experience in the area being considered and uses a memory search to list the choices. A person with minimal experience will do an external search to list alternatives; this can involve commercial sources, noncommercial sources, and/or social sources. Often, once there is a list of choices, items (brands, companies, and so on) that are not on it do not receive further consideration.

The second phase of information search deals with the *characteristics of each alternative*. This information can also be generated internally or externally, depending on the expertise of the consumer and the perceived risk. As risk increases, more information is sought. Once an information search is completed, it must be determined whether the shortage or unfulfilled desire can be satisfied by any alternative. If one or more choices are satisfactory, the consumer moves to the next step. The process is delayed or discontinued when no alternative provides satisfaction.

The Web is now a major source for information. Among the helpful sites are:

- CNET (**http://www.cnet.com**)—"Product reviews and prices, software downloads, and tech news"
- Epinions.com (**http://www.epinions.com**)—"Unbiased reviews by real people"
- mySimon (**http://www.mysimon.com**)—"Price comparison shopping"
- Pricing Central (**http://www.pricingcentral.com**)—"Indexes all the best price search engines and online shopping bots into a comprehensive directory"
- StartSpot (**http://www.shoppingspot.com**)—"Simplifies the search for the best shopping-related content on the Web"
- Yahoo! Shopping (**http://shopping.yahoo.com**)—"Compare, shop, and save"

8-4d Evaluation of Alternatives

> **Evaluating alternatives** consists of weighing features and selecting the desired product.

There is now enough information for a consumer to select one alternative from the list of choices. This is easy if one option is clearly the best across all attributes: A product with excellent quality and a low price will be a sure choice over an average-quality, expensive one. The choice is usually not that simple, and a consumer must carefully engage in an *evaluation of alternatives* before making a decision. If two or more alternatives seem attractive, a person needs to determine which criteria to evaluate and their relative importance. Alternatives would then be ranked and a choice made.

Decision criteria are the features a person deems relevant—such as price, style, quality, safety, durability, status, and warranty. A consumer sets standards for these features and forms an attitude on each alternative according to its ability to meet the standards. In addition, each criterion's importance is set because the multiple attributes of products are usually of varying weight. For example, a consumer may consider shoe prices to be more important than style and select inexpensive, nondistinctive shoes.

A consumer then *ranks alternatives* from most to least desirable and selects one. This may be hard because alternatives might have technical differences or be poorly labeled, new, or intangible (such as two political candidates). On these occasions, options may be ranked on the basis of brand name or price, which is used to indicate overall quality.

In situations where no alternative is satisfactory, a decision to delay or not make a purchase is made.

Marketing and the Web

Businesses Embrace Blogging

A blog is an online, interactive, frequently updated Web journal. Blogging started with everyday people developing and updating easy-to-use Web sites where they could share their thoughts and interact with others. Many consumers used blogging as a means of posting their thoughts and opinions.

Recently, many businesses have begun to use blogging as part of their corporate communications or social media programs. One study found that 12 percent of *Fortune 500* corporations run a corporate blog, including Dell (**http://www.dell.com**), Kodak (**http://www.koak.com**), IBM (**http://www.ibm.com**), and Intel (**http://www.intel.com**). Evidence of the growing popularity of corporate blogging is the increased use of "chief blogger" as a job title, and the application of standardized tools to measure the success of blogging.

Dell has a main corporate blog (**http://www.direct2Dell.com**), as well as specialized blogs aimed at information technology users and small businesses.

A major challenge for the Dell blog relates to the firm's globalization and the associated need to communicate in the various languages that cover roughly 95 percent of the world's population.

Peruvian Connection, a retailer that specializes in handcrafted and knitted sweaters, has a blog called "Common Threads" (**http://blog.peruvianconnection.com**). This blog includes shopping tips and information on the latest artisan textiles trends. This information enables consumers to make better buying decisions.

Several firms deploy two-way blogs that ask users to post feedback about their experiences with those firms' goods and services. Though some companies are leery of posts with negative comments, others feel that this can be an early warning signal of a potential problem area.

Sources: Based on material in Rich Karpinski, "Businesses Embrace Blogging," *B to B* (July 9, 2008), pp. 1, 48; and Samantha Murphy, "The Blogging Bandwagon," *Chain Store Age* (March 2008), p. 68.

8-4e   Purchase

After choosing the best alternative, a person is ready for the *purchase act*: an exchange of money, a promise to pay, or support in return for ownership of a specific good, the performance of a specific service, and so on. Three considerations remain: place of purchase, terms, and availability.

> The **purchase act** means picking where to buy, agreeing to terms, and checking availability.

The *place of purchase* is picked the same way as a product. Choices are noted, attributes are detailed, and a ranking is performed. The best locale is chosen. Although most items are bought at stores, some are bought at school, work, and home. *Purchase terms* involve the price and method of payment. Generally, a price is the amount (including interest, tax, and other fees) a person pays to gain ownership or use of a good or service. It may also be a person's vote, time investment, and so on. The payment method is the way a price is paid (cash, short-term credit, or long-term credit). *Availability* refers to the timeliness with which a consumer receives a product that he or she buys. It depends on stock on hand (or service capacity) and delivery. Stock on hand (service capacity) relates to a seller's ability to provide a good or service when requested. For items requiring delivery, the period from when an order is placed by a consumer until it is received and the ease with which an item is transported to its place of use are crucial.

A consumer will purchase if these elements are acceptable. That is why companies such as American Girl (**http://www.americangirl.com**), highlighted in Figure 8-10, want to be seen as consumer friendly. However, sometimes, dissatisfaction with any one of the elements may cause a person to delay or not buy, even though there is no problem with the good or service itself. If a store is closed or a salesperson is unfriendly, the consumer might not come back.

8-4f   Post-Purchase Behavior

Once a purchase is made, a person may engage in *post-purchase behavior*, via further purchases and/or re-evaluation. Many times, one purchase leads to others: A house purchase leads to the acquisition of fire insurance. A PC purchase leads to the acquisition of computer software. In addition, displaying complementary products near one another may encourage related purchases.

> **Post-purchase behavior** often involves further buying and/or re-evaluation. **Cognitive dissonance** can be reduced by proper consumer after-care.

Figure 8-10

American Girl: Bringing a Relationship Marketing Philosophy to the Youth Marketplace

American Girl (**http://www. americangirl.com**)—which markets books and other products "that help girls grow up in a wholesome way"—certainly get it. In order to develop and sustain customer relationships, the company not only offers excellent products, it also makes the shopping experience as convenient as possible.

Source: Reprinted by permission.

A person may also re-evaluate a purchase after making it: Are expectations matched by performance? Satisfaction often means a repurchase when a good or service wears out, a charity holds a fundraising campaign, and so on, and leads to positive communication with other people interested in the same item. Dissatisfaction can lead to brand switching and negative communication. It is often due to *cognitive dissonance*—doubt that a correct decision has been made. A person may regret a purchase or wish another choice had been made. To overcome dissonance, a firm must realize the process does not end with a purchase. Follow-up calls, extended warranties, and ads aimed at buyers can reassure people.

8-4g Factors Affecting the Final Consumer's Decision Process

Demographic, social, and psychological factors affect the way final consumers make choices and can help a firm understand how people use the decision process. For example, an affluent consumer would move through the process more quickly than a middle-income one due to less financial risk. An insecure consumer would spend more time making a decision than a secure one.

By knowing how these factors influence decisions, a firm can fine-tune its marketing strategies to cater to the target market and its purchase behavior, and answer these questions: Why do two or more people use the decision process in the same way? Why do two or more people use it differently?

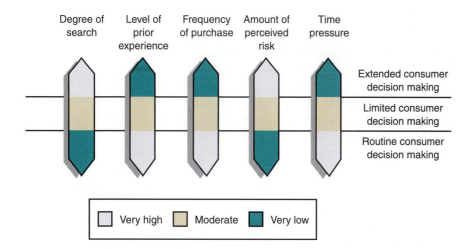

Figure 8-11

The Three Types of Final Consumer Decision Processes

8-4h Types of Decision Processes

Each time a person buys a good or service, donates to a charity, and so on, he or she uses the decision process. This may be done subconsciously, with the person not aware of using it. Some situations let a person move through the process quickly and de-emphasize or skip steps; others require a thorough use of each step. A consumer may use extended, limited, or routine decision making—based on the search, level of experience, frequency of purchase, amount of perceived risk, and time pressure. See Figure 8-11.

With *extended consumer decision making*, a person fully uses the decision process. Much effort is spent on information search and evaluation of alternatives for expensive, complex items with which a person has little or no experience. Purchases are made infrequently. Perceived risk is high, and the purchase is important. A person has time available to make a choice. Purchase delays often occur. Demographic, social, and psychological factors have their greatest impact. Extended decision making is often involved in picking a college, a house, a first car, or a location for a wedding.

Limited consumer decision making occurs when a person uses every step in the purchase process but does not spend a great deal of time on some of them. The person has previously bought a given good or service, but makes fresh decisions when it comes under current purchase consideration—due to the relative infrequency of purchase, the introduction of new models, or an interest in variety. Perceived risk is moderate, and a person is willing to spend some time shopping. The thoroughness with which the process is used depends on the amount of prior experience, the importance of the purchase, and the time pressure facing the consumer. Emphasis is on evaluating a list of known choices, although an information search may be done. Factors affecting the decision process have some impact. A second car, clothing, gifts, home furnishings, and an annual vacation typically need limited decision making.

In *routine consumer decision making*, a person buys out of habit and skips steps in the process. He or she spends little time shopping and often repurchases the same brands (or those bought before). This category includes items with which a person has much experience. They are bought regularly, have little or no perceived risk, and are rather low in price. Once a person realizes a good or service is depleted, a repurchase is made. Time pressure is high. Information search, evaluation, and post-purchase behavior are normally omitted, as long as a person is satisfied. Impulse purchases, where consumers have not thought of particular items until seeing displays for them, are common. Factors affecting the process have little impact because problem awareness usually leads to a purchase. Examples of items routinely purchased are the daily paper, a haircut by a regular stylist, and weekly grocery items.

There are differences between consumers in industrialized nations and those in less-developed and developing ones. Generally, consumers in less-developed and developing countries

> Final consumer decision making can be categorized as **extended, limited,** or **routine.**

- are exposed to fewer commercial and noncommercial cues.
- have access to less information.
- have fewer goods and services from which to choose.
- are more apt to buy a second choice if the first one is not available.
- have fewer places of purchase and may have to wait on long lines.
- are more apt to find that stores are out of stock.
- have less purchase experience for many kinds of goods and services.
- are less educated and have lower incomes.
- are more apt to repurchase items with which they are moderately satisfied (due to a lack of choices).

Most purchases are made by routine or limited decision making because many consumers—in both industrialized nations and less-developed nations—want to reduce shopping time, the use of complex decision making, and risk. Consumers often employ low-involvement purchasing and/or brand loyalty.

With *low-involvement purchasing*, a consumer minimizes the time and effort expended in both making decisions about and shopping for those goods and services he or she views as unimportant. Included are "those situations where the consumer simply does not care and is not concerned about brands or choices and makes the decision in the most cognitively miserly manner possible. Most likely, low involvement is situation-based, and the degree of importance and involvement may vary with the individual and with the situation."[16] In these situations, consumers feel little perceived risk, are passive about getting information, act fast, and may assess products after (rather than before) buying.

Firms can adapt to low-involvement purchasing by using repetitive ads to create awareness and familiarity, stressing the practical nature of products, having informed salespeople, setting low prices, using attractive displays, selling in all types of outlets, and offering coupons and free samples. Table 8-5 compares the traditional high-involvement view of consumer behavior with the low-involvement view. AdCracker.com has good examples at its Web site (**http://www.adcracker.com/involvement**).

> **Low-involvement purchasing** occurs with unimportant products.

Table 8-5	High-Involvement View of Active Consumers Versus Low-Involvement View of Passive Consumers
Traditional High-Involvement View of Active Consumers	**Newer Low-Involvement View of Passive Consumers**
1. Consumers are information processors.	1. Consumers learn information at random.
2. Consumers are information seekers.	2. Consumers are information gatherers.
3. Consumers are an active audience for ads and the effect of ads on them is *weak*.	3. Consumers are a passive audience for ads and the effect of ads on them is *strong*.
4. Consumers evaluate brands before buying.	4. Consumers buy first. If they do evaluate brands, it is done after the purchase.
5. Consumers seek to maximize satisfaction. They compare brands to see which provide the most *benefits* and buy based on detailed comparisons.	5. Consumers seek an acceptable level of satisfaction. They choose the brand least apt to have *problems* and buy based on few factors. Familiarity is key.
6. Lifestyle characteristics are related to consumer behavior because the product is closely tied to a consumer's identity and belief system.	6. Lifestyle characteristics are not related to consumer behavior because the product is closely tied to a consumer's identity and belief system.
7. Reference groups influence behavior because of the product's importance to group norms.	7. Reference groups have little effect on behavior because the product is unlikely to be related to group norms.

Source: Henry Assael, *Consumer Behavior and Marketing Action*, 6th ed. (Cincinnati: South-Western Publishing , 1998), p. 155. Reprinted by permission.

[16] "Dictionary," **http://www.marketingpower.com/_layouts/Dictionary.aspx?dLetter=L** (March 22, 2009).

After a consumer tries one or more brands of a good or service, ***brand loyalty***—the consistent repurchase of and preference toward a particular brand—may take place. With it, a person can reduce time, thought, and risk whenever buying a given good or service. Brand loyalty can occur for simple items such as gasoline (due to low-involvement purchasing) and for complex items such as autos (to minimize the perceived risk of switching brands).

<aside>**Brand loyalty** involves consistent repurchases and preferences of specific brands.</aside>

According to one study of 50 product categories, these were the top 10 categories in brand loyalty (U.S. adults saying they were very loyal to one brand): soft drinks (34 percent), insurance (33 percent), hair products (31 percent), bath soap (31 percent), health and beauty aids (29 percent), automobiles (26 percent), coffee (29 percent), mayonnaise (28 percent), laundry products (26 percent), and over-the-counter medicines (26 percent).[17]

How can firms generate and sustain customer loyalty? Here's the way Whirlpool (**http://www.whirlpool.com**), the home appliance company, does it:

> We know that loyal customers are recommending our brands to others, that they are requesting and repurchasing our brands over those of competitors, and that they are beginning to upgrade their appliances because they trust the innovation and value that our brands deliver. Initiatives that lead to higher levels of customer loyalty, such as our innovation process, result in improved revenue growth, margin expansion, and trade support for our brands. Because innovation is such an important driver of customer loyalty, we are expanding our efforts to transfer innovation capabilities and skills to employees everywhere. Innovation is ingrained in the Whirlpool culture, with employees from around the world—trained and actively involved in innovation initiatives. Another key aspect of customer loyalty involves the experiences that touch customers before, during, and long after the initial purchase. Each of our brands is putting in place a complete set of experiences—including brand advertising, the in-store purchase, call center interactions, and ongoing customer communications—that will help forge lifelong relationships with our customers.[18]

8-4i Marketing Applications of the Final Consumer's Decision Process

Over the years, the final consumer's decision process has been studied and applied in many settings, as these illustrations indicate:

- According to a study of female fashion shoppers in the United States, Europe, and Asia, 27 percent of those shoppers can be categorized as information seekers. These are "women who are willing to put considerable effort into researching fashions by consulting books and magazines." They are "very information-oriented and more open to considering new brands, or brands with which they do not have prior experience, than the conspicuous consumer." They look for "information to keep up with fashion trends. As a result, they show a high level of interest in advertising for fashion products."[19]
- Just over one-half of the respondents age 12 and younger to a Harris Interactive YouthPulse survey "said they had to abandon a purchase because of parent interference, making it the top reason for online shopping-cart abandonment in that group." In addition, "27 percent of those ages 13 and older said their parents had forced them to abandon an online purchase. But while tween online purchasers might have been stopped in their tracks by parents, the survey also reports that

---

[17] "Complete Listing of 50 Brand Products for Loyalty Study," **http://americasresearchgroup.com/brand_loyalty.html** (July 24, 2008).

[18] "Building Customer Loyalty," **http://www.whirlpoolcorp.com/about/vision_and_strategy/loyalty.asp** (April 30, 2009).

[19] Charles R. Taylor, "Lifestyle Matters Everywhere," *Advertising Age* (May 19, 2008), p. 24.

young consumers spend $20 billion a year on shopping sprees that they initially researched online."[20]

- When consumers use the Web during the decision process, they often look for particular information. A study by the Service Excellence Research Group found that 79 percent of shoppers look for pricing information, 59 percent look for product descriptions, 42 percent want to learn about product availability, 30 percent seek out product reviews, and 27 percent want purchase recommendations."[21]

- Brand loyal customers are quite apt to make referrals to their friends. A *Parago Customer Loyalty Research Report* found that "Eighty-two percent of Americans participating in customer loyalty programs have actively referred friends and family to their favorite programs. On average, active members refer about three friends or family members to their favorite programs. High-income earners—household incomes of $125,000 or higher—tend to be the most active in referrals since they are typically more involved in loyalty and rewards programs. Consumers are using referral and word-of-mouth more than we ever expected. It's clear customers want to be loyal."[22]

8-4j Limitations of the Final Consumer's Decision Process

The limitations of the final consumer's decision process for marketers lie in the hidden (unexpressed) nature of many elements of the process; the consumer's subconscious performance of the process or a number of its components; the impact of demographic, social, and psychological factors on the process; and the differences in decision making among consumers in different countries.

Web Sites You Can Use

One of the best features of the Web is that it gives us access to so much varied information. Thus, there are Web sites devoted to virtually every consumer lifestyle topic imaginable. Just type in a lifestyle topic in your favorite search engine, and away you go. Here is a sampling of the Web sites devoted to mainstream consumer lifestyle topics.

- Alloy Access (**http://www.alloy-access.com/ what_we_know/articles.shtml**)—A site with articles focusing on the Hispanic, Black, Asian, and urban markets.
- American Association of Retired People (**http://www.aarp. org**)—Provides tips for people ages 50 and older.
- Consumer Behavior and Marketing (**http://www. consumerpsychologist.com**)—Focuses on the psychology of consumers.
- Diabetic Lifestyle (**http://www.diabetic-lifestyle.com**)—Geared toward people with diabetes.

- Excel International Sports (**http://www.excelsports.net**)—Offers custom-designed vacation trips to sporting events in Europe.
- Food & Brand Lab (**http://www.foodpsychology.cornell. edu**)—Research into why consumers buy what they buy and eat what they eat.
- F.U.N. Place (**http://www.thefunplace.com**)—Devoted, in a colorful way, to parenting.
- Google Groups (**http://groups.google.com**)—Discussion groups on a wide range of lifestyle topics.
- Trendwatching.com (**http://www.trendwatching.com**)—"Scans the globe for the most promising consumer trends, insights, and related hands-on business ideas."
- Ubercool (**http://www.ubercool.com**)—"Bringing Trends to Life."

---

[20] "All in the Family," *Marketing Management* (May-June 2005), p. 4.

[21] "Online Reviews Sway Shoppers," **http://www.emarketer.com/Articles/Print.aspx?id=1006404** (May 14, 2008).

[22] "Majority of Americans Refer Friends to Favorite Loyalty Programs," **http://www.promomagazine.com/premiums/ wordofmouth_loyalty_051105** (May 11, 2005).

Summary

1. To *show the importance and scope of consumer analysis*   By analyzing consumers, a firm can better determine the most appropriate audience to which to appeal and the combination of marketing factors to satisfy this audience. This is a critical task given the diversity of the global marketplace. The scope of consumer analysis includes who, what, why, how, when, where, and how often. Chapter 8 examines final consumers, while Chapters 9 and 10 cover organizational consumers, developing a target market strategy, and sales forecasting.

2. To *define and enumerate important consumer demographics for the U.S. population and other countries*   Consumer demographics are objective and quantifiable population statistics. They include population size, gender, and age; population location, housing, and mobility; population income and expenditures; population occupations and education; population marital status; and population ethnicity/race. Profiles can be derived.

   The world has nearly 7 billion people, rising by 1.1 percent annually. By 2020, the United States will have 336 million people, increasing by less than 0.9 percent each year. In many nations, a large proportion of births involve firstborns. Worldwide, the number of men and women is roughly equal; however, women generally live longer than men. The average age of populations in industrialized nations is higher than in less-developed and developing countries.

   Urbanization varies by country, with about four-fifths of the U.S. population living in urban and suburban areas. In many countries, the majority of people own the home in which they live. Each year, millions of people immigrate from one country to another, and hundreds of millions move within their countries.

   The 2008 U.S. median household income was between $48,000 and $50,000. Many nations measure their cost of living and rate of inflation via a consumer price index. Differences in consumption patterns exist between people in industrialized nations and ones in less-developed and developing countries. When assessing consumption patterns, the distinction between disposable-income spending and discretionary-income expenditures should be kept in mind.

   For industrialized nations, the labor force is continuing its movement to white-collar and service occupations; many more jobs in less-developed and developing nations still entail manual work and are agriculture-based. Throughout the world, women comprise a significant part of the labor force. Unemployment varies widely among nations, based on economies and industry shifts. Globally, education has improved in recent decades.

   Marriage and family are strong institutions, although less dominant than before for some nations. A family consists of relatives living together. A household consists of a person or persons, related or not, occupying a housing unit. In many nations, both family and household size have declined, due to the growth in single-person households and other factors.

   Demographically, ethnicity/race is important as it pertains to the diversity of people among and within nations. Most countries have populations representing different ethnic and racial groups.

3. To *show why consumer demographic analysis is not sufficient in planning marketing strategies*   Demographics have limitations: Data may be obsolete; data may be unavailable for some nations; there may be hidden trends or implications; and demographics do not explain the factors affecting behavior, consumer decision making, and motivation.

   Because demographic data do not answer such questions as why consumers act as they do, why demographically similar consumers act differently, how motives and risks affect decisions, and how long it takes people to make purchase decisions, many firms now analyze the social and psychological aspects of final consumer lifestyles, as well as the way in which consumers make decisions, in conjunction with demographics.

4. To *define and describe consumer lifestyles and their characteristics, examine selected lifestyles, and consider the limitations of lifestyle analysis*   A final consumer's lifestyle is the way in which a person lives and spends time and money. It is a function of the social and psychological factors internalized by that person, along with his or her demographic background. Consumer social profiles consist of several elements, including culture, social class, social performance, reference groups, opinion leaders, the family life cycle, and time expenditures. Psychological profiles are based on a combination of personality, attitudes (opinions), level of class consciousness, motivation, perceived risk, innovativeness, and purchase importance.

   Seven lifestyle types are expected to continue, with their popularity often differing by country: family values, voluntary simplicity, getting by, the "me" generation, blurring gender roles, poverty of time, and component lifestyles.

   Many lifestyle concepts are hard to measure, rather subjective, based on consumer self-reports, and sometimes hidden from view. Disputes continue over terms, misuse of data, and reliability.

5. To *define and describe the final consumer's decision process and consider the limitations of final consumer decision-making analysis*   Through the decision process, people collect and analyze information and make choices among alternatives. There is the process itself and the factors affecting it (demographic, social, and psychological). A consumer can delay or terminate the process at any point.

   The process has six steps: stimulus, problem awareness, information search, evaluation of alternatives, purchase, and post-purchase behavior. There are three types of process: extended, limited, and routine. The way people make decisions varies widely between industrialized nations and less-developed and developing nations.

Consumers often reduce shopping time, thought, and risk via low-involvement purchasing and brand loyalty.

The limitations of the decision process for marketers lie in the unexpressed nature of many aspects of the process; the subconscious nature of many consumer actions; the impact of demographic, social, and psychological factors; and the differences between countries in consumer decision making.

Key Terms

final consumers (p. 225)
organizational consumers (p. 225)
consumer demographics (p. 225)
cost of living (p. 229)
disposable income (p. 229)
discretionary income (p. 229)
family (p. 231)
household (p. 231)
ethnicity/race (p. 231)
lifestyle (p. 233)
culture (p. 234)
social class (p. 235)
social performance (p. 235)
reference group (p. 235)
opinion leaders (p. 235)

family life cycle (p. 235)
joint decision making (p. 235)
household life cycle (p. 235)
time expenditures (p. 237)
personality (p. 237)
attitudes (opinions) (p. 237)
class consciousness (p. 238)
motivation (p. 239)
motives (p. 239)
perceived risk (p. 239)
innovativeness (p. 239)
importance of a purchase (p. 239)
final consumer's decision process (p. 242)
stimulus (p. 243)

problem awareness (p. 243)
information search (p. 244)
evaluation of alternatives (p. 244)
purchase act (p. 245)
post-purchase behavior (p. 245)
cognitive dissonance (p. 246)
extended consumer decision making (p. 247)
limited consumer decision making (p. 247)
routine consumer decision making (p. 247)
low-involvement purchasing (p. 248)
brand loyalty (p. 249)

Review Questions

1. How does the use of consumer demographics aid marketing decision making?
2. Cite several reasons why it is difficult to contrast personal income data by country.
3. Why are demographic data alone frequently insufficient for marketing decisions?
4. Distinguish between the traditional family life cycle and the household life cycle.
5. Distinguish between actual risk and perceived risk. How may a firm reduce each type of perceived risk for a new computer operating system?
6. Compare the poverty-of-time lifestyle with the getting-by lifestyle.
7. What could cause a consumer to *not* make a purchase even when he or she really likes a product?
8. Define low-involvement purchasing and explain its use by consumers. Give an example.

Discussion Questions

1. Develop a demographic profile of the people residing in your metropolitan area, using the *Census of Population*. What are the marketing overtones of this profile?
2. American culture emphasizes achievement and success, activity, efficiency and practicality, progress, material comfort, individualism, freedom, external conformity, humanitarianism, youthfulness, and fitness and health. What are the implications of this for firms marketing the following goods and services?

   a. Motorcycles
   b. Energy drinks
   c. Personal-care products for women
   d. Digital cameras

3. A leading apparel design firm has hired you as a marketing consultant. It is particularly interested in learning more about the concept of a component lifestyle and developing an appropriate strategy.

a. Explain the relevance of the component lifestyle concept for the apparel industry.

b. Suggest various ways in which an apparel designer can appeal to component lifestyles.

4. How may Hyundai (**http://www.hyundaiusa.com**), the maker of inexpensive autos, reduce both perceived risk *and* cognitive dissonance through its marketing efforts?

Web Exercise

Visit the Web site of the Personality Test Center (**http://www. personalitytest.net/cgi-bin/q.pl**) and take your own free personality test by answering the questions. What can a person learn about himself or herself from this site? Do you agree with the profile generated about you from the survey? Explain your answer.

Practice Quiz

1. *Census of Population* data
   a. are gathered annually.
   b. are a major source of demographics.
   c. include retail sales by merchandise category.
   d. are limited to cities.

2. Projections of the size of the U.S. population reveal that
   a. the number of people is decreasing.
   b. the Midwest is expanding more rapidly than other regions.
   c. population growth is increasing at a rapid rate.
   d. the rate of population growth is slow.

3. Approximately what percent of people in the United States reside in urban areas and their suburbs?
   a. 15
   b. 25
   c. 64
   d. 82

4. Among U.S. residents, about what percentage of all people move annually?
   a. 14
   b. 25
   c. 35
   d. 45

5. A family is
   a. one or more people residing together.
   b. a husband, wife, and children, regardless of whether living together.
   c. all relatives, including cousins, regardless of whether living together.
   d. two or more related people residing together.

6. According to the U.S. Bureau of the Census, which of the following is *not* a major racial group?
   a. Asian
   b. Black
   c. Hispanic
   d. White

7. Which of the following is *not* an attribute upon which social classes are based?

a. Education
b. Language
c. Occupation
d. Type of dwelling

8. The concept of the household life cycle is taking on greater importance because of the
   a. growing number of people who do not marry.
   b. growing number of families with only one working spouse.
   c. declining number of people who do not have children.
   d. declining number of people getting divorced.

9. Self-confidence, dominance, autonomy, sociability, defensiveness, adaptability, and emotional stability are selected
   a. attitudes.
   b. personality traits.
   c. social classes.
   d. lifestyle attributes.

10. The risk that a product will not perform adequately is an example of which type of perceived risk?
    a. Safety
    b. Time
    c. Financial
    d. Functional

11. If a husband stays home and takes care of the children and a wife works full-time outside the home, which type of lifestyle is being exhibited?
    a. Voluntary simplicity
    b. Blurring of gender roles
    c. Getting by
    d. Component

12. Unlike demographics, many of the social and psychological aspects of consumer lifestyles are
    a. objective.
    b. easy to measure.
    c. based primarily on observation.
    d. hidden from view.

13. Listing alternatives that will solve the problem at hand and determining the characteristics of each occurs during which stage of the final consumer's decision process?
    a. Stimulus
    b. Information search
    c. Evaluation of alternatives
    d. Purchase

14. Follow-up telephone and service calls, ads aimed at purchasers, and extended warranties can all be used to help reduce
    a. perceived risk.
    b. the number of criteria used in the evaluation of alternatives.
    c. the period from when an order is placed by a consumer until it is received.
    d. cognitive dissonance.

15. In low-involvement purchasing situations, consumers
    a. act quickly.
    b. use extended decision making.
    c. have a relatively high degree of functional perceived risk.
    d. are active about acquiring information.

For the answers to these questions, please visit the online site for this book at **http://www.atomicdog.com.**

Chapter 9

Organizational Consumers

Boeing (**http://www.boeing.com**) is the world's largest aerospace firm, typically "neck-and-neck" with Airbus (**http://www.airbus.com**) in market share for commercial jets. In one recent year, Boeing logged 1,413 orders for commercial jets and delivered 441 planes, and Airbus logged 1,341 orders and delivered 453 planes.

The large-jet commercial manufacturing business is characterized by slow growth. Demand is historically affected by airlines' profitability, final consumer demand for air travel, and airlines' retirement cycles for planes. None of these factors suggests high growth: airline profitability has been poor due to high jet fuel costs; and worldwide air travel is growing at an average rate of about 4 percent. Boeing is predicting that world airlines will order more than 27,000 new long-haul and regional planes over the next 20 years. Forty-five percent of these orders are predicted to come from North America, 24 percent from Europe, and 29 percent from the Asia Pacific region.

Commercial airlines usually purchase planes from Boeing via long-term, fixed-price contracts. The fixed-piece contracts include escalator clauses tied to labor and materials costs increases over the period it takes to build a commercial plane. Contracts generally specify specific delivery dates. If Boeing cannot deliver the planes on the agreed date, it faces a large penalty. However, if an airline requests to cancel, modify, or reschedule all or part of an order, it will not lose its deposit.

Boeing's sales are very dependent on the general economy, as well as the financial condition of the commercial airline industry. As a result of rising jet fuel prices during 2008, both Boeing and Airbus were concerned that as much as one-third of their orders for new jets might be cancelled. Since the combined orders for Boeing and Airbus commercial jets exceed $500 billion, cancellations send a powerful ripple effect throughout manufacturers of jet engines and other parts. Airlines such as JetBlue and Delta have already deferred or cancelled deliveries due to their poor financial state. These airlines prefer to fly more fuel efficient aircraft but cannot afford to buy or lease new planes.[1]

In this chapter, we will study much more than the characteristics and behavior of organizational (b-to-b) consumers. We will also discuss the different types of b-to-b consumers (including wholesalers and retailers) and their buying objectives, buying structure, and purchase constraints.

Chapter Objectives

1. To introduce the concept of industrial (b-to-b) marketing
2. To differentiate between organizational consumers and final consumers and look at organizational consumers from a global perspective
3. To describe the different types of organizational consumers and their buying objectives, buying structure, and purchase constraints
4. To explain the organizational consumer's decision process
5. To consider the marketing implications of appealing to organizational consumers

9-1 OVERVIEW

Organizations purchase goods and services for further production, use in operations, or resale to others—as noted in Chapter 8. In contrast, final consumers buy for personal, family,

[1] Various company and other sources.

or household use. Organizational consumers are manufacturers, wholesalers, retailers, and government and other nonprofit institutions. When firms deal with organizational consumers, they engage in **industrial (b-to-b) marketing**. Purchasing executives around the world spend trillions of dollars annually for the goods and services their companies require. Throughout this chapter, we use the term "b-to-b" (business-to-business) to refer to activities and transactions involving organizations. Here are some b-to-b examples.

Firms involved with organizational consumers use **industrial (b-to-b) marketing**.

Calico Cottage (http://www.calicocottage.com) is a highly successful company involved in b-to-b marketing. Calico "is the world's largest provider of fudge ingredients, equipment, and merchandising expertise—serving customers worldwide, including New Zealand, Australia, Europe, Canada, the Caribbean, and the United States." The company offers more than 400 flavors of fudge mix, as well as seasonal promotional specialties and a variety of gourmet make-at-home mixes that customers sell under their own names. Calico's customers include local and tourist gift shops, gourmet candy stores, casinos, hotels, and the largest amusement and recreational parks in the world.[2] See Figure 9-1.

The Principal Financial Group, PFG (http://www.principal.com), is a leader in financial services for businesses. Its b-to-b insurance division serves 100,000 small- and medium-size employers by offering retirement plans (including investment management, employee education, enrollment, consulting services, government reporting, compliance testing, and asset allocation); group life and health insurance; business protection plans (in case an owner or key employee dies, becomes disabled, retires, or leaves the client); and employee benefit plans (to help recruit, reward, and retain key employees).[3]

For a long time, Dell (http://www.dell.com) earned its reputation, and considerable profits, by making and marketing PCs for final consumers. But, in recent years, Dell has

Figure 9-1

Calico Cottage: Providing Superior Service to Its Business Customers

Source: Reprinted by permission.

[2] "About Us and Our Fudge Ingredients," http://www.calicocottage.com/about_us.shtml (May 14, 2009).
[3] "For Businesses," http://www.principal.com/biz.htm (May 14, 2009).

placed more emphasis on b-to-b marketing. For instance, "Boston Medical Center (http://www.bostonmedicalcenter.com) is the largest safety net hospital in the area and has the largest 24-hour level-one trauma center in the area. Employees rely on the high availability of applications that help manage both hospital operations and patient care. As a patient care tool, information technology has become as commonplace in the hospital as a blood pressure cuff. However, a few years ago, an aging and disjointed infrastructure began to slow operations and hinder access to vital administrative and patient care systems." The medical center chose "Dell OptiPlex when standardizing the desktops that provide nurses, physicians, and hospital operations staff access to the many patient care and administration applications that are needed." As a hospital administrator noted, "We need desktop computers that are user friendly, compact, and reliable. Dell OptiPlex fits the bill."[4]

American Greetings (http://www.americangreetings.com) makes cards and other personal-communications products. It is the second-largest firm in the field, behind Hallmark, and markets products globally, with its best markets being the United States, Canada, Great Britain, Mexico, Australia, New Zealand, and South Africa. It is in more than 70 nations. Although its products are ultimately sold to final consumers, American Greetings must first get support from organizational consumers—the 125,000 retail stores (70,000 in the United States) that stock its cards and related items. Thus, American Greetings provides research on greeting-cards customers to stores, devises and sets up in-store displays, helps computerize transactions, runs special promotions to draw consumers to stores, and so on.[5]

Booz Allen Hamilton (http://www.boozallen.com) is a b-to-b consulting firm with yearly revenues of $4 billion, 21,000 employees, and offices in 35 nations. It is a "global strategy and technology consulting firm that works with clients to deliver results that endure." The company serves "the world's leading corporations, government, and other public agencies, emerging growth companies, and institutions." Its expertise includes corporate finance and business analysis, information technology, marketing and sales, mergers and restructuring, operations and logistics, organization and change, product innovation, public-sector mission effectiveness, strategy and leadership, and systems engineering and integration.[6]

Two emerging trends merit special attention: the growth of the Internet in b-to-b marketing and the rise in outsourcing. As we noted in Chapter 7, the b-to-b use of the Internet is having a major impact on the way companies deal with their suppliers and customers. It fosters closer relationships, better communications, quicker transaction times, cost efficiencies, and greater flexibility. Consider the situation at Staples (http://www.staples.com), where the Internet is driving its b-to-b efforts:

> StaplesLink.com (http://www.stapleslink.com) is our proprietary Web site expressly for Staples Contract (http://www.staplescontract.com) customers. Created to provide a fast, easy, and cost-effective way to purchase office supplies, this site set the industry standard from day one—and continues to raise the bar. StaplesLink.com gives you access to over 80,000 products, along with company-specific contract pricing and delivery dates. You can order and return online, minimizing the time for procurement. With StaplesLink.com, you maintain control of the approval and purchasing process. More than 66,000 companies and over 5 million users turn to StaplesLink.com for 85 percent of their orders.[7]

With **outsourcing**, client firms farm out nonessential functions.

Outsourcing occurs when one company provides services for another company that could also be or usually have been done in-house by the client firm.[8] Global outsourcing now accounts for hundreds of billions of dollars in annual revenues; and it is gaining

---

[4] "Engineering Good Health," http://www.dell.com/downloads/global/casestudies/231_2007_BostonMedical.pdf (February 2007).

[5] "About Us," http://corporate.americangreetings.com/aboutus.html (April 30, 2009).

[6] "About Booz Allen," http://www.boozallen.com/about (May 4, 2009).

[7] "Learn About StaplesLink," http://www.staplescontract.com/stapleslinktour/index.asp (May 4, 2009).

[8] "Outsourcing," http://www.searchcio.techtarget.com/sDefinition/0,,sid182_gci212731,00.html (June 5, 2007).

momentum as companies look to "farm out" to third parties some of the functions that they consider to be nonessential, as highlighted in Figure 9-2. The functions most likely to be outsourced include human resources, information technology, facilities and real-estate management, and accounting. Some firms "also outsource customer support and call center functions, customer service, marketing research, manufacturing, Web development, and engineering."[9] For more information, visit Outsourcing Center (**http://www.outsourcing-center.com**)—which has a video overview (**http://www.outsourcing-faq.com/1.html**)— Global Sources (**http://www.globalservicesmedia.com**); and International Association of Outsourcing Professionals (**http://www.outsourcingprofessional.org**).

In the next section, organizational consumers are distinguished from final consumers and a global perspective is provided. Various b-to-b consumers are described. Major factors in b-to-b consumer behavior are presented. The b-to-b consumer's decision process is outlined. Marketing implications are offered.

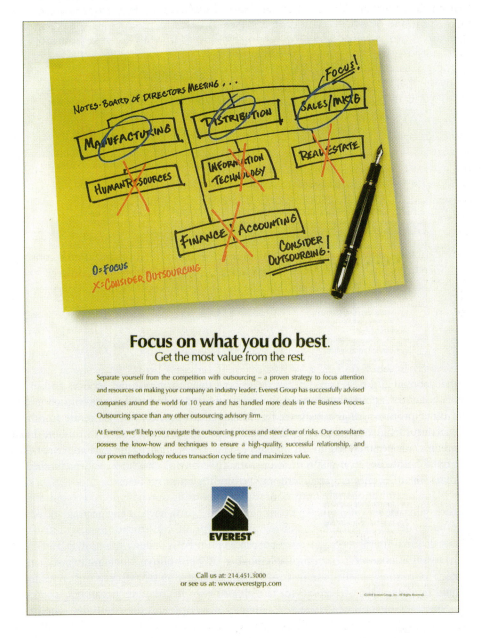

Figure 9-2

The Outsourcing Option for B-to-B Firms

Source: Reprinted by permission.

---

[9] "Outsourcing," **http://en.wikipedia.org/wiki/Outsourcing** (March 16, 2009).

Ethical Issues in Marketing

Nike's Green Sneakers: Air Jordan XX3

Although Nike's (http://www.nike.com) new Air Jordan XX3 sneakers do not have the color green anywhere on them, they are Nike's first truly green products. The sneakers are made with earth-friendly materials, non-toxic chemicals, and recycled materials. As the client (customer) for the materials used in the Air Jordan XX3, Nike worked very closely with many of its suppliers and subcontractors.

Nike's development team and its suppliers designed the Air Jordan XX3 as sneakers that would use a water-based bonding process in place of the toxic cements and glues that are often used by other firms. To further reduce the use of cements and glues, the Air Jordan XX3 uses outsole, midsole, and other components that fit together in a similar manner to pieces in a jigsaw puzzle. Many of these elements are stitched together. In addition, many of the components in the Air Jordan XX3 come from waste materials used in manufacturing outsoles and recycling used sneakers.

Somewhat surprising to some observers is that the Air Jordan XX3, priced at $230, is not really aimed at ecologically-minded consumers. Instead, it has been targeted at athletes, sports fans, and "sneaker heads" (collectors of limited-edition shoes), who are more attracted by the sneakers' performance attributes. To show how the new shoes will hold up, Nike signed Phoenix All-Star basketball guard Steve Nash, who introduced the shoe in a game against the Dallas Mavericks.

Nike's green products are in sharp contrast to a time 10 years ago when Nike's subcontractors were accused of using child labor to produce its sneakers, as well as forcing employees to work excessive hours to meet consumer demand.

Sources: Based on material in Nicholas Casey, "New Nike Sneaker Targets Jocks, Greens, Wall Street," *Wall Street Journal* (February 15, 2008), p. B1; and Reena Jana, "Quality Over Green: Nike's New Air Jordan," http://www.businessweek.com/innovate, *Business Week* (January 25, 2008).

9-2 THE CHARACTERISTICS OF ORGANIZATIONAL CONSUMERS

In undertaking industrial marketing, a firm must recognize that organizational consumers differ from final consumers in several ways. As shown in Table 9-1, differences are due to the nature of purchases and the nature of the market. A firm must also see that b-to-b consumer characteristics vary by nation.

9-2a Differences from Final Consumers Due to the Nature of Purchases

Organizational and final consumers vary in how they use goods and services and in the items bought. Organizations buy capital equipment, raw materials, semifinished goods, and other products for use in further production or operations or for resale to others. Final consumers usually buy finished items (and are not involved with million-dollar purchases) for personal, family, or household use. Thus, organizations are more apt than are final consumers to use specifications, multiple-buying decisions, value and vendor analysis, leased equipment, and competitive bidding and negotiation.

Many organizations rely on product specifications in purchase decisions and do not consider alternatives unless they meet minimum standards, such as engineering and architectural guidelines, purity, horsepower, voltage, type of construction, and construction materials. Final consumers more often purchase on the basis of description, style, and color.

Organizations often use **multiple-buying responsibility**, whereby two or more employees formally participate in complex or expensive purchase decisions. A decision to buy computerized cash registers may involve input from computer personnel, marketing personnel, the operations manager, a systems consultant, and the controller. The firm's president might make the final choice about system features and the supplier. Although final consumers use multiple-buying responsibility (joint decision making), they employ it less frequently and less formally.

Multiple-buying responsibility may be shared by two or more employees.

Table **9-1**	Major Differences Between Organizational and Final Consumers

Differences in Purchases

Organizations

1. Buy for further production, use in operations, or resale to others. Final consumers buy only for personal, family, or household use.
2. Commonly purchase installations, raw materials, and semifinished materials. Final consumers rarely purchase these goods.
3. Often buy on the basis of specifications and technical data. Final consumers frequently buy based on description, fashion, and style.
4. Utilize multiple-buying and team-based decisions more often than final consumers.
5. Are more apt to apply formal value and vendor analysis.
6. More commonly lease equipment.
7. More frequently employ competitive bidding and negotiation.

Differences in the Market

Organizations

1. Derive their demand from that of final consumers.
2. Have demand states that are more subject to cyclical fluctuations than final consumer demand.
3. Are fewer in number and more geographically concentrated than final consumers.
4. Often employ buying specialists.
5. Require a shorter distribution channel than do final consumers.
6. May require special relationships with sellers.
7. Are more likely than final consumers to be able to make goods and undertake services as alternatives to purchasing them.

Many entities use value analysis and vendor analysis. In *value analysis*, organizational consumers thoroughly compare the costs and benefits of alternative materials, components, designs, or processes so as to reduce the cost/benefit ratio of purchases. They seek to answer such questions as: What is the purpose of each good or service under consideration? What are the short-run and long-run costs of each alternative? Is a purchase necessary? Are there substitute goods or services that could be more efficient? How long will a good or service last before it must be replaced? Can uniform standards ease reordering? In *vendor analysis*, organizational consumers thoroughly assess the strengths and weaknesses of current or new suppliers in terms of quality, customer service, reliability, and price.[10] Satisfaction with current vendors often means customer loyalty. Figures 9-3 and 9-4 illustrate value analysis and vendor analysis.

Organizations of all sizes frequently lease major equipment. The Equipment Leasing and Finance Association (**http://www.elfaonline.org**) estimates that U.S. firms spend $300 billion each year in leasing equipment (measured by the original equipment cost). Commonly leased equipment includes aircraft, computers, office machinery, and trucks and trailers. The worldwide use of commercial leasing is rising rapidly. Final consumers are less involved with leasing; it is most common in apartment and auto leasing.

Organizations often use competitive bidding and negotiation. In *competitive bidding*, two or more sellers submit independent price quotes for specific goods and/or

> **Value analysis** reduces costs; **vendor analysis** rates suppliers.

> In **competitive bidding**, sellers submit price bids; in **negotiation**, buyers bargain to set prices.

---

[10] "Dictionary," **http://www.marketingpower.com/_layouts/Dictionary.aspx?dLetter=V** (March 22, 2009).

Figure 9-3

Value Analysis by a Purchaser of an Electric Pump

	Definitely Yes	Probably Yes	Uncertain	Probably No	Definitely No
• Can plastic pipe be substituted to reduce costs?	____	____	____	____	____
• Can a standardized 1/3-horsepower motor be used?	____	____	____	____	____
• Can an external float-triggered switch be used instead of an internal one?	____	____	____	____	____
• Can a noncorrosive base replace the current base that is easily corroded?	____	____	____	____	____
• Is a Westinghouse motor more reliable than a GE motor?	____	____	____	____	____
• Is a 5-year warranty acceptable?	____	____	____	____	____

services to a buyer, which chooses the best offer. In **negotiation**, a buyer uses bargaining ability and order size to get sellers' best possible prices. Bidding and negotiation most often apply to complex, custom-made goods and services.

9-2b Differences from Final Consumers Due to the Nature of the Market

Derived demand occurs for organizational consumers because the quantity of the items they purchase is often based on the anticipated level of demand by their subsequent customers for specific goods and services. For example, the demand for the precision rivets used in cruise ships is derived from the demand for new cruise ships, which ultimately is derived from the demand for cruises. Firms know that unless demand is generated at the end-user level, distribution pipelines become clogged and resellers will not buy fresh goods and services. Organizational consumers' price sensitivity depends on end-user demand. If end users are willing to pay higher prices, organizations will not object much to increases. If end-user demand is low, organizations will reduce purchases, even if prices to them are lowered. Figure 9-5 illustrates derived demand for major household appliances.

> Organizational consumers **derive demand** from their own customers. With the **accelerator principle**, final consumer demand impacts on many organizational consumers.

Figure 9-4

Vendor Analysis of a Sweater Supplier by a Purchaser

	Superior	Average	Inferior
• Speed of normal delivery	____	____	____
• Speed of rush delivery	____	____	____
• Distinctiveness of merchandise	____	____	____
• Availability of styles and colors in all sizes	____	____	____
• Handling of defective merchandise	____	____	____
• Percent of merchandise defective	____	____	____
• Ability for organizational consumer to make a profit when reselling merchandise	____	____	____
• Purchase terms	____	____	____

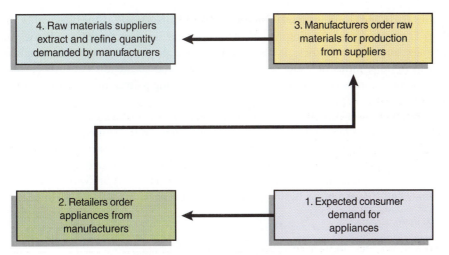

Figure 9-5

Derived Demand for Major Appliances

All intermediate levels of demand are derived
from final consumer demand.

The demand of organizations tends to be more volatile than that of final consumers. A small change in the final demand for highly processed goods and services can yield a large change in organizational consumers' demand. This is due to the *accelerator principle*, whereby final consumer demand affects many layers of organizational consumers. For example, a drop in auto demand by final consumers reduces dealer demand for cars, auto maker demand for steel, and steel maker demand for iron ore. In addition, capital purchases by organizations are highly influenced by the economy.

There are far fewer organizations than final consumers. In the United States, there are 340,000 manufacturing establishments, 440,000 wholesaling establishments (including manufacturer-owned facilities), and 3.1 million retailing establishments (including small family businesses), as compared with nearly 120 million final consumer households. In some industries, large organizations dominate, and their size and importance give them bargaining power in dealing with sellers. Organizations tend to be geographically concentrated. Eight states (California, New York, Texas, Ohio, Illinois, Pennsylvania, Michigan, and Florida) contain almost one-half of U.S. manufacturing plants. Some industries (such as steel, petroleum, rubber, auto, and tobacco) are even more geographically concentrated.

Due to their size and the types of purchases, many organizations use buying specialists. These people often have technical backgrounds and are trained in supplier analysis and negotiating. Their full-time jobs are to purchase goods and services and analyze purchases. Expertise is high.

Inasmuch as many organizations are large and geographically concentrated, purchase complex and custom-made goods and services, and use buying specialists, distribution channels tend to be shorter than for final consumers. For example, a laser-printer maker would deal directly with a firm buying 100 printers; a salesperson would call on its purchasing agent. A company marketing printers to final consumers would distribute them via stores and expect final consumers to purchase there.

Organizations may require special relationships. They may expect to be consulted as new products are devised; want extra services such as extended warranties, liberal returns, and free or inexpensive credit; and want close communications with vendors. That is why firms like Oracle (**http://www.oracle.com**), the information technology company, devote much attention to their sales force and customer relations.

Systems selling and reciprocity are two specific tactics used in b-to-b marketing. In *systems selling*, a combination of goods and services is provided to a buyer by one vendor. This gives a buyer one firm with which to negotiate and consistency among

> Organizational consumers tend to be large and geographically concentrated.

> **Systems selling** offers single-source accountability.

various parts and components. For example, Fluid Management (**http://www.fluidman. com**) is the worldwide leading maker of mixing and tinting equipment for the paint, coatings, and ink industries. It also markets specialized equipment and engineered systems to other industries, such as food, chemicals, and cosmetics. The firm's products increase the accuracy and efficiency of tinting and mixing paints, inks, and other fluids.[11] See Figure 9-6.

Reciprocity is a procedure by which organizational consumers select suppliers that agree to purchase goods and services, as well as sell them. In the United States, the Justice Department and the FTC monitor reciprocity due to its potential lessening of competition. However, in their international marketing efforts, sellers may sometimes be required to enter into reciprocal agreements—known as "countertrade." Worldwide, countertrade accounts for 15 percent of business transactions between countries; and hundreds of

In reciprocity, suppliers purchase, as well as sell.

Figure 9-6

Fluid Management's TintMaster: A Systems Approach

For retailers such as Ace Hardware, "When you're being flooded with large custom paint orders and need to get that long string of tint tasks completed quickly, Fluid Management's TintMaster system gets the job done right the first time, every time."

Source: Reprinted by permission.

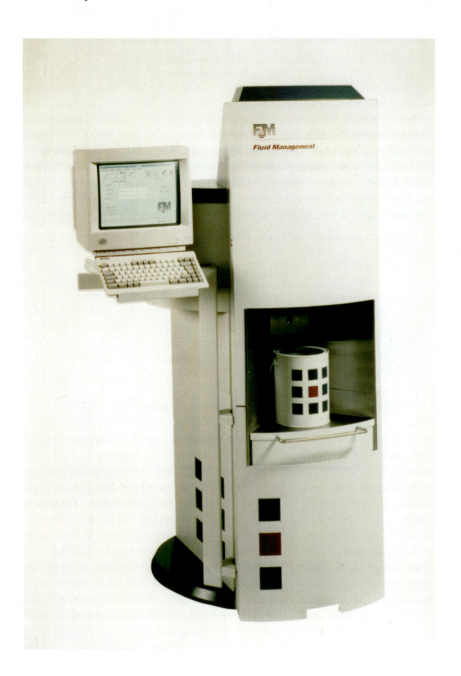

thousands of companies participate in it.[12] The Global Offset and Countertrade Association (http://www.globaloffset.org) promotes trade and commerce between companies and their foreign customers who engage in countertrade as a form of doing business.

Last, organizations may produce goods and services themselves if they find unacceptable the purchase terms, the way they are treated, or the available choices. They may sometimes suggest to suppliers that they will make their own goods or perform services so as to improve bargaining positions.

9-2c   A Global Perspective

As with final consumers, dissimilarities exist among organizational consumers around the world, and sellers must understand and respond to them. We discuss these topics here: attitudes to foreign firms as suppliers, the effects of culture on negotiating styles and decision making, the impact of economic development, the need for an adaptation strategy, and the opportunities available due to new technology.

> Foreign organizations must be carefully studied.

Firms that do business in foreign markets need to know how organizations there perceive the goods and services of firms from various countries. The attitudes of purchasing agents in foreign nations toward U.S. products are often quite positive for high-technology items, professional services, and industrial machinery. Likewise, many U.S. firms believe product quality and/or prices for some foreign goods and services are better than with American suppliers. That is why Ortho Biotech (http://www.orthobiotech.com), a Johnson & Johnson subsidiary, has bought water-purification equipment from Finland and Limited Brands (http://www.limited.com) buys clothing from Hong Kong, Taiwan, and other countries.

Nations' cultures have a large impact on the way their organizational consumers negotiate and reach decisions. Here is an illustration:

> *Doing Business in Argentina*: Argentines are tough negotiators. Concessions will not come quickly or easily. Good relationships with counterparts will shorten negotiations. A contract is not final until all elements are signed. Any portion can be re-negotiated. An Argentine contact is essential to wade through government bureaucracy. Be punctual, but prepare to wait 30 minutes for your counterpart, especially if you are meeting an important person. A meeting that is going well could last much longer than intended, even if it means postponing the next engagement. Personal relationships are necessary before doing business. Argentines often need several meetings to make deals. Decisions are made at the top. Try to meet with senior personnel. Guests at a meeting are greeted and escorted to their chairs. The visiting senior executive is seated opposite the Argentine senior executive. At meetings, sustain a relaxed manner, maintain eye contact, and restrict the use of gestures. Don't take a hard sell approach. Be prepared for some small talk before getting down to business.[13]

The stage of economic development in foreign countries affects the types of goods and services bought by organizations there. Many less-developed and developing nations may not yet have the infrastructure (electricity, roads, transportation systems, skilled workers) to properly use state-of-the-art machinery and equipment. In addition, such machinery and equipment may be too expensive for organizations in those markets to afford. On the other hand, there is substantial long-term growth potential in those nations due to their scarcity of industrial goods and services. Firms marketing to less-developed and developing nations need to be understanding and flexible in dealing with organizations.

Firms have to consider how much to adapt their strategies—and their goods and services—to address the unique characteristics and needs of organizations in foreign markets. Because large organizations can account for a significant part of any firm's overall revenues, sellers often will have to be responsive to the organizations' desires—by

---

[12] "2004 Global Reciprocal Trade Statistics," http://www.irta.com/Page.asp?Script=56 (September 28, 2005).

[13] "Argentina," http://www.cyborlink.com/besite/argentina.htm (July 31, 2008).

Figure 9-7

Types of Organizational Consumers

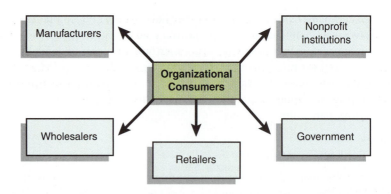

hiring personnel who fluently speak the language of the foreign markets, utilizing the most appropriate negotiating styles, and adapting product features and customer service as requested. In general, it is more likely that selling firms will engage in meaningful adaptation of their marketing efforts if a potential order is big, the good or service is complex, and the business cultures and stage of economic development in the domestic and foreign markets are dissimilar.

Due to the new technology now available, more opportunities are now available to market to foreign organizational consumers than ever before. The Internet, E-mail, satellite TV, and video conferencing all facilitate buyer-seller communications—and tear down the barriers caused by weak technological infrastructures, differences in time zones, and other factors.

9-3 TYPES OF ORGANIZATIONAL CONSUMERS

These attributes should be researched in devising a marketing plan aimed at organizations: areas of specialization, size and resources, location, and goods and services purchased. As shown in Figure 9-7, organizations can be placed into five broad major categories: manufacturers, wholesalers, retailers, government, and nonprofit.

Marketing and the Web

Grainger's Top-Notch B-to-B Web Site

W.W. Grainger (http://www.grainger.com) markets maintenance products such as motors and safety gear. The navigation system at its Web site originally was based on its business divisions. It replaced that system with one keyed to consumer behavior. The new design lets customers enter keywords organized by Grainger item number, manufacturer or brand, manufacturer model number, or cross reference numbers.

To maintain a successful b-to-b Web site, firms such as Grainger know they must keep this in mind:

- Pay special attention to content. Customers want to know a product's features, pricing, availability, and customer reviews.
- Make sure the Web pages are search-engine friendly. In many instances, sites that contain a lot of Adobe Flash animation get blocked by search engines.

- Organize the site's search engine using terminology used by consumers. Also consider using key word advertising used by Google, Yahoo!, and other mega search engines.
- Use trusted sources of E-mail lists of potential customers. Make sure these names are opt-in so that consumers on the list are really interested in your goods and services.
- Consider purchasing banner ads on Web sites that are used by the targeted audience.
- Use Web analytics to determine where users have come from, what is driving Web traffic, and what's generating sales volume. This can generally be implemented through simple software.

Sources: Based on material in Sean Carton, "Web Sites: Ask the Experts," *B to B* (April 3, 2007), p. 10; and Sharon Rutberg, "How Do We Reach Our Target Market," http://money.cnn.com/2008/01/24/smbusiness/target_customers.fsb (January 25, 2008).

The *North American Industry Classification System*, also known as *NAICS* (**http://www.census.gov/epcd/www/naics.html**), may be used to derive information about most organizational consumers. The NAICS, which has replaced the outdated Standard Industrial Classification (SIC), was introduced a decade ago. The NAICS is the official classification system for the United States, Canada, and Mexico (the members of NAFTA). It assigns organizations to 20 industrial classifications:

> The **North American Industry Classification System (NAICS)** provides information on U.S., Canadian, and Mexican organizations.

- Agriculture, forestry, fishing, and hunting
- Mining
- Utilities
- Construction
- Manufacturing
- Wholesale trade
- Retail trade
- Transportation and warehousing
- Information
- Finance and insurance
- Real-estate and rental and leasing
- Professional, scientific, and technical services
- Management of companies and enterprises
- Administrative and support and waste management and remediation services
- Educational services
- Health care and social assistance
- Arts, entertainment, and recreation
- Accommodation and food services
- Other services (except public administration)
- Public administration

Within these groups, 1,175 more specific industry classifications exist, such as farm machinery and equipment manufacturing.

U.S. data by industry code are available from various government and commercial publications. The *U.S. Industry & Trade Outlook* (**http://www.ita.doc.gov/td/industry/otea/outlook**) and the *Manufacturing, Mining, and Construction Statistics* (**http://www.census.gov/mcd**) are U.S. government reports with data on hundreds of industries. *Standard & Poor's Industry Surveys* (**http://www.standardandpoors.com**) and *D&B Reference Book of American Business* (**http://www.dnb.com**) also provide data by industry code and/or geographic area. Data on government institutions are available on local, state, and federal levels from the *Census of Governments* (**http://www.census.gov/govs/www**).

Although the NAICS is a North American classification system, considerable data on industrial activity and firms in other nations are available in the context of industry codes. The U.S. Department of Commerce's *U.S. Foreign Trade Highlights* (**http://www.ita.doc.gov/td/industry/otea/usfth**) has information on numerous international industries. Dun & Bradstreet's *Selectory International Data Base* service (**http://selectory.com/Selectory/ExternalPages/InternationalData.aspx**) lists more than 8 million firms in more than 200 countries.

End-use analysis is one way in which NAICS data can be employed. With it, a seller determines the proportion of sales made to organizational consumers in different industries.[14] Table 9-2 shows end-use analysis for a glue manufacturer (in this case, the seller). First, the firm learns the current relative importance of various categories of customers (section A of Table 9-2). It then applies end-use analysis to make an overall sales forecast by estimating the expected growth of each customer category in its area (section B of Table 9-2).

> With **end-use analysis**, a seller studies sales made in different industries.

---

[14] For a more in-depth discussion, see "End User Analysis," **http://www.biessentials.com/top10/EndUserAnalysis.html**. Be sure to click on the interactive charts.

Table 9-2 | End-Use Analysis for a Regional Glue Manufacturer

(A) Simple End-Use Analysis

NAICS Code	Industry Classification of Customers	Current Total Sales (in Percent)[a]
321	Wood product manufacturing	25
337	Furniture and related product manufacturing	20
323	Printing and related support activities	17
326	Plastics and rubber products manufacturing	15
316	Leather and allied product manufacturing	10
339	Miscellaneous manufacturing	13
	Total	100

(B) Applying End-Use Analysis to Sales Forecasting

NAICS Code	Industry Classification of Customers	Current Total Sales (in Percent)	Estimated Annual Percentage Growth Rate of Industry[b]	Overall Sales Growth Percentage for a Glue Manufacturer[c]
321	Wood product manufacturing	25	+1.8	+0.45
337	Furniture and related product manufacturing	20	+3.2	+0.64
323	Printing and related support activities	17	+1.9	+0.32
326	Plastics and rubber products manufacturing	15	+3.0	+0.45
316	Leather and allied product manufacturing	10	−2.0	−0.20
339	Miscellaneous manufacturing	13	+2.0	+0.26
	Total estimated sales increase			+1.92

[a] Firm examines its sales receipts and categorizes them by NAICS group.
[b] Firm estimates growth rate of each category of customer (in its geographic area) on the basis of trade association and government data.
[c] Firm multiplies percent of current sales in each NAICS group by expected growth rate in each industry to derive its expected sales for the coming year. It expects sales to rise by 1.92 percent during the next year.

Next, several characteristics of manufacturers, wholesalers, retailers, government, and nonprofit organizations as consumers are described.

9-3a   Manufacturers as Consumers

Manufacturers produce products for resale to other consumers. The NAICS lists three 2-digit industry groups in manufacturing. Each may be divided into 3-digit groups, 4-digit groups, 5-digit groups, and 6-digit groups. Thus, NAICS 33 is a manufacturing classification; 333 refers to machinery manufacturing; 3331 refers to agricultural, construction, and mining machinery manufacturing; 33311 refers to agricultural implement manufacturing; and 333111 refers to farm machinery and equipment manufacturing. Table 9-3 shows the 21 3-digit groups.

In the United States, 40 percent of manufacturers have 20 or more workers. The annual costs of their materials are $2.5 trillion. Their capital expenditures for plant and equipment (from trucks to generator sets) are $200 billion each year. They annually use trillions of BTUs of energy. The annual value of manufacturing shipments (including shipments between firms in the same industry category) exceeds $5 trillion, with the largest 500 industrial firms accounting for the majority of this amount.

By knowing where different industries are located, a seller can concentrate efforts and not worry about dispersed markets. Because manufacturers' purchasing decisions

Manufacturers make items for resale to others.

Table 9-3	U.S. Manufacturing Industries
NAICS Code	**Industry Name**
31, 32, 33	Manufacturing
311	Food manufacturing
312	Beverage and tobacco product manufacturing
313	Textile mills
314	Textile product mills
315	Apparel manufacturing
316	Leather and allied product manufacturing
321	Wood product manufacturing
322	Paper manufacturing
323	Printing and related support activities
324	Petroleum and coal products manufacturing
325	Chemical manufacturing
326	Plastics and rubber products manufacturing
327	Nonmetallic mineral product manufacturing
331	Primary metal manufacturing
332	Fabricated metal product manufacturing
333	Machinery manufacturing
334	Computer and electronic product manufacturing
335	Electrical equipment, appliance, and component manufacturing
336	Transportation equipment manufacturing
337	Furniture and related product manufacturing
339	Miscellaneous manufacturing

Source: "2007 NAICS Codes and Titles," http://www.census.gov/epcd/naics07/naics07.xls.

tend to be made centrally at headquarters or at divisional offices, the seller must identify the location of the proper decision makers.

As consumers, manufacturers buy a variety of goods and services, including land, capital equipment, machinery, raw materials, component parts, trade publications, accounting services, supplies, insurance, advertising, and delivery services. For example, Boeing (http://www.boeing.com) has long- and short-term contracts with suppliers that total several billion dollars; and it buys equipment, raw materials, component parts, finished materials, and services from thousands of subcontractors and other businesses.

9-3b Wholesalers as Consumers

> **Wholesalers** buy or handle merchandise and its resale to nonfinal consumers.

Wholesalers buy or handle merchandise and its subsequent resale to organizational users, retailers, and other wholesalers. They do not sell significant volume to final users but are involved when services are marketed to organizations. Table 9-4 lists the major industry groups in wholesaling, as well as transportation industries and business services. Chapter 16 has a broad discussion of wholesaling.

U.S. wholesalers are most prominent in California, New York, Texas, Florida, Illinois, New Jersey, Pennsylvania, and Ohio. Annual wholesaling and related sales (excluding manufacturer wholesaling) are $5 trillion. Sales are largest for groceries and related products; petroleum products; drugs and related products; professional and commercial equipment and supplies; machinery, equipment, and supplies; motor vehicles and related parts and supplies; electrical goods; lumber and other construction materials; and farm-product raw materials.

As consumers, wholesalers buy or handle many goods and services, including warehouse facilities, trucks, finished products, insurance, refrigeration and other equipment, trade publications, accounting services, supplies, and spare parts. A major task in dealing with wholesalers is getting them to carry the selling firm's product line for further resale, thereby placing items into the distribution system. For new sellers or those with new

Table 9-4	U.S. Wholesaling and Related Industries
NAICS Code	**Industry Name**
42	Wholesale trade
423	Merchant wholesalers, durable goods
424	Merchant wholesalers, nondurable goods
425	Wholesale electronic markets and agents and brokers
48, 49	Transportation and warehousing
481	Air transportation
482	Rail transportation
483	Water transportation
484	Truck transportation
486	Pipeline transportation
488	Support activities for transportation
491	Postal service
492	Couriers and messengers
493	Warehousing and storage
54	Professional, scientific, and technical services
541	Professional, scientific, and technical services

Source: "2007 NAICS Codes and Titles," http://www.census.gov/epcd/naics07/naics07.xls.

products, gaining cooperation may be difficult. Even well-established manufacturers may have problems with their wholesalers due to the competitive marketplace, wholesalers' perceptions that they are not being serviced properly, or wholesalers' lack of faith in the manufacturers' products.

9-3c Retailers as Consumers

Retailers buy or handle goods and services for sale (resale) to the final (ultimate) consumer. They usually obtain goods and services from both manufacturers and wholesalers. Table 9-5 lists the major industry groups in retailing, as well as several related service businesses that cater to final consumers. Chapter 17 has a broad discussion of retailing.

Retailers sell to the final consumer.

Table 9-5	U.S. Retailing and Retailed Industries
NAICS Code	**Industry Name**
44, 45	Retail trade
441	Motor vehicle and parts dealers
442	Furniture and home furnishings stores
443	Electronics and appliance stores
444	Building materials and garden equipment and supplies dealers
445	Food and beverage stores
446	Health and personal care stores
447	Gasoline stations
448	Clothing and clothing accessories stores
451	Sporting good, hobby, book, and music stores
452	General merchandise store
453	Miscellaneous store retailers
454	Nonstore retailers
52	Finance and insurance
522	Credit intermediation and related activities
523	Securities, commodity contracts, and other financial investments and related activities
524	Insurance carriers and related activities
53	Real-estate and rental and leasing
531	Real-estate
532	Rental and leasing services
71	Arts, entertainment, and recreation
711	Performing arts, spectator sports, and related industries
712	Museums, historical sites, and similar institutions
713	Amusements, gambling, and recreational industries
72	Accommodation and food services
721	Accommodations
722	Food services and drinking places
81	Other services, except public administration
811	Repair and maintenance
812	Personal and laundry services

Source: "2007 NAICS Codes and Titles," **http://www.census.gov/epcd/naics07/naics07.xls**.

Annual U.S. retail sales (both store and nonstore) for firms in NAICS codes 44, 45, and 722 exceed $5 trillion. Chains account for around two-thirds of total retail sales. About 800,000 retail stores are operated by franchisees. A large amount of retailing involves auto dealers, general merchandise stores, food and beverage stores, eating and drinking places, gas stations, apparel stores, health and personal care stores, and furniture and home furnishings stores.

As consumers, retailers buy or handle a variety of goods and services, including store locations, facilities, interior design, advertising, resale items, insurance, and trucks. Unlike wholesalers, they are usually concerned about both product resale and the composition of their physical facilities (stores)—because final consumers usually shop at stores, whereas wholesalers frequently call on customers. Retailers often buy fixtures, displays, and services to decorate and redecorate stores.

Getting retailers to stock new items or continue handling current ones can be difficult because store and catalog space is limited and retailers have their own goals. Many retail chains have evolved into large and powerful customers, not just "shelf stockers." Some are so powerful that they may even charge *slotting fees* just to carry manufacturers' products in their stores:

> Slotting fees—upfront fees to get items on shelves and ongoing fees to stay in stores—have become common since they were instituted in supermarkets in the 1980s to cover marketing and other costs. They have spread to more products, from greeting cards to over-the-counter drugs. Small firms argue that steep payments for shelf placement, mostly hidden from public view, make it hard to compete with larger companies. The FTC estimates that retailers collect $9 billion in the fees annually.[15]

Retailers (wholesalers) sometimes insist that suppliers make items under the retailers' (wholesalers') names. For private-label manufacturers, the continued orders of these customers are essential. If a large retailer (wholesaler) stops doing business with a private-label manufacturer, that firm has to establish its own identity with consumers. It may even go out of business due to the lack of recognition.

9-3d Government as Consumer

Government consumes goods and services in performing its duties and responsibilities. Federal (1), state (50), and local (88,000) units together account for the greatest volume of purchases of any consumer group in the United States—with all branches spending $3 trillion (excluding employee wages) on goods and services each year. The federal government accounts for 40 percent of that spending. The biggest budget shares (including employee wages) go for operations, capital outlays, military services, postal services, education, highways, public welfare, health care, police, fire protection, sanitation, and natural resources. Data on all levels of U.S. government expenditures are compiled by the Census Bureau (**http://www.census.gov/govs/www**). Table 9-6 shows the major NAICS codes for government.

> **Government** purchases and uses a variety of routine and complex products.

Governmental consumers buy a wide mix of goods and services, including food, military equipment, office buildings, subway cars, office supplies, clothing, and vehicles. Some purchases involve standard products offered to traditional consumers; others, such as highways, are specially made. Although many big firms—such as Boeing (**http://www.boeing.com**) and Lockheed Martin (**http://www.lockheed.com**) derive major percentages of their sales from government contracts, small sellers now account for several billion dollars in federal purchases. In fact, one-quarter of federal agency purchase contracts are with small firms.

Some small sellers are unaccustomed to the bureaucracy, barriers, political sensitivities, and financial constraints of dealing with government consumers. To aid them, the

---

[15] Rachel Brown, "Pay-to-Shelve Grocery Store Practices Called Too Pricey," *Los Angeles Business Journal Online* (April 11, 2005).

| Table **9-6** | U.S. Federal, State, and Local Government (Public Administration) |

NAICS Code	Industry Name
92	Public administration
921	Executive, legislative, and other general government support
922	Justice, public order, and safety activities
923	Administration of human resource programs
924	Administration of environmental quality programs
925	Administration of housing programs, urban planning, and community development
926	Administration of economic programs
927	Space research and technology
928	National security and international affairs

Source: "2007 NAICS Codes and Titles," http://www.census.gov/epcd/naics07/naics07.xls.

federal General Services Administration operates regional Small Business Utilization Centers (http://www.gsa.gov/smallbusiness) to issue directories, reference data, and technical reports on contracts and contracting procedures, bidding documents, and specifications.

9-3e Nonprofit Institutions as Consumers

Nonprofit institutions act in the public interest or to foster a cause and do not seek financial profits. Public hospitals, museums, most universities, civic organizations, and parks are nonprofit institutions. They buy goods and services in order to run their organizations and also buy items for resale to generate additional revenues to offset costs. There are many national and international nonprofit institutions, such as the American Cancer Society (http://www.cancer.org), the Boy Scouts (http://www.scouting.org) and Girl Scouts (http://www.girlscouts.org), and the International Committee of the Red Cross (http://www.icrc.org/eng). Hospitals, museums, and universities, due to fixed locations, tend to be local nonprofit institutions.

No separate NAICS codes exist for nonprofit- versus profit-oriented firms. Yet, firms in these NAICS categories are often nonprofit: 61 (educational services); 62 (health care and social assistance); 712 (museums, historical sites, and similar institutions); and 813 (religious, grant-making, civic, professional, and similar organizations).

> **Nonprofit institutions** function in the public interest.

9-4 KEY FACTORS IN ORGANIZATIONAL CONSUMER BEHAVIOR

Organizations' purchase behavior depends on their buying objectives, buying structure, and purchase constraints.

9-4a Buying Objectives

Organizations have several distinct goals in purchasing goods and services. Generally, these objectives are important: availability of items, reliability of sellers, consistency of quality, delivery, price, and customer service. See Figure 9-8.

Availability means a buyer can obtain items as needed. An organization's production or resales may be inhibited if products are unavailable at the proper times. *Seller*

> Organizational buying objectives relate to availability, reliability, consistency, delivery, price, and service.

Figure 9-8
Goals of Organizational
Consumers

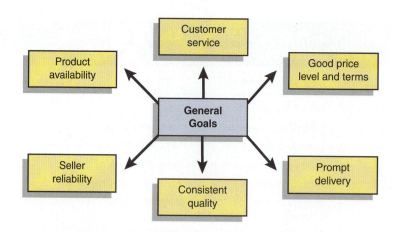

reliability is based on the fairness in allotting items in high demand, nonadversarial relationships, honesty in reporting bills and shipping orders, and reputation. *Consistency of quality* refers to buyers' interest in purchasing items of proper quality on a regular basis. Thus, drill bits should have the same hardness each time they are bought. *Delivery goals* include minimizing the time from ordering to receiving items, minimizing the order size required by the supplier, having the seller responsible for shipments, minimizing costs, and adhering to an agreed-on schedule. *Price considerations* involve purchase prices and the flexibility of payment terms. *Customer service* entails the seller's satisfying special requests, having a staff ready to field questions, promptly solving problems, and having a good relationship. For example, Hewlett-Packard works with small and medium businesses (**http://www.hp.com/sbso**), large businesses (**http://www.hp.com/go/enterprise**), and government, education, and health customers (**http://government.hp.com/index.asp**). See Figure 9-9.

B-to-b marketers must recognize that price is only one of several considerations for organizations. It may be lower in importance than availability, quality, service, and other factors. Consider this: "Everyone thinks you have to offer the lowest prices, but that simply isn't the case. Governments are getting more sophisticated about specifying bids for the lowest total cost of ownership through the product's life cycle, so such things as maintenance and repair costs are major factors."[16]

With regard to more specific goals, manufacturers are concerned about quality standards for raw materials, component parts, and equipment. Some like dealing with many suppliers to protect against shortages, foster price and service competition, and be exposed to new products. Others have been reducing the number of suppliers from which they buy to foster better relationships, cut ordering inefficiencies, and have more clout with each supplier.

Wholesalers and retailers consider further saleability (their customers' demand) to be the highest priority. If possible, they seek buying arrangements whereby the number of distribution intermediaries that can carry goods and services in a geographic area is limited. They also seek manufacturers' advertising, transportation, and warehousing support.

Government buyers frequently set exact specifications for some products they purchase; as large-volume buyers, they can secure them. Governments may consider the economic conditions in the geographic areas of potential sellers. Contracts may sometimes be awarded to the firms with the higher unemployment in their surrounding communities.

Nonprofits stress price, availability, and reliability. They may seek special terms in recognition of their nonprofit status.

> Saleability and exclusivity are keys for wholesalers and retailers.

---

[16] Roger Slavens, "How to Market to Government," **http://www.btobonline.com/article.cms?articleId=24152** (May 2, 2005).

If you're not at capacity, don't pay for capacity.

With the new hp superdome, you can pay less when you use less, or buy more when you need more. By adjusting capacity with a simple phone call, you pay only for what you use—not unlike how you pay for electricity. You can run IA-64, you can run multiple operating systems, and because comprehensive service is included, you can run your business instead of your server. hp.com/superdome

hp invent

©2000 Hewlett-Packard Company

Figure 9-9

Hewlett-Packard: Striving to Meet Buyers' Objectives

HP really tries to work with its business and government accounts. As this ad for an always-on, high-end computer server states, "You can pay less when you use less, or buy more when you need more. By adjusting capacity with a simple phone call, you pay only for what you use."

Source: Reprinted by permission.

9-4b   Buying Structure

The buying structure refers to the formality and specialization used in the purchase process. It depends on the organization's size, resources, diversity, and format. The structure is apt to be formal (separate department) for a large, corporate, resourceful, diversified, and departmentalized organization. It will be less formal for a small, independently owned, financially limited, focused, and general organization.

> The organization's buying structure depends on its attributes.

Large manufacturers normally have specialized purchasing agents who work with the firms' engineers or production department. Large wholesalers tend to have a purchasing department or a general manager in charge of operations. Large retailers tend to be quite specialized and have buyers for each narrow product category. Small manufacturers, wholesalers, and retailers often have their buying functions completed by the owner-operator.

Each government unit (federal, state, and local) typically has a purchasing department. The General Services Administration, known as the GSA (**http://www.gsa.gov**), is the federal office responsible for centralized procurement and coordination of purchases. Each federal unit may buy via the GSA's Federal Acquisition Service or directly from suppliers; either way, it must adhere to printed rules. In a nonprofit organization, there is often one purchasing department, or a member of the operations staff performs buying functions.

9-4c Constraints on Purchases

> Derived demand is the key constraint on organizational purchases.

For manufacturers, wholesalers, and retailers, derived demand is the major constraint on purchase behavior. Without the demand of consumers, production halts and sales drop as the backward chain of demand comes into play (final consumers→retailers→wholesalers→manufacturers).

Manufacturers also are constrained by the availability of raw materials and their ability to pay for big-ticket items. Wholesalers and retailers are limited by the funds available to make purchases, as well as by the level of risk they are willing to take. In this case, risk refers to the probability that wholesalers or retailers can sell the products they buy in a reasonable time and at a satisfactory profit. Products such as fashion apparel have higher risks than such staple items as vitamins and disposable diapers.

Government buyers are constrained by the budgeting process. Approval for categories of purchases must normally be secured well in advance, and deviations must be explained. Budgets must be certified by legislative bodies. For many nonprofit consumers, cash flow (the timing of the money they have coming in versus the money they spend) is the major concern.

9-5 THE ORGANIZATIONAL CONSUMER'S DECISION PROCESS

> An **organizational consumer's decision process** is like that of a final consumer.

Organizations use a decision-making procedure in much the same way as final consumers. Figure 9-10 shows the **organizational consumer's decision process**, with its four components: expectations, buying process, conflict resolution, and situational factors.[17]

Figure 9-10

The Organizational Consumer's Decision Process

Source: Adapted from Jagdish N. Sheth, "A Model of Industrial Buyer Behavior," *Journal of Marketing*, Vol. 37 (October 1973), p. 51. Reprinted by permission of the American Marketing Association.

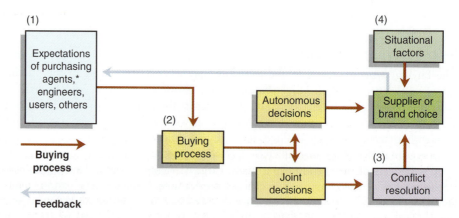

*In retailing, the term "buyer" is utilized.

---

[17] The material in this section is drawn from Jagdish N. Sheth, "A Model of Industrial Buyer Behavior," *Journal of Marketing*, Vol. 37 (October 1973), pp. 50–56. See also Leonidas C. Leonidou, Dayananda Palihawadana, and Marios Theodosiou, "An Integrated Model of the Behavioral Dimensions of Industrial Buyer-Seller Relationships," *European Journal of Marketing*, Vol. 40 (Number 1-2, 2006), pp. 145–173; and Tao M. Gao, M. Joseph Sirgy, and Monroe M. Bird, "Reducing Buyer Decision-Making Uncertainty in Organizational Purchasing: Can Supplier Trust, Commitment, and Dependence Help?" *Journal of Business Research*, Vol. 58 (April 2005), pp. 397–405.

9-5a Expectations

Purchasing agents, engineers, and users bring a set of organizational expectations to any buying situation: "These expectations refer to the perceived potential of alternative suppliers and brands to satisfy a number of explicit and implicit objectives."[18]

For purchases to occur, buyers must have positive expectations on such supplier attributes as product availability and quality, vendor reliability, delivery time, price, and customer service. Expectations are based on the backgrounds of those participating in the buying process, the information received, perceptions, and satisfaction with past purchases.

> Expectations are based on buyers' backgrounds, information, perceptions, and experience.

9-5b Buying Process

In the buying process, a decision as to whether to consider making a purchase is initiated, information gathered, alternative suppliers rated, and conflicts among different buyer representatives resolved. The process is similar to the final consumer buying process. Because of the Internet, information gathering—at sites such as Grainger.com (http://www.grainger.com) and ThomasNet (http://www.thomasnet.com)—has been simplified for many buyers.

The buying process may involve autonomous (independent) or joint decisions based on product and company factors. *Product-specific buying factors* include perceived risk, purchase frequency, and time pressure. Autonomous decisions occur mostly with low perceived risk, routine products, and high time pressure. Joint ones are more likely with high perceived risk, seldom-bought products, and low time pressure. *Company-specific buying factors* are a firm's basic orientation, size, and level of decision-making centralization. Autonomous decisions most often occur with a high technology or production orientation, small organization, and high centralization. Joint decisions are more likely with a low technology or production orientation, large organization, and little centralization in decision making.

> Autonomous or joint decision making is based on product and company buying factors.

Global Marketing in Action

Specialty Malls for Wholesale Buyers

International Home Deco Park (IHDP) (http://www.indp-india.com) is a 350,000-square-foot business-to-business mall located near Delhi, India. IHDP serves as a center where organizational buyers can visit with permanent exhibitors throughout the year. IHDP hosts the sales offices, as well as permanent showrooms, of prominent manufacturers of floor coverings, textiles, gifts and handicrafts, and furniture and fittings. It also houses office space for buying houses and retailers. Integral to IHDP's strategy is the space devoted to providers of such support services as a designers' library, a graphic design and online marketing agency, an in-house photo studio, and a service center for packaging, labeling, testing, inspecting, and shipping goods.

A similar Indian b-to-b mall is Ishanya (http://www.ishanya.com), a specialty mall that focuses on interior and exterior products for home and office builders and for architects. Ishanya sells such products as furniture, kitchen goods, bathroom accessories, and flooring. The mall also devotes space to specialists in illumination services; landscaping design; heating, ventilating, and air-conditioning (HVAC); and real-estate consulting. In addition to traditional space, there are meeting rooms for seminars and conferences, and a 500-seat amphitheater. At night, the amphitheater is used for corporate events and cultural events.

These b-to-b malls are differentiated from traditional trade shows, which use facilities on a temporary basis and do not have adequate space for many samples. However, the b-to-b malls are similar to typical shopping centers for final consumers: They provide industrial buyers with one-stop shopping and the ability to easily compare offerings.

Sources: Based on material in http://www.ihdp-india.com (January 9, 2009); and http://www.ishanya.com (January 9, 2009).

---

[18] Sheth, "A Model of Industrial Buyer Behavior," p. 52.

As noted earlier, competitive bidding is often used by organizational buyers: Potential sellers specify in writing all terms of a purchase in addition to product attributes; the buyer then selects the best bid. With *open bidding*, proposals can be seen by competing sellers. With *closed bidding*, contract terms are kept secret, and sellers are asked to make their best presentation in their first bids. Bidding is used in government purchases to avoid charges of unfair negotiations, and government bids tend to be closed.

9-5c   Conflict Resolution

Joint decision making may lead to conflicts due to the diverse backgrounds and perspectives of purchasing agents, engineers, and users. **Conflict resolution** is then needed to make a decision. Four methods of resolution are possible: problem solving, persuasion, bargaining, and politicking.

Problem solving occurs if purchasing team members decide to acquire further information before making a decision. This is the best procedure. *Persuasion* takes place when each team member presents reasons why a given supplier or brand should be picked. In theory, the most logical presentation should be chosen. Yet, the most dynamic (or powerful) person may persuade others to follow his or her lead.

With *bargaining*, team members agree to support each other in different situations, with less attention paid to the merits of a purchase. One member may select the supplier of the current item; in return, another member would choose a vendor the next time. The last, and least desired, method of conflict resolution is *politicking*. In this method, team members try to persuade outside parties and superiors to back their positions, and seek to win at power plays.

> Problem solving, persuasion, bargaining, and politicking lead to **conflict resolution**.

9-5d   Situational Factors

A number of **situational factors** can interrupt the decision process and the actual selection of a supplier or brand. These include "temporary economic conditions such as price controls, recession, or foreign trade; internal strikes, walkouts, machine breakdowns, and other production-related events; organizational changes such as merger or acquisition; and ad hoc changes in the marketplace, such as promotional efforts, new-product introduction, price changes, and so on, in the supplier industries."[19]

> **Situational factors** affect organizational consumer decisions.

9-5e   Purchase and Feedback

After the decision process is completed and situational factors are taken into account, a purchase is made (or the process terminated) and a product is used or experienced. The level of satisfaction with a purchase is then fed back to a purchasing agent or team, and the data are stored for future use.

To keep customers satisfied and ensure continued purchases, regular service and follow-up calls by sellers are essential:

> A beer salesperson became very busy and stopped calling on a small retail chain. The operator called him; the rep said he'd been swamped, but would get to the retailer as soon as he could. Another month passed. Frustrated, the retailer bought a bereavement card, scribbled a message on it, and sent it to the salesperson's boss. The card read: "I know Pat must have either passed away or is in a coma, or he certainly wouldn't have neglected me for so long." The boss was not amused. He called the retailer and said he didn't appreciate the sarcasm. In response, the retailer faxed a copy of a recent letter naming a competitor the chain's "Top Sales Professional" in the beer category. Within minutes, the boss called the retailer back and said, "I can't quarrel with a person who sees both sides of the matter!" The next year, the once-neglectful beer salesperson received the chain's recognition.[20]

---

[19] Ibid., p. 56.

[20] Barbara Grondin Francella, "The Ties That Bind," *Convenience Store News* (May 5, 2003), p. 31.

9-5f Types of Purchases

A *new-task purchase process* is needed for expensive products an organizational consumer has not bought before. A lot of decision making is undertaken, and perceived risk is high. This is similar to extended decision making for a final consumer. A *modified-rebuy purchase process* is employed for medium-priced products an organizational consumer has bought infrequently before. Moderate decision making is needed. This is similar to limited decision making for a final consumer. A *straight-rebuy purchase process* is used for inexpensive items bought regularly. Reordering, not decision making, is applied because perceived risk is very low. This is similar to a routine purchase for a final consumer.

> Organizational buyers use a **new-task process** for unique items, **modified rebuys** for infrequent purchases, and **straight rebuys** for regular purchases.

9-6 MARKETING IMPLICATIONS

Although organizations and final consumers have substantial differences in their purchasing behavior (as mentioned earlier), they also have similarities:

- Both can be described demographically; statistical and descriptive data can be gathered and analyzed.
- Both have different categories of buyers, each with separate needs and requirements.
- Both can be defined by using social and psychological factors, such as operating style, buying structure, purchase use, expectations, perceived risk, and conflict resolution.
- Both use a decision process, employ joint decision making, and face various kinds of purchase situations.

> Similarities, as well as differences, exist between organizational and final consumers.

This means that b-to-b marketers must have plans reflecting the similarities, as well as the differences, between organizations and final consumers. In their roles as sellers, manufacturers and wholesalers may also need two marketing plans: one for intermediate buyers and one for final consumers.

Finally, it must be recognized that purchasing agents or buyers have personal goals, as well as organizational goals. They seek status, approval, promotions, bonuses, and other rewards. And as shown in Figure 9-10, they bring distinct expectations to each buying situation, just as final consumers do.

> Industrial marketing strategies should be insightful.

One leading consultant offers these suggestions for b-to-b marketers:

- *Understand how your customers run their business.*
- *Show how your good or service fits into your customer's business.*
- *Make sure the benefits you sell stay current.*
- *Know how customers buy, and fit your selling to their buying process.*
- *When selling, reach everyone on the customer's side involved in the buying decision.*
- *Communicate to each decider the message that will address his or her chief concerns.*
- *Be the person or firm with whom your customers prefer to have a relationship.*
- *Be sure everything is consistent with your chosen level of quality, service, price, and performance.*
- *Understand your competitors' strengths and weaknesses.*
- *Strive to dominate your niche.*
- *Train your people in each aspect of your business and that of your customers.*
- *Have a distribution system that meets your needs and those of your customers.*
- *Seek new markets and new applications for your existing products.*
- *Enhance your products with customer service.*
- *Have your goals clearly in mind.*[21]

[21] F. Michael Hruby, "17 Tips (Not Just) for Industrial Marketers," *Sales & Marketing Management* (May 1990), pp. 68–76.

Web Sites You Can Use

Many Web sites are devoted exclusively to industrial marketing. One of the best such sites is *BtoBonline.com* (**http://www. btobonline.com**), "The Magazine for Marketing Strategists." It covers a wide range of topics and has many special sections.

Visit the site and look at the left toolbar. Both the "Features" and "Resources" sections of the toolbar have a lot of useful information, such as "10 Great Web Sites," "Marketers' Resource Guide," and "White Papers."

Summary

1. *To introduce the concept of industrial (b-to-b) marketing* When firms market goods and services to manufacturers, wholesalers, retailers, and government and other nonprofit institutions, industrial (b-to-b) marketing is used.

2. *To differentiate between organizational consumers and final consumers and look at organizational consumers from a global perspective* Organizations buy goods and services for further production, use in operations, or resale to others; they buy installations, raw materials, and semifinished materials. They often buy based on specifications, use joint decision making, apply formal value and vendor analysis, lease equipment, and use bidding and negotiation. Their demand is generally derived from that of their consumers and can be cyclical. They are fewer in number and more geographically concentrated. They may employ buying specialists, expect sellers to visit them, require special relationships, and make goods and undertake services rather than buy them.

   There are distinctions among organizational consumers around the globe.

3. *To describe the different types of organizational consumers and their buying objectives, buying structure, and purchase constraints* Organizations may be classified by area of specialization, size and resources, location, and goods and services purchased. Major organizations are manufacturers, wholesalers, retailers, government, and nonprofits. The North American Industry Classification System (NAICS) provides much data on organizations in the United States, Canada, and Mexico.

   B-to-b consumers have general buying goals, such as product availability, seller reliability, consistent quality, prompt delivery, good prices, and superior customer service. They also have more specific goals, depending on the type of firm involved. An organization's buying structure refers to

its level of formality and specialization in the purchase process. Derived demand, availability, further saleability, and resources are the leading purchase constraints.

4. *To explain the organizational consumer's decision process* This process includes buyer expectations, the buying process, conflict resolution, and situational factors. Of prime importance is whether an organization uses joint decision making and, if so, how. Some form of bidding may be employed with organizational consumers (most often with government).

   If conflicts arise in joint decisions, problem solving, persuasion, bargaining, or politicking is used to arrive at a resolution. Situational factors can intervene between decision making and a purchase. They include strikes, economic conditions, and organizational changes.

   New task, modified rebuy, and straight rebuy are the different purchase situations facing organizational consumers.

5. *To consider the marketing implications of appealing to organizational consumers* Organizational buyers and final consumers have many similarities and differences. B-to-b marketers must understand them and adapt marketing plans accordingly. Dual marketing campaigns may be necessary for manufacturers and wholesalers that sell to intermediate buyers and have their products resold to final consumers.

   Purchasing agents and buyers have personal goals, such as status, promotions, and bonuses; these may have a large impact on decision making.

   B-to-b marketers can do many things to enhance their chances for success. A number of them are outlined in this chapter.

Key Terms

industrial (b-to-b) marketing (p. 257)
outsourcing (p. 258)
multiple-buying responsibility (p. 260)

value analysis (p. 261)
vendor analysis (p. 261)
competitive bidding (p. 261)

negotiation (p. 262)
derived demand (p. 262)
accelerator principle (p. 263)

systems selling (p. 263)

reciprocity (p. 264)

North American Industry Classification System (NAICS) (p. 267)

end-use analysis (p. 267)

manufacturers (p. 269)

wholesalers (p. 270)

retailers (p. 271)

government (p. 272)

nonprofit institutions (p. 273)

organizational consumer's decision process (p. 276)

conflict resolution (p. 278)

situational factors (p. 278)

new-task purchase process (p. 279)

modified-rebuy purchase process (p. 279)

straight-rebuy purchase process (p. 279)

Review Questions

1. Describe five of the most important differences between organizational and final consumers.
2. What is outsourcing? In what situation must it *always* be avoided?
3. How is the North American Industry Classification System a useful marketing tool?
4. What are the most important general organizational consumer-buying objectives?
5. For manufacturers, retailers, and government, what is the major constraint on their purchase behavior? Why?
6. How do product-specific and company-specific buying factors affect the use of autonomous or joint decision making?
7. What is the best form of conflict resolution? Explain your answer.
8. Cite several suggestions that b-to-b marketers should keep in mind when developing and enacting their strategies.

Discussion Questions

1. As a university's purchasing agent, what criteria would you use for competitive bidding in the selection of a new, on-campus food service provider?
2. A packaging firm knows its current sales are allocated as follows: 20 percent to animal food manufacturers (NAICS code 3111), 20 percent to sugar and confectionery products manufacturers (NAICS code 3113), 15 percent to dairy products manufacturers (NAICS code 3115), 20 percent to bakeries (NAICS code 3118), and 25 percent to other food manufacturers (NAICS code 3119). The firm expects next year's industry sales growth in these categories to be as follows: 3111, 5 percent; 3113, 4 percent; 3115, 6 percent; 3118, 1 percent; and 3119, 7 percent. According to end-use analysis, by how much should the packaging firm's sales increase next year? Explain your answer.
3. Describe a motorcycle maker's decision process with regard to which tire manufacturer to use for a new car. Does this process entail a new task, modified rebuy, or straight rebuy? Explain your answer.
4. "The least desired method of conflict resolution is politicking." Comment on this statement.

Web Exercise

The Business Marketing Association focuses on business-to-business marketing. Visit its Web site (**http://www.marketing.org**) and click on "Resources." What do you think are the most valuable resources? Why?

Practice Quiz

1. Which of the following is an example of industrial marketing?
   a. A consumer buying a bathing suit at the end of a season due to an attractive price
   b. A government agency purchasing a police car
   c. A college student leasing a personal computer
   d. A retailer selling TVs at the end of a season for a special promotion
2. Derived demand tends to be
   a. related to the accelerator principle.
   b. sensitive to price changes.
   c. not very volatile.
   d. independent of final consumers.

3. A combination of goods and services is provided to a buyer by a single source in
   a. negotiation.
   b. reciprocity.
   c. systems buying.
   d. systems selling.

4. Which statement concerning the North American Industry Classification System (NAICS) is correct?
   a. The NAICS is the official classification system for the members of NAFTA.
   b. The NAICS assigns organizations to 7 main industrial classifications.
   c. NAICS data is further classified into over 5,000 more specific classifications.
   d. There is no data on the NAICS outside of the U.S. government.

5. North American Industry Classification System data would most likely be employed in
   a. systems selling.
   b. countertrade.
   c. end-use analysis.
   d. value analysis.

6. Unlike wholesalers, retailers are more concerned with their
   a. physical facilities.
   b. resale items.
   c. trucks.
   d. refrigeration and other equipment.

7. Which statement about nonprofit institutions is *not* correct?
   a. They buy goods and services in order to run their organizations.
   b. They often sell items to generate additional revenues.
   c. There are no separate NAICS codes for nonprofit-versus profit-oriented firms.
   d. There are few international nonprofit institutions.

8. Which of the following is *not* a major component of the organizational consumer's decision process?
   a. Expectations
   b. Conflict resolution
   c. Problem awareness
   d. Buying process

9. For organizational consumers,
   a. the buying process always involves joint decisions.
   b. vendor reliability is not very important.
   c. satisfaction with past purchases is not important in current purchase decisions.

d. expectations refer to the perceived potential of alternative suppliers and brands to satisfy a number of explicit and implicit objectives.

10. Product-specific buying factors leading to joint decision making usually include
    a. low perceived risk.
    b. low time pressure for purchases.
    c. routine products.
    d. technology orientation.

11. Which of the following is *not* a method of conflict resolution?
    a. Politicking
    b. Persuasion
    c. Lobbying
    d. Bargaining

12. In which form of conflict resolution does each member of a purchasing team present his or her reasons why a particular supplier or brand should be selected?
    a. Politicking
    b. Persuasion
    c. Problem solving
    d. Bargaining

13. Reordering, *not* decision making, is usually applied when
    a. a firm has not previously purchased the product.
    b. medium-priced products previously bought infrequently by the firm now need to be purchased.
    c. competitive bidding is used.
    d. perceived risk is very low.

14. Which of the following is *not* a similarity between organizational consumers and final consumers?
    a. They both use a decision process.
    b. They both employ joint decision-making.
    c. They both purchase products for resale to others.
    d. They both can be defined by using social and psychological factors.

15. When dealing with organizational purchasing agents, sellers have to realize that these buyers
    a. rarely get involved with the final purchase decision.
    b. have personal, as well as company, goals.
    c. are only interested in price.
    d. usually have very little technical knowledge.

For the answers to these questions, please visit the online site for this book at **http://www.atomicdog.com.**

Chapter 10

Developing a Target Market Strategy

More than 120 years ago, John Pemberton, an Atlanta pharmacist, invented a new soft drink. The beverage was named Coca-Cola (**http://www.coca-cola.com**), based on its two primary ingredients: coca leaves (the product does not have any narcotics) and kola nuts. Over the years, Coca-Cola expanded its operations overseas so that it currently operates in over 200 countries. The Coca-Cola Company markets more than 2,800 beverage products, including four of the world's top five nonalcoholic sparkling beverage brands: Coca-Cola, Diet Coke, Sprite, and Fanta. In addition to its cola-based beverages, Coca-Cola owns or licenses bottled water, juices and juice drinks, coffees, and energy and sports drinks.

For decades, Coca-Cola practiced undifferentiated marketing, using one product and brand name throughout the world. This provided Coca-Cola with economies in planning and enacting its marketing program, as well as a uniform image. In 1982, Roberto Goizueta, Coca-Cola's chairman, changed that by introducing Diet Coke. Although prior Coca-Cola management had refused to use the Coke name on any new product, Diet Coke ultimately became one of the world's most successful new products.

Since then, Coca-Cola has introduced a number of new brands, including caffeine-free versions of Coca-Cola Classic and Diet Coke. Vanilla Coke, introduced in 2002, quickly became one of the firm's biggest new product ventures. In total, Coca-Cola now has ten diet cola products: Tab, Diet Coke, Diet Coke Sweetened with Splenda, Coca-Cola Zero, Diet Coke Plus, Diet Cherry Coke, Diet Coke Black Cherry Vanilla, Diet Coke with Lime, Vanilla Coke Zero, and Caffeine-Free Diet Coke. Each of these brands has a different target market and a different ad message. Diet Coke, American's number 1 diet soft drink, focuses on a late 20s to early 30s audience that is slightly more female than male, with an upscale, sophisticated message. Coca-Cola Zero appeals to 18- to 34-year-olds and is promoted as "the pause that lets them re-center in this fast-paced, time-warped world and keep going."

Coca-Cola's multibrand, multiflavor approach has moved the firm to a differentiated marketing strategy. The firm can now more effectively appeal to multiple consumer groups with distinctive offerings. Differentiated marketing also enables the company to control more shelf space in retail stores.[1]

In this chapter, we will examine each step involved in planning a target market strategy, including concentrated versus differentiated marketing. We will also explore the related topic of sales forecasting.

Chapter Objectives

1. To describe the process for planning a target market strategy
2. To examine alternative demand patterns and segmentation bases for both final and organizational consumers
3. To explain and contrast undifferentiated marketing (mass marketing), concentrated marketing, and differentiated marketing (multiple segmentation)
4. To show the importance of positioning in developing a marketing strategy
5. To discuss sales forecasting and its role in target marketing

---

[1] Various company and other sources.

10-1 OVERVIEW

After a firm has gathered data on consumer traits, desires, and decision making; industry attributes; and environmental factors, it is ready to select the target market(s) to which it will appeal and for which it will develop a suitable strategy. The total *market* for a particular good or service consists of all the people and/or organizations who desire (or potentially desire) that good or service, have sufficient resources to make purchases, and are willing and able to buy. Firms often use *market segmentation*—dividing the market into distinct subsets of customers that behave in the same way or have similar needs. Each subset could possibly be a target market, such as a specialty apparel store catering to young adult women shopping for mid-priced casual clothing.

Developing a *target market strategy* consists of three general phases: analyzing consumer demand, targeting the market, and developing the marketing strategy. This comprises the seven specific steps shown in Figure 10-1 and described in Chapter 10. First, a firm determines the demand patterns for a given good or service, establishes bases of segmentation, and identifies potential market segments. For example, do prospective consumers have similar or dissimilar needs and desires? What consumer characteristics, desires, and behavior types can be best used to describe market segments?

Second, a firm chooses the target market approach and selects its target market(s). It can use *undifferentiated marketing (mass marketing)*—targeting the whole market with a single basic marketing strategy intended to have mass appeal; *concentrated marketing*—targeting one well-defined market segment with one tailored marketing strategy; or *differentiated marketing (multiple segmentation)*—targeting two or more well-defined market segments with a marketing strategy tailored to each segment.[2] Business Resource Software has a good synopsis of market segmentation at its Web site (**http://www. businessplans.org/Segment.html**).

Third, a firm positions its offering relative to competitors and outlines the proper marketing mix(es). Of particular importance here is attaining *product differentiation*, whereby the consumer perceives a product's physical or nonphysical characteristics, including price, as differing from competitors. When differentiation is favorable, it yields a competitive advantage. A firm may be able to achieve a key differential advantage by

> A **market** is all possible consumers for a good or service. Through **market segmentation**, it can be subdivided.

> In a **target market strategy**, a firm first studies demand.

> Targeting approaches are **undifferentiated**, **concentrated**, and **differentiated marketing**.

> The marketing strategy is developed with an emphasis on **product differentiation**.

Figure 10-1

The Steps In Planning a Target Market Strategy

1. Determine demand patterns	
2. Establish possible bases of segmentation	Analyze consumer demand
3. Identify potential market segments	
4. Choose a target market approach	
5. Select the target market(s)	Target the market
6. Position the company's offering in relation to competition	
7. Outline the appropriate marketing mix(es)	Develop the marketing strategy

---

[2] "Dictionary," **http://www.marketingpower.com/_layouts/Dictionary.aspx** (March 22, 2009).

emphasizing how its offering satisfies existing consumer desires and needs better than competitors do. Sometimes, demand patterns may have to be modified for consumers to perceive a firm's product differentiation as worthwhile. Thus, Tylenol (**http://www. tylenol.com**) is promoted as an alternative to aspirin for persons who cannot take aspirin (appealing to existing consumer needs), whereas Dove (**http://www.dove.com**) is marketed as a nonsoap bar cleanser with moisturizing qualities (modifying consumer perceptions of soap's role). If targeted consumers do not believe that moisturizing is a meaningful product attribute, then they will probably not buy Dove—no matter how much better a job of moisturizing it does compared to competing soaps. Because Dove is an industry leader in sales, moisturizing is clearly a desirable attribute.

In this chapter, we detail the steps in a target market strategy as they pertain to final and organizational consumers.[3] Sales forecasting and its role in target marketing are also examined.

10-2 ANALYZING CONSUMER DEMAND

The initial phase in planning a target market strategy (analyzing consumer demand) has three steps: determining demand patterns, establishing possible bases of segmentation, and identifying potential market segments.

10-2a Determining Demand Patterns

A firm must first determine the **demand patterns**—which indicate the uniformity or diversity of consumer needs and desires for particular categories of goods and services—it faces in the marketplace. A firm would encounter one of the three alternative demand patterns shown in Figure 10-2 and described here for each good or service category it markets.

With **homogeneous demand**, consumers have rather uniform needs and desires for a good or service category. A firm's marketing tasks are straightforward: to identify and satisfy the basic needs of consumers in a superior way. For instance, business customers in the express-mail-delivery market are most interested in rapid, reliable delivery and reasonable prices. UPS (**http://www.ups.com**) appeals to customers by convincing them it is better than competitors in these areas. As competition picks up, firms may try to alter consumer demand so new product features become desirable and homogeneous demand turns to clustered demand, with only one or a few firms marketing the new features.

> **Demand patterns** show if consumer desires are similar for a good or service. People may have **homogeneous, clustered,** or **diffused demand.**

Figure 10-2

Alternative Consumer Demand Patterns for a Good or Service Category

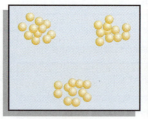
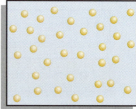

Homogeneous demand

Consumers have relatively similar needs and desires for a good or service category.

Clustered demand

Consumer needs and desires can be grouped into two or more identifiable clusters (segments), each with its own set of purchase criteria.

Diffused demand

Consumer needs and desires are so diverse that no clear clusters (segments) can be identified.

---

[3] An excellent overview of target marketing is Virtual Advisor's "Targeting Your Market," found at **http://va-interactive.com/inbusiness/editorial/sales/ibt/target_market.html**.

With *clustered demand*, consumer needs and desires for a good or service category can be divided into two or more clusters (segments), each having distinct purchase criteria. A firm's marketing efforts must be geared toward identifying and satisfying the needs and desires of a particular cluster (or clusters) in a superior way. See Figure 10-3. For example, in the golf equipment market, people can be grouped by their interest in performance and price. Thus, Golfsmith (**http://www.golfsmith.com**) sells a pre-owned set of Lynx irons for about $150 and the newest Callaway set of irons for $1,500—with each set of clubs appealing to a particular cluster of consumer needs and desires. Clustered demand is the most prevalent demand pattern. See Figure 10-3.

With *diffused demand*, consumer needs and desires for a good or service category are so diverse that clear clusters (segments) cannot be identified. Marketing efforts are complex because product features are harder to communicate and more product versions may be desired. For example, consumers have diverse preferences for lipstick colors; even the same person may desire several colors, to use on different occasions or to avoid boredom. Thus, cosmetics firms offer an array of lipstick colors. It would be nearly impossible for them to succeed with only a handful of colors. To make marketing strategies more efficient, firms generally try to modify diffused demand into clusters of at least moderate size.

Firms today often try to perform a balancing act regarding demand patterns. Just as the global marketplace is getting closer due to more open borders and enhanced communications, there is also more information available to companies on marketplace diversity via customer data bases, point-of-sale scanning in stores, and other data-collection techniques. On the one hand, some firms look for demand patterns that let them standardize (perhaps even globalize) their marketing mixes as much as possible—to maximize efficiency, generate a well-known image, and use mass media. On the other hand, some firms search for demand patterns that let them pinpoint more specific market segments—to better address consumer needs. For example, after getting feedback from the customers of its organic food products, Newman's Own now markets organic pet food for health-conscious pet owners (**http://www.newmansownorganics.com/pet/home**).

10-2b Establishing Possible Bases of Segmentation

A firm next studies possible bases for segmenting the market for each product or product line. See Table 10-1. It must decide which of these segmentation bases are most relevant for its particular situation.

Figure 10-3

Segmentation Based on Identifiable Clusters of Demand

Source: Reprinted by permission.

Global Marketing in Action

Coach Drives into China

Coach (http://www.coach.com), the maker of fine leather goods and custom fabrics, currently derives about 25 percent of its $2.6 billion in annual sales from overseas markets. Eighteen percent of total sales are in Japan, where Coach has 147 retail stores.

Coach is eyeing China as its next major growth opportunity. Coach recently purchased its Chinese distributor with 24 locations in China; and it also opened a new 9,400-square-foot flagship store in Hong Kong (its largest store outside of the United States). It plans to open an additional 50 retail outlets in China over the next 5 years. Although Coach now has a 3 percent market share of the overall handbag and women's accessories market in China, its target is to achieve a 10 percent market share within the next 5 years. Coach expects the handbag-and-accessories market in China to grow from $1.2 billion to $2.5 billion annually over that time period.

Coach's primary target market in China is not the super rich, who comprise only a fraction of one percent of the Chinese population. Instead, it is targeting the emerging middle class—which consists of engineers, physicians, bankers, lawyers, and executives who are reaping large pay raises. Coach positions itself as an alternative to such luxury European brands as Louis Vuitton (http://www.louisvuitton.com), Gucci (http://www.gucci.com), and Prada (http://www.prada.com). Many of the products under these brand names are made in France and Italy, where labor costs are $50 per hour. Coach's labor costs are 10 percent of that due to its manufacturing in lower-cost countries. It can take as much as 5 hours to make a handbag.

Sources: Based on material in Frederik Balfour, "Coach Builds Its Brand in China," http://www.businessweek.com/globalbiz (June 4, 2008); and Vanessa O'Connell, "Coach Targets China—and Queens," *Wall Street Journal* (June 3, 2008), pp. B1–B2.

Geographic demographics describe towns, cities, states, regions, and countries.

Geographic Demographics *Geographic demographics* are basic identifiable characteristics of towns, cities, states, regions, and countries. A firm may use one or a combination of the geographic demographics cited in Table 10-1 to describe its final or organizational consumers.

Because a segmentation strategy can be geared to geographic differences, it is useful to know such facts as these: Per-capita chocolate consumption in Western Europe is several times that in the United States; and per-capita consumption of bottled water in Italy is many times that in the United States. Germans want laundry detergents that are gentle on rivers, and will pay more for them; Greeks want small packages to keep down the cost per store visit. Canada and Mexico account for more than one-half of steel-mill products exported by U.S. firms. Many Brazilian, German, Korean, and Chinese consumers like to buy books and magazines online.

Here are some geographic household differences in the United States (all in percentages):

- Gender (male/female)—50/50 in the West, 47/53 in the Midwest, 45/55 in the North, and 44/56 in the South
- Home ownership—70 in the Midwest and in the South, 65 in the Northeast, and 63 in the West
- At least one vehicle owned or leased—90 in the West and in the Midwest, 89 in the South, and 79 in the Northeast.
- Proportion of income spent on housing and related goods and services—36 in the Northeast, 35 in the West, 33 in the Midwest, and 32 in the South.
- Proportion of income spent on transportation—19 in the South, 18 in the West, 17 in the Midwest, and 16 percent in the Northeast.[4]

Figure 10-4 indicates the population size, urbanization, and per-capita GDP ranking of the ten most populated nations of the world. Figure 10-5 shows a demographic map of the United States.

[4] *Consumer Expenditure Survey 2007* (Washington, DC: U.S. Bureau of Labor Statistics).

Table **10-1**	Possible Bases of Segmentation
Bases	**Examples of Possible Segments**
Geographic Demographics	
Population (people or organizations)	
Location	North, South, East, West; domestic, global
Size	Small, medium, large
Density	Urban, suburban, rural
Transportation network	Mass transit, vehicular, pedestrian
Climate	Warm, cold
Type of commerce	Tourist, local worker, resident; NAICS codes
Retail establishments	Downtown shopping district, shopping mall
Media	Local, regional, national, global
Competition	Underdeveloped, saturated
Growth pattern	Stable, negative, positive
Legislation	Stringent, lax
Cost of living/operations	Low, moderate, high
Personal Demographics	
A. Final Consumers	
Age	Child, young adult, adult, older adult
Gender	Male, female
Education	Less than high school, high school, college
Mobility	Same residence for 2 years, moved in last 2 years
Income	Low, middle, high
Occupation	Blue-collar, white-collar, professional
Marital status	Single, married, divorced, widowed
Household size	1, 2, 3, 4, 5, 6, or more
Ethnicity or race	European, American; black, white
B. Organizations	
Industry designation	NAICS codes; end-use analysis
Product use	Further production, use in operations, resale to others
Institutional designation	Manufacturer, wholesaler, retailer, government, nonprofit
Company size	Small, medium, large
Industry growth pattern	Slow, moderate, high
Company growth pattern	Slow, moderate, high
Age of company	New, 5 years old, 10 years old or more
Language used	English, French, Japanese
Consumer Lifestyles	
Social class (final consumers)	Lower-lower to upper-upper
Family life cycle (final consumers)	Bachelor to solitary survivor
Buying structure	Informal to formal, autonomous to joint

(continued)

Usage rate	Light, medium, heavy
Usage experience	None, some, extensive
Brand loyalty	None, some, total
Personality	Introverted-extroverted, persuasible-nonpersuasible
Attitudes	Neutral, positive, negative
Class consciousness	Inner-directed, outer-directed
Motives	Benefit segmentation
Perceived risk	Low, moderate, high
Innovativeness	Innovator, laggard
Opinion leadership	None, some, a lot
Importance of purchase	Little, a great deal

Personal demographics describe people and organizations. They should be used in studying final and organizational consumers.

Personal Demographics *Personal demographics* are basic identifiable characteristics of individual final consumers and organizational consumers, and groups of final consumers and organizational consumers. They are often used as a basis for segmentation because groups of people or organizations with similar demographics may have similar needs and desires that are distinct from those with different backgrounds. Personal demographics may be viewed singly or in combinations.

Final Consumers As noted in Table 10-1, several personal demographics for final consumers may be used in planning a segmentation strategy.

Applications of personal demographic segmentation are plentiful, as these examples indicate: In the United States and other Western nations, Clairol and many other companies now place greater emphasis on wooing consumers in the early stages of middle age. This group is quite large and particularly interested in slowing the aging process. Procter & Gamble has a special Web site for teenage girls (**http://www.beinggirl.com**) sponsored by its feminine-care products division. Godiva Chocolatier (**http://www.godiva.com**)

Figure 10-4

Comparing the Ten Most Populated Countries in the World, 2010

Source: Compiled by the authors from the U.S. Bureau of the Census, International Data Base (July 25, 2008); United Nations, *World Population Prospects: The 2007 Revised Population Database*, **http://esa.un.org/unup** (June 19, 2008); and *World Factbook 2008*, **https://www.cia.gov/library/publications/the-world-factbook/index.html** (June 10, 2008).

	Total population	Urbanization percentage[a]	Top ten GDP ranking per capita
China	1.35 billion	45	5
India	1.20 billion	30	7
United States	309 million	82	1
Indonesia	243 million	54	6
Brazil	201 million	87	4
Pakistan	180 million	37	8
Bangladesh	160 million	28	10
Nigeria	152 million	50	3
Russia	140 million	73	9
Japan	127 million	67	2

[a] % of population living in urban areas.

States	Population ranking	Median household income ranking	Population density ranking[a]
Alabama	24	45	27
Alaska	47	6	50
Arizona	14	27	33
Arkansas	32	48	34
California	1	12	11
Colorado	22	11	37
Connecticut	29	5	4
Delaware	45	14	6
Florida	4	35	8
Georgia	9	26	18
Hawaii	42	3	13
Idaho	39	28	44
Illinois	5	18	12
Indiana	16	32	17
Iowa	30	23	35
Kansas	33	36	40
Kentucky	26	46	22
Louisiana	23	47	23
Maine	41	31	38
Maryland	19	2	5
Massachusetts	13	8	3
Michigan	8	25	16
Minnesota	21	7	31
Mississippi	31	50	32
Missouri	18	33	28
Montana	44	44	48
Nebraska	38	21	43
Nevada	34	17	42
New Hampshire	40	4	19
New Jersey	11	1	1
New Mexico	36	40	45
New York	3	20	7
North Carolina	10	39	15
North Dakota	49	38	47
Ohio	7	29	9
Oklahoma	28	43	36
Oregon	27	30	39
Pennsylvania	6	22	10
Rhode Island	43	15	2
South Carolina	25	41	21
South Dakota	46	34	46
Tennessee	17	42	20
Texas	2	37	26
Utah	35	9	41
Vermont	48	16	30
Virginia	12	10	14
Washington	15	13	25
West Virginia	37	49	29
Wisconsin	20	19	24
Wyoming	50	24	49

[a] Population per square mile.

Figure 10-5

A Demographic Map of the United States, 2010

Source: Compiled by the authors from U.S. Bureau of the Census and U.S. Bureau of Economic Analysis data.

has separate Valentine's Day promotions aimed at men and women; in the past, all ads were oriented at gift-giving by men. Nike (**http://www.nikewomen.com**), Reebok (**http://www.reebok.com/US/#/womens**), and others are devoting more attention to women's sports shoes and apparel. Why? Women annually buy billions of dollars worth of these products—more than men spend![5]

Dollar General (**http://www.dollargeneral.com**), a discount "neighborhood" store chain, attracts value-conscious consumers with low prices; many items are $10 or less. It locates in smaller communities, sells many irregulars and factory overruns, and has few employees per store. In contrast, American Express attracts upper-income consumers with its platinum card (**http://www.americanexpress.com/platinum**). They pay an annual fee of $450 and charge tens of thousands of dollars per year; in return, they get special services (such as a worldwide concierge service to help them shop, plan trips, etc.) and a high credit line.

Marketing efforts aimed at U.S. ethnic groups have been growing. To serve its clients, at its Web site, Global Advertising Solutions (**http://www.ethnicusa.com/en/market_data/markets**) presents data on a number of ethnic markets in the United States, including these: Brazilian, Bulgarian, Chinese, Czech, Egyptian, Filipino, German, Greek, Israeli, Polish, Romanian, Russian, Serbian, South Asian, Turkish, Ukrainian, and Vietnamese. By visiting the site, a company could learn that the Brazilian-American population is about 1.6 million people. The major areas of concentration are New York, New Jersey, Connecticut, Massachusetts, Florida, and California. Their median household income is $38,200. One-fourth of Brazilian-American adults are married with children under 18 years of age.[6]

Organizational Consumers Table 10-1 also shows several personal demographics for b-to-b consumers that may be used in planning a segmentation strategy.

The easiest way to segment organizations is by their industry designation. As an illustration, if a firm studies the U.S. consumer goods rental industry sector (NAICS code 5322), it would learn the sector comprises 35,000 businesses with 260,000 employees, and generates $25 billion in annual sales. Among the business segments in this category are consumer electronics and appliances rental, formal wear and costume rental, video tape and disc rental, home health equipment rental, and recreational goods rental.[7]

To access potential b-to-b consumers by institutional type, some sellers rely on trade directories—such as the *Blue Book of Building & Construction* (**http://www.thebluebook.com**), with more than 1 million U.S. construction firms; *SA Yellow Online* (**http://www.sayellow.com**), with more than 600,000 firms doing business in South Africa; *BizEurope* (**http://www.bizeurope.com**), "Europe's leading import and export directory"; and *Scott's Directories* (**http://www.scottsinfo.com**), with 140,000 Canadian manufacturers and service firms. Mailing lists of organizations may also be bought. InfoUSA's (**http://www.infousa.com**) business lists have information on millions of U.S. manufacturers, wholesalers, retailers, professional service businesses, membership organizations, and others.

Organizations may be divided into small, medium, and large categories. Some firms prosper by marketing goods and services to smaller b-to-b customers, whereas others focus on medium and/or large accounts. For example, Brother (**http://www.brother.com**) has a line of inexpensive fax machines for small businesses that cost $75 or less, while Muratec's (**http://www.muratec.com**) top-line fax machines are priced at several thousand dollars; they can store 2,500 pages or more of text in memory, collate, and scan pages in under one second. Blackbourn (**http://www.blackbourn.com**), which makes plastic packaging for audio and video products, has a primary market of large *Fortune 500* companies but also sells to small businesses.

---

[5] Anthony Vagnoni, "Ads Are from Mars, Women Are from Venus," *Print* (March-April 2005), pp. 52–55.

[6] Global Advertising Strategies, "The Brazilian-American Population," **http://www.ethnicusa.com/en/market_data/markets/brazilian** (August 1, 2008).

[7] *2007 Service Annual Survey* (Washington, DC: U.S. Bureau of the Census).

Industry growth patterns may indicate a firm's future potential in marketing to businesses in those industries and provide a good segmentation base. The International Trade Administration of the U.S. Department of Commerce (**http://www.ita.doc.gov**) cites electronic information services, health services, semiconductors, and surgical and medical instruments as fast-growth industries. Paper industries machinery, personal leather goods, farm machinery, and newspapers are low-growth industries.

Consumer Lifestyles Lifestyles are the ways in which people live and spend time and money, and many lifestyle factors can be applied to both final and organizational consumers. Table 10-1 lists several lifestyle segmentation bases; except where indicated, these factors are relevant when segmenting either final or organizational consumer markets.

> Final consumer and organizational consumer segments each can be described on the basis of lifestyle factors.

Applications of lifestyle segmentation are abundant, as these examples show: Final consumers may be segmented by social class and stage in the family life cycle. The posh Four Seasons hotel chain (**http://www.fourseasons.com**) appeals to upper-middle-class and upper-class guests with luxurious accommodations, while the Hampton Inn chain (**http://www.hampton-inn.com**) appeals to middle-class and lower-middle-class consumers with low rates and limited services (such as no restaurant). Such diverse retailers as Tiffany (**http://www.tiffany.com**), Bloomingdale's (**http://www.bloomingdales.com**), Williams-Sonoma (**http://www.williams-sonoma.com**), and Crate and Barrel (**http://www.crateandbarrel.com**) offer online wedding gift registry services through Wedding-Channel.com (**http://www.weddingchannel.com**). To attract families with children, some Club Med resorts (**http://www.clubmed.com**) have day camps.

Final and organizational consumer market segments may be based on their usage rate, the amount of a product they consume. People or organizations can use very little, some, or a great deal. A *heavy-usage segment* (at times known as the *heavy half*) is a consumer group that accounts for a large proportion of a good's or service's sales relative to the size of the market. Women buy 85 percent of all greeting cards. Heavy yogurt consumers eat nearly double the amount as average yogurt consumers. Manufacturers, wholesalers, and retailers account for over 90 percent of all U.S. b-to-b equipment leasing; government and nonprofit organizations make less than 10 percent of equipment leases. Sometimes, a heavy-usage segment may be attractive due to the volume it consumes; other times, the competition for consumers in that segment may make other opportunities more attractive. Consider Kodak (**http://www.kodak.com**):

> A **heavy usage segment** has a rather large share of sales.

> When film ruled home photography, women took about two-thirds of all pictures and ordered most of the prints. But things changed when digital cameras began horning in on film's turf. More men got behind the camera—and many of the shots ended up trapped inside a computer. It was a disaster for Eastman Kodak (**http://www.kodak.com**). Sales of film and paper, its biggest sources of profit, tumbled. The long-successful strategy of courting women, emphasizing not so much gee-whiz technology as the chance to capture "Kodak moments," was in deep trouble. Today, Kodak is clawing its way to the top of the digital world by catering to its best customers. Starting a few years ago, Kodak set out to make digital photography female-friendly. Its research showed that women wanted digital photography to be simple, and they desired high-quality prints to share with family and friends. Kodak revamped its digital cameras, stressing simple controls and larger display screens. It invented a new product category, the compact, stand-alone photo printer, to easily make prints without a PC. And it pushed to make digital-image printing simpler through retail kiosks and an online service. Kodak isn't saying that women lack the aptitude to deal with digital photography. Women simply aren't that interested in fiddling with cables and complex camera-computer interfaces. So Kodak keeps things simple, while many rivals focus on high-tech features and marketing them to techies.[8]

---

[8] William M. Bulkeley, "Softer View: Kodak Sharpens Digital Focus on Its Best Customers: Women," *Wall Street Journal* (July 6, 2005), p. A1.

Benefit segmentation groups consumers based on their reasons for using products.

Consumer motives may be used to establish benefit segments. *Benefit segmentation* is a procedure for grouping people into segments on the basis of the different benefits sought from a product. It was first popularized when Russell Haley divided the tooth-paste market into four segments: sensory—people wanting flavor and product appearance; sociable—people wanting brighter teeth; worrier—people wanting decay prevention; and independent—people wanting low prices. Since then, benefit segmentation has been applied in many final and organizational consumer settings.[9] Figure 10-6 shows how benefit segmentation may be used to market children's toothpaste.

Blending Demographic and Lifestyle Factors

VALS and the **Social Styles model** describe market segments in terms of a broad range of factors.

It is generally advisable to use a mix of demographic and lifestyle factors to set up possible bases of segmentation. A better analysis then takes place. See Figure 10-7. Two broad classification systems are the *VALS (Values and Lifestyles) program*, which divides final consumers into lifestyle categories; and the *Social Styles model*, which divides the personnel representing organizational consumers into lifestyle categories.

In the United States, the current VALS 2 typology (**http://www.sric-bi.com/VALS**) explains why and how people make purchases, and places them into segments based on resources and innovativeness. Thinkers and believers are guided by their ideals; achievers and strivers are achievement-oriented; and experiencers and makers are guided by a desire for self-expression. People's resources include their education, income, self-confidence, health, eagerness to buy, intelligence, and energy level; and resources rise from youth to middle age and fall with old age. Here are descriptions of the basic VALS 2 segments (in terms of adult characteristics):

Figure 10-6

Applying Benefit Segmentation to Children's Toothpaste

Colgate and Oral-B realize that, as with adult toothpaste users, children are attracted to products that offer particular benefits—especially good-tasting flavors and packaging showing their favorite characters.

Source: Reprinted by permission of TNS Retail Forward.

---

[9] Russell I. Haley, "Benefit Segments: Backwards and Forwards," *Journal of Advertising Research*, Vol. 24 (February-March 1984), pp. 19–25; P. J. O'Connor and Gary L. Sullivan, "Market Segmentation: A Comparison of Benefits/Attributes Desired and Brand Preference," *Psychology & Marketing*, Vol. 12 (October 1995), pp. 613–635; Rizal Ahmad, "Benefit Segmentation: A Potentially Useful Technique of Segmenting and Targeting Older Consumers," *International Journal of Market Research*, Vol. 45 (Quarter 3, 2003), pp. 373–388; Chaim Ehrman, "On Using Benefit Segmentation for a Service Industry: A Study on College Career Counseling Services," *Journal of American Academy of Business*, Vol. 8 (March 2006), pp. 179–185; and Richard J. Harrington and Anthony K. Tjan, "Transforming Strategy One Customer at a Time," *Harvard Business Review*, Vol. 86 (March 2008), pp. 62–67.

Figure 10-7

Segmentation Based on Both Demographic and Lifestyle Factors

Dove (**http://www.dove.com**) markets its products to various customer segments based on a combination of demographic and lifestyle factors. For example, Dove shampoos come in several types: Dove Beautifully Clean Shampoo, Dove Extra Volume Shampoo, Dove Intensive Moisture Shampoo, Dove Moisture Rich Color Shampoo, and Dove Volumizing Color Shampoo.

Source: Reprinted by permission.

- *Innovators*—successful, sophisticated, take-charge people with high self-esteem. Abundant resources. Can indulge in any of the three primary motivations. Act as change leaders who are most receptive to new things. Active consumers; often interested in upscale, niche goods and services.
- *Thinkers*—Mature, satisfied, comfortable, and reflective. Value order, knowledge, and responsibility. Well educated; actively seek information in decision making. Alert to opportunities to broaden knowledge. Practical consumers interested in durability, functionality, and value.
- *Believers*—Conservative, conventional people with beliefs based on family, religion, community, and the nation. Follow established routines. Choose familiar products and established brands. Favor American products and are generally loyal.
- *Achievers*—Goal-oriented lifestyles and a deep commitment to career and family. Conventional lives, politically conservative, and respectful to authority. Active as consumers and favor established, prestige goods and services that show success to their peers.
- *Strivers*—Trendy and fun loving. Concerned about the opinions and approval of others. Money as a symbol of success. Income not high enough to meet their desires. Active, impulsive consumers who favor stylish products that emulate the purchases of those with more material wealth.
- *Experiencers*—Young and enthusiastic. Quickly become enthusiastic about new possibilities but are equally quick to cool. Seek variety and excitement, the offbeat, and the risky. Socially active. Spend a high proportion of their income on fashion and entertainment.

- *Makers*—Express themselves and experience the world by building a house, raising children, fixing a car, or canning vegetables. Have enough skill and energy to carry out practical projects successfully. Unimpressed by material possessions. Prefer value to luxury.
- *Survivors*—Narrowly focused. Limited resources. Often believe the world is changing too quickly. Comfortable with the familiar and mostly concerned with safety and security. Work to meet needs rather than fulfill desires. Cautious consumers. Loyal to favorite brands.[10]

GeoVALS is a high-tech way to use the U.S. VALS 2 model. Through GeoVALS, the VALS 2 market segments can be broken down by metropolitan area, city, and ZIP code.

The VALS system is also used in Japan (**http://www.sric-bi.com/VALS/JVALS. shtml**), and tailored to people there. For example, ryoshiki ("socially intelligent") innovators are career-oriented, middle-aged innovators; ryoshiki adapters are shy and look to ryoshiki innovators; tradition adapters are young and affluent; and low pragmatic are attitudinally negative and oriented to inexpensive products.

The Social Styles model popularized by Wilson Learning (**http://www.portalcenter. wilsonlearning.com**) and Tracom (**http://www.tracomcorp.com**), shown in Figure 10-8, indicates how social styles affect people's reactions to stimuli on and off the job. The model studies two traits—assertiveness and responsiveness—and divides organizational personnel into analyticals, drivers, amiables, and expressives. Assertiveness is the degree to which a person states views with assurance, confidence, and force, and the extent to which he or she tries to direct others' actions. Responsiveness is the extent to which a person is affected by appeals, influence, or stimulation and how feelings, emotions, or impressions are shown to others:

- *Analyticals*—Low in both assertiveness and responsiveness. Like facts and details. Money- and numbers-oriented. Work well alone. Stay under control. Interested in processes. Risk avoiders.
- *Expressives*—High in both assertiveness and responsiveness. The opposite of analyticals. Use hunches to make decisions. Need to be with people. Focus on generalities. Thrive on freedom from outside control. Risk takers, but seek approval for themselves and their firms.

Figure 10-8

The Social Styles Model for Organizational Consumers

Source: Wilson Learning Corporation and Tracom Corporation. Reprinted by permission of Crain Communications Inc., from Tom Eisenhart, "How to Really Excite Your Prospects," *Business Marketing* (July 1988).

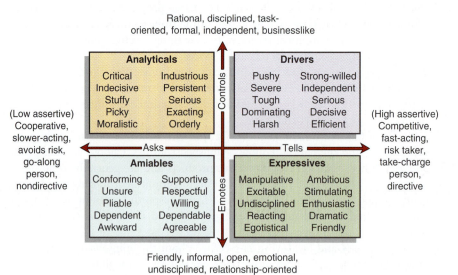

[10] SRI Consulting Business Intelligence, "The VALS Segments," **http://www.sric-bi.com/VALS/types.shtml** (May 12, 2009).

- *Drivers*—Low responsiveness and high assertiveness. Get right to the point. Limited time. "Hard chargers." Self-motivated and impatient. Work well alone. Risk takers. Success-oriented.
- *Amiables*—Low assertiveness and high responsiveness. Team players. Relationship builders. Friendly and loyal. Need support from others. Careful. Less time-oriented. Can be indecisive. Risk avoiders.[11]

The Social Styles model has been used to classify personnel in such industries as banking, computers and precision instruments, chemicals, pharmaceuticals, telecommunications, aerospace, utilities, and industrial and farm equipment. In all cases, the analyticals segment is the largest.

10-2c Identifying Potential Market Segments

Once it has established possible segmentation bases, a firm is ready to construct specific consumer profiles that identify potential market segments for the firm by aggregating consumers with similar traits and needs and separating them from those with different traits and needs. Following are some examples.

A supermarket can segment female and male shoppers in terms of their in-store behavior. In general, on each visit, women spend more time shopping, buy more items, are more apt to bring children, and more often use a shopping list than men; and they are equally apt to shop in the evening.

In appealing to the "senior" marketplace, "firms need to realize they can't approach them en masse. Firms tend to lump seniors into the 'old-old' category. That's a big mistake. Most observers say mature adults can break down into three different groups: (1) Leading-edge boomers or pre-retirees—younger seniors in their late 40s to late 50s still in the workplace. (2) In-betweeners or active retirees—range from their late 50s to early 70s, often in the beginning stages of retirement. (3) Seniors—'old' defined by most Americans as around the mid-70s (although most 70-year-olds would probably take exception to that)."[12]

A photocopier manufacturer could group the office-copier market into benefit segments, such as: basic copying (satisfied via simple, inexpensive machines that make up to 99 black-and-white copies of a single page at a time); extensive copying (satisfied via mid-priced machines that make up to 100 or more one- or two-sided copies of multiple pages and then collate them); and desktop publishing (satisfied via expensive, sophisticated machines that make high-quality color copies in large quantities).

> Consumer profiles are used in identifying market segments.

10-3 TARGETING THE MARKET

The second phase in planning a target market strategy (targeting the market) entails choosing the proper approach and selecting the target market(s).

10-3a Choosing a Target Market Approach

A firm now selects undifferentiated marketing, concentrated marketing, or differentiated marketing. We show these options in Figure 10-9 and Table 10-2, and discuss them next.

Undifferentiated Marketing (Mass Marketing) With an undifferentiated marketing (mass marketing) approach, a firm aims at a large, broad consumer market via one basic marketing plan. It believes consumers have very similar desires regarding product

> With undifferentiated marketing, a firm appeals to a broad range of consumers with one basic marketing plan.

[11] Wilson Learning, "Social Styles as a Global Phenomenon," http://portalcenter.wilsonlearning.com/pls/portal/url/page/wlc_web_site/resources (1999); and Tracom, "Social Style Model," http://www.tracomcorp.com/products_services/social_style/model.html (2006).

[12] Matt Kinsman, "Forever Young," *Promo* (October 2003), p. 22.

Figure 10-9

Figure 10-9

Contrasting Target Market Approachess

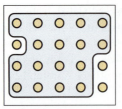

Undifferentiated marketing (Mass marketing)
The firm tries to reach a wide range of consumers with one basic marketing plan. These consumers are assumed to have a desire for similar good and service attributes.

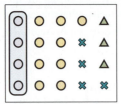

Concentrated marketing
The firm concentrates on one group of consumers with a distinct set of needs and uses a tailor-made marketing plan to attract this single group.

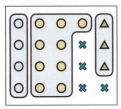

Differentiated marketing (Multiple segmentation)
The firm aims at two or more different market segments, each of which has a distinct set of needs, and offers a tailor-made marketing plan for each segment.

attributes or opts to ignore differences among segments. An early practitioner of mass marketing was Henry Ford, who sold one standard car at a reasonable price to many people. The original Model T had no options and came only in black.

Mass marketing was popular when large-scale production started, but the number of firms using a pure undifferentiated marketing approach has declined markedly in recent

Table 10-2	Contrasting Target Market Approaches		
	Approaches		
Strategic Factors	**Undifferentiated Marketing**	**Concentrated Marketing**	**Differentiated Marketing**
Target market	Broad range of consumers	One well-defined consumer group	Two or more well-defined consumer groups
Product	Limited number of products under one brand for many types of consumers	One brand tailored to one consumer group	Distinct brand or version for each consumer group
Distribution	All possible outlets	All suitable outlets	All suitable outlets—differs by segment
Promotion	Mass media	All suitable media	All suitable media—differs by segment
Price	One "popular" price range	One price range tailored to the consumer group	Distinct price range for each consumer group
Strategy emphasis	Appeal to a large number of consumers via a uniform, broad-based marketing program	Appeal to one specific consumer group via a highly specialized, but uniform, marketing program	Appeal to two or more distinct market segments via different marketing plans catering to each segment

years. Among the factors behind the drop are the following: competition has grown, consumer demand may be stimulated by appealing to specific segments, improved marketing research can better pinpoint different segments' desires, and total production and marketing costs can be reduced by segmentation.

Before engaging in undifferentiated marketing, a firm must weigh several factors. High total resources are needed to mass produce, mass distribute, and mass advertise. Yet, there may be per-unit production and marketing savings because a limited product line is offered and different brand names are not employed. These savings may allow low competitive prices.

A major goal of undifferentiated marketing is to maximize sales; a firm tries to sell as many units as possible. Regional, national, and/or international goals are set. Diversification is not undertaken.

For a firm to succeed with mass marketing, a large group of consumers must have a desire for the same product attributes (homogeneous demand) so one basic marketing program can be used. Or demand must be so diffused that it is not worthwhile for a firm to aim marketing plans at specific segments; the firm would try to make demand more homogeneous. In undifferentiated marketing, different consumer groups are not identified and sought. For example, suppose all consumers buy Morton's salt for its freshness, quality, storability, availability, and fair price. Mass marketing is then proper. If various shoppers want regular salt, iodized salt, low-sodium salt, seasoned salt, and popcorn salt (as they now do), Morton (**http://www.mortonsalt.com**) could not appeal to everyone with one marketing mix.

In undifferentiated marketing, a firm sells via all possible outlets. Some resellers may be displeased if a brand is sold at nearby locations and insist on carrying additional brands to fill out their product lines. It may be hard to persuade them not to carry competing brands. The shelf space a firm gets is based on its brand's popularity and the promotion support it provides.

An undifferentiated marketing strategy should take both total and long-run profits into account. Firms sometimes may be too involved with revenues and lose sight of profits. For example, for several years, A&P's sales rose as it competed with Safeway (**http://www.safeway.com**) for leadership in U.S. supermarket sales. A&P (**http://www.aptea.com**) incurred large losses during that period. Only when it began to close some unprofitable stores and stop pursuing sales at any cost did it regain profits. A&P is much smaller today.

A firm and/or its products can ensure a consistent, well-known image with a mass-marketing approach. Consumers have only one image when thinking of a firm (or a brand), and it is retained for a number of years. Think of Wal-Mart (**http://www.walmart.com**) and Target (**http://www.target.com**), discount department store chains that have a broad customer following.

USA Today (**http://www.usatoday.com**) is an example of undifferentiated marketing in action. As its Web site notes: "At a time when the vast majority of news organizations are suffering from decreased readership, *USA Today* is growing. We have a circulation of over 2 million and a readership of 3.6 million. USAToday.com has over 10.5 million unique visitors a month. And the reason is simple. *USA Today* readers find our brand approachable and friendly while still being smart and informed. In short, we invite everyone to the table. This inclusiveness is what sets us apart from our competition."

Concentrated Marketing

A concentrated marketing approach enables a firm to aim at a narrow, specific consumer segment with one specialized marketing plan catering to the needs of that segment. This is proper to consider if demand is clustered or if diffused demand can be clustered by offering a unique marketing mix.

Concentrated marketing has become more popular, especially for smaller firms. A firm does not have to mass produce, mass distribute, or mass advertise. It can succeed with limited resources and abilities by focusing efforts. This method does not usually maximize sales; the goal is efficiency—attracting a large part of one segment at controlled costs. The firm wants recognition as a specialist and does not diversify.

Via concentrated marketing, a firm appeals to one segment with a tailored marketing plan.

A firm must do better than competitors in tailoring a strategy for its segment if concentrated marketing is used. Areas of competitor strength should be avoided and weaknesses exploited. A new vendor selling standard office stationery would have a harder time distinguishing itself from competitors than a new vendor that provides customers with free recycling services for the stationery it sells.

When there are two or more attractive market segments from which a firm may choose, it should select the one with the greatest opportunity—while being alert to these two factors: (1) The largest segment may not be the best option, due to heavy competition or high consumer satisfaction with competitor offerings. A firm entering this segment may regret it due to the *majority fallacy*, which causes some firms to fail if they go after the largest market segment because competition is intense. See Figure 10-10. (2) A potentially profitable segment may be one ignored by other firms. As an example, Perdue (**http://www.perdue.com**) is a multibillion dollar company in the poultry business, due to its being the first chicken processor to see a market segment desiring superior quality, an identifiable brand name, and a guarantee—and having a willingness to pay premium prices. Previously, chicken was sold as an unbranded commodity.

Through concentrated marketing, a firm can maximize per-unit profits, but not total profits, because only one segment is sought. In addition, a firm with low resources can vie effectively for specialized markets. Many local and regional firms profitably compete in their own markets with national and international companies, but they do not have the finances to compete on a larger scale. Furthermore, minor shifts in population or consumer tastes can sharply affect a firm using concentrated marketing.

By carving out a distinct niche via concentrated marketing, a firm may foster a high degree of brand loyalty for a current offering and also be able to develop a product line under a popular name. As long as the firm stays within its perceived area of expertise, the image of one product will rub off on another: Porsche (**http://www.porsche.com**) aims only at the upscale segment of the auto market—people interested in styling, handling, acceleration, and status—even though it makes multiple vehicles (including a sports

> To avoid the **majority fallacy**, a company can enter a smaller, but untapped, segment.

Figure 10-10

How the Majority Fallacy Occurs

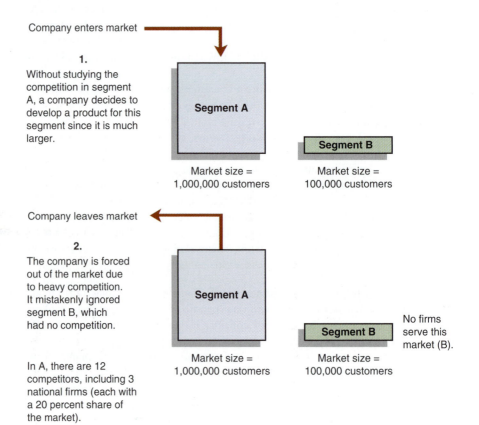

Company enters market

1.
Without studying the competition in segment A, a company decides to develop a product for this segment since it is much larger.

Segment A

Market size = 1,000,000 customers

Segment B

Market size = 100,000 customers

Company leaves market

2.
The company is forced out of the market due to heavy competition. It mistakenly ignored segment B, which had no competition.

In A, there are 12 competitors, including 3 national firms (each with a 20 percent share of the market).

Segment A

Market size = 1,000,000 customers

Segment B

Market size = 100,000 customers

No firms serve this market (B).

utility vehicle). Jack's 99¢ Stores offers products only for consumers interested in the lowest possible prices. See Figure 10-11.

Differentiated Marketing (Multiple Segmentation)

A firm can utilize differentiated marketing (multiple segmentation) to appeal to two or more distinct market segments, with a different marketing plan for each. This strategy combines the best aspects of undifferentiated marketing and concentrated marketing: A broad range of consumers may be sought and efforts focus on satisfying identifiable consumer segments. Differentiated marketing is appropriate to consider if there are two or more significant demand clusters, or if diffused demand can be clustered into two or more segments and satisfied by offering unique marketing mixes to each one.

Some firms appeal to each segment in the market and achieve the same market coverage as with mass marketing. Kyocera Mita (**http://www.kyoceramita.com**) markets copiers ranging from simple and inexpensive to sophisticated and expensive, thus separately appealing to small and large businesses. Other firms appeal to two or more, but not all, segments. Marriott International (**http://www.marriott.com**) operates Marriott Hotels & Resorts, Fairfield Inn, Courtyard by Marriott, Marriott Vacation Club, Residence Inn, Renaissance Hotels & Resorts, and other hotel chains. It aims at several—but not all—hospitality segments. Switzerland's Swatch Group (**http://www.swatchgroup.com**) markets Swatch watches for teens and young adults, Hamilton watches for adults lured by classic styles, and upscale Blancpain, Omega, and Tissot brands. Home Depot (**http://www.homedepot.com**) targets to small businesses, other b-to-b customers, and final consumers. See Figure 10-12.

Firms may use both mass marketing and concentrated marketing in their multiple segmentation strategies. They could have one or more major brands aimed at a wide range of consumers (the mass market) and secondary brands for specific segments. Time Inc. publishes *Time* (**http://www.time.com**) and *People* (**http://www.people.com**) for very broad audiences and *Fortune* (**http://www.fortune.com**) and *Sports Illustrated for Kids* (**http://www.sikids.com**) for more specialized segments.

Differentiated marketing requires thorough analysis. Resources and abilities must be able to produce and market two or more different sizes, brands, or product lines. This can be costly, as with high-tech products. However, if a firm sells similar products under its own and retailer brands, added costs are low.

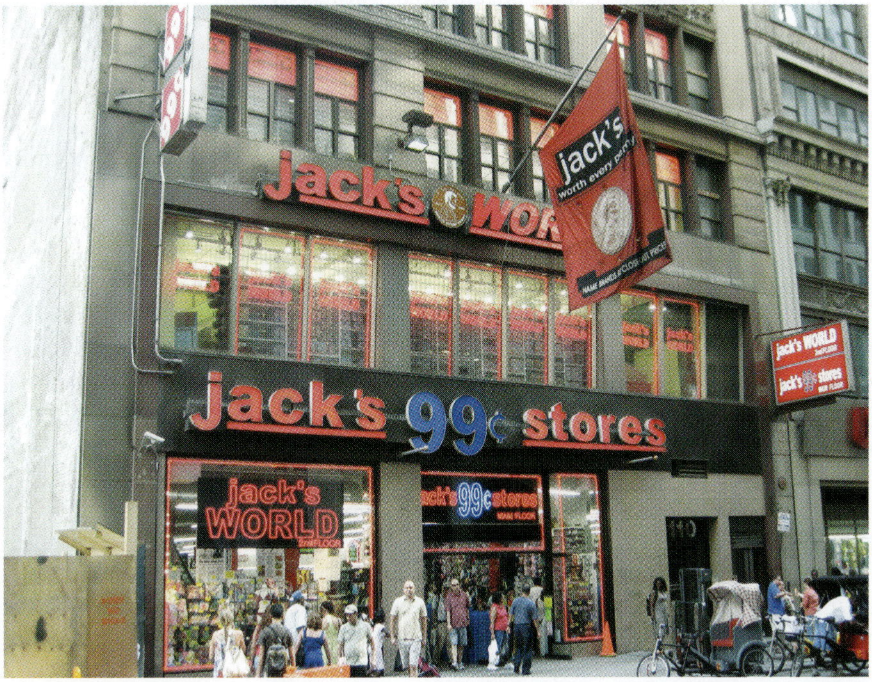

> In differentiated marketing, two or more marketing plans are tailored to two or more consumer segments.

Figure 10-11

Concentrated Marketing in Action: Deep Discounting for Extreme-Value Shoppers

Source: Reprinted by permission.

Figure 10-12

Differentiated Marketing in Action

At Home Depot, "We cater to both do-it-yourselfers and professional customers who serve the home improvement construction and building maintenance market segments."

Source: Reprinted by permission.

A firm can attain many goals with differentiated marketing. It can maximize sales: Procter & Gamble (**http://www.pg.com**) is the world leader in laundry products with such brands as Tide, Dreft, Cheer, Gain, Era, and Ivory. Boeing (**http://www.boeing.com**) leads in the global commercial aircraft business—offering planes with different sizes and configurations (including the 737, 747, 767, 777, and 787). Recognition as a specialist can be sustained if a firm has separate brands for distinct segments: Whirlpool has a clear image under its own name (**http://www.whirlpool.com**); few people know it also makes products under Sears' Kenmore brand (**http://www.kenmore.com**). Multiple segmentation lets a firm diversify and minimize risks because all emphasis is not on one segment: Honda's (**http://www.honda.com**) motorcycles and small engines (for lawn mowers and outboard motors) provide an excellent hedge against a drop in the sales of its cars.

Differentiated marketing does not mean a firm has to enter segments where competition is intense and face the majority fallacy. Its goals, strengths, and weaknesses must be weighed against competitors'. A firm should target only segments it can handle. The majority fallacy can work in reverse. If a firm enters a segment before a competitor, it may prevent the latter from successfully entering that segment.

Although differentiated marketing requires the existence of at least two consumer segments (with distinct desires by each), the more potential segments exist, the better the opportunity for multiple segmentation. Firms that start with concentrated marketing often turn to multiple segmentation and pursue other segments after they become established in one segment.

Wholesalers and retailers usually find differentiated marketing by suppliers to be attractive. It lets them reach multiple segments, offers some exclusivity, allows orders to be placed with fewer suppliers, and may enable them to carry their own private brands. For the selling firm, several benefits exist. Items can be placed with competing resellers under different brands. Space is given to display various sizes, packages, and/or brands. Price differentials among brands can be kept. Competitors may be discouraged from entering a channel. Overall, differentiated marketing places the seller in a good bargaining position.

Multiple segmentation can be quite profitable because total profits should rise as a firm increases the number of segments it services. Per-unit profits should also be high if a firm does a good job of enacting a unique marketing plan for each segment. Consumers

Marketing and the Web

Consumer Satisfaction with Online Sales

Internet researcher ForeSee Results (http://www.foreseeresults.com) conducts an Online Retail Satisfaction Index study which measures the performance of the top 100 online retailers and predicts consumers' future behavior and brand loyalty. The results are based on responses from 24,000 consumers. Scores of 80 or higher are interpreted as high satisfaction, while scores of under 70 show dissatisfaction.

In a recent online satisfaction study, ForeSee found that the top-ranked firm was Netflix, with a score of 86. The next five highest retailers were QVC.com (http://www.qvc.com), 84; Amazon.com (http://www.amazon.com), 83; Shutterfly (http://www.shutterfly.com), 80; Netegg (http://www.netegg.com), 80; and Apple (http://www.apple.com), 80. Scores for some other firms were J.C. Penney (http://www.jcpenney.com), 77; Wal-Mart (http://www.walmart.com), 75; Target (http://www.target.com), 73; and Costco (http://www.costco.com), 72.

ForeSee reported that online consumer and electronics retailers had the lowest overall satisfaction scores. Scores in these two segments were lower than those in the apparel, food and drug, sporting goods, and books, movies, and music categories. This was a very significant finding as highly satisfied shoppers are two-thirds more likely to purchase from the same retailer the next time for similar goods, and 75 percent are more apt to recommend the retailer.

ForeSee's research has discovered that lowering prices would not make consumers more loyal. Instead, consumer electronics and information technology retailers would get better results by offering free shipping, adding product reviews to their Web sites, and better coordinating their multichannel retailing strategies.

Source: Based on material in Alan Wolf, "CE, IT E-Tailers Score Lowest in Customer Satisfaction Study," *Twice* (July 6, 2008), p. 14.

---

in each segment would then be willing to pay a premium price for the tailor-made offering.

Although risks from a decline in any one segment are lessened, when a firm serves diverse segments, extra costs may be incurred by making product variations, selling in more channels, and promoting more brands. The firm must weigh the revenues gained from selling to multiple segments against the costs.

A company must be careful to maintain product distinctiveness for each market segment and guard its overall image. Some consumers perceive various General Motors' divisions as having "look-alike" cars. And IBM's image was affected by its past weak performance in the home PC segment (causing IBM's PC division to be sold to China's Lenovo, http://www.lenovo.com).

10-3b Selecting the Target Market(s)

At this point, a firm has these decisions: Which segment(s) offer the best opportunities? How many segments should it pursue? In assessing market segments, a firm should review goals and strengths, competition, segment size and growth potential, distribution requirements, the necessary expenditures, profit potential, company image, the ability to create and sustain differential advantages, and other factors.[13]

Based on the approach chosen, a firm would decide whether to pursue one or more segments (or the mass market). Due to the high costs of entering the HD-TV market and the existence of well-defined demand clusters, it is most likely that a firm new to that industry would start with concentrated marketing. On the other hand, a new sweater

> A company now chooses which and how many segments to target.

---

[13] See Karsten Sausen, Torsten Tomczak, and Andreas Herrmann, "Development of a Taxonomy of Strategic Market Segmentation: A Framework for Bridging the Implementation Gap between Normative Segmentation and Business Practice," *Journal of Strategic Marketing*, Vol. 13 (September 2005), pp. 151–173; Sally Dibb, "Market Segmentation Implementation Barriers and How to Overcome Them," *Marketing Review*, Vol. 5 (Spring 2005), pp. 13–30; and Johann Füller and Kurt Matzler, "Customer Delight and Market Segmentation: An Application of the Three-Factor Theory of Customer Satisfaction on Lifestyle Groups," *Tourism Management*, Vol. 29 (February 2008), pp. 116–126.

maker could easily use differentiated marketing to target boys, girls, men, and women. Pep Boys (**http://www.pepboys.com**), the auto repair and parts giant, aims to serve two distinct segments: do-it-yourselfers and professional mechanics. Industrywide, in the United States, each segment represents several billion dollars in annual sales—with the sales in the professional segment being twice as large.

Requirements for Successful Segmentation For concentrated marketing or differentiated marketing plans to succeed, the selected market segment(s) have to meet five criteria:

1. *Differences* must exist among consumers, or mass marketing would be an appropriate strategy.
2. Within each segment, there must be enough consumer *similarities* to develop an appropriate marketing plan for that segment.
3. A firm must be able to *measure* consumer attributes and needs in order to form groups. This may be hard for some lifestyle attributes.
4. A segment must be *large enough* to produce sales and cover costs.
5. The members of a segment must be *reachable* in an efficient way. For example, young women can be reached via *Teen* magazine (**http://www.teenmag.com**). It is efficient because males and older women do not read the magazine.

Limitations of Segmentation Segmentation is often consumer-oriented, efficient, and profitable; but it should not be abused. Firms can fall into one or more of these traps, which they should avoid. They may

- appeal to segments that are too small.
- misread consumer similarities and differences.
- become cost inefficient.
- spin off too many imitations of their original products or brands.
- become short-run instead of long-run oriented.
- be unable to use certain media (due to the small size of individual segments).
- compete in too many segments.
- confuse people.
- become locked into a declining segment.
- be too slow to seek innovative possibilities for new products.

10-4   DEVELOPING THE MARKETING STRATEGY

The third phase in planning a target market strategy (developing the marketing strategy) includes these steps: positioning the firm's offering relative to competitors and outlining appropriate marketing mix(es).

10-4a   Positioning the Company's Offering in Relation to Competition

Once a firm selects its target market(s), it must identify the attributes and image of each competitor and select a position for its own offering.

For example, a firm considering entry into the office PC market could describe the key strengths of some major competitors as follows:

- Acer—Good pricing, reliability, durability, product variety.
- Apple—Ease of use, graphics, desktop publishing, innovativeness.
- Dell—Made-to-order products, range of accessories carried, direct marketing experience.
- Hewlett-Packard—Innovativeness, construction, monitor quality, competitive pricing.

Ethical Issues in Marketing

Tips for Marketing to the Hispanic Market

Nearly one in six people currently living in the United States is of Hispanic origin, an increase from one in 8 as of 2000. Hispanics account for 9 percent of U.S. consumer buying power, up from 5 percent in 1990. As of 2011, annual Hispanic buying power is expected to reach nearly $1.2 trillion. Nonetheless, the Hispanic market is poorly understood by many marketers.

One common error is that too many marketers view Hispanics as one single market when they actually have immigrated to the United States from such diverse countries as Mexico, Cuba, Peru, Colombia, and Ecuador. Each of these nationalities has unique customs, cultural sensitivities, and holidays. A second blunder is to ignore the impact of acculturation because first-, second-, and third-generation people exhibit very different behavior as consumers. A

third problem occurs if firms translate commercials initially made for the Anglo-American market into Spanish without an understanding of their relevance or the possibility of a cultural taboo.

Heineken has been cited as an example of a firm that understands the Hispanic market. Its "Translations" radio campaign won a "Best of Show" Hispanic Creative Advertising Award. In each commercial, a Heineken beer drinker told a simple story using the accents and slang expressions of different nationalities: Argentine, Mexican, Dominican, and Puerto Rican. The ads' humor was from a second voice which translated each colloquial sentence into standard Spanish.

Source: Based on material in Salvatore Cavalieri, "Engaging the Hispanic Market: Three Commandments," *Television Week* (January 14, 2008), p. 12.

In positioning itself against these competitors, the firm would need to present a combination of customer benefits that are not being offered by them and that are desirable by a target market. Customers must be persuaded that there are clear reasons for buying the new firm's computers. It is not a good idea for the firm to go head-on against such big, well-known competitors.

As one alternative, the firm could focus on small businesses that have not yet bought a computer and that need a personal touch during both the purchase process and the initial use of the product. It could thus market fully configured PC systems, featuring Windows Vista-based clones that are installed by the seller (complete with software libraries and customized programs), in-office training of employees, and a single price for a total system. The positioning emphasis would be "to provide the best ongoing, personalized customer service possible to an underdeveloped market segment, small-business owners with little computer knowledge."

A fuller discussion of product positioning appears in Chapter 11.

10-4b Outlining the Appropriate Marketing Mix(es)

The last step in the target-marketing process is for a firm to outline a marketing-mix plan for each customer group sought. Marketing decisions relate to product, distribution, promotion, and price factors.

> The marketing mix must be attractive to the target market.

Here is a logical marketing-mix plan for a firm newly entering the office PC market and concentrating on small-business owners:

- Product—Good-quality, Windows Vista operating system, Intel Pentium chip, expansion capability; user friendly, simple keyboard layout; high-resolution color monitor; high-speed DVD player/rewriter and suitable speakers; 250-gigabyte hard drive; basic software library; customized software; and more.
- Distribution—Direct calls and installations at customers' places of business; follow-up service calls.
- Promotion—Focus on personal selling and direct mail; hands-on, on-site training; customer referrals.

- Price—Average to above average; customers presented with nonprice reasons to buy; positioning linked to high value for the price; price of computer, software, and service bundled together.

10-5   SALES FORECASTING

> A **sales forecast** predicts company sales over a specified period.

A firm should forecast short-run and long-run sales to the chosen market as it plans a target market strategy. A **sales forecast** outlines expected company sales for a specific good or service to a specific consumer group over a specific period of time under a specific marketing program. By accurately projecting sales, a firm can better set a marketing budget, allot resources, measure success, analyze sales productivity, monitor the environment and competition, and modify marketing efforts.[14]

First, industry forecasts should be studied; they can strongly affect any company's sales. Next, sales potential outlines the upper limit for the firm, based on marketing and production capacity. A sales forecast then enumerates a firm's realistic sales. The forecast is also based on the expected environment and company performance. Figure 10-13 shows this sales forecasting process.

A sales forecast should take into account demographics (such as per-capita income), the economy (such as the inflation rate), the competitive environment (such as promotion levels), current and prior sales, and other factors. When devising a forecast, precision is required. A forecast should break sales down by good or service (model 123), consumer group (adult female), time period (July through September), and type of marketing plan (intensive advertising).

10-5a   Data Sources

Several external secondary sources can be consulted to obtain the data needed for a forecast. Government agencies provide data on global, national, regional, and local

Figure 10-13

Developing a Sales Forecast

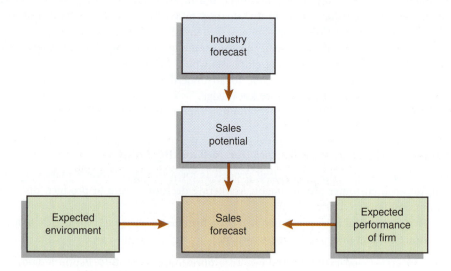

[14] See "Sales Forecasting," **http://www.tutor2u.net/business/marketing/sales_forecasting.asp** (May 19, 2009); "Three Methods of Sales Forecasting," **http://sbinfocanada.about.com/od/cashflowmgt/a/salesforecast.htm** (May 19, 2009); *Forecast Pro Trends Newsletter*, **http://www.forecastpro.com/resources/trends/index.html**; and Robert D. Kugel, "Six Steps to Better Sales Forecasting and Demand Planning," **http://www.intelligententerprise.com/showArticle.jhtml?articleID=209000118** (July 14, 2008).

demographic trends; past sales by industry and product category; and the economy. Trade associations publish statistics and often have libraries. General and specialized media, such as *Business Week* (**http://www.businessweek.com**) and *Ward's Automotive Reports* (**http://www.wardsauto.com**) do forecasts.

A firm can also get data from present and future customers, executives, salespeople, research studies and market tests, and internal records. These data often center on company, not industry, predictions.

10-5b Methods of Sales Forecasting

Sales forecasting methods range from simple to sophisticated. Among the simple methods are trend analysis, market share analysis, jury of executive (expert) opinion, sales force surveys, and consumer surveys. Among the more complex methods are the chain-ratio technique, market buildup method, and statistical analyses. Table 10-3 illustrates each. By combining two or more techniques, a firm can better forecast and minimize the weaknesses in any one method.

With simple trend analysis, a firm forecasts sales on the basis of recent or current performance. If sales have risen an average of 10 percent annually over the last five years, it will forecast next year's sales to be 10 percent higher than the present year's. Although

Table 10-3	Applying Sales Forecasting Techniques	
Technique	**Illustration**	**Selected Potential Shortcomings**
Simple trend analysis	This year's sales = $2 million; company trend is 5% growth per year; sales forecast = $2,100,000.	Industry decline not considered
Market share analysis	Current market share = 18%; company seeks stable market share; industry forecast = $10,000,000; company sales forecast = $1,800,000.	New competitors and greater marketing by current ones not considered
Jury of executive opinion	Three executives see strong growth and three see limited growth; they agree on a 6% rise on this year's sales of $11 million; sales forecast = $11,660,000.	Change in consumer attitudes not uncovered
Jury of expert opinion	Groups of wholesalers, retailers, and suppliers meet. Each group makes a forecast; top management utilizes each forecast in forming one projection.	Different beliefs by groups about industry growth
Sales force survey	Sales personnel report a competitor's price drop of 10% will cause company sales to decline 3% from this year's $7 million; sales forecast = $6,790,000.	Sales force unaware a competitor's price cut will be temporary
Consumer survey	85% of current customers indicate they will repurchase next year and spend an average of $1,000 with the firm; 3% of competitors' customers indicate they will buy from the firm next year and spend an average of $800; sales forecast = $460,000.	Consumer intentions possibly not reflecting real behavior
Chain-ratio method	Unit sales forecast for introductory marketing text = (number of students) × (% annually enrolled in marketing) × (% buying a new book) × (expected market share) = (10,000,000) × (0.07) × (0.87) × (0.11) = 66,990.	Inaccurate estimate of enrollment in introductory marketing course made
Market buildup method	Total sales forecast = region 1 forecast + region 2 forecast + region 3 forecast = $2,000,000 + $7,000,000 + $13,000,000 = $22,000,000.	Incorrect assumption that areas will behave similarly in future
Test marketing	Total sales forecast = (sales in test market A + sales in test market B) × (25) = ($1,000,000 + $1,200,000) × (25) = $55,000,000.	Test areas not representative of all locations
Detailed statistical analyses	Simulation, complex trend analysis, regression, and correlation.	Lack of understanding by management; all factors not quantifiable

the technique is easy to use, the problems are that sales fluctuations, changing consumer tastes, changing competition, the economy, and market saturation are not considered. A firm's growth may be affected by these factors.

Market share analysis is similar to simple trend analysis, except that a company assumes that its share of industry sales will be constant. However, all firms in an industry do not progress at the same rate. Market share analysis has the same weaknesses as simple trend analysis, but uses more industry data–and it would let an aggressive or declining firm adjust its forecast and marketing efforts.

> A **jury of executive (expert) opinion** has informed people estimate sales.

A *jury of executive (expert) opinion* is used if the management of a firm or other well-informed persons meet, discuss the future, and set sales estimates based on the group's experience and interaction. By itself, this method relies too much on informal analysis. In conjunction with other methods, it is effective because it enables experts to directly interpret and respond to concrete data. Because management lays out goals, sets priorities, and guides a firm's destiny, its input is crucial.

The employees most in touch with consumers and the environment are sales personnel. A sales force survey allows a firm to obtain input in a structured way. Salespeople are often able to pinpoint trends, strengths and weaknesses in a firm's offering, competitive strategies, customer resistance, and the traits of heavy users. They can break sales forecasts down by product, customer type, and area. However, they can have a limited perspective, offer biased replies, and misinterpret consumer desires.

Many marketers feel the best indicators of future sales are consumer attitudes. By conducting consumer surveys, a firm can obtain data on purchase intentions, future expectations, consumption rates, brand switching, time between purchases, and reasons for purchases. Yet, consumers may not reply to surveys and may act differently from what they say.

> With the **chain-ratio method**, general data are broken down. The **market buildup method** adds segment data.

In the *chain-ratio method*, a firm starts with general market information and then computes a series of more specific information. These combined data yield a sales forecast. A maker of women's casual shoes can first look at a trade association report to learn the industry sales estimate for shoes, the percentage of sales from women's shoes, and the percentage of women's shoe sales from casual shoes. It would then project its own sales of casual women's shoes to its target market. This method is only as accurate as the data plugged in for each market factor. It is useful because it gets management to think through a forecast and obtain different information.

Opposite to the chain-ratio method is the *market buildup method*, by which a firm gathers data from small, separate market segments and aggregates them. This method lets a firm operating in four urban areas devise a forecast by first estimating sales in each area and then adding them. A firm must note that consumer tastes, competition, population growth, and media do differ by area. Equal-size segments may present dissimilar opportunities; they should not be lumped together without careful study.

Test marketing is a form of market buildup analysis in which a firm projects a new product's sales based on short-run, geographically limited tests. With it, a company usually introduces a new product into one or a few markets for a short time and enacts a full marketing campaign there. Overall sales are forecast from test market sales. Yet, test areas may not be representative of all locales; and test-market enthusiasm may not carry into national distribution. Test marketing is covered more fully in Chapter 13.

Many detailed statistical methods are used for sales forecasting. Simulation lets a firm enter market data into a computer model and forecast under varying conditions and marketing plans. In complex trend analysis, the firm includes past sales fluctuations, cyclical factors (such as economic conditions), and other factors when looking at sales trends. Regression and correlation techniques explore mathematical links between future sales and market factors, such as annual income or derived demand. These methods rely on good data and the ability to use them well. Further discussion is beyond the scope of our text.

10-5c   Additional Considerations

The method and accuracy of sales forecasting greatly depend on the newness of a firm's offering. A forecast for a continuing good or service could be based on trend analysis, market share analysis, executive (expert) opinion, and sales force surveys. Barring major alterations in the economy, industry, competition, or consumer tastes, the forecast should be relatively accurate.

A forecast for an item new to the firm but continuing in the industry could be based on trade data, executive (expert) opinion, sales force and consumer surveys, and test marketing. The first year's forecast should be somewhat accurate; the ensuing years more so. It is hard to project first-year sales precisely because consumer interest and competition may be tough to gauge.

A forecast for a good or service new to both the firm and the industry should rely on sales force and consumer surveys, test marketing, executive (expert) opinion, and simulation. The forecast for the early years may be highly inaccurate because the speed of consumer acceptance cannot be closely estimated. Later forecasts will be more accurate. Though an initial forecast may be imprecise, it is still needed for setting marketing plans, budgeting, monitoring the environment and competition, and measuring success.

A firm must consider *sales penetration*—the degree to which a firm is meeting its sales potential—in forecasting sales. It is expressed as:

Sales penetration = Actual sales/Sales potential

A firm with high sales penetration needs to realize that *diminishing returns* may occur if it seeks to convert remaining nonconsumers; the costs of attracting them may outweigh revenues. Other products or segments may offer better potential. Table 10-4 illustrates sales penetration and diminishing returns.

Factors may change and cause a wrong forecast, unless revised. These include economic conditions, industry conditions, firm performance, competition, and consumer tastes.

> A forecast for a continuing product should be the most accurate.

> **Sales penetration** shows whether a firm has reached its potential. **Diminishing returns** may result if the firm seeks nonconsumers.

Table 10-4	Illustrating Sales Penetration and Diminishing Returns		
Year 1		**Year 2**	
Sales potential	= $1,000,000	Sales potential	= $1,000,000
Actual sales	= $600,000 (60,000 units)	Actual sales	= $700,000 (70,000 units)
Selling price	= $10/unit	Selling price	= $10/unit
Total marketing costs	= $100,000	Total marketing costs	= $150,000
Total production costs (at $8/unit)	= $480,000	Total production costs (at $8/unit)	= $560,000
Sales penetration	$= \dfrac{\$600,000}{\$1,000,000} = 60\%$	Sales penetration	$= \dfrac{\$700,000}{\$1,000,000} = 70\%$
Total profit	= $600,000	Total profit	= $700,000
	− ($100,000 + $480,000)		− ($150,000 + $560,000)
	= $20,000		= −$10,000

In year 1, sales penetration is 60% and the firm earns a $20,000 profit. In year 2, the firm raises marketing expenditures to increase sales penetration to 70%; as a result, it suffers diminishing returns—the additional $100,000 in actual sales is more than offset by a $130,000 rise in total costs (from $580,000 in year 1 to $710,000 in year 2).

Web Sites You Can Use

There are many valuable Web sites related to target marketing. Let us highlight several of them:

- Bank of America has an insightful, animated workshop on "Target Marketing" (**http://www.va-interactive.com/bankofamerica/resourcecenter/workshops/targetmarket/targetmarket.html**).
- Business Resource Center (**http://www.businessplans.org/Segment.html**) has a section of its site dedicated to market segmentation.
- Claritas markets lifestyle segmentation programs to business clients. At its Web site, Claritas discusses market segmentation (**http://www.claritas.com**) and enables visitors to try out its PRIZM NE program (**http://www.claritas.com/MyBestSegments/Default.jsp**). The segments are described at the Web site.
- Easy Analytic Software (**http://www.easidemographics.com**) makes available a number of free demographic and

lifestyle reports. This enables firms to study consumer backgrounds in different states and communities.

- *Target Marketing* has an online version of its magazine (**http://www.targetonline.com**) devoted to this topic from the perspective of direct marketing.
- The U.S. Small Business Administration has a section of its site devoted to target marketing (**http://www.sba.gov/starting_business/marketing/target.html**).
- Yankelovich MindBase (**http://www.yankelovich.com/products/MindBase_PS.pdf**) identifies eight major consumer groups based on attitudes and motivations. Each group is broken down into three distinct sub-segments, which enable client firms to create high-impact marketing programs and develop high-value customer relationships. The segments are described at its Web site.

Summary

1. *To describe the process for planning a target market strategy* After collecting information on consumers and the environment, a firm can pick the target market(s) to which to appeal. A potential market has people with similar needs, enough resources, and a willingness and ability to buy.

   There are three general phases in developing a target market strategy, with seven specific steps: analyzing consumer demand—determining demand patterns (1), establishing bases of segmentation (2), and identifying potential market segments (3); targeting the market—choosing a target market approach (4) and selecting the target market(s) (5); and developing the marketing strategy—positioning the company's offering relative to competitors (6) and outlining the appropriate marketing mix(es) (7). Of particular importance is product differentiation, whereby a product offering is perceived by the consumer to differ from its competition on any physical or nonphysical product characteristic, including price.

2. *To examine alternative demand patterns and segmentation bases for both final and organizational consumers* Demand patterns indicate the uniformity or diversity of consumer needs and desires for particular categories of goods and services. With homogeneous demand, consumers have relatively uniform needs and desires. With clustered demand, consumer needs and desires can be classified into two or more identifiable clusters (segments), with each having distinct purchase requirements. With diffused demand, consumer needs and desires are so diverse that clear clusters cannot be identified.

   The possible bases for segmenting the market can be placed into three categories: geographic demographics—

basic identifiable traits of towns, cities, states, regions, and countries; personal demographics—basic identifiable traits of individual final consumers and organizations and groups of final consumers and organizations; and lifestyles—patterns in which people (final consumers and those representing organizational consumers) live and spend time and money. It is generally advisable to use a combination of demographic and lifestyle factors to form possible segmentation bases. Although the distinctions between final and organizational consumers should be kept in mind, the three broad segmentation bases could be used in both cases.

   After establishing possible segmentation bases, a firm is ready to develop consumer profiles, which identify potential market segments by aggregating those with similar attributes and needs.

3. *To explain and contrast undifferentiated marketing (mass marketing), concentrated marketing, and differentiated marketing (multiple segmentation)* Undifferentiated marketing aims at a large, broad consumer market via a single basic marketing plan. In concentrated marketing, a firm aims at a narrow, specific consumer group via one specialized marketing plan catering to the needs of that segment. Under differentiated marketing, a firm appeals to two or more distinct market segments, with a different marketing plan for each. When segmenting, a firm must understand the majority fallacy: The largest segment may not offer the best opportunity; it often has the most competitors.

   In selecting its target market(s), a firm should consider its goals and strengths, competition, segment size and growth potential, distribution needs, required expenditures, profit potential, company image, and its ability to develop and sustain a differential advantage.

Successful segmentation requires differences among and similarities within segments, measurable consumer traits and needs, large enough segments, and efficiency in reaching segments. It should not be abused by appealing to overly small groups, using marketing inefficiently, overly emphasizing imitations of original company products or brands, confusing consumers, and so on.

4. *To show the importance of positioning in developing a marketing strategy* In positioning its offering against competitors, a firm needs to present a combination of customer benefits that are not being provided by others and that are desirable by a target market. Customers must be persuaded that there are clear reasons for buying the firm's products rather than those of its competitors.

The last step in the target marketing process is for a firm to develop a marketing mix for each customer group to which it wants to appeal.

5. *To discuss sales forecasting and its role in target marketing* Short- and long-run sales should be forecast in developing a target market strategy. This helps a firm compute budgets, allocate resources, measure success, analyze productivity, monitor the environment and competition, and adjust marketing plans. A sales forecast describes the expected company sales of a specific good or service to a specific consumer group over a specific time period under a specific marketing program.

A firm can obtain sales-forecasting data from internal and external sources. Forecasting methods range from simple trend analysis to detailed statistical analyses. The best results are obtained when methods and forecasts are combined. A sales forecast should consider the newness of a firm's offering, sales penetration, diminishing returns, and the changing nature of many factors.

Key Terms

market (p. 285)

market segmentation (p. 285)

target market strategy (p. 285)

undifferentiated marketing (mass marketing) (p. 285)

concentrated marketing (p. 285)

differentiated marketing (multiple segmentation) (p. 285)

product differentiation (p. 285)

demand patterns (p. 286)

homogeneous demand (p. 286)

clustered demand (p. 287)

diffused demand (p. 287)

geographic demographics (p. 288)

personal demographics (p. 290)

heavy-usage segment (heavy half) (p. 293)

benefit segmentation (p. 294)

VALS (Values and Lifestyles) program (p. 294)

Social Styles model (p. 294)

majority fallacy (p. 300)

sales forecast (p. 306)

jury of executive (expert) opinion (p. 308)

chain-ratio method (p. 308)

market buildup method (p. 308)

sales penetration (p. 309)

diminishing returns (p. 309)

Review Questions

1. Distinguish between the terms "market" and "market segmentation."
2. Explain this comment: "Sometimes, a firm can achieve a key differential advantage by simply emphasizing how its offering satisfies existing consumer desires and needs better than its competitors do. Sometimes, demand patterns must be modified for consumers to perceive a firm's product differentiation as worthwhile."
3. Differentiate among homogeneous, clustered, and diffused consumer demand. What are the marketing implications of each?
4. Describe five personal demographics pertaining to organizations.
5. What is the majority fallacy? How may a firm avoid it?
6. Cite the five key requirements for successful segmentation.
7. Why is sales forecasting important when developing a target market strategy?
8. Why are long-run sales forecasts for new products more accurate than short-run forecasts?

Discussion Questions

1. How could a regional magazine apply geographic demographic segmentation?
2. Develop a personal-demographic profile of the students at your school. For what goods and services would the class be a good market segment? A poor segment?
3. Describe several potential benefit segments for a firm marketing building security services to business clients.
4. A firm has a sales potential of $10,000,000 and attains actual sales of $4,000,000. What does this signify? What should the firm do next?

Web Exercise

At its Web site, *USA Today* has a highly interactive presentation related to market segmentation. Visit the site (**http://www. usatoday.com/news/graphics/whoweare/flash.htm**) and discuss what you learn.

Practice Quiz

1. What is the first general phase in developing a target market strategy?
   a. Facilitating the market
   b. Analyzing consumer demand
   c. Targeting the market
   d. Developing the marketing strategy

2. Personal demographics include
   a. benefit segments.
   b. usage experience.
   c. company size.
   d. class consciousness.

3. Which statement about benefit segmentation is correct?
   a. Consumer motives may be used to establish benefit segments.
   b. Consumer demographics may be used to establish benefit segments.
   c. Consumer education and income may be used to establish benefit segments.
   d. Consumer usage rates may be used to establish benefit segments.

4. According to the VALS 2 typology, within the ideals type are
   a. achievers.
   b. strivers.
   c. makers.
   d. thinkers.

5. Which of the following is *not* a lifestyle designation of the Social Styles model?
   a. Drivers
   b. Believers
   c. Expressives
   d. Amiables

6. In general, female shoppers in supermarkets, as compared to males,
   a. buy fewer items.
   b. spend more time shopping.
   c. use a shopping list less often.
   d. are less likely to bring children.

7. For a firm with limited resources and abilities, the *least* promising method of developing a target market is
   a. differentiated marketing.
   b. concentrated marketing.
   c. undifferentiated marketing.
   d. benefit segmentation.

8. Differentiated marketing is appropriate if
   a. benefit segmentation cannot be used.
   b. a firm wishes to maximize per-unit profits by appealing to only one segment.
   c. diffused demand can be satisfied by offering unique marketing mixes to each cluster.
   d. homogenous demand exists in a particular market.

9. A consumer goods marketer produces multiple brands of shampoo that are positioned for consumers with dyed hair, dandruff, oily hair, or dry hair. This strategy illustrates
   a. the majority fallacy.
   b. concentrated marketing.
   c. undifferentiated marketing.
   d. differentiated marketing.

10. Wholesalers and retailers usually find differentiated marketing on the part of their suppliers to be attractive because it
    a. can offer them some brand exclusivity.
    b. can allow them to avoid having to carry their own private brands.
    c. lets them avoid having to reach multiple segments.
    d. means that they cannot concentrate orders with fewer suppliers.

11. Which of the following is a criterion for successful market segmentation?
    a. There must not be differences among consumers.
    b. Each segment must be located within a small geographic area.
    c. There must not be consumer similarities within each segment identified.
    d. A segment must be large enough to cover costs.

12. A firm is abusing segmentation when it
    a. becomes too efficient.
    b. is consumer oriented.
    c. becomes short-run oriented rather than long-run oriented.
    d. is generating too much profit.

13. The upper sales limit for a company is defined as its
    a. sales ladder.
    b. sales penetration.
    c. sales potential.
    d. sales forecast.

14. Experience and interaction guide sales forecasting by
    a. sales force surveys.
    b. consumer surveys.
    c. juries of executives.
    d. test marketing.

15. The opposite approach to the market buildup method of sales forecasting is
    a. an experiment.
    b. projection.

c. simulation.
d. the chain-ratio method.

For the answers to these questions, please visit the online site for this book at http://www.atomicdog.com.

Case 1: J.C. Penney: Appealing to the Middle Market[c3-1]

J.C. Penney's (http://www.jcpenney.com) core female shoppers are "middle market" consumers. They are 35 to 54 years old, have a $70,000 median household income, and are married with children. Yet, Penney knows that although many of these consumers continue to shop for housewares and children's clothing at Penney's, some have to be won back for women's clothing, because they are increasingly shopping for their apparel at stores such as Target (http://www.target.com). To expand its customer base, Penney is also looking to attract more 18 to 35 year olds with its American Living (http://www.americanliving.com) and other private-label brands and its Sephora (http://www.sephora.com) cosmetics boutiques in selected stores.

Penney is devoting a lot of attention to developing new brands, many of which are at the high end of its current popular price points, to attract a younger, more affluent customer to the store. New brands include Dorm Life (for the back-to-school season), Linden Street (furniture and home accessories), Decree (jeans and T-shirts for teenage girls), and American Living (apparel and home furnishings). To make room for the new brands, Penney is consolidating or eliminating some of its secondary and tertiary brands, which generally consist of slow-selling merchandise.

As part of its repositioning strategy, Penney has worked with Global Brand Concepts, a division of Polo Ralph Lauren (http://www.polo.com), to develop the American Living brand exclusively for Penney. American Living features a wide range of apparel for women, men, and children—including footwear, fashion accessories, and home furnishings and textiles. In addition to the classic polo shirt, key items include cable-knit sweaters and cotton sundresses for women, pinpoint button-down shirts and sports coats for men, khaki pants for boys, and polo dresses for girls. Home-based items include bedding, bath accessories, and window treatments.

The American Living line was launched during the 2008 Academy Awards. The promotional effort for the brand includes TV and movie theater ads, print ads, direct mail, specialty catalogs, and weekly circulars. A Web site (http://www.americanliving.com) is being developed. However, as part of its licensing agreement, Penney may not refer to Ralph Lauren or Polo Ralph Lauren in its ads or displays.

To better focus on the American Living line, 11 Penney stores feature American Living "hubs," which can be readily observed through the use of white-wood fixtures. Other existing stores are diffusing American Living merchandise throughout various departments. New stores will feature expanded "hubs."

The American Living line is sold in all Penney stores, online, and via print catalogs. According to Penney's chief executive, "American Living truly differentiates J.C. Penney in the marketplace. Nowhere else but J.C. Penney will customers find this level of updates classic style and impeccable quality at such a smart price." Penney hopes that American Living will grow to constitute 5 percent of its total sales. Currently, it represents less than 3 percent of Penney's overall business. Some lines such as dresses and window coverings are strong sellers, while shorts and T-shirts have not sold particularly well.

The launch of private-label lines is a dual-edged sword. On the positive side, it offers retailers such as Penney the opportunity to sell distinctive merchandise, to gain store loyalty, and to have less direct price competition. Private-label merchandise traditionally also carries higher profit margins. On the negative side, most private-label agreements do not provide manufacturer-promotional support or markdown allowances for unsold merchandise.

Recently, Penney opened Sephora USA cosmetics and fragrance boutiques in 72 stores. It plans to expand these outlets to encompass 300 Penneys. Sephora products are targeted to 18- to 35-year-old women, who typically account for higher average sales than Penney's middle-aged female customers.

Questions

1. What other consumer demographic and lifestyle factors besides age and income should Penney analyze? How would you apply these factors in Penney's strategy?
2. Visit this section of the Penney Web site (http://www.jcpenneybrands.com) and discuss how American Living fits in with Penney's target market strategy.
3. How would you attract additional trendy young women to a Penney store?
4. Compare the positioning strategies of J.C. Penney and Target. Utilize secondary sources such as articles and each firm's Web site.

[c3-1] The data in the case are drawn from Cecile B. Corral, "Profits Halved, J.C. Penney Aims at 'Better' Zone," *Home Textiles Today* (May 19, 2008), pp. 1, 21; David Moin, "Penney's Recession Strategy," *Women's Wear Daily* (April 17, 2008), p. 3; and Jane Porter and Burt Helm, "Doing Whatever Gets Them in the Door," *Business Week* (June 30, 2008), pp. 60–61.

Case 2: What Does It Take to Be a B-to-B Value Merchant?[c3-2]

As a reseller, a "value merchant" recognizes that suppliers have their own costs and that consumers are interested in getting a good value from a purchase. The merchant works to obtain a fair return for both the supplier and customers. In contrast, a "value spendthrift" loses sight of its value to the two parties. In terms of behavior, a value spendthrift may routinely generate more business through low prices, offer price concessions, give services away to close a deal, or complain that a supplier's prices are too high.

To transform itself from a value spendthrift into a value merchant, a firm needs to assess and modify its compensation and training programs. The SKF Group (http://www.skf.com), a Swedish bearings company, bases one-half of its salesperson incentive compensation on specific targets, such as using a document solutions program to the value the firm generates for its customers. The remaining one-half of incentive compensation is based on net profit after capital costs for specific territories, businesses, and divisions.

Other b-to-b firms also stress gross margin profitability over sales targets. Territory gross margin profitability is commonly calculated as sales revenue less cost of goods sold equals gross profits. Expenses under a salesperson's control and allowance for bad debts are also generally deducted from gross profits to compute a territory's gross profit margin.

To reinforce the value merchant orientation, a firm's management also needs to provide its salespeople with more tools to document the superior value of its goods. This typically involves sales training and "hands-on" coaching and support. Applied Industrial Technologies (http://www.applied.com), a reseller of bearings and other industrial supplies, requires every salesperson to record all his/her efforts to demonstrate value as part of the firm's documented value added (DVA) program. Since it began, the DVA program has documented more than $1 billion in savings for Applied's customers. Demonstrating customer savings is helpful in instilling customer loyalty and reducing some resistance to price increases.

Grainger Industrial Supply (http://www.grainger.com), a wholesaler of maintenance, repair, and operating supplies (MRO), has a certified value seller program in which salespeople are taught and then practice value-selling skills. Salespeople also need to understand and communicate Grainger's value advantage in managing infrequent and small purchases of MRO supplies. Two weeks after the end of the course, each attendee must develop a value proposition for one customer. To become certified, a salesperson must develop a sales presentation relevant to a customer's business, as well as handle specific questions and objections. Grainger further reinforces its value advantage through local and national contests.

Value merchants try to make business more profitable by finding value drains and value leaks. Value drains consist of services that cost the supplier more than they are worth to its customers. Value leaks are customer activities that increase the cost of doing business for the customer and supplier but do not decrease costs or add value. An example of a value drain involves Tata Steel (http://www.tatasteel.com), a supplier of steel tubes used in the manufacture of boilers. Though Tata oiled the tubes to avoid rusting, a value analysis found that its customers favored tubes with rust. Removing the oiling process saved Tata's customers between $30 to $40 per metric ton; it also lowered Tata's costs.

In an example of a value leak, Tata Steel shipped steel reinforcing bars to its construction customers in 12 meter lengths, when its customers desired lengths of either 10 or 11 meters. As a result of a customer value process (CVP), Tata now delivers the bars in ready-to-use lengths. As a result of CVP, Tata's top customers accounted for 35 percent of its sales in 2005. In 2002, before CVP was implemented, this group of customers accounted for 15 percent of Tata's total revenues.

Questions

1. Develop a brief questionnaire to administer to a salesperson to show that he or she understands the difference between his or her firm's being a value merchant or a value spendthrift.
2. Conduct Web research on Grainger Industrial Supply. Identify how it generates value for its MRO (maintenance, repair, and operating supply customers).
3. Provide an example of a value drain for an industrial supplier, and state how you would handle it.
4. Provide an example of a value leak for an industrial supplier, and state how you would handle it.

[c3-2] The data in the case are drawn from James C. Anderson, Nirmalya Kumar, and James A. Narus, "Be a Value Merchant," http://www.salesandmarketing.com (May 6, 2008).

Case 3: Conducting Lifestyle Segmentation with PRIZM NE[c3-3]

Through Claritas Corporation's (http://www.claritas.com) PRIZM NE program, marketers can better understand the lifestyle behaviors of their customers, and they will learn how to best reach these customers and others with similar characteristics. PRIZM NE projections rely on the 2000 U.S. Census.

The PRIZM NE system classifies households into demographic and behavioral segments. Each segment is defined by product purchases (e.g., food and beverages, clothing, household goods, appliances, electronics, sports equipment, and autos); lifestyles (e.g., travel, vacations, hobbies, sports, and music); media used (e.g., cable, print, outdoor, broadcast television, radio, and Internet); and neighborhoods (maps showing high potential areas and highly penetrated areas).

PRIZM NE links a business client's customer data bases with data on a neighborhood's demographics, syndicated research data from firms such as Nielsen (http://www.nielsen.com), J.D. Power (http://www.jdpower.com), Polk (http://www.polk.com), IRI (http://www.infores.com), NPD (http://www.npd.com), and Simmons (http://www.smrb.com), and survey research. With these linkages, PRIZM NE determines the types of consumers most apt to buy a firm's goods or services. PRIZM NE works with geographic areas. This enables a marketer to determine where to promote products, where additional stores and distribution centers should be located, and which geographic regions require additional advertising and sales support.

The 66 different segments that PRIZM NE uses for U.S. consumer households are numbered according to socioeconomic rank (based on income, education, and home value). These groups are sorted in two different ways: by social groups (11 groups based on urbanization and socioeconomic rank) and by life-stage groups (11 groups based on age and presence of children at home and socioeconomic rank).

The groups live in diverse areas ranging from downtown in major cities to suburban and rural areas. Let's compare the characteristics of the midtown mix, "middleburbs," and rustic living groups. The midtown mix group is the most ethically diverse, consisting of singles, couples, homeowners, and renters. Households within this group are typically childless couples who pursue active social lives. The group frequents health clubs and restaurants, drives small imports, and buys the latest in consumer electronics.

Middleburb consumers comprise five segments that live in middle-class suburban communities. Two of these have very young residents, two have large compositions of seniors, and one is middle-aged. Middleburbs contain a mix of homeowners and renters. With good jobs, middleburbs visit nightclubs and casual dining restaurants, shop at mid-scale department stores, travel across the United States and Canada, and purchase CDs and DVDs in large quantities.

In contrast, the rustic living group lives in isolated towns and rural villages. As a group, it has modest income, aging homes, and blue-collar occupations. These consumers spend their leisure time fishing, hunting, attending church and veterans club functions, and enjoying country music.

Let's look at how direct marketers can be more effective by utilizing PRIZM NE:

- Direct marketers often advertise in traditional media to generate mailing lists for contact via catalog mailings and phone. PRIZM NE can help determine the media patterns of list members. For example, if a ZIP code has a large proportion of "Winner's Circle" consumers (wealthy suburbanites who live in new subdivisions, like to travel, and eat out), good media for advertising would be *Smithsonian Magazine* (http://www.smithsonianmag.com) and the *Wall Street Journal* (http://www.wsj.com).
- Direct marketers who use club-based lists (such as college alumni or fraternal organizations) can use PRIZM NE to select the best names for subsequent mailings.
- Direct marketers can use PRIZM NE to prioritize their response times and communication formats to a large number of inquiries. For example, high-priority customers could be contacted through a salesperson's call, whereas lower priority consumers may be contacted via E-mail.

Questions

1. Discuss the advantages of a stockbroker's use of PRIZM NE as compared to its using census data that contained detailed demographic data for geographic areas.
2. What goods and services are apt to be heavily used by the midtown mix group? Explain your answer.
3. What goods and services are apt to be heavily used by middleburb consumers? Explain your answer.
4. Describe ways that apparel retailers can use PRIZM NE.

[c3-3] The data in the case are drawn from "PRIZM NE: Lifestyle Segmentation System," http://www.claritas.com (February 11, 2006); "PRIZM NE: Successful Direct Marketing Applications," http://www.claritas.com (February 11, 2006); and "PRIZM NE: The New Evolution in Segmentation," http://www.claritas.com (July 3, 2008).

Case 4: Jumping on the Micro Segmentation Bandwagon[c3-4]

Department stores appeal to a wide range of shoppers, whereas niche stores selling women's clothing include bridal shops, clothing stores for girls and teenagers, clothing stores that specialize in given price points (such as every item under $25), and stores featuring maternity wear, petite-size clothing, and plus-size clothing. Let's examine the niche strategies of four successful firms: Designing Solutions (http://www.mydesigningsolutions.com), TLM Industries (http://www.tlmind.com), Jets.com (http://www.jets.com), and Bottlegreen (http://www.bottle-green.co.uk).

Deborah Wiener's firm, Designing Solutions, specializes in designing family-friendly, child-proof interiors for clients' homes. Wiener helps her clients choose stain-resistant fabrics, lamps that are less prone to breaking when dropped, and carpeting that can withstand heavy use by young children and pets. She formed her firm after talking to friends and acquaintances with young children who related that typical interior decorators were either too fancy or not practical enough in their selections. She began writing columns in local publications and advertised in religious organization weeklies to promote her niche-based decorating business. The firm's Web site now averages close to 9,000 visitors per month.

When Tim Mossberg started TLM Industries, he focused on distributing screen-printed cups and mugs with logos to convenience stores. Mossberg's clients then told him that they needed uniforms for their employees that would last through several washings. Many of these businesses expressed concern that current suppliers did not stock the larger sizes needed by many of their workers. After Mossberg traveled to clients in five southern states, he decided to switch to supplying uniforms. Mossberg's firm now supplies uniforms for chefs, security personnel, and factory workers. He also supplies dress shirts for ladies and men as well as smocks and polos.

Jets.com is a jet membership service that provides private jets for both individuals and corporations. The firm's technology includes a data base of aircraft located throughout the world. Using an online auction format, consumers receive instantaneous price quotes from selected aircraft based on point-to-point trip descriptions. The "hot deals" part of Jets.com's Web site lists open routes by destination and departure cities, aircraft, and time availability.

Potential clients can book a trip online or call for a quote. Frequent users of Jets.com receive additional benefits such as first-class concierge service and guaranteed fixed pricing. As part of its concierge service, files are maintained of specific likes and dislikes of customers. Ground transportation, specific catering options, and even product requests such as beach towels on certain flights are noted and fulfilled.

Bottlegreen's products consist of premium soft drinks aimed at 4 to 12 year olds. Called "Junior Cordials," these products consist of a mix of fruit juices made from natural ingredients that are free from additives, colorings, sweeteners, and preservatives. The cordials are available in three flavors: Awesome Apple & Elderberry, Brill Blackcurrant and Apple, and So Ho Orange & Mango Cordial. To reduce storage space and to facilitate handling, each bottle is designed to be diluted with ten parts of water.

In developing a marketing plan, care must be taken to properly define the niche. Too narrow a niche may limit demand, tie a business around a technology or product that can become obsolete, or make the firm highly vulnerable to changes in demand. A niche also cannot be so tightly defined that the market size cannot be profitable. On the other hand, too broad a definition would result in a small firm's competing in a general marketplace with many large competitors. One way of determining if a niche is properly defined is to examine the survival rate for older competitors in comparable markets.

Questions

1. What are the pros and cons of pursuing a niche strategy for an all-natural food store?
2. Discuss the potential pitfalls in defining a niche too broadly. Too narrowly.
3. Explain the relationship between niche marketing and concentrated marketing.
4. For one of the firms noted in this case, present a differentiated marketing strategy for it to expand.

[c3-4] The data in the case are drawn from Jemima Bokaie, "Soft-Drink Firm Eyes Premium Kids' Niche," *Marketing* (April 23, 2008), p. 8; "What Makes Us Different," http://www.mysedigningsolutions.com/different (August 3, 2008); "TLM Industries," http://www.tlmind.com (August 3, 2008); and "Jets.com," http://www.jets.com (August 3, 2008).

Two Target Markets for the Price of One[pc-3]

INTRODUCTION

Successful marketing communicates the message "this brand is for you" by product features, packaging, channels of distribution, advertising, or some combination of those signals. A challenge for many marketing managers, however, is communicating to more than one segment of "you." That's because identifying a brand with one segment might signal to another segment the message that it is not the intended buyer or would not want to be.

Such a problem might be handled with multiple brands offered by one company, which target different audiences. That solution solves the problem of communicating to different groups, but it has two downsides. Clearly, it raises per-unit costs to produce two or more marketplace offerings that might not have substantive differences, simply to create different images of who uses the brand. Likewise, it dilutes the marketing effect. Having twice the dollars to promote one brand permits those dollars to produce far greater impact than is achieved by splitting the budget. The solution suggested here is dual targeting: most pertinently, targeting two generations by directing the same ad for the same brand to young adults and their parents' age-50-and-older generation.

THE RATIONALE BEHIND DUAL MARKETING

Marketers can simultaneously attract young adults to build brand image and their age-50-and-older parents to pay the bill. Different branding for different age segments offers a conventional but expensive solution to the problem that 25-year-olds often reject offerings that clearly target their parents' baby boomer generation. By contrast, skillful dual targeting with one brand lets age-50-and-older buyers play subordinate but attractive roles in the advertising of everything from cell-phone service and beer to high-ticket items. The astute marketer gains the advantage of the baby boomers' greater purchasing power without sacrificing a youthful image.

Although this case will begin with examples from the marketing of a relatively inexpensive service and consumer packaged goods, it will move on to categories in which dual targeting is most important: high-ticket products.

T-MOBILE AND COORS LIGHT

It is easy to find not only ads targeting two generations but also consumer comments about them. For any marketing manager who wants to know how a given commercial or print ad is viewed, the "blogosphere" offers an anecdotal database. For this case, the blogosphere was employed to see what comments would be prompted by an unrelated pair of specific commercials targeting two generations. The commercials to which we sought reactions aired in June 2007 (and thereafter), sponsored by T-Mobile for a cell-phone plan and by Molson Coors Brewing Company.

T-Mobile

The T-Mobile (**http://www.tmobile.com**) TV commercial was one of several that promoted the company's "Fave [favorite] Five" plan: unlimited calls to any five individuals, a set that could not be changed more often than monthly. For teens and young adults, the plan provides the ability to talk often, or perhaps constantly, with "five best friends." For their parents' generation, it provides the ability to keep in touch with family members, including those same teens and young adults who might be their children.

T-Mobile's dual-targeting advertising approach showed parents asking a teenage son and daughter for the list of whom they picked for their "fave five."

After the daughter mentioned her five friends, the son named the same list of five that the daughter had named—saying that her friends are "hot."

The daughter looked at her father and said in dismay, "Are you going to do anything?"

The father replies, "Maybe you should have uglier friends," while the mother shrugs in acquiescence.

A female blogger (Web logger) commented: "I don't know why that commercial cracks me up so much, but the parents are hilarious." A marketing manager interested in dual targeting would note that in a message primarily aimed at teens, the parents—also potential cell-phone plan customers—were attractively included, although in a supporting role.

Note: By 2008, the "fave five" concept had become so popular that T-Mobile created numerous Individual myFaves plans (**http://www.t-mobile.com/shop/plans/#Individual+myFaves**) and Family myFaves plans (**http://www.t-mobile.com/shop/plans/#Family+myFaves**). T-Mobile promoted the individual plans at its Web site by saying: "Call the people who matter most to you—regardless of which carrier they use. myFaves plans give you unlimited calls to the five numbers you call most, as well as free domestic long distance and no digital roaming charges anywhere across the U.S." It promoted the family plans as "Family matters, and so do savings! You get both with two lines, up to three more lines at just

[pc-3] Adapted by the authors from Betsy D. Gelb, "Two for the Price of One," *Marketing Management* (November-December 2007), pp. 35–38. Reprinted by permission of the American Marketing Association.

$9.99 each, a shared pool of Whenever Minutes. The myFaves Family plans also include unlimited calls to the five numbers you call most—and everyone can choose their own top five."

Coors Light

Coors Light (http://www.coorslight.com) drew a blog notice for a commercial that likewise targeted two generations.

It was a father and adult-son talk in which the father commented that the son must be going to a lot of parties and meeting a lot of women—so he should think about "protection."

The son, horrified, said, "Dad, I'm 26 years old!"

The father then pulled out a can of Coors Light, referring with approval to the way the can's lining protected its chill.

As in the T-Mobile spot, the older adult played a supporting role in a tongue-in-cheek message targeting an audience one generation younger—but with a creative treatment taking into account that the age-50-and-older generation is also a potential customer for the brand.

Note: There are recent TV ads for Coors Light at its Web site. To be socially responsible, the site visitor is asked for his or her age to verify that the person is at least 21 years of age.

ZEROING IN ON PARENTS *AND* KIDS

As discussed by blogger Trent Hamm at the Simple Dollar Web site (http://www.thesimpledollar.com/2008/04/10/born-to-buy-nick-elodeon-and-the-anti-adult-bias), dual target marketing also has great potential in appealing to parents and their kids. For example, regular Alpha-Bits (http://www.kraftfoods.com/PostCereals/AlphaBitsHome.html) is "targeted to moms, because the letters are seen as educational and beneficial for kids and it has less sugar than Alpha-Bits with marshmallows, which is targeted only to kids. It's easy to see where this goes: the maker of Alpha-Bits is happy if either the parent or the child goes into the cereal aisle and picks out an Alpha-Bits product. So they simply make a 'mom' version and a 'kid' version and market each to that audience, focusing specifically on the attributes attractive to each. The version for moms is a pretty healthy cereal and a potential educational opportunity—seems good. The version for kids is a marshmallowy sugary fun time—seems good."

Hamm adds that: "This happens over and over again. McDonald's (http://www.mcdonalds.com) targets kids with Happy Meals and parents with the salad line and burgers. Kool-Aid (http://www.kraftfoods.com/koolaid) tells parents that it's an inexpensive way to get Vitamin C and shows kids partying with Kool-Aid Man. (How can I compete with Kool-Aid Man, really? He's big and red and bursts through walls!)"

MOM AND DAD HAVE THE MONEY

T-Mobile, Coors Light, and the other brands just highlighted do illustrate dual targeting. However, the concept appears most relevant not for the marketers of inexpensive goods and services but for those marketing relatively high-dollar products. For these firms, establishing separate brands targeted at separate generations of consumers will not help if most younger potential buyers simply cannot afford the product. Thus, without employing a dual-targeting approach, a marketing manager has a difficult decision to make:

- Do I go where the money is and target the age-50-and-older buyers with the economic power to well-afford the car, resort vacation, or flat-panel TV I am promoting?
- Or do I go where I want my brand image to be and target the age-30-and-younger buyer I want associated with my brand—painfully aware of how few such buyers can afford to buy compared with those a generation older?

Dual targeting seems to meet both marketing priorities. The proposition that the cohort of age-50-and-older consumers represents huge purchasing power is easily supported. In the United States, an Environmental Systems Research Institute (http://www.esri.com) report projecting to 2005 the data from the 2000 Census showed average household income of $146,672 for householders in the 45-54 age category (the highest of any group) and $130,738 for those ages 55-64. In Canada, a Tetrad Demographics (http://www.tetrad.com/pcensus/can/candata.html) report—based on that nation's 2001 Census—showed that the 57 percent of Canadian households headed by an individual age 45 or older make up 65 percent of the households with incomes of more than $150,000 [Canadian dollars] and 59 percent of those with incomes between $100,000 and $149,000.

In both the United States and Canada, then, age-50-and-older buyers show the highest income levels. But income is only the beginning of the story. Assets also provide purchasing power because retirees with savings are willing to "dis-save" (spend assets)—adding dollars to the revenue available to marketers from older consumers.

U.S. Bureau of the Census (http://www.census.gov) figures that categorize asset pools by age categories reveal the importance of that additional dimension. Based on panel data, they show roughly a 2:1 asset advantage for married-couple households with an age-55-and-older head of household—compared with parallel households headed by someone age 35-54. The *Wall Street Journal* describes "aging boomers" as commanding $2 trillion in annual spending power.

REASONS TO TARGET YOUNGER BUYERS

The financial picture suggests targeting age-50-and-older buyers when possible. However, many marketers believe that such buyers are stigmatized by those a generation younger, who might transfer that stigma by association to a brand that targets their parents. The young, those marketers reason, are worth more per buyer in lifetime profitability for three reasons:

1. Depending on the product category, they simply are more likely to need whatever it is the marketer wants to sell them. In many categories, almost all sales to age-50-and-older

households are replacement sales. By contrast, if younger households are buying for the first time, then their current version of a product doesn't need to wear out or become obsolete to tempt them to purchase.

2. Younger buyers are less likely to have a fixed brand preference if they don't yet own the product. Shifting a buyer away from his previous brand for a replacement purchase is, in a sense, expensive; switchers must be "bought" with product features, price cuts, sales promotions to retailers, large advertising budgets, or some combination of those attractions. A first-time buyer (easier to find in the age-30-and-younger pool) needs no such special incentives.

3. They will have more years to buy the brand if they can be attracted to it.

SOLVING THE PROBLEM

Those competing priorities—buying power versus image—provide a challenge best solved by targeting both generations simultaneously. Hypothetical illustrations of how to do so, for high-dollar items, are offered here. But expect that astute managers will soon be adopting approaches that are remarkably similar to them.

Picture a 30-second TV spot designed to let a marketer have it both ways. Viewers see a flashy red convertible and an attractive 20-something professionally dressed woman standing next to it, clicking to unlock the door. She flashes the audience a wide-eyed smile and says, "My parents changed my life when they bought me this [brand name here]! When I drive to work I'm telling the world I'm on my way up. And when I meet new people on weekends, they can see that I'm somebody special."

No younger viewer will think that this commercial promotes the equivalent of "your father's Oldsmobile" (an old-fashioned—and now defunct—brand that General Motors could not successfully marketer to younger adults). Will parents consider buying the car as a college graduation gift for a son or daughter, or as a gift for one who is newly hired, newly promoted, newly married, or has now provided a grandchild? Some parents will. Others will think, "Pat doesn't need a car that nice, but I do!"

Such a commercial exemplifies dual targeting. The one-generation-older viewer is not being ignored by the advertiser—for a change. That age-50-and-older viewer is shown as generous, and he can now associate that car (that youthful-image car) with his own generation. Meanwhile, a 28-year-old sees only a woman he'd like to meet and a car he'd like to own. And all of that happens in 30 seconds.

Note: At the time of Oldsmobile's demise, after more than 100 years on the market, this is what one business reporter said: "Oldsmobile, as a brand, never really fit in recent years. It was above Buick, but below Cadillac. It was above Pontiac but not considered as sporty or youthful as Chevrolet. It sold but one SUV and, despite ads proclaiming the opposite, never really succeeded in shedding its image as a magnet for older drivers. Try as it might,

GM's Oldsmobile couldn't seem to find its niche." (**http://www. money.cnn.com/2000/12/12/companies/oldsmobile_overview**)

APPLYING THE BASIC IDEA

Clearly, dual targeting can go much further. As it has become an advertising cliché to show multi-ethnic groups of young people enjoying cruises, social events, and athletic activities, the increasing fitness of the baby boomer generation will allow natural inclusion of a few receding hairlines in those ads.

A better imagination, however, moves a marketer from simply showing a wider age range of potential buyers to modifying a product to attract them, as often occurs. For example, more vacation resorts and trip packagers now feature not just activities for young children, but also for baby boomers/"echo boomers": golf, tennis, skiing, sailing, hiking, and/or rock climbing. Certainly, intriguing combinations (e.g., photography workshops and snowboarding) are the next step. Mom or Dad's credit card handles everything. But to preserve the youthful image, the ads show the snowboarder clearly—and the parent off to the side behind the lens.

Marketers of some of today's popular high-tech products can also benefit from that kind of thinking. Video games might permit intergenerational competition by offering customized variations to account for the equivalent of golf handicaps, allowing players mismatched in skill and sophistication to compete. Commercials promoting such games would target high-school-age users—pointing out that if Dad knows he can win once in a while, then "he'll be paying and he'll be playing."

An obvious question is whether dual targeting applies beyond age categories. Can the concept move a specialty ethnic food into a broader consumer marketplace without sullying its legitimacy for its core constituency? Can goods or services slide into a unisex image without alienating the men or the women usually associated with their purchase? As with so many issues in marketing, the answer is a firm "it depends." The success of dual targeting appears to depend on the plausibility and acceptability of the scenario that is presented.

Both work well in the commercial for the gift car—which does not blur the image of the desired consumer but supplements the visual youth of the driver with the vocal mention of the (older) buyer. And both the vacation site offering photography and rock climbing and the "handicap-friendly" video game present roughly the same prioritizing: younger person as "star," older person as admirer and/or enabler. In parallel fashion, one can imagine a successful ad showing a mainstream supermarket customer or restaurant patron learning from a Hispanic, Japanese, Indian, or Middle Eastern expert about authentic ethnic dishes. Such an approach elevates the importance of the ethnic buyer, but it can simultaneously attract an additional set of users.

Those examples suggest a checklist for deciding when the dual-targeting approach is most likely to prove successful. Dual targeting works best when a branded product is clearly a "natural" for one audience (e.g., young buyers), but a marketer wisely wants a second audience to share the experience and possibly pay the bill. That secondary audience, in turn, must be complimented by its association with the primary target group.

Consideration of those two factors—one primary audience with which the second is happy to be associated but also happy to be secondary—also indicates situations in which dual targeting will fail. For example, targeting both sexes for a product usually associated with one or the other seems problematic. An ad with a male expert showing the fine points of a power mower to a female might not disturb the mower's masculine image or perturb male buyers, but it is likely to annoy females who consider themselves an equally primary audience. An ad for a wok, reversing the typical gender roles by targeting males, offers a comparable problem: Neither female nor male cooks will see a reason to be relegated to a supporting role. It becomes clear, then, why such products are often advertised either in gender-targeted magazines and newspaper sections or on gender-targeted Web sites and TV channels—viewed by fewer consumers who might be resentful.

By contrast, dual-age targeting appears far more acceptable to both constituencies. Given skillful execution, it can offer the best of both generational worlds.

Questions

1. Comment on this statement: "A challenge for many marketing managers is communicating to more than one segment of 'you' because identifying a brand with one segment might signal to another segment the message that it is not the intended buyer or would not want to be."

2. Discuss the concept of "dual marketing." When is best to use this approach? When is it inappropriate?

3. Assess the T-Mobile target market efforts described in the case.

4. Assess the Coors Light target market efforts described in the case.

5. Do you agree that dual marketing is best suited for marketers of high-end products? Why or why not?

6. Present a current example of a firm that you believe is doing a good job of dual marketing and explain your reasoning.

7. Present a current example of a firm that you believe is doing a poor job of dual marketing and explain your reasoning.

Part 4

Product Planning

A firm needs a systematic marketing plan if it is going to practice the marketing concept. This plan centers on the four elements of the marketing mix: product, distribution, promotion, and price. We present these elements in Parts 4 through 7, with Part 4 devoted to product planning.

11 Basic Concepts in Product Planning

Here, we define tangible, augmented, and generic products and distinguish among different types of consumer and industrial products (both goods and services). We look at product mix strategies, product management organizations, and product positioning in detail. The roles of branding and packaging in product planning are also covered. The chapter concludes with a look at the global dimensions of product planning.

12 Goods Versus Services Planning

In this chapter, we look at the scope of goods and services, and present a goods/services continuum. We review goods and services classification systems. Then, we study the special considerations in the marketing of services. We also see that service marketing has lagged behind goods marketing and why this is changing. At this point, our discussion turns to nonprofit marketing and its distinction from profit-oriented marketing. We examine how nonprofits can be classified and the role of nonprofit marketing in the economy.

13 Conceiving, Developing, and Managing Products

To conclude Part 4, we look at products from their inception to their removal from the marketplace. We present the concept of the product life cycle and discuss types of new products, reasons for new-product failures, and the new-product planning process. We explain the growth of products in terms of the adoption and diffusion processes, and note several methods for extending the lives of mature products. Product deletion strategies are also offered.

After reading Part 4, you should understand element 10 of the strategic marketing plan outlined in Table 3-2 (page 74).

Chapter 11

Basic Concepts in Product Planning

Procter & Gamble (P&G) (http://www.pg.com) is the largest U.S. maker of household products and the largest advertiser in the world. P&G has a very strong portfolio of brands, with 300 or so brands marketed in more than 160 countries. Twenty-three of its brands have sales of at least $1 billion per year: Actonel, Always, Ariel, Bounty, Braun, Charmin, Crest, Dawn, Downy/Lenor, Duracell, Folgers, Gain, Gillette, Head & Shoulders, Iams, Olay, Oral-B, Pampers, Pantene, Prilosec, Pringles, Tide, and Wella. Other popular P&G brands are Cascade, Cover Girl, Mr. Clean, Scope, and Vicks 44.

P&G constantly adjusts its product mix to reflect industry growth, competition, and profit prospects. It recently sold off Spic and Span cleaning products, Jif peanut butter, Crisco shortening, and its juice business. To increase its presence in beauty care, it bought Clairol in 2001 and Wella in 2003. In its largest acquisition, P&G bought Gillette (http://www.gillette.com) in 2005 for $57 billion. This purchase gives P&G an even stronger presence in the male market and has led to advertising and distribution savings.

P&G traces its history to 1837, when William Procter, a candle maker, and James Gamble, a soap maker, merged their businesses. By 1859, the company had become one of the largest firms in Cincinnati with annual revenues of $1 million. Among its most successful products and their first introduction were Ivory soap (1879), Crisco shortening (1911), Tide detergent (1946), Crest toothpaste (1955), Charmin Paper (1957), Downy fabric softener (1960), Head & Shoulders shampoo (1961), Pampers disposable diapers (1961), Bounce fabric softener sheets (1972), and Febreze Air Effects (2004).

P&G has been associated with a number of marketing firsts. These include sponsorship of daytime radio and TV dramas (called soap operas due to P&G's role as an advertiser) and the development of the product management organization. When it introduced Camay, a soap with a different target market and features than its popular Ivory Soap (with its 99-and-44-one-hundredths percent pure positioning), P&G was concerned that Camay's marketing plan too closely resembled that of Ivory's. So, in 1927, P&G appointed a separate manager to oversee Camay, and the modern product management system was born.[1]

In this chapter, we will look at the product-planning decisions a firm must make, including product management organizations, product positioning, branding, and packaging strategies.

Chapter Objectives

1. To define product planning and differentiate among tangible, augmented, and generic products
2. To examine the various types of products, product mixes, and product management organization forms from which a firm may select
3. To discuss product positioning and its usefulness for marketers
4. To study branding and packaging, and their roles in product planning
5. To look at the global dimensions of product planning

---

[1] Various company and other sources.

11-1 OVERVIEW

Product planning is systematic decision making relating to all aspects of the development and management of a firm's products, including branding and packaging. Each *product* consists of a bundle of attributes (features, functions, benefits, and uses) capable of exchange or use, usually a mix of tangible and intangible forms. A product "may be an idea, a physical entity (a good), or a service, or any combination of the three. It exists for the purpose of exchange in satisfying individual and organizational objectives."[2]

A well-structured product plan lets a company pinpoint opportunities, develop appropriate marketing programs, coordinate the product mix, maintain successful products as long as possible, reappraise faltering products, and delete undesirable products. A firm should define products in three distinct ways: tangible, augmented, and generic. By considering all three definitions, consumer needs, competitive offerings, and distinctive product attributes can be better identified. This is illustrated in Figure 11-1.

A *tangible product* is a basic physical entity, service, or idea; it has precise specifications and is sold under a given description or model number. Examples of tangible products are Apple iPhone 3G (**http://www.apple.com/iphone**); a Cat 776D Off Highway Tractor (**http://www.cat.com/products**); a 75-minute Circle Line cruise to the Statue of Liberty (**http://www.circleline42.com**); and a proposal to cut state income taxes by 3.5 percent. Color, style, size, weight, durability, quality of construction, price, and efficiency in use are some tangible product features.

An *augmented product* includes not only the tangible elements of a product, but also the accompanying cluster of image and service features. One political candidate may receive more votes than another because of charisma (augmented product), despite identical platform issues (tangible product). Rolex watches (**http://www.rolex.com**) are popular chiefly due to the image of luxury and status they convey. At Cummins Engine (**http://www.cummins.com**), offering augmented products means helping customers to succeed, not just selling them quality engines. Cummins uses a value-added package of products, information systems, and support services to enhance customer performance.

> **Product planning** means devising and managing **products** that satisfy consumers.

> A tangible product has precise specifications; an augmented product includes image and service features; and a generic product centers on consumer benefits.

Tangible product
- Color
- Design
- Quality
- Size
- Weight
- Features
- Materials used in construction
- Efficiency in use
- Power source
- Brand name

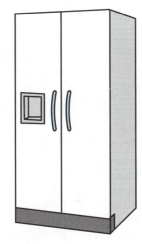

Augmented product
- Image of product and brand
- Status of product and brand
- Guarantee/warranty
- Delivery
- Installation
- Repair facilities
- Instructions and technical advice
- Credit
- Return policy
- Follow-up service

Generic product
- Stores, preserves, cools, and otherwise helps to satisfy home food-consumption needs

Figure 11-1

Illustrating the Three Product Definitions

---

[2] "Dictionary," **http://www.marketingpower.com/_layouts/Dictionary.aspx?dLetter=P** (March 22, 2009).

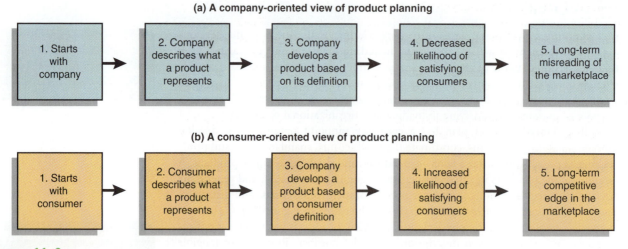

(a) A company-oriented view of product planning

| 1. Starts with company | → | 2. Company describes what a product represents | → | 3. Company develops a product based on its definition | → | 4. Decreased likelihood of satisfying consumers | → | 5. Long-term misreading of the marketplace |

(b) A consumer-oriented view of product planning

| 1. Starts with consumer | → | 2. Consumer describes what a product represents | → | 3. Company develops a product based on consumer definition | → | 4. Increased likelihood of satisfying consumers | → | 5. Long-term competitive edge in the marketplace |

Figure 11-2

Applying the Generic Product Concept

Source: Adapted by the authors from Leon G. Schiffman and Elaine Sherman, "Value Orientations of New-Age Elderly: The Coming of an Ageless Market," *Journal of Business Research*, Vol. 22 (March 1991), p. 193.

A *generic product* focuses on what a product means to the customer, not the seller. It is the broadest definition and is consistent with the marketing concept: "In the factory we make cosmetics, and in the drugstore we sell hope" (Charles Revson, founder of Revlon, **http://www.revlon.com**). "We know our customers come to us to buy more than bearings and steel. They come to us looking for solutions" (Timken Company, **http://www.timken.com**).

Two points should be kept in mind when applying the generic product concept. First, because a generic product is a consumer view of what a product represents, a firm should learn what the product means to the consumer before further planning—as shown in Figure 11-2. Second, inasmuch as people in various nations may perceive the same product (such as a car) in different generic terms (such as basic transportation versus comfortable driving), a firm should consider the impact of this on a global strategy.

Chapter 11 provides an overview of product planning. We study the areas in which a firm makes decisions: product type(s), product mix, product management organization, and product positioning. Branding and packaging, as well as considerations for international marketers, are also considered. Chapter 12 covers goods versus services planning. Chapter 13 discusses how to manage products over their lives, from finding new product ideas to deleting faltering products.

11-2 TYPES OF PRODUCTS

The initial product-planning decision is choosing the type(s) of products to offer. Products can be categorized as goods or services and as consumer or industrial. Classification is important because it focuses on the differences in the characteristics of products and the resulting marketing implications.

11-2a Fundamental Distinctions Between Goods and Services

Goods marketing entails the sale of physical products—such as furniture, heavy machinery, food, and stationery. **Service marketing** encompasses the rental of goods, servicing goods owned by consumers, and personal services—such as vehicle rentals, house painting, and accounting services.

> **Goods marketing** relates to selling physical products. **Service marketing** includes rented-goods services, owned-goods services, and nongoods services.

Four attributes generally distinguish services from goods: intangibility, perishability, inseparability from the service provider, and variability in quality. Their impact is greatest for personal services—which are usually more intangible, more perishable, more dependent on the skills of the service provider (inseparability), and have more quality variations than rented- or owned-goods services.

The sales of goods and services are frequently connected. For instance, a computer manufacturer may provide—for an extra fee—extended warranties, customer training, insurance, and financing. In goods marketing, goods dominate the overall offering and services augment them. In service marketing, services dominate the overall offering and goods augment them.

The distinctions between goods and services planning are more fully discussed in Chapter 12.

11-2b   Consumer Products

Consumer products are goods and services destined for the final consumer for personal, family, or household use. The purpose of a good or service designates it as a consumer product. A calculator, dinner at a restaurant, phone service, and an electric pencil sharpener are consumer products only if bought for personal, family, or household use. Consumer products may be classed as convenience, shopping, and specialty products—based on shoppers' awareness of alternative products and their characteristics prior to a shopping trip and the degree of search people will undertake. Placing a product into one of these categories depends on shopper behavior. See Table 11-1.

Convenience products are those bought with a minimum of effort because a consumer has knowledge of product attributes prior to shopping and/or is pressed for time. The person does not want to search for much information and will accept a substitute, such as Green Giant (**http://www.greengiant.com**) instead of Libby's (**http://www.consumer.senecafoods.com/product/branded/libby.cfm**) corn, rather than visit more than one store. Marketing tasks center on distribution at all available outlets, convenient store locations and hours, the use of mass advertising and in-store displays, well-designed store layouts, and self-service to minimize purchase time. Resellers often carry many brands.

> **Consumer products** are final-consumer goods and services that may be categorized as convenience products, shopping products, and specialty products.

Table **11-1**	Characteristics of Consumer Products		
	Type of Product		
Consumer Characteristics	**Convenience**	**Shopping**	**Specialty**
Knowledge prior to purchase	High	Low	High
Effort expended to acquire product	Minimal	Moderate to high	As much as needed
Willingness to accept substitutes	High	Moderate	None
Frequency of purchase	High	Moderate or low	Varies
Information search	Low	High	Low
Major desire	Availability without effort	Comparison shopping to determine best choice	Brand loyalty regardless of price and availability
Examples	(a) Staple: cereal (b) Impulse: candy (c) Emergency: tire repair	(a) Attribute-based: designer clothes (b) Price-based: budget hotel	Hellmann's mayonnaise

Convenience products include staples, impulse products, and emergency products. Staples are low-priced and routinely purchased on a regular basis, such as detergent and cereal. Impulse products are items or brands a person does not plan to buy on a specific store trip, such as candy or a lottery ticket. Nearly one-half of brand decisions at retail stores are made in-store.[3] Emergency products are bought out of urgent need, such as an umbrella in a rainstorm and aspirin for a headache.

Shopping products are those for which people feel they lack sufficient information about product alternatives and their attributes (or prices), and thus, must acquire more knowledge to make a decision. People exert effort because these items are bought infrequently, are expensive, or require comparisons. The marketing emphasis is on full assortments (many colors, sizes, and options), the availability of sales personnel, the communication of competitive advantages, informative ads, well-known brands (or stores), distributor enthusiasm, and customer warranties and follow-up service to reduce perceived risk. Shopping centers and downtown business districts ease shopping behavior by having many adjacent stores.

Shopping products may be attribute- or price-based. With attribute-based products, consumers get information on features, performance, and so forth. The items with the best combination of attributes are bought. Sony electronics (**http://www.sony.com**) and Tommy Hilfiger clothes (**http://www.tommy.com**) are marketed as attribute-based shopping products. With price-based products, people feel the choices are similar and shop for low prices. Budget hotels and low-end electronics are marketed in this way.

Specialty products are particular brands, firms, and persons to which consumers are loyal. People are fully aware of these products and their attributes prior to making a purchase decision. They make a significant effort to acquire the brand desired and will pay an above-average price. They will not buy if their choice is unavailable: Substitutes are not acceptable. The marketing emphasis is on maintaining the attributes that make products unique to loyal patrons; reminder ads; proper distribution (*Business Week* [**http://www.businessweek.com**] uses home subscriptions for loyal customers); brand extension to related products (such as Hellmann's [**http://www.hellmanns.com**] tartar sauce, in addition to the flagship mayonnaise); product improvements; customer contact (such as opt-in E-mail from the Hilton HHonors program [**http://www.hhonors.com**]); and monitoring reseller performance.

This classification is excellent for segmentation because many people may view the same products differently. Tylenol pain reliever (**http://www.tylenol.com**) is a convenience product for some people (who will buy another brand if Tylenol is unavailable), a shopping product for others (who read ingredient labels), and a specialty product for others (who insist on Tylenol). Johnson & Johnson, maker of Tylenol, understands how Tylenol fits into the various categories and markets accordingly.

11-2c Industrial Products

Industrial products are goods and services purchased for use in the production of other goods or services, in the operation of a business, or for resale to other consumers. Customers are manufacturers, wholesalers, retailers, government entities, and other nonprofit organizations.

Products may be grouped by the level of decision making in a purchase, costs, consumption rapidity, role in production, and change in form. Because industrial-products sellers often visit b-to-b customers, stores may not be not involved. Installations, accessory equipment, raw materials, component materials, fabricated parts, business supplies, and business services are types of industrial products. See Table 11-2.

Industrial products are organizational consumer goods and services that may be classified as installations, accessory equipment, raw materials, component materials, fabricated parts, industrial supplies, and industrial services.

---

[3] Jack Neff, "Pick a Product: 40% of Public Decide in Store," *Advertising Age* (July 28, 2008), pp. 1, 31.

Table 11-2	Characteristics of Industrial Products						
	Type of Product						
Characteristics	**Installations**	**Accessory Equipment**	**Raw Materials**	**Component Materials**	**Fabricated Parts**	**Supplies**	**Services**
Degree of consumer decision making	High	Moderate	Low	Low	Low	Very low	Low to high
Per-unit costs	High	Moderate	Low	Low	Low	Very low	Low to moderate
Rapidity of consumption	Very low	Low	High	High	High	High	Low to high
Item becomes part of final product	No	No	Sometimes	Yes	Yes	No	Sometimes
Item undergoes changes in form	No	No	Yes	Yes	No	No	Sometimes
Major consumer desire	Long-term facilities	Modern equipment	Continuous, low-cost, graded materials	Continuous, low-cost, specified materials	Continuous, low-cost, fabricated materials	Continuous, low-cost, efficient supplies	Efficient, expert services
Examples	Production plant	Forklift truck	Coal	Steel	Thermostat	Light bulb	Accounting

Installations and *accessory equipment* are capital goods. They are used in the production process and do not become part of the final product. Installations are nonportable, involve considerable decision making (usually by upper-level executives), are expensive, last many years, and do not change form. Key marketing tasks are direct selling to the purchaser, negotiations on features and terms, having complementary services such as maintenance and repair, tailoring products to buyers' desires, and offering technical expertise and team selling (whereby various salespeople have different expertise). Examples are buildings, assembly lines, major equipment, large machine tools, and printing presses.

Accessory equipment consists of movable goods that require moderate decision making, are less costly than installations, last many years, and do not become part of the final product or change form. The key marketing tasks are tying sales to those of installations; providing various choices in price, size, and capacity; having a strong distribution channel or sales force; stressing durability and efficiency; and having maintenance and technical support. Examples are drill presses, trucks, vans, and lathes.

Raw materials, *component materials*, and *fabricated parts* are used up in production or become part of final products. They are expense items. They require limited decision making, have low unit costs, and are rapidly consumed. Raw materials are unprocessed primary materials—such as minerals, coal, and crops. Component materials are semimanufactured goods that undergo changes in form—such as steel, textiles, and basic chemicals. Fabricated parts are placed in products without changes in form—such as electric motors, thermostats, and microprocessors. Marketing tasks for materials and parts are to ensure consistent quality, continuity in shipments, and prompt delivery; pursue reorders; have fair prices; seek long-term contracts; use assertive distributors or sales personnel; and meet buyer specifications.

Industrial supplies are convenience goods used in a firm's daily operation. They can be maintenance supplies, such as light bulbs, cleaning materials, and paint; repair supplies, such as rivets, nuts, and bolts; or operating supplies, such as stationery, pens, and business cards. They require little decision making, are very low cost on a per-unit basis, are rapidly consumed, and do not become part of the finished product. Marketing emphasis is on availability, promptness, and ease of ordering.

Industrial services are maintenance and repair services, and business advisory services. Maintenance and repair services (janitorial services and machinery repair) usually involve little decision making, are rather inexpensive, and are consumed quickly. They may become part of a final product (keeping for-sale equipment in good working condition) or involve a change in form (janitorial services converting a dirty office into a clean one). The key marketing thrust is on consistent, efficient service at a reasonable price. Business advisory services (accounting and legal services) may involve a moderate to high level of decision making when first bought. Ongoing costs tend to be low to moderate, while benefits may be long-lasting. These services do not become part of the final product. The major marketing task is to have an image of expertise and convey reasons for clients to use the service.

11-3   ELEMENTS OF A PRODUCT MIX

A **product item** is a specific model; a **product line** has related items; a **product mix** is all a firm's lines.

After determining the type(s) of products to offer, a firm needs to outline the variety and assortment of those products. A **product item** is a specific model, brand, or size of a product that a company sells, such as *Marketing, 11th edition* (**http://www.atomicdog. com**), an Apple iPod Shuffle (**http://www.apple.com/ipodshuffle**), or the Cadillac XLR roadster (**http://www.cadillac.com**). Usually, a firm sells a group of closely related product items as part of a **product line**. In each product line, items have some common characteristics, customers, and/or uses; they may also share technologies, distribution channels, prices, related services, and so on.[4] Revlon (**http://www.revlon.com**) markets lipstick, eye makeup, and other cosmetics. Visa (**http://www.visa.com**) offers several credit cards. Atomic Dog (**http://www.atomicdog.com**) publishes various marketing textbooks. Many local lawn-service firms offer mowing, landscaping, and tree-trimming services.

A **product mix** consists of all the different product lines a firm offers. Heinz (**http://www.heinz.com**) markets ketchup, low-calorie foods, frozen french fries, soup, barbeque sauces, and other food products in more than 200 nations. Metropolitan Life (**http://www.metlife.com**) operates North America's largest life insurer (MetLife), and focuses on insurance and related services. Tyco (**http://www.tyco.com**) is a global b-to-b manufacturer with five product lines: electronic security products and alarm-monitoring services, fire protection services, safety products, flow control products, and electrical and metal products.

A product mix can be described in terms of its width, depth, and consistency. The *width of a product mix* is based on the number of different product lines a company offers. A wide mix lets a firm diversify products, appeal to different consumer needs, and encourage one-stop shopping. A narrow mix requires lower resource investments and does not call for expertise in different product categories.

The *depth of a product mix* is based on the number of product items within each product line. A deep mix can satisfy the needs of several consumer segments for the same product, maximize shelf space, discourage competitors, cover a range of prices, and sustain dealer support. A shallow mix imposes lower costs for inventory, product alterations, and order processing; and there are no overlapping product items.

The *consistency of a product mix* is based on the relationship among product lines in terms of their sharing a common end-use, distribution outlets, consumer group(s), and price range. A consistent mix is generally easier to manage than an inconsistent one. It lets a firm focus on marketing and production expertise, create a strong image, and generate good distribution relations. Excessive consistency may leave a firm vulnerable to environmental threats, sales fluctuations, or less growth potential because emphasis is on

---

[4] "Dictionary," **http://www.marketingpower.com/_layouts/Dictionary.aspx?dLetter=P** (March 22, 2009).

a limited product assortment. Figure 11-3 shows product mix alternatives in terms of width and depth. Figure 11-4 highlights part of La-Z-Boy's (**http://www.lazboy.com**) product mix.

Product-mix decisions can have positive and negative effects, as these examples demonstrate:

- The highly successful Wrigley (**http://www.wrigley.com**)—which recently became a stand-alone subsidiary of Mars (**http://www.mars.com**)—focuses on chewing gum and confectionary items: "It has been over 110 years since Wrigley introduced its first two products, Juicy Fruit and Wrigley's Spearmint gums. Today, Wrigley brands are sold in over 180 countries and its portfolio of products includes dozens of innovative brands that provide consumers with a variety of benefits, including breath freshening, tooth whitening, and vitamin delivery." In recent years, it has moved into other confection categories through acquisitions: "Brands such as Altoids, Life Savers, Creme Savers, Pim Pom, and Solano provide consumers with a variety of fun, delicious products in numerous formats and flavors. From mints to candies to lollipops, these products help Wrigley reach consumers of all ages around the world and are a wonderful complement to Wrigley's great-tasting gum products."[5]
- WD-40 (**http://www.wd40company.com**) is a powerhouse in its product categories and has added a number of product lines over the past several years: "The same company you've trusted for years now offers a complete line of products to help you accomplish almost any household task, including the clean up afterward. Our products are found under the sink, in the garage, and in toolboxes of loyal fans around the world." Its products include lubricants (WD-40 and 3-In-One Oil), heavy-duty hand cleaners (Lava and Solvol), toilet bowl cleaners (X-14 and 2000

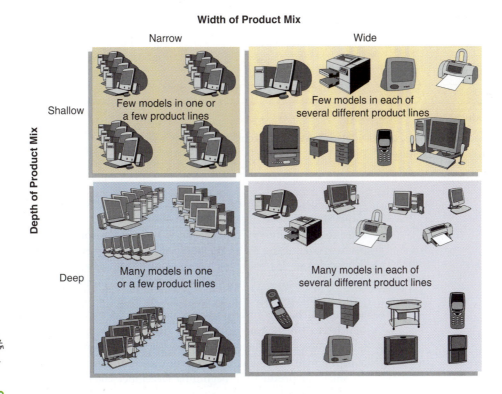

Width of Product Mix

Narrow | Wide

Shallow — Few models in one or a few product lines | Few models in each of several different product lines

Deep — Many models in one or a few product lines | Many models in each of several different product lines

Depth of Product Mix

Figure 11-3

Product Mix Alternatives

[5] "About Us," **http://www.wrigley.com/wrigley/about/about_index.asp** (August 1, 2008).

You're the kid
and we're the candy store.

Figure 11-4

La-Z-Boy's Deep Product Mix

Within its furniture product categories, La-Z-Boy (**http://www.lazboy.com**) offers a large selection.

Source: © La-Z-Boy Inc. Reprinted with permission.

Flushes), bathroom cleaners (X-14), rug and room deodorizers (Carpet Fresh), and carpet stain remover (Spot Shot and 1001).[6]

- After losing billions of dollars, Ford (**http://www.ford.com**) is undergoing a major restructuring "with the addition of several new fuel-efficient small vehicles in North America and a realignment of North American manufacturing. The actions represent a considerable shift in Ford's product plans toward smaller vehicles and fuel-efficient powertrains in both the near- and mid-term in line with rapid changes in customer preferences. In addition to bringing six small vehicles to North America from its European lineup, Ford is accelerating the introduction of the fuel-efficient EcoBoost and all-new four-cylinder engines, boosting hybrid production, and converting three existing truck and SUV plants for small car production, beginning December 2008. 'Ford is moving aggressively using our global product strengths to introduce additional smaller vehicles in

[6] "About WD-40 Company," http://www.wd40company.com/about (April 5, 2009); and "WD-40 Company Brands," http://www.wd40company.com/brands (April 5, 2009).

North America and to provide outstanding fuel economy with every new product,' said Ford's chief executive."[7]

11-4 PRODUCT MANAGEMENT ORGANIZATIONS

A firm may select from among these organizational forms of product management: marketing manager, product manager, product planning committee, new-product manager, and venture team.[8] See Table 11-3.

Under a ***marketing manager system***, an executive is responsible for overseeing a wide range of marketing functions (such as research, target marketing, planning existing and new products, distribution, promotion, pricing, and customer service) and for coordinating with other departments that do marketing-related activities (such as warehousing, order filling, shipping, credit, and purchasing). It works well for firms with a line of similar products or one dominant product line and for smaller firms that want centralized control of marketing tasks. It may be less successful if there are several product lines that require different marketing mixes—unless there are category marketing managers, each responsible for a broad product line. Pepsi-Cola North America (**http://www.pepsico.com**), Purex (**http://www.purex.com**), and Levi Strauss (**http://www.levi.com**) have used a marketing manager system at one point.

With a ***product (brand) manager system***, there is a level of middle managers, each of whom is responsible for planning, coordinating, and monitoring a single product (brand) or a small group of products (brands). Managers handle both new and existing products and are involved with all marketing activities related to their product or

> One person is responsible for a host of marketing tasks, including product planning, with a **marketing manager system**.

> Middle managers handle new and existing products in a category in the **product (brand) manager system**.

Table 11-3	Comparing Product Management Organizations		
	Characteristics		
Organization	**Staffing**	**Ideal Use**	**Permanency**
Marketing manager system	Key functional areas of marketing report directly to a senior marketer with a lot of authority.	A company makes one product line, has a dominant line, or uses broad category marketing managers.	The system is ongoing.
Product (brand) manager system	There is a layer of middle managers, with each focusing on a single product or a group of related products.	A company makes many distinct products, each requiring expertise.	The system is ongoing.
Product planning committee	Senior executives from various functional areas participate.	The committee should supplement another product organization.	The committee meets irregularly.
New-product manager system	Separate middle managers focus on new products and existing products.	A company makes several existing new products; and substantial time, resources, and expertise are needed for new products.	The system is ongoing, but new products are shifted to product managers after introduction.
Venture team	An independent group of company specialists guides all phases of a new product's development.	A company wants to create vastly different products than those currently offered, and needs an autonomous structure to aid development.	The team disbands after a new product is introduced, with responsibility going to a product manager.

[7] "Ford Accelerates Transformation Plan with Small Car Offensive, Manufacturing Realignment," Ford Motor Company Press Release (July 24, 2008).

[8] The definitions in this section are drawn from "Dictionary," **http://www.marketingpower.com/_layouts/Dictionary.aspx** (March 22, 2009).

product group. The system lets all products or brands get adequate attention. It works well if there are many distinct products or brands, each needing marketing attention. It also has two potential weaknesses: lack of authority for the product manager and inadequate attention to new products. Procter & Gamble (**http://www.pg.com**), Nabisco (**http://www.nabiscoworld.com**), and Black & Decker (**http://www.blackanddecker.com**) have used product managers.[9]

A **product-planning committee** is staffed by high-level executives from various functional areas in a firm, such as marketing, production, engineering, finance, and research and development. It handles product approval and development on a part-time basis. Once a product is introduced, the committee usually turns to other opportunities and gives the item over to a product manager. This system lets management have input into decisions; but the committee meets irregularly and passes projects on to line managers. It is best as a supplement to other methods, and is used by many large and small firms.

A **new-product manager system** has product managers supervise existing products and new-product managers develop new ones. It ensures the time, resources, enthusiasm, and expertise necessary for new-product planning. Once a product is introduced, it is given to the product manager, who oversees existing products of that line (or brand). The system can be costly, incur conflicts, and cause discontinuity when an item is introduced. Kraft Foods (**http://www.kraftfoods.com**), General Electric (**http://www.ge.com**), and Johnson & Johnson (**http://www.jnj.com**) have employed new-product managers.

A **venture team** is a small, independent department in a firm that has a broad range of specialists—drawn from that firm's marketing, finance, engineering, and other functional departments—who are involved with a specific new product's entire development process. Team members work full-time and act in a relatively autonomous manner. The team disbands when its new product is introduced, and the product is then managed within the firm's regular management structure. With a venture team, there are proper resources, a flexible environment, expertise, and continuity in new-product planning. It is valuable if a firm wants to be more far-sighted, reach out for truly new ideas, and foster creativity. It is also expensive to form and operate. Xerox (**http://www.xerox.com**), Monsanto (**http://www.monsanto.com**), and 3M (**http://www.3m.com**) are among the firms that have used venture teams.

The correct organization depends on the diversity of a firm's offerings, the number of new products introduced, the innovativeness sought, company resources, management expertise, and other factors. A combination organization may be highly desirable; among larger firms, this is particularly common.

A **product planning committee** has top executives involved part-time.

A **new-product manager system** has separate middle managers for new and existing products.

A **venture team** is an autonomous new-product department.

11-5 PRODUCT POSITIONING

Critical to a firm's product-planning efforts is how the items in its product mix are perceived in the marketplace. The firm must work quite hard to make sure that each of its products is perceived as providing some combination of unique features (product differentiation) and that these features are desired by the target market (thereby converting product differentiation to a differential advantage).

When a product is new, a company must clearly communicate its attributes: What is it? What does it do? How is it better than the competition? Who should buy it? The goal is to have consumers perceive product attributes as the firm intends. When a product has an established place in the market, a firm must regularly reinforce its image and communicate the reasons for its success. Once consumer perceptions are formed, they may be hard to alter. And it may also be tough later to change a product's niche in the market (for instance, from low price, low quality to high price, high quality).

---

[9] For a good overview of the challenges facing the product (brand) manager system, see James R. Stengel, Andrea L. Dixon, and Chris T. Allen, "Listening Begins at Home," *Harvard Business Review*, Vol. 81 (November-December 2003), pp. 106–115; and Marylyn Donahue, "Everything a Product Manager Needs To Know, But Might Not Know To Ask," *Pharmaceutical Executive* (March 2008), pp. 9–14.

Ethical Issues in Marketing

Addressing the Flood of Counterfeit Products

The International Chamber of Commerce (http://www.iccwbo.org) estimates that worldwide sales of counterfeit products exceed $650 billion per year. According to a U.S. Chamber of Commerce (http://www.uschamber.com) report, counterfeiting and piracy cost the U.S. economy between $250 billion and $300 billion a year—in addition to a cost of 750,000 jobs. Worldwide sales of counterfeit prescription and over-the-counter drugs alone are projected to be $75 billion as of 2010.

Besides the direct loss of jobs and revenues, firms whose goods have been counterfeited also face the loss of customer goodwill due to the poor quality of counterfeit merchandise and the diminution of brand exclusivity. And there are social costs due to unsafe products being sold. Often, the buyer may not know he/she is purchasing counterfeit merchandise.

Many experts view China as the main source of counterfeits, with Chinese counterfeiters becoming increasingly adept at copying holograms, "smart" chips, and other security devices that have traditionally been used to detect fake products. To avoid detection, some counterfeiters move their goods through several territories, including free trade zones. They even relocate from Asia to countries that are not known as a major source of counterfeiting activity.

Some counterfeit products look so much like the real thing that company executives with the affected brands cannot even distinguish them. There is a strong chance of finding counterfeit products for such popular items as Callaway golf clubs (http://www.callawaygolf.com), Kiwi shoe polish (http://www.kiwicare.com), and Bosch power drills (http://www.boschtools.com). In addition, there have been reported cases of counterfeit aircraft parts, auto brake parts, and popular software such as Windows.

Sources: Based on material in Jacob Barron, "Tough Competition," *Business Credit* (April 2008), pp. 10, 12; and Drew Buono, "Counterfeit Drugs a Growing Danger," *Drug Store News* (June 23, 2008), pp. 60, 62.

Through **product positioning**, a firm can map each of its products in terms of consumer perceptions and desires, competition, other company products, and environmental changes. Consumer perceptions are the images of products, both a firm's and competitors', in people's minds. Consumer desires refer to the attributes that people would most like products to have—their **ideal points**. If a group of people has a distinctive "ideal" for a product category, that group is a potential market segment. A firm will do well if its products' attributes are perceived by consumers as being close to their ideal.

Competitive product positioning refers to people's perceptions of a firm relative to competitors. The goal is for the firm's products to be viewed as "more ideal" than those of competitors. *Company product positioning* shows a firm how consumers perceive that firm's different brands (items) within the same product line and the relationship of those brands (items) to each other. The goal is for each of the firm's brands to be positioned near an ideal point, yet not clustered near one another in the consumer's mind—the brands should appeal to different ideal points (market segments). A firm must monitor the environmental changes that may alter the way its products are perceived. Such changes could include new technology, changing consumer lifestyles, new offerings by competitors, and negative publicity.

> **Product positioning** maps out consumer perceptions of product attributes. **Ideal points** show the most preferred attributes.

Product positioning is illustrated in Figure 11-5, which depicts the U.S. car marketplace—not including sports utility vehicles—in terms of the consumer desires regarding two key attributes: price and size. In this figure, there are nine ideal points (target markets)—I1 to I9, each associated with a specific type of car. Due to the economic difficulties facing the auto industry, some companies are downsizing. Thus, one or more of the models noted below may be consolidated into other brands or eliminated in the future. Here is a brief description of the segments of the U.S. auto industry as of early 2009:

- *I1—full-size luxury cars.* Large cars typically priced at $40,000 and up. Cadillac DTS (**http://www.cadillac.com/dts**), Infiniti M45 (**http://www.infiniti.com/m**), and Lincoln Town Car (**http://www.lincoln.com/towncar**) are in this grouping.
- *I2—full-size cars.* Large cars typically priced at $20,000 to $30,000. Chevrolet Impala (**http://www.chevrolet.com/impala**), Buick Lucerne (**http://www.buick.com/lucerne**),

and Mercury Grand Marquis (**http://www.mercuryvehicles.com/grandmarquis**) are in this category.

- *I3—full-size economy cars.* Large cars typically priced at less than $20,000. There are currently no significant brands in this category selling in the United States. Demand is virtually nonexistent.
- *I4—midsize luxury cars.* Midsize cars typically priced at $35,000 and up. BMW 3 Series sedans (**http://www.bmwusa.com**), Cadillac STS (**http://www.cadillac.com/sts**), and Lexus ES 300 (**http://www.lexus.com/models/es**) are positioned here.
- *I5—midsize cars.* Midsize cars typically priced from $18,000 to $27,000. Toyota Camry (**http://www.toyota.com/camry**), Pontiac G6 sedan (**http://www.pontiac.com/g6sedan**), and Volkswagen Passat (**http://www.vw.com/passat**) fit here.
- *I6—midsize economy cars.* Midsize cars typically priced at less than $18,000. Hyundai Sonata GL (**http://www.hyundaiusa.com/vehicle/sonata**), Saturn Aura sedan (**http://www.saturn.com**), and Kia Optima (**http://www.kia.com/optima**) are in this grouping.
- *I7—small luxury cars.* Small cars typically priced at $35,000 and up. BMW Z4 (**http://www.bmwusa.com**), Cadillac XLR (**http://www.cadillac.com/xlr**), and Porsche Boxster (**http://www.porsche.com/usa/models/boxster**) are in this category.
- *I8—small cars.* Small cars typically priced between $14,000 and $22,000. Volkswagen New Beetle (**http://www.vw.com/newbeetle**), Chevrolet Cobalt (**http://www.chevrolet.com/cobalt**), and Toyota Corolla (**http://www.toyota.com/corolla**) are positioned here.
- *I9—small economy cars.* Small cars typically priced at less than $14,000. Hyundai Accent (**http://www.hyundaiusa.com**), Kia Spectra (**http://www.kia.com/spectra**), and Chevrolet Aveo (**http://www.chevrolet.com/aveo**) are grouped here.

An examination of competitive product positioning reveals that competing products exist in each market niche except for I3 (full-size economy cars), which has virtually no

Figure 11-5

Product Positioning and the Auto Industry

Source: Data estimates and figure developed by the authors, based on statistics from *Motor Intelligence* (**http://www.motorintelligence.com**), as reported in "Auto Sales," **http://online.wsj.com** (August 1, 2008).

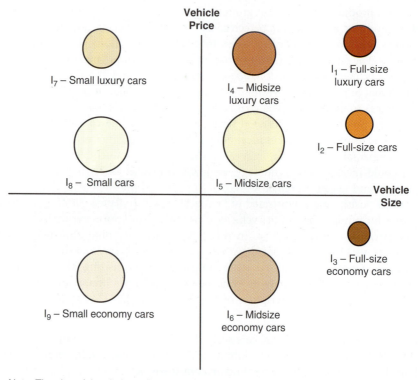

Note: The size of the circles reflects the relative sales volume for each segment (in units).

consumer demand in this era of high gas prices. In some instances, the marketplace is saturated. The companies in the industry have done a mixed job in addressing the needs of the various consumer segments and in differentiating the products offered to each segment. That is why there is a shift by auto makers away from large cars and toward midsize and small vehicles. Figure 11-6 shows the product positioning of the Acura (**http://www.acura.com**).

From an analysis of its 2009 company product positioning, it is clear that General Motors (**http://www.gm.com**) served all of the identified market segments except I3. The Cadillac DTS, Chevrolet Impala, Buick Lucerne, Cadillac STS, Pontiac G6 sedan, Saturn Aura, Cadillac SRX, Chevrolet Cobalt, and Chevrolet Aveo sedan were all marketed by General Motors. However, due to declining sales and a weak financial situation, in 2009, General Motors announced that it would be phasing out its Saturn division and cutting back on the offerings under the Pontiac brand, as well as enacting several other changes. Analysts still believe that General Motors has to differentiate carefully among its remaining brands and models to avoid confusion and a "fuzzy" perception by consumers.

By undertaking product-positioning analysis, a company can learn a great deal and plan its marketing efforts accordingly, as these examples indicate:

- "One can easily understand and accept positioning that's embodied in a single word because the positioning is obviously a single concept. In what has to be the quintessential positioning example, Volvo (**http://www.volvo.com**) has demonstrated that its own persuasive, enduring positioning can be stated in a single word: safety. Others have succeeded as well—Charmin (**http://www.charmin.com**) equals softness; Ivory soap (**http://www.ivory.com**) equals purity; Coke

LUXURY DESIGNED TO INTERFACE WITH
A WHOLE NEW GENERATION.

The Acura TL. Finally, a luxury sedan that offers all the conveniences of the modern world. From its sleek, boldly sculpted lines, to features like available voice-activated navigation and solar-sensing climate control, the TL sets the standard for style and innovation. While its thrilling 258-horsepower V-6 never lets you forget, it's a sport sedan at heart. Experience it at acura.com or call 1-800-To-Acura. **Advancing mobility.**

Figure 11-6
Acura's Positioning Message: Luxury for a New Generation

Source: Reprinted by permission.
© Peter Keil.

(**http://www.coke.com**) equals the real thing (OK, that's three words, but you get the idea). These are simple, singular concepts, well understood and remembered for that very reason. Many marketers fail when it comes to simplicity by injecting multiple concepts into their positioning statement until they've manufactured a multidimensional hodgepodge that isn't positioning at all."[10]

- "Harley-Davidson (**http://www.harley-davidson.com**) knows how to build ownership. For decades, the motorcycle company has attracted and retained a client base that shows no signs of waning. People purchase its products without solicitation, and they gladly spend millions of dollars to wear its advertising on clothes, attend national and international H.O.G. rallies, and even tattoo the Harley-Davidson logo on their body. As the tagline goes, Harley owners 'live by it.' For decades, Harley-Davidson has been 'engineering' customer expectations, says Lou Carbone, founder of Experience Engineering, a consulting firm. What Harley-Davidson gets—as do Starbucks (**http://www.starbucks.com**) and Disney (**http://www.disney.com**)—is that it is selling more than motorcycles (or coffee or entertainment). 'It is all about understanding the psychology of the customers,' Carbone says. 'It requires getting into the mind and heart and head of customers,' and ultimately, discovering the clues that make them loyal, sometimes irrationally so, to a brand."[11]

11-6 BRANDING

> **Brands** identify a firm's products.

Another key aspect of product planning is branding, the way a firm researches, develops, and implements its brands. A **brand** is a name, term, design, symbol, or any other feature that identifies the goods and services of a seller or group of sellers. The four types of brand designation are as follow:

1. A **brand name** is a word, letter (number), group of words, or letters (numbers) that can be spoken. Examples are Boeing (**http://www.boeing.com**), Century 21 (**http://www.century21.com**), and Lipton Cup-a-Soup (**http://www.cupasoup.com**).

> **Branding** involves **brand names, brand marks, trade characters,** and **trademarks.**

2. A **brand mark** is a symbol, design, or distinctive coloring or lettering that cannot be spoken. Examples are Lexus' (**http://www.lexus.com**) stylized L crest, McDonald's (**http://www.mcdonalds.com**) golden arch, Prudential's (**http://www.prudential.com**) rock, and Starbucks' (**http://www.starbucks.com**) mermaid. See Figure 11-7.
3. A **trade character** is a brand mark that is personified. Examples are Qantas Airlines' (**http://www.qantas.com**) koala bear, Metropolitan Life's (**http://www.metlife.com**) use of Snoopy, the Pillsbury Doughboy (**http://www.pillsbury.com**), and Kellogg's (**http://www.kelloggs.com**) Tony the Tiger.
4. A **trademark** is a brand name, brand mark, or trade character or combination thereof that is given legal protection. When used, a registered trademark is followed by ®, such as Scotch Brand ® tape.

Brand names, brand marks, and trade characters do not offer legal protection against use by competitors unless they are registered as trademarks (which all of the preceding examples have been). Trademarks ensure exclusivity for their owners or those securing permission, and provide legal remedies against firms using "confusingly similar" names, designs, or symbols. They are discussed more fully later in the chapter.

---

[10] Bill Robertson, "Ten Rules of Product Positioning," *Medical Marketing & Media* (May 2005), pp. 53–54.

[11] "Why Turning the Customer Experience into Emotional Engagement Adds Value to a Brand," **http://knowledge.emory.edu/article.cfm?articleid=1153** (June 12, 2008).

Figure 11-7

Starbucks' Popular Brand Mark

Source: Reprinted by permission.

Worldwide, millions of brand names exist. Each year, firms spend hundreds of billions of dollars globally to advertise their brands. Permanent media expenditures (such as logos, stationery, brochures, business forms and cards, and vehicular and building signs) for brands are another large marketing cost.

Brand loyalty is a key goal. This enables firms to maximize sales and maintain a strong brand image. As two experts noted: "Marketers must understand what brand loyalty is, bearing in mind that brand loyalty will be different for each brand managed. Research suggests that customers can demonstrate brand loyalty in a variety of ways. They can demonstrate loyalty by purchasing, by being willing to recommend, by providing advice to the company, and through an intention to repurchase."[12]

Some brands do so well that they gain "power" status—they are well known and highly esteemed. According to one recent study, the world's 10 most valuable brands are (in order) Google, GE (General Electric), Microsoft, Coca-Cola, China Mobile, IBM, Apple, McDonald's, Nokia, and Marlboro. Of the world's 100 most valuable brands, 51 are American, 8 are French, 8 are German, 8 are British, 6 are Japanese, 4 are Chinese, and 4 are Spanish.[13] The use of popular brands can also speed up public acceptance and gain reseller cooperation for new products.

Gaining and maintaining brand recognition and preference are often top priorities: "Why would P&G tinker with Tide (**http://www.tide.com**)? Long the detergent leader, Tide would seem best left alone as a profitable annuity. But P&G has tinkered, combining strong technology and consumer research to push sales up in a category that is growing very little. The secret: a widening family of detergents and cleaners that now includes everything from Tide Coldwater, for cold-water washing, to Tide HE, which works with less water." In addition, the firm has introduced the hugely popular Tide to Go portable-stain-removing pen, "the instant stain remover that helps eliminate many

---

[12] Rebekah Bennett and Sharyn Rundle-Thiele, "The Brand Loyalty Life Cycle: Implications for Marketers," *Journal of Brand Management*, Vol. 12 (April 2005), p. 258.

[13] Millard Brown Optimor, *Brandz Top Most Powerful Brands 08*, **http://www.millwardbrown.com/Sites/Optimor/ Media/Pdfs/en/BrandZ/BrandZ-2008-Report.pdf**.

fresh food and drink stains on the spot. Keep a Tide to Go in your briefcase, car, purse, and kitchen—everywhere you encounter stains."[14]

In recent years, a branding concept that more concretely recognizes brands' worth has emerged. It is known as ***brand equity***, which represents the revenue premium that a brand earns in the marketplace in comparison with an identical, but unbranded, alternative.[15] As one research company noted:

> There are many definitions of brand equity, but they have several commonalities: *Monetary Value*—The amount of additional income expected from a branded product over and above what might be expected from an identical, but unbranded product. Grocery stores frequently sell unbranded versions of name-brand products. Both branded and unbranded products are made by the same firms, but they carry a store brand label such as Kroger (**http://www.kroger.com**). Store brands sell for less than their name brand counterparts, even when the contents are identical. This price differential is the monetary value of the brand name. *Intangible*—The intangible value associated with a product that cannot be accounted for by price or features. Nike (**http://www.nike.com**) has created many intangible benefits for its athletic products by associating them with star athletes. Buyers are willing to pay extremely high price premiums over lesser known brands with the same, or better, product quality and features. *Perceived Quality*—The overall perceptions of quality and image attributed to a product, independent of its physical features. Mercedes (**http://www.mercedes.com**) has established its brand name as synonymous with high-quality, luxurious autos. Consumers are likely to perceive Mercedes as providing superior quality to other brand name autos, even when such a perception is unwarranted.[16]

These reasons summarize why branding is important:

- Product identification is eased. A customer can order a product by name instead of description.
- Customers are assured that a good or service has a certain level of quality and that they will obtain comparable quality if the same brand is reordered.
- The firm responsible for the product is known. Unbranded items cannot be as directly identified.
- Price comparisons are reduced when customers perceive distinct brands. This is most likely if special attributes are linked to different brands.
- A firm can advertise (position) its products and associate each brand in the buyer's mind. This aids the consumer in forming a *brand image*, which is the perception a person has of a particular brand.
- Branding helps segment markets by creating tailored images. By using two or more brands, multiple market segments can be attracted.
- For socially visible goods and services, a product's prestige is enhanced via a strong brand name.
- People feel less risk when buying a brand with which they are familiar and for which they have a favorable attitude. This is why brand loyalty occurs.

[margin note] Brand equity represents a brand's worth.

[margin note] Branding creates identities, assures quality, and performs other functions. Brand images are perceptions that consumers have of particular brands.

---

[14] Nanette Byrnes, Robert Berner, Wendy Zellner, and William C. Symonds, "Branding: Five New Lessons," *Business Week* (February 14, 2005), p. 28; and "Laundry Detergent Product Information," **http://www.tide.com/en_US/products/index.jsp** (February 12, 2009).

[15] See Matthew Yeung and Bala Ramasamy, "Brand Value and Firm Performance Nexus: Further Empirical Evidence," *Journal of Brand Management*, Vol. 15 (May 2008), pp. 322–335; Jorge M. Oliveira-Castro, Gordon R. Foxall, Victoria K. James, Roberta H. B. F. Pohl, Moema B. Dias, and Shing W. Chang, "Consumer-Based Brand Equity and Brand Performance," *Service Industries Journal*, Vol. 28 (June 2008), pp. 445–461; Michael K. Brady, J. Joseph Cronin, Gavin L. Fox, and Michelle L. Roehm, "Strategies to Offset Performance Failures: The Role of Brand Equity," *Journal of Retailing*, Vol. 84 (June 2008), pp. 151–164; and Morten Bach Jensen and Kim Klastrup, "Towards a B2B Customer-Based Brand Equity Model," *Journal of Targeting, Measurement & Analysis for Marketing*, Vol. 16 (March 2008), pp. 122–128.

[16] "Understanding Brand Equity," **http://www.dssresearch.com/toolkit/resource/papers/SR02.asp** (December 27, 2002).

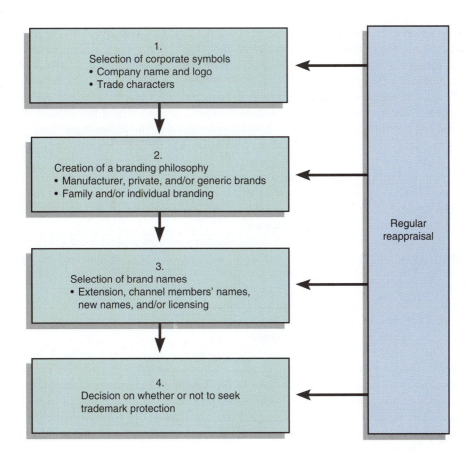

Figure 11-8

Branding Decisions

- Cooperation from resellers is greater for well-known brands. A strong brand also may let its producer exert more control in the distribution channel.
- A brand may help sell an entire line of products, such as Kellogg's (**http://www. kelloggs.com**) cereals.
- A brand may help enter a new product category, such as Nestlé Pure Life (**http:// www.nestle-purelife.com**) water.
- "People don't blow their noses on facial tissues, they use Kleenex. No one uses an Internet search engine, they Google it"[17]

There are four branding decisions a firm must undertake, involving corporate symbols, the branding philosophy, choosing a brand name, and using trademarks. See Figure 11-8.

11-6a   Corporate Symbols

Corporate symbols are a firm's name (and/or divisional names), logos, and trade characters. They are key parts of the overall image. When a firm begins a business; merges with another company; reduces or expands product lines; seeks new geographic markets; or finds its name to be unwieldy, nondistinctive, or confusing, it should assess and possibly change its symbols. Here are examples of each situation.

Google is a worldwide phenomenon after a little more than a decade: "Google's name is a play on the word googol, which refers to the number 1 followed by one hundred zeroes. Google's utility and ease of use have made it one of the world's best-known brands almost entirely through word of mouth from satisfied users. When you visit **http://www.google.com** or one of the dozens of other Google domains, you'll find

> **Corporate symbols** help establish a company-wide image.

---

[17] Jason Ubay, "5 Steps for Creating Brand Equity," **http://www.hawaiibusiness.com/Hawaii-Business/May-2008/ 5-Steps-for-Creating-Brand-Equity** (May 2008).

information in many different languages; check stock quotes, maps, and news headlines; lookup phonebook listings for every city in the United States; search billions of images; and peruse the world's largest archive of Usenet messages—more than 1 billion posts dating back to 1981."[18]

Due to mergers, defense contractors Lockheed and Martin Marietta are now Lockheed Martin (**http://www.lockheedmartin.com**), pharmaceutical firms Glaxo Wellcome and SmithKline Beecham are now GlaxoSmithKline (**http://www.gsk.com**), and satellite radio services Sirius and XM are now Sirius XM (**http://www.siriusxm.com**).

Because the nature of its business changed, International Harvester is now Navistar International (**http://www.navistar.com**), after selling its farm equipment business, and General Shoe Corporation is Genesco (**http://www.genesco.com**), a diversified retailer. When Andersen Consulting was spun off from Andersen Worldwide, it changed its name to Accenture (**http://www.accenture.com**).

As it expanded into new market areas, Allegheny Airlines was renamed US Airways (**http://www.usairways.com**); the old name suggested a small regional airline. More recently, America West merged with US Airways and the combined firm retained the more national US Airways name. The Exxon (**http://www.exxon.com**) name was developed globally because the firm's regional brands, including Esso and Humble, could not be used nationwide and other brands had unfortunate foreign connotations (for example, Enco means "stalled car" in Japanese).

The National Railroad Passenger Corporation was an unwieldy name; it became Amtrak (**http://www.amtrak.com**). Federal Express now promotes the FedEx name (**http://www.fedex.com**), since it is easier to say. United Telecommunications converted its nondistinctive name to Sprint (**http://www.sprint.com**), in recognition of its leading brand. The upscale Holiday Inn Crowne Plaza was changed to Crowne Plaza (**http://www.ichotelsgroup.com/h/d/cp/1/en/home**) to avoid confusion with the middle-class Holiday Inn name.

Developing and maintaining corporate symbols are not easy. When Nissan (**http://www.nissanusa.com**) changed the name of its U.S. car division from Datsun to Nissan (to have a global brand), sales fell, despite a major ad campaign. It took years for the Nissan name to reach the level of awareness that Datsun had attained. Along the way, Nissan had clashes with dealers not wanting the name change.

11-6b Branding Philosophy

In preparing a brand strategy, a firm needs to determine its branding philosophy. This outlines the use of manufacturer, private, and/or generic brands, as well as the use of family and/or individual branding.

Manufacturer, Private, and Generic Brands[19] *Manufacturer brands* use the names of their makers. They generate the vast majority of U.S. revenues for most product categories, including more than 80 percent of food, all autos, 75 percent of major appliances, and more than 80 percent of gasoline. They appeal to a wide range of people who desire good quality, routine purchases, status, convenience, and low risk of poor

> **Manufacturer brands** are well known and heavily promoted.

---

[18] "Corporate Information," **http://www.google.com/corporate/index.html** (April 7, 2009).

[19] See Rita Martenson, "Corporate Brand Image, Satisfaction, and Store Loyalty: A Study of the Store as a Brand, Store Brands, and Manufacturer Brands," *International Journal of Retail & Distribution Management*, Vol. 35 (Number 7, 2007), pp. 544–555; Gráinne M. Fitzsimons, Tanya L. Chartrand, and Gavan J. Fitzsimons. "Automatic Effects of Brand Exposure on Motivated Behavior: How Apple Makes You 'Think Different'," *Journal of Consumer Research*, Vol. 35 (June 2008), pp. 21–35; Natalia Rubio and María Jesús Yagüe, "Store Brand Management and Channel Dependence: A Model from the Manufacturer's Perspective," *Journal of Brand Management*, Vol. 15 (April 2008), pp. 272–290; and Sandra J. Milberg and Francisca Sinn, "Vulnerability of Global Brands to Negative Feedback Effects," *Journal of Business Research*, Vol. 61 (June 2008), pp. 684–690; Jill Jusko, "Consumer Packaged Goods: Muscling In," **http://www.industryweek.com/ReadArticle.aspx?ArticleID=10649** (September 1, 2005); "Private Label Widely Seen as 'Good Alternative' to Other Brands, According to A.C. Nielsen Global Survey," **http://us.acnielsen.com/news/20050811.shtml** (August 11, 2005); and Mary Beth Whitfield, "The Surging Growth of Private Brands," 2005 Strategic Outlook Conference (Columbus, OH: TNS Retail Forward).

product performance. The brands are often well known and trusted because quality control is strictly maintained. They are identifiable and present distinctive images. Producers may have a number of product alternatives under their brands.

Manufacturers have better channel control over their own brands, which may be sold through many competing intermediaries. Yet, individual resellers can have lower investments if the brands' pre-sold nature makes turnover high—and if manufacturers spend large sums promoting their brands and sponsor cooperative ads with resellers (so costs are shared). Prices are the highest of the three brands, with the bulk going to the manufacturer (which also has the greatest profit). The marketing goal is to attract and retain loyal consumers for these brands, and for their makers to direct the marketing effort for the brands.

Private (dealer) brands use names designated by their resellers, usually wholesalers or retailers—including service providers. They account for sizable U.S. revenues in many categories, such as 50 percent of both apparel and shoes, one-third of tires, one-sixth of food items, and one-quarter of major appliances. Unit market shares are higher. Private brands account for 20 percent of unit sales in supermarkets. Firms such as Limited Brands (**http://www.limitedbrands.com**) and McDonald's (**http://www.mcdonalds. com**) derive most revenues from their own brands. Private-brand foods are more popular in Europe than in the United States. They generate 35 percent of revenues in German food stores and one-quarter in French and British food stores.

Private brands appeal to price-conscious people who buy them if they feel the brands offer good quality at a lower price. They accept some risk as to quality, but reseller loyalty causes the people to see the brands as reliable. Private brands often have similar quality to manufacturer brands, with less emphasis on packaging. At times, they are made to dealer specifications. Assortments are smaller and the brands are unknown to people not shopping with a given reseller. Resellers have more exclusive rights for these brands and are more responsible for distribution and larger purchases. Inventory turnover may be lower than for manufacturer brands; and promotion and pricing are the reseller's job. Due to lower per-unit packaging and promotion costs, resellers can sell private brands at lower prices and still have better per-unit profits (due to their higher share of the selling price). The marketing goal is to attract people who become loyal to the reseller and for that firm to exert control over marketing. Large resellers advertise their brands widely. Some private brands, such as Sears' Kenmore (**http:// www.kenmore.com**), are as popular as manufacturer brands; and firms such as Sherwin-Williams (**http://www.sherwin-williams.com**) are manufacturers and retailers. As with all supermarket chains, Stop & Shop (**http://www.stopandshop.com**), which features manufacturer brands, also has its own private brand. Macy's (**http://www.macys.com**) has added an exclusive collection from Martha Stewart. See Figure 11-9.

Generic brands emphasize the names of the products themselves and not manufacturer or reseller names. They started in the drug industry as low-cost alternatives to expensive manufacturer brands. Today, generics have expanded into cigarettes, batteries, motor oil, and other products. One-half of U.S. prescriptions are filled with generics; but, due to their low prices, this is only 12 to 15 percent or so of prescription-drug revenues. Although 85 percent of U.S. supermarkets stock generic products, they account for less than 1 percent of supermarket revenues. Generics appeal to price-conscious, careful shoppers, who perceive them as being a very good value, are sometimes willing to accept lower quality, and often purchase for large families or large organizations.

Generics are seldom advertised and receive poor shelf locations; consumers must search out these brands. Prices are less than other brands by up to 50 percent due to quality, packaging, assortment, distribution, and promotion economies. The major marketing goal is to offer low-priced, lower-quality items to consumers interested in price savings. Table 11-4 compares the three types of brands.

Many companies—including service firms—use a *mixed-brand strategy*, thereby selling both manufacturer and private brands (and possibly generic brands). This benefits manufacturers and resellers: There is control over the brand bearing each seller's name. Exclusive rights to a brand can be gained. Multiple segments may be targeted. Brand and

Private (dealer) brands enable channel members to get loyal customers.

Generic brands are low-priced items with little advertising.

A **mixed-brand strategy** combines brand types.

Figure 11-9

Now at Macy's: An Exclusive Martha Stewart Collection

Source: Reprinted by permission.

Table **11-4**	Manufacturer, Private, and Generic Brands		
	Type of Brand		
Characteristics	**Manufacturer**	**Private**	**Generic**
Target market	Risk avoider, quality-conscious, brand loyal, status-conscious, quick shopper	Price-conscious, comparison shopper, quality-conscious, moderate risk taker, dealer loyal	Price-conscious, careful shopper, willing to accept lower quality, large family or organization
Product	Well known, trusted, best quality control, clearly identifiable, deep product line	Same overall quality as manufacturer, less emphasis on packaging, less assortment, not known to nonshoppers of the dealer	Usually less overall quality than manufacturer, little emphasis on packaging, very limited assortment, not well known
Distribution	Often sold at many competing dealers	Usually only available from a particular dealer in the area	Varies
Promotion	Manufacturer-sponsored ads, cooperative ads	Dealer-sponsored ads	Few ads, secondary shelf space
Price	Highest, usually suggested by manufacturer	Moderate, usually controlled by dealer	Lowest, usually controlled by dealer
Marketing focus	To generate brand loyalty and manufacturer control	To generate dealer loyalty and control	To offer a low-priced, lesser-quality item to those desiring it

Global Marketing in Action

The Globalization of Chinese Brands

Major Chinese brands include Lenovo (http://www.lenovo.com), Chery Automobile (http://www.cheryglobal.com), Tsingtao Brewery (http://www.tsingtaobeer.com), Huawei Technologies (http://www.huawei.com), and Haier (http://www.haieramerica.com). Let's look at these powerhouse brands.

Lenovo, which began in 1984 as Legend, acquired IBM's personal computer business in 2005. Chery markets cars in the Middle East, Africa, and Latin America. Tsingtao Brewery produces the 12th most popular beer brand in the world. Huawei Technologies' telecommunications goods and services are used by 1 billion people. Haier, a manufacturer of appliances, started with a single model of refrigerator in 1984; it now sells 96 categories of appliances in 100 countries.

In addition, there are a number of Chinese brands that are now seeking worldwide markets. These include Li Ning, a sportswear brand that is competing with Nike (http://www.nike.com) and Adidas (http://www.adidas.com); Chatea (http://www.chafortea.com), a tea brand that instills teahouse culture to young consumers; and Dragonfly (http://www.dragonfly.net.cn), a Shanghai-based day spa chain.

Some marketing observers believe there are strong parallels between these Chinese brands and such Japanese and South Korea brands as Sony (http://www.sony.com), Toyota (http://www.toyota.com), Honda (http://www.honda.com), LG (http://www.lge.com), and Samsung (http://www.samsung.com). They all started small but soon built a strong customer loyalty by focusing on continued product innovation and high levels of product quality. One potential obstacle to the growth of Chinese brands is a recent series of incidents involving product safety of Chinese-produced toys, pet foods, and pharmaceuticals.

Sources: Based on material in Stuart Smith, "Chinese Brands Must Fight to Be Winners," *Marketing Week* (January 17, 2008), p. 19; and Fara Warner, "Hidden Dragons," *Brandweek* (June 25, 2007), pp. 18–23.

dealer loyalty are fostered, shelf locations coordinated, cooperation in the distribution channel improved, and assortments raised. Production is stabilized and excess capacity used. Sales are maximized and profits are fairly shared. Planning is better. In Japan, Kodak (http://www.kodak.com) markets its own brand of film and COOP private-brand film (for the 2,500-store Japanese Consumer Cooperative Union, http://jccu.coop/eng). It wants to make a dent in Fuji's large share of the Japanese market. Kodak does not market private-brand film in the United States.

Manufacturer, private, and generic brands also repeatedly engage in a *battle of the brands*, in which each strives to gain a greater share of the consumer's dollar, control over marketing strategy, consumer loyalty, product distinctiveness, maximum shelf space and locations, and a large share of profits. In recent years, this battle has intensified. See Figure 11-10.

> In the **battle of the brands**, the three brand types compete.

Family and Multiple Branding

In *family (blanket) branding*, one name is used for two or more individual products. Many firms selling industrial goods and services, such as aircraft manufacturer Boeing (http://www.boeing.com) and global delivery service firm DHL (http://www.dhl.com), as well as those selling consumer services such as Teléfonos de México (http://www.telmex.com.mx), use some form of family branding for all or most of their products. Other companies employ a family brand for each category of products. For example, Sears has Kenmore appliances (http://www.kenmore.com) and Craftsman tools (http://www.craftsman.com). Family branding can be applied to both manufacturer and private brands and to both domestic and international (global) brands.

> **Family (blanket) branding** uses a single name for many products.

Family branding is best for specialized firms or ones with narrow product lines. Companies capitalize on a uniform, well-known image and promote a name regularly—keeping promotion costs down. The major disadvantages are that differentiated marketing opportunities may be low (if only one brand is used to target all customers), company image may be adversely affected if vastly different products (such as men's and women's cologne) carry one name, and innovativeness may not be projected to consumers.

Figure 11-10

The Battle of the Brands

Wal-Mart (**http://www.walmart. com**) sells its private-label Sam's American Choice brand for much less than Coke or Pepsi.

Source: Reprinted by permission of Susan Berry, Retail Image Consulting, Inc.

Brand extension gains quick acceptance.

Brand extension, whereby an established name is applied to new products, is an effective use of family branding. Quick customer acceptance may be gained since people are familiar with existing products having the same name, a favorable brand image can be carried over to a new product, and the risk of a failure is less. Brand extension may have a negative effect if people do not see some link between the original product and a new one. The majority of new products now use some form of brand extension.

These are examples of situations in which brand extension could be effective:

- Same product in a different form—Popsicle Snow Cone.
- Distinctive taste/ingredient/component in a new item—Arm & Hammer detergent.
- New companion product—Colgate Plus toothbrush.
- Same customer franchise for a new product (a different product offered to the same target market)—Visa traveler's checks aimed at Visa credit-card customers.
- Expertise conveyed to a new product—Canon laser-jet printers.
- Benefit/attribute/feature conveyed to a new product—Ivory shampoo (connoting mildness).
- Designer image/status conveyed to a new item—Pierre Cardin sunglasses.[20]

Individual (multiple) branding uses distinct brands.

With ***individual (multiple) branding***, separate brands are used for different items or product lines sold by a firm. For example, these are just some of the brands in Frito-Lay's (**http://www.fritolay.com**) product mix: Cheetos cheese-flavored snacks, Cracker Jack snacks, Doritos tortilla chips, Fritos corn chips, Funyuns onion-flavored rings, Grand-ma's cookies, Lay's potato chips, Munchies snack mix, Rold Gold pretzels, Ruffles potato chips, and SunChips snacks. This strong brand lineup enables Frito-Lay to dominate the snack food business with a more than 50 percent share of the market.

---

[20] Edward M. Tauber, "8 Types of Brand Extension," **http://www.brandextension.org/types.html** (2004). See also Eva Martinez, Yolanda Polo, and Leslie De Chernatony, "Effect of Brand Extension Strategies on Brand Image: A Comparative Study of the UK and Spanish Markets," *International Marketing Review*, Vol. 25 (Number 1, 2008), pp. 107–137; N. Thamaraiselvan and J. Raja, "How Do Consumers Evaluate Brand Extensions-Research Findings from India?" *Journal of Services Research*, Vol. 8 (April 2008), pp. 43–62; Mariachiara Colucci, Elisa Montaguti, and Umberto Lago, "Managing Brand Extension Via Licensing: An Investigation into the High-End Fashion Industry," *International Journal of Research in Marketing*, Vol. 25 (June 2008), pp. 129–137; and Henrik Sjödin, "Upsetting Brand Extensions: An Enquiry into Current Customers' Inclination to Spread Negative Word of Mouth," *Journal of Brand Management*, Vol. 15 (April 2008), pp. 258–271.

A firm can create multiple product positions (separate brand images) through individual branding and thereby attract various market segments, increase sales and marketing control, and offer both premium and low-priced brands. Manufacturers can also secure greater shelf space in stores. However, each brand requires a promotion budget, and there is no positive brand image rub-off. Economies from mass production may be lessened. New products may not benefit from an established identity. And there may be some cannibalization among company brands. Consumer-products firms are more likely than industrial products firms to engage in individual branding.

To gain the benefits of family and individual branding, many firms combine the two. A firm may have a flagship brand and secondary brands. Nearly 40 percent of Heinz's (http://www.heinz.com) sales are from products with the Heinz name; the rest have names such as Ore-Ida and Weight Watchers Foods. A family brand could be used with individual brands. At Honda, upscale Acura (http://www.acura.com) and mainstream Honda (http://automobiles.honda.com) are the two auto lines. The Honda line includes the Accord, Civic, and CR-V. It has an overall image and targets a specific market. New models gain from the Honda name, and a relationship exists among models. Individual brands are used with each model to highlight their differences.

11-6c Choosing a Brand Name

Several potential sources may be considered when a firm chooses brand names:

> Brand sources range from existing names to **licensing agreements** and **co-branding.**

1. Under brand extension, an existing name is used with a new product (Tylenol Extra Strength Rapid Release Gels, http://www.tylenol.com).
2. For a private brand, the reseller specifies the name (St. John's Bay—an apparel brand of J.C. Penney, http://www.jcpenney.com).
3. If a new name is sought, these alternatives are available:

    a. Initials (HBO, http://www.hbo.com).
    b. Invented name (Kleenex, http://www.kleenex.com).
    c. Numbers (WD-40, http://www.wd40.com).
    d. Mythological character (Samsonite luggage, http://www.samsonite.com).
    e. Personal name (Heineken, http://www.heineken.com).
    f. Geographical name (Air France, http://www.airfrance.com).
    g. Dictionary word (Scope mouthwash, http://www.scope-mouthwash.com).
    h. Foreign word (Nestlé, http://www.nestle.com).
    i. Combination of words, initials, numbers, etc. (Head & Shoulders shampoo, http://www.headandshoulders.com).

4. With a *licensing agreement*, a company pays a fee to use a name or logo whose trademark rights are held by another firm. Due to the high consumer recognition of many popular trademarks, sales for a product may be raised by paying a royalty fee to use one. Examples of names used in licensing are Coca-Cola, National Football League, and George Foreman. Salton Inc. (http://www.saltoninc.com) has sold millions of George Foreman grills. Licensing generates a total of $120 billion in yearly U.S. retail sales alone.
5. In *co-branding*, two or more brand names are used with the same product to gain from the brand images of each. Typically, a company uses one of its brands in conjunction with another firm's—sometimes via a licensing agreement. There are the Hilton American Express Card (http://www.americanexpress.com/hilton), Bath and Body Works (http://www.bbw.com) toiletries stocked in guest rooms at Renaissance Hotels (http://www.renaissancehotels.com), and various PC brands with "Intel Inside" (http://www.intel.com/pressroom/intel_inside.htm).

A good brand name has several attributes, depending on the situation: It suggests something about a product's use or attributes (Liquid-Plumr drain cleaners, http://www.liquid-plumr.com). It is easy to spell and recall and pronounceable in only one way (Bic, http://www.bicworld.com). It can be applied to a whole line of products (Deere tractors, http://www.deere.com). It is capable of legal protection from use by others (Perrier, http://www.perrierusa.com). It has a pleasant or at least neutral meaning internationally (Onvia—the b-to-b marketplace, http://www.onvia.com). It conveys a differential advantage (Pert Plus, http://www.pertplus.com).

As firms expand globally, branding takes on special significance. Regardless of whether brands are "global" or tailored to particular markets, their meanings must not have negative connotations or violate cultural taboos. To make sure that this does not happen, such specialized firms as Namestormers (http://www.namestormers.com) can devise names for clients that are acceptable around the world. But outside of the leading power brands, which firms may want to make into global brands, brands often must reflect the cultural and societal diversity in the way products are positioned and used in different nations.

When branding, a firm should plan for *the consumer's brand decision process*, as shown in Figure 11-11. For a new brand, a consumer begins with nonrecognition of the name; the seller must make a potential buyer aware of it. He or she then moves to recognition, where the brand and its attributes are known; the seller stresses persuasion. Next, the potential buyer develops a preference (or dislike) for a brand and buys it (or opts not to buy); the seller's task is to gain loyalty. Last, some customers show a brand insistence (or aversion) and become loyal (or never buy); the seller's role is to maintain loyalty. Often, people form preferences for several brands but do not buy or insist upon one brand exclusively.

A brand extension strategy enables a new product to begin at the recognition, preference, or insistence stage of the brand decision process due to the carryover effect of the established name. However, consumers who dislike the existing product line would be unlikely to try a new product under the same name, but they might try another company product under a different brand.

11-6d   The Use of Trademarks

Finally, a firm must decide whether to seek trademark protection. In the United States, it would do so under either the federal Lanham Act (updated by the Trademark Law Revision Act) or state law. A trademark gives a firm the exclusive use of a word, name, symbol, combination of letters or numbers, or other devices—such as distinctive packaging—to identify the goods and services of that firm and distinguish them from others for as long as they are marketed. Both trademarks (for goods) and service marks (for services) are covered by trademark law; and there are 300,000 U.S. filings each year through the U.S. Patent and Trademark Office (http://www.uspto.gov/main/trademarks.htm).

Trademarks are voluntary and require registration and implementation procedures that can be time consuming and expensive (challenging a competitor may mean high legal fees and years in court). A global firm must register trademarks in every nation in

> The consumer's brand decision process moves from nonrecognition to insistence (or aversion).

Figure 11-11

The Consumer's Brand Decision Process

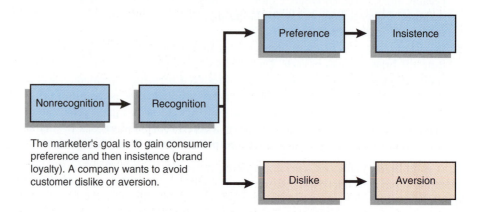

The marketer's goal is to gain consumer preference and then insistence (brand loyalty). A company wants to avoid customer dislike or aversion.

which it operates; even then, trademark rights may not be enforceable. To be legally protected, a trademark must have a distinct meaning that does not describe an entire product category, must be used in interstate commerce (for federal protection), must not be confusingly similar to other trademarks, and must not imply attributes a product does not have. A surname by itself cannot be registered because any person can generally do business under his or her name; it can be registered if used to describe a specific business (such as McDonald's restaurants). The U.S. Supreme Court has ruled that the color of a product can gain trademark protection, as long as it achieves "secondary meaning," whereby the color distinguishes a particular brand and indicates its "source."

When brands become too popular or descriptive of a product category, they risk becoming public property and losing trademark protection. Brands that have worked hard over the years to remain exclusive trademarks include L'eggs (**http://www.leggs. com**), Rollerblade (**http://www.rollerblade.com**), Formica (**http://www.formica.com**), and Teflon (**http://www.teflon.com**). Former trademarks now considered generic—thus, public property—are cellophane, aspirin, shredded wheat, cola, linoleum, and lite beer.

DuPont has used careful research to retain a trademark for Teflon. Its surveys have shown that most people identify Teflon as a brand name. On the other hand, the U.S. Supreme Court ruled that *Monopoly* was a generic term that could be used by any game maker; and a federal court ruled that Miller could not trademark the single word "Lite" for its lower-calorie beer.

11-7 PACKAGING

Packaging is the part of product planning where a firm researches, designs, and produces package(s). A *package* is a container used to protect, promote, transport, and/or identify a product. It may consist of a product's physical container, an outer label, and/or inserts:

> A **package** involves decisions as to a product's physical container, label, and inserts.

- The physical container may be a cardboard, metal, plastic, or wooden box; a cellophane, waxed paper, or cloth wrapper; a glass, aluminum, or plastic jar or can; a paper bag; Styrofoam; some other material; or a combination of these. Products may have more than one container: Cereal is individually packaged in small boxes, with inner waxed paper wrapping, and shipped in large corrugated boxes; watches are usually covered with cloth linings and shipped in plastic boxes.
- The label indicates a product's brand name, the company logo, ingredients, promotional messages, inventory codes, and/or instructions for use.
- Inserts are (1) instructions and safety information placed in drug, toy, and other packages or (2) coupons, prizes, or recipe booklets. They are used as appropriate.

About 10 percent of a typical product's final selling price goes for its packaging. The amount is higher for such products as cosmetics (as much as 40 percent or more). A complete package redesign for a major product might cost millions of dollars for machinery and production. Packaging decisions must serve both resellers and consumers. Plans are often made in conjunction with production, logistics, and legal personnel. Errors in packaging can be costly.

Package redesign is most likely if a firm's current packaging receives a poor response from channel members and customers or becomes too expensive; the firm seeks a new market segment, reformulates a product, or changes or updates its product positioning; there are difficulties in mass producing packages; or new technology is available. For instance,

> Take just one category—pharmaceutical products. There are prescription drugs, over-the-counter drugs, dietary supplements, and traditional and dietary foods. You can find products on the retail shelf that appear to be similar, but they're regulated differently, because one is considered a drug and the other a supplement. Companies constantly seek to expand their product mix. Future packaging will face the problem of differentiating similar products at an increasing rate. One of the biggest tests will be in meeting the needs of the senior market—and

that's not even mentioning the approaching deluge of baby boomers. Challenges include striking the right balance between the ease of opening a bottle and preserving child-resistance; using larger type for the visually impaired, without crowding the package; and using color and warning messages, without turning off other consumers.[21]

The functions of packaging, factors considered when making packaging decisions, and criticisms of packaging are described next.

11-7a   Basic Packaging Functions

> **Packaging functions** range from containment and protection to product planning.

The basic *packaging functions* are containment and protection, usage, communication, segmentation, channel cooperation, and new-product planning:

- *Containment and protection*—Packaging enables liquid, granular, and other divisible products to be contained in a given quantity and form. It protects a product while it is shipped, stored, and handled.
- *Usage*—Packaging lets a product be easily used and re-stored. It may even be reusable after a product is depleted. Packaging must also be safe for all, from a young child to a senior.
- *Communication*—Packaging communicates a brand image, provides ingredients and directions, and displays the product. It is a major promotion tool.
- *Segmentation*—Packaging can be tailor-made for a specific market group. If a firm offers two or more package shapes, sizes, colors, or designs, it may employ differentiated marketing.
- *Channel cooperation*—Packaging can address wholesaler and retailer needs with regard to shipping, storing, promotion, and so on.
- *New-product planning*—New packaging can be a key innovation for a firm and stimulate sales.

11-7b   Factors Considered in Packaging Decisions

> What image is sought?

Several factors must be weighed in making packaging decisions. Because package design affects the image a firm seeks for its products, the color, shape, and material all influence consumer perceptions. For instance: "Pennzoil (**http://www.pennzoil.com**) used its yellow motor oil container as a brand builder since the company launched under the Pennzoil name in 1963. The logo, the Liberty Bell stamped with 'Pennzoil' inside a black-rimmed oval, witnessed some changes but remained as steady a presence as the bottle. When the brand decided to change its message in 2008, from protection to performance with a campaign titled 'Feel the clean,' it wanted a label on the plastic bottle that made things more literal. So, it 'talked to consumers who said that they were aware that a clean piston means a clean engine.' The final design was 'familiar with a twist.' It showed the piston as the defining engine part to actively portray the cleaning concept. The look included 'brighter rays of light around the logo to make it stand out more and give it an active feel.' The tag line? 'No leading conventional oil helps keep engines cleaner.'"[22]

In family packaging, a firm uses a common element on each package in a product line. It parallels family branding. Campbell (**http://www.campbellsoup.com**) has virtually identical packages for its traditional soups, distinguished only by flavor or content identification. Johnson & Johnson (**http://www.jnj.com**), maker of Pepcid (**http://www.pepcid.com**) and Mylanta (**http://www.mylanta.com**) stomach pain medicines, does not use the same family packaging for these two brands; they have distinct packages to lure different segments.

A global firm must decide if a standardized package can be used worldwide (with only a language change on the label). Standardization boosts global recognition. Thus,

---

[21] "Future Packaging—What's Ahead?" *Brand Packaging Online* (May 2005).

[22] Steve Miller, "Pennzoil Fires on All Cylinders for Overhaul," *Brandweek* (February 18, 2008), p. 13.

Figure 11-12

Nonstandardized Packaging for Tide

Tide packaging adapts to the markets in which it is sold. In Shanghai, China, it is sold in tough plastic bags and labeled in Chinese.

Source: Reprinted by permission of TNS Retail Forward.

Coke (http://www.coke.com) and Pepsi (http://www.pepsi.com) have standard packages when possible. Yet, some colors, symbols, and shapes have negative meanings in some nations. For example, white can mean purity or mourning, two vastly different images. As shown in Figure 11-12, Tide detergent (http://www.tide.com) has different packaging in Shanghai, China, than in the United States.

Package costs must be considered on both a total and per-unit basis. As noted earlier, total costs can run into the millions of dollars, and per-unit costs can go as high as 40 percent or more of a product's selling price—depending on the purpose and extent of packaging.

A firm has many packaging materials from which to select, such as paperboard, plastic, metal, glass, Styrofoam, and cellophane. In the choice, trade-offs are probably needed: Cellophane allows products to be attractively displayed, but it is highly susceptible to tearing; paperboard is relatively inexpensive, but it is hard to open. A firm must also decide how innovative it wants its packaging to be. Aseptic packaging (for milk and juice boxes) allows beverages to be stored in special boxes without refrigeration. These beverages are more popular in Europe than in the United States. Figure 11-13 shows a typical display at Target (http://www.target.com)—with packaging that facilitates both the promotion and storage of products.

A wide range of package features is available from which to choose, depending on the product. These features include pour spouts, hinged lids, screw-on tops, pop-tops, see-through bags, tuck- or seal-end cartons, carry handles, product testers (for items like batteries), and freshness dating. They may provide a firm with a differential advantage.

A firm has to select the specific sizes, colors, and shapes of its packages. In picking a package size, shelf life (how long a product stays fresh), convenience, tradition, and competition must be considered. In the food industry, new and larger sizes have captured high sales. The choice of package color depends on the image sought. Mello Yello, a citrus soft drink by Coca-Cola (http://www.cocacola.com), has a label with bright orange and green lettering on a lemon-yellow background. Package shape also affects a product's image. Hanes (http://www.hanes.com) created a mystique for L'eggs pantyhose via the egg-shaped package. The number of packages used with any one product depends on competition and the firm's use of differentiated marketing. By selling small, medium, and large sizes, a firm may ensure maximum shelf space, appeal to different consumers, and make it difficult for a new company to gain channel access.

> **Should standard packages be used worldwide?**

> **What materials and innovations are right?**

> **What size(s), color(s), and shape(s) are used?**

Figure 11-13

Packaging Sells at Target

Source: Reprinted by permission of Susan Berry, Retail Image Consulting, Inc.

The placement, content, size, and prominence of the label must be set. Both company and brand names (if appropriate) need to appear on the label. The existence of package inserts and other useful information (some required by law) should be noted on the label. Sometimes, a redesigned label may be confusing to customers and hurt a product's sales.

Multiple packaging couples two or more product items in one container. It may involve the same product (such as razor blades) or combine different ones (such as a first-aid kit). The goal is to increase usage (hoarding may be a problem), get people to buy an assortment of items, or have people try a new item (such as a new toothpaste packaged with an established toothbrush brand). Many multiple packs, like cereal, are versatile—they can be sold as shipped or broken into single units.

Individually wrapping portions of a divisible product may offer a competitive advantage. It may also be costly. Kraft (**http://www.kraftfoods.com**) has done well with its individually wrapped cheese slices. Hammermill (**http://www.internationalpaper. com/Paper/Paper%20Products/Hammermill**) sells its paper in single packages with 500 sheets each, as well as in boxes with 12 packages of 500 sheets.

For certain items (such as shirts, magazines, watches, and candy), some resellers want pre-printed prices. They then can charge those prices or adhere their own labels. Other resellers prefer only a space for the price on the package and insert their own price labels automatically. With the growing use of computer technology by resellers in monitoring their inventory levels, more of them are insisting on pre-marked inventory codes on packages. The National Retail Federation (**http://www.nrf.com**) endorses the Universal Product Code (**http://www.gs1us.org**) as the voluntary U.S. vendor-marking standard.

With the *Universal Product Code (UPC)*, manufacturers pre-mark items with a series of thick and thin vertical lines. Price and inventory data barcodes are represented by these lines, which appear on outer package labels but are not readable by employees and customers. Lines are "read" by computerized scanning equipment at the checkout counter; the cashier does not have to ring up a transaction manually, and inventory data are instantly transmitted to the main computer of the retailer (or manufacturer). In the UPC system, human-readable prices must still be marked, either by the manufacturer or the reseller.

Last, a firm must be sure the package design fits in with the rest of its marketing mix. A prestige perfume may be extravagantly packaged, distributed in select stores, advertised in upscale magazines, and sold at a high price. In contrast, a firm making perfumes that

Should items be individually wrapped?

Should a package have a pre-printed price and use the Universal Product Code (UPC)?

Marketing and the Web

How to Enhance a Brand Image on the Internet

With consumers spending more time on the Web, it has become more important than ever for marketers to develop and reinforce a strong online image. Here are nine tips to consider:

- Define your brand upfront—Beware of using so many graphics that viewers lose sight of your business. Be sure to state your business in the opening paragraph.
- Begin with what you do, not your brand name— In addition to the firm's name, consider using a tag line that describes your business.
- Use a corporate spokesperson—This person could be the chief executive, the vice-president of marketing, or a public relations executive. Avoid asking people to send E-mail to the "Webmaster."
- Implement a "fan-club" mentality—Get users to describe their positive product-related experiences. Hope that the correspondence resembles that of "fans" instead of "users."

- Pay close attention to verbal content—Have a conversational tone.
- Use visual elements as reinforcement—Carefully evaluate the use of specific fonts, colors, and design elements. Make sure these reinforce your image.
- Become a clearinghouse—Make your site a destination for product information, product-related experiences, and answers to frequently-asked questions.
- Publish an E-mail letter—Deliver your message via opt-in E-mail on an ongoing basis.
- Generate visibility through online forums— Regularly post messages on online forums, message boards, and discussion lists.

Source: Based on material in Bob Baker, "9 Ways to Communicate a Rock-Solid Identity," http://www.websitemarketingplan.com/online/Branding.htm (August 22, 2008).

imitate leading brands has more basic packages, distributes in discount stores, does not advertise, and uses low prices. The two brands may cost an identical amount to make, but the imitator would spend only a fraction as much on packaging.

> **How does the package interrelate with other marketing variables?**

The Business Owner's Toolkit (http://www.toolkit.cch.com/text/P03_5100.asp) has a good discussion on package design, including its relationship with brand positioning, the use of graphics, and reflecting target market values.

11-7c Criticisms of Packaging

The packaging practices of some industries and firms have been heavily criticized and regulated due to their impact (or potential impact) on the environment and scarce resources, the high expenditures on packaging, questions about the honesty of labels and the confusion caused by inconsistent designations of package sizes (such as large, family, super), and critics' perceptions of inadequate package safety.

> **Packaging is faulted for waste, misleading labels, and so on.**

Yet, consumers—as well as business—must bear part of the responsibility for the negative results of packaging. Throwaway bottles (highly preferred by consumers) use almost three times the energy of returnable ones. Shoplifting annually adds to packaging costs because firms must add security tags and otherwise alter packages to deter this.

In planning a packaging strategy, firms need to weigh the short-term and long-term benefits and costs of environmentally safer ("green"), less confusing, and more tamper-resistant packages. Generally, firms are responding quite positively to the criticisms raised here. These issues were examined in Chapter 5.

11-8 THE GLOBAL DIMENSIONS OF PRODUCT PLANNING

When a product plan is devised, these points should be kept in mind with regard to international marketing:

- Although a firm may offer the same products in countries around the globe, those products can have distinct generic meanings in different countries.

> Several factors should be considered with international product planning.

- In developing and less-developed countries, product "frills" are often less important than in industrialized countries.
- Due to their intangibility, perishability, inseparability, and variability, the international marketing efforts for services are often more complex than those on behalf of goods.
- The concept of convenience, shopping, and specialty products is less valid in markets where distribution is limited or consumers have few choices.
- Installations and accessory equipment may be hard to ship overseas.
- Marketing all of the items in a wide and/or deep product mix may not be appropriate or economically feasible on a global basis.
- The diversity of international markets may necessitate a decentralized product management organization, with some executives permanently assigned to foreign countries.
- For many products, there are differences in product positioning and consumer ideal points by country or region. Simple positioning messages travel better than more complicated ones.
- Even though global branding and packaging may be desirable, various nations may have special needs or requirements.
- Expectations about goods/services combinations (discussed in the next chapter) may differ by nation.
- A product modification or minor innovation in a home market may be a major innovation internationally, necessitating different marketing approaches.
- The characteristics of the market segments—innovators, early adopters, early majority, late majority, and laggards—in the diffusion process (covered in Chapter 13) often differ by country.
- Some products are in different stages of their life cycles in developing and less-developed countries than in industrialized countries.

Web Sites You Can Use

A number of Web sites provide expert advice on how to properly position company products and brands in the consumer's mind. Here is a sampling:

- "Brand Positioning" (**http://www.s-m-a-r-t.com/Exp_brandpos.htm**) from Strategic Marketing and Research Techniques
- "How to Strengthen Product Positioning" (**http://www.toolkit.cch.com/text/P03_1074.asp**) from Business Owner's Toolkit

- "Market Positioning" (**http://marketing.about.com/od/positioning**) from About.com
- "Positioning" (**http://www.quickmba.com/marketing/ries-trout/positioning**) from Quick MBA
- "Positioning: Marketing" (**http://en.wikipedia.org/wiki/Positioning_(marketing)**) from Wikipedia
- "Repositioning for a New Market" (**http://www.biz360.com/positioning**), a free positioning guide

Summary

1. *To define product planning and differentiate among tangible, augmented, and generic products*   Through product planning, a firm can pinpoint opportunities, develop marketing programs, coordinate a product mix, maintain successful products, reappraise faltering products, and delete undesirable products.

A tangible product is a basic physical entity, service, or idea with precise specifications that is offered under a given description or model. An augmented product includes tangible elements and the accompanying image and service features. A generic product focuses on the benefits a buyer desires; this concept looks at what a product means to the consumer rather than the seller.

2. *To examine the various types of products, product mixes, and product management organization forms from which a firm may select*   Goods marketing entails physical products. Service marketing includes goods rental, servicing consumer-owned goods, and personal services. Goods and services often differ in intangibility, perishability, inseparability from the provider, and variability in quality.

Consumer products can be classified as convenience, shopping, and specialty items—on the basis of consumer awareness of alternatives prior to the shopping trip and the degree of search and time spent shopping. Industrial products include installations, accessory equipment, raw materials, component materials, fabricated parts, business supplies, and business services. They are distinguished on the basis of decision making, costs, consumption, the role in production, and the change in form.

A product item is a model, brand, or size of a product sold by a firm. A product line is a group of closely related items sold by a firm. A product mix consists of all the different product lines a firm offers. Width, depth, and consistency of a product mix are important.

A firm may choose from or combine several product management structures, including marketing manager system, product (brand) manager, product-planning committee, new-product manager system, and venture team. Each has particular strengths and best uses.

3. *To discuss product positioning and its usefulness for marketers*   A firm must ensure that each of its products is perceived as providing some combination of unique features and that they are desired by the target market. In product positioning, a firm can map its offerings with regard to consumer perceptions, consumer desires, competition, its own products in the same line, and the changing environment. Competitive positioning, company positioning, and consumers' ideal points are key.

4. *To study branding and packaging, and their roles in product planning*   Branding is the procedure a firm follows in planning and marketing its brand(s). A brand is a name, term, design, or symbol (or a combination) that identifies a good or service. A brand name is a word, letter (number), or group of words or letters (numbers) that can be spoken. A brand mark is a symbol, design, or distinctive coloring or lettering. A trade character is a personified

brand mark. A trademark is a brand name, brand mark, or trade character given legal protection.

Millions of brand names are in circulation worldwide. Ad spending on them is billions and billions of dollars annually. Through strong brands, brand loyalty can be secured. Popular brands also speed up the acceptance of new products. Gaining and keeping brand recognition is essential, as is the development of brand equity and a brand image. Branding benefits all parties: manufacturers and service providers, distribution intermediaries, and consumers.

Four primary decisions are necessary in branding. First, corporate symbols are determined and, if applicable, revised. Second, a branding philosophy is set, which includes the proper use of manufacturer, private, and/or generic brands, as well as family and/or individual branding. At this stage, a mixed-brand strategy, the battle of the brands, and brand extension (a popular approach) are also assessed. Third, a brand name is chosen from one of several sources, including brand extension from existing names, private brands, licensing a name from another firm, and co-branding. With a new brand, the consumer's brand decision process moves from nonrecognition to recognition to preference (dislike) to insistence (aversion). Fourth, the use of trademarks is evaluated and planned.

Packaging is the procedure a firm follows in planning and marketing product package(s). A package has a physical container, label, and/or inserts. Ten percent of a typical product's final selling price goes for packaging. The six basic functions are containment and protection, usage, communication, market segmentation, channel cooperation, and new-product planning.

Packaging decisions involve image; family packaging; standardization; package costs; packaging materials and innovativeness; package features; package size, color, and shape; the label and package inserts; multiple packaging; individual wrapping; pre-printed prices and inventory codes (such as the UPC); and integration with the marketing plan. Packaging has been criticized on the basis of environmental, safety, and other issues.

5. *To look at the global dimensions of product planning*   If a firm intends to market products internationally, the distinctive generic meanings of products in different nations and the complexity of marketing services in foreign markets should be kept in mind.

Key Terms

product planning (p. 327)
product (p. 327)
goods marketing (p. 328)
service marketing (p. 328)
consumer products (p. 329)
industrial products (p. 330)
product item (p. 332)

product line (p. 332)
product mix (p. 332)
marketing manager system (p. 335)
product (brand) manager system (p. 335)
product-planning committee (p. 336)
new-product manager system (p. 336)

venture team (p. 336)
product positioning (p. 337)
ideal points (p. 337)
brand (p. 340)
brand name (p. 340)
brand mark (p. 340)
trade character (p. 340)

trademark (p. 340)

brand equity (p. 342)

corporate symbols (p. 343)

manufacturer brands (p. 344)

private (dealer) brands (p. 345)

generic brands (p. 345)

mixed-brand strategy (p. 345)

battle of the brands (p. 347)

family (blanket) branding (p. 347)

brand extension (p. 348)

individual (multiple) branding (p. 348)

licensing agreement (p. 349)

co-branding (p. 349)

consumer's brand decision process (p. 350)

package (p. 351)

packaging functions (p. 352)

Universal Product Code (UPC) (p. 354)

Review Questions

1. Why is it so important to understand the concept of a generic product?
2. Distinguish between a consumer product and an industrial product.
3. How can the same product be a convenience, shopping, *and* specialty product? What does this mean to marketers?
4. Under what circumstances is a marketing manager appropriate? A product manager system?
5. What is the role of product positioning for a new product? A continuing product?
6. Why do manufacturer brands have such a large percentage of sales in so many product categories? Will private and generic brands eventually displace manufacturer brands? Explain your answers.
7. What are the three components of a package?
8. Describe the six major functions of packaging. Give an example of each.

Discussion Questions

1. For each of the following, describe the tangible, augmented, and generic product:
   a. The Graduate Management Aptitude Test (GMAT).
   b. A *Batman* movie on DVD.
   c. A commercial lawn mower.
2. What product positioning would you recommend for a small firm that makes, installs, and services bookcases for residential homes? Explain your answer.
3. Present two successful and two unsuccessful examples of brand extension. Discuss why brand extension worked or did not work in these cases.
4. Evaluate the recent package redesigns of three products. Base your analysis on several specific concepts covered in this chapter.

Web Exercise

Visit the Web site of Smart Draw and read the article on "Working Smarter with Product Positioning Matrix Diagrams" (**http://www.smartdraw.com/learn/worksmarter/diagrams/** **Working-Smarter-with-Positioning-Matrix.pdf**). Devise a positioning map for notebook computers based on what you learn from this article.

Practice Quiz

1. The broadest definition of a product is
   a. intangible.
   b. tangible.
   c. extended.
   d. generic.

2. The marketing emphasis for convenience products is on maintaining
   a. an ample sales force.
   b. selective distribution.
   c. brand loyalty.
   d. nearby locations and long hours.

3. Raw materials are
   a. expenses rather than capital items.
   b. semimanufactured goods that undergo further changes in form during manufacturing.
   c. re-engineered parts used in production.
   d. parts placed in products without further changes in form.

4. A wide/deep mix is characterized by a
   a. small number of product lines and a large number of product items within each line.
   b. large number of product lines and a small number of product items within each line.

c. large number of product lines and a large number of product items within each line.

d. small number of product lines and a small number of product items within each line.

5. The product management organizational form that functions best when the firm has one main product line is the
    a. marketing manager system.
    b. product-planning committee.
    c. new-product manager system.
    d. brand manager system.

6. Which is a characteristic of a venture team organization format?
    a. The venture team is inexpensive to utilize.
    b. The team disbands when a new product is introduced.
    c. Product managers supervise existing products.
    d. One executive oversees a wide range of functions.

7. A trademark is defined as a
    a. symbol or design that is distinctive.
    b. word or letters that can be spoken.
    c. corporate brand or symbol that is legally protected.
    d. brand mark that is personified.

8. Which of the following is *not* a reason why branding is important?
    a. Product identification is eased.
    b. Price comparisons are reduced.
    c. The firm responsible for the product is known.
    d. Consumers' perceived risk increases.

9. When manufacturer, private, and generic brands each attempt to gain a greater share of the consumer's dollar, they engage in
    a. a mixed-brand strategy.
    b. a battle of the brands.
    c. family branding.
    d. co-branding.

10. Which of the following is an advantage of family branding?
    a. Maximization of multiple segmentation
    b. Distinctive image for each company product

c. Lower promotion costs
d. No need to introduce new products

11. Which of the following is *not* an advantage of individual branding?
    a. New products benefit from an established identity.
    b. A firm can create multiple product positions.
    c. A firm can attract multiple market segments.
    d. Manufacturers can secure more shelf space in retail stores.

12. A new product that is a brand extension is *least* likely to start at which stage of the consumer's brand decision process?
    a. Nonrecognition
    b. Recognition
    c. Insistence
    d. Preference

13. For a trademark to be legally protected, it must
    a. have a distinctive meaning that describes an entire product category.
    b. be used only in intrastate commerce.
    c. only imply characteristics that a product actually possesses.
    d. be confusingly similar to other trademarks.

14. Multiple packaging often
    a. shortens shelf life.
    b. gets a consumer to buy an assortment of items.
    c. hurts a brand's image.
    d. reduces consumption.

15. The Universal Product Code
    a. is readable by humans and by machines.
    b. is not endorsed by any industry trade associations.
    c. is only used in the food industry.
    d. requires prices to be marked on merchandise.

For the answers to these questions, please visit the online site for this book at **http://www.atomicdog.com**.

Chapter 12

Goods Versus Services Planning

Oprah Winfrey (http://www.oprah.com) has built a service empire that includes a TV talk show, satellite radio show, magazine, book club, film division, and a Broadway musical. In 2008, *Forbes* magazine listed Oprah as the world's most powerful celebrity, ahead of Tiger Woods, Angelina Jolie, and Beyonce Knowles. *Forbes* estimates Oprah Winfrey's wealth at $2.5 billion. Her success is so staggering that she has been called the "most powerful woman on the planet."

Oprah's TV show, *The Oprah Winfrey Show*, the cornerstone of her empire, has been on the air for more than 25 years. It has an estimated audience of 46 million viewers a week in the United States and is broadcast in 135 countries. The show began locally as a Chicago talk program in 1984. In 1986, when the show entered national syndication, it became the highest-rated talk show in the history of television. This show has remained as the number one talk show for more than two decades.

Oprah's monthly magazine, *O, the Oprah Magazine*, has a monthly circulation of 2.3 million readers. In 2002, Oprah launched the first international edition of *O Magazine* in South Africa. And in 2004, she launched *O at Home*, a quarterly magazine that focuses on home furnishings.

Like her other ventures, Oprah's book club has been a tremendous success: During its first year, it became the largest book club in the world, with about 1.8 million members. The club features in-depth reading guides, online discussion groups, and question and answer sessions with literary experts.

In 1988, Oprah started her production company, Harpo ("Oprah" spelled backwards). Harpo specializes in producing films based on classic and contemporary literature. Harpo productions include *Tuesdays with Morrie* (starring Jack Lemmon), *Their Eyes Were Watching God* (starring Halle Berry), and *Mitch Albom's One More Day* (starring Michael Imperioli of *The Sopranos*).

Through her foundation, Oprah has given grants to organizations that support education and the empowerment of women, children, and families in the United States and around the world—with scholarships, school development, and funding for libraries and teacher education. She contributed more than $40 million to create the Oprah Winfrey Leadership Academy for Girls in South Africa.[1]

In this chapter, we will study key concepts pertaining to the marketing of services. We will focus on the differences and similarities between goods and services marketing, as well as nonprofit marketing.

Chapter Objectives

1. To examine the scope of goods and services, and explain how goods and services may be categorized
2. To discuss the special considerations in the marketing of services
3. To look at the use of marketing by goods versus services firms and provide illustrations of service marketing
4. To distinguish between nonprofit and profit-oriented marketing
5. To describe a classification system for nonprofit marketing, the role of nonprofit marketing in the economy, and applications of nonprofit marketing

---

[1] Various company and other sources.

12-1   OVERVIEW

A firm must fully comprehend the distinctions between goods and services when devising and enacting product plans—beyond the brief coverage in Chapter 11. Although the planning process is the same for goods and services, their differences need to be reflected by the decisions made in the process.

Chapter 12 covers the scope of goods and services, a goods/services continuum, goods and services classifications, special considerations in service marketing, and the use of marketing by goods and services firms. We also include information on nonprofit marketing because most nonprofits (such as colleges, health facilities, and libraries) are involved with services.

12-2   THE SCOPE OF GOODS AND SERVICES

As noted in Chapter 11, *goods marketing* entails the sale of physical products. *Durable goods* are physical products that last for an extended period, such as furniture and heavy machinery. *Nondurable goods* are physical products made from materials other than metals, hard plastics, and wood; they are rather quickly consumed or worn out; or they become dated, unfashionable, or otherwise unpopular. Examples are food and office supplies.

Service marketing includes the rental of goods, the alteration or maintenance/repair of goods owned by consumers, and personal services. *Rented-goods services* involve the leasing of goods such as autos, hotel rooms, office space, and tuxedos for a specified time. *Owned-goods services* involve alterations or maintenance/repairs of goods owned by consumers. These services include house painting, clothing alterations, lawn care, and equipment maintenance. *Nongoods services* involve personal service on the part of the seller, such as accounting, legal, and tutoring services; they do not involve goods.

Overall, the value of manufacturers' shipments of U.S.-made durable goods exceeds that of nondurable goods. The leading durable products are transportation equipment, computer and electronic products, fabricated metal products, and machinery. Among U.S. final consumers, nondurables comprise two-thirds of all goods purchases—led by food products. Because nondurables are bought more often and consumed more quickly, revenues are more affected by ads and sales promotions.

In industrialized nations, services account for a substantial share—generally well over one-half—of the gross domestic product. In developing and less-developed nations, services account for a lower share of the GDP; goods production (including agricultural items and extracted resources) is more dominant. Yet, even there, the role of services is growing rapidly.

The United States is the world's leading service economy: Services account for $10 trillion in annual spending (including government services). As noted in Chapter 6, on a global level, the United States is by far the biggest service exporter. Seventy percent of U.S. service spending is by final consumers; the rest is by businesses, government, and other nonprofits. Among the leading U.S. service industries are housing and household operations, medical care, personal services, transportation services, and repair services. Nearly 80 percent of the U.S. labor force is in service jobs. Other nations with at least one-half of the labor force in service jobs include Australia, Canada, France, Great Britain, Japan, and Germany.[2]

These reasons have been cited for the global growth of final consumer services: the rising standard of living, the complex goods that require specialized installation and repair, the lack of consumer technical skills, the high purchase prices of items that can be

Goods marketing involves the sale of **durable** and **nondurable goods**.

Service marketing covers **rented-goods**, **owned-goods**, and **nongoods** services.

Service marketing is huge in industrialized nations, with the U.S. the world leader.

---

[2] Estimated by the authors based on data from *Survey of Current Business*, **http://www.bea.gov/scb** (September 2008); and *Comparative Civilian Labor Force Statistics, Ten Countries*, **http://www.bls.gov/fls/lfcompendium.pdf** (Fall 2008).

rented rather than bought, and the greater need for health care, child care, and educational services. In the b-to-b sector, among the services experiencing the greatest growth are business services, computer repair and training, and equipment leasing.

The scope of services is sometimes underestimated because services may be lumped with goods in assigning revenues. The ***hidden service sector*** encompasses the delivery, installation, maintenance, training, repair, and other services provided by firms that emphasize goods sales. For instance, IBM is considered a manufacturer, although its Global Technology Services and Global Business Services units (**http://www.ibm.com/ services**) now account for nearly 60 percent of revenues: "Today's networked economy has created a global business landscape and a mandate for change. Integrated global economies have opened markets of new opportunity and new sources of skills. The Internet has enabled communication and collaboration across the world and brought with it a new computing model premised on continuous global connection. In that landscape, companies can distribute work and technology anywhere in the world. Given these opportunities, IBM is working with clients to develop new business designs and technical architectures to give their businesses the flexibility needed to compete in this new landscape."[3]

> The **hidden service sector** refers to services offered by goods-oriented firms.

12-3   CATEGORIZING GOODS AND SERVICES

Goods and services can be categorized in two ways. They can be located on a goods/services continuum, and they can be placed into separate classification systems.

12-3a   A Goods/Services Continuum

> Products are positioned from pure goods to pure services in a **goods/services continuum**.

A ***goods/services continuum*** categorizes products along a scale from pure goods to pure services. With pure goods, the seller offers consumers only physical goods without any accompanying services. With pure services, the seller offers consumers only nongoods services without accompanying physical goods. Between the two extremes, the seller would offer good/service combinations.

Figure 12-1 shows a goods/services continuum with four different examples. In each one, a pure good is depicted on the far left and a pure service is depicted on the far right. Moving from left to right, within each example, the combined good/service offerings become more service-oriented. Here is the reasoning behind the continuum examples in Figure 12-1:

- A computer flash drive (memory stick) is usually sold as a pure good—a product free from defects. With most computer software, a Web site is available for questions. A PC is often configured by the seller, pre-loaded with software, and accompanied by on-site service. Computer programming entails labor-intensive service on a physical good. Systems design entails professional consultation as to a client's information system needs; the seller offers a pure service and does not sell or service goods.
- When a consumer buys such exercise equipment as a stationary bike, he or she owns a pure good. If a person rents a stationary bike for the home, that individual obtains the use of a physical product. When a person uses a stationary bike at a hotel, he or she obtains the use of a physical product and the related facilities. If a person joins a health-and-fitness club, he or she not only gets to use the physical facilities but also can participate in exercise classes. When a person hires a personal trainer, he or she acquires the pure service of an expert teacher in exercise and motivation.
- Off-the-rack office furniture may be marketed as a pure good—with the buyer responsible for delivery and set-up. Custom-made office furniture is based on buyer specifications and buyer/seller consultations; delivery and set-up are included.

---

[3] "Background," **http://www.ibm.com/press/us/en/background.wss** (August 31, 2008).

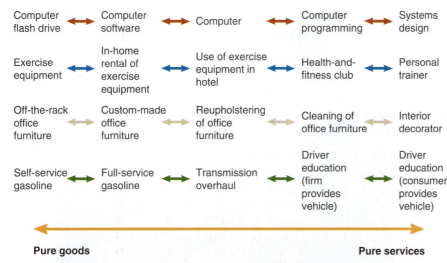

Figure 12-1

Illustrating the Goods/Services Continuum

Please note: The above continuum should be viewed from left to right. Within each row, there is a consistent pattern from pure good to pure service. When comparing different rows, there is somewhat less consistency due to the diversity of the examples shown.

Furniture reupholstering involves labor-intensive service on a physical good; the seller markets a service along with a physical good (the fabric used in the reupholstering). Cleaning office furniture is a labor-intensive service on a physical good; the seller markets a service (the value of the cleaning solution is minor). An interior decorator offers professional consultation regarding a client's office furniture, wall coverings, flooring materials, layout, and so on; the seller provides a pure service and does not sell or service goods.

- Self-service gasoline is marketed as a pure good, with no accompanying service. With full-service gasoline, an attendant pumps the gas—sometimes washing the windshield and doing other minor tasks. A transmission overhaul is a labor-intensive service on a physical good; the seller markets both a physical product (new parts) and service. In driver education, where the driving school provides the vehicle, the seller teaches a potential driver how to drive in a school car; the major offering is the education provided. In driver education where the trainee supplies his or her own vehicle, the driving school markets a pure service; it is not offering the use of a vehicle.

We can learn several lessons from this continuum. One, it applies to both final consumer and b-to-b products. Two, most products embody goods/services combinations; the selling firm must remember this. Three, each position along the continuum represents a marketing opportunity. Four, the bond between a goods provider and customers becomes closer as the firm moves away from marketing pure goods. Five, a firm must decide if it is to be perceived as goods- or services-oriented. See Figure 12-2.

Whether a firm is goods- or services-oriented, it must specify which are core services and which are peripheral—and the level of peripheral services to offer. *Core services* are the basic services that firms provide to their customers to be competitive. At Casio (**http://www.casio.com**), core services include prompt delivery, credit, advertising support, and returns handling for the far-flung retailers that carry its products around the globe. At Federal Express (**http://www.fedex.com**), core services involve taking phone orders, picking up packages, tracking them, shipping on time, and providing proof of delivery.

Peripheral services are supplementary (extra) services that firms provide to customers. Casio's peripheral services are extended credit and advice on how to set up displays for retailers, and a toll-free phone number for consumer inquiries. FedEx's peripheral services include shipping advice for clients, packaging materials, and package tracking. Although these services may increase costs, require added employee skills, and take time, they may also help a company create and sustain a competitive advantage.

> Firms can create a competitive advantage by adding **peripheral services** to their **core services**.

Figure 12-2

A Goods *and* Services Strategy

Home Depot is steadily moving away from the left side of the goods/services continuum toward the center. It is more heavily involved with the marketing of home improvement services than ever before. The firm hand-picks the licensed and insured contractors it recommends.

Source: Reprinted by permission.

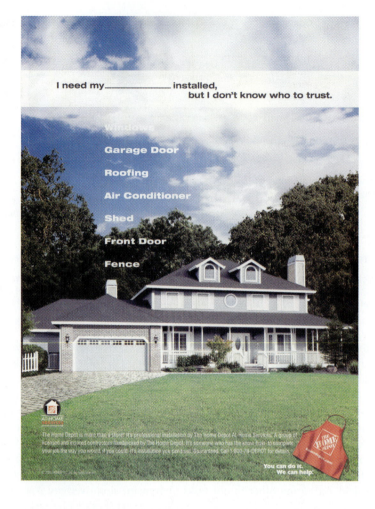

> Goods may be classified as to market, durability, value added, goals, regulation, distribution channel, and customer contact.

12-3b Goods and Services Classification Systems

Figure 12-3 shows a detailed, seven-way classification system for goods. It highlights the diversity of goods marketing.

In selecting a market segment, a goods seller should remember that final and organizational consumers have similarities and differences. The same good may be offered to each segment. The major distinctions between segments are the reasons for purchases, the amount bought, and the features desired.

Durable-goods firms have a particular challenge. On the one hand, they want to stress the defect-free, long-running nature of their products. On the other hand, in as much as they need to generate repeat sales from current customers, they continually try to add unique features and enhance the performance of new models—and then convince people to buy again while the goods they own are still functional. For nondurable-goods firms, the key task is to engender brand loyalty, so consumers rebuy the same brands.

High-value-added goods are those where manufacturers convert raw materials or components into distinctive products. The more value firms add to the goods they sell, the better the chance for a goods-based differential advantage. Low-value-added goods are those where manufacturers do little to enhance the raw materials or components they extract or buy. These firms often must compete on price because their goods may be seen as commodities. Superior customer service can be a major differential advantage and enable marketers of low-value-added goods to avoid commodity status.

For the most part, goods-oriented firms are profit-oriented. Sometimes, as noted in Figure 12-3, goods are marketed by nonprofit organizations—usually as a way of generating revenue to support the organizations' activities. Nonprofit marketing is discussed in depth in Section 12-6 of this chapter.

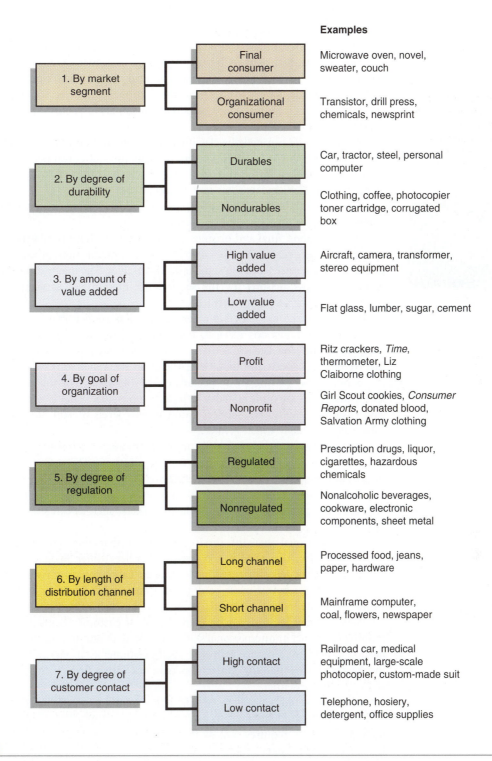

Examples

| 1. By market segment | Final consumer | Microwave oven, novel, sweater, couch |
| | Organizational consumer | Transistor, drill press, chemicals, newsprint |

| 2. By degree of durability | Durables | Car, tractor, steel, personal computer |
| | Nondurables | Clothing, coffee, photocopier toner cartridge, corrugated box |

| 3. By amount of value added | High value added | Aircraft, camera, transformer, stereo equipment |
| | Low value added | Flat glass, lumber, sugar, cement |

| 4. By goal of organization | Profit | Ritz crackers, *Time*, thermometer, Liz Claiborne clothing |
| | Nonprofit | Girl Scout cookies, *Consumer Reports*, donated blood, Salvation Army clothing |

| 5. By degree of regulation | Regulated | Prescription drugs, liquor, cigarettes, hazardous chemicals |
| | Nonregulated | Nonalcoholic beverages, cookware, electronic components, sheet metal |

| 6. By length of distribution channel | Long channel | Processed food, jeans, paper, hardware |
| | Short channel | Mainframe computer, coal, flowers, newspaper |

| 7. By degree of customer contact | High contact | Railroad car, medical equipment, large-scale photocopier, custom-made suit |
| | Low contact | Telephone, hosiery, detergent, office supplies |

Figure 12-3

A Classification System for Goods

Goods may be grouped by the extent of government regulation. Some items, such as those related to the health and safety of people and the environment, are highly regulated. Others, generally those not requiring special health and safety rules, are subject to less regulation.

Distribution channel length refers to the number of intermediaries between goods producers and consumers. Final consumer goods tend to have more intermediaries than b-to-b goods due to the size and importance of the latter. Furthermore, goods that are complex, expensive, bulky, and perishable are more apt to have shorter channels.

Goods may be classified by the degree of customer contact between sellers and buyers. Contact is greater for sophisticated equipment, items requiring some training, and custom-made goods. In these instances, proper employee training is needed. Low customer contact is required for goods that consumers are able to buy and use with little assistance from sellers.

A good would normally be classified on a combination of the factors in Figure 12-3. *Time* magazine (**http://www.time.com**) appeals to final consumers, is nondurable, has high value added, is profit-oriented, faces few regulations, is sold at newsstands and through home delivery, and has low customer contact.

Figure 12-4 displays a detailed, seven-way classification system for services. It demonstrates the diversity of service marketing.

As with goods, final and organizational consumers have similarities and differences, so the same basic service may be offered to each segment. Both groups can counter high prices or poor service by doing some tasks themselves. The major differences between the segments are the reasons for the service, the quantity of service required, and the complexity of the service performed.

In general, the less tangible a service, the less service marketing resembles goods marketing. For nongoods services, performance can be judged only after a service is completed, and consistency is hard to maintain. Rentals and owned-goods services involve physical goods and may be marketed in a manner somewhat similar to goods.

Services may be offered by persons of varying skills. For those requiring high skill levels, customers are quite selective in picking a provider. That is why professionals often gain customer loyalty. For services requiring low levels of skill, the range of acceptable substitutes is usually much greater.

Service firms may be profit- or nonprofit-oriented. Nonprofit service marketing may be undertaken by government or private organizations. The major distinctions between profit- and nonprofit-oriented marketing are noted in Section 12-5 of this chapter.

Services may be classed by level of government regulation. Some firms, such as insurance companies, are highly regulated. Others, such as caterers and house painters, face limited regulation.

The traditional view of services has been that they are done by one person for another. Yet, this view is too narrow. Services differ in labor intensity—such as automated versus teller-oriented bank services. Labor intensity rises if skilled personnel are used and/or services must be done at a customer's home or business. Also, do-it-yourself consumers may undertake some services, such as home repair.

Services may be grouped by their degree of customer contact. If contact is high, training personnel in interpersonal skills is essential, in addition to the technical schooling needed to perform a service properly. Such personnel as appliance repairpeople and car mechanics may be the only contact a person has with a firm. If contact is low, technical skills are most essential.

A service would typically be classified on a combination of the factors in Figure 12-4. A firm tutoring students for college entrance exams appeals to final consumers, has an intangible service, requires skill by the service provider, is profit-oriented, is not regulated, has many trainers, and has high customer contact. A company may also operate in more than one part of a category (this also applies to goods marketers): A CPA may have both final consumer and b-to-b clients.

> Services may be classified as to market, tangibility, skill, goals, regulation, labor intensity, and customer contact.

12-4 SPECIAL CONSIDERATIONS IN THE MARKETING OF SERVICES

Services have four attributes that typically distinguish them from goods (as noted in Chapter 11): higher intangibility, greater perishability, inseparability of the service from

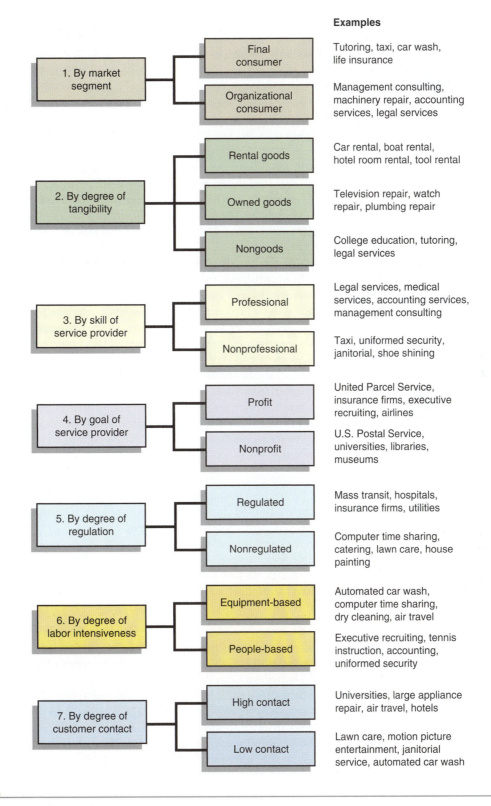

Examples

1. By market segment	Final consumer	Tutoring, taxi, car wash, life insurance
	Organizational consumer	Management consulting, machinery repair, accounting services, legal services
2. By degree of tangibility	Rental goods	Car rental, boat rental, hotel room rental, tool rental
	Owned goods	Television repair, watch repair, plumbing repair
	Nongoods	College education, tutoring, legal services
3. By skill of service provider	Professional	Legal services, medical services, accounting services, management consulting
	Nonprofessional	Taxi, uniformed security, janitorial, shoe shining
4. By goal of service provider	Profit	United Parcel Service, insurance firms, executive recruiting, airlines
	Nonprofit	U.S. Postal Service, universities, libraries, museums
5. By degree of regulation	Regulated	Mass transit, hospitals, insurance firms, utilities
	Nonregulated	Computer time sharing, catering, lawn care, house painting
6. By degree of labor intensiveness	Equipment-based	Automated car wash, computer time sharing, dry cleaning, air travel
	People-based	Executive recruiting, tennis instruction, accounting, uniformed security
7. By degree of customer contact	High contact	Universities, large appliance repair, air travel, hotels
	Low contact	Lawn care, motion picture entertainment, janitorial service, automated car wash

Figure 12-4

A Classification System for Services

the service provider, and greater variability in quality. Their effect is greatest for personal services.

Intangibility of services means they often cannot be displayed, transported, stored, packaged, or inspected before buying. This occurs for repair services and personal

> Services differ from goods in terms of **intangibility, perishability, inseparability,** and **variability.**

services; only the benefits derived from the service experience can be described. *Perishability of services* means many of them cannot be stored for future sale. If a painter who needs eight hours to paint a single house is idle on Monday, he or she will not be able to paint two houses on Tuesday; Monday's idle time is lost. A service supplier must try to manage consumers so there is consistent demand for various parts of the week, month, and/or year.

Inseparability of services means a service provider and his or her services may be inseparable. When this occurs, the service provider is virtually indispensable, and customer contact is often an integral part of the service experience. The quality of machinery repair depends on a mechanic's skill, and the quality of legal services depends on a lawyer's ability. *Variability in service quality*—differing service performance from one purchase occasion to another—often occurs even if services are completed by the same person. This may be due to a firm's difficulty in problem diagnosis (for repairs), customer inability to verbalize service needs, and the lack of standardization and mass production for many services.

In planning its marketing strategy, a service firm needs to consider how intangible its offering is, how perishable its services are, how inseparable performance is from specific service providers, and the potential variability of service quality. Its goal would be to prepare and enact a marketing strategy that lets consumers perceive its offering in a more tangible manner, makes its services less perishable, encourages consumers to seek it out but enables multiple employees to be viewed as competent, and makes service performance as efficient and consistent as possible.

Service intangibility can make positioning harder. Unlike goods positioning, which often stresses tangible factors and consumer analysis (such as touching and tasting) prior to a purchase, much service positioning must rely on performance promises (such as how well a truck handles after a tune-up), which can only be measured once a purchase is made. But, there are ways to use positioning to help consumers perceive a service more tangibly. A firm can

> **Service intangibility makes positioning decisions more complex.**

- associate an intangible service with tangible objects better understood by the customer. Figure 12-5 shows how a local pizza restaurant does this.
- focus on the relationship between the company and its customers. It can sell the competence, skill, and concern of employees.
- popularize the company name.
- offer tangible benefits, such as Northwest Airlines' (**http://www.nwa.com**) promoting specific reasons for people to fly with it. See Figure 12-6.
- achieve a unique product position, such as 24-hour, on-site service for office equipment repair.[4]

Consider this example of how to reduce service intangibility: Publishing Business Systems, a service provider to the newspaper industry, "upgraded its sales presentations to make it easier for prospects to 'touch and feel' the company's follow-on services," says Joe Cardosi of Timberlake Consulting. "Prospects are now shown examples of training materials, documentation, and newsletters, and they get a tour of the Web support site. The presentation also highlights the expertise of staff on the help desk and shows that we have all the pieces in place to ensure quick and effective help when they need it. The presentation also shows off specific consulting services, such as tune-ups and solutions to customer problems, that help maximize customer value."[5]

[4] Gordon H. G. McDougall and Douglas W. Snetsinger, "The Intangibility of Services: Measurement and Competitive Perspectives," *Journal of Services Marketing*, Vol. 4 (Fall 1990), pp. 27–40. See also Michel Laroche, Gordon H. G. McDougall, Jasmin Bergeron, and Zhiyong Yang, "Exploring How Intangibility Affects Perceived Risk," *Journal of Service Research*, Vol. 6 (May 2004), pp. 373–389; David D. C. Tarn, "Marketing-Based Tangibilization for Services," *Service Industries Journal*, Vol. 25 (September 2005), pp. 747–772; and Dwane H. Dean and Jane M. Lang, "Comparing Three Signals of Service Quality," *Journal of Services Marketing*, Vol. 22 (Number 1, 2008), pp. 48–58.

[5] Association of Support Professionals, *How to Grow Professional Services* (2006), p. 3.

Marketing and the Web

Online Reservations: An Effective Tool for Hotels

According to TravelClick (**http://www.travelclick.net**), about one-half of hotel reservations are made online by consumers directly and one-third are made online through travel agents. PricewaterhouseCoopers (**http://www.pwc.com**) says that one-third of all reservations come from hotel-owned proprietary Web sites.

A hotel's well-run online reservation system can be especially effective in reducing costs and increasing occupancy rates. As one hotel marketing consultant noted, "A person sitting at a desk can handle 20 reservations an hour. A Web site can easily handle 200 an hour." In addition, there are no commissions due to travel agents with proprietary Web sites. Expedia.com generally will pay a chain $67 for a room it would charge a consumer $100.

Most of Hilton's (**http://www.hilton.com**) online sales come from its proprietary Hilton.com and Embassysuites.com Web sites. In contrast, less than one-fifth of the company's online bookings come from outside online distributors. And its online bookings from its proprietary sites have grown by 250 percent over the past five years, while the online distributors' growth has been stagnant.

The Hilton and Embassy Suites Web sites offer special features to encourage travelers to use them. These include the ability to store detailed information on guests' preferred room locations, newspaper requests, and so on. The hotelier also lets groups of clients develop Web pages. In this way, guests to a wedding can choose among a cluster of rooms and even indicate if they will attend a special dinner for friends of the bride or groom.

Sources: Based on material in "Hotel Bookings by Channel," **http://www.travelclick.net/information-center/bookings-by-channel.cfm** (2008); and Stan Luxenberg, "Wooing Hotel Customers Online," *National Real Estate Broker* (February 2007), pp. 86–89.

Repair and servicing firms operate in a variety of product categories, including motor vehicles, computers, TVs and appliances, industrial equipment, watches and jewelry, and a host of others. These firms fix malfunctioning products, replace broken parts, and provide maintenance. Let us highlight the auto repair and servicing industry.

Auto repairs and servicing are carried out at manufacturer-owned or manufacturer-sponsored dealers and independent service centers. New-car dealers generate most of their profits from parts and servicing. In total, more than $200 billion is spent annually on U.S. auto and truck repairs and servicing (including parts and labor), $85 billion at new-car dealers, and the rest at independents.[12] General Motors cars can be repaired and serviced through its GM Goodwrench program (**http://www.goodwrench.com**), available at approved GM dealerships; independent repair and maintenance shops; tire, muffler, and battery outlets; mass merchants (such as Sears); and service stations. Independents handle many makes and models. Among the largest independents are Pep Boys (**http://www.pepboys.com**), general service; Jiffy Lube (**http://www.jiffylube.com**), oil and lubricating fluids; Meineke (**http://www.meineke.com**), mufflers; and Aamco (**http://www.aamco.com**), transmissions.

How has the auto repair and servicing business changed? Consider this:

Dealerships face increasing competition from service stations and quick-lube centers, but continue to attract customers with competitive pricing and upgraded facilities. New-car dealers have made major investments in service and parts to beef up sales and customer satisfaction. To boost customer convenience and make full use of their facilities, 71 percent of dealers offer evening service hours, weekend hours, or both. The average dealership service department is open for business 56 hours a week. In recent years, more dealerships have opted to remain out of the body-shop business.[13]

The Internet is also having a major impact. Consider Jonko.com (**http://www.jonko.com**), which "is an automobile reference and opinion site that offers a variety of auto

---

[12] Bureau of Economic Analysis, U.S. Commerce Department; and "NADA Data 2008," *AutoExec* (May 2008), pp. 43–63.

[13] "NADA Data 2008," p. 54.

repair tips, tricks, and tutorials. The Jonko.com staff is comprised of a handful of motivated individuals who volunteer their time to create and manage the site. At present, Jonko.com is a completely volunteer effort that pulls together folks who all share a love of cars and the community that can be built on the Web."[14]

A little more than 30 years ago, the U.S. Supreme Court ruled that lawyers could not be barred from advertising. Since then, legal services advertising has risen significantly, and many marketing innovations have been enacted. And today, all U.S. professionals are able to advertise their services. As one observer noted: "With thousands of mid-sized law firms and hundreds of thousands of lawyers all competing for the same pool of clients and prospects, differentiation is one of the most important ways to gain recognition and build brand awareness. Communicating your firm's unique characteristics, expertise, strengths, and successes to a large number of prospects can be achieved through advertising. This is not about selling the skill of your firm, but about promoting the qualities that differentiate your firm from so many others. Differentiation is your brand, and advertising is about positioning that brand by promoting and communicating your firm's differentiators to a targeted mass audience."[15]

The American Bar Association (**http://www.abanet.org**) says two-thirds of members engage in advertising. Industry experts estimate that 20 to 30 percent of new clients now choose attorneys on the basis of the latter's marketing efforts; the rest rely on referrals. Thus, many attorneys advertise in the Yellow Pages and have printed brochures. Some advertise in newspapers and magazines; certain ones use TV and radio ads; and a growing number have Web sites. Various law firms send out newsletters, hire public relations agencies, and have sessions for partners and associates to practice selling services to clients. Many firms hire jury consultants to advise them on the characteristics to look for in potential jurors.

Law clinics and franchised law firms have grown. They concentrate on rather routine legal services. They have large legal staffs, convenient locations (such as in shopping centers), standardized fees and services ($100 or so for a simple will), and plain fixtures. The largest franchised firms have hundreds of attorneys, cover a wide geographic area, advertise heavily, and set fees in advance and in writing.

Legal services marketing has been met with resistance from a number of attorneys. They criticize some advertising for stressing price at the expense of quality and mass-marketing techniques as eliminating personal counseling. They feel the public's confidence in the profession is falling, information in ads may be inaccurate, and overly high consumer expectations are created. A great many lawyers still do not advertise in mass media; they rely totally on referrals.

12-6 NONPROFIT MARKETING

> **Nonprofit marketing** serves the public interest and does not seek financial profits.

Nonprofit marketing is conducted by organizations and individuals that operate in the public interest or that foster a cause and do not seek financial profits. It may involve organizations (charities, unions, trade associations), people (political candidates), places (resorts, convention centers, industrial sites), and ideas ("stop smoking"), as well as goods and services. See Figure 12-9.

Although nonprofit organizations conduct exchanges, they do not have to be in the form of dollars for goods and services. Politicians request votes in exchange for promises of better government. The U.S. Postal Service (**http://www.usps.com**) wants greater use of ZIP codes in exchange for improved service and fewer rate hikes. The American Red Cross (**http://www.redcross.org**) seeks funds to help victims of disasters.

---

[14] "About Jonko," **http://www.jonko.com/about** (May 1, 2009).

[15] Terry Isner, "Creating a Brand Through Advertising," *Law Journal Newsletters Online* (May 2005).

L IKE HUMANS, WOLVES LIVE IN FAMILIES.

LIKE HUMANS, WOLVES NEED FRIENDS.

WOLVES DISPLAY A HIGH DEGREE OF INTELLIGENCE,
EXPRESSIVENESS AND OTHER CHARACTERISTICS THAT ENABLE THEM TO
MAINTAIN SOPHISTICATED, FAMILY-BASED SOCIAL BONDS. BUT WITHOUT FRIENDS
LOOKING OUT FOR THEM, THESE FAMILIES WILL BE BROKEN APART. TO LEARN HOW YOU
CAN BECOME A FRIEND AND HELP FRIENDS OF ANIMALS PROTECT ALASKA'S WOLVES,
PLEASE CALL 203.656.1522 OR VISIT WWW.FRIENDSOFANIMALS.ORG.
BE A FRIEND FOR LIFE.

Friends of Animals 🐾

Figure 12-9

Illustrating the Breadth of Nonprofit Marketing

Source: Reprinted by permission.

The prices charged by nonprofit organizations often have no relation to the cost or value of their services. The Girl Scouts of the USA (**http://www.girlscouts.org**) sells cookies to raise funds; only a small part of the price actually goes for the cookies. In contrast, the price of a chest X-ray at an overseas health clinic may be below cost or free.

Due to its unique attributes, marketing by nonprofit organizations rates a thorough discussion from a product-planning perspective. It is important that nonprofit organizations address the following:

Not enough nonprofit organizations have a comprehensive approach to marketing. While many nonprofits perform one or more marketing functions, few have embraced a marketing approach to operations. People are in charge of many marketing tasks, but their marketing responsibilities are secondary to other priorities. Organizations have added marketing tasks, but envision marketing in narrow terms. A majority of those performing marketing came into their jobs without formal training. While low salaries are a problem in attracting top talent, the larger problem may be nonprofit leaders who do not appreciate marketing as a comprehensive process and are not fully committed to incorporating the marketing approach into their marketing strategies.[16]

Next, nonprofit marketing is examined in terms of a comparison with profit-oriented marketing, a classification system, and its extent in the economy. Three detailed examples are also presented.

12-6a   Nonprofit Versus Profit-Oriented Marketing

A number of marketing similarities exist between nonprofit and profit-oriented firms. In today's uncertain and competitive arena, nonprofits must apply appropriate marketing concepts and strategies if they are to generate adequate support—financial and otherwise.

With both nonprofit and profit-oriented organizations, there is usually a choice among competing entities; the benefits provided by competitors differ; consumer segments may have distinct reasons for their choices; people are lured by the most desirable product positioning; and they are either satisfied or dissatisfied with performance. Figure 12-10 shows how a political candidate could seek various voter segments via a well-conceived marketing mix and careful product positioning (party platform, past record, and personal traits). This approach is similar to the one a profit-oriented firm would use.

Doesn't this message from the nonprofit Dallas Symphony Orchestra (**http://www. dallassymphony.org**) sound like one from a profit-oriented firm? "Our mission is to entertain, inspire, and change lives through musical excellence. Our core values are: Uncompromising excellence. Teamwork. Ensuring that every concert is an event. A community of passionate music lovers making more music lovers. Risk-taking and innovativeness. Committing to fiscal responsibility. Integrity. The members of our musical community build upon a rich 107-year tradition of artistic excellence and masterful musicianship.[17]

There are also some basic differences in marketing between nonprofit and profit-oriented organizations. They are highlighted in Table 12-1 and described next.

Nonprofit marketing includes organizations, people, places, and ideas, as well as goods and services. It is more apt to be involved with social programs and ideas than is profit-oriented marketing. Examples are AIDS prevention, recycling, highway safety, family planning, and conservation. Using marketing to gain the acceptability of social ideas is referred to as *social marketing*. See Figure 12-11. Two good Web sites on this topic are the Social Marketing Institute (**http://www.social-marketing.org**) and Social Marketing Links (**http://www.social-marketing.com/SMLinks.html**).[18]

The nonprofit exchange process can include nonmonetary and monetary transactions. Nonmonetary transactions can be votes, volunteers' time, blood donations, and so forth. Monetary transactions can be contributions, magazine subscriptions, tuition, and so on. Some nonprofit marketing does not generate revenues in daily exchanges, relying instead on infrequent fundraising efforts. A successful marketing campaign may even lose money if services or goods are provided at less than cost. Operating budgets must be big enough to serve the number of anticipated clients, so none are poorly treated or turned away.

Goals may be complex because success or failure cannot be measured just in financial terms. A nonprofit might have this combination of goals: raise $250,000 from

> Nonprofit marketing has both similarities with and distinctions from profit-oriented marketing.

> Nonprofit marketing is broad in scope and frequently involved with **social marketing**.

---

[16] Don Akchin, "Nonprofit Marketing: Just How Far Has It Come?" *Nonprofit World* (January-February 2001), p. 33.

[17] "About Us," **http://dallassymphony.com/About_Us.aspx** (May 1, 2009).

[18] See also Stephen Dann, "Adaptation and Adoption of the American Marketing Association (2007) Definition for Social Marketing," *Social Marketing Quarterly*, Vol. 14 (June 2008), pp. 92–100; Sameer Deshpande and Francois Lagarde, "International Survey on Advanced-Level Social Marketing Training Events," *Social Marketing Quarterly*, Vol. 14 (June 2008), pp. 50–66; Sara Bird and Alan Tapp, "Social Marketing and the Meaning of Cool," *Social Marketing Quarterly*, Vol. 14 (March 2008), pp. 18–29; and Christine T. Domegan, "Social Marketing: Implications for Contemporary Marketing Practices Classification Scheme," *Journal of Business & Industrial Marketing*, Vol. 23 (Number 2, 2008), pp. 135–141.

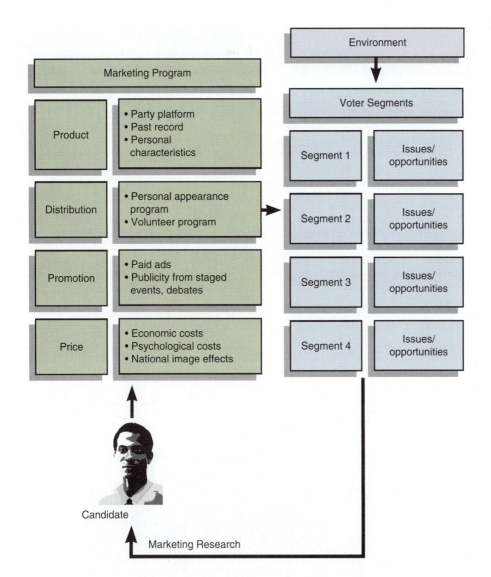

Figure 12-10

The Political Marketing Process

Source: Adapted by the authors from Phillip B. Niffenegger, "Strategies for Success from the Political Marketers," *Journal of Consumer Marketing*, Vol. 6 (Winter 1989), p. 46. Reprinted by permission of MCB University Press Ltd.

government grants, increase client usage, find a cure for a disease, change public attitudes, and raise $750,000 from private donors. Goals must include the number of clients to be served, the amount of service to be rendered, and the quality of service to be provided.

The benefits of nonprofits may not be allotted on the basis of consumer payments. Only a small portion of the population contracts a disease, requires humanitarian services, visits a museum, uses a public library, or goes to a health clinic in a given year; yet, the general public pays to find cures, support fellow citizens, or otherwise assist nonprofit organizations. Many times, those who would benefit most from a nonprofit's activities may be the ones least apt to seek or use them. This occurs for libraries, health clinics, remedial programs, and others. With profit-oriented firms, benefits are usually distributed equitably, based on consumers' direct payments in exchange for goods or services.

Nonprofits may be expected, or required, to serve markets that profit-oriented firms find uneconomical. The U.S. Postal Service (**http://www.usps.com**) must have rural post offices, and Amtrak (**http://www.amtrak.com**) must offer passenger rail service over some sparsely populated areas. This may give profit-oriented firms an edge; they can concentrate on the most lucrative market segments.

Profit-oriented firms have one major target market—clients (customers)—to whom they offer goods and services and from whom they receive payment; a typical nonprofit has two: *clients*—to whom it offers membership, elected officials, locations, ideas, goods,

> Consumer benefits may not be related to their payments.

> Nonprofit organizations must satisfy **clients** and **donors**.

Table **12-1**	The Basic Differences Between Nonprofit and Profit-Oriented Marketing
Nonprofit Marketing	**Profit-Oriented Marketing**
1. Nonprofit marketing is concerned with organizations, people, places, and ideas, as well as goods and services.	1. Profit-oriented marketing is largely concerned with goods and services.
2. Exchanges may be nonmonetary or monetary.	2. Exchanges are generally monetary.
3. Objectives are more complex because success or failure cannot be measured strictly in financial terms.	3. Objectives are typically stated in terms of sales, profits, and recovery of cash.
4. The benefits of nonprofit services are often not related to consumer payments.	4. The benefits of profit-oriented marketing are usually related to consumer payments.
5. Nonprofit organizations may be expected or required to serve economically unfeasible market segments.	5. Profit-oriented organizations seek to serve only those market segments that are profitable.
6. Nonprofit organizations typically have two key target markets: clients and donors.	6. Profit-oriented organizations typically have one key target market: clients.

and services—and *donors*—from whom it receives resources (which may be time from volunteers or money from foundations and individuals). There may be little overlap between clients and donors.

Figure 12-11

Gap Embraces Social Marketing

The Gap (http://www.gap.com) has been involved with the worldwide "Red" campaign, which has raised funds for HIV/AIDS prevention, care, and treatment in Africa.

Source: Reprinted by permission of Susan Berry, Retail Image Consulting, Inc.

Ethical Issues in Marketing

Improving the Integrity of Banking Practices

Federal regulators at the Federal Reserve (**http://www. federalreserve.gov**), the Office of Thrift Supervision (**http://www.ots.treas.gov**), and the National Credit Union Administration (**http://www.ncua.gov**) have proposed a series of laws that would prohibit banks, savings associations, and credit unions from engaging in practices that could be viewed as unfair and deceptive. According to a manager at Consumers Union Financial Services (**http://www.consumersunion.org**), "It's about time federal regulators offered some relief from unfair bank practices. This proposed rule finally acknowledges that some practices just aren't fair."

Let's look at the proposed rules:

- No late fees could be charged if a bill was sent to the customer less than 21 days before the due date.
- If a person has balances with different interest rates, payments will be allocated among the balances.

- Finance fees on credit cards would be restricted where the fees use up the majority of the available credit on that account.
- Interest rates could not be increased on money already borrowed unless (1) the money was borrowed on a variable rate card; (2) the promotional rate expired (then the rate could go to the regular rate but not a penalty rate); or (3) the minimum payment is made more than 30 days late.
- If a bank wishes to raise the rates on a category of transactions for all customers (such as cash advances), consumers who owe money in that category at a lower rate must be given five years to pay off the balance.

Source: Based on material in "Feds Propose New Rules on Unfair Banking Practices," *Tellervision* (July 2008), p. 5.

Private nonprofits have been granted many legal advantages. These include tax-deductible contributions, exemptions from most sales and real-estate taxes, and reduced postal rates. Profit-oriented firms often feel they are harmed competitively by these legal provisions.

12-6b Classifying Nonprofit Marketing

Nonprofits may be classified in terms of tangibility, structure, goals, and constituency. This is shown in Figure 12-12. An organization would be classed by a combination of factors. For example, postage stamps for collectors are tangible, distributed by the federal government, intended to reduce the Postal Service's deficit, and aimed at the general public.

Nonprofit marketing involves organizations, people, places, ideas, goods, and services. Organizations include foundations, universities, religious institutions, and government; people include politicians and volunteers; places include resorts and industrial centers; ideas include family planning and patriotism; goods include postage stamps and professional journals; and services include medical care and education.

Nonprofits may have a government-affiliated, private, or cooperative structure. The federal government markets military service to recruits, postal services, and other goods and services; state governments market universities and employment services; local governments market colleges, libraries, and sports arenas. Government marketing is also used to increase voter registration, secure bond approval, and gain passage of school budgets. Private organizations market hospitals, charities, social services, and other goods and services. They also use marketing to increase membership and donations. Cooperative organizations (such as the Better Business Bureau, **http://www.bbb.org**) aid consumers and/or businesses; success depends on their securing a large membership base and efficiently performing functions.

Overall nonprofit marketing goals may be divided into health (increase the number of nonsmokers), education (increase usage of the local library), welfare (list more job openings at a state employment office), and other (increase membership in the Boy Scouts) components.

> The classification of nonprofit marketing may be based on tangibility, structure, goal, and constituency.

Figure 12-12

A Classification System for Nonprofit Marketing

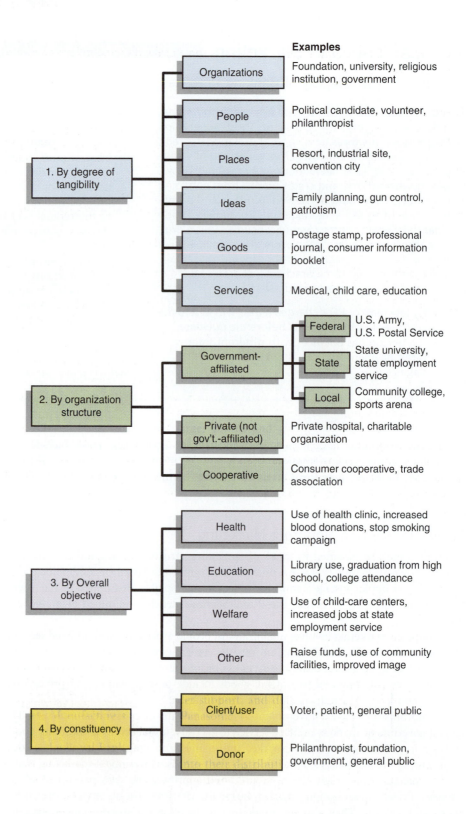

Nonprofits usually require the support of both clients/users and donors. Clients/users are interested in the direct benefits they get by participating in an organization, such as their improved health, education, or welfare. Donors are concerned about the efficiency of operations, success rates, the availability of goods and services, and the recognition of their contributions. For each constituency, an organization must pinpoint its target market. For example, the League of Women Voters (**http://www.lwv.org**) might focus on unregistered voters during an enrollment drive and seek funds from corporate foundations. Figure 12-13 shows some of the differing interests between clients and donors.

12-6c The Extent of Nonprofit Marketing in the Economy

Worldwide, millions of organizations and individuals engage in nonprofit marketing. There are about 1.5 million U.S. nonprofits (30,000 of which are national or international in scope) with millions of paid employees. They annually generate revenues of $3 trillion and receive $375 billion in private contributions, three-quarters from individual donors. Eighty-five percent of U.S. households make a donation each year. The U.S. mass media provide billions of dollars in free advertising space for public-service messages. Half of U.S. adults do some form of volunteer work.[19]

> There are millions of nonprofit organizations in the world.

This further demonstrates the scope of nonprofit marketing:

- The American Foundation for Aids Research (amFAR) is just one of the thousands of nonprofit organizations that operates an Internet site (**http://www.amfar.org**). Its site describes the organization, encourages online contributions, and provides a treatment directory.
- Many countries use tourism boards to market foreign travel to those nations. India's Ministry of Tourism (**http://www.tourisminindia.com**) actively promotes visits to that country. Visit Britain (**http://www.visitbritain.com**) works with airlines, hotels, and credit-card firms to create and publicize special offers. The German National Tourist Board (**http://www.germany-tourism.de**) has an elaborate Web site with colorful information on cities throughout the country.
- Newman's Own (**http://www.newmansown.com**), a nonprofit company founded by the late actor Paul Newman and his business partner A. E. Hotchner, makes and markets salad dressing, popcorn, lemonade, and other food products. All after-tax profits are donated to charities. Since the company's founding in the early 1980s, it has contributed more than $200 million to thousands of charitable groups worldwide.

12-6d Illustrations of Nonprofit Marketing

This section looks at marketing by the U.S. Postal Service (USPS), colleges and universities, and the United Way. The activities differ due to the level of tangibility, structure, objectives, and constituencies.

Figure 12-13

Clients Versus Donors

Clients Desire		Donors Desire	
→	Convenient services	→	Accountability on the part of the organization
→	Inexpensive services	→	Recognition of their contributions
→	Access to services	→	Efficient operations
→	Tangible benefits	→	High success rates

[19] National Center for Charitable Statistics, "Facts and Figures from the Nonprofit Almanac 2008: Public Charities, Giving, and Volunteering," **http://nccsdataweb.urban.org/kbfiles/797/Almanac2008publicCharities.pdf** (2008); Johns Hopkins Center for Civil Society Studies, **http://www.jhu.edu/~cnp** (September 5, 2008); and authors' estimates.

The U.S. Postal Service (USPS, http://www.usps.com) is an independent federal agency with yearly revenues of $75 billion and 685,000 career employees. It delivers more than 210 million pieces of mail—letters, cards, ads, bills, payments, and packages—each year. USPS serves nearly 150 million homes, offices, and post office boxes. It handles 46 percent of the world's card and letter mail volume. It is a self-supporting agency that uses the revenues generated to pay expenses.[20] Competition is intense, and it must deliver all mail—no matter how uneconomical. The Postal Service often runs an annual deficit, and all rate increases must be approved by a Board of Governors.

To protect itself against competitors and stimulate consumer demand, the Postal Service has enacted a strong marketing program—comprising a mix of continuing and new offerings and extensive advertising. It has a full-featured Web site, complete with mail tracking. Customers can buy stamps at more than 33,000 retail outlets, 17,000 ATMs, and other locations. With Express Mail, packages and letters are delivered overnight; the items can be dropped at special boxes or picked up for a small fee. Priority Mail is an inexpensive service, with two- to three-day average delivery anywhere in the United States. ZIP + 4 is an improved ZIP-code service that offers cost savings for both the Postal Service and its business customers, but it has not been used by customers as much as the Postal Service desires. The Postal Service has an agreement with Federal Express for the latter to use its planes to ship USPS Express and Priority Mail.

The Postal Service does hundreds of millions of dollars of business in commemorative stamps each year. It has featured celebrities such as Frank Sinatra, sports heroes such as Jackie Robinson, and social marketing causes such as breast cancer awareness. Many post offices now sell hand-held scales, padded envelopes for packages, air mail markers, and devices to adhere stamps to envelopes. Some post offices are "postal stores"—with interior space divided into two sections, one for specialized postal services and one for retail sales. The retail part of the stores carries stamps, envelopes, packing material, posters, T-shirts, coffee mugs, pen-and-pencil sets, and earrings. USPS has a multimillion dollar annual ad budget.

Colleges and universities know that population trends in many industrialized nations (such as smaller households and a relatively low birthrate) affect their enrollment pools, especially with the number of 18- to 24-year-olds falling in some areas. From 1977 to 1991, the number of U.S. high school graduates fell steadily and did not begin to rise until 1992. Since 1992, overall U.S. college enrollment has only gone up 1.4 percent annually. Thus, new markets are being targeted and marketing strategies are being used by more educational institutions than ever before.

Many schools actively seek nontraditional students: Today, 40 percent of U.S. college students attend part-time; and nearly one-quarter of college students are at least 35 years old. In addition, millions of people are now in adult higher-education programs at U.S. colleges, universities, and private firms.[21] The adult market needs convenient sites and classes not infringing on work hours. At New York University, the School of Continuing and Professional Studies (http://www.scps.nyu.edu) offers 4,000 courses to thousands of students each year.

Traditional students are also being sought vigorously. Schools often spend several hundred dollars—or more—on recruitment efforts for each new student who enrolls. Many buy direct-mailing lists of prospective students from the Educational Testing Service (http://www.ets.org), which administers college board examinations. A number of colleges distribute recruiting films, CDs, and DVDs—which cost tens of thousands of dollars (and up) to produce, to high schools. And the vast majority of schools have a significant presence on the Web.

---

[20] "Postal Facts 2008," http://www.usps.com/communications/newsroom/facts/postalfacts2008.pdf.

[21] U.S. Department of Education, National Center for Education Statistics, *Projections of Education Statistics to 2016,* http://nces.ed.gov//pubs2008/2008060.pdf (December 2007).

The heightened use of marketing is not limited to poor- or average-quality schools. For example, New York's Hofstra University has an award-winning Web site (**http://www.hofstra.edu**), as highlighted in Figure 12-14. Bryn Mawr, Duke, Harvard, and Stanford are among the huge number of colleges and universities that let prospective students submit applications via the Internet through FastWeb (**http://www.fastweb.com**) software, which enables applicants to enter standardized data just once and add customized information for each college. Johns Hopkins (**http://apply.jhu.edu/visit/tour.html**) in Maryland offers an online "virtual" college tour. It "allows you to get a feel for our campus through an interactive Flash piece with photos and descriptions of the campus. Click here to start our virtual tour."

The United Way of America (**http://www.liveunited.org**), with 1,300 affiliated local organizations and annual fundraising of $4 billion, is one of the leading nonprofit organizations in the world. It supports such groups as Boys & Girls Clubs of America (**http://www.bgca.org**), centers for children with learning disabilities, immigration centers, and mental health and drug rehabilitation programs. Most United Way donations come from deductions made from worker paychecks. In contrast, the Salvation Army USA (**http://www.salvationarmyusa.org**) receives most donations from nonworkplace sources. It gets $1.5 billion in yearly contributions (of money and "donations in kind"), and earns hundreds of millions of dollars more from its stores.[22]

For years, the United Way has had an outstanding marketing orientation. It is well known for its long-run association with the National Football League (**http://www.liveunited.org/nfl**) and the touching ads that appear during each game. Employees in affiliated chapters are trained in marketing. Periodic conferences on business topics are held. Affiliated chapters present United Way videos, films, and slide-show programs to potential contributors and volunteers. The United Way even published a book, *Competitive Marketing*, so other charitable groups could learn from it.

Figure 12-14

The Marketing of Higher Education

Source: Reprinted by permission.

---

[22] *United Way 2007 Annual Report*; and *Salvation Army 2007 Annual Report*.

Web Sites You Can Use

Service firms cover a very broad spectrum of businesses. Here is a sampling of them—from insurance to PC-based phone calls:

- Aetna (http://www.aetna.com)
- H&R Block (http://www.handrblock.com)
- Blockbuster Inc. (http://www.blockbuster.com)
- Century 21 Real Estate (http://www.century21.com)
- Choice Hotels International (http://www.hotelchoice.com)
- Club Med (http://www.clubmed.com)
- Cort Furniture Rental (http://www.cort1.com)
- Jenny Craig (http://www.jennycraig.com)
- Discovery Communications (http://www.discovery.com)
- ESPN (http://espn.go.com)
- E* Trade (http://www.etrade.com)
- FedEx Office (http://www.fedex.com/us/office)
- FTD (http://www.ftd.com)
- Hertz (http://www.hertz.com)
- Hilton (http://www.hilton.com)
- InterContinental Hotels Group (http://www.ichotelsgroup.com)
- Jazzercise (http://www.jazzercise.com)
- Knott's Berry Farm (http://www.knotts.com)
- Madison Square Garden (http://www.thegarden.com)
- MapQuest (http://www.mapquest.com)
- Marriott (http://www.marriott.com)
- MasterCard (http://www.mastercard.com)
- Prudential (http://www.prudential.com)
- Schwab (http://www.charlesschwab.com)
- ServiceMagic (http://www.servicemagic.com)
- Sheraton (http://www.starwood.com/sheraton)
- Sir Speedy (http://www.sirspeedy.com)
- Supercuts (http://www.supercuts.com)
- Thrifty Car Rental (http://www.thrifty.com)
- Ticketmaster.com (http://www.ticketmaster.com)
- Travelocity (http://www.travelocity.com)
- Universal Studios (http://www.universalstudios.com)
- Vindigo (http://www.vindigo.com)
- Visa (http://www.usa.visa.com)
- visitalk.com (http://www.visitalk.com)

Summary

1. *To examine the scope of goods and services, and explain how goods and services may be categorized*   Goods marketing encompasses the sales of durable and nondurable physical products; service marketing involves goods rental, goods alteration and maintenance/repair, and personal services. In the United States, the revenues from nondurable goods are higher than those from durable goods—and final consumers spend several times as much on nondurables as on durables. Services account for a very large share of the GDP in industrialized nations and account for a smaller share in developing and less-developed nations. The United States has the world's largest service economy. Both final consumer and business services have seen significant growth in recent years. The scope of services is sometimes underestimated due to the hidden service sector.

   With a goods/services continuum, products can be positioned from pure goods to goods/services combinations to pure services. Much can be learned by studying the continuum, including its use for final consumer and b-to-b products, the presence of unique marketing opportunities, and the changing relationship between sellers and buyers as pure goods become goods/services combinations. Both goods- and services-oriented firms need to identify core and peripheral services.

   Goods can be classed by market, product durability, value added, company goal, regulation, channel length, and customer contact. Services can be classed by market, tangibility, service provider skill, service provider goals, regulation, labor intensiveness, and customer contact. A firm would be categorized on the basis of a combination of these factors.

2. *To discuss the special considerations in the marketing of services*   Services are generally less tangible, more perishable, less separable from their provider, and more variable in quality than goods that are sold. The effect of these factors is greatest for personal services. Service firms need to enact strategies that enable consumers to perceive their offerings more tangibly, make their offerings less perishable, encourage consumers to seek them out but enable multiple employees to be viewed as competent, and make performance as efficient and consistent as possible. Such approaches as the industrialization of services, the service blueprint, and gap analysis enable service firms to better devise and implement marketing plans by improving their performance.

3. *To look at the use of marketing by goods versus services firms and provide illustrations of service marketing*   Many service firms have lagged behind manufacturers in marketing because of their small size, the larger geographic coverage

of goods-oriented companies, their technical emphasis, less competition and the lack of need for marketing, the high esteem of consumers for certain service providers, past bans on advertising, a dislike of marketing by some service professionals, and the reluctance of some manufacturers to view services as profit centers. Yet, for a number of reasons, this has been changing, and the marketing of services is now expanding greatly.

The marketing practices of hotels, repair and servicing firms, and lawyers are highlighted.

4. *To distinguish between nonprofit and profit-oriented marketing*   Nonprofit marketing is conducted by organizations and individuals operating for the public good or to foster a cause and not for financial profit. It is both similar to and different from profit-oriented marketing. These are some differences: Nonprofit marketing is more apt to involve organizations, people, places, and ideas. Nonprofit exchanges do not have to involve money, and goals can be hard to formulate. The

benefits of nonprofit firms may be distributed unequally, and economically unfeasible segments may have to be served. Two target markets must be satisfied by nonprofit organizations: clients and donors.

5. *To describe a classification system for nonprofit marketing, the role of nonprofit marketing in the economy, and applications of nonprofit marketing*   Nonprofits can be classed on the basis of tangibility, organization structure, objectives, and constituency. A nonprofit would be categorized by a combination of these factors.

Worldwide, millions of organizations and individuals engage in nonprofit marketing. There are 1.5 million nonprofit organizations in the United States, generating $3 trillion in annual revenues (including contributions). Their marketing efforts have increased greatly in a short time, and they play a key role in the U.S. economy. The marketing practices of the U.S. Postal Service, colleges and universities, and the United Way are highlighted.

Key Terms

goods marketing (p. 363)
durable goods (p. 363)
nondurable goods (p. 363)
service marketing (p. 363)
rented-goods services (p. 363)
owned-goods services (p. 363)
nongoods services (p. 363)
hidden service sector (p. 364)

goods/services continuum (p. 364)
core services (p. 365)
peripheral services (p. 365)
intangibility of services (p. 369)
perishability of services (p. 370)
inseparability of services (p. 370)
variability in service quality (p. 370)
industrialization of services (p. 373)

service blueprint (p. 374)
service gap (p. 374)
nonprofit marketing (p. 378)
social marketing (p. 380)
clients (p. 381)
donors (p. 382)

Review Questions

1. Differentiate among rented-goods services, owned-goods services, and nongoods services.
2. What is a goods/services continuum? How do pure goods and pure services differ?
3. Distinguish between core and peripheral services. What is the marketing role of each?
4. How can a service be positioned more tangibly?

5. Describe how hard, soft, and hybrid technologies may be used to industrialize services.
6. What are some of the similarities and differences involved in the marketing efforts used by nonprofit and profit-oriented organizations?
7. Discuss the factors that may be used to classify nonprofit marketing.
8. How do the goals of clients and donors differ?

Discussion Questions

1. Present a goods/services continuum related to a public library. Discuss the implications of this continuum for a public library interested in better marketing itself.
2. State several ways that a university could attract more students to its summer sessions.
3. Draw and discuss a weekly service blueprint for a residential lawn care service.

4. Discuss several innovative fund-raising programs that could be used by the ALS Association (**http://www.alsa. org**), the "only national not-for-profit voluntary health organization dedicated solely to the fight against **A**myotrophic **L**ateral **S**clerosis (often called Lou Gehrig's disease)."

Web Exercise

Visit this Web site and read "Tips for Marketing Your Service Business" (**http://www.entrepreneur.com/marketing/** **marketingcolumnistkimtgordon/article191850.html**). What are the most important lessons of this article? Why?

Practice Quiz

1. Which of the following is *not* among the leading service industries in terms of revenues generated?
   a. Recreation activities
   b. Housing
   c. Medical care
   d. Transportation services

2. Which of the following is part of the hidden service sector for a PC maker such as Lenovo?
   a. PCs
   b. PC accessories
   c. PC DVD drives
   d. PC repair

3. Peripheral services
   a. are the basic services that companies provide for their customers.
   b. decrease a service firm's investment.
   c. can be used to create and sustain a competitive advantage.
   d. combine hard and soft technologies.

4. Which type of good is characterized by a low level of price competition?
   a. Low-value-added
   b. Nondurable
   c. Durable
   d. High-value-added

5. When services are classified by their degree of customer contact, they are based on
   a. technical or interpersonal skills training.
   b. professionals or nonprofessionals.
   c. machinery or people.
   d. final consumers or industrial consumers.

6. To overcome high costs and low reliability, many firms involved in services rely on
   a. computer marketing.
   b. peripheral services.
   c. industrialization of services.
   d. hidden service sectors.

7. An example of a soft technology is the
   a. electronic credit authorization system.
   b. pre-packaged vacation tour.
   c. muffler repair shop.
   d. parking service at a hotel.

8. Which of the following is a reason why service firms have typically lagged behind manufacturing firms in developing marketing plans?
   a. Service firms do not stress technical expertise.
   b. Many firms are so big that marketing is not necessary.
   c. The customers of service firms tend to reject any marketing efforts.
   d. Strict licensing provisions sometimes limit competition and the need for marketing.

9. Which of the following is *not* a result of the Supreme Court decision that allows attorneys to advertise their services?
   a. The spread of legal clinics
   b. The growth of prepaid legal services
   c. The decline of legal services marketing
   d. The availability of services to new consumer groups

10. Which of the following is often *not* an aspect of nonprofit marketing?
    a. Relating pricing to costs
    b. Being in the public interest
    c. Spreading social ideas
    d. Fostering a cause

11. A municipality developed an advertising campaign designed to increase recycling of newspapers by homeowners. This illustrates
    a. sympathetic marketing.
    b. superficial marketing.
    c. social marketing.
    d. blue marketing.

12. Donors
    a. are those from whom nonprofit organizations receive resources.
    b. are those for whom nonprofit organizations provide services.
    c. do not engage in exchanges with nonprofit organizations.
    d. are most likely to benefit from nonprofit organizations' activities.

13. Which group is most likely to be either a client or a donor to the American Red Cross?
    a. NAFTA
    b. WTO
    c. Hurricane victims
    d. Public schools

14. College and university marketing
    a. actively seeks adults.
    b. ignores traditional students.
    c. is confined to average-quality institutions.
    d. is on the decline.

15. Which of the following has published a marketing-oriented book to enable other charitable groups to learn from it?
    a. The Salvation Army
    b. The Girl Scouts
    c. The United Way
    d. The Red Cross

For the answers to these questions, please visit the online site for this book at **http://www.atomicdog.com**.

Chapter 13

Conceiving, Developing, and Managing Products

DuPont (**http://www.dupont.com**) is the second-largest U.S. chemical manufacturer (after Dow Chemical). It pursues five key business segments: agriculture and nutrition, coating and color technologies, electronic and communication technologies, performance materials, and safety and protection.

DuPont began in 1802 with a Delaware gunpowder plant. Within 10 years, the plant was the largest of its kind in the United States. DuPont added dynamite and nitroglycerine in 1880, guncotton (an explosive substance) in 1892, and smokeless powder in 1894. As of 1906, DuPont controlled most of the U.S. market for explosives. After World War I, DuPont diversified into paints, plastics, and dyes.

Its rich history of product innovation continued with its production of neoprene synthetic rubber in 1931, Lucite in 1937, nylon in 1938, Teflon in 1938, Dacron in 1945, Tyvek in 1955, Kevlar in 1965, and Corian in 1967. Each year, DuPont invests more than $1 billion in research and development, about 5 percent of sales. In 2007 alone, it received about 600 U.S. patents and 1,500 international patents.

DuPont's innovations can be classified as either scientific (where the impetus for a new product is based on a laboratory finding) or market-driven (where a new product is based on consumer input that identifies unmet needs). Although scientific innovations can become major marketing successes (such as nylon, Teflon, and Dacron), DuPont must demonstrate the benefits for consumers. Because marketing innovations are often easier to understand by consumers, they may require lower marketing costs.

Let's look at two recent DuPont marketing-based innovations involving Kevlar, a DuPont material technology that in the past has been used by firefighters and military personnel. Kevlar is five times stronger than steel on an equal-weight basis. DuPont developed Kevlar-based materials to help mattress manufacturers meet new flammability standards. The Consumer Product Safety Commission estimates that the new federal standard will prevent as many as 270 deaths and 1,330 injuries annually. Kevlar has also been successfully used in DuPont's Storm Room tornado shelters. These shelters use Kevlar-reinforced wall panels that stop and deflect debris.[1]

Next, we will study how new products are developed, the factors causing rapid or slow growth for new products, how to manage mature products, and what to do when existing products falter.

Chapter Objectives

1. To study how products are created and managed, with an emphasis on the product life cycle
2. To detail the importance of new products and describe why new products fail
3. To present the stages in the new-product planning process
4. To analyze the growth and maturity of products, including the adoption process, the diffusion process, and extension strategies
5. To examine product deletion decisions and strategies

[1] Various company and other sources.

13-1 OVERVIEW

In this chapter, we discuss the conception and development of new products, the management of growing and mature products through their life cycle, and the termination of undesirable products.

Though any product combines tangible and intangible features to satisfy consumer needs, a ***new product*** involves a modification of an existing product or an innovation the consumer perceives as meaningful. To succeed, a new product must have desirable attributes, be unique, and have its features communicated to consumers. Marketing support is necessary.

Modifications are alterations in or extensions of a firm's existing products and include new models, styles, colors, features, and brands. ***Minor innovations*** are items not previously marketed by a firm that have been marketed by others (such as a Sony personal computer). ***Major innovations*** are items not previously sold by any firm (such as the first cell phone). If a firm works with major innovations, the costs, risks, and time required for profitability all rise. Overall, most new products are modifications; few are major innovations.

A company may conceive and develop new products by itself or purchase them from another firm. With the latter, a company may buy a firm, buy a specific product, or sign a licensing agreement (whereby it pays an inventor a royalty fee based on sales). Acquisitions may reduce risks and time demands, but they rely on outsiders for innovations and may require large investments.

There is usually strong sales growth early in a product's life, as more people purchase and repurchase. This is an exciting time; and if a product is popular, it can last for quite a while. Next, the market becomes more saturated and competition intensifies. At that point, a firm can keep sales high by adding features that provide convenience and durability, using new materials in construction, offering more models, stressing new packaging, and/or adding customer services. It can also reposition a product, enter untapped geographic markets, demonstrate new uses, offer new brands, set lower prices, use new media, and/or appeal to new segments. For many products, at some point down the road, firms must decide whether those items have outlived their usefulness and should be dropped.

> Product planning involves new and existing products.

> **New products** may be modifications, minor innovations, or major innovations.

13-2 THE PRODUCT LIFE CYCLE

The ***product life cycle*** is a concept that seeks to describe a product's sales, competitors, profits, customers, and marketing emphasis from its beginning until it is removed from the market.

From a product-planning perspective, the product life cycle is valuable for these reasons: (1) Some product lives are shorter than ever. (2) New products often require high marketing and other investments. (3) An understanding of the concept lets a firm anticipate changes in consumer tastes, competition, and support from resellers and adjust its marketing plan accordingly. (4) The concept enables a firm to consider the product mix it should offer; many firms seek a ***balanced product portfolio***, whereby a combination of new, growing, and mature products is maintained.[2]

The life-cycle concept can be applied to a product class (watches), a product form (quartz watches), and a brand (Seiko quartz watches). Product forms generally follow the traditional life cycle more faithfully than product classes or brands.

> The **product life cycle** describes each stage in a product's life.

> Companies often desire a **balanced product portfolio**.

---

[2] For good overview articles on how to extend the product life cycle, see Youngme Moon, "Break Free from the Product Life Cycle," *Harvard Business Review*, Vol. 83 (May 2005), pp. 86–94; and Peter Cebon, Oscar Hauptman, and Chander Shekhar, "Product Modularity and the Product Life Cycle: New Dynamics in the Interactions of Product and Process Technologies," *International Journal of Technology Management*, Vol. 42 (Number 4, 2008), pp. 365–386; and Bharat N. Anand, "The Value of a Broader Product Portfolio," *Harvard Business Review*, Vol. 86, (January 2008), pp. 20–22.

Figure 13-1

Selected Product Life-Cycle Patterns

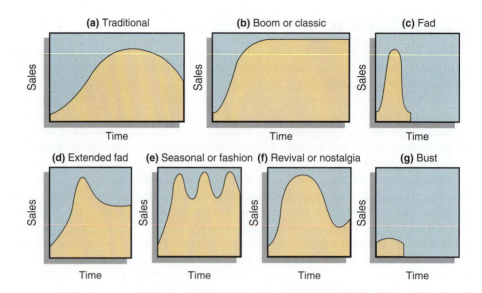

Product life cycles may be traditional, boom, fad, extended fad, seasonal, revival, or bust.

Product life cycles may vary a lot, both in length of time and shape. See Figure 13-1. A *traditional cycle* has distinct periods of introduction, growth, maturity, and decline. A *boom*, or *classic*, *cycle* describes a very popular product that sells well for a long time. A *fad cycle* represents a product with quick popularity and a sudden decline. An *extended fad* is like a fad, but residual sales continue at a lower level than earlier sales. A *seasonal*, or *fashion*, *cycle* results if a product sells well in nonconsecutive periods. With a *revival*, or *nostalgia*, *cycle*, a seemingly obsolete product achieves new popularity. A *bust cycle* occurs for a product that fails.

13-2a   Stages of the Traditional Product Life Cycle

The stages and characteristics of the traditional product life cycle are shown in Figure 13-2 and Table 13-1, which both refer to total industry performance during the cycle. The performance of an individual firm may vary from that of the industry, depending on its specific goals, resources, marketing plans, location, competitive environment, level of success, and stage of entry.

Figure 13-2

The Traditional Product Life Cycle

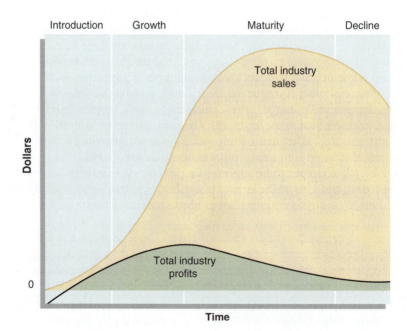

Table **13-1**	The Characteristics of the Traditional Product Life Cycle			
	Stage in Life Cycle			
Characteristics	**Introduction**	**Growth**	**Maturity**	**Decline**
Marketing goal	Attract innovators and opinion leaders to new product	Expand distribution and product line	Maintain differential advantage as long as possible	(a) Cut back, (b) revive, or (c) terminate
Industry sales	Increasing	Rapidly increasing	Stable	Decreasing
Competition	None or small	Some	Substantial	Limited
Industry profits	Negative	Increasing	Decreasing	Decreasing
Customers	Innovators	Resourceful mass market	Mass market	Laggards
Product mix	One or a few basic models	Expanding line	Full product line	Best-sellers
Distribution	Depends on product	Rising number of outlets/ distributors	Greatest number of outlets/ distributors	Decreasing number of outlets/ distributors
Promotion	Informative	Persuasive	Competitive	Informative
Pricing	Depends on product	Greater price range	Full line of prices	Selected prices

During the ***introduction stage of the product life cycle***, a new product is introduced to the marketplace and the goal is to generate customer interest. The rate of sales growth depends on a product's newness and desirability. Generally, a product modification gains sales faster than a major innovation. Only one or two firms have entered the market, and competition is minimal. Losses occur due to high production and marketing costs; and cash flow is poor. Initial customers are innovators who are willing to take risks, can afford to take them, and like the status of buying first. Because one or two firms dominate and costs are high, only one or a few basic product models are sold. For a routine item such as a new cereal, distribution is extensive. For a luxury item such as a new yacht, distribution is limited. Promotion must be informative, and samples may be desirable. Depending on the product and target market, a firm may start with a high status price or low mass-market price.

> In **introduction**, the goal is to establish a consumer market.

In the ***growth stage of the product life cycle***, a new product gains wider consumer acceptance, and the marketing goal is to expand distribution and the range of available product alternatives. Industry sales increase rapidly as a few more firms enter a highly profitable market that has substantial potential. Total and unit profits are high because an affluent (resourceful) mass market buys distinctive products from a limited group of firms and is willing to pay for them. To accommodate the growing market, modified versions of basic models are offered, distribution is expanded, persuasive mass advertising is utilized, and a range of prices is available.

> During **growth**, firms enlarge the market and offer alternatives.

During the ***maturity stage of the product life cycle***, a product's sales growth levels off, and firms try to maintain a differential advantage (such as a lower price, improved features, or extended warranty) for as long as possible. Industry sales stabilize as the market becomes saturated, and many firms enter to appeal to the still sizable demand. Competition is at its highest. Thus, total industry and unit profits drop because discounting is popular. The average-income mass market makes purchases. A full product line is available at many outlets (or by many distributors) and at many prices. Promotion is very competitive.

> In **maturity**, companies work hard to sustain a differential advantage.

At the ***decline stage of the product life cycle***, a product's sales fall as substitutes enter the market or consumers lose interest. Firms have three options. They can cut back on

> In **decline**, firms reduce marketing, revive a product, or drop it.

marketing, thus reducing the number of product items they make, the outlets they sell through, and the promotion used; they can revive a product by repositioning, repackaging, or otherwise remarketing it; or they can drop the product. As industry sales decline, many firms exit the market because customers are fewer and as a group, they have less money to spend. The product mix keys on best-sellers, selected outlets (distributors) and prices, and promotion stressing—informatively—availability and price.

The bulky, electric-powered portable calculator is an example of a product form that moved through the life cycle. It went from an exclusive, expensive item to a widespread, moderately priced item to a mass-marketed, inexpensive item to an obsolete item. Today, earlier versions of the calculator have been replaced by technologically advanced forms—such as credit-card sized, solar-powered calculators.

13-2b Evaluating the Product Life-Cycle Concept

The product life cycle provides a good framework for product planning; but, it has not proven very useful for forecasting:

- The stages, time span, and shape of a cycle (such as flat, erratic, or sharply inclined) vary by product.
- The economy, inflation, consumer lifestyles, and other external factors may shorten or lengthen a product's life cycle.
- A firm may do better or worse than the industry "average" at any stage in the cycle. An industry's being in the growth stage for a product does not mean success for every firm in the market, nor does its being in the decline stage for a product necessarily mean lower sales for every firm.
- A firm may not only be able to manage a product life cycle, it may also be able to extend it or reverse a decline. Effective marketing may lure a new market segment, find a new product use, or foster better reseller support.
- Many firms may engage in a **self-fulfilling prophecy**, whereby they predict falling sales and then ensure this by reducing or removing marketing support. See Figure 13-3. With proper marketing, some products might not fail.

> A **self-fulfilling prophecy** may occur when a firm reduces marketing.

13-3 THE IMPORTANCE OF NEW PRODUCTS

A firm's product policy should be future-oriented and recognize that products, no matter how successful, tend to be mortal—they usually cannot sustain peak sales and profits indefinitely. So, product line additions and replacements should be constantly

Figure 13-3

A Self-Fulfilling Prophecy

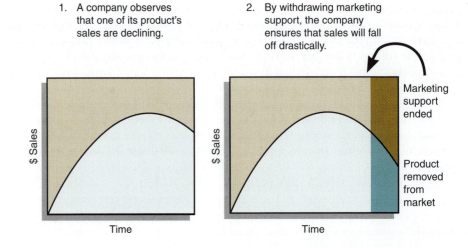

1. A company observes that one of its product's sales are declining.

2. By withdrawing marketing support, the company ensures that sales will fall off drastically.

Marketing support ended

Product removed from market

$ Sales

$ Sales

Time

Time

planned and a balanced product portfolio pursued by both large and small firms. Consider this: "The key is for companies to identify the unmet and unarticulated needs of the customer and align their innovation processes to those insights. Companies must discover what innovations customers are willing to pay a premium for, identify their own competitive strengths, and free up innovation capacity by removing or managing complexity within the organization's goods, services, and operations. The potential reward is a better bottom line and increased visibility with customers, as companies invest in understanding customers' needs while shedding the excess clutter that can bring down their rivals."[3]

Introducing new products is important for several reasons. Desirable differential advantages can be attained. Consider red espresso (**http://www.redespresso.com**), the revolutionary new line of tea:

> The "red espresso" brand is 100 percent premium espresso ground Rooibos tea that has been produced under patent for use in espresso appliances. Its revolutionary patented cut, coupled with its method of preparation, enables tea—for the first time—to perform like coffee: delivering an intense Rooibos espresso shot coated with crema that is the basis for a range of coffee-style Rooibos drinks, including the popular "red cappuccino," "red latte," and "fresh red" (a freshly expressed, natural iced tea). Naturally caffeine-free, with 5 times more antioxidants than green tea and 10 times more than traditional Rooibos tea, red espresso fuses the two growing global trends of health and café culture in genuine innovation. A mere two-and-a-half years since its launch in South Africa, red espresso has made a significant impact on local coffee culture—and is set to do the same overseas. Red espresso is currently launching in and being exported to several countries around the world, including the USA, Canada, Great Britain, Denmark, Sweden, Switzerland, Portugal, and parts of Asia.[4]

New products may be needed for continued growth. That is why ESPN created ESPN360.com (**http://www.espn360.com**) as an "interactive home for sports fans to watch live sporting events and programs through a simple interface. ESPN360.com harnesses the quality ESPN has built through its TV networks. Fans control their sports viewing schedule. Plus you get a fully interactive experience with real time in-game stats, extended press conferences, and more."[5] It is also why Apple introduced the iPod Nano (**http://www.apple.com/ipodnano**), a smaller version of the original iPod. See Figure 13-4.

For firms with cyclical or seasonal sales, new products can stabilize revenues and costs. Dow Chemical (**http://www.dow.com**) makes medical equipment, and other stable product categories, to reduce dependence on cyclical chemicals. Black & Decker (**http://www.blackanddecker.com**) has cut back on lawn-care items and looks for opportunities in less seasonal products, such as power tools for the home.

Planning for growth must take into account the total time to move from the idea stage to commercialization. Consider the lengthy process Boeing (**http://www.boeing.com**) must undergo: "Boeing Commercial Airplanes' new airplane is the super-efficient Boeing 787 Dreamliner. The Boeing board of directors granted authority to offer the airplane for sale in late 2003. Program launch occurred in April 2004. The program signed on 43 of the world's most capable top-tier supplier partners and together finalized the airplane's configuration in September 2005. The 787 program opened its final assembly plant in May 2007. First flight was anticipated during the fourth quarter of 2008 with certification, delivery, and entry into service occurring in the third quarter of 2009."[6]

New products offer differential advantages.

New products lead to sales growth or stability.

New products can take time.

---

[3] "'Smart Growth': Innovating to Meet the Needs of the Market without Feeding the Beast of Complexity," **http://knowledge.wharton.upenn.edu/mobile/article.cfm?articleid=1585** (October 25, 2006).

[4] "World's First Tea Espresso Wins 'Best New Product' at World's Largest Coffee Show," **http://www.redespresso.com/press/TueMay132008103902.pdf** (May 13, 2008).

[5] "ESPN360.com FAQs," **http://broadband.espn.go.com/espn360/faq** (August 31, 2008).

[6] "787 Dreamliner Background," **http://www.boeing.com/commercial/787family/background.html** (August 31, 2008).

Figure 13-4

The Growing Family of iPods

Source: Reprinted by permission of Susan Berry, Retail Image Consulting, Inc.

New products can increase profits and control.

New products can lead to larger profits and give a firm more control over its marketing strategy. New models of luxury cars such as Lexus (**http://www.lexus.com**) and Mercedes (**http://www.mercedes.com**) are often popular. And when they are, the cars sell at or close to the "sticker" price, with dealers earning gross profits of several thousand dollars on each car. Because there are fewer luxury dealers relative to ones selling lower-priced cars, they do not discount as much and have command over their marketing efforts.

Risk may be lessened through diversity.

To limit risk, many firms seek to reduce dependence on one product or product line. Thus, many movie theaters are now multiplexes, so their revenues are not tied to any one film's performance. Hewlett-Packard's (**http://www.hp.com**) offerings span business and consumer PCs, mobile computing devices, workstations, commercial printing, printing supplies, digital photography, managed services, and software; and it regularly adds new products. Turtle Wax (**http://www.turtlewax.com**), the world's leader in car-care products, now has a product mix that goes beyond car wax. It makes glass cleaners, leather cleaners, carpet cleaners, and upholstery cleaners—all for the car.

New products may improve distribution.

Firms may improve the efficiency of their established distribution systems by placing new products in them. They can then spread advertising, sales, and distribution costs among several products, gain dealer support, and discourage others from entering the market. Manufacturers such as Panasonic (**http://www.panasonic.com**) and Revlon (**http://www.revlon.com**) can place new products in many outlets quickly. Service firms such as the Royal Bank of Canada (**http://www.royalbank.com**) also can efficiently add new products (financial services) into their distribution networks.

Technology can be exploited.

Firms often seek technological breakthroughs. Makers of computer storage devices constantly introduce faster, better products—at lower prices. A Western Digital (**http://www.westerndigital.com**) 15-gigabyte hard drive sold for $200 in 2000. By 2009, the firm was selling 1-terabyte drives (equal to 1,000 gigabytes) for under $250. Titleist (**http://www.titleist.com**) "is committed to satisfying golfers with golf products of superior performance and quality." See Figure 13-5. General Electric highlights many of its breakthroughs at its Web site (**http://www.ge.com/files/usa/commitment/innovation/flash.html**).

Waste materials can be used.

Firms sometimes want to find uses for waste materials from existing products—to aid productivity or be responsive to recycling: O'Brien & Gere (**http://www.obg.com**),

Figure 13-5

Titleist: Using Technology to Drive New Golf Equipment

Source: Reprinted by permission.

an engineering company, has several clients that want to make energy out of waste products. It utilizes technology from Ecovation (**http://www.ecovation.com**) "to help companies harness the potential of their byproducts." O'Brien & Gere "has built and installed systems to convert wine, cheese, and yogurt byproducts into biogas that in turn is used to make steam and electricity. Kraft Foods (**http://www.kraft.com**) uses the process in its cream cheese processing plant in Lowville, Lewis County, and in its cheese plant in Campbell, Steuben County. At the Hood dairy plant in Oneida, biogas is sent to a cogeneration plant, where it is made into electricity."[7]

Companies may bring out new products to respond to changing consumer demographics and lifestyles. Single-serving pre-packaged foods are aimed at smaller households. Kodak (**http://www.kodak.com**) and Fuji (**http://www.fujifilm.com**) have single-use disposable cameras that appeal to people interested in convenience.

> New products respond to consumer needs.

---

[7] Meghan Rubado, "The Waste of One Manufacturer Can Be the Raw Material of Another," **http://www.syracuse.com/progress/index.ssf** (February 8, 2008).

Ethical Issues in Marketing

Do Consumers Really Care About "Ethical" Products?

From media reports, it seems clear that there has been a recent increase in the availability of ethically made products. Such products include Starbucks' (http://www.starbucks.com) coffee, produced by farmers who receive higher prices and do not use child labor; Toyota's Prius (http://www.toyota.com/prius-hybrid) hybrid car that runs on a gas and electricity mix; and American Apparel's (http://www.americanapparel.net) clothing line produced in nonsweatshop conditions. According to a study by the National Association of Home Builders (http://www.nahb.org) and McGraw-Hill Construction (http://www.construction.com), homes built with ecologically friendly features will rise to as much as 10 percent of all new U.S. homes in 2010.

Despite all of the publicity, marketers have often had limited success in selling "green" products. KB Home (http://www.kbhome.com), one of the nation's largest builders, recently opened a subdivision in Northern California that uses wood harvested in a manner based on the guidelines of the Forest Steward-ship Council (http://www.fscus.org). Although this added only about $3,500 to the price of a $700,000 home, these homes could not be sold at a premium price. In 2007, far less than 1 percent of KB home buyers chose environmentally-friendly benign bamboo for flooring. And when home buyers were offered front-loading washing machines that use 60 percent less water and electricity than top-loading models, only 3 percent of home buyers chose the energy-efficient model.

To increase acceptance of green options, KB planned a marketing campaign called "myEarth." This program featured sales presentations on energy-saving appliances and lighting fixtures, and on tankless water heaters, which are designed to heat water as needed.

Sources: Based on material in Christopher Palmeri, "Green Homes: The Price Still Isn't Right," http://www.businessweek.com/print/magazine/content/07_07 (February 12, 2007); and Rikki Stanich, "Recession Ethics: CSR in a Downturn—Recession-Proof Ethics Can Weather the Storm," http://www.ethicalcorp.com/content.asp?ContentID=5751 (March 5, 2008).

Microsoft (http://www.microsoft.com/hardware) offers computer keyboards that are easier on the wrist. The Hain Celestial Group (http://www.hain-celestial.com) markets foods that appeal to consumers interested in natural, specialty, organic, and snack foods under brand names such as Earth's Best organic foods, Celestial Seasonings teas, and Terra chips.

> **Government mandates are addressed.**

New products may be devised in response to government mandates. To address growing concerns about battery disposal (and the carcinogenic properties of nickel cadmium batteries), battery makers such as Rayovac (http://www.rayovac.com/recharge) have introduced rechargeable batteries that can be recharged up to 25 times or more. With the growing popularity of such power-draining products as digital cameras, rechargeable battery sales are expected to go up greatly in the future.

Good long-run, new-product planning requires systematic research and development—to match the requirements of new-product opportunities with company abilities, to determine consumer desires, to properly allocate time and money, and to consider both defensive and offensive plans. Some criticism exists about the negative effects of many U.S. firms' short-run, bottom-line orientation on their level of innovativeness (and willingness to take risks). A progressive firm accepts that some new products may have problems or even fail; it will take risks: Sherwin-Williams' Dutch Boy (http://www.dutchboy.com) has been very successful with its all-plastic gallon containers with a twist-off lid, side handle, and pour spout. Yet, "before launching this innovative packaging, the company had to deal with production problems, like changing from all-magnetic conveyor belts designed for metal cans. It also encountered retail problems, like retrofitting paint shakers in stores to accept the new container. But the efforts are paying off. 'Sales are far exceeding our expectations.' "[8]

---

[8] Lawrence A. Crosby, Sheree L. Johnson, and Karen D. Winslow, "Innovation—Not for the Fainthearted," *Marketing Management* (March-April 2003), pp. 10–11.

WHY NEW PRODUCTS FAIL

Despite better product-planning practices today than ever before, the failure rate for new products is quite high. According to various sources, 35 percent *or more* of all new industrial and consumer products fail.[9] The marketplace can be quite tough on new products.

We can define product failure in both absolute and relative terms. ***Absolute product failure*** occurs if a firm is unable to regain its production and marketing costs. It incurs a financial loss. ***Relative product failure*** occurs if a firm makes a profit on an item but that product does not reach profit goals and/or adversely affects a firm's image. In computing profits and losses, the impact of the new product on the sales of other company items must be measured. Arbor Strategy Group cites a list of product failures at its Web site (**http://www.arborstrategy.com/asg/newproductworks/failures.html**).

Even firms with good new-product records have had failures. These include "light" pizza (Pizza Hut), Noxema Skin Fitness (Procter & Gamble), Pepsi Edge (PepsiCo), Bic perfume, McLean Deluxe (McDonald's), Surge (Coca-Cola), Telaction interactive cable-TV shopping service (J.C. Penney), Premier smokeless cigarettes (R.J. Reynolds), and *Gigli* (the Jennifer Lopez and Ben Affleck movie).

Numerous factors may cause new-product failure:

> With **absolute product failure**, costs are not regained. With **relative product failure**, goals are not met.

- *Lack of a strong enough differential advantage:* Consumers had little interest in HD DVD players, which quickly lost the format war to Blu-Ray (**http://www.blu-ray.com**) players: "Both formats were designed as successors to DVD, capable of higher-quality video and audio playback, and of greater capacity when used to store video, audio, and computer data. Blu-ray and HD DVD shared most of the same methods of encoding media onto disks, resulting in equivalent levels of audio and visual quality; but they differed in other aspects such as interactive capabilities, Internet integration, usage control and enforcement, and the degree to which specifications were fixed. Storage size also varied. A dual-layer HD DVD held a maximum of 30 GB of data; a dual-layer Blu-ray carried 50 GB."[10]

> Leading to failure are lack of an advantage, poor planning and timing, and excess enthusiasm.

- *Poor planning:* "Ford [**http://www.ford.com**] introduced two cars to take the place of the highly successful Taurus. The company replaced its perennial best-selling car with the Fusion, which was slightly smaller than the Taurus, and the 500, which was slightly larger. Combined sales for the two vehicles were a fraction of those for the Taurus at the height of its market domination. But rest assured that Ford went to exhaustive lengths in marketing research, focus group testing, and development of a multimillion-dollar ad campaign before it decided to replace its top-selling car. By the end of 2007, the Ford 500 was transformed back into the Ford Taurus—only the nameplate was changed."[11]

- *Poor timing:* "Some products are just ahead of their time. Richard Simmons Salad Spray flopped when it was introduced as a way to encourage healthier salad dressing portions in 1989" because consumers were not as health-conscious then. "But by 2006, when Wishbone [**http://www.wish-bone.com**] introduced its spray-on salad dressing—Salad Spritzers—consumers were apparently ready to quit drowning their lettuce. In 2007, Ken's Foods [**http://www.kensfoods.com**] followed suit with the Ken's Lite Accents line of spray-on dressings. A trend was born."[12]

[9] See Richard Osborne, "New Product Development—Lesser Royals," **http://www.industryweek.com/ReadArticle.aspx?ArticleID=1049** (April 1, 2002); "A Creative Corporation Toolbox," **http://images.businessweek.com/ss/05/07/toolbox/index_01.htm** (August 1, 2005); and Rob Smart, "Assuming Doesn't Feed the Bulldog!" **http://www.inventvermont.com/RobSmartPresentation.pdf** (June 9, 2005).

[10] "HD DVD," **http://en.wikipedia.org/wiki/HD_DVD** (July 27, 2008).

[11] Neale Martin, "How Habits Undermine Marketing," **http://www.ftpress.com/articles/article.aspx?p=1223844** (July 1, 2008).

[12] Amy Whitesall, "New Product Works," **http://www.concentratemedia.com/features/AnnArborNewProductWorks0010.aspx** (May 28, 2008).

- *Excessive enthusiasm by the sponsor.* "The XFL was conceived to build on the success of the NFL [**http://www.nfl.com**] and professional wrestling [**http://www.wwe.com**]. It was hyped as 'real' football without penalties for roughness and with fewer rules in general. The loud games featured players and coaches with microphones and cameras in the huddle and in locker rooms. Although the XFL began with reasonable TV ratings, the audience declined sharply due to a number of factors including the poor quality of play. The XFL folded after one season, with one NBC broadcast receiving the lowest-ever market share for a major network prime time show. NBC originally signed a two-year broadcasting contract. The XFL was estimated by both the WWF and NBC to have lost about $70 million."[13]

13-5 NEW-PRODUCT PLANNING

> The **new-product planning process** moves from ideas to commercialization.

The *new-product planning process* consists of a series of steps from idea generation to commercialization. A firm generates ideas, evaluates them, weeds out poor ones, gets consumer feedback, devises the product, tests it, and brings it to market. An idea can be terminated at any time; costs rise as the process goes on. The process could be used by any firm, and applies to goods and services. See Figure 13-6. In the United States alone, Productscan Online (**http://www.productscan.com**) reports that more than 30,000 new products are introduced into supermarkets every year.

Firms need to endeavor to balance competing goals during new-product planning:

- A systematic process should be followed; however, there must be flexibility to adapt to each unique opportunity.
- The process should be thorough, yet not unduly slow down introductions.
- True innovations should be pursued, yet fiscal constraints must be considered.
- An early reading of consumer acceptance should be sought, but the firm must not give away too much information to potential competitors.
- There should be an interest in short-run profitability, but not at the expense of long-run growth.

Figure 13-6

The New-Product Planning Process

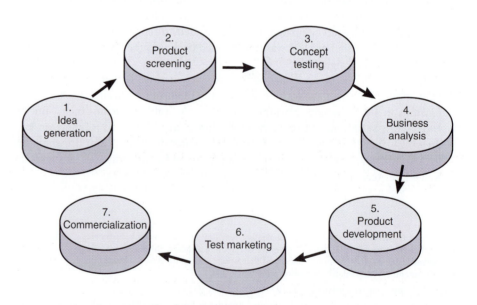

---

[13] "XFL," **http://en.wikipedia.org/wiki/XFL** (April 17, 2006).

Many companies do all the new-product planning activities themselves. Others outsource various tasks. A number of consulting firms specialize in this area, such as Cheskin (**http://www.cheskin.com**), Ideo (**http://www.ideo.com**), and Products 2 Market (**http://www.products2market.com**).

13-5a Idea Generation

Idea generation is a continuous, systematic search for new product opportunities. It involves new-idea sources and ways to generate ideas.

Sources of ideas may be employees, channel members, competitors, outside inventors, customers, government, and others.[14] *Market-oriented sources* identify opportunities based on consumer needs and wants; laboratory research is used to satisfy them. Light beer, many ice cream flavors, and easy-to-open soda cans have evolved from market-oriented sources. *Laboratory-oriented sources* identify opportunities based on pure research (which seeks to gain knowledge and indirectly leads to specific new-product ideas) or applied research (which uses existing scientific techniques to develop new-product ideas). Penicillin, antifreeze, and synthetic fibers have evolved from laboratory sources.

Methods for generating ideas include brainstorming (small-group sessions to come up with a variety of ideas), analyzing current products, reading trade publications, visiting suppliers and dealers, and doing surveys. An open perspective is key: Different people should be consulted; many ideas should be offered; and ideas should not be criticized, no matter how offbeat:

> Revolutionary products and strategies start with the same thing—a brilliant idea. But the smartest, most innovative companies don't stop with one inspiration. They know how to keep churning out new breakthroughs. After all, creativity isn't just a matter of waiting for the muse to strike. The more brainpower you bring to bear on a problem, the smarter the solutions you're likely to get. But that's easier said than done: Nothing stifles creativity faster than a heavy-handed boss who shoots down ideas before they're even properly aired.[15]

> **Idea generation** is the search for opportunities.

13-5b Product Screening

Once a firm spots potential products, it must screen them. In **product screening**, poor, unsuitable, or otherwise unattractive ideas are weeded out from further consideration. Today, many firms use a new-product screening checklist for preliminary analysis. In it, they list the attributes deemed most important and rate each idea on those attributes. The checklist is standardized and allows ideas to be compared.

Figure 13-7 shows a new-product screening checklist with three major categories: general characteristics, marketing characteristics, and production characteristics (which can be applied to both goods and services). Several product attributes must be assessed in each category. They are scored from 1 (outstanding) to 10 (very poor) for each product idea. In addition, the attributes would be weighted because they vary in their impact on new-product success. For every idea, the checklist would yield an overall score. Here is an

> **Product screening** weeds out undesirable ideas.

---

[14] See Ruediger Klein, "Smart World: Breakthrough Creativity and the New Science of Ideas by Richard Ogle and the Medici Effect: What Elephants & Epidemics Can Teach Us About Innovation by Frans Johansson," *Journal of Product Innovation Management*, Vol. 25 (September 2008), pp. 519–521; Robert C. Litchfield, "Brainstorming Reconsidered: A Goal-Based View," *Academy of Management Review*, Vol. 33 (July 2008), pp. 649–668; Kalotina Chalkiti and Marianna Sigala, "Information Sharing and Idea Generation in Peer-to-Peer Online Communities: The Case of 'Dialogoi,' " *Journal of Vacation Marketing*, Vol. 14 (April 2008), pp. 121–132; and Casimer DeCusatis, "Creating, Growing, and Sustaining Efficient Innovation Teams," *Creativity & Innovation Management*, Vol. 17 (June 2008), pp. 155–164.

[15] Bridget Finn, "Brainstorming for Better Brainstorming," *Business 2.0* (April 2005), pp. 109–114.

Figure 13-7

A New-Product Screening
Checklist

	Rating
General characteristics of new product	
Profit potential	_____
Existing competition	_____
Potential competition	_____
Size of market	_____
Level of investment	_____
Patentability	_____
Level of risk	_____
Marketing characteristics of new product	
Fit with marketing capabilities	_____
Effect on existing products (brands)	_____
Appeal to current consumer markets	_____
Potential length of product life cycle	_____
Existence of differential advantage	_____
Impact on image	_____
Resistance to seasonal factors	_____
Production characteristics of new product	
Fit with production capabilities	_____
Length of time to commercialization	_____
Ease of production	_____
Availability of labor and material resources	_____
Ability to produce at competitive prices	_____

example of how a firm could develop overall ratings for two ideas. Remember, in this example, the best rating is 1 (so, 3 is worse than 2):

1. Idea A gets an average rating of 2.5 on general characteristics, 2.9 on marketing characteristics, and 1.4 on production characteristics. Idea B gets ratings of 2.8, 1.4, and 1.8, respectively.

2. The firm assigns an importance weight of 4 to general characteristics, 5 to marketing characteristics, and 3 to production characteristics. The best overall rating is 12 [$(1 \times 4) + (1 \times 5) + (1 \times 3)$]. The poorest possible average rating is 120 [$(10 \times 4) + (10 \times 5) + (10 \times 3)$].

3. Idea A gets an overall rating of 28.7 [$(2.5 \times 4) + (2.9 \times 5) + (1.4 \times 3)$]. B gets an overall rating of 23.6 [$(2.8 \times 4) + (1.4 \times 5) + (1.8 \times 3)$].

4. Idea B's overall rating is better than A's due to its better marketing evaluation (the characteristics judged most important by the firm).

> A **patent** gives exclusive selling rights to an inventor.

During screening, patentability must often be determined. A ***patent*** grants an inventor of a useful product or process exclusive selling rights for a fixed period. An invention may be patented if it is a "useful, novel, and nonobvious process, machine, manufacture, or composition of matter" and not patented by anyone else. Separate applications are needed for protection in foreign markets. Many nations have simplified matters via patent cooperation treaties; however, some do not honor such treaties. Today, in the United States and the other members of the World Trade Organization, patents last for 20 years from the date that applications are filed. The U.S. Patent and Trademark Office (**http://www.uspto.gov**) receives more than 450,000 patent applications and grants 185,000 patents annually. Nearly one-half of U.S. patents involve foreign firms; in contrast, one-sixth of Japanese patents are held by foreigners.

A firm should answer these questions in screening: Can the proposed new product be patented? Are competitive items patented? When do competitors' patents expire? Are patents on competing items available under a licensing agreement? Would the company be free of patent liability (infringement) if it introduces the proposed new product?

13-5c   Concept Testing

Next, a firm needs consumer feedback about the new-product ideas that pass through screening. *Concept testing* presents the consumer with a proposed product and measures attitudes and intentions at an early stage of the new-product planning process.

Concept testing is a quick, inexpensive way to assess consumer enthusiasm. It asks potential customers to react to a picture, written statement, or oral product description. This lets a firm learn initial attitudes prior to costly, time-consuming product development. Heinz (**http://www.heinz.com**), Kodak (**http://www.kodak.com**), Sony (**http://www.sony.com**), and Sunbeam (**http://www.sunbeam.com**) are among those using concept testing. Figure 13-8 shows a brief concept test for a proposed fee-based online music service.

> **Concept testing** determines customer attitudes before product development.

A leading music company is considering the introduction of a new online music service. The company would make its whole catalog of 10,000 recorded songs available under two different subscription plans. With plan 1, customers would pay a monthly fee of $10.00 for up to 50 downloads per month. With plan 2, customers would pay a fee of 30 cents for each song that is downloaded. All songs would have the same fee.

1. React to the overall concept described above.

2. What do you like most about the proposed concept? Why?

3. What do you like least about the proposed concept? Why?

4. What suggestions do you have for improving the proposed concept?

5. What else would you like to know about the proposed concept?

6. How likely would you be to participate in the proposed music service?

Very likely ___ ___ ___ ___ ___ Very unlikely

Why?

Figure 13-8

A Brief Concept Test for a Proposed New Online Music Service

Concept testing generally asks consumers these types of questions:

- Is the idea easy to understand?
- Would this product meet a real need?
- Do you see distinct benefits for this product over those on the market?
- Do you find the claims about this product believable?
- Would you buy the product?
- How much would you pay for it?
- Would you replace your current brand with this new product?
- What improvements can you suggest in various attributes of the concept?
- How frequently would you buy the product?
- Who would use the product?[16]

13-5d Business Analysis

> **Business analysis** looks at demand, costs, competition, etc.

At this point, a firm does business analysis for the new-product concepts that are deemed attractive. **Business analysis** involves the detailed review, projection, and evaluation of such factors as consumer demand, production costs, marketing costs, break-even points, competition, capital investments, and profitability for each proposed new product. It is much more detailed than product screening.

Here are some considerations at this planning stage:

Criteria	Selected Considerations
Demand projections	Short- and long-run sales potential; speed of sales growth; price/sales relationship; seasonality; rate of repurchases
Production cost projections	Total and per-unit costs; startup versus continuing costs; estimates of raw materials and other costs; economies of scale; break-even points
Marketing cost projections	Product planning (patent search, product development, testing); promotion; distribution; marketing research; break-even points
Competitive projections	Short-run and long-run market shares of company and competitors; competitors' strengths and weaknesses; potential competitors; likely strategies by competitors in response to firm
Capital investment projections	Need for new equipment and facilities versus use of existing facilities and resources
Profitability projections	Time to recoup initial costs; short- and long-run total and per-unit profits; reseller needs; control over price; return on investment; risk

The next step is expensive and time-consuming product development; thus, critical use of business analysis is needed to eliminate marginal items. Go to "New Concept Analysis" (**http://www.businessplansoftware.org/qidemo/qidemo.asp**) for an online demonstration of business analysis; click on the arrow key that appears in the upper right portion of the screen. Keep clicking until you have finished the demonstration.

13-5e Product Development

> **Product development** focuses on devising an actual product and a broad marketing strategy.

In **product development**, an idea for a new product is converted into a tangible form and a basic marketing strategy is identified. Depending on the product involved, this

---

[16] Adapted by the authors from Philip Kotler and Kevin Lane Keller, *Marketing Management*, Thirteenth Edition (Upper Saddle River, NJ: Pearson Education, 2009).

planning stage encompasses product construction, packaging, branding, product positioning, and consumer attitude and usage testing.

Product construction decisions include the type and quality of materials comprising the product, the method of production, production time, production capacity, the assortment to be offered, and the time needed to move from development to commercialization. Packaging decisions include the materials used, the functions performed, and alternative sizes and colors. Branding decisions include the choice of a name, trademark protection, and the image sought. Product positioning involves selecting a target market and positioning the new good or service against competitors and other company offerings. Consumer testing studies perceptions of and satisfaction with the new product.

Product-development costs may be relatively low with a modification. However, an innovation may be costly (up to several million dollars or more), time consuming (up to four years for a new car), and complex. This is true of services, as well as goods: "At a cost of $3.8 billion, the Emirates Palace [**http://www.emiratespalace.com/en/hotel**] was designed to become a landmark for the Middle East and the entire world. According to the hotel, 'Each of the exceptional rooms and suites provide guests with uncompromising indulgence. Decoration includes acres of gold leaf and the finest marble.' The architecture and design include 114 domes, of which the Grand Atrium dome is higher than the dome of St. Peter's Basilica in Rome; 1,002 Swarovski crystal chandeliers; 6,000 square meters of interior covered in 22-carat gold leaf; over one million square feet of the world's finest marble imported from Italy, Spain, China, and India; 200 fountains spread throughout 600 acres of exotic grounds;" and more.[17]

Many firms are working diligently to make product development more efficient: "In an ongoing effort to improve its product development process, Boeing (**http://www.boeing.com**) is standardizing on Siemens' (**http://www.siemens.com**) Teamcenter product life-cycle management software, a move that affects tens of thousands of employees. Boeing has been a Siemens PLM customer for some newer projects for more than a year, but now it plans to make it the de facto software for managing data related to each part and every engineering change for commercial and military aircraft, including replacing legacy product life-cycle management systems used for older-model aircraft."[18]

13-5f Test Marketing

Test marketing involves placing a fully developed new product (a good or service) in one or more selected areas and observing its actual performance under a proposed marketing plan. The purpose is to evaluate the product and planned marketing efforts in a real setting prior to a full-scale introduction. Rather than just study intentions, test marketing lets a firm monitor actual consumer behavior, competitor reactions, and reseller interest. After testing, the firm could go ahead, modify the product and then go ahead, modify the marketing plan and then go ahead, or drop the product. Anheuser-Busch (**http://www.anheuser-busch.com**), Georgia-Pacific (**http://www.gp.com**), John Hancock Funds (**http://www.jhfunds.com**), Home Depot (**http://www.homedepot.com**), Levi Strauss (**http://www.levistrauss.com**), McDonald's (**http://www.mcdonalds.com**), and Procter & Gamble (**http://www.pg.com**) are among the firms that use test marketing. Consumer-products firms are more apt to engage in test marketing than industrial-products firms, which often do product-use testing with key customers.

Test marketing requires several decisions: when to test, where to test, how long to test, what test information to acquire, and how to apply test results. Figure 13-9 shows the criteria in making choices.

> **Test marketing** occurs in selected areas and observes real performance.

---

[17] Brett Siegel, "Emirates Palace: 7 Stars For Abu Dhabi!" **http://uaemegaprojects.blogspot.com/2008/05/emirates-palace-7-stars-for-abu-dhabi.html** (May 20, 2008).

[18] Mary Hayes Weier, "Boeing Standardizes Software for Product Development," **http://www.informationweek.com** (August 2, 2008).

Figure 13-9

Test Marketing Decisions

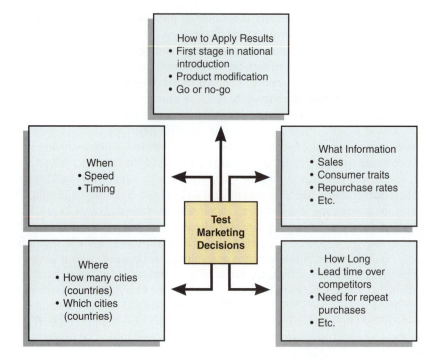

Although test marketing has often been beneficial, some firms now question its effectiveness and downplay or skip this stage in new-product planning. Dissatisfaction arises from test marketing's costs, the time delays before full introduction, the information being provided to competitors, the inability to predict national (global) results based on limited test-market areas, and the impact of such external factors as the economy and competition on test results. Test marketing can even allow nontesting competitors to catch up with an innovative firm by the time a product is ready for a full rollout.

Sometimes, consumer panels are used to simulate test market conditions—even online. For example, Nielsen's BASES (**http://www2.acnielsen.com/products/crs_newproduct. shtml**) is the "leader in simulated test marketing, having tested nearly 35,000 new product initiatives in over 55 countries. BASES' sales forecasting record is the most accurate in the industry. On average, our sales estimates are within 9 percent of actual in-market results."

13-5g Commercialization

At this point, a firm is ready to introduce a new product to its full target market. This involves *commercialization* and corresponds to the introductory stage of the product life cycle. During commercialization, the firm enacts a total marketing plan and works toward production capacity. Among the factors to be considered are the speed of acceptance by consumers and distribution intermediaries, the intensity of distribution (how many outlets), production capabilities, the promotion mix, prices, competition, the time until profitability, and commercialization costs.

Commercialization may require large outlays and a long-term commitment. Manufacturers often spend millions of dollars for a typical national rollout in U.S. supermarkets—nearly half on consumer promotion and the rest on product costs, marketing research, and promotions for supermarkets. Yet, commercialization costs can go much higher. When the Venus shaver for women was introduced, it had a $150 million marketing budget—for TV and print ads, a Web site, contests, in-store promotions, and other activities. Look at how dynamic and detailed the Web site (**http://www. gillettevenus.com/us**) is today.

Commercializing a new product sometimes must overcome consumer and reseller reluctance because of ineffective prior company offerings. This occurred with Texas

Commercialization involves a major marketing commitment.

Instruments (http://www.ti.com) in the business computer market, after it bowed out of the home computer market. And many resellers were upset with Sony when it had significant shortages of the Sony PlayStation 3 (http://www.us.playstation.com) during the product's first year on the market. This was a key reason why Nintendo's Wii (http://www.wii.com) did so well upon its introduction and overtook the sales of the PlayStation by a significant amount.

13-6 GROWING PRODUCTS

Once a product is commercialized, the goal is for consumer acceptance and company sales to rise rapidly. Sometimes, this occurs quickly; other times, it may take awhile. The growth rate and total sales of new products rely on two consumer behavior concepts: the adoption process and the diffusion process. In managing growing products, a firm must understand these concepts and plan its marketing accordingly.

The *adoption process* is the mental and behavioral procedure an individual consumer goes through when learning about and purchasing a new product. It consists of these stages:

> The **adoption process** explains the new-product purchase behavior of individual consumers.

1. *Knowledge*—A person (firm) learns of a product's existence and gains some understanding of how it functions.
2. *Persuasion*—A person (firm) forms a favorable or unfavorable attitude about a product.
3. *Decision*—A person (firm) engages in actions leading to a choice to adopt or reject a product.
4. *Implementation*—A person (firm) uses a product.
5. *Confirmation*—A person (firm) seeks reinforcement and may reverse a decision if exposed to conflicting messages.[19]

Global Marketing in Action

Successful Branding Practices in China

Though Chinese customers typically switch among brands, it is not due to Chinese culture. Instead, these shoppers change brands due to the many more available options as compared with 10 years ago. In addition, many firms have yet to properly identify and target their core Chinese consumer markets.

Popular home-grown Chinese brands include Tencent's (http://www.tencent.com.hk/index_e.shtml) QQ instant message service, Belle International's (http://www.belleintl.com) Belle shoes, and Shaghai Whitecat's (http://www.stof.com.cn) White Cat detergent and Shanghai Guanshengyuan Food's White Rabbit Candy. These marketers have built trust among Chinese consumers. Likewise, among the multinational firms that are thriving in China are Yum Brands' KFC (http://www.kfc.com), with more than 2,200 restaurants in China, and Omega Watches (http://www.omega-watches.com), which has a 70 percent market share for luxury watches sold in China. These firms properly define their brand positions, understand their customer base,

and target China's younger generation—which has both product sophistication and disposable income.

As in other countries, firms cannot be complacent in China. They also have to be creative in changing their brand image and target markets. To effectively market Buicks in China, General Motors (http://www.gm.com) promoted images of China's last emperor and key Chinese leaders being driven in Buicks. As a result, GM sold more Buicks in China than in the United States, despite their higher relative costs there. Then, to take advantage of the large market growth in China, GM decided to sell lower-end Buick models that were priced at about $12,000. This diluted Buick's image, causing its Chinese market share to drop. Business executives did not want to drive the same brand as first-time car buyers. And many first-time car buyers were unhappy that the new Buicks did not meet their expectations.

Source: Based on material in Shaun Rein, "The Key to Successful Branding in China," http://www.businessweek.com/globalbiz/content/sep2007 (September 25, 2007).

---

[19] Everett M. Rogers, *Diffusion of Innovations*, Fifth Edition (New York: Free Press, 2003), Chapter 5.

The speed of adoption depends on consumer traits, the product, and the firm's marketing effort. It is faster if people have high discretionary income and are willing to try new offerings; the product has low perceived risk; the product has an advantage over others on the market; the product is a modification, not an innovation; the product is compatible with current lifestyles or ways of operating a business; product attributes can be easily communicated; product importance is low; the product can be tested before a purchase; the product is consumed quickly; the product is easy to use; mass advertising and distribution are used; and the marketing mix adjusts as the person (organization) moves through the adoption process.

The ***diffusion process*** describes the manner in which different members of the target market often accept and purchase a product. It spans the time from product introduction through market saturation and affects the total sales level of a product as it moves through the life cycle:

> The **diffusion process** describes when different segments are likely to purchase.

1. *Innovators* are the first to try a new product. They are venturesome, willing to accept risk, socially aggressive, communicative, and worldly. It must be learned which innovators are opinion leaders—those who influence others. This group is about 2.5 percent of the market.
2. *Early adopters* are the next to buy a new product. They enjoy the prestige, leadership, and respect that early purchases bring—and tend to be opinion leaders. They adopt new ideas but use discretion. This group is about 13.5 percent of the market.
3. The *early majority* is the initial part of the mass market to buy. They have status among peers and are outgoing, communicative, and attentive to information. The group is about 34 percent of the market.
4. The *late majority* is the second part of the mass market to buy. They are less cosmopolitan and responsive to change, and include people (firms) with lower economic and social status, those past middle age (or set in their jobs), and skeptics. This group is about 34 percent of the market.
5. *Laggards* purchase last, if at all. They are price-conscious, suspicious of change, low in income and status, tradition bound, and conservative. They do not adopt a product until it reaches maturity. Some sellers ignore them because it can be hard to market a product to laggards. Thus, concentrated marketing may do well by focusing on products for laggards. This group is about 16 percent of the market.[20]

Growth for a major innovation often starts slowly because there is an extended adoption process and the early majority may be hesitant to buy. Sales may then rise quickly. For minor innovations or product modifications, growth is much faster right from the start.

The first high-definition television (HDTV) sets—a major innovation—were marketed in 1996; yet, by the end of 2002, only 4 percent of U.S. households had a set. During 2004, only 5 million of the 30 million TV sets purchased were HDTV sets. Consumers were hesitant to buy due to the high initial prices (several thousand dollars), the complexities of HDTV technology, the lack of programming in the HDTV format, and skepticism about how much better HDTV viewing really was. In recent years, sales have risen because of much lower prices, greater programming, and Federal Communications Commission support for the HDTV format (and the U.S. conversion to all-digital programming in 2009). Today, HDTV sets are in more than 40 percent of U.S. households—and growing.[21] See Figure 13-10.

These products are among those now in the growth stage, and they represent good opportunities for firms: HD DVD burners; cell phones with Internet capabilities and advanced graphics, text messaging, and camera features; high-capacity MP3 players;

---

[20] Ibid., Chapter 7.

[21] *CE Ownership and Market Potential* (Arlington, VA: Consumer Electronics Association, 2005); and Digital America 2008 (Arlington, VA: Consumer Electronics Association, 2008).

Figure 13-10
Encouraging Consumers to Want HDTV

Source: Reprinted by permission.

men's personal care products; generic drugs; flat-screen PC monitors; online banking; and self-scanning equipment for retailers.

13-7   MATURE PRODUCTS

Products are in the maturity stage of the life cycle when they reach the late majority and laggard markets. Goals turn from growth to maintenance. Because new products are so costly and risky, more firms are placing marketing emphasis on mature products with steady sales and profits, and with minimal risk.

> Proper marketing can let mature products maintain high sales.

In managing mature products, a firm should study the size, attributes, and needs of the current market; untapped market segments; competition; the potential for product modifications; the likelihood of new company products replacing mature ones; profit margins; the marketing effort for each sale; reseller attitudes; the promotion mix; the impact of specific products on the product line; each product's effect on company image; the remaining years for the products; and the management effort needed.

There are many benefits if a firm has a popular brand in a mature category: (1) The life cycle may be extended almost indefinitely. Budweiser beer (**http://www.budweiser.com**), Coke soda (**http://www.coke.com**), Goodyear tires (**http://www.goodyeartires.com**), Life Savers candy (**http://www.candystand.com/lifesavers**), and Sherwin-Williams paints (**http://www.sherwin-williams.com**) are leaders in their categories; each is well over 80 years old.[22] (2) A mature brand has a loyal customer base and a stable, profitable marketplace position. (3) The likelihood of future low demand is reduced; this is a real risk for new products. (4) A firm's overall image is enhanced. This may allow it to extend a popular name to other items. (5) There is more control of marketing and more precise forecasts. (6) Mature products can be cash cows and support new-product spending. Some marketing support must be continued for a mature product to stay popular.

Successful products can stay in maturity for long periods, as Figures 13-11 and 13-12 and the following illustrate:

- Although the paper clip was invented in the late 1800s, today it is more popular than ever due to its ease of use, flexible applications, and large customer following: "A variety of uses exist, ranging from bookmark, money clip, and staple remover to the item that holds a hem that needs sewing or serves as a hanger for curtains, lights, and pictures. Because of its price and availability, it is easy to see why the paper clip is one of the most versatile of inventions." It seems that, after more than 100 years, there is still nothing to match a paper clip. Twenty billion are sold yearly.[23]

- Chlorine is a chemical produced by the electrolysis of brine. It is used to process organic chemicals and in the production of pulp, paper, and other industrial goods. In industrialized nations, chlorine is a mature product—with stable sales in the United States and negative sales growth in Canada, Japan, and Europe. Sales are growing in Asia, Latin America, Africa, and the Middle East. Thus, chlorine producers' marketing efforts are now quite aggressive in developing and less-developed nations. There is even an active trade association, the Chlorine Chemistry Division of the American Chemistry Council (**http://www.americanchemistry.com/chlorine**).

- Lycra (**http://www.lycra.com**), the trademark for spandex fiber, began life in the 1950s as a rubber substitute in girdles. After sales stagnated, the fiber gained attention in the 1980s with the advent of cycling pants and leggings, and new technology that let Lycra fibers be used in sheer hosiery. Lycra is now included in all sorts of garments. To ensure continued success, Invista (**http://www.invista.com**)—a company that was spun off from DuPont in 2004—steadily invests in the brand: "Lycra has been able to continuously evolve and grow to meet the demanding needs of the apparel and home interiors industries. In the apparel context, consumers love Lycra for the pure pleasure of the way you look and feel when you wear a garment made with Lycra. In the home interiors context, consumers appreciate that products made with Lycra breathe better, look better, and fit better."[24]

- Since the 1930s, Hormel Foods (**http://www.hormel.com**) has marketed canned chili. To keep the line as the best-selling chili in the United States, the firm regularly introduces new versions—including ones that are fat-free and that have less sodium, as well as ones in easy-to-open cartons. Its online digital recipe book gives dozens of ways to use chili in casseroles, dips, sandwiches, pizza, and a lot more.

- Campbell's V8 juice has been around for 75 years. After a lull, Campbell has rejuvenated V8 by promoting its healthfulness (**http://www.v8juice.com/v8.aspx**): "V8 100% Vegetable Juice provides an easy way to help you get the vegetable nutrition you need every day. V8 is the delicious daily habit! Whether you crave an

---

[22] See Jack Trout, "Solid Foundations," *Advertising Age* (March 14, 2005), p. 28.

[23] "Paper Clip," **http://en.wikipedia.org/wiki/Paperclip** (April 24, 2009).

[24] "Lycra Fiber," **http://www.invista.com/page_product_lycra_en.shtml** (April 24, 2009).

interesting flavor twist on the original V8 or a variety with added nutrition, we have a V8 to please your body and your taste buds. One eight-ounce serving of V8 100% Vegetable Juice contains HALF THE CARBS of a glass of orange juice—plus two full servings of vegetables."

Many options are available for extending the mature stage of the product life cycle. Table 13-2 shows seven strategies and examples of each.

Not all mature products can be revived or extended. Consumer needs may disappear, as when frozen juice replaced juice squeezers. Lifestyle changes may lead to less interest in products, such as teller services in banks. Better, more convenient products may be devised, such as CD (and now, DVD) players replacing record players. The market may be saturated and marketing efforts may not garner enough sales to justify time and costs, which is why Japan's NEC reduced its consumer electronics presence.

Figure 13-12

Growing the Sales of Papermate After More Than 50 Years on the Market

Source: Reprinted by permission.

13-8 PRODUCT DELETION

> Products need to be deleted if they have consistently poor sales, tie up resources, and cannot be revived.

Products should be deleted if they offer limited sales and profit potential, reflect poorly on the firm, tie up resources that could be used for other opportunities, involve lots of management time, create reseller dissatisfaction due to low turnover, and divert attention from long-term goals.

However, many points must be weighed before deleting a product: As a product matures, it blends in with existing items and becomes part of the total product line (mix). Customers and distribution intermediaries may be hurt if an item is dropped. A firm may not want competitors to have the only product for customers. Poor sales and profits may be only temporary. The marketing strategy, not the product, may cause the poor results. Thus, in-depth analysis should be used with faltering products.[25]

Low-profit or rapidly declining products are often dropped or de-emphasized:

- The once popular VHS tape is winding down: "The format that debuted in 1977 and created a new industry has been in decline since the arrival of DVD in 1997. With sales dwindling, Best Buy (**http://www.bestbuy.com**) and Circuit City (**http://www.circuitcity.com**) were the first to put VHS out to pasture." VHS tape

---

[25] See "The Hard Sell: How to Market Products That Are No Longer Popular," **http://knowledge.wharton.upenn.edu/articlepdf/1950.pdf** (April 30, 2008).

Table **13-2** Selected Strategies for Extending the Mature Stage of the Product Life Cycle	
Strategy	**Examples**
1. Develop new uses for products	Jell-O used in garden salads
	WD-40 used in the maintenance of kitchen appliances
2. Develop new product features and refinements	Zoom lenses for 35mm cameras
	Battery-powered televisions
3. Increase the market	American Express accounts for small businesses
	International editions of major magazines
4. Find new classes of consumers for present products	Nylon carpeting for institutional markets
	Johnson & Johnson's baby shampoo used by adults
5. Find new classes of consumers for modified products	Industrial power tools altered for do-it-yourself market
	Inexpensive copy machines for home offices
6. Increase product usage among current users	Multiple packages for soda and beer
	Discounts given for increased long-distance phone calls
7. Change marketing strategy	Greeting cards sold in supermarkets
	Office furniture promoted via mail-order catalogs

sales declined from a peak of $6.3 billion in 1998 to $400 million in 2006. By then, "most major film studios had stopped releasing new movie titles in VHS format, opting for DVD-only releases. And most leading retailers have stopped selling pre-recorded movies on VHS, although VHS cassettes are still popular with collectors, mainly because there are thousands of titles that are still unavailable on DVD or other newer formats."[26]

Marketing and the Web

Photo-Sharing Web Sites Revolutionize the Picture Business

Kodak Gallery (http://www.kodakgallery.com), a division of Kodak, is a free photo-sharing Web site. It not only prints photos but also enables users to store and post pictures online. Consumers who want reprints simply click on their favorite photos and then enter their credit card number. For a fee of about $25, consumers can securely store their photos on Kodak Gallery's Web site with a unique Web address.

Various photo-sharing Web sites offer different features. Some allow users to lighten or darken images to correct lighting. Others let users improve their pictures by cropping, changing colors, and adjusting contrast. With one site, Flickr (http://www.flickr.com), friends, family, and even strangers can label photos that have been uploaded to its site with key words or notes so the files can be more easily searched or better organized into albums. Users can also specify who has access to pictures. Wal-Mart recently developed a system whereby users can create personalized gift cards at home. These cards can then be picked up at a local Wal-Mart for a charge of 88 cents plus the cost of the card.

Photo-sharing is also a popular feature in online social networking. Through Photobucket (http://www.photobucket.com), more than 40 million registered users can post their photos on such sites as Facebook (http://www.facebook.com), Friendster (http://www.friendster.com), craigslist (http://www.craigslist.org), Xanga (http://www.xanga.com), and MySpace (http://www.myspace.com). Photobucket provides free online storage tools so that registered users are able to save photos, videos, and digital slideshows on their social networking sites. As of late 2008, Photobucket already hosted 6 billion images. It also accounts for close to 40 percent of the online U.S. photo market.

Sources: Based on material in "MySpace to Acquire Photo-Sharing Site," *Chain Store Age* (June 2007), p. 48; and "About Photobuckbet," http://photobucket.com/about (December 6, 2008).

[26] Doug Desjardins, "Retailers and Studios to Bid Farewell to VHS," *DSN Retailing Today* (July 25, 2005), pp. 1, 27; and "VHS," http://en.wikipedia.org/wiki/VHS (May 30, 2009).

- After nearly 90 years, the upscale Helena Rubinstein cosmetics brand was pulled from the U.S. marketplace in 2003. The brand had lost its cachet and distinctiveness; and it was carried by very few stores. Parent company L'Oreal (**http://www.loreal.com**) decided to place more U.S. emphasis on its other brands: "We have ceased marketing the Helena Rubinstein (**http://www.helenarubinstein.com**) brand in North America and the United States, and the Spa has also closed. Given the current economic climate, we have decided to concentrate efforts and resources in markets where the Helena Rubinstein brand is experiencing exceptional growth (Asia, Europe, and South America). Naturally, we understand how disappointed you may be on learning that about products you have enjoyed using and we share your feelings. However, Helena Rubinstein products are still available in over 50 countries around the world, in many duty free shops, and in all countries in Europe."[27]
- In late 2000, General Motors decided to gradually phase out its then 103-year-old Oldsmobile division (**http://www.oldsmobile.com**): "Under General Motors (**http://www.gm.com**), Oldsmobile enjoyed years of success. But the past two decades saw stiff competition and overlapping models for the company, and the brand was eventually phased out. The last Alero that rolled off the assembly line in Lansing, Michigan, in April 2004 marked the end of the line for Oldsmobile."[28]
- "If business is a jungle, then the rise and fall of the typewriter is a demonstration of evolution, of the little creature that could. When Smith Corona filed for bankruptcy in 1995, one of the final signals in the triumph of PCs and software over the typewriter [originally patented in 1868] was at hand." Brother International (**http://www.brother-usa.com/typewriters**) is the only major firm still selling new typewriters in the United States.[29]

> During deletion, customer and distributor needs must be considered.

A firm must decide about replacement parts, the notification time for customers and resellers, and the honoring of warranties/guarantees when discontinuing a product. For example, a company planning to delete its line of office telephones must resolve these questions: (1) Replacement parts—Who will make them? How long will they be made? (2) Notification time—How soon before the actual deletion will an announcement be made? Will distributors be alerted early enough so they can contact other suppliers? (3) Warranties—How will warranties be honored? After they expire, how will repairs be done?

Web Sites You Can Use

These are just a few of the many helpful Web sites dealing with various aspects of product management:

- "Ask a Good Product Manager" (**http://www.ask.goodproductmanager.com**)
- Association of International Product Marketing & Management (**http://www.aipmm.com**)
- Forrester Blog for Technology Product Management & Marketing Professionals (**http://blogs.forrester.com/product_management**)
- "How to Be a Good Product Manager" (**http://www.goodproductmanager.com**)
- "Learn More About a Company by Examining Its Products" (**http://www.virtualpet.com/industry/howto/preview.htm**)
- National Inventors Hall of Fame (**http://www.invent.org**)
- "Product Articles" (**http://www.aipmm.com/html/newsletter/article.php**)
- Product Development & Management Association (**http://www.pdma.org**)
- "Product Life Cycles" (**http://www.marketing-magic.biz/archives/archive-management/product-life-cycles.htm**)

[27] "Dear Customer," **http://www.helenarubinstein.co.uk/_en/_us/whatsnew/whatsnew_edito.aspx** (May 30, 2009).

[28] Adele Woodyard, "Olds Heritage Lives on in Florida," *AutoWeek* (April 25, 2005), p. 24.

[29] Francis X. Clines, "An Ode to the Typewriter," *New York Times* (July 10, 1995), p. D5; and Reveuven Fenton, "Typewriter's Last Word Not Written Yet," **http://www.boston.com** (November 7, 2007).

- "Product Management and Packaging" (**http://www.knowthis.com/management/product-management-and-packaging.htm**)
- Product *News* Network (**http://www.productnews.com**)

- Ready 2 Launch (**http://www.ready2launch.com**)
- *Visions* Magazine (**http://www.pdma.org/knowledge_visions.cfm**)

Summary

1. *To study how products are created and managed, with an emphasis on the product life cycle*   Product management creates and oversees products over their lives. New products are modifications or innovations that consumers see as substantive. Modifications are improvements to existing products. Minor innovations have not been previously sold by the firm but have been sold by others. Major innovations have not been previously sold by anyone.

    The product life cycle seeks to describe a product's sales, competitors, profits, customers, and marketing emphasis from inception until removal from the market. Many firms seek a balanced product portfolio, with products in various stages of the cycle. The product life cycle has several derivations, from traditional to fad to bust. The traditional cycle consists of four stages: introduction, growth, maturity, and decline. During each stage, the marketing goal, industry sales, competition, industry profits, customers, and marketing mix change. Though the life cycle is useful in planning, it should not be a forecasting tool.

2. *To detail the importance of new products and describe why new products fail*   New products may foster differential advantages, sustain sales growth, require a lot of time for development, generate large profits, enable a firm to diversify, make distribution more efficient, lead to technological breakthroughs, allow waste products to be used, respond to changing consumers, and address government mandates.

    If a firm has a financial loss, a product is an absolute failure. If it has a profit but does not attain its goals, a product is a relative failure. Failures occur due to such factors as a lack of a significant differential advantage, poor planning, poor timing, and excessive enthusiasm by the product sponsor.

3. *To present the stages in the new-product planning process*   New-product planning involves a comprehensive, seven-step process. During idea generation, new opportunities are sought. In product screening, unattractive ideas are weeded out via a new-product screening checklist. At

concept testing, the consumer reacts to a proposed idea. Business analysis requires a detailed evaluation of demand, costs, competition, investments, and profits. Product development converts an idea into a tangible form and outlines a marketing strategy. Test marketing, a much-debated technique, involves placing a product for sale in selected areas and observing performance under actual conditions. Commercialization is the sale of a product to the full target market. A new product can be terminated or modified at any point in the process.

4. *To analyze the growth and maturity of products, including the adoption process, the diffusion process, and extension strategies*   After commercialization, the firm's goal is for consumer acceptance and company sales to rise as rapidly as possible. However, the growth rate and level for a new product are dependent on the adoption process—which describes how a single consumer learns about and purchases a product—and the diffusion process—which describes how different members of the target market learn about and purchase a product. These processes are faster for certain consumers, products, and marketing strategies.

    As products mature, goals turn from growth to maintenance. Mature products can provide stable sales and profits and loyal consumers. They do not require the risks and costs of new products. There are several factors to consider and alternative strategies from which to choose when planning to sustain mature products. It may not be possible to retain aging products if consumer needs disappear, lifestyles change, new products make them obsolete, or the market becomes too saturated.

5. *To examine product deletion decisions and strategies*   At some point, a firm may have to determine whether to continue a faltering product. Deletion may be hard due to the interrelation of products, the impact on customers and resellers, and other factors. It should be done in a structured manner; and replacement parts, notification time, and warranties should all be considered in a deletion plan.

Key Terms

new product (p. 395)

modifications (p. 395)

minor innovations (p. 395)

major innovations (p. 395)

product life cycle (p. 395)

balanced product portfolio (p. 395)

introduction stage of the product life cycle (p. 397)

growth stage of the product life cycle (p. 397)

maturity stage of the product life cycle (p. 397)

decline stage of the product life cycle (p. 397)

self-fulfilling prophecy (p. 398)

absolute product failure (p. 403)

relative product failure (p. 403)

new-product planning process (p. 404)

idea generation (p. 405)

product screening (p. 405)

patent (p. 406)

concept testing (p. 407)

business analysis (p. 408)

product development (p. 408)

test marketing (p. 409)

commercialization (p. 410)

adoption process (p. 411)

diffusion process (p. 412)

Review Questions

1. Distinguish among a product modification, a minor innovation, and a major innovation. Present an example of each for a golf equipment manufacturer.
2. Explain the basic premise of the product life cycle. What is the value of this concept?
3. Give four reasons why new products are important to a company.
4. How does product screening differ from concept testing?
5. What are the pros and cons of test marketing?
6. How can a firm speed a product's growth?
7. Cite five ways in which a firm could extend the mature stage of the product life cycle. Provide an example of each.
8. Why is a product deletion decision so difficult?

Discussion Questions

1. Comment on the following statement: "We never worry about relative product failures because we make a profit on them. We only worry about absolute product failures."
2. Develop a ten-item new-product screening checklist for an eyeglass manufacturer interested in new eyeglass frames made with titanium. How would you weight each item?
3. Differentiate between the commercialization strategies for a minor innovation and a major innovation. Relate your answers to the adoption process and the diffusion process.
4. Select a long-running product that was recently removed from the market and explain why it was removed.

Web Exercise

At the Web site of the U.S. Patent and Trademark Office (**http://www.uspto.gov**), there is a data base of current patents and trademarks. Go here (**http://patft.uspto.gov/netahtml/ PTO/search-bool.html**) and enter the term "MP3 Player." Then, select two patents that you believe have strong sales potential and state why.

Practice Quiz

1. An example of a major product innovation is
   a. the original Windows operating system for personal computers.
   b. Black & Decker's current production of an electric-powered lawn mower.
   c. a minivan produced by Ford (based on Chrysler's success).
   d. the Honda Accord station wagon (introduced in the 1990s).

2. During which stage of the product life cycle does the average-income mass market make purchases?
   a. Introduction
   b. Growth
   c. Maturity
   d. Late majority

3. Which of the following is a key point that should be kept in mind when using the product life cycle?
   a. The shape and length of the product life cycle do not vary much by product.
   b. External factors may have little impact on the performance of a product and rarely shorten or lengthen its life cycle.
   c. A company usually cannot manage the product life cycle and extend it or reverse a decline.
   d. It is not useful in forecasting.

4. A major reason for the importance of new products is to
   a. increase foreign competition.
   b. copy a competitor's innovation.
   c. reduce dependence on one product or product line.
   d. match a competitor's prices.

5. Although a firm made a profit with a new product, the new product's return on investment did not meet the firm's targeted level. The new product was subsequently discontinued. The product can be best classified as a(n)
   a. marginal product failure.
   b. absolute product failure.
   c. relative product failure.
   d. total product failure.

6. Which of the following products evolved from laboratory-oriented sources?
   a. Roll-on deodorants
   b. Easy-opening soda cans
   c. Swiss-almond chocolate ice cream
   d. Synthetic fibers

7. Which of these is the *least* expensive stage in new-product development?
   a. Idea generation
   b. Product development
   c. Test marketing
   d. Commercialization

8. In the business analysis stage of the new-product planning process,
   a. a sales forecast is important.
   b. consumer acceptance is determined.
   c. a prototype product is developed.
   d. a brand name and product package are determined.

9. Which of the following is *not* a type of decision usually made during the product development stage?
   a. Branding
   b. Packaging
   c. Concept testing
   d. Product positioning

10. In test marketing, which of the following is determined?
    a. Consumer attitudes
    b. Consumer and reseller product acceptance
    c. Product development costs
    d. Long-term product modifications

11. The commercialization stage corresponds to which stage of the product life cycle?
    a. Introduction
    b. Growth
    c. Maturity
    d. Decline

12. The rate of adoption is faster if a product
    a. is incompatible with a consumer's current lifestyle.
    b. is a modification.
    c. has high perceived risk.
    d. cannot be tried in small quantities.

13. In the diffusion process, laggards can be characterized as
    a. opinion leaders, and high in income and status.
    b. cosmopolitan, and attentive to information cues.
    c. tradition bound, and conservative.
    d. past middle age, and skeptics.

14. An appropriate marketing goal for a mature product is
    a. maintenance of product lines.
    b. expanding the market.
    c. product deletion.
    d. orderly withdrawal from the market.

15. A product should be deleted when it
    a. has a poor outlook for short-run sales and profit.
    b. complements other company offerings.
    c. attracts a small, loyal market.
    d. diverts attention from the firm's long-term goals.

For the answers to these questions, please visit the online site for this book at **http://www.atomicdog.com.**

Case 1: What Practices Are OK in the Product Positioning of Diamonds, Gemstones, and Pearls?[c4-1]

According to the Diamond Promotion Service (http://www.dps.org), disclosing gemstone treatments and synthetics isn't just good ethical business practice, it's the law. The World Jewellery Confederation (CIBJO, http://www.cibjo.org) and the Federal Trade Commission (http://www.ftc.gov) require that jewelers disclose all treatments on colored gemstones, diamonds, and pearls. The disclosures must clearly indicate whether a treatment is permanent or of limited duration, whether the treatment requires special care by the consumer, and whether the treatment affects the stone's value.

Nonpermanent treatments or treatments that require special care include coating, impregnation, irradiation, and dyeing. Though heating and irradiation are permanent treatments that do not require special care, the Jewelers Vigilance Committee (JVC, http://www.jvclegal.org) recommends disclosure. Applications of colored or colorless oils or epoxy resins, wax, plastic, and glass should also be disclosed.

Let's examine some of the more common treatments and special care requirements:

- Heat treatment—This is routinely used on most gemstones, and it's difficult or impossible to detect. Heat treatment results in a gem having more even color distribution and reduced visible flaws.
- Irradiation—High-energy particles or electromagnetic waves alter the color of gems. Gamma ray treatment of tourmaline can make the stone red in color. High-energy treatments can be detected.
- Fracture filling—Fractures and voids in emeralds and diamonds are often treated by fracture filling.
- Coatings—Foreign-colored substances are applied to stones to alter their color. A green coating on a pale-colored beryl will give the stone the color of a darker emerald stone.
- Special care requirements—While treated gemstones generally do not require treatment, oiled gemstones should never be cleaner in solvents or in ultrasonic cleaners.

The FTC requires that full disclosure should be made before each sale. Sales associates need to be trained to explain exactly how each stone was treated, as well as special care requirements. If stones are sold via direct marketing, the disclosure as to treatment and care must be part of the online ad, direct mail catalog, or televised shopping program. In order to prevent misrepresentation, jewelers should submit stones to a gemological laboratory to detect synthetics and treatments. The JVC recommends this procedure for suspicious stones. It also suggests that testing be performed on a random basis as part of a jeweler's overall quality control procedure.

Andrea Hopson, a vice-president at Tiffany Canada (http://www.tiffany.ca), says that "the heat treatment of gemstones at the mine is very common" and "globally accepted—so most sapphires and rubies go through it; all tanzanites do—it really enhances the gemstone. Just as pearls go through a bleaching and dyeing process that's very standard, and you can't make a bad pearl a good pearl through this process; heat-treating simply draws out the true beautiful hues." According to Hopson, unenhanced gemstones and pearls are particularly special and rare and need careful documentation. Similarly, one online jeweler states that close to 99 percent of the more popular gemstone varieties are treated.

According to *Today Gem* (http://www.todaygem.com), it is ethical to apply treatment to gemstones if the treatment is globally accepted, it is a stable type of treatment, it is disclosed to the customer prior to the sale, the treated or enhanced gemstone is honestly described, and the treated or enhanced gem is fairly priced. A certified untreated stone can be worth 150 percent of the value of a treated stone. Emeralds that have not been treated are extremely rare and can be worth several times more than treated emeralds.

Questions

1. What would you recommend that a jeweler do to ensure that customers fully understand the quality of the merchandise they are considering?
2. Would you recommend using a printed statement or a verbal description to describe enhancing diamonds? Explain your choice.
3. Develop a training program for sales associates in a small jewelry store so that they can adequately comply with the letter and the spirit of the law.
4. Why should a trade association of jewelers be so concerned with honest representation?

[c4-1] The data in the case are drawn from Natalie Atkinson, "Jewels for the Gem Set; Tiffany Collection Shows Why Semi-Precious Stones Can Shine as Brightly as the Big Three," *National Post* (Canada) (May 12, 2007), p. TO17; "Clarify Your Merchandise," Diamond Promotion Service http://www.dps.org/promotingyourreputation (August 21, 2008); "The Treatment of Gemstones," http://www.ganoksin.com/borisat/neman/gems-treatments.htm (August 21, 2008); and "Globally Accepted Gemstone Treatments," http://www.todaygem.com/gemstone_treatment.html (August 21, 2008).

Case 2: Private Brands Move Upscale[c4-2]

A common perception is that private brands trade on the success of manufacturer brands. This perspective suggests that private brands are lower-cost, lower-quality alternatives to manufacturer brands and that they are not supported with research and development, marketing, or promotional funds. Private brands now account for about one-seventh of U.S. retail sales and as much as 40 percent of retail sales in some major European markets. A key factor contributing to the success of private brands is the 25 percent or so price differential with comparable-quality manufacturer brands.

Product managers of manufacturer brands often assume that their brands are viewed by final consumers as more legitimate than store brands. In reality, private brands such as Craftsman (**http://www.craftsman.com**), Gap (**http://www.gap.com**), and Martha Stewart (**http://www.marthastewart.com**) enjoy significant trust in terms of quality and style that are the envy of many manufacturer brands. The success of major retailers such as Wal-Mart (**http://www.walmart.com**), Target (**http://www.target.com**), Costco (**http://www.costco.com**), and Trader Joe's (**http://www.traderjoes.com**) is also tied to their strong private brands. Wal-Mart generally positions its private brand next to the strongest-selling manufacturer brand and does not even stock second-level, "me-too" manufacturer brands.

All brands (including private brands) must be managed so that they can connect with consumers on a personal and emotional level. Brands also need to innovate, offer value, establish confidence, and generate pride of ownership. These connections cannot be based on a low price or a brand name alone. Brands have to offer an experience that is both meaningful and differentiated from other brands. This experience bonds a customer to the brand.

One way to determine how well a brand connects with its consumers is to look at its level of customer engagement, which examines what a brand designation means to a customer, not a manufacturer or a retailer. There are four levels of customer engagement: fully engaged, engaged, not engaged, and actively disengaged. These categories apply equally to manufacturer and private brands. Let's examine the characteristics of each of these levels.

Fully engaged customers are extremely loyal to a brand and will not accept a substitute. If a desired brand is not available, this shopper will go elsewhere or elect to buy at a later date. Fully engaged customers tend to be a firm's most profitable customers due to their large purchases on a consistent basis. They also serve as brand ambassadors due to their positive word-of-mouth influence with others.

Even though engaged customers are emotionally attached to a brand, they are not as loyal as fully engaged customers. Though they may like a firm's brands, they may also switch to other brands based on price, convenience, or additional customer service. An example of an engaged customer is one who is loyal to one brand of soda but will switch to another brand when it is on sale.

Not engaged customers are disconnected emotionally and are neutral to a brand. They often have a "take-it-or-leave-it" mentality about purchases. Actively disengaged customers are completely detached from a brand. They quickly switch to another brand and may even become angry if switching is difficult or even impossible. Like fully engaged customers, actively disengaged customers often tell others about their experiences with a brand. However, this group will focus on negative experiences.

One way to increase engagement is through superior product packaging that addresses a customer's aspirations as opposed to their functional needs. Private-label brand managers need to answer the question: "What does this product say about me?" Contemporary packaging and sales promotions may accomplish the goal of higher consumer engagement.

Questions

1. Discuss this statement: "All brands need to innovate, offer value, establish confidence, and generate pride of ownership. These connections cannot be based on a low price or a brand name alone."
2. Describe your degree of product engagement regarding your choice of gasoline, greeting cards, and facial tissues. What factors contribute to your degree of engagement?
3. Compare and contrast the degree of product engagement notion described in this case with the consumer's brand decision process covered in Figure 8.
4. How has Costco's Kirkland brand built trust among consumers as a brand name?

[c4-2] The data in the case are drawn from Donna C. Babson, "Private Label Grows Up," *Marketing Matters* (February 2008), p. 35; Chad Chadwick, "Your Store Is Your Brand," *Retail Merchandiser* (September-October 2007), pp. 38–39; and Mark Ritson, "Why Brands Are at a Premium," *Marketing* (July 2008), p. 19.

Case 3: Reckitt Benckiser's Keys to Speeding Innovations in Household and Personal-Care Products[c4-3]

Reckitt Benckiser (RB, http://www.reckittbenckiser.com) is one of the top marketers of household and personal-care products in Great Britain. Its Vanish brand laundry detergent has a 60 percent share of the $400 million market and its Finish dishwasher detergent remains a leading brand despite efforts by competitors Procter & Gamble (P&G, http://www.pg.com), Unilever (http://www.unilever.com), and Henkel (http://www.henkel.com). Other powerful RB brands include Calgon (http://www.calgon.com) disinfectants, Dettol bath and beauty products, and Airwick (http://www.airwick.com) air fresheners.

RB's formula for success is based on a combination of the effective use of marketing research in developing and maintaining products, strong new-product planning programs, and an excellent execution of marketing campaigns. One measure of the success of RB's new-product planning efforts is that 40 percent of total revenue comes from products launched in the prior three years.

Phil Thomas, an RB marketing director, explains that the firm can consistently develop successful new products both faster and less expensively than its competitors. RB's organization has fewer layers of management (a flatter organization) than its typical competitors. This means that marketing personnel are closer to top management and that decisions can be implemented faster. There are only two people between Thomas and RB's chief executive: a regional vice-president and the head of RB Europe. In a comparably sized firm, there could be five or six levels between Thomas' equivalent position and the firm's chief executive. According to Thomas, "There are simply fewer people to talk to and fewer people to argue with. We don't have endless meetings because there's no one to have them with."

At RB, brand and marketing managers participate in new-product planning programs as part of their overall job description, in addition to managing current products. At most firms, such managers work either on managing a firm's existing products or on new-product planning. An advantage to a brand or marketing manager working on both types of products is that he or she often sees opportunities for new products based on marketing research for existing products or when revitalizing an existing product. RB's brand and marketing managers also have a tremendous knowledge base to draw upon, consisting of a product's target market, market needs, competitive developments, and technical information.

RB's expertise also extends to marketing communications. It is one of Great Britain's top five advertisers. Communication between RB and its advertising agencies goes through a core team of RB personnel that reflects the firm's organizational structure. The communication strategy is built on its ability to clearly understand what customers want and to develop this information in a compelling manner. Sam Southey, who is responsible for RB's business at its advertising agency, says: "Like most of these things, the beauty is in the simplicity."

The company's formula for success has been extended to its health-care brands. As in the United States, over-the-counter medications in Great Britain are heavily regulated and have to be cleared on the basis of clinical trials before they are marketed. When RB purchased Boots' healthcare division in February 2006, RB acquired Nurofen (http://www.nurofen.co.uk) pain management medication, Strepsils (http://www.strepsils.com) cough medicine, and Optrex (http://www.optrex.com) eye treatment. For the most part, these over-the-counter medications, such as Nurofen, had seen little product development or innovation in nearly a decade. Nurofen Express, launched in July 2007, was based on research which found that customers who use a pain management pill want it to work quickly. As one industry observer remarked, this brand received the "RB treatment."

Questions

1. Explain the significance of 40 percent of Reckitt Benckiser's revenue coming from products that were not available three years ago.
2. Describe the pros and cons of flat organizations from the perspective of new product planning.
3. Comment on the advantages and disadvantages of product managers working both on new-product planning and on the management of a firm's existing products.
4. Discuss the introduction of Nurofen Express from the perspective of the product life cycle, brand equity, and brand extension.

[c4-3] The data in the case are drawn from "The Speed of Innovation," *Marketing Week* (May 8, 2008), pp. 16–17.

Case 4: Under Armour: Trying to Keep the Hits Coming[c4-4]

Under Armour (http://www.underarmour.com) was founded in 1996 by Kevin Plank, a former University of Maryland football player. The firm produces apparel, footwear, and accessories that are specially designed to keep athletes cool, dry, and light during games, practice activities, and workouts. Products include HeatGear products to use when it is warm, ColdGear for when it is cold, and AllSeasonGear (http://www.allseasongear.com) for normal weather conditions. These products incorporate moisture-wicking synthetic fabrics to help regulate body temperature by keeping perspiration away from the athlete's skin.

Under Armour also sells performance cleats for use in football, baseball, and softball, as well as headwear, eyewear, and wristbands. During Super Bowl XLII, Under Armour aired a 60-second TV ad launching its performance footwear. This new line represents the firm's first entry into the noncleated footwear business, a market dominated by Nike (http://www.nike.com), Reebok (http://www.reebok.com), and others. Under Armour's annual revenues are $700 million.

To better manage its product-life-cycle process, Under Armour recently replaced a number of manual and outdated systems with Dassault Systems' Enovia MatrixOne Apparel Accelerator (http://www.enovia.com) program. This software can better link product development and sourcing processes to streamline procedures. As an example of its effectiveness, a Swedish manufacturer of outdoor equipment that uses the system reported better quality control and faster product development. That manufacturer was able to reduce product development times from their normal 16 to 18 months to 12 months. It also reported improved communications, fewer errors, and more accurate product samples.

In contrast to other software installations than take 1 year to 18 months to be fully operational, the MatrixOne program was operational at Under Armour in less than 20 weeks. Under Armour initially used this software to launch its line of football and baseball cleats for men, and its softball and its lacrosse cleats for women. Dassault's three-dimensional design software has been used extensively by aircraft manufacturers. According to Under Armour's chief information officer, "if you can use a product to create 757s, we believe their product can help us with the design of technical footwear."

Under Armour also uses TEXbase (http://www.texbase.com) software to better manage lab testing by suppliers. TEXbase allows Under Armour's suppliers to work together on a new product's performance specifications. Under Armour can effectively automate the product certification process, create an online library of approved materials, and publish approved materials for key customers. Without such a program, Under Armour would have to continuously send E-mails, track spreadsheets, and exchange phone calls through different time zones. As Bill Mickle, Under Armour's director of material innovation, notes, "TEXbase provides us with a stable Web-based platform for vendor communication and project management from concept through commercialization. Data are easily and efficiently managed, which allows our teams to dedicate more time to material innovation."

A third system Under Armour uses to manage its product development activities is TradeCard (http://www.tradecard.com), which synchronizes financial transactions with physical events (such as a purchase order, shipping, and delivery) in a firm's global supply chain. This software helps customers such as Under Armour automate purchase orders, payments, and chargebacks (price reductions due to incorrect merchandise or late shipments). Because Under Armour has doubled the number of countries from which its materials are sourced, the accounting environment is much more complex. Under Armour's vice-president of finance says, "Prior to integration with TradeCard we were dealing with E-mail, faxes, different time zones, lack of visibility, potentially losing invoices, and invoice discrepancies." TradeCard now provides online access to a network of 3,500 trading partners in 40 countries with 32 languages.

Questions

1. Explain how outsourcing complicates the product development process.
2. Describe potential time and cost savings from better synchronizing financial transactions with physical events.
3. Should Under Armour use individual or family branding for its new footwear? Explain your answer.
4. What are the pros and cons of Under Armour's private labeling some of its mature products to retailers like Sports Authority?

[c4-4] The data in the case are drawn from "Under Armour Inc.," *Apparel Magazine* (May 2008), pp. 9–10; and "Shorter Development Cycles, Greater Efficiency Expected from PLM Solution," *Apparel Magazine* (September 2007), p. 4.

How to Survive in Today's Marketplace[pc-4]

INTRODUCTION

Industry research shows that up to 75 percent of new-product launches fail in the marketplace. That number does not even include product concepts that never successfully enter the market. There are many reasons for such failures, but lack of demand for new products introduced is the most important one. According to an AMR Research (**http://www.amrresearch.com**) report, out of 20 large manufacturers polled about poor performance of product launches, 47 percent cited failing to understand and meet customer needs exactly—compared with 33 percent citing being late to market and 20 percent citing poor pricing.

No company will develop and introduce a new product if it knows beforehand that there will be no market demand. Unfortunately, most firms try to justify new-product development (NPD) expenditures by doing some market analysis—only to find out later that projected market demand has failed to materialize. Thus, a critical question to industry players is how they can become more effective in their market assessment efforts. This case offers a practical methodology that answers the question.

DEFINING "NEW PRODUCT"

For the purpose of this case, "new product" refers to one of the following:

- A product that creates or implements a new technology.
- A product that implements an existing technology on a new platform.
- A product that integrates multiple technologies or functions into a single product for the first time.
- A product that provides significant enhancements to an existing product category.

The focus of our discussion is the overall market, not company-specific issues that can also lead to failures. There are many cases in which market demand for a new-product category exists but a particular company's product—falling into that category—fails in the market because of poor internal execution. Although internal execution is critical, companies must understand whether there will be a market for their new products being conceived or developed. Market investigation, in other words, remains highly relevant.

We will also assume that when a new product is introduced, it works and its functionality conforms to original design requirements

or intentions. Product failures attributed to unintended design flaws or quality problems are excluded from the scope of discussion. Again, such issues are internal, not market-related.

COMMON PITFALLS

Because so many new-product failures can be attributed to lack of market demand, it is necessary to understand why companies fail to foresee them. Granted that market forecasting is sometimes very difficult, companies can significantly reduce risks of failures if they do some basic market assessment homework the right way. In general, these are market assessment pitfalls into which companies fall:

- Blind faith in one's capability to drive or create market demand.
- Looking at technological merits only.
- Selective use of incomplete, biased, or deceiving market data and feedback in line with product concepts or initial decisions.
- Taking input from direct customers only, without looking at demand from customers' customers (when applicable).
- Relying on feedback or data of customer/consumer interest only, without looking at many other market factors that drive actual purchase decisions.
- Depending on third-party market forecasts only, without looking at or fully understanding the methodology used and assumptions made.

Some companies might achieve market success even if they fall into one of these pitfalls, but such success requires really good luck and can hardly be duplicated in different settings.

ASSESSING THE MARKET

Market assessment can be viewed as a science or an art. The challenge to market research professionals: Although some commonly used research techniques and tools exist, they might not be adequate to address the complete scope of market assessment required for sound business decision making. The challenge to senior executives is that they don't have the time to do detailed market investigations themselves. In addition, they might not have an effective framework for judging the quality and reliability of their subordinates' market assessments.

Both dedicated market research professionals and senior executives can use the methodology suggested here. The former can use it to investigate all the key aspects of a new product's market potential; the latter can use it to evaluate their subordinates' work. The methodology, if used the right way, can help companies avoid the aforementioned pitfalls.

[pc-4] Adapted by the authors from Hongjun Li, "Surveyor of the Fittest," *Marketing Management* (September-October 2007), pp. 39–44. Reprinted by permission of the American Marketing Association.

Individual elements in the suggested assessment framework are not new. See Figure 1. What might be new are identifying all major market-related factors affecting demand for a new product, categorizing these factors within a systematic framework, and setting up an easy step-by-step process: (1) define target segment and needs, (2) analyze relative value, and (3) evaluate food-chain and ecosystem risks.

DEFINING TARGET AND NEEDS

With rare exceptions, a particular new product serves only a particular market segment. This is especially true with consumer-technology. If a new product simply targets "everybody," then it will most likely have a tough road ahead—because different segments have different needs. There is a direct correlation between clarity of market-segment definition and ability to meet target customers' specific needs. Not surprisingly, the phenomenon of "shoot and aim" can explain why so many new products fail.

Defining the target market entails a detailed analysis of key segment characteristics such as size, demographics, and purchasing behavior. Without a clear understanding of the target segment, it will be difficult to identify the needs that a new product can meet.

Associating a generic need with a product is easy, and it can mislead companies into believing that their new product meets target customers' needs. To avoid that pitfall, companies can ask a simple question: What, exactly, is the problem that the new product solves?

Take the failed WebTV (a set-top box that consumers connect to their television sets, which allowed dial-up Internet connection), for example. Consumers with a PC at home did not need it for Internet access. WebTV did allow non-PC households to access the Internet; unfortunately, the amount of non-PC households with such a need was very small. Moreover, WebTV could not address that need well because of poor display of Web content on a standard-definition TV.

Even if the specific need for a new product is identified, companies must assess the strength of that need, as different strength levels mean different market sizes. In general, two variables influence the relative strength of the need for a product: cognizance and perceived importance.

Cognizance. This determines to what extent target customers are aware of a particular need. There are two levels: Explicit needs are well-recognized and can be clearly articulated. They normally indicate a high level of need strength. Only new products with meaningful differentiation (to be discussed next) can turn these needs into market demand. Implicit needs, on the other hand, are not well-recognized or clearly articulated. They often represent a new market that takes time, resources, and education to develop.

Perceived importance. Depending on how strong the perceived importance of a particular need is, products meeting that need can fit into three categories: must-have, nice-to-have, and can-live-without. Must-have products meet the needs with the highest level of perceived importance and have the broadest market reach. Nice-to-have products address less-important needs and therefore have lower market demand. Can-live-without products generally have the lowest market-penetration rate.

Although measuring need strength can be difficult and subjective, it is a key element of analysis. A common method of need-strength assessment is conducting a quantitative survey to ask consumers their interest level in a particular new product. The challenge, however, is that different survey designs can yield significantly different results even if the same topic is addressed. Thus, as mentioned, understanding methodologies used and assumptions made is vital to appropriate interpretation of survey results.

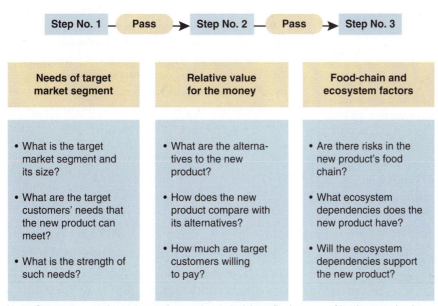

Figure 1
A Framework for Market Assessment

Note: Customers are those that make purchase decisions (in the case of business-to-business and business-to-consumer). Customers might be different from end users in the case of business-to-business-to-consumer.

One example of different survey results on the same topic is a study on consumers' interest in watching video on mobile devices. A survey by RBC Capital Markets (**http://www.rbccm.com**) showed that only 24 percent were interested, whereas a study by the Diffusion Group (**http://www.thediffusiongroup.com**) showed that 32 percent were interested. The results can be attributed to differences in measurement scales and age groups of survey respondents.

Regardless of which is right (or closer to being correct), consumer interest is only one variable; other factors also drive market demand for a new product. This is why completing the following second step is essential, too.

ANALYZING RELATIVE VALUE

Because new technologies are rapidly emerging, consumers have more choices that meet the same needs. For a new product to succeed, it must deliver a more compelling value proposition than alternative solutions by (a) being a better product for a similar price and/or (b) having a better price for a similar product. The higher the market penetration that alternatives have achieved, the more vital it is for new products to have strong differentiation in features/performance or cost.

The main reason voice over Internet protocol (VoIP) has been able to gain traction in both business and consumer markets is that it can deliver the same service as traditional wireline voice but at a lower cost. VoIP also enables certain features not available from "plain old telephone service" (POTS), but lower cost is the main driver of market adoption.

On the other hand, independent VoIP-over-broadband operators (at least in the United States) have had difficulties quickly penetrating the consumer market without spending tons of marketing dollars. That is because of the availability of four primary alternatives: existing POTS, mobile phone service, Skype-type (a peer-to-peer Internet telephone network) services, and inexpensive VoIP phone cards. Those services make voice communications a fulfilled need or deliver cost savings similar to VoIP over broadband.

The same can be said of telecoms' Internet protocol television (IPTV) service. In many markets, especially the United States, cable and satellite TV have made home-video entertainment a fulfilled need. If telecoms' IPTV offers only me-too video services, then the most effective way to gain market share from cable and satellite TV firms is to offer a lower price—as part of a discounted service bundle or a lower cost, stand-alone service. Alternatively, telecoms can devise new applications: true video on demand and other innovative, compelling services to leverage the Internet protocol network.

Alternative solutions are not limited to similar products from direct competitors. They also include various substitutes that address the same need. For example, the use of hands to turn lights on or off is an alternative to a lighting-control home-automation solution that requires a purchase—even though the former is less convenient. Substitutes create a negative impact on demand for a particular product.

Even if a cool new product has no or few existing alternatives and addresses a specific need, affordability will determine its market penetration. A good example is high-end home-control (also called home-automation) systems. They are not truly new products today, as a category, but they were when introduced about three decades ago. Those systems address consumers' need for comfort, convenience, safety, and prestige. However, because of high price tags (typically tens of thousands of dollars), high-end home-control systems have found success only in the custom-installed electronics market. And today's household penetration rate in the United States is still less than 2 percent.

EVALUATING RISKS

Suppose a new-product concept passes the previous two steps; there is still no guarantee of success. This third step prompts companies to identify market risks from a new product's food chain and its ecosystem. "Ecosystem" refers to the interdependency of a certain set of infrastructure elements, platforms, devices, and other components that function as a whole to meet a particular customer need.

From a market perspective, food-chain risks arise from direct customers' business model issues or uncertainty of demand from customers' customers. Although these risks do not apply to all, they can be significant in certain sectors. Food-chain issues can explain the failure of some telecom firms—and their products—that specifically targeted competitive local exchange carriers (CLECs) in the 1990s in the United States. Various newly developed products for CLECs could certainly pass the test of the previous two steps. But they failed because their CLEC customers did not have a sustainable business model.

Food-chain risks can also apply to a firm in the business-to-business-to-consumer market. Assume that a service provider has just approached a vendor of videophones for the deployment of a new service. To assess how many units the vendor can actually sell, it needs to carefully assess consumers' potential take rate, partially based on the service provider's marketing and pricing plans. If the provider cannot sign many subscribers to the service that involves the use of a videophone, then the vendor will not be able to sell many units either—no matter how rosy the service provider's deployment plan appears to be.

A new product might also face significant market risks if it has too much dependency on certain ecosystem elements beyond the product developer's control. Products that enable delivery of online video to the TV represent a good example. The main device that has such capability is the digital media adapter (DMA), a special set-top box that connects to both the television and a home network. For DMA to succeed as a product category, it will need support from at least the following ecosystem elements:

- Wide availability of high-quality online video content, which is subject to Hollywood's receptivity to digital-content distribution and compatible digital-rights management solutions.
- Attractive pricing from content owners.

- High penetration of robust, no-new-wire home-networking solutions for multimedia distribution.
- Wide deployment of higher bandwidth broadband-access networks.

DMA devices first appeared on the consumer market around 2003. Over the past few years, however, few units have been sold. The poor showing of DMA as a product category can be attributed to not only factors illustrated in the previous two steps but also poor ecosystem support (e.g., limited availability of quality online video content, various home networking issues). Going forward, though, the DMA market is expected to gain stronger momentum—this time driven by positive developments of the ecosystem.

IMPLEMENTING THE PROCESS

The person or team responsible for market intelligence should (1) develop detailed output based on the key questions in the three aforementioned steps and then (2) provide an overall assessment. See Table 1. The market intelligence function should present to executives not only the overall assessment but also a summary of the detailed output—so they can see how conclusions are reached.

To judge the quality and reliability of the market intelligence function's work, executives can ask themselves three questions: Is there clear definition of the market segment, the specific needs of target customers, and the strength of their needs? Is there adequate assessment of the impact from alternatives and customers' price elasticity? Are food-chain and ecosystem risks clearly identified and evaluated?

How should the three-step market assessment process be used for new-product development purposes? As different companies have different business models, financial objectives, market power, and so forth, perhaps there is no clear-cut answer that applies to everybody. However, executives might find Figure 2's risk-assessment framework (based on the three-step process) a useful tool for distilling output from the market intelligence function and making decisions on new projects.

If yellow lights are associated with a new-product concept, executives will need careful assessment of the value proposition and market positioning before making a "go" decision on product development. If a concept faces one or more red lights, there will be high risks of market failure, and executives might be better off allocating development resources to an alternative new product with a more viable market.

How often should the process be used? In fast-changing industries or markets, it is probably necessary for the market assessment framework to be used more than once for the entire development process. That will allow companies to not only reduce new-product introduction failure risks but also identify new market opportunities in a timely fashion.

Although the market intelligence function and executives are direct users of the market assessment framework, other functions should be included: product management, sales, marketing, strategic planning, and engineering managers. Their inclusion can take the form of providing input, reviewing output, and passing on findings to team members. The more synchronized the internal communication, the more capabilities firms will have for developing and selling new products that meet market needs.

Table 1	The Market Intelligence Function's Implementation
Steps	**Detailed Output**
Step No. 1: Needs of target market segment	• Definition of the target market segment and estimate of the total size of the target segment • Definition of the specific needs that the new product can address • Categorization of the strength of the identified needs: level of cognizance and importance
Step No. 2: Relative value for the money	• List of alternatives to the new product and their market penetration rate • Feature and price comparison between alternatives and the new product • Target customers' price elasticity and estimated market adoption rate at specific price points
Step No. 3: Food-chain and ecosystem factors	• Analysis of viability of target customers' business model specific to the new product • List of ecosystems elements that the new product depends on • The current status and projected future developments of the identified ecosystem elements
Overall assessment	• Qualitative assessment of the viability of the new product's market • Quantitative projections of the total available market in terms of units and revenues (if feasible and needed)

Note: Certain items of the output list can be omitted only if relevant facts (1) are already common knowledge to everybody or (2) do not apply to a particular new product.

Figure 2
**New Product Development
Risk Assessment**

Market assessment results		Yellow light	Red light
Needs of target market segment	Difficult-to-define target market segment		X
	Difficult-to-define specific needs of target customers		X
	Implicit needs	X	
	Nice-to-have product	X	
	Can-live-without product		X
Relative value for the money	Presence of alternatives with a high market penetration rate	X	
	High price elasticity of target customers	X	
Food-chain and ecosystem factors	Questionable business model of target customers		X
	Too much ecosystem dependency	X	
	Lack of ecosystem support		X

Yellow light: Market demand is limited or has substantial uncertainties.
Red light: Market demand is very limited or has very high uncertainties.

AVOIDING THE TRAP

There have been too many cases in which companies developed new technologies or products looking for problems to solve. To avoid falling into such a trap, companies can complete the aforementioned three simple steps. Afterward, they will be in a much better position to assess the market viability of a new-product concept and whether product development resources should be committed.

Questions

1. In the survey of large manufacturers noted in the case, why do you think that 47 percent cited failing to understand and meet customer needs as the most important cause of poor performance during new-product launches—compared with 33 percent citing being late to market and 20 percent citing poor pricing?
2. Discuss the framework for market assessment shown in Figure 1.
3. What could a small toy maker learn from Table 1?
4. How could a company convert a "red light" opportunity into a desirable opportunity?
5. What is the significance of "relative value" for a firm ready to introduce a new product into the marketplace? What is the significance of "relative value" for a firm with a popular mature product?
6. Comment on this statement: "There have been too many cases in which companies developed new technologies or products looking for problems to solve."
7. What concepts from this case could be applied to a company's branding strategy?

5

Distribution Planning

Part 5 deals with distribution, the second major element of the marketing mix.

14 Value Chain Management and Logistics

Here, we study the value chain and value delivery chain, which encompass all the activities and parties that create and deliver a given level of customer value. This requires careful planning as to the physical movement and transfer of ownership of a product from producer to consumer. We explore distribution functions, types of channels, supplier/distribution intermediary contracts, channel cooperation and conflict, the industrial channel, and international distribution. We also look at logistics, especially transportation and inventory management issues.

15 Wholesaling

In this chapter, we examine wholesaling—buying and/or handling goods and services and their subsequent resale to organizational users, retailers, and/or other wholesalers. We show wholesaling's impact on the economy, its functions, and its relationships with suppliers and customers. We describe the major company-owned and independent wholesalers and note trends in wholesaling.

16 Retailing

Here, we concentrate on retailing, which consists of those business activities involved with the sale of goods and services to the final consumer. We show the impact of retailing on the economy, its functions in distribution, and its relationship with suppliers. We categorize retailers by ownership, store strategy mix, and nonstore operations. We also describe several retail planning considerations and note trends in retailing.

 After reading Part 5, you should understand element 11 of the strategic marketing plan outlined in Table 3-2 (page 74).

Chapter 14

Value Chain Management and Logistics

Dell (http://www.dell.com) is the world's largest direct seller of computers. In addition to desktop and notebook PCs, Dell sells servers, networking products, third-party software, systems support, and other technology-related products. It has annual revenues of more than $61 billion.

Twenty-year-old Michael Dell founded PC Limited in 1984, when he started selling computer chips and disk drives from his University of Texas dormitory room. Dell bought these products at cost from retailers who were forced to purchase more units than they could sell due to IBM's quota system. Soon, his computer business was grossing $80,000 a month due to his ability to underprice traditional dealers by 10 to 15 percent. Dell then dropped out of college and began making IBM clones that he sold directly to consumers at a significant discount. In 1987, Dell renamed PC Limited "Dell Computer," went public, and added international offices. In 1988, Dell Computer began selling to large corporate customers. In 1999, Dell became the largest marketer on the Web with greater sales than Amazon.com, eBay, and Yahoo! combined. In 2008, *Forbes* estimated Michael Dell's net worth at about $16.4 billion.

Much of Dell's initial and continuing success is due to a combination of factors: Dell's direct-to-consumer model, mass customization, sales to large corporate customers, and recognition of consumer value. The direct-to-consumer model gives Dell greater control over pricing and customer service. Mass customization fulfills customers' specific needs while reducing inventory requirements for Dell. Sales to large corporate customers mean lower sales and customer support costs due to large orders and the customers' well-informed information technology staff. Finally, Dell recognizes customer value by installing software and providing the same configuration for all orders from the same corporate customer.

To increase its overall market presence, Dell has recently begun to sell selected computers, monitors, printers, ink, and toner in Wal-Mart, Sam's Club, Best Buy, and Staples. This strategy will enable consumers to compare Dell and competitive offerings, try out Dell products in the store, and immediately take home their purchases. This dual channel strategy addressed a major concern among many consumers that a "hands on" experience was particularly important in the sale of notebooks.[1]

In this chapter, we will learn about the decisions made in distribution planning—including direct and dual channels—and the activities involved in physical distribution.

Chapter Objectives

1. To discuss the role of the value chain and the value delivery chain in the distribution process
2. To explore distribution planning and review its importance, distribution functions, the factors used in selecting a distribution channel, and the different types of distribution channels
3. To consider the nature of distribution intermediary contracts, cooperation and conflict in a channel of distribution, the special aspects of a distribution channel for industrial products, and international distribution
4. To examine logistics and demonstrate its importance
5. To discuss transportation alternatives and inventory management issues

[1] Various company and other sources.

14-1 OVERVIEW

In recent years, the distribution process has witnessed a dramatic transformation, one that is expected to continue in the future. Consider the following:

> Shipper expectations and the role of airfreight firms are swiftly adapting to the needs of the marketplace. Consequently, creating value goes well beyond simply matching capacity with demand. Changing trade patterns driven by new manufacturing centers and burgeoning consumer markets have created a vacuum for airfreight firms that can deliver value-added services beyond commoditized capacity and customs brokerage services. Airfreight firms discern customer demand for services and technologies that help shippers gain better control of information and product flow farther back in the supply chain, work with vendors and carriers more collaboratively, and leverage these synergies to consolidate shipments, rationalize equipment utilization, and reduce costs.[2]

> An order for a Dell PC (**http://www.dell.com**) might go out by E-mail to the Dell notebook factory in Malaysia, where the parts are immediately ordered from the supplier logistics centers (SLCs) next to the Penang factory. Surrounding every Dell factory in the world are these supplier logistics centers, owned by the different suppliers of Dell parts. "If you are a Dell supplier anywhere in the world, your job is to keep your SLC full of your specific parts so they can constantly be trucked over to the Dell factory for just-in-time manufacturing. In an average day, we sell 140,000 to 150,000 computers," explained Dick Hunter, one of Dell's three global production managers. "Those orders come in over Dell.com or over the telephone. As soon as those orders come in, our suppliers know about it. They get a signal based on every component in the machine you ordered, so the supplier knows just what he has to deliver. If you are supplying power cords for desktops, you can see minute by minute how many power cords you are going to have to deliver. Every two hours, the Dell factory in Penang sends an E-mail to the various SLCs nearby, telling each one what parts and what quantities of those parts it wants delivered within the next 90 minutes—and not one minute later. Within 90 minutes, trucks from the various SLCs around Penang pull up to the Dell manufacturing plant and unload the parts needed for all those notebooks ordered in the last two hours. As soon as those parts arrive at the factory, it takes 30 minutes to unload the parts, register their barcodes, and put them in bins for assembly. We know where every part in every SLC is in the Dell system at all times."[3]

> In a survey of large firms, nearly all respondents said that improving customer experience is either critical or very important. But too often, their efforts are hype-heavy—delivering little improvement to a subpar set of customer interactions. What's wrong? **Fragmented responsibilities:** Customers interact with firms across a number of different touchpoints to meet a variety of different needs. And while customers view these interactions as pieces of a single "relationship," firms often don't look at it the same way. **Pushy marketing:** Firms regularly promote explicit and implicit promises about their brands. But they often forget to shift gears and deliver on the promises. Some telltale signs of the problem: Retailers that send coupons for products that are out of stock in the store, and Web site home pages overrun with product pictures that obscure the customer's path to achieving her goals.[4]

This chapter presents an in-depth look at the value chain and the value delivery chain, distribution planning, and logistics. Chapter 15 covers wholesaling. Chapter 16 discusses retailing.

---

[2] Joseph O'Reilly, "Airfreight Forwarders Perspectives 2008," **http://www.inboundlogistics.com/articles/features/0608_feature02.shtml** (June 2008).

[3] Maynard Hershon, "The World Is Flat (And Way Smaller Than You Think)," **http://maynardnet.blogspot.com/2008/02/world-is-flat-and-way-smaller-than-you.html** (February 9, 2008).

[4] Bruce D. Temkin, *The Customer Experience Value Chain* (Cambridge, MA: Forrester Research, March 15, 2005).

14-2   THE ROLE OF THE VALUE CHAIN AND THE VALUE DELIVERY CHAIN IN THE DISTRIBUTION PROCESS[5]

> The distribution process has four stages, from setting goals to the level of satisfaction for each party in the process.

The four stages of the distribution process are depicted in Figure 14-1: goals, value chain and value delivery chain, total delivered product, and level of satisfaction. Here are the key points to consider:

- The goals of the various parties are considered as inputs to the value chain and value delivery chain.
- The value chain and value delivery chain are parallel processes.
- The total delivered product is the *actual* result of the value chain and value delivery chain.
- Satisfaction is based on the *perceived* value received from the value chain and value delivery chain.
- Feedback regarding service gaps and breakdowns must be handled systematically in the process.

Let us now discuss the stages in the distribution process.

14-2a   Goals

The distribution process may be viewed from multiple perspectives, and the goals represented by these perspectives must be in sync for the distribution process to succeed in the long run. Many channels have three basic participants: suppliers/manufacturers, distribution intermediaries, and customers. Before enacting a distribution strategy, the goals of each party must be determined, exchanged, and reconciled. These goals then set the direction for the value chain and value delivery chain. As enumerated in Table 14-1, the three parties typically have distinct distribution goals.

14-2b   Value Chain and Value Delivery Chain

A value chain has two aspects: the value chain itself and the value delivery chain. A **value chain** represents the series of business activities that are performed to design, produce,

Figure 14-1

The Distribution Process

Source: Loosely adapted by the authors from Joel R. Evans and Barry Berman, "Conceptualizing and Operationalizing the Business-to-Business Value Chain," *Industrial Marketing Management*, Vol. 30 (February 2001), p. 138. Copyright Elsevier Science. Reprinted by permission.

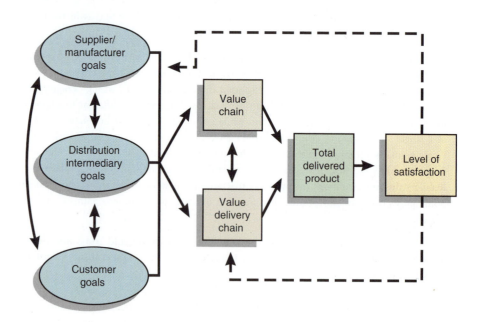

---

[5] The material in this section is loosely adapted by the authors from Joel R. Evans and Barry Berman, "Conceptualizing and Operationalizing the Business-to-Business Value Chain," *Industrial Marketing Management*, Vol. 30 (February 2001), pp. 135–148. Copyright Elsevier Science. Reprinted by permission.

Table 14-1	Selected Distribution Goals by Party

Party	Distribution Goals
Suppliers/ Manufacturers	To gain access to the distribution channel
	To ensure that all distribution functions are performed by one party or another
	To hold down distribution and inventory costs
	To foster relationship marketing with distribution intermediaries and customers
	To obtain feedback from distribution intermediaries and customers
	To have some control over the distribution strategy
	To optimize production runs and achieve economies of scale
	To secure some exclusivity with distribution intermediaries
	To resist the payment of slotting allowances (the fees charged by some distribution intermediaries to secure shelf space)
	To receive a fair share of profits
Distribution Intermediaries	To have on-time deliveries and quick turnaround time for orders
	To ensure that all distribution functions are performed by one party or another
	To service multiple suppliers/manufacturers in order to present a choice for customers
	To meet customer needs
	To foster relationship marketing with manufacturers/suppliers and customers
	To obtain feedback from distribution manufacturers/suppliers and customers
	To have some control over the distribution strategy
	To be as efficient as possible in shipping and inventory management
	To secure some exclusivity with suppliers/manufacturers
	To receive a fair share of profits
Customers	To have an assortment of products from which to choose
	To have a variety of resellers from which to choose
	To purchase in small quantities
	To shop at convenient locations
	To find items in-stock, including those on sale
	To have a number of payment options
	To be able to easily return products that are unsatisfactory
	To be treated in a respectful manner
	To have enough information to make informed decisions
	To pay fair prices

market, deliver, and service a product for customers.[6] These value chain activities are often performed: order fulfillment, product development, research and development, quality control, cost management, information interchange, facilities management, customer service, procurement, product commercialization, and returns (reverse logistics). The value chain is task-based.

A *value delivery chain* encompasses all of the parties who engage in value chain activities. It is performer-based and involves three factors: the specific parties in a given value chain, their relationships, and the activities undertaken by each party. The effectiveness of a value chain is greatly affected by the caliber of the value delivery

The **value chain** consists of activities that design, produce, market, deliver, and service a product for customers. The **value delivery chain** includes all the parties in a value chain.

[6] "Dictionary," http://www.marketingpower.com/_layouts/Dictionary.aspx?dLetter=V (March 22, 2009).

chain. Value is added by each participant, and differentiation is enhanced by the delivery chain, because each party adds something to the mix. A delivery chain is only as strong as its weakest link. If a supplier has quality control problems, this hurts the manufacturer. If a manufacturer is late with shipments, this hurts the wholesaler. If a wholesaler does not keep its facilities well maintained, this hurts the supplier and manufacturer. Win-win-win is a delivery chain goal. For the value delivery chain to work properly, the supplier/manufacturer, distribution intermediary, and customer must each feel its needs are satisfied. Firms must do everything possible to avoid value delivery chain breakdowns.

As an illustration, these are some activities that must be performed in a value chain for fresh-cut flowers: growing and harvesting the flowers, selecting the best flowers and storing them as they await shipment, shipping the flowers to resellers, displaying and preserving the flowers in florists' shops, wrapping flowers for customers, delivering customer orders when requested, and providing instructions for extending the life of the flowers. Through the value delivery chain, the supplier undertakes certain tasks and outsources others, such as using a local delivery firm to ship flowers throughout the city in which it operates, and selling at florists rather than at an on-site shop. The consumer is responsible for keeping the flowers in water and making sure they are not in direct sunlight.

14-2c   Total Delivered Product

The **total delivered product** comprises the bundle of tangible and intangible product attributes actually provided to consumers through a value chain and its related value delivery chain. This concept reflects how well activities in the distribution process are performed: Is the product shipped on time? Does it arrive intact without breaking or spoiling? Are store shelves fully stocked? Is the product properly price-marked? Is the return policy clearly stated and reasonable? Is the waiting time to make a purchase short enough? In the case of the fresh-cut flowers, the total delivered product is affected by delivery time, the refrigeration of delivery vehicles, the use of proper shipping containers, and other activities. See Figure 14-2.

The Web is a very promising tool for marketers to enhance the total delivered product, sometimes by adding value and other times by reducing costs. Through the Web, firms can access competitive intelligence, better communicate with one another, provide faster customer service, facilitate inventory planning, process orders, and reach channel members around the world.

> The **total delivered product** is the bundle of product attributes actually provided to consumers and depends on how well distribution functions are performed.

14-2d   Level of Satisfaction

The last stage in Figure 14-1 is the level of satisfaction with the distribution process, whereby the contentment of each party is determined and related to its goals. When the total delivered product is below expectations, gaps exist—due to poor performance, high prices, low profits, channel conflicts, and other factors. Value gaps should become integrated with future goals (as indicated by the top feedback arrow). If there are breakdowns in the delivery chain, they must be resolved by the parties in the chain (as shown by the bottom feedback arrow) and return policies must be clear. Only in this unlikely scenario would full satisfaction ever be reached: "Someone once described a truly integrated supply chain as one in which any time a Florida customer buys a bag of potato chips, an Idaho farmer plants two potatoes."[7]

---

[7] Joseph Bonney, "Missing Link in Supply Chain," *Journal of Commerce* (February 10, 2003), p. 6.

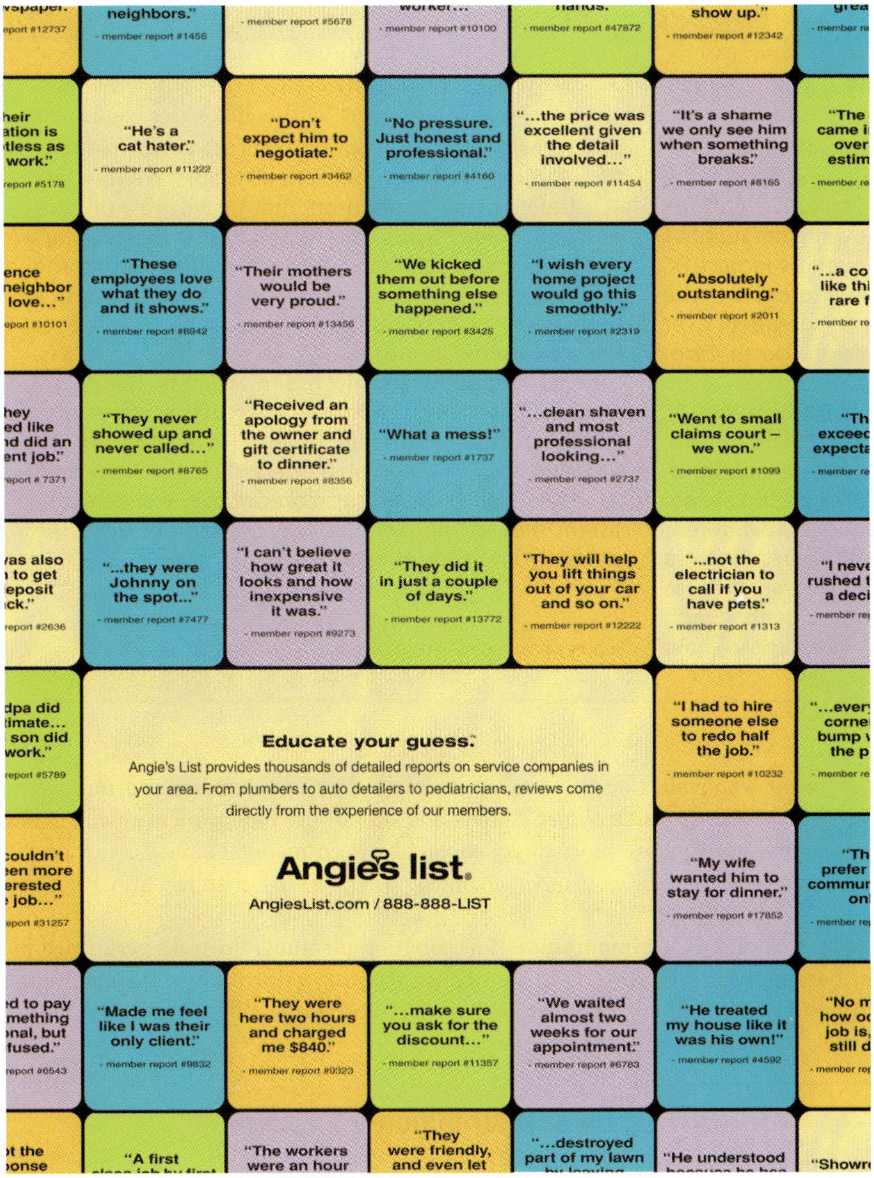

Figure 14-2

Adding Value to the Total Delivered Product

"The days of neighbors helping neighbors have not passed. The truth is that those days are still alive in Angie's List (**http://www.angieslist.com**), a grassroots organization that helps consumers find good contractors and service providers. Founded by Angie Hicks in Columbus, Ohio, in 1995, Angie's List takes the 'ask your neighbor' approach to a higher level. Using detailed reports, submitted by members, Angie's List provides reliable, unbiased ratings on local service providers and contractors. Because members submit reports each time they hire a service provider, ratings are current and reliable, and reflect the most recent feedback received on a particular company."

Source: Reprinted by permission. Advertising agency: Young and Laramore.

14-3 DISTRIBUTION PLANNING

Distribution planning is systematic decision making regarding the physical movement of goods and services from producer to consumer, as well as the related transfer of ownership (or rental) of them. It encompasses such diverse functions as transportation, inventory management, and customer transactions.

These functions are carried out by a *channel of distribution*, which comprises all the organizations or people involved in the distribution process. Those organizations or people are known as *channel members* and may include manufacturers, service providers, wholesalers, retailers, marketing specialists, and/or consumers.

When the term *distribution intermediaries* is used, it refers to wholesalers, retailers, and marketing specialists (such as transportation firms) that act as facilitators (links) between manufacturers/service providers and consumers.

A channel of distribution can be simple (based on a handshake between a small manufacturer and a local reseller) or complex (requiring detailed written contracts among numerous parties). Some firms seek widespread distribution and need

Distribution planning involves movement and ownership in a **channel of distribution**. It consists of **channel members**.

Distribution intermediaries often have a channel role.

Distribution arrangements vary widely.

Global Marketing in Action

Making Lenovo's Supply Chain a Key Asset

Lenovo Group (http://www.lenovo.com), a Chinese-based computer manufacturer, acquired IBM's (http://www.ibm.com) PC division for $1.75 billion in 2005. As a result of this purchase, Lenovo moved from number eight to number three among the world's largest PC manufacturers. At the time of the acquisition, the combined company's supply chain was spread all over the globe, with major offices in Raleigh, North Carolina; Beijing, China; and Singapore.

In its new supply chain model, called "worldsourcing," Lenovo has no real headquarters. William Amelio, the chief executive officer, works out of Singapore; Lenovo's chairman Yang Yuanqing has relocated to Raleigh; and the firm's top executives hold meetings in a different location each month. Lenovo recruited Gerry Smith, a Dell (http://www.dell.com) supply chain executive, as senior vice-president of global supply chain. Smith describes Lenovo as a "fully integrated supply chain

organization" because logistics, procurement, manufacturing, planning, and fulfillment all report to him.

Unlike many competitors that heavily rely on outsourcing, about three-quarters of Lenovo's manufacturing is done at its own 10 plants located around the world. Lenovo uses contract manufacturers only until a Lenovo plant can be built, or in locations where it does not make sense to run a plant due to taxes or tariffs. Lenovo's suppliers are given annual goals (based on input from Lenovo's chief executive officer, chief purchasing officer, and chief financial officer), and the suppliers are evaluated on a quarterly basis. According to Smith, "With consistent scorecarding, you get consistent metrics that send a clear message of what we expect from our suppliers."

Source: Based on material in David Hannon, "Lenovo Does Global Supply Chain Right," *Purchasing* (October 18, 2007), pp. 53–54.

independent wholesalers and/or retailers to carry their merchandise and improve cash flow. Others want direct customer contact and do not use independent resellers. Industrial channels usually have more direct contact between manufacturers/service providers and customers than final consumer channels. International channels also have special needs.

We next discuss the importance of distribution planning, the tasks performed in the distribution process, the criteria to consider in selecting a distribution channel, supplier/distribution intermediary contracts, channel cooperation and conflict, the industrial channel, and international distribution.

14-3a The Importance of Distribution Planning

Distribution decisions have a great effect on a company's marketing efforts. Because intermediaries can perform a host of functions, a firm's marketing plan will differ if it sells direct rather than via intermediaries; and a decision to sell in stores rather than through the mail or the World Wide Web requires a different marketing orientation and tasks.

One of the most critical decisions a firm makes is the choice of a distribution channel. Close ties with intermediaries and/or customers may take time to develop; if there are existing bonds among channel members, it may be hard for a new firm to enter. Once alliances are achieved, suitable new products can be put into distribution more easily. Channel members need to act in a coordinated way. Strong resellers enhance manufacturers' marketing abilities. Consumers like to buy products the same way over time.

More firms now recognize the value of good relationships throughout the distribution channel. See Figure 14-3. Thus, many companies engage in relationship marketing and seek to develop and maintain continuous long-term ties with suppliers, distribution intermediaries, and customers. These firms ensure a more consistent flow of goods and services from suppliers, encourage intermediaries to act more as partners than as adversaries, and increase the likelihood of customer loyalty. They foster good employee morale by empowering them to respond positively to reasonable requests from suppliers, intermediaries, and customers. They get earlier and better data on new products and the

> In relationship marketing, firms seek ongoing ties with suppliers, intermediaries, and customers.

Figure 14-3

Piggly Wiggly Supermarkets Progressively Add New Value-Added Elements to the Channel

Source: Reprinted by permission.

best strategies for continuing ones. They lower operating and marketing costs, thus improving efficiency. As the supply chain director for apparel firm Hugo Boss (**http://www.hugoboss.com**) noted: "We think of ourselves as being embedded in a network of supply chain partners, with warehousing operators, logistics service providers, forwarders, and manufacturers. We have to manage that network to get the shortest lead times and the best costs."[8]

This is how effective relationship marketing in a distribution channel may be achieved:

- There should be a continuous and systematic process that incorporates both buyer and seller needs.
- Top management support is required, and relationship marketing principles should permeate a firm's corporate culture.
- At a minimum, a firm needs to understand consumer expectations, build service partnerships, empower employees, and utilize total quality management.
- Suppliers, intermediaries, and customers should be surveyed—by category—to determine the aspects of relationship marketing to be emphasized for them.
- Although increased profitability is a desirable result, other important measures of success are customer satisfaction, customer loyalty, and product quality.
- Both positive and negative feedback (going far beyond just passively receiving customer complaints) can provide meaningful information.
- Sellers need to communicate to their customers that relationship marketing involves responsibilities, as well as benefits, for both parties.
- There should be mutually agreeable (by buyer and seller) contingency plans if anything goes awry.[9]

---

[8] "Air Freight Attractive for Hugo Boss," *Supply Chain Europe* (February 2005), p. 36.

[9] Joel R. Evans and Richard L. Laskin, "The Relationship Marketing Process: A Conceptualization and Application," *Industrial Marketing Management*, Vol. 23 (December 1994), p. 451.

Both costs and profits are affected by the selection of a distribution channel. A firm doing all functions must pay for them itself; in return, it reaps all profits. A firm using intermediaries reduces per-unit distribution costs; it also reduces per-unit profits because those resellers receive their share. With intermediaries, a firm's total profits would rise if there are far higher sales than it could attain itself.

Distribution formats are long-standing in some industries. For example, in the beverage and food industry, manufacturers often sell through wholesalers that then deal with retailers. Auto makers sell through franchised dealers. Mail-order firms line up suppliers, print catalogs, and sell to consumers. As a result, firms must frequently conform to the channel patterns in their industries.

A firm's market coverage is often influenced by the location and number, market penetration, image, product selection, services, and marketing plans of the wholesalers, retailers, and/or marketing specialists with which it deals. In rating its options, a firm should note that the more intermediaries it uses, the less customer contact it has and the lower its control over marketing.

These examples show the scope of distribution planning:

- Sherwin-Williams (http://www.sherwin-williams.com) distributes its paints via more than 3,300 company-owned stores and through independent paint stores, mass merchandisers, auto supply stores, wholesale distributors, and others. It has a direct sales force for certain industrial markets and employs distributors in many foreign nations.[10]

- Shoppers Advantage (http://www.shoppersadvantage.com) is a shopping service operating exclusively on the Web: "Who is Shoppers Advantage? We're the one-stop shopping site where members and nonmembers can browse diverse superstores to find thousands of products, and 1,100 name brands at deep discounts every day. Members enjoy extra benefits including 3.5% Shoppers Advantage Cash back on qualifying purchases, up to a 2-year extended warranty, and a 200% low price guarantee."[11]

- Century 21 (http://www.century21.com) is the "the franchisor of the world's largest residential real-estate sales organization, with more than 8,400 independently owned and operated franchised broker offices in over 57 countries and territories worldwide. We are dedicated to providing buyers and sellers of real-estate with the highest quality services possible."[12]

- Apple Inc. (http://www.apple.com) sells its products in three ways to facilitate shopping: (1) "Buy Online: Open 24-7, the Apple Store online lets you shop anytime from the comfort of your favorite chair. From built-to-order Macs to iPods to printers to cameras, you'll find everything you need and more at the Apple Store online." (2) "Shop Retail: The Apple Store is the best place to learn everything there is to know about the Mac or iPod. Let the Mac Specialists answer all your questions. Visit the Genius Bar for one-on-one support and advice. Attend free workshops—for beginners and pros—and learn how to bring your ideas to life. (3) "Resellers: Thousands of Apple resellers can help you discover the Apple product that's right for you." These resellers include AT&T (http://www.att.com), Best Buy (http://www.bestbuy.com), Radio Shack (http://www.radioshack.com), Target (http://www.target.com), and many others.[13]

---

[10] *Sherwin-Williams Company 2008 Annual Report.*

[11] "Shoppers Advantage: Who We Are," http://www.shoppersadvantage.com (May 9, 2009).

[12] "Company Profile," http://www.century21.com/aboutus (May 9, 2009).

[13] "Where Can I Buy Apple Products?" http://www.apple.com/buy (May 9, 2009).

14-3b Channel Functions and the Role of Distribution Intermediaries

The *channel functions* shown in Figure 14-4 must be undertaken for most goods and services. They need to be completed somewhere in a distribution channel and responsibility for them assigned.

Distribution intermediaries can play a vital role in marketing research. Due to their closeness to the market, they generally have good insights into the characteristics and needs of customers.

In buying products, intermediaries sometimes pay as items are received; other times, they accept items on consignment and do not pay until after sales are made. Purchase terms for intermediaries may range from net cash (payment due at once) to net 60 days (payment not due for 60 days) or more. If intermediaries do not pay until after resale, manufacturers risk poor cash flow, high product returns, obsolescence and spoilage, multiple transactions with intermediaries, and potentially low customer sales.

Manufacturers and service firms often take care of national (international) ads in assigning promotion roles. Wholesalers may coordinate regional promotions among retailers, and motivate and train retail salespeople. Many retailers undertake local ads, personal selling, and events.

Customer services include delivery, credit, in-office and in-home purchases, training, warranties, and return privileges. Again, these services can be offered by one channel member or a combination of them.

Distribution intermediaries can contribute to product planning in several ways. They often provide advice on new and existing products. Test marketing requires their cooperation. And intermediaries can be helpful in positioning products against competitors and suggesting which products to drop.

Wholesalers and retailers often have strong input into pricing decisions. They state their required markups and then price-mark products or specify how they should be marked. Court rulings limit manufacturers' ability to control final prices. Intermediaries thus have great flexibility in setting them.

Distribution involves three major factors: transportation, inventory management, and customer contact. Goods must be shipped from a manufacturer to consumers;

> Intermediaries can perform **channel functions** and reduce costs, provide expertise, open markets and lower risks

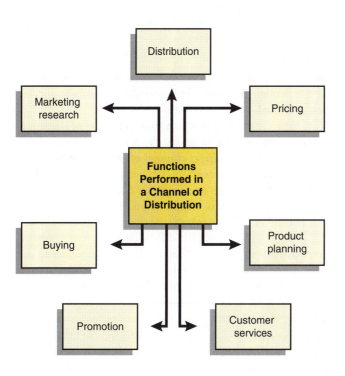

Figure 14-4

Channel Functions

intermediaries often do this. Because production capabilities and customer demand often differ, inventory levels must be properly managed (and items may require storage in a warehouse before being sold). Consumer transactions may require a store or other seller location, long hours of operation, and store fixtures (such as dressing rooms).

Manufacturers typically like to make a limited variety of items in large quantities and have as few transactions as possible to sell their entire output. However, consumers tend to want a variety of brands, colors, sizes, and qualities from which to select—and opt to buy a small amount at a time. Manufacturers might also prefer to sell products from a factory, have 9-to-5 hours and spartan fixtures, and use a limited sales force. Yet, b-to-b customers may want salespeople to visit them, and final consumers may want to shop at nearby locales and visit attractive, well-staffed stores on weekends and evenings.

To resolve these differences, intermediaries can be used in the *sorting process*, which consists of four distribution functions: *Accumulation* is collecting small shipments from several firms so shipping costs are lower. *Allocation* is apportioning items to various consumer markets. *Sorting* is separating products into grades, colors, and so forth. *Assorting* is offering a range of products so the consumer has choices.

The **sorting process** coordinates manufacturer and consumer goals.

14-3c   Selecting a Channel of Distribution

Several key factors must be considered in choosing a distribution channel:

- *The consumer:* (a) characteristics—number, concentration, average purchase size; (b) needs—shopping locations and hours, assortment, sales help, credit; (c) segments—size, purchase behavior.
- *The company itself:* (a) goals—control, sales, profit, timing; (b) resources—level, flexibility, service needs; (c) expertise—functions, specialization, efficiency; (d) experience—distribution methods, channel relationships.
- *The product:* (a) value—price per unit; (b) complexity—technical nature; (c) perishability—shelf life, frequency of shipments; (d) bulk—weight per unit, divisibility.
- *The competition:* (a) characteristics—number, concentration, assortment, customers; (b) tactics—distribution methods, channel relationships.
- *Distribution channels:* (a) alternatives—direct, indirect; (b) characteristics—number of intermediaries, functions performed, tradition; (c) availability—exclusive arrangements, territorial restrictions.
- *Legalities*—(a) current laws; (b) pending laws.

Channel choice depends on consumers, the company, the product, competition, existing channels, and legalities.

While it assesses the preceding factors, a firm would decide about the type of channel, contractual arrangements or administered channels, channel length and width, channel intensity, and dual channels.

There are two basic types of channels. A *direct channel of distribution* involves the movement of goods and services from producer to consumers without the use of independent intermediaries. An *indirect channel of distribution* involves the movement of goods and services from producer to independent intermediaries to consumers. Figure 14-5 shows the transactions necessary for the sale of 200,000 men's umbrellas under direct and indirect channels. Figure 14-6 shows the most common indirect channels for final consumer and organizational consumer products.

If a manufacturer or service provider sells to consumers at company-owned outlets (for example, Shell-owned gas stations), this is a direct channel. In an indirect channel, a manufacturer may use several layers of independent wholesalers (for example, regional, state, and local) and sell at different kinds of retailers (such as discount, department, and specialty stores). A direct channel is most often used by firms that want control over their entire marketing efforts, desire close customer contact, and have limited markets. An indirect channel is most often used by firms that want to enlarge their markets, raise sales, and give up distribution functions and costs; they will surrender some control and customer contact.

In a **direct channel,** one firm performs all tasks. An **indirect channel** has multiple firms.

(a) Direct channel

Manufacturer

In this direct channel, an umbrella manufacturer sells directly to final customers. It makes 200,000 separate transactions, one for each customer.

200,000 customers

(b) Indirect channel

Manufacturer

In this extended channel, the manufacturer makes four transactions, distributing 50,000 umbrellas to each wholesaler. In turn, each wholesaler distributes 1,000 umbrellas to the 50 retailers in its regions. The wholesalers each make 50 transactions. Every retailer makes 1,000 transactions, selling one umbrella to each final consumer.

Wholesaler (East U.S.)	Wholesaler (South U.S.)	Wholesaler (North U.S.)	Wholesaler (West U.S.)
50 retailers	50 retailers	50 retailers	50 retailers
1,000 customers per retailer	1,000 customers per retailer	1,000 customers per retailer	1,000 customers per retailer

Figure 14-5

Transactions in a Direct Versus an Indirect Channel

Because an indirect channel has independent members, a method is needed to plan and assign marketing responsibilities. With a *contractual channel arrangement*, all the terms regarding distribution tasks, prices, and other factors are stated in writing for each member. A manufacturer and a retailer could sign an agreement regarding promotion

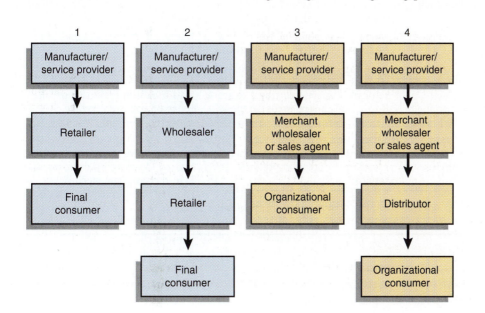

1	2	3	4
Manufacturer/ service provider	Manufacturer/ service provider	Manufacturer/ service provider	Manufacturer/ service provider
Retailer	Wholesaler	Merchant wholesaler or sales agent	Merchant wholesaler or sales agent
Final consumer	Retailer	Organizational consumer	Distributor
	Final consumer		Organizational consumer

Figure 14-6

Typical Indirect Channels of Distribution

support, delivery and payment dates, and product handling, marking, and displays. In an *administered channel arrangement*, the dominant firm in the distribution process plans the marketing program and itemizes and coordinates each member's duties. Depending on its relative strength, a manufacturer/service provider, wholesaler, or retailer could be a channel leader. Accordingly, a manufacturer with a strong brand could set its image, price range, and selling method.

Channel length refers to the levels of independent members along a distribution channel. In Figure 14-5, *A* is a short channel and *B* is a long channel. Sometimes, a firm shortens its channel by acquiring a company at another stage, such as a manufacturer merging with a wholesaler. This may let the firm be more self-sufficient, ensure supply, control channel members, lower distribution costs, and coordinate timing throughout the channel. Critics of the practice believe it limits competition, fosters inefficiency, and does not result in lower consumer prices.

Channel width refers to the number of independent members at any stage of distribution. In a narrow channel, a manufacturer or service provider sells via few wholesalers or retailers; in a wide channel, it sells via many. If a firm wants to enhance its position at its stage of the channel, it may buy other companies like itself, such as one janitorial services firm buying another. This lets a firm increase its size and market share, improve bargaining power with other channel members, and utilize mass promotion and distribution techniques more efficiently.

A firm must decide on the intensity of its distribution coverage in selecting a channel. A firm severely limits the number of resellers utilized in a geographic area under **exclusive distribution**, perhaps having only one or two resellers within a specific shopping location. It seeks a prestige image, channel control, and high profit margins and accepts lower total sales than in other types of distribution. With **selective distribution**, a firm employs a moderate number of resellers. It wants to combine some channel control and a solid image with good sales volume and profits. A firm uses a large number of resellers in **intensive distribution**. Its goals are wide market coverage, channel acceptance, and high total sales and profits. Per-unit profits are low. It is a strategy aimed at the most consumers. See Table 14-2.

> **Channel length** describes the levels of independents. **Channel width** refers to the independents at one level.

> **Exclusive, selective, and intensive distribution** depend on goals, sellers, customers, and marketing.

Table 14-2   Intensity of Channel Coverage

Attributes	Exclusive Distribution	Selective Distribution	Intensive Distribution
Objectives	Prestige image, channel control and loyalty, price stability and high profit margins	Moderate market coverage, solid image, some channel control and loyalty, good sales and profits	Widespread market coverage, channel acceptance, high volume sales and total profits
Resellers	Few in number, well established, reputable firms (outlets)	Moderate in number, well established, better firms (outlets)	Many in number, all types of firms (outlets)
Customers	Final consumers: fewer in number, trend setters, willing to travel to store, brand loyal B-to-b consumers: focus on major accounts, service expected from manufacturer	Final consumers: moderate in number, brand conscious, somewhat willing to travel to store B-to-b consumers: focus on many types of accounts, service expected from manufacturer or intermediary	Final consumers: many in number, convenience-oriented B-to-b consumers: focus on all types of accounts, service expected from intermediary
Marketing emphasis	Final consumers: personal selling, pleasant shopping conditions, good service B-to-b consumers: availability, regular communications, superior service	Final consumers: promotional mix, pleasant shopping conditions, good service B-to-b consumers: availability, regular communications, superior service	Final consumers: mass advertising, nearby location, items in stock B-to-b consumers: availability, regular communications, superior service
Major weakness	Limited sales potential	May be difficult to carve out a niche	Limited channel control
Examples	Autos, designer clothes, capital equipment, complex services	Furniture, clothing, mechanics' tools, standardized services	Household products, groceries, office supplies, routine services

Some additional factors are noteworthy in selecting a channel. First, a firm may use a *dual channel of distribution* (also known as *multichannel distribution*), whereby it appeals to different market segments or diversifies business by selling through two or more separate channels. A company could use selective distribution for a prestige brand of watches and intensive distribution for a discount brand, or use both direct and indirect channels (such as an insurance firm selling group health insurance directly to large businesses and individual life insurance indirectly to final consumers via independent agents). Consider the strategy of Office Depot (**http://www.officedepot.com**). It has 1,200 stores in 24 nations, annually conducts 1,100 catalog mailings, operates 9 U.S. E-commerce and 33 sites outside the United States, and employs a 2,500-person corporate account sales force. As one observer notes, "Merchants that large and diverse must coordinate their various channels to present an integrated brand and message to customers."[14] At our book Web site, see a multichannel distribution slide show by TNS Retail Forward (**http://www.retailforward.com**).

Second, a firm may go from exclusive to selective to intensive distribution through the product life cycle. Yet, it would be hard to go from intensive to selective to exclusive distribution. Designer jeans moved from prestige stores to better stores to all types of outlets. This process would not have worked in reverse. Third, a firm may distribute products in a new way and achieve great success. See Figure 14-7.

At its Web site (**http://www.toolkit.cch.com/text/P03_6000.asp**), the Business Owner's Toolkit gives some excellent advice for "Choosing Distribution Methods."

> A **dual channel (multichannel distribution)** lets a firm reach different segments or diversify.

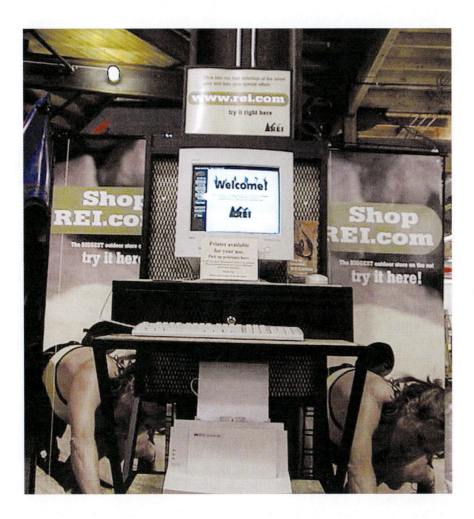

Figure 14-7

New Forms of Multichannel Distribution at REI

REI (**http://www.rei.com**) has marketed its products through stores for years. Today, it also uses in-store computerized kiosks and a Web site to sell its products.

Source: Reprinted by permission of TNS Retail Forward.

[14] Brian Quinton, "Office Depot's Multichannel Challenge," *Direct* (May 1, 2005), p. 10.

14-3d   Supplier/Distribution Intermediary Contracts

> Distribution contracts cover prices, sale conditions, territories, commitments, timing, and termination.

Distribution contracts focus on price policies, conditions of sale, territorial rights, the services/responsibility mix, and contract length and conditions of termination. The highlights of a contract follow.

Price policies largely deal with the discounts given to intermediaries for their functions, quantity purchases, and cash payments, and with commission rates. Functional discounts are deductions from list prices for performing storage, shipping, and other jobs. Quantity discounts are deductions for volume purchases. Cash discounts are deductions for early payment. Some intermediaries get paid commissions.

Conditions of sale cover price and quality guarantees, payment and shipping terms, reimbursement for unsaleable items, and returns. A guarantee against a price decline protects one intermediary from paying a high price for an item that is then offered to others at a lower price; the original buyer then receives a rebate so its costs are like those of competitors. Otherwise, it could not meet the competitors' resale prices. Suppliers sometimes use full-line forcing and require intermediaries to carry an entire product line. This is legal if they are not prevented from also buying items from other suppliers.

Territorial rights outline the geographic areas (such as greater Paris) in which resellers may operate and/or the target markets (such as small business accounts) they may contact. Sometimes, they have exclusive territories, as with McDonald's (**http://www.mcdonalds.com**) franchisees; in other cases, many firms gain territorial rights for the same areas, as with retailers selling Sharp (**http://www.sharpusa.com**) calculators.

The *services/responsibility mix* describes the role of each channel member. It outlines who delivers products, holds inventory, trains salespeople, writes ad copy, and sets up displays; and it sets performance standards. If included, a hold-harmless clause specifies that manufacturers or service providers—not resellers—are liable in lawsuits arising from poor design or negligence in production.

Contract length and conditions of termination protect an intermediary against a manufacturer or service provider prematurely bypassing it after a territory has been built up. The manufacturer or service provider is shielded by limiting contract duration and stating the factors leading to termination.

Although some firms rely on verbal agreements, without a written contract, there is a danger of misunderstandings as to goals, compensation, tasks performed, and the length of the agreement. A constraint of a written contract may be its inflexibility under changing market conditions.

14-3e   Channel Cooperation and Conflict

> Channel-member goals need to be balanced.

All firms in a distribution channel have similar general goals: profitability, access to goods and services, efficient distribution, and customer loyalty. Yet, the way these and other goals are achieved often leads to differing views, even if the parties engage in relationship marketing: How are profits allocated along a channel? How can manufacturers sell products via many competing resellers and expect the resellers not to carry other brands? Which party coordinates channel decisions? To whom are consumers loyal—manufacturers/service providers, wholesalers, or retailers?

Natural differences among the firms in a distribution channel exist by virtue of their channel positions, the tasks performed, and the desire of each firm to optimize its profits and control its strategy. A successful channel maximizes cooperation and minimizes conflict. In the past, manufacturers dominated channels because they had the best market coverage and recognition; resellers were small and local. With the growth of large national (and global) distribution intermediaries, the volume accounted for by them, and the popularity of private brands, the balance of power has shifted more to resellers. Table 14-3 cites causes of conflict. Table 14-4 shows how cooperation can reduce these conflicts.

If conflicts are not resolved cooperatively, confrontations may occur. A manufacturer or service provider may then ship late, refuse to deal with certain resellers, limit

Table 14-3	Potential Causes of Channel Conflict	
Factors	**Manufacturer's/Service Provider's Goals**	**Distribution Intermediary's Goals**
Pricing	To establish final prices consistent with product image	To establish final prices consistent with the intermediary's image
Purchase terms	To ensure prompt, accurate payments and minimize discounts	To defer payments as long as possible and secure discounts
Shelf space	To obtain plentiful shelf space with good visibility so as to maximize brand sales	To allocate shelf space among multiple brands so as to maximize total product sales
Exclusivity	To hold down the number of competing brands each intermediary stocks while selling via many intermediaries	To hold down the number of competing intermediaries carrying the same brands while selling different brands itself
Delivery	To receive adequate notice before deliveries are required	To obtain quick service
Advertising support	To secure ad support from intermediaries	To secure ad support from manufacturers/service providers
Profitability	To have adequate profit margins	To have adequate profit margins
Continuity	To receive orders on a regular basis	To receive shipments on a regular basis
Order size	To maximize order size	To have order size conform with consumer demand to minimize inventory investment
Assortment	To offer a limited variety	To secure a full variety
Risk	To have intermediaries assume risks	To have manufacturers/service providers assume risks
Branding	To sell products under the manufacturer's/service provider's name	To sell products under private brands, as well as manufacturers'/service providers' brands
Channel access	To distribute products wherever desired by the manufacturer/service provider	To carry only those items desired by intermediaries
Importance of account	To not allow any one intermediary to dominate	To not allow any one manufacturer/service provider to dominate
Consumer loyalty	To have consumers loyal to the manufacturer/service provider	To have consumers loyal to the intermediary
Channel control	To make key channel decisions	To make key channel decisions

Table 14-4	Methods of Channel Cooperation	
Factors	**Manufacturer's/Service Provider's Actions**	**Distribution Intermediary's Actions**
New-product introduction	Thorough testing, adequate promotional support	Good shelf location and space, enthusiasm for product, assistance in test marketing
Delivery	Prompt filling of orders, adherence to scheduled dates	Proper time allowed for delivery, shipments immediately checked for accuracy
Marketing research	Data provided to resellers	Data provided to manufacturers/service providers
Pricing	Prices to intermediaries let them gain reasonable profits, intermediary flexibility encouraged	Infrequent sales from regular prices, maintaining proper image
Promotion	Training reseller's salespeople, sales force incentives, developing appropriate ad campaign, cooperative ad programs	Attractive store displays, knowledgeable salespeople, participation in cooperative programs
Financing	Liberal financial terms	Adherence to financial terms
Product quality	Product guarantees	Proper installation and servicing of products for customers
Channel control	Shared and specified decision making	Shared and specified decision making

financing, withdraw promotional support, or use other tactics. Similarly, a reseller may make late payments, give poor shelf space, refuse to carry items, return many products, and apply other tactics. A channel cannot function well in a confrontational framework. Yet, in some instances, channel conflict seems to be growing:

> Multiple channel strategies are a way of life for manufacturers today. Whether you are managing a mix of direct and indirect channels or a spectrum of high-support to low-support resellers, channel conflict will be an ongoing issue. Some channel conflict is healthy. It indicates you have adequate market coverage. However, once the balance between coverage and conflict is lost, channel conflict can quickly undermine your channel strategy, market position, and profitability. Conflict can show up in the market in a variety of ways. A point of confusion for many manufacturers is whether problems are symptoms of destructive channel conflict or of other marketing issues. Channel conflict is managed by a combination of economics and controls. Economic solutions compensate channels fairly for functions performed and direct channels away from actions that create destructive conflict. Controls put structure around a channel strategy to limit the potential for destructive conflict.[15]

A thriving manufacturer or service provider can often secure reseller support and enthusiasm when it introduces new products and continues popular ones. This occurs because resellers know the manufacturer's or service provider's past sales track record, the promotion support to be provided, and delivery reliability. Thus, a ***pushing strategy*** is used, whereby the various firms in a distribution channel cooperate in marketing a product. With this approach, relationship marketing is involved.

As a rule, it is harder for a new manufacturer or service provider to break into an existing channel. Resellers are unfamiliar with the firm, not able to gauge its sales potential, and wonder about its support and future deliveries. So, a new firm often needs a ***pulling strategy***, whereby it first stimulates consumer demand and then gains dealer support. This means heavy promotion spending, fully paid by the manufacturer or service provider; the firm may have to offer guarantees of minimum sales or profits to resellers—and make up shortfalls. Figure 14-8 contrasts pushing and pulling strategies.

In today's highly competitive marketplace, with so many new domestic and foreign products being introduced each year, even leading firms must sometimes use pulling strategies. They need to convince resellers that demand exists for their products before the resellers will agree to tie up shelf space.

In a **pushing strategy**, there is cooperation. With **pulling**, a firm generates demand before channel support.

Figure 14-8

Pushing Versus Pulling Strategies

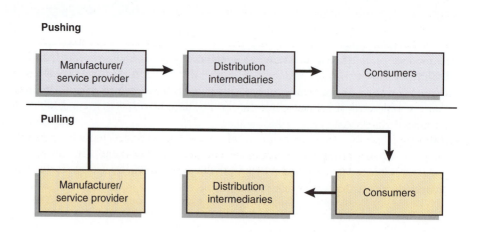

---

[15] Karl Edmunds, "How to Tell When Channel Conflict Is Destructive," http://www.mondaq.com/article.asp?articleid=57914 (March 6, 2008).

14-3f   The Industrial Channel of Distribution

The distribution channel for industrial (b-to-b) products differs from that for consumer products in these significant ways:

An industrial channel has unique characteristics.

- Retailers are typically not utilized.
- Direct channels are more readily employed.
- Transactions are fewer and orders are larger.
- Specification selling is more prevalent.
- Intermediaries are more knowledgeable.
- Team selling (two or more salespeople) may be necessary.
- Distinct intermediaries specialize in industrial products.
- Leasing, rather than selling, is more likely.
- Customer information needs are more technical.
- Activities such as shipping and warehousing may be shared.

Industrial Distribution magazine (**http://www.inddist.com**) is a good source for further information on this topic. To learn more about industrial distribution leaders, click "Industry Resources" on the top toolbar.

14-3g   International Distribution Planning

When devising an international distribution plan, a number of factors should be kept in mind.[16] Here are several of them.

International distribution requires particular planning.

Channel length often depends on a nation's stage of economic development and consumer patterns. Less-developed and developing nations tend to use shorter, more direct channels than do industrialized ones. They have many small firms marketing goods and services to nearby consumers, and limited transportation and communications networks foster local shopping. At the same time, cultural norms in nations—both developing and industrialized—affect expected interactions between sellers and consumers. For instance, in Japan, people treasure personal attention when making purchases, especially of expensive products. Unlike American shoppers, Japanese consumers are not used to buying by phone.

Distribution practices and formats vary by nation, as these examples show:

- Many European countries have been dominated by independent retailers rather than large chains. However, with the expansion of the European Union, the growth of chains will speed up throughout Europe in the future.
- Some Mexican supermarkets shut off electricity overnight to reduce costs. Perishable items such as dairy products have a shorter shelf life and require more frequent deliveries than in the United States.
- Large Japanese firms often set up *keiretsus*. A vertical keiretsu is an integrated network of suppliers, manufacturers, and resellers. A horizontal keiretsu typically consists of a money-center bank, an insurance company, a trust banking company, a trading company, and several major manufacturers. U.S. firms have some channels that resemble vertical keiretsus, but they do not have networks that emulate horizontal keiretsus.
- Although it has four times as many people as the United States, India has roughly the same number of retail establishments, and just one-quarter of them are in metropolitan areas. The leading retailers are the popular neighborhood grocery and general stores that offer very low prices.

---

[16] See Rob Martinez, "Getting Your Goods Across the Globe," *Multichannel Merchant* (March 2008), pp. 44–45; Robert Auerbach, "International Distribution Agreement Checklist," **http://www.marketnewzealand.com/common/files/auerbach-intdistribution.pdf** (May 2006); and "Checklist: International Distributorship Agreement," **http://www.internationalbusinesslawyers.org/disCheck_inter.shtml** (March 15, 2009).

If a firm enters a foreign market for the first time, it must resolve these questions: Should products be made domestically and shipped to the foreign market or made in the foreign market? If products are made domestically, what form of transportation is best? What kind of distribution intermediaries should be used? Which specific intermediaries should be used? Through its International Trade Administration (**http://www.ita.doc. gov**), the U.S. Department of Commerce has a Commercial Service (**http://www.ita.doc. gov/cs**) division to assist small and medium-size firms seeking advice on international distribution. There is a network of export and industry specialists in 107 U.S. cities and more than 80 nations worldwide. Along with Unz & Company (**http://www.unzco.com**), the U.S. Department of Commerce offers an online manual that covers "Methods/ Channels" in devising an export strategy (**http://www.unzco.com/basicguide/c4.html**).

Legal requirements for distribution differ by country—some have strict laws as to hours, methods of operation, and sites. In France, there are severe limits on Sunday retail hours. In Germany, there are strict limits on store size and Sunday hours. Many nations have complex procedures for foreign firms to distribute there. Thus, firms interested in standardized (global) distribution may be stymied.

What causes a company to be more or less satisfied with its international distribution channel? If a firm's domestic channel performs better than its international channel, it is likely that the firm will be dissatisfied with the international channel. If a firm has experience and expertise in foreign markets, it is likely that the firm will be satisfied with its international channel. If a firm has several distribution choices in entering a foreign market, it is likely to be more satisfied with the channel it selects. If environmental uncertainty is high, it is likely the firm will be less satisfied with its international channel.

14-4   LOGISTICS

> **Logistics (physical distribution)** involves the location, timing, and condition of deliveries. An order cycle covers many activities.

Logistics (also known as *physical distribution*) encompasses the broad range of activities concerned with efficiently delivering raw materials, parts, semifinished items, and finished products to designated places, at designated times, and in proper condition. It may be undertaken by any member of a channel, from producer to consumer. Logistics involves such functions as customer service, shipping, warehousing, inventory control, private trucking-fleet operations, packaging, receiving, materials handling, and plant, warehouse, and store location planning. The logistics activities involved in a typical *order cycle*—the period of time that spans a customer's placing an order and its receipt—are illustrated in Figure 14-9.

14-4a   The Importance of Logistics

Logistics is important due to its costs, the value of customer service, and its relationship with other functions. At our book Web site, view the Council of Supply Chain Management Professionals (**http://www.cscmp.org**)—formerly known as the Council of Logistics Management—slide show.

Figure 14-9

Selected Physical Distribution Activities Involved in a Typical Order Cycle

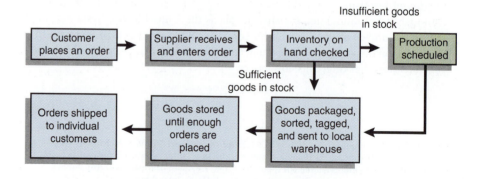

Costs Logistics costs amount to 10 percent of the U.S. GDP, with transportation (freight) accounting for about 62 percent of that total.[17] To contain costs, firms have been working hard to improve efficiency. Today, logistics tasks are completed faster, more accurately, and with fewer people than 30 years ago. Due to computerization and improved transportation, firms have reduced their annual inventory levels by tens of billions of dollars, thus saving on warehousing and interest expenses.

> Cost control is a major goal.

Distribution costs vary by industry and company type. Total logistics costs for individual firms depend on the nature of the business, the geographic area covered, the tasks done by other channel members, and the weight/value ratio of the items. Though petroleum refiners spend almost one-quarter of their sales just on inbound and outbound transportation, many retailers spend under 5 percent of their sales on transportation from vendors and receiving, marking, storing, and distributing goods. When the U.S. Postal Service (http://www.usps.com) raises rates, shipping costs are affected for all kinds of firms.

Firms must identify the symptoms of poor distribution systems and strive to be more efficient. Up to one-fifth of the perishable items carried by U.S. grocers, such as fish and dairy items, are lost to spoilage due to breakdowns in shipping or too much time on store shelves. To reduce losses, many grocers insist on small, frequent deliveries and have upgraded their storage facilities. Many firms engaged in E-commerce are still finding their way. This is the challenge:

> Supply-chain operations continually feel the pressure to manage the cost equation, while meeting the strategic objectives of providing superior customer service and driving growth within the business. If we consider the modern enterprise's entire value proposition and value chain, leadership must balance a precarious profitability equation—hoping product development, marketing, and distribution partners can drive revenue while they lean heavily on areas like logistics and procurement to control costs. The supply chain operations of many firms often find themselves one step forward in operational effectiveness as the industry environment pushes them one step back. Improvements in operational efficiency and working smarter seem to only offset the challenges companies face in managing rising expenses and stepping up to customer expectations.[18]

Table 14-5 shows several cost ramifications of poor distribution.

Table 14-5	Selected Symptoms and Cost Ramifications of a Poor Physical Distribution System
Symptoms	**Cost Ramifications**
1. Slow-turning and/or too-high inventory	Excessive capital is tied up in inventory. The firm has high insurance costs, interest expenses, and high risks of pilferage and product obsolescence. Merchandise may be stale.
2. Inefficient customer service	Costs are high relative to the value of shipments; warehouses are poorly situated; inventory levels are not tied to customer demand.
3. A large number of interwarehouse shipments	Merchandise transfers raise physical distribution costs because items must be handled and verified at each warehouse.
4. Frequent use of emergency shipments	Extra charges add significantly to physical distribution costs.
5. Peripheral hauls and/or limited backhauling	The firm uses its own trucking facilities; but many hauls are too spread out and trucks may only be full one way.
6. A large number of small orders	Small orders often are unprofitable. Many distribution costs are fixed.
7. Excessive number of returns	The firm incurs high handling costs and may lose disgruntled customers.

---

[17] Patrick Burnson, "19th Annual State of Logistics Report: Under the Weather," http://www.logisticsmgmt.com/article/CA6576165.html (July 1, 2008).

[18] IBM and the Grocery Manufacturers Association, "The GMA 2008 Logistics Survey," http://www.gmabrands.com/publications/GMALogisticsStudy2008.pdf (2008).

Customer Service A chief concern in planning a firm's logistics program is the level of customer service it should provide. Decisions involve delivery frequency, speed, and consistency; the use of emergency shipments; whether to accept small orders; warehousing; coordinating assortments; whether to provide order progress reports (and when to do so online); the return policy (known as *reverse logistics*); and other factors. Weak performance may lose customers.

To provide the proper customer service, distribution standards—clear and measurable goals as to service levels in logistics—must be devised. Examples are filling 90 percent of orders from existing inventory, responding to customer requests for order information within two hours, filling orders with 99 percent accuracy, and limiting goods damaged in transit to 1 percent or less.

One way to set the proper customer service level is the ***total-cost approach***, whereby the distribution service level with the lowest total costs—including freight (shipping), warehousing, and lost business—is the best service level. Figure 14-10 illustrates the total-cost approach. An ideal system seeks a balance between low expenditures on distribution and high opportunities for sales. Seldom will that be at the lowest level of distribution spending; lost sales would be too great.

Through superior customer service, a firm may gain a major competitive advantage. The opposite is also true. For example, in the Middle East's Qatar, shortages of medicine are due to its weak logistics infrastructure. As one observer notes, "international manufacturers rely too heavily on local distributors who do not have the tools, training, finances, or software infrastructure to handle ever-increasing logistics requirements." Often, local distributors in Qatar are undercapitalized and inefficient in addressing customer needs. Professional logistics providers such as Pharma World Holdings "although prevalent abroad, are new to the Middle East. They allow for more effective and efficient operations to better meet customers' requirements."[19]

Logistics and Other Functional Areas There is an interaction between logistics and every aspect of marketing, as well as other functional areas in the firm, as the following indicate.

Product variations in color, size, features, quality, and style impose a burden on a firm's distribution network. Greater variety means lower volume per item, which increases unit shipping and warehousing costs. Stocking a broader range of replacement parts also becomes necessary.

> The **total-cost approach** considers both costs and opportunities.

> Logistics must be coordinated with other areas.

Figure 14-10

An Illustration of the Total-Cost Approach in Distribution

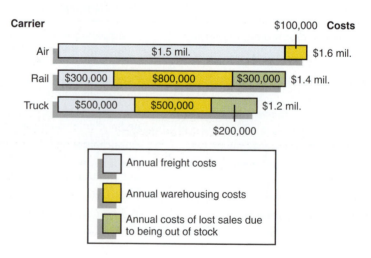

[19] "Burgeoning Logistic Demands Causing Qatar's Medicine Shortage," http://www.gulf-news.com/business/Commodities/10232216.html (July 27, 2008).

Logistics planning is related to the overall channel strategy. A firm seeking extensive distribution needs dispersed warehouses. One involved with perishables must be sure that most of a product's selling life is not spent in transit.

Promotion campaigns are often planned well in advance, so it is essential that resellers receive goods at the proper times. Resellers may get consumer complaints for not having sufficient quantities of advertised items, although the manufacturer is really at fault. Some new products fail or lag behind sales projections due to poor initial distribution. As noted in Chapter 13, this occurred when Sony PlayStation 3 (**http://www.us.playstation.com**) was introduced; the firm ran out of merchandise due to a parts shortage.

Logistics plays a part in pricing. A firm with fast, reliable delivery and in-stock replacement parts—that handles small orders and emergency shipments—can charge more than one with less service.

A logistics strategy is linked with production and finance functions. High freight costs motivate firms to put plants closer to markets. Low average inventories in stock allow firms to reduce finance charges. Warehouse receipts may be used as collateral for loans.

Overall, many decisions must be made and coordinated in planning a logistics strategy: the transportation form(s) used, inventory levels and warehouse form(s), and the number and sites of plants, warehouses, and shopping facilities. A strategy can be simple: A firm may have one plant, focus on one geographic market, and ship to resellers or customers without the use of decentralized warehouses. On the other hand, a strategy may include multiple plants, assembly and/or warehouse locations in each market, thousands of customer locations, and several transportation forms.

We now look at two central aspects of a logistics strategy: transportation and inventory management.

14-4b Transportation

Five basic *transportation forms* are used for shipping products, parts, raw materials, and so forth: railroads, motor carriers, waterways, pipelines, and airways. Table 14-6 shows the share of U.S. mileage and revenue for each. Table 14-7 ranks them on seven operating characteristics.

The deregulation of U.S. transportation industries has expanded the competition in and among these industries. Deregulation generally allows transportation firms to have greater flexibility in entering markets, expanding businesses, products carried, price setting, and functions performed. It also means more choice for those shipping. Each transportation form and three transport services are studied next.

> Transportation is rated on speed, availability, dependability, capability, frequency, losses, and cost. There are five major **transportation forms**: railroads, motor carriers, waterways, pipelines, and airways.

Table **14-6**	The Relative Share of U.S. Shipping Mileage and Revenue by Transportation Form	
Transportation Form	**Share of Ton-Miles Shipped**	**Share of Shipping Value**[a]
Railroads	38%	11%
Motor carriers	28	82
Waterways	14	1
Pipelines	20	3
Airways	less than 1	3

[a] Does not include multimodal shipping

Source: Computed by the authors from *National Transportation Statistics*, **http://www.bts.gov/publications/national_transportation_statistics** (Washington, DC: U.S. Bureau of Transportation Statistics, July 2008).

Table 14-7	The Relative Operating Characteristics of Five Transportation Forms				
Operating Characteristics	Ranking by Transportation Form[a]				
	Railroads	**Motor Carriers**	**Waterways**	**Pipelines**	**Airways**
Delivery speed	3	2	4	5	1
Number of locations served	2	1	4	5	3
On-time dependability[b]	3	2	4	1	5
Range of products carried	1	2	3	5	4
Frequency of shipments	4	2	5	1	3
Losses and damages	5	4	2	1	3
Cost per ton mile	3	4	2	1	5

[a] 1 = highest ranking.
[b] Relative variation from anticipated delivery time.

Source: Adapted by the authors from Donald J. Bowersox, David J. Closs, and M. Bixby Cooper, *Supply Chain Logistics Management*, Second Edition (NY: McGraw-Hill, 2006); Ronald H. Ballou, *Business Logistics/Supply Chain Management*, Fifth Edition (Upper Saddle River, NJ: Prentice Hall, 2004); James R. Stock and Douglas Lambert, *Strategic Logistics Management*, Fourth Edition (NY: McGraw-Hill, 2001); and *CSCMP Toolbox* (Oak Brook, IL: Council of Supply Chain Management Professionals, 2006).

Railroads *Railroads* usually carry heavy, bulky items that are low in value (relative to weight) over long distances. They ship items too heavy for trucks. Despite their position in ton-miles shipped, railroads have had problems. Fixed costs are high due to facility investments. Shippers face railroad car shortages in high-demand months for agricultural goods. Some tracks and railroad cars are in need of repair. Trucks are faster, more flexible, and packed more easily. In response, railroads are relying on new shipping techniques, operating flexibility, and mergers to improve efficiency.

Motor Carriers *Motor carriers* mostly transport small shipments over short distances. They handle the majority of U.S. shipments weighing less than 500 or 1,000 pounds. Seventy percent of all motor carriers are used for local deliveries and two-thirds of total truck miles are local. For these reasons, motor carriers account for a huge share of shipping revenue. Motor carriers are more flexible than rail because they can pick up packages at a factory or warehouse and deliver them to the customer's door. They often supplement rail, air, and other forms that cannot deliver directly to customers. In addition, trucks are faster than rail for short distances. Like railroads, the trucking industry has been deregulated since 1980. See Figure 14-11.

Waterways U.S. *waterways* are involved with the movement of goods on barges via inland rivers and on tankers and general-merchandise freighters through the Great Lakes, intercoastal shipping, and the St. Lawrence Seaway. They are used mostly for transporting low-value, high-bulk freight (such as coal, iron ore, gravel, grain, and cement). Waterways are slow and may be closed by ice in winter, but rates are quite low. Various improvements in vessel design have occurred over the years. For example, many "super-vessels" now operate on the Great Lakes and other waterways. They can each carry up to 60,000 gross tons or more of iron-bearing rock (or similar heavy materials) in one trip. Their conveyor systems are twice as efficient as the ones on older boats. Navigation is computer-controlled.

Pipelines Within *pipelines*, there is continuous movement and there are no interruptions, inventories (except those held by a carrier), and intermediate storage sites. Handling and labor costs are minimized. Although pipelines are very reliable, only certain commodities can be moved through them. In the past, emphasis was on gas and

Figure 14-11

Motor Carriers: Driving Most Distribution Channels

In terms of shipping value, motor carriers dominate the U.S. transportation network.

Source: Reprinted by permission.

petroleum products. Pipelines now handle coal and wood chips, which are sent as semiliquids. Still, the lack of flexibility limits their potential. Some pipelines are enormous. The Trans-Alaska Pipeline System (TAPS) is 48 inches in diameter and 800 miles long. In total, since TAPS began operations in 1977, it has transported 16 billion barrels of crude oil. It can discharge up to 2 million barrels daily. Oil is loaded from the pipeline to supervessels and then sent by water to the lower 48 states.

Airways *Airways* are the fastest, most expensive transportation form. High-value, perishable, and emergency goods dominate air shipments. Although air transit is costly, it may lower other costs, such as the need for outlying or even regional warehouses.

Ethical Issues in Marketing

Chargebacks and Markdown Money: Suppliers Fight Back Members

Chargebacks are deductions that retailers make from suppliers' bills. According to a study by the Credit Research Foundation (http://www.crfonline.org), the top five chargebacks relate to freight and routing issues, early or late deliveries, concealed shortages, errors associated with advance shipping notification or electronic data interchange (EDI), and ticketing and labeling issues.

In a related practice, many retailers require that vendors provide them with markdown money to reimburse them for goods sold below full price. Markdown monies can be effectively used by a supplier to entice a major retailer to stock an unproven designer's clothing line.

When used fairly, chargebacks reimburse retailers for extra costs or reduced sales opportunities associated with supplier errors, such as late deliveries. In practice, however, chargebacks and markdown monies are often used as a bargaining mechanism by powerful retailers. A number of abuses also are associated with these practices, such as a clothing designer that was charged

$750 for shipping goods by FedEx (http://www.fedex.com) instead of UPS (http://www.ups.com).

Kohl's (http://www.kohls.com) was sued by Fu Da International (http://www.fuda888.com.cn), a sportswear firm. Fu Da claimed that Kohl's held back payments for goods and stopped buying from Fu Da after it complained. London Fog (http://www.londonfog.com), a coat manufacturer, also filed a suit against Kohl's. In a similar action, International Design Concepts (IDC) (http://www.idc-design.com) filed a chargeback case asserting that Saks (http://www.saksfifthavenue.com) levied chargebacks and allowances on IDC's Oscar de la Renta women's sportswear line (http://www.oscardelarenta.com).

Sources: Based on material in William Atkinson, "Get in Charge of Your Chargebacks," *Multichannel Merchant* (January 2007), pp. 39–40; Doris Hajewski, "Supplier Sues Kohl's Over Markdown Deal; Clothing Maker Says Retailer Held Back Money," *The Milwaukee Sentinel* (July 9, 2008), p. D1; and "Saks Inc. Chargeback Case to Move Forward," *Home Textiles Today* (April 9, 2007), p. 10.

The costs of packing, unpacking, and preparing goods for shipping are lower than for other transportation forms. Airfreight has been deregulated since the late 1970s. Thus, many firms have stepped up their air cargo operations. Some now use wide-bodied jets for large containers. Modern communications and sorting equipment have also been added to airfreight operations. Firms specializing in air shipments stress speedy, guaranteed service at acceptable prices.

Transportation Services   Transportation service companies are marketing specialists that chiefly handle the shipments of small and moderate-sized packages. Some pick up at the sender's office and deliver direct to the addressee. Others require packages to be brought to a service company outlet. The major kinds of transportation service firms are government parcel post, private parcel, and express.

> These transportation service companies ship packages: government parcel post, private parcel, and express.

Parcel post from the U.S. Postal Service (**http://www.usps.com**) operates out of post offices and has rates based on postal zones, of which there are eight in the United States. Parcel post can be insured and it can be sent COD (collect on delivery). Regular service is completed in a few days. Special handling (at an extra cost) can expedite shipments. Express mail is available for next-day service from a post office to most addresses.

Private parcel services specialize in small-package delivery, usually less than 50 pounds. Most shipments go from businesses to their customers. Regular service generally takes two to three days. More expensive next-day service is also available from many carriers. The largest firm is United Parcel Service (**http://www.ups.com**), a multi-billion-dollar, global company that dominates the Internet delivery business.

Specialized express companies, such as Federal Express (**http://www.fedex.com**), do a lot of their business by providing guaranteed delivery of small packages within one or two days. The average express delivery is less than 10 pounds.

Coordinating Transportation   Because a single shipment may involve a combination of transportation forms, a practice known as *intermodal shipping*, coordination is needed. A firm can enhance its ability to coordinate shipments via containerization and freight forwarding.

With **containerization**, goods are placed in sturdy containers that can be loaded on trains, trucks, ships, or planes. The marked containers are sealed until delivered, thereby reducing damage and pilferage. Their progress and destination are monitored. The containers are mobile warehouses that can be moved from manufacturing plants to receiving docks, where they remain until the contents are needed.

> **Containerization** and **freight forwarding** simplify intermodal shipping.

In **freight forwarding**, specialized firms (freight forwarders) collect small shipments (usually less than 500 pounds each) from several companies. They pick up merchandise at each shipper's place of business and arrange for delivery at buyers' doors. Freight forwarders prosper because less than carload (lcl) shipping rates are sharply higher than carload (cl) rates. They also provide traffic management services, such as selecting the best transportation form at the most reasonable rate. The online *Directory of Freight Forwarding Services* (**http://www.forwarders.com**) has a good listing of freight forwarders by name. Menlo Worldwide (**http://www.menloworldwide.com**) is an industry leader in this aspect of logistics.

The Legal Status of Transportation Firms   Transportation firms are categorized as common, contract, exempt, and/or private carriers. **Common carriers** must transport the goods of any company (or individual) interested in their services; they cannot refuse shipments unless their rules are broken (such as packing requirements). Common carriers provide service on a fixed, publicized schedule between designated points. Fees are published. All railroads and petroleum pipelines and some air, motor vehicle, and water transporters are common carriers.

> Carriers are classified as **common, contract, exempt, or private.**

Contract carriers provide transportation services to one or more shippers, based on individual agreements. Contract carriers do not have to maintain set routes or schedules and may negotiate rates. Many motor vehicle, inland waterway, and airfreight firms are contract carriers. Firms can operate as both common and contract carriers, depending on their services.

Exempt carriers are excused from legal regulations and must only comply with safety rules. They are specified by law. Some commodities moved by water and most agricultural goods are exempt carriers.

Private carriers are firms with their own transportation facilities. They are subject to safety rules. In the United States, there are more than 100,000 private carriers.

14-4c   Inventory Management

The intent of *inventory management* is to provide a continuous flow of goods and to match the quantity of goods kept in inventory as closely as possible with customer demand. When production or consumption is seasonal or erratic, this can be particularly difficult.

Inventory management has broad implications: A manufacturer or service firm cannot afford to run out of a crucial part that could halt its business. Yet, inventory on hand should not be too large because the costs of storing raw materials, parts, and/or finished products can be substantial. If models change yearly, as with autos, large inventories can adversely affect new-product sales or rentals. Excessive stock may also lead to stale goods, cause a firm to mark down prices, and tie up funds. Thus, a pulling strategy by a manufacturer may be hard for a reseller to react to quickly.

A lot of companies are now applying either or both of two complementary concepts to improve their inventory management: a just-in-time inventory system and electronic data interchange. With a *just-in-time (JIT) inventory system*, a purchasing firm reduces the amount of inventory it keeps on hand by ordering more often and in lower quantity. This means better planning and data on the part of the buyer, collaborative computer systems, geographically closer sellers, improved buyer-seller relationships, and better production and distribution facilities. To retailers, a JIT system is known as a *quick response (QR) inventory system*—a cooperative effort between retailers and suppliers to reduce retail inventory while providing a merchandise supply that more closely addresses the actual buying patterns of consumers.

JIT and QR systems are being used by virtually all auto makers, Black & Decker (**http://www.blackanddecker.com**), Boeing (**http://www.boeing.com**), DuPont (**http://www.dupont.com**), General Electric (**http://www.ge.com**), Hewlett-Packard (**http://www.hp.com**), Levi Strauss (**http://www.levistrauss.com**), Limited Brands (**http://www.limited.com**), Motorola (**http://www.motorola.com**), Wal-Mart (**http://www.walmart.com**), and numerous other large and small firms. For example, when a Camry (**http://www.toyota.com/camry**) lands at Toyota's Kentucky paint shop, a seat order—color, fabric, and type (bench or bucket)—is sent by computer to a nearby Johnson Controls (**http://www.johnsoncontrols.com**) factory. Just hours later, the seat can be installed in the Camry. Johnson Controls provides similar service for a dozen other auto makers.

Through *electronic data interchange (EDI)*, suppliers and their manufacturers/service providers, wholesalers, and/or retailers exchange data via computer linkups. This lets firms maximize revenues, reduce markdowns, and lower inventory-carrying costs by speeding the flow of data and products. For EDI to work well, each firm in a distribution channel must use the Universal Product Code (UPC) and electronically exchange data. To learn more about electronic data interchange, visit "What Is EDI?" (**http://www.wisegeek.com/what-is-edi.htm**).

Four specific aspects of inventory management are examined next: stock turnover, when to reorder, how much to reorder, and warehousing.

Stock Turnover

Stock turnover—the number of times during a stated period (usually one year) that average inventory on hand is sold—shows the relationship between a firm's sales and the inventory level it maintains. It is calculated in units or dollars (in selling price or at cost):

> **Inventory management** deals with the flow and allocation of products.

> **Just-in-time (JIT)** and **quick response (QR) inventory systems** monitor inventory levels.

> With **electronic data interchange (EDI)**, computers are used to exchange information between suppliers and their customers.

> **Stock turnover** shows the ratio between sales and average inventory.

Marketing and the Web

eBay and Its Sellers: Big Firms Happy, Small Firms Not So Much

During January 2008, eBay (http://www.eBay.com) announced major changes in its pricing strategy with its sellers. The new structure reduced fees by as much as 25 percent for listing items in an auction and as much as 50 percent for items with fixed prices. And eBay's fees now decrease as an item's price goes up. Also, eBay gives its Power Sellers, those rated highest, a discount of up to 15 percent on the final fee. However, smaller merchants that sell goods priced at $100 or less have had their rates increased.

Some marketing analysts say they were not surprised at eBay's seeking to enhance its appeal to large merchants that sell items at fixed prices. They view eBay's new pricing structure as a way to better compete with Amazon.com (http://www.amazon.com) and Google (http://www.google.com), as well as merchants with their own Web sites. As an example of eBay's shift in strategy to favor large sellers, eBay now allows Buy.com (http://www.buy.com) to sells its books, DVDs, electronics, and other items

through 5 million fixed-price listings at a significantly reduced fee. Though details of Buy.com's deal are confidential, some observers believe that the extent of Buy.com's listings on eBay indicate that Buy.com is probably not paying any listing fees to eBay, only commission fees.

There is little doubt that eBay's revised pricing strategy was designed to stimulate demand. Before the changes took place, eBay had experienced only a one percent increase in its year-old active user count of 83.9 million. eBay also wants to attract more large merchants that offer services such as free shipping in order to improve eBay's customer feedback ratings.

Sources: Based on material in Stacy Cowley, "eBay CEO: Tough Seller Rules Here to Stay," http://money.cnn.com/2008/04/16/smbusiness/ebay_q1.fsb (April 17, 2008); Catherine Holahan, "eBay Courts 'Power Sellers,'" http://www.businessweek.com/technology (January 29, 2008); and Brad Stone, "Buy.com Deal with eBay Angers Sellers," *New York Times* (July 18, 2008), p. B8.

$$\text{Annual rate of stock turnover} = \frac{\text{Number of units sold during year}}{\text{Average inventory on hand (in units)}}$$

or

$$= \frac{\text{Net yearly sales}}{\text{Average inventory on hand (valued in sales dollars)}}$$

or

$$= \frac{\text{Cost of goods sold}}{\text{Average inventory on hand (valued at cost)}}$$

For example, in retailing, average annual stock turnover ranges from less than 2 in jewelry stores to 45 or more in gasoline service stations.

A high turnover rate has many advantages: inventory investments are productive, items are fresh, losses from style changes are reduced, and inventory costs (such as insurance, breakage, warehousing, and credit) are lower. Turnover can be improved by reducing assortments, dropping slow-selling items, keeping only small amounts of some items, and buying from suppliers that deliver on time. On the other hand, too high a turnover rate may have adverse effects: small purchases may cause a loss of volume discounts, low assortment may reduce sales volume if consumers do not have enough choice or related items are not carried, discounts may be needed to lift sales, and chances of running out of stock go up if average inventory size is low. Figure 14-12 shows how people can act should a firm run out of stock.

Knowing when to reorder helps protect against stockouts while minimizing inventory investments.

When to Reorder Inventory A firm sets the inventory levels at which to place new orders by having a specified *reorder point* for each of its products (or raw materials or parts). A reorder point depends on order lead time, the usage rate, and safety stock.

> The **reorder point** is based on lead time, usage, and safety stock.

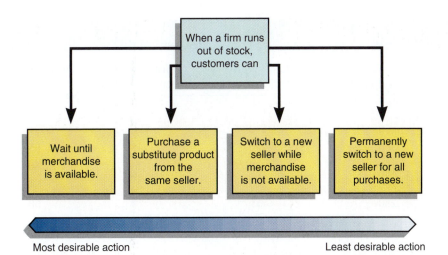

Figure 14-12

What Happens When a Firm Has Stock Shortages

Order lead time is the period from the date of an order until the date items are ready to sell or use (received, checked, and altered, if needed). *Usage rate* is the average unit sales (for a reseller) or the rate at which a product is used in production (for a manufacturer). *Safety stock* is extra inventory to guard against being out of stock due to unexpectedly high demand or production and delivery delays.

The reorder point formula is

$$\text{Reorder point} = (\text{Order lead time} \times \text{Usage rate}) + (\text{Safety stock})$$

A wholesaler that needs 4 days for its purchase orders to be placed and received, sells 10 items per day, and wants to have 10 extra items on hand in case a delivery is delayed by one day, has a reorder point of 50 [$(4 \times 10) + (10)$]. Without safety stock, the firm would lose 10 sales if it orders when inventory is 40 items and the items are received in 5 days.

How Much to Reorder   A firm must decide on its *order size*—the right amount of products, parts, and so on, to buy at one time. This depends on volume discounts, the firm's resources, the stock turnover rate, the costs of processing each order, and the costs of holding goods in inventory. If a firm places large orders, quantity discounts are often available, a large part of its finances are tied up in inventory, its stock turnover rate is relatively low, per-order processing costs are low, and inventory costs are generally high. The firm is also less apt to run out of goods. The opposite is true for small orders.

Many firms seek to balance order-processing costs (filling out forms, computer time, and product handling) and inventory-holding costs (warehouse expenses, interest charges, insurance, deterioration, and theft). Processing costs per unit fall as orders get bigger, but inventory costs rise. The *economic order quantity (EOQ)* is the order volume corresponding to the lowest sum of order-processing and inventory-holding costs. Table 14-8 shows three ways to compute EOQ for a firm with an annual demand of 3,000 units for a product; the cost of each unit is $1; order-processing costs are $3 per order; and inventory-holding costs equal 20 percent of each item's cost. As shown in the table, the economic order quantity is 300 units. Thus, the firm should place orders of 300 units and have 10 orders per year.

Economic order quantity (EOQ) balances ordering and inventory costs.

Warehousing   *Warehousing* involves the physical facilities used to store, identify, and sort goods in expectation of their sale and transfer within a distribution channel. Warehouses can be used to store goods, prepare goods for shipment, coordinate shipments, send orders, and aid in product recalls.

Private warehouses are owned and operated by firms that store and distribute their own products. They are most likely to be used by those with stable inventory levels and long-run plans to serve the same geographic areas.

Warehousing involves storing and dispatching goods.

Table 14-8   Computing an Economic Order Quantity

A.

Order Quantity (Units)	Average Inventory Maintained (Units)[a]	Annual Inventory- Holding Costs[b]	Annual Order- Processing Costs[c]	Annual Total Costs
100	50	$10	$90	$100
200	100	20	45	65
EOQ→ 300	150	30	30	60
400	200	40	24	64
500	250	50	18	68

B.

Graph: Total costs (vertical axis, 0 to 100) vs. Order quantity (Units) (horizontal axis, 100 to 500), showing Total costs, Holding costs, and Order-processing costs curves, with EOQ arrow pointing to order quantity 300.

C.

$$EOQ = \sqrt{\frac{2DS}{IC}} = \sqrt{\frac{2(3,000)(\$3)}{0.20(\$1)}} = 300$$

where   EOQ = Order quantity (units)

D = Annual demand (units)

S = Costs to place an order ($)

I = Annual holding costs (as a % of unit costs)

C = Unit cost of an item ($)

[a] The average inventory on hand = 1/2 × Order quantity.

[b] Inventory-holding costs = Annual holding costs as a percent of unit cost × Unit cost × Average inventory.

[c] Order-processing costs = Number of annual orders × Costs to place an order. Number of orders = Annual demand/Order quantity.

Public warehouses provide storage and related distribution services to any interested firm or individual on a rental basis. They are used by small firms without the resources or desire to have their own facilities, larger firms that need more storage space (if their own warehouses are full), or any size of firm entering a new area. They offer shipping economies by allowing carload shipments to be made to warehouses in local markets; then short-distance, smaller shipments are made to customers. Firms can also reduce their investments in facilities and maximize flexibility by using public warehouses. If products must be recalled, these warehouses can be used as collection points, where items are separated, disposed of, and/or salvaged. There are thousands of public warehouses in the United States.

Public warehouses can accommodate both bonded warehousing and field warehousing. In bonded warehousing, imported or taxable goods are stored and can be released for sale only after applicable taxes are paid. This enables firms to postpone tax payments until they are ready to make deliveries to customers. Cigarettes and liquor are often stored in bonded warehouses. In field warehousing, a receipt is issued by a public warehouse for goods stored in a private warehouse or in transit to consumers. The goods are put in a special area, and the field warehouser is responsible for them. A firm may use field warehousing because a warehouse receipt serves as collateral for a loan.

The most high-tech distribution center is automated and uses computer technology to replace people with machines. Both private and public warehouses are now more automated.

Web Sites You Can Use

These Web sites offer a lot of information pertaining to the value chain and distribution planning.

- *Inbound Logistics* (**http://www.inboundlogistics.com**)
- *IndustryWeek's Value/Supply Chain* (**http://www. industryweek.com/section.aspx?sectionid=11**)
- Logistics Online (**http://www.logisticsonline.com**)

- QuickMBA (**http://www.quickmba.com/strategy/ value-chain**)
- Supply Chain Management articles (**http://www.bpubs. com/Management_Science/Supply_Chain_Management**)
- *Supply Chain Management Review* (**http://www.scmr.com**)

Summary

1. *To discuss the role of the value chain and the value delivery chain in the distribution process*   The distribution process has four stages: goals, value chain and value delivery chain, total delivered product, and level of satisfaction.

   In many channels, there are three participants: suppliers/manufacturers, distribution intermediaries, and customers. The goals of each must be determined, exchanged, and reconciled.

   A value chain has two components: the value chain itself and the value delivery chain. A value chain represents the series of business activities that are performed to design, produce, market, deliver, and service a product for customers. A value delivery chain encompasses all of the parties who engage in value chain activities. It is performer-based and involves three factors: the specific parties in a given value chain, their relationships, and the activities undertaken by each party. A delivery chain is only as strong as its weakest link. Win-win-win is a delivery chain goal.

   The total delivered product comprises the tangible and intangible product attributes that are actually provided to consumers. From a distribution perspective, the total delivered product reflects how well the activities in the distribution process are performed. The Web is a promising tool to enhance the total delivered product, sometimes by adding value and other times by reducing costs.

   The final stage is the level of satisfaction with the distribution process, whereby the satisfaction of each party is determined and related to its goals.

2. *To explore distribution planning and review its importance, distribution functions, the factors used in selecting a distribution channel, and the different types of distribution channels*   Distribution planning systematically deals with the physical movement of goods and services from producer to consumer, as well as the related transfer of ownership (or rental). A channel of distribution consists of the organizations

or people—known as channel members or distribution intermediaries—involved in the distribution process.

Distribution decisions often affect a firm's marketing plans. For many firms, the choice of a distribution channel is one of their most important decisions. More companies now realize the value of relationship marketing and strive for long-term relations with suppliers, intermediaries, and customers. Both costs and profits are affected by the channel chosen. Firms may have to conform to existing channel patterns, and their markets' size and nature are also affected by the channel used.

No matter who performs them, channel functions include research, buying, promotion, customer services, product planning, pricing, and distribution. Intermediaries can play a key role by doing various tasks and resolving differences in manufacturer and consumer goals via the sorting process.

These factors must be considered in selecting a method of distribution: the consumer, the company, the product, the competition, the distribution channels themselves, and legal requirements.

A direct channel requires that one party do all distribution tasks; in an indirect channel, tasks are done by multiple parties. In comparing methods, a firm must weigh its costs and abilities against control and total sales. An indirect channel may use a contractual or an administered agreement. A long channel has many levels of independents; a wide one has many firms at any stage. A channel may be exclusive, selective, or intensive, based on goals, resellers, customers, and marketing. A dual channel (multichannel distribution) lets a company operate via two or more distribution methods.

3. *To consider the nature of distribution intermediary contracts, cooperation and conflict in a channel of distribution, the special aspects of a distribution channel for industrial*

products, and international distribution In supplier/ distribution intermediary contracts, price policies, sale conditions, territorial rights, the services/responsibility mix, and contract length and termination conditions are specified.

Cooperation and conflict may occur in a channel. Conflicts must be settled fairly; confrontation can cause hostility and negative acts by all parties. Frequently, a pushing strategy—based on channel cooperation—can be used by established firms. A pulling strategy—based on proving that demand exists prior to gaining intermediary support or acceptance—must be used by many new companies.

An industrial channel normally does not use retailers; it is more direct, entails larger orders and fewer transactions, requires specification selling and knowing resellers, uses team selling and special intermediaries, includes more leasing, provides more technical data, and embraces shared activities.

Channel length depends on a nation's stage of economic development and consumer behavior. Distribution practices and structures differ by nation. International decisions must be made as to shipping and intermediaries. Each country has distinct legal provisions pertaining to distribution.

4. *To examine logistics and demonstrate its importance* Logistics (physical distribution) involves efficiently delivering products to designated places, at designated times, and in proper condition. It may be undertaken by any member of a channel, from producer to consumer.

There are various reasons for studying logistics: its costs, the value of customer service, and its relationship with other functional areas in a firm. With the total-cost approach, the service level with the lowest total cost (including freight, warehousing, and lost business) is the best one. In a logistics strategy, choices are made as to transportation, inventory levels, warehousing, and facility locations.

5. *To discuss transportation alternatives and inventory management issues* Railroads usually carry bulky goods for long distances. Motor carriers dominate small shipments over short distances. Waterways ship low-value freight. Pipelines provide ongoing movement of liquids, gases, and semiliquids. Airways offer fast, costly shipping of perishables and high-value items. Transportation specialists mostly handle small and medium-sized packages. Coordination can be improved by containerization and freight forwarding. There are common, contract, exempt, and private carriers.

Inventory management needs to provide a continuous flow of goods and match the stock kept in inventory as closely as possible with demand. In a just-in-time (JIT) or quick response (QR) system, the purchasing firm reduces the stock on hand by ordering more often and in lower quantity. With electronic data interchange (EDI), channel members exchange information via computer linkages.

The interplay between a firm's sales and the inventory level it keeps is expressed by stock turnover. A reorder point shows the inventory level when goods must be reordered. The economic order quantity (EOQ) is the optimal amount of goods to order based on order-processing and inventory-holding costs. Warehousing decisions include selecting a private or public warehouse and examining the availability of public warehouse services.

Key Terms

value chain (p. 436)

value delivery chain (p. 437)

total delivered product (p. 438)

distribution planning (p. 439)

channel of distribution (p. 439)

channel members (p. 439)

distribution intermediaries (p. 439)

channel functions (p. 443)

sorting process (p. 444)

direct channel of distribution (p. 444)

indirect channel of distribution (p. 444)

exclusive distribution (p. 446)

selective distribution (p. 446)

intensive distribution (p. 446)

dual channel of distribution (multichannel distribution) (p. 447)

pushing strategy (p. 450)

pulling strategy (p. 450)

logistics (physical distribution) (p. 452)

total-cost approach (p. 454)

transportation forms (p. 455)

containerization (p. 458)

freight forwarding (p. 458)

common carriers (p. 458)

contract carriers (p. 458)

exempt carriers (p. 459)

private carriers (p. 459)

inventory management (p. 459)

just-in-time (JIT) inventory system (p. 459)

quick response (QR) inventory system (p. 459)

electronic data interchange (EDI) (p. 459)

stock turnover (p. 459)

reorder point (p. 460)

economic order quantity (EOQ) (p. 461)

warehousing (p. 461)

Review Questions

1. Distinguish between the terms *value chain*, *value delivery chain*, and *total delivered product*. Provide an example in your answer.
2. Explain the sorting process. Provide an example in your answer.
3. Which factors influence the selection of a distribution channel?
4. Under what circumstances should a company engage in direct distribution? Indirect distribution?
5. Explain how a product could move from exclusive to selective to intensive distribution.
6. Compare motor carrier and airfreight deliveries on the basis of the total-cost approach.
7. The average stock turnover rate in jewelry stores is less than 2. What does this mean? How could a jewelry store raise its turnover rate?
8. Two wholesalers sell identical merchandise. Yet, one plans a safety stock equal to 50 percent of expected sales, while the other plans safety stock of 25 percent of expected sales. Comment on this difference.

Discussion Questions

1. What distribution decisions would a leading manufacturer that leases video equipment to small businesses have to make?
2. Devise distribution channels for the sale of video games, magazines, and women's shoes. Explain your choices.
3. Present a checklist that a firm could use in making international distribution decisions on a country-by-country basis.
4. Develop a list of distribution standards for a firm delivering barbeque grills for Father's Day.

Web Exercise

Logistics Management (**http://www.logisticsmgmt.com**) calls itself the Web site for "News and Business Practices for the Logistics and Supply Chain Profession." Visit the site and then describe what kinds of valuable information could be acquired by logistics managers.

Practice Quiz

1. Which statement concerning the value chain is *not* correct?
   a. Value is added by each participant.
   b. A valid delivery chain goal is for one channel member to win at another member's expense.
   c. A value delivery chain involves all the parties and their respective tasks.
   d. A value delivery chain is only as strong as its weakest link.

2. A common characteristic of a value chain is
   a. outsourcing activities to selected channel members.
   b. channel conflict among channel members.
   c. a win-lose relationship.
   d. the search for low-cost, low-quality alternatives.

3. Which of the following is an aspect of distribution planning?
   a. Product management
   b. Advertising
   c. Manufacturing
   d. Customer transactions

4. Which of the following is the intermediary task of apportioning items to various consumer markets?
   a. Accumulation
   b. Allocation
   c. Assorting
   d. Sorting

5. Indirect channels of distribution are most frequently used by firms that
   a. want to increase sales volume.
   b. wish to maximize their customer interactions.
   c. absorb many distribution costs.
   d. service limited target markets.

6. In describing a channel of distribution, *width* refers to
   a. the levels of independent members along a channel.
   b. the number of independent members that are at any stage of distribution.
   c. ownership of companies at different stages in the channel.
   d. acquisition of businesses at the same stage in the channel.

7. Broadening its distribution channel enables a firm to
   a. be more self-sufficient.
   b. eliminate intermediary costs.
   c. coordinate the timing of products through the channel.
   d. increase its market share.

8. With exclusive distribution, a firm
   a. seeks the best possible customer service by resellers.
   b. seeks mass market appeal.
   c. maximizes total sales.
   d. reduces per-unit profit margins.

9. Logistics costs amount to about what percent of the U.S. GDP?
   a. Under 5
   b. 10
   c. 15
   d. 20

10. Many retailers spend what percent of revenues on physical distribution activities?
    a. Under 5
    b. 11-20
    c. 21-30
    d. 31-40

11. Heavy, bulky items that are low in value (relative to their weight) and transported over long distances are usually carried by
    a. airways.
    b. pipelines.
    c. railroads.
    d. trucks.

12. Stock turnover is the balance between
    a. reorder point and economic order quantity.
    b. usage rate and order-processing costs.
    c. sales and inventory on hand.
    d. order lead time and safety stock.

13. Which of these is an attribute of a high inventory turnover rate?
    a. Items are more likely to be stale.
    b. Losses from style changes are greater.
    c. Inventory investments are greater.
    d. The chances of running out of stock are greater.

14. Which of the following is *not* used in the calculation of a reorder point?
    a. Order style
    b. Order lead time
    c. Safety stock
    d. Usage rate

15. Firms with stable inventory levels and long-run plans to serve the same geographic areas tend to use
    a. public warehousing.
    b. private warehousing.
    c. generic warehousing.
    d. defined warehousing.

For the answers to these questions, please visit the online site for this book at **http://www.atomicdog.com**.

Chapter 15

Wholesaling

McKesson Corporation (**http://www.mckesson.com**), with annual sales exceeding $100 billion, is the largest and oldest U.S. pharmaceutical distributor. It traces its roots to 1833, when John McKesson opened a drugstore in New York City. McKesson conducts its business in two business groups: distribution solutions and technology solutions.

McKesson's distribution solutions business accounts for 97 percent of total revenues. To best service customers, its distribution centers are all equipped with a proprietary Acumax Plus software system that tracks the receipt of merchandise—and orders—using barcode technology, wrist-mounted computer hardware, and radio frequency signals. This system achieves 99.9 percent accuracy in order fulfillment. Technology solutions offers software and related support services to healthcare organizations.

McKesson's distribution solutions unit serves multiple groups of customers, including: retail chains (such as drugstores, food/drug combination stores, mail-order pharmacies, and mass merchandisers with drugstores), independent retail pharmacies, and institutional healthcare providers (including hospitals, clinics, and long-term care providers). Each segment requires a different combination of services from McKesson. Retail chains often want to reduce their labor costs by having prescriptions for multiple stores filled by a pharmacist in a central location. Chains also want to reduce their inventory-carrying costs by using McKesson's sophisticated inventory and automatic replenishment system.

In contrast, independent pharmacies want to (a) combine their purchases to obtain quantity discounts, (b) use McKesson's software to better process managed-care reimbursements, (c) be given a selection of generics from one source at significant savings, and (d) have access to profitability analysis tools. Pharmacies that are affiliated with McKesson's franchise program receive signage that identifies their stores as part of McKesson's Health Mart network. McKesson also offers these pharmacies in-store promotions.

Institutional healthcare providers are more concerned with electronic ordering and supply chain management programs to save labor costs, and with software that accelerates reimbursement from insurance companies and government agencies.[1]

In this chapter, we will further study wholesalers' relationships with their suppliers and customers. We will also examine the different types of firms that perform wholesaling activities and their strategies.

Chapter Objectives

1. To define wholesaling and show its importance
2. To describe the three broad categories of wholesaling (manufacturer/service provider wholesaling, merchant wholesaling, and agents and brokers) and the specific types of firms within each category
3. To examine recent trends in wholesaling

15-1 OVERVIEW

Wholesaling is the buying/handling of products and their resale to organizational buyers.

Wholesaling encompasses the buying and/or handling of goods and services and their subsequent resale to organizational users, retailers, and/or other wholesalers—but not the sale of significant volume to final consumers. It assumes many functions in a distribution channel, particularly those in the sorting process.

---

[1] Various company and other sources.

Manufacturers and service providers can be their own wholesalers or employ independent firms. Independents may or may not take title to or possession of products, depending on the type of wholesaling. Some independents have limited tasks; others do many functions.

Industrial, commercial, and government institutions are wholesalers' leading customers, followed closely by retailers. Sales from one wholesaler to another also represent a significant proportion of wholesaling activity. The following list shows the diversity of transactions considered as wholesaling:

- Sales of goods and services to manufacturers, service providers, oil refiners, railroads, public utilities, and government departments.
- Sales of office or laboratory equipment, supplies, and services to professionals such as doctors, chiropractors, and dentists.
- Sales of materials and services to builders of offices and homes.
- Sales to grocery stores, restaurants, hotels, apparel stores, stationery stores, and all other retailers.
- Manufacturer/service provider sales to wholesalers, and wholesaler sales to other wholesalers.

In this chapter, the importance of wholesaling, the different types of wholesaling, and recent trends in wholesaling are all discussed in depth.

15-2 THE IMPORTANCE OF WHOLESALING

Wholesaling is a vital aspect of distribution because of its impact on the economy, its functions in the distribution channel, and its relationships with suppliers and customers.

> Wholesale sales are high, and wholesalers greatly affect final prices.

15-2a Wholesaling's Impact on the Economy

In the United States, there are about 440,000 wholesale establishments with total annual sales of $6.5 trillion (including manufacturers with wholesale facilities); yet, although wholesale revenues are higher than those in retailing, there are several times as many retail establishments as wholesale.[2] According to the National Association of Wholesaler-Distributors (**http://www.naw.org**), U.S. wholesalers generate more than one-fifth of their total revenues from foreign markets.

Revenues are high because wholesaling entails any purchases by businesses and other organizations. Some products also move through multiple levels of wholesalers (such as regional and then local); an item can be sold two or three times at the wholesale level. There are far more retailers because they serve individual, dispersed final consumers; wholesalers handle fewer, larger, more concentrated customers.

From a cost perspective, many wholesalers have a big impact on prices. Table 15-1 shows the percent of wholesale selling prices that go to wholesalers to cover operating expenses and pre-tax profits. For example, 28.1 percent of the prices a hardware wholesaler charges its retailers cover that wholesaler's operating expenses and profits. Expenses include inventory handling, sales force salaries, ads, and rent.

Wholesaler costs and profits depend on inventory turnover, the dollar value of products, the functions performed, efficiency, and competition.

---

[2] Authors' estimates based on *Statistical Abstract of the United States 2008*, http://www.census.gov/compendia/statab/2008edition.html (June 3, 2008); and other sources.

Table 15-1	Gross Profit Data for U.S. Wholesalers by Product Category (Excluding Manufacturer Wholesaling)
Product Category of Wholesaler	**Gross Profit (As % of Sales)**
Total	18.9[a]
Durable Goods	23.5
Motor vehicle and motor vehicle parts and supplies	16.3
Furniture and home furnishings	31.0
Lumber & other construction materials	22.0
Professional and commercial equipment and supplies	25.9
Computer and peripheral equipment and software	16.8
Metals and minerals, except petroleum	23.4
Electrical goods	22.8
Hardware, and plumbing and heating equipment & supplies	28.1
Machinery, equipment, and supplies	28.1
Miscellaneous durable goods	21.5
Nondurable Goods	14.5
Paper and paper products	22.7
Drugs and druggists' sundries	8.6
Apparel, piece goods, and notions	30.9
Groceries and related products	15.4
Farm product raw materials	13.5
Chemicals and allied products	23.2
Petroleum and petroleum products	6.5
Beer, wine, and distilled alcoholic beverages	25.9
Miscellaneous nondurable goods	17.5

[a]Total costs of wholesaling, which include expenses and profit.

Source: 2006 Annual Wholesale Trade Report (Washington, DC: U.S. Census Bureau, February 21, 2008).

15-2b   The Functions of Wholesalers

Wholesalers can:

> Wholesalers perform tasks ranging from distribution to risk taking.

- enable manufacturers and service providers to distribute locally without making customer contacts.
- provide a trained sales force.
- offer marketing and research support for manufacturers, service providers, retailers, and other organizations.
- gather assortments for customers and let them make fewer transactions.
- purchase and/or handle large quantities, thus reducing total physical distribution costs.
- maintain warehousing and delivery facilities.
- put forward financing for manufacturers and service providers (by paying for products when shipped, not when sold) and retailer and other organizations (by granting credit).
- handle financial records.
- process returns and make adjustments for defective merchandise.
- take risks by being responsible for theft, deterioration, and obsolescence of inventory.

Wholesalers that take title to and possession of products usually perform several or all of these tasks. Agents and brokers that facilitate sales, but do not take title or possession, have more limited duties.

Independent wholesalers vary by industry. Most consumer products, food items, replacement parts, and office supplies are sold by independents. Yet, for heavy equipment, mainframe computers, gasoline, and temporary employment, manufacturers and service providers may bypass independent resellers.

Without independent wholesalers, b-to-b consumers have to develop their own supplier contacts, deal with a number of suppliers and coordinate shipments, do more distribution functions, stock greater quantities, and place more emphasis on an internal purchasing agent or department. Many small retailers and other firms might be avoided as customers because they might not be profitably reached by a manufacturer or service provider, and they might not be able to buy necessary items elsewhere.

An illustration of wholesaling's value is the U.S. auto parts industry, in which there used to be thousands of firms making a wide range of products and marketing them through a multitude of sales organizations. At that time, customers (mostly specialty stores and service stations) faced constant interruptions by salespeople, and manufacturers' sales costs were high. A better system exists today with the organized use of a much smaller number of independent distributors.

15-2c   Wholesalers' Relationships with Suppliers and Customers

Independent wholesalers are often caught "in the middle," not knowing whether their allegiance is more to manufacturers/service providers or their own customers. This is the challenge wholesalers face: "'I have a hard time trying to understand the value [wholesalers] are bringing,'" says the marketing director at Express Manufacturing (**http://www.eminc.com**), a $50 million (sales) maker of circuit boards for telecom

> Wholesalers have obligations to both suppliers and customers.

Marketing and the Web

Source 1: Selling Aftermarket Products to Distributors

Source 1 (**http://www.source1parts.com**) is a full-line wholesaler of replacement parts and supplies for heating, ventilation, and air-conditioning equipment (HVAC). Frank Kern of Source 1 says, "We offer the brands and breadth of products to make us a one-stop supplier." The products fit into specific groups, including installation-related, service-related, and consumables (such as refrigerants and sealants).

Although Source 1 is a full-line wholesaler, it does not sell every possible HVAC product. Kern notes, "We identify products that we can supply at competitive prices with the brands and breadth of offerings that our customers tell us they require. We also identify those products that are beyond our competency either from a pricing, freight, or brand perspective, and in some cases, we elect not to offer those products."

Source 1 has an integrated marketing communications program. This consists of a coordinated use of signage, a counter salesperson training program, and a Web site (**http://www.source1parts.com**). This site includes an online product catalog, a listing of distributor news and events, and a library of downloadable publications. There is also a secure members-only Web site for confidential information.

The Web site is designed to encourage Source 1's customers to continually use it. The online catalog is organized so customers can look up parts by specific categories. The news and events section includes key product information and monthly specials. And the publications section includes training materials in PowerPoint format, product specification sheets, and calendars with important dates from a marketing perspective.

Sources: Based on material in "Building a Partnership with Distributors," *Air Conditioning, Heating & Refrigeration News* (August 20, 2007), pp. 12, 14.

and water systems. Express tried letting a big wholesale distributor manage its component inventory on-site but eventually dropped the service because it figured it could manage on its own."[3]

Many wholesalers feel they get scant support from manufacturers/service providers. They desire training, technical assistance, product literature, and advertising. They dislike it when vendors alter territories, add new distributors to cover an existing geographic area, or decide to change to a direct channel and do wholesale tasks themselves. Wholesalers want manufacturers/service providers to sell to them and not through them. *Selling to the wholesaler* means a distributor is viewed as a customer to be researched and satisfied. *Selling through the wholesaler* means retailers or consumers are objects of manufacturers'/service providers' interest and wholesalers are less important. See Figure 15-1.

To remedy the situation, the best wholesalers are aggressively adapting to the marketplace:

> If they aren't selling to new markets, chances are distributors [wholesalers] have made themselves invaluable to their existing customer base. That's the case at Consumers Interstate (**http://www.cicgo.com**), a janitorial, safety, paper products, and office supplies distributor based in Connecticut. The company president says his customer base has not changed drastically in recent years, despite the poor health of the manufacturing industry in the United States. Though he has picked up business selling to Connecticut's casinos, which have emerged in the last 10 years or so, manufacturers still remain his company's emphasis: "We've remained focused on the manufacturing industry—and that's been terrible. But there's still a lot of market share for us. We're growing every year, and we're enjoying it." Consumers Interstate has grown because it's found ways to make those customers run more efficiently. The firm has helped manufacturers find better ways of ordering supplies, for one thing—specifically, by using an Internet procurement method that saves time and money. It also has added to its product base, enabling customers to buy more from one source.[4]

See Figure 15-2.

Figure 15-1

Selling TO Versus Selling THROUGH the Wholesaler

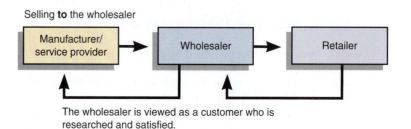

Selling **to** the wholesaler

The wholesaler is viewed as a customer who is researched and satisfied.

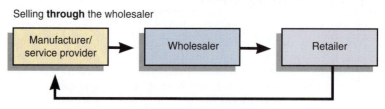

Selling **through** the wholesaler

The retailer (or final consumer) is the object of the manufacturer's/service provider's interests. The needs of the wholesaler are considered unimportant.

---

[3] Nelson Brett, "Stuck in the Middle," *Forbes* (August 15, 2005), pp. 88–89.

[4] Victoria Fraza Kickham, "Distributors Change with the Times," *Industrial Distribution* (August 2005), pp. 15–16.

Figure 15-2

Maintaining a Strong Wholesaling Business

As Menlo Worldwide (**http://www.menloworldwide.com**) says at its Web site, "Top-tier companies around the world look to Menlo for innovative solutions that help plan business strategies, improve customer service, accelerate order cycle times, and tighten control of the supply chain—all while reducing costs in transportation, inventory, and order fulfillment." Menlo "helps firms attain operational excellence across their global supply chains."

Source: Reprinted by permission.

15-3 TYPES OF WHOLESALING

Figure 15-3 outlines the three broad categories of wholesaling: manufacturer/service provider wholesaling, merchant wholesaling, and agents and brokers. Table 15-2 contains detailed descriptions of every type of independent wholesaler and shows their functions and special features.

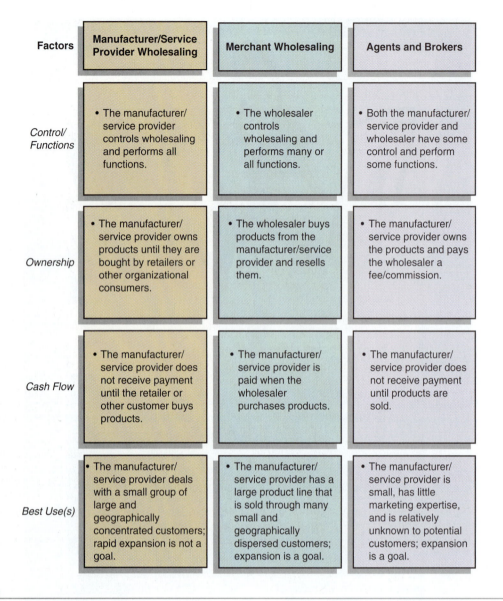

Factors	Manufacturer/Service Provider Wholesaling	Merchant Wholesaling	Agents and Brokers
Control/ Functions	• The manufacturer/ service provider controls wholesaling and performs all functions.	• The wholesaler controls wholesaling and performs many or all functions.	• Both the manufacturer/ service provider and wholesaler have some control and perform some functions.
Ownership	• The manufacturer/ service provider owns products until they are bought by retailers or other organizational consumers.	• The wholesaler buys products from the manufacturer/service provider and resells them.	• The manufacturer/ service provider owns the products and pays the wholesaler a fee/commission.
Cash Flow	• The manufacturer/ service provider does not receive payment until the retailer or other customer buys products.	• The manufacturer/ service provider is paid when the wholesaler purchases products.	• The manufacturer/ service provider does not receive payment until products are sold.
Best Use(s)	• The manufacturer/ service provider deals with a small group of large and geographically concentrated customers; rapid expansion is not a goal.	• The manufacturer/ service provider has a large product line that is sold through many small and geographically dispersed customers; expansion is a goal.	• The manufacturer/ service provider is small, has little marketing expertise, and is relatively unknown to potential customers; expansion is a goal.

Figure 15-3

Broad Categories of Wholesaling

15-3a Manufacturer/Service Provider Wholesaling

In *manufacturer/service provider wholesaling*, a producer does all wholesaling functions itself. This occurs if a firm feels it is best able to reach b-to-b customers by doing wholesaling tasks. The format yields 25 percent of U.S. wholesale revenues and 6 percent of establishments. Manufacturer/service provider wholesalers include Citigroup (http://www.citigroup.com), Frito-Lay (http://www.fritolay.com), General Motors (http://www.gm.com), Hanes (http://www.hanes.com), IBM (http://www.ibm.com), Pitney Bowes (http://www.pb.com), and Prudential (http://www.prudential.com).

Wholesale activities by a manufacturer or service provider may be done at sales offices and/or branch offices. A *sales office* is located at a firm's production facilities or close to the market. No inventory is kept there. In contrast, a *branch office* has facilities for warehousing products, as well as for selling them.

Manufacturer/service provider wholesaling works best if independent intermediaries are unavailable, existing intermediaries are unacceptable, the manufacturer or service provider wants control over marketing, customers are few in number and each is a key account, customers desire personal service from the producer, customers are near the firm

> In **manufacturing/service provider wholesaling**, a firm has its own sales or branch offices.

| Table **15-2** | Characteristics of Independent Wholesalers |

Wholesaler Type	Major Functions						
	Provides Credit	Stores and Delivers	Takes Title	Provides Merchandising and Promotion Assistance	Provides Personal Sales Force	Performs Research and Planning	Special Features
I. Merchant wholesaler							
A. Full service							
1. General merchandise	Yes	Yes	Yes	Yes	Yes	Yes	Carries nearly all items a customer usually needs
2. Specialty merchandise	Yes	Yes	Yes	Yes	Yes	Yes	Specializes in a narrow product range, extensive assortment
3. Rack jobber	Yes	Yes	Yes	Yes	Yes	Yes	Furnishes racks and shelves, consignment sales
4. Franchise	Yes	Yes	Yes	Yes	Yes	Yes	Use of common business format, extensive management services
5. Cooperative							
a. Producer-owned	Yes	Yes	Yes	Yes	Yes	Yes	Farmer controlled, profits divided among members
b. Retailer-owned	Yes	Yes	Yes	Yes	Yes	Yes	Wholesaler owned by several retailers
B. Limited service							
1. Cash and carry	No	Stores, no delivery	Yes	No	No	No	No outside sales force, wholesale store for business needs
2. Drop shipper	Yes	Delivers, no storage	Yes	No	Yes	Sometimes	Ships items without physically handling them
3. Truck/wagon	Rarely	Yes	Yes	Yes	Yes	Sometimes	Sales and delivery on same call
4. Mail order	Sometimes	Yes	Yes	No	No	Sometimes	Catalogs used as sole promotion tool
II. Agents and brokers							
A. Agents							
1. Manufacturers' (service providers')	No	Sometimes	No	Yes	Yes	Sometimes	Sells selected items for several firms
2. Selling	Sometimes	Yes	No	Yes	Yes	Yes	Markets all the items of a firm

(continued)

3. Commission (factor) merchants	Sometimes	Yes	No	No	Yes	Yes	Handles items on a consignment basis
B. Brokers							
1. Food	No	Sometimes	No	Yes	Yes	Yes	Brings together buyers and sellers
2. Stock	Sometimes	Sometimes	No	Yes	Yes	Yes	Brings together buyers and sellers

or clustered, computerized ordering links a firm with customers, and/or laws (particularly in foreign markets) limit arrangements with independent resellers. See Figure 15-4.

For instance, because it seeks close contact with its retailers and control over its marketing strategy, manufacturer wholesaling is a must for PepsiCo's Frito-Lay (**http://www.fritolay.com**). But, it sure is complex: "Frito-Lay North America is the dominant player in the salty snack category in the United States, with a 65 percent share of the market. Frito-Lay boasts no fewer than 15 brands, whose sales each year exceed $100 million, including Lay's, Ruffles, Cheetos, Fritos, Tostitos, Doritos, Sun Chips, and Rold Gold. Frito-Lay North America runs about 50 food manufacturing and processing plants and approximately 1,700 warehouses, distribution centers, and offices." Distribution efficiencies enable thousands of route salespeople to "spend more time merchandising and selling snack products in retail stores as opposed to loading and sorting the products in their trucks."[5]

15-3b Merchant Wholesaling

Merchant wholesalers buy, take title, and take possession of products for further resale. This is the largest U.S. wholesaler type in sales (65 percent of the total) and establishments (85 percent of the total).

> **Merchant wholesalers** buy products and are **full** or **limited service**.

As an example, Sysco (**http://www.sysco.com**) is a merchant wholesaler that buys and handles 375,000 products from thousands of producers of food and other products from around the world. It carries fresh and frozen meats, seafood, poultry, fruits and vegetables, bakery products, canned and dry foods, paper and disposable products, sanitation items, dairy foods, beverages, kitchen and tabletop equipment, medical and surgical supplies, and more. The firm operates throughout the contiguous United States and in parts of Alaska, Hawaii, and Canada. Sysco has nearly 180 distribution facilities, and it serves about 400,000 restaurants, hotels, schools, hospitals, retirement homes, and other locations.[6]

Full-service merchant wholesalers perform a full range of distribution tasks. They provide credit, store and deliver products, offer merchandising and promotion assistance, have a personal sales force, offer research and planning support, pass along information to suppliers and customers, and give installation and repair services. They are prevalent for grocery products, pharmaceuticals, hardware, plumbing equipment, tobacco, alcoholic beverages, and television program syndication.

Limited-service merchant wholesalers do not perform all the functions of full-service merchant wholesalers. They may not provide credit, merchandising assistance, or marketing research data. They are popular for construction materials, coal, lumber, perishables, equipment rentals, and specialty foods.

On average, full-service merchant wholesalers require more compensation than limited-service ones because they perform greater functions.

---

[5] "Company History: Frito-Lay Inc.," **http://www.answers.com/topic/frito-lay** (April 9, 2009).

[6] *Sysco Corporation Report 2008.*

The BRICK STORE
CUSTOMER SUCCESS STORY

"WHEN WE FIRST bought the store seven years ago, fudge sales were slow. We made some of the changes Calico suggested and moved the fudge closer to the register. Sales improved a little. Then we said, let's do the whole program to the letter and see what happens. That's when our sales doubled."

Fill it up! These days, the Brick Store does a lot of things differently. Nancy admits that the fudge case wasn't always filled. As the fudgemaker and store owner, she worried that if she made too much fudge, it would harden. She discovered the opposite was true — the more fudge she put out, the more she sold and the fresher it was. That led her to enlarge her display, which now boasts twelve to fourteen full slabs.

Nancy found that even with FRESH FUDGE signs in the store, many people didn't see the fudge because the store was visually busy. Once she and her staff offered customers a taste of fudge, sales immediately followed.

Remind yourself to sample.

The Brick Store is an old-fashioned General Store filled with interesting things that take you back in time.

"We constantly have to remind ourselves & each other to sample. It's easy to get complacent. Sampling is a little thing that makes a huge difference. In our case, following the program meant an additional $12,000 in profits."

Nancy Lusby, Store Owner and Fudgemaker

If you'd like to realize similar increases in your fudge program, just fill in the information below and mail or fax to Calico.

Your Name _____ Store Name _____

Address _____ Phone # ( ) _____

CALICO COTTAGE, INC. 210 New Highway • Amityville, NY 11701-1116
Phone 800-645-5345 (USA & Canada) • 516-841-2100 • Fax 516-841-2401

Figure 15-4

Calico Cottage: Manufacturer Wholesaling

Calico Cottage (http://www.calicocottage.com) manufactures fudge ingredients for more than 400 flavors of fudge, seasonal promotional specialties, and gourmet make-at-home mixes such as brownie mix, fudge pie mix, and hot cocoa mix. The company sells directly to its retailers—many of which are small—and provides them with considerable training, operations support, and promotion ideas.

Source: Reprinted by permission.

Full-Service Merchant Wholesalers Full-service merchant wholesalers can be divided into the following types.

General-merchandise (full-line) wholesalers carry a wide product assortment—nearly all the items needed by their customers. Some general-merchandise hardware, drug, and clothing wholesalers stock many product lines, but not much depth in any one line. They seek to sell their retailers or other organizational customers all or most of their products and foster strong loyalty and exclusivity.

Specialty-merchandise (limited-line) wholesalers concentrate on a rather narrow product range and have an extensive selection in that range. They offer many sizes, colors, and models—and provide functions similar to other full-service merchant wholesalers. They are popular for health foods, seafood, retail store displays, frozen foods, and video rentals.

Rack jobbers furnish the racks or shelves on which products are displayed. They own the products on the racks, selling them on a consignment basis—so their clients pay after goods are resold. Unsold items are taken back. Jobbers set up displays, refill shelves,

> **General-merchandise wholesalers** sell a range of items.

> **Specialty-merchandise wholesalers** sell a narrow line.

> **Rack jobbers** set up displays and are paid after sales.

price-mark goods, maintain inventory records, and compute the amount due from their customers. Heavily advertised, branded merchandise that is sold on a self-service basis is most often handled. Included are magazines, health and beauty aids, cosmetics, drugs, hand tools, toys, housewares, and stationery.

In *franchise wholesaling*, independent retailers affiliate with an existing wholesaler to use a standardized storefront design, business format, name, and purchase system. Suppliers often produce goods and services according to specifications set by a franchise wholesaler. This form of wholesaling is used for hardware, auto parts, and groceries. Franchise wholesalers include Independent Grocers Alliance (IGA, **http://www.iga.com**) and Ben Franklin Stores (**http://www.benfranklinstores.com**).

Wholesale cooperatives are owned by member firms to economize functions and provide broad support. Producer-owned cooperatives are popular in farming. They market, transport, and process farm products—as well as make and distribute farm supplies. These cooperatives often sell to stores under their own names, such as Farmland (**http://www.farmlandfoods.com**), Land O'Lakes (**http://www.landolakes.com**), Ocean Spray (**http://www.oceanspray.com**), Sunkist (**http://www.sunkist.com**), and Welch's (**http://www.welchs.com**). With retailer-owned cooperatives, independent retailers form groups that buy, lease, or build wholesale facilities. The cooperatives own products, handle cooperative ads, and negotiate with suppliers. They are used by hardware and grocery stores. At Ace Hardware, as described at its Web site (**http://www.myace.com**): "Since the cooperative structure allows our buyers to negotiate with combined buying-power of over 4,800 locations, our store owners have a significant advantage over nonaffiliated stores. Our regional and state-of-the-art distribution centers and computerized ordering give you efficient access to more than 70,000 items in every major hardware category. Your Ace Hardware store will also be equipped with a proprietary computerized management system, which will provide accurate sales transaction processing, detailed sales and expense information, and extensive inventory management and ordering features to help you run a 'tight ship.' But being a part of the Ace family has other advantages—national advertising, proven business models, and a corporate culture driven by service and innovation." See Figure 15-5.

Limited-Service Merchant Wholesalers

Limited-service merchant wholesalers can be classified as follows.

In *cash-and-carry wholesaling*, people from small businesses drive to wholesalers, order products, and take them back to a store or business. These wholesalers offer no credit or delivery, no merchandising and promotion help, no outside sales force, and no research or planning aid. They are good for fill-in items, have low prices, and allow immediate product use. They are used for construction materials, electrical supplies, office supplies, auto supplies, hardware products, and groceries.

Drop shippers (desk jobbers) buy goods from manufacturers or suppliers and arrange for their shipment to retailers or industrial users. They take ownership but do not physically possess products and have no storage facilities. They buy items, leave them at manufacturers' plants, contact customers by phone, set up and coordinate shipments from manufacturers directly to customers, and are responsible for unsold items. Trade credit, a sales force, and some research and planning are offered; merchandising and promotion support are not. Drop shippers are used for coal, coke, and building materials. Because these goods have high freight costs relative to their value, direct shipping from suppliers is needed.

Truck/wagon wholesalers generally have a regular sales route, offer items from a truck or wagon, and deliver goods when they are sold. These wholesalers provide merchandising and promotion support; they are considered limited service because they usually do not extend credit and offer little research and planning help. Operating costs are high due to the services performed and low average sales. These wholesalers often deal with goods requiring special handling or with perishables such as bakery products, tobacco, meat, candy, potato chips, and dairy products.

With **franchise wholesaling,** retailers join with a wholesaler.

Producers or retailers can set up **wholesale cooperatives.**

In **cash-and-carry wholesaling,** the customer drives to a wholesaler.

Drop shippers (desk jobbers) buy goods, but do not take possession.

Truck/wagon wholesalers offer products on a sales route.

Figure 15-5

Ace Hardware: The Power of a Cooperative for Small Retailers

Independent market research indicates that 8 out of every 10 American consumers know Ace as the "Helpful Hardware Place."

Source: © Ace Hardware. Reprinted by permission.

Mail-order wholesalers use catalogs, instead of a personal sales force, to promote products and communicate with customers. They may provide credit but do not generally give merchandising and promotion support. They store and deliver goods, and offer some research and planning assistance. These wholesalers are found with jewelry, cosmetics, auto parts, specialty food product lines, business supplies, and small office equipment.

> **Mail-order wholesalers** sell through catalogs.

15-3c Agents and Brokers

Agents and *brokers* perform various wholesale tasks but do not take title to products. Unlike merchant wholesalers, which make profits on the sales of products they own, they work for commissions or fees as payment for their services. They account for 10 percent of wholesale sales and 9 percent of wholesale establishments. The main difference between agents and brokers is that agents are apt to be used on a permanent basis, whereas brokers often are temporary.

> **Agents** and **brokers** do not take title to products.

Agents and brokers enable a manufacturer or service provider to expand sales volume despite limited resources. Their selling costs are a predetermined percent of

Ethical Issues in Marketing

Protecting Legitimate Film Wholesaling

The illegal copying of movies remains rampant— through both retail stores and the Web. Aside from pirated DVD copies of major film releases, illegal copies of popular movies are available as illegal downloads, mostly through peer-to-peer file sharing networks. In other instances, illegal copies are based on copies made by high-definition camcorders. Although there are divergent estimates as to the amount of illegal copying of films and videos, according to a study by the Motion Picture Association of America (MPAA, http://www.mpaa.org), producers, distributors, theaters, video stores, and pay-per-view operators lose nearly $20 billion globally as the result of piracy each year.

There are a number of technologies in place to detect pirated copies, as well as those responsible for pirated versions. According to a vice-president of the MPAA, 90 percent of new movie releases are recorded with a camcorder. The industry seeks to catch those

responsible for pirating by hiring employees with night-vision equipment who can see pirates in the act of illegal copying. Theater owners pay employees as much as $500 for each pirate who is arrested. Other technologies enable police to identify the specific theaters in which pirated copies were created. Furthermore, other firms are now able to identify the E-mail address of individuals who illegally downloaded pirated files.

New York State is seeking to upgrade the penalty for illegally recording a live performance or a film for commercial purposes to a Class-A misdemeanor. Under the proposed law, a first-time offender could receive up to one year in jail and a $1,000 fine; a repeat offender would be charged with a felony.

Sources: Based on material in "State Senator Padavan, Cuomo, Movie, TV Industry Team Up to Fight Film Piracy," *US Fed News Service, Including US State News* (May 5, 2008); and Eric A. Taub, "Off New York Streets, Film Piracy Is Online," *New York Times* (April 14, 2008), p. C7.

> **Manufacturers'/service providers' agents** work for many firms, selling noncompeting items.

sales, and they have trained salespeople. There are manufacturers'/service providers' agents, selling agents, and commission (factor) merchants.

Manufacturers'/service providers' agents work for several manufacturers/service providers and carry noncompetitive, complementary products in exclusive territories. By selling noncompetitive items, there are no conflicts of interest. By selling complementary items, they stock a fairly complete line of products for their markets. They do not offer credit, but may store and deliver products and give limited research and planning aid. Merchandising and promotional support are provided. These agents may enhance clients' sales efforts, help introduce new products, enter dispersed markets, and handle items with low average sales. They may carry only some of a firm's products; a manufacturer/service provider may hire many agents. Large firms may hire a separate one for each product line. Agents have little say on marketing and pricing. They earn commissions of 5 to 10 percent of sales, and are popular for auto products, iron, steel, footwear, textiles, and commercial real-estate and insurance. The Manufacturers' Agents National Association (http://www.manaonline.org) has 3,300 rep firms as members.

> **Selling agents** market all the products of a manufacturer or service provider.

Selling agents are responsible for marketing the entire output of a manufacturer/service provider under a contractual agreement. They become the marketing department for clients and negotiate price and other conditions of sale, such as credit and delivery. They do all wholesale tasks except taking title. Though a firm may use several manufacturers'/service providers' agents, it may hire only one sales agent. These agents are more apt to work for small firms. They are common for textile manufacturing, canned foods, metals, home furnishings, apparel, lumber, and metal products. Because they do more tasks, they often get higher commissions than manufacturers'/service providers' representatives.

> **Commission (factor) merchants** assemble goods from local markets.

Commission (factor) merchants receive goods on consignment, accumulate them from local markets, and arrange for their sale in a central location. They may offer credit; they do store and deliver goods, provide a sales force, and offer research and planning help. They normally do not assist in merchandising and promotion, but can negotiate prices—provided the prices are not below sellers' stated minimums. They may act in an auction setting; commissions vary. These wholesalers are used for agricultural and seafood products, furniture, and art.

Brokers are common in food and financial services. They are well informed about market conditions, terms of sale, sources of credit, price setting, potential buyers and sellers, and the art of negotiating. They do not take title and usually are not allowed to complete a transaction without approval.

Food brokers introduce buyers and sellers of food and related general-merchandise items to one another and bring them together to complete a sale. They operate in specific locales and work for a limited number of food producers. Their sales staff calls on chain-store buyers, store managers, and purchasing agents. They work closely with ad agencies. They often represent the seller, who pays a commission. They do not actually provide credit but may store and deliver. Commissions are typically 3 to 5 percent of sales. Two examples of food brokers with active Web sites are Cebco (**http://www.cebco.com/ indexframes.html**) and Wyman Foorman (**http://www.wymanfoorman.com**).

Commercial stock brokers are licensed sales representatives who advise business clients, take orders, and then acquire stocks and/or bonds for the clients. They may aid firms selling stocks or bonds, represent either buyers or sellers (with both paying commissions), and offer some credit. Although they operate in particular areas, they usually sell stocks and bonds of firms from around the United States—even around the world. They do a lot of business over the phone and may help publicize new stock or bond offerings. Commissions average 1 to 10 percent of sales, based on volume and stock prices.

> **Food brokers** and **commercial stock brokers** unite buyers and sellers, as well as conclude sales.

15-4 RECENT TRENDS IN WHOLESALING

During the last 25 to 30 years, wholesaling has changed dramatically, with independent wholesalers striving to protect their place in the channel. Among the key trends are those related to the evolving wholesaler mix, productivity, customer service, international opportunities, and target markets.

Since the early 1980s, the proportion of total sales volume contributed by manufacturer wholesaling, merchant wholesaling, and agents and brokers has seen a slight shift toward merchant wholesaling. Manufacturer wholesalers now have fewer establishments (due to consolidation of facilities) and merchant wholesalers have many more (to provide better customer service). Overall, 250,000 firms currently engage in some form of U.S. wholesaling, down from 364,000 firms in 1987. Today, average annual sales for the 25,000 U.S. manufacturer wholesaling establishments are $65 million—compared with $11 million for the 375,000 merchant wholesaling establishments and $16 million for the 40,000 agent/broker establishments. The trend toward bigger firms is expected to continue well into the future.[7]

> Firms are becoming larger and more cost-conscious.

The Internet is also having a major impact on the wholesaler mix: "The biggest negative influence on wholesalers and the wholesaling industry may be the growth of the Web, which enables sellers and buyers to bypass wholesalers and interface directly with each other. This new medium has been a major factor in products such as books, CDs, and airline tickets."[8] Yet, some wholesalers are flourishing on the Web. They understand how to use it to their advantage.

Wholesalers are constantly looking for productivity gains to benefit their customers and themselves and to protect their position in the marketplace. As highlighted in Figure 15-6, consider the approach of United Stationers (**http://www.unitedstationers.com**):

> It's not enough that we are North America's largest broad line wholesale distributor of business products. Our mission is to become a high-performance organization, delivering

---

[7] Estimated by the authors from "Monthly and Annual Wholesale Trade," **http://www.census.gov/wholesale** (April 9, 2009).

[8] "Wholesaling Industry," **http://www.activemedia-guide.com/wholesaling_industry.htm** (April 6, 2004).

Figure 15-6

United Stationers: How a Wholesaler Helps Its Customers Be More Productive

Source: Reprinted by permission.

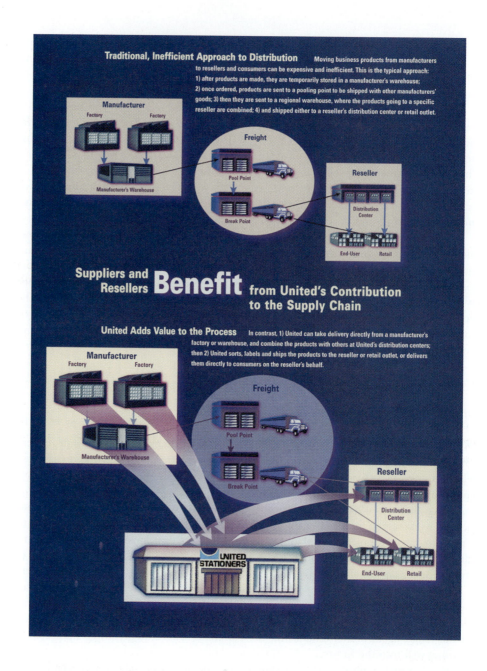

exceptional value through superior execution of innovative marketing and logistics services. I am pleased to report that we are making progress. You can see it in our team structure, which lets us draw on the expertise of associates at all levels to improve every aspect of our business—from making it easy for customers to work with us, to strengthening our partnerships with suppliers. You can see it in our initiatives, where we are working hard to find products that meet the needs of all of our resellers and designing programs to help our independent resellers more effectively build their businesses. You can see it in our efforts on cost and value leadership, where we are driving operating costs out of our company—to the tune of $20 million a year—while remaining the best value provider of logistical services. You can see it in our use of information technology, as we upgrade our systems platform to do a better job of mining data to improve our business processes while strengthening our service to customers.[9]

---

[9] "Message from Our President," http://www.unitedstationers.com/profile/message.html (April 5, 2006).

Global Marketing in Action

Product Safety: Purchasing Products Made in China

In 2007, Mattel (http://www.mattel.com) initiated a series of product recalls involving 20 million items. A number of its toy cars and Barbie accessories were covered with lead-based paint. Mattel dismissed the contractors responsible for the lead paint and immediately increased its pre- and post-production manufacturing inspections. The Mattel incident was one of many involving Chinese goods, which also included pet food tainted with melamine, toothpaste with an ingredient used in antifreeze, and unsafe tires. According to the U.S. Consumer Product Safety Commission (http://www.cpsc.gov), about one half of the products it recalled in 2006 were made in China.

One of the major factors that may have contributed to the large number of recalls of Chinese goods was the low costs associated with outsourcing of goods to China. The president of China Manufacturing Network (http://www.sourceglobally.com), a firm that matches U.S. firms with a network of about 100 factories in China, noted that some foreign businesses may inadvertently push the wrong buttons with their Chinese suppliers, "If you accept a price below material cost [Chinese manufacturers] expect to make a profit, so they have an incentive to substitute materials." With the cost of energy and other materials rising, many Chinese factory owners attempted to cut costs by using less costly ingredients, purchasing goods from unreliable sources, and even reducing the thickness of certain metals. For example, the problem of lead paint was due to the use of noncertified paint suppliers by Mattel's subcontractors.

Sources: Based on material in Christopher Palmeri, "Mattel Takes the Blame for Toy Recalls," http://www.businessweek.com (September 21, 2007); and Jeremy Quittner, "The China Code," http://www.businessweek.com/smallbiz (August 17, 2007).

Wholesalers know customer service is very important in securing a competitive advantage, developing client loyalty, and attaining acceptable profit margins. Here is what two firms are doing:

> Wholesalers are emphasizing customer service and looking to international markets.

- Procter & Gamble (http://www.pg.com) often acts as a manufacturer wholesaler: "We provide retailers with consumer and shopper research, supply chain solutions, branding and marketing expertise, and more. Our products are sold in more than 180 countries primarily through retail operations including mass merchandisers, grocery stores, membership club stores, drug stores, and high-frequency stores. We have on-the-ground operations in over 80 countries. We have tremendous knowledge scale in consumer understanding, research and development, and marketing. We drive out costs and complexities that do not add value for consumers or retail customers. We do this by leveraging P&G's significant manufacturing and purchasing scale, by maximizing the return on marketing investments, and by constantly improving organizational effectiveness and productivity."[10]
- Grainger (http://www.grainger.com) is a merchant wholesaler of maintenance, repair, and operating supplies. It assists customers "by stocking hundreds of thousands of items—from motors to mops to material-handling equipment—and making them available quickly." The wholesaler serves such customers as commercial establishments, contractors, hotels, government agencies, retailers, hospitals, educational facilities, mining operations, and agricultural businesses. It "links manufacturers and end users through a dedicated sales force, a vast logistics system, integrated information technology, and 18,000 employees intent on delivering great service. The firm uses multiple channels—a branch network, sales representatives, service centers, catalogs, other direct marketing materials, and the Internet—to help customers find and buy products efficiently."[11]

[10] *Procter & Gamble 2007 10-K.*
[11] *Grainger 2008 Fact Book.*

More U.S. wholesalers are turning to foreign markets for growth, but many are not necessarily moving quickly enough. Consider this comment from an industry expert:

> One day it happens. Your first international order. You didn't market to that country. You didn't solicit the business. But here it is. And you have to figure out a way to ship it. As U.S. markets continue to expand abroad, distribution managers are being thrust into the strange new world of international distribution. But shipping overseas is more complex *and* constrained than domestic distribution. It involves factors such as multiple service providers and language and cultural barriers, as well as delays due to time differences. Each government has specific documentation requirements to monitor the entry of goods into its country. Commodity restrictions, currencies, duties, and taxes vary from one country to the next. With increased trading partners and transit times, there's also a greater chance that something will go wrong, if it hasn't already. There are many reasons why distributors want to sell products overseas, but delivering the goods is another matter. Many steps are required to prepare an international logistics strategy.[12]

In large numbers, wholesalers are diversifying the markets they serve or the products they carry: Farm and garden machinery wholesalers now sell to florists, hardware dealers, and garden supply stores. Plumbing wholesalers have added industrial accounts, contractors, and builders. Grocery wholesalers deal with hotels, airlines, hospitals, schools, and restaurants. Large food wholesalers such as Supervalu (**http://www.supervalu.com**) have moved more actively into retailing. See Figure 15-7.

> Target market strategies are more complex.

Figure 15-7

Supervalu: From Merchant Wholesaling to Retailing

Supervalu is one of the leading food wholesalers in the United States. It provides distribution services to nearly 4,000 stores of all sizes and formats, including regional and national chain supermarkets, mass merchandisers, and E-tailers. It has also become one of the largest U.S. supermarket chains, with more than 1,400 outlets in 40 states. Among the retail stores it operates are Bigg's, Cub Foods, Save-A-Lot, Shop 'n Save (shown here), and Shoppers Food Warehouse.

Source: Reprinted by permission.

[12] Rob Martinez, "Getting Your Goods Across the Globe," *Multichannel Merchant* (March 2008), pp. 44–45.

Web Sites You Can Use

Here are a variety of useful Web sites related to wholesaling:

- *Annual Wholesale Trade Report* (**http://www.census.gov/wholesale**)
- *Electrical Wholesaling* (**http://www.ewweb.com**)
- Healthcare Distribution Management Association (**http://www.healthcaredistribution.org**)

- International Furniture Suppliers Association (**http://www.ifsa-info.com**)
- WholesaleCentral.com (**http://www.sumcomm.com**)
- *Wholesale Source* (**http://www.wsmag.com**)
- Wholesale Trade Definitions (**http://www.census.gov/svsd/www/wnaicsdef.html**)

Summary

1. *To define wholesaling and show its importance* Wholesaling involves the buying and/or handling of goods and services and their resale to organizational users, retailers, and/or other wholesalers—but not the sale of significant volume to final consumers. In the United States, about 440,000 wholesale establishments distribute $6.5 trillion in goods and services annually.

    Wholesale functions encompass distribution, personal selling, marketing and research assistance, gathering assortments, cost reductions, warehousing, financing, returns, and risk taking. They may be assumed by manufacturers/service providers or shared with independent wholesalers. The latter are sometimes in a precarious position because they are located between manufacturers/service providers and customers and must determine their responsibilities to each.

2. *To describe the three broad categories of wholesaling (manufacturer/service provider wholesaling, merchant wholesaling, and agents and brokers) and the specific types of firms within each category* In manufacturer/service provider wholesaling, a producer undertakes all wholesaling functions itself. This form of wholesaling can be done by sales or branch offices. The sales office has no inventory.

    Merchant wholesalers buy, take title to, and possess products for further resale. Full-service merchant wholesalers gather product assortments, provide trade credit, store and deliver products, offer merchandising and promotion assistance, provide a personal sales force, offer research and planning support, and complete other functions as well. They fall into general merchandise, specialty merchandise, rack jobber, franchise, and cooperative types. Limited-service merchant wholesalers take title to products but do not provide all wholesale functions. They are divided into cash-and-carry, drop shipper, truck/wagon, and mail-order types.

    Agents and brokers provide such wholesale tasks as negotiating purchases and expediting sales, but they do not take title. They are paid commissions or fees. Agents are used on a more permanent basis than brokers. Types of agents are manufacturers'/service providers' agents, selling agents, and commission (factor) merchants. Food brokers and commercial stock brokers are two key players in wholesale brokerage.

3. *To examine recent trends in wholesaling* The nature of wholesaling has been changing. Trends involve the evolving wholesaler mix, productivity, customer service, international openings, and target markets.

Key Terms

wholesaling (p. 468)

manufacturer/service provider wholesaling (p. 474)

merchant wholesalers (p. 476)

full-service merchant wholesalers (p. 476)

limited-service merchant wholesalers (p. 476)

general-merchandise (full-line) wholesalers (p. 477)

specialty-merchandise (limited-line) wholesalers (p. 477)

rack jobbers (p. 477)

franchise wholesaling (p. 478)

wholesale cooperatives (p. 478)

cash-and-carry wholesaling (p. 478)

drop shippers (desk jobbers) (p. 478)

truck/wagon wholesalers (p. 478)

mail-order wholesalers (p. 479)

agents (p. 479)

brokers (p. 479)

manufacturers'/service providers' agents (p. 480)

selling agents (p. 480)

commission (factor) merchants (p. 480)

food brokers (p. 481)

commercial stock brokers (p. 481)

Review Questions

1. Differentiate between selling *to* a wholesaler and selling *through* a wholesaler.
2. Under what circumstances should a manufacturer or service provider *not* undertake wholesaling?
3. Distinguish between a manufacturer's/service provider's branch office and a manufacturer's/service provider's sales office.
4. Which wholesaling functions are performed by merchant wholesalers? Which are performed by agents and brokers?
5. Distinguish between limited-service merchant wholesalers and full-service merchant wholesalers.
6. What are the unique features of wholesale cooperatives and rack jobbers?
7. Why are drop shippers frequently used for coal, coke, and building materials?
8. How do manufacturers'/service providers' agents and selling agents differ?

Discussion Questions

1. "Wholesalers are very much in the middle, often not fully knowing whether their first allegiance should be to the manufacturer/service provider or the customer." Comment on this statement. Can they rectify this situation? Why or why not?
2. The marketing vice-president of Hyundai USA (**http://www.hyundaiusa.com**) has asked you to outline a support program to improve relations with the dealers that see its products. Prepare this outline.
3. Develop a short checklist that a small greeting-card publisher could use in determining whether to use merchant wholesalers or agents/brokers in different countries around the world.
4. Discuss how and why a watchmaker might use a combination of manufacturer/service provider wholesaling, merchant wholesaling, and agents/brokers.

Web Exercise

The National Association of Wholesaler-Distributors (**http://www.naw.org**) "encompasses over 100 national line-of-trade associations, representing virtually all products that move to market via wholesaler-distributors—including 30 regional, state, and local wholesale distribution associations; 40,000 wholesale distribution companies; and 85,000 wholesale distribution company personnel." What could a member of this organization learn by visiting its Web site?

Practice Quiz

1. High wholesale sales occur because
   a. there are so few retailers.
   b. there is only one level of retailing.
   c. items can be sold twice on the wholesale level.
   d. wholesalers service small, final consumer groups.

2. Which statement about the functions of wholesalers is false?
   a. They do not enable manufacturers to distribute locally unless those firms make customer contacts.
   b. They provide a ready-made sales force.
   c. They provide warehouse and delivery facilities.
   d. They process returns and make adjustments for defective merchandise.

3. Without independent wholesalers, organizational consumers would have to
   a. stock smaller quantities.
   b. place less emphasis on an internal purchasing agent or department.

   c. perform fewer distribution functions.
   d. deal with a number of suppliers and coordinate shipments.

4. Which statement about wholesalers is true?
   a. Wholesalers do not want training, technical assistance, product literature, and advertising.
   b. Wholesalers dislike it when vendors alter territory assignments.
   c. Wholesalers want manufacturers to sell through them and not to them.
   d. Wholesalers like it when vendors decide to change to a direct channel and perform wholesale functions themselves.

5. The use of sales offices and/or branch offices is associated with which type of wholesaling?
   a. Agent wholesalers
   b. Broker wholesalers

    c. Manufacturer/service provider wholesalers

    d. Merchant wholesalers

6. Channel control is maximized through which form of wholesaling?

    a. Indirect wholesalers

    b. Global wholesalers

    c. Merchant wholesalers

    d. Manufacturer wholesalers

7. The largest category of wholesalers in terms of sales is

    a. agent wholesalers.

    b. broker wholesalers.

    c. manufacturer wholesalers.

    d. merchant wholesalers.

8. Which of the following is *not* a full-service merchant wholesaler?

    a. Wholesale cooperatives

    b. Specialty-merchandise wholesalers

    c. Franchise wholesalers

    d. Mail-order wholesalers

9. Rack jobbers

    a. do not own the merchandise on their racks.

    b. sell products on a consignment basis.

    c. have standardized storefronts, business formats, and purchase systems.

    d. do not take back unsold merchandise.

10. Land O'Lakes, Ocean Spray, Sunkist, and Welch's are all examples of

    a. retailers.

    b. franchise wholesaling.

    c. cash-and-carry wholesaling.

    d. producer-owned wholesale cooperatives.

11. The principal difference between agents and brokers is that

    a. agents take title to goods, whereas brokers do not.

    b. brokers receive profits from the sales of goods they own, whereas agents work for commissions.

    c. agents are more likely to participate in wholesales cooperatives.

    d. brokers are very common in the food industry, whereas agents are not.

12. Which of these is *not* an advantage offered by agents and brokers?

    a. They enable a manufacturer or service provider to expand sales volume despite limited resources.

    b. Their selling costs are a predetermined percent of sales.

    c. They take title to goods.

    d. They have trained salespeople.

13. Commission merchants do *not*

    a. assist in merchandising and promotion.

    b. accumulate goods from local markets.

    c. arrange for the sale of goods in a central market location.

    d. receive goods on consignment from producers.

14. Which statement concerning food brokers is correct?

    a. They work for a large number of competing food producers.

    b. They generally offer credit.

    c. They often represent the seller.

    d. They usually earn commissions in excess of 7 percent of sales.

15. When farm and garden machinery wholesalers begin to sell to florists, hardware dealers, and garden supply stores, which recent trend in wholesaling is being demonstrated?

    a. Diversification of the markets served

    b. Emphasis on service

    c. The decline in the size of independent wholesalers

    d. Gains in productivity

For the answers to these questions, please visit the online site for this book at **http://www.atomicdog.com.**

establishments (including those staffed by the owners and their families)—and a higher amount in some foreign nations—are run by independents, including many dry cleaners, beauty salons, furniture stores, gas stations, and neighborhood stores. This large number is due to the ease of entry because various kinds of retailing require low investments and little technical knowledge. So, competition is plentiful. Numerous firms do not succeed due to the ease of entry, poor management skills, and inadequate resources. The U.S. Small Business Administration says that one-third of new retailers do not last one full year and two-thirds do not make it past three years. About one-third of U.S. retail store sales are accounted for by independents.

A *retail chain* involves common ownership of multiple outlets. It usually has central purchasing and decision making. Although independents have simple organizations, chains tend to rely on specialization, standardization, and elaborate control systems. Chains can serve a large, dispersed target market and have a well-known company name. They operate one-quarter of U.S. retail outlets but account for two-thirds of all retail store sales. The 150 largest U.S.-based retailers account for more than $1.75 billion in worldwide sales and operate 176,000 stores. Chains are common for department stores, supermarkets, and home improvement stores, among others. Examples are Dillard's (**http://www.dillards.com**), Kroger (**http://www.kroger.com**), and Home Depot (**http://www.homedepot.com**).

Retail franchising is a contractual arrangement between a franchisor (a manufacturer, wholesaler, or service sponsor) and a retail franchisee, which allows the latter to run a certain form of business under an established name and according to specific rules. It is a form of chain retailing that lets owner-operators benefit from the experience, buying abilities, and name of large multiunit retailers. The franchisee often gets training and engages in cooperative buying and advertising. The franchisor benefits from franchise fees and royalties, faster payments, strict operating controls, consistency among outlets, and motivated owner-operators. Franchises annually account for $1.7 trillion in U.S. retail sales at 800,000 outlets. A growing number of U.S. franchisors now have stores in foreign markets. Franchising is popular for auto dealers, gas stations, fast-food chains, hotels and motels, and service firms. Examples are Chevrolet dealers (**http://www.chevrolet.com**), Pizza Hut (**http://www.pizzahut.com**), and H&R Block (**http://www.hrblock.com**).

A *leased department* is a section of a retail store rented to an outside party. The lessee operates a department—under the store's rules—and pays a percentage of sales as rent. Lessors gain from the reduced risk and inventory investment, expertise of lessees, lucrative lease terms, increased store traffic, and appeal to one-stop shopping. Lessees gain from the location in established stores, lessors' name awareness, overall store traffic, the customers attracted to stores, and the services (such as ads) that lessors provide. Leased departments are popular for beauty salons, jewelry, photo studios, shoes and shoe repairs, and cosmetics. In U.S. department stores, they generate $15 to $20 billion in annual sales. Meldisco (**http://www.footstar.com/meldisco.html**) operates leased shoe departments in Kmart (**http://www.kmart.com**) stores nationwide and select Rite Aid Pharmacies (**http://www.riteaid.com**).

Table 16-1 compares the retail ownership forms.

16-3b   By Store Strategy Mix

Firms can be classed by the store strategy mix they undertake. A typical *retail store strategy mix* consists of an integrated combination of hours, location, assortment, service, advertising, prices, and other factors retailers employ. Store strategy mixes vary widely, as the following indicate.

A *convenience store* is usually a well-situated, food-oriented store with long hours and a limited number of items. In the United States, these stores have annual sales of $170 billion, excluding gasoline, and account for 7 to 8 percent of all grocery sales. Annual per-store sales are a fraction of those at a supermarket. Consumers use

> **Retail franchising** uses an established name and operates under certain rules.

> A **leased department** is one rented to an outside party.

> A **retail store strategy mix** combines the hours, products, and so on, that are offered.

> A **convenience store** stresses fill-in items.

Global Marketing in Action

Retailing in Russia: Opportunities, But Be Cautious

A.T. Kearney's (http://www.atkearney.com) Global Retail Development Index (GRDI) regularly ranks the top 30 emerging countries for retail development. Its 2008 index listed Russia as the third-best emerging country for retail development after Vietnam (ranked first) and India (ranked second), but ahead of China (ranked fourth) and Egypt (ranked fifth). The 30 countries were scored on the basis of four key variables: country and business risk, market attractiveness, market saturation, and time pressure.

Likewise, analysts at both Deutsche UFG (http://www.deutsche-bank.de) and Renaissance Capital (http://www.renaissance.co.nz) predicted that Russia's retail sector would grow at an average annual rate of 18 percent through 2010. Prospects for the overall Russian economy have improved due to record high prices for crude oil and natural gas, two of Russia's key exports. Another opportunity is that Russia is expected to join the World Trade Organization (http://www.wto.org), which will increase its world trade.

Despite the positive economic trends, it is still difficult to do business in Russia due to licensing issues, high real-estate costs, and an inflation rate higher than many other countries. According to one research executive, retailers that seek to expand in Russia "often deal with hundreds of landlords who are unwilling to sell properties and who expect that rents will keep going higher." Another problem is the scarcity of professional retail managers, especially in outlying areas beyond major cities. Last, Russia has a poor road system; this hampers deliveries and distances customers are willing to travel.

Sources: Based on material in *Emerging Opportunities for Global Retailers: 2008 A.T. Kearney Retail Development Index* (Chicago: A.T. Kearney, 2008); and "Russia, A Treacherously Attractive Retail Market," http://www.foodinternational.net/articles/country-profile/480 (January 2, 2007).

convenience stores for fill-in items—such as gasoline, milk, groceries, papers, soda, cigarettes, beer, and fast food, often at off-hours. 7-Eleven (http://www.7-eleven.com), Circle K (http://www.circlek.com), and Speedway SuperAmerica (http://www.speedway.com) operate such stores.

Table 16-1   Key Characteristics of Retail Ownership Forms

| Ownership Form | Characteristics | | |
	Distinguishing Features	Major Advantages	Major Disadvantages
Independent	Operates one outlet, easy entry	Personal service, convenient location, customer contact	Much competition, poor management skills, limited resources
Retail chain	Common ownership of multiple units	Central purchasing, strong management, specialization of tasks, larger market	Inflexibility, high investment costs, less entrepreneurial
Retail franchising	Contractual arrangement between central management (franchisor) and independent businesspersons (franchisees) to operate a specified form of business	To franchisor: investments from franchisees, faster growth, entrepreneurial spirit of franchisees To franchisee: established name, training, experience of franchisor, cooperative ads	To franchisor: some loss of control, franchisees not employees, harder to maintain uniformity To franchisee: strict rules, limited decision-making ability, payments to store
Leased department	Space in a store leased to an outside operator	To lessor: expertise of lessee, little risk, diversification To lessee: lower investment in store fixtures, customer traffic, store image	To lessor: some loss of control, poor performance reflects on store To lessee: strict rules, limited decision-making ability, payments to store

A *conventional supermarket* is a departmentalized food store with minimum annual sales of $2 million; it emphasizes a wide range of food and related products—general merchandise sales are limited. It originated many decades ago, when food retailers realized a large-scale operation would let them combine volume sales, self-service, low prices, impulse buying, and one-stop grocery shopping. The car and refrigerator aided the supermarket's success by lowering travel costs and adding to perishables' life spans. These stores account for one-quarter of U.S. supermarket sales (which are $500 billion yearly). Kroger (**http://www.kroger.com**), Albertson's (**http://www.albertsons.com**), and Safeway (**http://www.safeway.com**) are among the large chains with some conventional supermarkets. See Figure 16-4.

A *food-based superstore* is a diversified supermarket that sells a broad range of food and nonfood items. The latter account for 20 to 25 percent of sales. This store usually has greeting cards, floral products, DVDs, garden supplies, some apparel, wine, film developing, and small appliances—besides a full line of supermarket items. While a conventional U.S. supermarket has 15,000 to 20,000 square feet of space and annual sales of $6 million to $10 million, a food-based superstore has 25,000 to 50,000 square feet and $20 million to $25 million in sales. Food-based superstores account for more than 40 percent of U.S. supermarket sales. Several factors have caused many conventional supermarkets to become superstores: consumer interest in one-stop shopping, the leveling of food sales due to competition from fast-food stores and restaurants, and higher profits on general merchandise. For most large chains, the superstore is the preferred format.

A *combination store* unites food/grocery and general merchandise sales in one facility, with general merchandise providing 25 to 40 percent or more of sales. It goes further than a food-based superstore in appealing to one-stop shoppers and occupies 30,000 to 100,000 square feet or more. It lets a retailer operate efficiently, expand the number of people drawn to a store, raise impulse purchases and the size of the average transaction, sell both high-turnover/low-profit food items and lower-turnover/high-profit general merchandise, and offer fair prices. A *supercenter* (known as a *hypermarket* in Europe) is a combination store that integrates an economy supermarket with a discount department store, with at least 40 percent of sales from nonfood items. It is 75,000 to 150,000 square feet in size or larger and carries 50,000 or more items. Among those with combination stores are Wal-Mart (**http://www.walmartstores.com**),

A **conventional supermarket** is a large, self-service food store.

A **food-based superstore** stocks food and other products for one-stop shoppers.

A **combination store** offers a large assortment of general merchandise, as well as food. One type is a **supercenter (hypermarket)**.

Figure 16-4

Kroger: Putting the "Super" in Supermarket

Source: Reprinted by permission of Susan Berry, Retail Image Consulting, Inc.

Fred Meyer (**http://www.fredmeyer.com**), and France's Carrefour (**http://www.carrefour.com**).

A *specialty store* concentrates on one product line, such as stereo equipment or hair-care services. Consumers like these stores because they are not faced with racks of unrelated products, do not have to search in several departments, are apt to find informed salespeople, can select from tailored assortments, and may avoid crowding. Specialty stores are quite successful with apparel, appliances, toys, electronics, furniture, personal care products, and personal services. See Figure 16-5. The total annual sales of the 25 largest U.S. specialty chains are hundreds of billion of dollars. They include Best Buy (**http://www.bestbuy.com**), Gap (**http://www.gap.com**), and Radio Shack (**http://www.radioshack.com**).

A *category killer* is an especially large specialty store. It features an enormous selection in its product category and relatively low prices, and shoppers are drawn from wide geographic areas. Auto Zone (**http://www.autozone.com**), Bed Bath & Beyond (**http://www.bedbathandbeyond.com**), Foot Locker (**http://www.footlocker.com**), and Sports Authority (**http://www.sportsauthority.com**) are among the specialty chains largely based on the category-killer store concept.

> A **specialty store** emphasizes one kind of product, with a **category killer** store being a larger version.

Figure 16-5

The Diamond Cellar: A Jewelry Specialty Store

The Diamond Cellar (**http://www.diamondcellar.com**) is a two-store jewelry company based in Ohio. It carries "some of the finest brands in the world." To stimulate business, the jewelry specialty retailer uses promotions such as the gift card mailing featured here.

Source: Reprinted by permission of Susan Berry, Retail Image Consulting Inc.

A department store usually sells a general line of apparel for the family, household linens and textile products, and some mix of furniture, home furnishings, appliances, and consumer electronics. It is organized into functional areas for buying, promotion, service, and control. There are two types: the traditional department store and the full-line discount store.

A ***traditional department store*** has a great assortment of goods and services, provides many customer services, is a fashion leader, and often serves as an anchor store in a shopping district or shopping center. Prices are average to above average. It has high name recognition and uses all forms of media in ads. In recent years, traditional department stores have set up more boutiques, theme displays, and designer departments to compete better. They face intense competition from specialty stores and discounters. Annual U.S. sales, which have been falling, are $85 billion (excluding leased departments). Leading chains include Macy's (**http://www.macys.com**), J.C. Penney (**http://www.jcpenney.com**), and Saks Fifth Avenue (**http://www.saks.com**).

A ***full-line discount store*** is a department store with lower prices, a broad product assortment, a lower-rent location, more emphasis on self-service, brand-name merchandise, wide aisles, shopping carts, and more goods displayed on the sales floor. U.S. full-line discounters (including supercenters) sell more than $400 billion in goods and services yearly. They are among the largest retailers of apparel, toys, housewares, electronics, health and beauty aids, auto supplies, sporting goods, photographic products, and jewelry. Wal-Mart (**http://www.walmart.com**) and Target (**http://www.target.com**) account for three-quarters of U.S. full-line discount store sales. See Figure 16-6.

With a ***membership warehouse club***, final consumers and businesses pay small yearly dues for the right to shop in a huge, austere warehouse. Products are often displayed in their original boxes, large sizes are stocked, and some product lines vary by time period (since clubs purchase overruns and one-of-a-kind items that cannot always be replaced). Consumers buy items at deep discounts. In the United States, warehouse clubs generate $55 billion in annual retail sales. The two dominant chains are Costco (**http://www.costco.com**) and Sam's Club (**http://www.samsclub.com**).

Other popular forms of low-price retailing also exist. Among them are warehouse-style food stores, off-price specialty chains, discount drugstore chains, and

> A **traditional department store** is a fashion leader with many customer services.

> A **full-line discount store** has self-service and popular brands..

> A **membership warehouse club** offers deep discounts to its member customers.

Figure 16-6

Wal-Mart: The Leader Stays Ahead

Wal-Mart (**http://www.walmart.com**) is regularly on the lookout for tools to keep it on top, such as its in-store TV network for advertising.

Source: Reprinted by permission of Susan Berry, Retail Image Consulting Inc.

Table 16-2	Comparing Retail Strategy Mixes: A Discount Store Versus a Traditional Department Store
Discount Store Strategy	**Traditional Department Store Strategy**
1. Less expensive rental location—lower level of pedestrian traffic. (Note: Some discount stores are using more expensive locations.)	1. More expensive rental location in shopping center or district—higher level of pedestrian traffic.
2. Simpler fixtures, linoleum floor, central dressing room, fewer interior and window displays.	2. More elaborate fixtures, carpeted floor, individual dressing rooms, many interior and exterior displays.
3. Promotional emphasis on price. Some discounters do not advertise brand names, but say "famous brands."	3. Promotional emphasis on full service, quality brands, and store image.
4. Fewer alterations; limited phone orders, delivery, and gift wrapping; less availability of credit.	4. Many alterations included in prices, phone orders accepted, and home delivery at little or no fee; credit widely available.
5. More reliance on self-service, plain displays with piles of merchandise; most merchandise visible.	5. Extensive sales assistance, attractive merchandise displays, a lot of storage in back room.
6. Emphasis on branded products; selection may not be complete (not all models and colors). Some discounters feature "seconds," remove labels from goods if asked by manufacturers, and stock low-price, little-known items.	6. Emphasis on a full selection of branded and privately branded first-quality products; does not stock closeouts, discontinued lines, or seconds.
7. Year-round use of low prices.	7. Sales limited to end-of-season clearance and special events.

factory outlet stores. These retailers hold prices down by carrying mostly fast-selling items, using plain fixtures, locating at inexpensive sites, using few ads, and offering less service. They attract price-sensitive shoppers. Examples are Marshalls, an off-price apparel chain (**http://www.marshallsonline.com**), and Tanger Factory Outlet Centers (**http://www.tangeroutlet.com**), which operates shopping centers with manfacturers' outlet stores in 22 states.

Table 16-2 shows the differences between discount store and traditional department store strategies.

16-3c   By Nonstore Operations

With *nonstore retailing*, a firm uses a strategy mix that is not store-based to reach consumers and complete transactions. It does not involve conventional store facilities.

Direct marketing occurs when a consumer is first exposed to a good or service by a nonpersonal medium (such as direct mail, TV, radio, magazine, newspaper, or PC) and then orders by mail, phone, or PC. The majority of U.S. households do at least some direct shopping each year—mostly due to convenience. The popularity of manufacturer brands and the private brands of direct marketers (and consumer confidence in them), the number of working women, and the belief that direct marketing is a good way to shop all fuel its growth: "Today, more than ever before, most of us count time as one of our most valuable assets. Direct marketing allows consumers to gather information about goods and services, to make educated buying decisions, and to acquire the

Nonstore retailing is nontraditional.

In **direct marketing,** a seller first communicates with consumers via nonpersonal media.

necessities and pleasures of life when and where we decide to do so—even from our kitchen tables at 3 A.M."[8]

Direct marketing provides lower operating costs, a wider geographic area, and new market segments for retailers. It is used both by specialized firms and by store-based retailers that apply it to supplement their regular business. Among the most popular direct-marketing items are books, DVDs and CDs, clothing, magazines, insurance, home accessories, and sporting goods. Yearly U.S. retail sales (including the Web) are hundreds of billions of dollars. Spiegel (**http://www.spiegel.com**), QVC (**http://www.qvc.com**), and L.L. Bean (**http://www.llbean.com**) are major direct marketers.

Globally, the United States, Europe, and Japan account for most of the world's mail-order business. The United States alone is responsible for almost one-half of the total. Among the leading Internet retailers are Amazon.com (**http://www.amazon.com**), Buy.com (**http://www.buy.com**), eBay (**http://www.ebay.com**), Dell (**http://www.dell.com**), and 1-800-flowers.com (**http://www.800flowers.com**).

A *vending machine* uses coin- or card-operated machinery to dispense goods (such as beverages) or services (such as life insurance policies at airports). It eliminates the need for salespeople, allows 24-hour sales, and can be placed in many nontraditional settings. Beverages and food items account for 95 percent of total U.S. sales. Machines may need intensive servicing due to breakdowns, stock-outs, and vandalism. Newer technology lets vending machines make change for larger bills, "talk" to consumers, use video screens to show products, brew coffee, and so on. Yearly U.S. sales are about $50 billion.

Direct selling involves personal contact with consumers in their homes (and other nonstore locations) and phone solicitations initiated by the retailer. Cosmetics, vacuum cleaners, encyclopedias, household services (such as carpet cleaning), dairy products, and newspapers are sometimes marketed via direct selling. In a cold canvass, a salesperson calls people or knocks on doors to find customers. With referrals, past buyers recommend friends to the salesperson. In the party method, one consumer acts as host and invites people to a sales demonstration in his or her home (or other nonstore site). To some consumers, direct selling has a poor image. In addition, sales force turnover is high and many people are not home during the day. To increase business, salespeople for firms such as Avon now target working women via office presentations during breaks and lunch hours. Direct selling has yearly U.S. revenues of $34 billion; and the Worldwide Federation of Direct Selling Associations (**http://www.wfdsa.org**) estimates foreign global sales at $80 billion.[9] Avon (**http://www.avon.com**), Mary Kay (**http://www.marykay.com**), and Amway (**http://www.amway.com**) are leading direct-selling firms.

> **Vending machines** allow 24-hour, self-service sales.

> **Direct selling** encompasses personal contacts with consumers in nonstore settings.

16-4   CONSIDERATIONS IN RETAIL PLANNING

Retailers must weigh many factors in devising marketing plans—and manufacturers, service providers, and wholesalers also must keep these factors in mind. Five key factors are store location, atmosphere, scrambled merchandising, the wheel of retailing, and technological advances.

16-4a   Store Location

A retail store's location helps determine the customer mix and competition faced. Once selected, it is also relatively inflexible. The basic forms of store location are the isolated store, the unplanned business district, and the planned shopping center.

An *isolated store* is a freestanding retail outlet located on a highway or street. There are no adjacent stores with which the firm competes, but there are also no stores to help draw shoppers. Customers may hesitate to travel to an isolated store unless it has a good

> An **isolated store** is a freestanding outlet on a highway or side street.

---

[8] "Frequently Asked Questions From Consumers," **http://www.dmachoice.org/consumerfaqs.php** (May 17, 2009).

[9] "Direct Selling by the Numbers," **http://www.dsa.org/pubs/numbers** (May 17, 2009); and "What Is Direct Selling?" **http://www.wfdsa.org/about_dir_sell/index.cfm?fa=whatisds** (May 17, 2009).

product assortment and an established image. This site may be used by discount stores due to low rent and supplier desires for them to be far enough away from stores selling goods and services at full prices. For example, some Kmart (**http://www.kmart.com**) and 7-Eleven (**http://www.7-eleven.com**) stores are isolated.

An *unplanned business district* exists where multiple stores are located close to one another without prior planning as to the number and composition of stores. The four unplanned sites are central business district, secondary business district, neighborhood business district, and string.

The hub of retailing in a city is the *central business district (CBD)*, often called "downtown." It has the most commercial, employment, cultural, entertainment, and shopping facilities in a city—with at least one major department store and a broad grouping of specialty and convenience stores. CBDs have had some problems with crowding, a lack of parking, older buildings, limited pedestrian traffic when offices close, nonstandardized store hours, crime, and other elements. Yet, in many urban areas, CBD sales remain strong. Among the tactics being used to strengthen CBDs are modernizing storefronts, improving transportation, closing streets to vehicles, developing strong merchant associations, planting trees to make areas more attractive, and integrating the commercial and residential environment.

A *secondary business district (SBD)* is a shopping area bounded by the intersection of two major streets. Cities tend to have several SBDs, each with at least one branch department store, a variety store, and/or some larger specialty stores, as well as several smaller shops. Compared to a CBD, an SBD has less assortment and a smaller trading area (the geographic area from which customers are drawn), and sells more convenience-oriented items.

A *neighborhood business district (NBD)* satisfies the convenience-shopping and service needs of a neighborhood. It has several small stores, with the major retailer being a supermarket, a large drugstore, or a variety store. An NBD is located on the major street in a residential area.

A *string* typically comprises a group of stores with similar or compatible product lines that situate along a street or highway. Because this location is unplanned, various store combinations are possible. Car dealers, antique stores, and clothing stores are retailers often locating in strings.

A *planned shopping center* has centrally owned or managed facilities; it is planned and operated as an entity, ringed by parking, and based on balanced tenancy. With *balanced tenancy*, the number and composition of stores are related to overall shopper needs—stores complement each other in the variety and quality of their offerings. Thus, a center may limit the products a store carries. Planned centers account for 40 percent of total U.S. store sales; unplanned business districts and isolated stores generate the rest. Centers are categorized as regional, community, and neighborhood.

A *regional shopping center* sells mostly shopping goods to a geographically dispersed market. It has at least one or two department stores and up to 100 or more smaller stores. People will drive up to a half hour to reach such a center. As with CBDs, some regional centers (especially those built awhile ago) need renovation. Enhancements include adding new retailers, erecting new store directories, redesigning storefronts, adding trees and plants, and replacing concrete in parking lots. The largest regional center in the United States is Minnesota's Mall of America (**http://www.mallofamerica.com**).

A *community shopping center* has a branch department store and/or a large specialty store as its major retailer, with several smaller stores. It sells both convenience- and shopping-oriented items. A *neighborhood shopping center* sells mostly convenience-oriented goods and services. It has a supermarket and/or drugstore, and a few smaller stores.

As discussed in Chapter 7, one of the biggest challenges facing retailers is the transition to a bricks-and-clicks strategy, whereby firms operate both traditional stores and Web sites. Consider the following:

> The "shop online, purchase in-store" phenomenon is driven by two primary consumer-shopping needs: efficiency and convenience. Shoppers are using the efficiency of the Internet to research products on retailer, manufacturer, and comparison shopping sites; and they are

---

In an **unplanned business district**, stores locate together with no prior planning.

A **planned shopping center** is centrally planned and has balanced tenancy.

using the convenience of the local store to see, touch, and ultimately buy the product. The top multichannel retailers have taken notice of this trend and have responded to it both on their own Web sites and in their online advertising. Furthermore, retailers are delivering and blending local promotions and components of the in-store experience into their Web sites. In-store sales and weekly circular ads, as well as store locators, are typically available and highly visible on most multichannel retailer sites.[10]

16-4b   Atmosphere

Atmosphere (also known as *atmospherics*) is the sum total of the physical attributes of a retailer, whether in a store or a nonstore format, that are used to develop an image and draw customers. It affects the target market attracted, the customer's shopping mood and time spent with the retailer, impulse purchases, and retailer positioning; and it is related to the strategy chosen.[11] As shown in Table 16-2, a discount store usually has simple fixtures, linoleum floors, and crowded displays. A full-service store usually has elaborate fixtures, carpeted floors, and attractive displays.

> **Atmosphere (atmospherics)** consists of a retailer's exterior, general interior, layout, and displays.

A retailer's atmosphere consists of four basic components:

- Exterior—includes the storefront, the marquee, entrances, display windows, store visibility, store design, the surrounding area, and traffic. For a Web retailer, the exterior is the home page.
- General interior—includes flooring, colors, scents, lighting, fixtures, wall textures, temperature, aisle width, vertical transportation, personnel, cash registers, and overall cleanliness. For a Web retailer, the use of colors and descriptive text are quite important, as are the links to product departments.
- Store layout—includes the floor space allotted for customers, selling, and storage; product groupings; and department locations. For a Web retailer, this involves the physical layout of each Web page and the way the customer accesses pages with specific products; the shopping process must also be clear.
- Interior (point-of-sale) displays—includes merchandise cases and racks, mobiles, in-store ads, posters, and mannequins. For a Web retailer, product displays can reflect the choices offered and even rotate items for 360-degree views.

Figure 16-7 highlights the image-oriented interior of a Gap store.

Consider how Ikea (**http://www.ikea.com**) has carved out a niche based on its distinctive atmosphere:

> Sweden's Ikea is already the world's largest furniture retailer. But it's still in growth mode. It doesn't matter how lofty your tastes: If you live near an Ikea, the store's low-price and high-style wares will draw you in eventually. Once there, expect to be the target of extensive in-store marketing. Ikea's strategy: Get you to follow a winding pathway that goes through each and every department. Entice you with sleek design. Ikea puts a premium on making things look good. The restaurant/bistro sells cheap, tasty food to rev you up for more shopping! The $5 medium Swedish meatball meal is all part of the "experience." The bounty of über-cheap small housewares is "very much for impulse buys." Baskets of them block the path. Ikea also woos you with free child care.[12]

[10] Bob Armour, "From Clicks to Bricks." *Multichannel Merchant* (May 2008), pp. 37–38.

[11] For a more in-depth discussion of atmosphere, see Lenita Davis, Sijun Wang, and Andrew Lindridge, "Culture Influences on Emotional Responses to Online Store Atmospheric Cues," *Journal of Business Research*, Vol. 61, (August 2008), pp. 806–812; Christoph Teller, Thomas Reutterer, and Peter Schnedlitz, "Hedonic and Utilitarian Shopper Types in Evolved and Created Retail Agglomerations," *International Review of Retail, Distribution & Consumer Research*, Vol. 18 (July 2008), pp. 283–309; and Nusser A. Raajpoot, Arun Sharma, and Jean-Charles Chebat, "The Role of Gender and Work Status in Shopping Center Patronage," *Journal of Business Research*, Vol. 61 (August 2008), pp. 825–833.

[12] Ismat Sarah Mangla, "Ikea Field Guide," *Money* (August 2008), pp. 136–137.

16-4c Scrambled Merchandising

> In **scrambled merchandising**, a retailer adds items to obtain one-stop shopping, higher profit margins, and impulse purchases.

A retailer engages in **scrambled merchandising** if it adds goods and services that are unrelated to each other and the firm's original business. Examples are supermarkets adding video rentals, consumer electronics stores offering computer software, drugstores carrying newspapers, and car washes stocking postcards.

Several reasons account for the popularity of scrambled merchandising: Retailers want to make their stores into one-stop shopping centers. Scrambled merchandise is often fast-selling, generates store traffic, and yields high profit margins. Impulse purchasing is increased. Different target markets can be attracted. And the effects of seasonality and competition may be lessened.

On the other hand, scrambled merchandising can spread quickly and cause competition among unrelated firms. When supermarkets branch into nonfood personal-care items, drugstore sales fall. This forces the drugstores to scramble into stationery and other product lines, which has a subsequent impact on specialty store sales. The situation is illustrated in Figure 16-8.

There are limits to how far a firm should go with scrambled merchandising, especially if adding unrelated items would reduce buying, selling, and service effectiveness. Stock turnover might also be low for certain product lines should a retailer enter too many diverse product categories. And, due to scrambled merchandising, a firm's image may become fuzzy to consumers.

16-4d The Wheel of Retailing

> The **wheel of retailing** shows how strategies change, leaving opportunities for new firms.

The **wheel of retailing** describes how low-end (discount) strategies can evolve into high-end (full service, high-price) strategies and thus provide opportunities for new firms to enter as discounters. According to the wheel, retail innovators often begin as low-price operators with low profit-margin requirements and low costs. As time passes, the innovators look to increase their sales and customer base. They upgrade product offerings, facilities, and services and become more traditional. They may expand the sales force, move to better sites, and offer delivery, credit, and alterations. These improvements lead to higher costs, which in turn cause higher prices. As a result, openings exist for a new

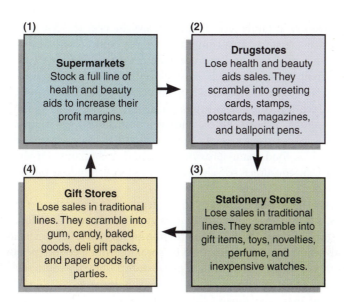

Figure 16-8

The Self-Perpetuating Nature of Scrambled Merchandising

generation of retailers to emerge by appealing to the price-conscious shoppers who are left behind as existing firms move up the wheel. Figure 16-9 shows the wheel in action.

There are some limitations in applying the wheel-of-retailing theory too literally, these two in particular: (1) many retailers do not follow the pattern suggested, and (2) trying to move along the wheel may cause a firm to lose its loyal customers. The best use of the wheel is in understanding that distinct low-end, medium, and high-end strategies can be pursued by retailers.

16-4e   Technological Advances

In recent years, many technological advances related to retailing have emerged. The most dramatic involve the Web (which we highlighted in Chapter 7), checkout systems, video kiosks, atmospherics, computer-aided site selection, electronic banking, and enhanced operating efficiency.

Most retailers use a computerized-checkout (electronic point-of-sale) system, whereby a cashier rings up a sale or passes an item over or past an optical scanner; a

> Technological advances range from computerized checkout systems to enhanced operating efficiency.

Figure 16-9

The Wheel of Retailing in Action

computerized register instantly records and displays the sale. The customer gets a receipt, and inventory data are stored in a computer memory bank. This reduces checkout time, employee training, misrings, and the need for price marking on all products. It also generates a current list of the items in stock without a physical inventory, improves inventory control, reduces spoilage, and aids ordering. Some retailers are also turning to *self-scanning*, which lets consumers bypass cashiers: "At a growing number of retailers, including gas stations, airports, hotels, and even post offices, self-scanning is becoming more popular. Self-scan machines can now be found at Home Depot and Wal-Mart." The majority of U.S. food chains provide self-scanning checkouts for shoppers. Annual revenues from U.S. consumer self-checkouts are several hundred billion dollars.[13] See Figure 16-10.

Video kiosks let retailers efficiently, conveniently, and promptly present information, receive orders, and process transactions—in a store or nonstore location. Consider this convenience store example: "Self-service ordering kiosks enable customers to order made-to-order sandwiches more efficiently than by speaking with a counterperson. Customers begin at the ordering kiosk, walk throughout the store to shop for additional items, pickup the sandwich, and end at the cashier. The system is simple to use and offers custom choices. If the buyer desires extra mayonnaise, the sandwich can be ordered as such. Chains such as Wawa (**http://www.wawa.com**) and Sheetz (**http://www.sheetz.com**) have been using self-service kiosks for years with extraordinary success."[14]

Figure 16-10

Self-Scanning Gains in Popularity

Kroger (**http://www.kroger.com**), which operates 2,500 supermarkets under various names, is a big advocate of self-scanning for its customers who choose to use this technology.

Source: Reprinted by permission of Susan Berry, Retail Image Consulting, Inc.

[13] "Americans Embrace Self-Scanning Checkout, Other Self-Serve Transactions," **http://72.3.136.90/NACS/News/ Daily_News_Archives/February2005/nd0201053.htm** (February 1, 2005); and Steve Martinez and Phil Kaufman, "Twenty Years of Competition Reshape the U.S. Food Marketing System," **http://www.ers.usda.gov/AmberWaves/ April08/Features/FoodMarketing.htm** (April 2008).

[14] Greg Rapport, "The Time Is Right for Self-Service Kiosks," **http://www.retailtechnologyreview.com/absolutenm/ templates/retail_kiosk_terminals.aspx?articleid=102&zoneid=11** (December 2008).

Technology lets retailers enhance their atmospherics by using electronic point-of-purchase displays with frequently updated scrolling messages, electronic coupons, Internet ("Wi-Fi") connections, and video monitors with programming or sales presentations. At Starbucks (**http://www.starbucks.com**), "we are focused on the in-store experience for customers. As we continue to build ways that both enhance and expand the *Starbucks Experience*, we decided to expand our relationship with technology partner AT&T (**http://www.att.com**) to include Wi-Fi." In addition, "T-Mobile HotSpot (**http://hotspot.t-mobile.com**) customers can continue to access Wi-Fi services at no added cost, via an agreement between AT&T and T-Mobile. Our enhanced partnership with AT&T will permit us to deliver a compelling in-store entertainment experience for Starbucks customers as well as AT&T customers."[15]

The availability of inexpensive, computerized site-selection software is so prevalent that retailers of any size and type can now use it. For as little as a few hundred dollars, a retailer can buy geographic information systems software that graphically depicts population characteristics, location attributes, roadways, and more—for potential or existing store sites. Vendors include Caliper (**http://www.caliper.com**), Claritas (**http://www.claritas.com**), ESRI (**http://www.esri.com**), and Tetrad (**http://www.tetrad.com**). They make their software available through downloads from the Internet or by DVD.

Electronic banking involves the use of automatic teller machines (ATMs) and the instant processing of purchases. It provides central record keeping and lets customers conduct transactions 24 hours a day, seven days a week at many bank and nonbank locations (such as supermarkets). Deposits, withdrawals, and other banking and retailing functions can be done. There are 425,000 ATMs in the United States—150,000 at bank locations and 265,000 in shopping centers, stores, airports, and other sites. Each year, Americans engage in billions of ATM transactions.[16] To allow customers to make financial transactions over wider geographic areas, many banks have formed ATM networks. Numerous local and regional networks, as well as national (global) locations, exist.

As electronic banking spreads, more firms are encouraging *debit transactions*; when purchases are made, the amount is immediately charged against buyer accounts. There is no delayed billing without an interest charge. A debit-card system differs from credit-card policy, in which consumers are sent bills and then remit payment. Debit cards have wide acceptance as a substitute for checks.

> With debit transactions, payments are immediately deducted from customers' accounts.

Technological advances are also leading to greater retailer efficiency by:

- increasing the use of self-service operations by firms marketing gasoline, airline tickets, and rental cars, and for hotel registrations and payment.
- linking manufacturers, warehouses, and transportation firms.
- producing antishoplifting merchandise that sets off an alarm if not properly removed by employees.
- automating energy-control systems to monitor store temperature carefully and reduce fuel costs.
- computerizing in-store promotions.
- enabling touchpad order entry in restaurants.

16-5   RECENT TRENDS IN RETAILING

Retailing faces challenging times, as firms seek to defend or expand their positions in a fast-changing marketplace. Many consumers no longer want to spend as much time shopping as they once did, various retail sectors are saturated, a number of large retailers

> This is a tough period for many retailers, due to customer lifestyles, competition, and other factors.

---

[15] "Starbucks to Expand Technology Relationship with AT&T High-Speed Wireless Internet Access," **http://www.starbucks.com/aboutus/pressdesc.asp?id=826** (February 11, 2008).

[16] ATM & Debit News, "U.S. Banking, Mortgages & Credit Industry Overview," **http://www.plunkettresearch.com** (August 13, 2008).

have heavy debt (typically due to leveraged buyouts or overexpansion), and some retailers—after running frequent sales—find it difficult to maintain "regular prices." This observation about retailing shows where we're at:

> Every retail leader confronts the inevitable. Over time, the brand achieves a level of maturity and reliability. With it comes less surprise and relevance. Imitators dilute the differential advantage. Shopper behavior changes and the tastes retailers have helped educate grow more sophisticated. How do retailers that have reached this plateau develop a renewed shopping experience with enough depth and emotional resonance to triumph? As if that weren't daunting enough, toss in a sluggish economy. Re-imagining a successful business is challenging when times are good. In tougher times, a firm will rein in expenditures and squeeze everything it can out of current assets. It's the rare retailer that gets beyond defensive measures. An engaging, exciting second act depends on the strength and flexibility of a brand to overcome complications. It's the difference between pressure and opportunity.[17]

To succeed in the long run, retailers must respond properly to the trends they face. Among the most prominent are those relating to consumer demographics and lifestyles, competitive forces, operating costs, the labor force, and foreign opportunities. Here is how various retailers are dealing with them.

The aging U.S. population, geographic population shifts, and widespread market saturation have led to innovative retailing actions. In addition to its online catalog, Wardrobe Wagon (**http://www.wardrobewagon.com**) uses "traveling clothing stores" to visit nursing homes for the elderly in 16 states. The Bloomingdale's chain (**http://www.bloomingdales.com**) has opened stores in growing areas such as California, Florida, Georgia, and Nevada to reduce emphasis on its Northeast base. Nontraditional locales, which have been underserved, are being used—Baskin-Robbins (**http://www.baskin-robbins.com**) has outlets in U.S. Navy exchanges (**http://www.navy-nex.com**), and Godiva (**http://www.godiva.com**) has stores at various airports.

Retailers are adapting to the shopping needs and time constraints of working women and dual-earner households, and the increased consumer interest in quality and customer service. They are stocking such laborsaving products as ready-to-eat foods and pre-loaded PCs; lengthening store hours and opening additional days; expanding Web, catalog, and phone sales efforts; re-emphasizing personal selling; pre-wrapping gift items to eliminate waiting lines; setting up comprehensive specialty boutiques to minimize the number of departments a consumer must visit; including special services, such as fashion coordinators; marketing high-quality private brands; and using more attractive displays.

Retailing's intense competition often requires proactive company actions. For example, 99 Cents Only (**http://www.99only.com**) is a "dollar store" chain which has reached $1 billion in annual sales. It is a "unique deep-discount retailer of primarily name-brand consumable general merchandise, where nothing is over 99 cents, ever! Our mission is to provide an exciting shopping destination for price-sensitive consumers, and a fun treasure-hunt shopping experience for other value-conscious consumers. We offer only excellent values on a wide selection of quality food and basic household items with a focus on name brands and an exciting assortment of surprises." Pier 1 (**http://www.pier1.com**), the home furnishings and accessories chain, is quicker to freshen its product mix: "As much as 75 percent of our assortment includes new product introductions each year. The process begins with our buyers, who import goods from more than 50 countries. All merchandise is carefully selected in order to offer our customers exclusive, one-of-a-kind product that reflects excellent quality at a great value. Our Visual Merchandising team works to create merchandise displays that appeal to Pier 1 customers through easy-to-navigate store layouts and idea-generating vignettes."[18]

---

[17] "Trouble in the Second Act," *Chain Store Age* (August 2005), p. 3A.

[18] "99¢ Only Stores—About Our Stores," **http://www.99only.com/about** (May 14, 2009); and "About Pier 1: The Merchandise," **http://www.pier1.com** (May 14, 2009).

Figure 16-11

Multiformat Retailing

To better address the needs of multiple market segments, more food retailers are sharing space.

Source: Reprinted by permission.

Due to the large number of firms in many sectors, the price sensitivity of a large segment of consumers, and firms' interest in improving efficiency (and profit margins), retailers are more concerned with cost control. Several fast-food firms now use a format whereby different outlets occupy the same building (as food courts have done for years in malls). This format allows common costs and some workers to be shared. See Figure 16-11. Most small hardware stores belong to buying cooperatives to get quantity discounts and "buy smarter." Many supermarkets use more bulk selling, by which consumers select items such as candy and dried fruit from open displays. Most mail-order firms are better targeting customers and containing their catalog costs. Furthermore, the use of self-service in retailing has steadily increased.

Some U.S. retailers have trouble attracting and retaining a quality labor force. According to surveys, retailers rank the labor shortage as one of the most crucial issues for them to address. Among the reasons why the shortage exists are that the number of interested young people has declined; full-time career opportunities in other industries have lured away a number of part-time retail workers; many retail workers are inexperienced and have overly high job expectations, leading to employee dissatisfaction and turnover; hours can be long and irregular; some people do not like the pressure of interacting with customers on a regular basis; and the pay in other industries has been relatively higher.

Among the actions undertaken by retailers to resolve the labor shortage are recruiting more at high schools and colleges, hiring retired persons, offering child care for working mothers, raising starting salaries (at times, well above the minimum wage),

Ethical Issues in Marketing

Barnes & Noble "Discovers" New and Underappreciated Authors

Barnes & Noble (http://www.barnesandnoble.com), the world's largest bookseller, began its Discover Great New Writers awards program (Discover) about 20 years ago. This program has been highly regarded in the industry as a sign of the retailer's commitment to new and previously underappreciated authors. The Discover program enables excellent writers to receive recognition that would otherwise be overlooked.

To be eligible for the program, a writer has to have produced fewer than three previously published books, had net sales of less than 10,000 copies, and not won any major literary awards. Each year, Barnes & Noble awards $35,000 in Discover prize money. Winners in each category (fiction and nonfiction) receive $10,000 and a full year of additional promotion from Barnes & Noble. Second place winners receive $5,000, and third-place winners receive $2,500. The winners are chosen by two panels of distinguished authors.

Many of the books featured through the Discover program have been from small publishers. Being selected as a Discover selection not only helps in increasing orders from wholesalers and other retailers; it also increases the visibility of an author and his or her work. In addition to the cash prize, Discover book selections are featured at over 700 Barnes & Noble stores. Additional exposure for these titles is from special Discover displays (with a 12-week duration), a 20 percent discount on Discover titles, individual reviews of each Discover title in the seasonal Discover brochure, and special events (such as book group discussions of Discover titles).

Source: Based on material in "Discover Great New Writers," http://www.barnesandnoble.com/awards/home.asp?PID=21573 (August 9, 2008).

rotating employees among tasks to lessen boredom, rewarding good performance with bonuses, and encouraging good workers to pursue retailing careers.

For retailers with the proper resources and management prowess, numerous retailing opportunities exist in foreign markets. These are a few examples:

> **Foreign opportunities are plentiful.**

- "With projected retail spending of more than $1.4 trillion in 2012, China will surpass Japan and move up one spot from its current ranking by 2012 to become the second-largest retail market following the United States. China's upward movement on the list is being driven by continuing high growth rates despite somewhat higher inflation."[19]

- "Brazil topped the 2008 Retail Apparel Index due to the country's total expenditures on apparel, higher per-capita spending on the sector, and level of clothing imports. Brazil is among the world's fastest-growing clothing markets. The population is young, with more than 60 percent under the age of 29. The young Brazilian is fashion-conscious and ready to devote a significant portion of income to apparel. Also, Brazilians use more credit when buying apparel than their market counterparts."[20]

- Worldwide, McDonald's (http://www.mcdonalds.com) "is the leading food-service retailer with more than 30,000 local restaurants serving 52 million people in more than 100 countries each day. More than 70 percent of McDonald's restaurants are owned and operated by independent local men and women." The firm "holds a leading share in the globally branded, quick-service restaurant segment of the informal eating-out market in virtually every country in which it does business."[21]

---

[19] *Global Retail Outlook* (Columbus, OH: Retail Forward, March 2008), p. 7.

[20] *Emerging Opportunities for Global Retailers: 2008 A.T. Kearney Retail Development Index* (Chicago: A.T. Kearney, 2008), pp. 16–17.

[21] "About McDonald's," http://www.mcdonalds.com/corp/about.html (May 15, 2009).

Web Sites You Can Use

There are trade associations covering almost every aspect of retailing. Most have detailed Web sites. Here is a sampling of them:

- Direct Marketing Association (**http://www.the-dma.org**)
- Directory of International Retail Trade Associations (**http://www.retailcouncil.org/aboutus/ind_direc.asp**)
- Direct Selling Association (**http://www.dsa.org**)
- Electronic Retailing Association (**http://www.retailing.org**)
- International Association of Department Stores (**http://www.iads.org**)
- International Council of Shopping Centers (**http://www.icsc.org**)

- International Franchise Association (**http://www.franchise.org**)
- National Association of Convenience Stores (**http://www.nacsonline.com**)
- National Automatic Merchandising Association (**http://www.vending.org**)
- National Retail Federation (**http://www.nrf.com**)
- Retail Industry Leaders Association (**http://www.retail-leaders.org**)
- Retail Merchants Association (**http://www.retailmerchants.com**)

Summary

1. *To define retailing and show its importance* Retailing encompasses the business activities involved with selling goods and services to the final consumer for personal, family, or household use. It is the last stage in a distribution channel. Average sales are small, yet use of credit is widespread. Final consumers generally visit a store to make a purchase, and they also make many unplanned purchases.

   Retailing affects the economy due to its total sales and the number of people employed. Retailers provide various functions, including gathering a product assortment, providing information, handling merchandise, and completing transactions. They deal with suppliers that sell products the retailers use in operating their businesses, as well as suppliers selling items the retailers will resell.

2. *To discuss the different types of retailers, in terms of ownership, store strategy mix, and nonstore operations* Retailers may be classified in several ways. Basic ownership formats are independent, a retailer operating one outlet; chain, a retailer operating two or more outlets; franchise, a contractual arrangement between a franchisor and a franchisee; and leased department (a department in a store leased to an outside party). The ease of entry into retailing fosters competition and results in the failure of many new firms.

   Different strategy mixes are used by convenience stores, well-situated food-oriented retailers; conventional supermarkets, departmentalized food stores with minimum annual sales of $2 million; food-based superstores, diversified supermarkets that sell a broad range of food and nonfood items; combination stores (including supercenters/hypermarkets), outlets that go further than food-based superstores in carrying both food and general merchandise; specialty stores (including category killers), outlets that concentrate on one merchandise or service line; traditional department stores, outlets that have a great

assortment, provide customer services, are fashion leaders, often dominate surrounding stores, and have average to above-average prices; full-line discount stores, department stores with a low-price, moderate-service orientation; membership warehouse clubs, stores that offer very low prices in austere settings; and other discounters.

   In nonstore retailing, a firm uses a strategy mix that is not store-based. Direct marketing occurs when consumers are exposed to goods and services through nonpersonal media and then order by mail, phone, or PC. It is now a large part of retailing. Vending machines use coin- or card-operated machinery to dispense goods and services. Direct selling involves both personal contact with consumers in their homes (or other places) and phone solicitations initiated by retailers.

3. *To explore five major aspects of retail planning: store location, atmosphere, scrambled merchandising, the wheel of retailing, and technological advances* A firm may select from three forms of location: an isolated store, a freestanding outlet on a highway or street; an unplanned business district, in which two or more stores locate near one another without prior planning as to their number and composition; and a planned shopping center, which is centrally managed, as well as planned and operated as an entity. Only planned centers utilize balanced tenancy.

   Atmosphere is the sum total of a retailer's physical characteristics that help develop an image and attract customers. It depends on the exterior, general interior, layout, and interior displays.

   In scrambled merchandising, a retailer adds products unrelated to its original business. The goals are to encourage one-stop shopping, increase sales of high-profit items and impulse purchases, attract different target markets, and balance sales throughout the year.

   The wheel of retailing explains low-end and high-end strategies and how they emerge. As low-cost, low-price innovators move along the wheel, they leave opportunities for newer, more cost-conscious firms to enter the market.

Several technological advances have emerged. These include electronic checkout systems, video kiosks, atmospherics, computer-aided site selection, electronic banking, and enhanced operating efficiency.

4. *To examine recent trends in retailing*   The nature of retailing has changed dramatically in recent years. Among the trends that retailers are adapting to are those relating to consumer demographics and lifestyles, competitive forces, operating costs, the work force, and global opportunities.

Key Terms

retailing (p. 491)

independent retailer (p. 494)

retail chain (p. 495)

retail franchising (p. 495)

leased department (p. 495)

retail store strategy mix (p. 495)

convenience store (p. 495)

conventional supermarket (p. 497)

food-based superstore (p. 497)

combination store (p. 497)

supercenter (hypermarket) (p. 497)

specialty store (p. 498)

category killer (p. 498)

traditional department store (p. 499)

full-line discount store (p. 499)

membership warehouse club (p. 499)

nonstore retailing (p. 500)

direct marketing (p. 500)

vending machine (p. 501)

direct selling (p. 501)

isolated store (p. 501)

unplanned business district (p. 502)

planned shopping center (p. 502)

atmosphere (atmospherics) (p. 503)

scrambled merchandising (p. 504)

wheel of retailing (p. 504)

Review Questions

1. Describe the four basic functions performed by retailers.
2. What are the disadvantages of an independent retailer in competing with retail chains?
3. What are the benefits of retail franchising to the franchisee? To the franchisor?
4. Compare the strategies of traditional department stores and full-line discount stores.
5. Distinguish between direct marketing and direct selling. Which has greater sales? Why?
6. What are the pros and cons of scrambled merchandising?
7. Explain the wheel of retailing from the perspective of the battle between upscale specialty stores and discount specialty stores for market share.
8. Differentiate between credit cards and debit cards. What is the benefit of debit cards to retailers?

Discussion Questions

1. As a prospective franchisee for a Fantastic Sams beauty salon (**http://www.fantasticsams.com**), what criteria would you use in deciding whether Fantastic Sams is right for you? What criteria do you think Fantastic Sams should use in assessing potential franchisees? Explain the differences in your answers to these two questions.
2. Develop an upscale-store strategy for a major appliance store. How would the strategy differ from that for a discount major appliance store?
3. Select a planned shopping center near your college or university and evaluate it.
4. How can Amazon.com (**http://www.amazon.com**) create a good shopping atmosphere for its customers?

Web Exercise

Costco is one of the world's leading store-based retailers. Visit the firm's Web site (**http://www.costco.com**) and evaluate it.

Compare Costco's Web site with that of Sam's Club (**http://www.samsclub.com**), a leading competitor.

Practice Quiz

1. Which of the following is a characteristic of retailing?
   a. A low percent of consumer sales on credit
   b. Many unplanned purchases by final consumers
   c. Many sales to business customers
   d. The high average sale by final consumers

2. Unlike independents, retail chains
   a. operate at least 20 outlets.
   b. have simple organizations.
   c. tend to rely on elaborate control systems.
   d. are the most common form of retail ownership.

3. Conventional supermarkets
   a. emphasize the sale of general merchandise.
   b. have minimum annual sales of $2 million.
   c. originated in the late 1800s.
   d. account for the greatest portion of total U.S. supermarket sales.

4. Which of the following is *not* a reason why many conventional supermarkets are switching to food-based superstores?
   a. Improved transportation networks
   b. The leveling of food sales due to competition from fast-food stores and restaurants
   c. The higher profits on general merchandise
   d. Declining consumer interest in one-stop shopping

5. Wal-Mart operates
   a. full-line specialty stores.
   b. convenience stores.
   c. retail cooperatives.
   d. combination stores.

6. Which of the following is *not* true about full-line discount stores?
   a. They rely more heavily on credit sales than do traditional department stores.
   b. They emphasize self-service.
   c. They are among the largest retailers of apparel, housewares, and electronics.
   d. They offer a broad merchandise assortment.

7. Which of these is *not* a form of nonstore retailing?
   a. Internet retailing
   b. Direct selling
   c. Mail-order retailing
   d. Membership warehouse club

8. Where there are no adjacent stores with which a firm competes, the location is most appropriately described as a(n)
   a. distressed site.
   b. isolated store.
   c. planned shopping center.
   d. unplanned business district.

9. A shopping area bounded by the intersection of two major streets is a
   a. secondary business district.
   b. central business district.
   c. neighborhood business district.
   d. neighborhood shopping center.

10. A regional shopping center sells mostly
    a. unbranded goods.
    b. discount items.
    c. shopping goods.
    d. catalog merchandise.

11. Atmosphere is most closely related to a store's
    a. nonstore operations.
    b. location.
    c. interior displays.
    d. advertisements.

12. Which of the following is a reason for the popularity of scrambled merchandising?
    a. One-stop shopping
    b. Confusing store image
    c. High inventory turnover
    d. Less impulse purchasing

13. Differences between department-store and discount-store strategies are explained by the
    a. scrambled merchandising concept.
    b. off-price optimization concept.
    c. unbalanced tenancy concept.
    d. wheel-of-retailing concept.

14. Computer-based checkouts
    a. require price marking on merchandise.
    b. increase employee training time.
    c. improve ordering decisions.
    d. increase checkout time.

15. Baskin-Robbins outlets in U.S. Navy exchange facilities and Godiva stores at airports are examples of retailers' response to the
    a. decline of online retailing.
    b. increased consumer sophistication about purchases.
    c. increase in overall population growth.
    d. time constraints on working women.

For the answers to these questions, please visit the online site for this book at **http://www.atomicdog.com.**

Case 1: Making a Multichannel Strategy Work Better[c5-1]

Numerous firms now offer multichannel shopping options. Nonetheless, some of them have not properly developed synergies across their channels. One general problem is that many companies have separate organizational units that handle in-store, catalog, Web, and mail-order shoppers. In certain cases, individual units of the same company may be competitive with one another, such as a Web product manager not wanting to lose a sale to a shopper that prefers picking up the item in the store. A second issue is that computer systems are often not integrated across channels. The editor of *Retail Customer Experience* (**http://www.retailcustomerexperience.com**) reports: "Companies often still have wholly separate in-store, online, and mail-order departments, from data sets to customer service staff to product selection."

One firm with a superior multichannel strategy is Saks Fifth Avenue (**http://www.saksfifthavenue.com**), which uses its Web site to get more information from consumers about their preferences. Gift cards and wedding registries are available online. To encourage cross-shopping, Saks provides Web customers with an exclusive toll-free service phone number, invitations to in-store events, and free valet parking when they visit a Saks Fifth Avenue store.

An important development is the effort to promote multichannel migration by measuring key customer groups and then influencing each group to interact with the optimal channel. Best Buy (**http://www.bestbuy.com**), through its multichannel migration strategy, attempts to get last-minute holiday season shoppers to buy goods online due to its large inventories. Best Buy's "Geek Squad" is available to set up or troubleshoot electronics equipment at customers' homes or offices. Best Buy also carefully observes trends in shopping behavior in both in-store and online environments. It uses this information to improve its assortment and merchandising across channels.

Similarly, Select Comfort (**http://www.selectcomfort.com**), a Minneapolis-based mattress retailer, has 450 stores, a contact center, and a sophisticated Web site. Its site ascertains the type of mattress a consumer wants, based on responses to the chain's sleep personality quiz. The test asks people a series of questions, such as how long they sleep, what side they sleep on, how much they weigh, and whether they toss and turn. Based on their responses, consumers are referred to a store to try out specific mattresses. "This is an experiential product. We want customers to come to the site and spend a lot of time on the site, but then we want them to go to a store and try the mattress out," says a Select Comfort executive.

To foster greater multichannel coordination, Sephora (**http://www.sephora.com**), the worldwide retail beauty chain, recently shifted its loyalty card operations from an outsourcing firm to in-house. It can now mine its extensive customer data base and better identify different opportunities between online and in-store operations. One such opportunity is to inform a Web shopper of the opening of a new store close to her home. Through better channel coordination, Sephora has increased response rates to specific promotions by 70 percent.

Customers must be allowed to use the proper channel based on their individual needs and values. Each company's channel preferences also need to be balanced with customer needs. A shopper who buys a lot of goods online, for instance, could be encouraged to come to the store for extra customer service or to try out a product he or she would ordinarily purchase online. On the other hand, a customer who loves online shopping should not be pushed to come to the store (if he or she truly enjoys the convenience, 24/7 timing, and the ability to more easily research a product through the Web).

Questions

1. Describe five possible sources of synergies for a camera retailer that offers both a Web site and store facilities for shoppers. The store specializes in the sale of used, high-quality camera equipment.
2. Should a retailer charge the same prices online as compared to in-store? Discuss both sides to this question.
3. Discuss five potential pitfalls associated with a small bricks-and-mortar retailer undertaking a multichannel strategy.
4. Cite five ways that a multichannel retailer can encourage its store shoppers to visit its Web site.

[c5-1] The data in the case are drawn from Partick McHugh, "Has Your Multichannel Strategy Become Frankenstein's Monster?" *DM News* (December 3, 2007), p. S8; "Report: Retailers Must Go Multichannel or Lose Customers," **http://www.prnewswire.com** (June 26, 2008); and Michael Stich, "Ring Up E-Commerce Gains with a True Multichannel Strategy," *Advertising Age* (March 10, 2008), p. 15.

Case 2: Verizon's FiOS Technology Moves to Enterprise Clients[c5-2]

Verizon Business (http://www.verizonbusiness.com) recently developed an enterprise version of its popular residential FiOS high-speed Internet service. Verizon designed this version in response to a request by the U.S. Defense Department for a network technology that can meet its bandwidth requirements for the next 25 years while reducing electricity usage. The FiOS residential broadband service (combining Internet, phone, and TV service) is sent over a fiber-optic network. As of mid-2008, Verizon had 1.8 million FiOS Internet and 1.2 million FiOS television customers.

The enterprise service, aimed at business clients, involves installing the same passive optical network (PON) to government, corporate, and university customers. Verizon's target market for this product consists of organizations that are heavy users of computer-assisted-design (CAD) applications, streamlined video, and/or real-time work group collaboration services. Some analysts believe that FiOS technology will be very attractive with government markets due to its enhanced security over copper-based systems, which are much easier to access. They also assume that due to high upfront costs, FiOS will more likely be used in owned versus leased buildings. As one marketing analyst observed, "When you wire a building for anything other than Cat 5 (Category 5 copper), it's like trying to sell Betamax to somebody. Copper is the standard." It is also not cost effective to convert to FiOS unless a building is undergoing a major renovation project.

The FiOS enterprise service for businesses has some major advantages to customers over the traditional services that rely on copper-based technology:

- Floor-space requirements are reduced. According to Verizon's director of technology and operations for its Business Federal Network Systems group, "[Racks of equipment] that normally took over 15 feet are now compressed to 1 foot." There is also no need to have wiring closets on every floor of an office building or college campus.
- Electricity usage in office buildings can be reduced by as much as 95 percent. The major savings occurs because the FiOS systems do not require workgroup switches and repeaters: "Nothing between the end user and the wiring closet is powered at all."
- Due to the lower use of electricity, less heat is generated: The system "consumes as much power and generates as much heat as a small data center did 10 years ago."
- Upfront equipment costs are reduced by 50 percent. Some of these savings are due to the fact that the new technology uses fiber-optic networking instead of Category 5 or Category 6 cable, which is much more costly.
- Installation time is reduced by 50 percent.
- System maintenance is easier since the new system has fewer moving parts.
- The system can accommodate greater capacity as a user's requirements change.
- Unlike older systems, fiber technology has greater security.

The major disadvantage of the enterprise system, aside from its relatively limited target market (new construction and major building renovations) is that there will be no phone service if the electricity to a building or area is disrupted. Verizon recommends that firms have battery-based backup systems.

Questions

1. What type of wholesaling is best suited for sales to customers of the FiOS enterprise system?
2. Develop a proposal to offer to a potential FiOS enterprise customer.
3. What customer service standards must be set for the performance of FiOS enterprise systems?
4. Discuss two other hi-tech services that Verizon should think about offering to large businesses.

[c5-2] The data in the case are drawn from Carolyn Duffy Marsan, "Verizon FiOS Tech Heading to Enterprises," http://www.idg.com (May 30, 2008).

Case 3: Costco: Carving Out a Strong Retail Niche[c5-3]

Costco (**http://www.costco.com**) is the nation's leading membership club chain, with about 54 percent of the overall market. This compares favorably with Sam's Club (**http://www.samsclub.com**), a Wal-Mart subsidiary, which has a 38 percent share. Costco's U.S. stores each average about $130 million in annual sales versus $75 million for each Sam's Club. Costco has been very successful in attracting and keeping its affluent shopper base. The average household income for a Costco shopper is $75,000, and about one-third of its shoppers have household incomes of more than $100,000.

Despite the firm's success, Jim Sinegal—Costco's chief executive—has been criticized by some industry analysts as being overgenerous to both workers (with the company's relatively high salaries and fringe benefits) and its customers (by providing great deals). Costco's average employee earns 40 percent more than the average Sam's Club's employee. And 82 percent of all Costco workers are covered by its health care plan, compared to less than one-half at Wal-Mart. Sinegal firmly believes that there are significant benefits to these compensation practices, including the low rates of employee turnover and theft. In addition, some of Costco's customers shop there due to its fair treatment of employees.

Sinegal rejects analysts' advice to raise prices. Costco uses a 14 percent markup on all of its goods (except for 15 percent on private-label items), while many supermarkets have 25 percent markups, and some department stores use 40 percent or even higher markups. Sinegal is passionate about Costco's pricing: "When I started, Sears (**http://www.sears.com**) was the Costco of the country, but they allowed someone else to come in under them. We don't want to be a casualty. We don't want to turn around and say, 'We got so fancy we've raised our prices,' and all of a sudden, a new competitor comes in and beats our prices. We understand our members don't come and shop with us because of fancy window displays or the Santa Claus or the piano player. They come and shop with us because we offer great values."

Several factors are essential in Costco's overall retail strategy: its low building and fixture costs, the small inventory on hand, the relentless search for the best prices, and the "treasure hunts" for shoppers. Costco's warehouse facilities are bare-bone structures with cement floors, high ceilings, visible pallets, and industrial-strength fixtures loaded to the ceiling with merchandise. A Costco store can stock up to 4,000 items and possibly four brands of toothpaste; a Wal-Mart store stocks more than 100,000 items and can carry dozens of different sizes and brands of toothpaste. Costco's lean stock on hand maximizes its inventory turnover while keeping stockouts low. By concentrating its purchases on fewer items, Costco is also able to receive substantial quantity discounts and purchase special buys.

Sinegal has been known to be a tough negotiator with Costco's suppliers and to warn them of the consequences of selling the same item to competitors at a lower price. When he discovered that a supplier sold frozen foods to Wal-Mart at lower prices, Sinegal dropped the offending supplier. Sinegal also warned Starbucks (**http://www.starbucks.com**) to reduce its prices, after coffee bean prices were reduced, at the risk of losing Costco's business.

With Costco's treasure hunts, Costco members can purchase items such as Coach (**http://www.coach.com**) leather bags, LCD TVs, and Waterford (**http://www.waterford.com**) crystal that are offered on a temporary, "as available" basis. Many of the offers are specifically targeted to Costco's affluent customer base. Because the selection of these items varies daily and cannot be replaced, shoppers are encouraged to return periodically to Costco to take advantage of special offers.

Questions

1. Discuss the pros and cons of Costco's affluent customer base versus Wal-Mart's less-affluent customer base.
2. As a buyer for Costco, how would you decide whether to stock a new line of barbeque grills?
3. Develop a program to enable Costco to further reduce its inventory on hand without having stockouts.
4. Apply the wheel of retailing to Costco.

[c5-3] The data in the case are drawn from Steven Greenhouse "How Costco Became the Anti Wal-Mart," **http://www.nytimes.com/2005/07/17/business/yourmoney/17costco.html** (July 17, 2005); and "Costco Appeals to Affluent," *Video Business* (May 26, 2008), pp. 20, 22.

Case 4: Walgreens: Competing in a Tougher Retail Drugstore Environment[c5-4]

Walgreens (http://www.walgreens.com) is the nation's largest drugstore chain based on sales. In the 2007 fiscal year, it recorded its 33rd year of consecutive growth in both earnings and sales. Walgreens operates about 6,000 locations throughout the lower 48 states and in Puerto Rico. A major strategic advantage for Walgreens is that its store locations are extremely accessible. About 140 million people live within two miles of a Walgreens, and 5 million shoppers walk into a Walgreens store on a daily basis.

In September 2007, Walgreens made the largest acquisition in its history with the purchase of Option Care Inc., a provider of specialty pharmacy services, for $850 million. This was in addition to its purchase of Medmark Specialty Pharmacy (http://www.medmark.org) in August 2006. The combined acquisitions make Walgreens one of the largest specialty pharmacies in the United States. Operators of specialty pharmacies sell high-cost prescriptions aimed at people with cancer, HIV/AIDS, and hepatitis C who require special care. The average prescription cost per patient with one or more of these diseases is $15,000. That amount is more than 20 times the annual prescription costs for a traditional patient.

Another source of revenue is Walgreens' Take Care Health Systems (http://www.takecarehealth.com) subsidiary. Take Care Health operates clinics in 14 states and plans to have more than 400 clinics by the beginning of 2009. Many of Take Care Health's patients would have to go to an emergency room or would not seek treatment for their conditions if their Take Care Health clinic is closed. About 30 percent of Take Care patients do not have a primary health-care provider.

Even though Walgreens has enjoyed a high level of financial performance, some industry analysts are concerned about the intense competitive environment. First, Walgreens and other store-based pharmacies now face a competitive threat from mail-order and online pharmacies. Prescription sales from mail-order and online pharmacies have been growing sharply and now generate nearly one-quarter of total prescription revenues. Chain pharmacy stores still account for more than 40 percent of prescription sales. However, the market share of mail-order pharmacies is greater than that for any of the major sources of prescription drugs: independent pharmacies, mass merchandisers, and supermarkets.

A second, but related, threat is that mail-order and online pharmacy customers have less need to visit a Walgreens store at all. Less store traffic can affect Walgreens' sale of highly profitable front-end merchandise (such as health and beauty aids, candy, tobacco, and film products and processing). Because mail-order and online pharmacies are highly automated, operate in low-cost areas, and do not require a store location, they can fill and mail a prescription at a lower cost compared to Walgreens. Third-party sales at Walgreens, where reimbursement is received from managed care organizations, government, and private insurance, accounts for close to 95 percent of Walgreens' prescription drug sales.

A third threat comes from Wal-Mart (http://www.walmart.com), Target (http://www.target.com), and Kroger (http://www.kroger.com) stores that offer hundreds of different generic versions of prescription drugs for $4 for a 30-day supply. Large drugstore chains such as Walgreens and CVS (http://www.cvs.com) have not yet matched this offer because a large percentage of their prescription drug sales are made to consumers who are reimbursed by insurance companies.

Last, marketing experts are concerned about the effect on Walgreens of CVS' significant recent acquisition of Caremark (http://www.caremark.com), a pharmacy benefit-management business (PBM) that offers mail-order services, specialty pharmacy services, and claims administration services to unions, managed care organizations, and government agencies. This acquisition resulted in CVS saving at least $660 million in 2008. Furthermore, Caremark's mail-order customers can get access to a pharmacist and be offered special deals at a local CVS store.

Questions

1. Discuss the pros and cons of Walgreens operating specialty pharmacy services.
2. Describe Walgreens' competitive advantages and disadvantages relative to Wal-Mart.
3. Discuss other ways that Walgreens can fight back against the mail-order and online pharmacies.
4. Discuss the pros and cons of Walgreens matching the generic drug prices at Wal-Mart, Target, and Kroger.

[c5-4] The data in the case are drawn from Joseph Agnese, *Standard & Poor's Industry Surveys: Supermarkets & Drugstores* (January 24, 2008); "Take Care Patient Count Hits Half-Million," *Drug Store News* (June 23, 2008), p. 8; and *Walgreen Company 2007 10-K*.

Is Channel Collaboration Feasible?[pc-5]

INTRODUCTION

As the world of business has become more complex and interdependent, so has marketing. Participating in cross-functional business teams is important; but it no longer is the means for solving complex problems or successfully pursuing rapidly moving and often fleeting market opportunities. This is simply because the knowledge, expertise, and information no longer primarily resides in the firm (no matter how large it might be), but is dispersed throughout the firm's entire value network or constellation to include suppliers, distributors, customers, and sometimes competitors. And it increasingly includes a model of working collaboratively through close relationships with customers and partners to co-create solutions to complex problems and/or jointly pursue marketplace opportunities.

Marketing collaborations with customers, suppliers, and even competitors are becoming more commonplace. Witness the following examples:

- 7-Eleven (**http://www.7-eleven.com**) collaborated with Anheuser-Busch (**http://www.anheuser-busch.com**) to develop various innovative marketing programs, such as a co-branded NASCAR (**http://www.nascar.com**) promotion and a Major League Baseball (**http://www.mlb.com**) promotion campaign targeting 7-Eleven's core customers.
- Honda (**http://www.honda.con**) engineers looked to collaborative relationships with their suppliers for extended joint improvement efforts, encouraging enhanced communication and sharing cost benefits.
- As a key part of its marketing strategy, Scholastic Inc. (**http://www.scholastic.com**), publisher of the Harry Potter books in the United States, collaborates with printers, logistics providers, and retail customers to ensure its books go on sale at midnight throughout the United States on the same day.
- Lockheed Martin Aeronautics (**http://www.lockheedmartin.com**) collaborated with historical competitor Northrop Grumman (**http://www.northropgrumman.com**) and BAE Systems (**http://www.baesystems.com**) to develop a proposal to win the right to jointly manufacture a strike fighter for the U.S. Department of Defense.

Organizations have been increasingly motivated to work collaboratively because of three primary factors: (1) greater interconnectedness of global commerce, (2) the rise in outsourcing, and (3) the ascendance of highly specialized organizations. Unfortunately, as any marketer who has been a part of a collaboration project with another organization will tell you, there is an alarmingly high failure rate associated with collaboration efforts. Frustrated marketing professionals are asking, "How do we collaborate successfully to achieve desired outcomes?" That is precisely the issue focused on in this case.

DEFINING COLLABORATION

Often, collaboration is a strategy for managing a long-term relationship. Firms form collaborative alliances to share their resources and combine their knowledge, skills, and physical assets to create strategic advantage and enhance profits. However, as Sandy Jap and Erin Anderson reported in the *Sloan Management Review*, there might also be a dark side to close, collaborative relationships. Often, the parties involved become too familiar with each other (e.g., they feel safer and are more likely to engage in conflict, or as each party learns what the other knows, the relationship becomes less valuable).

Business relationships are not likely to endure indefinitely, and a better perspective might be to move in and out of collaborative initiatives with a network of companies over time. In brief, given the high turbulence in markets today, an adaptive and often shorter-term approach to collaboration with different types of firms might be required. In fact, in our field interviews, we found that more and more firms were moving toward short-term collaborative projects to solve particular problems or pursue specific market opportunities. Predictably, collaboration projects might be intertwined with longer-term relationships, but the central focus is the project and its management. Each project is increasingly managed across functional departments within the firm and across organizations in a collaborative manner.

Consequently, we focused on a more adaptive form of collaboration, with the premise being that a firm will engage in specific collaborative projects as needed, whether with a close partner or with a loosely connected firm. Based on extensive secondary research, focus groups, and field interviews, we found that collaboration managed interdependencies to maximize shared goals and enhance individual goals through open exchange of information with joint decision-making and planning. Both our field interviews and the results from a large-scale survey showed that collaboration is an intense process, and is most useful when problems are complex and the solution is dependent on knowledge and insights from another firm.

[pc-5] Adapted by the authors from Nancy Nix, Robert Lusch, Zach Zacharia, and Wesley Bridges, "Competent Collaborations," *Marketing Management* (March-April 2008), pp. 18–24. Reprinted by permission of the American Marketing Association.

WHEN SHOULD FIRMS COLLABORATE?

The collaborative approach is for situations in which a more straightforward approach will not suffice: The individual firms are not capable of solving the problem, and the solution improves when the knowledge and skills of the two firms are considered collectively. For example, a collaborative effort would be required to evaluate and reduce a customer's total cost of ownership. Both firms would need to understand the complete set of activities and other factors affecting the cost of acquisition, receipt, use, recovery, and/or disposal of material—and to identify and implement opportunities for improvement.

A key characteristic of collaboration is joint planning or problem solving. For example, early supplier involvement in product design is important to ensure information about the supplier's process is considered. Also, the supplier's knowledge of various system components and processes can spur innovation that can have a significant influence on the overall cost, quality, or availability of the final product. However, if each party to a collaborative effort is not open to alternative solutions, the intensive information exchange and knowledge sharing required for collaboration is a waste of time. Too often, firms engage in collaboration to get the other party to adopt the answer they have already developed. Importantly, to indicate a desire to collaborate and then show a lack of willingness to do so will signal that a partner cannot be trusted, which may damage the quality of the relationship between the firms.

WHAT ARE THE BENEFITS?

There are at least two categories of benefits from successful project-specific collaboration efforts. The first and most important is tangible task performance, or the effectiveness of the project or problem resolution. Organizations collaborate because they want some combination of lower costs, improved product or service quality, better customer service, quicker project results, reduced cycle-time, or the ability to make more compelling value propositions to customers. Collaboration allows firms to pool knowledge and resources to develop innovative solutions that outperform those developed individually.

There is strong evidence that a second major benefit from effective collaboration is improved relationships with collaborating partners. It is widely recognized that commitment, trust, and credibility are important factors contributing to successful collaborations. Only over time, however—based on firms' experiences with each other—do commitment, trust, and credibility accrue. As firms engage seriously and intensely in collaboration, each has the opportunity to demonstrate capabilities, willingness to contribute, and commitment to the relationship. Thus, an important side benefit of collaboration across firms is greater trust and credibility—resulting in a more effective relationship with greater mutual commitment.

CRITICAL SUCCESS FACTORS

Using a secondary data review, coupled with focus group discussions and field interviews, we identified a set of factors associated with successful marketing supply chain collaborations and then validated these factors with broad survey data across many industries. The success factors included a willingness to collaborate with high intensity, coupled with organizational capabilities in three areas: (1) collaborative capability (the skills, capabilities, and supporting processes required to manage the collaboration process well); (2) absorptive capability (the ability to learn and apply new knowledge); and (3) project-specific capability (the skills and abilities required to accomplish the specific objectives of the task).

Firms that do well in these areas achieve better results, in terms of both task performance and improved relationship quality. See Figure 1. The differences in collaboration results were striking, in

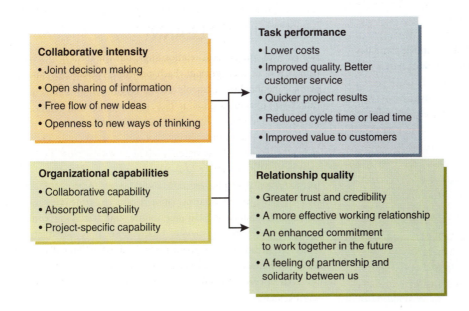

Collaborative intensity
- Joint decision making
- Open sharing of information
- Free flow of new ideas
- Openness to new ways of thinking

Organizational capabilities
- Collaborative capability
- Absorptive capability
- Project-specific capability

Task performance
- Lower costs
- Improved quality. Better customer service
- Quicker project results
- Reduced cycle time or lead time
- Improved value to customers

Relationship quality
- Greater trust and credibility
- A more effective working relationship
- An enhanced commitment to work together in the future
- A feeling of partnership and solidarity between us

Figure 1

Collaborative Intensity, Organizational Capabilities, and Collaboration Benefits

comparison with companies that did not focus on these critical success factors.

DOING THE RESEARCH

The research consisted of valid and reliable scales administered via a mail survey to 1,037 qualified respondents. The response rate was 46 percent (473 useable surveys were returned). Table 1 shows the broad characteristics of the sample in terms of type of the organization of the respondent and the collaboration partner, the role of the collaboration partner (supplier, customer, alliance partner, competitor, other), years involved with the collaboration partner, duration of the specific collaboration, and success of the collaboration project.

Based on our review of the literature and interviews, multi-item measures using a seven-point scale were adapted or developed for key constructs. The measures were incorporated into a 7-page survey instrument to test the hypothesized relationships shown in Figure 1. Potential respondents were prequalified, based on recent involvement in a complex collaboration project. To help ensure a high response rate, the potential respondents were contacted by phone to obtain their agreement to respond to the survey questionnaire. They were thus only mailed a survey if they agreed to participate.

To test the generalizability of our findings, we analyzed responses from both high-tech industries (where rapid technology developments would require frequent innovation) and traditional industries (which would be somewhat less dynamic). Hypothesized relationships were supported in both cases. We also analyzed responses for buyer-supplier collaborations vs. all other types of collaborations. In both cases, statistical tests supported the hypothesized relationships, reinforcing that collaboration can be an important tool in any industry and critical success factors are applicable in multiple settings.

SUPPLY CHANGE MANAGER INTERVIEWS

We gave considerable thought to who should be the key informant on collaborative efforts between firms. Many spanning processes involve supply chain activities, such as order fulfillment, purchasing, customer service, and outsourcing activities. In fact, as we interviewed supply chain managers, we found they engaged in many collaborative projects that interfaced with a multitude of marketing processes—especially product development and innovation activities. Because supply chain managers are increasingly involved in collaborations that link marketing to suppliers and customers, they were the target group we surveyed. More than 60 percent of responses reflected initiatives focused on innovation, such as new product, service, or packaging development (28 percent); new process design (27 percent); new supplier development (11 percent); or new technology implementation (6 percent). Other initiatives included resolving problems, negotiating agreements, and ongoing relationship development initiatives.

WHAT DID WE LEARN?

The research findings can be summarized in line with the model presented in Figure 1. In brief, we discuss and report the empirical findings related to the influence of collaboration intensity and organizational capabilities on task performance and relationship quality.

Collaboration Intensity

Successful collaboration requires a willingness to engage intensely in such behavior as sharing information, meeting face-to-face, making decisions and planning jointly, and resolving conflicts. Although this sounds obvious, many companies say that they want to collaborate, but they don't devote the time, energy, or resources required. Participants must be willing to engage in an interactive process that allows for new solutions, based on knowledge exchanged in the collaboration. This kind of exchange occurs

Table 1	Summary of Survey Respondents
Relevant Dimension	**Profile**
Type of organization: respondent	57% Manufacturer
	17% Service company
	9% Wholesale/distributor
	5% Retailer
	11% Other
Type of organization: collaboration partner	51% Manufacturer
	24% Service company
	13% Wholesale/distributor
	4% Retailer
	8% Other
Role of collaboration partner	61% Supplier
	12% Customer
	10% Alliance partner
	7% Another division within the firm
	4% Competitor
	6% Other
Years involved with collaborative partner	12% less than 1 year
	35% 1-5 years
	25% 5-10 years
	19% 10-20 years
	9% more than 20 years
Duration of collaboration	12 months (average)
Success of collaboration	66% Successful
	29% Unsuccessful
	5% Neither successful or unsuccessful

when firms invest in face-to-face meetings, and personal relationships are established.

Unfortunately, many firms engage in initiatives, but only give "lip service" to the collaboration. They withhold important information, or fail to take the time to listen and consider important information. Not only will this result in an unsuccessful marketing collaboration, but it will also damage the relationship between the parties. Collaboration requires face-to-face meetings and joint decisions, based on the full set of information available from both parties. This requires a "give and take" approach to understanding and managing the conflicting objectives and trade-offs. Part of the problem in unsuccessful collaboration is that firms do not collaborate seriously, with a proper level of resource commitment and intense information exchange.

The key empirical finding was that collaboration intensity enhances both task performance and relationship quality.

Organizational Capabilities

Successful collaboration also requires having the right organizational capabilities in place. These capabilities might be difficult to develop, but can be an important source of competitive advantage.

Collaborative Capability

Collaborative capability is having the skills, attitude, and mindset to manage the process well. This includes understanding the resources required, having strong communication and conflict management skills, knowing when and with whom to collaborate, and being able to select the right people to make the collaboration work. From the outset, organizations with these capabilities have support from senior management, and a realistic understanding of both the time commitment and risks involved. Such organizations recognize opportunities to collaborate, select partners they can successfully collaborate with, and select the right individuals for collaborative assignments. They also recognize, learn from, and resolve conflicts as they arise—and establish processes to monitor and manage collaboration efforts.

The empirical results strongly support the positive link between collaborative capability and both task performance and relationship quality.

Absorptive Capability

A common barrier to successful collaboration is the "not invented here" syndrome: Employees believe they are supposed to solve their own problems and that others have nothing to teach them. However, some organizations have a special ability to recognize, assimilate, and exploit new knowledge from external sources or high levels of absorptive capability. Organizations with strong absorptive capability have a commitment to looking for new ideas and creating an environment that encourages putting new ideas into practice to improve business performance.

Firms that recognize the importance of identifying and using relevant new ideas are much more likely to capitalize on the open sharing of information. They are also more likely to participate successfully in joint decision making, based on the shared set of knowledge resident in the two firms.

In our empirical research, there was a strong positive relationship between absorptive capability and task performance and relationship quality.

Project-Specific Capability

Organizations that engage in collaborations but do not bring a strong capability related to the specific project are unlikely to be successful. The temptation is to collaborate with a strong partner to compensate for a lack of necessary knowledge or capabilities. Unfortunately, if you cannot contribute some unique capability to the effort, you are not a very good collaboration partner and, perhaps worse, you might become too dependent on the other firm. In our empirical research, a strong positive relationship was seen between project-specific capability and task performance and relationship quality.

DOING IT RIGHT

The ability to collaborate successfully with other firms is a strategic imperative in today's dynamic and interdependent environment. However, successful collaborations do not come easily. They require a commitment to intense collaboration and organizational capabilities that drive success. Although the results of this research cannot offer a panacea, they do indicate that marketing managers and their firms should seriously ask themselves the following:

1. Can our firm recognize when collaboration is needed on a project, and can we see when a more straightforward solution is best? Don't try to collaborate on every single marketing effort, but focus the collaborative efforts where a difference in task performance and relationship quality is significant.

2. Does our firm have the commitment of senior management to invest the necessary time, resources, and effort for marketing collaborations? In our large-scale survey and field interviews, we found warnings about taking on collaborations between firms when a top-level commitment was not present.

3. Can we improve on whom we select as collaborators, the people in the organization we put on collaborative teams, and our willingness to exchange information and ideas? If collaboration is important, then put the best team together. This might involve not only marketers in your firm, but other functional areas as needed to bring the needed knowledge and expertise to the effort.

4. Do we have an organizational capability that allows us to learn from collaboration partners and utilize the knowledge to improve performance, or are we encumbered by the "not invented here" syndrome? Have we put in place the systems, procedures, and incentives that encourage the application of new ideas within the firm? Importantly, if we think we are a great marketing organization, are we willing to admit we can still learn more and benefit from marketing collaborations across firms?

5. Are we committed to collaborating in a way that improves relationship quality with our partners? Are we developing a relationship that thrives on mutual commitment, mutual respect, trustworthiness, and unity of purpose? If that is the situation, then the firm will not only be able to improve short- to intermediate-marketing performance but also build social capital for future marketing collaborations.

If an organization can answer "yes" to these basic questions, it can dramatically improve collaboration outcomes. If the answers to these questions are negative, a firm might waste a great deal of time and energy in unsuccessful collaborations. It is important to develop the internal capabilities that enable successful collaboration, before engaging in collaborative projects with supply chain partners, customers, and even competitors.

Questions

1. Generally speaking, how would you answer this question: "Is channel collaboration feasible?"
2. In your own words, explain what "collaboration" means from a distribution channel perspective.
3. What is the value of the flowchart shown in Figure 1?
4. In an ideal distribution channel, what is the role of the manufacturer, the wholesaler, the retailer, and the customer?
5. Under what circumstances should firms *not* collaborate?
6. What could a large manufacturer learn from the material in this case?
7. What could a small retailer learn from the material in this case?

6

Promotion Planning

Part 6 covers promotion, the third major element of the marketing mix.

17 Integrated Marketing Communications

Here, we broadly discuss promotion planning—all communication used to inform, persuade, and/or remind people about an organization's or individual's goods, services, image, ideas, community involvement, or impact on society. We describe the basic types of promotion and the stages in a channel of communication. Next, we present the steps in developing an overall promotion plan. We conclude the chapter with global promotion considerations, and the legal environment and criticisms of promotion.

18 Advertising and Public Relations

In this chapter, we examine two of the four types of promotion: advertising and public relations. Advertising is paid, nonpersonal communication by an identified sponsor, and public relations is any form of image-directed communication by an identified sponsor or the independent media. We detail the scope and attributes of advertising and public relations, and describe the role of publicity. We discuss developing advertising and public relations plans in depth.

19 Personal Selling and Sales Promotion

Now, we focus on the two other key elements of a promotion mix: personal selling and sales promotion. Personal selling is oral communication with one or more prospective buyers by paid representatives for the purpose of making sales, and sales promotion is the paid marketing communication activities (other than advertising, publicity, or personal selling) that stimulate consumer purchases and dealer effectiveness. We describe the scope, characteristics, and stages in planning for both personal selling and sales promotion.

After reading Part 6, you should understand element 12 of the strategic marketing plan outlined in Table 3-2 (page 74).

Chapter 17

Integrated Marketing Communications

American Express (AmEx) (**http://www.americanexpress.com**) is a payments-and-travel services firm that offers charge cards, credit cards, and travel-related services to consumers and businesses around the world. Its credit-card operations account for over one-half of total revenues, although AmEx has more than 2,200 locations for its travel agency operations and is the world's largest issuer of traveler's checks.

The three cornerstones of AmEx's credit-card strategy are to: attract and retain more affluent customers, increase the number of firms accepting its cards, and engage in local credit-card programs. The strategy requires a combination of advertising, public relations, personal selling, and sales promotions. To attract wealthy consumers, AmEx has partnerships with financial institutions in 125 countries. These partnerships give AmEx access to the banks' valuable customers.

AmEx's average spending per card by customers is substantially higher than for its competitors. And, even though it offers a selection of Blue cards with no annual fee, it recently launched a Bank of America Accolades American Express Card and the ultra-premium Citi Chairman American Express Card aimed at wealthy and ultra-wealthy banking clients.

AmEx realizes that it can expand its revenues by both increasing the number of establishments that accept its cards and increasing the average customer purchase. It is using a substantial amount of advertising and personal selling to expand the number of gasoline and grocery stores that honor its cards. It also offers a no-annual-fee Costco card that functions as a Costco membership card.

The firm has many local promotions. It sponsors these no-annual-fee special credit cards: IN:New York City, IN:Chicago, and IN:Los Angeles. These cards offer members one Inside reward point on general purchases and double points for "City Essentials" such as magazines, movie theaters, and dining.

Image-based advertising and public relations are also vital aspects of AmEx's overall promotional strategy. The firm sponsors a number of sporting events (such as the U.S. Open tennis series), as well as events such as New York's Tribeca Film Festival (**http://www.tribecafilmfestival.org**).[1]

In this chapter, we will study the many dimensions of promotion planning, including developing an integrated approach to promotion planning.

Chapter Objectives

1. To define promotion planning, show its importance, and demonstrate the value of integrated marketing communications
2. To describe the general characteristics of advertising, public relations, personal selling, and sales promotion
3. To explain the channel of communication and how it functions
4. To examine the components of a promotion plan
5. To discuss global promotion considerations, and the legal environment and criticisms and defenses of promotion

---

[1] Various company and other sources.

17-1 OVERVIEW

Promotion is any communication used to inform, persuade, and/or remind people about an organization's or individual's goods, services, image, ideas, community involvement, or impact on society. *Promotion planning* is systematic decision making relating to all aspects of an organization's or individual's communications efforts.

Communication occurs through brand names, packaging, company marquees and displays, personal selling, customer service, trade shows, sweepstakes, and messages in mass media (such as newspapers, TV, radio, direct mail, billboards, magazines, and transit). It can be company sponsored or controlled by independent media. Messages may emphasize information, persuasion, fear, sociability, product performance, humor, and/or comparisons with competitors.

In this chapter, we cover the context of integrated promotion planning. Included are discussions on promotion's importance, integrated marketing communications, promotion types, the channel of communication, promotion planning, global considerations, the legal environment, and general criticisms and defenses of promotion. Chapter 18 covers advertising and public relations. Chapter 19 deals with personal selling and sales promotion.

> **Promotion planning** focuses on a total **promotion** effort—informing, persuading, and reminding.

17-2 THE IMPORTANCE OF PROMOTION

Promotion is a vital element of the marketing mix. For new products, people must be informed about items and their features before they can develop favorable attitudes toward them. For products with some consumer awareness, the focus is on persuasion: converting knowledge to liking. For very popular products, the focus is on reminding: reinforcing existing consumer beliefs.

The people and organizations at whom a firm's promotional efforts are aimed may fall into various categories: consumers, stockholders, consumer advocates, government, channel members, employees, competitors, and the public. Communication often goes on between a firm and each group, not just with consumers; and it may differ because the groups have distinct goals, knowledge, and needs.

Within an audience category (such as consumers), a firm needs to identify and appeal to the opinion leaders who influence others' decisions. It also needs to understand *word-of-mouth communication*, the process by which people express opinions and product-related experiences to one another. It is hard to succeed without sustained, positive word of mouth. With such communication, popularity can grow:

> **Word-of-mouth communication** occurs as people state opinions to others.

> You could break your small business bank account on flashy ads. Or, you can follow the lead of successful entrepreneurs who know one sure-fire marketing tool: There's no shame in asking a friend to tell a friend. You're encouraging your happiest customers to create a buzz about you. When Mia Jackson, president of Doro Marketing (**http://www.doromarketing. com**)—which produces marketing materials for companies and nonprofit organizations— launched her firm, she counted on friends and former colleagues to chat up her services. As her clientele grew, she began asking her favorites to pass along her name and card to others in need of her expertise. "If you don't have that word of mouth, it's very seldom a brochure will get you the clients you want," says Jackson, who landed her largest client when a woman she once worked with suggested Doro for a marketing project.[2]

> According to eMarketer (**http://www.emarketer.com**), more than 25 million U.S. adults regularly share advice about goods or services online. And a study by BIGresearch (**http:// www.bigresearch.com**) shows that 91 percent of U.S. adults regularly or occasionally seek advice about goods or services and 94 percent give advice to others. Recent research from

---

[2] Stacy Gilliam, "Closing the Sale," *Black Enterprise* (September 2005), p. 56.

ForeSee Results (http://www.foreseeresults.com) found that 17 percent of all visitors to the 100 top-grossing retail Web sites came because of a recommendation. Those that came because of word of mouth were much more likely to buy, recommend, return to the site, and remain loyal to the company than those that came in through a shopping comparison site, search engine, promotional E-mail, or advertisement. All-in-all, word of mouth is an incredibly powerful marketing strategy when understood and harnessed correctly.[3]

These Web sites offer advice on how to stimulate positive word-of-mouth communication among consumers: "Word of Mouth Marketing Articles" (http://www.mnav.com/womtitlepage.htm) and "Essentials of Word of Mouth Marketing" (http://www.soho.org/Marketing_Articles/word_of_mouth.htm).

A company's promotion plan usually stresses individual goods and services, with the intent of moving people from awareness to purchase. Yet, the firm may also convey its overall image (industry innovator), views on ideas (free trade), community service (funding a new hospital), or impact on society (the size of its work force).

A good promotion plan complements the product, distribution, and price aspects of marketing, and it is well designed. Allen Edmonds (http://www.allenedmonds.com)—a maker of quality shoes—distributes products at finer stores and sets premium prices. It advertises in such magazines as *GQ* and *Fortune* and expects retailers to do first-rate personal selling. Ads are in color and stress product features, not prices.

Superior promotion plans are feasible even if companies have limited resources. Here are 10 tips:

1. "Create a brochure for your business. Include testimonials from customers and focus on your unique and special expertise."
2. "Publish a newsletter. Many people will toss out the flyers or advertisements but will take a moment to read an interesting newsletter."
3. "Develop a Web site and get an E-mail address."
4. "Attend trade shows or exhibits related to your industry, product, or business. Bring along your brochures, sales flyers, and newsletters."
5. "Join and participate in community business groups such as your local chamber of commerce."
6. "Write articles for the local paper. Each time one is published, you gain credibility and visibility."
7. "Set up a 'take-one' box in your place of business. Put flyers, brochures, and letters there."
8. "Send out congratulatory notes for customers' personal events such as birthdays."
9. "Ask your customers for referrals."
10. "Send out press releases when you introduce new goods or services."[4]

Promotion's importance is also evident from the spending and jobs in this area. The world's ten largest ad agencies have overall annual billings of nearly $50 billion. The International Advertising Association (http://www.iaaglobal.org) has thousands of members from 76 nations. In the United States alone, each year, auto makers and retailers each spend $19 billion on measured advertising media; 15 million people work in sales; 300 billion coupons are given out; and there are thousands of trade shows.[5]

---

[3] Larry Freed, Foresee Results, "Measuring Word of Mouth Online: Six Key Considerations," http://www.foreseeresults.com/_downloads/whitepaper/WordofMouth_BestPractices.pdf (2008).

[4] Kate Schultz, "Top 10 Tips for Marketing a Small Business," http://www.marketingsurvivalkit.com/sbmarketing.htm (May 4, 2006).

[5] "World's Top 50 Agency Companies," *Advertising Age* (May 5, 2008); "U.S. Ad Spending by Category," *Advertising Age* (June 23, 2008); U.S. Department of Labor, Bureau of Labor Statistics; "Promotion Industry Trends Report," *Promo* (September 2008); and authors' estimates.

17-3 AN INTEGRATED APPROACH TO PROMOTION PLANNING

When it develops and applies a well-coordinated promotion plan, a firm should use *integrated marketing communications (IMC)*. IMC "recognizes the value of a comprehensive plan that evaluates the strategic roles of a variety of communication disciplines—advertising, public relations, personal selling, and sales promotion—and combines them to provide clarity, consistency, and maximum communication impact."[6] For example, PepsiCo (**http://www.pepsico.com**) has a sales force that visits stores stocking its products, advertises in consumer media, and offers cents-off coupons. Xerox (**http://www.xerox.com**) has a technical sales force, advertises in business publications, and sends representatives to trade shows to promote its document management technology. Table 17-1 shows the value of integrated marketing communications.

A superior IMC plan properly addresses these points:

- *It is synergistic*, taking into account the multiple ways to reach potential consumers at different points during their decision process.
- *There is tactical consistency*, so various promotion tools complement each other and communicate the same basic themes.
- *There is interactivity with consumers*, so messages are better tailored to specific market segments.
- *Every company message positively influences the target audience*, so each contact builds on the contacts before it.
- *The company's basic promotion themes and differential advantages are clearly understood by all employees who interface with the targeted audience* to avoid the

> **Integrated marketing communications (IMC)** evaluates the strategic roles of various communication disciplines and combines them for clarity, consistency, and impact.

> IMC efforts should be synergistic, tactically consistent, interactive, positive influences, and so forth.

Table 17-1 The Value of Integrated Marketing Communications
Through an integrated marketing communications strategy, a firm can: • Coordinate all of its promotional activities.   • Establish and maintain a consistent image for the company and its goods and services.   • Communicate the features of goods and services.   • Create awareness for new goods and services.   • Keep existing goods and services popular.   • Reposition the images or uses of faltering goods and services.   • Generate enthusiasm from channel members.   • Note where goods and services can be purchased.   • Persuade consumers to trade up from one product to a more expensive one.   • Alert consumers to sales.   • Justify (rationalize) the prices of goods and services.   • Answer consumer questions.   • Close transactions with customers.   • Provide service for consumers after transactions are completed.   • Reinforce consumer loyalty.   • Place the company and its goods and services in a favorable light, relative to competitors.   • Encourage cross-marketing, whereby each element of the promotion mix reinforces the other (such as including a Web address on shopping bags, in the store, on the sales receipt, and in ads).

[6] Adapted by the authors from Janet Smith, "Integrated Marketing," *Marketing Tools* (November-December 1995), p. 64.

negative impact of misinformed employees passing on the wrong information to potential customers.

- *Advertising, public relations, sales, and sales promotion personnel cooperate with one another*, and view each other as partners rather than as adversaries.
- *Detailed data bases are maintained*, so that promotion efforts can be regularly reviewed.[7]

Frito-Lay (**http://www.fritolay.com**), a leading IMC practitioner, was recently honored by the Promotion Marketing Association (**http://www.pmalink.org**) for an integrated campaign it ran for newly acquired Stacy's Pita Chips (**http://www.pitachips.com**):

Stacy Madison created Stacy's from a street sandwich cart in Boston in the late 1990s. People lined up for her gourmet sandwiches, so Stacy started serving homemade pita chips to appease them. Soon the pita chips became more popular than the sandwiches. We believed that Stacy Madison's unique spirit would resonate with women. So, the "Welcome To Stacy's" campaign was born. We wanted to personally introduce Stacy's to the country and facilitate an ongoing conversation to tell her story, share her passion for the chips, invite people to try them, and inspire a healthier way to snack. A gift box was sent just before Super Bowl XLI (February 2007) to every woman in America named Stacy. Rachael Ray and several news shows reported on our direct mail program, giving our brand a push as we began national introduction. During the launch, we created a site dubbed "Calling All Stacy's." This gave consumers another way to request a gift box if their name had a different spelling, or if they wanted to be a "Stacy-For-The-Day." A print campaign in lifestyle publications such as *People, Real Simple, Health, Cooking Light*, and *New Yorker* kept the brand fresh, while the copy kept the brand topical. Stacy celebrated the Academy Awards with an Oscar Party, took us to pool parties, beach picnics, and yoga classes. Trade ads got the attention of key retailers by promising we'd reach 10 million shoppers with our marketing program. In-store branded displays in unexpected places like the grocery deli (rather than the chip aisle) captured the attention of consumers.[8]

Figures 17-1 and 17-2 highlight the integrated marketing communications approaches of the Apple iPod (**http://www.apple.com/itunes**) and Celestial Tea (**http://www.celestialtea.com**), respectively.

17-4   TYPES OF PROMOTION

Organizations use one or more of four basic types of promotion in their communications programs:

> Advertising, public relations (publicity), personal selling, and sales promotion are the four key promotion types.

- *Advertising* is paid, nonpersonal communication regarding goods, services, organizations, people, places, and ideas that is transmitted through various media by business firms, government and other nonprofit organizations, and individuals who are identified in the advertising message as the sponsor. The message is generally controlled by the sponsor.
- *Public relations* includes any communication to foster a favorable image for goods, services, organizations, people, places, and ideas among their publics—such as consumers, investors, government, channel members, employees, and the general public. It may be nonpersonal or personal, paid or nonpaid, and sponsor controlled

---

[7] Adapted by the authors from Kim Bartel Sheehan and Caitlin Doherty, "Re-Weaving the Web: Integrating Print and Online Communications," *Journal of Interactive Marketing*, Vol. 15 (Spring 2001), pp. 47–59; Anders Gronstedt, *The Customer Century: Lessons from World-Class Companies in Integrated Marketing and Communications* (London: Routledge, 2000); and Michael Render, "IMC Gets Better with Inflow Marketing," *Marketing News* (September 11, 2000), p. 23.

[8] "Stacy's Pita Chips: Premium CPG Salty Snacks," **http://www.pmalink.org/awards/default.asp?p=2008reggie_winners** (2008).

Figure 17-1

Integrated Marketing Communications and the Apple iPod

In all of its communications about the iPod, Apple (**http://www.apple.com**) delivers a consistent message: fun, innovative, trendsetting, stretching the limits, personal.

Source: Reprinted by permission.

or not controlled. *Publicity* is the form of public relations that entails nonpersonal communication passed on via various media but not paid for by an identified sponsor. Wording and placement of publicity messages are generally media controlled.

- *Personal selling* involves oral communication with one or more prospective buyers by paid representatives for the purpose of making sales.
- *Sales promotion* involves paid marketing communication activities (other than advertising, publicity, or personal selling) that are intended to stimulate consumer purchases and dealer effectiveness. Included are trade shows, premiums, incentives, giveaways, demonstrations, and various other efforts not in the ordinary promotion routine.[9]

The general characteristics of each type of promotion are shown in Table 17-2. As discussed later in the chapter, many firms in some way combine them into an integrated promotional blend. This lets them reach their entire target market, present both persuasive and believable messages, have personal contact with customers, sponsor special events, and balance the promotional budget.

17-5 THE CHANNEL OF COMMUNICATION

To develop a proper promotion mix and interact effectively with a target audience, the *channel of communication (communication process)* shown in Figure 17-3 must be understood. Through such a channel, a source develops a message, transmits it to an

> A message is sent to an audience via a **channel of communication**.

[9] Adapted by the authors from "Dictionary," **http://www.marketingpower.com/_layouts/Dictionary.aspx** (March 22, 2009).

Figure 17-2

Integrated Marketing Communications and Celestial Tea

At Celestial Tea (**http://www. celestialseasonings.com**), from Hain Celestial (**http://www.hain-celestial.com**): "We've long prided ourselves on the beautiful artwork and inspiring quotes that are the backbone of our packaging. That hasn't changed. Our new look retains all the beauty and originality tea drinkers have come to expect, while focusing on what makes our tea so special: high-quality, all-natural ingredients from the finest farms and tea estates around the world, crafted into distinctive blends that burst with aroma and flavor."

Source: Reprinted by permission.

audience via some medium, and gets feedback from the audience. The components of a communication channel are discussed next.

17-5a The Source

A **source** presents a message.

The **source** of communication is usually a company, an independent institution, or an opinion leader seeking to present a message to an audience. A firm communicates through a(n) spokesperson, celebrity, actor playing a role, representative consumer, and/or salesperson. A company spokesperson is typically a long-time employee who represents the firm in communications. The spokesperson has an aura of sincerity, commitment, and expertise. Sometimes, the spokesperson is a top executive, such as George Zimmer, founder and chief executive of the Men's Wearhouse (**http://www.menswearhouse.com**) apparel chain, or Dan Hesse, chief executive of Sprint (**http://www.sprint.com**). Other times, front-line workers are used, such as a Verizon (**http://www.verizon.com**) customer service representative or a Sheraton (**http://www.starwoodhotels.com/sheraton**) hotel chef. In general, this source has been quite effective.

Table 17-2	Characteristics of Promotional Types			

Factor	Advertising	Publicity Form of Public Relations[a]	Personal Selling	Sales Promotion
Audience	Mass	Mass	Small (one-to-one)	Varies
Message	Uniform	Uniform	Specific	Varies
Cost	Low per viewer or reader	None for media space and time; can be some costs for media releases and publicity materials	High per customer	Moderate per customer
Sponsor	Company	No formal sponsor (media not paid)	Company	Company
Flexibility	Low	Low	High	Moderate
Control over content and placement	High	None (controlled by media)	High	High
Credibility	Moderate	High	Moderate	Moderate
Major goal	To appeal to a mass audience at a reasonable cost, and create awareness and favorable attitudes	To reach a mass audience with an independently reported message	To deal with individual consumers, to resolve questions, to close sales	To stimulate short-run sales, to increase impulse purchases
Example	Television ad for an Apple iPhone	Magazine article describing an Apple iPhone's unique features	Salesperson explaining how an Apple iPhone works	An Apple iPhone exhibited at trade shows

[a] Please note: When public relations embodies advertising (an image-related message), personal selling (a salesperson describing his or her firm's public service efforts to college students), and/or sales promotion (distributing special discount coupons to low-income consumers), it takes on the characteristics of those promotional types. However, the goal would be more image-related than sales-related.

Marketing and the Web

Spyware and Adware Undermine Online Communications

Spyware and adware consist of programs that can monitor a computer user's behavior without his or her knowledge or permission. Spyware runs on a consumer's PC and displays ads in response to the consumer's Web-based activities. Programs that enable spyware to operate are often bundled with freeware and computer games. The bundled software is typically downloaded by a consumer from an adware vendor's site or from an affiliated Web site. In addition to tracking personal data, adware programs can slow a computer to a virtual crawl due to their use of its memory.

Among those that profit from spyware and adware are ad brokers, search engines that sell ads based on key words, and software bundlers that distribute adware. In one adware case, the New York Attorney General (AG) said Priceline.com. (**http://www.priceline.com**), Travelocity.com (**http://www.travelocity.com**), and Cingular Wireless (now part of

AT&T) were responsible for ads displayed via adware. The AG found that Direct Revenue-installed adware programs had delivered advertising, tracked people's use of specific Web sites, and collected data typed into online forms on computers around the world. According to settlement terms, Priceline, Travelocity, and Cingular each paid small penalties.

Antispyware legislation has been introduced in several states and enacted in Arkansas and Virginia. These laws make it a crime to hijack a user's computer to show ads or collect personal information. Some opponents of the proposed legislation argue that tracking software helps users gain access to more personalized Web sites.

Sources: Based on material in "Advertisers Settle Claims for Adware Distributed by Intermediaries," *The Computer & Internet Lawyer* (April 2007), p. 48; and "Aaron Ricadela, "Congress Takes Aim at Spyware," **http://www.businessweek.com/technology** (June 18, 2007).

Figure 17-3

A Channel of Communication

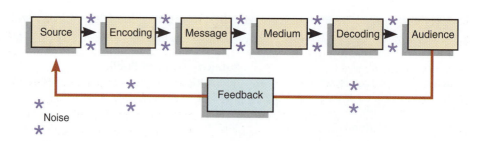

A celebrity is used to gain the audience's attention and improve product awareness. Problems can arise if a celebrity is seen as insincere or unknowledgeable. Popular celebrities include Michael Jordan for Hanes (**http://www.hanes.com**), Reese Witherspoon for Avon (**http://www.avon.com**), Snoopy and other *Peanuts* characters for MetLife (**http://www.metlife.com**), and Tiger Woods for Tag Heuer (**http://www.tagheuer.com**). See Figure 17-4.

Many ads have actors playing roles rather than celebrity spokespeople. The emphasis then is on presenting a message about a good, service, or idea rather than on the consumer recognizing a celebrity. The hope is that the consumer will learn more about product attributes.

A representative consumer is one who likes a product and recommends it in an ad. The intent is to present a real consumer in an actual situation, such as Jared Fogle for Subway (**http://www.subway.com**). The person is sometimes shown with his or her name and hometown. A hidden camera or blind taste test may be used with this source. Today, some viewers are skeptical about how "representative" the endorser is.

Finally, a firm may use a salesperson to communicate with consumers. Many salespeople are knowledgeable, assertive, and persuasive. However, consumers may doubt their objectivity and tactics. Auto salespeople rate particularly low in consumer surveys.

An independent institution is not controlled by the firms on which it reports. It presents information in a professional, nonpaid (by the firms) manner. Consumers Union (**http://www.consumersunion.org**), the publisher of *Consumer Reports* (**http://www.consumerreports.org**), and a local newspaper restaurant critic are examples of

Figure 17-4

Tiger Woods: A Tag Heuer Endorser

Source: Reprinted by permission of Susan Berry, Retail Image Consulting, Inc.

independent sources. They have great credibility for readers because they discuss both good and bad points, but some population segments may not be exposed to these sources. The information presented may differ from that contained in a firm's commercials or sales-force presentations.

An opinion leader has face-to-face contact with and influences potential consumers. Because he or she deals on a personal level, an opinion leader often has strong persuasive impact and believability, and can offer social acceptance for followers. Firms often address initial messages to opinion leaders, who then provide word-of-mouth to others. Many marketers believe opinion leaders not only influence, but also are influenced by, others (opinion receivers); even opinion leaders need approval for their choices.

In assessing a source, these questions are critical: Is he/she believable? Is he/she convincing? Does he/she present an image consistent with the firm? Do consumers value the message of the source? Is he/she seen as knowledgeable? Does the source complement the product he/she communicates about, or does the source overwhelm it? Do significant parts of the market dislike the source?

17-5b Encoding

Encoding is the process whereby a thought or idea is translated into a message by the source. Preliminary decisions are made as to message content, such as the use of symbolism and wording. It is vital that the thought or idea be translated exactly as the source intends. A firm wanting to stress its product's prestige would include the product's status, exclusive ownership, and special features in a message. It would not stress a low price, availability in discount stores, or the millions of people who have already purchased.

> In **encoding**, a source translates a thought into a message.

17-5c The Message

A *message* is a combination of words and symbols transmitted to an audience. It depends on whether the goal is to inform, persuade, or remind. Almost all messages include some information on the firm's name, the product name, the desired image, differential advantages, and product attributes. A firm would also give information on availability and price at some point in the consumer's decision process. With integrated marketing communications, message consistency is important. As highlighted in Figure 17-5, the Almond Board of California (http://www.almondsarein.com) understands this.

> A **message** combines words and symbols.

Most communication involves one-sided messages, in which only the benefits of a good, service, or idea are cited. Few firms use two-sided messages, in which both benefits and limitations are noted. Companies are not anxious to point out their shortcomings, although consumer perceptions of honesty may be improved via two-sided messages.

Many messages use symbolism and try to relate safety, social acceptance, or sexual appeal to a purchase. In symbolic messages, a firm stresses psychological benefits rather than tangible product performance. Clothing ads may offer acceptance by peers; toothpaste may brighten teeth and make a person more sexually attractive. One type of symbolism, fear appeals (such as anti-drug ads), has had mixed results. People respond to moderate fear appeals, but strong ones may not be as well received.

Humor may be used to gain audience attention and retain it. Dove (http://www.dove.com) has done this quite creatively, as shown in Figure 17-6. About.com (http://humor.about.com/cs/advertisinghumor) has several popular examples and related materials. Yet, a firm needs to be careful to get across the intended message when using humor—which should not make fun of the firm, its goods, or its services; and humor should not dominate a message so the brand name or product attributes go unnoticed. Because humor has cultural underpinnings, successful ads in one country may not work well in another nation:

Figure 17-5

A Creative, Well-Conceived Message from the Almond Board of California

Source: Reprinted by permission.

Besides understanding why/how humor works, knowing why it fails is also important. This concern is best illustrated by how some humorous ads have not only failed to evoke laughter, but have also provoked negative viewer reactions. For marketers, such failure is costly, since it essentially means failure at two levels: first, the inappropriate humor itself, and second, the lack of sensitivity and knowledge about the consumer market to understand the inappropriateness of failed humor.[10]

> **Comparative messages** position a firm versus competitors.

Comparative messages implicitly or explicitly contrast a firm's offerings with those of competitors. Implicit comparisons use an indirect brand-X or leading-brand approach ("Our industrial glues are more effective than other leading brands"). Explicit comparisons use a direct approach (such as DirecTV, **http://www.directv.com**, promoting the availability of all NFL games—via its "NFL Sunday Ticket" package—for viewers in

---

[10] Yih Hwai Lee and Elison Ai Ching Lim, "What's Funny and What's Not," *Journal of Advertising*, Vol. 37 (Summer 2008), pp. 71–84.

campaignforrealbeauty.com

Say goodbye to stickiness. Say hello to movement.

Turn unruly hair into foxy momma hair. Dove Anti-Frizz Cream with our Weightless Moisturizers™ makes hair smooth, shiny and doesn't leave it greasy. Welcome to blue heaven.

unstick your style.

Figure 17-6

A Clever Use of Humor

Source: Reprinted by permission.

contrast to the lesser NFL coverage by the leading cable TV operators). Comparative messages are used in some TV and radio commercials, print ads, and other media; and salespeople often compare their products' attributes with those of competitors. In using comparative messages, a firm must be careful not to turn off consumers, place too much emphasis on a competitor's brand, or lose sight of its own differential advantages to promote.

A message must be presented in a desirable, exclusive, and believable way. The good, service, or idea must be perceived as something worth buying or accepting. It also must be seen as unique to the seller—that is, it cannot be gotten elsewhere. Finally, the message must make believable claims.

> **Massed** or **distributed promotion** and the **wearout rate** must be carefully planned.

Message timing must also be carefully planned. First, during what times of the year should a firm advertise, seek publicity, add salespeople, or run promotions? In *massed promotion*, communication efforts are concentrated in peak periods, such as holidays. In *distributed promotion*, communication efforts are spread throughout the year. Figure 17-7 compares massed and distributed promotion.

Second, the *wearout rate*—the time it takes for a message to lose effectiveness—must be determined. Some messages wear out quickly; others last for years. Wearout depends on communications frequency, message quality, the number of different messages used, and other factors. Allstate (**http://www.allstate.com**) has done such a good job with its decades-old "You're in good hands" message that it is still popular.

17-5d The Medium

> A **medium** is a personal or nonpersonal channel for a message.

The *medium* is the personal or nonpersonal means used to send a message. Personal media are company salespeople and other representatives, as well as opinion leaders. Nonpersonal (mass) media include newspapers, television, radio, direct mail, billboards, magazines, and transit.

Personal media offer one-to-one audience contact, are flexible, and can adapt messages to individual needs and handle questions. They appeal to a small audience and are best with a concentrated market. Nonpersonal media have a large audience and low per-customer costs, and are not as flexible and dynamic as one-to-one contacts. They work best with a dispersed target market.

Figure 17-7

Massed Versus Distributed Promotion

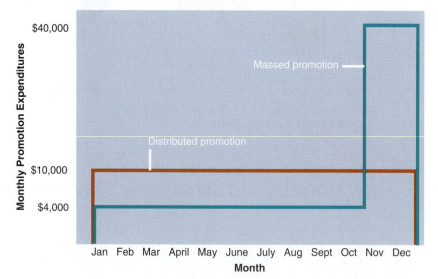

With a total promotion budget of $120,000, a hosiery manufacturer employs distributed promotion and spends $10,000 each month throughout the year. With the same budget, a toy manufacturer uses massed promotion and spends $80,000 from November 1 through December 31 (the remaining $40,000 is spent over the other 10 months). In both cases, monthly promotion expenditures are linked to monthly sales.

A firm should consider both total and per-unit costs, product complexity, audience attributes, and communication goals in deciding between personal and nonpersonal media. The two kinds of media go well together because nonpersonal media generate consumer interest and personal media help close sales.

17-5e   Decoding

Decoding is the process by which a message sent by a source is interpreted by an audience. The interpretation is based on the audience's background, as well as message clarity and complexity. For example, a homemaker and a working woman might have different interpretations of a message on the value of child-care centers. As symbolism and complexity increase, clarity usually decreases. As noted earlier, it is vital that a message be decoded in the manner intended by the source (encoding = decoding): "People have trouble remembering someone's name, let alone a complicated message. Every ad element should support the headline message, whether that message is 'price,' 'selection,' 'quality,' or any other concept. Find a likable style and personality and stay with it for at least a year, to avoid confusing buyers. Be credible. If you say your quality or value is 'best' and it clearly is not, advertising will speed your demise, not increase your business. Identifying and denigrating the competition should also be avoided. It is potentially distracting and may backfire."[11] Is an ad too provocative or merely attention grabbing? Is a serious message buried in the imagery or quite clear to the targeted audience?

Subliminal advertising is a highly controversial kind of promotion because it does not enable the audience to consciously decode a message. Visual or verbal messages are presented so quickly that they are not consciously seen, heard, or remembered. The assumption is that people will buy products due to subconscious impulses stimulated by the messages. Yet, overwhelming evidence shows that fully subliminal ads cannot get people to buy items they do not want. And because these ads are often misinterpreted, clearly perceived ads work much better. In the United States, state laws and self-regulation have all but eliminated fully subliminal ads. However, the growing use of *product placement*, a practice whereby products/brands are placed into the story lines of TV shows, movies, or some other media for marketing purposes, is also controversial—because the viewer is often not aware that the product/brand is placed for commercial purposes.[12] This practice is growing as a means of keeping viewers from bypassing traditional commercial breaks.

17-5f   The Audience

An *audience* is the object of a source's message. In marketing, it is generally the target market. However, a source may also want to communicate an idea, build an image, or give information to stockholders, independent media, the public, government officials, and others.

The way a communication channel is used depends on the size and dispersion of the audience, demographic and lifestyle audience traits, and the availability of appropriate media. Because the communication process needs to be keyed to the audience, AIDS

> In **decoding**, the audience translates the message sent by the source.

> **Subliminal advertising** and **product placement** are questionable tactics.

> The **audience** is usually the target market; but it can also be others.

---

[11] Susan Jacksack, "Advertising Ideas on a Small Budget," in *Start Run & Grow a Successful Small Business—CCH Business Owner's Toolkit Series*, 5th Edition (Riverwoods, IL: CCH Incorporated, 2005). See also Alexandra J. Kenyon, Emma H. Wood, and Anthony Parsons, "Exploring the Audience's Role: A Decoding Model for the 21st Century," *Journal of Advertising Research*, Vol. 48 (June 2008), pp. 276–286.

[12] See Sony Ta and Dominick L. Frosch, "Pharmaceutical Product Placement: Simply Script Or Prescription for Trouble?" *Journal of Public Policy & Marketing*, Vol. 27 (Spring 2008), pp. 98–106; Chris Hackley, Rungpaka Amy Tiwsakul, and Lutz Preuss, "An Ethical Evaluation of Product Placement: A Deceptive Practice?" *Business Ethics: A European Review*, Vol. 17 (April 2008), pp. 109–120; and Simon Hudson, David Hudson, and John Peloza, "Meet the Parents: A Parents' Perspective on Product Placement in Children's Films," *Journal of Business Ethics*, Vol. 80 (June 2008), pp. 289–304.

prevention organizations have spent a lot of time trying to get their message across to the diverse groups they are targeting. For example:

> The LOVE LIFE STOP AIDS campaign is a major element in the national AIDS prevention strategy being pursued by the Swiss Federal Office of Public Health (SFOPH). It aims to empower people to protect themselves against infection with HIV. The objective is to reinforce people's awareness of the risk, to modify their behavior, and to make them protect themselves effectively. In addition, the LOVE LIFE STOP AIDS campaign promotes solidarity with people affected by HIV and AIDS. Information is communicated to the general public through various channels: TV and cinema spots; posters and advertisements; media releases; a Web site (**http://www.lovelife.ch**); a partnership with the Swiss AIDS Association and its regional offices; and other partner marketing. There are now new challenges: HIV and AIDS have become less threatening and less relevant ever since it has become possible to treat HIV. However, AIDS continues to be a potentially fatal disease. The long-term success of therapy remains uncertain. Fewer resources are available for prevention. The STOP AIDS campaign has to succeed in making the younger generation aware of an apparently familiar issue.[13]

To make matters still tougher for marketers, global consumer surveys have found that many people are rather disapproving of promotion messages. The majority of those questioned believe marketers exaggerate health benefits, do not respect consumers' intelligence, aim too many messages toward children, do not always provide accurate information, and try to make some promotion look like "news."

17-5g   Feedback

> **Feedback (channel of communication)** consists of purchase, attitude, or nonpurchase responses to a message.

Feedback (channel of communication) is the response an audience has to a message. It may be a purchase, an attitude change, or a nonpurchase. A firm must realize that all of these responses are possible and devise a way to monitor them.

The most desirable feedback occurs if a consumer buys a good or service (or accepts an idea) after communication with or from a firm. The message is effective enough to stimulate a transaction. A second type of feedback occurs if a firm finds promotion elicits a favorable attitude toward it or its offerings. For new goods or services, positive attitudes must often be formed before purchases (awareness->attitude->purchase). For existing products, people may have bought another brand just before receiving a message or be temporarily out of funds; generating their favorable attitudes may lead to future purchases.

The least desirable feedback is if the audience neither makes a purchase nor develops a favorable attitude. This may happen for one of several reasons: There is no recall of the message. There is contentment with another brand. The message is not believed. No differential advantage is perceived.

17-5h   Noise

> **Noise** may interfere with the communication process at any stage.

Noise is interference at any point along a channel of communication. It can cause messages to sometimes be encoded or decoded incorrectly or have weak audience responses. Examples are:

- A phone call interrupting a marketing manager while he or she is developing a promotional theme
- A salesperson misidentifying a product and giving incorrect information
- An impatient customer interrupting a sales presentation
- A broken page link at a Web site
- A conversation between two consumers during a TV commercial

[13] "Love Life Stop Aids," **http://www.bag.admin.ch/hiv_aids/00833/index.html?lang=en** (November 27, 2008).

- A direct-mail ad being opened by the wrong person
- A consumer seeing a competitor's item on sale while waiting in line at a checkout counter

17-6 PROMOTION PLANNING

A firm is ready to develop an overall promotion plan once it understands the communication process. Such a plan consists of three parts: objectives, budgeting, and the promotion mix.

17-6a Objectives

Promotion objectives can be divided into two main categories: stimulating demand and enhancing company image.

The *hierarchy-of-effects model* should be used in setting demand goals. It outlines the sequential short-term, intermediate, and long-term promotion goals for a firm to pursue—and works in conjunction with the consumer's decision process we discussed in Chapter 8:

> The **hierarchy-of-effects model** outlines demand goals.

1. *Provide information*—Gain consumer product recognition and then consumer knowledge of product attributes.
2. *Develop positive attitudes and feelings*—Obtain favorable attitudes and then preference for the company's brand(s) over those of competitors.
3. *Stimulate purchases and repeat purchases*—Achieve strong consumer preference toward a good or service and generate purchases; encourage continued purchases (brand loyalty).

By using this approach, a firm can go from informing to persuading and then to reminding consumers about its offerings. When a good or service is little known, *primary demand* should be sought. This is consumer demand for a *product category*. Later, with preference the goal, *selective demand* should be sought. This is consumer demand for a *particular brand*. Sometimes, organizations may try to sustain or revitalize interest in mature products and revert to a primary demand orientation. Thus, the Florida Department of Citrus (**http://www.floridajuice.com**) sponsors ads to generate primary demand for oranges, while Florida's Natural (**http://www.floridasnatural.com**) promotes its brand to stimulate selective demand.

> **Primary demand** is for a product category; **selective demand** is for a brand.

With image-related promotion goals, a firm engages in public relations—via suitable advertising, publicity, personal selling, and/or sales promotion (as noted in Table 17-2). *Institutional advertising* is used when the advertising goal is to enhance company image—and not to sell specific goods or services. More than one-half of the leading advertisers in the United States run such ads.

> **Institutional advertising** is involved with image goals.

17-6b Budgeting

Five basic methods are available in setting a total promotion budget: all-you-can-afford, incremental, competitive parity, percentage-of-sales, and objective-and-task. The choice depends on the individual firm. Budgets often range from 1 to 5 percent of sales for industrial-products firms to up to 10 percent or more of sales for some consumer-products firms.

> Budgeting methods are **all-you-can-afford, incremental, competitive parity, percentage-of-sales**, and **objective-and-task**.

In the *all-you-can-afford method*, a firm first allots funds for other elements of marketing; any remaining marketing funds then go to the promotion budget. It is the weakest technique and is used most often by small, production-oriented firms. It gives little importance to promotion, spending is not linked to goals, and there is a risk of having no promotion budget if finances are low.

With the *incremental method*, a company bases its new promotion budget on the previous one. A percentage is added to or subtracted from this year's budget to determine next year's. The technique is also used by small firms. It has these advantages: a reference point, a budget based on a firm's feelings about past performance and future trends, and easy calculations. Key disadvantages do exist: budget size is rarely tied to goals, "gut feelings" are overemphasized, and it is hard to evaluate success or failure.

In the *competitive parity method*, a firm's promotion budget is raised or lowered according to competitors' actions. It is useful to both large and small firms. Benefits are that it is keyed to a reference point, market-oriented, and conservative. Shortcomings are that it is a following and not a leadership approach, it is difficult to get competitors' promotion data, and there is an assumption of a similarity between the firm and its competitors (as to years in business, goods or services, image, prices, and so on). However, firms usually have basic differences from competitors.

With the *percentage-of-sales method*, a firm ties its promotion budget to sales revenue. In the first year, a promotion-to-sales ratio is set. During succeeding years, the ratio of promotion to sales dollars is constant. Benefits are the use of sales as a base, the adaptability, and the link of revenues and promotion. However, there is no relation to promotion goals; promotion is a sales follower, not a sales leader; and promotion cuts occur in poor sales periods (when increases could help). The technique yields too large a budget in high sales periods and too small a budget in low sales periods.

Under the *objective-and-task method*, a firm sets promotion goals, determines the activities needed to satisfy them, and then establishes the proper budget. It is the best method. Advantages are that goals are clearly stated, spending is related to goal-oriented tasks, adaptability is offered, and it is rather easy to evaluate performance. The major weakness is the complexity of setting goals and specific tasks, especially for small firms. Most large companies use some form of objective-and-task technique.

A firm should keep the concept of marginal return in mind during promotional budgeting. The *marginal return* is the amount of sales each increment of promotion spending will generate. It tends to be high for a new product because the market is expanding. When a product is established, the marginal return tends to be lower because each additional increment of promotion has less of an impact on sales (due to a saturated target market).

> The **marginal return** refers to the sales generated through incremental promotional spending.

17-6c   The Promotion Mix

After establishing a total promotion budget, a company must determine its *promotion mix*—the firm's overall and specific communication program, including its involvement with advertising, public relations (publicity), personal selling, and/or sales promotion. Seldom does a firm use just one type of promotion—such as a mail-order firm relying on ads, a hospital on publicity, or a flea-market vendor on personal selling. A promotion mix is typically used. These Web sites have good online resources regarding the promotion mix: tutor2u (**http://www.tutor2u.net/business/marketing/promotion_mix.asp**) and eSmallOffice (**http://www.esmalloffice.com/SBR_template.cfm?DocNumber=PL12_3600.htm**).

> A **promotion mix** somehow combines advertising, public relations, personal selling, and/or sales promotion.

Within an integrated marketing communications program, each type of promotion has a distinct function and complements the other types. Ads appeal to big audiences and create awareness; without them, selling is more difficult, time consuming, and costly. Publicity provides credible information to a wide audience, but content and timing cannot be controlled. Selling has one-to-one contact, flexibility, and the ability to close sales; without it, the interest caused by ads might be wasted. Sales promotion spurs short-run sales and supplements ads and selling.

Selection of a promotion mix depends on company attributes, the product life cycle, media access, and channel members. A small firm is limited in the ads it can afford or use efficiently; it may have to stress personal selling and a few sales promotions. A large firm covering a sizable geographic area could combine many ads, personal selling, and

Ethical Issues in Marketing

Are Pharmaceutical Firms Overspending on Promotion?

According to a controversial recent study by two researchers at York University in Canada, the U.S. pharmaceutical industry spends nearly twice as much on promotion to doctors, hospitals, and consumers as it does for research-and-development efforts. The study found that the industry spends nearly one-quarter of each dollar of sales for promotion and slightly more than one-eighth on research and development. This study contradicts industry-supported research which shows that the amount spent on research and development is somewhat higher than the amount spent on promotion.

In the York study, the authors examined data from both industry reports by IMS Health (IMS, http://www.imshealth.com) and doctor surveys by CAM Group (http://www.camgroupinternational.com): "By selectively using both sets of figures provided by IMS and CAM, in order to determine the most relevant data for each category, and adjusting for methodological differences between the ways IMS and CAM collect data, the authors arrived at $57.5 billion for the total amount spent on pharmaceutical promotion in 2004" (the latest year with comparable data). Thus, the authors concluded that the U.S. pharmaceutical industry spent about $61,000 per physician in promotion.

The York researchers further concluded that: "Even our revised promotion figure is apt to be understated, as there are other promotion avenues that are not likely to be taken into consideration by IMS or CAM, such as ghost-writing and off-label promotion. Also, seeding trials, which are designed to promote the prescription of new drugs, may be allocated to other budget categories."

The new study's findings are consistent with estimates of promotion spending by Consumers International (http://www.consumersinternational.org), a nongovernmental organization.

Source: Based on material in York University, "Big Pharma Spends More on Advertising than Research and Development, Study Finds," http://www.sciencedaily.com/releases/2008/01/080105140107.htm (January 7, 2008).

frequent promotions. As products move through the life cycle, promotion emphasis goes from information to persuasion to reinforcement; different media and messages are needed at each stage. Some media may not be accessible (no cigarette ads on TV) or require lead time (Yellow Pages). Channel members may demand promotions, sales support, and/or ad allowances.

It is the job of a firm's marketing director (or vice-president) to set up a promotion budget and a promotion mix, as well as to allocate resources to each aspect of promotion. In large firms, there may be separate managers for advertising, public relations, personal selling, and sales promotion. They report to, and have their efforts coordinated by, the marketing director.

Figure 17-8 contrasts promotion mixes in which advertising and personal selling would dominate.

17-7 GLOBAL PROMOTION CONSIDERATIONS

While preparing a promotion strategy for foreign nations, the channel of communication, promotion goals, budgeting, and the promotion mix should be carefully reviewed as they pertain to each market.

With regard to the channel of communication, a firm should recognize that:

> International promotion decisions should not be made until each market is carefully studied.

- Source recognition and credibility vary by nation or region. As celebrities, golfers such as recently retired Annika Sorenstam have high recognition rates around the world. On the other hand, baseball celebrities such as Derek Jeter are mostly popular in the United States.
- Encoding messages can be quite challenging, particularly if the messages must be translated into another language.

Figure 17-8

Contrasting Promotion Mixes

Advertising Dominates When		Personal Selling Dominates When
• The market is large and dispersed, and final consumers are involved.	**Consumers**	• The market is small and concentrated and organizational consumers are involved.
• The budget is large enough to cover regular promotion in mass media.	**Budget**	• The budget is limited or tailored to the needs of specific customers.
• Products are simple and inexpensive, and differential advantages are clear.	**Products**	• Products are complex and expensive, and differential advantages are not obvious.
• Competitors stress it in their promotion mixes.	**Competition**	• Competitors stress it in their promotion mixes.
• A wide range of media are available.	**Media**	• Media are unavailable or inefficient.
• Customers are satisfied with self-service in stores or shop through the mail or the internet.	**Place of purchase**	• Customers expect sales assistance and service in stores.

- Because the effects of message symbolism depend on the nation or region, care must be taken if fear-related, humorous, and/or sexual messages are used. Themes have to correspond to local customs. French print ads are more apt to have emotional, humorous, and sexual themes than U.S. ones.
- In some locales, few residents have TVs, there are a limited number of newspapers and magazines, and programs (channels) limit or do not accept ads.
- Ensuring that messages are decoded properly can be demanding: Some advertising "can travel across any borders. The categories are simple and obvious: hi-tech products (computers, mobile phones), hi-touch products (beauty, fashion), functional offers (promotions, features), and brands that exploit national heritage (airlines and national icons, for example)." However, "Would you normally try to communicate the same message in the same way to different groups of people who don't speak the same language, don't believe in the same values, don't share cultural or religious roots, don't share the same sense of humor or emotion—and who don't want to be spoken to in the same way?"[14]
- Making assumptions about audience traits in foreign markets without adequate research may lead to wrong assumptions, such as this one: "The Chinese market has huge income divergences between first- and second-tier cities. Let alone the third- and fourth-tier cities and rural areas. The difference exists not only in different areas, but also among different population sectors within a city. These distinctions substantiate one conclusion: do not treat China as one market. Marketing targeted at

[14] Chris Jaques and David Guerrero, "Do 'Regional' Concepts Exist?" *Media Asia* (June 17, 2005), p. 6.

all consumers is usually short-lived; promotion aimed at particular groups can often break through."[15]

- Global techniques for measuring promotion effectiveness are emerging, particularly on the Web.

In terms of promotion goals, budgeting, and the promotion mix, these points should be considered:

- For nations where a firm and its brands are unknown, there must be a series of promotion goals as people are taken through the hierarchy-of-effects model. For nations in which a product category is new, primary demand must be created before selective demand is gained. To show goodwill, image ads may be even more important in foreign than in domestic markets.
- The promotion budgets in foreign countries must be keyed to the size of the markets and the activities required to succeed there. The objective-and-task method is highly recommended in setting international promotion budgets.
- Due to cultural, socioeconomic, infrastructure, and other differences, promotion mixes must be consistent with the nations served. In Western Europe, Germans listen to the most radio; the Dutch and British watch the most TV.

Two Web sites that can help marketers better understand global promotion are Advertising World International (**http://advertising.utexas.edu/world/PROD75_017380.html**) and International Advertising Resource Center (**http://www.bgsu.edu/departments/tcom/faculty/ha/intlad1.html**).

17-8 THE LEGAL ENVIRONMENT OF PROMOTION

In the United States and other nations around the globe, federal, state, and local governmental bodies have laws and rules regarding promotion practices. These regulations range from banning billboards in some locales to requiring celebrity endorsers to use products if they say they do. The U.S. agencies most involved with promotion are the Federal Trade Commission (**http://www.ftc.gov**) and the Federal Communications Commission (**http://www.fcc.gov**). Table 17-3 shows selected U.S. regulations.

Five major enforcement tools protect consumers and competing firms from undesirable practices: full disclosure, substantiation, cease-and-desist orders, corrective advertising, and fines.

Full disclosure requires that all data necessary for a consumer to make a safe and informed decision be provided in a promotion message. That is why three lenders recently agreed to settle Federal Trade Commission charges that their Internet advertising did not disclose the annual percent rate (APR) of their loans. For example, one of the firms advertised a $20 fee for a $100 14-day loan without disclosing that the loan would cost consumers 460 percent interest on an annualized basis."[16]

Substantiation requires a firm to be able to prove all the claims it makes in promotion messages. This means thorough testing and evidence of performance are needed before making claims. If a tire maker says a brand will last for 70,000 miles, it must be able to verify this with test results. Recently, the Federal Trade Commission announced a consent agreement with Herbs Nutrition Corporation, a seller of hormone replacement therapy products. The FTC complaint stated that the firm could not substantiate any of its claims relating to the prevention, treatment, or cure of

> **Full disclosure, substantiation, cease-and-desist orders, corrective advertising,** and fines are major governmental limits on promotion activities.

---

[15] Miranda Li, "Brand Planning in China," *Brand Strategy* (November 2002), p. 12.

[16] "FTC Charges Three Internet Payday Lenders with Not Disclosing Required APR Information in Ads," **http://www.ftc.gov/opa/2008/02/amercash.shtm** (February 27, 2008).

Table 17-3	Selected U.S. Regulations Affecting Promotion
Factor	**Legal Environment**
Access to media	Cigarettes and liquor have restricted access. Legal, medical, and other professions have been given the right to advertise.
Deception	It is illegal to use messages that would mislead reasonable consumers and potentially harm them.
Bait-and-switch	It is illegal to lure a customer with an ad for a low-priced item and then, once the customer talks to a salesperson, to use a strong sales pitch intended to switch the shopper to a more expensive item.
Door-to-door selling	Many locales restrict door-to-door sales practices. A cooling-off period allows a person to cancel an in-home sale up to three days after an agreement is reached.
Promotional allowances	Such allowances must be available to channel members in a fair and equitable manner.
Comparative advertisements	Claims must be substantiated. The Federal Trade Commission favors naming competitors in ads (not citing a competitor as brand X).
Testimonials or endorsements	A celebrity or expert endorser must actually use a product if he or she makes such a claim.

osteoporosis, uterine cancer, or breast cancer. Under terms of the order, all future claims from this company about its product health benefits, safety, and effectiveness need to be based on "competent and reliable scientific evidence."[17]

Under a *cease-and-desist order*, a firm must stop a promotion practice that is deemed deceptive and modify a message accordingly. The firm is often not forced to admit guilt or pay fines, as long as it obeys an order to stop running a particular message. In one 2007 case, the actions of the firm were egregious enough that it was closed down. According to the FTC, a firm known as "Home Business System" placed classified ads throughout the United States stating that participants would earn a guaranteed weekly income of up to $1,400 if they operated an envelope-stuffing business. Most consumers, who paid a $45 registration deposit, never heard from the company. A federal judge closed the operation and froze the defendants' assets. Home Business System and its principal owner are also barred from making future misrepresentations involving sales and earnings that its consumers are likely to achieve.[18]

Corrective advertising requires a firm to run new ads to correct the false impressions left by previous ones. Although this enforcement tool is not used very often, it has been applied effectively. A few years ago, the Food and Drug Administration requested that Amgen pull an ad for Enbrel, a prescription drug that supposedly treated psoriasis, a skin condition. In addition, Amgen was ordered to disseminate "truthful" and "complete corrective messages" to the same television audience to correct any false impressions of the drug's effectiveness.[19]

The last major remedy is fines, which are dollar penalties for deceptive promotion paid to the government or consumers. A short time ago, Pacific Liberty, a firm based in Ontario, Canada, was fined a total of $5 million dollars, the total net sales it achieved

[17] "Sellers of Alternative Hormone Replacement Therapy Products Settle with FTC for Failing to Substantiate Health Claims," http://www.ftc.gov/opa/2008/01/hrt.shtm (January 17, 2008).

[18] "Work-At-Home Marketer Settles FTC Charges in Envelope-Stuffing Scheme," http://www.ftc.gov/opa/2008/04/workathome.shtm (April 28, 2008).

[19] Julie Schmit, "FDA Races to Keep Up with Drug Ads That Go Too Far," http://www.usatoday.com/mone (May 30, 2005).

Global Marketing in Action

The Long-Term Effects of Buy-One Get-One Free Offers

Intentional branding is based on a marketer's use of integrated marketing communications, while holistic branding considers all interactions that consumers have with a brand. Unfortunately, too often a firm's short-sighted use of intentional branding comes at the expense of long-term holistic brand building. As the director of one major advertising agency noted, "A multibuy [such as buy one, get one free], on average, yields a 70 percent uplift in short-term volume sales. That uplift is considerably smaller in value terms, and you get post-promotional dips, because the net effect of most promotions is to bring sales forward—people just keep more in their cupboard."

Cadbury (http://www.cadbury.co.uk), a British-based confectionery and beverage manufacturer, employed a $24 million advertising campaign that focused on the theme "You dream it, we make it" to stress its chocolate bar's richness. At the same time, Cadbury ran a "buy-one-get-one free" (BOGOF) pro-

motion for its Dairy Milk brand of chocolate at a leading British general merchandise retailer. The two campaigns had opposite—and somewhat conflicting—goals. Although the image-based campaign stressed Cadbury's richness, the BOGOF promotion totally focused on price and value.

The BOGOF promotion also had other potential problems for Cadbury, such as the sales of Dairy Milk declining significantly after the promotion ended. Consumers stocking up on Dairy Milk during the BOGOF promotion would not need to buy additional candy for weeks or even months. In addition, the BOGOF promotion could get nonparticipating retailers angry with Cadbury as its Dairy Milk products appeared to be drastically overpriced at those stores.

Sources: Based on material in Jane Simms, "Scant Value in BOGOFs," *Marketing* (November 7, 2007), p. 18; and Mark Ritson, "Cadbury's Decision to BOGOF Is a Strategic Error," *Marketing* (May 25, 2005), p. 24.

through a cross-border telemarketing scheme. For an advance fee of $319, defendants promised they would deliver credit cards as well as free gifts, such as cell phones. None of the consumers received either the credits cards or free phones.[20]

Besides government rules, the media have their own voluntary standards for promotion practices. The National Association of Broadcasters (http://www.nab.org) monitors TV and radio ads. General industry groups, such as the Better Business Bureau (http://www.bbb.org), the American Association of Advertising Agencies (http://www.aaaa.org), and the International Advertising Association (http://www.iaaglobal.org), also participate in the self-regulation of promotion.

17-9 CRITICISMS AND DEFENSES OF PROMOTION

For many years, industry trade groups have campaigned to improve the overall image of promotion. This is illustrated in Figure 17-9. As the International Advertising Association notes at its Web site: "Our focus is to advocate freedom of commercial speech and defend a responsible communications industry against unwarranted advertising bans and restrictions; use our global network as a leading platform for sharing knowledge on industry issues, best practices, and insights in a rapidly changing business environment; and provide and develop education and professional initiatives that serve the industry, and contribute to bringing in and training talent."

Nonetheless, promotion is the most heavily criticized area of marketing. Here are a number of criticisms and the defenses of marketers to them:

> Promotion controversies center on materialism, honesty, prices, symbolism, and consumer expectations.

---

[20] "Court Orders Cross-Border Telemarketers to Pay Nearly $5 Million," http://www.ftc.gov/opa/2008/05/pacliberty.shtm (May 1, 2008).

Detractors Feel That Promotion	Marketing Professionals Answer That Promotion
Creates an obsession with material possessions.	Responds to consumer desires for material possessions. In affluent societies, these items are plentiful and bought with discretionary income.
Is basically dishonest.	Is basically honest. The great majority of firms abide by all laws and set strict self-regulations. A few dishonest firms give a bad name to all.
Raises the prices of goods and services.	Holds down prices. By increasing consumer demand, promotion enables firms to use mass production and mass distribution and reduce per-unit costs. Employment is higher if demand is stimulated.
Overemphasizes symbolism and status.	Differentiates goods and services by symbolic and status appeals. Consumers desire distinctiveness and product benefits.
Causes excessively high expectations.	Keeps expectations high; it thereby sustains consumer motivation and worker productivity so expectations can be satisfied.

Figure 17-9

A Strong Defense of Promotion by the American Association of Advertising Agencies

Source: Reprinted by permission.

Figure 17-9

(Continued)

Web Sites You Can Use

Many specialized service firms work with clients to devise and enact integrated marketing communications strategies. These service firms help their clients establish goals, coordinate promotion efforts, and devise the best mix of promotion tools. The following integrated marketing communications service firms have attractive Web sites that highlight their capabilities and successes:

- Bottom Line Communications (**http://www. bottomlinecom.com**)
- Carbonhouse (**http://www.carbonhouse.com**)
- Cornerstone Word Company (**http://www. cornerstoneword.com**)
- Godbe Communications (**http://www.godbe.com**)

- Hale Integrated Marketing Communications (**http://www. haleinc.com**)
- Pacifico (**http://www.pacifico.com**)
- Paragon Marketing Communications (**http://www. paragonmc.com**)
- Phelps Group (**http://www.thephelpsgroup.com/ our_work.asp**)
- SGW Integrated Marketing Communications (**http:// www.sgw.com**)
- Silver Creative Group (**http://www.silvercreativegroup. com**)
- TMP Worldwide (**http://www.integrated.tmp.com**)
- Wallrich Landi (**http://www.wallrichlandi.com**)

Summary

1. *To define promotion planning, show its importance, and demonstrate the value of integrated marketing communications* Promotion involves any communication that informs, persuades, and/or reminds people about an organization's or individual's goods, services, image, ideas, community involvement, or impact on society. Promotion planning systematically relates to all communication.

Promotion efforts are needed for both new and existing products. The audience may be consumers, stockholders, consumer advocacy groups, government, channel members, employees, competitors, and the public. Through word of mouth, people express opinions and product-related experiences to one another. A firm may communicate its image, views on ideas, community involvement, or impact on society—as well as persuade people to buy. Good promotion enhances the other elements of the marketing mix. Promotion is a major activity around the world.

With well-coordinated promotion plans, a firm applies integrated marketing communications. This means the strategic roles of a variety of communication disciplines are evaluated and combined for clarity, consistency, and maximum communication impact. A proper plan is synergistic. It has tactical consistency and fosters interactivity with consumers. Every company message positively influences the target audience. The company's basic promotion themes and differential advantages are clearly understood by all employees who interface with the targeted audience. Promotion personnel cooperate with one another. Data bases are maintained.

2. *To describe the general characteristics of advertising, public relations, personal selling, and sales promotion*   Advertising is paid, nonpersonal communication transmitted through various media by identified sponsors. Public relations includes any communication (paid or nonpaid, nonpersonal or personal, sponsored by a firm or reported by an independent medium) designed to foster a favorable image. Publicity is the nonpaid, nonpersonal, nonsponsored form of public relations. Personal selling involves oral communication with one or more prospective buyers by paid representatives for the purpose of making sales. Sales promotion involves paid marketing activities to stimulate consumer purchases and dealers.

3. *To explain the channel of communication and how it functions*   A source sends a message to its audience via a channel of communication. A channel consists of a source, encoding, the message, the medium, decoding, the audience, feedback, and noise.

A source is a company, an independent institution, or an opinion leader that seeks to present a message to an audience. Encoding is the way in which a thought or an idea is translated into a message by the source. A message is a combination of words and symbols transmitted to the audience. A medium is a personal or nonpersonal channel used to convey a message. Decoding is the way in which a message sent by a source is translated by the audience. The audience is the object of a source's message. Feedback is the response the audience makes to a message: purchase, attitude change, or nonpurchase. Noise is interference at any stage.

4. *To examine the components of a promotion plan*   Goals may be demand- or image-oriented. Demand goals should correspond to the hierarchy-of-effects model, moving a consumer from awareness to purchase. Primary demand is total demand for a product category; selective demand refers to interest in a particular brand. Institutional advertising is used to enhance company image.

Five ways to set a promotion budget are all-you-can-afford (the weakest method), incremental, competitive parity, percentage-of-sales, and objective-and-task (the best method). Marginal return should be considered when budgeting.

A promotion mix is the overall and specific communication program of a firm, including its use of advertising, public relations (publicity), personal selling, and/or sales promotion. Many factors need to be considered in developing a promotion mix.

5. *To discuss global promotion considerations, and the legal environment and criticisms and defenses of promotion*   In devising an international promotion plan, the channel of communication, promotion goals, budgeting, and promotion mix should be studied for and applied to each market.

Many laws and rules affect promotion. The major ways to guard against undesirable promotion are full disclosure, substantiation, cease-and-desist orders, corrective ads, and fines. Critics are strong in their complaints about promotions. Marketers are equally firm in their defenses.

Key Terms

promotion (p. 527)

promotion planning (p. 527)

word-of-mouth communication (p. 527)

integrated marketing communications (IMC) (p. 529)

advertising (p. 530)

public relations (p. 530)

publicity (p. 531)

personal selling (p. 531)

sales promotion (p. 531)

channel of communication (communication process) (p. 531)

source (p. 532)

encoding (p. 535)

message (p. 535)

comparative messages (p. 536)

massed promotion (p. 538)

distributed promotion (p. 538)

wearout rate (p. 538)

medium (p. 538)

decoding (p. 539)

subliminal advertising (p. 539)

product placement (p. 539)

audience (p. 539)

feedback (channel of communication) (p. 540)

noise (p. 540)

hierarchy-of-effects model (p. 541)

primary demand (p. 541)

selective demand (p. 541)

institutional advertising (p. 541)

all-you-can-afford method (p. 541)

incremental method (p. 542)

competitive parity method (p. 542)

percentage-of-sales method (p. 542)   promotion mix (p. 542)   cease-and-desist order (p. 546)

objective-and-task method (p. 542)   full disclosure (p. 545)   corrective advertising (p. 546)

marginal return (p. 542)   substantiation (p. 545)

Review Questions

1. Why is integrated marketing communications so important?
2. Distinguish among advertising, public relations, personal selling, and sales promotion.
3. What is a two-sided message? Why do few companies use such messages?
4. What should be the relationship between encoding and decoding messages? Why?

5. A consumer listens to a sales presentation but does not make a purchase. Has the presentation failed? Explain your answer.
6. Explain the hierarchy-of-effects model. How is it related to demand objectives?
7. Describe each of the methods of promotional budgeting.
8. When should advertising dominate the promotion mix?

Discussion Questions

1. What are the advantages and disadvantages of maintaining messages (themes) over a long period of time?
2. Present a promotion campaign to increase attendance at G-rated movies.
3. As the marketing manager for a small U.S.-based toy maker that is entering the European market for the first time, devise a promotion budget relying on the objective-and-task method.

4. Develop a promotion mix for:
   a. a local cable television channel.
   b. an ice-cream store chain.
   c. a 20-attorney legal practice.
   d. a small, business-to-business maintenance services firm.

Web Exercise

"For over 40 years, Marketing Evaluations' Q Scores have provided clients with data to aid in their marketing, advertising, and media efforts. Q Scores are the industry standard for measuring familiarity and appeal of performers, characters, sports and sports personalities, and broadcast and cable programs—as well as company and brand names. Based on our 'One of My Favorites' concept, Q Scores actually summarize the various perceptions and feelings that consumers have, into a single, but revealing, 'likeability' measurement." Visit the firm's Web site (**http://www.qscores.com**) and discuss what you learn there.

Practice Quiz

1. People express opinions and product-related experiences to one another through
   a. free speech communication.
   b. word-of-mouth communication.
   c. public relations.
   d. institutional advertising.

2. An integrated marketing communications plan is based upon which fundamental premise?
   a. A well-coordinated promotion plan
   b. An ethical framework
   c. Low overhead costs
   d. Extensive use of public relations

3. Consumers Union and a local newspaper restaurant critic are examples of
   a. opinion leaders.
   b. representative consumers.
   c. independent institutions.
   d. industry spokespersons.

4. A firm wanting to stress its product prestige would emphasize
   a. mass ownership.
   b. competitive prices.
   c. status.
   d. availability in discount stores.

5. Which promotional concept most closely resembles depreciation?
   a. Decoding
   b. Encoding
   c. Wearout rate
   d. Clutter

6. Which of the following statements about subliminal advertising is true?
   a. It is rarely misinterpreted.
   b. It enables a consumer to consciously decode a message.
   c. It is used by most firms in the United States.
   d. It is not effective in getting consumers to buy products they do not want.

7. Which of these statements on consumer attitudes about promotion is correct?
   a. The majority believe marketers give accurate information.
   b. The majority believe ads do not exaggerate health claims.
   c. The majority believe marketers respect consumers' intelligence.
   d. The majority believe marketers target children too much.

8. Which of the following is *not* an objective found in the hierarchy-of-effects model?
   a. Informing consumers
   b. Personalizing consumers
   c. Persuading consumers
   d. Reminding consumers

9. Which of these is the weakest method for setting a total promotion budget?
   a. Percentage-of-sales technique
   b. Incremental technique
   c. All-you-can-afford technique
   d. Competitive parity technique

10. Which of the following is a benefit of the competitive parity method?
    a. It is internally driven.
    b. It is useful only for small firms.

c. It is keyed to a reference point.
d. It considers firms in the same industry to be similar.

11. Which of these is the best method for setting a total promotion budget?
    a. Objective-and-task technique
    b. Percentage-of-sales technique
    c. Incremental technique
    d. All-you-can-afford technique

12. Which statement about the types of promotion is *not* true?
    a. Sales promotion stimulates short-run sales.
    b. Personal selling can best be used to reach large audiences with a uniform message.
    c. Without personal selling, initial interest caused by ads might be wasted.
    d. Personal selling advertising can best be used to close sales.

13. A firm must be able to prove its promotional claims under which promotional enforcement rule?
    a. A cease-and-desist order
    b. Corrective advertising
    c. Full disclosure
    d. Substantiation

14. An example of corrective advertising is
    a. Alka-Seltzer's mentioning that it is an antacid.
    b. Lewis Galoob Toys' agreement not to promote its products as doing things of which they were incapable.
    c. Listerine's disclaimer that it is not a cold remedy.
    d. Pfizer's payment of a large sum to a number of states.

15. Which of the following is *not* a common criticism of promotion?
    a. It is basically dishonest.
    b. It overemphasizes symbolism and status.
    c. It creates an obsession with material possessions.
    d. It causes excessively low expectations.

For the answers to these questions, please visit the online site for this book at **http://www.atomicdog.com**.

Chapter 18

Advertising and Public Relations

A powerful example of a successful celebrity-based promotion campaign is George Foreman's endorsement of Salton (http://www.salton.com) grilling machines bearing his name. Well over 100 million George Foreman Lean, Mean, Fat-Reducing Grilling Machines have been sold since the mid-1990s. The Foreman grills have been Salton's largest sellers. For his endorsement, George Foreman has received greater than $150 million, more money than he earned in his entire boxing career.

Foreman's success in the ring, coupled with a friendly ("cuddly") persona, made Foreman a highly sought-after endorser. Unlike other athletes, who have endorsed only sports-related items, Foreman's endorsements have included Meineke (http://www.meineke.com) and Doritos (http://www.doritos.com). He always tries products prior to allowing his name to be used; and his endorsements include an ethics clause prohibiting a sponsor from being sold to a firm that sells alcohol, tobacco, pornography, or gambling items. In 2008, he began starring in the reality show *Foreman Family* on TV Land (http://www.tvland.com).

Under the initial arrangement negotiated with Salton, Foreman received 45 percent of the profits on grills with his name and Salton got 40 percent. The balance was divided between a marketing expert and an attorney. Foreman received nothing up front. In March 1995, just after the contract was signed, the Gourmet Housewares Show (http://www.thegourmetshow.com) took place in Las Vegas. There, Foreman clearly showed his upbeat personality. Whenever he showed up at the trade show, he was so popular that security personnel had to surround him. Still, the grill did not sell well.

Almost a year later, Foreman went on QVC to sell the grills; and sales took off so rapidly that every available QVC employee was summoned to handle the phone orders. The "magic moment" occurred when the TV audience saw Foreman grab a hamburger from the grill and start eating it. According to Salton's chief executive officer at the time, "It was so spontaneous. It was a real reaction. People saw that he eats what he sells." In 1999, Salton agreed to pay Foreman and his partners $137.5 million over five years for the right to use Foreman's name in perpetuity for cooking appliances.[1]

In this chapter, we will study both the advertising and public relations aspects of promotion, including the use of creative strategies in developing advertisements and the role of advertising agencies.

Chapter Objectives

1. To examine the scope, importance, and characteristics of advertising
2. To study the elements in an advertising plan
3. To examine the scope, importance, and characteristics of public relations
4. To study the elements in a public relations plan

18-1 OVERVIEW

> Advertising and public relations are two major forms of promotion.

Chapter 18 covers advertising and public relations. As defined in Chapter 17, *advertising* is paid, nonpersonal communication regarding goods, services, organizations, people, places, and ideas; it may be used by businesses, government and other nonprofit

---

[1] Various company and other sources.

organizations, and individuals. Its distinguishing features are that a sponsor pays for its message, a set format is sent to an entire audience via mass media, the sponsor's name is clearly presented, and the sponsor controls the message.

In contrast, *public relations* involves communication that fosters a favorable image for goods, services, organizations, people, places, and ideas among their various publics. Its unique features are that it is more image- than sales-oriented; it embodies image-oriented advertising, personal selling, and sales promotion; and it often seeks to generate favorable publicity for a firm. As an aspect of public relations, publicity entails non-personal communication that is transmitted via mass media but not paid for by an identified sponsor. The media usually control the wording and placement of publicity messages.

The distinctions between advertising and publicity are in part revealed by this statement: "Advertising is paid for, publicity is prayed for." We examine the scope and importance, characteristics, and planning considerations for both advertising and public relations in Chapter 18. InfoTech Marketing has an excellent Web site (**http://www. smsource.com/sitemap.htm**) with a lot of resources on advertising and public relations. Visit the site, scroll down, and click "Advertising" or "Public Relations."

18-2   THE SCOPE AND IMPORTANCE OF ADVERTISING

In 2010, $725 billion is expected to be spent on advertising globally—about 42 percent in the United States (including direct mail) and the rest elsewhere.[2] Table 18-1 shows global spending by medium (not including direct mail), as well as U.S. media spending.

Table 18-1	Global Advertising Expenditures by Region and Medium—2010 Projections				
Global Advertising[a]				**U.S. Advertising**	
Region	**Percent of Total Global Ad Expenditures**	**Medium**	**Percent of Total Global Ad Expenditures**	**Medium**	**Percent of Total U.S. Ad Expenditures**
North America	36.6	Television	37.6	Television	23.8
Europe	30.3	Newspapers	23.9	Direct mail	21.6
Asia/Pacific	22.2	Magazines	11.3	Newspapers	14.3
Latin America	6.2	Radio	7.6	Internet	12.0
Africa/Middle East	4.7	Outdoor	6.9	Radio	6.2
Total	100.0	Internet	12.3	Yellow Pages	5.0
		Cinema	0.2	Magazines	4.8
		Total	100.0	Outdoor	1.4
				Miscellaneous	10.9
				Total	100.0

[a] Includes only the major media shown in the table. A lot of direct-mail advertising is done in the United States, which is not reflected in the breakout in the global section of the table.

Sources: Compiled and estimated by the authors from data reported in "Advertising Boom in Developing Ad Markets Compensates for Credit-Crunch Boom in the West," *Zenith Optimedia Press Release* (March 31, 2008); and Universal McCann, "Robert Coen Presentation on Advertising Expenditures," **http://www.universalmccann.com** (July 2008).

Note: There are minor rounding errors in this table.

---

[2] Authors' estimate based on Universal McCann, "Robert Coen Presentation on Advertising Expenditures," **http://www.universalmccann.com** (July 2008).

Globally, the leading three media account for nearly three-quarters of ad expenditures. In the United States, the leading three media account for 60 percent of ad expenditures, due to the level of U.S. media choice. Direct mail is a key U.S. medium; and globally, Internet advertising has gone from virtually zero a decade ago to become a growing presence.

Advertising as a percent of sales varies by industry and firm, and company advertising as a percent of sales is low. During 2007, expenditures were less than 2.5 percent of sales in 57 percent of U.S. industries; 2.5 to 4.9 percent of sales in 22 percent of U.S. industries; and at least 5.0 percent of sales in 21 percent of U.S. industries.[3] Among the leading advertisers, such as Procter & Gamble, the percentages often far exceed industry averages. Table 18-2 shows ad expenditures by selected industry category, while Table 18-3 indicates the highest-spending advertisers in the world.

An advertising emphasis is most likely if products are standardized, have easily communicated features, appeal to a large market, have competitive prices, are marketed via independent resellers, and/or are new. Leading brands often get large ad budgets to hold their positions. At Charles Schwab (**http://www.schwab.com**), the discount stockbroker, ads stress two themes: quality service and competitive prices. It has an in-house ad agency and runs ads on traditional and cable TV, as well as the Internet. By advertising, it raises awareness and introduces new products.

Consider this: "No, it's not your imagination. The amount of advertising and marketing [we] are exposed to daily has exploded over the past decade. At the gas pumps, in the movie theater, in a washroom stall, during sporting events—advertising is impossible to avoid. Even outer space isn't safe from commercialization: The Russian space program launched a rocket bearing a 30-foot Pizza Hut (**http://www.pizzahut. com**) logo, and some companies have investigated placing ads in space that will be visible from earth. The challenge of the future may be finding public and private spaces that are free of advertising. Marketers are pressed to find even more innovative and aggressive ways to cut through the 'ad clutter' or 'ad fatigue' of modern life."[4]

> The vast majority of U.S. firms spend less than 5 percent of sales on advertising. Ads are most important for standardized products aimed at large markets.

Table 18-2   Advertising by Selected U.S. Industries, 2007

Industry	Advertising as Percent of Sales	Industry	Advertising as Percent of Sales
Perfume and cosmetics	13.7	Household furniture	5.2
Books	11.7	Department stores	4.7
Dolls and stuffed toys	10.2	Footwear	3.8
Food products	10.0	Eating places	3.1
Watches and clocks	9.3	Household appliances	2.4
Soaps and detergents	9.1	Accident and health insurance	1.3
Jewelry stores	8.2	Auto dealers	0.8
Cable TV services	7.4	Management consulting services	0.8
Cutlery, hand tools, general hardware	1.4	Computer and office equipment	0.7
Sugar and confectionary products	5.9	Motion picture theaters	0.7

Sources: Derived from Schonfeld & Associates, "2007 Advertising-to-Sales Ratios for 200 Largest Spending Industries," **http://www.adage.com/datacenter/article?article_id=106575**.

[3] Computed by the authors from Schonfeld & Associates, "2007 Advertising-to-Sales Ratios for 200 Largest Spending Industries," **http://www.adage.com/datacenter/article?article_id=106575**.

[4] "Advertising: It's Everywhere," **http://www.media-awareness.ca/english/parents/marketing/advertising_everywhere.cfm** (April 5, 2009).

Table 18-3	The Leading 25 Advertisers in the World	
U.S.-Based Firms	**Firms Based Outside the United States**
Procter & Gamble	Unilever (Great Britain/Netherlands)
General Motors	L'Oreal (France)
Ford	Toyota (Japan)
Time Warner	Nestlé (Switzerland)
Johnson & Johnson	Daimler (Germany)
Coca-Cola	Honda (Japan)
Walt Disney	GlaxoSmithKline (Great Britain)
McDonald's	Nissan (Japan)
PepsiCo	Sony (Japan)
Kraft Foods	Volkswagen (Germany)
General Electric	Reckitt Benckiser (Great Britain)
Yum! Brands	Danone (France)
News Corp.	

Sources: Table developed by the authors based on worldwide measured media spending data in "Top 100 Global Marketers," *Advertising Age* (November 19, 2007), p. 4.

These general observations can be made as to the usefulness of advertising:

- With low-involvement purchases, consumer behavior may be easier to change than attitudes.
- One ad can have a strong effect on brand awareness.
- By advertising, it is easier to raise people's opinions on a little-known item than a well-known one.
- Effectiveness often rises with long-term campaigns.

18-3   THE CHARACTERISTICS OF ADVERTISING

On the positive side, advertising reaches a large, geographically dispersed market; and, for print media, circulation is supplemented by the passing of a copy from one reader to another. Costs per viewer or listener are low. A single TV ad may cost $360,000 to air and reach 30 million people—a cost of $0.012 per person (for media time). A broad range of media is available: from national (global) TV to local newspapers. Thus, a firm's goals and resources may be matched with the most appropriate medium.

A sponsor can control message content, graphics, timing, and size or length, as well as the audience targeted. A uniform message is sent to the whole audience. With print media, people can study and restudy messages. Editorial content (a news story or segment of a broadcast show) often borders an ad. This can raise readership or viewing/listening, enhance an image, and create the proper mood. A firm may even seek specialized media or sections of media (such as a sports section for a men's clothing ad).

Ads ease the way for personal selling by creating audience awareness and liking for brands. They also enable self-service wholesalers and retailers to operate, and they sustain an industry—mail order. With a pulling strategy, advertising enables a firm to show its resellers that consumer demand exists.

On the negative side, because messages are standardized, they are rather inflexible and not responsive to questions. This makes it hard to satisfy the needs of a diverse audience. And because many media appeal to broad audiences, a large portion of viewers

> Advertising attracts an audience, has low per-customer costs, offers varied media, is surrounded by information, and aids selling.

> Advertising is inflexible and can be wasteful, costly, and limit information and feedback.

or readers may be wasted for a sponsor. A single-unit health spa might find that only one-fifth of a newspaper's readers live in its shopping area.

Advertising sometimes requires high total expenditures, although costs per viewer or reader are low. This may keep smaller firms from using some media. In the example earlier in this section, it was said that a TV ad might cost only $0.012 per viewer. Yet, media time alone for that ad would be $360,000—for one ad, placed once. Also, because high costs lead to brief messages, most ads do not provide much information. TV commercials are short, mostly 15 or 30 seconds; few are as long as one minute. Further, because ads are impersonal, feedback is harder to get and it may not be immediately available.

Mass media are used by many people who do not view or listen to ads. It is estimated that the typical American is exposed to 3,500 to 5,000 advertising messages per day![5] Of added concern to TV advertisers is "zapping," whereby a viewer uses a remote-control device to switch programs when an ad comes on. A newer phenomenon, known as the "TiVo (**http://www.tivo.com**) factor," lets consumers use their personal and digital video recorders (PVRs and DVRs) to skip ads. PVR and DVR owners skip ads most of the time: "Device-assisted ad-skipping is widespread. One-quarter of consumers surveyed already own a digital video recorder (DVR), with another 20 percent planning to buy one soon. As many as 85 percent of those viewers skip 75 percent or more of commercials. Only 5 percent do not skip any ads."[6]

18-4 DEVELOPING AN ADVERTISING PLAN

An advertising plan consists of the nine steps shown in Figure 18-1. These steps are now highlighted.

Figure 18-1

Developing an Advertising Plan

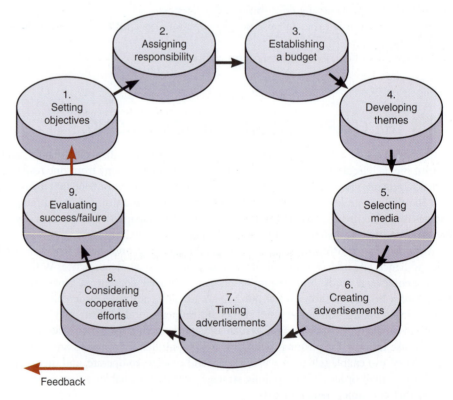

[5] Karla Jo Helms, "Marketing Outside-the-Box = Getting Ahead," **http://www.articleset.com/ Marketing_articles_en_Marketing-Outside-the-Box-Getting-Ahead.htm** (August 19, 2007).

[6] Darren Murph, "DVR Owners Do Indeed Skip Ads Study Affirms," **http://www.switched.com/2008/08/07/ dvr-owners-do-indeed-skip-ads-study-affirms** (August 7, 2008).

18-4a   Setting Objectives

Advertising goals can be divided into demand and image types, with image-oriented ads being part of a public relations effort. Table 18-4 cites several goals.

Usually, a number of goals are pursued: "You need to decide if you want your ad to generate leads, generate sales, move somebody to the next step in the buying process, or a combination of these things. You need to make sure that you know exactly what you're trying to accomplish before you start. So think about your ads. What are you trying to accomplish? How can you get more people to raise their hand and at least say they're interested? Can you offer something to lower the risk or to give information?"[7]

18-4b   Assigning Responsibility

In assigning advertising responsibility, a firm can rely on its internal marketing personnel, use an in-house advertising department, or hire an outside advertising agency. Although many firms use internal personnel or in-house departments, most companies involved with advertising on a regular or sizable basis hire outside agencies (some in addition to their own personnel or departments). Diversified firms may hire a different agency for each product line. A firm's decision to use an outside agency depends on its own expertise and resources and on the role of advertising for the firm.

An *advertising agency* is an organization that provides a variety of advertising-related services to client firms. It often works with clients in devising their advertising plans—including themes, media choice, copywriting, and other tasks. A large agency may also offer market research, product planning, consumer research, public relations, and more. The two largest U.S.-based ad agencies are Omnicom Group (**http://www.omnicomgroup.com**) and Interpublic Group (**http://www.interpublic.com**).

> An **advertising agency** may work with a firm to develop its ad plan, conduct research, or provide other services.

Table 18-4	Illustrations of Specific Advertising Objectives
Type of Objective	**Illustrations**
Demand-Oriented	
Information	To create target market awareness for a new brand
	To acquaint consumers with new business or store hours
	To reduce the time salespeople take to answer basic questions
Persuasion	To gain brand preference
	To increase store traffic
	To achieve brand loyalty
Reminding (retention)	To stabilize sales
	To maintain brand loyalty
	To sustain brand recognition and image
Image-Oriented	
Industry	To develop and maintain a favorable industry image
	To generate primary demand
Company	To develop and maintain a favorable company image
	To generate selective demand

[7] Ross Parks, "Biz Tips: Do You Know Your Advertising Objective?" **http://www.novascotiabusinessjournal.com/index.cfm?sid=157436&sc=107** (July 29, 2008).

18-4c   Establishing a Budget

After computing overall spending by the all-you-can-afford, incremental, competitive parity, percentage-of-sales, or objective-and-task method, a firm sets a detailed ad budget—to specify the funds for each type of advertising (such as product and institutional messages) and each medium (such as newspapers and radio). Because demand-oriented ads generate revenues, firms should be cautious about reducing these budgets. A better campaign, not a lower budget, may be the answer if goals are not reached.

These points should be addressed: What do various alternatives cost for time or space (a 30-second TV spot versus a full-page magazine ad)? How many placements are needed to be effective (if it takes four telecasts of a single ad to make an impact, a budget must allow four placements)? How have media prices risen recently? How should a firm react during an industry sales slump? What channel members are assigned which promotion tasks? Do channel members require contributions toward advertising? What does it cost to produce an ad? How should a budget be allocated for domestic versus foreign ads? Consider that the cost of producing one 30-second national TV commercial in the United States is now about $350,000 (not including the cost for airtime).[8]

From a global perspective, companies can use three major methods to establish their advertising budgets: (1) They can allow personnel in each pan-geographic region to determine their needs and petition headquarters for a budget. (2) They can let each individual market have its own advertising strategy and budget. (3) They can control budgeting decisions from their world headquarters.

18-4d   Developing Themes

> Basic **advertising themes** are product, consumer, and/or institutional appeals.

A firm next develops *advertising themes*, the overall appeals for its campaign. A good or service appeal centers on the item and its attributes. A consumer appeal describes a product in terms of consumer benefits rather than its features. An institutional appeal

Marketing and the Web

Web-Based Advertising Comes of Age

Web advertising, which includes keyword-based searches and streaming video and audio, has begun to challenge traditional media such as television and radio. And in 2012, annual U.S. Internet advertising revenues are expected to reach $51 billion, double the 2008 amount. By 2008, Internet ad spending was already equal to one-third of the ad spending on national broadcast and cable TV, according to the Interactive Advertising Bureau (http://www.iab.net) and Robert Coen Insider's Report (http://www.mccannworldwidegroup.com). As of 2011, Internet advertising will surpass newspapers as the largest advertising medium in the United States.

Three important reasons for the growth of Internet advertising are the greater use of broadband, the ease of targeting an audience, and the ability to track effectiveness. Broadband enables advertisers to use exciting video formats. In some instances, an ad made for television can be broadcast over the Internet. A car dealership ad, for example, can appear at the same time a consumer is searching for a car online. And Web marketers typically pay for Web advertising based on dollar sales, not the presentation of the ad.

Many Web-based advertisers are small companies seeking a highly targeted audience. Disaboom.com (http://www.disaboom.com) is a site aimed at people with disabilities and functional limitations. The site combines some of the social networking aspects of Facebook (http://www.facebook.com) with specialized information on medical news, career information, and vacation tips. Disaboom.com also has attracted large firms such as RE/MAX (http://www.remax.com), Ford (http://www.ford.com), and Johnson & Johnson (http://www.jnj.com) as sponsors.

Sources: Based on material in Randall Rothenberg, "The Internet Runs on Ad Billions," http://www.businessweek.com/managing (April 10, 2008); and "Online Ad Spending Holding Strong," http://www.emarketer.com (May 23, 2008).

---

[8] American Association of Advertising Agencies, "Results of AAAA 2007 Television Production Cost Survey," http://www.aaaa.org (2008).

Table 18-5	Advertising Themes
Theme	**Example**
Good or Service Related	
Dominant features described	Whirlpool washers emphasize dependability and durability.
Competitive advantages cited	Aiwa stresses the superior quality of its portable stereos.
Price used as dominant feature	Private-label beauty products advertise low prices.
News or information domination	New-model laser printers point out enhancements in color and fonts.
Size of market detailed	Hertz emphasizes its leading position in car rentals.
Primary demand sought	Grapes are advertised.
Consumer Related	
Good or service uses explained	Pillsbury ads have cake recipes.
Cost benefits of good or service shown	Owens-Corning states how consumers reduce heating bills with Fiberglas insulation.
Emphasis on how good or service helps consumer	The Regent Beverly Wilshire hotel says that its customer service is so good that it gives clients complete peace of mind.
Threatening situation	The American Heart Association points out the risks of smoking.
Incentives given to encourage purchases	An ad mentions $1 off a purchase as an introductory offer for a new brand of coffee.
Institutional Related	
Favorable image sought	ExxonMobil explains how it is searching for new energy sources.
Growth, profits, and potential described to attract investors	Companies regularly take out full-page ads in business sections of major newspapers.

deals with a firm's image. Table 18-5 presents a full range of advertising themes from which a firm may select. Figures 18-2 and 18-3 show thematic ads for Skinny Cow (http://www.skinnycow.com) and Macy's (http://www.macys.com).

18-4e Selecting Media

Many media choices are available, as noted in Table 18-6. Costs, reach, waste, message permanence, persuasive impact, narrowcasting, frequency, clutter, lead time, and media innovations should be reviewed when choosing among them.

Advertising media costs are outlays for media time or space. They are related to ad length or size, and media attributes. First, the total costs to place an ad in a medium are computed—such as $30,000 for a full-page color magazine ad. Second, per-reader or per-viewer costs are derived (stated in cost per thousand). If a $30,000 ad goes in a magazine with a circulation of 500,000, the cost per thousand is $60.

Reach refers to the number of viewers, readers, or listeners in a medium's audience. For TV and radio, it is the total number of people who watch or listen to an ad. For print media, it has two aspects: *circulation* and *passalong rate*. Circulation is the number of copies sold or distributed to people. The passalong rate is the number of times each copy is read by another reader. For instance, each copy of *Newsweek* (http://www.newsweek.com) is read by several people. The magazine passalong rate is much higher than that for daily papers.

> **Advertising media costs** include total and per-person costs.

> **Reach** includes circulation and passalongs.

Figure 18-2

Skinny Cow: Highlighting Competitive Advantages

Source: Reprinted by permission.

> **Waste** is the audience segment not in the target market.

> **Message permanence** refers to exposures per ad.

> **Persuasive impact** is highest for TV.

Waste is the part of a medium's audience not in a firm's target market. Because media appeal to mass audiences, waste can be a big factor. We can show this with the magazine example cited in media costs. If a special-interest magazine with 500,000 readers appeals to amateur photographers, a camera maker knows 450,000 of the readers might be interested in a new digital camera; 50,000 would have no interest. The latter is the wasted audience. The real cost is $66.67 ($30,000/450,000 × 1,000 = $66.67) per thousand readers. The firm also knows a general-interest magazine runs camera ads, attracts 1 million readers, and prices a full-page ad at $40,000—$40 per thousand. The firm expects only 200,000 of those readers to be interested in photography. So, the real cost is $200 ($40,000/200,000 × 1,000 = $200) per thousand. See Figure 18-4.

Message permanence refers to the number of exposures one ad generates (repetition) and how long it remains available to the audience. Outdoor ads, transit ads, and phone directories yield many exposures per message; and many magazines are retained by consumers for long periods. On the other hand, radio and TV ads typically last only 5 to 60 seconds and are over.

Persuasive impact is the ability of a medium to stimulate consumers. TV often has the most persuasive impact because it combines audio, video, color, and action.

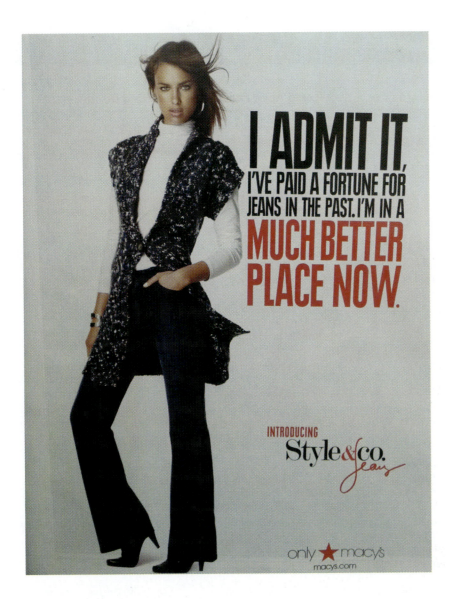

Figure 18-3

Macy's: A Value Proposition for the Value-Oriented Shopper

Source: Reprinted by permission of Susan Berry, Retail Image Consulting, Inc.

Magazines and the Internet also have high persuasive impact. Many newspapers have improved their technology so as to feature color ads and increase their persuasive impact.

Narrowcasting—advertising messages presented to rather limited and well-defined audiences—is a way to reduce the audience waste with mass media. It may be done via direct mail, cable TV, specialty magazines, the Internet, and other targeted media. In narrowcasting, a firm gets less waste in return for a smaller reach. And due to the advances in technology, the potential is great. As one observer noted: "The History channel, Sci-Fi channel, and Animal Planet channel are examples of the fundamental shift from broadcasting to narrowcasting in cable network TV. Narrowcasting has also found useful applications in malls, airports, and other public facilities where visitors use touch screens to find flight schedules, shop locations, restaurants, or other information. This is known as *interactive narrowcasting*. Today, even a teenager can use an Internet café and a free Web site to reach his or her own niche audience."[9]

Frequency refers to how often a medium can be used. It is greatest for the Internet, newspapers, radio, and TV. Different ads may appear daily, and a strategy may be easily

> In **narrowcasting**, advertisers seek to reduce waste.

> **Frequency** is highest for daily media.

---

[9] R. Kayne, "What Is Narrowcasting?" http://www.wisegeek.com/what-is-narrowcasting.htm (June 1, 2009).

Table 18-6 Advertising Media

Medium	Market Coverage	Best Uses	Selected Advantages	Selected Disadvantages
Commercial television	Regional, national, or international	Regional, national, and international manufacturers, service firms, and retailers	Reach, low cost per viewer, persuasive impact, creative options, flexible, high frequency, surrounded by programs	High minimum costs, general audience, lead time for popular shows, short messages, limited availability
Cable television	Local, regional, national, or international	Local, regional, and national manufacturers, service firms, and retailers	More precise audience and more creative than commercial television	Not all consumers hooked up; ads not yet fully accepted on programs
Direct mail	Advertiser selects market	New products, book clubs, financial services, catalog sales	Precise audience, flexible, personal approach, less clutter from other messages	High throwaway rate, receipt by wrong person, low credibility
Daily newspaper	Entire metropolitan area; local editions used sometimes	Medium and large manufacturers, service firms, and retailers	Short lead time, concentrated market, flexible, high frequency, passalongs, surrounded by content	General audience, heavy ad competition, limited color, limited creativity
Weekly newspaper	One community	Local firms	Same as daily	Heavy ad competition, very limited color, limited creativity, small market
Radio	Entire metorpolitan area	Local or regional firms	Low costs, selective market, high frequency, immediacy of messages, surrounded by content	No visual impact, commercial clutter, channel switching, consumer distractions
Telephone directories	Entire metropolitan area (with local supplements)	All types of retailers, professionals, service companies, and others	Low costs, permanence of messages, repetition, coverage of market, specialized listings, action-oriented messages	Clutter of ads, limited creativity, very long lead time, low appeal to passive consumers
Magazines	Local, national, or international (with regional issues)	Local service firms and mail-order firms; major manufacturers, service firms, and retailers	Color, creative options, affluent audience, permanence of messages, passalongs, flexible, surrounded by content	Long lead time, poor frequency (if monthly), ad clutter, geographically dispersed audience
Outdoor	Entire metropolitan area or one location	Brand-name products, nearby retailers, reminder ads	Large size, color, creative options, repetition, less clutter, message permanence	Legal restrictions, consumer distractions, general audience, inflexible, limited content, lead time
Internet	Local, national, or international	All types and sizes of firms	Low costs, huge potential audience, vast geographic coverage, amount of information conveyed, interactivity	Clutter of ads, viewed as a novelty by some, goals unclear (advertising vs. entertainment and education), no set rate structure
Business publications	Regional, national, or international	Corporate advertising, b-to-b firms	Selective market, high readability, surrounded by content, message permanence, passalongs	Restricted product applications, may not be read by proper decision maker, not final consumer-oriented
Transit	Urban community with a transit system	Firms located along transit route	Concentrated market, message permanence, repetition, action-oriented messages, color, creative options	Clutter of ads, consumer distractions, geographically limited audience
Flyers	Single neighborhood	Local firms	Low costs, market coverage, little waste, flexible	High throwaway rate, poor image

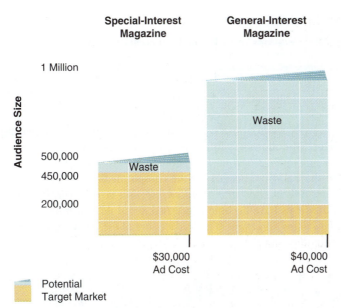

Special-Interest Magazine

General-Interest Magazine

Figure 18-4

Waste in Advertising

Even though the general-interest magazine attracts a much larger overall audience than the special-interest magazine (at little additional cost), a large portion of its audience is wasted—many people are not part of the potential target market.

changed. Phone directories, outdoor ads, and magazines have the worst frequency. A printed Yellow Pages ad can be placed only once per year.

Clutter involves the number of ads found in a single program, issue, and so forth, of a medium. It is low when few ads are presented, such as Hallmark (**http://www.hallmark. com**) placing only scattered commercials on the TV specials it sponsors. It is high when there are many ads, such as the large number of supermarket ads in a newspaper's Wednesday issue. Overall, magazines have the most clutter. And TV is criticized for assigning more time per hour to commercials (about 15 to 20 minutes) and for letting firms show brief messages (15 seconds or shorter). More than one-third of TV ads are 15-second spots.

Lead time is the period required by a medium for placing an ad. It is shortest for newspapers and longest for magazines and phone directories. Popular TV shows may also require a lengthy lead time because the number of ads they can carry is limited. Because a firm must place ads well in advance, with a long lead time, it risks improper themes in a changing environment.

There have been many media innovations. These include online computer services such as Google AdWords (**https://www.adwords.google.com**) and other offerings that let people "surf the Web" and be exposed to advertising; regional editions and special one-sponsor issues ("advertorials") to revitalize magazines; targeted Yellow Pages; TV ads in retail stores, movie theaters, and planes; digital outdoor signs; and full-length advertising programs ("infomercials").

According to one major research report, in the United States, one-seventh of the people ages 12 and older listened to Internet radio in the prior week, one-fifth watched an Internet video in the prior week, and one-tenth listened to audio podcast in the prior month. Furthermore, "Users of digital radio are early adopters who represent a broad variety of attractive qualitative attributes. Advertisers who want to go where the trend is leading should get more involved with new forms of 'audio media' while they expand. Consumers will respond to the advertisers who meet them on these new frontiers."[10]

Clutter occurs when there are many ads.

Lead time is needed for placing an ad.

[10] Arbitron/Edison Media Research, *The Infinite Dial 2008*, **http://www.edisonresearch.com/home/archives/2008/04/ internet_multim_5.php.**

> Ad creation involves content, scheduling, media placement, and variations.

18-4f Creating Advertisements

Four fundamental decisions must be made in creating ads:

1. *Determine message content and devise ads.* Each ad needs a headline or opening to create interest, and copy that presents the message. Content decisions also involve the use of color and illustrations, ad size or length, the source, the use of symbolism, and foreign market adaptations. Decisions depend on a firm's goals and resources. Figure 18-5 shows a provocative ad from Charles Penzone salons (**http://www.charlespenzone. com**). Figure 18-6 shows a stylish ad for a Liz (**http://www.liz.com**) fragrance.
2. *Outline a promotion schedule.* This should allow for all copy and artwork and be based on the lead time needed for the chosen media.
3. *Specify each ad's location in a broadcast program or print medium.* As costs have risen, more firms have become concerned about ad placement.
4. *Choose how many variations of a basic message to use.* This depends on the frequency of presentations and the ad quality.

Figure 18-5

Stopping Traffic

Source: Reprinted by permission of Susan Berry, Retail Image Consulting, Inc.

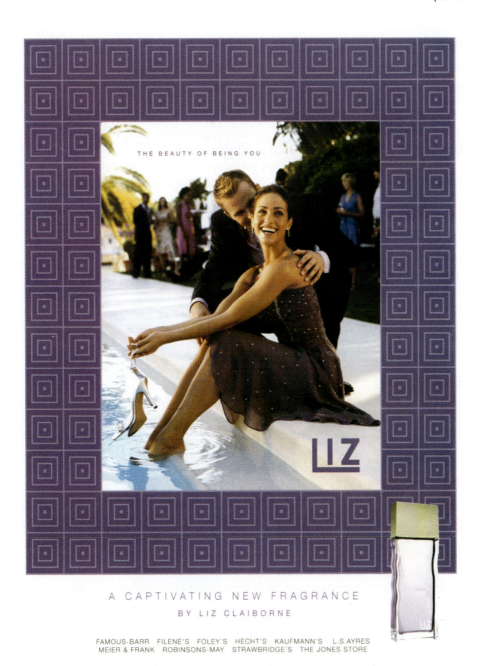

Figure 18-6

A Stylish Ad from Liz Fragrances

Source: Reprinted by permission.

THE BEAUTY OF BEING YOU

LIZ

A CAPTIVATING NEW FRAGRANCE
BY LIZ CLAIBORNE

FAMOUS-BARR   FILENE'S   FOLEY'S   HECHT'S   KAUFMANN'S   L.S.AYRES
MEIER & FRANK   ROBINSONS-MAY   STRAWBRIDGE'S   THE JONES STORE

18-4g   Timing Advertisements

Two key decisions must be made about the timing of ads: how often an ad is run and when to advertise during the year. First, a firm must balance audience awareness and knowledge versus irritation if it places an ad several times in a short period. McDonald's (http://www.mcdonalds.com) runs ads often but changes them repeatedly. Second, a firm must choose whether to advertise over the year or in certain periods. *Distributed ads* hold on to brand recognition and increase sales in nonpeak periods. They are used by many manufacturers, service firms, and general-merchandise retailers. *Massed ads* are used in peak times to foster short-run interest; they ignore nonpeak periods. Specialty and seasonal firms use this method.

Other timing considerations include when to advertise new products, when to stop advertising existing products, how to coordinate advertising and other promotional tools, when to change basic themes, and how to space messages during the hierarchy-of-effects process.

> Timing refers to how often an ad is shown and when to advertise during the year.

18-4h   Considering Cooperative Efforts

To stimulate channel member advertising and/or to hold down its own ad budget, a firm should consider cooperative efforts. With *cooperative advertising*, two or more firms share some advertising costs. In *vertical cooperative advertising*, firms at different stages in a distribution channel (such as a manufacturer and a wholesaler) share costs. In *horizontal cooperative advertising*, two or more independent firms at the same stage in a distribution channel share costs (such as retailers in a mall).

Good agreements state the share of costs paid by each party, the functions and responsibilities of each party, the ads covered, and the basis for termination. They benefit all.

Each year, $15 to $20 billion in vertical-cooperative advertising support is made available by manufacturers in the United States. Yet, distribution intermediaries actually use only two-thirds of this amount. The nonuse by so many resellers is due to their perceptions of manufacturer inflexibility with messages and media, the costs of cooperative advertising to the resellers, restrictive provisions (such as high minimum purchases to be eligible), and the emphasis on manufacturer names in ads. To remedy this, many manufacturers are more flexible as to the messages and media they support, pay a larger share of advertising costs, have eased restrictive provisions, and feature reseller names more prominently in ads.

18-4i   Evaluating Success or Failure

The success of advertising depends on how well it helps to reach promotion goals. Gaining awareness and expanding sales are distinct goals; success or failure in reaching them must be measured differently. Advertising can also be quite difficult to isolate as the one factor leading to a certain image or sales level.

Here are various examples dealing with the evaluation of advertising's success or failure:

- Many "marketers have long known that repetition of an advertisement is critical if people are later to recall the advertised good or service. It also matters, however, how and when an ad is repeated. Spacing the repetitions of an ad, for example, rather than massing them, can increase later recall–and, hence, advertising effectiveness—quite dramatically."[11]
- The consumer's attention span tends to be rather brief, perhaps no more so than in locations such as airports: "Few people spend more than one to three seconds viewing airport advertising—unless they are waiting in line, for example. Thus, it appears that ads should be brief, should use simple appeals, and/or should have multiple placements in the concourse. However, certain situations may warrant advertisers incorporating more information into the ad's execution than would otherwise be recommended, as when the ad is placed in a location where passengers are known to spend more idle time, such as standing in line at retail or food outlets" at airports.[12]
- The use of fear is only effective in certain circumstances: It is an "age-old" practice. "But compared with milder fare in the past ('This is your brain on drugs'), today's imagery is like a sledgehammer. For instance, an anti-drunk-driving ad for Arrive Alive (**http://www.arrivealive.org**) featured a scantily clad girl collapsing in a men's bathroom. Experts called it muddled and provocative. Yet, deterrence by fear can work. Volkswagen (**http://www.volkswagen.com**) safety ads drew attention for

---

[11] Sara L. Appleton-Knapp, Robert A. Bjork, and Thomas D. Wickens, "Examining the Spacing Effect in Advertising: Encoding Variability, Retrieval Processes, and Their Interaction," *Journal of Consumer Research*, Vol. 32 (September 2005), p. 266.

[12] Rick T. Wilson and Brian D. Till, "Airport Advertising Effectiveness," *Journal of Advertising*, Vol. 37 (Spring 2008), pp. 59–72.

Global Marketing in Action

MTV: Worldwide Powerhouse

MTV Networks (http://www.mtv.com) is the world's largest television network with about 135 channels globally. The channels include MTV (http://www.mtv.tv), Nick at Nite (http://www.nickatnight.com), Comedy Central (http://www.comedycentral.com), Noggin (http://www.noggin.com), and Nickelodeon (http://www.nick.com). In addition to cable television, consumers can watch and listen to MTV via online, wireless, and interactive formats. MTV Networks International (http://www.mtv.com/mtvinternational) is the largest global network. Its brands are seen in 500 million households in 161 nations representing 28 different languages.

Many global advertisers understand the power of MTV in reaching young audiences. MTV recently launched a global retail partnership with Body Shop (http://www.thebodyshop.com) to increase the public's awareness of HIV and AIDS prevention. The campaign entitled "Spray to Change Attitudes" involved developing a fragrance called Rougeberry Eau de Toilette, which was sold in 44 Body Shop outlets in 44 countries. All proceeds went to the Staying Alive Foundation (http://www.staying-alive.org).

Sears (http://www.sears.com) also realized the potential of MTV in appealing to young shoppers through its use of cross-promotions with MTV's movie *The American Mall*. The movie was shot in a Sears store, the actors wore Sears clothing, and all of the actors subsequently appeared in Sears ads. According to Sears' chief merchandising officer, "While mom may decide what the acceptable place is to shop, kids are deciding what clothes they want and what places have it. If we come out of our season with more relevance with this group, and improving our sales and profitability with this group, it's a big win."

Sources: Based on material in Nicola Clark, "MTV in Global Body Shop Tie to Push HIV Message," *Marketing* (January 24, 2007), p. 13; and Ashley M. Heher, "Sears Targets Teens with MTV Film, LL Cool J Gear," *Marketing News* (July 15, 2008), p. 32.

showing its cars in heart-stopping accidents; within weeks, sales inquiries were up. An ad for Canadian workplace safety showed a glowing young chef describing her fiancé, whom she'll never marry, she says, because she's about to have a 'terrible accident.' She then slips and scorches her face with a cauldron of boiling water. The series of ads got 1.7 million YouTube (http://www.youtube.com) views."[13]

• In about 40 countries around the world, EFFIE Awards (http://www.effie.org) are presented annually for outstanding ad efforts: "Effie honors ideas that work—the great ideas that achieve real results and the strategy that goes into creating them. Effie winners represent client and agency teams who tackled a marketplace challenge with a big idea and knew exactly how to communicate their message to their customer. Since 1968, winning an Effie has become a global symbol of achievement."[14]

18-5 THE SCOPE AND IMPORTANCE OF PUBLIC RELATIONS

Each firm would like to foster the best possible relations with its publics and receive favorable publicity about its offerings or the firm itself. Sometimes, as with restaurant or theater reviews, publicity can greatly increase sales or virtually put a firm out of business.

> Public relations efforts can have a major impact.

In the United States, thousands of firms and hundreds of trade associations have their own public relations departments, and there are 1,800 public relations agencies. The leading U.S. organization in the field is the Public Relations Society of America (http://www.prsa.org), which has almost 22,000 professional members around the globe. The International Public Relations Association (http://www.ipra.org) has more than 1,000

[13] Jessica Bennett, "This Is Your Brain on Scary Ads," http://www.newsweek.com/id/114737 (March 3, 2008).

[14] "About the EFFIEs," http://www.effie.org/about (June 3, 2009).

members from 96 nations; nevertheless, the role of public relations varies greatly by nation:

> Most PR people get ahead in their careers by making themselves expert in a particular geography, and usually in the nuances of a specific demographic group—for example, the youth market on the West Coast. Yet, today, more clients are looking to their public relations directors and consultancies to coordinate cross-border programs in order to achieve control of messaging, rapid response to issues and crises, best-in-class creative solutions, and insurance against local errors becoming global problems. There is a large and growing demand for professionals who can take responsibility for a multicountry PR program. There is not, however, a large and growing pool of practitioners with the needed experience and training.[15]

The competition to gain media attention for publicity is intense. In the United States, there are rather few national TV networks and less than 100 magazines and newspapers with circulations of one million or more. However, there are many opportunities for publicity—with 4,800 AM radio stations, 6,200 FM radio stations, 1,750 conventional TV stations, 1,450 daily newspapers, and 20,000 periodicals around the United States. In addition, there are 10,000 cable TV systems and millions of Web sites.[16]

Some firms have poor policies to deal with their publics and the media and do not have a sustained public relations approach. Table 18-7 shows public relations-related situations and how a firm could deal with them. Because unfavorable publicity can happen to any firm, a successful one will have a plan to handle it. A firm may foster media fairness by being candid and communicating promptly; media communications may be used to explain complex issues; and preconceived ideas may be dispelled by cooperating with reporters.

> Public relations encompasses image-directed ads, selling, and sales promotion—as well as publicity.

The interrelationship of public relations and other promotion forms must be understood. If advertising, personal selling, and sales promotion are image-oriented, public relations is involved. If they are demand-oriented, it is not. Figure 18-7 shows the interface between public relations and other promotion tools. These observations apply to organizations of all sizes and types:

> Public relations is the art and science of proactive advocacy on the part of a company, individual, or brand. It requires strategic management of your position statement and key messages in order to reach your target audiences, and through various tactics, establish goodwill and a mutual understanding. In short, effective use of public relations tools allows us to shape public opinion, attitudes, and beliefs. The public relations portion of your firm's marketing must be a strategic part of a carefully considered marketing plan so that it complements the branding, advertising, business development, client services, sponsorships, and other communication initiatives. The role of public relations is to help build the firm's brand equity by delivering key messages to target audiences to elicit a particular response and thus shape public opinion, attitudes, and beliefs. In other words, PR is the method by which we communicate messages about ourselves and our firms.[17]

18-6 THE CHARACTERISTICS OF PUBLIC RELATIONS

> Public relations engenders good feelings; publicity has no time costs, a large audience, high credibility, and attentiveness.

Public relations offers several benefits. Because it is image-oriented, good feelings toward a firm by its external publics can be fostered. In addition, employee morale (pride) is enhanced if the firm is community and civic minded.

[15] Adrian Wheeler, "Citizens of the World," http://www.ipra.org (June 2005).

[16] Authors' estimates based on *2008 Statistical Abstract of the United States,* http://www.census.gov/compendia/statab/2008edition.html.

[17] Gina Rubel, "PR for Lawyers Tip # 1: Understand Public Relations," http://www.theprlawyer.com/2008/01/everyday-public-relations-for-lawyers.html (January 2, 2008).

Table 18-7	Public Relations-Related Situations and How a Firm Could Respond to Them	
Situation	**Poor Response**	**Good Response**
Fire breaks out in a company plant	Requests for information by media are ignored.	Company spokesperson explains the fire's causes and the precautions to avoid it, and answers questions.
New product introduced	Advertising is used without publicity.	Pre-introduction news releases, product samples, and testimonials are used.
News story about product defects	Media requests for information are ignored, blanket denials are issued, and there is hostility to reporters.	Company spokesperson says tests are being done, describes the procedure for handling defects, and takes questions.
Competitor introduces new product	A demand-oriented advertising campaign is stepped up.	Extensive news releases, statistics, and spokespeople are made available to media to present firm's competitive features.
High profits reported	Profits are justified and positive effects on the economy are cited.	Profits are explained, comparative data are provided, and profit uses are noted: research and community development.
Overall view of public relations	There is an infrequent need for public relations; crisis fighting is used when bad reports are circulated.	There is an ongoing need for public relations, strong planning, and plans to counter bad reports.

When publicity is involved, no costs are incurred for message time or space. A prime-time TV ad may cost up to $300,000 or more per 30 seconds; a 5-minute report on a network newscast does not cost anything for media time. Yet, there are costs for news releases, a public relations department, and so on. Publicity reaches a mass audience. In a short time, new products or company policies are well known.

Message believability is higher with publicity because stories are in independent media. A newspaper's movie review is more credible than an ad in that paper—the reader links independence with objectivity. Similarly, people may pay more attention to news than to ads. *Women's Wear Daily* (**http://www.wwd.com**) has both fashion reports and ads; people read the stories, but flip through ads. A dozen or more ads appear in a half-hour TV show and hundreds in a typical magazine; feature stories are fewer and stand out.

Compared to other promotion forms, public relations also has limitations. Some firms question the value of image-oriented messages and are disinterested in activities not directly tied to sales and profits. They may give the poor responses that were indicated in Table 18-7.

With publicity, a firm has less control over messages and their timing, placement, and coverage by the media. It may issue detailed press releases and find only parts cited in the media; and media may be more critical than a firm would like. The media tend to find disasters, scandals, and product recalls more newsworthy than press releases. And consider this:

> Public relations may be downplayed by some firms; publicity cannot be controlled or timed accurately by a company.

Figure 18-7

The Relationship Between Public Relations and the Other Elements of the Promotion Mix

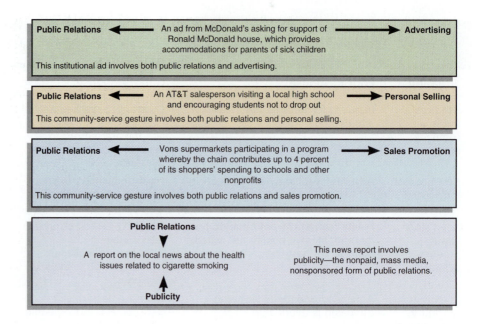

Web sites with elaborate information to counterbalance negative reports in the press may miss the target, because only highly aware consumers will have the patience to read and the skills to comprehend this information. Mass media campaigns with one simple countervailing message may also miss their target, because many unaware consumers will be reached who were not even aware of the negative reports in the press in the first place, whereas in the meanwhile highly aware citizens will reject over simplistic messages. Some firms try to compensate for negative publicity by raising their ad budget, whereas others keep silent. Advertisers might wait until a storm of negative news dies down. Companies do have many means to prevent such a storm. They may monitor their own phone communications and complaints services, as well as public Web sites, discussion groups, Weblogs, and podcasts to learn the concerns of interest groups and the word of mouth of their consumers to enable anticipation, either by feeding the ongoing discussions with new words, new propositions, and new topics, or by staging a "stealing thunder" operation to admit shortcomings and failures frankly, for example, by announcing the withdrawal of a product from the market, while at the same time announcing an improved product, or even a new policy, or a new takeover.[18]

A firm may want publicity during certain periods, such as when a new product is introduced or a new store opens, but the media may not provide coverage until much later. Similarly, the media determine a story's placement; it may follow a crime or sports report. Finally, the media choose whether to cover a story at all and the amount of coverage for it. A firm-sponsored jobs program might go unreported or get three-sentence coverage in a local paper.

Publicity may be hard to plan in advance because newsworthy events occur quickly and unexpectedly. Thus, short-run and long-run public relations plans should differ in approach. Publicity must complement advertising and not be a substitute. The assets of each (credibility and low costs for publicity, control and coverage for ads) are needed for a good communications program.

To optimize their public relations efforts, at many companies:

• public relations personnel have regular access to senior executives.
• the publicity value of annual reports is recognized.

---

[18] May-May Meijer and Jan Kleinnijenhuis, "News and Advertisements: How Negative News May Reverse Advertising Effects," *Journal of Advertising Research*, Vol. 47 (December 2007), pp. 507–517.

- public relations messages are professionally prepared (with the same care as used in writing ad copy) and continuously given to media.
- internal personnel and media personnel interaction is fostered.
- public-service events are planned to obtain maximum media coverage.
- part of the promotion budget goes to publicity-generating tasks.
- there is a better understanding of the kinds of stories the media are apt to cover and how to present stories to the media.

18-7 DEVELOPING A PUBLIC RELATIONS PLAN

Developing a public relations plan is much like devising an advertising plan. It involves the steps shown in Figure 18-8 and described next.

18-7a Setting Objectives

Public relations goals are image-oriented (firm and/or industry). The choice guides the entire public relations plan. These are some possible goals:

- Gain placement for news releases and appearances for company spokespersons with a variety of media.
- Have the media report on the accomplishments of the company.
- Have the company's viewpoint presented when controversy arises.
- Coordinate publicity with advertising.
- Obtain more media coverage than competitors.
- Sustain favorable publicity as long as possible.
- Reach out to community groups.
- Have publics view the firm and its industry favorably.

In setting goals, this truism should be kept in mind: "While journalists complain that people who work in public relations do not understand news, public relations

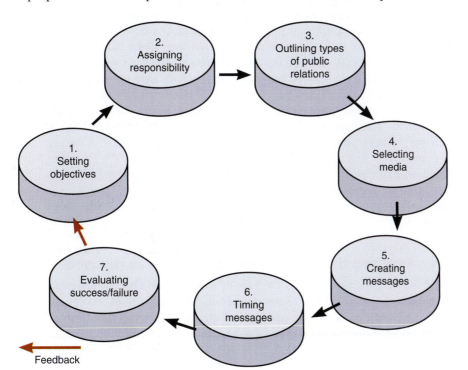

Figure 18-8

Developing a Public Relations Plan

Ethical Issues in Marketing

What's the Proper Approach to Negative Publicity?

What type of publicity program should a firm conduct when a key product is recalled, the financial media accuse it of mismanagement, or it is the subject of a government investigation? Until recently, most firms would not comment on these issues, hoping that the public would soon forget about them. Now, more firms have become proactive by having their chief executives interviewed on key talk shows, increasing their advertising, and sending E-mail messages to their important consumers. Let's see how Merck (**http://www.merck.com**), Shering-Plough (**http://www. shering-plough.com**), Coca-Cola (**http://www.coca-cola. com**), and PepsiCo (**http://www.pepsico.com**) have handled negative publicity.

Vytorin (**http://www.vytorin.com**), a one-pill combination of Zocor and Zetia, is a leading cholesterol product jointly marketed by Merck and Shering-Plough. In 2008, widely publicized research showed that Vytorin was no better than the same dose of Merck's Zocor alone at keeping fatty plaque from building at arteries located in the neck. As a result,

Merck and Shering-Plough suspended TV ads, saying this was due to the public's "misinterpretation" of research data. At the time, *Advertising Age* (**http://www.adage.com**) reported that Vytorin ads were among the most heavily recalled by viewers.

Coca-Cola and PepsiCo are using different strategies in response to reports that Coca-Cola's Dasani and PepsiCo's Aquafina are purified water that come from public reservoirs rather than spring water. PepsiCo now states "Public Water Source" on Aquafina's labels. In contrast, Coca-Cola is posting information online about its quality-control procedures. Groups critical of bottled water say that plastic bottles contribute to pollution and that bottled water undermines confidence in local tap water.

Sources: Based on material in Jacob Goldstein, "Merck and Shering-Plough Silence Vytorin TV Ads," **http://blogs.wsj.com/2008/01/23/merck-schering-plough-silence-vytorin-tv-ads** (January 23, 2008); and "Aquafina Labels to Spell Out Source—Tap Water," **http://www.cnn.com/2007/HEALTH/07/27/pepsico.aquafina.reut** (July 27, 2007).

practitioners complain that sometimes the journalists do not understand well enough the public relations role nor do they understand general business principles."[19]

18-7b Assigning Responsibility

> A firm can use an in-house department, hire an outside ad agency, or hire a specialist.

A firm has three options in assigning public relations responsibility: it may use its existing marketing personnel, an in-house public relations department, or an in-house publicity department; it may have an outside advertising agency handle public relations; or it may hire a specialized public relations firm. Internal personnel or an in-house department ensure more control and privacy. An outside firm often has better contacts and expertise. Each approach is popular, and they may be combined.

Procter & Gamble (**http://www.pg.com**) has an in-house publicity department and outside public relations agencies. In contrast, some smaller firms rely on specialists, which may charge annual fees of $25,000 to $50,000. Computer software, such as Automated Press Releases (**http://www.automatedpr.com**) and PR Free (**http://www. prfree.com/index.php**), also enable small firms to reach media contacts. A wealth of information on the public relations industry may be found at 101publicrelations.com (**http://www.101publicrelations.com**) and Online Public Relations (**http://www.online-pr.com**).

18-7c Outlining the Types of Public Relations to Be Used

In this step, a firm first chooses the mix of institutional advertising, image-oriented personal selling, image-oriented sales promotion, and publicity to incorporate into an overall promotion plan. Public relations efforts must then be coordinated with the demand-oriented promotion activities of the firm.

---

[19] Lee Bollinger, "Public Relations, Business, and the Press," *Public Relations Quarterly*, Vol. 48 (Summer 2003), pp. 20–23.

Finally, the general *publicity types* must be understood. Each can play a role in an integrated public relations program:

- *News publicity* deals with global, national, regional, or local events. Planned releases can be prepared and regularly given out by a firm.
- *Business feature articles* are detailed stories about a firm's offerings that are given to business media.
- *Service feature articles* are lighter stories focusing on personal care, household items, and similar topics that are sent to newspapers, TV stations, magazines, and Internet sites.
- *Finance releases,* such as quarterly earnings, are stories aimed at the business sections of newspapers, TV news shows, magazines, and other media.
- *Product releases* deal with new products and product improvements; they aim at all media forms.
- *Sponsorship releases* report that firms support particular causes or charities.
- *Pictorial releases* are illustrations or pictures sent to the media.
- *Video news releases* are videotaped segments supplied to the media.
- *Background editorial material* is extra information (such as the biography of the chief executive of a firm) given to media writers and editors; it enhances standard releases and provides filler for stories.
- *Crisis publicity* consists of special spontaneous news releases keyed to unexpected events.[20]

> **Publicity types** include news, features, releases, background material, and emergency information.

18-7d Selecting the Media for Public Relations Efforts

For institutional ads, personal selling, and sales promotion, traditional nonpersonal and/ or personal media would be used. For publicity, a firm would typically focus on newspapers, TV, magazines, radio, business publications, and the Internet. Due to the infrequent nature of many magazines and some business publications, publicity-seeking efforts may be aimed at daily or weekly media.

Public relations executives rank newspapers and business publications the highest. The *Wall Street Journal* (**http://www.online.wsj.com/public/us**), *New York Times* (**http://www.nytimes.com**), and *USA Today* (**http://www.usatoday.com**) are preferred newspapers. *Business Week* (**http://www.businessweek.com**), *Fortune* (**http://money. cnn.com/magazines/fortune**), and *Forbes* (**http://www.forbes.com**) are preferred business publications. *Time* (**http://www.time.com**), *Newsweek* (**http://www.newsweek. com**), and *U.S. News & World Report* (**http://www.usnews.com**) are preferred general news magazines.

18-7e Creating Messages

Public relations messages entail the same factors as other communication—content, variations, and a production schedule. Messages can be sent in one or a combination of forms, such as news conferences, media releases, phone calls or personal contacts, media kits (a group of materials on a story), special events (such as Macy's Thanksgiving Parade—**http://www.macys.com/campaign/parade/parade.jsp**), or videos.

Because it is essential that the media find a firm to be cooperative and its publicity messages to be useful, these tips should be followed:

1. "Know the reporter and the publication before picking up the phone. First, build a targeted media list of the publications that may have an interest in what you're

---

[20] Adapted by the authors from Gordon C. Bruner II, "Public Relations," **http://www.siuc.edu/~mktg363/ppts/pr/ frame.htm** (2002).

pitching, and then determine which journalists you should be talking to at those publications."

2. "Always know how and when a reporter wants to be contacted. Some reporters want phone calls, others prefer E-mail, and still others want news the old-fashioned way—by snail mail."

3. "Clarify your message before delivering your pitch. There is nothing worse for a reporter than receiving an E-mail that is a carbon copy of a press release, or getting a call from someone who is not familiar with the company they are pitching or the news they are announcing."

4. In a press release, "it is important to make the reporter's job as easy as possible so make sure to provide the most important news in the first paragraph. You should also include the company's URL, as a reporter will often times visit the company's Web site before calling back."

5. "Never send unsolicited E-mail attachments, as some reporters will be wary of opening them due to virus concerns, and others simply won't take the time."

6. "When calling a reporter, introduce yourself fully, reference previous conversations to jog the reporter's memory on who you are and why you're calling, and ask if this is a good time to talk."

7. "When you get a reporter on the phone, ask what they are working on and how you can help."

8. "Never make promises you cannot keep."

9. "Follow up aggressively. Although some reporters will provide coverage after one phone interview, that is often not enough."

10. "Whenever possible, pitch by phone. This will get you better results and allow you to build the relationships you need to ensure consistent success."[21]

18-7f Timing Messages

Public relations efforts should precede new-product introductions and generate excitement for them. For emergencies, media releases and spokespeople should be immediately available. For ongoing public relations, messages should be spaced during the year. As already noted, a firm may find it hard to anticipate media coverage for both unexpected and planned publicity because the media control timing.

18-7g Evaluating Success or Failure

Several straightforward ways are available to rate a public relations campaign:

- With institutional ads, image-oriented personal selling, and image-oriented sales promotion, a firm can conduct simple surveys to see how well these communications are received and their impact on its image.
- With publicity, a firm can count the stories about it, analyze coverage length and placement, review desired with actual timing of stories, evaluate audience reactions, and/or compute the cost of comparable advertising.
- Firms such as Wal-Mart (**http://www.walmart.com**) track the *quality*, as well as the quantity, of media coverage. Wal-Mart sorts items as news stories, letters to the editor, editorials, or opinion articles.
- Through the Internet, companies can track media stories. For example, 1st Headlines (**http://www.1stheadlines.com**) can do a topical search for stories appearing in media around the world.

---

[21] Peter Granat, "Top 10 Tips to Improve Your Media Relations Skills," **http://www.b2bpublicrelations.org/ media_skills.html** (May 30, 2009).

Web Sites You Can Use

Numerous Web sites provide access to current and past advertisements. Many offer real-time video commercials. Here is a cross-section of sites where you can view or read ads. (Please note: TV ads are best viewed through a high-speed connection.):

- Ad*Access (**http://www.scriptorium.lib.duke.edu/adaccess**)—Classic print ads from 1911 to 1955
- Adflip (**http://www.adflip.com**)—Print ads
- Advertising Council (**http://www.adcouncil.org/default.aspx?id=15**)—Multimedia public service announcements (PSAs)
- Clio Award Winners (**http://www.clioawards.com**)—Annual global competition in many media formats
- Coca-Cola Television Ads (**http://www.memory.loc.gov/ammem/ccmphtml/colahome.html**)—50 Years of Coke commercials

- Creativity (**http://www.creativity-online.com/?action=adcritic:home**)—TV, video, and print ads
- Eisner Museum of Advertising & Design (**http://www.eisnermuseum.org/exhibits/index.shtm**)—Multimedia online exhibits
- General Electric Ads (**http://www.ge.com/company/advertising**)—Latest online ads, prints ads, TV ads, and popular campaigns
- Super Bowl TV Commercials (**http://www.ifilm.com/superbowl**)
- Very Funny Ads (**http://www.veryfunnyads.com**)—TV ads from around the world

Summary

1. *To examine the scope, importance, and characteristics of advertising*   Advertising is paid, nonpersonal communication sent through various media by identified sponsors. Worldwide ad spending is $725 billion annually, 42 percent in the United States via such media as TV, direct mail, newspapers, radio, Yellow Pages, magazines, outdoor (billboards), the Internet, and business publications. U.S. advertising is under 5.0 percent of sales in four-fifths of industries.

   Ads are most apt with standardized products and when features are easy to communicate, the market is large, prices are low, resellers are used in distribution, and/or products are new. In general, behavior is easier to change than attitudes; one ad can have an impact; ads do well with little-known products; and effectiveness rises during extended campaigns.

   Among advertising's advantages are its appeal to a geographically dispersed audience, low per-customer costs, the availability of a broad variety of media, the firm's control over all aspects of a message, the surrounding editorial content, and how it complements personal selling. Disadvantages include message inflexibility, some viewers or readers not in the target audience, high media costs, limited information provided, difficulty in getting audience feedback, and low audience involvement.

2. *To study the elements in an advertising plan*   An advertising plan has nine steps: setting goals—demand and image types; assigning duties—internal and/or external; setting a budget; developing themes—good/service, consumer, and institutional; selecting media—based on costs, reach, waste, message permanence, persuasive impact, narrowcasting, frequency, clutter, lead time, and media innovations; creating ads—including content,

placement, and variations; timing ads; considering cooperative efforts—both vertical and horizontal; and evaluating success or failure.

3. *To examine the scope, importance, and characteristics of public relations*   Public relations includes any communication that fosters a favorable image among a firm's various publics. It is more image- than sales-oriented; embodies image-oriented ads, personal selling, and sales promotion; and seeks favorable publicity—the nonpersonal communication sent via various media but not paid for by identified sponsors. Thousands of companies have their own public relations departments, and many specialized public relations firms exist. Companies try to get positive publicity and avoid negative publicity. Competition is intense for placing publicity releases. Some firms have ineffective policies to deal with independent media or develop a sustained publicity campaign.

   Among its advantages are the image orientation, the positive effects on employee morale, and—for publicity—the lack of costs for message time, the high credibility, and audience attentiveness. The relative disadvantages of public relations include the lack of interest by some firms in image-oriented communications and the lesser control of publicity placements by the firm, the media interest in negative events, and the difficulty of planning publicity in advance.

4. *To study the elements in a public relations plan*   A public relations plan has seven steps: setting goals—company and/or industry; assigning duties—internally and/or externally; outlining types of public relations—the mix of image-oriented promotion forms and the categories of publicity (news publicity, business and service feature

articles, finance releases, product and pictorial releases, video news releases, background editorial releases, and

emergency publicity); choosing media; creating messages; timing messages; and weighing success or failure.

Key Terms

advertising agency (p. 559)

advertising themes (p. 560)

advertising media costs (p. 561)

reach (p. 561)

waste (p. 562)

message permanence (p. 562)

persuasive impact (p. 562)

narrowcasting (p. 563)

frequency (p. 563)

clutter (p. 565)

lead time (p. 565)

cooperative advertising (p. 568)

publicity types (p. 575)

Review Questions

1. Explain the statement "Advertising is paid for, publicity is prayed for."
2. List five objectives of advertising and give an example of how each may be accomplished.
3. A small firm has an overall annual budget of $125,000 for advertising. What specific decisions must it make in allocating the budget?
4. Differentiate among these advertising concepts: lead time, reach, waste, clutter, and frequency.
5. What are the pros and cons of cooperative advertising?
6. Describe the role of public relations.
7. According to public relations executives, which are the two most preferred media for receiving publicity?
8. State three ways for a firm to evaluate the success or failure of its public relations efforts.

Discussion Questions

1. Devise an advertising plan for generating primary demand for American-made cars.
2. A motel chain knows a full-page ad in a general-interest magazine would cost $150,000; the magazine's total audience is 5 million—750,000 of whom are part of the chain's target market. A full-page ad in a travel magazine would cost $40,000; its total audience is 325,000—290,000
   of whom are part of the chain's target market. Which magazine should be selected? Why?
3. Present and evaluate current examples of companies using institutional advertising, image-oriented personal selling, image-oriented sales promotion, and publicity.
4. How would you obtain publicity for a small company that has developed a recordable HD-DVD player that would sell for $100?

Web Exercise

Go to the Web site of *Advertising Age* (**http://www.adage.com**) and visit the "Data Center." Discuss five interesting facts that

you obtain from the Web site, and state their implications for marketers. Note: Look for the free content at this site.

Practice Quiz

1. Which of the following is common to both advertising and publicity?
   a. Paid presentation
   b. Mass audience
   c. Source control of presentation
   d. Known sponsorship of presentation

2. The leading medium for U.S. advertising is
   a. the Internet.
   b. direct mail.
   c. television.
   d. newspapers.

3. Which of the following is a positive characteristic attributed to advertising?
   a. Low costs for prime-time TV commercials
   b. Limited control over editorial content
   c. The ability to tailor a message to each reader or viewer
   d. A broad range of media to choose among

4. Which of the following is *not* a negative characteristic of advertising?
   a. It often requires high total expenditures.
   b. Messages are standardized.

c. A large portion of viewers or readers may be considered waste for an advertiser.
d. Messages in print media can be reread and restudied.

5. The first step in developing an advertising plan is
a. assigning responsibility.
b. setting objectives.
c. establishing a budget.
d. developing themes.

6. For print media, reach has two components: circulation and
a. psychographics.
b. frequency.
c. passalong rate.
d. clutter.

7. Frequency is lowest for
a. printed phone directories.
b. outdoor ads.
c. magazines.
d. radio.

8. The highest level of clutter exists with
a. magazines.
b. newspapers.
c. television.
d. telephone directories.

9. Which of the following statements concerning distributed ads is *incorrect*?
a. They increase sales in nonpeak periods.
b. They are used by very few manufacturers.
c. They increase brand recognition.
d. They balance the advertising budget.

10. Public relations does *not* encompass
a. sales-oriented advertising.
b. personal selling.
c. publicity.
d. sales promotion.

11. With publicity,
a. credibility is generally high.
b. a firm has complete control over messages.
c. a firm can ensure that the media will cover only positive events.
d. there are costs for message time or space.

12. The first step in developing a public relations plan is
a. assigning responsibility.
b. outlining the types of publicity to be used.
c. setting objectives.
d. selecting media.

13. Assigning public relations responsibility to internal personnel or an in-house department
a. is not a popular approach to assigning responsibility.
b. ensures more control and secrecy.
c. results in better contacts and expertise than using an outside public relations firm.
d. cannot be combined with any other option for assigning the publicity responsibility.

14. Business feature articles are
a. concerned with new products and product improvements.
b. stories dealing with finance found in business sections of newspapers and magazines.
c. detailed stories about a firm's products.
d. extra information provided to media writers and editors.

15. Lighter stories focusing on personal care, household items, and similar topics are examples of
a. background editorial material.
b. news releases.
c. product releases.
d. service feature articles.

For the answers to these questions, please visit the online site for this book at **http://www.atomicdog.com**.

Chapter 19

Personal Selling and Sales Promotion

Anheuser-Busch (A-B) (http://www.anheuser-busch.com) is the leading U.S. beer maker, with a market share of 48 percent. It was recently acquired by InBev and renamed Anheuser-Busch InBev. A-B alone makes more than 30 beers, including Budweiser, Michelob, Busch, and Bud Light—the best-selling U.S. beer. It also imports beers such as Bass, Becks, Grolsch, and Stella Artois. A large part of its success is due to its use of independent sales reps and its sales promotions. Let's examine the roles of each of these.

A-B's beer is sold to retailers (stores, bars, restaurants, etc.) through its more than 600 independent wholesalers. Each wholesaler has a written agreement with A-B that covers its territory, the brands it can sell, specific performance standards, and conditions for terminating the agreement. About 60 percent of A-B's volume is sold by distributors that only sell A-B's brands. A-B recently changed its exclusivity agreement with wholesalers to let distributors carry a small amount of beer (up to 3 percent of total sales) from approved sources—such as a local craft beer. An exclusivity incentive gives wholesalers 6 days of additional credit, a 2 cent per case discount, and a $2,500 painting allowance for their delivery trucks.

Each wholesaler gets national and local media advertising support, point-of-sale advertising materials, and sales promotion material from A-B. One channel where sales promotions have been quite effective is convenience stores, which sell nearly one-third of all U.S. beer. Because only 76 percent of convenience stores sell beer, the per-store beer sales of those that do are $175,000. "The convenience store is ideal for our 'freshness' platform, and most convenience stores work with us to use that as a competitive advantage," said an A-B executive. Many sales promotions involve new products, single-serving packages, and multi-packs. A-B also cross-markets beer via joint promotions with snack items.

A-B and its wholesalers have been quite effective in targeting the Hispanic community. A-B has the top two brands among U.S. Hispanics: Bud Light and Budweiser. In areas with a high Hispanic population, A-B and its wholesalers have recruited bilingual employees and sponsored soccer leagues by providing T-shirts to players, special equipment, and facilities for coaches.[1]

Next, we will study the personal selling and sales promotion aspects of promotion and see how these tools can be used effectively.

Chapter Objectives

1. To examine the scope, importance, and characteristics of personal selling
2. To study the elements in a personal selling plan
3. To examine the scope, importance, and characteristics of sales promotion
4. To study the elements in a sales promotion plan

19-1   OVERVIEW

Personal selling is one-on-one with buyers. Sales promotion includes paid supplemental efforts.

We examine the scope and importance, characteristics, and planning considerations for both personal selling and sales promotion in this chapter.

As defined in Chapter 17, *personal selling* involves oral communication with prospective buyers by paid representatives for the purpose of making sales. It relies on

[1] Various company and other sources.

personal contact, unlike ads and publicity. Goals are similar to other promotion forms: informing, persuading, and/or reminding.

Sales promotion involves paid marketing communication activities (other than advertising, publicity, or personal selling) that stimulate consumers and dealers. Coupons, trade shows, contests and sweepstakes, and point-of-purchase displays are among the marketing tools classified as sales promotion.

19-2   THE SCOPE AND IMPORTANCE OF PERSONAL SELLING

In the United States, 15 million people work in the sales positions defined by the Department of Labor (**http://www.dol.gov**); millions more in other nations are also employed in sales jobs. Professional salespeople generate new customers, ascertain needs, interact with customers, emphasize knowledge and persuasion, and offer service. They include stockbrokers, insurance agents, manufacturer sales representatives, and real-estate brokers. Top ones can earn well over $100,000 per year. Clerical salespeople answer simple queries, retrieve stock from inventory, recommend the best brand in a category, and complete orders by receiving payments and packing products. They include retail, wholesale, and manufacturer sales clerks.

From a marketing perspective, "personal selling" goes far beyond the people in identified sales positions because every contact between a company representative and a customer entails some personal interaction. Lawyers, hair stylists, and cashiers are not defined as salespeople. Yet, they have lots of customer contact. Basin (**http://www.basin.com**), the bath-and-beauty-products chain, and ConAgra (**http://www.conagra.com**), the food giant, know the value of customer contact. See Figures 19-1 and 19-2.

In varying situations, a strong personal-selling emphasis may be needed. Large-volume customers require special attention. Geographically concentrated consumers may be more efficiently served by a sales force than with ads in mass media. Custom-made,

> Selling is stressed when orders are large, consumers are concentrated, items are expensive, and service is required.

Figure 19-1

Highlighting a Personal Touch

As its Web site (**http://www.basin.com**) states: "The experience presented by Basin, as well as its products, set the store apart from the rest. Basin customers have the feeling that they are a part of the process. The store's atmosphere even becomes a draw, as people enjoy watching the soaps being cut and shampoos being mixed."

Source: Reprinted by permission of Susan Berry, Retail Image Consulting, Inc.

Figure 19-2

Personal Selling Throughout the Channel

ConAgra recognizes that it has two customers: the stores that purchase its food products and the final customers who buy them. To enhance its relationship marketing efforts, the firm has increased its in-store sales force. This is part of an overall program to provide greater ordering and display support for resellers, as well as to encourage more frequent communication with store personnel.

Source: Reprinted by permission.

expensive, and complex goods or services require in-depth consumer information, demonstrations, and follow-up calls. Tangential sales services—such as gift wrapping and delivery—may be requested. If ads are not informative enough, questions can be resolved by personal selling. New products may rely on personal selling to gain reseller acceptance. Foreign-market entry may be best handled by personal contacts with potential resellers and/or consumers. Finally, many b-to-b customers expect a lot of personal contact. Generally, a decision to stress personal selling depends on such factors as costs, audience size and needs, and a desire for flexibility.

Selling costs are often greater than advertising costs. Auto-parts suppliers, office and equipment firms, and major appliance makers all spend far more on selling than on ads. Direct marketer Fuller Brush's (**http://www.fullerbrush.com**) sales commissions range up to 50 percent or more of sales. The average cost of a single b-to-b field sales call is several hundred dollars; and it may take multiple visits for a sale.

A number of strategies have been devised to keep selling costs down and improve the efficiency of the sales force, as these examples show:

- Many firms are more effectively routing salespeople to minimize travel time and expenses. Some firms are bypassing smaller customers in their personal selling efforts and specifying minimum order sizes for personalized service. This means opportunities for sellers willing to serve small accounts.
- With *telemarketing*, telephone communications are used to sell or solicit business or to set up an appointment for a salesperson to sell or solicit business. Salespeople can talk to several consumers per hour, centralize operations and lower expenses, screen prospects, process orders and arrange shipments, provide customer service, assist the field sales staff, speed communications, and increase repeat business. A lot of companies rely on telephone personnel to contact customers; outside sales personnel (who actually call on customers) are then more involved with customer service and technical assistance. A broad range of small and large firms use some form of telemarketing. The American Teleservices Association (**http://www.ataconnect.org**) is dedicated exclusively to telemarketing issues. One impediment is

High selling costs have led to a concern for efficiency. In **telemarketing**, phone calls initiate sales or set up sales appointments.

the "Do Not Call Registry," which prohibits most companies from calling U.S. consumers who list themselves on that registry (**http://www.donotcall.gov**).

- Computerization improves efficiency by providing salespeople with detailed and speedy data, making ordering easier, coordinating orders by various salespeople, and identifying the best prospects and their desires (such as preferred brands)—based on prior purchases. Many salespeople use their laptop computers to communicate with the home office to get the latest product data, learn about inventory status, and so on. Firms are also using the Internet to train salespeople. In nearly every issue, *Sales & Marketing Management* (**http://www.salesandmarketing.com**) reports on computerization and selling.

- A lot of firms now view computerized customer data bases as among their most valuable sales resources. These data bases enable the firms to focus efforts better, make sure key accounts are regularly serviced, and use direct mailings to complement telephone calls and salesperson visits.

19-3 THE CHARACTERISTICS OF PERSONAL SELLING

On the positive side, personal selling provides individual attention for each consumer and passes on a lot of information. There is a dynamic interplay between buyer and seller. This lets a firm use a ***buyer-seller dyad***, the two-way flow of communication between both parties. See Figure 19-3. That is not possible with advertising. Personal selling can be flexible and adapted to specific consumer needs. Thus, a real-estate broker can use one sales presentation with a first-time buyer and another with a person who has already bought a home. A salesperson can also apply as much persuasion as needed and balance it against the need for information.

> Selling uses a **buyer-seller dyad** and is flexible and efficient, closes sales, and provides feedback.

Through the buyer-seller dyad, *relationship selling* is possible, whereby long-term customer bonds are developed. Consider this example: "The retail banking division of Massachusetts-based Rockland Trust [**http://www.rocklandtrust.com**] has been bustling with training, coaching practices, and sales and service techniques aimed at creating a process for boosting customer retention and customer growth." As a Rockland executive vice-president put it, "Our focus is to service customers by satisfying their real financial needs rather than trying to hit sales quotas. The process we use is rooted in good questioning and listening skills and strong, technical product knowledge. Branch staff ask open-ended questions, listen to the answers to understand, and respond by presenting appropriate product recommendations."[2]

Personal selling targets a more defined and concentrated audience, which means less waste than with ads. In addition, people who enter a store or who are contacted by a salesperson are more apt to buy than those watching a TV ad. Because ads stimulate

1. Salesperson determines consumer needs.

2. Salesperson presents information and answers consumer's questions.

3. Salesperson and consumer conclude transaction.

Salesperson   Consumer

Figure 19-3

The Buyer-Seller Dyad

---

[2] "Rockland Trust Co., Cross-Selling Is About Relationship Building," *Bank Marketing* (October 2005), p. 36. See also Stephen F. King and Thomas F. Burgess, "Understanding Success and Failure in Customer Relationship Management," *Industrial Marketing Management*, Vol. 37 (June 2008), pp. 421–431.

interest, those who make it to the personal selling stage are often in the target market. When unsolicited, direct selling has the most waste in personal selling.

Selling clinches sales and is usually conducted during the purchase stage of the consumer's decision process, taking place after information search. It holds repeat customers and those already convinced by advertising—and resolves any concerns of undecided consumers by answering questions about price, warranty, and other factors. It addresses service issues, such as delivery and installation. Feedback is immediate and clear-cut: Consumers may be asked their feelings about product features or they may complain; and salespeople may unearth a marketing program's strengths and weaknesses.

On the negative side, selling is ineffective for generating awareness because sales-people can handle only a limited number of consumers. A retail furniture salesperson may be able to talk to fewer than 20 people per day if the average length of a customer contact is 15 minutes to a half hour. Sales personnel who call on customers can handle even fewer accounts, due to travel. In addition, many consumers drawn by advertising may want self-service. This is discouraged by some aggressive salespeople.

> **Selling has a limited audience, high costs per customer, and a poor image.**

Personal selling costs per customer can be very high due to the one-on-one nature of selling. An in-store furniture salesperson who talks to 20 customers daily might cost a firm $8 per presentation ($160/day compensation divided by 20), an amount much higher than an ad's cost per-customer contact. For outside salespeople, hotel stays, meals, and transportation can amount to $400 or more—especially in larger cities—daily per salesperson, and compensation must be added to these costs.[3]

Finally, personal selling, especially among final consumers, has a poor image. It needs to overcome criticisms regarding a lack of honesty and pressure tactics:

> Unwilling to listen. Won't take no for an answer. Lacking knowledge about their products. Pushy. Deceptive. One-way street. You would cringe if this was how your customers described your company's sales reps. Yet, despite all the time and money spent over the past few years to transform salespeople into trusted business advisors, descriptors such as these still reflect customer perceptions of the sales profession. DDI surveyed 2,705 corporate buyers across six countries to understand how they feel about their interactions with salespeople. These buyers represented a wide range of industries, job levels, and age groups. What we really wanted to know was how they viewed their buyer-seller relationships. We uncovered that: Buyers have a poor perception of salespeople. Buyers have increasingly high expectations—and they are not being met. Salespeople are not making inroads toward becoming business partners. What can your firm do to turn the tide? Take a lesson from the pharmaceutical industry where salespeople are increasingly assigned based on the relationship the *physicians* want. Physicians who want to participate in clinical trials and have dialogues are paired with knowledgeable, seasoned reps who are patient-focused. Others who only want copies of efficacy studies or their sample bins filled are served by recent college graduates just learning their craft.[4]

The problem can be tackled through better sales-force training and use of consumer-oriented rather than seller-oriented practices. Industry organizations such as the Direct Selling Association (**http://www.dsa.org**), Manufacturers' Agents National Association (**http://www.manaonline.org**), and National Association of Sales Professionals (**http://www.nasp.com**) are also striving to improve the image of personal selling.

19-4 DEVELOPING A PERSONAL SELLING PLAN

A personal selling plan can be divided into the seven steps shown in Figure 19-4 and highlighted here.

---

[3] "The Cost of the Average Sales Call Today Is More Than $400," **http://www.businesswire.com** (February 28, 2006).

[4] Bradford Thomas, Simon Mitchell, and Jeff Del Rossa, *Sales: Strategic Partnership or Necessary Evil? 2007-2008 Global Sales Perceptions Report*, **http://www.ddiworld.com/pdf/globalsalesperceptionsreport_br_ddi.pdf** (2007).

Global Marketing in Action

Selling Camrys in China

Lin Baojia is among Toyota's (http://www.toyota.com) top-producing salespeople in China, responsible for selling about 60 Camry autos per month. Even though overall car sales in China have been growing at 20 to 30 percent annually, selling Camrys in China is far from easy. The Camry sold in China is somewhat similar to the version sold in the United States. However, it is priced from $27,000 to $37,000 in China. That's an exceptionally high price in a country where many residents can buy a car priced at $4,000.

Baojia and his fellow sales associates are happy to answer any questions about the cars they sell, but they are also are careful not to pressure prospective customers. Unlike in the United States, there is no haggling over a car's price. If Baojia can get a customer to order such extras as insurance and a GPS navigation

system, he is eligible to receive a $14 commission per car. The commission drops to $7 without these options. To Baojia's credit, he earns the $14 commission on 90 percent of his sales.

Baojia excels at customer support. As an example of exemplary customer service, Baojia arranged to have a customer's car towed for free at 2:30 A.M. after the car would not start. Baojia even had two cases of mandarin oranges delivered to the car's driver, just in case he was hungry. At other times, Baojia has been awakened by drivers who have called him after they drank too much. According to Baojia, "Good service is an investment."

Source: Based on material in David Rocks and Ian Rowley, "He Works Hard for the Money," *Business Week* (February 4, 2008), pp. 64–65.

19-4a Setting Objectives

Selling goals can be demand- and/or image-oriented. Image-oriented goals involve public relations. Although many firms have some interest in information, reminder, and image goals, the major goal usually is persuasion: converting consumer interest into a sale. Examples appear in Table 19-1.

19-4b Assigning Responsibility

The personal selling function may be assigned to a marketing or sales manager who oversees all areas of selling, from planning to sales force management. A small or

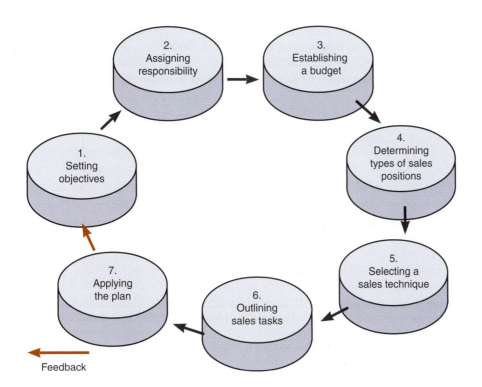

Figure 19-4

Developing a Personal Selling Plan

Table 19-1	Specific Personal Selling Objectives
Type of Objective	**Illustrations**
Demand-Oriented	
Information	Fully explain all attributes of goods and services Answer any questions Probe for any further questions
Persuasion	Differentiate the attributes of goods or services from those of competitors Maximize the number of purchases relative to the presentations made Convert undecided consumers into buyers Sell complementary items—such as a telephoto lens with a camera Placate dissatisfied customers
Reminding	Ensure delivery, installation, etc. Follow up after a good or service has been purchased Follow up when a repurchase is near Reassure previous customers as they make a new purchase
Image-Oriented	
Industry and company	Have a good appearance for all personnel having customer contact Follow acceptable (ethical) sales practices Be respected by customers, employees, and other publics

specialized firm is likely to have its marketing manager oversee selling or use one general sales manager. A large or diversified firm may have multiple sales managers—assigned by product line, customer type, and/or region.

> **A manager must oversee selling functions.**

These are the basic responsibilities of a sales manager:

- Understand the firm's goals, strategies, market position, and basic marketing plan and convey them to the sales force.
- Determine and outline a sales philosophy, sales-force characteristics, selling tasks, a sales organization, and methods of customer contact.
- Prepare and update sales forecasts.
- Allocate selling resources based on sales forecasts and customer needs.
- Select, train, assign, compensate, and supervise sales personnel.
- Synchronize selling tasks with advertising, product planning, distribution, marketing research, production, and other activities.
- Assess sales performance by salesperson, product line, customer group, and geographic area.
- Continuously monitor competitors' actions.
- Make sure the sales force acts ethically.
- Convey the image sought by the company.

19-4c Establishing a Budget

> **A sales-expense budget assigns spending for a specific time.**

A ***sales-expense budget*** allots selling costs among salespeople, products, customers, and geographic areas for a given period. It is usually tied to a sales forecast and relates selling tasks to sales goals. It should be somewhat flexible in case expected sales are not reached or are exceeded.

These items should be covered in a budget: sales forecast, overhead (manager's compensation, office costs), sales-force compensation, sales expenses (travel, lodging, meals, entertainment), sales meetings, selling aids (including computer equipment), and sales management (employee selection and training) costs. Table 19-2 shows a budget for a small manufacturer of business machinery.

The budget is larger if customers are geographically dispersed and a lot of travel is required. Complex products need costly, time-consuming sales presentations and result

Table **19-2**	An Annual Sales-Expense Budget for a Small Manufacturer Specializing in Business Machinery	
Item	**Estimated Annual Costs (Revenues)**
Sales Forecast	$1,950,000
Overhead (1 sales manager, 1 office)	$100,000
Sales-force compensation (2 salespeople)	110,000
Sales expenses	50,000
Sales meetings	5,000
Selling aids	20,000
Sales management costs	15,000
Total personal selling budget	$300,000
Personal selling costs as a percentage of sales forecast	15.4

in fewer calls per salesperson. An expanding sales force needs expenditures for recruiting and training salespeople.

19-4d Determining the Type(s) of Sales Positions

Salespeople can be broadly classed as order takers, order getters, or support personnel. Some firms employ one type of salesperson; others use a combination.

An *order taker* processes routine orders and reorders. This person does more clerical tasks than creative selling, typically for pre-sold goods or services. He or she arranges displays, restocks items, answers simple questions, writes up orders, and completes transactions. He or she may work in a warehouse (manufacturer clerk) or store (retail clerk) or call on customers (a field salesperson). An order taker has these advantages for a firm: compensation is rather low, little training is required, both selling and nonselling tasks are done, and a sales force can be expanded or contracted quickly. Yet, an order taker is an improper choice for goods and services that need creative selling or extensive information for customers. Personnel turnover is high. Enthusiasm may be limited due to the low salary and routine tasks.

An *order getter* generates customer leads, provides information, persuades customers, and closes sales. He or she is the creative salesperson used for high-priced, complex, and/or new products. Less emphasis is placed on clerical tasks. The person may be inside (car salesperson) or outside (Xerox—**http://www.xerox.com**—salesperson). He or she is expert and enthusiastic, grows sales, and can convince undecided customers to buy or decided customers to add peripheral items—such as appliances along with a newly built house. Yet, for many customers, the order getter has a high-pressure image. He or she may also need expensive training. Such nonsales tasks as writing reports may be avoided because they take away from a salesperson's time with customers and are seldom rewarded. Compensation can be very high for salespersons who are effective order getters. Figure 19-5 contrasts order takers and order getters.

Support personnel supplement a sales force. A *missionary salesperson* gives out information on new goods or services. He or she does not close sales but describes items' attributes, answers questions, and leaves written materials. This paves the way for later sales and is often used with prescription drugs. A *sales engineer* accompanies an order getter if a very technical or complex item is involved. He or she discusses specifications and long-range uses, while the order getter makes customer contacts and closes sales.

An **order taker** handles routine orders and sells items that are pre-sold.

An **order getter** obtains leads, provides information, persuades customers, and closes sales.

Missionary salespersons, **sales engineers**, and **service salespersons** are support personnel.

Figure 19-5

Contrasting Order Takers and Order Getters

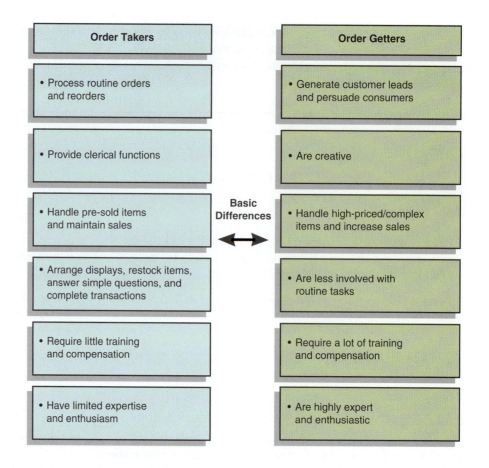

Order Takers		Order Getters
• Process routine orders and reorders		• Generate customer leads and persuade consumers
• Provide clerical functions		• Are creative
• Handle pre-sold items and maintain sales	**Basic Differences** ⟷	• Handle high-priced/complex items and increase sales
• Arrange displays, restock items, answer simple questions, and complete transactions		• Are less involved with routine tasks
• Require little training and compensation		• Require a lot of training and compensation
• Have limited expertise and enthusiasm		• Are highly expert and enthusiastic

A **service salesperson** ordinarily deals with customers after sales. Delivery, installation, and other follow-up tasks are done.

19-4e   Selecting a Sales Technique

Two basic selling techniques are the canned sales presentation and the need-satisfaction approach. The **canned sales presentation** is a memorized, repetitive presentation given to all customers interested in a given item. It does not adapt to customer needs or traits but presumes that a general presentation will appeal to everyone. Though criticized for its inflexibility and a nonmarketing orientation, it does have value for companies that employ inexperienced salespeople and have little time or interest in training them in creative selling techniques. With this approach, salespeople have a consistent sales presentation and a structured order of topics to discuss; and basic customer questions-and-answers can be scripted.

The **need-satisfaction approach** is a high-level selling method based on the principle that each customer has different attributes and wants, and therefore the sales presentation should be adapted to the individual consumer. With this technique, a salesperson first asks: What type of product are you looking for? Have you ever bought this product before? What price range are you considering? Then the sales presentation is more responsive to the particular person, and a new shopper is treated differently from an experienced one. The need-satisfaction approach is more customer-oriented; yet, it requires better training and skilled sales personnel. Here are some hints for using this approach:

The **canned sales presentation** is memorized and nonadaptive.

The **need-satisfaction approach** adapts to individual consumers.

- "Be sincere with people. Too many salespeople are fake and feign interest in their prospects. People are smart and see right through such insincerity."
- "It is vitally important to constantly hone your sales and communications skills. Continuous growth and training in formal professional selling techniques is also very important."
- "First listen to your customer, understand his or her wants and needs, and then try to learn whether or not you can deliver the goods or services to meet those wants and needs. If you approach a prospect with a solution before understanding the problem, you are likely to be wrong about the solution."
- "The best salespeople ask many questions and genuinely listen to answers before speaking again."
- "Your prospects and customers are all different, so you should treat them differently."
- "The best salespeople listen much more than they talk."
- "If you cannot give your prospects what they want, tell them so and help them find what they are looking for elsewhere."[5]

The canned sales presentation works best with inexpensive, routine items that are heavily advertised and relatively pre-sold. The need-satisfaction approach works best with more expensive, more complex items that have moderate advertising and require substantial additional information for consumers.

19-4f Outlining Sales Tasks

The tasks to be performed by the personal sales force need to be outlined. The **selling process** consists of prospecting for leads, approaching customers, determining consumer wants, giving a sales presentation, answering questions, closing the sale, and following up.[6] See Figure 19-6.

Outside selling requires a procedure, known as **prospecting**, to generate a list of customer leads. Blind prospecting uses phone directories, the Internet, and other general listings of potential customers; with it, a small percentage of those contacted will be interested in a firm's offering. Lead prospecting depends on past customers and others for referrals; thus, a greater percentage of people will be interested because of the referral from someone they know. Inside selling does not involve prospecting because customers have already been drawn to a store or office through ads or prior purchase experience.

Approaching customers is a two-stage procedure: pre-approach and greeting. During pre-approach, a salesperson tries to get information about the customer from the firm's data base, census materials, and/or other secondary data—as well as from referrals. The salesperson is then better equipped to interact with that customer. Inside retail salespeople may be unable to use a pre-approach; they often know nothing about a consumer until he or she enters the store. During the greeting, a salesperson begins a conversation. The intention is to put the customer at ease and build rapport.

The **selling process** consists of seven steps.

Prospecting creates customer leads.

The pre-approach and greeting are the two parts of **approaching customers**.

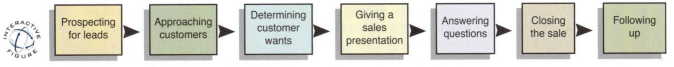

Figure 19-6
The Selling Process

[5] Dave Dolak, "Sales and Personal Selling," http://www.davedolak.com/psell.htm (May 31, 2009).

[6] For a good checklist of sales tasks, see Barry Farber, "Step by Step," http://www.entrepreneur.com/sales/salestechniques/article59802.html (March 2003).

The **sales presentation** converts an uncertain consumer.

The next step is to ascertain customer wants by asking the person a variety of questions regarding past experience with the product category, price, product features, intended uses, and the kinds of information still needed.

The *sales presentation* includes a verbal description of a product, its benefits, options and models, price, associated services such as delivery and warranty, and a demonstration (if needed). A canned sales presentation or need-satisfaction method may be used. The purpose of a sales presentation is to convert an undecided consumer into a purchaser.

After a presentation, the salesperson usually answers consumer questions. They are of two kinds: the first request more information; the second raise objections that must be settled before a sale is made.

The **closing** clinches a sale.

Once questions have been answered, a salesperson is ready for *closing the sale*. This means getting a person to agree to a purchase. The salesperson must be sure no key questions remain before trying to close a sale, and the salesperson must not argue with a customer.

With a big purchase, the salesperson should follow up after a sale to be sure the customer is pleased. The person is then better satisfied, referrals are obtained, and repurchases are more likely. "Here's the bottom line. You can easily differentiate yourself from your competition by making the effort to follow up with your prospects and customers. Don't take it for granted that they will call you. Be proactive and contact them."[7]

Besides the tasks in the selling process, a firm must clearly enumerate the nonselling tasks it wants sales personnel to perform. Among the nonselling tasks that may be assigned are setting up displays, writing up information sheets, marking prices on products, checking competitors' strategies, doing test marketing analysis and consumer surveys, and training new employees.

19-4g Applying the Plan

Sales management tasks range from employee selection to supervision.

Sales management—planning, implementing, and controlling the personal sales function—should be used in applying a personal selling plan. It covers employee selection, training, territory allocation, compensation, and supervision.

In selecting salespeople, a combination of personal attributes should be assessed: mental (intelligence, ability to plan), physical (appearance, speaking ability), experiential (education, sales/business background), environmental (group memberships, social influences), personality (ambition, enthusiasm, tact, resourcefulness, stability), and willingness to be trained and to follow instructions.[8] What makes a superior sales force?

(1) *Optimism*—Ever notice how the best reps tend to look on the bright side? Optimism also may determine how resilient a rep will be. (2) *Resilience*—This is the "ability to take 15 no's before you get a yes." (3) *Self-Motivation*—Most managers and experts believe this is a trait that cannot be taught. The best reps tend to have an inherent competitive drive for money or recognition or simply pride. (4) *Personability*—You can't sell if your customers don't like you. Being friendly and sociable is a hallmark of reps who maintain long-term customer relationships. (5) *Empathy*—This underlies virtually all other emotional intelligence skills, because it involves truly understanding the customer. Empathetic reps tend to have good listening and communication skills.[9]

---

[7] Kelley Robertson, "The Impact of Follow Up," **http://www.businessknowhow.com/marketing/follow-up.htm** (December 14, 2005).

[8] Adapted by the authors from Rosann L. Spiro, William J. Stanton, and Greg A. Rich, *Management of a Sales Force*, Twelfth Edition (New York: McGraw-Hill/Irwin, 2008).

[9] Julia Chang, "Born to Sell?" *Sales & Marketing Management* (July 2003), p. 36. See also Paul Sloan and Alan Key, "The Sales Force That Rocks," *Business 2.0* (June 2005), pp. 102–107.

The traits of potential salespeople must be compatible with the customers with whom they will interact and the requirements of the good or service being sold. The buyer-seller dyad operates better when there are some similarities in salesperson and customer characteristics. And certain product categories require much different education, technical training, and sales activities than others (such as jewelry versus computer sales).

Once the preceding factors are reviewed, the firm would develop a formal procedure that specifies the personal attributes sought, sources of employees (such as colleges and employment agencies), and methods for selection (such as interviews and testing). It would be based on the overall selling plan.

Salesperson training may take many forms. A formal program uses a trainer, a classroom, lectures, and printed materials. It may also include role playing (in which trainees act out parts) and case analysis. Field trips take trainees on actual calls so they can observe skilled salespeople. On-the-job training places trainees in their own selling situations under the close supervision of a trainer or senior salesperson. Training often covers a range of topics; it should teach selling skills and include information on the firm and its offerings, the industry, and employee duties. For example, Century 21 (**http://www.century21.com**) has several sales training initiatives, including CREATE 21 (Career Real Estate Agent Training and Education), whereby new salespeople "participate in a live, affordable, online six-week training course; BLAST! (Bottom Line Advanced Sales Training), whereby experienced salespeople receive training to "boost their bottom line and take their career to the next level"; and Virtual Solution Series (VSS), a free online program for members of Century 21 which covers "a range of such relevant topics as business planning, managing business activities, and real-estate photography."[10] As many firms (including Century 21) recognize, in addition to initial training, continuous training or retraining of sales personnel may be necessary to teach new techniques, explain new products, or improve performance.

Territory size and salesperson allocation are decided next. A *sales territory* consists of the geographic area, customers, and/or product lines assigned to a salesperson. If territories are assigned by customer type or product category, two or more salespeople may cover the same area. Territory size depends on customer locations, order size, travel time and expenses, the time per sales call, the yearly visits for each account, and the number of hours per year each salesperson has for selling tasks. The mix of established versus new customer accounts must also be considered. Allocating salespeople to specific territories depends on their ability, the buyer-seller dyad, the mix of selling and non-selling tasks (such as one salesperson training new employees), and seniority. Proper territory size and allocation provide adequate coverage of customers, minimize overlap, recognize geographic boundaries, minimize travel expenses, encourage solicitation of new accounts, provide enough sales potential for good salespeople to be well rewarded, and are fair to everyone. Sales territory software, such as that marketed by Territory Mapper (**http://www.territorymapper.com**) and AlignStar (**http://www.alignstar.com**), can facilitate planning.

> A **sales territory** contains the area, customers, and/or products assigned to a salesperson.

Salespeople are compensated by straight salary, straight commission, or a combination of salary and commission or bonus. With a *straight salary plan*, a salesperson is paid a flat amount per time period. Earnings are not tied to sales. Advantages are that both selling and nonselling tasks can be specified and controlled, salespeople have security, and expenses are known in advance. Disadvantages are the low incentive to increase sales, expenses not being tied to productivity, and the continuing costs even if there are low sales. Order takers are usually paid straight salaries.

> Sales compensation may be **straight salary, straight commission**, or a **combination** of the two.

With a *straight commission plan*, a salesperson's earnings are directly related to sales, profits, customer satisfaction, or some other performance measure. The commission rate is often keyed to a quota, which is a productivity standard. Advantages of this

---

[10] "Get Training," **http://www.century21.com/careerfranchise/career/gettraining.jsp** (May 31, 2009).

plan are the use of motivated salespeople, no fixed sales compensation costs, and expenses being tied to productivity. Disadvantages are the firm's lack of control over nonselling tasks, the instability of a firm's expenses, and salesperson risks due to variable pay. Insurance, real-estate, and direct-selling order getters often earn straight commissions. A real-estate salesperson might receive a 2 percent commission of $8,000 for selling a $400,000 house.

To gain the advantages of both salary- and commission-oriented methods, many firms use elements of each in a *combination sales compensation plan*. This balances control, flexibility, and employee incentives; and some companies award bonuses for superior individual or firm performance. All types of order getters work on a combination basis. Two-thirds of U.S. firms compensate sales personnel by some form of combination plan, one-fifth use a straight salary plan, and the rest use straight commissions. Smaller firms are more apt to use a straight salary plan and less apt to use a combination plan.

Supervision encompasses four aspects of sales management:

- *Sales personnel must be motivated*. Their motivation depends on such factors as the clarity of the job (what tasks must be performed), the salesperson's desire to achieve, the variety of tasks performed, the incentives for undertaking each task, the style of the sales manager, flexibility, and recognition.
- *Performance must be measured*. To do this, achievements must be gauged against such goals as sales and calls per day. The analysis should take into account territory size, travel time, and experience. Salesperson failure is often related to poor listening skills, the failure to concentrate on priorities, a lack of effort, the inability to determine customer needs, a lack of planning for presentations, promising too much, and inadequate knowledge.
- *The sales manager must ensure that all nonselling tasks are completed*, even if sales personnel are not rewarded for them.
- *Some action may be needed to modify behavior* if performance does not meet expectations.[11]

In sales management, these key factors should also be taken into account: the evolving role of women in selling and the special nature of selling in foreign markets.

With regard to women in personal selling, a dramatic increase has taken place in the proportion of sales personnel and sales managers who are female. According to the U.S. Bureau of Labor Statistics (**http://www.bls.gov**), women now comprise 50 percent of the total sales force in the United States and nearly 40 percent of sales supervisors (up from 25 percent in the mid-1980s).[12]

When firms go international, sales managers must recognize that sales personnel have to deal with vastly different cultures: "As businesses increasingly seek to market across international borders, they face the challenge of finding people who can successfully communicate to customers of multiple nations. Not only do salespeople need to understand another language, but they must also understand the complex web of social, cultural, and rhetoric features to which customers respond."[13] In particular, the attributes of salespeople; salesperson training, compensation, and supervision; the dynamics of the buyer-seller dyad; and the selling process may need to be tailored to distinct foreign markets.

[11] See Andris A. Zoltners, Prabhakant Sinha, and Sally E. Lorimer, "Sales Force Effectiveness: A Framework for Researchers and Practitioners," *Journal of Personal Selling & Sales Management*, Vol. 28 (Spring 2008), pp. 115–131.

[12] See Nikala Lane, "Strategy Implementation: The Implications of a Gender Perspective for Change Management," *Journal of Strategic Marketing*, Vol. 13 (June 2005), pp. 117–131.

[13] "Global Selling and Sales Management: Cross-Cultural Issues—National Character," *Journal of Personal Selling & Sales Management*, Vol. 22 (Summer 2002), pp. 204–205.

19-5 THE SCOPE AND IMPORTANCE OF SALES PROMOTION

As a result of intense competition in their industries, numerous firms are aggressively seeking every marketing edge possible. Thus, sales promotion activities worldwide are at a high level. In the United States alone, spending exceeds $400 billion a year, including some sales promotion activities (such as direct mail and promotion-oriented ads) that may also be viewed as advertising.

The extent of sales promotion activities can be shown by the following:

- About 85 percent of U.S. households use coupons, half on a regular basis. Each year, about $3 billion worth of coupons are redeemed. Yet, people redeem only a small fraction of distributed coupons.[14]
- There are thousands of trade shows around the world each year. One is the Automotive Aftermarket Products Expo (AAPEX). It attracts 2,000 exhibitors and 120,000 visitors—including 60,000 b-to-b customers from 150 countries.[15] The TSNN.com Web site (**http://www.tsnn.com**) contains information on more than 15,000 trade shows and conferences worldwide.
- According to International Events Group (**http://www.sponsorship.com**), firms spend $45 billion annually worldwide (including $18 billion in North America) to sponsor special events—two-thirds on sports-related events. Among the leading sponsors are Anheuser-Busch (**http://www.anheuser-busch.com**), Coca-Cola (**http://www.coca-cola.com**), Nike (**http://www.nike.com**), and PepsiCo (**http://www.pepsico.com**).[16]
- Safeway (**http://www.safeway.com**), the California-based supermarket chain, has 1.5 million members in its Club Card frequent-shopper program. Customers are rewarded with special discounts, and Safeway is able to build customer loyalty. Loyalty programs are extremely popular. Figure 19-7 shows a Tesco (**http://www.tesco.com**) Green Clubcard promotion to foster customer loyalty.
- $20 billion is spent on point-of-purchase displays in U.S. stores each year.[17] These displays stimulate impulse purchases and provide information. Besides traditional cardboard, metal, and plastic displays, more stores now use digital electronic signs and video displays.

Several reasons account for sales promotion's strength as a marketing tool. As noted earlier, firms look for any competitive edge they can get, and this often involves some kind of sales promotion. The various forms of sales promotions are more acceptable to firms and consumers than in the past. Rapid results are possible, and numerous firms want to improve short-run profits. Today, more shoppers seek promotions before buying, and resellers put pressure on manufacturers for promotions. In economic slowdowns, more shoppers look for value-oriented sales promotions. Due to rising costs, advertising and personal selling have become more expensive relative to sales promotion. Technological advances make aspects of sales promotion, such as coupon redemption, easier to administer.

Sales promotion efforts are now quite extensive.

Sales promotion lures customers, maintains loyalty, creates excitement, is often keyed to patronage, and appeals to channel members.

19-6 THE CHARACTERISTICS OF SALES PROMOTION

Sales promotion has many advantages. It helps attract customer traffic and keep brand or company loyalty: New-product samples and trial offers draw customers. A manufacturer

[14] "All About Coupons," **http://www.couponmonth.com/pages/allabout.htm** (May 27, 2009).

[15] "AAPEX Show," **http://www.aapexshow.com** (December 21, 2008).

[16] "Promotion Industry Trends Report," *Promo* (September 2008); and *IEG Sponsorship Report* (Chicago, IL: IEG: December 24, 2007 and January 21, 2008 issues).

[17] "Promotion Industry Trends Report," *Promo* (September 2008).

Figure 19-7

Generating Customer Loyalty Through Sales Promotion

Great Britain's Tesco (**http://www. tesco.com**) appeals to shoppers' environmental awareness by offering a Green Clubcard: "One way you can collect Green Clubcard Points is by reusing bags in-store, rather than taking new ones—we'll give you at least one point for each bag reused, depending on its size. They don't even have to be Tesco bags—Asda, Sainsbury's, or the shop down the road; it doesn't matter—as long as you're reusing them when you shop with us, you get the points."

Source: Reprinted by permission of Susan Berry, Retail Image Consulting, Inc.

Marketing and the Web

The Boom in Online Coupon Usage

As recently as 2004, many retailers were reluctant to place E-coupons on their Web sites. Now, the use of E-coupons from various types of retailers has significantly grown. While the overall use of coupons in the United States has stagnated, considerable growth is attributed to online coupons. Instead of using newspapers and scissors, online coupons are accessed via computers and even mobile phones. The number of page views on Web sites that feature money-off coupons increased to 281 million in 2008, an increase of 38 percent from one year earlier. These visitors spent 145 million minutes on these sites.

Coupons.com (**http://www.coupons.com**) and RetailMeNot.com (**http://www.retailmenot.com**) are the largest firms in the online coupon industry. Coupons.com provides marketers with unique serial numbers for each of the coupon offers the marketers create. These coupons are then printed and redeemed at retail stores or at Web sites. The redemption rate for coupons distributed through Coupons.com is about 17 percent, versus a 1 percent redemption rate for a typical newspaper-based coupon. At RetailMeNot.com, consumers can post and share digital coupons.

In March 2008, AOL began an online coupon service, Shortcuts.com (**http://www.shortcuts.com**), with Kroger (**http://www.kroger.com**) as its first major account. In this instance, consumers needed to first set up an individual account using a Kroger loyalty card. Next, shoppers would search Shortcuts.com's coupons by brand, products, or category and indicate which coupons they wished to select. Coupon discounts would be automatically applied to a consumer's purchases upon scanning his/her loyalty card at a Kroger store.

Sources: Based on material in "Coupon-Clicking Replaces Clipping," *Chain Store Age* (April 2008), p. 90; Catherine Holahan, "Cutting Costs with Online Coupon Sites," **http://www.businessweek.com/technology** (May 6, 2008); and Paul Sloan, "Listening to the Coupon Clickers," *Fortune* (June 23, 2008), p. 114.

can sustain brand loyalty by giving gifts to regular customers and coupons for its brands. A reseller can retain loyal customers by having incentives for frequent shoppers and using store coupons.

Quick customer responses can be gained. Some promotions provide value and are kept by customers (such as calendars, matchbooks, T-shirts, pens, and posters with the firm's name); they provide a reminder function. Impulse purchases can be stimulated via in-store displays. An attractive supermarket display for batteries can dramatically raise sales. In addition, a good display may lead a shopper to buy more than originally intended.

Excitement is created by certain short-run promotions involving gifts, contests, or sweepstakes; and high-value items or high payoffs encourage consumers to participate. Contests offer the further benefit of customer involvement (through the completion of some skill-oriented activity). Many promotions are tied to customer patronage—with coupons, frequent-shopper gifts, and referral gifts directly related to purchases. In these cases, promotions can be a fixed percentage of sales and their costs not incurred until transactions are completed. And resellers may be stimulated if support is provided in the form of displays, manufacturer coupons, manufacturer rebates, and trade allowances.

Sales promotion also has limitations. A firm's image may be lessened if it always runs promotions. People may view discounts as representing a decline in product quality and believe a firm could not sell its offerings without them. Profit margins are often lower for a firm if sales promotion is used. When coupons, rebates, or other special deals are offered frequently, people may not buy when products are sold at regular prices; they will stock up each time there is a promotion. Shoppers may even interpret a regular price as an increase for items that are heavily promoted.

Some promotions shift the marketing focus away from the product itself to secondary factors. People may be lured by calendars and sweepstakes instead of product quality and features. In the short run, this generates consumer enthusiasm. In the long run, it may adversely affect a brand's image and sales because a product-related advantage has not been communicated. Sales promotion should enhance—not replace—advertising, personal selling, and public relations.

> Sales promotion many hurt image, cause consumers to wait for special offers, and shift the focus from the product.

19-7 DEVELOPING A SALES PROMOTION PLAN

A sales promotion plan consists of the steps shown in Figure 19-8 and is explained next.

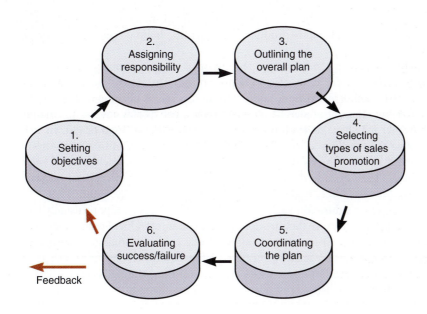

Figure 19-8

Developing a Sales Promotion Plan

19-7a   Setting Objectives

Goals are usually demand-oriented. They may be related to channel members and to consumers.

Objectives associated with channel-member sales promotions include gaining distribution, receiving adequate shelf space, increasing dealer enthusiasm, raising sales, and getting cooperation in sales promotion expenditures. Objectives pertaining to consumer sales promotions include boosting brand awareness, increasing product trials, hiking average purchases, encouraging repurchases, obtaining impulse sales, emphasizing novelty, and supplementing other promotional tools.

19-7b   Assigning Responsibility

Duties are often shared by advertising and sales managers, with each directing the sales promotions in his or her area. An advertising manager would work on coupons, customer contests, calendars, and other mass promotions. A sales manager would work on trade shows, cooperative promotions, special events, demonstrations, and other efforts involving individualized attention for channel members or consumers.

Some companies have their own sales promotion departments or hire outside promotion firms, such as PromoWorks (**http://www.promoworkspromotions.com**). Outside firms often work with specific tools—such as coupons, contests, or gifts—and often can devise a sales promotion campaign at less cost than the user company could. These firms offer expertise, swift service, flexibility, and, when requested, distribution.

19-7c   Outlining the Overall Plan

At this juncture, a sales promotion plan should be outlined and include a budget, an orientation, conditions, media, duration and timing, and cooperative efforts. In setting a budget, it is important to include all costs. The average face value of a U.S. coupon is now $1.30; retailers get a handling fee for each coupon they redeem; and there are costs for printing, mailing, and advertising coupons.

Sales promotion orientation refers to its focus—channel members or consumers—and its theme. Promotions for channel members should improve their product knowledge, provide sales support, offer rewards for selling a promoted product, and foster better cooperation and efficiency. Consumer promotions should induce impulse and larger-volume sales, sustain brand name recognition, and gain participation. A promotion theme refers to its underlying channel member or consumer message—such as a special sale, new-product introduction, holiday celebration, or customer recruitment.

Sales promotion conditions are requirements channel members or consumers must meet to be eligible for a specific sales promotion. These may include minimum purchases, performance provisions, and/or minimum age. A channel member may have to stock a certain amount of merchandise to receive a free display case from a manufacturer. A consumer may have to send in proofs of purchase for a refund or gift. In some cases, strict time limits are set as to the closing dates for participation in a promotion.

Media are the vehicles through which sales promotions reach channel members or consumers. They include direct mail, displays, billboards, newspapers, magazines, TV, the Web, the sales force, trade shows, and group meetings. See Figure 19-9.

A promotion's duration varies, depending on its goals. Coupons usually have short-term closing dates because they are used to increase store traffic. Frequent-shopper points often can be redeemed for at least one year; the goal is to maintain loyalty. As noted earlier, if promotions are lengthy or offered often, consumers may expect them as part of a purchase. Some promotions are seasonal, and for these timing is crucial. They must be tied to such events as fall school openings or model changes.

> **Sales promotion orientation** may be toward channel members or final consumers.

> **Sales promotion conditions** are eligibility requirements.

Figure 19-9

A Sidewalk Sales Promotion Display

Jamba Juice (**http://www.jambajuice.com**) stores market "a range of freshly blended beverages, on-the-go breakfasts, and snacks in our stores." The company uses attractive promotional displays to draw passersby into stores.

Source: Reprinted by permission.

Finally, the use of shared promotions should be decided. With cooperative efforts, each party pays some costs and gets benefits. Promotions can be sponsored by trade associations, manufacturers and/or service firms, wholesalers, and retailers. Consider this example:

Nike (**http://www.nike.com**) and Apple (**http://www.apple.com**) may seem unlikely partners. Yet, they launched a cooperative advertising campaign to sell common benefits and reduce overall costs. "Cooperative advertising occurs when two brands appear in one ad because their lifestyles match," said Harish Bijoor (**http://www.harishbijoor.blogspot.com**), an Indian marketing consultant. "It's kind of like a marriage between two people from different backgrounds with a common goal." For Nike and iPod (which pioneered the concept in this segment), the commonality lies in the fact that most runners listen to music while running. So, Nike and Apple launched the Nike+ shoes, which have a sleeve to fit a pedometer and an iPod Nano—which picks up signals from the pedometer apart from playing music; then, the two firms launched a campaign. "The response to this product has been so overwhelming that we plan to make more products Nike+ ready," said a Nike spokesperson.[18]

---

[18] Priyanka Mehra, "Companies Embrace Cooperative Advertising, But Hitches Remain," **http://www.livemint.com/2007/04/23003525/Companies-embrace-cooperative.html** (April 23, 2007).

19-7d Selecting the Types of Sales Promotion

A wide range of sales promotion tools is available. The attributes of promotion tools oriented to channel members are shown in Table 19-3. The attributes of promotion tools oriented to consumers are noted in Table 19-4. Examples for each tool are also provided in these tables. The selection of sales promotions should be based on such factors as company image, company goals, costs, participation requirements, and the enthusiasm of channel members or customers. See Figure 19-10.

19-7e Coordinating the Plan

> Advertising and sales promotion should be integrated.

It is essential for sales promotion activities to be well coordinated with other elements of the promotion mix. In particular:

- Advertising and sales promotion plans should be integrated.
- The sales force should be notified of all promotions well in advance and trained to implement them.
- For special events, such as the appearance of a major celebrity, publicity should be generated.
- Sales promotions should be consistent with channel members' activities.

19-7f Evaluating Success or Failure

> The success or failure of some sales promotions is simple to measure.

Measuring the success or failure of many sales promotions is straightforward because the promotions may be closely linked to performance or sales. By analyzing before-and-after

Table 19-3 Selected Types of Sales Promotion Directed at Channel Members

Type	Characteristics	Illustration
Trade shows or meetings	One firm or a group of firms invites channel members to attend sessions where products are displayed and explained.	The annual National Hardware Show attracts more than 3,500 exhibitors and tens of thousands of attendees.
Training	A firm provides training for personnel of channel members.	Apple trains AT&T retail salespeople in how to operate and use its iPhone.
Trade allowances or special offers	Channel members are given discounts or rebates for performing specified functions or purchasing during certain time periods.	A local distributor receives a discount for running its own promotion for Whirlpool appliances.
Point-of-purchase displays	A firm gives channel members fully equipped displays for its products and sets them up.	Coca-Cola provides display cases with its name on them to retailers carrying minimum quantities of Coca-Cola products.
Push money	Channel members' salespeople are given bonuses for pushing the brand of a certain firm. Channel members may not like this if their salespeople shift loyalty to the supplying firm.	A salesperson in an office-equipment store is paid an extra $50 for every desk of a particular brand that is sold.
Sales contests	Prizes or bonuses are distributed if certain performance levels are met.	A wholesaler receives $2,500 for selling 1,000 microchips in a month.
Free merchandise	Discounts or allowances are provided in the form of merchandise.	A retailer gets one case of ballpoint pens free for every 10 cases purchased.
Demonstration models	Free items are given to channel members for demonstration purposes.	A hospital-bed manufacturer offers demonstrator models to its distributors.
Gifts	Channel members are given gifts for carrying items or performing functions.	During one three-month period, a book publisher gives computerized cash registers to bookstores that agree to stock a specified quantity of its books.
Cooperative promotions	Two or more channel members share the costs of a promotion.	A manufacturer and retailer each pay part of the costs for T-shirts with the manufacturer's and retailer's names embossed.

Type	Characteristics	Illustration
Coupons	Firms advertise special discounts for customers who redeem coupons.	P&G mails consumers a coupon for Gillette Fusion razor blades, which can be redeemed at any supermarket.
Refunds or rebates	Consumers submit proof purchases (often to the manufacturer) and receive an extra discount.	First Alert provides rebates to consumers submitting proofs of purchase for its fire alarms.
Samples	Free merchandise or services are given to consumers, generally for new items.	Adobe offers a free Internet trial of its Flash software.
Contests or sweepstakes	Consumers compete for prizes by answering questions (contests) or filling out forms for random drawings of prizes (sweepstakes).	Publishers Clearing House sponsors various sweepstakes and awards cash and other prizes.
Bonus packs or multipacks	Consumers receive discounts for purchasing in quantity.	A furniture store runs a "buy one, get one free" sale on desk lamps.
Shows or exhibits	Many firms co-sponsor exhibitions for consumers.	The Auto Show is annually scheduled for the public in New York.
Point-of-purchase displays	In-store displays remind customers and generate impulse purchases.	*People* sales in supermarkets are high due to checkout counter displays.
Special events	Firms sponsor the Olympics, fashion shows, and other activities.	Visa USA is a worldwide sponsor of the Olympics.
Product placements	Branded goods and services are depicted in movies and TV shows.	BMW cars appear in movies.
Gifts	Consumers get gifts for making a purchase or opening a new account.	Savings banks offer gifts for consumers opening new accounts or expanding existing ones.
Frequent-shopper gifts	Consumers get gifts or special discounts, based on cumulative purchases. Points are amassed and exchanged for gifts or money.	Airline travelers accumulate mileage and receive free trips or gifts when enough miles are earned.
Referral gifts	Existing customers are given gifts for referring their friends to the company.	Tupperware awards gifts to the woman hosting a Tupperware party in her home.
Demonstrations	Goods or services are shown in action.	Different models of barbeque grills are demonstrated in a free lesson.

Table **19-4** Selected Types of Sales Promotion Directed at Consumers

data, the impact of these promotions is clear. Trade show effectiveness can be gauged by counting the number of leads generated, examining sales from those leads and the cost per lead, getting customer feedback about a show from the sales force, and determining the amount of literature given out at a show. Companies can verify sales increases as a result of dealer-training programs. Firms using coupons can review sales and compare redemption rates with industry averages. Surveys of channel members and consumers can indicate satisfaction with promotions, suggestions for improvements, and the effect of promotions on image.

Some sales promotions—such as event sponsorships and T-shirt giveaways—are more difficult to evaluate. Objectives are less definitive.

Here are two examples relating to the effectiveness of sales promotion:

- Coca-Cola recently won an Interactive Marketing Award for its My Coke Rewards (**http://www.mycokerewards.com**) program: "My Coke Rewards has set a benchmark for all marketers considering an online loyalty program. But Coca-Cola Co. hasn't rested on its laurels. In April 2007, it rolled out an enhanced MyCokeRewards.com Web site that now covers all 13 client brands, as opposed to the first version, which debuted in 2006 and allowed consumer redemption only for franchise products: Coke, Diet Coke, and Coke Zero. Each member's experience is customized, based on up to 400 pieces of information captured about each member. That data is crunched, then spit back out in highly individualized messaging, reward recommendations, partner information, and promotions. By

Ethical Issues in Marketing

Are Frequent-Flier Programs Still a Good Deal for Consumers?

According to some estimates, consumers have earned 17 trillion frequent-flier miles over the past 30 years. Yet, despite the popularity of these programs, some experts question their use. These programs are costly for the airlines in that they must first promote membership among consumers and then promote the programs to get members to use their points.

Some consumers have also become less enamored with frequent-flier programs. They believe airline miles are difficult to redeem, causing them to travel at inconvenient times or to make multiple stops instead of taking direct flights. Due to recent cutbacks in the number of flights because of high jet fuel costs, redeeming frequent-flier miles is even more difficult. Some airlines such as Delta (**http://www.delta.com**) have added fuel surcharges (of $25 to $50) for flights taken by frequent fliers. On American (**http://www.aa.com**), United (**http://www.**

united.com), and US Airways (**http://www.usair.com**), frequent flier members can lose airline miles if their account has been inactive for 18 months (down from 36 months).

Frequent-flier programs are highly profitable to the airlines. In comparison to other loyalty programs, where a firm provides a customer with a product having a wholesale cost that is high in relation to the retail price, the cost of placing a passenger in an unsold airline seat is very low. American Airlines and other major carriers earn large amounts from partners such as hotels, car-rental firms, and credit-card companies who purchase airlines miles in bulk as part of their loyalty programs.

Sources: Based on material in Dean Foust, "Maybe You Can Trade Them for Peanuts," *Business Week* (June 30, 2008), p. 17; and Micheline Maynard, "Delta Adds Fuel Fee to Frequent-Flier Tickets," **http://www.nytimes.com** (June 28, 2008).

Figure 19-10

Pentax: Generating Buzz and Enthusiasm for Its Cameras

Both resellers and their customers benefit from the mobile sales displays of Pentax (**http://www.pentax.com**). Resellers appreciate the business that Pentax drives their way; and customers like the professional information they receive by Pentax-trained representatives.

Source: Reprinted by permission.

mid-2008, close to 6 million rewards had been redeemed by the more than 9 million members since the site first launched in 2006. And registration continues to grow."[19]

- How successful is sampling? According to a recent study on food sampling, it can be quite effective: "Presenting consumers with cues that are high in incentive value (e.g., a tasty food or beverage item, a pleasant odor) in a store environment can

---

[19] "Rewarding Redemption," **http://www.promomagazine.com/awards/iaawards/IMA_Awards08.pdf** (2008).

induce a general motivational state that increases the likelihood of engaging in a broad array of reward-seeking behaviors. This is likely not only to increase the subsequent desirability and purchase of that particular food or beverage but also to affect the desirability of other rewarding items, such as indulgent nonfood and on-sale products. This leads to the possibility that marketers could actually benefit from stationing several food and beverage sampling booths at various locations in the store, particularly at the entrance to the store."[20]

Web Sites You Can Use

Looking for a bargain? Try one of these sales promotion Web sites:

- All Online Coupons (**http://www.allonlinecoupons.com**)
- ContestListings.com (**http://www.contestlistings.com**)
- Cool Savings (**http://www.coolsavings.com**)
- Coupon Mountain (**http://www.couponmountain.com**)
- Daily eDeals (**http://www.dailyedeals.com**)
- Deal Catcher (**http://www.dealcatcher.com**)
- DealofDay.com (**http://www.dealofday.com**)
- Deals Digger (**http://www.dealsdigger.com**)

- Deals2buy (**http://www.deals2buy.com**)
- Hot Coupons (**http://www.hotcoupons.com**)
- MyCoupons (**http://www.mycoupons.com**)
- MyPoints (**http://www.mypoints.com**)
- Simply Best Coupons (**http://www.simplybestcoupons.com**)
- StartSampling (**http://www.startsampling.com**)
- UltimateCoupons.com (**http://www.ultimatecoupons.com**)
- Val-Pak (**http://www.valpak.com**)

Summary

1. *To examine the scope, importance, and characteristics of personal selling* Personal selling involves oral communication with prospective buyers by paid representatives for the purpose of making sales. About 15 million people work in U.S. selling jobs; millions more work in sales jobs outside the United States. These numbers understate the value of personal selling because every contact between a company employee and a customer involves some degree of selling.

   Selling is used with high-volume clients, geographically concentrated customers, expensive/complex products, customers wanting sales services, and entries into foreign markets. It also resolves questions and addresses other issues. Selling costs are higher than advertising costs at many firms. Thus, efficiency is important.

   Selling fosters a buyer-seller dyad (a two-way communication flow), is flexible and adaptable, adds to relationships with customers, results in less audience waste, clinches sales, and provides immediate feedback. Yet, personal selling can handle only a limited number of customers, is rather ineffective for creating awareness, and has high costs per customer and a poor image among some shoppers.

2. *To study the elements in a personal selling plan* A selling plan has seven steps: setting goals—demand- and/or image-related; assigning oversight—to one manager or to several managers; setting a budget; choosing the type(s) of sales positions—order takers, order getters, and/or support salespeople; selecting a sales technique—the canned sales presentation or the need-satisfaction approach; outlining tasks—including each of the relevant steps in the selling process and nonselling tasks; and applying the plan—which centers on sales management.

3. *To examine the scope, importance, and characteristics of sales promotion* Sales promotion encompasses paid marketing communication activities (other than advertising, publicity, or personal selling) that stimulate consumer purchases and dealer effectiveness. In the United States, such expenditures exceed $400 billion annually.

   The growth of sales promotion is due to firms looking for a competitive edge, the greater acceptance of sales promotion tools by both firms and consumers, quick returns, the pressure by consumers and channel members for promotions, the popularity during economic downturns, the high costs of other promotional forms, and technological advances.

---

[20] Monica Wadhwa, Baba Shiv, and Stephen M. Nowlis, "A Bite to Whet the Reward Appetite: The Influence of Sampling on Reward-Seeking Behaviors," *Journal of Marketing Research*, Vol. 45 (August 2008), p. 411.

A sales promotion helps attract customer traffic and loyalty, provides value and may be retained by people, increases impulse purchases, creates excitement, is keyed to patronage, and improves reseller cooperation. On the other hand, it may hurt a firm's image, encourage consumers to wait for promotions before making purchases, and shift the focus away from product attributes. Sales promotion cannot replace other forms of promotion.

4. *To study the elements in a sales promotion plan*   A promotion plan has six steps: setting goals—ordinarily demand-oriented; assigning responsibility—to advertising and sales managers, company departments, and/or outside specialists; outlining the overall plan—including orientation, conditions, and other factors; selecting the types of sales promotion; coordinating the plan with the other elements of the promotion mix; and evaluating success or failure.

Key Terms

telemarketing (p. 584)
buyer-seller dyad (p. 585)
sales-expense budget (p. 588)
order taker (p. 589)
order getter (p. 589)
missionary salesperson (p. 589)
sales engineer (p. 589)
service salesperson (p. 590)

canned sales presentation (p. 590)
need-satisfaction approach (p. 590)
selling process (p. 591)
prospecting (p. 591)
approaching customers (p. 591)
sales presentation (p. 592)
closing the sale (p. 592)
sales management (p. 592)

sales territory (p. 593)
straight salary plan (p. 593)
straight commission plan (p. 593)
combination sales compensation plan (p. 594)
sales promotion orientation (p. 598)
sales promotion conditions (p. 598)

Review Questions

1. Under what circumstances should personal selling be emphasized? Why?
2. Draw and explain the buyer-seller dyad.
3. Distinguish among order taker, order getter, and support sales personnel.
4. When is the need-satisfaction approach to selling most appropriate?
5. Outline the steps in the selling process.
6. Why is sales promotion growing as a marketing tool?
7. What are the limitations associated with sales promotion?
8. Differentiate between the orientation and conditions of sales promotion.

Discussion Questions

1. As an executive with the Direct Selling Association (http://www.dsa.org), how would you improve the image of direct selling firms?
2. How would you handle these objections raised at the end of a sales presentation for a $1,000 watch?
   a. "How do I know that this watch is authentic and not a counterfeit?"
   b. "I saw the same price at a competing store, but that store also offered lifetime free battery replacement."
   c. "None of the alternatives you showed me is satisfactory."
3. List several sales promotion techniques that would be appropriate for the American Cancer Society (http://www.cancer.org). List several that would be appropriate for a local health clinic. Explain the differences in your two lists.
4. How could a sales promotion be *too* successful? What are the potential risks with too much success?

Web Exercise

Visit the *Sales & Marketing Management* Web site (http://www.salesandmarketing.com), scroll down to the "In This Issue" section, and read one of the current articles in the "Sales Strategy" subsection. Offer several tips based on the information in the story you read.

Practice Quiz

1. Which of these is a characteristic of personal selling?
   a. Personal selling is usually the first stage in the consumer's decision process.
   b. Personal selling is a very effective tool for generating consumer awareness.
   c. Personal selling costs per customer can be very high.
   d. There is more waste with most forms of selling than with advertising.

2. Which statement about the drawbacks of personal selling is false?
   a. Only a small number of consumers can be accommodated at a given time.
   b. Feedback is more difficult to ascertain than with advertising.
   c. It is an ineffective tool for addressing consumer objections.
   d. It has a poor image in the eyes of a number of consumers.

3. The major goal for personal selling is
   a. image.
   b. information.
   c. persuasion.
   d. reminding.

4. Which of the following is *not* a normal function of an order taker?
   a. Arranging displays
   b. Completing transactions
   c. Generating customer leads
   d. Writing up orders

5. The need-satisfaction approach works best with
   a. simple items that have moderate advertising.
   b. inexpensive items.
   c. items that are pre-sold through heavy advertising.
   d. items for which customers require additional information.

6. The first stage in the selling process for outside salespeople is
   a. hiring sales personnel.
   b. prospecting for customer leads.
   c. approaching customers.
   d. researching the product.

7. Which of the following is *not* a nonselling task that may be carried out by a firm's sales force?
   a. Checking competitors' strategies
   b. Marking prices on products
   c. Looking through trade publications for customer leads
   d. Writing up information sheets

8. Which of the following is a fundamental part of sales management?
   a. Price setting
   b. Advertising
   c. Marketing research
   d. Territory allocation

9. A salesperson's earnings are completely tied to sales with a
   a. straight commission plan.
   b. straight salary plan.
   c. combination compensation plan.
   d. sales territory assigned on the basis of product type.

10. Which of the following is *not* a part of sales supervision?
    a. Hiring sales personnel
    b. Motivating sales personnel
    c. Completing nonselling tasks
    d. Modifying behavior changes

11. Which of the following is a contributing factor to the rapid growth of sales promotion as a marketing tool?
    a. Fewer shoppers seek promotions before buying.
    b. Various sales promotions are less acceptable to firms and consumers.
    c. Firms are turning away from a short-run orientation and are seeking to improve long-term profits.
    d. Advertising and personal selling have become more expensive.

12. Sales promotion may have an adverse effect on
    a. new-product introduction.
    b. a firm's image.
    c. impulse purchasing.
    d. brand functionality.

13. In contrast to a sales manager, the advertising manager's sales promotion responsibility would focus on
    a. customer contests.
    b. special events.
    c. demonstrations.
    d. trade shows.

14. An example of the conditions of sales promotion is a
    a. Thanksgiving theme.
    b. purchase of three bars of soap to get one free.
    c. free sample of a new deodorant.
    d. direct-mail solicitation.

15. Which is *not* usually a type of promotion directed at channel members?
    a. Training
    b. Point-of-purchase displays
    c. Coupons
    d. Sales contests

For the answers to these questions, please visit the online site for this book at **http://www.atomicdog.com.**

Case 1: The Growth of Web Advertising[c6-1]

Internet Protocol TV (IPTV) technology joins TV viewing and the Internet. Many different types of communications firms have begun to use IPTV technology, including telecommunications, cable, and satellite companies, as well as Microsoft (**http://www.microsoft. com**). For example, cable and satellite firms now offer highly targeted and on-demand ads via technology contained in viewers' set-top boxes.

IPTV converts video content into digital files and makes TV watching an interactive experience. Through IPTV, viewers can chat on their screens or even use their phones to remotely program their digital video recorders. Other important capabilities of IPTV include a consumer's ability to watch a baseball game while simultaneously searching the Web for information about a player and the ability to receive videos at a time when they are wanted by viewers, as opposed to when they are aired by a network. IPTV can also target specific audiences with unique ads that best appeal to each group. According to an IPTV business development manager at Tandberg (**http://www.tandberg.com**), part of Ericcson, IPTV adds personalization and interaction capabilities to the television watching experience.

Because IPTV is a point-to-point service (unlike television, it is not broadcast), every home and even every TV set in a home could receive different programming as well as different ads specifically targeted at the household's entertainment needs and lifestyle. Through IPTV's interactive capabilities, a consumer can buy a PC shown in an ad by clicking on a box, instead of having to order the unit via phone. In addition to the convenience in ordering, a shopper could use IPTV to better understand the options and features available with each model, as well as to gain access to user reviews. Another application is Mediaroom's MyPad (**http://www. mypad.net**), which connects viewers to online communities that can discuss a current TV show, answer a poll, or surf the Web.

According to a survey by In-Stat (**http://www.instat.com**), a marketing research firm that specializes in digital programming, consumers most desire the following IPTV applications: digital video recording (DVR), multiroom DVR, TV access to personal computer content, on-screen caller ID, and interactive information about the program they are currently watching.

Some marketing analysts believe that the future of TV advertising may depend on the success of IPTV. Television advertising has been hard hit by the DVR's capability of skipping commercials. And with cable and satellite television stations, there are a lot more channels competing for the same viewers.

Television costs have substantially increased on a relative basis. A 30-second spot commercial that reached 97.5 million viewers on the 2005 Super Bowl cost $2.7 million. An ad for the 2009 Super Bowl was priced at $3 million. IPTV can generate more ad spending due to its highly targeted and interactive nature. One challenge for IPTV providers is that many media buyers are accustomed to buying ad time based on the number of viewers reached. As the chief executive of blinkBox (**http://www.blinkbox.com**), a film clip and download Web service, says: "Only when these values change—and brands become ready to pay a premium for targeting specific groups—can revenue potential be realized." The chief executive of Inuk Networks (**http://www.inuknetworks.com**) adds, "Though most advertisers claim they want their messages to be targeted, none are geared up to exploiting the platform's true personalization potential."

Consumer pricing for IPTV can vary on a customer-to-customer basis due to its capability of customization. Some observers believe that sites with a lot of advertising could be free, while other consumers who are not willing to receive banner ads would pay a fee. There could also be a graduated scale for consumers who want different levels of advertising. One IPTV provider is exploring the possibility of "pay as you go IPTV" aimed at students who would pay for IPTV by the hour.

Questions

1. Describe the role of IPTV in a manufacturer's integrated marketing communications (IMC) program.
2. Explain the significance of this statement: "Because IPTV is a point-to-point service, every home and even every TV set in a home could receive different ads."
3. Discuss how an IPTV advertiser could best utilize its interactive capabilities.
4. What factors have contributed to the decline in importance of TV advertising over the past 10 years?

[c6-1] The data in the case are drawn from Meg Carter, "Online TV: Why Advertisers Love Tailor-Made Television," *Guardian* (June 30, 2008), p. 3; Ben Rooney, "Super Bowl Ads: $2.7 Million and Worth It," **http://www.money.cnn. com** (January 25, 2008); and Sarah Reddy, "To IPTV and Beyond," *Telephony* (March 17, 2008), pp. 28–29.

Case 2: In-Store Marketing: An Integral Part of the Promotion Mix[c6-2]

A recent Point-of-Purchase Advertising (POPAI, http://www.popai.com) study found that shoppers are exposed to 1.6 items of in-store marketing materials every second they are in a store. Customers are also expected to look at or interact with a display every three seconds they are in a store. A Deloitte (http://www.deloitte.com) study concluded that in-store advertising is, in the United States, growing at a faster pace than Internet advertising. The Deloitte research also uncovered that the manufacturers surveyed expect in-store advertising to comprise 8 percent of their overall marketing budgets in 2010.

As of 2008, in-store marketing became a measurable medium with Nielsen (http://www.nielsen.com) providing data on usage. By placing counting devices in every part of a group of stores, shopper behavior can be recorded as the devices measure specific areas by hour and day of the week. Nielsen's research covers all in-store media, including retail TV and radio networks, shelf talkers, digital signs, and traditional point-of-purchase displays. As a result of this research, marketers can now determine the size of specific market segments, the ideal timing of in-store promotions, and the effect of in-store promotions on sales.

As an example of the usefulness of this project, Nielsen found that for a major retailer during a one month period, more than 1.7 million shoppers (including 1 million women) passed by the hair-care aisle on the way to the carbonated soft drink section. Of this group, more than 500,000 shoppers were ages 24 to 54, an important segment for marketers of hair-care products. By using the data, a hair-care manufacturer can evaluate optimal locations for displays within a store and the value of alternative retailers. The Nielsen data will further enable a marketer to compare the cost of using in-store displays with other media. For example, though the popular TV show *American Idol* reached 246,000 females ages 25 to 54 in San Francisco-Oakland, Nielsen was able to show that more than 1.1 million females of the same ages passed through the lobby of select retail stores located in San Francisco-Oakland.

Another promising technological development for in-store marketing is the increased amount of interactivity between consumers and promotions. Tourism New Zealand's NZ Spring Pass (http://www.newzealand.com/travel/USA) campaign in Australia used Flash animated-advertising with a Bluetooth component. Mobile phone customers were given free ringtones when they passed the screens. More than 280,000 Bluetooth-enabled consumers received the campaign's message with an opt-in rate of 13.4 percent. Another interesting new in-store program allows cell phone customers to charge their phones for free. The program, by Kwik-Fix (http://www.kwikfix.co.nz), uses kiosks in high-traffic areas. Users have the option to view in-store ads during the 15 minutes or so it takes to charge their mobile phone.

Although there is not much conclusive data on the increased effectiveness of digital screens and interactive kiosks, an Ogilvy Interactive (http://www.ogilvy.com) executive says: "Consumers expect to see it. This increases recall of the brand and the price the retailer is charging, and it's an effective way of capturing foot-traffic attention and directing it through the store."

A study by Moving Tactics (http://www.movingtactics.com), an in-store media firm, found that after seeing in-store digital ads, 34 percent of the respondents were encouraged to browse the store, and 24 percent were reminded of products they wanted to buy. Overall, 72 percent rated digital advertising as either effective or very effective. As Moving Tactics' general manager concludes: "The main driver of value behind digital in-store media is the concept of 'recency.'" Recall of digital ads is higher because the time between viewing the ad and the opportunity to purchase the product is so short in an in-store environment as opposed to traditional radio and TV ads.

Questions

1. Discuss the concept of clutter as it relates to in-store marketing.
2. Develop a brief promotional program for a new hair spray that integrates in-store marketing with other media.
3. Explain the value of Nielsen's in-store marketing research from the perspective of the concepts of reach and frequency.
4. What is the impact of "recency" as applied to in-store marketing?

[c6-2] The data in the case are drawn from "The Power of POP," *Ad Media* (March 2008), pp. 34–38; "Research Will Take P-O-P to the Next Level Says POPAI," *In-Store* (January 2008), p. 5; and George Wishart, "Ratings Gone Shopping: Measuring In-Store Marketing Effectiveness," http://www.nielsen.com/consumer_insight/ci_story4.html (June 2008).

Case 3: Attracting Generation Y Consumers to Music Festivals?[c6-3]

During the past 10 years, music festivals held in Australia and New Zealand—such as Big Day Out (**http://www.bigdayout. com**), Future Music Festival (**http://www.futuremusicfestival. com.au**), and V Festival (**http://www.vfestival.com**)—have annually attracted more than one million 18- to 30-year-olds (Generation Y). According to Fuzzy (**http://www.fuzzy.com.au**), the organizer of seven annual events, about 27 percent of its typical attendees are 18 to 20 years old, 33 percent are 21 to 25, 24 percent are 26 to 30, and 11 percent are 31 to 35. The balance (5 percent) are 36 and older. Not all festivals attract the same demographics, however. Some, such as the Great Escape, can target a younger market or maybe even market families.

One of the largest festival events in Australia and New Zealand is Big Day Out, which attracts about 250,000 festival goers. The Future Music Festival attracts attendance of 130,000 people, and the V Festivals attracts 100,000 people. Marketers such as Coca-Cola (**http://www.coca-cola.com**), Smirnoff (**http://www.smirnoff. com**), Red Bull (**http://www.redbull.com**), V energy drink (**http:// www.v.co.nz**), and Pump (**http://www.thepumpenergyfood.com**) tend to invest between $30,000 and $1 million per festival, roughly between $1 and $2 per festival attendee, for a non-naming rights sponsorship at these festivals.

Research by Naked Communications (**http://www.nakedcomms. sbcom**), a British advertising agency, found that brands which target the youth market usually spend between 5 and 20 percent of their overall marketing budgets on music-themed communications. A Nokia (**http://www.nokia.com**) marketing manager says, "Nothing else other than music gives you the broad scope of appeal and the ability to tailor your message based on genre, venue, and media." Another industry spokesperson adds, "Music is becoming something that brands want to be associated with more and more and it's the universal youth passion."

To be successful at a music festival, advertisers need to enhance the attendees' experience by creating a memorable impression. Nokia, a sponsor of the Good Vibrations concert, used a "Sound Lounge" to demonstrate the features of its new mobile phone models. Festival attendees are invited to listen to music via an MP3-enabled device, get free messages, receive free cold drinks, and take photos of themselves on the mobile phone and then print the photos.

Naked Communications' head of special projects warns marketers that "brands are becoming like wallpaper at music festivals and consumers are screening them out. Festival sponsorship is a bit overexposed, and the best music marketing initiatives are done at standalone brand experiences outside the festival space."

Many marketers view music festivals as just one part of their overall marketing communications efforts and that they need to be supplemented by other media. Some advertisers are concerned about the promotional clutter at festivals due to the large number of sponsors. Others feel that the experience at a music festival needs to be reinforced in other media. For example, *Vodaphone Live at the Chapel* (**http://music.vodafone.com.au/live-at-the-chapel/**) is a live music show delivered across nine platforms, including subscription TV, radio, CD, Qantas (**http://www.qantas.com**) in-flight, online, mobile, and as a live event. Similarly, Nokia targets its *Take 40* lounge market with broadcasts on MTV, live events, and streaming Web videos. Nokia provides festival attendees with behind-the-scenes footage of featured artists and music downloading capability.

An MCM Entertainment (**http://www.mcmentertainment. com**) marketing executive says it is not sufficient to spend monies on event sponsorship. The typical rule of thumb should be that for every dollar spent on a sponsorship deal, an additional dollar should be invested in leverage (support activities using other media). Nokia's marketing manager comments, "We would not market Nokia through music if we couldn't demonstrate a music device or our Nokia Music Service before, during, or after the event."

Questions

1. Show how music festival sponsorship can fulfill short-intermediate and long-term promotional goals that are identified in the hierarchy of effects model.
2. What other media work best to complement sponsorship in a music festival? Explain your answer.
3. What techniques for budgeting are best for a music festival sponsor? Explain your answer.
4. Comment on this observation: "The typical rule of thumb should be that for every dollar spent on a sponsorship deal, an additional dollar should be invested in leverage (activities using other media)."

[c6-3] The data in the case are drawn from "Do Brands Hit the Right Note with Gen Y? **http://www.bandt.com.au** (April 2008), pp. 22–25.

Case 4: Are Rebates Running Out of Steam?[c6-4]

Some firms have been increasing their use of rebates. Why? They are a very flexible form of sales promotion that can be adjusted in terms of dollar value, applicable time period, and conditions (such as whether a consumer must buy a printer along with a digital camera to qualify for a $50 rebate). Rebates are an effective way of clearing out inventory prior to the introduction of a new model. Unlike reductions in a product's list price, rebates provide full profit margins for wholesalers and retailers. Rebates also enable a retailer to record the sales of discounted merchandise based on the product's full price. In this way, rebates do not reduce retailers' total sales, sales per square foot, and same-store sales levels that are closely watched by security analysts and investors. Last, cynics feel that some manufacturers develop rebate offers knowing that many purchasers will not redeem them.

Yet, despite the potential savings, many consumers do not view the rebate experience as a pleasant one. Typically, shoppers must remove barcodes (remembering to be careful so that the label comes off in one piece), keep applicable receipts, fill out required forms, make copies of all of the materials (in case they get lost in the mail), and mark the calendar to remember to look for their checks. The process is so time consuming that a study found that one-half of consumers never submit rebate forms.

There have been so many complaints about rebates that a Web site, Rebate Report Card (**http://www.rebatereportcard.com**), is now devoted to this topic. Of the hundreds of firms whose rebate policies are graded, several have received an "F." These include Amazon.com (**http://www.amazon.com**), Bed Bath & Beyond (**http://www.bedbathandbeyond.com**), Canon (**http://www.canonusa.com**), Garmin Electronics (**http://www.garmin.com**), Linksys (**http://www.linksys.com**), McAfee (**http://www.mcafee.com**), Norton Anti Virus (**http://www.norton.com**), Samsung (**http://www.samsung.com**), and Toshiba (**http://www.toshiba.com**).

Another troublesome sign is that rebates were recently featured in a *PC World* report on "The 10 Most Annoying Habits of Technology Companies." Numerous consumers have also passed along horror stories of firms telling them that a rebate form was never received, the proof of purchase was inadequate, or the rebate confirmation company thought the person returned the item after submitting the rebate form.

One way for a shopper to better ensure compliance with a rebate offer is to follow a series of steps: carefully follow all directions on the rebate form, make copies of all documentation prior to mailing the rebate, and sending the rebate materials via registered mail. Again, this is a labor-intensive process.

In response to consumer concerns, some marketers have dramatically improved their rebate programs. Staples (**http://www.staples.com**), the office supply chain, offers Easy Rebates (**http://www.staplesrebates.com**), a simplified rebate redemption program that requires its consumers to just enter receipt information online (eliminating the need to remove barcodes, photocopy information, and mail items to qualify for a rebate). At Staples, consumers with rebates enter two numbers from their receipt at their home or office computer or at a store's kiosk to qualify. To reduce the possibility of a consumer receiving the rebate and then returning the merchandise, Staples mails out a Visa prepaid card that can be used anywhere a Visa debit card is accepted. The card is mailed out four to six weeks after receipt. At that time, the retailer will not accept the item for return. Other retailers, including Rite Aid (**http://www.riteaid.com**) and Ace Hardware (**http://www.acehardware.com**), offer similar online redemption programs but issue a check instead of a debit card.

Such retailers as Best Buy (**http://www.bestbuy.com**) and Office Max (**http://www.officemax.com**) have eliminated their use of traditional rebates. Instead, they use an instant savings program whereby prices are immediately reduced at the time of sale.

Questions

1. Differentiate between a rebate, a coupon, and a reduction in a manufacturer's suggested list price as sales promotion techniques.
2. Describe the pros and cons of a manufacturer using a rebate versus a coupon offer.
3. Visit Staples' Easy Rebates (**http://www.staplesrebates.com**) site and discuss what you find there.
4. Why are some firms still expanding their use of rebates despite the issues identified in this case? Do you think this will continue? Why or why not?

[c6-4] The data in the case are drawn from "Are Mail-In Rebates Headed for Extinction?" *PC World* (April 2007), p. 36; and "The 10 Most Annoying Habits of Technology Companies," *PC World* (July 2008), pp. 82–88.

Campaign Trail[pc-6]

INTRODUCTION

How can firms effectively connect to customers in today's cluttered media environment? Managers are asking this question constantly, as connecting to customers through traditional mass media becomes more and more difficult. One such approach is the use of below-the-line (BTL) advertising. Although traditional above-the-line (ATL) advertising uses mass-media (such as television, radio, magazines, and newspapers), BTL advertising campaigns use direct media (such as direct mailings, E-mails, and short message service messages).

BTL VERSUS ATL ADVERTISING

Recent figures from Winterberry Group (**http://www.winterberrygroup. com**) show that BTL spending grows approximately 8 percent annually in the United States. Similar figures can be retrieved in Europe. Dutch companies have increased their interactive marketing expenditures by more than 8 percent in the last year. Moreover, companies are moving budgets from ATL advertising to BTL advertising campaigns. The Dutch incumbent telecom provider KPN (**http://www.kpn.com/corporate/en.htm**) lowered its ATL spending by 30 percent, reallocating these expenditures to BTL ads with a focus on interactive media.

BTL advertising includes all advertising where no media commissions are paid, such as direct media, sales promotions, and public relations. Here we will primarily focus on the interactive or direct media (i.e., direct mail, E-mail, and telemarketing) within BTL advertising and not consider public relations, event marketing, and so on. According to the Direct Marketing Association (**http:// www.the-dma.org**), U.S. spending on direct or interactive marketing advertising was $166.5 billion in 2006, a 6 percent gain over 2005. An increase of 5 percent occurred for 2007, leading to direct marketing spending of $172.5 billion.

The increasing use of interactive media within BTL advertising creates a new discipline within companies: interactive campaign management. However, firms struggle with the discouraging response to their campaigns. Low response rates around 1 percent are not uncommon. At the same time, McLean, Virginia-based Capital One (**http://www.capitalone.com**) has achieved a competitive advantage with successful interactive campaign management practices. Why was this financial services company so successful with its interactive marketing campaigns, while many other companies do not achieve positive results?

In this case, we present a study on the success factors of campaign management. We provide guidelines for successful campaign management at the campaign and organizational level. Please note that this study includes data from Dutch firms only. But we feel the prescriptive elements can be applied in other venues. We hope more studies will be done on this topic in the United States, Asia, and Europe.

CAMPAIGN MANAGEMENT

An interactive marketing campaign is used to acquire prospects or potential customers, and to retain and reward existing customers. It involves a series of interconnected interactive promotional efforts to reach precise goals. Interactive campaign management includes campaign planning, development, execution, and analysis of results. Four factors drive the importance of interactive campaign management.

1. Greater media fragmentation. Forrester Research (**http://www. forrester.com**) reports that the number of TV channels per U.S. home has increased to nearly one hundred—up from six in 1960, while the number of radio stations has more than doubled. There are now more than 25,000 Internet broadcast stations and billions of Web pages indexed in Google. This clutter and channel fragmentation means huge problems in getting connected to customers. People easily skip commercials, and attention for ads is lacking. The Internet is replacing TV. Teenagers spend a lot of time on the Internet chatting with friends.

2. Increasing availability of customer data. This creates more opportunities for targeted campaigns and target selection. The growing use of customer relationship management (CRM) systems and software creates huge customer data bases. A good example of this is Harrah's Entertainment's (**http://www. harrahs.com**) large customer data base, which is used extensively as part of its successful marketing strategy.

3. Short-term thinking. This trend also implies a shift from longer-term-oriented strategies (such as brand advertising) to more sales-oriented tactics (such as direct mail and sales promotions).

4. A call for more accountability. This leads to a shift toward BTL advertising. Results of interactive marketing campaigns can be measured almost immediately, and with significant confidence. In contrast, marketers still face difficulties assessing the performance of ATL campaigns.

[pc-6] Adapted by the authors from Peter C. Verhoef, Christiaan Ph. Koenders, and Marijn Knaack, "Campaign Trail," *Marketing Management* (March-April 2008), pp. 38–43. Reprinted by permission of the American Marketing Association.

ASSESSING CURRENT PRACTICES

We studied campaign management practices at 19 Dutch companies in such industries as financial services, telecom, pharmaceuticals, and entertainment. The participating firms were either clients of Netherlands-based VODW Marketing (**http://www.vodw.com**, click the bottom toolbar for English) or members of the knowledge center on customer insights at the University of Groningen.

Although the U.S. market is much larger than the Dutch market, there are multiple similarities. First, in the Dutch market, companies spend 39 percent of their marketing budget on direct marketing (DM) advertising. According to the Dutch Direct Marketing Association (**http://www.ddma.nl/?taal=uk**), Dutch firms spend between 5 billion and 7.5 billion Euros on DM advertising. Although this is much less than total DM advertising spending in the United States, the DM advertising budget as a percent of gross national product is 1.5 percent for the Netherlands and 2.0 percent for the United States. Thus, correcting for size effects, DM advertising expenditures are pretty comparable.

Second, like U.S. companies, Dutch firms have been confronted with increased media fragmentation. The number of television channels has increased substantially in the last years. There is also a drop in TV viewing among Dutch consumers, recently measuring a 10 percent decline in number of hours watched. Third, like many U.S. companies, Dutch firms have invested heavily in CRM systems for the management of their customer contacts. Fourth, we observe that as in many Western economies, the service sector and its increasing number of customer touch points are very important in the Dutch economy.

We first assessed the intensity of campaign management practices, and found convincing evidence for its growing importance. All the companies had increased the number of targeted campaigns, and aimed to increase that in the next years as well.

Next, we assessed the general campaign management execution with two metrics. First, we measured the percentage of the revenue generated with campaigns. This shows how important campaigns are for the business of a firm. Second, we measured the percentage of the marketing capacity in terms of staff allocated toward interactive BTL campaigns. If we combine these two metrics in a two-by-two matrix, we can assess which firms executed interactive campaign management successfully and which executed interactive campaign management problematically. Figure 1 shows this matrix. We classified companies into four groups: non-campaigners, problem campaigners, core campaigners, and stars.

We found a large number of problem campaigners. These companies allocate too much capacity to interactive BTL campaigns in comparison with the related revenue results. They should become more efficient and/or generate more revenues with their campaigns. There were only a few stars, which need only limited marketing capacity to generate a large part of the company's revenue. The core campaigners seem to have their capacity and revenue results in line.

Using our two-by-two matrix, firms can easily assess the performance of their campaign management execution. Problem campaigners in particular should reconsider their campaign management practices.

EXECUTING MORE SUCCESSFUL CAMPAIGNS

We identified four potential success factors of a campaign. These characteristics concern elements of the campaign itself, and do not concern organizational issues.

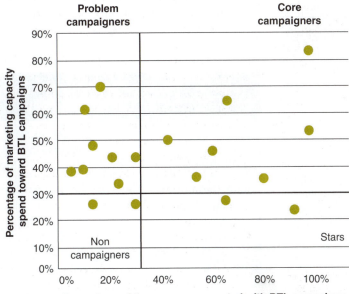

Figure 1

Capacity Allocation and Revenue Percentage

Target Group Size

It is essential to select the right customer at the right time with the right product offer. Small target groups reflect the firm's ability to select specific, defined groups of customers with specific needs that match the provided offer.

Testing

With testing, the changes in performance due to changes in the campaign elements can be assessed. Moreover, testing can be used to select the right customers. Capital One is an excellent example. It adopted a testing and learning strategy, with each new interactive campaign being extensively tested before execution. Based on testing results and prior experience (the learning part), the company develops the optimal campaign and selects the right customers.

Multistep Vs. Single-Step Campaigns

In a single-step campaign, the customer gets the offer with a call for action immediately. In a multi-step campaign, the firm first communicates to the customer to get attention and interest. In a next step, the offer is sent to the customer, which involves a call for action. This method follows the well-known AIDA-process model (attention, interest, desire, and action) in communication research. Multi-step campaigns following this AIDA process garner more response.

Differentiation

Customizing the offer to specific needs of customers creates more response to a campaign. Different customers might be approached with different messages and offers, and through different channels, because their needs differ.

Many interactive campaigns fall short on one or more of these success factors. Consider the campaign of a Dutch bank focusing on the creation of more attention and interest among intermediaries for mortgage loans. Each intermediary was approached via direct mail, with a winning code referring to the specific campaign Web site. After viewing a non-customized commercial at the Web site, the intermediary received a message saying whether he or she had won a VIP ticket for a racing event on a Dutch car racing circuit. This campaign had a multi-step approach involving multiple media. However, it lacked differentiation, as it assumed that all intermediaries were interested in car racing.

But what is the net impact of each of these potential success factors on campaign performance? To address this question, we further investigated 70 executed campaigns of the participating 19 companies. Each firm provided information on potential success factors for multiple, recently executed campaigns with different objectives: customer acquisition, customer retention, cross-selling, and winning back customers. On average, we garnered approximately 3.5 campaigns per firm.

An important insight concerned the existing campaign management practices. Only 31 percent of the campaigns were tested,

even though 38.8 percent involved a multi-step campaign. An average campaign was differentiated on 2.6 elements. The low percentage of campaigns being tested was remarkable! We used the provided conversion ratio of each campaign as a performance metric. Depending on the objective of the campaign, the conversion ratio was the number of acquired customers/retained customers/cross-sell successes/win-back customers divided by the target group size. The average conversion percentage of the interactive campaigns was 7 percent.

We used statistical models to assess the impact of the identified success factors on the conversion ratio of each campaign. This conversion ratio was defined as the number of buyers, divided by the number of respondents, multiplied by 100. In Table 1, we show our model results. The first column shows the factors included. The second column indicates the impact on the conversion rate. The third column shows whether the found effect has significant impact.

The estimated model explained 49 percent of the variance. As we had data at one point in time for multiple firms, an explained variance of 49 percent is satisfactory. Usually, higher explained variances (e.g., approximately 90 percent) are only achieved when there are data over time and one is comparing current performance with past performance.

We confirmed the importance of the majority of the identified success factors. Having a small target group was essential, while testing led to significantly higher conversion ratios. Multi-step campaigns had a significantly higher performance than single-step campaigns, stressing the relevance of campaigns following the AIDA principle. Surprisingly, we did not find a significant effect from differentiation. Perhaps the differentiation methods used were not meaningful for customers.

Our study shows the relevance of the majority of identified success factors. To further understand the implications of our results, we developed scenarios for firms to improve conversion ratios: (1) Decrease target group size by 10 percent, (2) Test all campaigns, (3) Make all campaigns multi-step. If we simulate these scenarios with our model, our results indicate that the conversion ratios improve substantially. See Figure 2. If all campaigns had been tested, our model indicates that the conversion should have

Table 1	Influence of Campaign Characteristics on Conversion Ratio	
Potential success factor	**Impact on conversion ratio**	**Significant**
Target group size	−	Yes
Testing of campaign	+	Yes
Multi-steps vs. single steps	+	Yes
Differentiation of campaign	−	No

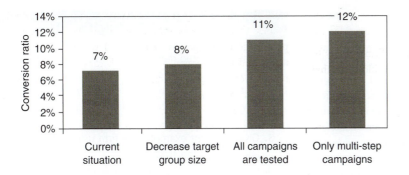

Figure 2

The impact of Improving
Campaign Characteristics

increased by 4 percent to 11 percent, while using only multi-step campaigns would increase the conversion ratio by 5 percent to 12 percent. Thus, by adjusting only one campaign characteristic, a conversion ratio of more than 50 percent is achieved. Moreover, combining multiple adjustments could potentially more than double the conversion ratio. Using these insights, problem campaigners might become core campaigners.

OVERCOMING HURDLES

The preceding insights can be used to improve the performance of individual campaigns. But, even knowing this, companies still struggle with effective campaign management. We identified four hurdles for effective campaign management at the organizational level.

1. Lack of systematic campaign knowledge. There are only a few companies building up campaign management knowledge data bases with information on the performance and characteristics of past campaigns. An excellent example of this is Capital One, which has built a large data base of executed campaigns. This data base is crucial in its campaign management testing and learning strategy. However, we also observed that, in many instances, the campaigns were often separate ad-hoc processes without any learning. This can damage the return on investment (ROI) of campaigns. This problem is more severe when campaign marketers have a short turnaround time; they often come and go within organizations.

2. Lack of flexibility. Imagine that a telecom company has implemented strict procedures, whereby the campaign marketer must show the effectiveness of the campaign with formal procedures and testing. In general, this leads to improved campaigns. However, at some point, a major competitor surfaces with an aggressive pricing-oriented campaign aimed at attracting the telecom's customers. This triggers an immediate aggressive reaction. The campaign marketer wants to start a campaign immediately, but knows it will take weeks to go through the formal procedures. At that point, the competitor might already attract a significant number of customers. The lesson is that companies need quick standardized procedures for campaign execution in place, with sufficient flexibility for specific environmental situations.

3. Lack of capabilities. Companies often lack campaign management capabilities. The major problem they face is a lack of analytical/statistical skills. They face difficulties in attracting well-trained statistical employees for good testing and target group selection. Capital One has multiple employees with a strong statistical background that enable it to be successful in its testing and learning strategy. Another firm also known for hiring such employees is *Readers Digest* (**http://www.rd.com**). With more attention on campaign management, hiring these employees is more critical. Firms have started to invest in training programs. The Dutch telecom KPN has a two-year marketing intelligence academy to train new employees.

4. Clash between marketing and sales. As the use of campaign management increases, brand marketers will want to use campaigns for long-term, brand-building purposes. At the same time, sales managers will want campaigns to achieve short-term sales goals. This leads to a clash between sales and marketing with the campaign marketer in between. Campaign marketers might be tempted to serve two masters, leading to unclear campaigns. We believe a firm should clearly state the goals it wants to achieve with different communication methods. Most campaigns are best suited for sales-oriented purposes.

REMEMBER ACCOUNTABILITY

Interactive campaign management is an approach to reconnecting with customers. Yet, only a few companies are interactive campaign management stars. We have discussed potential success factors at the campaign and organizational levels. At the campaign level, companies can improve performance by having smaller target group sizes, improving testing practices, and using multi-step campaigns.

At the organizational level, different structural changes should be implemented. The most important change is that marketers should be forced to calculate pre- and post-ROI (return on investment) before executing an interactive campaign. Nowadays, too many firms lack a solid accountability of interactive marketing campaigns and tend to implement the great ideas of campaign marketers too soon without considering the ROI of the campaign. When calculating ROI, companies should not only consider the direct response on a mailing, but also possible long-term effects and cannibalization effects. For example, having a campaign to sell a new savings account with high interest rates might cannibalize existing savings accounts—leading to a loss in value. To achieve these ROI calculations, firms should invest in improving the analytical and accounting skills of interactive campaign marketers. Companies might have to develop on-the-job training programs, as good campaign marketers are hard to find.

In our experience, we found marginal evidence for the brand-building effects of campaigns. Implementing formal ROI procedures before campaign execution should not result in a lack of flexibility and creativity. If we consider the experiences of companies that applied ROI principles, we see that analytically examining the drivers of successful campaigns leads to more and deeper thinking on how this success can be improved.

Questions

1. What integrated marketing communications lessons can be learned from this case?
2. Distinguish between traditional above-the-line (ATL) advertising and below-the-line (BTL) advertising. Discuss the role of each.
3. Give a current example of a firm using ATL advertising and critique the strategy.
4. Give a different current example involving a firm using BTL advertising and critique the strategy.
5. Describe the four factors that drive the importance of interactive campaign management.
6. Comment on Figure 1.
7. How can each of the communications hurdles highlighted in the case be overcome?

Part 7 covers pricing, the fourth and final element of the marketing mix.

20 Considerations in Price Planning

In this chapter, we study the role of price, its importance, and its interrelationship with other marketing variables. Price-based and nonprice-based approaches are contrasted. We also look at each of the factors affecting price decisions in depth: consumers, costs, government, channel members, and competition.

21 Developing and Applying a Pricing Strategy

Here, we explain how to construct and enact a pricing strategy. First, we distinguish among sales, profit, and status quo objectives. Next, the role of a broad price policy is discussed. Then, we introduce three approaches to pricing (cost-, demand-, and competition-based) and show how they may be applied. We also explain why cost-, demand-, and competition-based pricing methods should be integrated. A number of pricing tactics, such as customary and odd pricing, are examined. The chapter concludes by noting methods for adjusting prices.

After reading Part 7, you should understand element 13 of the strategic marketing plan outlined in Table 3-2 (page 75).

Chapter 20

Considerations in Price Planning

Ask people to identify the most prestigious jewelry stores in the world and many will probably mention Tiffany (**http://www.tiffany.com**)—and have a tough time thinking about another store.

Tiffany started in New York as Tiffany & Young, a stationery and costume jewelry store, in 1837. Unlike other stores, where bargaining was common, it was known for marking items with specific prices and for its strict one-price policy (no bargaining). In the 1840s, the firm started to sell fine jewelry, entered catalog sales, and expanded into silverware, pocket watches, and other high-quality goods. In 1851, the store was renamed Tiffany & Co., after Charles Lewis Tiffany bought out his partners.

Tiffany now has about 70 stores in the United States (in addition to its New York City main store), more than 50 stores in Japan, 34 stores elsewhere in Asia Pacific, 17 stores in Europe, and 10 stores in Canada and Central/South America. About 86 percent of total sales are from Tiffany brand jewelry.

Despite the perception that Tiffany only sells jewelry at higher price levels, the firm offers jewelry, sterling silver, china, crystal, stationery, and fragrances over a wide range of prices. However, the bulk of its merchandise is sold at premium prices that reflect distinctiveness, high quality, a sophisticated image, and high levels of customer service.

To keep its jewelry unique, Tiffany is the sole licensee for jewelry designed by Elsa Peretti, Paloma Picasso, Frank Gehry, and the late Jean Schlumberger. These designers account for about 20 percent of Tiffany's sales. Tiffany makes about 60 percent of the finished goods it sells in its own plants. And to keep control over the quality of its diamonds, Tiffany has a financial interest in a firm that purchases, sorts, cuts, and polishes rough diamonds.

Tiffany's mission is clear: "The Company competes on the basis of reputation for high-quality products, brand recognition, customer service, and distinctive value-priced merchandise and does not engage in price promotional advertising."[1]

In this chapter, we will learn more about the effect of image on price, the importance of price and nonprice approaches to marketing strategy, and the role of consumers in pricing. We will also look at other factors affecting price decisions: costs, government, channel members, and competition.

Chapter Objectives

1. To define the terms price and price planning
2. To demonstrate the importance of price and study its relationship with other marketing variables
3. To differentiate between price-based and nonprice-based approaches
4. To examine the factors affecting pricing decisions

20-1 OVERVIEW

> Through **price planning**, each **price** places a value on a good or service.

A **price** represents the value of a good or service for both the seller and the buyer. **Price planning** is systematic decision making by an organization regarding all aspects of pricing.

---

[1] Various company and other sources.

The value of a good or service can involve both tangible and intangible factors. A tangible factor is the cost saving a soda distributor obtains from buying a new bottling machine; an intangible factor is a consumer's pride in owning a Lexus (**http://www. lexus.com**) rather than another car brand. For an exchange to occur, both the buyer and seller must feel a price represents an equitable ("fair") value. To the buyer, the payment of a price reduces the purchasing power available for other items. To the seller, the receipt of a price is a source of revenue and a key determinant of sales and profit levels.

Many words are substitutes for the term *price*, including admission fee, membership fee, rate, tuition, service fee, donation, rent, salary, interest, retainer, and assessment. No matter what it is called, a price refers to all terms of purchase: monetary and non-monetary charges, discounts, handling and shipping charges, credit charges and other forms of interest, and late-payment penalties. A nonmonetary exchange would be a department store awarding a gift to a person who gets a friend to shop at that store or an airline offering tickets as payment for advertising space and time. Monetary and nonmonetary exchanges may be combined. This is common with autos, where the buyer gives the seller money plus a trade-in. That combination leads to a lower monetary price.

From a broader perspective, price is the mechanism that allocates goods and services among potential buyers and ensures competition among sellers in an open marketplace. If demand exceeds supply, prices are usually bid up by consumers. If supply exceeds demand, prices are usually reduced by sellers. See Figure 20-1.

In this chapter, we look at the importance of price and its relationship to other marketing variables, price-based and nonprice-based approaches, and the factors affecting price decisions. Chapter 21 deals with devising and enacting a price strategy, and applying techniques for setting prices.

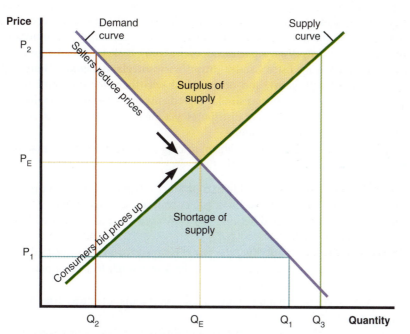

Figure 20-1

The Role of Price in Balancing Supply and Demand

At equilibrium (P_E Q_E), the quantity demanded equals the supply.
At price P_1, consumers demand Q_1 of an item. However, at this price, suppliers will make available only Q_2. There is a shortage of supply of $Q_1 - Q_2$. The price is bid up as consumers seek to buy greater quantities than offered at P_1.
At price P_2, suppliers will make available Q_3 of an item. However, at this price, consumers demand only Q_2. There is a surplus of supply of $Q_3 - Q_2$. Suppliers reduce the price to attract greater consumer demand.

20-2 THE IMPORTANCE OF PRICE AND ITS RELATIONSHIP TO OTHER MARKETING VARIABLES

The prominence of price decisions has risen because more firms recognize their far-reaching impact.

The importance and complexity of price decisions have risen considerably in recent decades: (1) Because price in a monetary or nonmonetary form is a component of the exchange process, it appears in every marketing transaction. More companies now realize the impact of price on their image, sales, and profits. (2) Deregulation in several industries has led to more price competition among firms. (3) To increase profit levels, many firms are more cost-conscious and more focused on operating as efficiently as possible. (4) The growth of the global economy has led to greater interest in currency valuations and exchange rates. Many firms adapt their marketing strategies to reflect international currency fluctuations. (5) Rapid technological advances have led to intense price competition for such items as computers, printers, HD-TV sets, and DVD players. (6) Service-based firms now place more emphasis on how they set prices. (7) Worldwide energy prices have been volatile, which impacts most goods and services. (8) In slow economies, it is hard for firms to raise prices.

Consider this observation about the complexity of restaurant pricing:

> When food and overhead costs escalate, many chains raise menu prices cautiously. "We're in the penny business," says Chris Contino, vice-president of marketing for Prairie du Sac, Wisconsin-based Culver's ButterBurgers & Frozen Custard (**http://www.culvers.com**). And these days, chains are counting and watching pennies ever more closely. Besieged by rising food and energy costs, restaurant operators continually do battle with the threat of margin shrinkage. And although menu-price hikes are inevitable, operators must consider the potential fallout of asking customers to bear some of the increased costs. "The biggest challenge we face is how to deal [with rising expenses] without passing too much of the cost on to the consumer," Contino explains.[2]

Inasmuch as a price places a value on the overall marketing mix offered to consumers (such as product features, product image, store location, and customer service), pricing decisions must be made in concert with product, distribution, and promotion plans. Parfums de Coeur (**http://www.parfumsdecoeur.com**) makes "designer imposters" of expensive perfumes from Estée Lauder (**http://www.esteelauder.com**), Giorgio (**http://www.giorgiobeverlyhills.com**), and others—and sells them for one-third to one-fifth the price of those perfumes. It uses similar ingredients but saves on packaging, advertising, and personal selling costs. It distributes via such mass merchants as Wal-Mart (**http://www.walmart.com**) and online.

These are some basic ways in which pricing is related to other marketing and company variables:

- Prices ordinarily vary over the life of a product category, from high prices to gain status-conscious innovators to lower prices to lure the mass market.
- Customer service is affected because low prices are often associated with less customer service.
- From a distribution perspective, the prices charged to resellers must adequately compensate them for their functions, yet be low enough to be competitive with other brands at the wholesale or retail level.
- There may be conflict in a distribution channel if a manufacturer tries to control or suggest prices.
- Product lines with different features—and different prices—can attract different market segments.
- A sales force may need some flexibility in negotiating prices and terms, particularly with large business accounts.

[2] Kate Leahy, "Pricing Under Pressure," *Restaurants & Institutions* (July 2008), p. 97.

- The roles of marketing and finance personnel must be coordinated. Marketers often begin with the prices that customers are willing to pay and work backward to ascertain acceptable company costs. Finance people typically start with costs and add desired profits to set prices.
- As costs change, decisions must be made as to whether to pass these changes on to consumers, absorb them, or modify product features.

If firms market products internationally, they must consider the following: "In what currency will prices be set? What payment options will you offer? How will you clear and collect payments? Whatever your distribution channel, make payment a convenient exercise for your customers."[3] The complexity of pricing in foreign markets is often due to the divergent company goals in different markets, the varying attributes of each market, and other factors. Furthermore, the ability to set prices in foreign markets may be affected by varying government rules, competition, antidumping laws, operating costs, the rate of inflation, the standard of living, and so forth.

> Pricing internationally can be quite complicated.

20-3 PRICE-BASED AND NONPRICE-BASED APPROACHES

Sellers influence consumer demand primarily through changes in price levels with a *price-based approach*. Sellers downplay price as a factor in consumer demand by creating a distinctive good or service via promotion, packaging, delivery, customer service, availability, and other marketing factors with a *nonprice-based approach*. The more unique a product offering is perceived by consumers, the greater a firm's freedom to set prices above competitors'. See Figure 20-2.

In a price-based approach, sellers move along a demand curve by raising or lowering prices. This is a flexible marketing technique because prices can be adjusted quickly and easily to reflect demand, cost, or competitive factors. Yet, of all the controllable marketing variables, price is the easiest for a competitor to copy. This may result in "me-too"

> A **price-based approach** occurs when sellers stress low prices; a **nonprice-based approach** emphasizes factors other than price.

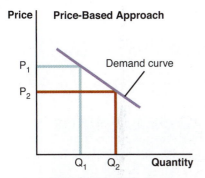

A company operating at P₁ Q₁ may increase sales by lowering its price to P₂. This increases demand to Q₂.

A firm relying on a price-based approach must lower its prices to increase sales.

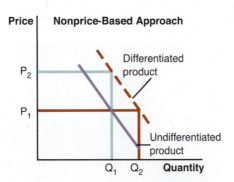

Through a nonprice-based approach, the firm shifts the consumer demand curve to the right by successfully differentiating its products from competitors. This enables the firm to:

(a) increase demand from Q₁ to Q₂ at price P₁, or

(b) raise the price from P₁ to P₂ while maintaining a demand of Q₁.

Figure 20-2

Price-Based and Nonprice-Based Approaches

[3] Renee Frappier, "Hit Close to Home," *Target Marketing* (July 2000), p. 48. See also John Quelch and Gordon Swartz, "Prepare Your Company for Global Pricing," *Sloan Management Review*, Vol. 42 (Fall 2000), pp. 61–70; and Ruth N. Bolton and Matthew B. Myers, "Price-Based Global Market Segmentation for Services," *Journal of Marketing*, Vol. 67 (July 2003), pp. 108–128.

strategies or even in price wars. Furthermore, the government may monitor anticompetitive aspects of price-based strategies.

In a nonprice-based approach, sellers shift demand curves by stressing the distinctive attributes of products. This lets firms increase unit sales at a given price or sell their original supply at a higher price. The risk is that people may not perceive a seller's product as better than a competitor's. People would then buy the lower-priced item believed to be similar to the higher-priced one.

These are examples of price- and nonprice-oriented strategies:

- At Daffy's (**http://www.daffys.com**) apparel stores, "Our mantra is high fashion, low prices—so that you can find the styles that speak to you and perfectly reflect your taste and personality. You can rely on us to find and bring you the most stunning and unique styles we find—at irresistible prices." See Figure 20-3.
- Since being introduced in 1983, hundreds of millions of low-price Swatch (**http://www.swatch.com**) watches have been sold worldwide. They are fashionable, yet have fewer working parts than costlier models. To learn more about the Swatch story, visit the "About Swatch" section of the Web site.
- Countess Mara (**http://www.countessmara.com**) appeals to upscale shoppers: It "has successfully established itself as the special-occasion solution for men of distinction. Countess Mara's vision of European style and conduct has helped define the modern American gentleman." See Figure 20-4.
- Lenox makes fine china and crystal. Ads rarely mention price, but focus on quality and design. As its Web site (**http://www.lenox.com**) notes, "Since 1889, Lenox has created gifts, tableware, and collectibles for U.S. presidents, dignitaries—and families like yours across America. In fact, Lenox was the first American china to be used in the White House. Over the years, our original focus on fine tableware has broadened to include casual collections in stoneware and earthenware, crystal stemware, and flatware. Our gifts in china, crystal, and precious metals have been part of family celebrations for generations. And our collectibles continue to win awards—and the hearts of collectors everywhere."

Figure 20-3
Daffy's Price-Oriented Strategy

Source: Reprinted by permission.

Figure 20-4
Countess Mara's Nonprice-Oriented Strategy
Source: Reprinted by permission.

20-4 FACTORS AFFECTING PRICING DECISIONS

Before developing its pricing strategy (described in Chapter 21), a firm should analyze the outside factors affecting decisions. As with distribution planning, pricing depends heavily on elements external to the company. This contrasts with product and promotion decisions, which are more controlled by a company (except for publicity). Sometimes, outside elements greatly influence the ability to set prices; in other cases, they have little impact. Figure 20-5 outlines the major factors, which are discussed next.

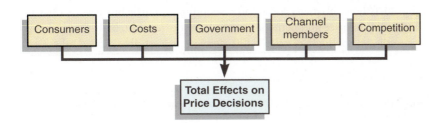

Figure 20-5

Factors Affecting Price Decisions

20-4a   Consumers

Company personnel involved with pricing decisions must understand the relationship between price and consumer purchases and perceptions. This relationship is explained by two economic principles—the law of demand and the price elasticity of demand—and by market segmentation.

According to the *law of demand*, consumers usually purchase more units at a low price than at a high price. The *price elasticity of demand* indicates the sensitivity of buyers to price changes in terms of the quantities they will purchase.[4] Price elasticity represents the percentage change in the quantity demanded relative to a specific percentage change in the price charged. This formula shows the percentage change in demand for each 1 percent change in price:

$$\text{Price elasticity} = \frac{\dfrac{\text{Quantity 1} - \text{Quantity 2}}{\text{Quantity 1} + \text{Quantity 2}}}{\dfrac{\text{Price 1} - \text{Price 2}}{\text{Price 1} + \text{Price 2}}}$$

Because the quantity demanded usually falls as price rises, elasticity is a negative number. However, for purposes of simplicity, elasticity calculations are usually expressed as positive numbers.

Elastic demand occurs if relatively small changes in price result in large changes in quantity demanded. Elasticity is more than 1. Total revenue goes up when prices are decreased and goes down when prices rise. *Inelastic demand* takes place if price changes have little impact on the quantity demanded. Elasticity is less than 1. Total revenue goes up when prices are raised and goes down when prices decline. *Unitary demand* exists if price changes are exactly offset by changes in the quantity demanded, so total sales revenue remains constant. Price elasticity is 1.

Demand elasticity is based mostly on two criteria: availability of substitutes and urgency of need. If people *believe* there are many similar goods or services from which to choose or have no urgency to buy, demand is elastic and greatly influenced by price changes: Price increases lead to purchases of substitutes or delayed purchases, and decreases expand sales as people are drawn from competitors or move up the date of their purchases. For some people, the airfare for a vacation is highly elastic. If prices go up, they may switch to a cheaper airline, travel to a nearer location by car, or postpone a trip.

If consumers believe a firm's offering is unique or there is an urgency to buy, demand is inelastic and little affected by price changes: Neither price increases nor declines will have much impact on demand. In most locales, when heating oil prices go up or down, demand remains relatively constant because there is often no feasible substitute, and homes and offices must be heated. Brand loyalty also generates inelastic demand; consumers then feel their brands are distinctive and do not accept substitutes. Finally, emergency conditions increase demand inelasticity. A truck driver with a flat tire would pay more for a replacement than one who had time to shop around. Figure 20-6 illustrates elastic and inelastic demand.

Elasticity usually varies over a wide range of prices for the same good or service. At very high prices, even revenues for essential goods and services may fall (mass-transit ridership would drop a lot if fares rise from $2 to $4; driving would become a more reasonable substitute). At very low prices, demand cannot be stimulated further; saturation is reached and shoppers may begin to perceive quality as inferior.

Table 20-1 shows elasticity for an office-equipment repair business. A clear relationship exists between price and demand. At the lowest price, $60, daily demand is greatest: 10 service calls. At the highest price, $120, demand is least: five service calls. Demand is

According to the **law of demand**, more is bought at low prices; **price elasticity** explains reactions to changes.

Demand may be **elastic**, **inelastic**, or **unitary**. It depends on the availability of substitutes and urgency of need.

---

[4] For further information, visit these Web sites: "Economics Basics: Elasticity" (**http://www.investopedia.com/university/economics/economics4.asp**); and "Price Elasticity of Demand" (**http://www.quickmba.com/econ/micro/elas/ped.shtml**).

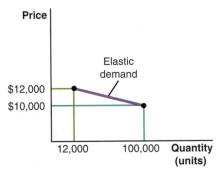

Figure 20-6

Demand Elasticity for Two Models of Automobiles

Economy Car (Model A)
The purchasers of an economy car are highly sensitive to price. They perceive many models as interchangeable, and demand will suffer significantly if the car is priced too high. At $10,000, 100,000 models may be sold (revenues are $1 billion). A small increase to $12,000 will cause demand to fall to 12,000 units (revenues are $144 million).

Luxury Car (Model B)
The purchasers of a luxury car have little sensitivity to price. They perceive their model as quite distinctive and will pay a premium price for it. At $40,000, 20,000 models may be sold (revenues are $800 million). A large increase in price, to $50,000, will have only a small effect on demand, reducing it to 18,000 units (revenues are $900 million).

inelastic between $60 and $84; total service-call revenues rise as price increases. Demand is unitary between $84 and $96; total service-call revenues remain the same ($672). Demand is elastic between $96 and $120; total service-call revenues decline as the price rises within this range. Although a fee of either $84 or $96 yields the highest service-call revenues, $672, other criteria must be evaluated before selecting a price. The repair firm should consider costs per call; the number of servicepeople required at different levels; the overall revenues generated by each service call, including parts and added labor charges; travel time; the percentage of satisfied customers at different prices (expressed by repeat business); and the potential for referrals.

Table **20-1**	Price Elasticity for Service Calls by an Office-Equipment Repair Business			
Price of Service Call	Service Calls Demanded Per Day	Revenues from Services Calls	Price Elasticity of Demand[a]	Type of Demand
$60.00	10	$600.00		
			0.76	Inelastic
$72.00	9	$648.00		
			0.76	Inelastic
$84.00	8	$672.00		
			1.00	Unitary
$96.00	7	$672.00		
			1.31	Elastic
$108.00	6	$648.00		
			1.73	Elastic
$120.00	5	$600.00		

[a] Expressed as positive numbers.

Price sensitivity varies by market segment because all people are not equally price-conscious. Consumers can be divided into such segments as these:

- *Price shoppers*—They are interested in the "best deal" for a product.
- *Brand-loyal customers*—They believe their current brands are better than others and will pay "fair" prices for those products.
- *Status seekers*—They buy prestigious brands and product categories and will pay whatever prices are set; higher prices signify greater status.
- *Service/features shoppers*—They place a great value on customer service and/or product features and will pay for them.
- *Convenience shoppers*—They value ease of shopping, nearby locations, long hours by sellers, and other approaches that make shopping simple; they will pay above-average prices.

A firm must decide which segment or segments are represented by its target market and plan accordingly.

The consumer's (market segment's) perception of the price of a good or service as being high, fair, or low—its **subjective price**—may be more important than its actual price. A consumer may feel a low price represents a good buy or inferior quality—or a high price represents status or poor value, depending on his/her perception. Such factors as these affect a consumer's (market segment's) subjective price:

- *Purchase experience with a particular good or service*—"How much have I paid in the past?"
- *Purchase experience with other, rather similar goods or services*—"What's a fair price for an item in the same or adjacent product category that I bought before?"
- *Self-image*—"How much should a person like me pay for something like this?"
- *Social situation*—"How much do my friends expect me to pay for something like this?"
- *Context of the purchase*—"What should this cost in these circumstances?"[5]

KB Home (**http://www.kbhome.com**) is a leading U.S. home developer that seeks to offer prices perceived as fair by its target market: "With KB Home, you'll have new Whirlpool (**http://www.whirlpool.com**) and KitchenAid (**http://www.kitchenaid.com**) appliances, quality flooring, energy-efficient insulation and double-pane windows, and modern heating/cooling systems that are low-maintenance and easy to operate. And that's just scratching the surface. Plus, new products often come with warranties you won't find in an older home. When you move into a used home, you may have to begin worrying about the dishwasher breaking down or central air-conditioning giving out. The results can be a hassle and terribly expensive."[6]

20-4b Costs

The costs of raw materials, supplies, labor, transportation, and other items are commonly beyond a firm's control. Yet, they have a great impact on prices. Since the early 1980s, overall U.S. cost increases have been rather low. Though the 1980 inflation rate was 13.5 percent, the recent annual rate has typically been 3 to 5 percent. This means better cost control and more stable prices for most firms. Nonetheless, the costs of some goods and services have risen rapidly or fluctuated a lot in recent years. For example,

[5] G. Ray Funkhouser, "Using Consumer Expectations as an Input to Pricing Decisions," *Journal of Product & Brand Management*, Vol. 1 (Spring 1992), p. 48. See also Justin Kruger and Patrick Vargas, "Consumer Confusion of Percent Differences," *Journal of Consumer Psychology*, Vol. 18 (January 2008), pp. 49–61; and Juha Munnukka, "Customers' Purchase Intentions as a Reflection of Price Perception," *Journal of Product & Brand Management*, Vol. 17 (Number 3, 2008), pp. 188–196.

[6] "Home Buying Tips," **http://www.kbhome.com/Page~PageID~184.aspx** (June 2, 2009).

Global Marketing in Action

Are You Attracted by easyGroup's Anti-Luxury Approach?

easyGroup (http://www.easy.com) is the brainchild of Greek shipping heir Stelios Haji-Ioannou, who founded the budget airline easyJet (http://www.easyjet.com) at the age of 28. Among the goods and services under the "easy" brand umbrella are easyHotel (http://www.easyhotel.com), easyCar (http://www.easycar.com), easyBus (http://www.easybus.co.uk), easyCruise (http://www.easycruise.com), easyMusic (http://www.easymusic.com), and easyMoney (http://www.easymoney). Most of easyGroup's ventures use a common model based on low costs, few frills, and the use of the Web as a primary promotional vehicle. Among easyGroup's offerings, easyJet (http://www.easyjet.com) has been highly successful. easyJet is one of the largest low-fare airlines in Europe, with 400 routes between more than 100 European and North African airports.

Let's look at easyHotel, which opened its first hotel in London in 2005. As of late 2008, 8 easyHotels were open, with 5 locations in Great Britain, 2 in Switzerland, and 1 in Hungary. To reduce booking costs, easyHotel is only marketed online. In fact, its Web site does not include any phone number. At its easyHotel Victoria in London, the lowest room rate is the equivalent of $50, much less than a comparable hotel. To reduce costs, many conveniences that consumers expect are add-ons at additional expense. For example, the remote control on a television costs about $10 extra, housekeeping is an optional $20 per day, and luggage storage for guests who have checked out is $10 for two items. The rooms are also very spartan; they are windowless and have no closets or drawers.

Sources: Based on material in Luan Goldie, "easyHotel to Overhaul Web Site Ahead of Global Hotel Openings," *New Media Age* (April 27, 2007), p. 7; John Reynolds, "When the Going's Not So Easy," *Marketing Week* (February 2, 2007), pp. 26–27; and "About Us," http://www.easyhotel.com/about_us.htm (August 27, 2008).

- During July 2008, the average U.S. price for a gallon of regular unleaded gasoline reached an all-time high of $4.05 per gallon, compared with $3.15 per gallon for the same period in 2007 and $2.29 per gallon in July 2005. The price then dropped to less than $2.00 per gallon a few months later.
- The cost of prime-time TV ads for major events has gone up dramatically. A 30-second ad on the 1996 Super Bowl telecast cost $1.3 million. In 2009, the cost was approaching $3 million.
- Gold and silver prices have been volatile. Gold went from $325 per ounce in mid-1999 to $250 per ounce in early 2001, to $420 per ounce in 2004, to more than $1,000 per ounce in early 2008 before falling to $800 per ounce in August 2008. Silver went from $7.00 per ounce in 1998 to $4.50 an ounce in 2001, back to $6.00 in 2004, to $12.00 in 2006, and to $20 in 2008. High gold and silver prices adversely affect dentists and jewelers, among others.

During periods of rising costs, firms can react in one or more ways: They can leave products unchanged and pass along all of their cost increases to consumers, leave products unchanged and pass along part of their increases and absorb part of them, modify products to hold down costs and maintain prices (by reducing size, using lesser-quality materials, or offering fewer options), modify products to gain consumer support for higher prices (by increasing size, using better-quality materials, offering more options, or upgrading customer service), and/or abandon unprofitable products.

Consider the U.S. furniture industry:

With ongoing pricing pressure on items ranging from foam to fuel, many companies that avoided passing along price hikes say they can no longer absorb the costs. Some have already raised prices on finished goods, while others expect to do so soon. Several factors are driving up prices, according to manufacturers: Foam producers have requested an increase, in response to higher costs of chemicals used to produce the material. Crude oil prices are high. This affects the price of fuel and also a range of items, ranging from packaging materials to finishes. Some wood prices are rising, although not all. Prices of certain grades of red oak have actually fallen over the past year. But prices of kiln-dried ash have risen. Prices on steel components have gone up several times. As one manufacturer noted: "It has been an incredible run-up. We're just passing along some of our increased costs."[7]

> **Cost decreases have mostly positive benefits for marketing strategies.**

If costs decline, firms can drop prices or raise margins, as these examples show: Using microchips has reduced PC costs by requiring less wiring and assembly time, improving durability, and enlarging information-processing capability. PC prices have gone down steadily, thus expanding the market. On the other hand, low sugar prices let candy makers increase profits without raising prices.

Sometimes, low costs can actually have a negative long-run impact: "Lowering prices is all well and good as long as sales levels remain high, but the problem comes when times become more challenging. Retailers have to sell higher volumes to compensate for lower prices just to maintain the level of cash flowing through their tills. Store owners have to look for even more cost cuts and further efficiencies. There must be concerns about just how much more pressure retailers can put on themselves and their suppliers to gain further price reductions. There are only so many times you can go to the well."[8]

20-4c   Government

U.S. government (federal and/or state) actions related to pricing can be divided into the five major areas shown in Figure 20-7 and discussed next.

> **Horizontal price fixing is illegal and results from agreements along companies at the same stage in a channel.**

Price Fixing   There are horizontal and vertical price-fixing restrictions. *Horizontal price fixing* results from agreements among manufacturers, among wholesalers, or among retailers to set prices at a given stage in a channel of distribution. Such agreements are illegal according to the federal Sherman Antitrust Act and the Federal Trade Commission Act, regardless of how "reasonable" prices are.

If violations occur, federal penalties may be severe: A firm can be fined up to $10 million per violation, and individuals can be fined up to $350,000 each and imprisoned for up to three years. The U.S. Department of Justice (**http://www.usdoj.gov/atr/public/ guidelines/guidelin.htm**) investigates and prosecutes price-fixing cases. In 2007 and 2008, it reached plea agreements with several foreign airlines for "conspiring to fix prices on air cargo rates" and other infractions. Cumulatively, Air France-KLM (**http:// www.airfranceklm-finance.com/EN**), British Airways (**http://www.britishairways.com**), Korean Air Lines (**http://www.koreanair.com**), Australia's Qantas Airways (**http://www. qantas.com.au**), Cathay Pacific (**http://www.cathayairlines.com**), Scandinavian Air (**http://www.flysas.com**), and the Netherlands' Martinair (**http://www.martinair.com**)

Figure 20-7

Selected U.S. Government Actions Affecting Price Decisions

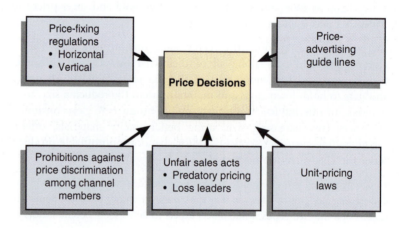

[7] Thomas Russell, "Pricing Pressure Continues to Escalate on Producers," *Furniture Today* (June 16, 2008), p. 2.

[8] Helen Dickinson, "Price Cutters Will Soon Count the Cost," *Marketing* (UK) (October 5, 2005), p. 11.

were fined more than $1 billion. In addition, executives at SAS and Qantas received jail sentences.[9]

To avoid price-fixing charges, a firm must be careful not to

- coordinate discounts, credit terms, or conditions of sale with competitors.
- talk about price levels, markups, and costs at trade association meetings.
- plan with competitors to issue new price lists on the same date.
- plan with competitors to rotate low bids on contracts.
- agree with competitors to limit production to keep high prices.
- exchange information with competitors, even informally.

Vertical price fixing occurs when manufacturers or wholesalers seek to control the final selling prices of their goods or services. In the United States, from 1937 until 1975, these firms were legally allowed to set and strictly enforce resale prices if they so desired. This practice was known as *fair trade*. It protected small resellers and maintained brand images by forcing all resellers within fair-trade states to charge the same price for affected products. It was also criticized as noncompetitive—keeping prices too high and rewarding reseller inefficiency. The Consumer Goods Pricing Act ended all interstate use of resale price maintenance, and it was fully in effect from 1976 until 2007. During that time, resellers could not be forced to adhere to manufacturer or wholesaler list prices. Most times, they could set their prices.

Then, in 2007, the U.S. Supreme Court (**http://www.supremecourtus.gov/opinions/06pdf/06-480.pdf**) issued a new ruling "that it was not automatically unlawful for manufacturers and distributors to agree on minimum retail prices. The decision will give producers significantly more, though not unlimited, power to dictate retail prices and to restrict the flexibility of discounters. The Court instructed judges considering vertical-pricing agreements for possible antitrust violations to apply a case-by-case approach, known as a 'rule of reason,' to assess their impact on competition."[10]

A manufacturer or wholesaler may also control final prices by one of these methods:

- Manufacturer or wholesaler ownership of sales facilities.
- Consignment selling. The manufacturer or wholesaler owns items until they are sold and assumes costs normally associated with the reseller, such as advertising and selling.
- Careful screening of the channel members that resell goods or services. A supplier can bypass or drop distributors if they are not living up to the supplier's performance standards, as long as there is no collusion between the supplier and other distributors. (A firm must be careful not to threaten channel members that do not adhere to suggested prices.)
- Suggesting realistic selling prices.
- Pre-printing prices on products.
- Establishing customary prices (such as 75 cents for a newspaper) that are accepted by consumers.

Price Discrimination The ***Robinson-Patman Act*** prohibits manufacturers and wholesalers from price discrimination in dealing with different channel-member purchasers of products with "like quality" if the effect of such discrimination is to injure competition. Covered by the act are prices, discounts, rebates, premiums, coupons, guarantees, delivery, warehousing, and credit rates. Terms and conditions of sale must

> Under **vertical price fixing**, manufacturers or wholesalers try to control resale prices. This practice has some limits.

> The **Robinson-Patman Act** prohibits price discrimination in selling to channel members.

[9] Department of Justice, "Former Top SAS Cargo Group A/S Executive Agrees to Plead Guilty to Participating in Price-Fixing Conspiracy," **http://www.usdoj.gov/atr/public/press_releases/2008/235514.pdf** (July 28, 2008).

[10] Steve Labaton, "Century-Old Ban Lifted on Minimum Retail Pricing," **http://www.nytimes.com/2007/06/29/washington/29bizcourt.html** (June 29, 2007).

Ethical Issues in Marketing

Whom Do Below-Cost Laws Protect?

Many states, including Colorado, have sales-below-cost laws that forbid retailers from selling gasoline below the wholesale cost or that require gasoline stations to charge a minimum markup on the sales of gasoline. Many of the laws were originally drafted to protect small retailers from indiscriminate price cutting by larger firms. The laws were based on the fear that rampant price cutting could drive smaller retailers out of business.

Prior to the huge 2008 run up in gasoline prices, King Soopers (http://www.kingsoopers.com) and City Market (http://www.citymarket.com), both owned by Kroger (http://www.kroger.com), were sued by independent gas stations for violating Colorado's Unfair Practices Act, which makes selling gasoline below cost illegal. The supermarkets were ultimately hit with a $1.4 million judgment. A jury found that City Market's below-cost gasoline sales injured two local Colorado-based distributors. City Market sold gasoline below cost for 505 days. It admitted that it lost $500,000 on gas sales, but customers who bought the specially priced gasoline were required to make $100 worth of grocery purchases in the store.

Due to fear of a similar lawsuit, Safeway (http://www.safeway.com) discontinued its gas program in Colorado. Wal-Mart (http://www.walmart.com) and Target (http://www.target.com) announced that the unfair-sales-act judgments would cause them to drop their $4 generic prescription plans. Responding to the public's concern about these programs being dropped, Colorado's Attorney General introduced a bill to allow retailers to sell gasoline and prescription drugs for below cost if this was part of a loyalty program.

Sources: Based on material in Jim Isgar, "Selling Below-Cost Gas Has Downside," http://www.durangoherald.com (March 18, 2007); and Leo Jakobson, "Lawsuit Ends Gas Loyalty Program, and Discounts," *Incentive* (February 2007), p. 33.

be made available to all competing channel-member customers on a proportionately equal basis.[11]

The Robinson-Patman Act was enacted in 1936 to protect small retailers from unfair price competition by large chains. It was feared that small firms would be driven out of business due to the superior bargaining power (and the resultant lower selling prices) of chains. This act requires that the price differences charged to competing resellers be limited to the supplier's cost savings in dealing with the different resellers. It remains a legal restraint on pricing.

There are exceptions to the Robinson-Patman Act. Price discrimination within a channel is allowed if each buyer purchases items with substantial physical differences, if noncompeting buyers are involved, if prices do not injure competition, if price differences are justified by costs, if market conditions change (such as production costs rising), or if the seller reduces prices in response to another supplier.

Discounts are permissible if a seller shows they are available to all competing resellers on a proportionate basis, sufficiently graduated so both small and large buyers can qualify, or cost-justified. A seller must also prove that discounts for cumulative purchases (total volume during the year) or multistore purchases by chains are based on cost savings.

Although the Robinson-Patman Act is geared toward sellers, it has specific liabilities for purchasing firms under Section 2(F): "It shall be unlawful for any person engaged in commerce, in the course of such commerce, knowingly to induce or receive a discrimination in price which is prohibited in this section." Accordingly, resellers should try to get the lowest prices charged to any competitor in their class, but not bargain so hard that their discounts cannot be explained by one of the acceptable exceptions to the act.

---

[11] See Roger Dickinson, "The Robinson-Patman Act: An Important Conundrum," *Journal of Macromarketing*, Vol. 23 (June 2003), pp. 31–41; and "Robinson-Patman: Further Readings," http://law.jrank.org/pages/9901/Robinson-Patman-Act.html (May 9, 2009).

Minimum Prices Many states have *unfair-sales acts (minimum price laws)* to prevent firms from selling products for less than their cost plus a fixed percentage that includes overhead and profit. About one-half of the states have unfair-sales acts covering all kinds of products and retail situations; two-thirds have laws involving specific products, such as bread, dairy items, and liquor. These acts are intended to protect small firms from predatory pricing by larger competitors and to limit the use of loss leaders by retailers.

With *predatory pricing*, large firms cut prices on products to below their cost in selected geographic areas so as to eliminate small, local competitors. At the federal level, predatory pricing is banned by the Sherman and Clayton Acts. Manufacturers, wholesalers, and retailers are all subject to these acts. However, predatory pricing is extremely difficult to prove.[12]

Loss leaders, items priced below cost to attract customers to a seller—usually in a store setting—are also restricted by some state unfair-sales acts. Sellers use loss leaders, typically well-known and heavily advertised brands, to increase their overall sales. They assume customers drawn by loss leaders will also buy nonsale items. Because consumers benefit, loss-leader laws are not often enforced.

Unit Pricing The lack of uniformity in package sizes has led to unit-pricing laws in several states. *Unit pricing* lets consumers compare price per quantity for competing brands and for various sizes of the same brand.[13]

Food stores are most affected by unit-pricing laws; they often must show price per unit of measure, as well as total price. For example, through unit pricing, a shopper could learn that a 12-ounce can of soda selling for 40 cents is priced at 3.3 cents per ounce, whereas a 67.6-ounce (2-liter) bottle of the same brand selling for $2.09 is priced at 3.1 cents per ounce. The larger size is cheaper than the smaller one.

Retailers' unit-pricing costs include computing per-unit prices, printing shelf labels, and maintaining computer records. The costs are affected by the number of stores in a chain, the sales per store, the number of items under unit pricing, and the frequency of price changes.

When U.S. unit-pricing laws were first enacted more than 30 years ago, research found that people generally did not use the data and that low-income consumers (for whom the laws were most intended) were unlikely to look at unit prices. Critics felt the laws were costly without providing benefits. More recent research shows unit pricing to be effective and suggests that consumer learning and subsequent behavioral changes take time. Upscale suburban residents are still more prone to use the data than others.

Price Advertising Price advertising guidelines have been set by the FTC and various trade associations, such as the Better Business Bureau (**http://www.bbb.org**). The FTC's guidelines (**http://www.ftc.gov/bcp/guides/decptprc.htm**) specify standards of permissible conduct in several categories:

- A firm may not claim or imply that a price has been reduced from a former level unless the original price was offered to the public on a regular basis during a reasonable, recent period of time.
- A firm may not claim its price is lower than that of competitors or the manufacturer's list price without verifying, via price comparisons involving large quantities of merchandise, that an item's price at other companies in the same trading area is in fact higher.

> **Unfair-sales acts** protect small firms from **predatory pricing** by large companies and restrict the use of **loss leaders**.

> With **unit pricing**, consumers can compare prices for different-sized packages.

> FTC guidelines establish standards for price ads.

[12] See Patrick Greenlee, David Reitman, and David S. Sibley, "An Antitrust Analysis of Bundled Loyalty Discounts," *International Journal of Industrial Organization*, Vol. 26 (September 2008), pp. 1132–1152; and Joe Nocera, "Predatory Pricing or Old-Fashioned Competition?" **http://www.iht.com/articles/2008/06/20/business/wbjoe21.php** (June 21, 2008).

[13] See National Conference on Weights and Measures, "Uniform Unit Pricing Regulation," **http://www.ts.nist.gov/WeightsAndMeasures/Publications/upload/12_IVC_UnitPricReg_08_H130_FINAL.pdf** (2008).

- A suggested list price or a pre-marked price cannot be advertised as a reference point for a sale or a comparison with other products unless the advertised product has really been sold at that price.
- Bargain offers ("free," "buy one, get one free," and "half-price sale") are deemed deceptive if terms are not disclosed at the beginning of a sales presentation or in an ad, the stated regular price of an item is inflated to create an impression of savings, or the quality or quantity of a product is lessened without informing consumers. A firm cannot continuously advertise the same item as being on sale.
- *Bait-and-switch advertising* is an illegal practice whereby customers are lured to a seller that advertises items at very low prices and then told the items are out of stock or of poor quality. Salespeople try to switch shoppers to more expensive substitutes, and there is no intent to sell advertised items. Signs of bait-and-switch are refusals to demonstrate sale items, the belittling of sale items, inadequate quantities of sale items on hand, refusals to take orders, demonstrations of defective items, and the use of compensation plans encouraging salespeople to use the tactic.

Under **bait-and-switch advertising**, sellers illegally draw customers by deceptive pricing.

20-4d   Channel Members

Each channel member typically seeks a major role in setting prices so as to generate sales volume, obtain adequate profit margins, have a proper image, ensure repeat purchases, and meet specific goals.

A manufacturer can gain greater control over prices by using an exclusive distribution system or avoiding price-oriented resellers; pre-marking prices on products; owning sales outlets; offering products on consignment; providing adequate margins to resellers; and, most importantly, by having strong brands to which people are brand loyal and for which they will pay premium prices.

A wholesaler or retailer can gain better control over prices by stressing its importance as a customer to the supplier, linking resale support to the profit margins allowed by the supplier, refusing to carry unprofitable items, stocking competing items, having strong private brands so people are loyal to the seller and not the supplier, and purchasing outside traditional channels.

To increase private-brand sales, some channel members **sell against the brand**.

Wholesalers and retailers may engage in *selling against the brand*, whereby they stock well-known brands, place high prices on them, and then sell other brands for lower prices. This is done to increase sales of their private brands and is disliked by manufacturers because sales of their brands decline.

Sometimes, wholesalers and retailers go outside traditional distribution channels and buy *gray market goods*—foreign-made products imported into countries such as the United States by distributors (suppliers) that are not authorized by the products' manufacturers. Personal stereos, DVD players, car stereos, watches, and cameras are just some of the items handled in this way. If wholesalers and retailers buy gray market goods, their purchase prices are less than they would be otherwise, and they have greater control over their own selling prices. The result is often discounted prices for consumers, which may be upsetting to both manufacturers and their authorized dealers.[14]

Gray market goods bypass authorized channels.

To maximize channel-member cooperation, these factors should be incorporated in pricing decisions: channel-member profit margins, price guarantees, special deals, and the impact of price increases. Wholesalers and retailers require appropriate profit margins to cover their costs (such as shipping, storage, credit, and advertising) and earn reasonable profits. Thus, the prices charged to them must take these profit margins into account. An attempt to reduce traditional margins for channel members may lose their

[14] See Barry Berman, "Strategies to Combat the Sale of Gray Market Goods," *Business Horizons*, Vol. 47 (July-August 2004), pp. 51–60; John P. Koch, "Using Copyright to Police Gray Market Goods in Canada," *Licensing Journal*, Vol. 25 (October 2005), pp. 8–14; Hsiu-Li Chen, "Gray Marketing and Its Impacts on Brand Equity," *Journal of Product & Brand Management*, Vol. 16 (August 2007), pp. 247–256; and Mina Kimes, "How Middlemen Can Discredit Your Goods," *FSB: Fortune Small Business* (May 2008), pp. 75–78.

Marketing and the Web

Comparison Shopping Web Sites: On Target for Careful Shoppers

BizRate (http://www.bizrate.com), PriceGrabber (http://www. pricegrabber.com), Shopping.com (http://www.shopping.com), Shopzilla (http://www.shopzilla.com), and Yahoo! Shopping (http://shopping.yahoo.com) are among the leading comparison Web sites. According to eBizMBA (http://www.ebizmba.com), based on a compilation of data from several sources, the top 20 Web-based comparison shopping sites draw about 75 million visitors each month.

Studies show that these sites are used both by online shoppers and by shoppers who wish to be better informed when visiting a traditional bricks-and-mortar store. For example, a store shopper who wants to be knowledgeable about the features of alternative models or prices can access one of these sites prior to going on a traditional shopping trip.

Most of these sites offer similar features. Consumers can review both expert and final consumer reviews of products; and merchants are also rated regarding customer past transactions on such attributes as return privileges, speed of delivery, and resolution of complaints. Most also list total costs, which include purchase price, shipping, and sales tax. Some include rebate and coupon offers.

There are some potential problems with the use of these sites by consumers. Because most of the sites charge retailers every time potential customers click on a listing, not all merchants list every product. Other merchants may have lower prices. Some retailer reviews may even be bogus. Friends or associates of an online retailer can easily write positive reviews. Last, some merchants seem to offer low prices on goods and then report they are out of stock on these specials. Ultimately, shoppers may be switched to more costly products.

Sources: Based on material in "20 Most Popular Comparison Shopping Sites," http://www.ebizmba.com/articles/comparison-shopping (June 2008); and Wilson Rothman, "The Search Engines of Commerce," http://money.cnn.com (March 22, 2007).

cooperation and perhaps find them unwilling to carry a product. Pricing through a distribution channel is discussed further in Chapter 21.

Channel members may seek price guarantees to maintain inventory values and profit. Such guarantees assure resellers that the prices they pay are the lowest available. Any discount given to competitors will also be given to the original purchasers. Guarantees are most frequently requested of new firms or for new products that want to gain entry into an established channel.

Special deals—consisting of limited-time discounts and/or free products—are often used to stimulate reseller purchases. The deals may require channel members to share their savings with final consumers to increase the latter's demand. For example, soda bottlers normally give retailers large price discounts on new products to encourage them to make purchases and then offer low introductory prices to consumers.

The impact of price increases on channel members' behavior must also be assessed. When firms raise prices to resellers, these increases tend to be passed along to consumers. This practice is more difficult for items with customary prices, such as candy, where small cost rises may be absorbed by the resellers. In any event, cooperation depends on an equitable distribution of costs and profit within the channel.

20-4e Competition

Another factor contributing to the degree of control a firm has over prices is the competitive environment within which it operates. See Figure 20-8.

A *market-controlled price environment* is characterized by a high level of competition, similar goods and services, and little control over prices by individual firms. Those trying to charge much more than the going price would attract few customers, because demand for any single firm is weak enough that customers would switch to competitors. There would similarly be little gained by selling for less because competitors would match price cuts.

> A firm may face a **market-controlled, company-controlled,** or **government-controlled price environment.**

A *company-controlled price environment* is characterized by moderate competition, well-differentiated goods and services, and strong control over prices by individual firms. Companies can succeed with above-average prices because people view their offerings as unique. Differentiation may be based on brand image, features, associated services, assortment, or other elements. Discounters also can carve out a niche in this environment by attracting consumers interested in low prices.

A *government-controlled price environment* is characterized by prices being set or strongly influenced by some level of government. Examples are public utilities, mass transit, insurance, and state universities. In each case, government bodies determine or affect prices after getting input from relevant firms, institutions, and/or trade associations, as well as other parties such as consumer groups.

Companies may have to adapt to a changing competitive environment in their industries. Firms in the transportation, telecommunications, and financial industries have seen their price environment shift from government- to market-controlled, although some strong firms in these industries have managed to develop a company-controlled price environment.

Because price strategies are rather easy and quick to copy, competitors' reactions are predictable if the firm initiating a price change does well. Thus, marketers must view price from both short- and long-run perspectives. Excessive price competition may lead to lengthy and costly *price wars*, in which various firms continually try to undercut each other's prices to draw customers. These wars often result in low profits or even losses for the participants and in some companies being forced out of business.

In recent years, there have been price wars among some electronics manufacturers, PC makers, semiconductor manufacturers, supermarkets, insurance firms, and others. Though more price wars have occurred in the United States (due to fierce competition in some industries), they have spread overseas—particularly to Europe and, to a lesser extent, to Japan. The impact of price wars can be dramatic:

> Travel agents spend too much time competing among themselves and not enough on growing the market. Fred Olsen Cruise Lines' (**http://www.fredolsencruises.com**) marketing director says that cruise lines have successfully raised the profile of the industry but that too often retailers focus solely on price. "Retail has not done enough to grow the market. Rather, too much effort is spent on competition which distills down to stories about price. This presupposes that consumers already know what cruising is. Together, we must identify target markets, which can vary from brand to brand, demographically and geographically." He warns agents that cruise customers' propensity to book online will increase as they become more familiar and confident with using online payment methods. So, agents need to work hard to capture customers and to keep them loyal by overcoming their objections to taking a cruise holiday.[15]

Price wars occur when competitors constantly lower prices.

Figure 20-8

The Competitive Environment of Pricing

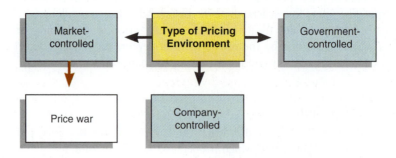

[15] Damian Horner, "Stop Price War, Agents," *Travel Trade Gazette UK & Ireland* (May 23, 2008), p. 6.

Web Sites You Can Use

As the chief U.S. government agency involved with pricing issues, the Federal Trade Commission's Web site has a lot of excellent information—beneficial for both consumers and businesses:

- At various sections of the site, you will find *Consumer Alerts*, such as "Free and Low-Cost PC Offers. Go Figure" (**http://www.ftc.gov/bcp/conline/pubs/alerts/pcalrt. shtm**); "Holiday Shopping: Is a Sale Price Your Best Deal?" (**http://www.ftc.gov/bcp/conline/pubs/alerts/salealrt. shtm**); "Ads Promising Debt Relief May Be Offering Bankruptcy" (**http://www.ftc.gov/bcp/edu/pubs/ consumer/alerts/alt015.shtm**); "Medical Discount Plans: They're Not Health Insurance" (**http://www.ftc.gov/bcp/ conline/pubs/alerts/medplanalrt.shtm**); "Long Distance Deals" (**http://www.ftc.gov/bcp/conline/pubs/alerts/ lgdisalrt.shtm**); and "Taking the 'Bait' Out of Rebates" (**http://www.ftc.gov/bcp/conline/pubs/alerts/rebatealrt. shtm**).

- At the *For Business: Advertising Guide* section of the site (**http://www.ftc.gov/bcp/guides/guides.htm**), several guides for business are available, such as "FTC Guides Against Deceptive Pricing," "FTC Guide Concerning the Use of the Word 'Free'," "FTC Guides Against Bait Advertising," "Joint FTC/FCC Guides on Long Distance Advertising," and "Guides for the Jewelry, Precious Metals, and Pewter Industries."

Summary

1. *To define the terms price and price planning*   A price represents the value of a product for both the seller and the buyer. Price planning is systematic decision making relating to all aspects of pricing by a firm; it involves tangible and intangible factors, purchase terms, and the nonmonetary exchange of goods and services. Exchange does not take place unless the buyer and seller agree that a price represents an equitable value. Price also balances supply and demand.

2. *To demonstrate the importance of price and study its relationship with other marketing variables*   Price decisions have become more important and complex. This is due to price (monetary or nonmonetary) being part of every type of exchange, deregulation, cost increase, currency rates, technological advances, the greater emphasis by service companies, volatile energy prices, and periodic economic slowdowns.

   Price decisions must be made in sync with other marketing-mix elements. And pricing is often related to the product life cycle, customer service levels, and other specific marketing and company variables. In addition, setting prices for foreign markets can be complex and influenced by country factors.

3. *To differentiate between price-based and nonprice-based approaches*   Under a price-based approach, sellers influence demand primarily via changes in price levels; they move consumers along a demand curve by raising or lowering prices. With a nonprice-based approach, sellers downplay price and emphasize such other marketing attributes as image, packaging, and features; they shift the demand curves of consumers by stressing product distinctiveness.

4. *To examine the factors affecting pricing decisions*   Several factors affect pricing decisions: consumers, costs, government, channel members, and competition. The law of demand states that consumers usually buy more units at a low price than at a high price. The price elasticity of demand explains the sensitivity of buyers to price changes in terms of the amounts they buy. Demand may be elastic, inelastic, or unitary; and it is impacted by the availability of substitutes and urgency of need. Consumers can be divided into segments based on their level of price sensitivity. Subjective price may be more important than actual price.

   The costs of raw materials, supplies, labor, ads, transportation, and other items affect prices. Large increases often lead firms to raise prices, modify products, or abandon some offerings. Cost declines benefit marketing strategies by improving firms' ability to plan prices.

   Government restrictions affect a broad variety of pricing areas. Horizontal price fixing is always illegal, while vertical pricing is allowable in some situations. The Robinson-Patman Act bans most price discrimination to resellers that is not justified by costs. A number of states have unfair-sales acts (minimum price laws) to protect small firms against predatory pricing. Unit-pricing laws require specified retailers to post prices in terms of quantity. The FTC has a series of guidelines for price advertising.

   Often, each channel member seeks a role in pricing. Manufacturers exert more control via exclusive distribution, pre-ticketing, opening their own outlets, offering goods on consignment, providing adequate margins, and having strong brands. Resellers exert more control by making large purchases, linking sales support to margins, refusing to carry items, stocking competing brands, developing private brands, and purchasing outside traditional channels. Reseller profit margins, price guarantees, special deals, and the ramifications of price increases all need to be considered.

   A market-controlled price environment has a lot of competition, similar products, and little control over prices by individual firms. A company-controlled price environment has a moderate level of competition, well-differentiated products, and strong control over prices by individual firms. In a government-controlled price environment, the government sets or influences prices. Some competitive actions may result in price wars, in which firms try to undercut each other's prices.

Key Terms

price (p. 618)
price planning (p. 618)
price-based approach (p. 621)
nonprice-based approach (p. 621)
law of demand (p. 624)
price elasticity of demand (p. 624)
elastic demand (p. 624)
inelastic demand (p. 624)
unitary demand (p. 624)
subjective price (p. 626)

horizontal price fixing (p. 628)
vertical price fixing (p. 629)
Robinson-Patman Act (p. 629)
unfair-sales acts (minimum price laws) (p. 631)
predatory pricing (p. 631)
loss leaders (p. 631)
unit pricing (p. 631)
bait-and-switch advertising (p. 632)
selling against the brand (p. 632)

gray market goods (p. 632)
market-controlled price environment (p. 633)
company-controlled price environment (p. 634)
government-controlled price environment (p. 634)
price wars (p. 634)

Review Questions

1. Explain the role of price in balancing supply and demand. Refer to Figure 20-1.
2. What is the risk with using a nonprice-oriented strategy?
3. Distinguish between elastic and inelastic demand. Why is it necessary for a firm to understand these differences?
4. At a price of $60, a firm could sell 1,000 units. At a price of $45, it could sell 1,750 units. Calculate the elasticity of demand and state what price the firm should charge—and why.

5. If costs rise rapidly, how could a company react?
6. Is horizontal price fixing always illegal? Explain your answer.
7. Does the buyer have any potential liability under the Robinson-Patman Act? Why or why not?
8. How can a firm turn a market-controlled price environment into a company-controlled one?

Discussion Questions

1. How could a firm estimate price elasticity for a new product? A mature product?
2. When would you pass along a cost decrease to consumers? When would you not pass the decrease along?

3. You are the marketing vice-president of a firm that sells extended warranties for used cars. What would you do to persuade consumers that you offer fair prices?
4. Present five examples of price advertising by a consumer electronics store that would violate FTC guidelines.

Web Exercise

The Hilton Hotels Corporation operates about 2,800 hotels around the world under such names as Conrad Hotels, Doubletree, Embassy Suites, Hampton Inn, Hilton Hotels, Hilton Garden Inn, and Homewood Suites (**http://www.hilton.com/en/** hi/brand/about.jhtml**). Visit the firm's Web site and review the prices charged by the various brands. Comment on what you find. Does the firm's strategy make sense to you? Why or why not?

Practice Quiz

1. The one element found in every marketing transaction is
   a. credit.
   b. final consumer.
   c. price.
   d. service.

2. The law of demand
   a. defines the insensitivity of buyers to price changes.
   b. relates purchase units to price.
   c. concerns only nonprice competition.
   d. involves government regulation of price.

3. Brand loyalty tends to generate
   a. elastic demand.
   b. price wars.
   c. inelastic demand.
   d. frequent sales.

4. The type of shopper most interested in the "best deal" for a product is a
   a. gotcha shopper.
   b. service shopper.
   c. convenience shopper.
   d. price shopper.

5. Horizontal price fixing has been outlawed by the
   a. Sherman Antitrust Act.
   b. Consumer Pricing Act.
   c. McGuire Act.
   d. Miller-Tydings Act.

6. Fair trade practices refer to
   a. price controls.
   b. price promotion.
   c. vertical price fixing.
   d. unfair-sales acts.

7. The Robinson-Patman Act was enacted in 1936 to directly protect
   a. consumers.
   b. small retailers.
   c. large manufacturers.
   d. state government.

8. Which of the following is an exception to the Robinson-Patman Act?
   a. Directly competing buyers are involved.
   b. Each buyer in a channel purchases products with similar physical attributes.
   c. Price differences are not justified by costs.
   d. A seller raises price to satisfy suppliers.

9. Which of the following statements about loss leaders is correct?
   a. Loss leaders are not restricted by some state unfair-sales acts.
   b. Sellers assume customers drawn by loss leaders will not buy nonsale items.
   c. Loss-leader laws are not vigorously enforced.
   d. Loss leaders rarely attract customers to a seller.

10. Which of the following statements about price advertising is true?
    a. A suggested list price can be advertised as a reference point for a sale, even though the product was never sold at that price.
    b. A firm can claim that a price has been reduced from an original price that was never before offered to the public.
    c. A firm cannot claim that its price is lower than that of competitors or the manufacturer's list price, even if it verifies that the price of an item at other companies in the same trading area is in fact higher.
    d. A firm cannot continuously advertise the same item as being on sale.

11. When wholesalers and retailers stock well-known brands, place high prices on them, and then sell other brands for lower prices, they engage in
    a. horizontal price fixing.
    b. vertical price fixing.
    c. price discrimination.
    d. selling against the brand.

12. Price guarantees
    a. prohibit entry into established channels of distribution.
    b. help channel members maintain inventory value and profit.
    c. usually grant discounts to purchasers who are not competitors.
    d. encourage passing price increases along to consumers.

13. A market-controlled price environment is characterized by
    a. little competition.
    b. well-differentiated goods and services.
    c. not much control over prices by individual firms.
    d. prices being strongly influenced by some level of government.

14. By attracting consumers interested in low prices, discounters can carve out a niche in a
    a. fluid-demand price environment.
    b. company-controlled price environment.
    c. market-controlled price environment.
    d. government-controlled price environment.

15. Firms in the transportation, telecommunications, and financial industries have seen their price environments shift from
    a. market- to company-controlled.
    b. company- to market-controlled.
    c. government- to market-controlled.
    d. market- to government-controlled.

For the answers to these questions, please visit the online site for this book at **http://www.atomicdog.com**.

Chapter 21

21

Developing and Applying a Pricing Strategy

Club Méditerranée (Club Med, http://www.clubmed.com) was started by Gérard Blitz in Alcudia Beach, Spain, in 1950. Although the 300 vacationers had to sleep in tents and cook their own food, they enjoyed the community spirit and the sports and activities provided by 20 or so organizers. During the first summer, Club Med attracted 2,300 customers and had to turn away 10,000 potential guests. The use of exotic destinations, all-inclusive prices, and simple accommodations has continued at Club Med today.

Club Med has had a colorful history. Polynesian huts replaced tents at the Greece location in 1954, and the firm opened its first ski resort in Switzerland in 1956. Club Med went public in 1966 and rapidly expanded through a number of mergers and acquisitions in the 1970s. Throughout the 1970s and 1980s, Club Med was associated with a "free-wheeling, anything goes" image. In 1989, Club Med 1, the largest 5-mast passenger sail ship with a capacity of 450 began in service. Today, there are more than 80 Club Med villages across five continents. To appeal to diverse holiday preferences, Club Med offers five different styles of vacations. For example, its Luxury Collections features 14 resorts with gourmet cuisine. It is also in the process of upgrading all of its villages to attract more affluent vacationers.

Club Med is commonly considered to be the originator of the all-inclusive vacation. In typical vacations, consumers are charged separately for meals, beverages, lessons, and equipment usage. In contrast, Club Med's pricing includes continuous buffets, beverages, and a wide variety of leisure, sporting, and recreational activities for the entire family. Club Med's ski programs include lodging, meals, drinks, and snacks, as well as ski lessons and ski passes.

All-inclusive resorts have a number of significant attractions for vacationers. Guests can sample a number of activities such as sailing, snorkeling, or tennis to determine their interest without concern for lesson or equipment usage fees. Vacationers can also better plan their budgets, as well as engage in activities they would ordinarily not. The all-inclusive pricing strategy provides Club Med with a unique pricing strategy among vacation resorts, a high-value-for-the-money image among its guests, and success in reaching and satisfying a target market seeking an active lifestyle vacation.[1]

In this chapter, we will look at the overall process of developing and applying a pricing strategy—including the use of various pricing approaches such as bundled pricing.

Chapter Objectives

1. To present an overall framework for developing and applying a pricing strategy
2. To analyze sales-based, profit-based, and status quo-based pricing objectives, and to describe the role of a broad price policy
3. To examine and apply the alternative approaches to a pricing strategy
4. To discuss several specific decisions that must be made in implementing a pricing strategy
5. To show the major ways that prices can be adjusted

---

[1] Various company and other sources.

21-1   OVERVIEW

A pricing strategy has the five steps shown in Figure 21-1: objectives, broad policy, strategy, implementation, and adjustments. All of them are affected by the outside factors we note in this chapter. Like any planning activity, a pricing strategy begins with a clear statement of goals and ends with an adaptive or corrective mechanism. Pricing decisions are integrated with the firm's overall marketing program during the broad price-policy step. At the Small Business Administration Web site (**http://www.sba.gov/tools/ resourcelibrary**), you can find an excellent discussion on how to plan and implement a price strategy, complete with checklists and examples. Click on "Publications" and go to "Financial Management Series." Choose "Pricing Your Products and Services Profitably."

Development of a pricing strategy is not a one-time occurrence. The strategy needs to be reviewed when a new product is introduced, an existing product is revised, the competitive environment changes, a product moves through its life cycle, a competitor initiates a price change, costs rise or fall, the firm's prices come under government scrutiny, and/or other events take place.

These are indications a pricing strategy may be performing poorly:

- Prices are changed too frequently.
- The pricing policy is difficult to explain to consumers.
- Channel members complain that profit margins are inadequate.
- Price decisions are made without first conducting adequate marketing research.
- Too many different price options are offered.
- Excessive sales personnel time is spent in bargaining.
- Prices are inconsistent with the target market.

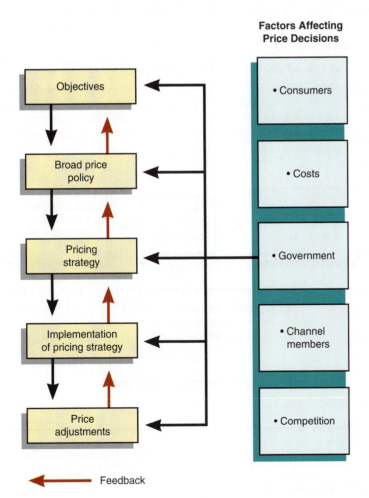

Figure 21-1

A Framework for Developing and Applying a Price Strategy

- A high percentage of goods is marked down or discounted late in the selling season to clear out surplus inventory.
- Too high a proportion of customers is price-sensitive and attracted by competitors' discounts. Demand is elastic.
- The firm has problems conforming to pricing legislation.

This chapter describes in detail the pricing framework outlined in Figure 21-1.

21-2   PRICING OBJECTIVES

A pricing strategy should be consistent with and reflect overall company goals. It is possible for different firms in the same industry to have dissimilar objectives and, therefore, distinct pricing strategies.[2]

Firms may select from three general objectives: sales-based, profit-based, and status quo-based. See Figure 21-2. With sales-based goals, a firm wants sales growth and/or to maximize market share. With profit-based goals, it wants to maximize profit, earn a satisfactory profit, optimize the return on investment, and/or secure an early recovery of cash. With status quo-based goals, it seeks to avoid unfavorable government actions, minimize the effects of competitor actions, maintain good channel relations, discourage the entry of competitors, reduce demands from suppliers, and/or stabilize prices.

A firm may pursue more than one pricing goal, such as increasing revenues by 5 to 10 percent each year, achieving a 15 percent return on capital investments, and keeping prices near those of competitors. It may also set distinct short- and long-run goals. In the short run, it may seek high profit margins on new products; in the long run, these profit margins would drop to discourage potential competitors.

21-2a   Sales-Based Objectives

A firm with *sales-based pricing objectives* is oriented toward high sales volume and/or expanding its share of sales relative to competitors. The company focuses on sales-based goals for any (or all) of three reasons: (1) It sees market saturation or sales growth as a major step leading to market control and sustained profits. (2) It wants to maximize unit sales and will trade low per-unit profits for larger total profits. (3) It assumes greater sales will enable it to have lower per-unit costs.

> **Sales based pricing objectives** seek high volume or market share.

Figure 21-2

Pricing Objectives

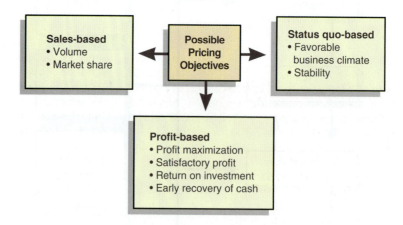

[2] See Richard A. Lancioni, "A Strategic Approach to Industrial Product Pricing: The Pricing Plan," *Industrial Marketing Management*, Vol. 34 (February 2005), pp. 177–183; Linda Lisanti, "The Price of Beauty," *Convenience Store News* (November 15, 2005), pp. 59–64; Scott Miller, "Pricing Power: Using Price Strategy Road Maps and Tools to Maximize Bottom-Line Results," *CMA Management* (May 2008), pp. 26–32; and Ruiliang Yan, "Pricing Strategy for Companies with Mixed Online and Traditional Retailing Distribution Markets," *Journal of Product & Brand Management*, Vol. 17 (February 2008), pp. 48–56.

To gain high sales volume, ***penetration pricing*** is often employed, whereby low prices are used to capture the mass market for a good or service. It is a proper approach if customers are highly sensitive to price, low prices discourage actual and potential competitors, there are economies of scale (per-unit production and distribution costs fall as sales rise), and a large consumer market exists. Penetration pricing also recognizes that a high price may leave a product vulnerable to competition.

Penetration pricing is used by such firms as NetZero, Malt-O-Meal, and Costco. For $9.95 monthly, NetZero (**http://www.netzero.com**) markets a dialup Internet connection with these features: unlimited access, spam and E-mail virus protection, 1 gigabyte of E-mail storage, nationwide coverage, and 24/7 support. Malt-O-Meal (**http://www.malt-o-meal.com**) makes no-frills cereals and sells many of them in bags rather than boxes. Its prices are far less than those of better-known brands. Kirkland is the low-priced private brand of discounter Costco (**http://www.costco.com**) that is used with apparel, food, and many other products.

Penetration pricing may tap markets not originally anticipated. For example, few people forecast that cordless phones would reach the sales attained during their peak. The market expanded rapidly after prices fell below $100. It grew again as new models were sold for $50 and less, and then for $25 and less.

> **Penetration pricing** aims at the mass market.

21-2b   Profit-Based Objectives

A firm having ***profit-based pricing objectives*** orients its strategy toward some type of profit goals. With profit-maximization goals, high dollar profits are sought. With satisfactory-profit goals, stability over time is desired, rather than maximum profits in a given year (which could cause a fall in nonpeak years); steady profits for many years are sought. With return-on-investment goals, profits are related to outlays; these goals are often sought by regulated utilities to justify rate increases. With early-recovery-of-cash goals, high initial profits are sought because firms are short of funds or uncertain about their future.

Profit may be expressed in per-unit or total terms. Per-unit profit equals the revenue a seller receives for one unit sold minus its costs. A product such as custom-made furniture has a high unit profit. Total profit equals the revenue a seller receives for all

> **Profit-based pricing objectives** range from maximization of profit to recovery of cash. Goals can be per unit or total.

Marketing and the Web

What Pricing Approach Is Best for Online Music Downloads?

Apple Computer, the maker of the iPod music player (**http://www.apple.com/ipodstore**), has sold 5 billion song downloads through its online iTunes Music Store (**http://www.apple.com/itunes**) which began in 2003. It charges 99 cents per song. With a catalog of 6 million songs, it appeals to music lovers who no longer buy CDs. Apple is the second-largest U.S. music retailer, behind only Wal-Mart (**http://www.walmart.com**).

To date, Apple has been a clear winner over Napster (**http://www.napster.com**), eMusic (**http://www.emusic.com**), and Rhapsody (**http://www.rhapsody.com**), which sell subscriptions to download music. These firms enable users to download unlimited amounts of music on a subscription basis.

Napster has 800,000 subscribers who pay about $13 per month to download its library of 6 million songs. However, it keeps only about 30 percent of its subscription sales revenues and about 10 percent on its download sales. eMusic has 400,000 subscribers who pay as little as 33 cents to download each song. eMusic has no contracts with major labels. It has deals with 33,000 independent labels. Rhapsody is a subscription music service jointly owned by RealNetworks (**http://www.realnetworks.com**) and Viacom (**http://www.viacom.com**). In 2008, Yahoo! moved its existing Yahoo! Music Unlimited subscribers (who paid $8.99 per month) to Rhapsody. Yahoo! discontinued its subscription service due to the high costs of making music downloads compatible over a wide range of electronic devices. RealNetworks has 3 million subscribers to its various music services, including Rhapsody.

Sources: Based on material in Jim Dalrymple, "Apple Is the Number-Two Music Retailer in the United States," *Macworld* (May 2008), p. 27; Devin Leonard, "How eMusic Hopes to Keep Its Groove," **http://money.cnn.com/2008/07/15/technology/emusic.fortune/index.htm** (July 16, 2008); and Nick Wingfield, "Music Unlimited No More—Yahoo! Aims to End Subscription Service, Promote Rhapsody," *Wall Street Journal* (February 4, 2008), p. B2.

items sold minus total costs. It is computed by multiplying per-unit profit times the number of units sold. A product such as mass-marketed furniture has a low unit profit; success is based on the number of units sold (turnover). Products with high per-unit profits may have lower total profits than ones with low per-unit profits if the discount prices of the latter generate a much greater level of consumer demand. This depends on the elasticity of demand.

Skimming pricing uses high prices to attract the market segment more concerned with product quality, uniqueness, or status than price. It is proper if competition can be minimized (via patent protection, brand loyalty, raw material control, or high capital requirements); funds are needed for early cash recovery or further expansion; consumers are insensitive to price or willing to pay a high initial price; and unit costs remain equal or rise as sales increase (economies of scale are absent).

Skimming prices are used by such firms as Genentech, Cartier, and British Airways. Genentech (**http://www.gene.com**) makes Activase, a patented brand of TPA (tissue plasminogen activator), which quickly clears the blood clots associated with heart attacks and effectively treats certain strokes. Activase sells for $1,700 for one 50-mg dose and $3,400 for one 100-mg dose. One version of Cartier's (**http://www.cartier.com**) Tank Américaine ladies watch retails for $25,000 or so. The watch has an 18-karat yellow gold bracelet, a case set in diamonds, and other luxury features. British Airways' (**http://www. britishairways.com**) first-class cabins provide passengers with fully reclining seats: "We'll prepare your bed when you're ready to sleep with our turndown service. Then sink into total comfort with a soft undermatress, cozy duvet [comforter], and plump pillow, all covered in the finest 100 percent Egyptian cotton." It targets those who will pay about $15,000 for a roundtrip between London and New York.

Firms may first use skimming pricing and then penetration pricing, or they may market both a premium brand and a value brand. There are many advantages to this:

- High prices are charged when competition is limited.
- High prices help cover development and introductory advertising costs.
- The first group of customers to buy a new product is usually less price-sensitive.
- High initial prices portray a high-quality image.
- Raising initial prices may be resisted by consumers; lowering them is viewed favorably.
- After the initial market segment is saturated, penetration pricing can appeal to the mass market and expand total sales volume.
- Multiple segments can be reached.

21-2c   Status Quo-Based Objectives

Status quo-based pricing objectives are sought by a firm interested in continuing a favorable business climate for its operations or in stability. The pricing strategy is used to minimize the impact of such outside parties as government, competitors, and channel members—and to avoid sales declines.

It should be not inferred that status quo goals require no effort. A firm must instruct salespeople not to offer different terms to competing channel members or it may face a Robinson-Patman Act violation. It may have to match competitors' price cuts to keep customers—while trying to avoid price wars. It may have to accept lower profit margins in the face of rising costs to hold channel cooperation. It may have to charge penetration prices to discourage competitors from marketing certain product lines.

21-3   BROAD PRICE POLICY

A **broad price policy** sets the overall direction (and tone) for a firm's pricing efforts and makes sure pricing decisions are coordinated with the firm's choices as to a target market, an image, and other marketing-mix factors. It includes short- and long-term

---

Skimming pricing is aimed at the segment interested in quality or status.

Status quo-based pricing objectives seek good business conditions and stability.

A **broad price policy** links prices with the target market, image, and other marketing elements.

pricing goals. Pricing can play a passive role—with customer purchases based on service, convenience, and quality—or it can play an active role—with purchases based on low prices. A high-income segment buying status brands would expect premium prices. A moderate-income segment buying private brands would expect low prices.

A firm outlines a broad price policy by integrating individual decisions. It then decides on the interrelationship of prices for items within a product line, how often discounts are used, how prices compare to competition, the frequency of price changes, and the method for setting new-product prices.

Utilizing an integrated broad price policy is not effortless:

> To do pricing right, you need a basic indication of what the customer is willing to pay, and you've got to know the benefits a product will provide. But how do you do it if you're starting from scratch? And how do you decide whether to lower a price you've already established when you find yourself in a competitive situation? Consider this scenario: Your firm is in a heated selling bake-off. Your competition's pricing is similar, but you have better profit margins. You know you can offer a price way under the competition. Should you? (1) Be aware of what differentiates you from competitors. If you have a tangible differentiator, don't lower your price. (2) Know the right price point. Getting a foot in the door is key. (3) Make it clear if you're a specialist or a commodity provider. A specialist can charge more, but a commodity provider can learn to differentiate on service.[3]

21-4 PRICING STRATEGY

A pricing strategy may be cost-, demand-, and/or competition-based. When the approaches are integrated, combination pricing is involved. See Figure 21-3. Next, we explain each method and provide illustrations.

21-4a   Cost-Based Pricing

In *cost-based pricing*, a firm sets prices by computing merchandise, service, and overhead costs and then adding an amount to cover its profit goal. Table 21-1 defines the key concepts in cost-based pricing and shows how they may be applied to big-screen television sets.

Cost-based prices are rather easy to derive because there is no need to estimate elasticity of demand or competitive reactions to price changes. There is also greater certainty about costs than demand or competitor responses to prices. Finally, cost-based pricing seeks reasonable profits because it is geared to covering all types of costs. It is often used by firms whose goals are stated in terms of profit or return on investment. A *price floor* is the lowest acceptable price a firm can charge and attain its profit goal.

When used by itself, cost-based pricing does have some significant limitations. It does not consider market conditions, the full effects of excess plant capacity, competitive prices, the product's phase in its life cycle, market share goals, consumers' ability to pay, and other factors.

Sometimes, it is hard to figure how such overhead costs as rent, lighting, personnel, and other general expenses should be allocated. These costs are often assigned in terms of product sales or the personnel time associated with each item. If product A accounts for 10 percent of sales, it may be allotted 10 percent of overhead costs. If product B gets 20 percent of personnel time, it may be allotted 20 percent of overhead costs. Problems may arise because different ways of assigning costs may yield varying results: How are costs allotted if a product yields 10 percent of sales and needs 20 percent of personnel time?

> Under **cost-based pricing**, expenses are computed, profit is projected, and a **price floor** is set.

---

[3] Christine Comaford-Lynch, "The Fine Art of Pricing Your Product," **http://www.businessweek.com/smallbiz** (December 17, 2007).

Figure 21-3

The Alternative Ways of Developing a Pricing Strategy

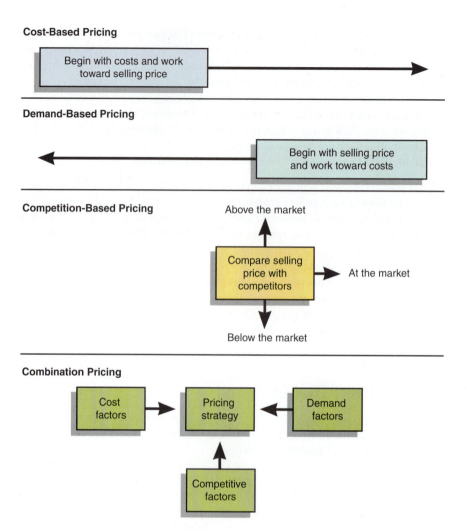

Cost-Based Pricing

Begin with costs and work toward selling price

Demand-Based Pricing

Begin with selling price and work toward costs

Competition-Based Pricing

Above the market

Compare selling price with competitors

At the market

Below the market

Combination Pricing

Cost factors → Pricing strategy ← Demand factors

Competitive factors ↑

In the following subsections, we cover five cost-based pricing techniques: cost-plus, markup, target, price-floor, and traditional break-even analysis. Figure 21-4 gives a synopsis of each technique. And at the end of these subsections, Table 21-2 contains numerical examples of them. See page 649.

Cost-Plus Pricing For *cost-plus pricing*, prices are set by adding a predetermined profit to costs. It is the simplest form of cost-based pricing. Generally, the steps for computing cost-plus prices are to estimate the number of units to be produced, calculate fixed and variable costs, and add a desired profit to costs. The formula is

$$\text{Price} = \frac{\text{Total fixed costs} + \text{Total variable costs} + \text{Projected profit}}{\text{Units produced}}$$

This method is easy to compute; yet, it has shortcomings. Profit is not expressed in relation to sales but in relation to costs, and price is not tied to consumer demand. Adjustments for rising costs are poorly conceived, and there are no plans for using excess capacity. There is little incentive to improve efficiency to hold down costs, and marginal costs are rarely analyzed.

Cost-plus pricing is most effective when price fluctuations have little influence on sales and when a firm is able to control prices. The prices of custom-made furniture, ships, heavy machinery, and extracted minerals typically depend on the costs incurred in producing these items; thus, companies set prices by computing costs and adding a reasonable profit. Cost-plus pricing often allows firms to get consumer orders, produce items, and then derive prices after total costs are known. This protects sellers.

> **Cost-plus pricing** is the easiest form of pricing, based on units produced, total costs, and profit.

Table 21-1 Key Cost Concepts and How They May Be Applied to Big-Screen Television Sets

Cost Concept	Definition	Examples[a]	Sources of Information	Method of Computation
Total fixed costs	Ongoing costs not related to volume. They are usually constant over a given range of output for a specified time.	Rent, salaries, electricity, real-estate taxes, plant, and equipment.	Accounting data, bills, cost estimates.	Addition of all fixed cost components.
Total variable costs	Costs that change with increases or decreases in output (volume).	Parts (such as tuners and speakers), hourly employees who assemble sets, and sales commissions.	Cost data from suppliers, estimates of labor productivity, sales estimates.	Addition of all variable cost components.
Total costs	Sum of total fixed and total variable costs.	See above.	See above.	Addition of all fixed and variable cost components.
Average fixed costs	Average fixed costs per unit.	See above under total fixed costs.	Total fixed costs and production estimates.	Total fixed costs/ Quantity produced in units.
Average variable costs	Average variable costs per unit.	See above under total variable costs.	Total variable costs and production estimates.	Total variable costs/ Quantity produced in units.
Average total costs	Sum of average fixed costs and average variable costs.	See above under total fixed and total variable costs.	Total costs and production estimates.	Average fixed costs + Average variable costs or Total costs/Quantity produced in units.
Marginal costs	Costs of making an additional unit.	See above under total fixed and total variable costs.	Accounting data, bills, cost estimates of labor and materials.	(Total costs of producing current quantity + one unit) – (Total costs of producing current quantity).

[a] Such marketing costs as advertising and distribution are often broken down into both fixed and variable components.

Markup Pricing A firm uses *markup pricing* when it sets prices by computing the per-unit costs of producing (buying) goods and/or services and then determining the markup percentages needed to cover selling costs and profit. It is most commonly used by wholesalers and retailers, although it is employed by all types of organizations. The formula for markup pricing is:[4]

> **Markup pricing** considers per-unit product costs and the markups required to cover selling costs and profits. Markups should be expressed in terms of price rather than cost.

$$\text{Price} = \frac{\text{Product cost}}{(100 - \text{Markup percent})/100}$$

Several reasons explain why markups are commonly stated in terms of selling price instead of cost: (1) Because expenses, markdowns, and profits are computed as a percentage of sales, when markups are also cited as a percentage of sales, they aid in profit planning. (2) Firms quote their selling prices and trade discounts to channel members as percentage reductions from final list prices. (3) Competitive price data are

[4] Markup can be calculated by transposing the formula into

$$\text{Markup percentage} = \frac{\text{Price} - \text{Product cost}}{\text{Price}} \times 100$$

Figure 21-4

Cost-Based Pricing Techniques

Cost-Plus Pricing
• Adds pre-determined profit to costs

Traditional Break-Even Analysis
• Determines sales quantity needed to break even at a given price

Price-Floor Pricing
• Determines lowest price at which to offer additional units for sale

Markup pricing
• Calculates percentage markup needed to cover selling costs and profit

Cost-Based Pricing Techniques

Target Pricing
• Seeks specified rate of return at a standard volume of production

A **variable markup policy** responds to differences in selling costs among products.

more readily available than cost data. (4) Profitability appears smaller if based on price rather than on cost. This may be useful to avoid criticism over high earnings.

Markup size depends on traditional profit margins, selling and operating expenses, suggested list prices, inventory turnover, competition, the extent to which products must be serviced, and the effort needed to complete transactions. Due to differences in selling costs among products, some firms use a **variable markup policy**, whereby separate categories of goods and services receive different percentage markups. Variable markups recognize that some items require greater personal selling, customer service, alterations, and end-of-season markdowns than others. Expensive cosmetics need more personal selling and customer service than paperback books, suits need greater custom alterations than shirts, and fashion items are marked down more than basic clothing late in the selling season.

Markup pricing, though having many of cost-plus pricing's limitations, is popular. It is fairly simple, especially for firms with uniform markups across several items. Channel members get fair profits. Price competition is less if firms have similar markups. Resellers can show their actual prices compared to suggested prices. Adjustments can be made as costs rise. Variable markups are responsive to selling-cost differences among products or channel members.

Target pricing enables a rate of return on investment to be earned for a standard volume of production.

Target Pricing

In **target pricing**, prices are set to provide a particular rate of return on investment for a standard volume of production—the level of production a firm anticipates achieving. In the paper industry, prices are usually based on the standard volume of production being set at 90 to 92 percent of plant capacity. For target pricing to operate properly, a company must sell its entire standard volume at specified prices.

Target pricing is used by capital-intensive firms (such as auto makers) and public utilities (such as water companies). The prices charged by utilities are based on fair rates of return on invested assets and must be approved by regulatory commissions. Mathematically, a target price is computed as

$$\text{Price} = \frac{\text{Investment costs} \times \text{Target return on investment (\%)}}{\text{Standard volume}}$$
$$+ \text{Average total costs (at standard volume)}$$

Target pricing has five major shortcomings: (1) It is not useful for firms with low capital investments; it understates selling price. (2) Because prices are not keyed to demand, the entire standard volume may not be sold at the target price. (3) Production problems may hamper output, and standard volume may not be attained. (4) Price cuts to handle overstocked inventory are not planned. (5) If the standard volume is reduced due to unexpected poor sales performance, the price would have to be raised.

Table 21-2 Examples of Cost-Based Pricing Techniques

Cost-Plus Pricing—A custom-bed maker has total fixed costs of $200,000, variable costs of $1,500 per bed, desires $100,000 in profits, and plans to produce 1,000 beds. What is the selling price per bed?

$$\text{Price} = \frac{\text{Total fixed costs} + \text{Total variable costs} + \text{Projected profit}}{\text{Units produced}} = \underline{\$1,800}$$

Markup Pricing—A retailer pays $25 for full-featured cordless telephones and wants a markup on selling price of 40 percent (30 percent for selling costs and 10 percent for profit). What is the final selling price?

$$\text{Price} = \frac{\text{Merchandise costs}}{(100 - \text{Markup percent})/100} = \underline{\$41.67}$$

Target Pricing—A manufacturer of mid-sized economy cars has spent $160,000,000 for a new plant. It has a 25 percent target return on investment. Standard production volume for the year is 5,000 units. Average total costs, excluding the new plant, are $14,000 for each car (at a production level of 5,000 cars). What is the selling price to the firm's retail dealers?

$$\text{Price} = \frac{\text{Investment costs} \times \text{Target return on investment}(\%)}{\text{Standard volume}} + \text{Average total costs (at standard volume)} = \underline{\$22,000}$$

Price-Floor Pricing—A big-screen HD-TV manufacturer's plant capacity is 1,000 units. Its total fixed costs are $500,000 and variable costs are $375 per unit. At full production, average fixed costs are $500 per unit. The firm sets a price of $1,100 to retailers and gets orders for 800 TVs at that price. It must operate at 80 percent of capacity, unless it re-evaluates its pricing strategy. With price-floor pricing, it can sell the 200 additional sets to retailers. How?

The firm could let resellers buy one TV at $425 for every four they buy at $1,100. Then, it earns a profit of $90,000 [revenues of ($1,100 × 800) + ($425 × 200) less costs of ($875 × 1,000)]. If it just makes and sells 800 TVs at full price, it earns $80,000 [revenues of ($1,100 × 800) less variable costs of ($375 × 800) and fixed costs of ($500,000)]. The higher profits are due to marginal revenue > marginal cost.

Traditional Break-Even Analysis—A small candy maker has total fixed costs of $150,000 and variable costs per unit of $0.25. It sells to retailers for $0.40 per bar. What is the break-even point in units? In sales dollars?

$$\text{Break-even point (units)} = \frac{\text{Total fixed costs}}{\text{Price} - \text{Variable costs (per unit)}} = \underline{1,000,000}$$

$$\text{Break-even point (sales dollars)} = \frac{\text{Total fixed costs}}{1 - \dfrac{\text{Variable costs (per unit)}}{\text{Price}}} = \underline{\$400,000}$$

Price-Floor Pricing A firm's usual goal is to set prices to cover the sum of average fixed costs, average variable costs, and profit per unit. But when a firm has excess (unused) capacity, it may use *price-floor pricing* to find the lowest price at which it is worthwhile to increase the amount of goods or services it makes available for sale. The general principle is that the sale of additional units can be used to increase profits or help pay for fixed costs (which exist whether or not these items are made), as long as marginal revenues are greater than marginal costs. Although a firm cannot survive in the long run unless its average total costs are covered by prices, it may improve performance through price-floor pricing. The formula is

> Price-floor price = Marginal revenue per unit > Marginal cost per unit

Price-floor pricing may be used if there is excess capacity.

Traditional Break-Even Analysis As with target pricing, traditional break-even analysis looks at the relationship among costs, revenues, and profits. Whereas target pricing yields the price that results in a specified return on investment, *traditional break-even analysis* finds the sales quantity in units or dollars that is needed for total revenues (price × units sold) to equal total costs (fixed and variable) at a given price. If sales exceed the break-even quantity, a firm earns a profit. If sales are less than the break-even quantity, it loses money. Traditional break-even analysis does not consider return on investment, but can be extended to take profit planning into account. It is used by all kinds of sellers.

Traditional break-even analysis computes the sales needed to break even at a specific price.

The break-even point can be computed in terms of units or sales dollars:

$$\text{Break-even point (units)} = \frac{\text{Total fixed costs}}{\text{Price} - \text{Variable costs (per unit)}}$$

$$\text{Break-even point (sales dollars)} = \frac{\text{Total fixed costs}}{1 - \dfrac{\text{Variable costs (per unit)}}{\text{Price}}}$$

The preceding formulas are derived from the equation: Price × Quantity = Total fixed costs + (Variable costs per unit × Quantity).

Break-even analysis can be adjusted to take into account the profit sought by a firm:

$$\text{Break-even point (units)} = \frac{\text{Total fixed costs} + \text{Projected profit}}{\text{Price} - \text{Variable costs (per unit)}}$$

$$\text{Break-even point (sales dollars)} = \frac{\text{Total fixed costs} + \text{Projected profit}}{1 - \dfrac{\text{Variable costs (per unit)}}{\text{Price}}}$$

There are limitations to traditional break-even analysis: (1) As with all cost-based pricing, demand is not considered. It is presumed that wide variations in quantity can be sold at the same price; this is highly unlikely. (2) It is assumed that all costs can be divided into fixed and variable categories. Yet, some, such as advertising, are difficult to define; advertising can be fixed or a percent of sales. (3) It is assumed that variable costs per unit are constant over a range of quantities, but purchase discounts or overtime wages may alter the costs. (4) It is assumed that fixed costs remain constant; but increases in production may lead to higher costs for new equipment, new full-time employees, and other items.

By including demand considerations, each of the cost-based techniques can be improved. Demand-based pricing techniques are discussed next.

21-4b Demand-Based Pricing

Under **demand-based pricing**, consumers are researched and a **price ceiling** is set.

With *demand-based pricing*, a firm sets prices after studying consumer desires and ascertaining the range of prices acceptable to the target market. This approach is used by firms that believe price is a key factor in consumer decision making. These firms identify a *price ceiling*, which is the maximum amount consumers will pay for a given good or service. If the ceiling is exceeded, consumers will not make purchases. Its level depends on the elasticity of demand (availability of substitutes and urgency of need) and consumers' subjective price regarding the particular good or service.

Demand-based methods require consumer research as to the quantities that will be bought at various prices, sensitivity to price changes, the existence of market segments, and consumers' ability to pay. Demand estimates tend to be less precise than cost estimates. Also, firms that do inadequate cost analysis and rely on demand data may end up losing money if they make unrealistically low cost assumptions.

Under demand-based pricing, very competitive situations may lead to small markups and lower prices because people will buy substitutes; costs must be held down or prices will be too high—as might occur via cost-based pricing. For noncompetitive situations, firms can set large markups and high prices because demand is rather inelastic. Less emphasis is placed on costs when setting prices in these situations. Firms are more apt to set overly low prices in noncompetitive markets with cost-based pricing.

Four demand-based pricing techniques are reviewed next: demand-minus, chain-markup, modified break-even analysis, and price discrimination. Figure 21-5 gives a synopsis of each technique. And at the end of these subsections, Table 21-3 contains numerical examples of them. See page 652.

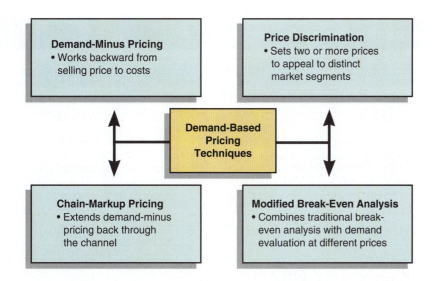

Figure 21-5

Demand-Based Pricing
Techniques

Demand-Minus Pricing Through *demand-minus (demand-backward) pricing*, a firm finds the proper selling price and works backward to compute costs. This approach requires that price decisions revolve around consumer demand rather than company operations. It is used by firms selling directly to consumers.

Demand-minus pricing has three steps: Selling price is determined via consumer surveys or other research. The required markup percentage is set based on selling expenses and desired profits. The maximum acceptable per-unit cost for making or buying a product is computed. This formula is used, and it shows that product cost is derived after selling price and markup are set:

$$\text{Maximum product cost} = \text{Price} \times [(100 - \text{Markup percent})/100]$$

The difficulty in demand-minus pricing is that research may be time consuming or complex, especially if many items are involved. Also, new-product pricing research may be particularly inaccurate.

Chain-Markup Pricing *Chain-markup pricing* extends demand-minus calculations all the way from resellers back to suppliers (manufacturers). With it, final selling price is determined, markups for each channel member are examined, and the maximum acceptable costs to each member are computed.

In a typical consumer-goods channel, the markup chain is composed of

1. Maximum selling price to retailer = Final selling price ×
   $$[(100 - \text{Retailer's markup})/100]$$

2. Maximum selling price to wholesaler = Selling price to retailer ×
   $$[(100 - \text{Wholesaler's markup})/100]$$

3. Maximum product cost to manufacturer = Selling price to wholesaler ×
   $$[(100 - \text{Manufacturer's markup})/100]$$

By using chain-markup pricing, price decisions can be related to consumer demand, and each reseller is able to see the effects of price changes on the total distribution channel. The interdependence of firms becomes clearer; they cannot set prices independently of one another.

Modified Break-Even Analysis *Modified break-even analysis* combines traditional break-even analysis with an evaluation of demand at various levels of price. Traditional

In **demand-minus (demand-backward) pricing,** selling price, then markup, and finally maximum product costs are computed.

Chain-markup pricing traces demand-minus calculations from channel members to suppliers.

Modified break-even analysis melds traditional break-even analysis with demand evaluation at various prices.

| Table 21-3 | Examples of Demand-Based Pricing Techniques |

Demand-Minus Pricing—A hardware manufacturer has done consumer research and found that contractors are willing to spend $60.00 for its flagship electric drill. Selling expenses and profits are expected to be 35 percent of the selling price. What is the maximum the manufacturer can spend to develop and produce each drill?

Maximum merchandise costs = Price × [(100 – Markup percent)/100] = <u>$39.00</u>

Chain-Markup Pricing—A ladies' shoe maker knows women will pay $100.00 for a pair of its shoes. It sells via wholesalers and retailers. Each requires a markup of 30 percent; the manufacturer wants a 25 percent markup. (a) What is the maximum price that retailers and wholesalers will spend for a pair of shoes? (b) What is the maximum the manufacturer can spend to make each pair of shoes?

(a) Maximum selling price to retailer = Final selling price × [(100 – Retailer's markup)/100] = <u>$70.00</u>

Maximum selling price to wholesaler = Selling price to retailer × [(100 – Wholesaler's markup)/100] = <u>$49.00</u>

(b) Maximum merchandise costs to manufacturer = Selling price to wholesaler × [(100 – Manufacturer's markup)/100] = <u>$36.75</u>

Modified Break-Even Analysis—An aspirin maker has total fixed costs of $2,000,000 and variable costs of $1.50 per bottle. Research shows the following demand schedule. At what price should the company sell its aspirin?

Selling Price	Quantity Demanded	Total Revenue	Total Cost	Total Profit (Loss)	
$3.00	2,000,000	$ 6,000,000	$5,000,000	$1,000,000	Maximum
2.50	3,200,000	8,000,000	6,800,000	1,200,000	← profit at
2.00	5,000,000	10,000,000	9,500,000	500,000	price of <u>$2.50</u>

Price Discrimination—A sports team knows people will pay different prices for tickets, based on location. It offers 5,000 tickets at $50 each, 25,000 at $20 each, and 20,000 at $12 each. What are profits if total costs per game are $750,000?

Profit = (Revenues from segment A + segment B + segment C) – Total costs = <u>$240,000</u>

analysis focuses on the sales needed to break even at a given price. It does not indicate the likely level of demand at that price, examine how consumers respond to different levels of price, consider that the break-even point can vary greatly depending on the price the firm happens to select, or calculate the price that maximizes profits.

Modified analysis reveals the price-quantity mix that maximizes profits. It shows that profits do not inevitably rise as the quantity sold increases because lower prices may be needed to expand demand. It also verifies that a firm should examine various price levels and select the one with the greatest profits. Finally, it relates demand to price, rather than assuming that the same volume could be sold at any price.

Price Discrimination

With a *price discrimination* approach, a firm sets two or more distinct prices for a product so as to appeal to different final consumers or organizational consumer segments. Higher prices are offered to inelastic segments and lower prices to elastic ones. Price discrimination can be customer-based, product-based, time-based, or place-based.[5]

In *customer-based price discrimination*, prices differ by customer category for the same good or service. Price differentials may relate to a consumer's ability to pay (doctors, lawyers, and accountants partially set prices in this manner), negotiating ability (the price of an office building is usually set by bargaining), or buying power (discounts are given for volume purchases).

> **Price discrimination** entails setting distinct prices to reach different market segments.

---

[5] See Paul W. Dobson and Michael Waterson, "Chain-Store Pricing Across Local Markets," *Journal of Economics & Management Strategy*, Vol. 14 (March 2005), pp. 93–119; Dipayan Biswas and Stacy Landreth Grau, "Consumer Choices Under Product Option Framing: Loss Aversion Principles Or Sensitivity to Price Differentials?" *Psychology and Marketing*, Vol. 25 (May 2008), pp. 399–415; and Andrew Cohen, "Package Size and Price Discrimination in the Paper Towel Market," *International Journal of Industrial Organization*, Vol. 26 (March 2008), pp. 502–516.

Global Marketing in Action

The $100 Computer Finally Comes to the Marketplace

Rajesh Jain's latest product is NetPC, a computer with a Web browser and E-mail, word processing, and spreadsheet capabilities. What sets NetPC apart from its competitors is its $100 purchase price or $10 a month leasing fee. The development of an inexpensive computer is seen as essential to increase PC usage in such nations as Brazil, China, India, and Russia. In many of these markets, traditional PCs are viewed by most potential consumers as either too expensive, too difficult to use, and/or too difficult to maintain.

Jain's firm, Novatium (http://www.novatium.com), is able to produce its computers at a fraction of the cost of many competitors. These firms have tried to reduce costs by using older and slower microprocessors, less memory, and smaller hard drives. On the other hand, to reduce its costs, the Novatium computer uses the same inexpensive microprocessor as found in a wireless phone. Its $100 model is little more than a keyboard, a screen, and a couple of USB ports. A central network is used to run software and to store a user's data. Another Novatium model, NetTV, is similar to the NetPC but is connected to a user's television instead of a PC monitor.

The notion of Web-hosted software and data storage has caused many software providers, including Microsoft (http://www.microsoft.com), to begin rethinking their traditional model of selling software that is installed on a consumer's own computer. Some analysts feel that if Novatium's model is successful in developing countries, other major computer manufacturers will copy its strategy.

The first NetPCs were introduced in Mauritius (an island off the coast of southern Africa) in mid-2008. Novatium's goal is to sell units to 1 million households worldwide by 2012.

Sources: Based on material in Jason Overdorf, "The $100 Un-Pc," http://www.newsweek.com/id/42955 (February 12, 2007); and "Novatium NetPC Goes International!," http://www.efytimes.com/efytimes/fullnews.asp?edid=27735 (July 25, 2008).

Through *product-based price discrimination*, a firm markets a number of features, styles, qualities, brands, or sizes of a product and sets a different price for each product version. Price differentials are greater than cost differentials for the various versions. A dishwasher may be priced at $500 in white and $550 in brown, although the brown color costs the manufacturer only $10 more. There is inelastic demand by customers desiring the special color, and product versions are priced accordingly.

Through *time-based price discrimination*, a firm varies prices by day versus evening (movie theater tickets), time of day (telephone and utility rates), or season (hotel rates). Consumers who insist on prime-time use pay higher prices than those who are willing to make their purchases during nonpeak times.

In *place-based price discrimination*, prices differ by seat location (sports events), floor location (office buildings), or geographic location (resort cities). Demand for locations near the field, elevators, or warm climates drives the prices of these locations up. General admission tickets, basement offices, and moderate-temperature resorts are priced lower to attract consumers to otherwise less desirable purchases.

When a firm engages in price discrimination, it should use ***yield management pricing***—whereby it determines the mix of price-quantity combinations that generates the highest level of revenues for a given time. A company should give itself every opportunity to sell as many goods and services at full price as possible, while also seeking to sell as many units as it can. It should not sell so many low-price items that it jeopardizes full-price sales. A 1,000-seat theater offering first-run plays must decide how many tickets to sell as preferred seating (at $100 each) and how many as general admission (at $40 each). If it tries to sell too many preferred seating tickets, there may be empty seats. If it looks to sell too many general admission tickets, the theater may be full—but total revenues may be unsatisfactory. Yield management pricing is now easier to utilize due to the availability of inexpensive computer software. It is especially popular with airlines and hotels, and widely used by Internet firms.[6] These Web sites

> **Yield management pricing** lets firms optimize price discrimination efforts.

---

[6] See Barry Berman, "Applying Yield Management Pricing to Your Service Business," *Business Horizons*, Vol. 48 (March-April 2005), pp. 169–179.

are good sources for information on yield management pricing: Veritec Solutions (**http://www.veritecsolutions.com/Articles.htm**) and Managing Change (**http://www.managingchange.com/dynamic/yieldmgt.htm**).

Before engaging in price discrimination, a firm should address these questions: Are there distinct market segments? Do people talk to each other about prices? Can product versions be differentiated? Will some people choose low-priced versions when they might buy high-priced versions if those are the only ones sold? How do the marginal costs of adding product alternatives compare with marginal revenues? Will channel members stock all models? How hard is it to explain product differences to consumers? Under what conditions is price discrimination legal (so as to not violate the Robinson-Patman Act)?

21-4c   Competition-Based Pricing

> **Competition-based pricing** is setting prices relative to other firms.

Competition-based pricing is involved when a firm uses competitors' prices rather than demand or cost considerations as its primary pricing guideposts. That firm may not respond to changes in demand or costs unless those changes also affect competitors' prices. It can set prices below the market, at the market, or above the market, depending on its customers, image, marketing mix, consumer loyalty, and other factors. This approach is used by firms contending with others selling similar items (or those perceived as similar).

Because it is simple and does not rely on demand curves, price elasticity, or costs per unit, competition-based pricing is popular. The ongoing market price is often assumed to be fair for both consumers and firms. Pricing at the market level does not disrupt competition or lead to retaliations. It may lead to complacency, and different firms may not have the same demand and cost structures.

We now discuss two aspects of competition-based pricing: price leadership and competitive bidding.

Price Leadership   *Price leadership* exists in situations where one firm (or a few firms) is usually the first to announce price changes and others in the industry follow. The price leader's role is to set prices that reflect market conditions, without disrupting the marketplace—it must not turn off consumers with price increases perceived as too large or precipitate a price war with competitors by excessive price cuts.

> **Price leadership** occurs when one or a few firms initiate price changes in an industry; they are effective when others follow.

Price leaders are often firms with significant market shares, well-established positions, respect from competitors, and a desire to initiate price changes. Consider Southwest Airlines (**http://www.southwest.com**):

> Today, Southwest operates over 500 Boeing 737 aircraft in 64 cities. Southwest has the lowest operating-cost structure in the domestic airline industry and consistently offers the lowest and simplest fares. Southwest also has one of the best overall customer service records. The airline has been ranked the top U.S. domestic airline (in terms of number of passengers). Southwest dominates the markets it serves, ranking first in market share in approximately 90 percent of its top 100 city pairs. Its strong market position is driven not just by consistent delivery of low fares but also due to reliable service, frequent and convenient flights, comfortable cabins, in-flight experience, frequent flyer programs, hassle-free airports, and friendly customer service.[7]

Today, the role of price leaders has diminished in many industries, including steel, chemicals, glass containers, and newsprint, as more firms have sought greater independence. Many times, an industry leader has announced higher prices but had to backtrack after competitors decided not to go along.

Announcements of price changes by industry leaders must be communicated through the media. It is illegal for firms in the same industry or in competing ones to confer regarding their prices.

---

[7] "Company Profile," **http://www.southwest.com/investor_relations/fs_ir_index.html** (December 3, 2008); and *Southwest Airlines Co. Company Profile* (New York: Datamonitor USA, May 10, 2007), p. 10.

Competitive Bidding Through *competitive bidding* (discussed in Chapter 9), two or more firms independently submit prices to a customer—usually b-to-b—for a specific good, project, and/or service. Sealed bids may be requested by some government or organizational consumers; each seller then has one chance to make its best offer.

Mathematical models have been applied to competitive bidding. All use the expected profit concept, which states that as the bid price increases, the profit to a firm increases but the probability of its winning a contract decreases. The potential profit (loss) at a given bid can usually be estimated accurately, but the probability of getting a contract (underbidding all other qualified competitors) is hard to determine.

21-4d Combination Pricing

Although we have separately discussed cost-, demand-, and competition-based pricing methods, aspects of the three approaches should be integrated into a **combination pricing** approach. This is done often in practice. A cost-based approach sets a price floor and outlines the costs incurred in doing business. It establishes profit margins, target prices, and/or break-even quantities. A demand-based approach finds the prices consumers will pay, and the ceiling prices for each channel member. It develops the price-quantity mix that maximizes profits and lets a firm reach different market segments (if it so desires). A competition-based approach examines the proper price level for the firm in relation to competitors.

Critical issues may be overlooked unless the approaches are integrated. Table 21-4 shows a list of questions a firm should consider in setting prices.

> It is essential that companies integrate cost, demand, and competitive pricing techniques via **combination pricing.**

21-5 IMPLEMENTING A PRICING STRATEGY

Implementation of a pricing strategy involves many distinct—but related—specific decisions, in addition to the broader concepts just discussed. Decisions involve whether and how to use customary versus variable pricing, a one-price policy versus flexible pricing, odd pricing, the price-quality association, leader pricing, multiple-unit pricing, price lining, price bundling, geographic pricing, and purchase terms.

21-5a Customary Versus Variable Pricing

Customary pricing occurs when a firm sets prices and seeks to maintain them for an extended time. Prices are not changed during this period. Customary pricing is used for items such as candy, gum, magazines, restaurant food, and mass transit. Rather than modify prices to reflect cost increases, firms may reduce package size, change ingredients, or have a more restrictive transfer policy among bus lines. The assumption is that consumers prefer one of these alternatives to constantly changing prices.

Variable pricing lets a firm intentionally alter prices in response to cost fluctuations or differences in consumer demand. When costs change, prices are lowered or raised; the fluctuations are not absorbed and product quality is not modified to maintain customary prices. Through price discrimination, a firm offers distinct prices to appeal to different market segments. The prices charged to diverse consumers are not based on costs, but on consumer price sensitivity. Many firms use some form of variable pricing.

It is possible to combine customary and variable pricing. For example, a magazine may be $3 per single copy and $24 per year's subscription ($2 an issue); thus, two customary prices are available to consumers. The reader then selects the offer he or she finds most attractive. See Figure 21-6.

> One price is maintained over an extended period with **customary pricing.** Prices reflect costs or differences in demand under **variable pricing.**

21-5b A One-Price Policy Versus Flexible Pricing

A *one-price policy* lets a firm charge the same price to all customers seeking to purchase a good or service under similar conditions. Prices may differ according to the quantity

> All those buying the same product pay the same price under a **one-price policy.** Different customers may pay different prices with **flexible pricing.**

Table 21-4	Selected Issues to Consider When Combining Pricing Techniques

Cost-Based

What profit margin does a particular price level permit?

Do markups allow for differences in product investments, installation and servicing, and selling effort and merchandising skills?

Are there accurate and timely cost data by good, service, project, process, and/or store?

Are cost changes monitored and prices adjusted accordingly?

Are there specific profit or return-on-investment goals?

What is the price-floor price for each good, service, project, process, and/or store?

What are the break-even points for each good, service, project, process, and/or store?

Demand-Based

What type of demand does each good, service, project, process, and/or store face?

Has price elasticity been estimated for various price levels?

Are demand-minus, chain-markup, and modified break-even analyses utilized?

Has price discrimination been considered?

How loyal are customers?

Competition-Based

How do prices compare with those of competitors?

Is price leadership used in the industry? By whom?

How do competitors react to price changes?

How are competitive bids determined?

Is the long-run expected profit concept used in competitive bidding?

bought, time of purchase, and services obtained (such as delivery and installation), but all consumers are given the opportunity to pay the same price for the same combinations of goods and services. This builds consumer confidence, is easy to administer, eliminates bargaining, and permits self-service and catalog sales. Today, throughout the United States, one-price policies are the rule for most retailers. In industrial marketing, a firm with a one-price policy would not allow sales personnel to deviate from a published price list.

Through *flexible pricing*, a firm sets prices based on the consumer's ability to negotiate or on the buying power of a large customer. People who are knowledgeable or are good bargainers pay less than those who are not knowledgeable or are weaker bargainers. Jewelry stores, car dealers, real-estate brokers, and many industrial marketers tend to use flexible pricing. Commissions may be keyed to profitability to encourage salespeople to obtain higher prices. Flexible prices to resellers are subject to Robinson-Patman limits. Flexible pricing is more likely outside the United States, where "haggling" may be culturally ingrained. To remedy consumer insecurities about bargaining, Web sites now have guides to educate people. The Woman Motorist site offers a free *New Car Buying Guide* that includes a chapter on "Dealing with Dealers: Negotiating a New Car Purchase," as well as a *Used Car Buying Guide* that has a chapter on "Negotiating a Good Deal." Navigate the Woman Motorist home page to access these guides (**http://www.womanmotorist.com**).

One result of flexible pricing is that some people gather data from full-service sellers, shop for the best price (often on the Internet), and then challenge discount sellers to "beat the lowest price." This practice hurts full-service firms, lets discounters hold down selling costs, and encourages bargaining.

Figure 21-6

Combining Customary and Variable Pricing

Source: Reprinted by permission.

21-5c   Odd Pricing

Odd pricing is used when selling prices are set at levels below even dollar values, such as 49 cents, $4.95, and $199. It is popular for several reasons: People like getting change. Because the cashier must make change, employers ensure that cash sales are recorded and money is placed in the register. Consumers gain the impression that a firm thinks carefully about prices and sets them as low as possible. They may also believe odd prices represent price reductions; a price of $8.95 may be viewed as a discount from $10. See Figure 21-7.

Odd prices 1 or 2 cents below the next even price (29 cents, $2.98) are common up to $4 or $5. Beyond that point and up to $50 or so, 5-cent reductions from the highest even price ($19.95, $49.95) are more usual. For expensive items, odd endings are in dollars ($499, $5,995).

Odd prices may help consumers stay within their price limits and still buy the best items available. A shopper willing to spend "less than $30" for a tie will be attracted to a $29.95 tie and might be as apt to buy it as a $24 tie since it is within the defined price range. The sales tax in 45 states has the effect of raising odd prices into higher dollar levels and may reduce the impact of odd pricing as a selling tool (**http://salestaxinstitute. com/sales_tax_rates.php**).

> **Odd prices** are set below even-dollar values.

Ethical Issues in Marketing

Challenging Visa and MasterCard over Credit Card Fees

In May 2008, a U.S. House Judiciary Committee held a hearing concerning a proposed law that would stop credit-card firms from charging unfair transaction fees. According to one report, the interchange fee (the charge to a merchant every time a credit or debit card is used for a transaction) was rising at an average rate of 17 percent per year. Though these fees are paid by merchants to Visa (http://www.visa.com) and Master-Card (http://www.mastercard.com), the merchants usually pass the fees on to consumers in the form of higher prices. The average U.S. family paid $425 in fees in 2008, up from $159 in 2001.

Credit-card companies have defended their fee increases as necessary for their continuing investments in technology. They also say their fees reflect the value of the cards, which provide access to cardholders, as well as guaranteed payments for authorized purchases.

Interchange fees vary, with the typical fee being slightly less than 2 percent of the total purchase amount. Even though a 2 percent fee may seem low to some casual observers, it represents a high proportion of some retailers' overall profits. The National Retail Federation (http://www.nrf.org) reported that credit-card fees paid by convenience stores in 2007 amounted to $7.6 billion. In contrast, convenience stores' total profits in 2007 equaled $3.4 billion. To increase profits, some gas stations have begun to post both cash and credit prices. The credit price in some markets is up to 6 cents per gallon—or more—above the cash price.

Sources: Based on material in Brian Burnsed, "To Save Money at the Gas Pump, Pay Cash," http://www.businessweek.com/bwdaily (June 20, 2008); and Michael Sanson, "Fighting the Credit Card Companies," *Restaurant Hospitality* (June 2008), p. 6.

21-5d   The Price-Quality Association

> The **price-quality association** deals with perceptions. **Prestige pricing** indicates that consumers may not buy when a price is too low.

According to the **price-quality association**, consumers may believe high prices represent high quality and low prices represent low quality. This association tends to be most valid when quality is difficult to judge on bases other than price, buyers perceive large differences in quality among brands, buyers have little experience or confidence in assessing quality (as with a new product), high prices exclude the mass market, brand names are unknown, or brand names require certain price levels to sustain their images.[8]

If brand names are well known and/or people are confident of their ability to compare brands on nonprice factors, the price-quality association may be less valid. Consumers may then be more interested in the perceived value they receive for their money—and not necessarily believe a higher price represents better quality. It is imperative that prices properly reflect both the quality and the image of the firm.

Prestige pricing is a theory drawn from the price-quality association that assumes consumers will not buy goods or services at prices they consider too low. Most people set price floors and will not buy at prices below those floors—they feel quality and status would be inferior at extremely low prices. Most people also set ceilings as to the prices they consider acceptable for particular goods or services. Above those ceilings, items are seen as too expensive. For each good or service, a firm should set prices in the target market's acceptable range between the floor and ceiling. See Figure 21-8.

21-5e   Leader Pricing

> **Leader pricing** is used to attract customers to low prices.

A firm uses **leader pricing** to advertise and sell key items in its product assortment at less than usual profit margins. The wholesaler's or retailer's goal is to increase customer traffic. The manufacturer's goal is to gain greater consumer interest in its overall product

---

[8] Anthony D. Miyazaki, Dhruv Grewal, Ronald C. Goodstein, Dawn Iacobucci, and Kent Monroe, "The Effect of Multiple Extrinsic Cues on Quality Perceptions: A Matter of Consistency," *Journal of Consumer Research*, Vol. 32 (June 2005), pp. 146–153; and Emin Babakus and Ugur Yavas, "Does Customer Sex Influence the Relationship between Perceived Quality and Share of Wallet?," *Journal of Business Research*, Vol. 61 (September 2008), pp. 974–981.

Figure 21-7

Odd Pricing: A Popular Psychological Pricing Tool

Source: Reprinted by permission.

line. In both cases, it is hoped that consumers will buy regularly priced products in addition to the specially priced items that attract them.

Leader pricing is most used with well-known, high-turnover, frequently bought products. In supermarkets, one best-selling item is soda. To stimulate customer traffic, Coke or Pepsi may be priced very low; in some cases, it is sold at close to cost. Soda is a good item for leader pricing because consumers are able to detect low prices and they are attracted into a store by a discount on the item.

There are two kinds of leader pricing: loss leaders and prices higher than cost but lower than regular prices. As stated in Chapter 20, the use of loss leaders is regulated or illegal in a number of states.

21-5f   Multiple-Unit Pricing

Multiple-unit pricing is a practice whereby a firm offers discounts to consumers to encourage them to buy in quantity, so as to increase overall sales volume. By offering items at two for 89 cents or six for $139, a firm attempts to sell more units than would be sold at 50 cents or $25 each.

> Quantity discounts are intended to result in higher sales volume with **multiple-unit pricing.**

Figure 21-8

Demand for Designer Jeans Under Prestige Pricing

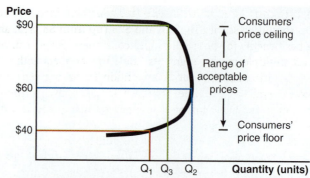

When designer jeans are priced under $40, consumers believe the jeans are labeled incorrectly, are an old style, are seconds, or are of poor quality. Demand is negligible.

When designer jeans are priced at $40, consumer demand is Q_1. A small group of discount-oriented consumers will buy the jeans. This is the minimum price they will pay for a good pair of designer jeans.

As the price goes from $40 to $60, demand rises continuously as more consumers perceive the jeans as a high-quality, status product. At $60, sales peak at Q_2.

As the price goes from $60 to $90, consumer demand drops gradually to Q_3. In this range, some consumers begin to see the jeans as too expensive. But many will buy the jeans until the price reaches $90, their ceiling price.

When designer jeans are priced over $90, consumers believe the jeans are too expensive and demand is negligible.

Four major benefits arise from multiple-unit pricing: (1) Customers may increase their immediate purchases if they feel they get a bargain. (2) They may boost long-term consumption by making larger purchases, as occurs with soda. (3) Competitors' customers may be attracted by the discounts. (4) A firm may be able to clear out slow-moving and end-of-season merchandise, as wholesaler Liquidity Services does through its Web site (**http://www.liquidation.com**), which sells overstocked and closeout items in bulk.

Multiple-unit pricing will not succeed if shoppers just shift purchases and do not hike consumption. Multiple-unit pricing for Heinz ketchup may not result in consumers using more ketchup with meals. Total revenues would not rise if consumers buy ketchup less often because it can be stored.

21-5g   Price Lining

Price lining involves selling products at a range of prices, with each representing a distinct level of quality (or features). Instead of setting one price for a single version of a good or service, a firm sells two or more versions (with different levels of quality or features) at different prices. Price lining involves two decisions: prescribing the price range (floor and ceiling) and setting specific price points in that range.

> **Price lining** sets a range of selling prices and price points within that range.

A price range may be low, intermediate, or high. Inexpensive radios may be priced from $8 to $20, moderately priced radios from $25 to $50, and expensive radios from $75 to $120. After the range is chosen, a limited number of price points are set. They must be distinct and not too close together. Inexpensive radios could be $8, $12, and $20. They should not be priced at $8, $9, $10, $11, $12, $13, $14, $15, $16, $17, $18, $19, and $20. This would confuse consumers and be inefficient for the firm.

A firm must consider these factors with price lining: Price points must be spaced far enough apart so customers perceive differences among product versions—otherwise, consumers might view the price floor as the price they should pay and believe there is no difference among models. Price points should be spaced farther apart at higher prices because consumer demand becomes more inelastic. Relationships among price points must be kept when costs rise, so clear differences are retained. If radio costs rise 25 percent, prices should be set at $10, $15, and $25 (up from $8, $12, and $20).

Price lining has benefits for both sellers and consumers. Sellers can offer a product assortment, attract multiple market segments, trade up shoppers within a price range, control inventory by price point, reduce competition by having versions over a price range, and increase overall sales volume. Shoppers are given an assortment from which to choose, confusion is lessened, comparisons may be made, and quality options are available within a given price range.

Price lining can also have constraints: Consumers may feel price gaps are too large—a $25 handbag may be too low, while the next price point of $100 may be too high. Rising costs may squeeze individual prices and make it hard for a firm to keep the proper relationships in its line. Markdowns or special sales may disrupt the balance in a price line, unless all items in the line are proportionately reduced in price.

21-5h Price Bundling

A firm uses ***bundled pricing*** to sell a basic product, options, and customer service for one total price. An industrial-equipment manufacturer may have a single price for a drill press, its delivery, its installation, and a service contract. Individual items, such as the drill press, would not be sold separately. With ***unbundled pricing***, a firm breaks down prices by individual components and allows the consumer to decide what to purchase. A discount appliance store may have separate prices for a refrigerator, its delivery, its installation, and a service contract. Many firms offer both pricing options and allow a slight discount for bundled pricing. See Figure 21-9.

> A firm can use **bundled** or **unbundled pricing**.

Figure 21-9

Unbundling Prices

To appeal to its price-conscious customers, Ikea (**http://www.ikea.com**) does not include a delivery charge in its basic prices. Delivery is an unbundled add-on for shoppers who want it.

Source: Reprinted by permission of Susan Berry, Retail Image Consulting, Inc.

21-5i Geographic Pricing

Geographic pricing outlines responsibility for transportation charges. Many times, it is not negotiated but depends on the traditional practices in the industry in which the firm operates, and all companies in the industry normally conform to the same geographic pricing format. Geographic pricing often involves industrial marketing situations.

The most common methods of geographic pricing are:

- *FOB (free-on-board) mill (factory) pricing*—The buyer picks a transportation form and pays all freight charges, the seller pays the costs of loading the goods (hence, "free on board"), and the delivered price to the buyer depends on freight charges.
- *Uniform delivered pricing*—All buyers pay the same delivered price for the same quantity of goods, regardless of their location; the seller pays for shipping.
- *Zone pricing*—This provides for a uniform delivered price to all buyers within a geographic zone; through a multiple-zone system, delivered prices vary by zone.
- *Base-point pricing*—Firms in an industry establish basing points from which the costs of shipping are computed; the delivered price to a buyer reflects the cost of transporting goods from the basing point nearest to the buyer, regardless of the actual site of supply.

21-5j Purchase Terms

Purchase terms are the provisions of price agreements. They include discounts, the timing of payments, and credit arrangements.

Discounts are the reductions from final selling prices available to resellers and consumers for doing certain functions, paying cash, buying large amounts, buying in off-seasons, or enhancing promotions. A wholesaler may buy goods at 40 percent off a manufacturer's suggested final selling price. This covers its expenses, profit, and the discount to the retailer. The retailer could buy for 25 percent off list (the wholesaler keeping 15 percent for its costs and profit). Discounts must be proportionately available to all competing channel members to avoid violating the Robinson-Patman Act.

Payment timing must be specified in a purchase agreement. Final consumers may pay immediately or upon delivery. In credit sales, payments are not made until bills are received; they may be made over time. B-to-b consumers negotiate for good terms: "Net 30" means products do not have to be paid for until 30 days after receipt. They must then be paid for in full. With "2/10, net 30," a buyer receives a 2 percent discount if the full bill is paid within 10 days after merchandise receipt. The buyer must pay the face value of a bill within 30 days after the receipt of products. Various time terms are available.

Sellers must sometimes be prepared to wait an extended period to receive payments when marketing internationally. It can take U.S. firms up to 100 days or more—from invoice to payment—to get paid by b-to-b consumers in Iran, Kenya, Argentina, Brazil, Greece, Italy, and elsewhere.

A firm that permits credit purchases may use open accounts or revolving accounts. With an *open credit account*, the buyer receives a monthly bill for the goods and services bought during the preceding month. The account must be paid in full each month. With a *revolving credit account*, the buyer agrees to make minimum monthly payments during an extended period of time and pays interest on outstanding balances. Today, various types of firms (from Xerox to many colleges) offer some form of credit plan. Auto makers provide their own cut-rate financing programs to stimulate sales and leasing.

21-6 PRICE ADJUSTMENTS

Once a price strategy is enacted, it often requires continuous fine-tuning to reflect changes in costs, competitive conditions, and demand. *Price adjustment tactics* include alterations in list prices, escalator clauses and surcharges, added markups, markdowns, and rebates.

List prices are the regularly quoted prices provided to customers. They may be pre-printed on price tags, in catalogs, and in dealer purchase orders. Modifications in list prices are necessary if there are sustained changes in labor costs, raw material costs, and market segments, and as a product moves through its life cycle. If these events are long-term in nature, they enable customary prices to be revised, new catalogs to be printed, and adjustments to be completed in an orderly fashion.

Costs or economic conditions may sometimes be so volatile that revised list prices cannot be printed or distributed efficiently. Escalator clauses or surcharges can then be used. With *escalator clauses*, a firm is contractually permitted to raise prices to reflect higher costs in essential materials without changing printed list prices. It may even be able to set prices at the time of delivery. *Surcharges* are across-the-board published price increases that supplement list prices. These may be used with catalogs because of their simplicity; an insert is distributed with the catalog. Several airlines now impose a fee on paper tickets to encourage travelers to use electronic ticketing (which cuts distribution costs).

When list prices are not involved, *additional markups* can be used to raise regular selling prices if demand is unexpectedly high or if costs rise. This involves some risk. For example, supermarkets get bad publicity for relabeling low-cost existing items at higher prices to match those of newer items bought at higher costs.

Markdowns are reductions from items' original selling prices. All types of sellers use them to meet the lower prices of competitors, counteract overstocking of merchandise, clear out shopworn merchandise, deplete assortments of odds and ends, and lift customer traffic.

Although manufacturers regularly give discounts to resellers, they may periodically offer **rebates** to customers to stimulate the purchase of an item or a group of items. Rebates are flexible, do not alter basic prices, involve direct communication between customers and manufacturers (because rebates are usually sent by the manufacturers), and do not affect reseller profits (as regular reductions do). Price cuts by individual resellers may not generate the same kind of consumer enthusiasm. Rebate popularity can be traced to its usage by auto makers to help reduce inventory surpluses. Rebates are regularly offered by Canon (**http://www.canon.com**), Linksys (**http://www.linksys.com**), and others. To ease rebate redemption processing, retailers such as Staples (**http://www.stapleseasyrebates.com**) have online rebate centers for customers. The major disadvantage of rebates is that so many firms use rebates that their impact may be lessened.

Channel members should cooperatively agree on their individual roles whenever adjustments are needed. Price hikes or cuts should not be unilateral.

Web Sites You Can Use

The Business Owner's Toolkit Web site offers a lot of information on price planning. Look at its "Pricing Your Product" section (**http://www.toolkit.cch.com/text/p03_5200.asp**). The Center for Business Planning's Web site (**http://www.businessplans.org/topic71.html**) provides access to a wide range of resources. You can also download a free book, *Make Your Price Sell* (**http://www.thatswise.com/free/e-books/pdf/price_sell/MYPS.pdf**). For a change of pace, take a look at the Price.com (**http://www.price.com**) and PriceScan.com (**http://www.pricescan.com**) comparison-shopping Web sites.

Summary

1. *To present an overall framework for developing and applying a pricing strategy*   The five stages in a pricing strategy are: objectives, broad policy, strategy, implementation, and adjustments. These stages are affected by outside factors and must be integrated with a firm's marketing mix.

2. *To analyze sales-based, profit-based, and status quo-based pricing objectives, and to describe the role of a broad price policy* Sales goals center on volume and/or market share. In penetration pricing, low prices capture a mass market. Profit goals focus on profit maximization, satisfactory profits, optimum return on investment, and/or early cash recovery. In skimming pricing, a firm seeks the segment less concerned with price than quality or status. Status quo goals seek to minimize the impact of outside parties and ensure stability. Two or more pricing objectives may be combined.

A broad price policy sets the overall direction for a firm's pricing efforts. Through it, a firm decides if it is price- or nonprice-oriented.

3. *To examine and apply the alternative approaches to a pricing strategy* A price strategy may be cost-based, demand-based, competition-based, or a combination of these.

With cost-based pricing, merchandise, service, and overhead costs are computed and then an amount to cover profit is added. Cost-plus pricing adds costs and a desired profit to set prices. Markup pricing sets prices by calculating the per-unit costs of producing (buying) goods and/or services and then finding the markup percentages to cover selling costs and profit; a variable markup policy has different markups for distinct products. In target pricing, prices provide a rate of return on investment for a standard volume of production. If a firm has excess capacity, it may use price-floor pricing, in which prices are set above variable costs rather than total costs. Traditional break-even analysis determines the sales quantity at which total costs equal total revenues for a chosen price.

With demand-based pricing, prices are set after doing consumer research and learning the range of acceptable prices to the target market. A firm uses demand-minus pricing to find the proper selling price and works backward to set costs. Chain-markup pricing extends demand-minus calculations from resellers back to suppliers (manufacturers). Modified break-even analysis combines traditional break-even analysis with an evaluation of demand at various prices. A firm uses price discrimination to set two or more distinct prices for a product so as to appeal to different market segments.

Competition is the main guidepost in competition-based pricing. Prices may be below, at, or above the market.

A firm would see whether it has the ability to be a price leader or price follower. With competitive bidding, two or more firms submit prices in response to precise customer requests.

The three approaches should be integrated via combination pricing, so a firm includes all necessary factors in its pricing strategy. Otherwise, critical decisions are likely to be overlooked.

4. *To discuss several specific decisions that must be made in implementing a pricing strategy* Enacting a price strategy involves several specific decisions. Customary pricing is used when a firm sets prices for an extended time. In variable pricing, prices coincide with cost or consumer demand fluctuations.

In a one-price policy, all those buying under similar conditions pay the same price. Flexible pricing lets a firm vary prices based on shopper negotiations or the buying power of a large customer.

With odd pricing, amounts are set below even-dollar values. The price-quality theory suggests people may feel there is a relation between price and quality. Prestige pricing assumes people do not buy products at prices that are considered too low. They set price floors, as well as price ceilings.

Under leader pricing, key items are sold at less than their usual amounts to increase consumer traffic. Multiple-unit pricing is a practice that offers discounts to consumers for buying in quantity.

Price lining involves the sale of products at a range of prices, with each embodying a distinct level of quality (or features). In bundled pricing, a firm offers a product, options, and customer service for a total price; unbundled pricing breaks down prices by individual components.

Geographic pricing outlines the responsibility for transportation. Purchase terms are the provisions of price agreements, including discounts, timing of payments, and credit.

5. *To show the major ways that prices can be adjusted* Once a pricing strategy is enacted, it often needs fine-tuning to reflect cost, competition, and demand changes. Prices can be adjusted by altering list prices, using escalator clauses and surcharges, marking prices up or down, and offering rebates.

Key Terms

sales-based pricing objectives (p. 642)
penetration pricing (p. 643)
profit-based pricing objectives (p. 643)
skimming pricing (p. 644)
status quo-based pricing objectives (p. 644)
broad price policy (p. 644)
cost-based pricing (p. 645)

price floor (p. 645)
cost-plus pricing (p. 646)
markup pricing (p. 647)
variable markup policy (p. 648)
target pricing (p. 648)
price-floor pricing (p. 649)
traditional break-even analysis (p. 649)
demand-based pricing (p. 650)

price ceiling (p. 650)
demand-minus (demand-backward) pricing (p. 651)
chain-markup pricing (p. 651)
modified break-even analysis (p. 651)
price discrimination (p. 652)
yield management pricing (p. 653)
competition-based pricing (p. 654)

price leadership (p. 654)

combination pricing (p. 655)

customary pricing (p. 655)

variable pricing (p. 655)

one-price policy (p. 655)

flexible pricing (p. 656)

odd pricing (p. 657)

price-quality association (p. 658)

prestige pricing (p. 658)

leader pricing (p. 658)

multiple-unit pricing (p. 659)

price lining (p. 660)

bundled pricing (p. 661)

unbundled pricing (p. 661)

geographic pricing (p. 662)

purchase terms (p. 662)

price adjustment tactics (p. 662)

rebates (p. 663)

Review Questions

1. When should a firm pursue sales-based pricing objectives? Status quo-based pricing objectives?
2. Why are markups usually computed on the basis of selling price?
3. A firm requires a 10 percent return on a $1.1 million investment in order to manufacture a new electric garage-door opener. If the standard volume is 50,000 units, fixed costs are $500,000, and variable costs are $45 per unit, what is the target price?
4. A company making office desks has total fixed costs of $2 million per year and variable costs of $350 per desk. It sells the desks to retailers for $750 apiece. Compute the traditional break-even point in both units and dollars.
5. Discuss chain-markup pricing from the perspective of a retailer.
6. Contrast customary pricing and variable pricing. How may the two techniques be combined?
7. Under what circumstances is the price-quality association most valid? Least valid?
8. How does price lining benefit manufacturers? Retailers? Consumers?

Discussion Questions

1. A movie theater has weekly fixed costs (land, building, and equipment) of $6,000. Variable weekly costs (movie rental, electricity, ushers, etc.) are $2,600. From a price-floor pricing perspective, how much revenue must a movie generate during a slow week for it to be worthwhile to open the theater? Explain your answer.
2. A retailer determines that customers are willing to spend $17.95 for a new children's book. The publisher charges the retailer $12.75 for each copy. The retailer wants a 35 percent markup. Comment on this situation.
3. a. A wholesaler of small industrial tools has fixed costs of $260,000, variable costs of $25 per tool, and faces this demand schedule from its hardware-store customers:

Price	Quantity Demanded
$31	100,000
$36	85,000
$41	65,000
$46	40,000

   At what price is profit maximized?
   b. If the firm noted in Question 3a decides to sell 40,000 small tools at $36 and 45,000 of these tools at $31, what will its profit be? What are the risks of this approach?
4. A wholesaler of plumbing supplies recently added a new line of kitchen sinks and priced them at $199 each (to plumbers). The manufacturer has just announced a 7 percent price increase on the sinks, due to higher materials and labor costs. Yet, for this wholesaler, the initial response of plumbers to the sinks has been sluggish. Also, some competing wholesalers are selling similar private-label sinks for $149 to plumbers. What should the wholesaler do next?

Web Exercise

Kelley Blue Book is the leading online source for information on the value of used cars—based on the make, model, year, features, condition, and so forth. Visit the Web site (**http://www.kbb.com/kbb/UsedCars/default.aspx**) and discuss how the information you find there could be applied by a used car dealer, a private party looking to resell his or her car, and a consumer looking to buy a used car.

Practice Quiz

1. Which statement is true?
   a. A firm may pursue more than one pricing goal at the same time.
   b. A pricing strategy should focus on short-run goals only.
   c. A firm still has a probability of succeeding even if it does not set pricing goals.
   d. Different firms in the same industry always have the same pricing strategies.

2. With sales-based objectives, a firm focuses on
   a. minimizing the effects of competitor actions.
   b. maintaining good channel relations.
   c. expanding its market share relative to competitors.
   d. reducing the return on investment.

3. Firms that desire high initial profits because they are short of funds or uncertain about their future use
   a. early-recovery-of-cash goals.
   b. return-on-investment goals.
   c. satisfactory-profit goals.
   d. status quo-based goals.

4. Which of the following is an advantage to firms that first employ skimming pricing and then apply penetration pricing?
   a. Low prices are charged when competition is limited.
   b. Lowering initial prices presents a poor image to the market.
   c. High prices are used to ignore competitors.
   d. Multiple segments can be reached.

5. The first step in outlining a broad price policy is
   a. examining brand image.
   b. integrating individual decisions.
   c. determining a pricing strategy.
   d. analyzing the marketing mix.

6. Price floors are frequently set in
   a. cost-based strategies.
   b. competition-based strategies.
   c. demand-based strategies.
   d. status quo-based strategies.

7. Price ceilings
   a. are the lowest acceptable prices firms can set to gain profit goals.
   b. are the minimum amounts consumers will pay for goods or services.
   c. do not take demand into account.
   d. depend on the elasticity of demand.

8. Under customary pricing, channel members
   a. alter prices to coincide with fluctuations in costs.
   b. adjust prices to levels of demand.

   c. try to maintain prices as long as possible.
   d. offer discounts to those who buy in quantity.

9. A one-price policy
   a. erodes customer confidence.
   b. eliminates bargaining.
   c. is difficult to administer.
   d. does not permit self-service and catalog sales.

10. With what pricing approach does a firm advertise and sell key items in its product assortment at less than their usual profit margins?
    a. Variable pricing
    b. Leader pricing
    c. Odd pricing
    d. Prestige pricing

11. Which of these is *not* a major reason for employing multiple-unit pricing?
    a. Greater consumption is encouraged.
    b. The firm can clear out slow-moving merchandise.
    c. Total dollar sales are maintained.
    d. Competitors' customers may be attracted.

12. Which of these is *not* a method of geographic pricing?
    a. Chain-markup pricing
    b. Uniform delivered pricing
    c. Base-point pricing
    d. Zone pricing

13. Purchase terms include discounts, the timing of payments, and
    a. delivery.
    b. installation.
    c. credit arrangements.
    d. warranty coverage.

14. In catalogs, to tie prices to rising costs, it is simplest to
    a. publish escalator clauses.
    b. add on surcharges.
    c. change list prices.
    d. reduce markups.

15. Which of the following statements about rebates is *not* true?
    a. They help cut down on inventory surpluses.
    b. They are used by a wide variety of firms.
    c. They are flexible.
    d. They reduce communication between consumers and manufacturers.

For the answers to these questions, please visit the online site for this book at **http://www.atomicdog.com.**

Case 1: **What's Ahead for iTunes' Video Pricing Strategy?[c7-1]**

Although iTunes (**http://www.itunes.com**) accounts for the majority of the online video resale market, the overall size of the market is still relatively small. In 2007, the total online video resale market was estimated at $300 million by Forrester Research (**http://www.forrester.com**).

Until recently, Apple's (**http://www.apple.com**) iTunes video store was strong enough that it was able to dictate pricing terms to both its suppliers of videos and consumers. As of mid-2008, the iTunes store had sold 150 million episodes from its library of approximately 800 television shows.

iTunes typically priced videos from ABC (**http://abc.go.com**), CBS (**http://www.cbs.com**), News Corporation's Fox (**http://www.fox.com**), CW Networks (**http://www.cwtv.com**), and from 50 cable networks at a flat rate of $1.99 per episode. In 2008, Time Warner's HBO channel (**http://www.hbo.com**) arranged a deal with Apple that would enable HBO to set different prices for its TV shows than the typical $1.99 rate. Some HBO videos, such as episodes of *Sex and the City*, *Deadwood*, *Rome*, *The Wire*, and *Flight of the Concords* would be priced at $2.99 per episode.

Apple announced no plans to offer discounts for a consumer's purchasing an entire season. A person who purchased *Sex and the City* episodes on a DVD from Amazon.com (**http://www.amazon.com**) would pay slightly more than the iTunes' price. In contrast, the *Sopranos*, which would cost $520 on Amazon.com for the 28 discs of the six-season show, at $2.99 per episode, would cost $260 to download.

The ability of Apple to dictate retail pricing was such a bone of contention for NBC (**http://www.nbc.com**) that during the Fall 2007 season, NBC announced that it would not renew its iTunes contract. Apple explained that NBC wanted to increase its wholesale price for each episode by so much that Apple would have had to charge consumers $4.99 per episode to download these videos (instead of its $1.99 customary price). NBC pulled its video content from iTunes after Apple refused to test several different price points among consumers to determine the price elasticity of demand. Instead of selling copies of its shows to Apple for downloading, NBC built a platform that enabled viewers to download shows for free. NBC receives revenues from advertising by sponsors. One marketing analyst estimates that these sponsorships will result in hundreds of millions of dollars from sponsorships and advertisers. Unlike with iTunes, NBC will not have to share this revenue stream with Apple.

A Forrester Research executive says that the NBC incident indicates "how paltry and uninfluential the video side of iTunes is. Few major music labels could similarly afford to pull out of iTunes, which dominates the online music industry."

The impact of the new two-tiered pricing system is significant for Apple, its suppliers, and consumers. The HBO arrangement marks the end of Apple's ability to fully dictate to TV networks and cable channels such as HBO that all videos be sold at the same price. No doubt, as contracts expire, other networks will demand increased revenues from their most popular shows. What is not known is what effect the increased costs and revenues will have on Apple's gross profit per video rental or the public's price elasticity of demand. Though Apple keeps about one-third of the retail price for each video and music download it sells, Apple's gross profit on videos is not public information.

The Enderle Group (**http://www.enderlegroup.com**), a technology consulting firm, believes that, "The pricing shift represents the reality that not all content is equal." Through further extending the tiered-pricing system, it may be possible for consumers to even download movies while they are still in theaters. Enderle suggests that, "Maybe a first-time movie will sell for $30. It's not going to sell for $2."

[c7-1] The data in the case are drawn from John Boudreau, "Apple's HBO Deal Signals Shift in iTunes Pricing," **http://www.mercurynews.com** (May 14, 2008); Nancy Gohring, "iTunes Pricing Spat with NBC Seen as Hurting Apple," **http://www.infoworld.com** (August 31, 2007); Michael Learmonth, "Apple Caves on iTunes Pricing for HBO," **http://www.alleyinsider.com** (May 12, 2008); and R. Thomas Unstead, "HBO Squeezes Apple for Higher iTunes Pricing," **http://www.multichannel.com** (May 13, 2008).

Questions

1. How can Apple estimate the price elasticity of demand between the market prices of $2.99 versus $1.99?
2. Explain the relevance of a price floor and a price ceiling to Apple.
3. How does multi-tiered pricing affect Apple's profitability? Answer this question using the chain-markup method.
4. In this instance, is multi-tiered pricing a form of customer- or product-based price discrimination? Explain your answer.

Case 2: How Should Parking Be Priced in Downtown Areas?[c7-2]

Parking on most the streets in downtown Gainesville, Florida, is free. During daytime hours, parking typically costs $1 per hour at a garage, with a flat fee of $5 after 6 P.M. As a result, most on-street parking is usually filled, and the downtown parking garage tends to be half empty. Instead of encouraging use of the garage, this pricig environment encourages motorists to drive around downtown or to illegally park at a hydrant hoping an on-street spot will open up. One parking specialist says this is evidence that the price of parking at the garage actually encourages congestion on the street.

One solution is to make parking in garages in downtown Gainesville free for a reasonable time (say 3 hours to encourage shoppers), but to charge visitors for stays beyond this time. The municipality could also place parking meters on streets, possibly making street parking more costly than the garage. As a result, more on-street parking spots would be available for those shoppers who desire the convenience of parking in front of a specific merchant. That practice would also encourage long-term visitors to use the parking garage.

Advocates believe the strategy just described would have several beneficial outcomes:

- Some motorists would use public transportation rather than pay to park.
- Emissions and gasoline consumption would be reduced.
- On-street parking spots would turn over at a faster rate.

Midtown Manhattan has a very different parking situation. Visitors can legally park after 6 P.M. on weekdays and all day Saturday and Sunday at parking meters that charge 50 cents per 15 minutes (with a maximum of 6 hours). Thus, a visitor going out to dinner and a Broadway show for 5 hours would have an expense of $10.00. The meters accept quarters, smart cards (that can be purchased from New York's Parking Authority), or credit cards, and produce receipts that indicate the expiration time for parking. The $10 or so charge is significantly less than a local garage (which might charge as much as $35 for the same time period). In addition, visitors have the added advantages of parking directly in front of a restaurant (if the spot is available) and being able to leave directly after the show (without having to wait for a car to be delivered by a parking attendant). Other than those stated times, metered parking is available only to commercial vehicles (such as delivery trucks and vehicles owned by electricians and plumbing concerns).

Municipalities can choose between two types of parking meters: single-space meters (that accept coins and smart cards) and multispace meters that can serve up to 10 parking spaces (and accept bills as well as credit cards). A traditional single-space parking meter costs between $300 and $500, while a multispace meter generally costs between $5,000 and $10,000, based on its features.

The average life span for a meter is 5 to 7 years. Some meters are automatically reset for each new vehicle. This prohibits a driver from using the remaining unused minutes from a previous auto. Computing the break-even point for installing meters needs to be based on the cost of the parking meters, the added parking revenues over the meters' life span, and the direct costs of emptying and servicing meters. Higher costs for the multispace meters can be partly offset because of the lower collection and servicing costs. Calculations are needed as to whether metering facilitates or reduces shopping activity. If it facilitates shopping, municipalities will generate additional income from sales tax from customers and state income taxes from retailers with higher sales.

Questions

1. Contrast the parking differences in demand between Gainesville and midtown Manhattan.
2. How would you develop break-even analysis for the installation of single-space parking meters in Gainesville? State your assumptions for the cost of meters, the extent of meter usage, meter revenue, collection costs, and meter-servicing costs. Assume that meters have a five-year life.
3. Does meter pricing exist in a market-, company-, or government controlled price environment? Explain your answer.
4. What are the pros and cons of New York City increasing its metering fees from 50 cents per 15 minutes to $1 per 15 minutes? Include the concept of price elasticity in your answer.

[c7-2] The data in the case are drawn from Vicky Gagliano, "The Price Is Right," *Planning* (May 2008), pp. 24–29.

Case 3: Trading Up Shoppers Through the Aggressive Use of Price Points[c7-3]

Mattress retailers tend to heavily promote low-priced mattresses. Currently, the starting retail price points for promotional mattresses are $299 to $399, depending on the brand and the retailer. In many instances, retailers promote low-end prices in order to trade up customers to more costly—and more profitable—products. In response to retailer requests, mattress manufacturer Simmons (http://www.simmons.com) recently reduced the starting price of its DeepSleep mattress line from $399 to $299. Anne Kozel, a brand director at DeepSleep, said, "Dealers have asked for $299. They want to advertise that price to get customers in."

A crucial decision for manufacturers, importers, and retailers is selecting the price point most appropriate for promotional pricing. The correct price point gets a consumer to consider purchasing the product, generates store traffic, and creates opportunity for trading the customer up. If the price point is too high, consumers will resist the offering. Too low a price point, on the other hand, can result in the consumer being overly concerned about the product's quality. According to Anne Kozel, "Forty percent of sales in the industry are at $500 or below."

Retailers often use a promotional price point to get a consumer into the store and as a starting point in assessing a buyer's needs. Retailers can then determine the buyer's desire for additional features (such as pillowtops), better construction (e.g., higher coils), and more costly fabrics. A customer examining a $299 promotional mattress might agree to buy a $699 model due to its higher quality and additional features. Simmons' DeepSleep line starts at $299, then has a Eurotop model at $399, and a pillowtop model priced at $599. The $699 model is DeepSleep's "top-of-the line" model.

Trading up consumers based on initial promotional pricing is an ethical business practice. However, bait-and-switch advertising is not. In trading up, a retailer ascertains a consumer's needs and may recommend a more costly product that is more suitable to the customer. However, the retailer will gladly sell the promotional product. In contrast, with bait-and-switch advertising, the retailer has no intention of selling the heavily promoted good.

One problem with some popular promotional price points is their impact on profitability. Though it may be easy to initially generate business at the promotional pricing point, it can be very difficult to maintain the same price for two years. Competitive pressures may force manufacturers to keep prices low, but they constantly have to be concerned with the impact of cost increases on profitability. In some cases, manufacturers have had to reduce features and product quality to keep their promotional price points intact. Another potential problem is whether the quality of promotionally priced mattresses is adequate.

There should be some relationship between the starting promotional price point and the trade-up price. It may be difficult to trade a customer up from a $299 to a $999 mattress. Both models would usually appeal to different target markets in terms of income and lifestyle or for different purposes (the $299 mattress might be used in a guest room, while the $999 mattress would be placed in the master bedroom).

In addition to promotional pricing, mattress manufacturers use bridge pricing to differentiate low-priced promotional goods from higher-priced merchandise. Part of the logic of bridge pricing is a "good," "better," and "best" pricing model. In this pricing model, "good" represents promotional pricing, "better" can be equated with bridge pricing, and "best" is the top-of-the-line model.

Questions

1. What should be the role of promotional pricing in a full-service retailer's overall pricing strategy?
2. Describe the relationship between trading up and the setting of promotional prices.
3. Discuss how the price-quality association affects promotional pricing.
4. Does the following statement apply to all goods and services? Explain your answer: "In this pricing model, 'good' represents promotional pricing, 'better' can be equated with bridge pricing, and 'best' is the top-of-the-line model."

[c7-3] The data in the case are drawn from David Perry, "Simmons Drops Starting Point for DeepSleep Line," *Furniture Today* (October 30, 2006), p. 24; and David Perry, "Therapedic Sharpens Pricing on Ireland Line," *Furniture Today* (February 18, 2008), p. 28.

Case 4: Is Cutting Down on the Use of Markdowns a Losing Battle?[c7-4]

For many years, December 5th marked the day that retailers began to mark down winter coats. What would happen if the date shifted to January 5th? There is a strong likelihood that retailers' gross profit would increase substantially.

Today, a number of retailers use automated markdown software to advise their staff when to take markdowns and what discounts are optimal. These retailers include American Eagle (http://www.ae.com), Bloomingdale's (http://www.bloomingdales.com), Casual Male (http://www.casualmale.com), Ann Taylor (http://www.anntaylor.com), Nordstrom (http://www.nordstrom.com), Loehmann's (http://www.loehmanns.com), J.C. Penney (http://www.jcpenney.com), and the Gap (http://www.gap.com).

To aid retailers' markdown planning and implementation, various firms, such as Oracle (http://www.oracle.com/profitlogic), SAP for Retail (http://www.sap.com), and Demand Tec (http://www.demandtec.com), have developed mathematical models to determine the relationship between an item's price, advertising expenditures, and sales. Many of these firms use a regionally based pricing model as opposed to a chain-wide approach.

One study of 18 retailers that use markdown software found that among those firms that were able to quantify the benefit, the average improvement in net profit margins was 2 to 3 percent. This is significant, because many retailers have net profits after tax of between 2 to 4 percent. Retailers that reported the greatest benefit sold goods with high turnover that had seasonality of 10 to 16 weeks. These firms also heavily relied on markdowns for specific groups of merchandise or specific groups of stores. Close to one-half of the companies surveyed used markdown software for all of their merchandise.

Generally, total costs for markdown software, the installation process, staff coaching, and the training of software personnel is in the range of $3 million to $5 million. The entire process takes 20 weeks or so, according to one consultant who has implemented the software in 10 U.S. companies and 2 foreign ones.

The recommended pricing strategies of markdown software are often contrary to the conventional wisdom of "off-the-cuff" pricing decisions. Among upscale apparel retailers, there are two important promotional periods: beginning-of-the-season pricing to establish the product and end-of-the-season pricing to clear out inventory: "The trick is to take the markdowns when there is still demand on the upward curve of the life cycle of the item. That's counterintuitive. But you want to extend the peak demand before it starts waning." Another common error among many retailers is that they may assume that a market is more price-sensitive than it really is. As a result, markdowns are sometimes greater than they need to be to clear out the merchandise.

Most software packages are based on the use of a highly variable pricing strategy in which customers are offered different prices at different times. This lets the retailer capitalize on changes in supply and demand. The models also allow a retailer to set different prices levels on a city, regional, or store-by-store basis. Many models are similar to the yield management pricing models used by airlines, hotels, and car-rental firms. In almost all markdown software models, a merchandise manager can override the software's recommendations based on his or her knowledge of local conditions. This could include a major storm that is forecast or the opening of a major competitor offering a special store-opening sales event.

One problem with variable pricing is that it violates the customer's notion of fairness. Some customers are more comfortable with a one-price policy where everyone pays pay the same price for items bought under similar conditions. A second potential problem is the difficulty in applying markdown software at the store level. This relates to getting personnel to understand the technology, the need to regularly change price tags, and the greater responsibility for store managers as a result of the software.

Questions

1. Contrast the use of markdown pricing software in retailing with the use of yield management pricing by hotels and airlines.
2. Why are many of the markdown pricing models regional versus chainwide?
3. List five situations (beyond those mentioned in the case) where a merchandise manager should override the markdown software's recommendations.
4. Under what circumstances would you recommend *not* using markdown software? Why?

[c7-4] The data in the case are drawn from David Moin, "Automating Markdowns: The Keys to Success," *Women's Wear Daily* (January 12, 2007), p. 14.

Launching the Proper Pricing Strategy[pc-7]

INTRODUCTION

Innovation is the fuel that drives growth. Any good sales executive can tell you that the quickest path to revenue growth is through new-product innovation rather than fighting for share in existing markets. Innovation offers immediate differentiation and the chance to command a premium price. Yet the risks of failure are high. A new-product launch enjoys many proud parents: the development team that followed a rigorous staged development process, the manufacturing organization that trained quality experts, the marketing team that developed creative promotions and toured with industry trade shows, the public relations team that built a compelling publicity campaign, and the sales team that enthusiastically extolled the product's virtues to customers. So why are there high failure rates?

THE ROLE OF PRICING IN PRODUCT FAILURES

Many companies' innovation efforts are inwardly focused. The results are billions of dollars wasted developing offerings that have little to no appeal to customers. In business-to-business markets, there are three principal reasons for that.

Failure to Connect Customer Needs to Value

The now-defunct PictureTel was an early innovator in the videoconferencing industry 20 years ago, developing a breakthrough technology enabling live videoconferences. Its product launch focused on its impressive technical capabilities. Yet, after PictureTel's great investment and product differentiation, the market did not beat a path to its door. The early value propositions failed to translate the cost of the system into clear value for customers: revenue benefits of reaching more customers or cost savings from travel. In 2000, PictureTel lost $100 million; in 2001, a smaller and more profitable rival purchased it.

Use of Product-Based Value Propositions Centering on Technical Ability Over Market Needs

Iridium (**http://www.iridium.com**) was a triumph of rocket science. In 1987, the wife of a senior Motorola technology leader fumed because she couldn't call home from a boat in the Bahamas. Eleven years and more than $2 billion later, Motorola (**http://www.motorola.com**) had successfully launched a necklace of 66 satellites linking

$3,000 phone sets for $7-a-minute calls. However, cell phone customers wanted increasingly small units, not 1-pound "shoe phones," and the market for people who needed a dedicated satellite system for $7 a minute calls was tiny. In 2000, the network was sold for around $25 million—about a penny on the dollar for Motorola's investment.

Overemphasis on the Role of Pricing in Driving Customer Adoption

Petrocosm launched as an oil industry transaction platform with a $100 million investment from Chevron (**http://www.chevron.com**) and top leadership from the oil equipment industry. It offered a cheap source of high-technology drilling equipment. But in an industry requiring billion-dollar offshore platforms poised over explosive hydrocarbon reservoirs, replacing the trust and experience that trained sales and service representatives offer with a low-cost transaction failed to gain a customer base. The customer base didn't want cheap; it wanted cost-effective. Petrocosm faded away.

The Good News

The pricing process is straightforward and will improve the returns on investment in innovations. Most successful innovators follow a few simple rules:

- Define the financial benefits that customers receive from adopting the new solution.
- Align price levels with financial and psychological drivers of customer value.
- Align pricing strategy with the specific nature of the innovation and the product category life cycle.
- Create outstanding launches—taking emphasis off price by reducing customers' perceived risk.

Companies that adhere to those principles enjoy significant benefits over competitors, including (1) a more effective screening process that enables them to focus resources only on innovations that provide superior value to customers, (2) compelling launches that communicate the business value of innovations, and (3) a coherent pricing strategy that prevents panic discounting to drive sales. Together, the benefits translate to greater success rates for new offerings and better pricing for those that make it to market.

THE VALUE-ON-INNOVATION PARADOX

In b-to-b markets, technological possibility often drives innovation, not defined customer needs. Living on the uncertain edge of technology, it should be less risky to focus on what's possible rather than

[pc-7] Adapted by the authors from Mark Burton and Steve Haggett, "Rocket Plan," *Marketing Management* (September-October 2007), pp. 32–38. Reprinted by permission of the American Marketing Association.

invest money in less-certain research based on customer wish lists. But the results show the drawbacks of a technology-driven approach.

Often, market research is focused on projections of market size and growth based on customer intent-to-purchase studies. Although this information can be important, it overlooks the most fundamental issue of whether an innovation will be successful: Is there a compelling business reason for customers to go through the upheaval of changing how they do things—to get the potential benefits of adopting your innovation? In short, what value does the customer expect to get, and how does value compare with the costs of switching? That question sets a much higher standard for research.

Great innovators do not finalize specifications until they understand the customer value that their innovations create, the barriers to successful launches, and the enablers of adoption. These insights are used to define high-impact value propositions and establish pricing models and price levels.

Defining barriers to adoption and identifying the likely adopters are critical. Companies commonly misread how their innovations change the buying center dynamics. Existing customer contacts might not be the right targets for an innovation when relationships with new decision makers and influencers need to be cultivated. Companies often call on the same old contacts and fail to anticipate that those contacts will not have the power to drive change and/or are very much invested in the status quo. When that happens, they find the relationships actually impede the ability to sell innovations to current customers.

The smartest road to profitable returns on innovations starts with an understanding of the customer; technology comes second.

USING VALUE INSIGHTS

Translating the results of customer value research into effective pricing for innovations requires answering some challenging questions about value to the customer. Importantly, it is not necessary to exhaustively answer these questions at the start of your customer research and innovation development processes. In fact, one defining characteristic of many leading innovators is that they are comfortable with a certain amount of ambiguity to start. The key is that they continue to ask hard questions about customers and value and refine their views on offering specifications, value positioning, and pricing. They do it early and they do it often.

A leading manufacturer of dental equipment (disguised), which has built its business by entering new markets with innovative offerings, does exactly this. Figure 1 shows a summary of its process.

It is tempting to look at the timeline and say "Our product life cycles are too short for this to be practical." But the fact is that all windows of innovative advantage are shortening. For all companies, it is critical to do value homework and get launch pricing right. Although your business might require far more compressed timelines, the process of establishing and refining your view of value to the customer is the foundational element for successful introduction, pricing, and positioning of innovations.

When the manufacturer was able to use new technologies, to replace reusable dental instruments with disposable ones, it knew it had a potentially valuable innovation to market. Through direct customer interviews and operational studies, it determined that such a device would improve procedure-room utilization by reducing cleanup time. The device also provided a market opportunity for oral surgeons seeking to differentiate themselves by advertising that they use the safest and most advanced equipment.

Using this information to establish a range for pricing is a three-step process: (1) Determine the total costs to the customer of his current solution options. (2) Define the financial benefits that your innovation delivers over and above current alternatives. (3) Identify the switching costs for customers who want to move to your solution.

In the case of our dental equipment manufacturer, that meant determining the following:

Figure 1
Preparing for Successful Launch Pricing

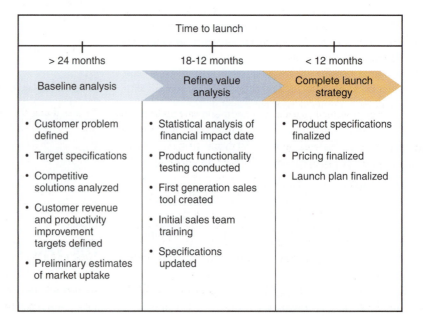

- The cost per procedure of current solutions—by amortizing the total lifetime costs of current and reusable equipment over the number of procedures performed.
- The cost savings due to greater procedure-room utilization.
- Revenue increases from patients attracted by oral surgeons advertising use of new equipment.
- Switching costs (in this instance, disposal and training costs).

Its findings are summarized in Figure 2.

The results of customer value research yield a band of customer value and establish upper and lower boundaries for price range. Using that information about financial value, the manufacturer was then able to set an initial price that captured a fair share of the value created for customers. To do that, it first defined its value advantage over existing solutions: in this case, $500 per procedure. Next, it added the cost of the current solution to define the maximum range of price options available: $180–$680 (the $180 cost of the current solution plus the $500 value advantage).

To narrow down the range, the manufacturer analyzed the psychological elements of value from the customer's perspective. That included negative perceptions (e.g., risk from adopting the new technology, concerns about moving from the comfortable old solution to something new) and psychological benefits (e.g., pride in being on the cutting edge). Finally, the manufacturer needed to set a price that offered some incentive to purchase. At the end of the process, it decided on $400 per instrument. Although that was at the lower end of the possible range, it ensured a significant profit and gave customers a reasonable incentive to switch.

How do companies best select the right price within the range of customer value? Let's turn to that by looking more closely at pricing strategy.

PRICING STRATEGY SELECTION

To really refine the pricing decision, evaluate price ranges against a defined pricing strategy for your innovation. This is an iterative process of checking pricing strategy against market research data and possible price points against your pricing strategy. The best way to get your arms around the pricing strategy element is to think about the following two variables.

What Is the Nature of the Innovation?

Is it a minor improvement, such as an interim software update? Is it a major one, such as the introduction of flat-panel TV sets? Or is it disruptive, such as the current move to solid-state flash memory for applications previously covered by high-speed disk drives?

Understanding the nature of the innovation defines the degrees of freedom that the innovator has in selecting a pricing strategy. Minor innovations (e.g., line extensions) are often necessary, but they do little to create advantage over the competition. As such, they provide little to increase pricing power. Innovations that are recognized as major breakthroughs present much greater flexibility in choosing a pricing strategy. This is because companies can keep prices high to skim value until the market develops—and then bring prices down to drive growth.

With disruptive innovations, the decision is a bit trickier. In the groundbreaking *Harvard Business Review* article "Disruptive Technologies: Catching the Wave," Clayton M. Christensen points out that such innovations fall into one of two categories.

Some, such as flash memory, offer significant performance advantages for niche markets (e.g., aerospace applications) but are too expensive for mainstream applications (e.g., laptop computers). The best approach for these products is to go up-market and use a skim pricing strategy—until costs and complementary technologies make it possible to enter mainstream markets. Alternately, some offer inferior performance on many key attributes but offer clear benefits in one or two areas for some customers. That was the case with 3.5-inch disk drives when they were introduced. In that instance, the best approach is to go down-market and use a penetration pricing strategy with prices set below established alternatives.

In What Stage of the Life Cycle Is the Product Category?

This element is critical but often overlooked. Failure to consider the life cycle dimension can result in disastrous financial consequences. That happened with flat-panel TVs. Early entrants initially played the game well. Prices for the early sets were high, reflecting both costs and the value that enthusiasts placed on them. As process technologies improved, prices dropped precipitously and customer adoption took off. Unfortunately, as the market started to show signs of maturity, most manufacturers were slow to take their feet off the pricing gas. The result has been terrible margin pressures due to low prices and overcapacity—at a time when consumers are becoming sophisticated enough to value and actively seek differentiation.

Summing Up

Taken together, those two variables point to default pricing strategies for each combination type and stage of the product category life cycle.

DRIVING CUSTOMER ADOPTION

Besides doing their homework on value to frame initial prices as fair and reasonable, great marketers take the focus off price by targeting the right customers, working to mitigate the risks of adopting a new technology, and making it easy for customers to see the value for themselves—as Figure 2 shows.

In rolling out a true innovation, marketers often focus on identifying and converting early adopters. Those customers are desirable because they become references for later adopters. The motivations for early adopters run the gamut from exploiting the latest technologies to get ahead of the competition, to desiring to satisfy the emotional need to be on the cutting edge. Regardless of the specific motivation, early adopters are traditionally less price-sensitive. However, they are still concerned about the potential challenges in adopting an innovation; even the most motivated aren't completely careless about how much risk they will take on. And if the price is too high for an unknown product and its unproven benefits, then the product might never get off the ground.

To address those concerns, marketers should build their launches on what does drive adoption of new technologies. And they should use that knowledge to support sales. Key drivers of customer adoption include the following:

- Compelling advantages over existing technology.
- The ability to observe and measure the impact of those advantages.
- The complexity of the new solution.
- Compatibility with existing processes and technologies.
- The ability to try out an innovation before making a full commitment.

Note that price is not on the list. What the list represents is customer desire to mitigate the risks inherent in adopting an innovative new technology. Too often, companies fail to take into account these drivers of adoption when launching an innovative new offering. Instead, the approach is: "Our specifications are set. Our product is so innovative that it's hard to prove value or understand risk until we get it into customers' hands. Once they have it, they'll see the genius of what we have created."

Consider how Azul Systems (**http://www.azulsystems.com**) addressed adoption drivers in the launch of an entirely new server for handling Java applications used in software development. In addition to being a new player in the business, Azul's product did not replace any existing customer equipment—further squeezing already tight information technology budgets. Yet it enjoyed a successful launch. Here's how:

- An economic advantage program: "A free, private consulting engagement helps customers quantify the financial gains their organization will realize through a computer pool deployment."

- Integration of its technology that required changing only one line of code.
- A relationship with IBM to provide global support, services, and spare parts to address customer concerns about ongoing support and maintenance.
- Documented adherence to industry standards for interfacing with existing platforms.
- A no-cost 45-day evaluation program for qualified accounts.

Successful introduction of new products is challenging, but some simple things can be done to greatly improve your chances. More than anything, companies need to understand what ease of adoption will mean to their customers.

An alternative method of enlightening customers is often absurdly low introductory price deals. That compounds the perception of risk by leading customers to think: "If this technology is so good, then why do they seem so desperate for customers?" Price dealing to get those early "reference accounts" can also dramatically affect future revenues. Once low prices are out on the street, it is very difficult to raise them.

PRICING FOR SUCCESS

Price strategy can be the lever that maximizes return on the risky investment or the velvet rope that bars customers from your service. Get it right and your firm enjoys a commanding market position, increased profits, and well-earned confidence across the team. Get it wrong and your company limits both sales and profitability and suffers from a weakened market position, financial performance, and team capabilities.

Lessons from successful new-product launches demonstrate an effective process for innovation price strategy.

First, implement a customer-value measurement process as rigorous as the technology development process. Offer a quantified value message as compelling as the technology, and estimate a price

Figure 2
Using Customer Value to Determine Your Price

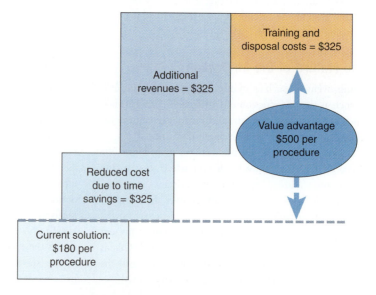

Training and disposal costs = $325

Additional revenues = $325

Value advantage $500 per procedure

Reduced cost due to time savings = $325

Current solution: $180 per procedure

range corresponding to customer value. Without a solid understanding of quantified customer value, the launch process is unnecessarily risky.

Second, within that range of customer value, set prices based on the interaction of the innovation's nature (minor, major, or disruptive) and the stage of product life cycle (introduction, maturity, growth, or decline). A simple matrix allows firms to plot a price point that maximizes both adoption and profitability.

The rules laid out here offer a guideline of where to set a price for a product or service innovation. That process can help companies overcome the long odds of new-product success—and fuel growth in both revenues and profitability.

Questions

1. How does pricing affect the success or failure of a new product?
2. Discuss the simple pricing rules followed by most successful innovators.
3. Do you think that Apple follows these rules when it introduces new products such as the iPod and the iPhone? Why or why not?
4. What is the "value-on-innovation" paradox?
5. Should a small firm use the pricing process shown in Figure 1? Explain your answer.
6. Describe how Procter & Gamble could apply the principles shown in Figure 2 to the introduction of a new detergent.
7. Relate the ideas covered in this case to the concept of elasticity of demand.

Marketing Management

In Part 8, we tie together the concepts introduced in Chapters 1 through 21 and discuss planning for the future.

22 Pulling It All Together: Integrating and Analyzing the Marketing Plan

We first note the value of developing and analyzing integrated marketing plans. Next, the elements in a well-integrated marketing plan are examined: clear organizational mission, long-term competitive advantages, precisely defined target market, compatible subplans, coordination among SBUs, coordination of the marketing mix, and stability over time. We then study five types of marketing plan analysis: benchmarking, customer satisfaction research, marketing cost analysis, sales analysis, and the marketing audit. These are valuable tools for evaluating the success or failure of marketing plans. We conclude with a look at why and how firms should anticipate and plan for the future.

After reading Part 8, you should understand elements 14 and 15 of the strategic marketing plan outlined in Table 3-2 (page 75).

Chapter 22

Pulling It All Together: Integrating and Analyzing the Marketing Plan

As *Business Week* said in an article on the great innovators of the past 75 years, "more than anyone else, he [Bill Gates, Microsoft's founder] can be credited with turning the disorganized PC tribes of the late 1970s into today's huge industry. Gates was among the first to recognize that all sorts of firms and products would be created if a computer's operating system and all the other software programs were separated from the hardware." Gates' most important strategic decision, however, was persuading IBM to allow his firm (Microsoft) to license its MS-DOS computer operations to other manufacturers of PCs.

This gave Microsoft (**http://www.microsoft.com**) a large source of potential revenues. The standardized operating system greatly expanded the market for PCs, as well as peripherals such as disk drives, memory, motherboards, hard drives, and printers. Also contributing to Microsoft's success was the support it gave developers by having technical conferences and its encouragement of software innovation by others to expand the dominance of its operating system. "Microsoft showed amazing determination to make Windows the standard and did everything it could to protect its dominance," said an analyst.

Recently, however, Microsoft's growth has slowed; the firm has been heavily fined by the European Union for the way it bundles Internet Explorer and Windows Media Player with Windows; and it has been looking for opportunities to further expand beyond operating system software. All of this, and Bill Gates recently retired from everyday management to run his foundation (**http://www.gatesfoundation.org**).

Microsoft is currently devising a new operating system—temporarily called Windows 7—to replace Windows Vista. Although 150 million copies of Vista had been sold by late 2008, many users were dissatisfied with that operating system. Nonetheless, Microsoft stopped selling its popular Windows XP to PC makers as of June 30, 2008.

In 2008, Microsoft made an unsuccessful $47 billion bid to purchase Yahoo! Microsoft hoped to increase its presence on the Web, build online advertising revenues, and provide itself with a search engine more competitive with Google. The deal fell apart as the two parties could not agree to terms.[1]

In this chapter, we will see the value of developing and implementing a clear, forward-looking, cohesive, and adaptable strategy.

Chapter Objectives

1. To show the value of an integrated marketing plan
2. To discuss the elements of a well-integrated marketing plan
3. To present five types of marketing plan analysis: benchmarking, customer satisfaction research, marketing cost analysis, sales analysis, and the marketing audit
4. To see the merit of anticipating and planning for the future

22-1 OVERVIEW

Chapters 1 and 2 introduced basic marketing concepts and described the marketing environment. Chapters 3 and 4 presented the strategic planning process as it applies to marketing and the role of marketing information systems and marketing research. Chapters 5 to 7 broadened our scope to include the societal, ethical, and consumer

---

[1] Various company and other sources.

implications of marketing; global marketing efforts; and marketing applications of the Internet. Chapters 8 to 21 centered on specific aspects of marketing: describing and selecting target markets, and the marketing mix (product, distribution, promotion, and price planning).

We tie things together in this chapter and describe how a marketing plan can be integrated and assessed. Chapter 22 builds on the strategic planning discussion in Chapter 3—particularly, the total quality approach (whereby a firm strives to fully satisfy customers in an effective and efficient way). With an integrated effort, individual marketing components are synchronized and everyone is "on the same page." When a firm wants to appraise performance, capitalize on strengths, minimize weaknesses, and plan for the future, marketing analysis (including benchmarking and customer satisfaction) is necessary. The overall process is shown in Figure 22-1. This is the challenge:

> To achieve exceptional performance, a firm must be an ever-evolving enterprise. Learning must lead to the implementation of a continuous stream of proactive changes that enable the firm to evolve. Ever-evolving enterprises will thrive in the years ahead because they recognize that what worked well yesterday will be less effective today, inappropriate tomorrow, and obsolete the day after. Firms that are not in sync with new realities will not survive. Random changes in companies rarely result in long-term advantages. Adaptations may initially emerge, but they must be deliberately developed and leveraged to provide significant benefits. Second, organizational changes must occur at an infinitely quicker pace than those appearing in nature. Future success will also be contingent on the firm's ability to be innovative. It must be able to offer goods and services that give it a competitive edge. It must also be able to develop and implement processes that enable it to be faster, provide higher and more consistent quality, be more efficient, and be more convenient to its target markets.[2]

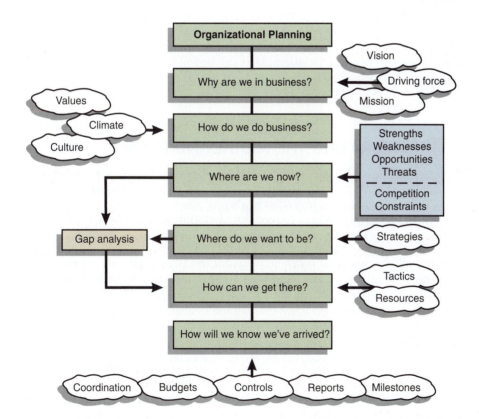

Figure 22-1

Integrating and Assessing Strategic Marketing Plans

Source: Clark Crouch, "A New Simplified Model for Planning," **http://crouchnet. com/planning.html** (May 5, 2001). Reprinted by permission. Copyright © 1991 by In-Com. Inc. Revision © 1999 by Clark E. Crouch. All Rights reserved.

---

[2] Stephen C. Harper and David J. Glew, "Becoming an Ever-Evolving Enterprise," *Industrial Management,* Vol. 50 (May 2008), p. 23.

Here is what three diverse companies are doing to optimize their marketing strategies:

- Green Hills Farms (**http://www.greenhills.com**) is an independent supermarket in Syracuse, New York. *Inc.* has called it "the best little grocery store in America." The store is renowned for its customer loyalty program. The firm tries out all sales promotions on employees before offering them to customers (to see what works best), monitors its customer data base, and exchanges ideas with noncompeting supermarkets. Its strategy is to offer "a wide assortment of specialty, international, gourmet, and high-quality fresh foods in a friendly, courteous shopping environment."[3]

- Japan's Toyota (**http://www.toyota.com**) is widely acknowledged to be one of the leading manufacturers in the world. What makes it tick? "At Toyota, whenever we're faced with a challenge, we ask ourselves the same question. Why not? Two words that are filled with possibilities. They can turn a challenge into an opportunity. An obstacle into an inspiration. We're continuously looking for new ways to improve what we do. By asking tough questions. Can we make a car that has zero emissions? Can we improve the economy of a community? Can we enrich the lives of people around us? And we endeavor to do this by creating jobs, pioneering new technologies that help make vehicles cleaner and safer, and involving ourselves in the communities where we live and work."[4]

- Wells Fargo (**http://www.wellsfargo.com**) has 11,000 outlets, more than 12,000 ATMs, and serves 48 million banking households. It recently acquired Wachovia Corporation as part of its long-term growth plan: "This merger creates what we believe will be a very compelling value proposition for our team members, customers, communities, and shareholders. Our team members can benefit from even more professional development opportunities across a much broader geography. Our customers can benefit from greater convenience and a better value for entrusting us with more of their business. Our communities can benefit because we want to be a leading contributor of financial, human, and social capital in every community in which we do business. Our shareholders can benefit because of the exciting growth opportunities created by this merger."[5]

22-2 INTEGRATING THE MARKETING PLAN

> From a total quality perspective, the many parts of a marketing plan should be unified, consistent, and coordinated.

When a marketing plan is properly integrated—all its various parts are unified, consistent, and coordinated—a total quality approach can then be followed. Although this appears to be an easy task, keep in mind that a firm may have long-run, moderate-length, and short-run plans; the different strategic business units in an organization may require separate marketing plans; and each aspect of the marketing mix requires planning:

- An overall plan would be poorly integrated if short-run profits are earned at the expense of long-term profits. This could occur if marketing research or new-product planning expenditures are reduced to raise profits temporarily. A firm might also encounter difficulties if plans are changed too frequently, leading to a blurred image for consumers and a lack of focus for executives.

- Resources must be allocated among SBUs so funds are given to those with high potential. The target market, image, prices, and so on, of each SBU have to be

---

[3] "Our Mission," **http://www.greenhills.com** (May 25, 2009).

[4] *Toyota: U.S. Operations 2008*, **http://www.toyota.com/about/our_business/operations/2008OperationsBrochure.pdf**.

[5] "Wells Fargo and Wachovia Merger Completed," **http://www.wellsfargo.com/press/2009/20090101_Wachovia_Merger** (January 1, 2009).

Ethical Issues in Marketing

The Rights of Whistle-Blowers Under the Sarbanes-Oxley Act

The Sarbanes-Oxley Act (http://www.soxlaw.com) was enacted to prevent unethical behavior by tightening accounting standards and requiring greater disclosure by public companies. It was devised in 2002, after the collapse of Enron and World.Com. Sarbanes-Oxley compliance is costly for a public corporation. One executive at a public company with $12 billion in annual revenues estimates that the cost for his firm to comply is about $40 million per year. Aside from relying on Sarbanes-Oxley, individual investors have the responsibility to be more diligent by carefully reading annual reports and checking out companies through multiple sources.

Whistle-blowers are employees who report unethical policies and strategies used by their current employer. Although Sarbanes-Oxley protects whistle-blowers at public companies from retaliation by their employers, it does not cover those employed by private firms. Groups such as the Consumer Federation of America (http://www.consumerfed.org) argue that whistle-blower rules need to apply to firms that sell privately held mutual funds that are sold to the public.

In a recent lawsuit against Fidelity Investments (http://www.fidelity.com), a former portfolio manager claimed he was fired for complaining about some of Fidelity's business practices, including how Fidelity discloses its fund managers' compensation policies. A second lawsuit against Fidelity was filed by a former senior director, who said she was forced to resign after questioning how Fidelity set its fees. In both cases, Fidelity stated that since it was not a public firm, it was not subject to Sarbanes-Oxley.

Source: Based on material in Ross Kerber, "Lawsuits May Expand Sarbanes-Oxley," *Boston Globe*, http://www.boston.com/business (May 8, 2008).

distinctive, yet not in conflict with one another. Physical distribution and channel member arrangements must be timed so the system and the total quality process are not strained by multiple SBUs making costly demands simultaneously.

- Although a promotion plan primarily deals with one strategic element, it must also be integrated with product, distribution, and pricing plans. It must reflect the proper positioning for a firm's products, encourage channel cooperation, and show that products are worth the prices set.

A well-integrated marketing plan incorporates the elements shown in Figure 22-2. We explain these elements next.

22-2a Clear Organizational Mission

A clear organizational mission outlines a firm's commitment to a type of business and a place in the market. It directs total quality efforts. The mission is involved if a firm seeks new customer groups or abandons existing ones, adds or deletes product lines, acquires other firms or sells part of its own business, does different marketing functions, and/or shifts technological focus (as noted in Chapter 3). See Figure 22-3.

> The organizational mission should be clear and directive.

Both top management and marketing personnel must be committed to a mission; and the mission must be communicated to customers, company employees, suppliers, and distribution intermediaries. If the mission is not on target, results can be poor.

Many experts think a firm should reappraise its mission if that company has values that do not fit a changing environment, its industry undergoes rapid changes, its performance is average or worse, it changes size (from small to large or large to small), or opportunities unrelated to its original mission arise. Some companies, such as Campbell, are especially proactive in assessing their mission:

> An identity provides executives with direction and focuses attention on opportunities and threats. For instance, in August 2007, Campbell [http://www.campbell.com] decided it would sell off its Godiva [http://www.godiva.com] business. The company didn't base the decision on financial performance; Godiva is a super-premium chocolate brand and a profitable business. Trouble is, Campbell's values, competencies, and aspirations focus on nutrition and simplicity—and Godiva chocolates don't fit in with that self-image. "Although the premium

Figure 22-2

Elements Leading to a Well-Integrated Marketing Plan

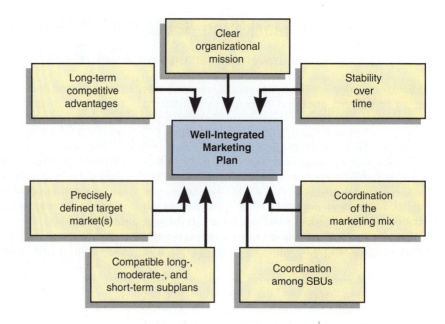

chocolate category is experiencing strong growth and Godiva is well-positioned for the future, the premium chocolate business does not fit with Campbell's focus on simple meals," explained Douglas R. Conant, Campbell's chief executive, while announcing the decision. [In January 2008, the sale of Godiva was completed.][6]

To learn more about devising superior organizational missions, visit the About.com Web site (**http://www.about.com**) and type "mission statement" in the "Search" box.

Figure 22-3

Target Stores: A Clear Company Vision

As Target (**http://www.target.com**) says at its Web site: "Step into any Target store in any city in the country, and you know exactly what to expect: high-quality, stylishly designed items plus all the essentials for your life, displayed in a clean, organized, and welcoming environment. The one-of-a-kind experience comes from our department store roots and ongoing commitment to great prices and stylish innovations; the one-of-a-kind feeling is why millions of guests visit every year."

Source: Reprinted by permission of Susan Berry, Retail Image Consulting, Inc.

[6] John C. Camillus, "Strategy as a Wicked Problem," *Harvard Business Review*, Vol. 86 (May 2008), p. 103.

22-2b Long-Term Competitive Advantages

Long-term competitive advantages are company, product, and marketing attributes whose distinctiveness and consumer appeal can be maintained over an extended period of time. A firm must capitalize on the attributes that are most important to consumers and prepare competitive advantages accordingly. For advantages to be sustainable, consumers must perceive a consistent positive difference in key attributes between the company's offerings and those of competitors; that difference must be linked to a capability gap that competitors will have difficulty in closing (due to patents, superior marketing skills, customer loyalty, and other factors); and the company's offerings must appeal to an enduring consumer need. This is highlighted in Figure 22-4 for Moen's (**http://www.moen.com**) line of faucets, whose slogan is "Buy it for looks. Buy it for life." While concentrating on its competitive advantages, a company should not lose sight of the role of customer service in a total quality program.

Pixar and Ikea are examples of firms that are successful due to well-articulated, well-implemented, long-term competitive advantages. Pixar (**http://www.pixar.com**) is the

> Competitive advantages should center on company, product, and marketing attributes with long-range distinctiveness.

Figure 22-4

Moen: Capitalizing on Its Long-Term Competitive Advantages

Source: Reprinted by permission.

IF YOU CONSIDER YOURSELF FLASHY

DO TURN THE PAGE.

Because you won't find it here. Only elegant and timeless designs that reflect good taste. Just like yours.

MOEN

Buy it for looks. Buy it for life.®

1-800-BUY-MOEN • www.moen.com

animation studio responsible for such hits as *Wall-e*, *Cars*, *Toy Story*, and more. Ikea (**http://www.ikea.com**) is the global retail furniture giant. "Pixar, one of the world's most innovative firms, 'combines proprietary technology and world-class creative talent to develop computer-animated feature films with memorable characters and heartwarming stories that appeal to audiences of all ages.' No films for mature audiences only. Lots of pushing the envelope. Ikea offers customers 'a wide range of well-designed, functional home furnishing products at prices so low that as many people as possible will be able to afford them.'"[7]

Smaller firms often cannot compete on the basis of low prices, so they tend to concentrate on other competitive advantages,[8] such as:

- Targeting underserved market niches, including foreign ones.
- Having unique offerings by specializing. Firms can be innovative, process customized orders, or otherwise adapt products for particular customers.
- Emphasizing product quality and reliability to reduce customers' price sensitivity.
- Working harder to attain shopper loyalty. Hands-on customer service is particularly effective.
- Emphasizing relationship marketing, whereby relationships with both suppliers and customers are viewed as important.

When implementing a marketing strategy, a firm should note that its competitive advantages may not apply in all situations. For instance, an advantage can lose its value when transferred to another nation, because it is not relevant in a different context or because it can easily be countered by local competitors.

22-2c Precisely Defined Target Market(s)

> The target market(s) should be indentified precisely.

By precisely defining its target market(s), a firm identifies the specific consumers to be addressed in its marketing plans. This guides current marketing efforts and future direction. When a firm engages in concentrated marketing or differentiated marketing, it is essential that each segment be understood. TCF Bank (**http://www.tcfbank.com**) has more than 450 branches in Minnesota, Illinois, Michigan, Colorado, Wisconsin, Indiana, and Arizona. TCF's main businesses are retail and commercial banking services, and investment and insurance services. It targets "a broad range of customers, individuals, families, and small to medium-size businesses." The firm also works "to ensure that credit is available to everyone, especially those in low- to moderate-income neighborhoods." Emphasis is on "convenience in banking; we're open 12 hours a day, seven days a week, 364 days per year. We provide customers innovative products through multiple banking channels, including traditional, supermarket, and campus branches, TCF Express Teller and other ATMs, debit cards, phone banking, and Internet banking."[9]

A firm's target market approach may have to be fine-tuned due to changing demographics and lifestyles—or declining sales. Consider the dinnerware industry:

> The consumer market is in transition. Moderate-income shoppers are gravitating to mass merchants and discounters as the preferred shopping venue for tableware and spending less money than in the past. Today's affluent consumers are increasing their spending on dinnerware, not necessarily in the luxury end, but more toward 'casual luxury' that they use and enjoy, not display in cabinets. These luxury consumers are attracted to dinnerware that offers new experiential attributes besides those provided by fine china and crystal. Pier 1 [**http://www.pier1.com**], Pottery Barn [**http://www.potterybarn.com**], Crate & Barrel

---

[7] Cynthia A. Montgomery, "Putting Leadership Back into Strategy," *Harvard Business Review*, Vol. 86 (January 2008), p. 58.

[8] See Alan Davis and Eric M. Olson, "Critical Competitive Strategy Issues Every Entrepreneur Should Consider Before Going into Business," *Business Horizons*, Vol. 51 (May 2008), pp. 211–221.

[9] "Philosophy" and "Community Relations," **http://www.tcfbank.com/About/index.jsp** (May 25, 2009).

[http://www.crateandbarrel.com], and many others have discovered a thriving market niche by offering seasonal, casual dinnerware. For $100 to $200, one can set a party table with creative, designer-look, and fully coordinating dishes, glasses, serving dishes, linens, centerpieces, and all the rest that are designed to enhance the moment and are strictly for the here and now. This is dinnerware to use once, twice, maybe three times, then toss it out or recycle it through a local charity. It is fun, frivolous, and total luxury—the equivalent of paper plates and cups for the luxury set.[10]

In this context, a total quality approach is especially crucial in attracting and retaining consumers. This is aided through the use of data-base marketing.

22-2d Compatible Long-, Moderate-, and Short-Term Subplans

The long-, moderate-, and short-term marketing subplans of a firm need to be compatible with one another. Long-term plans are the most general and set a broad framework for moderate-term plans. Short-term plans are the most specific, but they need to be derived from both moderate- and long-term plans. Unfortunately, adequate plans and subplans are not always set—or are not communicated to employees.

> Long-, moderate-, and short-term subplans must be compatible.

One important trend among many companies is the shrinking time frame of marketing plans. For example, Tag Heuer (http://www.tagheuer.com),

> ... has always been rooted in sport, but what we've tried to do and have done very successfully is position the brand from sports-inspired to sports- and glamour-directed. With the addition of actors Uma Thurman, Peter Ho, and Shah Rukh Khan, we've extended the position to more of a lifestyle position of active, successful people who want to win in their lives, whatever that means to them. We've also very recently made a much stronger push into the women's business. Tag Heuer was historically known as a male-skewed brand, but we realized through various surveys with consumers that our U.S. women's sales have been growing very fast. We have developed a huge business in the women's category without consciously trying to get that appeal to women in a large way. With Maria Sharapova and Uma Thurman, we think we're making an aggressive push into the women's market.[11]

22-2e Coordination Among SBUs

Coordination among an organization's SBUs is enhanced when the functions, strategies, and resources allotted to each are described in long-, moderate-, and short-term plans. For big firms, SBU coordination can be challenging. British-based Arcadia Group is a large apparel retailer, with more than 2,500 stores. It has several store divisions (SBUs), such as Evans for women, Miss Selfridge for women, Topman for men, and others. And Arcadia is growing internationally. To position its SBUs well, each division seeks distinct segments. As Arcadia's Web site (http://www.arcadiagroup.co.uk/about/brands.html) notes, Evans "offers great value" and appeals to "20- to 45-year-old women to women who want to celebrate their shapes," Miss Selfridge targets "stylish, individualistic, and self-assured customers aged 18 to 24," and Topman "is the leader on the high street for young men's fashion. It has won numerous awards and worked with leading young British designers."

> SBUs should be coordinated.

The coordination of SBUs by large multinational firms can be complex. For example, less than a decade ago, ABB (Asea Brown Boveri, http://www.abb.com) had 175 global managers at its Swiss headquarters, 200,000 employees, and more than 1,000 companies operating in 140 countries around the globe. Today,

---

[10] Michelle Moran and Pam Danziger, "Heading Toward Casual Luxury," *Gourmet Retailer* (October 2005), pp. 43–46.

[11] Sandra O'Loughlin, "Tag Heuer Makes Time for New Marketing Tactics," *Brandweek* (May 9, 2005), p.16; and "The Brand: Stars and Glamour," http://www.tagheuer.com/the-brand/stars-glamour/index.lbl?lang=en (September 5, 2008).

ABB is a global leader in power and automation technologies that enable utility and industry customers to improve performance while lowering environmental impact. With more than 115,000 employees, we are close to customers in around 100 countries. With our technology leadership, global presence, application knowledge, and local expertise, we offer products, systems, solutions, and services that allow our customers to improve their operations—whether they need to increase the reliability of a power grid or raise productivity in a factory. Focusing on our core strengths in power and automation technologies, we strive for organic profitable growth. Our global manufacturing base ensures consistent top-quality products and systems—made in ABB—for customers around the world. Our customers have broad and easy access to ABB's offerings—whether they buy from us directly or through distributors, wholesalers, system integrators, or other partners. Our people work together seamlessly to deliver benefits for our customers. Our way of doing business is values-based, leadership-driven, and performance-oriented.[12]

22-2f   Coordination of the Marketing Mix

> The marketing mix within each SBU must be coordinated.

Marketing mix components (product, distribution, promotion, and price) need to be coordinated and consistent with the organizational mission. Wal-Mart (**http://www.walmart.com**) is a discount retailer that has become the largest firm in the world. The key to its success is a superior marketing mix that adheres to a total quality philosophy. As the late founder Sam Walton said: "The secret of successful retailing is to give your customers what they want. And if you think about it from your point of view as a customer, you want everything: a wide assortment of good-quality merchandise; the lowest possible prices; guaranteed satisfaction with what you buy; friendly, knowledgeable service; convenient hours; free parking; a pleasant shopping experience." Today, Wal-Mart's marketing mix remains well coordinated:

- Product—Wal-Mart offers a wide range of manufacturer and private-label branded goods and services in categories ranging from apparel to consumer electronics to food to optical services to prescription drugs to toys, and much more. Over 1 million products are listed at its main Web site.
- Distribution—Wal-Mart operates multiple store formats for the shopping convenience of customers, including Wal-Mart stores (**http://www.walmartstores.com**), Sam's Club (**http://www.salesclub.com**), and the newest entry Neighborhood Markets. It also has multiple Web sites for shoppers. And Wal-Mart International is quite active with both stores and Web sites in its expanding foreign markets.
- Promotion—Compared to many other retail chains, Wal-Mart spends relatively little on advertising—about one-half of 1 percent of annual revenues. However, this still represents $2 billion or more in annual expenditures, mostly on print and TV ads. As a further reflection of its low-price image, stores are mostly self-service; but they do have floor staff to answer queries and help shoppers in other ways. Wal-Mart's slogan is "Save Money. Live Better."
- Price—Wal-Mart does everything it can to keep prices low in all of its retail formats. "Whether it is in the United States, Great Britain, Mexico, or Brazil, we position ourselves as the unbeatable price leader. Our customers appreciate it and our shareholders understand it."[13]

22-2g   Stability Over Time

> The stability of the basic plan should be maintained over time.

A marketing plan must have a degree of stability over time to be implemented and evaluated properly. This does not mean it should be inflexible and thus unable to adjust

---

[12] "Strategy," **http://www.abb.com** (July 25, 2008).

[13] *Wal-Mart 2008 Annual Report*; and various sections of **http://www.walmart.com** and **http://www.walmartstores.com**.

to a dynamic environment. Rather, it means a broad marketing plan, consistent with the firm's mission and total quality approach, should guide long-term efforts and be fine-tuned regularly; the basic plan should remain in effect for a number of years. Short-run marketing plans can be more flexible, as long as they conform to long-term goals and the organizational mission. Low prices might be part of a long-term marketing plan. However, in any particular year, prices might have to be raised in response to environmental forces.

U.S.-based Staples (highlighted in Figure 22-5) is a firm seeking to maintain a stable, but flexible, strategy. Here is how:

> Staples [http://www.staples.com], the world's largest office-products company, is committed to making it easy for customers to buy a wide range of office products, including supplies, technology, furniture, and business services. With $27 billion in sales, Staples serves businesses of all sizes and consumers in 27 countries throughout North and South America, Europe, Asia, and Australia. In July 2008, Staples acquired Corporate Express [http://www.corporateexpress.com], one of the world's leading suppliers of office products to businesses and institutions. Staples invented the office superstore concept in 1986 and is headquartered outside Boston.[14]

22-3 ANALYZING THE MARKETING PLAN

Marketing plan analysis involves comparing actual performance with planned or expected performance for a specified period of time. If actual performance is unsatisfactory, corrective action may be needed. Also, plans must sometimes be revised due to uncontrollable variables.

Five techniques to analyze marketing plans are discussed next: benchmarking, customer satisfaction research, marketing cost analysis, sales analysis, and the marketing audit. Although our discussion relates to these tools' utility in assessing marketing plans, they may also be used in devising and adjusting plans.

> **Marketing plan analysis** compares actual and targeted achievements.

Figure 22-5

Staples: Applying a Consistent, But Evolving Strategy

Everything that Staples (**http://www.staples.com**) does is intended to grow its business: "Today, we are the world's largest office products company. Our associates around the world are dedicated to making it easy for businesses of all sizes and consumers to buy office products."

Source: Reprinted by permission of Susan Berry, Retail Image Consulting, Inc.

---

[14] "Corporate Profile," **http://investor.staples.com/phoenix.zhtml?c=96244&p=irol-IRHome** (August 15, 2008).

22-3a   Benchmarking

A company must set performance standards to properly assess the effectiveness of its marketing plans. That is, it must specify what exactly is meant by "success." One way to do this is to utilize *benchmarking*, whereby a firm sets its own marketing performance standards based on prior actions by the firm itself, the prowess of direct competitors, the competence of the best companies in its industry, and/or the approaches of innovative companies in other industries anywhere around the world. As two observers recently noted: A firm's "capacity to flourish depends in part on its ability to capture and embed best practices from its own and other companies. Without mechanisms that facilitate the sharing of best-practice knowledge—such as visits to exemplar companies and the use of experts—organizations would be consigned to reliving the same mistakes day after day. Searching for and then articulating, refining, and embedding best-practice ideas brings companies in a sector to a level playing field. Those companies that fail to adopt best-practice processes rapidly become complacent laggards."[15] Among the firms that do benchmarking are Best Buy (http://www.bestbuy.com), DuPont (http://www.dupont.com), Hewlett-Packard (http://www.hp.com), IBM (http://www.ibm.com), Marriott (http://www.marriott.com), and Walt Disney (http://www.disney.com). According to a recent global study of senior executives by Bain & Company, about four-fifths of the responding firms regularly do benchmarking.[16]

There are two main types of external benchmarking—competitive and best practice:

The goal of *competitive benchmarking* is to assess your advantages and disadvantages by comparing them with those of direct competitors. *Best practice benchmarking*, by contrast, is designed to identify world-class performers and the specific underlying best practices they utilize that will enable your company to realize similar world-class results. It is natural for companies to want to benchmark their performance against a handpicked group of major competitors. However, depending on individual objectives and business strategy, different companies, even within the same industry, have different strategic goals. Assessing potentially effective best practices is possible only by looking at companies outside one's own industry to see what innovators are doing elsewhere.[17]

A good benchmarking process comprises these steps:

1. *Identify benchmarking needs:* Benchmarking should focus on the critical factors that truly impact on the success of the firm, and not be diverted into inconsequential or ill-defined areas.
2. *Develop performance metrics:* Performance standards and measures must be clear for each factor under review. What must occur for a firm to be rated as "excellent" in each area studied?
3. *Collect internal data:* Appropriate internal data must be compiled. Data categories should be consistent with commonly available and custom-generated data on external measures.
4. *Select comparison organizations:* Marketing research companies and independent consultants are often better able to collect external data, because they are not competitors, and they only report average and "best-in-class" performance information. They do not reveal individual data.
5. *Collect outside benchmarking data:* All of the firms participating in a benchmarking study must agree on the terminology for measures and provide data in the categories requested. Initially, this may be time consuming. The data are then compiled by the

[15] Lynda Gratton and Sumantra Ghoshal, "Beyond Best Practice," *Sloan Management Review*, Vol. 46 (Spring 2005), p. 49.

[16] Darrell Rigby and Barbara Bilodeau, *Bain & Company: Management Tools and Trends 2007*, http://www.bain.com/management_tools/Management_Tools_and_Trends_2007.pdf.

[17] Richard T. Roth, "Best Practice Benchmarking vs. Competitive Benchmarking," *Financial Executive* (July-August 2005), p. 58.

independent research firm or consultant, which is responsible for distributing a report with aggregate and "best-in-class" findings.

6. *Assess the competitive gap and develop an action plan:* During this step, based on its own situation and strategy, each firm must: (a) make direct comparisons of the measures; (b) assess the gap that exists between that firm and the best in class; (c) compare the activities that are used by all companies included in the report and that are used by the best-in-class companies; (d) set new performance goals; (e) adapt the marketing strategy and develop an action plan to attain the goals; and (f) be realistic about the firm's ability to change.

7. *Implement and regularly assess the action plan:* The action plan must be enacted in response to the findings of the benchmarking project. The key players in the firm must "buy in" to the action plan. And once implemented, the action plan needs to be reviewed and results measured. Are the gaps closing—or are they growing?[18]

When formulating a program, a company needs to consider its experience with benchmarking and act accordingly.[19] A *novice* firm should try to emulate direct competitors, not world-class companies. It should rely on customers for new-product ideas and choose suppliers mostly on price and reliability. The focus should be on cost reduction, with a "don't develop it, buy it" thrust. The firm should look for processes to add value, simplify those processes, and be faster responding to the marketplace.

A *journeyman* firm should encourage employees to find ways to do their jobs better and simplify operations. It should emulate market leaders and selected world-class companies. Consumer input, formal marketing research, and internal ideas should be used in generating new products. The firm should select good-quality suppliers, and then look at their prices. The firm should refine practices to improve value added per employee, time to market, and customer satisfaction.

A *master* firm should rely on self-managed, multiskilled teams that emphasize horizontal processes (such as product development). It should measure its marketing practices against the world's best. Consumer input, benchmarking, and internal research and development should be used in generating new products. The firm should select suppliers that are technologically advanced and offer superior quality. Executive compensation should be linked to teamwork and quality. The firm should continue refining its practices to improve the value added per employee, the time to market, and customer satisfaction.

Two especially useful benchmarks are the Malcolm Baldrige National Quality Award (**http://www.quality.nist.gov**) and *Fortune's* "Most Admired" corporate reputations surveys (**http://money.cnn.com/magazines/fortune/rankings**). A firm does not have to participate in either of these competitions to benefit from the benchmarks. Any organization can internally assess itself and compare its results with others.

The Baldrige Award rates U.S. firms in seven areas: leadership; strategic planning; customer and market focus; measurement, analysis, and knowledge management (such as competitive comparisons); workforce focus; process management; and results. Of the maximum 1,000 points a company can score, 255 points are assigned to marketing-related areas: customer and market focus, customer-focused outcomes, and product and service outcomes. *Fortune's* corporate reputations surveys (one for U.S. firms and one for global firms, including American firms) rate companies in such areas as quality of management; quality of goods and services; innovativeness; long-term investment value; financial soundness; the ability to attract, develop, and keep talented people; social responsibility; and wise use of corporate resources. The global survey also asks about international business acumen. Companies are rated within their own industry.

> There are three rungs in the benchmarking ladder: novice, journeyman, and master.

---

[18] Adapted by the authors from Kevin Reid, "Gaining a Competitive Advantage Using Benchmarking," *Paint & Coatings Industry* (April 2008), pp. 84–90.

[19] Otis Port, John Carey, Kevin Kelly, and Stephanie Anderson Forest, "Quality: Small and Midsize Companies Seize the Challenge—Not a Moment Too Soon," *Business Week* (November 30, 1992), pp. 66–72.

These Web sites provide further insights into benchmarking: Benchmarking Exchange (**http://www.benchnet.com**), Benchmarking Network (**http://www.well.com/user/benchmar**), and Best Practices (**http://www.best-in-class.com**).

22-3b Customer Satisfaction Research

As we defined it in Chapter 1, *customer satisfaction* is the degree to which there is a match between a customer's expectations of a good or service and the actual performance of that good or service, including customer service. Today, due to the intensely competitive global marketplace, it is more important than ever that companies regularly—and properly—measure the level of customer satisfaction. Here are some common mistakes that companies make in assessing customer satisfaction:

> *Asking only about your product.* If you ask only about your products, you're likely to miss the little things that actually drive choice in a competitive market. *Asking only about your company.* Customers ultimately choose among competing products. What drives their behavior is not their absolute satisfaction with your company, but their satisfaction relative to the competitive options available. *Asking only about satisfaction.* A key assumption underlying customer satisfaction research is that satisfaction leads to loyalty, but research suggests the strength of this link varies across business sectors and customer groups. *Not asking about price.* No matter how wonderful a product may be, price still has a tremendous impact on most customer decisions. This impact may remain hidden unless you ask about price directly. *Asking only your current customers.* If you talk only to current customers, you're likely to get an overly rosy picture of your situation.[20]

> Research is needed to gauge customer satisfaction. ACSI is a broad project that does so.

The largest ongoing customer satisfaction research project is the American Customer Satisfaction Index (ACSI, **http://www.theacsi.org**) sponsored by the University of Michigan (**http://www.bus.umich.edu**), the American Society for Quality (**http://www.asq.org**), and CFI Group (**http://www.cfigroup.com**). To compute ACSI, more than 65,000 consumers are surveyed annually on more than 200 firms and federal government agencies in 43 industries. ACSI is based on three measures: "*Customer expectations* is a measure of the customer's anticipation of the quality of a company's goods. Expectations represent both prior consumption experience, which includes some nonexperiential information such as advertising and word of mouth, and a forecast of the company's ability to deliver quality in the future. *Perceived quality* is a measure of the customer's evaluation via recent consumption experience of the quality of a company's goods or services. Quality is measured in terms of both customization, which is the degree to which a good or service meets the customer's individual needs, and reliability, which is the frequency with which things go wrong with the good or service. *Perceived value* is a measure of quality relative to price paid. Although price (value for money) is often very important to the customer's first purchase, it usually has a somewhat smaller impact on satisfaction for repeat purchases." See Figure 22-6.

With a maximum score of 100, these were the 2008 ratings for several firms: Federal Express (**http://www.fedex.com**), 85; UPS (**http://www.ups.com**), 83; Olive Garden (**http://www.olivegarden.com**), 82; Hilton Hotels (**http://www.hilton.com**), 78; AT&T (**http://www.att.com**), 75; Starbucks (**http://www.starbucks.com**), 75; McDonald's (**http://www.mcdonalds.com**), 69; American Airlines (**http://www.aa.com**), 62; and Comcast (**http://www.comcast.com**), 54. The average score for all companies was 75.[21]

Any firm can measure customer satisfaction:

> If you have only 20 clients, you can talk to each one personally. Focus groups are good ways to get informal input from a group of customers. You bring in 5 to 10 customers and ask them questions. You have a chance to gather ideas about customer needs, reactions to your

[20] Bruce H. Clark, "Bad Examples," *Marketing Management* (November-December 2003), pp. 34–38.

[21] Various sections, **http://www.theacsi.org** (August 25, 2008).

Figure 22-6

The American Customer Satisfaction Index

Source: Web screen from Dr. Claes Fornell, National Quality Research Center at the University of Michigan School of Business. Reprinted by permission.

company, suggestions for new services, and so forth. One way to get regular input from customers is to put together an advisory group. This can act like a focus group, but is set up to provide input over time. If you create a good group, members may enjoy meeting and interacting with each other. Advisory boards are a much underused way to improve customer service, develop new services, and encourage repeat business. Even the smallest businesses can use them effectively.

Customer surveys with standardized questions insure that you will collect the same information from everyone. Remember that few of your customers will be interested in "filling out a questionnaire." It's work for them without much reward. By casting any survey as an attempt to find out "how we can serve you better," your customers will feel less put upon. Up to about 10 minutes of questions can be done on the phone. By speaking directly with people, you have the flexibility to talk with them. But, of course, it takes more of your time. On a longer survey, here are a few of the possible dimensions you could measure: service quality and speed, pricing, complaints or problems, and your positioning in customers' minds. If you have a simple survey, E-mail can be the way to go.[22]

The Edward Lowe Foundation Web site (**http://www.edwardlowe.org**) has an excellent discussion about customer satisfaction measurement. At the home page, go to the "Entrepreneurs' Resource Center" (under "Second-Stage Entrepreneurs"), choose "Defining and Serving a Market," select "Customer Feedback," and then click on "How to Measure Customer Satisfaction."

22-3c   Marketing Cost Analysis

Marketing cost analysis is used to evaluate the cost efficiency of various marketing factors, such as different total quality configurations, product lines, order sizes, distribution methods, sales territories, channel members, salespersons, advertising media, and

> Cost efficiency is measured in **marketing cost analysis**.

---

[22] Rick Crandall, "Why Measure Customer Satisfaction?" **http://www.hostedsurvey.com/article-measure-survey.html** (August 28, 2008).

Global Marketing in Action

Repositioning Long-Time Companies and Their Brands

Each year, *Business Week* (http://www.businessweek.com) and Interbrand Group (http://www.interbrand.com)—a global branding consultant—compile a list of the "100 Best Global Brands." As part of the report on the 2007 list, brands that at one point in time had stumbled, but then recovered, were profiled. According to Interbrand's chief executive, "Benchmark brands should be studied, but solutions can seem a lot more accessible when you can see how someone fell and picked themselves up." Two of the comeback brands were Nintendo (http://www.nintendo.com) and Burberry (http://www.burberry.com).

Nintendo deliberately did not emphasize the Nintendo name on its new Wii (http://www.wii.com) player since it wanted to give a clear message that the Wii was a home entertainment system for all family members, not just serious gamers in a household. To demonstrate its wide potential usage, Nintendo hosted parties for individual families and for groups of moms' friends. Further, the Wii was priced for less than the PlayStation 3 (http://www.playstation.com) and the Xbox (http://www.xbox.com). In the first two years after its late 2006 launch, more than 30 million Wii game consoles were sold worldwide.

In celebration of its 150th anniversary, Burberry developed the Icons collection, comprising luxury handbags, boots, trench coats, and small leather goods. This collection combined Burberry's classic look with such new features as quilted linings. Burberry also stopped making stadium hats and scarves that typically sold at $50 or less. Today, it is focused on these company strengths: "Unique democratic positioning in the luxury sector. Multicategory competence—women's wear, men's wear, non-apparel—with innovative, functional outerwear at the core. Global reach with a balance across geographies. Channel expertise in retail, wholesale, and licensing. A unified, seasoned management team."

Sources: Based on material in David Kiley, "Best Global Brands," http://www.businssweek.com (August 6, 2007); James Sherwood, "Global Wii Sales Near 30 Million," http://www.reghardware.co.uk/2008/07/30/nintendo_sales (July 30, 2008); and "Overview," http://www.burberryplc.com/bbry/corporateprofile/overview (July 30, 2008).

---

customer types. Even if a firm is very profitable, it is unlikely that all products, distribution methods, and so on are equally cost efficient (or profitable).

Consider this scenario: "Through the late 1990s, marketing budgets spent more and more, promising larger market share, higher sales, and greater customer loyalty that would, in theory, generate greater cash flow for the corporation and its shareholders." But the results were not always clear: "Sometimes, but all too rarely, marketers could point to greater market share or higher unit profitability to claim success. But how efficiently was money being spent? Though good executives ask some questions in times of plenty, as corporations try to spend their resources more efficiently in the 21st century, marketing professionals often are having a tougher time adapting."[23]

With marketing cost analysis, a firm can determine which factors (classifications) are the most efficient and which are the least efficient, and make appropriate adjustments. It can also generate information that may be needed to substantiate price compliance with the Robinson-Patman Act.

For this type of analysis to work properly, a firm needs to obtain and use continuous and accurate cost data. Table 22-1 presents several examples of marketing cost analysis.

Marketing cost analysis consists of three steps: studying natural account expenses, reclassifying natural accounts into functional ones, and allocating functional accounts by marketing classification.

Studying Natural Account Expenses The first step is to determine the level of expenses for all *natural accounts*, which report costs by the names of the expenses and not by their purposes. Expense categories include salaries and fringe benefits, rent, advertising, supplies, insurance, and interest. These are the names most often entered in accounting records. Table 22-2 shows a natural-account expense classification.

Natural accounts are reported as salaries, rent, insurance, and other expenses.

---

[23] David W. Stewart, "How Marketing Contributes to the Bottom Line," *Journal of Advertising Research*, Vol. 48 (March 2008), p. 94.

Table 22-1	Examples of Marketing Cost Analysis		
Marketing Factor	**Strategy/Tactics Studied**	**Problem/Opportunity Discovered**	**Action Applied**
Customer type	What are the relative costs of selling X-rays to dentists, doctors, and hospitals?	Per-unit costs of hospital sales are lowest (as are prices); per-unit costs of dentist and doctor sales are highest (as are prices).	Current efforts are maintained. Each customer is serviced.
Product	Should a manufacturer accept a retailer's offer that it make 700,000 private-label sneakers?	A lot of excess capacity exists; the private label would require no additional fixed costs.	A contract is signed. Different features for private and manufacturer labels are planned.
Distribution	Should a men's suit maker sell direct to consumers, as well as through normal channels?	Startup and personal selling costs would be high. Additional sales would be minimal.	Direct sales are not undertaken.
Order size	What is the minimum acceptable order size for a hardware manufacturer?	Orders below $50 are not profitable; they are too costly to process.	Small orders are discouraged by surcharges and minimum order size.
Advertising media	Which is more effective, TV or magazine advertising?	TV ads cost 5 cents for every potential customer reached; magazine ads cost 7 cents.	TV ads are increased.
Personal selling	What are the costs of making a sale?	15 percent of sales covers compensation and selling expenses, 2 percent above the industry average.	Sales personnel are encouraged to phone customers before visiting them, to confirm appointments.

Reclassifying Natural Accounts into Functional Accounts In the second step, natural accounts are reclassified into *functional accounts*, which indicate the purposes or activities for which expenditures have been made. These costs include marketing administration, personal selling, advertising, transportation, warehousing, marketing research, and general administration. Table 22-3 reclassifies the natural accounts of Table 22-2 into functional ones.

> **Functional accounts** denote the purpose or activity of expenditures.

Once functional accounts are set, cost analysis is clearer. For instance, if salaries and fringe benefits increase by $25,000 from the prior year, natural account analysis cannot

Table 22-2	A Natural-Account Expense Classification	
Net sales (after returns and discounts)	$1,000,000	
Less: Costs of goods sold	450,000	
Gross profit		$550,000
Less: Operating expenses (natural account expenses)		
Salaries and fringe benefits	220,000	
Rent	40,000	
Advertising	30,000	
Supplies	6,100	
Insurance	2,500	
Interest expense	1,400	
Total operating expenses		300,000
Net profit before taxes		$250,000

Table 22-3 Reclassifying Natural Accounts into Functional Accounts

Natural Accounts	Total	Functional Accounts						
		Marketing Administration	Personal Selling	Advertising	Transportation	Warehousing	Marketing Research	General Administration
Salaries and fringe benefits	$220,000	$30,000	$50,000	$15,000	$10,000	$20,000	$30,000	$65,000
Rent	40,000	3,000	7,000	3,000	2,000	10,000	5,000	10,000
Advertising	30,000			30,000				
Supplies	6,100	500	1,000	500			1,100	3,000
Insurance	2,500		1,000			1,200		300
Interest expense	1,400							1,400
Total	$300,000	$33,500	$59,000	$48,500	$12,000	$31,200	$36,100	$79,700

allocate the rise to a functional area. Functional account analysis can pinpoint the areas of marketing having higher personnel costs.

Functional costs are assigned with each marketing classification becoming a profit center.

Allocating Functional Accounts by Marketing Classification The third step assigns functional costs by product, distribution method, customer, or other marketing classification. Each classification is reported as a profit center. Table 22-4 shows how costs can be allocated to different products, using the data in Tables 22-2 and 22-3. From Table 22-4, it is obvious that product A has the highest sales and total profit. Product C has the greatest profit as a percent of sales.

Table 22-4 Allocating Functional Expenses by Product

	Total	Product A	Product B	Product C
Net sales	$1,000,000	$500,000	$300,000	$200,000
Less: Cost of goods sold	450,000	250,000	120,000	80,000
Gross profit	$550,000	$250,000	$180,000	$120,000
Less: Operating expenses (functional account expenses)				
Marketing administration	33,500	16,000	10,000	7,500
Personal selling	59,000	30,000	17,100	11,900
Advertising	48,500	20,000	18,000	10,500
Transportation	12,000	5,000	5,000	2,000
Warehousing	31,200	20,000	7,000	4,200
Marketing research	36,100	18,000	11,000	7,100
General administration	79,700	40,000	23,000	16,700
Total operating expenses	300,000	149,000	91,100	59,900
Net profit before taxes	$250,000	$101,000	$88,900	$60,100
Profit as percent of sales	25.0	20.2	29.6	30.1

These two points should be kept in mind in assigning functional costs. One, assigning some costs—such as marketing administration—to different products, customers, or other classifications is often somewhat arbitrary. Two, the elimination of a poorly performing classification would lead to overhead costs—such as general administration—being allotted among the remaining product or customer categories. This may lead to lower overall total profit. A firm should distinguish between the separable costs directly associated with a given classification category that can be eliminated if a category is dropped and the common costs shared by various categories that cannot be eliminated if one is dropped.

Before making strategic changes suggested by marketing cost analysis, a firm must be sure its cuts do not damage the value (price-quality) proposition offered to customers: "Many companies take a quick-fix approach by cutting costs to save this quarter's profit margin. This can cause permanent harm due to lost know-how and less control over innovation and quality. The puzzle is how to do more for less."[24]

22-3d Sales Analysis

Sales analysis is the detailed study of sales data to appraise the appropriateness and effectiveness of a marketing strategy. Without it, a poor response to the firm's total value chain may not be seen early enough, the strength of certain market segments and territories may be overlooked, sales effort may be poorly matched with market potential, trends may be missed, or support for sales personnel may not be forthcoming. Sales analysis enables plans to be set in terms of revenues by product, product line, salesperson, region, customer type, time period, price line, method of sale, and so on. It also compares actual sales against planned sales. More firms engage in sales analysis than in marketing cost analysis.

The main source of sales analysis data is the sales invoice, which may be written, printed, or computer generated. An invoice may contain such data as the customer's name and address, the quantity ordered, the price paid, purchase terms, all of the items bought at the same time, the order date, shipping arrangements, and the salesperson. Summary data are generated by adding invoices. Computerized marking, cash register, and inventory systems speed data recording and improves accuracy.

Proper control units must be selected in conducting sales analysis. *Control units* are the sales categories for which data are gathered, such as boys', men's, girls', and women's clothing. Although a marketing executive can broaden a control system by adding sales categories together, wide categories cannot be broken down into components. Thus, a narrow sales category is preferable to one that is too wide. It is also helpful to select control units consistent with other company, trade association, and government data. A stable classification system is necessary to compare data from different time periods.

A key concept when undertaking sales analysis is that summary data, such as overall sales or market share, are usually insufficient to diagnose a firm's strength and weakness. More intensive investigation is needed. Two techniques that offer in-depth probing are the 80-20 principle and sales exception reporting.

According to the *80-20 principle*, in many organizations, a large proportion of total sales (profit) is likely to come from a small proportion of customers, products, or territories. To function as efficiently as possible, firms need to determine sales and profit by customer, product, or territory. Marketing efforts can then be allocated accordingly. Firms err if they do not isolate and categorize data, and they then may place equal effort into each sale instead of concentrating on key accounts. These errors are due to a related concept, the *iceberg principle*, which states that superficial data are insufficient to make sound evaluations. This is how Illinois Tool Works (**http://www.itw.com**) applies the 80-20 principle:

Sales analysis looks at sales data to assess the effectiveness of a marketing strategy.

Control units are an essential aspect of sales analysis.

The 80-20 principle notes that a large share of sales (profits) often comes from few customers, products, or territories. Analysis errors may be due to the **iceberg principle**.

---

[24] Geoffrey Somary, "Cutting Costs While Doing More—Is It Possible?" *Industrial Paint & Powder* (November 2003), p. 10.

A driving force behind much of our success at ITW is our 80-20 business process. Too often, companies do not spend enough time on the critical 20 percent of their key customers and products and spend too much time on the less important 80 percent. Our view is that once you know your high-volume customers, you can understand what drives your growth and what your true costs are. At the same time, we don't typically walk away from low-volume customers; we just treat them differently, via outsourcing and specialty pricing. Our proven techniques guide our business process and help us find new ways to enhance customer satisfaction and drive margin growth and profits. Specific strategies that help us reach our goals include: product line simplification, segmentation, cellular manufacturing, and outsourcing, as well as manufacturing to the market rate of demand.[25]

> **Sales exception reporting** centers on unmet goals or special opportunities.

Sales exception reporting, which highlights situations where goals are not met or opportunities are present, can further enhance analysis. The firm can evaluate the validity of forecasts and make the proper modifications in them. A slow-selling item report cites products whose sales are below forecasts. It could suggest such corrective actions as price reductions, promotions, and sales incentives to increase sales. A fast-selling item report cites items whose sales exceed forecasts. It points out opportunities, as well as items that need more inventory to prevent stockouts. Figure 22-7 presents examples of the 80-20 principle, the iceberg principle, and sales exception reporting.

Organizations also may use sales analysis to identify and monitor consumer buying patterns by answering such questions as these:

- *Who purchases?* B-to-b versus final consumer, geographic region, end use, purchase history, customer size, customer demographics
- *What is sold?* Product line, price, brand, country of origin, package size, options purchased

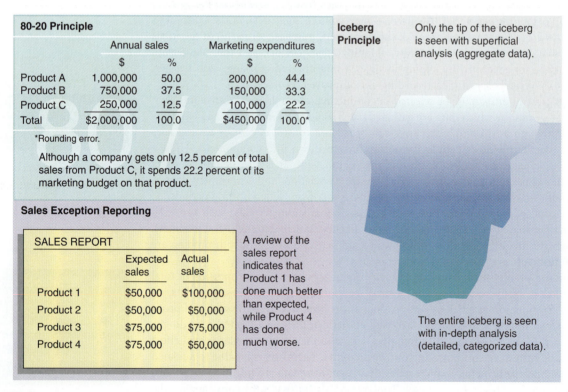

80-20 Principle

	Annual sales		Marketing expenditures	
	$	%	$	%
Product A	1,000,000	50.0	200,000	44.4
Product B	750,000	37.5	150,000	33.3
Product C	250,000	12.5	100,000	22.2
Total	$2,000,000	100.0	$450,000	100.0*

*Rounding error.

Although a company gets only 12.5 percent of total sales from Product C, it spends 22.2 percent of its marketing budget on that product.

Sales Exception Reporting

SALES REPORT	Expected sales	Actual sales
Product 1	$50,000	$100,000
Product 2	$50,000	$50,000
Product 3	$75,000	$75,000
Product 4	$75,000	$50,000

A review of the sales report indicates that Product 1 has done much better than expected, while Product 4 has done much worse.

Iceberg Principle

Only the tip of the iceberg is seen with superficial analysis (aggregate data).

The entire iceberg is seen with in-depth analysis (detailed, categorized data).

Figure 22-7

Sales Analysis Concepts

[25] "80-20," http://www.itwinc.com/itw/this_is_itw/guiding_principles/80_20_Process (May 25, 2009).

- *Where are sales made?* Place of customer contact, purchase location, warehouse location
- *How are items sold?* Form of payment, billing terms, delivery form, packaging technique
- *When are sales heaviest and lightest?* Season, day of week, time of day
- *How much is sold?* Unit sales volume, dollar sales volume, profit margin
- *What types of promotion get the best sales results?* Advertising, personal selling, sales promotion
- *What prices do customers pay?* List prices versus discounted prices

22-3e   The Marketing Audit

A *marketing audit* is a systematic, critical, impartial review and appraisal of the basic goals and policies of the marketing function, and of the organization, methods, procedures, and personnel employed to implement the policies and achieve the goals. The purpose of a marketing audit is to determine (1) how well a firm's marketing efforts are being conducted, and (2) how they can be improved. Audits should be conducted on a regular basis.

> A **marketing audit** examines a firm in a systematic, critical, and unbiased manner.

The marketing audit process involves the six steps shown in Figure 22-8:

1. A marketing audit may be conducted by company specialists, by company division or department managers, or by outside specialists. Expertise, access to information, costs, and potential biases are some of the factors to be considered when choosing audit personnel.

2. An audit may be undertaken at the end of a calendar year, at the end of a firm's annual reporting year, or when conducting a physical inventory. It should be done at least annually, although some firms prefer more frequency. The same time period should be used each year to allow comparisons. Unannounced audits may be useful to keep employees alert and to ensure spontaneous answers.

3. A *horizontal audit* (a marketing-mix audit) studies the overall marketing performance of a firm with particular emphasis on the interrelationship of variables and their relative importance. A *vertical audit* (a functional audit) is an in-depth analysis of one aspect of a firm's marketing strategy, such as product planning.

> A **horizontal audit** studies overall marketing performance; a **vertical audit** analyzes one aspect of marketing.

Figure 22-8

The Marketing Audit Process

1. Determining who does the audit
2. Determining when and how often the audit is conducted
3. Determining the areas to be audited
4. Developing audit forms
5. Implementing the audit
6. Presenting the results to management

The two audits should be used in conjunction with one another because a horizontal audit often reveals areas needing further study.

4. Audit forms list the topics to be examined and the exact information required to evaluate each topic. Forms usually resemble questionnaires, and they are completed by the auditor. Figures 22-9 and 22-10 are examples of audit forms.

Does Your Department, Division, or Firm...	**Answer yes or no to each question**
Planning, organization, and control	
1. Have specific objectives?	— — — — —
2. Devise objectives to meet changing conditions?	— — — — —
3. Study customer needs, attitudes, and behavior?	— — — — —
4. Organize marketing efforts in a systematic way?	— — — — —
5. Have a market planning process?	— — — — —
6. Engage in comprehensive sales forecasting?	— — — — —
7. Integrate buyer behavior research in market planning?	— — — — —
8. Have strategy and tactics within the marketing plan?	— — — — —
9. Have clearly stated contingency plans?	— — — — —
10. Monitor environmental changes?	— — — — —
11. Incorporate social responsiblity as a criterion for decision making?	— — — — —
12. Control activities via marketing cost analysis, sales analysis, and the marketing audit?	— — — — —
Marketing research	
13. Utilize marketing research for planning, as well as problem solving?	— — — — —
14. Have a marketing information system?	— — — — —
15. Give enough support to marketing research?	— — — — —
16. Have adequate communication between marketing research and line executives?	— — — — —
Products	
17. Utilize a systematic product-planning process?	— — — — —
18. Plan product policy relative to the product life-cycle concept?	— — — — —
19. Have a procedure for developing new products?	— — — — —
20. Periodically review all products?	— — — — —
21. Monitor competitive developments in product planning?	— — — — —
22. Revise mature products?	— — — — —
23. Phase out weak products?	— — — — —
Distribution	
24. Motivate channel members?	— — — — —
25. Have suffcent market coverage?	— — — — —
26. Periodically evaluate channel members?	— — — — —
27. Evaluate alternative shipping arrangements?	— — — — —
28. Study warehouse and facility locations?	— — — — —
29. Compute economic order quantities?	— — — — —
30. Modify channel decisions as conditions warrant?	— — — — —
Promotion	
31. Have an overall promotion plan?	— — — — —
32. Balance promotion components within the plan?	— — — — —
33. Measure the effectiveness of advertising?	— — — — —
34. Seek out favorable publicity?	— — — — —
35. Have a procedure for recruiting and retaining sales personnel?	— — — — —
36. Analyze the sales-force organization periodically?	— — — — —
37. Moderate the use of sales promotions?	— — — — —
Prices	
38. Have a pricing strategy that is in compliance with government regulations?	— — — — —
39. Have a pricing strategy that satisfies channel members?	— — — — —
40. Estimate demand and cost factors before setting prices?	— — — — —
41. Plan for competitive developments?	— — — — —
42. Set prices that are consistent with image?	— — — — —
43. Seek to maximize total profits?	— — — — —

Figure 22-9

A Horizontal Marketing Audit Form

Figure 22-10

A Total-Quality Vertical-Audit Form

Source: Dick Berry, "How Healthy Is Your Company?" *Marketing News* (February 15, 1993), p. 2. Reprinted by permission of the American Marketing Association.

Total quality health check-up questionnaire

After filling out questionnaire, return to: _____

The purpose of this questionnaire is to provide a means for companies to conduct a study of their employees, to determine the degree of involvement and commitment to the principles and practices of Total Quality Management.

The questionnaire is based on the criteria embodied in the Baldridge Quality Award categories (being employed by many companies as an integrated management system and to conform to requirements in attaining the award).

INDIVIDUAL INSTRUCTIONS

Identify your position title and company department in the spaces below, then respond to each of the following ten statements, indicating your personal opinion as to the degree of compliance with the criteria in company operations. When completed, return to the individual identified at the top of the sheet for tabulation and reporting of results.

Your Position: _____   Department: _____

QUALITY HEALTH CRITERIA (Circle numbers at right to indicate agreement)	HOW ARE WE DOING? Not true Very true
1. External customer expectations define the quality of our goods and services.	0 1 2 3 4 5
2. Cross-functional and inter-departmental cooperation are encouraged and supported.	0 1 2 3 4 5
3. There is active leadership for quality improvement at all levels of management.	0 1 2 3 4 5
4. Employees have the authority to act on goods and service quality problems.	0 1 2 3 4 5
5. A team approach is used to solve quality problems and to meet customer expectations.	0 1 2 3 4 5
6. Measures of internal and external customer expectations are well understood.	0 1 2 3 4 5
7. Employees are brought into decisions that affect the quality of their work.	0 1 2 3 4 5
8. There is major emphasis on the prevention and solving of quality problems.	0 1 2 3 4 5
9. Individuals and teams are given recognition for contributions to quality improvement.	0 1 2 3 4 5
10. Systems are in place to assess and respond to changing customer expectations.	0 1 2 3 4 5

5. When implementing an audit, decisions need to be made as to its duration, whether employees are to be aware of the audit, whether the audit is performed while a firm is open or closed for business, and how the final report is to be prepared.

6. The last step is to present findings and recommendations to management. However, the auditing process is complete only after suitable responses are taken by management. It is the responsibility of management, not the auditor, to determine these responses.

Despite the merits, many firms still do not use formal marketing audits. Three factors mostly account for this. One, success or failure is difficult to establish in marketing. A firm may have poor performance despite the best planning if environmental factors intervene; and good results may be based on a firm's being at the right place at the right time. Two, if marketing audits are done by company personnel, they may not be detailed enough to be considered audits. Three, the pressures of other activities often mean that only a small part of a marketing strategy is audited or that audits are done infrequently.

22-4 ANTICIPATING AND PLANNING FOR THE FUTURE

> Planning efforts for the future must consider external factors and company abilities.

The future will be complex for firms around the globe as they try to anticipate trends and plan their long-run marketing strategies. On the positive side, there will be a larger middle class in many countries, advances in technological capabilities, expanded worldwide trade, further industry deregulation, and other opportunities. On the negative side, there will be greater competition among firms based in different countries, relatively moderate growth in U.S. and European markets, some resource instability with regard to supply and prices, and an uncertain worldwide economy, among other potential problems.

Long-range plans must take into account both the external factors a firm faces and its capacity for change. What variables will affect the firm? What trends are forecast for these variables? Is the firm able to respond to these trends because it has the needed resources and lead time? For example, manufacturers that have recognized the retailing trend toward self-service have successfully redesigned their packaging to provide more information for shoppers.

A firm that does not anticipate and respond to future trends has a good possibility of falling into the marketing myopia trap and losing ground to more farsighted competitors:

> Suppose you work at a firm that has been in business for years. Sometimes you "pulled yourself up by your own bootstraps" to survive. In other cases, you worked your way up through the ranks. You have an employee base that can be as small as one person or as large as thousands of people. You represent the many faces of success in your profession—and you are ripe for failure. Success breeds arrogance, and arrogance leads to complacency. Complacency can come in many forms. One is the one-trick pony: You ride your success well beyond the effective lifespan. For example, why deal with all of that confusing Internet and E-commerce stuff when you have done just fine without it? Why think of the impact of diversity on your service, product selection, or store layout? Why change now? Great question. The key to getting beyond the one-trick pony is to be honest with yourself and recognize that, possibly, the way you conduct business is out of date. Perhaps customers would like services you don't provide. Join the club. To remain the same (successful!), we must all change.[26]

To prepare for the future, organizations can engage in the following:

- *Company vision planning* articulates the firm's future mission.
- *Scenario planning* identifies the range of events that may occur in the future.
- *Contingency planning* prepares alternative strategies, each keyed to a specific scenario.
- *Competitive positioning* outlines where a firm will be positioned versus competitors.

---

[26] Doug Lipp, "Why Change?" *Leadership Excellence* (April 2005), p. 15.

Marketing and the Web

Assessing E-Commerce Web Sites

Penton Media (http://www.penton.com), a publisher of trade magazines and the host of Web sites and trade shows, recently completed a research study of subscribers of its *Multichannel Merchant* magazine for a "Benchmark Report on E-Commerce." The report examined the practices and performance data for both business-to-consumer (b-to-c) and business-to-business (b-to-b) Web sites.

Here are some of the findings of the study:

- 60 percent of the b-to-b respondents stated that their online sales volume had increased during the past 12 months. Only 8 percent stated that online sales decreased, while 25 percent said that Web sales remained the same. (The balance did not know if online sales had changed.)
- On average, 47.8 percent of sales came from the Web, up from 43.4 percent in 2006, the last time this survey was conducted.
- 81 percent of b-to-b respondents who collected data from buyer registrations used this data to

E-mail customers about special offers; 45 percent added the registrants to their print catalogs' mailing lists; and 22 percent used these data to better customize their Web sites, based on past purchases.

- 20 percent of b-to-b respondents stated that they were considering integrating the Web site with their catalog system. 23 percent said they had no plans for this linkage.
- 44 percent of b-to-b respondents stated that the marketing department was in charge of running the Web site. Just over one-half (51 percent) of those respondents said an in-house staff designed the Web site. 37 percent used a combination of in-house and outsourced Web service providers.

Source: Based on material in Melissa Dowling, "Benchmark Report on E-Commerce," *Multichannel Merchant* (March 2008), pp. 23–29.

- *Competitive benchmarking* keeps a firm focused on how well it is doing versus competitors.
- *Ongoing marketing research* entails consumer and other relevant research.[27]

As we look ahead, it is clear that "Marketing has changed. Once, you could use 'seat of the pants marketing' with some success. However, with the speed of change in demands and budgets, a well-defined plan must be in place to increase the chances of success. Because you will hit some home runs and you will strike out sometimes, it is crucial to develop, at least once a year, an aggregate roadmap for marketing; and regular adjustments should be made."[28] For instance, with the use of advanced computer data bases, market segmentation efforts will be even more focused and responsive than ever before.

Let us conclude with these observations from marketing executives at Toyota (http://www.toyota.com), the new global leader in the auto marketplace:

How do you come up with new marketing ideas? "We often hold off-site planning days with the team, to help inspire fresh thinking. We always monitor our competitors and carry out various forms of research to ensure we engage our audience with a strong brand message. We also hold agency 'Big Ideas Days' during which we give a free rein to all our agencies, to encourage them to think about the consumer research, regardless of their sphere of expertise." *What Is the main marketing challenge you face?* "Launching 12 new or minor change models within 13 months." *Can you describe the marketing team in three words?* Dedicated, passionate, enthusiastic."[29]

---

[27] Adapted by the authors from Bernard Taylor, "The New Strategic Leadership: Driving Change, Getting Results," *Long Range Planning*, Vol. 28 (Number 5, 1995), pp. 71–81.

[28] David G. Malkowski, "Planning Well: Creating a Marketing Plan," *Rural Telecommunications* (July–August 2003), pp. 34–38.

[29] "What's It Really Like Inside Toyota?" *Marketing* (May 21, 2008), p. 71.

Web Sites You Can Use

Here are several good Web sites related to the integration and assessment of marketing strategies:

- Business Owner's Toolkit—"Small Business Tools" (**http://www.toolkit.cch.com/tools/tools.asp**)
- "Finding Hidden Profits Using a Marketing Audit" (**http://www.wilsonconsultants.com/Articles/marketing_audit.htm**)
- InfoTech—"Marketing Strategy" (**http://www.infotechmarketing.net/marketing_strategy.htm**)
- iSixSigma—"Benchmarking" (**http://www.isixsigma.com/me/benchmarking**)

- Maritz Loyalty Marketing—Why Loyalty Marketing (**http://www.maritzloyalty.com/loyalty-why.html**)
- Marketing Scope—"Free Marketing Articles" (**http://www.marketingscoop.com/articles.htm**)
- PlanMagic Marketing 6.0 (**http://planmagic.com/tourmar/tourmar.htm**)
- Prophet—"Insights and Articles" (**http://www.prophet.com/insights/articles**)
- The Marketing Audit (**http://www.marketingaudit.com**)

Summary

1. *To show the value of an integrated marketing plan* Integrated planning builds on a firm's strategic planning efforts and its use of a total quality approach. Thus, everyone is "on the same page." With an integrated marketing plan, all of its various parts are unified, consistent, and coordinated.

2. *To discuss the elements of a well-integrated marketing plan* A clear organizational mission outlines a firm's commitment to a type of business and a place in the market. Long-term competitive advantages are company, product, and marketing attributes—whose distinctiveness and appeal to consumers can be maintained over an extended period of time. A precisely defined target market enables a firm to identify the specific consumers it addresses in a marketing plan. Long-, moderate-, and short-term marketing subplans need to be compatible with one another. Coordination among SBUs is enhanced when the functions, strategies, and resources of each are described and monitored by top management. Marketing mix components need to be coordinated within each SBU. The plan must have a certain degree of stability over time.

3. *To present five types of marketing plan analysis: benchmarking, customer satisfaction research, marketing cost analysis, sales analysis, and the marketing audit* Marketing plan analysis compares a firm's actual performance with planned or expected performance for a specified period of time. If actual performance is unsatisfactory, corrective action may be needed. Plans may have to be revised because of the impact of uncontrollable variables.

   Through benchmarking, a company can set its own marketing performance standards by studying the best firms in its industry, innovative firms in any industry, direct competitors, and/or itself. There are process benchmarks and strategic benchmarks. In general, firms progress through three stages as they engage in benchmarking: novice, journeyman, and master. The Malcolm Baldrige National Quality Award and *Fortune's* corporate reputations surveys are good benchmarking tools.

   In customer satisfaction research, a firm determines the degree to which customer expectations regarding a good or service are actually satisfied. The largest research project in this area is the American Customer Satisfaction Index (ACSI), which rates thousands of goods and services. In 2008, the average ACSI score for all companies was 75 (out of 100).

   Marketing cost analysis evaluates the efficiency of various marketing factors, such as different total quality configurations, product lines, order sizes, distribution methods, sales territories, channel members, salespersons, advertising media, and customer types. Continuous and accurate cost data are needed. Marketing cost analysis involves studying natural account expenses, reclassifying natural accounts into functional accounts, and allocating accounts by marketing classification.

   Sales analysis is the detailed study of sales data to appraise the appropriateness and effectiveness of a marketing strategy. It enables plans to be set in terms of revenues by product, product line, salesperson, region, customer type, time period, price line, or method of sale. It also monitors actual sales against planned sales. More firms use sales analysis than marketing cost analysis. The main source of sales data is the sales invoice; control units must be specified. Sales analysis should take the 80-20 principle, the iceberg principle, and sales exception reporting into account.

   The marketing audit is a systematic, critical, impartial review and appraisal of a firm's marketing objectives, strategy, implementation, and organization. It has six steps: determining who does the audit, establishing when and how often the audit is conducted, deciding what the audit covers, developing audit forms, implementing the audit, and presenting the results. A horizontal audit studies the overall marketing performance of a firm. A vertical audit is an in-depth analysis of one aspect of marketing strategy.

4. *To see the merit of anticipating and planning for the future* Long-range plans must take into account both the external variables facing a firm and its capacity for change. A firm that does not anticipate and respond to future trends has a good chance of falling into the marketing myopia trap—which should be avoided.

Key Terms

marketing plan analysis (p. 689)

benchmarking (p. 690)

marketing cost analysis (p. 693)

natural accounts (p. 694)

functional accounts (p. 695)

sales analysis (p. 697)

control units (p. 697)

80-20 principle (p. 697)

iceberg principle (p. 697)

sales exception reporting (p. 698)

marketing audit (p. 699)

horizontal audit (p. 699)

vertical audit (p. 699)

Review Questions

1. Explain Figure 22-1, which deals with a well-integrated marketing plan.
2. Why might competitive advantages not travel well internationally?
3. What is benchmarking? How should a *novice* firm use it differently from a *master* firm?
4. Explain the American Customer Satisfaction Index (**http://www.theacsi.org**).
5. Why is natural account analysis less useful than functional-account cost analysis?
6. Distinguish between marketing cost analysis and sales analysis.
7. Differentiate between a vertical and a horizontal marketing audit.
8. What are some of the positive and negative trends firms are likely to face over the coming decade?

Discussion Questions

1. Do you think your college or university on-campus bookstore is applying an integrated marketing approach? Why or why not? What marketing recommendations would you make for the bookstore?
2. Develop a customer satisfaction survey for a national drugstore chain. Discuss the kinds of information you are seeking. What possible difficulties may arise in administering the survey and analyzing the results?
3. Develop a vertical marketing audit form for Apple (**http://www.apple.com**) to appraise its relationship with the retailers that carry its products.
4. As the marketing vice-president for a newspaper publisher, how would you prepare for the future? What key trends do you foresee over the next decade? How would you address them?

Web Exercise

The Marketing Source offers a number of "Do It Yourself Resources" at its Web site (**http://www.fixyourmarketing.com/resources**). One of the resources is a marketing audit questionnaire, "Is Your Marketing Working?"

(**http://www.fixyourmarketing.com/resources/marketing.htm**). What could a local movie theater learn by answering the questions in this audit?

Practice Quiz

1. Organizational mission is most likely to be reappraised when
   a. the industry undergoes rapid changes.
   b. company values suit a changing environment.
   c. the firm's performance is above average.
   d. marketing myopia is practiced.

2. Smaller firms *cannot* usually compete on the basis of
   a. location.
   b. customer loyalty.
   c. low prices.
   d. customer service.

3. Which of the following statements about marketing subplans is correct?
   a. It does not matter if long-, moderate-, and short-term subplans are compatible with one another.
   b. Such plans are always communicated to employees.
   c. Long-term plans set a broad framework for moderate-term plans.
   d. Short-term plans are the least specific.

4. For it to be implemented and evaluated properly, a marketing plan must
   a. be inflexible.
   b. have stability.
   c. be narrow.
   d. concern the short run.

5. Which of the following is a technique used to analyze marketing plans?
   a. Marketing cost analysis
   b. Differentiated marketing
   c. Marketing segmentation
   d. Mass marketing

6. As it relates to benchmarking, which type of firm should emulate market leaders and selected world-class companies?
   a. A journeyman firm
   b. A novice firm
   c. A master firm
   d. A market-leading firm

7. The final step in marketing cost analysis is
   a. allocating functional accounts by marketing classification.
   b. assigning natural accounts to functional accounts.
   c. determining natural account expenses.
   d. monitoring results of marketing costs through natural accounts.

8. Which of the following is an example of a functional expense?
   a. Salaries
   b. Overhead
   c. Floor pricing
   d. Warehousing

9. The main source of sales analysis data is the
   a. horizontal audit.
   b. vertical audit.
   c. salesperson.
   d. sales invoice.

10. Sales categories for which data are gathered are known as
    a. order-processing costs.
    b. control units.

c. market accounts.
d. SBUs.

11. According to the 80-20 principle, firms should
    a. allocate revenues according to how items relate to sales forecasts.
    b. place equal effort into every sale.
    c. determine sales and profit by customer, product, and territory.
    d. use total sales data to diagnose their strengths and weaknesses.

12. The first step in a marketing audit is
    a. deciding who does the audit.
    b. determining areas to be audited.
    c. developing audit forms.
    d. determining when the audit is done.

13. An audit is complete after
    a. data are analyzed.
    b. the final report is prepared.
    c. management receives the findings and recommendations.
    d. management responds.

14. Situations where sales forecasts are exceeded are reported in
    a. natural account expenses.
    b. functional account expenses.
    c. sales invoices.
    d. fast-selling item reports.

15. Which of the following is a reason why formal marketing audits have been adopted by relatively few firms?
    a. Many companies do not label their analyses as audits.
    b. Marketing audits conducted by company personnel are detailed enough to be considered audits.
    c. Success or failure is easy to determine.
    d. Company personnel allocate considerable time for conducting audits.

For the answers to these questions, please visit the online site for this book at **http://www.atomicdog.com.**

Case 1: Apple: The King of Innovation Marches On[c8-1]

Consider this: In 1997, when co-founder Steve Jobs regained control as Apple's (http://www.apple.com) chief executive, the firm was in poor financial condition. However, ever since Apple introduced its first iPod in late 2001, the firm has done extremely well. From 2002 to 2005, Apple literally changed the way consumers purchase, record, and listen to music, and its sales revenues grew from $5.7 billion in fiscal 2002 to $13.9 billion in fiscal 2005. In fiscal year 2008, Apple's sales have continued to grow, approaching $30 billion.

As one reporter said, "The iPod ranks as one of the greatest consumer electronics scores of all time—and may stand as the ultimate champ before all is said and done." Apple's sales of about 10 million iPods (http://www.apple.com/ipod) in the three years after its introduction were more than three times greater than Sony's (http://www.sony.com) sales of its Walkman in a comparable three-year time period. iTunes is also one of the largest music retailers in the world, featuring a music catalog with more than 8 million songs. In July 2008, Apple announced that its music customers had bought and downloaded over 5 billion songs from its iTunes (http://www.apple.com/itunes) store. In addition, iTunes customers now rent and purchase thousands of movies every day. This makes iTunes the world's most popular online movie store.

Apple's iPhone has also been an innovation leader. Although an industrywide total of 1 billion cell phones were sold globally in 2007, Apple's iPhone (http://www.apple.com/iphone), a device combining a mobile phone, a widescreen iPod, and an Internet communications device in one product, captured the market's attention. The firm's new iPhone 3G model, introduced in 2008, was so hot that 1 million units were sold during the first three days after it hit the market. The 3G model has a global positioning chip and it can run business programs and games. Marketing analysts predicted that Apple would sell 10 million units in the first year. According to Steve Jobs, "It took 74 days to sell the first million original iPhones, so the new iPhone 3G is clearly off to a great start around the world."

Although the new iPhone 3G is priced significantly less than the initial model, Apple still has high profits based on subsidies from the phone's carriers, including AT&T (http://www.att.com). Some industry observers suggest that these subsidies may exceed $300 per phone. Unlike the older models, Apple now requires that consumers purchase a service contract at the time of sale. This eliminates consumers who have their iPhone "unlocked" and then use unauthorized cell services. One estimate is that 25 percent of older iPhone models were unlocked, preventing partner AT&T from getting its $70 to $130 monthly subscription fee.

Apple also maintains strong innovations in other electronic markets with products such as its desktop and portable Apple computers and Apple TV. Apple's computer products now use the Leopard operating system (Mac OS X Leopard), which became available in October 2007, and iLife software to create and manage digital photography, movies, DVDs, and the Web. Leopard enables Apple Mac owners to start their PC using either Leopard or Windows. Mac users can run Windows through an application called "Boot Camp" that's included with each Mac computer. Windows applications have full access to 3D graphics, USB connections, and Wi-Fi. The Apple TV offers two models. The 40-gigabyte model stores as much as 50 hours of video TV; and the 160-gigabyte model stores up to 200 hours. Movie rentals last 30 days, at which time they are deleted from the hard drive. Apple TV can also store songs and photos and can display content on a high definition television and connect to a home theater system.

Questions

1. Outline Apple's short-term and long-term competitive advantages.
2. Discuss how Apple can better coordinate its iPod, iTunes, iPhone, and PC businesses.
3. Describe how Apple can use benchmarking.
4. Develop a vertical marketing audit to assess Apple's new-product planning efforts.

[c8-1] The data in the case are drawn from Emi Endo, "Three Days, 1 Million iPhones," *Newsday* (July 15, 2008), p. A6; Ben Charny, "New iPhones: More Apple Revenue, Fewer Unlocked Phones," *Dow Jones News Service* (July 2, 2008); Matt Hamblen, "iPhone: One Year Later," *Computer World* (June 2, 2008), pp. 24–29; and "iTunes Store Tops Five Billion Songs Sold," *PR Newswire* (June 19, 2008).

Case 2: Marketing Effectiveness and the Small Accounting Firm[c8-2]

One way to increase the effectiveness of a small accounting firm is to focus on a niche market. Though a small CPA firm does not have the overall resources to successfully compete with a "Big Four" accounting firm, a niche-oriented marketing campaign involves some advertising, publicity, and personal selling.

To determine the most appropriate niche to target, a small CPA firm (just like other small firms) could conduct a systematic marketing audit. The audit can examine the firm's strengths, weaknesses, opportunities, and threats; the profiles of partners; and the importance of various types of clients (in terms of hours billed, profits, profits per hour, and so forth). The analysis could also list the industry classification of each key client, clients by geographical area, clients by size, and/or clients by form of business organization (individual proprietor, partnership, or corporation).

After determining what niches to explore, many CPA firms have found that they do not have the proper staff to effectively meet the needs of the sought-after niche market. In some cases, they have attracted personnel with specific talents from other CPA firms; in other instances, they have merged with a CPA firm having complementary capabilities.

Tauber & Balser PC (**http://www.tbcpa.com**), a small Atlanta-based CPA firm, specializes in accounting and business consulting for such niches as family businesses and forensic (legal) accounting. Promotion is aimed at each niche via newsletters and articles published by the firm's partners, and through networking. The firm's "niche teams" also regularly meet to review the status of marketing programs.

Friedman LLP (**http://www.friedmanllp.com**) specializes in accounting and business consulting for real-estate developers. In 1969, the firm had a few real-estate clients; now, the real-estate business constitutes 45 percent of its total revenues. To appeal to its current clients and to attract new ones, Friedman sponsors 3 seminars each year, exhibits at trade shows, and actively participates in local and national trade associations. The chairman of the firm's real-estate practice says: "To really grow a niche, know the problems your clients face, provide suggestions regarding accounting, tax, and organizational issues—how they run their business. It's far better today not to be a jack-of-all-trades but to be a firm with particular expertise in a number of significant areas."

Let's examine some of the basic marketing strategies used by small CPA firms to successfully appeal to niche markets:

- Develop a champion for each niche. The niche champion is the spokesperson, chief marketing person, and niche advocate. He or she represents the niche in public forums.
- Prepare staff with the required skills. Sometimes, accountants will have to obtain additional certifications and training to achieve the required knowledge base. In other cases, staff development may be through mergers with other firms whose partners have the appropriate experience.
- Have a niche team that regularly reviews its market planning, implementation, and performance. The niche team can be viewed as a separate profit center of the accounting firm.
- Gain valuable publicity by writing articles, sponsoring seminars, and underwriting relevant events attended by current and prospective clients.
- Work with other professionals, such as tax attorneys and specialized business consultants, on joint projects.
- Be an active member of relevant trade and professional associations.
- Use networking to expand the number of firms that know about your specialized services.
- Circulate articles written by principals in the firm to current and prospective clients.

Questions

1. For a small CPA firm, what are the pros and cons of a niche market strategy in contrast to a mass market strategy?
2. How can a small CPA firm utilize benchmarking?
3. Explain the role of marketing cost analysis in a small CPA firm's choosing and evaluating a niche market.
4. What environmental factors should a small CPA firm regularly monitor? How?

[c8-2] The data in the case are drawn from Jean Marie Caragher, "Expand Your Horizons: Niche Marketing Success Stories," *Journal of Accountancy* (April 2008), pp. 56–58.

Formulating Your Company's Next Big Innovation and Growth Strategy[pc-8]

INTRODUCTION

The most successful companies of our times face a significant problem. Sony (http://www.sony.com), which invented the Walkman, totally blew the MP3 opportunity and the PlayStation 3 launch. Motorola (http://www.motorola.com) had a huge opportunity with the RAZR phone and could not ride its success to sustainable growth and leadership. Gillette (http://www.gillette.com) had all the capabilities to reinvent oral care. It knew how to build and design wonderful small devices through its Braun division, it had the leading battery division with Duracell, and it had a world-class capability in toothbrushes with Oral-B.

Yet, it was Procter & Gamble (http://www.pg.com) that saw the opportunity, licensed it through so-called open innovation, and launched the hugely successful Crest SpinBrush. In 2005, Procter & Gamble bought Gillette. How is it that those firms could not see their biggest and greatest opportunities in plain sight?

Table 1	Inside-Out Management Practices	
In search of products	**In search of customers**
Disruptive innovation	Customer orientation
Technology innovation	CRM
TQM	Segmentation
New product development	Customer delight
Brand extension	Customer co-creation
Competitive strategy	Ethnography, market research
Design innovation	Customer satisfaction
Jobs to be done	Customer centricity
Stage-gate process	Voice of the customer
Quality function deployment	Listening to the customer

THE PROBLEM IS US

Marketers and strategists in search of growth tend to adopt practices or reapply approaches that worked long ago—in the hope that this time around they will help. Unfortunately, more often than not, those approaches don't help. As Table 1 shows, there are many approaches to growth covering a wide range of management practices. They fall into two types.

The Product Perspective

This view suggests that consumers cannot know what they have not experienced. Thus, research and development, product management, and engineering create and design in search of the next product not based on customer input. That thinking was the foundation of Motorola's satellite phone, introduced in the late 1990's: a brick-sized phone, with an antenna the size of a baseball bat, that would work only in wide-open spaces and never in a building. The pricing plan called for a $3,000 upfront payment and a $7-a-minute charge for calling.

The Customer Perspective

This perspective is often adopted by today's marketers. It suggests that listening and observing customers while conducting insightful and in-depth research leads to successful products. Yet, observation does not necessarily equate to understanding consumers. If it did, then several thousand products and brands would not be filling the graveyard of products that "did not live up to expectations" and only a small percent of new products remaining on the shelf after one year.

The Problem with the Product and Customer Perspectives

Both perspectives lead executives to view the world from the inside out. It doesn't matter if product engineers look at consumers with their latest technologies tucked under their arms or use the latest methodologies in consumer research. It also doesn't matter whether marketers decide to split consumers into smaller segments and develop fanciful consumer portraits. Following those perspectives still involves looking at opportunities from the inside out—with our own biases and preconceptions about markets and from the confines and perimeters of the company, its capabilities, and its past successes.

The inside-out world view blurs our vision, and it distorts our ability to see the biggest and most obvious opportunities objectively and comprehensively. Worse, it permeates everything we do: how we innovate new products or services, how we define good brand extensions, how we develop marketing plans, and how we activate

---

[pc-8] Adapted by the authors from Erich Joachimsthaler, "Room to Grow," *Marketing Management* (November-December 2007), pp. 39–44. Reprinted by permission of the American Marketing Association.

them. More than 50 years ago, the American marketing industry adopted that inside-out view by establishing need fulfillment as the dominant paradigm. That paradigm is still followed today. But it often does not work when consumers are oversaturated with product choices and brands.

ECOSYSTEM OF DEMAND

It is time to retire the simplistic need-fulfillment paradigm and replace it with the ecosystem-of-demand paradigm. The latter aims to establish a comprehensive portrayal of the complex and changing nature of consumer behavior in context first—and then define means by which a company, brand, or product might change and transform the behavior and realities it has identified. The new paradigm does not aim to identify a need and satisfy it or delight customers with a product better, faster, or cheaper than competitors do. It aims to temporarily deemphasize our assumptions and knowledge about consumers and their needs, wants, and demands so that we set aside our brand or product altogether.

In the ecosystem-of-demand paradigm, we first identify a relevant set of behaviors, rituals, activities, or tasks occurring in the 1,440 minutes that encompass a consumer's day. We look at the episodic, daily occurrences that matter most to consumers and how they experience them. We then insert a new good or service, create a new business model or pricing plan, or define a new brand to change the way people go about their lives. Lesser-used products require studying whole-life experiences and change of life routines.

The goal is to fit a good, service, or brand into a consumer's daily life or whole life—or into the workflow processes of an industrial customer—and create a transformative experience.

DEMAND-FIRST INNOVATION AND GROWTH

The ecosystem-of-demand paradigm gives rise to a new outside-in process for dramatic innovation and growth opportunities: the demand-first innovation and growth (DIG) model. Instead of trying to understand consumers broadly, by delving into differences in their psychological or socioeconomic makeup or their needs, the DIG model aims to dig deeper into the serial realities of people's routines, rituals, and ways of going about what really matters. The DIG model starts with behavior and draws on consumers' episodic knowledge—not merely semantic recall of product features, needs, and wants.

The DIG model is a third perspective and, again, a very novel alternative to finding opportunities for innovation and growth. Implementation follows a simple three-step process: mapping the demand landscape, reframing the opportunity space, and formulating the strategic blueprint for growth.

MAPPING THE DEMAND LANDSCAPE

The first step is to comprehensively understand the ecosystem of demand without bias, independent from the current product or feature set. We begin by reconstructing the relevant daily or life episodes or rituals in a consumer's life by recalling the memory of recent episodes (e.g., setting up the breakfast table or taking a vacation). The research follows an adapted version of the "day reconstruction methodology" and measures the goals, activities, and priorities or the GAP. See Figure 1.

Figure 1

Capturing the Ecosystem of Demand

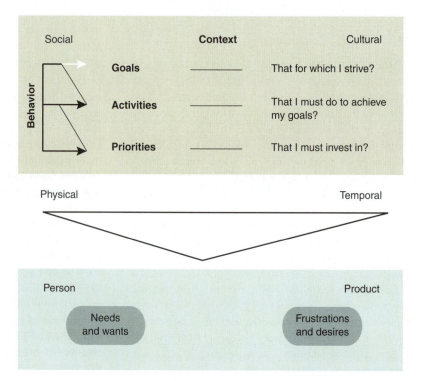

It captures all relevant episodes and associated affective experiences. Goals are very specific things for which a person strives daily, such as getting home early to spend more time with the children. Activities are the means to achieve goals, such as taking the subway or listening to music in the park. Priorities are the time and effort allocated to activities. The GAP depends on the context: temporal (time of day, week, or month), cultural (life setting), and social and physical (at home or at work).

Centering on the GAP in the contexts in which people live, work, or play provides a new way to understand consumers. The DIG model focuses innovation on similarities in people's behaviors and episodes in their lives rather than on differences in attribute or brand perceptions. Instead of merely eliciting an understanding of the differing needs or wants of high-fidelity music lovers versus those of "Joe Six-Pack," research elicits the activities that people go through in living around music: how they find out about music and how they evaluate, select, buy, listen, store, and discard music. The DIG model calls for understanding the specific goals that people seek in each of those activities and then deeply exploring how consumers experience those activities. Only after that is a marketer in a position to explore moods, urges, fantasies, frustrations, and passions. It can lead to the next iPod (**http://www.ipod.com**), but it will more likely lead to a breakthrough such as the iPod-iTunes-iMusicStore ecosystem of products or a new business model (as Netflix, **http://www.netflix.com**, has done). It doesn't aim to just create customer satisfaction or fulfill needs and wants. It also doesn't try to just make competition irrelevant or find uncontested market spaces. Those inside-out objectives are from the dominant need-fulfillment paradigm. Instead, the objective is to achieve a transformative experience of a daily or life episode that matters.

The new leader in male grooming, Axe (**http://www.unilever.com/ourbrands/personalcare/Axe.asp**) from Unilever, is illustrative of what that new approach delivers. Young men's needs and wants have little to do with staying dry in the armpits or sampling "flavors" of the latest deodorant or antiperspirant. Those needs and wants are already fulfilled by many other deodorants or antiperspirants. When one deeply explores the ecosystem of demand, the real motivations of young men emerge. Many of their activities, daily goals, and priorities focus on one thing: getting the girl. Thus, Unilever studied the daily episodes around dating and mating and the sequences of activities that led to a successful date: how young men prepare themselves for a date, the various ways they date, and when and how they succeed and fail. One finding from the research was that men are not very good at dating.

So Axe did not position itself as the better fragrance or body spray. It positioned itself as the brand that helps young men get an edge in the mating game. Instead of looking into research and development for new fragrances or asking consumers to go through sniff tests, Unilever dug deeper into the activities and daily rituals of guys. It sent brand managers, as live-ins, to fraternities at U.S. universities for more than a month and asked them to map young men's activities around the house, on parties, during a night at a club, and at school. Research showed that success in the frequent ritual of dating on campus requires playing the good-guy/bad-guy persona that some girls like. That led to the launch of Essence body spray.

When Unilever studied males' various methods of making first contact, research also showed that some pickup lines are better than others and that most men are pretty bad at the pickup. So Unilever launched a Web site to help teach young men the many different ways of meeting girls. It launched the Unlimited variant to remind guys of the unlimited possibilities in playing the mating game. Today, Axe has taken over 10 percent of the global grooming market and is available in 69 countries. In the United States, it has replaced the longtime category leader in just four years in key retail markets.

REFRAMING THE OPPORTUNITY SPACE

Understanding the ecosystem of demand by mapping life experiences is important. But, again, it is only the first step. A company needs to have a process to really see the biggest and most obvious opportunities in plain sight, even beyond what can be learned from consumers. That process needs to be as structured and as thoroughly pursued as companies presently benchmark competitors, drive themselves crazy disrupting competitors, analyze competitive advantages, and aim to make competitors irrelevant.

Consider Axe. Reframing the opportunity space of Axe involves extending its positioning beyond the episodes of dating itself. One new frame could be the episodes that matter after successful dating, when a couple engages. That reframes the opportunity space of Axe into a potentially huge and entirely different product market—ranging from jewelry to real-estate to savings accounts to life insurance. Those innovation and growth opportunities explore radically and highly relevant consumer directions; they are not merely incremental changes in the feature or product attribute set or more nuanced and finely crafted brand benefits and message points.

Think Apple (**http://www.apple.com**) right after launching the iPod. The need-fulfillment paradigm's natural direction for seizing new opportunities would have been to think through differences among consumers in terms of age, sophistication, or preferences for music and then segment. Different consumers would have been offered slight variants of the iPod. Instead, Apple thought about the comprehensive integration of behaviors before, during, and after listening to music: learning, evaluating, choosing, purchasing, and storing music. That course of action radically changed its innovation agenda. It launched iTunes, iMusicStore, downloadable music for a dollar a song, and more—instead of just creating different product variants for different segments. Moreover, it involved launching thousands of accessories with collaborator companies (such as Bose, **http://www.bose.com**, for stereo speakers) to help consumers assimilate and absorb the iPod into their lives when listening to music in various contexts. CEO Steve Jobs reinvented Apple as a music/entertainment company, not merely as a world-class computer maker with accessories for sale.

Reframing the opportunity space requires creativity, in addition to structured thinking, to explore the ecosystem of demand from many different angles. There are three major ways of reframing:

1. Examine the demand landscape from an individual consumer's perspective. Axe's looking at a consumer's episodes after a period of successful dating is an example of that type of structured thinking. The research question is what opportunities exist to help young men in the activities beyond the dating game?

2. Examine the demand landscape around dating from a market perspective. What activities or episodes exist if dating is not an option? What do consumers substitute for dating? What goods and services complement?

3. Examine the demand landscape from the industry perspective. How is the mating game changing overall? What is the role of MySpace (**http://www.myspace.com**) and Facebook (**http://www.facebook.com**)? What are the larger societal trends that are changing the mating game?

The reframed opportunity space then has to be structured into meaningful episodic or behavior-based, consumer-relevant growth platforms. In a typical study, initial quantification involves about 30 people mapping their activities over three months. They do so using various forms of methodologies, diaries, journals, and reconstruction tools that generate around 35,000 activities—including 120 hours from four hours of one-on-one conversations with each person. The data base quickly becomes enormous and increasingly valuable for structuring the demand landscape, exploring the opportunity space, and developing a compelling business case for innovations and growth.

FORMULATING THE GROWTH BLUEPRINT

A big benefit of the DIG model is that it lets marketers build strategies for profitable growth from an unbiased view of the greatest opportunities in the future, rather than from only the existing business scope. Instead of building a marketing strategy or plan around a new product, marketers define their business and growth agenda and decisively influence it. Another benefit is the focus on the similarities of daily routines, episodes, and activities that really matter to consumers—not on the differences among products, technologies, or fleeting purchase motivations. Those benefits translate into completely new ways of reinventing a company or category, building strong brands, and connecting with customers.

Reinventing a Company or Category

The iPod's success has created a different firm and refocused it on entirely new growth opportunities in consumer electronics, music, and our digital lives. And Axe has equally reinvented the category of male grooming. Other firms have achieved similar successes, such as Ikea (**http://www.ikea.com**) for home furnishing, Starbucks (**http://www.starbucks.com**) for coffee, and Netflix for movie rentals.

One way to understand reinvention successes is to examine them from the point of view of strategy, the ends or the objectives, and the means or the advantages they were creating. Those companies did not focus on competitive objectives. Starbucks did not think about serving better coffee. Rather, Chairman Howard Schultz's vision was to create the "third place for Americans," by which he meant the place to be after work and home. After the minutes consumers spend at home and at work, out of the total 1,440 minutes they live every day, Schultz wanted them to spend most of the discretionary time at Starbucks. That's why Starbucks uses "day parts" and looks for opportunities to get a bigger share of them. That is quite different than becoming the No. 1 coffee company in terms of market share. Starbucks looks at the customer advantage: how long they spend in the store and how often they come. The passionate consumer visits a Starbucks an average of 18 times a month and spends about 45 minutes per visit.

Apple was hardly thinking about creating a better Walkman. Do you know the biggest online music retailer today? It is Apple. Do you know the No. 2? Most likely you don't. Do you know the No. 1 MP3-player company? It is Apple. Do you know the No. 2? Most likely you don't. Consumers usually don't know because they have never been invited to compare the iPod with anything else. Have you ever seen an iPod ad that touted its better product features?

The iPod has defied the classic idea of strategic positioning and growth. Instead, Apple has rolled out numerous devices that help us absorb and assimilate the iPod into our lives. With every accessory sold and with every new launch, such as the iPhone, Apple generates profitable growth by capturing more of the 1,440 minutes we all live, work, and play. It pursued an intensive strategy by digging deeper into the relevant episodes and activities of passionate consumers, rather than with an extensive strategy of segmenting markets, proliferating a product portfolio, or racing competitors to the bottom of lower prices, lower margins, and commodity status. It created customer advantage, not just competitive advantage.

Building Strong Brands

Instead of building a brand around a product, the superiority of a feature, or an emotional benefit communicated to a broadly defined market, DIG-model marketers center on narrow but big opportunities and then go very deep. They focus on making the brand a cultural currency among a particular set of customers. They focus on those similar behaviors or activities among those customers and create a better transformative experience, which in turn creates authentic and real word-of-mouth communications.

Axe focused on the specific niche of those ages 17-24 and the activities of mating. It leveraged a deep understanding of the cultural codes of young men to exploit a large opportunity. The activation programs fit the context in which young men live so well that every effort of Axe to help them get better in the mating game was welcomed not only by college students but also by a huge number of men across all age ranges. The brand became a part of culture and conversation everywhere for men of any age.

Connecting with Customers

Existing communication theory suggests that the goal is to find a simple message that resonates with consumers and effectively moves them along the purchase funnel from awareness toward purchase and loyalty. A set of proof points and repetition ensures that the message is credible and believable to as many consumers as possible. That could be called the spray-and-pray model: Reach many consumers by spraying wherever you can and pray that they find their way to the store or your Web site.

The DIG model flips that upside down. Instead of widely spraying messages, the model aims to first focus on and change the behaviors, activities, or daily routines of a particular set of consumers. Messages become stories told in a contextually relevant way. The network and communities among the narrow targets become the brand builder. Think of how consumers learned about Google (**http://www.google.com**), Skype (**http://www.skype.com**), or Starbucks. All three of them have become billion-dollar brands by narrowly focusing on changing behaviors before spending a dime on advertising.

THINKING AHEAD

Opportunities for innovation and growth are abundant, and we often don't see them or pursue them. The DIG model is a systematic way to make sure that does not happen. It ensures that your company's next big innovation and growth are built on a full understanding of those opportunities, whether they are big or small. That is important so you never again have to say, "Why didn't we think of that?" when a rival company or a startup comes out with a wildly successful and innovative concept or idea, a marketing program, a breakthrough product, or a brand that your company could have introduced.

Questions

1. Why is sustainable growth so difficult?
2. Differentiate between the product perspective and the customer perspective to growth practices, as highlighted in Table 1. Why are both perspectives limited?
3. What is the ecosystem-of-demand paradigm? How could a company apply this paradigm? Relate your answer to Figure 1.
4. Discuss the premise of the DIG model.
5. Does the DIG model apply to all types of firms? Why or why not?
6. How could a book publisher reframe its opportunity space? Cover all three ways of reframing in your answer.
7. Recently, Starbucks ran into some difficulties and actually closed some stores. What should it do now to stay ahead of the curve in the future?

Appendix A

Careers in Marketing

Marketing career opportunities are extensive and diverse. Many marketing positions give a lot of responsibility to people early in their careers. For example, within six months to one year of being hired, assistant retail buyers are usually given budget authority for purchases involving hundreds of thousands of dollars. Beginning salespeople typically start to call on accounts within several weeks of being hired. Marketing research personnel develop preliminary questionnaires, determine sampling procedures, and interpret study results within a short time after their initial employment. A marketing career is excellent preparation for a path to top management positions in all types of organizations.

Marketing positions are often highly visible. These include salespeople, sales managers, retail buyers, product and brand managers, industrial traffic managers, credit managers, and advertising and public relations personnel. For instance, a product manager at Procter & Gamble (P&G, **http://www.pg.com**) develops localized marketing strategies for specific markets, interprets market research studies, evaluates the offerings of current and potential competitors, and continually reassesses the environment for both opportunities and threats. A P&G product manager works with advertising agencies, marketing research firms, consultants, and P&G's own sales force. In general, because most marketing positions are visible, effective persons can be readily recognized, promoted, and well compensated.

Marketing offers career opportunities for people with varying education. An associate's or a bachelor's degree is often needed for management training positions in retailing, inventory management, sales, public relations, and advertising. A master's degree is usually necessary for marketing research, consulting, brand management, marketing management, and industrial sales jobs. Consultants, research directors, and marketing professors commonly have Ph.D. degrees in marketing or related subjects.

A marketing background can also train a person to operate his or her own business. Among the entrepreneurial opportunities available are careers as retail store owners, manufacturers' agents, wholesalers, insurance and real-estate brokers, marketing consultants, marketing researchers, and free-lance advertising illustrators, copywriters, and Web-site developers.

Table 1 contains a detailed listing of jobs in marketing. Overall, these jobs are growing more rapidly than those in other occupational categories—and this is expected to continue. For example, today, those people who work in U.S. retailing and wholesaling activities represent about one-fifth of total nonfarm employment. And according to U.S. Bureau of Labor Statistics (**http://www.bls. gov/oco**) projections, employment in marketing research, advertising, sales, public relations, and securities and financial-services-sales positions will increase faster than average between now and the year 2016.

The strong demand for marketing personnel is based on several factors. More service firms, nonprofit institutions, political candidates, and others are applying marketing principles. The deregulation of several industries (such as banking, communication, and transportation) has encouraged firms in these industries to increase their marketing efforts. Although production can be mechanized and automated, many marketing activities require personal contact. The rise in foreign competition, the attraction of many international markets, and the maturity of several market segments in the United States are causing more U.S. firms to expand and upgrade their marketing programs.

Such new technologies as electronic checkouts, marketing-based computer software, data-base marketing techniques, and E-marketing are creating marketing opportunities for firms. The changes in U.S. and foreign societies (such as blurring gender roles, recreational activities, and the rise in single-person households) need to be monitored through marketing research and marketing information systems, and adapted to via careful marketing planning.

Figure 1 shows four potential marketing career paths. They are general and intended to give you a perspective about "moving up the ladder." Individual firms have their own versions of these career paths. Specialized opportunities also exist in each area shown (such as sales training, support sales, and final consumer versus organizational consumer sales in the sales area); these are not revealed in Figure 1.

Starting salaries for marketing personnel range from $18,000 to $33,000 for those with an associate's degree; $27,000 to $47,000 for those with a bachelor's degree; and $50,000 to $90,000+ for those with a master of business administration degree. In addition to salary, some marketing positions (especially in sales) provide a company car, bonus, and/or expense account that are not common to other professions.

Worldwide, and especially in the United States, marketing executives often become chief executive officers (CEOs) of major industrial and nonindustrial corporations. They each typically earn at least several hundred thousand dollars per year plus bonuses.

Table 2 shows the types of firms that employ people in marketing positions. Table 3 presents salary ranges for a number of marketing positions (with a focus on entry-level, middle-management, and top management jobs). Table 4 gives the Web site addresses of several sources with useful information relating to marketing careers.

Table 1   Selected Jobs in Marketing

Job Title	Description
Account executive	Liaison between an ad agency and its clients. This person is employed by the agency to study clients' promotion goals and create promotion programs (including messages, layout, media, and timing).
Advertising copywriter	Creator of headlines and content for ads.
Advertising layout person	Producer of illustrations or one who uses other artists' materials to form ads.
Advertising manager	Director of a firm's ad program. He or she determines media, copy, budget size, ad frequency, and the choice of an ad agency.
Advertising production manager	Person who arranges to have an ad filmed (for TV), recorded (for radio), or printed (for newspaper, magazine, Internet, etc.).
Advertising research director	Person who researches markets, evaluates alternative ads, assesses media, and tests reactions.
Agent (broker)	Wholesaler who works for a commission or fee.
Catalog manager	Person who determines target market, products, copy, displays, and pricing for sales catalogs.
Commercial artist	Creator of ads for TV, print media, the Internet, and product packaging. This artist selects photos and drawings, and determines the layout and type of print used in newspaper and magazine ads. Sample scenes of TV commercials are sketched for clients.
Consumer affairs specialist (customer relations specialist)	Firm's contact with consumers. The person handles consumer complaints and attempts to have the firm's policies reflect customer needs. Community programs, such as lectures on product safety, are devised.
Credit manager	Supervisor of the firm's credit process, including eligibility for credit, terms, late payments, consumer complaints, and control.
Customer service representative	Person responsible for order status inquiries, expediting deliveries, field sales support, and returns and claims processing.
Direct-to-home (or office) salesperson	Person who sells goods and services to consumers by personal contact at the consumer's home or office.
Display worker	Person who designs and sets up retail store displays.
Exporter	Individual who arranges for foreign sales and distribution, mostly for domestic firms having a small presence internationally.
Fashion designer	Designer of such apparel as beachwear, pants, dresses, scarves, shoes, and suits.
Franchisee	Person who leases or buys a business with many outlets and a popular name. A franchisee often has one outlet and engages in cooperative planning and ads. The franchisor sets operating rules for all.
Franchisor	Person who develops a company name and reputation and then leases or sells parts of a firm to independent businesspeople. The franchisor oversees the firm, sets policy, and often trains franchisees.
Freight forwarder	Wholesaler who consolidates small shipments from many companies.
Industrial designer	Person who enhances the appearance and function of machine-made products.
Industrial traffic manager	Arranger of transportation to and from firms and customers for raw materials, fabricated parts, finished goods, and equipment.
International marketer	Person who works abroad or in the international department of a domestic firm and is involved with some aspect of marketing. Positions are available in all areas of marketing.
Inventory manager	Person who controls the level and allocation of merchandise throughout the year. This manager evaluates and balances inventory amounts against the costs of holding merchandise.
Life insurance agent (broker)	Person who advises clients on the policy types available relative to their needs. Policies offer insurance and/or retirement income.
Manufacturers' representative (agent)	Salesperson representing several, often small, manufacturers that cannot afford a sales force. The person often sells to wholesalers and retailers.

(continued)

Marketing manager (vice-president)	Executive who plans, directs, and controls all of a firm's marketing functions. He or she oversees marketing decisions and personnel.
Marketing research project supervisor	Person who develops the research methodology, evaluates the accuracy of different sample sizes, and analyzes data.
Media analyst	Person who evaluates the characteristics and costs of available media. He or she examines audience size and traits, legal restrictions, types of messages used, and other factors. The effectiveness of company messages is also measured.
Media director (space or time buyer)	Person who determines the day, time (for radio and TV), media, location, and size of ads. The goal is to reach the largest desirable audience efficiently. This person negotiates contracts for ad space or air time.
Missionary salesperson	Support salesperson who provides information about new and existing products.
Order-fulfillment manager	Supervisor responsible for shipping merchandise. He or she verifies orders, checks availability of goods, oversees packing, and requests delivery.
Packaging specialist	Person responsible for package design, durability, safety, appeal, size, and cost. This specialist must be familiar with all key laws.
Political consultant	Person who advises political candidates on media relations, opinion polling, fundraising, and overall campaign strategy.
Pricing economist	Specialist who studies sources of supply, consumer demand, government restrictions, competition, and costs, and then offers short-run and long-run pricing recommendations.
Product manager (brand manager)	Person who supervises the marketing of a product or brand category. In some firms, there are product (brand) managers for existing items and new-product (brand) managers for new items. For a one-brand or one-product firm, this manager is really the marketing manager.
Property and casualty insurance agent (broker)	Person who evaluates client risks from such perils as fire, burglary, and accidents; assesses coverage needs; and sells policies to indemnify losses.
Public relations director	Manages firm's efforts to keep the public aware of its societal accomplishments and to minimize negative reactions to its policies and activities. He or she constantly measures public attitudes and seeks to keep a favorable public opinion of a firm.
Purchasing agent	Buyer for a manufacturer, wholesaler, or retailer. He or she purchases the items necessary for operating the firm and usually buys in bulk, seeks reliable suppliers, and sets precise specifications.
Real-estate agent (broker)	Liaison who brings together a buyer and a seller, lessor and lessee, or landlord and tenant. This salesperson receives a commission.
Retail buyer	Person responsible for purchasing items for resale. The buyer normally concentrates on a product area and develops a plan for proper styles, assortments, sizes, and quantities.
Retail department manager	Supervisor of one retail department, often at a branch store. This is often the first job a college graduate gets after initial training.
Retail merchandise manager	Supervisor of several buyers. He or she sets the retailer's direction in terms of styles, product lines, image, pricing, and other factors and allocates budgets among buyers.
Retail salesperson	Salesperson for a firm that sells to final consumers.
Retail store manager	Supervisor of day-to-day operations of a store. All in-store personnel report to this manager.
Sales engineer	Support salesperson involved with technical goods or services.
Sales manager	Sales force supervisor who is responsible for recruitment, selection, training, motivation, evaluation, compensation, and control.
Salesperson	Company representative who interacts with consumers. He or she may require limited or extensive skills, deal with final or organizational customers, work from an office or go out in the field, and be a career salesperson or progress in management.
Sales promotion director	Person involved with supplementary promotional activities, such as frequent-shopper programs, coupons, contests, and free samples.

(continued)

Securities and financial services sales agent (commodities broker)	Salesperson involved with buying and selling stocks, bonds, government securities, mutual funds, and other financial transactions.
Traffic manager	Supervisor of the purchase and use of alternative transportation methods. This manager routes shipments and monitors performance.
Travel agent	Salesperson who suggests travel arrangements, hotels, car rental, and tours for vacations and business-related travel.
Warehouser	Person responsible for storage and movement of goods within a firm's warehouse facilities. He or she keeps inventory records and makes sure older items are shipped before newer ones (rotating stock).
Wholesale salesperson	Salesperson representing a wholesaler to retailers and other firms.

Figure 1

Selected Marketing Career Paths

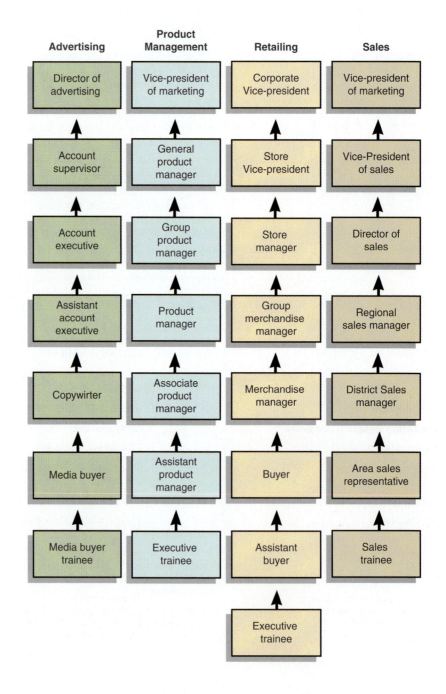

Table 2   Selected Employers of Marketing Personnel

Advertising agencies	Internet companies
Agents and brokers	Manufacturers
Charities	Marketing research firms
Common carriers	Marketing specialists
Computer service bureaus	Media firms
Consulting firms	Multinational firms
Credit bureaus	Nonprofit institutions
Credit card issuers	Product-testing laboratories
Delivery firms	Public relations firms
Direct marketing businesses	Raw material extractors
Educational institutions	Real-estate firms
Entertainment firms	Retailers
Exporting companies	Self-employed
Financial institutions	Service firms
Franchisees	Shopping centers
Franchisors	Sports teams
Fundraising organizations	Transportation firms
Government agencies	Universities
Health-care firms	Warehousers
Industrial firms	Web-site designers
International firms	Wholesalers

Table 3   Typical Annual Compensation for Personnel in Selected Marketing Positions (Including Bonus)

Advertising Positions	Compensation
Assistant media planner	$ 25,000–$ 40,000+
Media planner	$ 40,000–$ 70,000+
Chief copywriter	$ 50,000–$ 90,000+
Creative director	$ 75,000–$150,000+
Marketing Research Positions	**Compensation**
Junior analyst	$ 30,000–$ 45,000+
Senior analyst/project director	$ 45,000–$ 85,000+
IT/data-base specialist	$ 50,000–$ 85,000+
Research director	$ 80,000–$150,000+
Product Management Positions	**Compensation**
Senior marketing analyst	$ 35,000–$ 60,000+
Product manager	$ 65,000–$110,000+
Group product manager	$ 85,000–$175,000+
Public Relations Positions	**Compensation**
Account executive	$ 30,000- $45,000+
Account supervisor	$ 55,000- $80,000+

(continued)

Retailing Positions	Compensation
Assistant buyer	$ 28,000–$ 40,000+
Buyer	$ 45,000–$ 90,000+
General merchandise manager	$ 90,000–$200,000+
Sales Positions	**Compensation**
Sales trainee	$ 25,000–$ 45,000+
Real-estate agent (broker)	$ 35,000–$100,000+
Key account sales representative	$ 75,000–$100,000+
Regional sales manager	$ 75,000–$135,000+
Chief sales executive	$100,000–$175,000+
Miscellaneous Marketing Positions	**Compensation**
Customer service representative	$ 25,000–$ 35,000+
Customer service supervisor	$ 35,000–$ 65,000+
Search engine optimization specialist	$ 40,000–$ 85,000+
Distribution general manager	$ 45,000–$100,000+
Event planner	$ 50,000–$100,000+
Fund raising executive	$ 50,000–$100,000+
Sales promotion director	$ 55,000–$100,000+
International general sales executive	$ 75,000–$140,000+
Top Marketing Positions	**Compensation**
Branch office manager—advertising agency	$ 70,000–$200,000+
Senior public relations executive	$ 75,000–$175,000+
Senior sales executive	$ 85,000–$175,000+
President—distributor	$ 85,000–$200,000+
Executive vice-president—advertising agency	$ 90,000–$200,000+
Vice-president of sales	$100,000–$275,000+
Vice-president of marketing	$100,000–$500,000+
President—advertising agency	$125,000–$500,000+

Source: Compiled by the authors from various publications.

Table 4   Selected Online Sources of Marketing Career Information

Source	Web Address
Abbott, Langer & Associates Salary Survey	http://www.abbott-langer.com/amasumm.html
About Marketing Careers and Training	http://marketing.about.com/od/careersinmarketing
American Marketing Association	http://www.marketingpower.com/careers
Career Builder	http://sales-marketing.careerbuilder.com
Career Magazine	http://www.careermag.com
Career Marketing Online	http://www.careermarketingonline.com
Careers in Marketing	http://www.careers-in-marketing.com
CollegeGrad.com Marketing and Sales Careers	http://www.collegegrad.com/career/marketingcareer.shtml
Direct Marketing Association Job Bank	http://www.the-dma.org/jobbank
Hot Jobs: Marketing	http://hotjobs.yahoo.com/marketingjobs
InfoTech's Marketing Careers Center	http://www.smsource.com/careers.htm

(continued)

International Marketing Careers	http://www.careeroverview.com/international-marketing-careers.html
KnowThis.com's Careers in Marketing	http://www.knowthis.com/careers.htm
Marketing Career Network	http://www.marketingcareernetwork.com
Marketing Careers Overview	http://www.careeroverview.com/marketing-careers.html
MarketingHire.com	http://www.marketinghire.com
MarketingJobs.com	http://www.marketingjobs.com
Monster Sales	http://sales.monster.com
NationJob's Marketing and Sales Job Page	http://www.nationjob.com/marketing
Occupational Outlook Handbook	http://www.bls.gov/oco
Salary Wizard	http://www.salary.com/salary/layoutscripts/sall_display.asp
TigerJobs.com	http://www.tigerjobs.com
TopUSAJobs.com Sales/Marketing	http://www.topjobsusa.com/jobs-by-cat/sales
True Careers	http://www.truecareers.com

Appendix B

Marketing Mathematics

To properly design, implement, and review marketing programs, it is necessary to understand basic business mathematics from a marketing perspective. Accordingly, this appendix describes and illustrates the types of business mathematics with which marketers should be most familiar: the profit-and-loss statement, marketing performance ratios, pricing, and determining an optimal marketing mix.

The crucial role of marketing mathematics can be seen from the following:

- By utilizing marketing mathematics well, a firm can evaluate monthly, quarterly, and annual reports, and study performance on a product, market, SBU, division, or overall company basis.
- Marketing plans for all types of channel members (manufacturers, wholesalers, and retailers) and all time periods (short term through long term) should be based on marketing mathematics.
- Both small and large, goods and services, and profit and nonprofit organizations need to rely on marketing mathematics in making decisions.
- Marketing mathematics provide a systematic basis for establishing standards of performance, reviewing that performance, and focusing attention on opportunities and problem areas.
- By comprehending marketing mathematics, better marketing mix decisions can be made.
- By grasping marketing mathematics, decision making with regard to entering or withdrawing from a market, budgeting expenditures, and the deployment of marketing personnel can be aided.

The Profit-and-Loss Statement

The **profit-and-loss (income) statement** presents a summary of the revenues and costs for an organization over a specific period of time. Such a statement is generally developed on a monthly, quarterly, and yearly basis. The profit-and-loss statement enables a firm to examine overall and specific revenues and costs over similar time periods (for example, January 1, 2009 to December 31, 2009 versus January 1, 2008 to December 31, 2008), and to analyze its profitability. Monthly and quarterly statements enable a firm to monitor progress toward goals and revise performance estimates.

The profit-and-loss statement consists of these major components:

- **Gross sales**—The total revenues generated by a firm's goods and services.

- **Net sales**—The revenues received by a firm after subtracting returns and discounts (such as trade, quantity, cash, and special promotional allowances).
- **Cost of goods sold**—The cost of merchandise sold by a manufacturer, wholesaler, or retailer.
- **Gross margin (profit)**—The difference between net sales and the cost of goods sold; consists of operating expenses plus net profit.
- **Operating expenses**—The cost of running a business, including marketing.
- **Net profit before taxes**—The profit earned after all costs have been deducted.

When examining a profit-and-loss statement, it is important to recognize a key difference between manufacturers and wholesalers or retailers. For manufacturers, the cost of goods sold involves the cost of producing products (raw materials, labor, and overhead). For wholesalers or retailers, the cost of goods sold involves the cost of merchandise purchased for resale (purchase price plus freight charges).

Table 1 shows the projected fiscal year 2009 annual profit-and-loss statement (in dollars) for a manufacturer, the General Pillow Company. From this table, these observations can be made:

- Total company sales for fiscal year 2009 are $1 million. However, the firm gives refunds worth $10,000 for returned merchandise and allowances. Discounts of $50,000 are also provided. This leaves the firm with actual (net) sales of $940,000.
- As a manufacturer, General Pillow computes its cost of goods sold by adding the cost value of the beginning inventory on hand (items left in stock from the previous period) and the merchandise manufactured during the time period (costs included raw materials, labor, and overhead), and then subtracting the cost value of the inventory remaining at the end of the period. For General Pillow, this is $460,000 ($100,000 + $400,000 − $40,000).
- The gross margin is $480,000, calculated by subtracting the cost of goods sold from net sales. This sum is used for operating expenses, with the remainder accounting for net profit.
- Operating expenses involve all costs not considered in the cost of goods sold. Operating expenses for General Pillow include sales force compensation, advertising, transportation, administration, rent, office supplies, and miscellaneous costs, a total of $380,000. Of this amount, $225,000 is directly

Table 1	General Pillow Company, Projected Profit-and-Loss Statement for the Fiscal Year January 1, 2009 through December 31, 2009 (in Dollars)		
Gross sales			$1,000,000
Less: Returns and allowances		$10,000	
Discounts		50,000	
Total sales deductions			60,000
Net sales			$940,000
Less cost of goods sold:			
Beginning inventory (at cost)		$100,000	
New merchandise (at cost)[a]		400,000	
Merchandise available for sale		$500,000	
Ending inventory (at cost)		40,000	
Total cost of goods sold			460,000
Gross margin			$480,000
Less operating expenses:			
Marketing expenses			
Sales force compensation	$125,000		
Advertising	75,000		
Transportation	25,000		
Total marketing expenses		$225,000	
General expenses			
Administration	$75,000		
Rent	40,000		
Office supplies	20,000		
Miscellaneous	20,000		
Total general expenses		155,000	
Total operating expenses			380,000
Net profit before taxes			$100,000

[a]For a manufacturer, new-merchandise costs refer to the raw materials, labor, and overhead costs incurred in the production of items for resale. For a wholesaler or retailer, new-merchandise costs refer to the purchase costs of items (including freight) bought for resale.

allocated for marketing costs (sales force, advertising, transportation).

- General Pillow's net profit before taxes is $100,000, computed by deducting operating expenses from gross margin. This amount is used to cover federal and state taxes as well as company profits.

Performance Ratios

Performance ratios are used to measure the actual performance of a firm against company goals or industry standards. Comparative data can be obtained from trade associations, Dun & Bradstreet (http://www.dnb.com), Risk Management Association (http://www.rmahq.org), and other sources. Among the most valuable performance ratios for marketing analysis are the following:

(1) Sales efficiency ratio (percentage) $= \dfrac{\text{Net sales}}{\text{Gross sales}}$

The **sales efficiency ratio (percentage)** compares net sales against gross sales. The highest level of efficiency is 1.00; in that case, there would be no returns, allowances, or discounts. General Pillow has a sales efficiency ratio of 94 percent ($940,000/$1,000,000) in fiscal year 2009. This is a very good ratio; anything greater would mean General Pillow is too conservative in making sales.

(2) Cost-of-goods-sold ratio (percentage) $= \dfrac{\text{Cost of goods sold}}{\text{Net sales}}$

The **cost-of-goods-sold ratio (percentage)** indicates the portion of net sales used to make or buy the goods sold. When the ratio is high, a firm has little revenue left to use for operating expenses and net profit. This could mean costs are too high or selling price is too low. In fiscal year 2009, General Pillow has a cost-of-goods-sold ratio of 48.9 percent ($460,000/$940,000), a satisfactory figure.

(3) Gross margin ratio (percentage) $= \dfrac{\text{Gross margin}}{\text{Net sales}}$

The **gross margin ratio (percentage)** shows the proportion of net sales allotted to operating expenses and net profit. If the ratio is high, a firm has a lot of revenue left for these items. In fiscal year 2009, General Pillow has a gross margin ratio of 51.1 percent ($480,000/$940,000), a satisfactory figure.

(4) Operating expense ratio (percentage) =

$$\frac{\text{Operating expenses}}{\text{Net sales}}$$

The **operating expense ratio (percentage)** expresses these expenses in terms of net sales. When the ratio is high, a firm is spending a large amount on marketing and other operating costs. General Pillow has an operating expense ratio of 40.4 percent in fiscal year 2009 ($380,000/$940,000), meaning that about 40 cents of every sales dollar goes for operations, a moderate amount.

(5) Net profit ratio (percentage) = $\dfrac{\text{Net profit before taxes}}{\text{Net sales}}$

The **net profit ratio (percentage)** indicates the portion of each sales dollar going for profits (after deducting all costs). The net profit ratio greatly varies by industry. For example, in the supermarket industry, net profits are 2 percent or so of net sales; in the industrial chemical industry, net profits are about 5 percent or so of net sales. The fiscal 2009 net profit for General Pillow is 10.6 percent of net sales ($100,000/$940,000), well above the industry average.

(6) Stock turnover ratio = $\dfrac{\text{Net sales (in units)}}{\text{Average inventory (in units)}}$

or

$$\frac{\text{Net sales (in sales dollars)}}{\text{Average inventory (in sales dollars)}}$$

or

$$\frac{\text{Cost of goods sold}}{\text{Average inventory (at cost)}}$$

The **stock turnover ratio** shows the number of times during a specified period, usually one year, that average inventory on hand is sold. It can be calculated in units or dollars (in selling price or at cost). In the case of General Pillow, the fiscal year 2009 stock turnover ratio

can be calculated on a cost basis. The cost of goods sold during fiscal year 2009 is $460,000. Average inventory at cost = (Beginning inventory at cost + Ending inventory at cost)/2 = ($100,000 + $40,000)/2 = $70,000. The stock turnover ratio is ($460,000/70,000) = 6.6. This compares favorably with the industry average, which means General Pillow sells its goods more quickly than competitors.

(7) Return on investment = $\dfrac{\text{Net sales}}{\text{Investment}} \times \dfrac{\text{Net profit before taxes}}{\text{Net sales}}$

$$= \frac{\text{Net profit before taxes}}{\text{Investment}}$$

The **return on investment (ROI)** compares profitability with the investment necessary to manufacture or distribute merchandise. For a manufacturer, this investment includes land, plant, equipment, and inventory costs. For a wholesaler or retailer, it involves inventory, the costs of land, the outlet and its fixtures, and equipment. To find General Pillow's return on investment, total investment costs are culled from its **balance sheet**, which lists the assets and liabilities of a firm at a particular time.

There are two components to the return on investment measure—investment turnover ratio and net profit ratio (percentage):

Investment turnover ratio = $\dfrac{\text{Net sales}}{\text{Investment}}$

Net profit ratio (percentage) = $\dfrac{\text{Net profit before taxes}}{\text{Net sales}}$

The investment turnover ratio computes the sales per dollar of investment. The General Pillow management calculates that an overall investment of $600,000 is needed to yield fiscal year 2009 net sales of $940,000. Thus, its investment turnover ratio is 1.6 times ($940,000/$600,000). Because General Pillow's net profit ratio is 10.6 percent ($100,000/$940,000), the firm's return on investment equals 17.0 percent (1.6 × .106). This figure is above the industry norm.

Table 2 shows a percentage profit-and-loss statement for the General Pillow Company, using the same period as in Table 1. All figures in the table are computed on the basis of net sales equaling 100 percent. This table allows a firm to quickly observe such performance measures as the cost-of-goods-sold percentage, operating expense percentage, and net profit percentage.

Table 2	General Pillow Company, Projected Profit-and-Loss Statement for the Fiscal Year January 1, 2009 through December 31, 2009 (in Percent, with Net sales = 100.0)	
Net sales		100.0
Less cost of goods sold		48.9
Gross margin		51.1
Less operating expenses:		
Marketing expenses	23.9	
General expenses	16.5	
Total operating expenses		40.4
Net profit before taxes		10.7

Pricing

The material here complements Chapters 20 and 21. Five specific aspects of pricing are examined: price elasticity, fixed versus variable costs, markups, markdowns, and profit planning using markups and markdowns.

Price Elasticity

As defined in Chapter 20, **price elasticity** refers to the buyer sensitivity to price changes in terms of the quantities they will purchase. It is based on the availability of substitutes and the urgency of need, and expressed as the percentage change in quantity demanded divided by the percentage change in price:

$$\text{Price elasticity} = \frac{\dfrac{\text{Quantity 1} - \text{Quantity 2}}{\text{Quantity 1} + \text{Quantity 2}}}{\dfrac{\text{Price 1} - \text{Price 2}}{\text{Price 1} + \text{Price 2}}}$$

For purposes of simplicity, elasticity is often shown as a positive number (as it will be in this section).

Table 3 shows a demand schedule for women's blouses at several different prices. When selling price is reduced by a small percentage, from $40 to $35, the percentage change in quantity demanded rises materially, from 120 to 150 units. Maxine's Blouses then gains a strong competitive advantage. Demand is highly elastic (price sensitive). As price is reduced, total revenues go up:

$$\text{Price elasticity} = \frac{\dfrac{120 - 150}{120 + 150}}{\dfrac{\$40 - \$35}{\$40 + \$35}}$$

$$= 1.7 \text{ (expressed as a positive number)}$$

At a price of $25, the market becomes more saturated—the percentage change in price, from $25 to $20, is directly offset by the percentage change in quantity demanded, from 240 to 300 units:

$$\text{Price elasticity} = \frac{\dfrac{240 - 300}{240 + 300}}{\dfrac{\$25 - \$20}{\$25 + \$20}}$$

$$= 1.0 \text{ (expressed as a positive number)}$$

Total revenues remain the same at a price of $25 or $20. This is unitary demand, whereby total revenues stay constant as price changes.

At a price of $20, the market becomes extremely saturated, and further price reductions have little impact on demand. A large percentage change in price, from $20 to $15, results in a small percentage change in quantity demanded, from 300 to 350 units. Maxine's is able to sell relatively few additional blouses. Demand is inelastic (insensitive to price changes):

$$\text{Price elasticity} = \frac{\dfrac{300 - 350}{300 + 350}}{\dfrac{\$20 - \$15}{\$20 + \$15}}$$

$$= 0.5 \text{ (expressed as a positive number)}$$

Total revenue falls as demand goes from elastic to inelastic; at this point, price cuts are not effective.

Total revenue is maximized at the price levels where price and demand changes directly offset each other (in this example, $25 and $20). How does a firm choose between those prices? It depends on the marketing philosophy. At a price of $25, profit will probably be higher because the firm needs to produce and sell fewer products, thus reducing some costs. At a price of $20, more units are sold; this may increase the customer base for other products the firm offers and raise overall company sales and profits.

Table 3	Maxine's Blouses—A Demand Schedule		
Selling Price	**Quantity Demanded**	**Elasticity[a]**	**Total Revenue[b]**
$40	120		$4,800
		1.7	
35	150		5,250
		1.5	
30	190		5,700
		1.3	
25	240		6,000 ← Maximum total revenue
		1.0	
20	300		6,000 ←
		0.5	
15	350		5,250
		0.3	
10	390		3,900

[a]Expressed as positive numbers.

[b]Total revenue = Selling price × Quantity demanded.

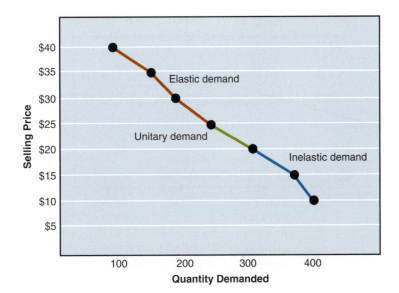

Figure 1

Maxine's Blouses, Demand Elasticity

Figure 1 graphically depicts demand elasticity for Maxine's Blouses. This figure indicates that a demand curve is not necessarily straight and that a single demand schedule has elastic, unitary, and inelastic ranges.

Remember: Elasticity refers to percentage changes, not to absolute changes. A demand shift from 120 to 150 units involves a greater percentage change than one from 300 to 350 units. In addition, each product or brand faces a distinct demand schedule. Milk and magazines have dissimilar schedules, despite similar price ranges, due to different availability of substitutes and urgency of need.

Fixed Versus Variable Costs

In making pricing decisions, it is essential to distinguish between fixed and variable costs. **Fixed costs** are ongoing costs that are unrelated to production or sales volume; they are generally constant for a given range of output for a specific period. In the short run, fixed costs cannot usually be changed. Examples are rent, full-time employee salaries, physical plant, equipment, real-estate taxes, and insurance.

Variable costs are directly related to production or sales volume. As volume increases, total variable costs increase; as volume declines, total variable costs decline. Per-unit variable costs often remain constant over a given range of volume (for example, total sales commissions go up as sales rise, while sales commissions as a percent of sales remain constant). Examples are raw materials, sales commissions, parts, salaries of hourly employees, and product advertising.

Figure 2 shows how fixed, variable, and total costs vary with production or sales for Eleanor's Cosmetics, a leased-department operator selling popular-priced cosmetics in a department store. Total fixed costs are $10,000. Variable costs are $5.00 per unit. Figure 2A depicts total costs: as volume rises, total fixed costs are constant at $10,000, while total variable costs and total costs go up by $5.00 per unit. At 1,000 units, total fixed costs are $10,000, total variable costs are $5,000, and total costs are $15,000. At 5,000 units, total fixed costs are $10,000, total variable costs are $25,000, and total costs are $35,000.

Figure 2B depicts average costs: as volume increases, average fixed costs and average total costs decline (because fixed costs are spread over more units), while average variable costs remain the same. At 1,000 units, average fixed costs are $10.00 ($10,000/1,000 units), average variable costs are $5.00, and average total costs are $15.00. At 5,000 units, average fixed costs are $2.00 ($10,000/5,000 units), average variable costs are $5.00, and average total costs are $7.00.

By knowing the relationship between fixed and variable costs, firms are better able to set prices. They recognize that average total costs usually decline as sales volume expands, which allows them to set skimming prices when volume is low and penetration prices when volume is high. They also realize that losses can be reduced with selling prices that are lower than average total costs—as long as prices are above average variable costs, transactions will contribute toward the payment of fixed costs. Finally, the break-even point can be shown on a total-cost curve graph. See Figure 3.

With a selling price of $10.00 per unit, Eleanor's Cosmetics loses money unless 2,000 units are sold. At that amount, the firm breaks even. For all sales volumes above 2,000 units, the company earns a profit of $5.00 per unit, an amount equal to the difference between selling price and average variable costs (fixed costs are assumed to be "paid off" when sales reach 2,000 units). A sales volume of 5,000 units returns a profit of $15,000 (total revenues of $50,000 − total costs of $35,000).

Markups

A **markup** is the difference between merchandise cost and selling price for each channel member. Markup is usually expressed as a percentage:

$$\text{Markup percentage (on selling price)} = \frac{\text{Selling price} - \text{Merchandise cost}}{\text{Selling price}}$$

$$\text{Markup percentage (at cost)} = \frac{\text{Selling price} - \text{Merchandise cost}}{\text{Merchandise cost}}$$

Table 4 shows markup percentages on selling price and at cost for an item selling for $10.00 under varying costs. Because firms often consider a markup percentage as the equivalent of the gross margin

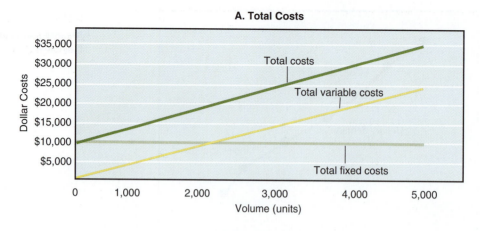

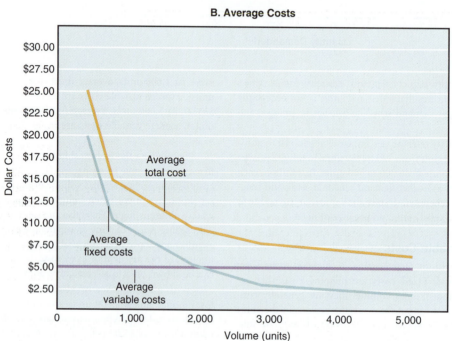

Figure 2

Fixed and Variable Costs for Eleanor's Cosmetics

percentage discussed earlier in this appendix, they use the markup percentage on selling price in their planning. As with gross margins, firms use their markups to cover operating expenses and net profit.

Channel members need to be aware of the discounts given to them by vendors (suppliers). Besides markups for providing regular marketing functions, they may also get quantity, cash, seasonal, and/or promotional discounts. Transportation costs are added to the price; they are not discounted.

Table 5 shows the computation of a purchase price by a TV retailer, based on a functional markup of 40 percent and individual discounts of 10 (quantity), 2 (cash), 5 (seasonal), and 5 (promotional) percent. The discounts do not total 62 percent off final selling price. They total 52.2 percent because the discounts are computed upon successive balances. For example, the 10 percent quantity discount is computed on $165, which is the purchase price after deducting the functional markup allowed by the vendor.

Markdowns

A key price adjustment made by most firms is a **markdown**, which is a reduction in the original selling price of an item so as to sell it. Markdowns are due to slow sales, model changes, and other factors.

Markdown percentages can be computed in either of two ways:

Markdown percentage (off-original price) =

$$\frac{\text{Original selling price} - \text{Reduced selling price}}{\text{Original selling price}}$$

Markdown percentage (off-sale price) =

$$\frac{\text{Original selling price} - \text{Reduced selling price}}{\text{Reduced selling price}}$$

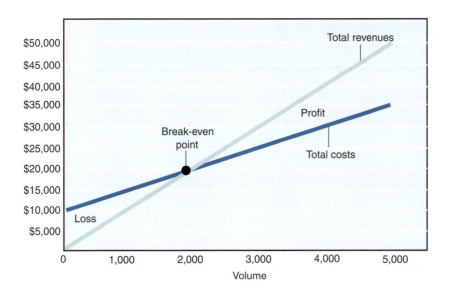

Figure 3

Break-Even Analysis for Eleanor's Cosmetics

The off-original markdown percentage for an item that initially sold for $20 and has been marked down to $15 is ($20 − $15)/$20 = 25. The off-sale markdown percentage is ($20 − $15)/$15 = 33. The off-original percentage is more accurate for price planning, but the off-sale percentage shows a larger price reduction to consumers and may generate increased interest.

Profit Planning Using Markups and Markdowns

Although lower markups (higher markdowns) generally result in higher unit sales, and higher markups (lower markdowns) generally result in lower unit sales, it is essential that a firm determine the effect of a change in selling price on its profitability. The impact of a price adjustment on total gross profit (also known as gross margin) can be determined through the use of this formula:

Unit sales required to earn the same total gross profit with a price adjustment

$$= \frac{\text{Original markup (\%)}}{\text{Original markup (\%)} \pm \text{Price change (\%)}}$$

$$\times \text{Expected unit sales at original price}$$

If a wholesaler pays $7 to buy one unit of an item and decides to reduce that item's selling price by 10 percent—from an original price of $10 to $9—its markup on selling price drops from 30 percent ($3/$10) to 22.2 percent ($2/$9). Because the wholesaler originally planned to sell 1,000 units at $10, it must now sell 1,500 units at $9 to keep the same gross profitability (30/20 × 1,000). Conversely, if it decides to raise its price by 10 percent—to $11—its new markup on selling price is 36.4 percent ($4/$11), and it

Table 4	Markups on Selling Price and at Cost		
Selling Price	**Merchandise Cost**	**Markup (% on Selling Price)**	**Markup (% at Cost)**
$10.00	$9.00	10	11
10.00	8.00	20	25
10.00	7.00	30	43
10.00	6.00	40	67
10.00	5.00	50	100
10.00	4.00	60	150
10.00	3.00	70	233
10.00	2.00	80	400
10.00	1.00	90	900

Formulas to convert markup percentages:

$$\text{Markup percentage (on selling price)} = \frac{\text{Markup percentage (at cost)}}{100\% + \text{Markup percentage (at cost)}}$$

$$\text{Markup percentage (at cost)} = \frac{\text{Markup percentage (on selling price)}}{100\% - \text{Markup percentage (on selling price)}}$$

Table 5	A TV Retailer's Final Purchase Price, After Deducting All Discounts—Model 123	
Discounts Offered by Manufacturer (in %)		
Functional	40	
Quantity	10	
Cash	2	
Seasonal	5	
Promotional	5	
Suggested Final Selling Price		$275.00
Shipping Charges		$15.30
Computation of Purchase Price Paid by Retailer		
List price		$275.00
Less functional markup ($275.00 × 0.40)		110.00
Balance		$165.00
Less quantity discount ($165.00 × 0.10)		16.50
Balance		$148.50
Less cash discount ($148.50 × 0.02)		2.97
Balance		$145.53
Less seasonal discount ($145.53 × 0.05)		7.28
Balance		$138.25
Less promotional discount ($138.25 × 0.05)		6.91
Balance after all discounts		$131.34
Plus shipping charges		15.30
Price to TV retailer		$146.64
Total of Discounts		$143.66
Total Discount % ($143.66/$275)		52.2

must sell only 750 units to keep the original gross profit level (30/40 × 1,000).

Determining an Optimal Marketing Mix

When devising, enacting, and assessing a marketing plan, a firm should consider alternative marketing mixes and find the most effective one. Because many marketing costs (such as packaging, distribution, advertising, and personal selling) can be both order generating and variable, marketers need to estimate and compare sales for various combinations at various levels of costs. Table 6 shows how a firm could set prices and allot its $3 million annual marketing budget among product, distribution, advertising, and personal selling—so as to maximize profit. In this situation, the firm would choose a mass marketing mix resulting in a low price, a lower-quality product, extensive distribution, and an emphasis on advertising.

The concepts of opportunity costs and sales response curves provide valuable information in determining an optimal marketing mix. **Opportunity costs** measure the foregone revenues (profit) from not using the optimal marketing mix. For example, it may

be possible for a firm to sell an additional 10,000 units in a selective marketing strategy by raising advertising expenditures by $100,000 and reducing distribution expenditures by $100,000. A firm that is unaware of this option would have opportunity costs—in terms of profit—of $110,000:

Opportunity costs

$$= (\text{Foregone unit sales} \times \text{Selling price}) - (\text{Added costs})$$

$$= (10,000 \times \$29.00) - (10,000 \times \$18.00) = \$110,000$$

At its optimal marketing strategy, a firm's opportunity costs equal zero.

Sales response curves show the expected relationships between sales revenue and functional marketing efforts. These curves are estimated on the basis of executives' judgment, surveys, industry data, and/or experiments (whereby marketing mix factors are systematically varied in a controlled way).

Figure 4 shows sales response curves for a firm examining four aspects of its marketing effort: depth of product line, number of outlets carrying products, advertising expenditures, and price level. For each of these factors, the expected impact of a strategy change

Table 6			Determining an Optimal Marketing Mix for a Company with a $3 Million Annual Marketing Budget						

Alternative Marketing Mix	Selling Price	Unit Sales	Sales Revenue	Total Product Costs[a]	Advertising Costs	Personal Selling Costs	Distribution Costs	Total Costs	Profit
Mass marketing	$11.00	2,507,000	$27,577,000	$22,563,00	$1,400,000	$ 300,000	$1,300,000	$25,563,000	$2,014,000
Selective marketing	29.00	432,000	12,528,000	7,776,000	900,000	1,200,000	900,000	10,776,000	1,752,000
Exclusive marketing	43.00	302,000	12,986,000	9,966,000	600,000	1,850,000	550,000	12,966,000	20,000

[a] Mass marketing = $9.00 per unit for labor, materials, and other production costs; selective marketing = $18.00 per unit for labor, materials, and other production costs; and exclusive marketing = $33.00 per unit for labor, materials, and other production costs.

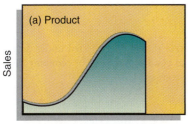

(a) Product

Sales

Depth of product line

With limited depth in the product line, consumers have few choices and many find none satisfactory. As the firm adds new brands, styles, options, etc., sales increase because customers have a better variety from which to choose. At some point, consumers believe there are enough choices and will not increase purchases if new brands/models are introduced.

Figure 4

Selected Sales Response Curves for Marketing Mix Functions

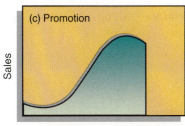

(b) Distribution

Sales

Number of outlets carrying products

With products distributed through too few outlets in a given area, many consumers find it inconvenient to shop for or purchase the firm's items. As the number of outlets increases, sales rise because it is easier for consumers to shop and purchase. At some point, there is saturation, as stores only draw each other's customers not new ones for the firm's products.

(c) Promotion

Sales

Advertising expenditures

With too little advertising, there is inadequate awareness of the firm's products. As advertising increases, more people become aware of and develop a preference toward the firm. At some point, there is saturation as media coverage is duplicated and ads are repeated too frequently.

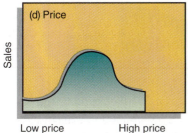

(d) Price

Sales

Low price   High price

With a low price, many consumers believe the firm's offering is of poor quality. At a medium price, many consumers feel there is a good value for their money. At a high price, many consumers think there is poor value for their money and consider other alternatives.

Figure 5

Sales Response Curves and Product/Market Maturity

(a) New Product/Growing Market

Sales / Marketing expenditures

Due to product/market newness, marketing expenditures have a large impact on sales. By adding product features, increasing distribution and promotion, and offering special credit terms or special introductory prices, sales will rise dramatically.

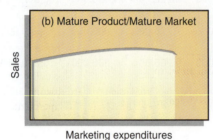

(b) Mature Product/Mature Market

Sales / Marketing expenditures

When a product/market is mature, marketing expenditures have a limited impact on sales. With no or little marketing effort, brand-loyal consumers continue to purchase. With extensive marketing effort, a small number of consumers may switch from competitors, buy earlier than intended, or increase consumption.

on sales is shown; it is clear that different actions will result in different sales responses.

When using sales response curves, these points should be considered:

- Sales responsiveness may vary by product and by market segment. Marketing expenditures have a much greater influence on new products/growing markets than on mature products/mature markets. See Figure 5.
- The range of efficient marketing efforts must be determined. At low levels, marketing activities may be insufficient to generate consumer interest. At high levels, these activities may be redundant and appeal to a saturated market. The range of marketing efforts having the greatest impact on sales is the appropriate one. See Figure 6.
- Sales response curves are related to the combination of marketing mix factors employed by a firm. To determine its overall sales response curve, a company would combine all the individual curves shown in Figure 4 (or use all the data in Table 6).
- Sales response curves examine revenue fluctuations. Before making marketing decisions, profit response curves should also be studied.

- Sales response curves should be projected under different conditions, such as good economy/poor economy or heavy competition/light competition.

Questions

1. What information can a firm obtain from a profit-and-loss statement (in dollars)?

2. Develop a profit-and-loss statement for the Home Furnishings Shop, a retail store, based on the following:

Beginning inventory (at cost)	$ 700,000
New merchandise (at cost)	850,000
Ending inventory (at cost)	600,000
Gross sales	2,000,000
Returns and allowances	200,000
Marketing expenses	450,000
General expenses	300,000

Figure 6

Optimal Marketing Expenditures

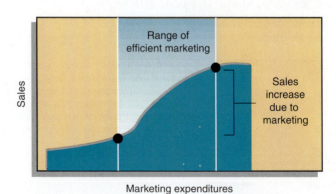

Sales / Marketing expenditures

Range of efficient marketing

Sales increase due to marketing

3. Using the profit-and-loss statement from Question 2, calculate:
   a. Return on investment. (Assume that investment equals $500,000 plus average inventory.)
   b. Stock turnover ratio.
   c. Net profit ratio (percentage).
   d. Operating expense ratio (percentage).
   e. Gross margin ratio (percentage).
   f. Cost-of-goods-sold ratio (percentage).
   g. Sales efficiency ratio (percentage).

4. How would the Home Furnishing Shop determine whether its performance ratios are satisfactory?

5. a. What is the impact on return on investment if a firm increases its investment turnover from four times to six times?
   b. List five ways for a firm to increase its investment turnover.

6. A wholesaler estimates that it can sell 10,000 inexpensive GPS systems at $100 each, or 7,500 at $115 each. The units cost the wholesaler $65 each.
   a. Calculate the price elasticity between the $100 and $115 price levels.
   b. What factors should determine the price to be set?

7. A full-service car wash has done research on customer sensitivity to price. These are the results:

Price	Number of Car Washes Demanded in Market Area per Year
$5.25	70,000
5.75	60,000
6.25	50,000
6.75	25,000
7.25	15,000
7.75	10,000

   a. Calculate price elasticity for all price levels.
   b. At what price is total revenue maximized?
   c. What price should be set? Why?
   d. What other information, not given in this question, is important in setting price?
   e. Which expenses for a car wash are fixed? Which expenses are variable?

8. The car wash in Question 7 can accommodate up to 30,000 cars per year with fixed costs of $90,000. Above 30,000 cars, fixed costs rise to $110,000. Variable costs are $2.50 per car wash.
   a. Compute average fixed costs, average variable costs, and average total costs for the car wash at each price.
   b. Why might the car wash set a price that does not maximize profit?

9. An appliance manufacturer has fixed costs of $1,100,000 and variable costs of $51.00 per electric espresso machine.
   a. Calculate total costs for volumes of 10,000, 25,000, and 50,000 units.

   b. Calculate average total, fixed, and variable costs for the same volumes.
   c. At a volume of 25,000 machines, would the firm make a profit or loss with a wholesale selling price of $68.00? What is the total profit or loss?

10. A supermarket retailer sells small-sized toothpaste for $1.49; they are purchased for $0.97. Medium-sized containers sell for $2.09; they are purchased for $1.55.
    a. For each size container, determine the markup percentage on selling price and at cost.
    b. Why would the retailer use a different markup percentage for small versus medium containers?
    c. If a toothpaste manufacturer offers the supermarket a 25 percent markup on selling price for small-sized containers, as well as a cash discount of 2 percent and a quantity discount of 5 percent, what is the purchase price to the supermarket? What is the overall discount? There are no transportation costs.

11. A wholesaler requires a 40 percent markup on selling price for profit projections to be met. The merchandise costs $47.00.
    a. What must the selling price be for the wholesaler to meet its markup goal?
    b. What would be the minimum selling price if the wholesaler has a markup goal of 50 percent on selling price?

12. Convert the following markups from selling price to cost:
    a. 30 percent markup on selling price.
    b. 40 percent markup on selling price.
    c. 50 percent markup on selling price.

13. Convert the following markups from cost to selling price:
    a. 110 percent markup at cost.
    b. 150 percent markup at cost.
    c. 180 percent markup at cost.

14. A clothing store is offered the following discounts: functional markup, 45 percent; quantity discount, 5 percent; cash discount, 2 percent; and seasonal discount, 3 percent. If the suggested final selling price of the total order is $1,250 and shipping charges are $50.00, compute the total order cost to the firm.

15. A hardware store originally sold electric heaters for $49. An end-of-season sale has reduced the price of these heaters to $25.
    a. Compute the off-original and off-sale markdown percentages.
    b. Why is there a difference in these calculations?

16. a. A firm expects to sell 1,000 advanced laptop computers yearly at a price of $900. At the $900 price, the company's markup is 15 percent. How many units would the firm need to sell to earn the same gross profit at a selling price of $1,100 as it would at a selling price of $900?
    b. How many units must the firm sell to earn the same gross profit at a selling price of $800 as it would at a selling price of $900?

17. A manufacturer estimates the following relationship between marketing expenses and sales:

Marketing Expenses	Unit Sales
$100,000	225,000
200,000	275,000
300,000	325,000
400,000	375,000
500,000	400,000

If a product has a gross profit of $4 per unit and general operating expenses are constant at $100,000, at what marketing expenditure level is profit maximized?

18. Calculate the opportunity costs associated with each marketing expenditure level in Question 17.

19. a. Why do most sales response curves have "S" shapes?
    b. Under what conditions would sales response curves have different shapes?
    c. Draw sales response curves based on the information in Table 6.

Appendix C

Computer-Based Marketing Exercises

An accompanying computer program enables you to engage in marketing decision making under simulated conditions and apply many of the concepts studied during your principles of marketing course. The exercises described in this appendix are designed to reinforce text material; to have you manipulate controllable marketing factors and see their impact on costs, sales, and profits; to have you better understand the impact of uncontrollable factors; and to have you gain experience using a computer to assess marketing opportunities and solve marketing problems. All 18 exercises are designed to be handed in for class assignments or for your own use. They are balanced in terms of subject and level.

Please note: A separate, more-detailed computer exercise, entitled *StratMktPlan*, covers the basic elements of a strategic marketing plan. It is tied to all eight parts in *Marketing*. An overview of this exercise is presented at the end of Chapter 3 ("Developing and Enacting Strategic Marketing Plans"). That exercise may be accessed from your Backpack at our Web site.

How to Use the Computer-Based Exercise Program

Program Downloading and Operation Using a Computer with a Hard Drive

This section explains how to install and operate your copy of *Computer-Based Marketing Exercises*, and how to permanently place your name, class, and section on your copy (so that assignments may be submitted with your name printed on them).

To run *Computer-Based Marketing Exercises*, you must first download the compressed installation program from your Backpack at the text's Web site. Save this program in a folder on your hard drive. It is recommended that you save this program in a folder labeled as TEMP. If you do not have this folder, make one with this title. (Because this program is compressed and then extracted, it cannot be run from a 3-1/2-inch floppy disk.) You must also download a program to unzip these compressed files. Download WINZIP Evaluation version 10.0 (or later) from **http:// www.winzip.com**. The evaluation version is for a 45-day trial period; a license fee is required for continued use beyond 45 days.

Complete the following steps to extract the installation program and install the exercise program on your hard drive:

1. Go to the TEMP file and highlight "ExerZIP.zip."
2. Open the zip file by clicking on it or by using the Run utility on your Start Menu. (See instructions below to use the Run utility.)

3. Activate the "Extract" function by clicking the "Extract" button or the "Unzip or Install" button on the Actions menu.
4. A dialog screen should appear providing actions for extraction. Select the drive and folder in which you would like to save the extracted files. The default drive and folder is C:\EXERCISE.
5. Complete the extraction by clicking "Extract," "Continue," or "OK."
6. The extracted files should be downloaded in the folder you specified.
7. Click on the set.up file to install the program.

If you prefer to open the zip file by using the Run utility, click the Start menu and select "Run." You can browse for the zip file or type in C:\TEMP\ExerZIP.zip and press "OK." Then go to step 3 above. In a few cases, the unzip program may not install the marketing exercises or strategic marketing plan program but will display a 'window' with the names of the files. Choose the file called "setup.exe" and run that file to install the program. Do not run setup1.exe or setup2.exe files that may be displayed. Should you receive a notice that downloading these files is blocked, select the Exercises zipped file, go to "Properties," select "General," choose "Unblock," and then select "Apply," and then "OK." This will unblock the program.

You are now ready to run *Computer-Based Marketing Exercises* from your hard drive. If you are still in the Windows environment, follow the screen prompts for the *Computer-Based Marketing Exercises* program. If you have exited your computer and then return at another time, initialize the Windows environment. Then, simply adhere to the preceding instructions 3 to 5.

The first time you run *Computer-Based Marketing Exercises*, the program requires you to insert your name, class, and section to identify your responses. If necessary, enter this information by choosing the Rest Name button. Once you enter this information, it will appear on each computer screen and printout—and become a permanent part of your exercise program. It will not have to be repeated. The program will do the rest and guide you to the main menu.

After running *Computer-Based Marketing Exercises*, you may wish to delete the "ExerZIP.zip" file from your "Temp" folder. The file was used in installation and will not be needed in the future. Some versions of WinZip will automatically delete the file and others will not.

Running the Program from a Network

Some colleges and universities have PC networks for student use. Please consult with your professor or someone in the computer lab with regard to using *Computer-Based Marketing Exercises*.

MAIN MENU

The Main Menu

All exercises can be accessed from the MAIN MENU. Use your mouse or trackball to select an exercise. You can also choose an exercise by repeatedly pressing the "Tab" key until the desired exercise is highlighted and then pressing the "Enter" key. Selecting "Exit" will enable you to quit the program.

The menu shown above is arranged in the order the topics appear in the text:

How to Operate Each Exercise

At the bottom of each exercise screen, a number of commands appear. They include the Exit button [E] to quit the program, the Menu button [M] to return to the main menu, the Next button [N] to proceed to the following screen, the Back button [B] to return to the prior screen, the Objectives button [O] to go to the Objectives section, the Questions button [Q] to go to the first page of the questions, the Print Screen button [P], and the Analysis button [A]. Some screens have an [E] button for Evaluation, a [C] button for Criteria, and a few other specialized buttons. All commands can be executed by either clicking your mouse (or trackball) or by holding down the [ALT] key and then pressing the respective letter key.

How to Print from the Exercise Program

While using the exercise program, you may print any screen for your own reference or for the submission of an assignment. Simply turn on the printer connected to the computer you are using. Then, click the Print Screen button at the bottom of each exercise screen (or hold down the [Alt] key and then press the [P] key). The screen appearing on your computer monitor will automatically be printed—including your name, class, and section. The printing option should not be selected if no printer is available.

The Exercises

In the following sections, the basic premise of each exercise is described.

Exercise 1: Marketing Orientation

As owner of a local camera shop, a table lets you enter your degree of agreement with 10 questions (on a 5-point scale ranging from strongly agree to strongly disagree). Questions relate to such areas as the importance of various markets, planning for seasonality, the impact of the Web, forecasting sales and profits, assessing customer needs, understanding competitors' strategies, and monitoring customer satisfaction. The exercise is keyed to "The Marketing Concept" in Chapter 1, pages 11–12 in the printed text.

Exercise 2: Boston Consulting Group Matrix

As a marketing executive for Packard Athletic Shoe Company, a table allows you to enter revised values for the relative market shares and industry growth rates for any or all of Packard's product categories (SBUs). The products are then displayed in a Boston Consulting Group matrix. The exercise is keyed to "The Boston Consulting Group Matrix" in Chapter 3, pages 65–67 in the printed text.

Exercise 3: Questionnaire Analysis

In this exercise, you are a market researcher who is requested to collect data for a consumer survey on boom boxes (portable, self-contained stereos with multiple speakers). The exercise screens explain how blank copies of the survey may be printed, as well as how the survey may be administered at the computer. The exercise is keyed to "Data Analysis" in Chapter 4, page 105 in the printed text.

Exercise 4: Ethics in Action

As a marketing executive for an industrial-goods manufacturer, a table allows you to enter your degree of agreement with 10 statements (on a 5-point scale ranging from strongly agree to strongly disagree). The statements offer various ethical situations regarding salespersons, marketing managers, buyers, retailers, and importers. The exercise is keyed to "Ethics" in Chapter 5, pages 133–135 in the printed text.

Exercise 5: Standardizing Marketing Plans

By answering a series of questions, you—as an international marketing consultant—are able to make decisions regarding the level of standardization for five factors: a product's brand name, its design, its manufacturing process, its advertising, and its pricing. You can vary each factor from pure standardized (global) to glocal to nonstandardized. This exercise is keyed to "Standardizing Plans" in Chapter 6, pages 171–172 in the printed text.

Exercise 6: Vendor Analysis

As the purchasing director for a firm, you are to assign weights to 8 important vendor attributes: delivery speed, delivery reliability, product quality, quality of final customer support, quality of intermediate customer support, purchase terms, pricing, and availability of styles and colors in all sizes. The exercise is keyed to "Differences from Final Consumers Due to Nature of Purchases" in Chapter 9, pages 260–262 in the printed text.

Exercise 7: Segmentation Analysis

A table allows you, the vice-president of marketing for a medium-sized local company, to allocate a $3 million annual marketing budget between final and organizational market segments. Varying the budget affects unit sales, sales revenues, manufacturing costs, total costs, and profit.. Different levels of marketing expenditures are required to be successful in each market segment. The exercise is keyed to "Targeting the Market" in Chapter 10, pages 297–304 in the printed text.

Exercise 8: Product Positioning

A product positioning map lets you—acting as an outside consultant—evaluate Hewlett Packard's (HP's) personal computer positioning relative to other major brands (Dell, Lenovo, Acer, and Toshiba). By rating HP's updated image on the basis of a series of statements, a revised product-positioning map for HP and other brands is generated and displayed. In addition, the computer program calculates revised market shares for HP and the other brands, leading to an adjusted market-share table. The exercise is keyed to "Product Positioning" in Chapter 11, pages 336–340 in the printed text.

Exercise 9: Services Strategy

By making a number of marketing decisions, you—as a manager of a hotel chain—are able to develop an overall services strategy. You are seeking to increase your hotel's occupancy rate and profits by offering free breakfasts, exercise facilities, and the use of a print shop. Each of these strategies can be offered at four different levels; cost data are provided for each level. By varying the level of each strategy, total revenues, costs, operating profit, and the hotel's occupancy rate are affected. You can revise your overall strategy by re-entering a new strategy. This exercise is keyed to "Special Considerations in Marketing of Services" in Chapter 12, pages 368–375 in the printed text.

Exercise 10: Product Screening Checklist

A new-product screening checklist lets you—acting as an outside consultant specializing in new-product concepts—weight the importance of various general, marketing, and production characteristics; and then you rate a new-product idea in terms of each characteristic. The software then computes separate indexes for general, marketing, and production factors—as well as an overall evaluation index. The exercise is keyed to "Product Screening" in Chapter 13, pages 405–406 in the printed text.

Exercise 11: Economic Order Quantity

As the purchasing manager for a firm, you can determine its economic order quantity under various assumptions by answering questions about expected annual demand for a product, its unit cost at wholesale, order-processing costs, and inventory-holding costs (as a percentage of a unit's wholesale cost). The computer program uses the EOQ formula, and a screen graphically displays the results. The exercise is keyed to "How Much to Reorder" in Chapter 14, page 461 in the printed text.

Exercise 12: Wholesaler Cost Analysis

As a consultant for a manufacturer, you have been retained to review that firm's selection of manufacturer wholesaling versus merchant wholesaling. The total costs of each wholesaling alternative differ on the basis of sales. The exercise is keyed to "Manufacturer/Service Provider Wholesaling" in Chapter 15, pages 474–476 in the printed text.

Exercise 13: Advertising Budget

As advertising director for Sunshine Cruise Lines, a leading cruise ship operator, one of your tasks is to allocate the firm's ad budget among various magazines via a computerized spreadsheet table. The exercise is keyed to "Establishing a Budget" in Chapter 18, page 560 in the printed text.

Exercise 14: Salesperson Deployment

As a regional sales manager, one of your more important responsibilities is to determine the required number of salespeople in your territory. Your firm has four types of industrial accounts ("A", "B", "C", and "D"). "A" accounts are key customers, "B" accounts have high potential but only moderate sales, "C" accounts are smaller firms with lower sales potential, and "D" are the smallest accounts. The exercise is keyed to "Establishing a Budget" in Chapter 19, pages 588–589 in the printed text.

Exercise 15: Price Elasticity

As the owner-operator of an auto-repair firm specializing in quick oil changes, you are concerned about what price to charge for an oil change. First, you answer a series of questions about the price range to be considered and the expected average amount of consumer demand (which may be expressed in fractions) at various prices. The computer program then calculates elasticity of demand for the various price intervals and graphically displays it. The exercise is keyed to "Consumers" in Chapter 20, pages 624–626 in the printed text.

Exercise 16: Key Cost Concepts

As a pricing consultant for Ultimate Audiovision, you answer questions about the fixed and variable costs of making the home-entertainment system at various production levels. Ultimate Audiovision contains a state-of-the-art 55-inch rear-projection TV, a hi-fi stereo VCR, a DVD player, a 500-watt digital receiver, and a six-speaker home theater stereo package. The exercise is keyed to "Cost-Based Pricing" in Chapter 21, pages 645–646 in the printed text.

Exercise 17: Performance Ratios

As a General Pillow Company executive vice-president, you are quite interested in using performance ratios to measure your company's relative success or failure across several criteria. The pre-set data in this exercise (those programmed into the exercise) are drawn from Appendix B in the text. By entering new data onto a profit-and-loss screen, you can see the impact of changes in General Pillow's sales efficiency, cost of goods sold, gross margin, operating expenses, net profit, stock turnover, and return on investment on the company's related performance ratios. For example, what would happen to ROI if General Pillow's assets rise by 5 percent? The exercise is keyed to "Performance Ratios" in Appendix B, pages A-10–A-11 in the printed text.

Exercise 18: Optimal Marketing Mix

A table allows you—the marketing director for a small industrial manufacturer—to make decisions regarding your firm's $3 million annual marketing budget. You have the ability to make decisions regarding the expenditures for advertising, personal selling, and distribution and to set the price for your product for each of three strategy alternatives: mass marketing, selective marketing, and exclusive marketing. Thus, you are involved with two distinct areas of decision making: (1) For each strategy alternative (mass marketing, selective marketing, and exclusive marketing), what is the best marketing mix? (2) Which strategy alternative should your firm pursue? Once you enter decisions, the computer program automatically calculates and displays unit sales, revenues, total product costs, total costs, and profit. The results will differ substantially for the three alternative strategies. The exercise is keyed to "Determining an Optimal Marketing Mix" in Appendix B, pages A-16–A-18 in the printed text.

Appendix D

Glossary

A

Absolute product failure   Occurs if a firm is unable to regain its production and marketing costs. The firm incurs a financial loss.

Accelerator principle   States that final consumer demand affects many layers of organizational consumers.

Adaptation   A firm's responses to the surrounding environment, while continuing to capitalize on differential advantages, including looking for new opportunities and responding to threats.

Adoption process   The mental and behavioral procedure an individual consumer goes through when learning about and purchasing a new product. It consists of five stages: knowledge, persuasion, decision, implementation, and confirmation.

Advertising   Paid, nonpersonal communication regarding goods, services, organizations, people, places, and ideas that is transmitted through various media by business firms, government and other nonprofit organizations, and individuals who are identified in the advertising message as sponsors.

Advertising agency   An organization that provides a variety of advertising-related services to client firms. It often works with clients in devising their advertising plans—including themes, media choice, copywriting, and other tasks.

Advertising media costs   Outlays for media time or space. They are related to ad length or size, as well as media attributes.

Advertising themes   The overall appeals for a campaign. Themes can be good or service, consumer, or institutional.

Agents   Wholesalers that do not take title to products. They work for commissions or fees as payment for their services and are comprised of manufacturers'/service providers' agents, selling agents, and commission (factor) merchants.

All-you-can-afford method   A promotional budget method in which a firm first allots funds for every element of marketing except promotion; remaining marketing funds go to the promotion budget.

Approaching customers   The stage in the selling process that consists of the pre-approach and greeting.

Atmosphere (atmospherics)   The sum total of the physical attributes of a retailer, whether in a store or a nonstore format, that are used to develop an image and draw customers.

Attitudes (opinions)   An individual's positive, neutral, or negative feelings about goods, services, firms, people, issues, and/or institutions.

Audience   The object of a source's message in a channel of communication.

B

Backward invention   An international product-planning strategy in which a firm appeals to developing and less-developed nations by making products less complex than those sold in its domestic market.

Bait-and-switch advertising   An illegal practice whereby customers are lured to a seller that advertises items at very low prices and then told the items are out of stock or of poor quality. There is no intent to sell advertised items.

Balanced product portfolio   A strategy by which a firm maintains a combination of new, growing, and mature products.

Barter era   Earliest use of the exchange process. With barter, people trade one resource for another.

Battle of the brands   Manufacturer, private, and generic brands each striving to gain a greater share of the consumer's dollar, control over marketing strategy, consumer loyalty, product distinctiveness, maximum shelf space and locations, and a large share of profits.

Benchmarking   A procedure used by a firm to set its marketing performance standards based on prior actions by the firm itself, the prowess of direct competitors, the competence of the best companies in its industry, and/or the approaches of innovative companies in other industries anywhere around the world.

Benefit segmentation   A procedure for grouping consumers into segments on the basis of the different benefits sought from a product.

Blanket branding   See *Family branding.*

Boston Consulting Group matrix   Lets a firm classify each strategic business unit (SBU) in terms of market share relative to major competitors and annual industry growth. The matrix identifies four types of SBUs: star, cash cow, question mark, and dog, and offers strategies for them.

Brand   A name, term, design, symbol, or any other feature that identifies the goods and services of one seller from those of other sellers.

Brand equity   A branding concept that recognizes the worth of brands. It reflects the revenue premium that a brand earns in the marketplace in comparison with an identical, but unbranded alternative.

Brand extension   A strategy by which an established brand name is applied to new products.

Brand loyalty   The consistent repurchase of and preference toward a particular brand. With it, people can reduce time, thought, and risk.

Brand manager system   See *Product manager system.*

Brand mark   A symbol, design, or distinctive coloring or lettering that cannot be spoken.

Brand name   A word, letter (number), group of words, or letters (numbers) that can be spoken.

Bricks-and-clicks firms   Companies that operate in both a traditional setting and on the Internet.

Bricks-and-mortar firms   Traditional companies that are not involved with the Internet.

Broad price policy   Sets the overall direction (and tone) for a firm's pricing efforts and makes sure pricing decisions are coordinated with the choices as to a target market, an image, and other marketing-mix factors. It incorporates short- and long-term pricing goals, and the role of pricing.

Brokers   Temporary wholesalers, paid by a commission or fee, who introduce buyers and sellers and help complete transactions.

B-to-b marketing   See *Industrial marketing.*

Bundled pricing   An offering of a basic product, options, and customer service for one total price.

Business analysis   The stage in the new-product planning process which involves the detailed review, projection, and evaluation of such factors as consumer demand, production costs, marketing costs, break-even points, competition, capital investments, and profitability for each new proposed product.

Buyer-seller dyad   A two-way flow of communication between buyer and seller.

C

Canned sales presentation   A memorized, repetitive presentation given to all customers interested in a given item. It does not adapt to customer needs or traits but presumes a general presentation will appeal to everyone.

Cash-and-carry wholesaling   A limited-service merchant wholesaler format in which people from small businesses drive to wholesalers, order products, and take them back to a store or business. No credit, delivery, merchandise, and promotional assistance are provided.

Category killer   An especially large specialty store that features an enormous selection in its product category and relatively low prices.

Cause-related marketing   A somewhat controversial practice in which profit-oriented firms contribute specific amounts to given nonprofit organizations for each consumer purchase of certain goods and services during a special promotion.

Cease-and-desist order   A consumer-protection legal concept requiring a firm to discontinue a promotion practice that is deemed deceptive and modify a message accordingly.

Chain-markup pricing   A form of demand-based pricing in which final selling price is determined, markups for each channel member are examined, and maximum acceptable costs to each member are computed. It extends demand-minus calculations from resellers back to suppliers (manufacturers).

Chain-ratio method   A method of sales forecasting in which a firm starts with general market data and then computes a series of more specific information. These combined data yield a sales forecast.

Channel functions   The functions completed by some member of a channel: marketing research, buying, promotion, customer services, product planning, pricing, and distribution.

Channel members   Those organizations or people participating in the distribution process. They may be manufacturers, service providers, wholesalers, retailers, and/or consumers.

Channel of communication (communication process)   The mechanism by which a source develops a message, transmits it to an audience via some medium, and gets feedback from the audience.

Channel of distribution   Composed of all the organizations or people in the distribution process.

Class consciousness   The extent to which a person seeks social status.

Class-action suit   A legal action on behalf of many affected consumers.

Clicks-only firms   Companies that do business just online. They do not have traditional facilities.

Clients   The constituency for which a nonprofit organization offers membership, elected officials, locations, ideas, goods, and services.

Closing the sale   The stage in the selling process that involves getting a person to agree to a purchase. The salesperson must be sure no major questions remain before trying to close a sale.

Clustered demand   A demand pattern in which consumer needs and desires for a good or service category can be classified into two or more clusters (segments), each with distinct purchase criteria.

Clutter   Involves the number of ads found in a single program, issue, and so forth, of a medium.

Co-branding   A strategy in which two or more brand names are used with the same product to gain from the brand images of each.

Cognitive dissonance   Doubt that a correct purchase decision has been made. To overcome dissonance, a firm must realize that the decision process does not end with a purchase.

Combination pricing   A pricing approach whereby aspects of cost-, demand-, and competition-based pricing methods are integrated.

Combination sales compensation plan   A format that uses elements of both salary and commission methods. Such plans balance company control, flexibility, and employee incentives.

Combination store   Unites food/grocery and general merchandise sales in one facility, with general merchandise providing 25 to 40 percent or more of sales.

Commercial data bases   Contain information on population traits, the business environment, economic forecasts, industry and companies' performance, and other items.

Commercial stock brokers   Licensed sales representatives who advise business clients, take orders, and then acquire stocks and/or bonds for the clients. They may aid the firms selling the stocks or bonds, represent either buyers or sellers, and offer some credit.

Commercialization   The final stage in the new-product planning process in which the firm introduces a product to its full target market. This corresponds to the introductory stage of the product life cycle.

Commission (factor) merchants   Agents that receive goods on consignment, accumulate them from local markets, and arrange for their sale in a central location.

Common carriers   Companies that must transport the goods of any company (or individual) interested in their services; they cannot refuse any shipments unless their rules are broken. They provide service on a fixed and publicized schedule between designated points. A fee schedule is published.

Communication process   See *Channel of communication.*

Company-controlled price environment   Characterized by moderate competition, well-differentiated goods and services, and strong control over prices by individual firms.

Comparative advantage   A concept in international marketing stating that each country has distinct strengths and weaknesses based on its natural resources, climate, technology, labor costs, and other factors. Nations can benefit by exporting the goods and services with which they have relative advantages and importing the ones with which they have relative disadvantages.

Comparative messages   Implicitly or explicitly contrast a firm's offerings with those of competitors.

Competition-based pricing   A pricing strategy approach whereby a firm uses competitors' prices rather than demand or cost considerations as its primary pricing guideposts. A firm can set prices below the market, at the market, or above the market.

Competitive bidding   A situation in which two or more sellers submit independent price quotes for specific goods and/or services to a buyer, which chooses the best offer.

Competitive parity method   A method by which a firm's promotion budget is raised or lowered according to competitors' actions.

Concentrated marketing   Exists when a company targets one well-defined market segment with one tailored marketing strategy.

Concept testing   The stage in the new-product planning process that presents the consumer with a proposed product and measures attitudes and intentions at an early stage of the process.

Conclusive research   The structured collection and analysis of data about a specific issue or problem.

Conflict resolution   A procedure in organizational buying for resolving disagreements in joint decision making. The methods of resolution are problem solving, persuasion, bargaining, and politicking.

Consumer bill of rights   A statement by President Kennedy saying that all consumers have four basic rights: to information, to safety, to choice in product selection, and to be heard.

Consumer demand   Refers to the attributes and needs of final consumers, industrial consumers, wholesalers and retailers, government institutions, international markets, and nonprofit institutions.

Consumer demographics   Objective and quantifiable population characteristics. They are rather easy to identify, collect, measure, and analyze—and show diversity around the globe.

Consumer products   Goods and services destined for the final consumer for personal, family, or household use.

Consumerism   Encompasses the wide range of activities of government, business, and independent organizations designed to protect people from practices that infringe upon their rights as consumers.

Consumer's brand decision process   Consists of nonrecognition, recognition, preference (or dislike), and insistence (or aversion) stages that consumers pass through.

Containerization   A coordinated transportation practice in which goods are placed in sturdy containers that can be loaded on trains, trucks, ships, or planes. The containers are mobile warehouses.

Continuous monitoring   Used to regularly study a firm's external and internal environment.

Contract carriers   Provide transportation services to shippers, based on individual agreements. Contract carriers do not have to maintain set routes or schedules and may negotiate rates.

Control units   The sales categories for which data are gathered, such as boys', men's, girls', and women's clothing.

Controllable factors   Decision elements internally directed by an organization and its marketers. Some of these factors are directed by top management; others are directed by marketers.

Convenience store   A retail store that is usually well situated and food-oriented, with long hours and a limited number of items. Consumers shop there for fill-in merchandise, often at off-hours.

Conventional supermarket   A departmentalized food store with minimum annual sales of $2 million that emphasizes a wide range of food and related products.

Cooperative advertising   Allows two or more firms to share some advertising costs. It can be vertical or horizontal.

Core services   The basic services that firms provide to their customers to be competitive.

Corporate culture   The shared values, norms, and practices communicated to and followed by those working for a firm.

Corporate symbols   A firm's name (and/or divisional names), logos, and trade characters. They are significant parts of an overall company image.

Corrective advertising   A consumer-protection legal concept that requires a firm to run new ads to correct the false impressions left by previous ones.

Cost of living   The total amount consumers annually pay for goods and services.

Cost-based pricing   A pricing strategy approach whereby a firm sets prices by computing merchandise, service, and overhead costs and then adding an amount to cover its profit goal.

Cost-plus pricing   A form of cost-based pricing in which prices are set by adding a predetermined profit to costs. It is the simplest form of cost-based pricing.

Culture   Consists of a group of people sharing a distinctive heritage.

Customary pricing   Occurs when a firm sets prices and seeks to maintain them for an extended time.

Customer satisfaction   The degree to which a match exists between a customer's expectations of a good or service and the actual performance of that good or service, including customer service.

Customer service   Involves the identifiable, but rather intangible, activities undertaken by a seller in conjunction with the basic goods and/or services it offers.

D

Data analysis   The coding, tabulation, and analysis of marketing research data.

Data mining   An in-depth, computerized search of available information to find profitable marketing opportunities that may otherwise be hidden.

Data warehousing   Involves retaining all types of relevant company records (sales, costs, personnel performance, etc.), and information collected by continuous monitoring and marketing research.

Data-base marketing   A computerized technique that compiles, sorts, and stores relevant information about customers and potential customers; uses that information to highlight opportunities and prioritize market segments; and enables the firm to profitably tailor marketing efforts for specific customers or customer groups.

Dealer brands See *Private brands.*

Decline stage of the product life cycle The period during which industry sales decline and many firms exit the market since customers are fewer and they have less money to spend.

Decoding The process in a channel of communication by which a message sent by a source is interpreted by an audience.

Demand patterns Indicate the uniformity or diversity of consumer needs and desires for particular categories of goods and services.

Demand-backward pricing See *Demand-minus pricing.*

Demand-based pricing A pricing strategy approach whereby a firm sets prices after studying consumer desires and ascertaining the range of prices acceptable to the target market.

Demand-minus (demand-backward) pricing A form of demand-based pricing whereby a firm finds the proper selling price and works backward to compute costs.

Derived demand Occurs for organizational consumers because the quantity of the items they buy is often based on anticipated demand by their subsequent customers for specific goods and services.

Desk jobbers See *Drop shippers.*

Developing countries Have a rising education level and technology, but a per-capita gross domestic product of about $4,000 to $9,000.

Differential advantages The unique features in a firm's marketing program that cause consumers to patronize that firm and not its competitors.

Differentiated marketing (multiple segmentation) Exists when a company targets two or more well-defined market segments with a marketing strategy tailored to each segment.

Diffused demand A demand pattern in which consumer needs and desires for a good or service category are so diverse that clear clusters (segments) cannot be identified.

Diffusion process Describes the manner in which different members of the target market often accept and purchase a product. It spans the time from product introduction through market saturation.

Diminishing returns May occur in a firm with high sales penetration if the firm seeks to convert remaining nonconsumers because the costs of attracting them may outweigh revenues.

Direct channel of distribution Involves the movement of goods and services from producer to consumers without the use of independent intermediaries.

Direct marketing Occurs when a consumer is first exposed to a good or service by a nonpersonal medium (direct mail, TV, radio, magazine, newspaper, PC, etc.) and orders by mail, phone, or PC.

Direct ownership A form of international marketing company organization in which a firm owns production, marketing, and other facilities in one or more foreign nations without any partners. The firm has full control over its international operations in those nations.

Direct selling A nonstore retail operation that involves both personal contact with consumers in their homes (and other nonstore locations) and phone solicitations initiated by the retailer.

Discretionary income What a person, household, or family has available to spend on luxuries, after necessities are purchased.

Disposable income A person's, household's, or family's total after-tax income to be used for spending and/or savings.

Distributed promotion Communication efforts spread throughout the year.

Distribution intermediaries Wholesalers, retailers, and marketing specialists (such as transportation firms) that are facilitators (links) between manufacturers/service providers and consumers.

Distribution planning Systematic decision making about the physical movement of goods and services from producer to consumer, and the related transfer of ownership (or rental) of them. It encompasses such diverse functions as transportation, inventory management, and customer transactions.

Domestic marketing Encompasses a firm's efforts in its home country.

Donors The constituency from which a nonprofit organization receives resources.

Drop shippers (desk jobbers) Limited-service merchant wholesalers that buy goods from manufacturers or suppliers and arrange for their shipment to retailers or industrial users. They have legal ownership, but do not take physical possession of products and have no storage facilities.

Dual channel of distribution (multichannel distribution) A strategy whereby a firm appeals to different market segments or diversifies business by selling through two or more separate channels.

Dumping Selling a product in a foreign country at a price much lower than that prevailing in the exporter's home market, below the cost of production, or both.

Durable goods Physical products that last for an extended period.

E

E-commerce Revenue-generating Internet transactions.

Economic community Promotes free trade among its member nations—but not necessarily with nonmember nations.

Economic order quantity (EOQ) The order volume corresponding to the lowest sum of order-processing and inventory-holding costs.

EDI See *electronic data interchange.*

80-20 principle States that in many organizations, a large proportion of total sales (profit) is likely to come from a small proportion of customers, products, or territories.

Elastic demand Occurs if relatively small price changes result in large changes in quantity demanded.

Electronic data interchange (EDI) Allows suppliers and their manufacturers/service providers, wholesalers, and/or retailers to exchange data via computer linkups.

E-marketing Any marketing activity that is conducted through the Internet, from customer analysis to marketing-mix components.

Embargo A form of trade restriction that disallows entry of specified products into a country.

Empowering employees When companies give their workers broad leeway to satisfy customer requests. Employees are encouraged and rewarded for showing initiative and imagination.

Encoding The process in a channel of communication whereby a thought or idea is translated into a message by the source.

End-use analysis The process by which a seller determines the proportion of its sales made to organizational consumers in different industries.

EOQ See *economic order quantity.*

Ethical behavior Based on honest and proper conduct.

Ethnicity/race Should be studied from a demographics perspective to determine the existence of diversity among and within nations in terms of language and country of origin or race.

European Union (EU) Also known as the Common Market. Rules call for no trade restrictions among members, uniform tariffs with nonmembers, common product standards, and a free flow of people and capital.

Evaluation of alternatives The stage in the final consumer's decision process in which criteria for a decision are set and alternatives ranked.

Exchange The process by which consumers and publics give money, a promise to pay, or support for the offering of a firm, institution, person, place, or idea.

Exclusive distribution A policy in which a firm severely limits the number of resellers utilized in a geographic area, perhaps having only one or two within a specific shopping district.

Exempt carriers Transporters that are excused from legal regulations and must only comply with safety rules. Exempt carriers are specified by law.

Experiment A type of research in which one or more factors are manipulated under controlled conditions. Experiments are able to show cause and effect.

Exploratory research Used when a researcher is uncertain about the precise topic to be investigated, or wants to informally study an issue. It is also called "qualitative research."

Exporting A form of international marketing company organization in which a firm reaches international markets by selling products made in its home country directly through its own sales force or indirectly via foreign merchants or agents. An exporting structure requires minimal investment in foreign facilities.

Extended consumer decision making Occurs when a person fully uses the decision process. Much effort is spent on information search and evaluation of alternatives for expensive, complex items with which a person has little or no experience.

F

Factor merchants See *Commission merchants.*

Family Two or more persons residing together who are related by blood, marriage, or adoption.

Family (blanket) branding A strategy in which one name is used for two or more individual products. It can be applied to both manufacturer and private brands, and to both domestic and international (global) brands.

Family life cycle Describes how a family evolves through various stages from bachelorhood to solitary retirement. At each stage, needs, experience, income, family composition, and the use of joint decision making change.

Feedback (channel of communication) The response an audience has to a message.

Feedback (uncontrollable environment) Information about the uncontrollable environment, the organization's performance, and how well the marketing plan is received.

Final consumer's decision process The way in which people gather and assess information and choose among alternative goods, services, organizations, people, places, and ideas. It has six stages: stimulus, problem awareness, information search, evaluation of alternatives, purchase, and post-purchase behavior. Demographic, social, and psychological factors affect this process.

Final consumers Buy goods and services for personal, family, or household use.

Flexible pricing Allows a firm to set prices based on the consumer's ability to negotiate or on the buying power of a large customer.

Food brokers Introduce buyers and sellers of food and related general-merchandise items to one another and bring them together to complete a sale.

Food-based superstore A diversified supermarket that sells a broad range of food and nonfood items.

Forward invention An international product-planning strategy in which a company develops new products for its international markets.

Franchise wholesaling A full-service merchant wholesaler format whereby independent retailers affiliate with an existing wholesaler to use a standardized storefront design, business format, name, and purchase system.

Freight forwarding A transportation service in which specialized firms (freight forwarders) collect small shipments (usually less than 500 pounds each) from several companies. They pick up merchandise at each shipper's place of business and arrange for delivery at buyers' doors.

Frequency How often a medium can be used.

Full disclosure A consumer-protection legal concept requiring that all data necessary for a consumer to make a safe and informed decision be provided in a promotion message.

Full-line discount store A department store with lower prices, a broad product assortment, a lower-rent location, more emphasis on self-service, brand-name merchandise, wide aisles, shopping carts, and more goods displayed on the selling floor.

Full-line wholesalers See *General-merchandise wholesalers.*

Full-service merchant wholesalers Perform a full range of distribution tasks. They provide trade credit, store and deliver products, offer merchandising and promotion assistance, have a personal sales force, offer research and planning support, pass along information to suppliers and customers, and give installation and repair services.

Functional accounts Occur when natural account expenses are reclassified by function to indicate the purposes or activities for which expenditures have been made. Included as functional expenses are marketing administration, personal selling, advertising, transportation, warehousing, marketing research, and general administration.

G

GDP See *Gross domestic product.*

General Electric business screen Categorizes strategic business units and products in terms of industry attractiveness and company business strengths.

General-merchandise (full-line) wholesalers Full-service merchant wholesalers that carry a wide product assortment—nearly all the items needed by their customers.

Generic brands   Emphasize names of the products themselves and not manufacturer or reseller names.

Geographic demographics   Basic identifiable characteristics of towns, cities, states, regions, and countries.

Geographic pricing   Outlines responsibility for transportation charges. The most common methods of geographic pricing are FOB (free on board) mill pricing, uniform delivered pricing, zone pricing, and base-point pricing.

Global marketing   An advanced form of international marketing in which a firm addresses global customers, markets, and competition.

Global marketing approach   See *Standardized marketing approach.*

Glocal marketing approach   An international marketing strategy in which combining standardized and nonstandardized efforts lets a firm attain production efficiencies, have a consistent image, have some home-office control, and still be sensitive and responsive to local needs.

Goods marketing   Entails the sale of physical products.

Goods/services continuum   Categorizes products along a scale from pure goods to pure services.

Government   Consumes goods and services in performing its duties and responsibilities. There are 1 federal, 50 state, and 87,000 local governmental units.

Government-controlled price environment   Characterized by prices being set or strongly influenced by some level of government.

Gray market goods   Foreign-made products imported into countries such as the United States by distributors (suppliers) that are not authorized by the products' manufacturers.

Gross domestic product (GDP)   The total annual value of goods and services produced in a country less net foreign investment.

Growth stage of the product life cycle   The period during which industry sales increase rapidly as a few more firms enter a highly profitable market that has substantial potential.

H

Heavy half   See *Heavy-usage segment.*

Heavy-usage segment (heavy half)   A consumer group that accounts for a large proportion of a good's or service's sales relative to the size of the market.

Hidden service sector   Encompasses the delivery, installation, maintenance, training, repair, and other services provided by firms that emphasize goods sales.

Hierarchy-of-effects model   Outlines the sequential short-term, intermediate, and long-term promotion goals for a firm to pursue—and works in conjunction with the consumer's decision process.

Homogeneous demand   A demand pattern in which consumers have rather uniform needs and desires for a good or service category.

Horizontal audit   Studies the overall marketing performance of a firm with particular emphasis on the interrelationship of variables and their relative importance. It is also called a marketing-mix audit.

Horizontal price fixing   Results from agreements among manufacturers, among wholesalers, or among retailers to set prices at a given stage in a channel of distribution. Such agreements are illegal according to the federal Sherman Antitrust Act and the Federal Trade Commission Act, regardless of how "reasonable" prices are.

Household   A person or group of persons occupying a housing unit, whether related or unrelated.

Household life cycle   Incorporates the life stages of both family and nonfamily households.

Hypermarket   The European term for a *supercenter.*

I

Iceberg principle   States that superficial data are insufficient to make sound marketing evaluations.

Idea generation   The stage in the new-product planning process which involves the continuous, systematic search for product opportunities. It involves new-idea sources and ways to generate ideas.

Ideal points   The combinations of attributes that people would most like products to have.

IMC   See *Integrated marketing communications.*

Importance of a purchase   Related to the degree of decision making, level of perceived risk, and amount of money to be spent/invested. The level of importance of a purchase affects the time and effort a person spends shopping for a product—and the money allotted.

Incremental method   A promotional budget method in which a firm bases a new budget on the previous one. A percentage is added to or subtracted from this year's budget to determine next year's.

Independent media   Communication vehicles not controlled by a firm; yet, they influence government, consumer, and publics' perceptions of that firm's products and overall image.

Independent retailer   Operates only one outlet and offers personal service, a convenient location, and close customer contact.

Indirect channel of distribution   Involves the movement of goods and services from producer to independent intermediaries to consumers.

Individual (multiple) branding   Separate brands used for different items or product lines sold by a firm.

Industrial (b-to-b) marketing   Occurs when firms deal with organizational consumers.

Industrial products   Goods and services purchased for use in the production of other goods or services, in the operation of a business, or for resale to other consumers.

Industrialization of services   Improves service efficiency and variability by using hard, soft, and hybrid technologies.

Industrialized countries   Have high literacy, modern technology, and per-capita income of several thousand dollars.

Inelastic demand   Takes place if price changes have little impact on the quantity demanded.

Information search   The stage in the final consumer's decision process that requires listing the alternatives that will solve the problem at hand and determining the characteristics of each option. Information search may be either internal or external.

Innovativeness   The willingness to try a new good or service that others perceive as risky.

Inseparability of services   Means a service provider and his or her services may be inseparable. Customer contact is often considered an integral part of the service experience.

Institutional advertising   Used when the advertising goal is to enhance company image—and not to sell specific goods or services.

Intangibility of services   Means that services often cannot be displayed, transported, stored, packaged, or inspected before buying.

Integrated marketing communications (IMC) Recognizes the value of a comprehensive plan that evaluates the strategic roles of a variety of communication disciplines—advertising, public relations, personal selling, and sales promotion—and combines them to provide clarity, consistency, and maximum communication impact.

Intensive distribution A policy in which a firm uses a large number of resellers in order to have wide market coverage, channel acceptance, and high total sales and profits.

International marketing Involves marketing goods and services outside a firm's home country, whether in one or several markets.

Internet A global electronic superhighway of computer networks—a network of networks in which users at one computer can get information from another computer (and sometimes talk directly to users at other computers).

Introduction stage of the product life cycle The period during which only one or two firms have entered the market, and competition is limited. Initial customers are innovators.

Inventory management Involved with providing a continuous flow of goods and matching the quantity of goods kept in inventory as closely as possible with customer demand.

Isolated store A freestanding retail outlet located on a highway or street.

Issue (problem) definition A statement of the topic to be looked into via marketing research. It directs the research process to collect and analyze appropriate data for the purpose of decision making.

Item price removal A practice whereby prices are marked only on store shelves or aisle signs and not on individual items.

J

JIT inventory system See *Just-in-time inventory system.*

Joint decision making The process whereby two or more people have input into purchases.

Joint venture (strategic alliance) A form of international marketing company organization in which a firm agrees to combine some aspect of its manufacturing or marketing efforts with those of a foreign company so as to share expertise, costs, and/or connections with important persons.

Jury of executive (expert) opinion A method of sales forecasting by which the management of a firm or other well-informed persons meet, discuss the future, and set sales estimates based on the group's experience and interaction.

Just-in-time (JIT) inventory system A procedure by which a purchasing firm reduces the amount of inventory it keeps on hand by ordering more often and in lower quantity.

L

Law of demand States that consumers usually purchase more units at a low price than at a high price.

Lead time The period required by a medium for placing an ad.

Leader pricing A firm's advertising and selling key items in its product assortment at less than their usual profit margins. For a wholesaler or retailer, the goal is to increase customer traffic. For a manufacturer, the goal is to gain greater consumer interest in its overall product line.

Leased department A section of a retail store rented to an outside party. The lessee operates a department—under the store's rules—and pays a percentage of sales as rent.

Less-developed countries Have low literacy, limited technology, and per-capita gross domestic product typically below $2,000 (sometimes less than $1,000).

Licensing agreement A situation in which a company pays a fee to use a name or logo whose trademark rights are held by another firm.

Lifestyle Represents the way in which a person lives and spends time and money. It is based on the social and psychological factors that have been internalized by that person, as well as his or her demographic background.

Limited consumer decision making Occurs when a person uses every step in the purchase process but does not spend a great deal of time on some of them. The person has previously bought a given good or service, but makes fresh decisions when it comes under current purchase consideration.

Limited-line wholesalers See *Specialty-merchandise wholesalers.*

Limited-service merchant wholesalers Buy and take title to products, but do not perform all the functions of full-service merchant wholesalers. They may not provide credit, merchandising assistance, or marketing research data.

Line of business Refers to the general goods/service category, functions, geographic coverage, type of ownership, and specific business of a firm.

Local content laws Require foreign firms to set up local plants and use locally made components. The goal of these laws is to protect the economies and domestic employment of the nations involved.

Logistics (physical distribution) Encompasses the broad range of activities concerned with efficiently delivering raw materials, parts, semifinished items, and finished products to designated places, at designated times, and in proper condition.

Loss leaders Items priced below cost to attract customers to a seller—usually in a store setting.

Low-involvement purchasing Occurs when a consumer minimizes the time and effort expended in both making decisions about and shopping for those goods and services he or she views as unimportant.

M

Macroenvironment Encompasses the broad demographic, societal, economic, political, technological, and other factors that an organization faces.

Mail-order wholesalers Limited-service merchant wholesalers that use catalogs, instead of a personal sales force, to promote products and communicate with customers.

Major innovations Items not previously sold by any firm.

Majority fallacy Concept stating that firms may fail when they go after the largest market segment because competition is intense. A potentially profitable segment may be one ignored by other firms.

Manufacturer brands Use the names of their makers and generate the vast majority of U.S. revenues for most product categories. The marketing goal for manufacturer brands is to attract and retain loyal consumers, and for their makers to direct the marketing effort for the brands.

Manufacturer/service provider wholesaling Occurs when a producer does all wholesaling functions itself. It may be carried out via sales offices and/or branch offices.

Manufacturers Produce products for resale to other consumers.

Manufacturers'/service providers' agents Agents who work for several manufacturers/service providers and carry noncompetitive, complementary products in exclusive territories. A manufacturer/service provider may use many agents.

Marginal return The amount of sales each increment of promotion spending will generate.

Market Consists of all the people and/or organizations who desire (or potentially desire) a good or service, have sufficient resources to make purchases, and are willing and able to buy.

Market buildup method A method of sales forecasting in which a firm gathers data from small, separate market segments and aggregates them.

Market segmentation Involves subdividing a market into clear subsets of customers that act in the same way or that have comparable needs.

Market-controlled price environment Characterized by a high level of competition, similar goods and services, and little control over prices by individual firms.

Marketing The anticipation, management, and satisfaction of demand through the exchange process.

Marketing audit A systematic, critical, impartial review and appraisal of the basic goals and policies of the marketing function, and of the organization, methods, procedures, and personnel employed to implement the policies and achieve the goals.

Marketing company era Recognition of the central role of marketing. The marketing department is the equal of others in the company. Company efforts are well integrated and regularly reviewed.

Marketing concept A consumer-oriented, market-driven, value-based, integrated, goal-oriented philosophy for a firm, institution, or person.

Marketing cost analysis Used to evaluate the cost efficiency of various marketing factors, such as different total quality configurations, product lines, order sizes, distribution methods, sales territories, channel members, salespersons, advertising media, and customer types.

Marketing department era Stage during which the marketing department shares in company decisions but remains in a subordinate position to the production, engineering, and sales departments.

Marketing environment Consists of controllable factors, uncontrollable factors, the organization's level of success or failure in reaching its objectives, feedback, and adaptation.

Marketing functions Include environmental analysis and marketing research, broadening the scope of marketing, consumer analysis, product planning, distribution planning, promotion planning, price planning, and marketing management.

Marketing information system (MIS) A set of procedures and methods for the regular, planned collection, analysis, distribution, and storage of information for use in making marketing decisions.

Marketing intelligence network The part of a marketing information system that consists of continuous monitoring, marketing research, and data storage.

Marketing manager system A product management organizational format under which a company executive is responsible for overseeing a wide range of marketing functions and for coordinating with other departments that perform marketing-related activities.

Marketing mix The specific combination of marketing elements used to achieve objectives and satisfy the target market. It encompasses decisions regarding four major variables: product, distribution, promotion, and price.

Marketing myopia A shortsighted, narrow-minded view of marketing and its environment.

Marketing organization The structural arrangement that directs marketing functions. It outlines authority, responsibility, and tasks to be done.

Marketing performers The organizations or individuals that undertake one or more marketing functions. They include manufacturers and service providers, wholesalers, retailers, marketing specialists, and organizational and final consumers.

Marketing plan analysis Involves comparing actual performance with planned or expected performance for a specified period of time.

Marketing research Involves systematically gathering, recording, and analyzing information about specific issues related to the marketing of goods, services, organizations, people, places, and ideas.

Marketing research process Consists of a series of activities: defining the issue or problem to be studied; examining secondary data; generating primary data, if necessary; analyzing information; making recommendations; and implementing findings.

Marketing strategy Outlines the way in which the marketing mix is used to attract and satisfy the target market(s) and achieve an organization's goals.

Markup pricing A form of cost-based pricing in which a firm sets prices by computing the per-unit costs of producing (buying) goods and/or services and then determining the markup percentages needed to cover selling costs and profit.

Mass customization A process by which mass-market goods and services are individualized to satisfy a specific customer need, at a reasonable price.

Massed promotion Communication efforts that are concentrated in peak periods, such as holidays.

Mass marketing See *Undifferentiated marketing*.

Maturity stage of the product life cycle The period during which industry sales stabilize as the market becomes saturated, and many firms enter to capitalize on the still sizable demand. Companies seek to maintain a differential advantage.

Medium The personal or nonpersonal means in a channel of communication used to send a message.

Membership warehouse club A retailing format in which final consumers and businesses pay small yearly dues to shop in a huge, austere warehouse. Consumers buy items at deep discounts.

Merchant wholesalers Buy, take title, and take possession of products for further resale. Merchant wholesalers may be full or limited service.

Message A combination of words and symbols sent to an audience via a channel of communication.

Message permanence Refers to the number of exposures one ad generates (repetition) and how long it remains available to the audience.

Microenvironment Encompasses the forces close to an organization that have a direct impact on its ability to serve customers, including distribution intermediaries, competitors, consumer markets, and the capabilities of the organization itself.

Minimum price laws See *Unfair-sales acts.*

Minor innovations Items not previously marketed by a firm that have been marketed by others.

MIS See *Marketing information system.*

Missionary salesperson A type of sales support person who gives out information on new goods or services. He or she does not close sales, but describes items' attributes, answers questions, and leaves written materials.

Mixed-brand strategy Occurs when a combination of manufacturer and private brands (and maybe generic brands) are sold by manufacturers, wholesalers, and retailers.

Modifications Alterations in or extensions of a firm's existing products. They include new models, styles, colors, features, and brands.

Modified break-even analysis A form of demand-based pricing that combines traditional break-even analysis with an evaluation of demand at various levels of price. It reveals the price-quantity mix that maximizes profits.

Modified-rebuy purchase process A moderate amount of decision making undertaken in the purchase of medium-priced products that an organizational consumer has bought infrequently before.

Monitoring results Involves comparing the actual performance of a firm, business unit, or product against planned performance for a specified period.

Monopolistic competition A situation in which there are several firms in an industry, each trying to offer a unique marketing mix—based on price or nonprice factors.

Monopoly A situation in which just one firm sells a given good or service and has a lot of control over its marketing plan.

Motivation Involves the positive or negative needs, goals, and desires that impel a person to or away from certain actions, objects, or conditions.

Motives The reasons for behavior.

Multichannel distribution See *Dual channel of distribution.*

Multiple branding See *Individual branding.*

Multiple-buying responsibility Two or more employees formally participating in complex or expensive purchase decisions.

Multiple segmentation See *Differentiated marketing.*

Multiple-unit pricing A practice whereby a firm offers discounts to consumers to encourage them to buy in quantity, so as to increase overall sales volume.

N

NAFTA See *North American Free Trade Agreement.*

NAICS See *North American Industry Classification System.*

Narrowcasting Presenting advertising messages to rather limited and well-defined audiences. It is a way to reduce the audience waste with mass media.

Nationalism Refers to a country's efforts to become self-reliant and raise its stature in the eyes of the world community. At times, a high degree of nationalism may lead to tight restrictions on foreign firms to foster the development of domestic industry at their expense.

Natural accounts Costs that are reported by the names of the expenses and not by their purposes. Such expense categories include salaries, rent, advertising, supplies, insurance, and interest.

Need-satisfaction approach A high-level selling method based on the principle that each customer has different attributes and wants; thus the sales presentation should adapt to the individual consumer.

Negotiation A situation in which a buyer uses bargaining ability and order size to get sellers' best possible prices.

New product A modification of an existing product or an innovation the consumer sees as meaningful.

New-product manager system A product management organizational format that has product managers to supervise existing products and new-product managers to develop new ones. Once a product is introduced, it is given to the product manager.

New-product planning process Consists of a series of steps from idea generation to commercialization. The firm generates ideas, evaluates them, weeds out poor ones, obtains consumer feedback, develops the product, tests it, and brings it to market.

New-task purchase process A large amount of decision making undertaken in the purchase of an expensive product an organizational consumer has not bought before.

Noise Interference at any point along a channel of communication.

Nondurable goods Physical products made from materials other than metals, hard plastics, and wood; are rather quickly consumed or worn out; or become dated, unfashionable, or otherwise unpopular.

Nongoods services Involve personal service on the part of the seller. They do not involve goods.

Nonprice-based approach A pricing strategy in which sellers downplay price as a factor in consumer demand by creating a distinctive good or service via promotion, packaging, delivery, customer service, availability, and other marketing factors.

Nonprofit institutions Act in the public interest or to foster a cause and do not seek financial profits.

Nonprofit marketing Conducted by organizations and individuals that operate in the public interest or that foster a cause and do not seek financial profits. It may involve organizations, people, places, and ideas, as well as goods and services.

Nonstandardized marketing approach An international marketing strategy in which a firm sees each nation or region as distinct and requiring its own marketing plan.

Nonstore retailing Occurs when a firm uses a strategy mix that is not store-based to reach consumers and complete transactions.

North American Free Trade Agreement (NAFTA) An agreement that created an economic community linking the United States, Canada, and Mexico. It will remove tariffs and trade restrictions among the three countries over the next several years.

North American Industry Classification System (NAICS) A coding system that may be used to derive information about most organizational consumers. The NAICS is the official classification system for the United States, Canada, and Mexico. It uses 20 industry categories.

O

Objective-and-task method A promotional budget method in which a firm sets promotion goals, determines the activities needed to satisfy them, and then establishes the proper budget.

Observation A research method whereby present behavior or the results of past behavior are observed and noted. People are not questioned and cooperation is unnecessary.

Odd pricing Used when selling prices are set below even dollar values, such as 49 cents and $199.

Oligopoly A situation in which a few firms—usually large ones—account for most industry sales and would like to engage in nonprice competition.

One-price policy Lets a firm charge the same price to all customers seeking to purchase a good or service under similar conditions.

Opinion leaders People to whom other consumers turn for advice and information via face-to-face communication. They normally have an impact over a narrow product range.

Opinions See *Attitudes*.

Opt-in (permission-based) E-mail A Web-based promotion tool whereby Internet users agree to receive targeted E-mail from a firm.

Order getter A type of salesperson who generates customer leads, provides information, persuades customers, and closes sales.

Order taker A type of salesperson who processes routine orders and reorders. The order taker typically handles goods and services that are pre-sold.

Organizational consumer's decision process Consists of expectations, the buying process, conflict resolution, and situational factors.

Organizational consumers Buy goods and services for further production, usage in operating the organization, or resale to other consumers.

Organizational mission A long-term commitment to a type of business and a place in the market. It can be expressed in terms of the customer group(s) served, the goods and services offered, the functions performed, and/or the technologies utilized.

Outsourcing When one company provides services for another company that could also be or usually have been done in-house by the client firm.

Owned-goods services Involve alterations or maintenance/repairs of goods owned by consumers.

P

Package A container used to protect, promote, transport, and/or identify a product.

Packaging functions Containment and protection, usage, communication, segmentation, channel cooperation, and new-product planning.

Patent Grants an inventor of a useful product or process exclusive selling rights for a fixed period.

Penetration pricing Uses low prices to capture the mass market for a good or service.

Perceived risk The level of uncertainty a consumer believes exists as to the outcome of a purchase decision; this belief may or may not be correct. Perceived risk can be divided into six major types: functional, physical, financial, social, psychological, and time.

Percentage-of-sales method A promotional budget method in which a firm ties its promotion budget to sales revenue.

Peripheral services Supplementary (extra) services that firms provide to customers.

Perishability of services Means that many services cannot be stored for future sale. A service firm must try to manage consumer usage so there is consistent demand over various times.

Permission-based E-mail See *Opt-in E-mail*.

Personal demographics Basic identifiable characteristics of individual final consumers and organizational consumers and groups of final consumers and organizational consumers.

Personal selling Involves oral communication with one or more prospective buyers by paid representatives for the purpose of making sales.

Personality The sum total of a person's enduring internal psychological traits making the person unique.

Persuasive impact The ability of a medium to stimulate consumers.

Physical distribution See *Logistics*.

Planned obsolescence A marketing practice that capitalizes on short-run material wearout, style changes, and functional product changes.

Planned shopping center A retail location that consists of centrally owned or managed facilities. It is planned and operated as an entity, ringed by parking, and based on balanced tenancy. The three types of planned center are regional, community, and neighborhood.

Porter generic strategy model Identifies two key marketing planning concepts and the options available for each: competitive scope (broad or narrow target) and competitive advantage (lower cost or differentiation).

Post-purchase behavior The stage in the final consumer's decision process when further purchases and/or re-evaluation of the purchase are undertaken.

Predatory pricing An illegal practice in which large firms cut prices on products to below their cost in selected geographic areas so as to eliminate small, local competitors.

Prestige pricing Assumes consumers will not buy goods or services at prices they consider too low.

Price Represents the value of a good or service for both the seller and the buyer.

Price adjustment tactics Alterations in list prices, escalator clauses and surcharges, added markups, markdowns, and rebates.

Price ceiling The maximum amount customers will pay for a given good or service.

Price discrimination A form of demand-based pricing in which a firm sets two or more distinct prices for a product so as to appeal to different final consumer or organizational consumer segments. Price discrimination can be customer-, product-, time-, or place-based.

Price elasticity of demand Indicates the sensitivity of buyers to price changes in terms of the quantities they will purchase. It is computed by dividing the percentage change in quantity demanded by the percentage change in price charged.

Price floor The lowest acceptable price a firm can charge and attain its profit goal.

Price leadership A form of competition-based pricing in which one firm (or a few firms) is usually the first to announce price changes and others in the industry follow.

Price lining Involves selling products at a range of prices, with each representing a distinct level of quality (or features).

Price planning Systematic decision making by an organization regarding all aspects of pricing.

Price wars Situations in which firms continually try to undercut each other's prices to draw customers.

Price-based approach A pricing strategy in which sellers influence consumer demand primarily through changes in price levels.

Price-floor pricing   A form of cost-based pricing whereby a firm determines the lowest price at which it is worthwhile to increase the amount of goods or services it makes available for sale.

Price-quality association   A concept stating that consumers may believe high prices represent high quality and low prices represent low quality.

Primary data   Consist of information gathered to address a specific issue or problem at hand.

Primary demand   Consumer demand for a product category.

Private (dealer) brands   Use names designated by their resellers, usually wholesalers or retailers, and account for sizable U.S. revenues in many product categories. Resellers have more exclusive rights for these brands, and are more responsible for distribution and larger purchases.

Private carriers   Shippers with their own transportation facilities.

Problem awareness   The stage in the final consumer's decision process during which a consumer recognizes that the good, service, organization, person, place, or idea under consideration may solve a problem of shortage or unfulfilled desire.

Problem definition   See *Issue definition.*

Process-related ethical issues   Involve the unethical use of marketing strategies or tactics.

Product   A bundle of attributes capable of exchange or use, usually a mix of tangible and intangible forms. It may be an idea, a physical entity (a good), or a service, or any combination of the three.

Product (brand) manager system   A product management organizational format under which there is a level of middle managers, each of whom is responsible for planning, coordinating, and monitoring the performance of a single product (brand) or a small group of products (brands). The managers handle both new and existing products and are involved with all the marketing activities related to their product or group of products.

Product adaptation   A product-planning strategy in which domestic products are modified to meet foreign language needs, taste preferences, climates, electrical requirements, laws, and other factors.

Product development stage of new-product planning   Converts an idea for a new product into a tangible form and identifies a basic marketing strategy.

Product differentiation   Occurs when a product offering is perceived by the consumer to differ from its competition on any physical or nonphysical product characteristic, including price.

Product item   A specific model, brand, or size of a product that a company sells.

Product life cycle   A concept that seeks to describe a product's sales, competitors, profits, customers, and marketing emphasis from its beginning until it is removed from the market. It is divided into introduction, growth, maturity, and decline stages.

Product line   A group of closely related product items.

Product mix   All the different product lines a firm offers. It can be described in terms of its width, depth, and consistency.

Product placement   A practice in which products/brands are placed into the story lines of TV shows, movies, or some other media for marketing purposes. It is controversial because the viewer is often not aware that the product/brand is placed for commercial purposes.

Product planning   Systematic decision making relating to all aspects of the development and management of a firm's products, including branding and packaging.

Product positioning   Enables a firm to map each of its products in terms of consumer perceptions and desires, competition, other company products, and environmental changes.

Product recall   The primary enforcement tool of the Consumer Product Safety Commission (CPSC), whereby the CPSC asks or orders firms to recall and modify (or discontinue) unsafe products.

Product screening   The stage in the new-product planning process when poor, unsuitable, or otherwise unattractive ideas are weeded out from further consideration.

Product/market opportunity matrix   Identifies four alternative marketing strategies to maintain and/or increase sales of business units and products: market penetration, market development, product development, and diversification.

Production era   Devotion to physical distribution of products due to high demand and low competition. Consumer research, product modifications, and adapting to consumer needs are not needed.

Product-planning committee   A product management organizational format with high-level executives from various functional areas in a firm, such as marketing, production, engineering, finance, and R&D. It does product approval, evaluation, and development on a part-time basis.

Product-related ethical issues   Involve the ethical appropriateness of marketing certain products.

Profit-based pricing objectives   Those that orient a firm's pricing strategy toward some type of profit goals: profit maximization, satisfactory profit, return on investment, and/or early recovery of cash.

Promotion   Any communication used to inform, persuade, and/or remind people about an organization's or individual's goods, services, image, ideas, community involvement, or impact on society.

Promotion mix   A firm's overall and specific communication program, including its involvement with advertising, public relations (publicity), personal selling, and/or sales promotion.

Promotion planning   Systematic decision making relating to all aspects of an organization's or individual's communications efforts.

Prospecting   The stage in the selling process that generates a list of customer leads. It is common with outside selling, and can be blind or lead in orientation.

Public relations   Includes any communication to foster a favorable image for goods, services, organizations, people, places, and ideas among various publics—such as consumers, investors, government, channel members, employees, and the general public.

Publicity   The form of public relations that entails nonpersonal communication passed on via various media but not paid for by an identified sponsor.

Publicity types   News publicity, business feature articles, service feature articles, finance releases, product releases, pictorial releases, video news releases, background editorial material, and emergency publicity.

Publics' demand   The attributes and needs of employees, unions, stockholders, the general public, government agencies, consumer groups, and other internal and external forces that affect a company.

Pulling strategy   Occurs when a firm first stimulates consumer demand and then gains dealer support.

Purchase act   The stage in the final consumer's decision process in which there is an exchange of money, a promise to pay, or support in return for ownership of a specific good, the performance of a specific service, and so on.

Purchase terms   The provisions of price agreements.

Pure competition   A situation in which many firms sell virtually identical goods or services and they are unable to create differential advantages.

Pushing strategy   Occurs when various firms in a distribution channel cooperate in marketing a product.

Q

Quick response (QR) inventory system   A cooperative effort between retailers and suppliers to reduce retail inventory while providing a merchandise supply that more closely addresses the actual buying patterns of consumers.

R

Rack jobbers   Full-service merchant wholesalers that furnish the racks or shelves on which products are displayed. They own the products on the racks, selling them on a consignment basis.

Reach   Refers to the number of viewers, readers, or listeners in a medium's audience. For TV and radio, it is the total number of people who watch or listen to an ad. For print media, it has two aspects: circulation and passalong rate.

Real income   The amount of income earned in a year adjusted by the rate of inflation.

Rebates   A form of price adjustment in which refunds are given directly from the manufacturer to the customer to stimulate the purchase of an item or a group of items.

Reciprocity   A procedure by which organizational consumers select suppliers that agree to purchase goods and services, as well as sell them.

Reference group   A group that influences a person's thoughts or actions.

Relationship marketing   Exists when marketing activities are performed with the conscious intention of developing and managing long-term, trusting relationships with customers.

Relative product failure   Occurs if a firm makes a profit on an item but that product does not reach profit goals and/or adversely affects a firm's image.

Rented-goods services   Involve the leasing of goods for a specified time.

Reorder point   Sets an inventory level at which new orders must be placed. It depends on order lead time, the usage rate, and safety stock.

Research design   Outlines the procedures for collecting and analyzing data. It includes decisions relating to the person collecting data, data to be collected, group of people or objects studied, data-collection techniques employed, study costs, method of data collection, length of study period and time, and location of data collection.

Retail chain   Involves common ownership of multiple outlets.

Retail franchising   A contractual agreement between a franchisor (a manufacturer, wholesaler, or service sponsor) and a retail franchisee, which allows the latter to run a certain form of business under an established name and according to specific rules.

Retail store strategy mix   An integrated combination of hours, location, assortment, service, advertising, prices, and other factors retailers employ.

Retailers   Buy or handle goods and services for sale (resale) to the final (ultimate) consumer.

Retailing   Encompasses those business activities involved with the sale of goods and services to the final consumer for personal, family, or household use. It is the final stage in a channel of distribution.

Robinson-Patman Act   Prohibits manufacturers and wholesalers from price discrimination in dealing with different channel-member purchasers of products with "like quality" if the effect of such discrimination is to injure competition.

Routine consumer decision making   Occurs when a person buys out of habit and skips steps in the decision process. In this category are items with which a person has much experience.

S

Sales analysis   The detailed study of sales data for the purpose of appraising the appropriateness and effectiveness of a marketing strategy.

Sales engineer   A type of sales support person who accompanies an order getter if a very technical or complex item is being sold. He or she discusses specifications and long-range uses.

Sales era   Involves hiring a sales force and sometimes advertising to sell inventory, after production is maximized. The goal is to make consumer desires fit the features of the products offered.

Sales exception reporting   Highlights situations where sales goals are not met or sales opportunities are present.

Sales forecast   Outlines expected company sales for a specific good or service to a specific consumer group over a specific period of time under a specific marketing program.

Sales management   Planning, implementing, and controlling the personal sales function. It covers employee selection, training, territory allocation, compensation, and supervision.

Sales penetration   The degree to which a firm is meeting its sales potential.

Sales presentation   The stage in the selling process that includes a verbal description of a product, its benefits, options and models, price, associated services such as delivery and warranty, and a demonstration (if needed).

Sales promotion   Involves paid marketing communication activities (other than advertising, publicity, or personal selling) that are intended to stimulate consumer purchases and dealer effectiveness. Included are trade shows, premiums, incentives, giveaways, demonstrations, and various other efforts not in the ordinary promotion routine.

Sales promotion conditions   Requirements channel members or consumers must meet to be eligible for a specific sales promotion.

Sales promotion orientation   Refers to its focus—channel members or consumers—and its theme.

Sales territory   The geographic area, customers, and/or product lines assigned to a salesperson.

Sales-based pricing objectives Goals that orient a company's pricing strategy toward high sales volume and/or expanding its share of sales relative to competitors.

Sales-expense budget Allots selling costs among salespeople, products, customers, and geographic areas for a given period.

Sampling The analysis of selected people or objects in a designated population, rather than all of them.

SBU See *Strategic business unit.*

Scientific method A research philosophy incorporating objectivity, accuracy, and thoroughness.

Scrambled merchandising Occurs if a retailer adds goods and services that are unrelated to each other and the firm's original business.

Secondary data Consist of information not collected for the issue or problem at hand but for some other purpose. The two types of secondary data are internal and external.

Selective demand Consumer demand for a particular brand.

Selective distribution A policy in which a firm employs a moderate number of resellers.

Self-fulfilling prophecy A situation in which a firm predicts falling sales and then ensures this by reducing or removing marketing support.

Selling against the brand A practice used by wholesalers and retailers, whereby they stock well-known brands, place high prices on them, and then sell other brands for lower prices.

Selling agents Responsible for marketing the entire output of a manufacturer/service provider under a contractual agreement. They perform all wholesale tasks except taking title to products.

Selling process Consists of prospecting for leads, approaching customers, determining consumer wants, giving a sales presentation, answering questions, closing the sale, and following up.

Semantic differential A survey technique using rating scales of bipolar (opposite) adjectives. An overall company or product profile is then devised.

Service blueprint A systematic, visual portrayal of all the service processes followed by a company.

Service gap The difference between customer expectations and actual service performance.

Service marketing The rental of goods, servicing goods owned by consumers, and personal services.

Service salesperson A type of sales support person who ordinarily deals with customers after sales. Delivery, installation, and other follow-up tasks are done.

Simulation A computer-based method to test the potential effects of various marketing factors via a software program rather than real-world applications.

Single-source data collection Allows research firms to track the activities of individual consumer households from the programs they watch on TV to the products they purchase at stores.

Situation analysis Identifies an organization's internal strengths and weaknesses and external opportunities and threats. It seeks to answer: Where is a firm now? In what direction is it headed?

Situational factors Those that can interrupt the organizational consumer's decision process and the selection of a supplier or brand. They include strikes, machine breakdowns, and so on.

Skimming pricing Uses high prices to attract the market segment more concerned with product quality, uniqueness, or status than price.

Social class A status hierarchy by which groups and individuals are classified on the basis of esteem and prestige. Social classes are based on income, occupation, education, and type of dwelling.

Social marketing The use of marketing to increase the acceptability of social ideas.

Social performance How one carries out his/her roles as a worker, family member, citizen, and friend.

Social responsibility A concern for the consequences of a person's or firm's acts as they might affect the interests of others. Corporate social responsibility balances a company's short-term profit needs with long-term societal needs.

Social Styles model A classification system for segmenting organizational consumers in terms of a broad range of demographic and lifestyle factors. The model divides the personnel representing those consumers into lifestyle categories.

Socioecological view of marketing Considers all the stages in a product's life span in developing, selling, purchasing, using, and disposing of that product. It incorporates the interests of everyone affected by a good's or service's use.

Sorting process The distribution activities of accumulation, allocation, sorting, and assorting. Through this process, intermediaries can resolve the differences in the goals of manufacturers and consumers.

Source A company, an independent institution, or an opinion leader seeking to present a message to an audience. It is part of the channel of communication.

Spam Unsolicited and unwanted E-mail.

Specialty store A retailer that concentrates on one product line.

Specialty-merchandise (limited-line) wholesalers Full-service merchant wholesalers that concentrate on a rather narrow product range and have an extensive selection in that range.

Standard of living Refers to the average quantity and quality of goods and services that are owned and consumed in a given nation.

Standardized (global) marketing approach A marketing strategy in which a firm uses a common marketing plan for all nations in which it operates—because it assumes worldwide markets are more homogeneous due to better communications, more open borders, free-market economies, etc.

Status quo-based pricing objectives Sought by a firm interested in continuing a favorable business climate for its operations or in stability.

Stimulus A cue (social, commercial, or noncommercial) or a drive (physical) meant to motivate a person to act.

Stock turnover The number of times during a stated period (usually one year) that average inventory on hand is sold. Stock turnover is calculated in units or dollars (in selling price or at cost).

Straight commission plan A sales compensation plan in which a salesperson's earnings are directly related to sales, profits, customer satisfaction, or some other type of performance.

Straight extension An international product-planning strategy in which a firm makes and markets the same products for domestic and foreign sales.

Straight salary plan A sales compensation plan in which a salesperson is paid a flat amount per period.

Straight-rebuy purchase process Routine reordering by organizational consumers for the purchase of inexpensive items bought regularly.

Strategic alliance   See *Joint venture.*

Strategic business plan   Describes the overall direction an organization will pursue within its chosen environment and guides the allocation of resources and effort. It integrates the perspectives of functional departments and operating units.

Strategic business unit (SBU)   A self-contained division, product line, or product department in an organization with a specific market focus and a manager with complete responsibility for integrating all functions into a strategy.

Strategic marketing plan   Outlines the marketing actions to undertake, why they are needed, who carries them out, when and where they will be completed, and how they will be coordinated.

Strategic planning process   Consists of seven interrelated steps: defining organizational mission, establishing strategic business units, setting marketing objectives, performing situation analysis, developing marketing strategy, implementing tactics, and monitoring results.

Subjective price   A consumer's perception of the price of a good or service as being high, fair, or low.

Subliminal advertising   A highly controversial kind of promotion because it does not enable the audience to consciously decode a message.

Substantiation   A consumer-protection legal concept that requires a firm to be able to prove all the claims it makes in promotion messages. This means thorough testing and evidence of performance are needed before making claims.

Supercenter (hypermarket)   A combination store that integrates an economy supermarket with a discount department store, with at least 40 percent of sales from nonfood items.

Survey   Gathers information by communicating with respondents in person, by phone, by mail, or through the Internet.

Systems selling   A combination of goods and services provided to a buyer by one vendor. This gives the buyer one firm with which to negotiate, as well as consistency among various parts and components.

T

Tactical plan   Specifies the short-run actions (tactics) that a firm undertakes in implementing a given market strategy.

Target market   The particular group(s) of customers a firm proposes to serve, or whose needs it proposes to satisfy, with a particular marketing program.

Target market strategy   Comprises three general phases: analyzing consumer demand, targeting the market, and developing the marketing strategy.

Target pricing   A form of cost-based pricing in which prices are set to provide a particular rate of return on investment for a standard volume of production—the level of production a firm anticipates achieving.

Tariff   The most common form of trade restriction, in which a tax is placed on imported products by a foreign government.

Technology   Refers to developing and using machinery, products, and processes.

Telemarketing   An efficient way of operating, whereby telephone communications are used to sell or solicit business or to set up an appointment for a salesperson to sell or solicit business.

Test marketing   The stage in the new-product planning process which involves placing a fully developed new product (a good or service) in one or more selected areas and observing its actual performance under a proposed marketing plan.

Time expenditures   The activities in which a person participates and the time allocated to them.

Total delivered product   The bundle of tangible and intangible product attributes actually provided to consumers through a value chain and its related value delivery chain

Total quality   A process- and output-related philosophy, whereby a firm strives to fully satisfy customers effectively and efficiently. It requires a customer focus, top management commitment, an emphasis on continuous improvement, and support from employees, suppliers, and intermediaries.

Total-cost approach   Determines the distribution service level with the lowest total costs—including freight (shipping), warehousing, and lost business. An ideal system seeks a balance between low expenditures on distribution and high opportunities for sales.

Trade character   A brand mark that is personified.

Trade deficit   The amount by which the value of imports exceeds the value of exports for a country.

Trade quota   A restriction that sets limits on the amounts of products imported into a country.

Trade surplus   The amount by which the value of exports exceeds the value of imports for a country.

Trademark   A brand name, brand mark, or trade character or combination thereof with legal protection.

Traditional break-even analysis   Finds the sales quantity in units or dollars that is needed for total revenues to equal total costs at a given price.

Traditional department store   A department store that has a great assortment of goods and services, provides many customer services, is a fashion leader, and often serves as an anchor store in a shopping district or shopping center.

Transportation forms   The modes for shipping products, parts, raw materials, and so forth. These include railroads, motor carriers, waterways, pipelines, and airways.

Truck/wagon wholesalers   Limited-service merchant wholesalers that generally have a regular sales route, offer items from a truck or wagon, and deliver goods when they are sold.

U

Unbundled pricing   Breaks down prices by individual components and allows the consumer to decide what to purchase.

Uncontrollable factors   The external elements affecting an organization's performance that cannot be fully directed by that organization and its marketers. These include consumers, competition, suppliers and distributors, government, the economy, technology, and independent media.

Undifferentiated marketing (mass marketing)   Exists when a company targets the whole market with a single basic marketing strategy intended to have mass appeal.

Unfair-sales acts (minimum price laws)   Legislation in a number of states that prevents firms from selling products for less than their cost plus a fixed percentage that includes overhead and profit.

Unit pricing   Lets consumers compare price per quantity for competing brands and for various sizes of the same brand. With it, prices are shown per unit of measure, as well as by total price.

Unitary demand Exists if price changes are exactly offset by changes in the quantity demanded, so total sales revenue remains constant.

Universal Product Code (UPC) A series of thick and thin vertical lines used to pre-mark items. Price and inventory data are represented by the lines, but are not readable by employees and customers.

Unplanned business district A retail location form that exists where multiple stores are located close to one another without prior planning as to the number and composition of stores. The unplanned sites are central business district, secondary business district, neighborhood business district, and string.

UPC See *Universal Product Code.*

V

VALS (Values and Lifestyles) program A classification system for segmenting consumers via a broad range of demographic and lifestyle factors. It divides final consumers into lifestyle categories.

Value analysis A comparison of the costs and benefits of alternative materials, components, designs, or processes so as to reduce the cost/benefit ratio of purchases.

Value chain Represents the series of business activities that are performed to design, produce, market, deliver, and service a product for customers.

Value delivery chain Encompasses all of the parties who engage in value chain activities.

Values and Lifestyles program See *VALS program.*

Variability in service quality Differing service performance from one purchase occasion to another. Variations may be due to the service firm's difficulty in problem diagnosis (for repairs), customer inability to verbalize service needs, and the lack of standardization and mass production.

Variable markup policy Cost-based markup pricing whereby separate categories of goods and services receive different percentage markups. Variable markups recognize that some items require greater personal selling, customer service, alterations, and end-of-season markdowns than others.

Variable pricing Allows a firm to intentionally alter prices in response to cost fluctuations or differences in consumer demand.

Vending machine A nonstore retail operation that uses coin- or card-operated machinery to dispense goods or services. It eliminates the need for salespeople, allows 24-hour sales, and can be placed outside rather than inside a store.

Vendor analysis An assessment of the strengths and weaknesses of current or new suppliers in terms of quality, customer service, reliability, and price.

Venture team A product management organizational format in which a small, independent department with a broad range of specialists is involved with a specific new product's entire development process. Team members work on a full-time basis and act in a relatively autonomous manner.

Vertical audit An in-depth analysis of one aspect of a firm's marketing strategy. It is also known as a functional audit.

Vertical price fixing When manufacturers or wholesalers seek to control the final selling prices of their goods or services.

W

Warehousing Involves the physical facilities used to store, identify, and sort goods in expectation of their sale and transfer within a distribution channel.

Warranty An assurance to consumers that a product meets certain standards.

Waste The part of a medium's audience not in a firm's target market.

Wearout rate The time it takes for a message to lose its effectiveness.

Wheel of retailing Describes how low-end (discount) strategies can evolve into high-end (full service, high price) strategies and thus provide opportunities for new firms to enter as discounters.

Wholesale cooperatives Full-service merchant wholesalers owned by member firms to economize functions and provide broad support. There are producer-owned and retailer-owned cooperatives.

Wholesalers Buy or handle merchandise and its subsequent resale to organizational users, retailers, and other wholesalers.

Wholesaling Includes buying and/or handling goods and services, and their subsequent resale to organizational users, retailers, and/or other wholesalers—but not the sale of significant volume to final consumers.

Word-of-mouth communication The process by which people express opinions and product-related experiences to one another.

World Trade Organization (WTO) An organization whose mission is to open up international markets even further and promote a cooperative atmosphere around the globe.

World Wide Web (WWW) Comprises all of the resources and users on the Internet using the Hypertext Transfer Protocol (HTTP). It is a way of accessing the Internet, whereby people work with easy-to-use Web addresses and pages. Users see words, colorful charts, pictures, and video, and hear audio.

WTO See *World Trade Organization.*

WWW See *World Wide Web.*

Y

Yield management pricing A form of demand-based pricing whereby a firm determines the mix of price-quantity combinations that generates the highest level of revenues for a given period.

Company Index

Name Index

Subject Index